MW01129114

1 MONTH OF
FREE
READING

at

www.ForgottenBooks.com

By purchasing this book you are eligible for one month membership to ForgottenBooks.com, giving you unlimited access to our entire collection of over 1,000,000 titles via our web site and mobile apps.

To claim your free month visit:

www.forgottenbooks.com/free860154

ISBN 978-0-331-96288-8
PIBN 10860154

THE

CAMBRIDGE

MEDIEVAL HISTORY

VOLUME I

THE MACMILLAN COMPANY
NEW YORK · BOSTON · CHICAGO
SAN FRANCISCO

MACMILLAN & CO., Limited
LONDON · BOMBAY · CALCUTTA
MELBOURNE

THE MACMILLAN CO. OF CANADA, Ltd.
TORONTO

THE
CAMBRIDGE
MEDIEVAL HISTORY

PLANNED BY

J. B. BURY, M.A.
REGIUS PROFESSOR OF MODERN HISTORY

EDITED BY

H. M. GWATKIN, M.A.
J. P. WHITNEY, B.D.

VOLUME I

THE CHRISTIAN ROMAN EMPIRE AND THE
FOUNDATION OF THE TEUTONIC KINGDOMS

New York
THE MACMILLAN COMPANY
1911

All rights reserved

GENERAL PREFACE

THE present work is intended as a comprehensive account of medieval times, drawn up on the same lines as *The Cambridge Modern History*, but with a few improvements of detail suggested by experience. It is intended partly for the general reader, as a clear and, as far as possible, interesting narrative; partly for the student, as a summary of ascertained facts, with indications (not discussions) of disputed points; partly as a book of reference, containing all that can reasonably be required in a comprehensive work of general history. A full bibliography is added to every chapter, and a portfolio of illustrative maps is published to accompany each volume.

There is nothing in the English language resembling the present work. Germany, indeed, has Heeren and Oncken, but in France even the great work of Lavisse and Rambaud deals with the Middle Ages on a much smaller scale than is here contemplated. The present volumes are intended to cover the entire field of European medieval history, so that in every chapter a specialist sums up recent research upon the subject. America, France, Germany, Austria, Bulgaria, Hungary, Italy, Spain and Russia are represented in the list of contributors.

The principles on which the work is constructed were laid down by the late Lord Acton for *The Cambridge Modern History*. Professor Bury, Lord Acton's successor as Regius Professor of Modern History, was invited by the Syndics of the Press to plan the *History* as a whole, and to draw up the scheme of each volume. The first editors appointed were the Rev. H. M. Gwatkin, M.A., Dixie Professor of Ecclesiastical History, Miss Mary Bateson and Mr G. T. Lapsley, M.A., Fellow of Trinity College. On Miss Bateson's death, the Rev. J. P. Whitney, B.D. of King's College, was appointed in her stead; but on Mr Lapsley's retirement through ill-health (happily only temporary) his place was not filled up. The present editors are, therefore, Professor Gwatkin and Mr Whitney. They wish to place on record their grateful thanks for the helpful advice which Professor Bury has always been ready to give them when requested; but it should be understood that the editors are alone responsible for the matter contained in each volume, for the selection of the writers of the various chapters and for the general treatment of the subjects discussed.

It is hoped to publish two volumes yearly in regular succession.

H. M. G.
J. P. W.

September 1911

PREFACE TO VOLUME I

THE present volume covers a space of about two hundred years beginning with Constantine and stopping a little short of Justinian. At its opening the Roman Empire is standing in its ancient majesty, drawing new strength from the reforms of Diocletian and the statesmanship of Constantine: at its close the Empire has vanished from the West, while the East is slowly recovering from the pressure of the barbarians in the fifth century, and gathering strength for Justinian's wars of conquest. At its opening heathenism is still a mighty power, society is built up on heathen pride of class, and Rome still seems the centre of the world: at its ending we see Christianity supreme, Constantinople the seat of power, and the old heathen order of society in the West dissolving in the confusion of barbarian devastations. At its opening Caesar's will is law from the Atlantic to Armenia: at its ending a great system of Teutonic and Arian kingdoms in the West has just been grievously shaken by the conversion of the Franks from heathenism direct to orthodoxy.

In our first chapter we trace the rise of Constantine, his reunion of the Empire, his conversion to Christianity, the political side of the Nicene Council, and the foundation of Constantinople. Then follows Dr Reid's account of the reforms of Diocletian and Constantine, which fixed for centuries the general outline of the administration. After this Mr Norman Baynes takes up the struggle with Persia under Constantius and Julian, and continues in a later chapter the story of the wars of Rome in East and West in the times of Valentinian and Theodosius. The victory of Christianity is treated by Principal Lindsay; and he describes also the rival systems of Neoplatonism and Mithraism, and gives an account of Julian's reaction and the last struggles of heathenism. The next chapter is devoted to Arianism. First the doctrine is described, in itself and in some of its relations to modern thought; then the religious side of the Nicene Council is given, and the complicated history of the reaction is traced down to the decisive overthrow of Arianism in the Empire by Theodosius. After this Mr C. H. Turner describes the organisation of the Church — clergy, creeds and worship — looking back to the beginning, but chiefly concerned with its development in the age of the great Councils.

We now pass to the Teutons.   Dr Martin Bang begins in prehistoric times, describing their migrations and their conquests westward and southward till the legions brought them to a stand on the Rhine and the Danube, and their long struggle of four centuries to break through the Roman frontier before the battle of Hadrianople settled them inside the Danube.   Then Dr Manitius carries down the story through the administrations of Theodosius and Stilicho to the great collapse — the passing of the Rhine, the overrunning of Gaul and Spain, the Roman mutiny of Pavia, and the sack of Rome by Alaric.   After this the great Teutonic peoples have to be dealt with severally.   Dr Ludwig Schmidt begins with the settlement of the Visigoths in Gaul, traces the growth and culmination of their kingdom of Toulouse, and ends with their expulsion from Aquitaine by Clovis.   Professor Pfister gives the early history of the Franks; but they are still a feeble folk when he leaves them, for the conquests of Clovis belong to another volume.   Then Dr Schmidt tells the little that is known of the Sueves and Alans in Spain, and more fully describes the history and institutions of the Vandal kingdom in Africa to its destruction by Belisarius.

Our next chapter differs from the rest in containing very little history.   It is Dr Peisker's account of Central Asia and the Altaian mounted nomads.   It is given as a general (and much needed) introduction to the chapters on the Huns, the Avars, the Turks, and the rest of the Asiatic hordes who devastated Europe in the Middle Ages.   To this is attached Dr Schmidt's short account of the Huns and Attila.   We next turn to our own country.   Professor Haverfield describes the conquest and organisation of Roman Britain, and the decline and fall of the Roman power in the island, while Mr Beck deals with the English in their continental home, and tells the story of their settlement in Britain from the English side.   After this Mr Barker records the last struggles of the Western Empire — the loyalty of Gaul and the disaffection of Africa — under Aëtius and Majorian, concluding with the barbarian mutiny at Pavia which overthrew the last Augustus of the West.   Then M. Maurice Dumoulin continues the history of Italy under the barbarian rule of Odovacar and Theodoric, describing the great king's policy, and shewing how he kept in check for awhile the feud of Roman and barbarian which had wrecked the Western Empire.   Turning now to the Eastern provinces, the fifth century, which falls to Mr Brooks, is upon the whole a prosaic period of second-rate rulers and dire financial strain.   Yet even here we have striking events, remarkable characters, and important movements — the fall of Rufinus and the failure of Gaïnas; Pulcheria ruling the Empire as a girl of sixteen, the romance of Athenais, and the catastrophe of Basiliscus; the Isaurian policy of Leo, and the reforms of Anastasius. Then Miss Alice Gardner traces the history of religious disunion in the East. The fall of Chrysostom brought to the front the rivalry of Constantinople and Alexandria, the defeat of Nestorianism at Ephesus and of Monophysitism at Chalcedon fixed the lines of orthodoxy, but left Egypt and Syria heterodox and disaffected, and the reconciling Henoticon of Zeno produced nothing but a new schism. In the next chapter Dom Butler traces the growth of monasticism and its various forms in East and West, including the Benedictine rule and the Irish monks. After this Professor Vinogradoff surveys the whole field of social and economic conditions in the declining Empire, and shews the part which rotten economics and bad taxation played in its destruction. Then Mr H. F. Stewart gives his account of the heathen and Christian literature of the time, and of the various lines of thought which seemed to converge upon the grand figure of Augustine. The volume concludes with Mr Lethaby's account of the beginnings and early development of Christian art.

Shortly: to the student of universal history the Roman Empire is the bulwark which for near six hundred years kept back the ever-threatening attacks of Teutonic and Altaian barbarism. Behind that bulwark rose the mighty structure of Roman Law, and behind it a new order of the world was beginning to unfold from the fruitful seeds of Christian thought. So when the years of respite ended, and the universal Empire went down in universal ruin, the Christian Church was able from the first to put some check on the northern conquerors, and then by the long training of the Middle Ages to mould the nations of Europe into forms which have issued in richer and fuller developments of life and civilisation than imperial Rome had ever known.

It remains for us to give our best thanks to Dr A. W. Ward for much counsel and assistance, and to all those who have kindly helped us by looking over the proofs of particular chapters.

H. M. G.
J. P. W.

September 1911

CHAPTER II

THE REORGANISATION OF THE EMPIRE

By J. S. Reid, Litt.D., Professor of Ancient
History, Cambridge

xi

TABLE OF CONTENTS

CHAPTER I

CONSTANTINE AND HIS CITY

By H. M. GWATKIN, M.A., Dixie Professor of Ecclesiastical History, Cambridge

CHAPTER II

THE REORGANISATION OF THE EMPIRE

By J. S. REID, Litt.D., Professor of Ancient History, Cambridge

CHAPTER III

CONSTANTINE'S SUCCESSORS TO JOVIAN: AND THE
STRUGGLE WITH PERSIA

By Norman H. Baynes, M.A. Oxon., Barrister-at-Law

CHAPTER IV

THE TRIUMPH OF CHRISTIANITY

By the Rev. T. M. Lindsay, D.D., LL.D., Principal of the
Glasgow College of the United Free Church of Scotland

CHAPTER V

ARIANISM

By Professor Gwatkin

CHAPTER VI

THE ORGANISATION OF THE CHURCH

By C. H. TURNER, M.A., F.B.A., Fellow of Magdalen
College, Oxford

CHAPTER VII

EXPANSION OF THE TEUTONS (TO A.D. 378)

By MARTIN BANG, Ph.D.

CHAPTER VIII

THE DYNASTY OF VALENTINIAN AND THEODOSIUS THE GREAT

By NORMAN H. BAYNES, M.A.

CHAPTER IX

THE TEUTONIC MIGRATIONS, 378-412

By Dr M. MANITIUS, Privatgelehrter in Radebeul bei Dresden

CHAPTER X

TEUTONIC KINGDOMS IN GAUL

(A) The Visigoths to the death of Euric

By Prof. Dr Ludwig Schmidt, Bibliothekar an der
Königl. Bibliothek Dresden

(B) The Franks before Clovis

By M. Christian Pfister, docteur ès lettres, professeur
à la Faculté des lettres de l'Université de Paris

CHAPTER XI

THE SUEVES, ALANS, AND VANDALS IN SPAIN, 409–429
THE VANDAL DOMINION IN AFRICA, 429–533

By Dr Ludwig Schmidt

CHAPTER XII

(A) THE ASIATIC BACKGROUND

By T. PEISKER, Ph.D., Privatdocent and Librarian, Graz

(B) ATTILA

By Dr LUDWIG SCHMIDT

CHAPTER XIII

(A) ROMAN BRITAIN

By F. J. HAVERFIELD, LL.D., F.B.A., Camden Professor
of Ancient History, Oxford

CHAPTER XIV

ITALY AND THE WEST, 410–476

By ERNEST BARKER, M.A., Fellow of St John's College,
Oxford

CHAPTER XV

THE KINGDOM OF ITALY UNDER ODOVACAR AND THEODORIC

By MAURICE DUMOULIN, Professeur de l'Université de France

CHAPTER XVI

THE EASTERN PROVINCES FROM ARCADIUS TO ANASTASIUS

By E. W. BROOKS, M.A., King's College, Cambridge

CHAPTER XVII

RELIGIOUS DISUNION IN THE FIFTH CENTURY

By ALICE GARDNER, Lecturer of Newnham College, Cambridge

CHAPTER XVIII

MONASTICISM

By Dom E. C. BUTLER, M.A., Hon. D.Litt. Dublin,
Abbot of Downside Abbey

CHAPTER XIX

SOCIAL AND ECONOMIC CONDITIONS OF THE ROMAN EMPIRE IN THE FOURTH CENTURY

By PAUL VINOGRADOFF, Hon. D.C.L., F.B.A., Corpus
Professor of Jurisprudence, Oxford

CHAPTER XX

THOUGHTS AND IDEAS OF THE PERIOD

By the Rev. H. F. STEWART, B.D., Fellow of St John's College, Cambridge

CHAPTER XXI

EARLY CHRISTIAN ART

By W. R. LETHABY, Architect, Professor of Design, Royal College of Art

LIST OF BIBLIOGRAPHIES

xxii

THE

CAMBRIDGE
MEDIEVAL HISTORY

VOLUME I

CHAPTER I

CONSTANTINE AND HIS CITY

THE first question that has to be considered in laying down the plan of a Medieval History is, Where to begin? Where shall we draw the line that separates it from Ancient History? Some would fix it at the death of Domitian, others at that of Marcus. Some would come down to Constantine, to the death of Theodosius, to the great barbarian invasion of 406, or to the end of the Western Empire in 476; and others again would go on to Gregory I, or even as late as Charlemagne. There is even something to be said for beginning with Augustus, or at the destruction of Jerusalem, though perhaps these epochs are not seriously proposed. However, they all have their advantages. If for example we consider only the literary merit of the historians, we must draw the line after Tacitus; and if we fix our eyes on the feud of Roman and barbarian, we cannot stop till the coronation of Charlemagne. Curiously enough, the epoch usually laid down at the end of the Western Empire in 476, is precisely the one for which there is least to be said. We should do better than this by dividing in the middle of the Gothic War (535–553). We have in quick succession the closing of the Schools of Athens, the Code of Justinian, the great siege of Rome, and the abolition of the consulship. The Rome which Belisarius delivered was still the Rome of the Caesars, while the Rome which Narses entered sixteen years later is already the Rome of the popes. It is the same in Gaul. The remains of the old civilization still found under the sons of Clovis are mostly obliterated in the next generation. Procopius witnessed as great a revolution as did Polybius.

But even this would not be satisfactory. We cannot cut in two the Gothic War and the reign of Justinian; and in any case we can draw no sharp division after Constantine without ignoring the greatest power of the world — that Eastern Roman Empire which carried down the old Graeco-Roman civilisation almost to the end of the Middle Ages. In truth, the precise beginning of Medieval History is as indefinite as the precise beginning of the fog. There is no point between Augustus and Charlemagne where we can say, The old is finished, the new not yet

begun.   Choose where we will, medieval elements are traceable before it,
ancient elements after it.   Thus Theodoric's government of Italy is on
the old lines, while the Frankish invasion of Gaul belongs to the new
order.   If in the present work we begin with Constantine, we do not
mean that there is any break in history at this point, though we see
important changes in the adoption of Christianity and the fixing of the
government in the form it retained for centuries.   The chief advantage
of choosing this epoch is that as the medieval elements were not strong
before the fourth century, we shall be able to trace nearly the whole of
their growth without encroaching too much on Ancient History.   At
the same time, we shall hold ourselves free to trace them back as far as
may be needful, and to point out the ancient elements as late as they
may appear.

We begin with an outline of Constantine's life.   Its significance we
can discuss later.

Flavius Valerius Constantinus was born at Naissus in Dacia, about
the year 274.   His father Constantius was already a man of some mark,
though still in the lower stages of the career which brought him to the
purple.   On his father's side Constantius belonged to the great families
of Dardania, the hilly province north of Macedonia, while his mother
was a niece of the emperor Claudius Gothicus.   But Constantine's own
mother Helena was a woman of low rank from Drepanum in Bithynia,
though there is no reason to doubt   d the legal (and quite
moral) position of *concubina* or mor   to Constantius.

Of Constantine's early years we know only that he had no learned
education; and we may presume from his hesitating Greek that he was
brought up in Latin lands, perhaps partly in Dalmatia, where his father
was at one time governor.   In 293 Constantius was made Caesar, and
practically master of Gaul, with the task assigned him of recovering
Britain from Carausius.   But as a condition of his elevation he was
required to divorce Helena and marry Theodora, a stepdaughter of
Maximian.   Constantine was taken to the court of Diocletian, partly as
a hostage for his father, and partly with a view to a future place for him
in the college of emperors.   So he went with Diocletian to Egypt in
296, and made acquaintance on the way with Eusebius, the future
historian and bishop of Caesarea.   Next year he seems to have seen
service with Galerius against the Persians.   About this time he must
have taken Minervina (most likely as a *concubina*), for her son Crispus
was already a young man in 317.   Early in 303 the Great Persecution
was begun with the demolition of the church at Nicomedia : and there
was a tall young officer looking on with thoughts of his own, like
Napoleon watching the riot of June 1792.

When Diocletian and Maximian abdicated (1 May 305) it was
generally believed that Constantine would be one of the new Caesars.
There was reason for this belief.   He had been betrothed to Fausta the

daughter of Maximian as far back as 293, when she was a mere child; and daughters of emperors were not common enough to be thrown away on outsiders. Moreover, money had recently been coined at Alexandria with the inscription CONSTANTINUS CAESAR. But at the last moment Diocletian passed him over. Perhaps he was over-persuaded by Galerius: more likely he was reserving him to succeed his father in Gaul. After this, however, the court of Galerius was no place for Constantine. Presently he managed to escape, and joined his father at Boulogne. After a short campaign in Caledonia, Constantius died at York (25 July 306) and the army hailed Constantine Augustus. He was a good officer, the sons of Theodora were only boys, and the army of Britain (always the most mutinous in the Empire) had no mind to wait for a new Caesar from the East. Its chief mover was Crocus the Alemannic king: and this would seem to be the first case of a barbarian king as a Roman general, and also the first case of barbarian action in the election of an emperor. Willingly or unwillingly, Galerius recognised Constantine, though only as Caesar. It mattered little: he had the power, and the title came a couple of years later.

Thus Constantine succeeded his father in Gaul and Britain. We hear little of his administration during the next six years (306–312), but we get a general impression that he was a good ruler, and careful of his people. Such fighting as he had to do was of the usual sort against the Franks, mostly inside the Rhine, and against the Alemanni and the Bructeri beyond it. The war however was merciless, for even heathen feeling was shocked when he gave barbarian kings to the beasts, along with their followers by thousands at a time. But Gaul had never recovered from the great invasions (254–285) and his remissions of taxation gave no permanent relief to the public misery. In religion he was of course heathen; but he grew more and more monotheistic, and the Christians always counted him friendly like his father.

The last act of Galerius (Apr. 311) was an edict of toleration for the Christians. It was not encumbered with any "hard conditions,"[1] but it was given on the heathen principle that every god is entitled to the worship of his own people, whereas the persecution hindered the Christians from rendering that worship. A few days after this Galerius died. There were now four emperors. Constantine held Gaul and Britain, Maxentius Italy, Spain and Africa, while Licinius (more properly Licinian) ruled Illyricum, Greece and Thrace, and Maximin Daza (or Daia) held everything beyond the Bosphorus. Their political alliances were partly determined by their geographical position, Constantine reaching over Maxentius to Licinius, while Maximin reached over Licinius to Maxentius; partly also by their relation to the Christians, for this was now the immediate question of practical politics. Constantine was

---

[1] One of the toleration laws alluded to by Licinius was so encumbered; but this appears to have been the rescript of Maximin Daza a little later.

CH. I.

friendly to them, and Licinius had never been an active persecutor; whereas Maximin was a cruel and malicious enemy, and Maxentius, standing as he did for Rome, could not but be hostile to them. So Maxentius was to crush Constantine, and Maximin to deal with Licinius.

Constantine did not wait to be crushed. Breaking up his camp at Colmar, he pushed rapidly across the Alps. In a cavalry fight near Turin, the Gauls overcame the formidable *cataphracti* — horse and rider clad in mail — of Maxentius. Then straight to Verona, where in Ruricius Pompeianus he found a foeman worthy of his steel. Right well did Pompeianus defend Verona; and if he escaped from the siege, it was only to gather an army for its relief. Then another great battle. Pompeianus was killed, Verona surrendered, and Constantine made straight for Rome. Still Maxentius gave no sign. He had baffled invasion twice before by sitting still in Rome, and Constantine could not have besieged the city with far inferior forces. At the last moment Maxentius came out a few miles, and offered battle (28 Oct. 312) at Saxa Rubra. A skilful flank march of Constantine forced him to fight with the Tiber behind him, and the Mulvian bridge for his retreat. His Numidians fled before the Gaulish cavalry, the Praetorian Guard fell fighting where it stood, and the rest of the army was driven head-long into the river. Maxentius perished in the waters, and Constantine was master of the West.

This short campaign — the most brilliant feat of arms since Aurelian's time — was an epoch for Constantine himself. To it belongs the story of the Shining Cross. Somewhere between Colmar and Saxa Rubra he saw in the sky one afternoon a bright cross with the words *Hoc vince*, and the army saw it too; and in a dream that night Christ bade him take it for his standard. So Constantine himself told Eusebius, and so Eusebius recorded it in 338; and there is no reason to suspect either the one or the other of deceit. The evidence of the army is in any case not worth much; but that of Lactantius [1] in 314 and of the heathen Nazarius in 321 puts it beyond reasonable doubt that something of the sort did happen. But we need not therefore set it down for a miracle. The cross observed may very well have been a halo, such as Whymper saw when he came down after the accident on the Matterhorn in 1865 — three crosses for his three lost companions. The rest is no more than can be accounted for by Constantine's imagination, inflamed as it must have been by the intense anxiety of the unequal contest. Yet after all, the cross was not an exclusively Christian symbol. The action was am-biguous, like most of Constantine's actions at this period of his life. He was quite clear about monotheism; but he was not equally clear about the difference between Christ and the Unconquered Sun. The Gauls had fought of old beneath the Sun-god's cross of light: so while the Christians

---

[1] Lactantius is not discredited by the similar vision he gives to Licinius. Why should not Licinius take a hint from Constantine, and have a vision of his own?

saw in the labarum the cross of Christ, the heathens in the army would only be receiving an old standard back again. Such was the origin of the Byzantine *Labarum.*

One enduring monument of the victory is the triumphal arch still standing at Rome, dedicated to him by the Senate and People in 315. Its inscription recites how INSTINCTU DIVINITATIS he inflicted just punishment on the tyrant and all his party. The expression has been set down as a later correction of some such heathen form as NUTU IOVIS O. M.: but it is certainly original, and must express Constantine's declared belief — for we may trust the Senate and the other panegyrists for knowing what was likely to please him.

Constantine remained two months in Rome, leaving in the first days of 313 for Milan, where he gave his sister Constantia in marriage to Licinius, and conferred with him on policy generally, and on the hostile attitude of Maximin in particular. That ruler had not published the edict of Galerius, but merely sent a circular to the officials that actual persecution was to be stopped for the present. A few months later (about Nov. 311) he resumed it, with less bloodshed and more statesmanship. It was far more skilfully planned than any that had gone before. Maximin's endeavour was to stir up the municipalities against the Christians, to organise a rival church of heathenism, and to give a definitely antichristian bias to education. Even the fall of Maxentius had drawn from him only a rescript so full of inconsistencies that neither heathens nor Christians could make head or tail of it, except that Maximin was a prodigious liar. He even denied that there had been any persecution during his reign. At all events, this was not the complete change of policy needed to save him. Constantine and Licinius saw their advantage, and issued from Milan a new edict of toleration. Its text is lost,[1] but it went far beyond the edict of Galerius. For the first time in history, the principle of universal toleration was officially laid down — that every man has a right to choose his religion and to practise it in his own way without any discouragement from the State. No doubt it was laid down as a political move, for neither Constantine nor Licinius kept to it. Constantine tried to crush Donatists and Arians, and Licinius fell back even from toleration of Christians. Still the old heathen principle, that no man may worship gods who are not on the official list, was rejected for the present, and toleration became the general law of the Empire, till the time of Theodosius.

The wedding festivities were rudely interrupted by the news that Maximin had made a sudden attack without waiting for the end of the

---

[1] The issue of the edict seems proved by Eus. *H. E.* x. 5 τῶν βασιλικῶν (incl. Constantine) διατάξεων. Its purport is recited in the *Litterae Licinii* which is the form in which it reached Maximin's dominions, and is therefore given in its place by Eus. and Lact.

winter, and met with brilliant success, capturing Byzantium and pushing on towards Hadrianople. There, however, Licinius met him with a very inferior force, and completely routed him (30 April 313). Maximin fled to Nicomedia, and soon found that it would be as much as he could do to hold the line of Mount Taurus. Now he had no choice — the Christians were strong in Egypt and Syria, and must be conciliated at any cost. So he issued a new edict, explaining that the officials had committed many oppressions very painful to a benevolent ruler like himself; and now, to make further mistakes impossible, he lets all men know that everyone is free to practise whatever religion he pleases. Maximin gives the same liberty as Constantine and Licinius — he could not safely offer less — but he states no principle of toleration. However, it was too late now. Maximin died in the summer, and Licinius issued a rescript carrying out the decisions of Milan, and restoring confiscated property to "the corporation of the Christians." It was published at Nicomedia 13 June 313. Constantine sent out similar letters in the West.

The defeat of Maximin ends the long contest of Church and State begun by Nero. Former persecutions had died out of themselves, and even Gallienus had only restored the confiscated property; but now the Christians had gained full legal recognition, of which they were never again deprived. Licinius and Julian might devise annoyances and connive at outrages, and work the administration in a hostile spirit; but they never ventured to revoke the Edict of Milan. Heathenism was still strong in its associations with Greek philosophy and culture, with Roman law and social order, and its moral character stood higher than it had done. It hardly looked like a beaten enemy: yet such it was. Its last real hope was gone.

Religious peace was assured, but the unity of the Empire was not yet restored. Constantine and Licinius were both ambitious, and war between them was only a question of time. They were not unequally matched. If Constantine had the victorious legions of Gaul, Licinius ruled the East from the frontier of Armenia to that of Italy, so that he was master of the Illyrian provinces, which furnished the best soldiers of the Roman army. Every emperor from Claudius to Licinius himself was an Illyrian, except Tacitus and Carus. And if Constantine had done a splendid feat of arms, Licinius was a fine soldier too, and (with all his personal vices) not less careful of his subjects.

Constantine was called away from Milan by some incursions of the Franks, who kept him busy during the summer of 313. When things were more settled, he proposed to institute a middle domain for his other brother-in-law Bassianus. The plan seems to have been that while Constantine gave him Italy, Licinius should give him Illyricum. Licinius frustrated it by engaging Bassianus in a plot for which he was put to death, and then refused to give up to Constantine his agent Senecio, the brother of Bassianus.   This meant war.   Constantine took the offensive as he had done before, pushing into Pannonia with no more than 20,000 men, and attacking Licinius at Cibalae, where he was endeavouring to cover Sirmium.   He had 35,000 against him, but a hard-fought battle (8 Oct. 314) ended in a complete victory, and the capture of Sirmium.   Licinius fled towards Hadrianople, deepening the quarrel on the way by giving the rank of Caesar to his Illyrian general Valens.   A new army was collected; but another great battle on the Mardian plain was indecisive.   Constantine won the victory; but Licinius and Valens were able to take up a threatening position in his rear at Beroea.   So peace had to be made.   First Valens was sacrificed : then Licinius gave up Illyricum from the Danube to the extremity of Greece, retaining in Europe only Thrace, which, however, in those days reached north to the Danube.   So things settled down.   Constantine returned to Rome in the summer to celebrate his Decennalia (25 July 315), and in 317 the succession was secured by the nomination of Caesars, Crispus and Constantine the sons of Constantine, and Licinianus the son of Licinius.   Crispus was grown up, but Constantine was a baby.

The treaty might be hollow, but it kept the peace for nearly eight years.   If Constantine was evidently the stronger, Licinius was still too strong to be rashly attacked.   So each went his own way.   It soon appeared which was the better statesman.   Constantine drew nearer to the Christians, while Licinius drifted into persecution, devising annoyances enough to make them enemies but not enough to make them harmless.   Thus Constantine allows manumission in church, judges the Donatists, closes the courts on Sundays, loads the churches with gifts, and, at last (May 323),[1] frees Christians from all pagan ceremonies of state.   Licinius drove the Christians from his court, forbade meetings of bishops, and meddled vexatiously with their worship.   This gave the war something of a religious character; but its occasion was not religious.   The Goths had been pretty quiet since Aurelian had settled them in Dacia.   It was not till 322 that Rausimod their king crossed the Danube on a foray.   Constantine drove them back, chased them beyond the Danube, slew Rausimod, and settled thousands of Gothic serfs in the adjacent provinces.   But in the pursuit he crossed the territory of Licinius; and this led to war.   Constantine's army was 130,000 strong, and his son Crispus had a fleet of 200 sail, in the Piraeus.   Licinius awaited him with 160,000 men near Hadrianople, while his admiral Amandus was to hold the Hellespont with 350 ships.   There was no idea of using the fleet to take Constantine in the rear.

[1] Recent opinion (Jonquet, Pears) seems to place the campaign in 324.   The question is difficult: but the Council of Nicaea seems firmly fixed for 325, the preparations for it cannot have begun till the war was ended, and no room seems left for them if the battle of Chrysopolis is placed in Sept. 324.

After some difficult manœuvres, Constantine won the first battle (3 July 323), but was brought to a stop before the walls of Byzantium. Licinius was safe there, so long as he held the sea; so he chose Martinianus his *magister officiorum* for the new Augustus of the West. Meanwhile Constantine strengthened his fleet, and his son Crispus completely defeated Amandus in the Hellespont. Licinius left Byzantium to defend itself — it had held out two years against Severus — and prepared to maintain the Asiatic shore. Constantine left Byzantium on one side and landed near Chrysopolis, where he found the whole army of Licinius drawn up to meet him. The battle of Chrysopolis (18 or 20 Sept. 323) was decisive. Licinius fled to Nicomedia, and presently Constantia came out to ask for her husband's life. It was granted, and Constantine confirmed his promise with an oath. Nevertheless Licinius was put to death in October 325 on a charge of treasonable intrigue. The charge is unlikely: but Licinius was quite capable of it, and his execution does not seem to have estranged Constantia from her brother. But perhaps the matter is best connected with the family tragedy which we shall come to presently.

As a general, Constantine ranks high among the emperors. Good soldiers as they mostly were, none but Severus and Aurelian could boast of any such career of victory as had brought Constantine from the shores of Britain to the banks of the Tiber and the walls of Byzantium. But after the "crowning mercy" of Chrysopolis there was no more fighting, except with the Goths. The last fourteen years of Constantine (323–337) were years of peace: and the first question which then confronted him was the question of religion. By what road did he approach Christianity, and how far did he come on the journey?

Two fables may be dismissed at once — the heathen fable told by Zosimus in the fifth century, that the Christians were complaisant when the philosophers refused to absolve him for the murder of his son Crispus; and the papal fable of the eighth century, that he was healed of leprosy by Pope Sylvester, and thereupon gave him dominion over "the palace, the city of Rome, and the entire West." These legends are summarily refuted by the fact that he was baptised in 337, not as they tell us in 326. Turning now to history, we have no reason to suppose that he owed Christian impressions to his mother's teaching: but Constantius was an eclectic of the better sort, and a man of some culture; and his memory contrasted well with that of his colleagues. Constantine seems to have begun where his father left off, as more or less monotheistic and averse to idols, and more or less friendly to the Christians; and all these things grew upon him. The last of them may not have meant much at first, for even hostile emperors like Severus and Diocletian had sense enough to keep on good terms with the Christians when they were not prepared to crush them. But Constantine was drawn to them personally as well as politically; by his pure life and genuine humanity as well as by his shrewd statesmanship. Their lofty monotheism and austere morals attracted the man, their strong organi-sation arrested the attention of the ruler. When Diocletian threw down his challenge to the Church, he made religion the urgent question of the time : and the persecution was a visible failure before Constantine was well settled in Gaul. If Diocletian had failed to crush the Church, others were not likely to succeed. Maximin or Licinius might hark back to the past; but Constantine saw clearly that the Empire would have to make some sort of terms with the Church, so that the only question was how far it would be needful or safe to go. For the moment, a little friendliness to the Gaulish bishops was enough to secure the good will of the Christians all over the Empire. Then came the wars of 312–3, which forced on Constantine and Licinius the championship of the Christians, and made it plain good policy to give them full legal toleration. Licinius stopped there, and Constantine did not make up his mind without anxiety. The God of the Christians had shown great power, and might be the best protector; and in any case a firm alliance with their strong hierarchy would not only remove a great danger, but give the very help which the Empire needed. On the other hand, it was a serious thing to break with the past and brave the terrors of heathen magic. Moreover, the Christians were a minority even in the East, and he could not openly go over to them without risk of a pagan reaction. So he moved cautiously. Christianity differed forsooth very little from the better sort of heathenism. They could both be brought under the broad shield of monotheism, if the heathens would give up their idols and immoral worships, and the Christians would not insist too rudely on that awkward doctrine of the deity of Christ. On these terms the lion of Christianity might lie down with the lamb of Eclecticism, and the guileless emperor would be the little child to lead them both.

The problem of Church and State was new, for the old religion of Rome was never more than a department of the State, and the worship-pers of Isis and Mithras readily "conformed to the ceremonies of the Roman people." But when Christianity made a practical distinction between Caesar's things and God's, the relation of Church and State became a difficult question. Constantine handled it with great skill and much success. He not only made the Christians thoroughly loyal, but won the active support of the churches, and obtained such influence over the bishops that they seemed almost willing to sink into a depart-ment of the State. But he forgot one thing. The surface thought of his time, Christian as well as heathen, tended to a vague monotheism which looked on Christ and the sun as almost equally good symbols of the Supreme : and this obscured the deeper conviction of the Christians that the deity of Christ is as essential as the unity of God. After all, Christianity is not a monotheistic philosophy, but a life in Christ.

When this conviction asserted itself with overwhelming power at the Council of Nicaea, Constantine gave way with a good grace. As it had been decided at Saxa Rubra that the Empire was to fight beneath the cross of God, so now it was decided at Nicaea that the cross was to be the cross of Christ, and not the Sun-god's cross of light.

We may doubt whether Constantine took in the full meaning of the decision: but at any rate it meant that the Christians refused to be included with others in a monotheistic state religion. If the Empire was to have their full friendship, it must become definitely Christian: and this is the goal to which Constantine seems to have looked forward in his later years, though he can hardly have hoped himself to reach it. Heathenism was still strong, and he continued to use vague monotheistic language. Only in his last illness did he feel it safe to throw off the mask and avow himself a Christian. "Let there be no ambiguity," said he, as he asked for baptism; and then he laid aside the purple, and passed away in the white robe of a Christian neophyte (22 May 337).

This would seem to be the general outline of Constantine's religious life and policy. We can now return to the morrow of Chrysopolis, and take it more in detail. Now that he was master of the Empire, he made his alliance with the Christians as close as he could without abandoning the official neutrality of his monotheism. His attitude is well shown by his coins. *Mars* and *Genius P. R.* disappear after Saxa Rubra, or at latest by 317: *Sol invictus* by 315, or at any rate 323. Coins of *Iuppiter Aug.* seem to have been struck only for Licinius. Later on, the heathen inscriptions are replaced by phrases as neutral as the cross itself, like *Beata tranquillitas* or *Providentia Augg.*, or *Instinctu Divinitatis* on his triumphal arch at Rome. His laws keep pace with the coins. In form they are mostly neutral; but they show an increasing leaning to Christianity. Thus his edict for the observance of "the venerable day of the Sun" only raised it to the rank of the heathen *feriae* by closing the law-courts; and the Latin prayer he imposed on the army (the first case known of prayer in an unknown tongue) is quite indeterminate as between Christ and Jupiter. So too when before 316 he sanctioned manumissions in churches, he was only taking a hint from the manumissions in certain temples. Yet again, when in 313 (and by later law) he exempted the clergy of the Catholic Church — not those of the sects — from the decurionate and other burdens, he gave them only the privileges already enjoyed by some of the heathen priests and teachers. But the relief was great enough to cause an ungodly rush for holy Orders, and with it such a loss of taxpayers that in 320 he had to forbid the ordination of anyone qualified for the *curia* of his city. None but the poor (and an occasional official) could now be ordained, and those only to fill vacancies caused by death. The second limitation may not have been enforced, but the first remained. To save the revenue, the Church was debased at a stroke.

Other laws however lean more to a side, like the edict of 319 which threatens to burn the Jews if they stone "a convert to the worship of God." No doubt such converts needed protection; and Roman law was not squeamish about burning criminals, if they were of low rank. Upon the whole, this policy of official neutrality and personal favour powerfully stimulated the growth of the churches. The time-servers were all Christians now, and Eusebius plainly denounces their "unspeak- able hypocrisy." At least in later years, Constantine himself had to rebuke bishops for flattery. The defeat of Licinius enabled him to come forward more openly as the patron of the churches. His letter to the provincials of the Empire (Eusebius naturally gives the copy which went to Palestine) begins with high praise of the confessors and strong denunciation of the persecutors, whose wickedness is shown by their miserable ends. They would have destroyed the republic, if the Divinity had not raised up me, Constantine, from the far West of Britain to destroy them. He then restores rank and property to all the victims of persecution in the islands, the mines, and the houses of forced labour, and finishes with an earnest exhortation to the worship of the one true God.

But after all, the Church was not quite what Constantine wanted it to be. He was not more attracted to it by its lofty monotheism than by the imposing unity which promised new life to the weary State. For six hundred years the world had been in quest of a universal religion. Stoicism was no more than a philosophy for the few, the worship of the emperor was debased by officialism, and by this time quite outworn, and even Mithraism had never shown such living power as Christianity. Here then was something that could realise the religious side of the Empire in a nobler form than Augustus or Hadrian had ever dreamed of — a universal Church that could stand beside the universal Empire and worthily support its labours for the peace and welfare of the world. But for this purpose unity was essential. If the Church was divided against itself, it could not help the Empire. Worse than this; it could hardly be divided against itself without being also divided against the Empire. One of the parties was likely to appeal to the emperor; and then he would have to decide between them and make an enemy of the defeated party; and if he tried to enforce his decision, they were likely to resist him as stubbornly as the whole Church had resisted the heathen emperors. This would bring back the whole difficulty of the perse- cutions, though possibly on a smaller scale. To put it shortly, the Christians had a conscience in matters of religion, and sometimes mis- took self-will for conscience.

Constantine had experience of Christian self-will in Africa soon after the defeat of Maxentius. When Diocletian commanded the Christians to give up their sacred books, all parties agreed in refusing to obey. Those who did obey were called *traditores*. But the officers did not

always care what books they took : might apocryphal books be given
up ?   So thought Mensurius of Carthage, while others counted it
apostasy to give up any books at all.   The controversy became acute at
the death of Mensurius in 311, when Felix of Aptunga consecrated his
successor Caecilian.   But that right was claimed by Secundus of Tigisis,
the senior bishop of Numidia, who consecrated a rival bishop of Carthage.
It was some time before the Donatists (as they soon came to be called)
got their position clear.   They held that Felix was a *traditor*, that the
ministrations of a *traditor* are null and void, and that a church which
has communion with a *traditor* is apostate.

After the battle of Saxa Rubra Constantine sent money to Caecilian
for the clergy "of the catholic church"; and as he "had heard that
some evil-disposed persons were troubling them," he directed Caecilian
to refer them to the civil authorities for punishment.   Thereupon they
appealed to him.   Constantine seems to have contemplated a small
court to try the case — Miltiades of Rome, three Gaulish bishops, and
apparently the archdeacon of Rome : but a small council met instead
(Oct. 313) at Rome, which pronounced for Caecilian.   The Donatists
were furious, and appealed again.   This time Constantine summoned as
many bishops as he could, directing each to bring so many clergy and
servants with him, and giving him power to use the state post (*cursus
publicus*) for the journey.   So a large council of the Western churches
met at Arles in August 314 (possibly 315).   Even Britain sent bishops
from London, York, and some other place.   It destroyed the Donatist
contention by deciding that Felix was not a *traditor*.   It also settled
some more outstanding controversies, in favour of the Roman date of
Easter, and the Roman custom of not repeating heretical baptism, if it
had been given in the name of the Trinity.   The decisions were sent to
Sylvester of Rome for circulation — not for confirmation.   We can recognise in Arles the pattern of the Nicene Council.   Still the Donatists
were not satisfied.   They asked the emperor to decide the matter
himself, and he unwillingly consented.   He heard them at Milan
(Nov. 316) and once more decided against them.   Then they turned
round and said, What business has the emperor to meddle with the
Church ?   A vigorous persecution was begun, but with small success.
A band of Donatist fanatics called *Circumcelliones* ranged the country,
committing disorders and defying the authorities to make martyrs of
them.   Even in 317 Constantine ordered that their outrages were not
to be retaliated; and when they sent him a message in 321 that they
would in no way communicate with "that scoundrel, his bishop," he
stopped the persecution as useless, and frankly gave them toleration.
Africa was fairly quiet for the rest of his reign.

After the defeat of Licinius, Constantine found several disputes in
the Eastern churches.   The old Easter question was still unsettled, the
Meletian schism was dividing Egypt, and there was no knowing how far

the Arian controversy would spread. Unity must be restored at once, and that by the old plan of calling a council. The churches had long been in the habit of conferring together when difficulties arose· They could refuse to recognise an unsatisfactory bishop; and *cir.* 269 a council ventured to depose Paul of Samosata, and Aurelian had enforced its decision. The weak point of this method was that rival councils could be got up, so that every local quarrel had an excellent chance of becoming a general controversy. Arianism in particular was setting council against council. Constantine determined to go a step beyond these local meetings. As he had summoned the Western bishops to Arles, so now he summoned all the bishops of Christendom. If he could bring them to a decision, it was not likely to be disputed; and in any case he could safely give it the force of law. An oecumenical council would be a grand demonstration, not only of the unity of the Church, but of its close alliance with the Empire. So he issued invita_ tions to all Christian bishops to meet him at Nicaea in Bithynia in the summer of 325, to make a final end of all the disputes which rent the unity of Christendom. The programme was even wider than at Arles; but the Donatists were not included in it. Constantine could let sleeping dogs lie. We note here the choice of Nicaea for its auspicious name — the city of victory — and convenience of access; and we see in it one of many signs that the true centre of the Empire was settling down somewhere near the Bosphorus.

We need not closely analyse the imposing list of bishops present from almost every province of the Empire, with a few from beyond its frontiers in the far East and North. Legend made them 318, the holy number (τιη) of the cross of Jesus. We have lists in sundry languages, none of them giving more than 221 names; but these are known to be incomplete. The actual number may have been near 300. All the thirteen great dioceses of the Empire were represented except Britain and Illyricum, though only single bishops came from Africa, Spain, Gaul and Dacia. Only one came in person from Italy, though two presbyters appeared for the bishop of Rome. So the vast majority came from the Eastern provinces of the Empire. The outsiders were four or five — Theophilus bishop of the Goths beyond the Danube, Cathirius (the name is corrupt) of the Crimean Bosphorus, John the Persian, and Restaces the Armenian, the son of Gregory the Illuminator, with perhaps another Armenian bishop. Eusebius is full of enthusiasm over his majestic roll of churches far and near, from the extremity of Europe to the furthest ends of Asia. It was a day of victory for both the Empire and the Church. The Empire had not only made peace with the stubbornest of its enemies, but been accepted as its protector and guide. The Church had won the greatest of all its victories when Galerius issued his edict of toleration: but its mission to the whole world has never been so vividly embodied as by that august assembly.

CH. I.

We miss half the meaning of the Council if we overlook the tremulous hope and joy of those first years of worldwide victory. Athanasius shows it even more than Eusebius. One thing at least was clear. The new world faced the old, and the spell of the Holy Roman Empire had already begun to work.

Constantine took up at once the position of a moderator. He began by burning unread the budget of complaints against each other which the bishops had presented to him. He then preached them a sermon on unity; and unity was his text all through. He was much more anxious to make the decisions unanimous than to influence them one way or another. His one object was to make an end of division in the churches. So whatever pleased the bishops pleased the emperor too. Easter was fixed according to the custom of Rome and Alexandria for the Sunday after the full moon following the vernal equinox. It is the rule we have now, and though it did not produce complete unity till the lunar cycle was quite settled, it secured that Easter should come after the Passover, for, said Constantine, How can we who are Christians keep the same day as those ungodly Jews? The Meletian schism was peacefully settled — to the disgust of Athanasius in later years — by giving the Meletian clergy a status next to the orthodox, with a right of succession if found worthy. So far well: but the condemnation of Arianism may have been something of a trial to Constantine, who could not quite see why they thought it worth while to be so hot on such a trifling question as the deity of Christ. However that may be, Arianism was politically impossible. He must have known already from Hosius that the West would not accept it, and the first act of the Council meant its almost unanimous rejection by the East. As soon as there was no doubt what the decision would be, he did his best to make it quite unanimous. All the arts of imperial persuasion were tried on the waverers, till in the end only two stubborn recusants remained to be sent into exile.

To some wider aspects of the Council we shall return hereafter. For the moment it may be enough to say that Constantine had won a great success. He had not only got his questions settled, but had himself taken a conspicuous part in settling them. More than this. He had established formal relations, no longer with bishops or groups of bishops, but with a great confederacy of churches. The churches had long been tending to organise themselves on the lines of the Empire, as we see in Cyprian's theories; and now Constantine made the Church an *alter ego* of the State, and gave it a concrete unity of the political sort which it never had before. Henceforth the holy Catholic Church of the creeds was more and more limited to the confederation of churches recognised by the State, so that it only remained to compel all men to come into these, and prevent the formation of any other religious communities. In this way the Church became much more useful to the State, and also perhaps fitter to resist the shock of the barbarian conquests which followed; but surely something was lost in freedom and spirituality, and therefore also in practical morality.

We pass from the Council of Nicaea to a family tragedy. So far Constantine may pass as fairly merciful to the plotters of his own house. Maximian, Bassianus and Licinius had all tried to assassinate him; and if he put to death Bassianus (see p. 8), he had spared Maximian till he plotted again, and so far he had spared Licinius also. But now in a few months from Oct. 325 he puts to death not only Licinius but his own son Crispus and the younger Licinius, then his own wife Fausta, and then a number of his friends. The facts are certain, but their exact meaning is obscure. It must however be noticed that the dynastic policy of Diocletian had given a new political importance to members of an imperial family. The widows of the third century emperors fall into obscurity; but the widow of Galerius is first sought in marriage by Maximin Daza, then executed by Licinius, who also put to death the children of Severus, Daza and Galerius. Now Constantine married twice; and there may well have been a bitter division in his family. Minervina was the mother of Crispus, whom we have seen greatly distinguishing himself in the war with Licinius: and there seems no serious doubt that the three younger sons were children of Fausta, though the eldest of them was not born till 315–6, eight years after her marriage. So we come to the questions we cannot answer. Was Constantine jealous of his eldest son, or anxious to get him out of the way of the others? Or was Crispus a plotter justly put to death? And how came Fausta to share his fate a little later? They are not likely to have been accomplices in a plot or connected by a guilty passion, though the story of Zosimus is not impossible, that she accused him falsely, and was herself put to death for it when Helena convicted her. We have not material enough for any decided opinion. The worst point, it may be, against Constantine is that he did not spare the young Licinius. If he was the son of Constantia, he cannot have been more than twelve years old. But the allusions to him suggest that he was something more than a boy, and we know that Constantia was on the best of terms with her brother when she died a couple of years later. If Constantine suspected the elder Licinius, the new sultanism would involve the younger in his fate; and if Crispus had married Helena his daughter, suspicion might attach to him too. Fausta's fate is the mystery. Or was Constantine more or less out of his mind that winter, as despots occasionally are? One or two of his laws may point that way, and the possibility may help to explain a good deal.

Constantine kept his Vicennalia at Rome in the summer of 326. It was an unhappy visit, even if the domestic tragedy had already taken place. Rome was the focus of heathenism, and of Roman pride. She expected to see her sovereigns at the ceremonies, and to treat them with something of republican familiarity. Constantine scandalised her with his Eastern pomp, and gave deep offence to the senate and people by refusing to join the immemorial procession of the knights of Rome to the Capitol.   When he left the city in September, he left it for ever.

Rome indeed had long ceased to be a good capital.   It was too far from the frontier for military purposes, too full of republican survivals for such sultans as the emperors had now become, too heathen for Christian Caesars.   So Maximian held his court at Milan, while Diocletian gradually shifted his chief resort eastward from Sirmium to Nicomedia.   There were many signs now that the seat of empire ought to be somewhere near the Bosphorus.   The chief dangers had always come from the Danube and the Euphrates; and about the Bosphorus was the only point which commanded both.   If these were watched by the emperor himself, the Rhine might be left in charge of a Caesar. This was much the best course for the present; but in the long run the problem was insoluble.   The Rhine and the Danube might be guarded, or the Danube and the Euphrates; but now that Rome had failed to make a solid nation of her empire, she could not permanently guard all three together.   Sooner or later it must come to a choice between the Rhine and the Euphrates, between Italy and Greece, between Europe and Asia.   Constantine is not likely to have seen clearly all this; but he did see that he commanded more important countries from the Bosphorus than he could from Rome or Milan.   These might control the Latin West and the upper Danube; but at the Bosphorus he had at his feet the Greek world from Taurus to the Balkans, flanked northward by the warlike peoples of Illyricum, and eastward by the great barbarian fringe of Egypt, Syria and Armenia, reaching from the Caucasus to the cataracts of the Nile.   Nobody could yet foresee that by the seventh century nothing but the Greek world would be left.   But where precisely was the new capital to be placed?   Nicomedia would have been Diocletian's city, not Constantine's, and in any case it lay at the far end of a gulf, some fifty miles from the main line of traffic.   Constantine may at one time have dreamed of his own birthplace Naissus, or of Sardica, and at another he began buildings on the site of Troy, before he fixed upon the matchless position of Byzantium.

Europe and Asia are separated by the broad expanses of the Euxine and Aegean seas, together stretching nearly a thousand miles from the Crimea to the mountains of Crete, and in ancient times almost fringed round with Greek cities.   It is not all a land of the vine and the olive, even in Aegean waters, for the Russian wind sweeps over the whole region except in sheltered parts, as where Trebizond is protected by the Caucasus, Philippi by the Rhodope, or Sparta by Taygetus, or where Ionia hides behind the Mysian Olympus and the Trojan Ida.   For all its heat in summer, Constantinople is quite as cold in winter as London, and the western ports of the Black Sea are more cumbered with ice than the north of Norway.   But the Aegean and the Euxine are not a single broad sheet of water.   In the narrows between them the coasts of Europe and Asia draw so close together that we can sail for more than two hundred miles in full view of both continents.   Leaving the warm South behind at Lesbos (Mitylene) we pass from the Aegean to the Propontis (Marmora) by the Hellespont (Dardanelles) a channel of some fifty miles in length to Gallipoli, and two or three miles broad. Then a voyage of a hundred and forty miles through the more open waters of the Propontis brings us to the Bosphorus, which averages only three-quarters of a mile wide, and has a winding course of sixteen miles from Byzantium to the Cyanean rocks at the entrance of the Euxine. It follows that a city on the Propontis is protected north and south by the narrow passages of the Bosphorus and the Dardanelles, and that all traffic between the Aegean and the Euxine must pass its walls.   More. over, the Bosphorus lay more conveniently than the Dardanelles for the ,passage from Europe to Asia.   Thus two of the chief trade-routes of the Roman world crossed each other at Byzantium.

The Megarians may have had some idea of these things when they colonised Chalcedon (B.C. 674) just outside the south end of the Bosphorus, on the Asiatic side of the Propontis.   But the site of Chalcedon has no special advantages, so that its founders became a proverb of blindness for overlooking the superb position of Byzantium across the water, which was not occupied till B.C. 657.   At the south end of the Bosphorus, but on the European side, a blunt triangle is formed by the Propontis and the Golden Horn, a deep inlet of the Bosphorus running seven miles to the north-west.   On the rising ground between them was built the city of Byzantium.   Small as its extent was in Greek times, it played a great part in history.   Its command of the corn trade of the Euxine made it one of the most important strategic positions in the Greek world, so that its capture by Alexander (it had repulsed Philip) was one of the chief steps of his advance to empire.   It formed an early alliance with the Romans, who freed it from its perpetual trouble with the barbarians of Thrace, whom neither peace nor war could keep quiet.   Vespasian (A.D. 73) took away its privileges and threw it into the province of Thrace.   In the civil wars of Septimius Severus it took the side of Pescennius Niger, and held out for two years after Niger's overthrow at Issus in 194.   Severus destroyed its walls, and made it a subject-village of Perinthus.   Caracalla made it a city again, but it was sacked afresh by Gallienus.   Meanwhile the Gothic vikings came sailing past its ruined walls to spread terror all over the Aegean and to the shores of Italy. Under the Illyrian emperors it was fortified again.   Even then it was taken first by Maximin Daza and then by Constantine in the first Licinian war, so that its full significance only came out in the second.   Licinius was a good general, and pivoted the whole war upon it after his defeat at Hadrianople.   He might have held his ground indefinitely, if the destruc-tion of his fleet in the Hellespont had not driven him from Byzantium.

The lesson was not lost on Constantine.   He began the work some
time after his visit to Rome, and pushed it forward with impatience.
He traced his walls to form a base two and a half miles from the apex
of the triangle.   Byzantium stood on a single hill, but he took in five,
and his successors counted seven, according to the number of the hills of
Rome.   The market-place was on the second hill, where his camp had
been during the siege.   He erected great buildings, and gathered works
of art from all parts to adorn it.   The temples of Byzantium remained,
though they were overshadowed by the great cathedral of the Twelve
Apostles.   Some heathen ceremonies also were used, for Constantinople
was the last and greatest colony of Rome, and for centuries retained the
flavour of a Latin city.   He gave it a senate also, and brought over
many of the senators of Rome to be senators of the New Rome — for such
was its official title, though it has always been known as the City of
Constantine.   The Northmen called it simply Miklagard, the Great
City.   It never had much in the way of amphitheatre or beast-fights:
amusement more Christian and humane was provided by a circus and
horse-races.   Its corn largesses were like those of Rome, and the corn of
Egypt was diverted to its use, leaving that of Sicily and Africa for Rome.
The New Rome stood next to the Old in rank and dignity, being
separated from the province of Europa, and governed by proconsuls till
it received a *Praefectus Urbi* like Rome in 359.   The bishop also soon
shook off his dependence on Perinthus, and was recognised as standing
next to the bishop of Rome, "because Constantinople is New Rome," by
the Council of 381.   This ousted Alexandria from the second place, and
the jealousy thereupon arising had important ecclesiastical consequences.
The work was complete, so far as the hasty building would allow, by
the spring of 330: and 11 May of that year is the official date for the
foundation of Constantinople.[1]

It would be hard to overestimate the strength given to the Empire
by the new capital.   So long as the Romans held the sea, the city was
impregnable.   If it was attacked on one side, it could draw supplies
from the other; and when it was attacked on both sides in 628, Persians
and Avars could not join hands across the Bosphorus.   Even when the
command of the sea was lost, it still remained a fortress of uncommon
strength.   So stood Constantinople for more than a thousand years.
Goths and Avars, Persians and Saracens, Bulgarians and Russians,
dashed in vain upon its walls, and even the Turks failed more than
once.   It was often enough taken in civil war by help from within;
but no foreign enemy ever stormed its walls till the Fourth Crusade
(A.D. 1204).   The Arian controversy first made it clear that the heart
of the Empire was in the Greek world, or more precisely in Asiatic
Greece between the Taurus and the Bosphorus; and of the Greek world
Constantinople was the natural capital.   It did not however at once

[1] The *city* will be described in Vol. IV. Ch. xx.

become the regular residence of the emperors. Constantine himself
died in a suburb of Nicomedia, Constantius led a wandering life, Jovian
never reached the city, and Valens in his later years avoided it. Theodosius was the first emperor who made it his usual residence. But the
commercial supremacy of Constantinople was assured from the outset.
The centre of gravity of Asia Minor had shifted northward since the
first century, and the Bosphorus gave an easier passage to Europe than
the Aegean. So the roads which had converged on Ephesus now converged on Constantinople. It dominated the Greek world; and the
Greek world was the solid part of the Empire which resisted all attacks
for ages. The loss was more apparent than real when first the Slavic
lands were torn away, then Syria and Egypt, and lastly Sicily and Italy.
The Empire was never struck in a vital part till the Seljuks rooted out
Greek civilization from the highland of Asia Minor in the eleventh
century. Even after that it was still a conquering power under the
Comnenians and the house of Lascaris; and its fate was never hopeless
till its last firm ground in Asia was destroyed by the corrupt and selfish
policy of Michael Palaeologus.

We know little of Constantine's declining years, except that they
were generally years of peace. The civil wars were ended at Chrysopolis:
now there was not even a pretender, unless we count as such Calocerus
the camel-driver in Cyprus, who was put down without much difficulty,
and duly burned in the market-place of Tarsus (335). If the Rhine was
not entirely quiet, the troubles there were not serious. The Jews, to be
sure, were never loyal, and the Christian Empire had already shown
marked hostility to them. A rising mentioned only by Chrysostom is
most likely a legend: but there may have been already some signs of
the great outbreak put down by Ursicinus in 352. However, upon the
whole there was peace. The old emperor never again took the field in
person. His last war was with the Goths; and that was conducted by
the younger Constantine.

On a broad view, the legions of the Danube faced the Germans in
its upper course and the Goths lower down, with the Sarmatians between
them; and each of these names stands for sundry tribes and groups of
tribes, whose mutual enmities were diligently fostered by the policy of
Rome. In 331 the Sarmatians and the Vandals had somehow got mixed
up together, and suffered a great defeat from the Goths. They asked
Constantine for help, and he was very willing to check the growth of the
Gothic power. Araric the Gothic king replied by carrying the war into
the Roman province of Moesia, from which he was driven out with
heavy loss. The younger Constantine gained a great victory over him,
20 April 332; and when peace was made, the Goths returned to their
old position as servants and allies of Rome. But when the Sarmatians
themselves made inroads on Roman territory, Constantine left them to
their fate. They were soon in difficulties with Geberic the new Gothic

king, and with their own slaves the Limigantes, who drove them out of
their country.   Some fled to the Quadi, some found refuge among the
Gothic tribes, but 300,000 of them sought shelter in the Empire, and
were given lands by Constantine, chiefly in Pannonia.

The most interesting circumstance of the Gothic war is the help
which Constantine received from Cherson, the last of the Greek re-
publics.   It stood where Sebastopol now stands.   The story is told only
by Constantine Porphyrogenitus (911–959), but the learned emperor
was an excellent antiquarian, and used original authorities.   Cherson
and the Goths were old enemies, Rome and Cherson old allies.   The
republic decided for war, and its first magistrate Diogenes struck a
decisive blow by attacking the rear of the Goths.   Cherson received
a rich reward from Constantine, and remained in generally friendly
relations to the Empire till its annexation in 829, and even till its capture
by the Russians in 988.

The settlement of the Danube was the last of Constantine's great
services to the Empire.   The Edict of Milan had removed the standing
danger of Christian disaffection in the East, the defeat of Licinius had
put an end to the civil wars, the reform of the administration completed
Diocletian's work of reducing the army to permanent obedience, the
Council of Nicaea had secured the active alliance of the Christian
churches, the foundation of Constantinople made the seat of power
safe for centuries; and now the consolidation of the northern frontier
seemed to enlist all the most dangerous enemies of Rome in her defence.
The Empire gained three hundred thousand settlers for the wastes of
the Gothic march, and a firm peace of more than thirty years with the
greatest of the northern nations.   Henceforth the Rhine was guarded
by the Franks, the Danube covered by the Goths, and the Euphrates
flanked by the Christian kingdom of Armenia.   The Empire was already
dangerously dependent on barbarian help inside and outside its frontiers;
but the Roman peace never seemed more secure than when the skilful
policy of Constantine had formed its chief barbarian enemies into a
covering ring of friendly client states.

At all events, the years of peace were not a time of healthful
recovery.   The Empire had not gained strength in the long peace of
the Antonines; and it had gone a long way downhill since the second
century.   When Diocletian came to the throne in 284, he found three
great problems before him.   The first was military — how to stop the
continual mutinies which cut off the emperors before they could do their
work.   This he solved, though at the cost of leaving behind him a period
of civil war.   The second was religious — how to deal with the Christians.
Diocletian went wrong on this, and left his mistake to be repaired by
Constantine.   The third and hardest was mainly economic — to restore
the dwindled agriculture, commerce, and population of the Empire.   On
this Diocletian and Constantine went wrong together.   They not only

failed to cure the evil, but greatly increased it.   Not much was gained
by remitting taxes that could not be paid, and settling barbarian
colonists and barbarian serfs in the wasted provinces.   Serious economic
difficulties have moral causes, and there was no radical cure short of a
complete change in the temper of society.   Yet much might have been
done by a permanent reduction of taxation and a reform of its incidence
and of the methods of collection.   Instead of this, the machinery of
government (and its expense) was greatly increased.   The army had to
be held in check by courts of Oriental splendour and a vast establishment of corrupt officials.   We can see the growth of officialism even in the
language, if we compare the Latin words in Athanasius with those in the
New Testament.   So heavier taxes had to be levied from a smaller and
poorer population.   Taxation under the Empire had never been light ; in
the third century it grew heavy, under Diocletian it was crushing, and
in the later years of Constantine the burden was further increased by the
enormous expenditure which built up the new capital like the city in a
fairy tale.   We are within sight of the time when the whole policy of
the government was dictated by dire financial need.   We have already
reached a state of things like that we see in Russia.   The strongest of
the emperors had never been able to put down brigandage ; and now
disorder was rampant in the mountains, and often elsewhere.   The great
army of officials was all-powerful for oppression, and very little controlled by the emperor.   He might displace an official at a moment's
notice, or "deliver him to the avenging flames" ; but he could enforce
no reform against the passive resistance of the officials and the landowners.   So things drifted on from bad to worse.

Nor can we doubt that Constantine himself grew slacker in the years
of peace.   Nature had richly gifted him with sound health, strong
limbs, and a stately presence.   His energy was untiring, his observation
keen, his decision quick.   He was a splendid soldier, and the best general
since Aurelian.   If he had no learned education, he was not without
interest in literature, and in practical statesmanship he may fairly rank
with Diocletian.   His general humanity stands out clear in his laws, for
no emperor ever did more for the slave, the foundling, and the oppressed.
If he began by giving the Frankish kings to the beasts, he went on (325)
to forbid the games of the amphitheatre.   In private life he was chaste
and sober, moderate and pleasant.   Yet he was given to raillery, and
his nearest friends could not entirely trust him.   His ambition was
great, and he was very susceptible to flattery.   So freely was it
ministered to him that he sometimes had to check it himself : but
in his later years he was more or less influenced by unworthy favourites,
as Ablabius and Sopater seem to have been.   No doubt his Christianity
is of itself an offence to Zosimus and Julian, so that we may discount
their charges of sloth and luxury : but upon the whole, the judgment of
Eutropius would seem impartial, that Constantine was a match for the

best emperors in the early part of his reign, and at its end no more than average.

As Constantine had won the Empire, so now he had to dispose of it. Constantine, Constantius, and Constans, his three sons by Fausta, were born in 316, 317, 320, and received the title of Caesar in 317, 323, 333. In 335 their inheritance was marked out. Constantine was to have the Gaulish prefecture, Constantius the Eastern, Constans the Italian and Illyrian. This is the partition actually made after the emperor's death; but for the present it was complicated by some obscure transactions. Constantine had made honourable provision for his half-brothers Delmatius and Julius Constantius, the sons of Theodora, and they never gave him political trouble. Of their sisters, he married Constantia to Licinius, Anastasia to Bassianus and Nepotianus, of whom the second certainly was a great Roman noble, so that they too suffered no disparagement. Basilina also, the wife of Julius Constantius and mother of the emperor Julian, belonged to the great Anician family. Now Delmatius left two sons, Delmatius and Hanniballianus. Of these Delmatius must have been a man of mark, for he held the high office of *magister militum*, and was made Caesar in 335, while Hanniballianus was the husband of Constantine's daughter Constantina. But they had no proper claim to any share in the succession, and we do not know why they were given it. There may have been parties in the palace; and if so, Ablabius is likely to have had a share in the matter, for he was put to death along with them in the massacre which followed Constantine's death. Certain it is that shares were carved out for them from the inheritance of their cousins. Delmatius was to have the Gothic march, while Hanniballianus received Pontus, with the astonishing title of *rex regum* — for no Roman since the Tarquins had ever borne the name ✓ of king.

The strange title may point to some design upon Armenia, for the whole Eastern Question of the day was raised when Persia threatened war. Four emperors in the third century had met with disaster on the Persian frontier, but there had been forty years of peace since the victory of Galerius in 297. The Empire gained Mesopotamia to the Aboras, and the five provinces which covered the southern slopes of the Armenian mountains; and in Armenia itself, Roman supremacy was fully recognised by its great king Tiridates (287–314). If his adoption of Christianity led to a short war with Maximin Daza, it only drew Armenia closer to Constantine. But if the royal house was Christian and leaned on Rome, there was a large heathen party which looked to Persia: and Persia was an aggressive power under Sapor II (309–380). A vigorous persecution of Christians was carried on, and war with Rome was only a question of time. Sapor demanded back the five provinces and attacked Mesopotamia, while a revolution in the palace threw Armenia into his hands.

How much of this was done during Constantine's lifetime is more than we can say : but at all events a Persian war was plain in sight by the spring of 337 ; and a war with Persia was too serious a matter to be left to Caesars like a Frankish foray or a Gothic inroad, so the old emperor prepared to take the field in person. He never set out. Constantine fell sick soon after Easter, and when the sickness grew upon him, he took up his abode at Ancyrona, a suburb of Nicomedia. As his end drew near, he received the imposition of hands, for up to that time he had not been even a catechumen. He then applied for baptism, explaining that he had hoped some day to receive it in the waters of the Jordan like the Lord himself. After the ceremony he laid aside the purple, and passed away in stainless white (22 May 337). As all his sons were absent, the government was carried on for three months in the dead emperor's name, till they had made their arrangements, and the soldiers had slaughtered almost the entire house of Theodora. Constantine was buried on the spot he had himself marked out in the cathedral of the Twelve Apostles in his own imperial city. The Greek Church still calls him ἰσαπόστολος — an equal of the Apostles.

CHAPTER II

THE REORGANISATION OF THE EMPIRE

IT is natural to think of Diocletian as the projector and of Constantine as the completer of a new system of government for the Roman Empire, which persisted with mere changes of detail until it was laid in ruins by the barbarians. But in reality the imperial institutions from the time of Augustus onwards had passed through a course of continuous development. Diocletian did but accelerate processes which had been in operation from the Empire's earliest days, and Constantine left much for his successors to accomplish. Still these two great organisers did so far change the world which they ruled as to be rightly styled the founders of a new type of monarchy. We will first sketch rapidly the most striking aspects of this altered world, and then consider them one by one somewhat more closely. But our survey must be in the main of a general character, and many details, especially when open to doubt, must be passed over. In particular, the minutiae of chronology, which in this region of history are specially difficult to determine, must often be disregarded.

The ideal of a balance of power between the Princeps and the Senate, which Augustus dangled before the eyes of his contemporaries, was never approached in practice. From the first the imperial constitution bore within it the seed of autocracy, and the plant was not of slow growth. The historian Tacitus was not far wrong when he described Augustus as having drawn to himself all the functions which in the Republic had belonged to magistrates and to laws. The founder of the Empire had studied well the art of concealing his political art, but the pressure of his hand was felt in every corner of the administration. Each princeps was as far above law as he chose to rise, so long as he did not strain the endurance of the Senate and people to the point of breaking. When that point was passed there was the poor consolation of refusing him his apotheosis, or of branding with infamy his memory. As the possibility of imperial interference was ever present in every section of the vast machine of government, all concerned in its working were anxious to secure themselves by obtaining an order from above. This anxiety is conspicuous in the letters written by Pliny to his master Trajan. Even those emperors who were most citizen-like (*civiles* as the phrase went) were carried away by the tide. Tacitus exhibits the Senate as eagerly pressing Tiberius to permit the enlargement of his powers — Tiberius who regarded every precept of Augustus as a law for himself. The so-called *lex regia Vespasiani* shews how constantly the admitted authority of the emperor advanced by the accumulation of precedents. Pliny gave Trajan credit for having reconciled the Empire with "liberty" ; but "liberty" had come to mean little more than orderly and benevolent administration, free from cruel caprice, with some external deference paid to the Senate. Developed custom made the rule of Marcus Aurelius greatly more despotic than that of Augustus. Even the emperors of the third century who, like Severus Alexander, made most of the Senate, could not turn back the current. It was long, however, before the subjects of the Empire realised that the ancient glory had departed. Down to the time of the Emperor Tacitus pretenders found their account in posing as senatorial champions, and rulers used the Senate's name as a convenient screen for their crimes. But the natural outcome of the anarchy of the third century was the unveiled despotism of Diocletian. He was the last in a line of valiant soldiers sprung from Illyrian soil, who accomplished the rescue of Rome from the dissolution with which it had been threatened by forces without and by forces within. To him more than to Aurelian, on whom it was bestowed, belonged by right the title "restorer of the world." For three centuries the legions had been a standing menace to the very existence of Graeco-Roman civilisation. They made emperors and unmade them, and devoured the substance of the State, exacting continually lavish largess at the sword's point. One hope of Diocletian when, following in the steps of Aurelian, he hedged round the throne with pomp and majesty, was that a new awe might shield the civil power from the lawless soldiery. In place of an Augustus, loving to parade as a bourgeois leader of the people, there comes a kind of Sultan, with trappings such as the men of the West had been used to associate with the servile East, with the Persians and Parthians. The ruler of the Roman world wears the oriental diadem, the mere dread of which had brought Caesar to his end. He is approached as a living god with that adoration from which the souls of the Greeks revolted when they came into the presence of the Great King, though Alexander bent them to endure it. Eunuchs are among his greatest officers. Lawyers buttress his throne with an absolutist theory of the constitution which is universally accepted.

From Augustus to Diocletian the trend of the government towards centralisation had been incessant. The new monarchy gave to the centralisation an intensity and an elaboration unknown before. In the early days of conquest, whether within Italy or beyond its boundaries, the Roman power had attempted no unification of its dominions. As rulers, the Romans had shewn themselves thorough opportunists. They tolerated great varieties of local privilege and partial liberty. Their government had followed, almost timidly, the line of least resistance, and had adapted itself to circumstance, to usage, and to prejudice-in every part of the Empire. Even taxation had been elastic. Before the age of despotism, few matters had ever been regulated by one unvarying enactment for every province. To this great policy the Romans chiefly owed the rapidity of their successes and the security of their ascendancy. The tendency towards unity was of course manifest from the first. But it sprang far less from the direct action of the central government than from the instinctive and unparalleled attraction which the Roman institutions possessed for the provincials, particularly in the West. In part by the extension of Roman and Italian rights to the provinces, in part by the gradual depression of Italy to the level of a province, and in part by interference designed to correct misgovernment, local differences were to a great extent effaced. Septimius Severus by stationing a legion in Italy removed one chief distinction between that favoured land and the subject regions outside. Under his successor, Caracalla, all communities within the Empire became alike Roman. By Diocletian and by Constantine, control from the centre was made systematic and organic. Yet absolute uniformity was not attained. In taxation, in legal administration, and in some other departments of government, local conditions still induced some toleration of diversities.

Centralisation brought into existence with its growth a vast bureaucracy. The organisation of the Imperial side of the administration, as opposed to the Senatorial, became more and more complex, while the importance of the Senate in the administrative machinery continually lessened. The expansion and organisation of the executive engaged the attention of many emperors, particularly Claudius, Vespasian, Trajan, Hadrian, and Septimius Severus. When the chaos of the third century had been overcome, Diocletian and his successors were compelled to reconstruct the whole service of the Empire, and a great network of officials, bearing for the most part new titles and largely undertaking new functions, was spread over it.

Along with the development of absolutism and the extension of bureaucracy, and the unification of administration had gone certain tendencies which had cut deeply into the constitution of society at large. The boundaries between class and class tended more and more to become fixed and impassable. As the Empire decayed society stiffened, and some approximations were made to the oriental institution of caste. Augustus had tried to give a rigid organisation to the circle from which senators were drawn, and had constituted it as an order of nobility passing down from father to son, only to be slowly recruited by imperial choice. Many duties owed to the State tended to become hereditary, and it was made difficult for men to rid themselves of the status which they acquired at birth. The exigencies of finance made membership of the local senates in the municipalities almost impossible to escape. The frontier legions, partly by encouragement and partly by ordinance, were largely filled with sons of the camp. Several causes, the chief of which was the financial system, gave rise to a kind of serfdom (*colonatus*) which at first attached the cultivators of the soil, and as time went on, approximated to a condition of actual slavery. The provisioning of the great capitals, Rome and Constantinople, and the transportation of goods on public account, rendered occupations connected with them hereditary. And many inequalities between classes became pronounced. The criminal law placed the *honestiores* and the *tenuiores* in different categories.

The main features of the executive government as organised by Diocletian and his successors, must now be briefly described. For the first time the difference between the prevalently Latin West and the prevalently Greek East was clearly reflected in the scheme of administration. Diocletian ordained (286) that two Augusti with equal authority should share the supreme power, one making his residence in the Eastern, the other in the Western portion. The Empire was not formally divided between them; they were to work together for the benefit of the whole State. This association of Augusti was not exactly new; but it had never been before formalised so completely. The separation of West from East had been foreshadowed from the early days of the Empire. In the first century it had been found necessary to have a Greek Secretary of State (*a libellis Graecis*) as well as a Latin Secretary (*a libellis Latinis*). The civilisation of the two spheres, in spite of much interaction, remained markedly different. The municipal life of the Eastern regions in which Greek influence predominated was fixed in its characteristics before the Romans acquired their ascendancy, and the impression they made on it was not on the whole great. But they spread their own municipal institutions all over Western lands. Although Diocletian's arrangement of the two Augusti was overthrown by Constantine, the inherent incompatibility between the two sections of the Empire continued to assert itself, and the separation became permanent in fact if not in form on the death of Theodosius. The establishment of Constantinople as the capital rendered the ultimate severance inevitable. Another problem which Diocletian attacked was that of the succession to the throne. Each "Augustus" was to have assigned to him (293) a "Caesar" who would assist him in the task of government and succeed him on his retirement or death. The transference of power would thus be peaceful and the violent revolutions caused by the claims of the legions to nominate emperors would cease. But in the nature of things this device could not prosper. The Empire followed the course it had taken from the beginning. The dynastic principle strove time after time to establish itself, but dynasties were ever threatened with catastrophe, such as had ensued on the deaths of Nero, of Commodus, and of Severus Alexander. But new emperors frequently did homage to

heredity by a process of posthumous and fictitious adoption, whereby
they grafted themselves on to the line of their predecessors. Apparently
even this phantom of legitimacy had some value for the effect it produced
on the public mind.

The theory of government now became, as has been said, frankly
autocratic. Even Aurelian, a man of simple and soldierly life, had
thought well to take to himself officially the title of "lord and god"
which private flattery had bestowed upon Domitian. The lawyers
established a fiction that the Roman people had voluntarily resigned
all authority into the hands of the monarch. The fable was as baseless
and as serviceable as that of the "social compact," received in the
eighteenth century. No person or class held any rights against the
emperor. The revenues were his private property. All payments from
the treasury were "sacred largesses" conceded by the divine ruler. So
far as the State was concerned, the distinction between the senatorial
exchequer (*aerarium*) and the imperial exchequer (*fiscus*) disappeared.
Certain revenues, as for instance those derived from the confiscated
estates of unsuccessful pretenders, were labelled as the emperor's private
property (*res privata*), and others as belonging to his "family estate"
(*patrimonium*).   But these designations were merely formal and administrative. The emperor was the sole ultimate source of all law and
authority. The personnel by which he was immediately surrounded in
his capital was of vast extent, and the palace was often a hotbed of
intrigue. Even in the time of the Severi the "Caesareans" (Καισάρειοι),
as Dio Cassius names them, were numerous enough to imperil often the
public peace. Another class of imperial servants, the workers at the
mint, had, in the reign of Aurelian, raised an insurrection which led to a
shedding of blood in Rome such as had not been witnessed since the age
of Sulla. The military basis of imperial power, partly concealed by the
earlier emperors, stood fully revealed. Septimius Severus had been the
first to wear regularly in the capital the full insignia of military
command, previously seen there only on days of triumph. Now every
department of the public service was regarded as "militia," and "camp"
(*castra*) is the official name for the court. All high officers, with the
exception of the *praefectus urbi*, wore the military garb. It is needless
to say that officials who were nominally the emperor's domestic servants
easily gathered power into their own hands and often became the real
rulers of the Empire. The line between domestic offices and those which
were political and military was never strictly drawn. All higher functions
whose exercise required close attention on the emperor's person were
covered by the description *dignitates palatinae*.   Under the early
emperors the great ministers of state were largely freedmen, whose
status was rather that of court servants than of public administrators.
The great departments of the imperial service were gradually freed from
their close attachment to the emperor's person. The natural result was

that direct personal influence over the ruler often passed into the hands of men whose duties were in name connected only with the daily life of the palace. From the third century onwards the Eastern custom of choosing eunuchs as the most trusted servants prevailed in the imperial household as in the private households of the wealthy. The greatest of these was the *praepositus sacri cubiculi* or Great Chamberlain. This officer often wielded the power which had been enjoyed by such men as Parthenius had been under Domitian. The office grew in importance, as measured by dignity and precedence, until in the time of Theodosius the Great it was one of four high offices which conferred on their holders membership of the Imperial Council (*Consistorium*), and a little later was made equal in honour to the other three. The "Palatine" servants, high and low, formed a mighty host, which required a special department for their provisioning and another for their tendance in sickness. But exactly how many of them were under the immediate direction (*sub dispositione*) of the *praepositus sacri cubiculi* cannot be determined. Some duties fell to him which are hardly suggested by his title. He was in control of the emperor's select and intimate bodyguard, which bore the name of *silentiarii*, thirty in number, with three *decuriones* for officers. Curiously, he superintended one division of the vast imperial domains, that considerable portion of them which lay within the province of Cappadocia. Dependent probably on the *praepositus sacri cubiculi* was the *primicerius sacri cubiculi*, who appears in the *Notitia Dignitatum* as possessing the quality of a proconsular. Whether the *castrensis sacri palatii* was independent or subordinate, cannot be determined. Under his rule were a host of pages and lower menials of many kinds, and he had to care for the fabric of the imperial palaces. Also he had charge of the private archives of the imperial family.

The service of the officers described was rather personal to the emperor than public in character. We now turn to the civil and military administration as it was refashioned under the new monarchy. The chaos of the period preceding Diocletian's supremacy had finally effaced some of the leading features of the Augustan Principate which had become fainter and fainter as the Empire ran its course. The Senate lost the last remnant of real power. Such of its surviving privileges and dignities as might carry back the mind to the days of its glory were mere shadows without substance. All provinces had become imperial. All functionaries of every class owed obedience to the autocrat alone, and looked to him for their career. The old state-treasury, the *aerarium*, retained its name, but became in practice the municipal exchequer of Rome, which ceased to be the capital of the Empire and was merely the first of its municipalities. The army and the civil service alike were filled with officers whose titles and duties would have seemed strange to a Roman of the second century of the Empire.

CH. II.

The aspect of the provincial government, as ordered by the new monarchy, differed profoundly from that which it had worn in the age of the early Principate. To diminish the danger of military revolutions Diocletian carried to a conclusion a policy which had been adopted in part by his predecessors. The great military commands in the provinces which had often enabled their holders to destroy or to imperil dynasties or rulers were broken up; and the old provinces were severed into fragments. Spain, for example, now comprised six divisions, and Gaul fifteen. Within these fragments, still named provinces, the civil power and the military authority were, as a rule, not placed in the same hands. The divisions of the Empire now numbered about a hundred and twenty, as against forty-five which existed at the end of Trajan's reign. Twelve of the new sections lay within the boundaries of Italy, and of the old contrast between Italy and the provinces of the Principate, few traces remained. Egypt, hitherto treated as a land apart, was brought within the new organisation. The titles of the civil administrators were various. Three, who ruled regions bearing the ancient provincial names of Asia, Africa, and Achaia were distinguished by the title of *proconsul*, which had once belonged to all administrators of senatorial provinces. About thirty-six were known as *consulares*. This designation ceased to indicate, as of old, the men who had passed the consulship: it was merely connected with the government of provinces. The *consularis* became technically a member of the Roman Senate, though he ranked below the ex-consul. So also with the provincial governors who bore the common title of *praeses*, and the rarer name of *corrector*. This last appellation belonged, in the fourth century, to the chiefs of two districts in Italy, Apulia, and Lucania, and of three outside. It denoted originally officers who began to be appointed in Trajan's reign to reform the condition of municipalities. The precedence of the *correctores* among the governors seems to have placed them, in the West, after the *consulares*, in the East after the *praesides*. Sometimes the title of *proconsul* was for personal reasons bestowed on a governor whose province was ordinarily ruled by an officer of lower dignity. But such an arrangement was temporary. The old expressions *legatus pro praetore* or *procurator*, in its application to provincial rulers, went out of use. After the age of Constantine new and fanciful descriptions of the provincial governors, as of other officers, tended to spring into existence. A few frontier districts were treated (as was the case under the Principate) in an exceptional manner. Their chiefs were allowed to exercise civil as well as military functions and were naturally described by the ordinary name for an army commander (*dux*).

The proconsuls possessed some privileges of their own. Two of them, the proconsul of Africa and the proconsul of Asia, were alone among provincial governors entitled to receive their orders from the emperor himself; and the Asian proconsul was distinguished by having under him two deputies, who directed a region known as *Hellespontus* and the *Insulae* or islands lying near the Asiatic coast. All other administrators communicated with the emperor through one or other of four great officers of state, the *Praefecti Praetorio*. Their title had been originally invented to designate the commander of the Praetorian Cohorts, whom Augustus called into existence. The control of these was usually vested in two men. Now and then three commanders were appointed. Some emperors, disregarding the danger to themselves, allowed a single officer to hold command. Men like Sejanus under Tiberius and Plautianus under Septimius Severus were practically vice-emperors. As time went on, the office gradually lost its military character. Sometimes one of the commanders was a soldier and the other a civilian. During the reign of Severus Alexander the great lawyer Ulpian was in sole charge, being the first senator who had been permitted to hold the post. The legal duties of the Praefect continued to grow in importance. When the Praetorian Cohorts brought destruction on themselves by their support of Maxentius against Constantine, the Praefectus Praetorio became a purely civil functionary. The four Praefecti were distinguished as Praefectus Praetorio, Galliarum, Italiae, Illyrici and Orientis respectively. The first administered not only the ancient Gaul, but also the Rhine frontier and Britain, Spain, Sardinia, Corsica and Sicily. The second in addition to Italy had under him Rhaetia, Noricum, Dalmatia, Pannonia, and some regions on the upper Danube, also most of Roman Africa; the third Dacia, Achaia, and districts near the lower Danube besides Illyricum, properly so called; the fourth all Asia Minor, in so far as it was not subjected to the proconsul of Asia, with Egypt and Thrace, and some lands by the mouth of the Danube. It will be seen that three out of the four had the direction of provinces lying on or near the Danube. Probably on their first institution and for some time afterwards all the Praefecti retained in their own hands the administration of some portions of the great territories committed to their charge. Later the Illyrian praefect alone had a district, a portion of Dacia, under his own immediate control. Apart from this exception, the Praefecti conducted their government through officials subordinated to them.

Each praefectal region was divided into great sections called *dioeceses*. Each of these was formed by combination of a certain number of provinces; and each was comparable to the more important of the old provinces of the age of the Republic and early Principate. The word *dioecesis* had passed through a long history before the time of Diocletian. The Romans found it existent in their Asiatic dominions, where it had been applied by earlier rulers to an administrative district, especially in relation to legal affairs. The Roman government extended the employment of the term both in the East and in the West and connected it with other sides of administration besides the legal. Diocletian marked

CH. II.

out ten great divisions of the Empire to be designated by this title. The number of the divisions and their limits were somewhat altered by his successors. At the head of each Dioecesis was placed an officer who bore the name *vicarius*, excepting in the Eastern praefecture. Here the Vicarius was after a while replaced by a *comes Orientis*, to whom the governor of Egypt was at first subject, though he acquired independent authority later. The treatment of Italy (in the new and extended sense) was peculiar. It constituted a single Dioecesis, but possessed two *vicarii*, one of whom had his seat at Milan, the other at Rome. This bisection of the Italian praefecture depended on differences in taxation, to which we must recur later. In the Dioecesis Asiana, and the Dioecesis Africae, the Vicarius was of course responsible not to the Praefectus, but to the proconsul.

Such were, in broad outline, the features which the civil administration of the Empire wore after Diocletian's reforms. Some rough idea must be conveyed of the mode in which the scheme was applied to the practical work of government. It must be premised that now, as heretofore, there was no point in the vast and complex machinery of bureaucracy at which the direct interposition of the emperor might not be at any moment brought into play. There was therefore no mechanical subordination of officer to officer, such as would produce an unbroken official chain, passing down from the emperor to the lowest official. And even apart from imperial intervention we must not conceive of the different grades of functionaries as arranged in absolutely systematic subjection one grade to another. This would have interfered with one principal purpose of the new organisation, which aimed at providing the emperor with information about the whole state of his dominions, through officers immediately in touch with him at the centre of the government. The emperor could not afford to restrict himself to such reports as might reach him through a Praefectus Praetorio or a proconsul. Thus the Vicarii were never regarded as mere agents or deputies of the Praefecti, and the same may be said of other officials. All might be called on to leave the beaten track. The Praefecti Praetorio, though each had his allotted sphere, were still in some sense colleagues, and were required on occasion to take common action. One great aim of the new system was to prevent administrators from accumulating influence by long continuance in the same post, or in any other way. Therefore functionaries were passed on rapidly from one position to another. Therefore, also, except in rare instances, no man was allowed to hold office in the province of his birth. All offices were now paid and the importance of many was discernible from the amount of the stipend received by the holder. As in earlier times, certain offices conferred on their incumbents what may be regarded as patents of nobility. The nobiliary status arising from office was not hereditary as in an earlier age; yet the halo of the title to some extent covered the official's family. New appellations were invented to decorate the higher offices, whose tenants were graded as *illustres, spectabiles,* and *clarissimi.* To the last designation all senators were entitled. Other expressions as *comes, patricius,* were less closely bound up with office. The use of these titles spread gradually. Before the end of the first century *vir clarissimus (v.c.* on inscriptions) began to denote the senator. The employment of distinctive titles for high officers of equestrian rank, *vir eminentissimus, vir perfectissimus, vir egregius,* began with Hadrian, and developed in the time of Marcus Aurelius. The designation *vir egregius* fell out of use during or soon after Constantine's reign. The tendency of the new organisation was to detach many offices from their old connexion with the equestrian body, whose importance in the State diminished and then rapidly died away. Many changes in the application of these titles to the different offices took place from time to time.

The Praefectus Praetorio was the most exalted civil officer in the new Empire. His duties were executive, legal, financial, of every description in fact excepting the military. His only service for the army lay in the supply of its material requirements in pay, food, and equipment. He became in the end one of the highest of the *viri illustres.* The Praefectus in whose district the emperor resided was for the time being of enhanced importance, and was denoted as *Praefectus Praetorio praesens.* The office had even before the time of Diocletian attracted to itself a good deal of criminal jurisdiction. The Praefectus was now not a judge of first instance, but heard appeals from the courts below, within his sphere of action, with the exception of the court of the Vicarius, from whom the appeal went straight to the emperor. On the other hand, after 331 there was in the ordinary way no appeal against a sentence passed by the Praefectus, who was held to sit as the *alter ego* of the emperor (*vice sacra iudicans*). No other official possessed this privilege. The whole administration of the regions committed to him was passed under review by the Praefectus. His supervision of the provincial governors was of the most general kind. Each was compelled to send in twice a year a report on the administration of his province, and particularly on his exercise of jurisdiction. In the selection of governors the Praefectus had a large share, and he exercised disciplinary power over them. Erring functionaries both military and civil could be suspended by him till the emperor's pleasure was known. He usually advised the emperor concerning appointments. His control of finance both on the side of receipts and on that of expenditure formed a most important part of his duties. All difficulties in the incidence of taxation and in the collection of the taxes came under his consideration, but no officer of the Empire, however highly placed, could diminish or increase taxation without the emperor's express sanction. The Praefectus was also responsible for the due transport of corn and other necessaries destined for the supply of Rome and Constantinople. Many other functions fell to his lot, among them the superintendence of the state Post (*cursus publicus*).

If we may adapt an ecclesiastical phrase which describes the Archdeacon as the *oculus Episcopi*, we may say that the Vicarius was the *oculus Praefecti*. He gave a closer eye to details than was possible for his superior within his Dioecesis. At first he was *perfectissimus*, afterwards *spectabilis*. The tendency of the rulers after Constantine was to increase his importance at the expense of the Praefectus; rather however in the field of jurisdiction than in other fields. The Vicarius had but little disciplinary power over the *rector provinciae*. The governor could in a difficult case seek advice from the emperor without having recourse to either of his superior officers, though he was bound to inform the Vicarius, and the latter could on occasion go straight to the monarch. The court of the Vicarius, like that of the Praefectus, was an appeal court only. The provincial governor was judge of first instance in all civil and criminal matters, except in the cases of some privileged persons, and in those minor affairs which were left to the magistrates of the municipalities within the province. The small size of the province made it unnecessary that its ruler should travel about to administer justice, as in the earlier time. Causes were heard at the seat of government. Much of the time of the governor was occupied in seeing that imposts were duly collected and that no irregularities were practised by subordinates. Responsibility for public order rested primarily with him.

The lower grades of civil servants in the provinces were to a very large extent in connexion with and controlled by the great departments of the imperial service whose chief offices were in the capital. Early in the imperial period three great bureaux were established, whose presidents were named *ab epistulis*, *a libellis*, and *a memoria*. These phrases survived into the age of Constantine and after, but denoted the offices and not their chiefs, whose title was *magister*. The departments themselves were now described by the word *scrinium*, which had originally denoted a box or desk for containing papers. The word had therefore undergone a change of meaning similar to that which had passed over *fiscus*, whereby from a basket for holding coin, it came to mean the imperial exchequer. The demarcation of business allotted to the three great *scrinia* was not always the same. The *magister memoriae* gradually encroached on the functions of the other two heads of departments and became much the most influential of the three. A fourth *scrinium*, called the *scrinium dispositionum*, was added. Its *magister* (later called *comes*) was at first inferior to the other three, who belonged to the class of the *spectabiles*, but was afterwards placed on a level with them. All these *magistri* on being promoted became *vicarii*. All four were subject to an exalted personage known as *magister officiorum*, who was a *vir illustris*.

The department known as *ab epistulis* was early divided into two sections distinguished as *ab epistulis Latinis* and *ab epistulis Graecis*. It was originally the great Secretariat of the Empire. Here were managed all communications touching _foreign affairs_, and the general corre_ spondence of the government, excepting in so far as it related to the legal and other multifarious petitions addressed to the emperor, appealing for his interference or his favour. These would come not only from officials, but also from private persons, and all fell within the functions of the office _a libellis_. This bureau absorbed into itself another which had been specially devoted to legal inquiries, and was called a _cognitionibus_. Hence the _magister libellorum_ is described in the Digest by the fuller title _magister scrinii libellorum et sacrarum cognitionum_. The depart_ ment had famous lawyers, like Papinian and Ulpian, connected with it, and it must often have sought the aid of specialists in other matters belonging to the public service, as revenue and finance: for many of the petitions addressed to the ruler sought relief from taxation.

The name of the department _a memoria_ implies that its head was the keeper of the "emperor's memory." It was therefore a Record Office, but it was much more. It assisted other offices in putting documents into their final shape, and not only recorded the documents but issued them. The accounts we have of the office make it clear that it took to itself much important business which originally was transacted by other departments. Thus the _Notitia_ describes the _magister memoriae_ as dictating and issuing _adnotationes_, that is to say brief pronouncements running in the emperor's name; also as giving answers to supplications (_preces_). Further he gave to the emperor's letters, speeches, and general announcements their final form, and sent them forth. The _magister libellorum_ and the _magister epistularum_ must have become in fact, though not in form, his inferiors. From his office emanated diplomas of appointments, the permission to use the imperial post, and countless other official permits. The _scrinium dispositionum_ kept in order all the emperor's engagements, and made the innumerable arrangements necessary for his journeys, and took count of many matters with which he was in touch, being of such a nature as not to come definitely within the purview of other bureaux.

All these _scrinia_ were under the control of one of the greatest functionaries of the Empire, the _magister officiorum_. His importance grew over a long space of time from small beginnings. His functions encroached greatly on those of the _Praefecti Praetorio_, and their develop ment is a measure of the jealousy entertained by the emperors for these great officers. The word _officium_ indicates a group of public servants placed at the disposal of a state functionary. The _magister officiorum_ is the general master of all such groups. Naturally he is _vir illustris_. He selected from the _scrinia_, in accordance with elaborate rules of service, the clerks who were required to carry out many sorts of business in the capital and in the provinces. His duties were of many different kinds, through which no connected thread of principle ran; they evidently reached their full compass by an agglomeration which followed lines of convenience merely.   One of the most prominent occupations of the *magister* lay in his direction of what may be called the Secret Service of the Empire.   He had under him the very important *schola agentum in rebus*, which was organised by Constantine or possibly by Diocletian, and replaced a body of men called *frumentarii*, drawn originally from the corps which had in charge the provisioning of the army.   These had acted as secret agents of the government.   They were the men by whose means Hadrian, as his biographer says, "wormed out all hidden things." The vast extension of the Secret Service in the age of Constantine and later was a consequence of the huge increase in the number of officials, and of the suspicion which an autocratic ruler naturally entertains towards his subordinates : in part also of a genuine but ineffectual desire to check misgovernment.   The term *schola* is closely connected with the army, and implies a service which is regarded as military in trend, like that of the other *scholae palatinae*.   The duties assigned to this *schola* opened of course wide doors through which corruption entered, and it became one of the greatest scourges from which the subjects of the Empire suffered.   All attempts to keep it in order failed.   The number of the officers attached to it was generally enormous.   Julian practically disbanded it, retaining only a few of its members; but it soon grew again to its former proportions.   The officers belonging to the *schola* were arranged in five classes, with more or less mechanical promotion, such as generally prevailed through the imperial service.   The members themselves seem to have had some voice in the selection of men for the highest and most responsible duties.   The standing of the *schola* became continually more honourable; and members of it rose to provincial governorships and even to still higher positions.   The *agens in rebus* was ubiquitous, but only some of the more momentous forms of his activity can be mentioned here.

An officer called *princeps*, drawn from the *schola*, was sent to every Vicarius and into every province, where he was the chief of the governor's staff of assistants (*officium*).   This officer had gone through a course of espionage in lower situations, and his relation to the *magister officiorum* made his proximity uncomfortable for his nominal superior.   Indeed the *princeps* came to play the part of a sort of Maire du Palais to the *rector provinciae*, who tended to become a merely nominal ruler.   The *princeps* and the *officium* were quite capable of conducting the affairs of the province alone.   Hence we hear of youths being corruptly placed in important governorships, and of these offices being purchased, as in the days of the Republic, only in a different manner.   After this provincial service, the *princeps* usually became governor of a province himself.

At an earlier stage of his career, the *agens in rebus* would be despatched to a province to superintend the imperial Post-service there, and see that it was not in any way abused.   This title was then *praepositus cursus publici,* or later *curiosus.* This service would enable him to play the part of a spy wherever he went. The burden of providing for the Post was one of the heaviest which the provincials had to bear, and those who contravened the regulations concerning it were often highly-placed officials. That the *curiosi* by their espionage could make themselves intolerable there is much evidence to show.

The *agentes in rebus* were also the general messengers of the govern‑ ment, and were continually despatched on occasions great or small, to make announcements in every part of the emperor's dominions. While performing this function they were often the collectors of special dona‑ tions to the imperial exchequer, and made illegitimate gains of their own, owing to the fear which they inspired. A regulation which is recorded forbidding any *agens in rebus* from entering Rome without special permission, is eloquent testimony to the reputation which the *schola* in general had earned.

Among the other miscellaneous duties of the *magister officiorum* was the supervision of formal intercourse between the Empire and foreign communities and princes. Also the general superintendence of the imperial factories and arsenals which supplied the army with weapons. The corps of guards (*scholae scutariorum et gentium*) who replaced the destroyed Praetorians were under his command, so that he resembled the Praefectus Praetorio of the earlier empire. And connected with this was a responsibility for the safety for the frontiers (*limites*) and control over the military commanders there. Further the servants who attended to the court ceremonial (*officium admissionis*) were under his direction, as were some others who belonged to the emperor's state. His civil and criminal jurisdiction extended over the immense mass of public servants at the capital, with few exceptions, and his voice in selecting officials for service there was potent. In short, no officer had more constant and more confidential relations with the monarch than the *magister officiorum.* He was the most important executive officer at the centre of government.

The greatest judicial and legal officer was the *quaestor sacri palatii.* The early history of this officer is obscure and no acceptable explanation has been found for the use of the title *quaestor* in connexion with it. The dignity of the Quaestor's functions may be understood from descrip‑ tions given in literature. Symmachus calls him "the disposer of petitions and the constructer of laws" (*arbiter precum, legum conditor*). The poet Claudian says that he "issued edicts to the world, and answers to suppliants," while Corippus describes him as "the Champion of justice, who under the emperor's auspices controls legislation and legal principles" (*iura*). The Quaestor's office, like many others, advanced in importance after its creation, which appears to have taken place not earlier than Constantine's reign. In the latter part of the fourth century he took precedence even of the *magister officiorum,* and with

CH. II.

one brief interruption, he maintained this rank. The requirements for the office were above all skill in the law and in the art of legal expression. On all legal questions, whether questions of change in law, or questions of its administration, the emperor gave his final decision by the voice of the Quaestor. No body of servants (*officium*) was specially allotted to him, but the *scrinia* were at his service. Indeed he may be said to have been the intermediary between the *scrinia* and the emperor. His relations with the heads of the departments *a libellis* and *a memoria*, and particularly with the latter, must have been very close; but their work was preparatory and subordinate to his so far as legal matters were concerned. The instances in which the *magister memoriae* succeeded in acting independently of the Quaestor were exceptional. A share in the appointment to certain of the lesser military offices was also assigned to the Quaestor, who kept a record of the names of their holders, which was known as *laterculum minus*. In this duty he was assisted by a high official of the *scrinium memoriae*, whose title was *laterculensis*.

There was another body called *tribuni et notarii*, not attached to the *scrinia*, which was of considerable importance. The service of these functionaries was closely connected with the deliberations of the great Imperial Council, the *Consistorium*, which is to be described presently. They had to see that the proper officers carried out the decisions of the Council. Their business often brought them into close and confidential relation with the emperor himself. The officer at the head is *primicerius* (literally, one whose name is written first on a wax tablet — *primâ cerâ*). The title is given to many officers serving in other departments and indicates usually, but not always, high rank. This particular *primicerius* ranked even higher than the chiefs of the *scrinia* and the *castrensis sacri palatii*. According to the *Notitia* he has "cognizance of all dignities and administrative offices both military and civil." He kept the great list known as *laterculum maius*, in which were comprised not only the actual tenants of the greater offices, but forms for their appointment, schedules of their duties, and even a catalogue of the different sections of the army and their stations, including the *scholae* which served as imperial guards.

The reorganisation of Finance brought into existence a host of officials who either bore new names or old titles to which new duties had been assigned. The great and complex system of taxation initiated by Diocletian and carried further by his successors can here be only sketched in broad outline. Although, like all the institutions of the new monarchy, the scheme of taxation had its roots in the past, the new development in its completed form stands in such marked contrast to old conditions, that there is not much to be gained by detailed references to the earlier Empire. Before Diocletian's time the old *aerarium Saturni* had ceased to be of imperial importance, and the *aerarium militare* of Augustus had disappeared. The general census of Roman citizens, carried out at Rome, is not heard of after Vespasian's time. Of the ancient revenues of the State very many were swept away by Diocletian's reform, even the most productive of all, the five per cent. tax on inherited property(*vicesima hereditatum*) by which Augustus had subjected Roman citizens in general to taxation. The separate provincial census, of which in Gaul, for example, we hear much during the early Empire, was rendered unnecessary. The great and powerful *societates publicanorum* had dwindled away, though *publicani* were still employed for some purposes. Direct collection of revenue had gradually taken the place of the system of farming. Where any traces of the old system remained, it was subject to strict official supervision. Before Diocletian the incidence of taxation on the different parts of the Empire had been most unequal. The reasons for this lay partly in the extraordinary variety of the conditions by which in times past the relation of different portions of the Empire to the central government had been fixed when they first came under its sway; partly in Republican or Imperial favour or disfavour as they afterwards affected the burdens to be endured in different places; partly by the evolutions of the municipalities of different types throughout the Roman dominions. Towns and districts which once had been immune from imposts or slightly taxed had become tributary and *vice-versa*. The reforms instituted by Augustus and carried further by his successors did something towards securing uniformity, but many diversities continued to exist. Some of these were produced by the gift of *immunitas* which was bestowed on many civic communities scattered over the Empire. Without this gift even communities of Roman citizens were not exempt from the taxation which marked off the provinces from Italy.

In order to understand the purpose of Diocletian's changes in the taxation of the Empire, it is necessary to consider the struggle which he and Constantine made to reform the imperial coinage. The difficult task of explaining with exactness the utter demoralisation of the currency at the moment when Diocletian ascended the throne cannot be here attempted. Only a few outstanding features can be delineated. The political importance of sound currency has never been more conspicuously shewn than in the century which followed on the death of Commodus[1] (A.D. 180). Augustus had given a stability to the Roman coinage which it had never before possessed. But he imposed no uniform system on the whole of his dominions. Gold (with one slight exception) he allowed none to mint but himself. But copper he left in the hands of the Senate. Silver he coined himself, while he permitted many local mints to strike pieces in that metal also as well as in copper. Subsequent history extinguished local diversities and brought about by gradual steps a general system which was not attained till the fourth century. Aurelian deprived the Senate of the power which Augustus had left it.

Although the imperial coins underwent a certain amount of deprecia-

CH. II.

tion between the time of Augustus and that of the Severi, it was not such
as to throw out of gear the taxation and the commerce of the Empire.
But with Caracalla a rapid decline set in, and by the time of Aurelian
the disorganisation had gone so far that practically gold and silver were
demonetised, and copper became the standard medium of exchange.
The principal coin that professed to be silver had come to contain no
more than five per cent of that metal, and this proportion sank
afterwards to two per cent.   What a government gains by making its
payments in corrupted coin is always far more than lost in the revenue
which it receives.   The debasement of the coinage means a lightening
of taxation, and it is never possible to enhance the nominal amount
receivable by the exchequer so as to keep pace with the depreciation.
The effect of this in the Roman Empire was greater than it would have
been at an earlier time, since there is reason to believe that much of the
revenue formerly payable in kind had been transmuted into money.
A measure of Aurelian had the effect of multiplying by eight such taxes
as were to be paid in coin.   As the chief (professing) silver coin had
twenty years earlier contained eight times as much silver as it had then
come to contain, he claimed that he was only exacting what was justly
due, but his subjects naturally cried out against his tyranny.   No
greater proof of the disorganisation of the whole financial system could
be given than lies in the fact that the treasury issued sackloads (*folles*)
of the *Antoniani*, first coined by Caracalla, which were intended to be
silver, but were now all but base metal only.   These *folles* passed
from hand to hand unopened.

Diocletian's attempts to remove these mischiefs were not altogether
fortunate.   He made experiment after experiment, aiming at that
stability of the currency which had, on the whole, prevailed for two
centuries after the reforms of Augustus, but never reaching it.   Finally,
discovering that the last change he had made led to general raising of
prices, he issued the celebrated edict of A.D. 301 by which the charges
for all commodities were fixed, the penalty for transgression being
death.

Constantine was forced to handle afresh the tangled problem of the
currency.   The task was rendered especially difficult by the fresh
debasement of coinage which was perpetrated by Maxentius while he
was supreme in Italy.   It may be said at once that the goal of Diocletian's
efforts was never reached by Constantine.   He did indeed alter the
weight of the gold piece, which now received the name of *solidus*, and it
continued in circulation, practically unchanged, for centuries.   But this
gold piece was to all intents and purposes not a coin, for when payments
were made in it, they were reckoned by weight.   The *solidus* was in effect
only a bit of bullion, the fineness of which was conveniently guaranteed
by the imperial stamp.   The same is true of Constantine's silver pieces.
The only coins which could be paid and received by their number,

without weighing, were those contained in the *folles*, of which mention was made above, and the word *follis* was now applied to the individual coins, as well as to the whole sack. It had proved to be impossible to restore the monetary system which had prevailed in the first and second centuries of the Empire. But the tide of innovation was at length stayed; and this in itself was no small boon.

The line taken by the reform of Diocletian in the scheme of taxation was partly marked out for him by the anarchy of the third century, which led to the great debasement of the coinage described above and to many oppressive exactions of an arbitrary character. The lowering of the currency had disorganised the whole revenue and expenditure of the government. Where dues were receivable or stipends payable of a fixed nominal amount, these had largely lost their value. A natural consequence was that payments both to be made and to be received were ordered by Diocletian to be reckoned in the produce of the soil, and not in coin. During the era of confusion a phrase, *indictio*, had come into use to denote a special requisition made upon the provincials over and above their stated dues. What Diocletian did was to make what had been irregular into a regular and general impost, subjecting all provincials to it alike, and abolishing the unequal tributes of different kinds which had been previously required. The result was an enormous levelling of taxation throughout the provinces. And to some extent the immunity of Italy itself was withdrawn. But the sum to be raised from year to year was not uniform. It depended on an announcement to which the word *indictio* was applied, issued by the emperor for each year. Hence the number of *indictiones* proclaimed by an emperor became a convenient means for denoting the years of his reign.

The assessment of communities and individuals was managed by an elaborate process. The newly arranged burdens fell on land. The *territorium* attached to every town was surveyed and the land classified according to its use for growing grain or producing oil or wine. A certain number of acres (*iugera*) of arable land was called a *iugum*. The number varied, partly according to the quality of the soil, which was roughly graded, partly according to the province in which it was situated. In the case of oil, the taxable unit was often arrived at by counting the number of olive trees; and this was sometimes the case with vines. The *iugum* was however supposed to be fixed in accordance with the limits of one man's labour, and therefore *caput* (person) and *iugum*, from the point of view of revenue, became convertible terms. But men and women and slaves and cattle were taxed separately, and in addition to the tax on the land. Each man or slave on a farm counted as one *caput* and each woman as half a *caput*. A certain number of cattle constituted also a *iugum* and thus there was no need to divide up the pasture lands as the arable lands were divided. Meadows were rated for

CH. II.

the supply of fodder. The total requirements of the government were stated in the *indictio*, and every community had to contribute in accordance with the number of taxable units which the survey had disclosed. All the produce which the taxpayers handed over was stored in great government barns (*horrea*).

The system of collection, though decentralised, was bad. The decurions-or senators of each town, or the ten chief men of each town (*decemprimi*) were responsible for handing over to the government all that was due. A revision took place every five years, and was generally carried through with much unfairness and oppression of the poorer landholders. Apparently a fresh survey was not made, but evidence taken by the town-officers in the town itself. From 312 onwards we find a fifteen-year indiction-period, which came to be largely used as a chronological instrument. It would seem that every fifteenth year a re-allotment of taxes was made which was based on actual survey. But evidence for this is scanty. An imperial revenue officer called *censitor* was restricted to the duty of receiving the dues from a community as a whole. Outside imperial officers were called in to assist in the collection of dues from recalcitrant taxpayers. This happened at first occasionally, then regularly. Naturally another door was thus opened to oppression, from which the rich would manage to escape more lightly than the poor. The special arrangement made by Diocletian for Italy will be explained later; also the exemptions accorded to privileged classes of individuals.

Along with the payment of government dues in kind went the payment of stipends in kind. A certain amount of corn, wine, meat, and other necessaries, grouped together, constituted a unit to which the name *annona* was applied, and salaries, military and civil, were largely calculated in *annonae*. Where allowance was made for horses,the amount granted for each was called *capitum*. When stability was in some degree secured for the currency, these *annonae* were again expressed in money, by a valuation called *adaeratio*. The government, to be on safety's side, of course exacted as a rule more produce from the soil than was needed for use, and the excess was turned into money, naturally at low prices.

In addition to the burdens on the land, many other imposts were levied. The maintenance of the Post Service along the main roads was most oppressive. In the towns every trade was taxed, the contribution bearing the name of *lustralis collatio* or *chrysargyrum*. The customs dues at the ports and transit dues at the frontier were maintained. Revenues were derived from government monopolies in mines, forests, salt factories, and other possessions. Some of the old Republican imposts, such as the tax on manumitted slaves, still survived. Persons of distinction were subject to special exactions. Imperial senators paid several dues, especially the so-called *aurum oblaticium*, which like many inevitable forms of taxation, professed in its name to be a free-will offering. Senators of municipal towns (*decuriones*) were weighted both by local and by imperial burdens. Every five years of his reign the emperor celebrated a festival, at which he dispensed large sums to the army and to civil functionaries. At the same time the *decuriones* of the municipalities had to pay an oppressive tax known as *aurum coronarium*, the beginnings of which go right back to the time of the Republic. As is shewn below, certain trading corporations were hereditarily bound to assist in the provisioning of the two capitals; and some other miscellaneous services were similarly treated.

From the third century the officer who in each province looked after the imperial revenue, whose earlier title was *procurator*, began to be called *rationalis*. But under Diocletian's system, each governor became the chief financial officer in his province. For each Dioecesis there was appointed a *rationalis summae rei*, in which name *summae rei* refers to the complex of provinces forming the Dioecesis. The great Imperial minister of finance at the centre bore the same name at first; *summa res* in his case indicated the whole Empire. But the title *comes sacrarum largitionum* came into use in the reign of Constantine. This officer advanced from the rank of *perfectissimus* to a high place among the *illustres*. The appellation *comes* came to be given to all the chief financial officers in the Dioeceses of the East and to some of those in the West, while others continued to bear the name *rationalis*. Disputes between taxpayers and the lower government financial officers were doubtless decided in the last resort by the *comes sacrarum largitionum*. A number of treasury officials and officers of the mint were under his orders. In certain places (Rome, Milan, Lugdunum, London and others) sub-treasuries of the government were maintained. There were also factories for the supply to the Court of many fabrics; all these the *comes* had under his charge. And he was in touch with the administrators of all public income and expenditure throughout the Empire.

The emperor had revenues which he distinguished as personal to himself rather than public, although they doubtless were largely expended on imperial administration. These personal revenues were derived from two sources distinguished as *res privata* and *patrimonium*, and administered to some extent by different staffs. In theory the *patrimonium* consisted of property which might be regarded as belonging to the emperor apart from the crown, while the *res privata* attached to the crown itself. But these distinctions were of no great practical value. The imperial estates and possessions had come to be enormous, and covered large parts of some provinces. We have seen that the control of the imperial domains in one province, Cappadocia, was entrusted to the *quaestor sacri cubiculi*. The concentration of these immense estates in the hands of the ruler had an important effect upon the general evolution of society in the Empire. These properties had largely accrued by confiscation, mainly as a consequence of struggles for the supreme power. The head of the administration of the *res privata*, designated as

comes rei privatae or *rerum privatarum*, had a whole army of subordinates
scattered over the provinces, and the staff which managed the *patrimonium* under an officer usually called *procurator patrimonii*, though
smaller, must have been considerable.

The new hierarchy of office was swollen in its dimensions also by
the reorganisation of the army, which placed a series of new *dignitates
militares* beside the *dignitates civiles*. Diocletian completed the severance
of military from civil duties, excepting in some frontier districts, where
they were still combined. The regular title for a commanding officer is
dux; and the army, like the Empire, was broken up into smaller sections
than of old, and for the same reason, jealousy of the concentration of
much power in private hands. The whole force of the army was
considerably increased. The distinction between the legions and the
auxilia was maintained. The senatorial *legatus* who had been the
commander of the legion since Caesar's day, was replaced by a *praefectus*
of equestrian rank, and other changes were made in the legionary officers.
To the older *auxilia* were added new detachments to which the same
name was given, but filled chiefly with soldiers from beyond the bounds
of the Empire, free Germans, Franks, and others. The barbarian chiefs
who came into the service became very prominent, and more and more
frequently as time went on rose to the highest commands in the whole
army. Other barbarian forces were within the Empire, recruited from
peoples who had been deliberately planted there to defend the frontiers,
and owing no other duty to the government. The general term for these
auxiliaries is *laeti*, but in the region of the Danube their designation
was *gentiles*. They were commanded sometimes by men of their own
race, sometimes by Roman *praefecti*. The tendency also to compose the
cavalry of barbarians was conspicuous, and new designations for the
different detachments came into use. The common title for the more
regular corps was *vexillationes*; the frontier forces passed under the
names of *cunei, alae,* or sometimes *equites* only.

The greatest military reform introduced by the new monarchy lay in
the construction of a mobile army. The want of this had been early felt
in the imperial period, when war on any frontier compelled the removal
of defensive forces from other frontiers. The difficulty had been one of
the causes which led Septimius Severus to station a legion at Alba
near Rome, thus breaking with the tradition that Italy was not governed
like the provinces. So long as the old Praetorian Cohorts existed, their
military efficiency as a field force was not great, and they were destroyed
in consequence of the rising of Maxentius. Diocletian created a regular
field army, the title for which was *comitatenses*. The name indicates the
practice under the new system, whereby the emperor himself took
command in all important wars, and therefore these troops were his
retinue (*comitatus*). The description *comitatenses* applied both to the
foot-soldiers (*legiones*), and the cavalry (*vexillationes*). In the later

fourth century a section of the *comitatenses* appear as *palatini*; and another body is named *pseudo-comitatenses*, probably detachments not forming a regular part of the field army, but united with it temporarily, and recruited from the frontier forces. The designation *riparienses* denotes the garrisons of the old standing camps on the outside of the Empire. These are distinct from the newer *limitanei*, who cultivated lands (*terrae limitaneae*, or *fundi limotrophi*) along the *limites*, and held them by a kind of military tenure. The *castriciani* and *castellani* seem to have held lands close to the *castra* and *castella* respectively, and did not differ essentially from the *riparienses* and *limitanei*. Their sons could not inherit the lands unless they entered the same service. The *comitatenses* were in higher honour than the soldiers stationed on the outmost edges of the Empire, and their quarters were usually in the inner regions. The whole strength of the army under Diocletian, Constantine, and their successors is difficult to calculate. The number of men in the legion seems to have steadily diminished and by the end of the fourth century to have sunk to two, or even one thousand. An estimate based on the *Notitia* gives 250,000 infantry and 110,000 cavalry on the frontiers, while the *comitatenses* comprise 150,000 foot and 46,000 horse. But the calculation is dubious, probably excessive. Generally speaking, the burden of army service fell chiefly on the lowest class. Though every subject of the Empire was in theory liable to service, the wealthier, when any levy took place, were not only allowed, but practically compelled, to find substitutes, lest the finances of the Empire should suffer.

In addition to the forces already mentioned, there grew up some corps which may be described as Imperial Guards. From the early Empire the practice of surrounding the emperor with an intimate bodyguard composed of barbarians, principally Germans, had prevailed. Augustus possessed such a force, which he disbanded after the disaster suffered by Varus in Germany, but it was reestablished by his successors down to Galba. A little later came the *equites singulares*, also mainly recruited from Germans, who had a special camp in the capital, and were an appendage to the Praetorians. Probably when Constantine abolished the Praetorians the *equites singulares* also disappeared. But before this happened, a new bodyguard had come into existence, bearing the name of the *protectores divini lateris*. It included Germans (often of princely origin), and Romans of several classes high and low. Diocletian added a new set of *protectores*, composed partly of infantry and partly of cavalry, which formed a sort of *corps d'élite*, and served for the training of officers. In it were found officers' sons, men of different ranks, promoted from the regular army, and young members of noble or wealthy families. The distinction between the two sets of *protectores* was not maintained, and the later title was *domestici* only. They served in close proximity to the emperor, who thus made personal acquaintance with men among them who were destined to hold commands, often important commands,

in the regular army.   The members of the body were raised far above
the ordinary soldier by their personnel, their privileges, their pay, in
some cases equal to that of civil officials of a high grade, by their equipment, and by the estimation in which they were held.   The historian
Ammianus Marcellinus served in their ranks.   They were divided into
sections called *scholae*.

Still another corps of Imperial Guards was created by Constantine,
consisting of *scholae palatinae*, distinguished as *scholae scutariorum*,
who were Romans, and *scholae gentilium*, who were barbarians.   They
were detached from the general army organisation and were under the
orders of the *magister officiorum*.   Their history was not unlike that of
the Praetorians; they became equally turbulent, and equally inefficient
as soldiers.

With the new organisation of the army, there sprang up new military
offices of high importance, with new names.   Constantine created two
high officers as chief commanders of the mobile army, a *magister equitum*
and a *magister peditum*.   Their position resembled that of the *Praefecti
Praetorio* of the early Empire in several respects.   They were immediately
dependent on the emperor, and also, from the nature of their commands,
on one another.   But circumstances in time changed their duties and
their numbers.   They had sometimes to take the field when the emperor
was not present, and the division between the infantry command and the
cavalry command thus broke down.   Hence the titles *magister equitum
et peditum*, and *magister utriusque militiae*, or *magister militum* simply.
The jealousy which the emperors naturally entertained for all high
officers caused considerable variations in the position and importance of
these *magistri*.   After the middle of the fourth century the necessary
connexion of the *magistri* with the emperor's person had ceased, and the
command of a *magister* generally embraced the Dioecesis, within which
war occurred or threatened.   Where the emperor was, there would be
two *magistri* called *praesentales*, either distinguished as commanders of
infantry and cavalry, or bearing the title of *magistri utriusque militiae
praesentales*.   But in the fifth century the emperor was generally in
practice a military nonentity, and was in the hands of one *magister* who
was not unfrequently the real ruler of the Empire.   As was the case with
all high officials the *magistri* exercised jurisdiction over those under
their *dispositio*, not only in matters purely military, but in cases of crime
and even to some extent in connexion with civil proceedings.   The lower
commanders also possessed similar jurisdiction, but the details are not
known.   Appeal was to the emperor, who delegated the hearing as a rule
to one or other of the highest civil functionaries.

No view of the great imperial hierarchy of officials would be complete
which did not take account of the new title *comes*.   Its application
followed no regular rules.   In the earlier Latin it was used somewhat
loosely to designate men who accompanied a provincial governor, and

were attached to his staff (*cohors*), especially such as held no definite office connected with administration, whether military or civil. Such unofficial members of the staff seem especially to have assisted the governor in legal matters, and in time they were paid, and were punishable under the laws against extortion in the provinces. In the early Empire the title *comes* begins to be applied in no very precise manner to persons attached to the service of the emperor or of members of the imperial family; but only slowly did it acquire an official significance. Inscriptions of the reign of Marcus Aurelius show a change; as many persons are assigned the title in this one reign as in all the preceding reigns put together. Probably at this time began the bestowal of the title on military as well as legal assistants of the emperor, and soon its possessors were chiefly military officers, who after serving with the emperor, took commands on the frontier. Then from the end of the reign of Severus Alexander to the early years of Constantine the description *comes Augusti* was abolished for human beings, but attached to divinities. Constantine restored it to its mundane employment, and used it as an honorific designation for officers of many kinds, who were not necessarily in the immediate neighbourhood of an Augustus or Caesar, but were servants of the Augustus or Augusti and Caesars generally, that is to say might occupy any position in the whole imperial administration. Constantine seems to have despatched *comites*, not all of the same rank or importance, to provinces or parts of the Empire concerning which he wished to have confidential information. Later they appear in most districts, and the ordinary rulers are in some degree subject to them, and they hear appeals and complaints which otherwise would have been laid before the Praefecti Praetorio. The *comites provinciarum* afford a striking illustration of the manner in which offices were piled up upon offices, in the vain attempt to check corruption and misgovernment.

In the immediate neighbourhood of the Court the name *comes* was attached to four high military officers; the *magister equitum* and *magister peditum*, and the commanders of the *domestici equites* and the *domestici pedites*. Also to four high civil officers, the High Treasurer (*comes sacrarum largitionum*) and the controller of the Privy Purse (*comes rerum privatarum*); also the *quaestor sacri palatii* and the *magister officiorum*. These high civil functionaries appear as *comites consistoriani*, being regular members of the Privy Council (*consistorium*). Before the end of Constantine's reign the words connecting the *comes* with the emperor and the Caesars drop out, possibly because the imperial rulers were deemed to be too exalted for any form of companionship. A man is now not *comes Augusti* but *comes* merely or with words added to identify his duties, as for instance when the district is stated within which a military or civil officer acts, on whom the appellation has been bestowed. The former necessary connexion of the *comes* with the Court having ceased, the name was vulgarised and connected with offices of many kinds, sometimes of a somewhat lowly nature. In many cases it was not associated with duties at all, but was merely titular. As a natural result, *comites* were classified in three orders of dignity (*primi, secundi, tertii ordinis*). Admission to the lowest rank was eagerly coveted and often purchased, because of the immunity from public burdens which the boon carried with it. Constantine also adapted the old phrase *patricius* to new uses. The earlier emperors, first by special authorisation, later merely as emperors, had raised families to patrician rank, but the result was merely a slight increase in social dignity. From Constantine's time onwards, the dignity was rarely bestowed and then the *patricii* became a high and exclusive order of nobility. They had precedence next to the emperor, with the exception of the consuls actually in office. Their titles did not descend to their sons. The best known of the *patricii* are some of the great generals of barbarian origin, who were the last hopes of the crumbling Empire. The title lasted long; it was bestowed on Charles Martel, and was known later in the Byzantine Empire.

At the centre of the great many-storeyed edifice of the bureaucracy was the *Consistorium* or Most Honourable Privy Council. There was deep rooted in the Roman mind the idea that neither private citizen nor official should decide on important affairs without taking the advice of those best qualified to give it. This feeling gave rise to the great advising body for the magistrates, the Senate, to the jury who assisted in criminal affairs, to the bench of counsellors, drawn from his staff, who gave aid to the provincial governor, and also to the loosely constituted gathering of friends whose opinion the *paterfamilias* demanded. To every one of these groups the word *consilium* was applicable. It was natural that the early emperors should have their *consilium*, the constitution of which gradually became more and more formal and regular. Hadrian gave a more important place than heretofore to the jurisconsults among his advisers. For a while a regular paid officer called *consiliarius* existed. In Diocletian's time the old name *consilium* was supplanted by *consistorium*. The old advisers of the magistrates sat on the bench with them and therefore sometimes bore the name *adsessores*. But it was impious to be seated in the presence of the new divinised rulers; and from the practice of standing (*consistere*) the Council derived its new name. From Constantine the Council received a more definite frame. As shewn above, certain officers became *comites consistoriani*. But these officers were not always the same after Constantine's reign, and additional persons were from time to time called in for particular business. The *Praefectus Praetorio praesens* or *in comitatu* would usually attend. The *Consistorium* was both a Council of State for the discussion of knotty imperial questions, and also a High Court of Justice, though it is difficult to determine exactly what cases might be brought before it. Probably that depended on the emperor's will.

It is necessary that something should be said of the position which the two capitals, Rome and Constantinople, held in the new organisation, and of the traces which still hung about Italy of its older historical privileges. The old Roman Senate was allowed a nominal existence, with a changed constitution and powers which were rather municipal than imperial. Of the old offices whose holders once filled the Senate, the Consulship, Praetorship, and Quaestorship survived, while the Tribunate and the Aedileship died out. Two *consulares ordinarii* were named by the emperor, who would sometimes listen to recommendations from the senators. The years continued to be denoted by the consular names, and, to add dignity to the office, the emperor or members of the imperial family would sometimes hold it. The tenure of the office was brief, and the *consules suffecti* during the year were selected by the Senate, with the emperor's approval. But to be *consul suffectus* was of little value, even from a personal point of view. A list of nominations for the Praetorship and Quaestorship was laid by the *Praefectus urbi* before the emperor for confirmation. Apart from these old offices, many of the new *dignitates* carried with them membership of the *ordo senatorius*. Ultimately all officials who were *clarissimi*, that is to say who possessed the lowest of the three noble titles, belonged to it. Thus it included not merely the highest functionaries, as the principal military officers, the civil governors, and the chiefs of bureaux, but many persons lower down in the hierarchy of office, for example all the *comites*. The whole body must have comprised some thousands. But a man might be a member of the *ordo* without being actually a senator. Only the higher functionaries and priests and the *consulares* described above, with possibly a few others, actually took part in the proceedings. The actual Senate and the *ordo* were distinguished by high-sounding titles in official documents, and emperors would occasionally send communications to the Senate about high matters, and make pretence of asking its advice, out of respect for its ancient prestige, but its business was for the most part comparatively petty, and chiefly confined to the immediate needs of the city. But every now and then it was convenient for the ruler to expose the Senate to the odium of making unpopular decisions, as in cases of high treason; and when pretenders rose, or changes of government took place, the favour of this ancient body still carried with it a certain value. Among the chief functions of the senators was the supervision of the supply of *panis et circenses*, provisions and amusements, for the capital. The games were chiefly paid for by the holders of the Consulship, Praetorship, and Quaestorship. The obligation resting on the Praetorship was the most serious, and therefore nomination to this magistracy took place many years in advance, that the money might be ready. Naturally these burdens became to a large extent compulsory;

and so even women who had inherited from a senator had to supply money for such purposes. Rich men of course exceeded the minimum largely with a view to display. The old privilege still attached to Rome of receiving corn from Africa. Diocletian divided Italy into two districts, of which the northern (*annonaria regio*) paid tribute for support of the Court at Milan, while the southern (*dioecesis Romae*, or *suburbicaria regio*) supplied wine, cattle, and some other necessaries for the capital.

Senators as such and the *senatorius ordo* were subject to special taxation, as well as the ordinary taxation of the provinces (with exception perhaps of the *aurum coronarium*). The *follis senatorius* was a particular tax on senatorial lands, and even a landless senator had to pay something. The *aurum oblaticium*, already mentioned, was specially burdensome.

The most important officer connected with the Senate was the *Praefectus urbi*. His office had grown steadily in importance during the whole existence of the Empire. From the time of Constantine its holder was *vir illustris*. He was the only high official of the Empire who continued to wear the *toga* and not the military garb. He was at the head of the Senate and was the intermediary between that body and the emperor. The powers of his office were extraordinary. The members of the Senate resident in Rome were under his criminal jurisdiction. There was an appeal to him from all the lesser functionaries who dealt with ·legal matters in the first instance, not only in the capital, but in a district extending 100 miles in every direction. His control spread over every department of business. He was the chief guardian of public security and had the *cohortes urbanae*, as well as the *praefectus vigilum* under his command. The provisioning of the city was an important part of his duty, and the *praefectus annonae* acted under his orders. A whole army of officials, many of them bearing titles which would have been strange to the Republic and early Empire, assisted him in looking after the water-supply, controlling trade and the markets, and the traffic on the river, in maintaining the river banks, in taking account of the property of senators and in many other departments of affairs. It is difficult to say how far his position was affected by the presence in the city of a Corrector, and a Vicarius of the Praefectus Praetorio. The material welfare of Rome was at least abundantly cared for by the new monarchy. The city had already grown accustomed to the loss of dignity caused by the residence of the emperors in cities more convenient for the purposes of government. But the foundation of Constantinople must have been a heavy blow. The institutions of the old Rome were to a great extent copied in the new. There was a Senate subject to the same obligations as in Rome. Most of the magistracies were repeated. But until 359 no *Praefectus urbi* seems to have existed at Constantinople. Elaborate arrangements were made for placing the new city on a level with the old as regards tributes of corn, wine, and other necessaries from the provinces. The more frequent presence of the ruler gave to the new capital a brilliance which the old must have envied.

So far the machinery of the new government in its several parts has been described. We must now consider in outline what was its total effect upon the inhabitants of the Empire. The inability of the ruler to assure good government to his subjects was made conspicuous by the frequent creation of new offices, whose object was to curb the corruption of the old. The multiplication of the functionaries in close touch with the population rendered oppression more certain and less punishable than ever. Lactantius declares, with pardonable exaggeration, that the number of those who lived on the taxes was as great as the number who paid them. The evidence of official rapacity is abundant. The laws thundered against it in vain. Oftentimes it happened that illegitimate exactions were legalised in the empty hope of keeping them within bounds. Penalties expressed in laws were plain enough and numerous enough. For corruption in a province not only the governor but his whole *officium* were liable to make heavy recompense. And the comparative powerlessness of the governor is shewn by the fact that the *officium* is more heavily mulcted than its head. But a down-trodden people rarely will or can bring legal proof against its oppressors. Nothing but extensive arbitrary dismissal and punishment of his servants by the emperor, without insistence on forms of law, would have met the evil. As it was, corruption reigned through the Empire with little check, and the illicit gains of the emperor's servants added to the strain imposed by the heavy imperial taxation. Thus the benefit which the provincials had at first received by the substitution of Imperial for Republican government was more than swept away. Their absorption into the Roman polity on terms of equality with their conquerors, brought with it degradation and ruin.

During the fourth century that extraordinary development was completed whereby society was reorganised by a demarcation of classes so rigid that it became extremely difficult for any man to escape from that condition of life into which he was born. In the main, but not altogether, this result was brought about by the fiscal system. When the local Senates or their leaders were made responsible for producing to the government the quota of taxation imposed on their districts, it became necessary to prevent the members (*decuriones* or *curiales*) from escaping their obligations by passing into another path of life, and also to compel the sons to walk in their fathers' footsteps. But the maintenance of the local *ordo* was necessary also from the local as well as the imperial point of view. The magistracies involved compulsory as well as voluntary payments for local objects, and therefore those capable of filling them must be thrust into them by force if need were. Every

CH. II.

kind of magistracy in every town of the Empire, and every official position
in connexion with any corporate body, whether priestly college or trade
guild or religious guild, brought with it expenditure for the benefit of
the community, and on this, in great part, the ordinary life of every
town depended.   The Theodosian Code shews that the absconding
decurio was in the end treated as a runaway slave; five gold pieces
were given to any one who would haul him back to his duties.

In time the members also of all or nearly all professional corporations
(*collegia* or *corpora*) were held to duties by the State, and the burden of
them descended from father to son.   The evolution by which these free
unions for holding together in a social brotherhood all those who
followed a particular occupation were turned into bodies with the stamp
of caste upon them, is to be traced with difficulty in the extant inscriptions and the legal literature.   Here as everywhere the fiscal system
instituted by Diocletian was a powerful agent.   A large part of the
natural fruits of the earth passed into the hands of government, and
a vast host of assistants was needed for transport and distribution.   And
the organisation for maintaining the food-supply at Rome and Constantinople became more and more elaborate.   For the *annona* alone
many corporations had to give service, in most cases easily divined from
their names, as *navicularii, frumentarii, mercatores, olearii, suarii, pecuarii,
pistores, boarii, porcinarii* and numerous others.   Similar bodies were connected with public works, with police functions, as the extinction of fires,
with government operations of numerous kinds, in the mints, the mines,
the factories for textiles and arms and so on.   In the early Empire the
service rendered to the State was not compulsory, and partly by rewards,
such as immunity from taxation, partly by pay, the government was
willingly served.   But in time the burdens became intolerable.   State
officers ultimately controlled the minutest details connected with these
corporations.   And the tasks imposed did not entirely proceed from the
imperial departments.   The *curiales* of the towns could enforce assistance
from the local *collegia* within their boundaries.   And the tentacles of the
great octopus of the central government were spread over the provinces.
In the fourth and later centuries the restrictions on the freedom of these
corporations were extraordinarily oppressive.   Egress from inherited
membership was inhibited by government except in rare instances.
Ingress, as into the class of *curiales*, was, directly or indirectly, compulsory.   The colleges differed greatly in dignity.   In some, as in that
of the *navicularii*, even senators might be concerned, and office-holders
might obtain, among their rewards, the rank of Roman knight.   On the
other hand, the bakers (*pistores*) approached near the condition of
slavery.   Marriage, for instance, outside their own circle was forbidden,
whereas, in other cases, it was only rendered difficult.   Property which
had once become subject to the duties required of a *collegium* could
hardly be released.   The end was that *collegiati* or *corporati* all over the

Empire took any method they could find of escaping from their servitude, and the law's severest punishments could not check the movement. If we may believe some late writers, thousands of citizens found life in barbarian lands more tolerable than in the Roman Empire.

The status of other classes in the community also tended to become hereditary. This was the case with the *officiales* and the soldiers, though here compulsion was not so severe. But the tillers of the ground (*coloni*) were more hardly treated than any other class. It became impossible for them, without breach of the law, to tear themselves away from the soil of the locality within which they were born. The evolution of this peculiar form of serfdom, which existed for the purposes of the State, is difficult to trace. Many causes contributed to its growth and final establishment, as the extension of large private and especially of vast imperial domains, the imitation of the German half-free land-tenure when barbarians were settled as *laeti* or *inquilini* within the Empire, the influence of Egyptian and other Eastern land-customs, but above all the drastic changes in the imperial imposts which Diocletian introduced. The cultivator's principal end in life was to insure a contribution of natural products for the revenue. Hence it was a necessity to chain him to the ground, and in the law-books *adscripticius* is the commonest title for him. The details of the scheme of taxation, given above, shew how it must have tended to diminish population, for every additional person, even a slave, increased the contribution which each holding must pay. The owners of the land were in the first instance responsible, but the burdens of course fell ultimately and in the main on the agricultural workers. The temporary loss of provinces to the invader, the failure of harvest in any part of the Empire, the economic effects of pestilence, and other accidents, all led to greater sacrifices on the part of those provinces which were not themselves affected. The exactions became heavier and heavier, the punishments for attempts to escape from duty more and more severe, and yet flight and disappearance of *coloni* took place on a large scale. By the end of the fourth century it was possible for lawyers to say of this unhappy class that they were almost in the condition of slaves, and a century or so later that the distinction between them and slaves no longer existed; that they were slaves of the land itself on which they were born.

In many other ways, under the new monarchy, the citizens of the Empire were treated with glaring inequality. The gradations of official station were almost as important in the general life of the Empire as they now are in China, and they were reflected in titular phrases, some of which have been given above. Etiquette became most complicated. Even the emperor was bound to exalted forms of address in his communications with his servants or with groups of persons within his Empire. "Your sublimity," "Your magnificence," "Your loftiness," were common salutations for the greater officers. The ruler did not disdain to employ the title *parens* in addressing some of them. The innumerable new titles which the Empire had invented were highly valued and much paraded by their possessors, even the titles of offices in the municipalities. Great hardship must have been caused to the lower ranks of the taxpayers by the extensive relief from taxation which was accorded to hosts of men in the service of the government (nominal or real) as part payment for the duties which they performed or were supposed to perform. With these immunities, as with everything else in the Empire, there was much corrupt dealing. The criminal law became a great respecter of persons. Not only was the jurisdiction over the upper classes separated at many points from that over the lower, but the lower were subject to punishments from which the upper were free. Gradually the Empire drifted farther and farther away from the old Republican principle, that crimes as a rule are to be punished in the same way, whoever among the citizens commits them. A sharp distinction was drawn between the "more honourable" (*honestiores*) and the "more humble" (*humiliores* or *plebeii*). The former included the imperial *ordo senatorius*, the *equites*, the soldier-class generally and veterans, and the local senators (*decuriones*). The *honestiores* could not be executed without the emperor's sanction, and if executed, were exempt from crucifixion (a form of punishment altogether abolished by the Christian emperors). They could not be sentenced to penal servitude in mines or elsewhere. Nor could they be tortured in the course of criminal proceedings, excepting for treason, magic, and forgery.

A general survey of Roman government in the fourth and later centuries undoubtedly leaves a strong impression of injustice, inequality, and corruption leading fast to ruin. But some parts of the Empire did maintain a fair standard of prosperity even to the verge of the general collapse. The two greatest problems in history, how to account for the rise of Rome and how to account for her fall, never have been, perhaps never will be, thoroughly solved.

CHAPTER III

CONSTANTINE'S SUCCESSORS TO JOVIAN: AND THE STRUGGLE WITH PERSIA

DEATH had surprised Constantine when preparing to meet Persian aggression on the Eastern frontier and it seems certain that the Emperor had made no final provision for the succession to the throne, though later writers profess to know of a will which parcelled out the Roman world among the members of his family. During his lifetime his three sons had been created Caesars and while for his nephew Hanniballianus he had fashioned a kingdom in Asia, to his nephew Delmatius had been assigned the Ripa Gothica. Possibly we are to see in these latter appointments an attempt to satisfy discontent at Court; it may be that Optatus and Ablabius, espousing the cause of a younger branch of the imperial stock, had forced Constantine's hand and that it was for this interference that they afterwards paid the penalty of their lives. But it would seem a more probable suggestion that the Persian danger was thought to demand an older and more experienced governor than Constantius, while the boy Constans was deemed unequal to withstand the Goths in the north. At least the plan would appear to have been in substance that of a threefold division of spheres itself suggested by administrative necessity; Constantine was true to the principle of Diocletian, and it was only a superficial view which saw in this devolution of the central power a partition of the Roman Empire.[1] Thus on the Emperor's death there followed an interregnum of nearly four months. Constantine had, however, been successful in inspiring his soldiers with his own dynastic views; they feared new tumult and internal struggle and in face of the twenty year old Constantius felt themselves to be the masters. The armies agreed that they would have none but the sons of Constantine to rule over them, and at one blow they murdered all the other relatives of the dead Emperor save only the child Julian and Gallus the future Caesar; in the latter's case men looked to his own ill health to spare the executioner. At the same time perished Optatus and Ablabius. On 9 September 337 Constantius, Constantine II, and Constans each assumed the title of Augustus as joint Emperors.

[1] Cf. Victor, *Caes.* XXXIX. 30, quasi partito imperio.

His contemporaries were unable to agree how far Constantius was
to be held responsible for this assassination.   He alone of the sons of
Constantine was present in the capital, it was he who stood to gain
most by the deed, the property of the victims fell into his hands, while
it was said that he himself regarded his ill-success in war and his
childlessness as Heaven's punishment and that this murder was one of
the three sins which he regretted on his death-bed.   In later times some,
though considering the slaughter as directly inspired by the Emperor,
have yet held him justified and have viewed him as the victim of
a tragic necessity of state.   Certainty is impossible but the circumstances
suggest that inaction and not participation is the true charge against
Constantius; the army which made and unmade emperors was determined
that there should be no rival to question their choice.   The massacre
had fatal consequences; it was the seed from which sprang Julian's
mistrust and ill-will: in a panegyric written for the Emperor's eye he
might admit the plea of compulsion, but the deep-seated conviction
remained that he was left an orphan through his cousin's crime.

In the summer of 338 the new rulers assembled in Pannonia (or
possibly at Viminacium in Dacia, not far from the Pannonian frontier)
to determine their spheres of government.   According to their father's
division, it would seem, Spain, Britain, and the two Gauls fell to
Constantine: the two Italies, Africa, Illyricum, and Thrace were subjected to Constans, while southward from the Propontis, Asia and the
Orient with Pontus and Egypt were entrusted to Constantius.   It was
thus to Constantius that, on the death of Hanniballianus, Armenia and
the neighbouring allied tribes naturally passed, but with this addition
the eastern Augustus appears to have remained content.   The whole of
the territory subject to Delmatius, *i.e.* the Ripa Gothica which probably
comprised Dacia, Moesia I and II, and Scythia (perhaps even Pannonia
and Noricum) went to swell the share of Constans who was now but
fifteen years of age.[1]   But though both the old and the new Rome were
thus in the hands of the most youthful of the three emperors, the balance
of actual power still seemed heavily weighted in favour of Constantine,
the ruler of the West; indeed, he appears to have assumed the position
of guardian over his younger brother.   It may be difficult to account
for the moderation of Constantius, but Julian points out that a war
with Persia was imminent, the army was disorganised, and the preparations for the campaign insufficient; domestic peace was the Empire's
great need, while Constantius himself really strengthened his own position
by renouncing further claims: to widen his sphere of government might
have only served to limit his moral authority.   Further he was perhaps
unwilling to demand for himself a capital in which his kinsmen had been

---

[1] In his eighteenth year, Eutrop. x. 9; cf. Seeck, *Zeitschrift für Numismatik*, XVII.
pp. 39 sqq.

so recently murdered : his self-denial should prove his innocence.[1] During
·the next thirteen years three great and more or less independent interests
absorbed the energies of Constantius : the welfare and doctrine of the
Christian Church,[2] the long drawn and largely ineffective struggle
against Persia and lastly the assertion and maintenance of his personal
influence in the affairs of the West.

It was to Asia that Constantius hastened after his meeting with his
co-rulers.   Before his arrival Nisibis had successfully withstood a Persian
siege (autumn 337 or spring 338), and the Emperor at once made
strenuous efforts to restore order and discipline among the Roman forces.
Profiting by his previous experience he organised a troop of mail-clad
horsemen after the Persian model — the wonder of the time — and raised
recruits both for the cavalry and infantry regiments; he demanded
extraordinary contributions from the eastern provinces, enlarged the
river flotillas and generally made his preparations for rendering effective
resistance to Persian attacks.   The history of this border warfare is
a tangled tale and our information scanty and fragmentary.   In
Armenia the fugitive king and those nobles who with him were loyal
to Rome were restored to their country, but for the rest the campaigns
resolved themselves in the main into the successive forays across
the frontier of Persian or Roman troops.   Though Ludi Persici
(13–17 May) were founded, though court orators could claim that the
Emperor had frequently crossed the Tigris, had raised fortresses on its
banks and laid waste the enemy's territory with fire and sword, yet the
lasting results of these campaigns were sadly to seek : now an Arab
tribe would be induced to make common cause with Rome (as in 338)
and to harry the foe, now a Persian town would be captured and its
inhabitants transported and settled within the Empire, but it was rare
indeed for the armies of both powers to meet face to face in the open
field.   Constantius persistently declined to take the aggressive; he
hesitated to risk any great engagement which even if successful might
entail a heavy loss in men whom he could ill afford to spare.   Of one
battle alone have we any detailed account.   Sapor had collected a vast
army ; conscripts of all ages were enlisted, while neighbouring tribesmen
served for Persian gold.   In three divisions the host crossed the Tigris
and by the Emperor's orders the frontier guards did not dispute the
passage.   The Persians occupied an entrenched camp at Hileia or Ellia
near Singara, while a distance of some 150 stades lay between them and
the Roman army.   Even on Sapor's advance Constantius true to his
defensive policy awaited the enemy's attack; it may be, as Libanius
asserts, that Rome's best troops were absent at the time.   Beneath their
fortifications the Persians had posted their splendid mailed cavalry

---

[1] For the above cf. Victor, *Epit.* xli. 20; Vita Artemii Martyris, *AS. Boll.* Tom. viii.
Oct. 20; Eutyches, *Chron. Alex. Ol.* 279; Seeck, *Zeits. f. Numismatik*, l.c.
[2] See Chap. v.

(*cataphracti*) and upon the ramparts archers were stationed.   On a midsummer morning, probably in the year 344 (possibly 348), the struggle
began.   At midday the Persians feigned flight in the direction of their
camp, hoping that thus their horsemen would charge upon an enemy
disorganised by long pursuit.   It was already evening when the Romans
drew near the fortifications.   Constantius gave orders to halt until the
dawn of the new day; but the burning heat of the sun had caused
a raging thirst, the springs lay within the Persian camp and the troops
with little experience of their Emperor's generalship refused to obey his
commands and resumed the attack.   Clubbing the enemy's cavalry, they
stormed the palisades.   Sapor fled for his life to the Tigris, while the
heir to his throne was captured and put to death.   As night fell, the
victors turned to plunder and excess, and under cover of the darkness
the Persian fugitives re-formed and won back their camp.   But success
came too late; their confidence was broken and with the morning the
retreat began.

Turning to the history of the West after the meeting of the Augusti
in 338, it would appear that Constantine forthwith claimed an authority
superior to that of his co-rulers;[1] he even legislated for Africa although
this province fell within the jurisdiction of Constans.   The latter, however, soon asserted his complete independence of his elder brother and
in autumn (338?) after a victory on the Danube assumed the title of
Sarmaticus.   At this time (339) he probably sought to enlist the support
of Constantius, surrendering to the latter Thrace and Constantinople.[2]
Disappointed of his hopes, it would seem that the ruler of the West now
demanded for himself both Italy and Africa.   Early in 340 he suddenly
crossed the Alps and at Aquileia rashly engaged the advanced guard of
Constans who had marched from Naissus in Dacia, where news had
reached him of his brother's attack.   Constantine falling into an ambush
perished, and Constans was now master of Britain, Spain, and the Gauls
(before 9 April 340).   He proved himself a terror to the barbarians
and a general of untiring energy who travelled incessantly, making light
of extremes of heat and cold.   In 341 and 342 he drove back an
inroad of the Franks and compelled that restless tribe "for whom
inaction was a confession of weakness" to conclude a peace: he disregarded the perils of the English Channel in winter, and in January 343
crossed from Boulogne to Britain, perhaps to repel the Picts and Scots.
His rule is admitted to have been at the outset vigorous and just, but
the promise of his early years was not maintained: his exactions grew
more intolerable, his private vices more shameless, while his favourites
were allowed to violate the laws with impunity.   It would seem, however,
to have been his unconcealed contempt for the army which caused his

[1] This is an inference drawn from his coinage.
[2] Cf. the language of the *ita Artemii*, l.c. ὁ δὲ Κωνστάντιος . . . τὸ τῆς ἑώας ἀσπά-
ζεται μέρος καὶ τότε . . . κ.τ.λ.

fall.   A party at Court conspired with Marcellinus, Count of the sacred largesses, and Magnentius, commander of the picked corps of Joviani and Herculeani, to secure his overthrow.   Despite his Roman name Magnentius was a barbarian : his father had been a slave and subsequently a freedman in the service of Constantine.   While at Augustodunum, during the absence of the Emperor on a hunting expedition, Marcellinus on the pretext of a banquet in honour of his son's birthday feasted the military leaders (18 January 350) ;   wine had flowed freely and the night was already far advanced, when Magnentius suddenly appeared among the revellers, clad in the purple.   He was straightway acclaimed Augustus : the rumour spread : folk from the country-side poured into the city : Illyrian horsemen who had been drafted into the Gallic regiments joined their comrades, while the officers hardly knowing what was afoot were carried by the tide of popular enthusiasm into the usurper's camp. Constans fled for Spain and at the foot of the Pyrenees by the small frontier fortress of Helene was murdered by Gaiso, the barbarian emissary of Magnentius.   The news of his brother's death reached Constantius when the winter was almost over, but true to his principle never to sacrifice the Empire to his own personal advantage he remained in the East, providing for its safety during his absence and appointing Lucillianus to be commander-in-chief.

The hardships and oppression which the provinces had suffered under Constans were turned by Magnentius to good account.   A month after his usurpation Italy had joined him and Africa was not slow to follow. The army of Illyricum was wavering in its fidelity when, upon the advice of Constantia sister of Constantius, Vetranio, *magister peditum* of the forces on the Danube, allowed himself to be acclaimed Emperor (1 March, at Mursa or Sirmium) and immediately appealed for help to Constantius.   The latter recognised the usurper, sent Vetranio a diadem and gave orders that he should be supported by the troops on the Pannonian frontier.   Meanwhile in Rome, the elect of the mob, Flavius Popilius Nepotianus, cousin of Constantius, enjoyed a brief and bloody reign of some 28 days until, through the treachery of a senator, he fell into the hands of the soldiers of Magnentius, led by Marcellinus the newly appointed *magister officiorum*.

In the East, Nisibis was besieged for the third and last time : Sapor's object was, it would seem, permanently to settle a Persian colony within the city.   The siege was pressed with unexampled energy ; the Mygdonius was turned from its course, and thus upon an artificial lake the fleet plied its rams but without effect.   At length under the weight of the waters part of the city wall collapsed ; cavalry and elephants charged to storm the breach, but the huge beasts turned in flight and broke the lines of the assailants.   A new wall rose behind the old, and though four months had passed, Jacobus, Bishop of Nisibis, never lost heart.   Then Sapor learned that the Massagetae were invading his own country and slowly the Persian host withdrew.   For a time the Eastern frontier was at peace (A.D. 350).

In the West while Magnentius sought to win the recognition of Constantius, Vetranio played a waiting game.   At last, the historians tell us, the Illyrian Emperor broke his promises and made his peace with Magnentius.   A common embassy sought Constantius : let him give Magnentius his sister Constantia to wife, and himself wed the daughter of Magnentius.   Constantius wavered, but rejected the proposals and marched towards Sardica.   Vetranio held the pass of Succi — the Iron Gate of later times — but on the arrival of the Emperor gave way before him.   In Naissus, or as others say in Sirmium, the two Emperors mounted a rostrum and Constantius harangued the troops, appealing to them to avenge the death of the son of the great Constantine.   The army hailed Constantius alone as Augustus and Vetranio sought for pardon.   The Emperor treated the usurper with great respect and accorded him on his retirement to Prusa in Bithynia a handsome pension until his death six years later.   Such is the story, but it can hardly fail to arouse suspicion.   The greatest blot on the character of Constantius is his ferocity when once he fancied his superiority threatened, and here was both treason and treachery, for power had been stolen from him by a trick.   All difficulties are removed if Vetranio throughout never ceased to support Constantius, even though the Emperor may have doubted his loyalty for a time when he heard that the prudent general had anticipated any action on the part of Magnentius by himself seizing the key-position, the pass of Succi.   It is obvious that their secret was worth keeping : it is ill to play with armies as Constantius and Vetranio had done ; while the clemency of an outraged sovereign offered a fair theme to the panegyrists of the Emperor.

Marching against one usurper in the West, Constantius was anxious to secure the East to the dynasty of Constantine : the recent success of Lucillianus may have appeared dangerously complete.   The Emperor's nephew Gallus had, it would seem, for some time followed the Court, and while at Sirmium Constantius determined to create him Caesar.   At the same time (15 March 351) his name was changed into Flavius Claudius Constantius, he was married to Constantia and became *frater Augusti*; forthwith the prince and his wife started for Antioch.   Meanwhile Magnentius had not been idle; he had raised huge sums of money in Gaul, while Franks, Saxons, and Germans trooped to the support of their fellow-countryman, whose army now outnumbered that of Constantius.   The latter however took the offensive in the spring of 351 and uniting Vetranio's troops with his own marched towards the Alpine passes.   An ambush of Magnentius posted in the defiles of Atrans inflicted severe loss on his advance guard and the Emperor was compelled to withdraw.   Elated by this success, the usurper now occupied Pannonia and passing Poetovio made for Sirmium.

Throughout his reign the policy of Constantius was marked by an anxious desire to husband the military forces of the Empire, and even now he was ready to compromise and to avoid the fearful struggle between the armies of Gaul and Illyricum. He dispatched Philippus, offering to acknowledge Magnentius as co-Augustus in the West, if he would abandon any claim to Italy. The ambassador was detained, but his proposals after some delay rejected; the usurper was so certain of victory that his envoy the Senator Titianus could even counsel Constantius to abdicate. An attack of Magnentius on Siscia was repulsed and an effort to cross the Save was also unsuccessful. Constantius then retired, preferring to await the enemy in open country where he could turn to the best advantage his superiority in cavalry. At Cibalae the army took up an entrenched position, while Magnentius advanced on Sirmium, hoping to meet with no resistance. Foiled in this he marched to Mursa in the rear of Constantius' army. The latter was forced to relieve the town and here on 28 September the decisive battle was fought. Behind Constantius flowed the Danube and on his right the Drave: for him flight must mean destruction. On both wings he posted mounted archers and in the forefront the mailed cavalry (*cataphracti*) which he had himself raised after the Persian model; in the centre the heavy armed infantry were stationed and in the rear the bowmen and slingers. Before the struggle Silvanus with his horsemen deserted Magnentius. From late afternoon till far into the night the battle raged; the cavalry of Constantius routed the enemy's right wing and this drew the whole line into confusion. Magnentius fled but Marcellinus continued the fight; the Gauls refused to acknowledge defeat; some few escaped through the darkness, but thousands were driven into the river or cut down upon the plain. It is said that Magnentius lost 24,000 men, Constantius 30,000.[1] The usurper took refuge in Aquileia and garrisoned the passes of the Alps; although his overtures were rejected and though his schemes to murder the Caesar Gallus and thus to raise difficulties for Constantius in the East were foiled, yet the exhaustion of his enemies and the approach of winter made pursuit impossible. Constantius forthwith proclaimed an amnesty for all the adherents of Magnentius except only those immediately implicated in his brother's murder; many deserted the pretender and escaped by sea to the victor. In the following year (352), Constantius forced the passes of the Julian Alps, while his fleet dominated the Po, Sicily, and Africa. At the news Magnentius fled to Gaul and by November the Emperor was already in Milan, abrogating all the fugitive's measures. In 353 Constantius crossed the Cottian Alps and at length, three years and a half after his assumption of the purple, Magnentius was surrounded in Lyons by his own troops, and finding his

---

[1] Zonaras states that Constantius had 80,000 men, Magnentius 36,000. Seeck has suggested that at this time Magnentius may have been besieging Sirmium.

cause hopeless committed suicide, while his Caesar Decentius also perished
by his own hand.

The importance and significance of this unsuccessful bid.for empire
may easily be overlooked. A Roman civil official at the head of some
discontented spirits at the Court hatches a plot against his sovereign,
and in order to win the support of the army alienated by the contempt
of Constans induces a barbarian general to declare himself Emperor.
But though the Roman world was willing enough that Germans should
fight the Empire's battles in their defence, they were not prepared to see
another Maximin upon the throne; they refused to be reconciled to
Magnentius even by the admitted justice of his rule. The lesson of his
failure was well learned: the barbarian Arbogast caused not himself but
the Roman civilian Eugenius to be elected Emperor. Further, while in
this struggle the eastern and western halves of the Empire are seen
falling naturally and almost unconsciously asunder, the most powerful
force working for unity is the dynastic sentiment: Constantius claims
support as the legitimate successor of the house of Constantine and as
the avenger of the death of his son. His claim is not merely as the
chosen of senate or army but far more as the rightful heir to the throne.
This struggle throws into prominence the growth of the hereditary
principle and the warmth of the response which it could evoke from the
sympathies of the subjects of the Empire. No student of the history
of the fourth century can indeed afford to neglect the battle of Mursa;
contemporaries were staggered at the appalling loss of life, for while
it is said that the Roman dead numbered 40,000 at Hadrianople
(A.D. 378), at Mursa 54,000 are reported to have been slain. It is
hardly too much to say that the defence of the Empire in the East was
crippled by this blow, and it must have been largely through the
slaughter at Mursa that Constantius was forced to make his fatal demand
that the troops of Gaul should march against Persia. Neither must the
military significance of the battle be forgotten: it lies in the fact that
this was the first victory of the newly formed heavy cavalry, and the
result of the impact of their charge, which carried all before it, showed
that it was no longer the legionary who was to play the most important
part in the campaigns of the future.

Meanwhile in Antioch Gallus was ruling as an oriental despot; there
was in his nature a strain of savagery, and his appointment as Caesar
seems to have awakened within him a brutal lust for a naked display of
unrestrained authority. His passions were only fed by the violence of
Constantia. The unsuccessful plot of Magnentius to assassinate the
Caesar aroused the latter's suspicions and a reign of terror began;
judicial procedure was disregarded and informers honoured, men were
condemned to death without trial and the members of the city council
imprisoned; when the populace complained of scarcity it was suggested
that the responsibility lay with Theophilus governor of Syria: the mob

took the hint and the governor perished. The feeling of insecurity was rendered more intense by a rising among the Jews, who declared a certain Patricius their King, and by the raids of Saracens and Isaurians upon the country-side. The loyalty of the East was jeopardised. The reports of Thalassius, the praetorian praefect, and of Barbatio, the Caesar's Count of the guard, at length moved Constantius to action. On the death of Thalassius (winter 353–4) Domitian was sent to Antioch as his successor, directions being given him that Gallus was to be persuaded to visit the Emperor in the West. The praefect's studied discourtesy and overbearing behaviour enraged the Caesar; Domitian was thrown into prison and the populace responding to the appeal of Gallus tore in pieces both the praefect and Montius the quaestor of the palace. The trials for treason which followed were but a parody of justice; fear and hate held sway in Antioch. Constantius himself now wrote to Gallus praying his presence in Milan. In deep foreboding the Caesar started; on his journey the death of his wife, the Emperor's masterful sister, further dismayed him, and after passing through Constantinople his guard of honour became his gaolers; stripped of his purple by Barbatio in Poetovio, he was brought near Pola before a commission headed by Eusebius, the Emperor's chamberlain, and bidden to account for his administration in the East. The Court came to the required conclusion, and Gallus was beheaded.

Thus of the house of Constantine there only remained the Emperor's cousin Julian. Born in all probability in April 332, the child spent his early years in Constantinople; his mother Basilina, daughter of the praetorian praefect Anicius Julianus, died only a few months after the birth of her son, while his father Julius Constantius, younger brother of Constantine the Great, perished in the massacre of 337. From this Julian was spared by his extreme youth and was thereupon removed to Nicomedia and entrusted to the charge of a distant relative, by name Eusebius, who was at the time bishop of the city. When seven years of age, his education was undertaken by Mardonius, a "Scythian" eunuch — perhaps a Goth — who had been engaged by Julian's grandfather to instruct Basilina in the works of Homer and Hesiod. Mardonius had a passionate love for the classical authors, and on his way to school the boy's imagination was fired by the old man's enthusiasm. Already Julian's love for nature was aroused; in the summer he would spend his time on a small estate which had belonged to his grandmother; it lay eight stades from the coast and contained springs and trees with a garden. Here, free from crowds, he would read a book in peace, looking up now and again upon the ships and the sea, while from a knoll, he tells us, there was a wide view over the town below and thence beyond to the capital, the Propontis and the distant islands. Suddenly (in 341?) both he and his brother Gallus were banished to Marcellum, a large and lonely imperial castle in Cappadocia, lying at the foot of Mount Argaeus.

Here for six years the two boys lived in seclusion, for none of their friends were allowed to visit them. Julian chafed bitterly at this isolation : in one of his rare references to this period he writes "we might have been in a Persian prison with only slaves for our companions." For a time the suspicions of Constantius seem to have gained the upper hand. At length Julian was allowed to visit his birthplace Constantinople. Here, while studying under Christian teachers as a citizen among citizens, his natural capacity, wit, and sociability rendered him dangerously popular : it was rumoured that men were beginning to look upon the young prince as Constantius' successor. He was bidden to return to Nicomedia (349 ?), where he studied philosophy and came under the influence of Libanius, although he was not allowed to attend the latter's lectures. The rhetorician dates Julian's conversion to Neoplatonism from this period :—
"the mud-bespattered statues of the gods were set up in the great temple of Julian's soul." At last, in 351, when Gallus was created Caesar, the student was free to go where he would, and the Pagan philosophers of Asia Minor seized their opportunity. One and all plotted to secure the complete conversion of the young prince. Aedesius and Eusebius at Pergamum, Maximus and Chrysanthius at Ephesus could hardly content Julian's hunger for the forbidden knowledge. It was at this time (351–2) when he was twenty years of age (as he himself tells us) that he finally rejected Christianity and was initiated into the mysteries of Mithras. The fall of Gallus, however, implicated the Caesar's brother and Julian was closely watched and conducted to Italy. For seven months he was kept under guard, and during the six months which he spent in Milan he had only one interview with Constantius which was secured through the efforts of the Empress Eusebia. When at length he was allowed to leave the Court and was on his way to Asia Minor, the trial of the tribune Marinus and of Africanus, governor of Pannonia Secunda, on a charge of high treason inspired Constantius with fresh fears and suspicions. Messages reached Julian ordering his return. But before his arrival at Milan Eusebia had won from the Emperor his permission for Julian to retire to Athens, love of study being a characteristic which might with safety be encouraged in members of the royal house. Men may have seen in this visit to Greece (355) but a banishment; to Julian, nursing the perilous secret of his new-found faith, the change must have been pure joy. In Hellas, his true fatherland, he was probably initiated into the Eleusinian mysteries, while he plunged with impetuous intensity into the life of the University. It was not to be for long, for he was soon recalled to sterner activities.

Since the death of Gallus, the Emperor had stood alone; although no longer compromised by the excesses of his Caesar, he was still beset by the old problems which appeared to defy solution. At this time the power of the central government in Gaul had been still further weakened. Here Silvanus, whose timely desertion of Magnentius had contributed to the Emperor's success at the battle of Mursa, had been appointed *magister peditum*.' He had won some victories over the Alemanni but, driven into treason by Court intrigues, had assumed the purple in Cologne and fallen after a short reign of some 28 days a victim to treachery (August–September 355 ?). In his own person Constantius could not take the command at once in Rhaetia and in Gaul, and yet along the whole northern frontier he was faced with danger and difficulty. He was haunted by the continual fear that some capable general might of his own motion proclaim himself Augustus, or like Silvanus be hounded into rebellion. A military triumph often advantaged the captain more than his master and might have but little influence to-wards kindling anew the allegiance of the provincials. A prince of the royal house could alone with any hope of success attempt to raise the imperial prestige in Gaul. It was thus statecraft and no sinister machi-nation against his cousin's life which led Constantius to listen to his wife's entreaties. He determined to banish suspicion and disregard the interested insinuations of the Court eunuchs: he would make of the philosopher scholar a Caesar, in whose person the loyalty of the West should find a rallying-point and on whom its devotion might be spent. In the Emperor's absence Julian once more arrived in Milan (summer 355), but to him imperial favour seemed a thing more terrible than royal neglect; Eusebia's summons to be of good courage was of no avail, only the thought that this was the will of Heaven steeled his purpose. Who was he to fight against the Gods ? — After some weeks on 6 November 355 Julian was clothed with the purple by Constantius and enthusias-tically acclaimed as Caesar by the army. Before leaving the Court the Caesar married Helena, the youngest sister of Constantius; the union was dictated by policy and she would seem never to have taken any large place in the life or thought of Julian. The position of affairs in Gaul was critical. Magnentius had withdrawn the armies of the West to meet Constantius, and horde after horde of barbarians had swept across the Rhine. In the north the Salii had taken possession of what is now the province of Brabant; in the south the Alemanni under Chnodomar had defeated the Caesar Decentius and had ravaged the heart of Gaul. The rumour ran that Constantius had even freed the Alemanni from their oaths and had given them a bribe to induce them to invade Roman territory, allowing them to take for their own any land which their swords could win. The story is probably a fabrication of Julian and his friends, but the fact of the barbarian invasion cannot be doubted. In the spring of 354 Constantius crossed the Jura and marched to the neighbourhood of Basel, but the Alemanni under Gundomad and Vadomar withdrew and a peace was concluded. In 355 Arbitio was defeated near the Lake of Constance and the fall of Silvanus had for its immediate consequence the capture of Cologne by the Franks. Forty-five towns, not to speak of lesser posts, had been laid waste and the valley of the Rhine was lost to the Romans. Three hundred stades, from the left bank of the river the barbarians were permanently settled and their ravages extended for three times that distance. The whole of Elsass was in the hands of the Alemanni, the heads of the municipalities had been carried into slavery, Strassburg, Brumath, Worms, and Mainz had fallen, while soldiers of Magnentius, who had feared to surrender themselves after their leader's death, roamed as brigands through the country-side and increased the general disorder. On 1 December 355, Julian left Milan with a guard of 360 soldiers; in Turin he learnt of the fall of Cologne and thence advanced to Vienne where he spent the winter training with rueful energy for his new vocation of a soldier. For the following year a combined scheme of operations had been projected: while the Emperor advancing from Rhaetia attacked the barbarians in their own territory, Julian was to act as lieutenant to Marcellus with directions to guard the approaches into Gaul and to drive back any fugitives who sought to escape before Constantius. The neutrality of the Alemannic princes in the north had been secured in 354, while internal dissension among the German tribes favoured the Emperor's plans. The army in Gaul was ordered to assemble at Rheims and Julian accordingly marched from Vienne, reaching Autun on 24 June. That the barbarians should have constantly harried the Caesar's soldiers as they advanced through Auxerre and Troyes only serves to show how completely Gaul had been flooded by the German tribesmen. From Rheims, where the scattered troops were concentrated, the army started for Elsass pursuing the most direct route by Metz and Dieuze to Zabern. Two legions of the rear-guard were surprised on the march and were only with difficulty saved from annihilation. At this time Constantius was doubtless advancing upon the right bank of the Rhine, for Julian at Brumath drove back a body of the Alemanni who were seeking refuge in Gaul. The Caesar then marched by Coblenz through the desolated Rhine valley to Cologne. This city he recovered and concluded a peace with the Franks. The approach of winter brought the operations to a close and Julian retired to Sens. Food was scarce and it was difficult to provision the army; the Caesar's best troops — the Scutarii and Gentiles — were therefore stationed in scattered fortresses. The Alemanni had been driven by hunger to continue their raids through Gaul and hearing of the weakness of the garrison they suddenly swept down upon Sens. In his heroic defence of the town Julian won his spurs as a military commander. For thirty days he withstood the attack, until the Alemanni retired discomfited. Marcellus had probably already experienced the ambition and vanity of the Caesar, his independence and intolerance of criticism: an imperial prince was none too agreeable a lieutenant. The general may even have considered that the Emperor would not be deeply grieved if the fortune of war removed a possible menace to the throne. Whatever his reasons may have been, he treacherously failed to come to the relief of the besieged. When the news reached the Court he was recalled and deprived of his command. Eutherius, sent by Julian from Gaul, discredited the calumnies of Marcellus, and Constantius silenced the malignant whispers of the Court; accepting his Caesar's protestations of loyalty, he created him supreme commander over the troops in Gaul. The actual gains won by the military operations of the year 356 may not have been great but that their moral effect was considerable is demonstrated by the campaign of 357 and by the spirit of the troops at the battle of Strassburg; above all, Julian was no longer an imperial figure-head, he now begins an independent career as general and administrator.

In the spring of 357 Constantius, wishing to celebrate with high pomp and ceremony the twentieth year of his rule since the death of Constantine, visited Rome for the first time (28 April–29 May). The city filled him with awe and wonder and he caused an obelisk to be raised in the Circus Maximus as a memorial of his stay in the capital. But to the historian the main interest of this visit lies in the fact that as a Christian Emperor Constantius removed from the Senate-house the altar of Victory.[1] To the whole-hearted Pagans this altar came to stand for a symbol of the Holy Roman Empire as they conceived it: it was an outward and visible sign of that bond which none might loose between Rome's hard-won greatness as a conquering nation and her loyalty to her historic faith. They clung to it with passionate devotion as to a time-honoured creed in stone — a creed at once political and religious — and thus again and again they struggled and pleaded for its retention or its restoration. The deeper meaning of what might seem a matter of trifling import must never be forgotten if we are to understand the earnest petition of Symmachus or the scorn of Ambrose. The Pagan was defending the last trench: the destruction of the altar of Victory meant for him that he could hold the fortress no longer.

From Rome the Emperor was summoned to the Danube to take action against the Sarmatians, Suevi, and Quadi; he was unable to co-operate with Julian in person, but dispatched Barbatio, *magister peditum*, to Gaul in command of 25,000 troops. Julian was to march from the north, Barbatio was to make Augst near Basel his base of operations, and between the two forces the barbarians were to be enclosed. The choice of a general, however, foredoomed the plan of campaign to failure. Barbatio, one of the principal agents in the death of Gallus, was the last man to work in harmony with Julian. The Caesar leaving Sens concentrated his forces only 13,000 strong at Rheims, and as in the previous year marched south to Elsass. Finding the pass of Zabern blocked, he drove the barbarians before him and forced them to take refuge in the islands of the Rhine. Barbatio had previously allowed a marauding band of Laeti laden with booty to pass his camp and to cross the Rhine

[1] Symm. *Rel.* iii. 6.

unscathed, and later by false reports he secured the dismissal of the tribunes Bainobaudes and the future emperor Valentinian, whom Julian had ordered to dispute the robbers' return. He now refused-to supply the Caesar with boats; light-armed troops, however, waded across the Rhine to the islands and seizing the barbarians' canoes massacred the fugitives. After this success Julian fortified the pass of Zabern and thus closed the gate into Gaul; he settled garrisons in Elsass along the frontier line and did all in his power to supply them with provisions, for Barbatio withheld all the supplies which arrived from southern Gaul. Having now secured his position, Julian received the amazing intelligence that Barbatio had been surprised by the Germans, had lost his whole baggage train and had retreated in confusion to Augst, where he had gone into winter quarters. It must be confessed that this defeat of 25,000 men by a sudden barbarian foray seems almost inexplicable, unless it be that Barbatio was determined at all costs to refuse in any way to co-operate with the Caesar and was surprised while on the march to Augst.   Julian's position was one of great danger: the Emperor was far distant on the Danube, the Alemanni previously at variance among themselves, were now re-united, Gundomad, the faithful ally of Rome, had been treacherously murdered and the followers of Vadomar had joined their fellow-countrymen. Barbatio's defeat had raised the enemy's hopes, while Julian was unsupported and had only some 13,000 men under his command.   It was at this critical moment that a host of Alemannic tribesmen crossed the Rhine under the leadership of Chnodomar and encamped, it would seem, on the left bank of the river, close to the city of Strassburg which the Romans had apparently not yet recovered. On the third day after the passage of the stream had begun, Julian learned of the movement of the barbarians, and set out from Zabern on the military road to Brumath, and thence on the highway which ran from Strassburg to Mainz towards Weitbruch; here after a march of six or seven hours the army would reach the frontier fortification and from this point they had to descend by rough and unknown paths into the plain. On sight of the enemy despite the counsels of the Caesar, despite their long march and the burning heat of an August day, the troops insisted on an immediate attack.   The Roman army was drawn up for battle, Severus on rising ground on the left wing, Julian in command of the cavalry on the right wing in the plain.   Severus from this point of vantage discovered an ambush and drove off the barbarians with loss, but the Alemanni in their turn routed the Roman horse; although Julian was successful in staying their flight, they were too demoralised to renew the conflict. The whole brunt of the attack was therefore borne by the Roman centre and left wing, and it was a struggle of footmen against footmen.   At length the stubborn endurance of the Roman infantry carried the day, and the Alemanni were driven headlong backwards toward the Rhine. Their losses were enormous — 6000 left dead on the field of battle and

countless others drowned : Chnodomar was at last captured, and Julian
sent the redoubtable chieftain as a prisoner to Constantius. The victory
meant the recovery of the upper Rhine and the freeing of Gaul from
barbarian incursions. There would even seem to have been an attempt
after the battle to hail Julian as Augustus, but this he immediately
repressed. The booty and captives were sent to Metz and the Caesar
himself marched to Mainz, being compelled to subdue a mutiny on the
way ; the army had apparently been disappointed in its share of the
spoil. Julian at once proceeded to cross the Rhine opposite Mainz and
to conduct a campaign on the Main. His aim would seem to have been
to strike still deeper terror into the vanquished, and to secure his
advantage in order that he might feel free to turn to the work which
awaited him in the north. Three chieftains sued for peace after their
land had been laid waste with fire and sword, and to seal this success
Julian rebuilt a fortress which Trajan had constructed on the right bank
of the Rhine. The great difficulty which faced the Caesar was the question
of supplies, and one of the terms of the ten months' armistice granted to
the Alemanni was that they should furnish the garrison of the Muni-
mentum Trajani with provisions. It was this pressing necessity which
demanded both an assertion of the power of Rome among the peoples
dwelling about the mouths of the Meuse and Rhine, and also the re-
establishment of the regular transport of corn from Britain. During the
campaign on the Main, Severus had been sent north to reconnoitre ; the
Franks now occupied a position of virtual independence in the district
south of the Meuse, and in the absence of Roman garrisons and with the
Caesar fully occupied by the operations against the Alemanni a troop of
600 Frankish warriors were devastating the country-side. They retired
before Severus and occupied two deserted fortresses. Here for 54 days
in December 357 and January 358 they were besieged by Julian who
had marched north to support the *magister equitum*. Hunger compelled
them at last to yield, for the relief sent by their fellow-tribesmen arrived
too late. Julian spent the winter in Paris, and in early summer advanced with great speed and secrecy, surprised the Franks in Toxandria
and forced them to acknowledge Roman supremacy. Further north the
Chamavi had been driven by the pressure of the Saxons in their rear to
cross the Rhine and to take possession of the country between that river
and the Meuse. The co-operation of Severus enabled Julian to force
them to submission, and it would appear that in consequence they retired to their former homes on the Yssel. The lower Rhine was now
once more in Roman hands ; the generalship of Julian had achieved what
the praefect Florentius had deemed that Roman gold could alone secure,
and the building of a fleet of 400 sea-going vessels was at once begun.
The lower Rhine secured, Julian forthwith (July–August) returned to his
unfinished task in the south. It was imperative that the ravaged provinces of Gaul should be repeopled : their desolation and the honour of

the Empire alike demanded that the prisoners in the hands of the barbarians should be restored. The remorseless ravaging of his land compelled Hortarius to yield, to surrender his Roman captives and to furnish timber for the rebuilding of the Roman towns. The winter past, Julian once more left Paris and with his new fleet brought the corn of Britain to the garrisons of the Rhine. Seven fortresses, from Castra Herculis in the land of the Batavi to Bingen in the south, were reconstructed, and then in a last campaign against the most southerly tribes of the Alemanni, those chieftains who had taken a leading part in the battle of Strassburg were forced to tender their submission. It was no easy matter to secure the release of the Roman prisoners, but Julian could claim to have restored 20,000 of these unfortunates to their homes. The Caesar's work was done: Gaul was once more in peace and the Rhine the frontier of the Empire.

When we turn to Julian's action in the civil affairs of the West, our information is all too scanty. It is clear that he approached his task with the passionate conviction that at all costs he would relieve the lot of the oppressed provincials. He took part in person in the administration of justice and himself revised the judgments of provincial governors; he refused to grant "indulgences" whereby arrears of taxation were remitted, for he well knew that these imperial acts of grace benefited the rich alone, for wealth when first the tribute was assessed could purchase the privilege of delay and thus in the end enjoy the relief of the general rebate. He resolutely opposed all extraordinary burdens, and when Florentius persistently urged him to sign a paper imposing additional taxation for war purposes he threw the document indignantly to the ground and all the remonstrances of the praefect were without avail. In Belgica the Caesar's own representatives collected the tribute and the inhabitants were saved from the exactions alike of the agents of the praefect and of the governor. So successful was his administration that where previously for the land-tax alone twenty-five aurei had been exacted seven aurei only were now demanded by the State. But reform was slow, and in Julian's character there was a strain of restless impatience: he was intolerant of delays and of the irrational obstacles that barred the highway of progress; it galled him that he could not appoint as officials and subordinates men after his own heart. Admitted that Constantius sent him capable civil servants, yet these men who were to be the agents of reform were themselves members of the corrupt bureaucracy which was ruining the provinces. Indeed, might these nominees of his cousin be withstood? The undefined limits of his office might always render it an open question whether the assertion of the Caesar's right were not aggression upon imperial privilege. Julian's conscious power and burning enthusiasm felt the cruel curb of his subordination. Constantius wished loyally to support his young relative, had given him the supreme command in Gaul after the first trial year and was determined that he should be supported by experienced generals, but Julian was far distant and his enemies at Court had the Emperor's ear; for them his successes and virtues but rendered him the more dangerous; the eunuch gang, says Ammianus, only worked the harder at the smithies where calumnies were forged. At times they mocked the Caesar's vanity and decried his conquests, at others they played upon the suspicions of Constantius: Julian was victor to-day, why not another Victorinus — an upstart Emperor of Gaul — to-morrow. Imperial messengers to the West were careful to bring back ominous reports, and Julian, who knew how matters stood and was not ignorant of his cousin's failings, may well have feared the overmastering influence of the Emperor's advisers. Thus constantly checked in his plans of reform alike religious and political, already, it may be, hailed as Augustus by his soldiery and dreading the machinations of courtiers, he began, at first perhaps in spite of himself, to long for greater independence; in 359 he was dreaming of the time when he should be no longer Caesar. The war in the East gave him his opportunity.

While Julian had been recovering Gaul, Constantius had been engaged in a series of campaigns on the Danube frontier, and for this purpose had removed his court from Milan to Sirmium. An unimportant expedition against the Suevi in Rhaetia in 357 was followed in 358 by lengthy operations in the plains about the Danube and the Theiss against the Quadi and various Sarmatian tribes who had burst plundering across the border. The barbarian territory was ravaged, and through the Emperor's successful diplomacy one people after another submitted and surrendered their prisoners. They were in most cases left in possession of their lands under the supremacy of Rome, but the Limigantes were forced to settle on the left instead of the right bank of the Theiss, while the Sarmatae Liberi were given a king by Constantius in the person of their native prince Zizais, and were themselves restored to the district which the Limigantes had been compelled to leave. The latter however in the following year (359), discontented with their new homes, craved that they might be allowed to cross the Danube and settle within the Empire. This Constantius was persuaded to permit, hoping thus to gain recruits for the Roman army and thereby to lighten the burdens of the provincials. The Limigantes, once admitted upon Roman territory, sought to avenge themselves for the losses of the previous year by a treacherous onslaught upon the Emperor. Constantius escaped and a general massacre of the faithless barbarians ensued. The pacification of the northern frontier was now complete.

Meanwhile in the East hostilities with Persia had ceased on any large scale since 351, and in 356–7 the praefect Musonianus had been carrying on negotiations for peace (through Cassianus, military commander in Mesopotamia) with Tampsapor a neighbouring satrap. But the moment was inopportune. Sapor himself had at length effected an alliance with the Chionitae and Gelani and now (spring 358) in a letter to the Emperor

CH. III.

demanded the restoration of Mesopotamia and Armenia; in case of refusal he threatened military action in the following year. Constantius proudly rejected the shameful proposal, but sent two successive embassies to Persia in the hope of concluding an honourable peace. The effort was fruitless. Court intrigue deprived Ursicinus, Rome's one really capable general in the East, of the supreme command, and in spite of the prayers of the provincials he was succeeded by Sabinianus, who in his obscure old age was distinguished only by his wealth, inefficiency and credulous piety. During the entire course of the war inactivity was the one prominent feature of his generalship. On the outbreak of hostilities in 359 the Persians adopted a new plan of campaign. A rich Syrian, Antoninus by name, who had served on the staff of the general commanding in Mesopotamia, was threatened by powerful enemies with ruin. Having compiled from official sources full information alike as to Rome's available ammunition and stores and the number of her troops he fled with his family to the court of Sapor; here, welcomed and trusted, he counselled immediate action: men had been withdrawn from the East for the campaigns on the Danube, let the King no longer be content with frontier forays, let him without warning strike for the rich province of Syria unravaged since the days of Gallienus! The deserter's advice was adopted by the Persians. On the advance of their army, however, the Romans, withdrawing from Charrae and the open country-side burned down all vegetation over the whole of northern Mesopotamia. This devastation and the swollen stream of the Euphrates forced the Persians to strike northward through Sophene; Sapor crossed the river higher in its course and marched towards Amida. The city refused to surrender, and the death of the son of Grumbates, king of the Chionitae, provoked Sapor to abandon his attack on Syria and to press the siege. Six legions formed the standing garrison, a force which probably numbered some 6000 men in all. But at the time of the Persian advance the country-folk had all assembled for the yearly market, and when the peasantry fled for refuge within the city walls Amida was densely overcrowded. None however dreamed of surrender; Ammianus, one of the besieged, has left us a vivid account of those heroic seventy-three days. In the end the city fell (6 Oct.) and its inhabitants were either slain or carried into captivity. Winter was now approaching and Sapor was forced to return to Persia with the loss of 30,000 men.

The sacrifice of Amida had saved the eastern provinces of the Roman Empire, but the fall of the city also convinced Constantius that more troops were needed if Rome was to withstand the enemy. Accordingly the Emperor sent by the tribune Decentius his momentous order that the auxiliary troops, the Aeruli Batavi Celtae and Petulantes, should leave Gaul forthwith, and with them 300 men from each of the remaining Gallic regiments. The demand reached Julian in Paris where he was spending the winter (January? 360); for him the serious feature of the

despatch was that the execution of the Emperor's command was entrusted
to Lupicinus and Gintonius,[1] while Julian himself was ignored. The
transference of the troops was probably an imperial necessity, but this
could not justify the form of the Emperor's despatch. The unrelenting
malice of the courtiers had carried the day; Constantius seems to have
lost confidence in his Caesar. At first Julian thought to lay down his
office; then he temporised: he professed that obedience to the Emperor
would imperil the safety of the province, he raised the objection that the
barbarians had enlisted on the understanding that they should never be
called upon to serve beyond the Alps, Lupicinus was in Britain fighting the
Picts and Scots, while Florentius, to whose influence rumour ascribed the
Emperor's action, was absent in Vienne. Julian summoned him to Paris
to give his advice, but the praefect pleaded the urgency of the supervision
of the corn supply and remained where he was. While Julian played
a waiting game, a timely broadsheet was found in the camp of the
Celtae and Petulantes. The anonymous author complained that the
soldiers were being dragged none knew whither, leaving their families to
be captured by the Alemanni. The partisans of Constantius saw the
danger; should Julian still delay, they insisted, he would but justify the
Emperor's suspicions. His hand was forced; he wrote a letter to
Constantius, ordered the soldiers to leave their winter quarters and gave
permission for their families to accompany them; Sintula, the Caesar's
tribune of the stable, at once set out for the East with a picked body
of Gentiles and Scutarii. Unwisely, as events proved, the court party
demanded that the troops should march through Paris: there, they
thought, any disaffection could be repressed. Julian met the men outside
the city and spoke them fair, their officers he invited to a banquet in the
evening. But when the guests had returned to their quarters, there
suddenly arose in the camp a passionate shout, and crowding tumultu-
ously to the palace the soldiers surrounded its walls, raising the fateful
acclamation, "Julianus Augustus." Without the army clamoured, within
his room its leader wrestled with the gods until the dawn, and with the
break of a new day he was assured of Heaven's blessing. When he
came forth to face his men he made attempt to dissuade them, but he
knew that he would bow to their will. Raised upon a shield and
crowned with a standard bearer's torque, the Caesar returned to his
palace an Emperor. But now that the irrevocable step was taken, his
resolution seemed to have failed, and he remained in retirement —
perhaps for some days. The adherents of Constantius took heart and
a group of conspirators plotted against Julian's life. But the secret was
not kept, and the soldiers once more encircled the palace and would not
be contented until they had seen their Emperor alive and well. From
this moment Julian stifled his scruples and accepted accomplished fact.
After the flight of Decentius and Florentius he despatched Eutherius

[1] Or Sintula. Amm. xx. 4. 3.

CH. III.

and his *magister officiorum* Pentadius as ambassadors to Constantius, while in his letter he proposed the terms which he was prepared to make the basis of a compromise.   He would send to the East troops raised from the *dediticii* and the Germans settled on the left bank of the Rhine — to withdraw the Gallic troops would be, he professed, to endanger the safety of the province — while Constantius should allow him to appoint his own officials, both military and civil, save only that the nomination of the praetorian praefect should rest with the elder Augustus, whose superior authority Julian avowed himself willing to acknowledge.   When the news from Paris reached Caesarea, Constantius hesitated : should he march forthwith against his rebellious Caesar and desert the East while the Persians were threatening to renew the attack of the previous year, or should he subordinate his personal quarrel to the interests of the State ?   Loyalty to his conception of an Emperor's duty carried the day and he advanced to Edessa.   The fact that the Persians in this year were able to recover Singara, once more fallen into Roman hands, and to capture and garrison Bezabdê, a fortress on the Tigris in Zabdicene, while the Emperor remained perforce inactive, serves to show how very earnest was his need of troops.   Even the attempt to recover Bezabdê in the autumn was unsuccessful.   Meanwhile Constantius, ignoring Julian's proposals, made several nominations to high officers in the West, and despatched Leonas to bid the rebel lay aside the purple with which a turbulent soldiery had invested him.   The letter, when read to the troops, served but to inflame their enthusiasm for their general, and Leonas fled for his life.   But Julian still hoped that un under-standing between himself and Constantius was even now not impossible. To save his army from inaction he led them — not towards the East, but against the Attuarian Franks on the lower Rhine.   The barbarians, unwarned of the Roman approach, were easily defeated and peace was granted on their submission.   The campaign lasted three months, and thence by Basel and Besançon Julian returned to winter at Vienne, for Paris, his beloved Lutetia, lay at too great a distance from Asia. Letters were still passing between himself and Constantius, but his task lay clear before him : he must be forearmed alike for aggression and defence.   By a display of power he sought to wrest from his cousin recognition and acknowledgment, while, with his troops about him, he could at least sustain his cause and escape the shame of his brother's fate.   Recruits from the barbarian tribes swelled his forces, and large sums of money were raised for the coming campaign.   In the spring of 361 Julian by the treacherous capture and banishment of Vadomar removed all fears of an invasion by the Alemanni, and about the month of July set out from Basel for the East.   By this step he took the aggressive and himself finally broke off the negotiations ; this was avowed by his appointment of a praefect of Gaul in place of Nebridius, the nominee of Constantius, who had refused to take the oath of allegiance to Julian. Germanianus temporarily performed the praefect's duties but retired in favour of Sallust, while Nevitta was created *magister armorum* and Jovius *quaestor*.

As soon as he was freed from the Persian War, Constantius had thought to hunt down his usurping Caesar and capture his prey while Julian was still in Gaul; he had set guards about the frontiers and had stored corn on the Lake of Constance and in the neighbourhood of the Cottian Alps. Julian determined that he would not wait to be surrounded, but would strike the first blow, while the greater part of the army of Illyricum was still in Asia. He argued that present daring might deliver Sirmium into his hands, that thereupon he could seize the Pass of Succi, and thus be master of the road to the West. Jovius and Jovinus were ordered to advance at full speed through North Italy, in command, it would appear, of a squadron of cavalry. They would thus surprise the inhabitants into submission, while fear of the main army, which would follow more slowly, might overawe opposition. Nevitta he commanded to make his way through Rhaetia Mediterranea, while he himself left Basel with but a small escort and struck direct through the Black Forest for the Danube. Here he seized the vessels of the river fleet, and at once embarked his men. Without rest or intermission Julian continued the voyage down the river, and reached Bononia on the eleventh day. Under the cover of night, Dagalaiphus with some picked followers was despatched to Sirmium. At dawn his troop was demanding admission in the Emperor's name; only when too late was the discovery made that the Emperor was not Constantius. The general Lucilianus, who had already begun the leisurely concentration of his men for an advance into Gaul, was rudely aroused from sleep and hurried away to Bononia. The gates of Sirmium, the northern capital of the Empire, were opened and the inhabitants poured forth to greet the victor of Strassburg. Two days only did Julian spend in the city, then marched to Succi,[1] left Nevitta to guard the pass and retired to Naissus, where he spent the winter awaiting the arrival of his army. Julian's march from Gaul meant the final breach with Constantius; his present task was to justify his usurpation to the world. Thus the imperial pamphleteer was born. One apologia followed another, now addressed to the senate, now to Athens as representing the historic centre of Hellenism, now to some city whose allegiance Julian sought to win. But he overshot the mark; the painting of the character of Constantius men felt to be a caricature and the scandalous portraiture unworthy of one who owed his advancement to his cousin's favours. Meanwhile Julian strained every nerve to raise more troops for the coming campaign. He was not yet strong enough to advance into Thrace to meet the forces under Count Martianus, and the news from the West forced him to realise how critical his position might become.

[1] Now *Kapulu-Derbend*: Bulgarian, *Trajanova Vrata.*

CH. III.

Two legions and a cohort stationed in Sirmium he did not dare to trust and so gave the command that they should march to Gaul to take the place of those regiments which formed part of his own army. On the long journey the men's discontent grew to mutiny : refusing to advance, they occupied Aquileia and were supported by the inhabitants who had remained at heart loyal to Constantius. The danger was very real ; the insurgents might form a nucleus of disaffection in Italy and thus imperil Julian's retreat. He gave immediate orders to Jovinus to return and to employ in the siege of Aquileia the whole of the main force now advancing through Italy.

In the East Constantius had marched to Edessa (spring 361), where he awaited information as to the plans of Sapor. It was only on the news of Julian's capture of the pass of Succi that he felt that the war in the West could be no longer postponed. At the same time Constantius learned of Sapor's retreat, since the auspices forbade the passage of the Tigris. The Roman army assembled at Hierapolis greeted the Emperor's harangue with enthusiasm, Arbitio was despatched in advance to bar Julian's progress through Thrace, and when Constantius had made provision in Antioch for the government of the East he started in person against the usurper. Fever however attacked him in Tarsus and his illness was rendered still more serious by the violent storms of late autumn. At Mopsucrenae, in Cilicia, he died on 3 November 361 at the age of 44. Ammianus Marcellinus has given us a definitive sketch of the character of Constantius. His faults are clear as day. To guard the Emperor from treason, Diocletian had made the throne unapproachable, but this severance of sovereign and people drove the ruler back on the narrow circle of his ministers. They were at once his informants and his advisers : their lord learned only that which they deemed it well for him to know. The Emperor was led by his favourites ; Constantius possessed considerable influence, writes Ammianus in bitter irony,with his eunuch chamberlain Eusebius. The insinuations of courtiers ultimately sowed mistrust between his Caesar Julian and himself. They played upon the suspicious nature of the Emperor, their whispers of treason fired him to senseless ferocity, and the services of brave men were lost to the Empire lest their popularity should endanger the monarch's peace. Even loyal subjects grew to doubt whether the Emperor's safety were worth its fearful price. To maintain the extravagant pomp of his rapacious ministers and followers, the provinces laboured under an overwhelming weight of taxes and impositions which were exacted with merciless severity, while the public post was ruined by the constant journeyings of bishops from one council to another. Yet though these dark features of the reign of Constantius are undeniable, below his inhuman repression of those who had fallen under the suspicion of treason lay a deep conviction of the solemnity of the trust which had been handed down to him from father and grandfather. For Constantius the consciousness that he was representative by the grace of Heaven of a hereditary dynasty carried with it its obligation, and the task of main-taining the greatness of Rome was subtly confused with the duty of self-preservation, since a usurper's reign would never be hallowed by the seal of a legitimate succession. With a sense of this responsibility Constantius always sought to appoint only tried men to important offices in the State, he consistently exalted the civil element at the expense of the military and rigidly maintained the separation between the two services which had been one of the leading principles of Diocletian's reforms. Sober and temperate, he possessed that power of physical endurance which was shared by so many of his house. In his early years he served as lieutenant to his father alike in East and West and gained a wide experience of men and cities. Now on this frontier, now on that, he was constantly engaged in the Empire's defence; a soldier by necessity and no born general, he was twice hailed by his men with the title of Sarmaticus, and in the usurpations of Magnentius and of Julian he refused to hazard the safety of the provinces and loyally sacrificed all personal interests in face of the higher claims of his duty to the Roman world. He was naturally cold and self-contained; he fails to awake our affection or our enthusiasm, but we can hardly withhold our tribute of respect. He bore his burden of Empire with high serious-ness; men were conscious in his presence of an overmastering dignity and of a majesty which inspired them with something akin to awe.

By the death of Constantius the Empire was happily freed from the horrors of another civil war: Julian was clearly marked out to be his cousin's successor, and the decision of the army did not admit of doubt; Eusebius and the Court party were forced to abandon any idea of putting forward another claimant to the throne. Two officers, Theolaifus and Aligildus, bore the news to Julian; fortune had inter-vened to favour his rash adventure, and he at once advanced through Thrace by Philippopolis to Constantinople. Agilo was despatched to Aquileia and at length the besieged were convinced of the Emperor's death and thereupon their stubborn resistance came to an end. Nigrinus, the ringleader, and two others were put to death, but soldiers and citizens were fully pardoned. When on 11 December 361 Julian, still but 31 years old, entered as sole Emperor his eastern capital, all eyes were turned in wondering amazement on the youthful hero, and for the rest of his life upon him alone was fixed the gaze of Roman historians; wherever Julian is not, there we are left in darkness, of the West for example we know next to nothing. The history of Julian's reign becomes perforce the biography of the Emperor. In that biography three elements are all-important: Julian's passionate determination to restore the Pagan worship; his earnest desire that men should see a new Marcus Aurelius upon the throne, and that abuses and maladministration should hide their heads ashamed before an Emperor who was also a philosopher; and, in the last place, his tragic ambition to emulate the achievements of Alexander the Great and by a crushing blow to assert over Persia the pre-eminence of Rome.

Innumerable have been the explanations which men have offered for the apostasy of Julian. They have pointed to his Arian teachers, have suggested that Christianity was hateful to him as the religion of Constantius whom he regarded as his father's murderer, while rationalists have paradoxically claimed that the Emperor's reason refused to accept the miraculous origin and the subtle theologies of the faith. It would be truer to say that Christianity was not miraculous enough — was too rational for the mystic and enthusiast. The religion which had as its central object of adoration the cult of a dead man was to him human, all too human: his vague longings after some vast imaginative conception of the universe felt themselves cabined and confined in the creeds of Christianity. With a Roman's pride and a Roman's loyalty to the past as he conceived it, the upstart faith of despised Galilaean peasants aroused at one moment his scorn, at another his pity: a Greek by education and literary sympathies, the Christian Bible was but a faint and distorted reflex of the masterpieces which had comforted his solitary youth: a mystic who felt the wonder of the expanse of the heavens, with a strain in his nature to which the ritual excesses of the Orient appealed with irresistible fascination, it was easy for him to adopt the speculations of Neoplatonism and to fall a victim to the thaumaturgy of Maximus. The causes of Julian's apostasy lie deep-rooted in the apostate's inmost being.

His first acts declared his policy: he ordered the temples to be opened and the public sacrifices to be revived; but the Christians were to be free to worship, for Julian had learned the lesson of the failure of previous persecutions, and by imperial order all the Catholic bishops banished under Constantius were permitted to return. Those privileges, however, which the State had granted to the churches were now to be withdrawn: lands and temples which had belonged to the older religion were to be surrendered to their owners, the Christian clergy were no longer to claim exemption from the common liability to taxation or from duties owed to the municipal senates. With Julian's accession Christianity had ceased to be the favoured religion, and it was therefore contended that reason demanded alike restitution and equality before the law. Meanwhile a Court was sitting at Chalcedon to try the partisans of Constantius. Its nominal president was Sallust (probably Julian's friend when in Gaul), but the commission was in reality controlled by Arbitio, an unprincipled creature of Constantius. Julian may perhaps have intended to show impartiality by such a choice, but as a result justice was travestied, and though public opinion approved of the deaths of Paul the notary and of Apodemius, who were principally responsible for the excesses committed in the treason trials of the late reign, and may have welcomed the fate of the all-powerful chamberlain Eusebius, men were horror-struck at the execution of Ursulus, who as treasurer in Gaul had loyally supported Julian when Caesar; his unpopularity with the troops was indeed his only crime, and the Emperor did not mend his error by raising the weak plea that he had been kept in ignorance of the sentence. Julian's next step was the summary dismissal of the horde of minor officials of the palace who had served to make the Court circle under Constantius a very hot-bed of vice and corruption. The purge was sudden and indiscriminate; it was the act of a young man in a hurry. The feverish ardour of the Emperor's reforming energy swept before it alike the innocent and the guilty. Such impatience appeared unworthy of a philosopher, and so far from awaking gratitude in his subjects served rather to arouse discontent and alarm.

But already Julian was burning to undertake his great expedition against Persia, and refused to listen to counsellors who suggested the folly of aggression now that Sapor was no longer pressing the attack. The Emperor's preparations could best be made in Antioch and here he arrived probably in late July 363. On the way he had made a détour to visit Pessinus and Ancyra; the lukewarm devotion of Galatia had discouraged him, but in Antioch where lay the sanctuary of Daphne he looked for earnest support in his crusade for the moral regeneration of Paganism. The Crown of the East (as Ammianus styles his native city) welcomed the Emperor with open arms, but the enthusiasm was short-lived. The populace gay, factious, pleasure-loving, looked for spectacles and the pomp of a Court; Julian's heart was set on a civil and religious reformation. He longed for amendment in law and administration, above all for a remodelling of the old cult and the winning of converts to the cause of the gods. He himself was to be the head of the new state church of Paganism; the hierarchy of the Christians was to be adopted — the country priests subordinated to the high priest of the province, the high priest to be responsible to the Emperor, the pontifex maximus. A new spirit was to inspire the Pagan clergy; the priest himself was to be no longer a mere performer of public rites, let him take up the work of preacher, expound the deeper sense which underlay the old mythology and be at once shepherd of souls and an ensample to his flock in holy living. What Maximin Daza had attempted to achieve in ruder fashion by forged acts of Pilate, Julian's writings against the Galilaeans should effect: as Maximin had bidden cities ask what they would of his royal bounty, did they but petition that the Christians might be removed from their midst, so Julian was ready to assist and favour towns which were loyal to the old faith. Maximin had created a new priesthood recruited from men who had won distinction in public careers: his dream had been to fashion an organisation which might successfully withstand the Christian clergy; here too Julian was his disciple: When pest and famine had desolated the Roman East in

CH. III.

Maximin's days, the helpfulness and liberality of Christians towards the starving and the plague-stricken had forced men to confess that true piety and religion had made their home with the persecuted heretics: it was Julian's will that Paganism should boast its public charity and that an all-embracing service of humanity should be reasserted as a vital part of the ancient creed. If only the worshippers of the gods of Hellas were once quickened with a spiritual enthusiasm, the lost ground would be recovered. It was indeed to this call that Paganism could not respond. There were men who clung to the old belief, but theirs was no longer a victorious faith, for the fire had died upon the altar. Resignation to Christian intolerance was bitter, but the passion which inspires martyrs was nowhere to be found. Julian made converts — the Christian writers mournfully testify to their numbers — but he made them by imperial gold, by promises of advancement or fear of dismissal. They were not the stuff of which missionaries could be fashioned. The citizens were disappointed of their pageants, while the royal enthusiast found his hopes to be illusions. Mutual embitterment was the natural result. Julian was never a persecutor in the accepted meaning of that word: it was the most constant complaint of the Christians that the Emperor denied them the glory of martyrdom, but Pagan mobs knew that the Emperor would not be quick to punish violence inflicted on the Galilaeans: when the Alexandrians brutally murdered their tyrannous bishop, George of Cappadocia, they escaped with an admonition; when Julian wrote to his subjects of Bostra, it was to suggest that their bishop might be hunted from the town. If Pessinus was to receive a boon from the Emperor, his counsel was that all her inhabitants should become worshippers of the Great Mother; if Nisibis needed protection from Persia, it would only be granted on condition that she changed her faith. In the schools throughout the Empire Christians were expounding the works of the great Greek masters; from their earliest years children were taught to scorn the legends which to Julian were rich with spiritual meaning. He that would teach the scriptures must believe in them, and given the Emperor's zealous faith, it was but reasonable that he should prohibit Christians from teaching the classic literature which was his Bible. If Ammianus criticised the edict severely, it was because he did not share the Emperor's belief; the historian was a tolerant monotheist, Julian an ardent worshipper of the gods. The Emperor's conservatism and love of sacrifice alike were stirred by the records of the Jews. A people who in the midst of adversity had clung with a passionate devotion to the adoration of the God of their fathers deserved well at his hands. Christian renegades should see the glories of a restored temple which might stand as an enduring monument of his reign. The architect Alypius planned the work, but it was never completed. The earth at this time was troubled by strange upheavals, earthquakes, and ocean waves, and by some such phenomenon Jerusalem would seem to have been visited; [1] perhaps during the excavations a well of naphtha was ignited. We only know that Christians, who saw in Julian's plan a defiance of prophecy, proclaimed a miracle, and that the Emperor did not live to prove them mistaken.

Thus in Antioch the relations between the sovereign and his people were growing woefully strained. Julian removed the bones of Saint Babylas from the precinct of Daphne and soon after the temple was burned to the ground. Suspicion fell upon the Christians and their great church was closed. A scarcity of provisions made itself felt in the city and Julian fixed a maximum price and brought corn from Hierapolis and elsewhere, and sold it at reduced rates. It was bought up by the merchants, and the efforts to coerce the senate failed. The populace ridiculed an Emperor whose aims and character they did not understand. The philosopher would not stoop to violence but the man in Julian could not hold his peace. The Emperor descended from the awful isolation which Diocletian had imposed on his successors; he challenged the satirists to a duel of wits and published the *Misopogon*. It was to sacrifice his vantage-ground. The chosen of Heaven had become the jest of the mob, and Julian's pride could have drained no bitterer cup. When he left the city for Persia, he had determined to fix his court, upon his return, at Tarsus, and neither the entreaties of Libanius nor the tardy repentance of Antioch availed to move him from his purpose.

Here but the briefest outline can be given of the oft-told tale of Julian's Persian expedition. Before it criticism sinks powerless, for it is a wonder-story and we cannot solve its riddle. The leader perished and the rest is silence: with him was lost the secret of his hopes. Julian left Antioch on 5 March 363 and on the 9th reached Hierapolis. Here the army had been concentrated and four days later the Emperor advanced at its head, crossed the Euphrates and passing through Batnae halted at Charrae. The name must have awakened gloomy memories and the Emperor's mind was troubled with premonitions of disaster; men said that he had bidden his kinsman Procopius mount the throne should he himself fall in the campaign. A troop of Persian horse had just burst plundering across the frontier and returned laden with booty; this event led Julian to disclose his plan of campaign. Corn had been stored along the road towards the Tigris, in order to create an impression that he had chosen that line for his advance; in fact the Emperor had determined to follow the Euphrates and strike for Ctesiphon. He would thus be supported by his fleet bearing supplies and engines of war. Procopius and Sebastianus he entrusted with 30,000 troops—almost half his army—and directed them to march towards the Tigris. They were for the present to act only on the defensive, shielding the eastern provinces from invasion and guarding his own forces from any Persian attack from the north. When he himself was once at grips

---

[1] Cf. Vita Artemii Mart. *AS. Boll.* Tom. VIII. p. 883, § 66.

with Persia in the heart of the enemy's territory, Sapor would be forced to concentrate his armies,and then,the presence of Julian's generals being no longer necessary to protect Mesopotamia, should a favourable opportunity offer, they were to act in concert with Arsaces, ravage Chiliocomum, a fertile district of Media, and advance through Corduene and Moxoene to join him in Assyria.   That meeting never took place : from whatever reason Procopius and Sebastianus never left Mesopotamia. Julian reviewed the united forces — 65,000 men — and then turned south following the course of the Belias (Belecha) until he reached Callinicum (Ar-Rakka) on 27 March.

Another day's march brought him to the Euphrates, and here he met the fleet under the command of the tribune Constantianus and the Count Lucillianus.   Fifty warships, an equal number of boats designed to form pontoon bridges, and a thousand transports—the Roman armada seemed to an eyewitness fitly planned to match the magnificent stream on which it floated.   Another 98 miles brought the army to Diocletian's bulwark fortress of Circesium (Karkisiya).   Here the Aboras (Khabūr) formed the frontier line; Julian harangued the troops, then crossed the river by a bridge of boats and began his march through Persian territory. In spite of omens and disregarding the gloomy auguries of the Etruscan soothsayers, the Emperor set his face for Ctesiphon; he would storm high Heaven by violence and bend the gods to his will.   From its formation the invading army was made to appear a countless host, for their marching column extended over some ten miles, while neither the fleet nor the land forces were suffered to lose touch with each other. Some of the enemy's forts capitulated, the inhabitants of Anatha being transported to Chalcis in Syria, some were found deserted, while the garrisons of others refusing to surrender professed themselves willing to abide by the issue of the war.   Julian was content to accept these terms and continued his unresting advance.   Historians have blamed this rash confidence, whereby he endangered his own retreat.   It is however to be remembered that a siege in the fourth century might mean a delay of many weeks, that the Emperor's project was clearly to dismay Persia by the rapidity of his onset and that it would seem probable that his plan of campaign had been from the first to return by the Tigris and not by the Euphrates.   The Persians had intended a year or two before to leave walled cities untouched and strike for Syria, Julian in his turn refused to waste precious time in investing the enemy's strongholds, but would deal a blow against the capital itself.   The march was attended with many difficulties : a storm swept down upon the camp, the swollen river burst its dams and many transports were sunk, the passage of the Narraga was only forced by a successful attack on the Persian rear which compelled them to evacuate their position in confusion, a mutinous and discontented spirit was shown by the Roman troops and the Emperor was forced to exert his personal influence and authority before discipline

was restored; finally the Persians raised all the sluices and, freeing the
waters, turned the country which lay before the army into a widespread
marsh.   Difficulties however vanished before the resource and prompti.
tude of the Emperor, and the advance guard under Victor brought him
news that the country up to the walls of Ctesiphon was clear of the
enemy.   On the fall of the strong fortress of Maiozamalcha, the fleet
followed the Naharmalcha (the great canal which united Euphrates and
Tigris), while the army kept pace with it on land.   The Naharmalcha,
however, flows into the Tigris three miles below Ctesiphon, and thus the
Emperor would have been forced to propel his ships *up stream* in his
attack on the capital.   The difficulty was overcome by clearing the dis.
used canal of Trajan, down which the fleet emerged into the Tigris
to the north of Ctesiphon.   From the triangle thus formed by the
Naharmalcha, the Tigris, and the canal of Trajan, Julian undertook the
capture of the left bank of the river.   Protected by a palisade, the
Persians offered a stubborn resistance to the Roman night attack.   The
five ships first despatched were repulsed and set on fire; on the moment
"it is the signal that our men hold the bank," cried the Emperor, and
the whole fleet dashed to their comrades' support.   Julian's inspiration
won a field of battle for the Romans.   Underneath a scorching sun the
armies fought until the Persians — elephants, cavalry, and foot — were
fleeing pell-mell for the shelter of the city walls; their dead numbered
some 2500.   Had the pursuit been pressed, Ctesiphon might perhaps
have been won that day, but plunder and booty held the victors fast.
Should the capital be besieged or the march against Sapor begun?   It
would almost seem that Julian himself wavered irresolute, while precious
days were lost.   Secret proposals of peace led him to underestimate the
enemy's strength, while men, playing the part of deserters, offered to lead
him through fertile districts against the main Persian army.   Should
he weary his forces and damp the spirit of his men by an arduous siege,
he might not only be cut off from the reinforcements under Procopius
and Sebastianus, but might find himself caught between two fires—Sapor's
advance and the resistance of the garrison.   To conclude a peace were
unworthy of one who took Alexander for his model — better with his
victorious troops to strike a final and conclusive blow, and possibly
before the encounter effect a junction with the northern army.   Crews
numerous enough to propel his fleet against the stream he could not
spare, and if he were to meet Sapor, he might be drawn too far from
the river to act in concert with his ships: they must not fall into the
enemy's hands, and therefore they must be burned.   The resolution was
taken and regretted too late; twelve small boats alone were rescued
from the flames.   Julian's plans miscarried, for the army of the north
remained inactive, perhaps through the mutual jealousy of its commanders, and Arsaces withheld his support from the foe of Sapor.
The Persians burned their fields before his advance, and the rich country

side which traitorous guides had promised became a wilderness of ash and smoke. Orders were given for a retreat to Corduene; amidst sweltering heat, with dwindling stores, the Romans beheld. to their dismay the cloud of dust upon the horizon which heralded Sapor's approach. At dawn the heavy-armed troops of Persia were close at hand and only after many engagements were beaten off with loss. After a halt of two days at Hucumbra, where a supply of provisions was discovered, the army advanced over country which had been devastated by fire, while the troops were constantly harassed by sudden onsets. At Maranga the Persians were once more reinforced; two of the king's sons arrived at the head of an elephant column and squadrons of mailed cavalry. Julian drew up his forces in semicircular formation to meet the new danger; a rapid charge disconcerted the Persian archers, and in the hand-to-hand struggle which followed the enemy suffered severely. Lack of provisions, however, tortured the Roman army during the three days' truce which ensued. When the march was resumed Julian learned of an attack upon his rear. Unarmed he galloped to the threatened point, but was recalled to the defence of the vanguard. At the same time the elephants and cavalry had burst upon the centre, but were already in flight when a horseman's spear grazed the Emperor's arm and pierced his ribs. None knew whence the weapon came, though rumour ran that a Christian fanatic had assassinated his general, while others said that a tribesman of the Taieni had dealt the fatal blow. In vain Julian essayed to return to the field of battle; his soldiers magnificently avenged their Emperor, but he could not share their victory. Within his tent he calmly reviewed the past and uncomplaining yielded his life into the keeping of the eternal Godhead. "In medio cursu florentium gloriarum hunc merui clarum e mundo digressum." Death in mercy claimed Julian. The impatient reformer and champion of a creed outworn might have become the embittered persecutor. Rightly or wrongly after generations would know him as the great apostate, but he was spared the shame of being numbered among the tyrants. He was born out of due time and therein lay the tragedy of his troubled existence; for long years he dared not discover the passionate desires which lay nearest his heart, and when at length he could give them expression, there were few or none fully to understand or sympathise. His work died with him, and soon, like a little cloud blown by the wind, left not a trace behind.

The next day at early dawn the heads of the army and the principal officers assembled to choose an Emperor. Partisans of Julian struggled with followers of Constantius, the armies of the West schemed against the nominee of the legions of the East, Christianity and Paganism each sought its own champion. All were however prepared to sink their differences in favour of Sallust, but when he pleaded ill-health and advanced age, a small but tumultuous faction carried the election of Jovian, the captain of the imperial guard. Down the long line of troops ran the Emperor's name, and some thought from the sound half-heard that Julian was restored to them. They were undeceived at the sight of the meagre purple robe which hardly served to cover the vast height and bent shoulders of their new ruler. Chosen as a whole-hearted adherent of Christianity, Jovian was by nature genial and jocular, a gourmand and lover of wine and women — a man of kindly disposition and very moderate education. The army by its choice had foredoomed itself to dishonour; its excuse, pleads Ammianus, lay in the extreme urgency of the crisis. The Persians, learning of Julian's death and of the incapacity of his successor, pressed hard upon the retreating Romans; charges of the enemy's elephants broke the ranks of the legionaries while on the march, and when the army halted their entrenched camp was constantly attacked. Saracen horsemen took their revenge for Julian's refusal to give them their customary pay by joining in these unceasing assaults. By way of Sumere, Charcha, and Dara the army retired, and then for four whole days the enemy harassed the rear-guard, always declining an engagement when the Romans turned at bay. The troops clamoured to be allowed to cross the Tigris: on the further bank they would find provisions and fewer foes, but the generals feared the dangers of the swollen stream. Another two days passed — days of gnawing hunger and scorching heat. At last Sapor sent Surenas with proposals of peace. The king knew that Roman forces still remained in Mesopotamia and that new regiments could easily be raised in the Eastern provinces: desperate men will sell their lives dearly and diplomacy might win a less costly victory than the sword. Four days the negotiations continued, and then when suspense had become intolerable the Thirty Years' Peace was signed. All but one of the five satrapies which Rome under Diocletian had wrested from Persia were to be restored, Nisibis and Singara were to be surrendered, while the Romans were no longer to interfere in the internal affairs of Armenia. "We ought to have fought ten times over," cries the soldier Ammian, "rather than to have granted such terms as these!" But Jovian desired (by what means it mattered not) to retain a force which should secure him against rivals — Was not Procopius who, men said, had been marked out by Julian as his successor, at the head of an army in Mesopotamia? Thus the shameful bargain was struck, and the miserable retreat continued. To the horrible privations of the march were added Persian treachery and the bitter hostility of the Saracen tribesmen. At Thilsaphata the troops under Sebastianus and Procopius joined the army, and at length Nisibis was reached, the fortress which had been Rome's bulwark in the East since the days of Mithridates. The citizens prayed with tears that they might be allowed single-handed to defend the walls against the might of Persia; but Jovian was too good a Christian to break his faith with Sapor, and Bineses, a Persian noble, occupied the city in the name of his master. Procopius, who had been content to

CH. III.

acknowledge Jovian, now bore the corpse of Julian to Tarsus for burial, and then, his mission accomplished, prudently disappeared. The army in Gaul accepted the choice of their eastern comrades, but Jovian's success was short-lived. In the depth of winter he hurried from Antioch towards Constantinople and with his infant son, Varronianus, assumed the consulship at Ancyra. At Dadastana he was found dead in his bedroom (16 Feb. 364), suffocated some said by the fumes of a charcoal stove. Many versions of his death were current, but apparently no contemporary suspected other than natural causes. On his accession the Pagan party had looked for persecution, the Christians for the hour of their retaliation. But though the Christian faith was restored as the religion of the Empire, Jovian's wisdom or good nature triumphed and he issued an edict of toleration: he had thereby anticipated the policy of his successor.

CHAPTER IV

THE TRIUMPH OF CHRISTIANITY

THE old or official religions of Greece and of Rome had lost most of their power long before Constantine first declared that Christianity was henceforth to be recognised as a *religio licita* and then proceeded to bestow the Imperial favour on the faith which his predecessors had persecuted. Hellenism had destroyed their influence over the cultivated classes, and other religions, coming from the East, had captivated the masses of the people. If temples, dedicated to the gods of Olympus, were still standing open; if the time-honoured rites were still duly and continuously celebrated; if the official priesthood, recognised and largely supported by the state, still performed its appointed functions; these things no longer compelled the devotion of the crowd. The Imperial cult of the *Divi* and *Divae*, once so popular, had also lost its power to attract and to charm; the routine of ceremonial worship was still performed; the well-organised priesthood spreading all over the Empire maintained its privileged position; but crowds no longer thronged the temples, and the rites were neglected by the great mass of the population.

Yet this did not mean, as has often been supposed, the universal triumph of Christianity. It may almost be said that Paganism was never so active, so assertive, so combative, as in the third century. But this paganism, for long the successful rival of Christianity and its real opponent, was almost as new to Europe as Christianity itself. Something must be known about it and its environment ere the reaction under Julian and the final triumph of Christianity can be sympathetically understood.

During the earlier centuries of the Roman Empire the process of disintegration was completed which had begun with the conquests of Alexander the Great. Instead of a system of self-contained societies, solidly united internally and fenced off from all external social, political, and religious influences, which characterised ancient civilisation, this age saw a mixing of peoples and a cosmopolitan society hitherto unknown.

If fighting went on continuously somewhere or other on the extended frontiers of the great Empire, peace reigned within its vast domains. A system of magnificent roads, for the most part passable all the year round, united the capitals with the extremities, from Britain and Spain on the west to the Euphrates on the east.   The Mediterranean had been cleared of pirates, and lines of vessels united the great cities on its shores.   Travelling, whether for business, health, or pleasure, was possible under the Empire with a certainty and a safety unknown in after centuries until the introduction of steam.   It was facilitated by a common language, a coinage universally valid, and the protection of the same laws.   Men could start from the Euphrates and travel onwards to Spain using one *lingua-franca* everywhere understood.   Greek could be heard in the streets of every commercial town — in Rome, Marseilles, Cadiz, and Bordeaux, on the banks of the Nile, of the Orontes, and of the Tigris.

With all these things to favour it, the movements of peoples within the Empire had become incalculably great, and all the larger cities were cosmopolitan.   Families from all lands, of differing religions and social habits, dwelt within the same walls.   National, social, intellectual, and religious differences faded insensibly.   Thinking became eclectic as it had never been before.

This growing community in habit of thought and even of religious belief was fed by something peculiar to the times.   The soldier of many lands, the travelled trader, the tourist in search of pleasure, and the invalid wandering in quest of health were common then as now. But a special characteristic of the end of the third and the beginning of the fourth century was the widely wandering student, the teacher far from the land of his birth, and the itinerant preacher of new religions.

The Empire was well provided with what we should now call universities.   Rome, Milan, and Cremona were seats of higher learning for Italy; Marseilles, Bordeaux, and Autun for Gaul; Carthage for North Africa; Athens and Apollonia for Greece; Tarsus for Cilicia; Smyrna for Asia; Beyrout and Antioch for Syria; and Alexandria for Egypt.   The number of foreign students to be found at each was remarkable.   Young Romans enrolled themselves at Marseilles and Bordeaux.   Greeks crossed the seas to attend lectures at Antioch, and found as their neighbours men from Assyria, Phoenicia, and Egypt.   At Alexandria the number of students from distant parts of the Empire exceeded largely those from the neighbourhood.   At Athens, whose schools were the most famous in the beginning of the fourth century, the crowds of *Barbarians* (for so the citizens called those foreign students) were so great that it was said that their presence threatened to spoil the purity of the language. Everywhere, in that age of wandering, the student seemed to prefer to study far from home and to flit from one place of learning to another.

Nor were the professors much different.   They commonly taught far

from their native land.   Even at Athens it became increasingly rare to
find a teacher who belonged by birth to Greece.   They too travelled from
one university seat to another.   Lucian, Philostratus, Apuleius, all who
portray the age and the class, describe their wanderings.

/ Missionaries of new cults went about in the same way.   Bands of
itinerant devotees, the prophets and priests of Syrian, Persian, possibly
of Hindu cults, passed along the great Roman roads.   Solitary preachers
of Oriental faiths, with all the fire of missionary enthusiasm, tramped
from town to town, drawn by an irresistible impulse to Rome, the centre
of power, the protectress of the religions of her myriad subjects, the
tribune from which, if a speaker could only ascend it, he might address
the world.   The end of the third and the beginning of the fourth
century was an age of religious excitements, of curiosity about strange
faiths, when all who had something new to teach about the secrets of
the soul and of the universe, hawked their theories as traders their
merchandise.

This mixture of peoples, this new cosmopolitanism, this hurrying to
and fro of religious teachers, brought it about that Oriental faiths, at first
only the religions of groups of families who had brought their cults with
them into the West, made numerous converts and spread themselves
over the Roman Empire.   These Oriental religions prospered the more
because from the middle of the third century onwards Rome was looking
to the East for many things.   From it came the deftest artizans and
mechanics who gave to life most of its material comforts.   It largely contributed to feed Rome with its grain.   Its philosophy (for most of
the greatest stoical thinkers were not Greeks but Orientals) gave the
substructure to Roman Law; and the most famous Law School in the
third, fourth, and fifth centuries was not in Rome but at Beyrout.
Ulpian came from Tyre and Papinian from Syria.   The greatest non-
Christian thinkers of these centuries were neither Greeks nor Romans
but Orientals.   Plotinus was an Egyptian; Iamblichus, Porphyry, and
Libanius were Syrians; Galen was an Asiatic.   Oriental ideas were
slowly changing Rome's political institutions themselves, and the
Princeps of a Republic, as was Octavius, became, in the persons of
Diocletian and Constantine, an Oriental monarch.   Rome, by the
discipline of its legions, by the mingled severity and generosity of its
rule, by the justice of its legislation, had conquered the East.   Eastern
thought, wedded to Hellenism, was in its turn subjugating the Empire.
Its religions had their share in the conquest.

Among those Oriental faiths which spread themselves over civilised
Europe some were much more popular than others.   All entered the
Empire at an early date and won their way very slowly at first.   Most
of them seem to have made some alliance with the survivals of such
Greek mysteries as those of Eleusis and of Dionysos.   All of them, save
that of Mithras, had been affected and to some extent changed by

CH. IV.

Hellenism before they entered into the full light of history in the beginning of the third century.

From Asia Minor came the worship of Cybele with its hymns and dances, its mysterious ideas of a deity dying to live again, its frenzies and trances, its soothsayings, and its blood-baths of purification and sanctification. From Syria came the cult of the Dea Syra, described by Lucian the sceptic, with its sacred prostitutions, its more than hints of human sacrifices, its mystics and its pillar saints. Persia sent forth the worship of Mithras, with its initiations, its sacraments, its mysteries, and the stern discipline which made it a favourite religion among the Roman legionaries. Egypt gave birth to many a cult. Chief among them was the worship of Isis. Before the end of the second century it had far outstripped Christianity and could boast of its thousands where the religion of the Cross could only number hundreds. It had penetrated everywhere, even to far-off Britain. A ring bearing the figure of the goddess' constant companion, the dog-headed Anubis, has been discovered in a grave in the Isle of Man. Votaries of Isis could be found from the Roman Wall to Land's End.

The worship of Isis may be taken as a type of those Oriental faiths before whose presence the official gods of Olympus were receding into the background. The cult had a body of clergy, highly organised, a book of prayers, a code of liturgical actions, a tonsure, vestments, and an elaborate impressive ceremonial. The inner circle of its devotees were called "the religious," like the monks of the Middle Ages; those who were altogether outside the faith were termed "pagans"; the service of the goddess was a "holy war," and her worshippers of all grades were banded together in a "militia." Apuleius, himself converted to the faith, has, in his *Metamorphoses*, described its ceremonies of worship and enabled us to see how desires after a better life drew men like himself to reverence the deity and enrol himself among her followers. He has described, with a vividness that makes us see them, the stately processions which moved with deliberate pace through the crowded narrow streets of oriental towns, and drew after them to the temple many a hitherto unattached inquirer. We can enter the temple with him and listen to the solemn exhortation of the high-priest; hear him dwell upon the past sins and follies of the neophyte and the unfailing goodness and mercy of the goddess whose eyes had followed him through them all and who now waited to receive him if he truly desired to become her disciple and worshipper. The initiation was a secret rite and Apuleius is careful not to profane it by description; but we learn that there was a baptism, a fast of ten days, a course of priestly instruction, sponsors given to the neophyte, and, in the evening, a reception of the new brother by the congregation, when every one greeted him kindly and presented him with some small gift. We can penetrate with him into the secret chamber reserved for the higher initiation where he was taught that he would endure a voluntary death which he was to look upon as the gateway into a higher and better life. We can dimly see him excited with wild anticipations, dizzy with protracted fasting, almost suffocated by surging vapours, blinded by sudden and unexpected flashes of light, undergo his hypnotic trance during which he saw unutterable things. "I trod the confines of death and the threshold of Proserpine; I was swept round all the elements and back again; I saw the sun shining at midnight in purest radiance; gods of heaven and gods of hell I saw face to face and adored in presence." We can understand how such an hypnotic trance marked a man for life.

Isis worship, humanised by Hellenism, extracted from the crude wild legends of Egypt the thought of a suffering and all-merciful Mother-Goddess who yearned to ease the woes of mankind. It raised the beast-gods of the Nile and the tales about them into emblems and parables. It captured the common man by its thaumaturgy. For the more cultured intelligences it had a more sublime theology which appealed to the philosophy of the day. In all this it was a type, perhaps the best, of those Oriental cults which were permeating the Empire.

All those religions, whatever their special form of teaching or variety of cult, brought with them thoughts foreign to the old official worships of Greece and Rome; though not altogether strange to the *Mysteries* which had for long been the real people's religion in Greece nor to the cult of Dionysos which in various forms had preserved its vitality.

They taught (or perhaps it would be more correct to say that the action of the subtle Greek intellect, playing upon the crude ideas which these Oriental religions presented to it, evolved from them) a series of religious conceptions foreign to the old paganism, and these became common parts of the newer non-Christian intelligence which was powerful in the third and fourth centuries.

A sharp distinction, much more definite than anything previous, was drawn between the soul and the body. The soul belonged to a different sphere and was more estimable than the body. The former was the inhabitant of a higher and better world and was therefore immortal. The thoughts of individuality and personality became much clearer. In the same way the thoughts of Godhead as a whole and of the world as a whole — conceptions scarcely separate before — were distinguished more or less clearly. Godhead became what the world was *not*, and yet Something good and great Which was the primal basis of all things.

The earlier philosophical depreciation of the world of matter became more emphatic, and raised the question whether the creation of the whole material world and of the body which belonged to it was not after all a mistake; whether the body was not a prison or at least a house of correction in which the soul was grievously detained; whether the soul could ever become what it really was until it had undergone a deliverance

CH. IV.

from the body. Such deliverance was called *salvation*, and much practical thinking was expended on the proper means of effecting it. Might not knowledge and the means it suggested of living purely or with as little bodily contamination as possible while this life lasted, be the beginnings of entrance into the real and eternal life of the soul? Was it not most likely that souls had been *gradually* confined in bodies, and must not the process of delivery be gradual also? The *gradual Way of Return* to God became a feature in almost all those Eastern cults, by whatever means they sought to accomplish it.

Perhaps however the most novel thought was the conviction that something more than knowledge, beyond any means of living purely which human wisdom could suggest, something outside man and belonging to the sphere of *divinity*, was needed to start the soul on this gradual *Way of Return* and sustain his faltering footsteps along the difficult path. Contact with the Godhead was needed to *save* and *redeem*. Such contact was to be found in a *consecration* (mysterium, sacramentum, initiation) wherein the soul, in some hypnotic trance, was possessed by the deity who overpowered it and for ever afterwards led it step by step along the path of salvation or *Way of Return*. Perhaps something more than any such consecration was needed; might not some surer way be found if only diligently sought for? It might be in one of the older cults whose inner meaning had never been rightly understood; or in some *mystery* not yet completely accessible; or in a divinely commissioned man who had not yet appeared. It might even be found within the soul itself, if men could only discover and use the true powers of the human soul (Higher Thought). At all events it was held that true religion really implied a detachment from the world, and included a strict discipline of soul and body while life lasted.

Such a paganism was very different from the polytheism with its furred, feathered, and scaly deities which first confronted Christianity and was attacked by the early Christian apologists. The later ones recognised its power. Firmicus Maternus, writing in the time of Constantine, dismisses with good-humoured scorn the deities of Olympus and their myths, but criticises with thorough earnestness the Oriental religions. It had, in spite of its external multiformity, a natural cohesion in virtue of the circle of common thoughts above described. It hardly deserves the name of polytheism; for its idea of one abstract divinity, separate from the world of matter, made it monotheism of a kind; and evidence shews that its votaries regarded Isis, Cybele, and the rest more as the representatives and impersonations of the one godhead than as individual deities. Inscriptions from tombstones reveal that worshippers did not attach themselves to one cult exclusively. The varying forms of initiation were all separate methods of attaining to union with the one divinity, the different ceremonies of purification were all ways of reaching the same end, and, as one might succeed where another failed, they could be all tried impartially. Just as we find men and women in the beginning of the sixteenth century enrolling themselves in several religious associations of different kinds (witness Dr Pfeffinger, a member of thirty-two religious confraternities), so in the third and fourth centuries members of both sexes were initiated into several cults and performed the lustrations prescribed by very different worships, in order to miss no chance of union with divinity and to leave no means of purification and sanctification untried. The tombstone of Vettius Agorius Praetextatus, the friend of Symmachus, who took part in the *Saturnalia* of Macrobius, records that he had been initiated into several cults and that he had performed the *taurobolium*. His wife, Aconia Paulina, was more indefatigable still. This lady, a member of the exclusive circle of the old pagan nobility of Rome, went to Eleusis and was initiated with baptism, fasting, vigil, hymn-singing into the several mysteries of Dionysos, of Ceres, and Koré. Not content with these, she went on to Lerna and sought communion with the same three deities in different rites of initiation. She travelled to Aegina, was again initiated, slept or waked in the porches of the small temples there in the hope that the divinities of the place in dream or waking vision might communicate to her their way of salvation. She became a hierophant of Hecate with still different and more dreaded rites of consecration. Finally, like her husband, she submitted herself to the dreadful, and to us disgusting, purification won in the *taurobolium*. A great pit was dug into which the neophyte descended naked; it was covered with stout planks placed about an inch apart; a young bull was led or forced upon the planks; it was stabbed by the officiating priest in such a way that the thrust was mortal and that the blood might flow as freely as possible. As the blood poured down on the planks and dripped into the pit the neophyte moved backwards and forwards to receive as much as possible of the red warm shower and remained until every drop had ceased to drip. Inscription after inscription records the fact that the deceased had been a *tauroboliatus* or a *tauroboliata*, had gone through this blood-bath in search of sanctification. Evidence from inscriptions seems to shew that in the declining days of paganism, the energy of its votaries drove them in greater numbers to accumulate initiations and to undergo the more severe rites of purification.

This multiform and yet homogeneous paganism had the further support of a system of philosophy expounded and enforced by the greatest non-Christian thinkers of the age. Neoplatonism, the last birth of Hellenic thought, not without traces of Oriental parentage, has the look of a philosophy of hesitation and expectancy. It had lost the firm tread of Plato and Aristotle, and feared that the human intelligence unaided could not penetrate and explain all things. The intellectual faculty of man was reduced to something intermediate between mere sense perception and some vague intuition of the supernatural, and the whole energy of the movement was concentrated on discovering the means to follow out this intuition and to attain by it not only communion but union with what was completely and externally divine.

Its great thinker was Plotinus (d. 269). His disciples Porphyry (233–304) and Iamblichus (d. *circa* 330) made it the basis and buttress of paganism when it was fighting for its life against a conquering Christianity. If the Universe of things seen and unseen be an emanation from Absolute Being, the Primal Cause of all things, the fountain from which all existence flows and the haven to which everything that has reality in it will return when its cycle is complete, then every heathen deity has its place in this flow of existence. Its cult, however crude, is an obscure witness to the presence of the intuition of the supernatural. The legends which have gathered round its name, if only rightly understood, are mystic revelations of the divine which permeates all things. Its initiations and rites of purification are all meant to help the soul on the same path of return by which it completes its cycle of wanderings. The new paganism can be represented to be the collected flower and fruit of all the older faiths presented and ready to satisfy the deeper desires of the spirit of man. Neoplatonism could present itself as a naturalistic, rational polytheism, retaining all the old structures of tradition, of thought and of social organisation. The "common man" was not asked to forsake the deities he was wont to reverence. The Roman was not required to despise the gods who, as his forefathers believed, had led them to the conquest of the world. The cultured Hellenist was taught to overstep, without disturbing, creeds which for him were worn out and to seek and find communion with the Divine which lies behind all gods. The very conjuror was encouraged to cultivate his magic. Pantheism, that wonder-child of thought and of the phantasy, included all within the wide sweep of its sheltering arms and made them feel the claim of a common kinship. Jesus Himself, had His followers allowed, might have had a place between Dionysos and Isis; but Christianity, which according to Porphyry had departed widely from the simple teaching of the mystic of Galilee, was sternly excluded from the Neoplatonist brotherhood of religions. Its idea of a creation in time seemed irreligious to Porphyry; its doctrine of the Incarnation introduced a false conception of the union between God and the world; its teaching about the end of all things he thought both irreverent and irreligious; above all things its claim to be the *one* religion, its exclusiveness, was hateful to him. He was too noble a man (*philosophus nobilis*, says Augustine) not to sympathise with much in Christianity, and seems to have appreciated it more and more in his later writings. Still his opinion remained unchanged: "The gods have declared Christ to have been most pious; he has become immortal, and by them his memory is cherished. Whereas the Christians are a polluted set, contaminated and enmeshed in error." Christianity was the one religion to be fought against and if possible conquered.

What Neoplatonism did theoretically the force of circumstances accomplished on the practical side. The Oriental creeds had not merely gained multitudes of private worshippers; they had forced their way among the public deities of Rome. Isis, Mithra, Sol Invictus, Dea Syra, the Great Mother, took their places alongside of Jupiter, Venus, Mars, etc., and the *Sacra peregrina* appeared on the calendar of public festivals. As most of these Oriental cults contained within them the monotheist idea it is possible that they might have fought for pre-eminence and each aspired to become *the* official religion of the Empire. But they all recognised Christianity to be a common danger, and M. Cumont has shewn that this feeling united them and made them think and act as one.

Such was the paganism which faced Christianity in the fourth century — a marvellous mixture of philosophy and religion, not without grandeur and nobility of thought, feeling keenly the unity of nature, the essential kinship of man with the Divine, and knowing something of the yearning in man's heart for redemption and for communion with God. It was able to fascinate and enthral many of the keenest intellects and loftiest natures of the time. It laid hold on Julian.

Christianity was the common opponent of all these cults. It had entered the field last and seemed easily outstripped in the race. In its beginning it was but a ripple on the surface of a Galilaean lake. Now, in the fourth century, it had compelled Imperial recognition and alliance. In strength and in weakness its claim had been always the same. It was the one, the only true, the universal religion.

From its beginning it had never lacked at least a few wealthy and cultured adherents, but during the first two centuries the overwhelming majority of its converts had come from the poorer classes — slaves, freedmen, labourers. It had early drawn upon itself the contempt of society and the hatred of the populace. It was held to be something inhuman. Its votaries were "the third race." They had all the un-social vices of the Jews and even worse vices of their own. Christians had appropriated the epithet flung at them in scorn. They *were* "the third race," a peculiar people, separate from the rest of mankind, a *natio* by themselves.

The last decade of the second century witnessed the beginnings of a change. Men of all ranks and classes became converts—members of the Senatorial and Equestrian Orders, distinguished pleaders, physicians, officers in the army, officials in the civil service, judges, even governors of provinces. Their wives, sisters, and daughters accompanied or more frequently preceded them. Then the tone of society began to change, gradually and insensibly. Scorn and contempt gave place to feelings of toleration. Before the end of the third century no one gave credit to the old scandalous reproaches which had been flung at the followers of Jesus, even when an Emperor tried to revive them. Statesmen were compelled to consider the movement — not now because it affected a town or a province, but as something pervading the Empire. They found that it possessed two characteristics which were enormous sources of strength—a peculiar power of assimilation and a compact organization.

From the first Christianity had proclaimed that the *whole* life of man belonged to it. This meant that everything that made man's life wider, deeper, fuller; whatever made it more joyous or contented; whatever sharpened the brain, strengthened and taught the muscles, gave full play to man's energies, could be taken up into and become part of the Christian life. Sin and foulness were sternly excluded; but, that done, there was no element of the Graeco-Roman civilisation which could not be appropriated by Christianity. So it assimilated Hellenism or the fine flower and fruit of Greek thought and feeling; it appropriated Roman law and institutions; it made its own the simple festivals of the common people. All were theirs; and they were Christ's; and Christ was God's.

Then the Christian churches were compactly organised. Their polity had been a natural growth. Its power of assimilation had enabled Christianity to absorb what was best in Roman civil and temple organisation, to exclude the worst elements of the bureaucracy, and to preserve much democratic popular life. Its local rulers belonged to the people they at once ruled and served. No over-centralisation crushed the local and provincial life. Christian societies formed themselves into groups, more or less compact, and made use of the *synod* to effect the grouping. One common life throbbed through the network of synods. The feeling of brotherhood did not exhaust itself in sentiment. If one part were attacked all the others were swift to help. Nothing within the Empire save the army could compare with the compact organisation of the Christian Church.

In the middle of the third century the Emperor and the Empire learnt to dread this organised force within their midst. The despised "third race" had become indeed a *natio* within the Empire. The first impulse was to exterminate what seemed to be a source of danger. One well-organised universal persecution followed another. From each Christianity emerged with sadly diminished numbers (for the lapsed were always a larger body than the martyrs), but with spirit unbroken and with organisation intact and usually strengthened.

Constantine himself had watched the last, the most prolonged and relentless of all — that under Diocletian and his successors — and had marked its failure. From his entrance into public life he made it plain that, while his rivals clung to the method of repression, he had completely abandoned it. Christianity won toleration and then Imperial patronage.

It cannot have been difficult for Constantine to carry out his policy towards the Christian religion. We cannot ascertain the proportion of

Christians to pagans at the close of the second decade of the fourth century, but it may be assumed that, when their organisation is taken into account, they were able to control public opinion in the most populous and important provinces of the Empire. All he had to do "was to let the leading provinces have the religion they desired"; the rest of the Empire would follow in their wake. He was content to adopt the principle of toleration; though for himself Christianity became more and more the one religion in which "crowning reverence is observed towards the holiest powers of heaven." He probably carried the public opinion of the Empire with him. The paganism of the fourth century was for the most part quiet and desired only to be left in peace. Perhaps Ammianus Marcellinus, himself a pagan, expressed the general opinion of his co-religionists when he praised the Emperor Valentinian because he tolerated all creeds, gave no orders that any one divinity should be worshipped, and did not strive to bend the necks of his subjects to adore what he did.

The sons of Constantine changed all this. They proposed to destroy paganism by legislation. Their laws, doubtless, inflicted much injury on individual pagans, and, in the hands of such unprincipled Imperial sycophants as Paulus and Mercurius, were the pretexts for many executions, banishments, and confiscation of goods; but they remained inoperative in all the greater pagan centres. The worship of the gods went on as before in Rome, Alexandria, Heliopolis, and in many other cities. But they could not fail to irritate. If the laws were inoperative, they remained to threaten. Proposed destruction of temples and prohibition of heathen ceremonies meant in many cases the abandonment of the games and spectacles to which the careless multitude were strongly attached. Scholars saw in the advancing power of the Church the destruction of the old learning which gave its charm to their lives. Christianity itself, troubled by the meddling of the heads of the State, seemed to be rent in pieces by its controversies, to have lost its original purity and simplicity, and to have degenerated into "old-wife superstitions" (Ammianus). So wherever paganism abounded, and in places too where it only lingered, there was a general feeling of discontent ready to welcome the first signs of a reaction and eagerly listening to whispers that the last of the race of Constantine, if he lived to assume to the Imperial purple, would undo what his kinsmen had accomplished.

At the death of Constantine his nephew, Flavius Claudius Julianus, was six years old. The child escaped, almost by accident, the massacre of his family connived at if not ordered by Constantius. He lived for more than twenty years in constant peril, in the power of that suspicious cousin who scarcely knew whether he wished to slay or to spare him. He was kept secluded, now in one or other of the great cities of the East, for long in a palace far from the haunts of men, solacing himself with hard uninterrupted studies. Then for seven brief years he startled the Roman world by his meteor-like career, and died from wounds received in battle against the Persians at the age of thirty-two. Two things about him filled the imagination of his contemporaries and have drawn the attention of succeeding generations: that he a recluse, suddenly snatched from his loved studies in poetry and philosophy, proved himself all at once not merely an intrepid soldier but a skilful general, and a born leader of men; and that he, a baptised Christian, who had actually been accustomed to read the lessons at public worship, threw off like a mask the Christianity he had professed and spent the last years of his short life in a feverish attempt to restore the old and expiring paganism. It is this last fact that made him the object of undying hate and unconquerable love to his contemporaries, and still excites the interest of mankind.

His own writings which have survived make it plain that from his earliest years he looked at Christianity and Christians through the blood-red mist of the massacre of his relations—father, brother, uncles, cousins. His education did little to remove the impression. The lonely, imaginative, lovable child had never known his mother's care, but he inherited her fondness for Homer, Hesiod, and the masters of Greek poetry. Mardonius, who had been his mother's tutor, was his also, and the boy went through the same course of study. The tutor was passionately fond of Greek literature and especially of Homer, and he imbued mother and son with his own tastes. For the rest he was something of a martinet. The young Julian had the strictest moral training and never forgot those early lessons. He was taught to be temperate and self-restrained; to look with dislike on pantomimes, races, and the other more or less licentious amusements of the populace. His tutor made him read in Plato, Aristotle, Theophrastus, and other pagan moralists, and was unwearied in enforcing pure living after these examples of antiquity. Julian was all his life a puritan pagan, and this puritanism of his was perhaps his greatest obstacle in accomplishing the task to which he subsequently dedicated himself. He never entered a theatre save when he was commanded to do so by the Emperor, and was seldom on a race-course in his life. He was naturally a dreamy, sensitive child, full of yearning fancies, which he kept to himself. He tells us that from early boyhood he felt a strange elevation of soul when he watched the sun and saw it dispensing light and heat; that he worshipped the stars and understood their whispered thoughts. He was filled with enthusiasm for everything Greek and the very word *Hellas* sent a thrill through him when he pronounced it. Seven years were spent under the care of the kindly, stern preceptor, and the impress they made was lasting.

In 344 Constantius suddenly sent Julian into obscurity. His elder brother, Gallus, who had escaped the massacre of 337 because he was so sickly that he was not expected to live, accompanied him. They were sent to Macellum, a palace in a remote part of Cappadocia — splendid enough with its baths, its springs, and its gardens, but which Julian looked upon as a prison. There he was supplied with teachers in abundance, Christian clergy who were supposed to teach the faith to the young princes, and from whose instructions Julian doubtless acquired that superficial knowledge of the Scriptures he afterwards shewed that he possessed. Books were granted him, and he seems to have been permitted to send to Alexandria for what Greek literature he desired. He mentions specially volumes from the library of Bishop George because, along with many treatises on Christianity for which he did not care, they included the writings of philosophers and rhetoricians. But he bitterly complained that neither he nor his brother were allowed to see any suitable companions, and he believed that all their attendants were imperial spies. The boy, reserved before, shrank further into himself. Outwardly he was a pattern of devotion. He received Christian instruction; was taught the "evidences of Christianity" and used the knowledge later to expose its weaknesses; was trained to give alms, to observe fasts, to venerate the shrines of saints to the extent of aiding to build them with his own hands; and occasionally to officiate as reader at public worship. Privately he fed his mind on the lessons of Mardonius and studied such books of philosophy and rhetoric as he could command. Ammianus Marcellinus, who knew him well, says that from his early years he felt attracted to the worship of the gods.

After six years in the gilded prison of Macellum the brothers were summoned to Constantinople — Gallus to be made Caesar or Vice-Emperor, to misgovern frightfully the province entrusted to his care, and in consequence to meet a not undeserved death, though to his brother it was another crime to be charged against Constantius, a Christian and the murderer of kinsmen; Julian to meet soon the supreme moment of his religious life. He was set at first to pursue his studies in the capital city and the scholar appointed to take charge of him was Hecebolius, the fourth century Vicar of Bray, whose religion was always that of the reigning Emperor. But too many admiring eyes followed the princely student, and Constantius ordered him to Nicomedia, the centre of the cultured paganism of the East and the home of its acknowledged leader, the great rhetorician Libanius. Julian had promised not to attend the lectures of Libanius; he kept his pledge in the letter and broke it in the spirit. He got notes written out for him and pored over them day and night. But more important than all lectures was the intercourse with men such as he had never met before. At Nicomedia, Julian first came in touch with those for whom the old gods were living, who had the gift of "seers," to whom prophecies and prodigies were matters of fact. He saw and conversed with men who "had easy access to the ears of the gods," who could "command winds, waves, and earthquakes." He knew Aedesius who was said to

CH. IV.

receive oracles from the deities by night, and whose wife Sosipatra had
"lived from girlhood amid prodigies of all kinds." He was told
of the wonderful *séances* presided over by Maximus and of the marvels
which occurred at them. This Maximus was one of the most celebrated theurgics or "mediums" of fourth century Neoplatonism. His
favourite occupation, he said, was to live in constant communion with the
gods. He had long white hair, brilliant magnetic eyes, and his disciples
boasted that his influence was irresistible over all those with whom he
came in contact. Eusebius of Myndus, also a Neoplatonist, told Julian
of his powers. "He made a number of us descend into the temple of
Hecate. There he saluted the goddess. Then he said: 'Be seated,
friends, see what happens, then judge whether I am not superior to
most men.' We all sat down. He burnt a grain of incense and chanted
a whole hymn in a low voice. The statue began to smile, then to laugh.
We were afraid at the sight. 'Do not be alarmed,' he said, 'you will
see that the lamps which the goddess holds in her hands will light of
themselves.' As he spoke the light streamed from the lamps." Julian
eagerly begged to be introduced to the man who was so powerful with
the gods, and Maximus was even more ready to gain one who stood so
near the Imperial throne. No accounts survive of the spiritualistic *séances*
at which he assisted; but their effect on the nervous, sensitive young
man was irresistible. Maximus converted him heart and soul to the
new paganism and was the confidential adviser of Julian from that time
onwards. The young man entered into a new life. The religion which
Homer and Hesiod had sung, which Plato and Aristotle had speculated
upon, which he had known as a student from books, became all at once
living to him. His day-dreams of the past vanished, or rather changed
into an actual present. The passion for Greece which had gradually
grown to be the ruling force in his character had now the support of
every-day experience. The gods sung by the old Greek poets, and
many a passionate Oriental deity unknown to them, could be seen and
their presence felt. He could himself have communion with them
through mysterious rites of divination. They had created the noblest
thing on earth, Greek civilisation; they were even now moulding and
controlling events; they could give courage and inspiration to their
votaries. From his sojourn at Nicomedia onwards, Julian believed
that all his actions were determined by divine voices which he heard
and obeyed. This natural religion was not the crude polytheism his
Christian teachers had said. Hellenism had made it a unity. A great
First Cause, the Father and King of all men, had parcelled out the lands
and peoples among the deities, His viceroys. They were the real rulers
of provinces and cities and governed them according to their natural
habits and dispositions. What was Christianity when compared with
this ancient and universal worship, supported by the wealth of civilisation which had come down from the past? It was a cult of barbarian

origin, born in an obscure province, ignorant of Hellenic culture, its very Scriptures written in a barbarous Greek offensive to the ears of educated men. Was Greece to abdicate in favour of Galilee? Perish the thought! So Julian believed, and longed to steep himself in Hellenism at its purest source — the Schools at Athens.

He gained his wish through the sisterly kindness of the Empress Eusebia. At Athens, as at all the schools of higher learning, the majority of the teachers were pagans, and Julian with more than his usual eagerness devoted himself to their lectures and to all the benefits of the place. "He was continually seen surrounded by crowds of youths, old men, philosophers, and rhetoricians." Outwardly he was still a Christian, for his life depended on his conformity to the Imperial creed; but inwardly he had consecrated himself heart and soul to paganism, had already became conscious that he had a divine mission, and that he was a favourite of the gods. The double life he had to live, the knowledge that he was surrounded by spies ready to report anything compromising to his Imperial cousin, must have acted upon his naturally nervous and emotional temperament and betrayed itself in many outward ways. His portrait drawn by a fellow-student, Gregory of Nazianzus, though the work of an enemy, needs only a little toning down—twitching shoulders, eyes glancing from side to side, something conceited in nostrils and face, feet that were never still, hasty laugh, sentences begun and never finished, irrelevant answers. Julian had more to do at Athens than study philosophy; he had to penetrate to the centre of Greek religion. He was secretly initiated into the ancient mysteries of Eleusis; and there are hints of other initiations either there or afterwards — of the worship of Mithras, of the purifying rite of the *taurobolium*.

Constantius was childless—the punishment of the gods whose temples he had despoiled, said the pagans; a retribution for the slaughter of his kinsmen, his own conscience sometimes whispered. The needs of the Empire demanded assistance. It is hard to say whether the Emperor or the student was the more unwilling, the one to summon and the other to obey the call. Julian was ordered to Milan where the Court was. He was made Caesar, was married to Helena, the Emperor's sister, and sent to Gaul to protect the province from invading Germans. The recluse bookworm, the man whose emotional nature had succumbed without suspicion to the suggestions of spiritualist *séances*, was suddenly confronted with one of the hardest tasks that practical life could offer. He had to restore a half-ruined province and to overcome an enemy grown bold by success. He was totally ignorant of the arts of war and of administration. It need not cause surprise that he proved an intrepid soldier. He was the last of a race of warriors, and the blood spoke. His studies had taught him the need of concentration and thoroughness; he set himself to learn and speedily mastered the elements of drill and discipline. But what the world did wonder at was that, hampered as he

CH. IV.

was by the assistants whom the jealousy of the Emperor had forced upon
him, he shewed himself a general who defeated his foes as much by
strategy as by fighting.

The Germans had been driven back; the administration of Gaul was
improved and its finances reformed, when the legions, irritated at commands from the distant Emperor, mutinied and called upon their general
to assume the purple (Jan. 360).   After long hesitation Julian consented.
It meant civil war.   But the gods encouraged him, his mission called
him, the soldiers rallied round him, and he marched against Constantius.
There was no battle.   Constantius died before the armies met, and
Julian became sole ruler over the Roman Empire.

During the whole of Julian's five years' stay in Gaul he publicly professed the Christian religion which privately he had repudiated.   He
allowed his name to be attached to the persecuting edicts of Constantius,
while in secret he began the day with a prayer to Hermes.   His
dissimulation went the length of joining with Constantius in threatening
anyone with torture who took part in the very ceremonies of divination
which he himself was all the while practising in private.   The only
trace of his real feelings is that no Christian emblems appear on the
coins which he struck in Gaul.   This double life did not cease when he
assumed the purple.   He ostentatiously joined in the public devotions of
the people during the festival of Epiphany (361), while in private he was
practising all manner of secret incantations and divinations aided by an
adept in the mysteries of Eleusis.   It may be that he waited until he was
sure of the sympathies of the army.   He seems to have taken care that
most of the soldiers who followed him from Gaul were pagans; and
that the Christian troops were left behind to guard the province.   At
all events it was not until he reached Sirmium on the lower Danube,
where the magistrates, citizens, and soldiers received him with acclama-
tions, that he declared himself a pagan, and could write to Maximus:
"We worship the gods openly; most of the soldiers who follow me
reverence them !   We have thanked the gods in the sight of men
with many hecatombs."   He entered Constantinople a professed pagan,
believing himself commissioned by the gods to restore the ancient religion,
a Dionysos and a Hercules in one, the prophet and king of a pagan
revival.

In his treatment of Christianity he believed that he shewed
impartiality and refrained from persecution, and, if due allowance be
made for his private hatred of those whom he contemptuously called
Galilaeans, it is possible to believe that he was sincere in his professions.

His first act was to issue an edict permitting all bishops, exiled by
Constantius for their attachment to the Nicene theology, to return and
resume possession of their confiscated property but not their sees.   More
than once the leaders, clerical and laic, of the various parties into which

Christianity was then divided, were summoned to his palace and told that they were at liberty to follow and advocate any form of belief they pleased. Ammianus Marcellinus, himself a pagan and a devoted admirer of Julian, declares that the Emperor did this in the firm belief that the Christians were so thoroughly divided that this liberty would end in their destroying each other by their mutual quarrels. If so the intention shows how little Julian understood the faith he despised. The bishops who had thronged the antechambers of Constantius and used backstairs intrigues against their rivals were very poor specimens of Christianity. The freedom of discussion which Julian permitted, the absence of Imperial interference, were the means of uniting not destroying the Church.

The greater part of the Emperor's edicts against Christianity were undoubtedly meant by him to make restitution to paganism and to the State of property and privileges which had been wrongly bestowed. The churches were commanded to restore the temple-sites and lands which had been given them for ecclesiastical purposes. If churches had been erected. they were ordered to be demolished and the temples rebuilt at the expense of the Christians. The clergy and Christian poor had been granted sums of money from municipal treasuries; and these grants were to cease. Constantine's legislation had given to the Christian clergy privileges enjoyed by the heathen priesthood. To Julian's mind paganism was the religion of the State and alone it carried privileges with it. So the special laws guaranteeing to the Church rights of inheritance, and laws exempting the clergy from personal taxation and freeing them from the obligation to serve on municipal councils, were abrogated. Ammianus Marcellinus probably expresses the popular opinion when he declares that this legislation, however just in theory, was harsh in practice from its cumulative weight and the haste with which it was enforced.

No edict of Julian's excited the indignation of the Christians so thoroughly as that upon education. It enacted that no Christian was to be allowed to teach in schools where the literature of Greece and Rome formed the basis of education; that all teachers must expound and insist upon the *religion* of the authors studied; but that Christian children might attend the schools. Perhaps the Emperor's reasons for his legislation increased their wrath; for pedantry is more irritating than force, and Julian's pedantic nature is displayed in his reasonings. "Homer, Hesiod, Demosthenes, Thucydides, Isocrates, Lysias, all founded their learning on the gods. Did not some of them believe themselves to be consecrated to Hermes and others to the muses? It seems therefore absurd to me that those who explain their works should not worship the gods they reverenced." He did not like to remember that Mardonius, his own honoured teacher, had been a Christian. His fixed idea was that Christianity could have no connexion with Hellenic thought or

CH. IV.

civilisation, that its affectation of interest in ancient Greek literature was hypocrisy, and that it was his duty as ruler to keep men from occasions of practising such a vice. From one point of view the edict seemed to affect the Christians but slightly. They had long been accustomed to send their children to schools in which the most famous teachers were pagans; but now they believed that the Emperor desired to use all the public schools throughout the Empire for proselytising purposes. In the end this edict did more good than harm to Christianity. It shewed in a striking way both the stedfastness and the resources of the Christians. The two most distinguished Christian teachers, Prohaeresius of Athens and C. Marius Victorinus of Rome, at once resigned their appointments. The former was the most esteemed teacher in the East, Libanius only excepted. Julian did his utmost to win him over to paganism. When he remained firm, the Emperor offered to make him an exception to his rule; but the Christian refused to accept any concession which was not to be shared by his humbler brethren. Christian teachers all over the East assiduously devoted themselves to acquire the elegancies of the Greek tongue and to write school-books in that language which could serve as substitutes for the authors they were forbidden to use.

The Emperor naturally abolished the *Labarum*, and changed all other Christian into pagan emblems. He permitted, encouraged, the worship of his statues; he purged the Praetorian guard (not the whole army) of Christians. He also dismissed from his service all Christian attendants, and endeavoured to make the civil service completely pagan.

At least one distinguished Christian had little cause to thank Julian for his toleration, and his treatment of Athanasius almost suggests that the Emperor felt that the great bishop was the opponent from whom his plans had most to fear. On Julian's edict restoring to their homes and properties Christian bishops who had been banished by Constantius, Athanasius naturally returned to Alexandria and was warmly welcomed by his people. Julian was indignant. He insisted that his edict had not authorised the banished bishops to resume their ecclesiastical work, and ordered Athanasius to be sent away from the city and then from Egypt. "By all the gods," he wrote to the governor of Egypt, "nothing could give me more pleasure than that thou shouldst expel from every corner of Egypt that criminal Athanasius, who has dared, during my reign, to baptise Greek wives of illustrious citizens. He must be persecuted."

Julian's efforts to restore and put new life into paganism are much more interesting than his attempts to damage Christianity. He called the religion he had so fervently adopted Hellenism, and his co-religionists Hellenes: Christianity was a barbarian cult, its supporters Galilaeans. But in reality the Christianity of the fourth century had absorbed much of what was best and most enduring in Hellenism; while the religion of Julian drew more of its contents from Oriental than from Hellenist sources. One cult into which he had been initiated and which he greatly esteemed, Mithraism, was the only one of those Oriental religions which seems to have been entirely unaffected by Hellenist thought.

The religion which Julian attempted to force on the Empire was a mosaic of decadent philosophy, bloody sacrifices, rituals old and new, "spiritualism," and divinations of all sorts. Its piety came from the cult of the *Mysteries*. It contained so much that was new that it was much more an attempted reconstruction or reformation than a revival of paganism.

Julian was quick to see that no religion could be universally accepted which had not behind it some common stable truths, and that Christianity had gained enormously from that compact system of doctrine which it had laboriously built up during the three centuries of its existence. If critics, like Celsus, had made capital out of the intellectual differences within Christianity, paganism was in a worse case. Heathenism had no basis of intellectual certainty; it had no universally accepted or acknowledged system of doctrine. If pagan philosophy were appealed to, it was anything but an harmonious system — one teacher said one thing only to be refuted by another. The *Hermotimus* of Lucian had somewhat wickedly shewn that the opinions of philosophy were as various as the thinkers were numerous. But the philosophic thinking of the age of Julian was eclectic, and Neoplatonism was supposed to reconcile all sorts of opinions. By ignoring some and rounding off the sharp corners of others it might be plausibly made out that all philosophies really meant to say the same things if they were only rightly understood. So Julian went to Neoplatonism for the intellectual basis or dogmatic theology of his new catholic State Religion. His philosophical acumen was by no means equal to that of his masters and he modestly confessed it. Iamblichus had taught him all that he knew, and that philosopher, in the opinion of Julian, had so explored the heights and depths of human and divine thought that nothing remained for any man save to accept his conclusions. The Neoplatonic thought of a Trinity of existence took the central place of the Christian in this new pagan theology.

Three worlds exist. First and highest is the realm of pure ideas where the Supreme Principle, the One, the Highest Good, the Great First Cause, lives and reigns. Below it is the intellectual world over which presides the same Supreme Principle, but now represented by an emanation from Itself, wholly spiritual, the Logos of the Platonic philosophy. The third is the world of sense existence, the universe of things seen and handled, and there, as beseems its surroundings, the ruler, the emanation from the Supreme Principle, assumes a visible form and can be seen while adored.

CH. IV.

The "common man," of course, could not be expected to understand or care for such high matters; but pagan philosophy had never thought much of the "common man" (which was its weakness), and he had always the gods nearest him to worship in that instinctive way which was alone possible for an intelligence such as his.   Yet Julian, with more sympathetic feeling for his needs than most pagan thinkers, made provision that even he should be taught the underlying unity and catholicity of his ancestral faith.   Just as in Christianity, Jesus was the revealer of the Father, and men were taught to see the One Supreme God in the Son Incarnate, the Mediator, so Julian called on all men to see in the great orb of day the visible manifestation of the Supreme Principle, the First Cause, Who has begotten him and placed him in the heavens, the medium through which He dispenses His benefits throughout the universe of men and things.   Even Christians, Julian thinks, might come to see this if their minds were not so darkened.   They believe in Jesus, whom neither they nor their fathers have ever *seen;* but they do not believe that the God Helios is the true revealer of God, Helios whom the whole human race from the beginning of time has *seen* and has honoured as their munificent and potent benefactor, Helios the living animated beneficent image of the Supreme Father, Who is exalted above all the powers of reason.   Man has body as well as soul, he has senses as he has capacities for intellectual thinking, therefore he needs visible gods to represent the gods invisible whom the Supreme Principle has sent forth from Himself and who suit the religious needs not merely of the different nations and tribes of mankind but also of the various divisions of men such as shopkeepers, tax-gatherers, dancers, etc.   These thousands of deities are all in their places representatives of the One Supreme Principle, Who has sent them forth and on Whom they depend.   The sun among the stars is an emblem of this divine unity in diversity.

Having thus demonstrated, as he believed, by exhortations and treatises, the unity which underlay the surface diversity of polytheism, Julian gave full scope to his desire to honour *every* manifestation of the one Supreme Principle, and to make use of every means whereby man could both shew his reverence for and seek communion with the divine. His first care was to make it clear to all that the worship of the old gods was to be the privileged cult.   Bishops were banished from the antechambers and audience halls of the palace and in their stead came pagan priests and Neoplatonic philosophers — chief among them being Maximus the "medium."   The Emperor was unwearied in issuing decrees that *all* the ancient temples were to be thrown open and that the ceremonies of *all* the ancient cults were to be duly performed.   It might be said that he converted his palace into a temple — so determined was he that every heathen festival should be observed and every detail of appropriate rite and sacrifice duly attended to — and it was said that his knowledge of the various rituals surpassed that of the priests themselves. His devotion to the whole sacrificial system of paganism has been recorded both by enemies and friends. We are told of one solemn sacrifice at which the victims included one hundred bulls, rams, sheep, and goats, as well as innumerable white birds from land and sea. He issued minute directions about the number of the sacrifices which were to be offered by day and by night in the reopened temples. He wished that all the old gods should be invoked — Saturn, Jupiter, Apollo, Mars, Pluto, Bacchus, Silenus, Aesculapius, Castor and Pollux, Rhea, Juno, Minerva, Latona, Venus, Hecate, the Muses, etc., etc.; but personally, like the pagans of the age he lived in, he was more devoted to the deities of Oriental origin — to the Attis cult, to Mithras, and most of all to Isis and Serapis. Dionysos, whose cult had many of the Oriental characteristics, seems to have been his most favoured among the gods of Greece.

The office of Pontifex Maximus was an Imperial prerogative and the one most prized by Julian. He was unwearied in the performance of all the duties it required and he used it in his attempt to create that Catholic Pagan State Church. The very conception is decisive proof that Julian aimed, not at the revival but at a thorough reconstruction of paganism. He had the thought of a great independent spiritual community, wide as the Empire — a community so holy and separated that men and women who abandoned Christianity could only be admitted into it after the performance of prescribed purifying rites. This community was to be ruled over by a priesthood set apart for the service and forming a graded hierarchy. At the head of all was the Pontifex Maximus; next came pagan metropolitans or the high-priests of provinces; under them were high-priests who had rule over the temples and priests within the districts assigned to them. It is improbable that Julian had completed the hierarchical organisation of the Empire before his death, but large parts of the East had been put in order. We have some briefs which he, as supreme pontiff, sent down to his metropolitans in which he regulated many things from the dress and morals of the clergy to the training of temple choirs — so minute was the interference of the Pontifex Maximus. Now it is *possible* that one form of paganism, the Imperial cult, had been strictly organised in the West and its provincial priests may have had some jurisdiction over the ministers of other cults; Maximin Daza had attempted to do something similar in the East; but the attempt to gather every cult of polytheism into one organised communion was not merely new; it was a startling novelty. Julian's conception of a pagan priesthood entirely devoted to the service of religion was certainly not Hellenist; nor was it Roman; it was Oriental; the cults of Egypt, of Syria, and of Asia had separated priesthoods. It was a new thing to be introduced into a universal State Church whose religion called itself Hellenism.

Julian thought a great deal about this priesthood of his and recognised its supreme importance for the reformation he dreamt of making.

CH. IV.

As the priest, from the office he fills, ought to be an example to all men, he should be selected with care — if possible a man of good family, neither very rich, nor very poor; but the indispensable qualifications are that he loves God and his neighbour. Love to God may be tested by observing whether the members of his family attend the temple services with regularity (Julian was very indignant when he discovered that the wives and daughters of some pagan priests were actually Christians), and love to one's neighbour by charity to the poor. Julian further insisted that the priest must be careful about what he reads. He is to shun all lascivious writings such as the old comedies or the contemporary erotic novels. He is to be equally circumspect in his conduct. He must not go to the theatre, nor to spectacles, and is not to frequent wine-shops. He is not to consort with actors nor to admit them to his house, he is even recommended not to accept too many invitations to dinner. On the other hand he is to see that he is master within his temple. He is to wear within it gorgeous vestments in honour of the gods whom he serves; but outside the sanctuary, when he mingles with men, he is to wear the ordinary dress. He is not to permit even the commander of the forces or the governor of the province to enter the temple with ostentation. He is to know the service thoroughly and to be able to repeat all the divine hymns. Occasionally he is to deliver addresses on philosophical subjects for the instruction of the multitude.

Julian also desired that the priests should organise schemes of charitable relief, more especially for the poor who attend the temple services. He thought that some such widely organised scheme might help to counteract the popularity of the "Galilaeans." He seems also to have contemplated the institution of religious communities of men and women vowed to a life of chastity and meditation — another proof that his so-called Hellenism was based much more on Oriental religions than on those of Greece.

The Emperor in all this legislation or advice was at pains to declare that he was acting, not as Emperor, but as "Pontifex Maximus of the religion of my country."

One feature of Julian's attempt to make the worship of the gods the universal and privileged religion of the Empire is too characteristic of the age to be entirely passed over. In the opening pages of this chapter, in which the living paganism of the third and fourth centuries is briefly described, it is shewn that the old official worships of Greece and Rome lingered as mere *simulacra* and that the real religious life of the times was fed by Oriental faiths which had introduced such thoughts as redemption, salvation, purification, the *Way of Return*, etc. It is not too much to say that whatever of the old pagan *piety* remained in the middle of the fourth century had attached itself to the worship of the *Mysteries*; and that pious men, if educated, looked on the different initiations and rites of purification taught in the various cults to be ways of attaining the same redemption, or finding the same *Way of Return.* Julian belonged to his age. He was a pure-hearted and deeply pious man. His piety was in a real sense heart religion, and, like that of his contemporaries, clothed itself in the cult of the *Mysteries* ; while his nervous, sensitive character inclined him personally to the theurgic or magical side of the cult, and especially to what re_ produced the old Dionysiac ecstasy. Hence the dominating thought in Julian's mind was to reform the whole public worship of paganism by impregnating it with the real piety and heart religion of the *Mysteries* cult. The one thing really reactionary in the movement he con_ templated was the return to the worship of the old official deities, but he proposed to attempt this in a way which can only be called revolu_ tionary. He endeavoured to put life into the old rituals by bringing to their aid and quickening them with that sincere fervour which the *Mysteries* cult demanded from its votaries. This is what makes Julian such an interesting figure in the history of paganism ; while it in part accounts for his complete failure to do what he attempted. He tried to unite two things which had utterly separate roots, whose ideals were different, and which could not easily blend. For the religion of the *Mysteries* was essentially a private cult, into which men and women were received, one by one, by rites of initiation which each had to pass through personally, and, when admitted, they became members of coteries, large or small, of like-minded persons. They had entered because their souls had craved something which they believed the initiations and purifications would give. It was a common saying among them that as sickness of the body needed medicine, so the sickness of the soul required those rites to which they submitted. What had this to do with the courteous recognition due to bright celestial beings which was the central thought of the official religion of Greece, or the punctilious performance of ceremonies which was believed to propitiate the sterner deities of Rome ? *Mysteries* and participation in their rites may exist along with a belief in the necessity and religious value of the public services of a state religion ; but whenever the latter can only be justified, even by its own votaries, on the ground of traditional and patriotic propriety, *Mystery* worship may take its place but can never quicken it. When the whole piety of paganism disappeared in the *Mysteries* cult, it estranged itself from the national and official religion ; and the *Mysteries* could never be used to recall the gods of Olympus for whose banishment they had been largely responsible.

No edicts of an Emperor could change the bright deities of Olympus into saviours, or transform their careless votaries into men who felt in their hearts the need of redemption and a way of return. Yet that was what Julian had to do when he proposed to impregnate the old official worship with the fervour of the *Mysteries* cult. It was equally in vain to think that the *Mysteries* cult, which owed its power to its spontaneity, to its independence, to its individuality, could be drilled and organised into the national religion of a great Empire. It was a true instinct that led Julian to see that the real and living pagan piety of his generation had taken refuge within the circles of the *Mysteries*, and that the hope of paganism lay in the spread of the fervour which kindled their votaries; his mistake lay in thinking that it could be used to requicken the official worship. It would have been better for his designs had he acted as did Vettius Agorius Praetextatus, the model of genuine pagan piety in the Roman senatorial circle (*princeps religiosorum*, Macrobius calls him). Praetextatus contented himself with a dignified and cool recognition of the official deities of Rome but sought outlet for his piety elsewhere, in initiations at Eleusis and other places and in the purifying rite of the *taurobolium*. The sentimental side of Julian's nature led him astray. He could not forget his early studies in Homer and Hesiod (he quotes Homer as frequently and as fervently as a contemporary Christian does the Holy Scriptures) and he had to introduce the gods of Olympus somewhere. He tried to unite the passionate Oriental worships with the dignified Greek and the grave Roman ceremonies where personal faith was superfluous. The elements were too incongruous.

In spite of all the signs of a reaction against Christianity Julian failed; and for himself the tragedy of his failure lay in the apathy of his co-religionists. In spite of his elaborate treatise against Christianity and his other writings; notwithstanding his public orations and his private persuasions, Julian did not succeed in making many converts. We hear of no Christians of mark who embraced Hellenism, save the rhetorician Hecebolius and Pegasius, a bishop with a questionable past. The Emperor boasted that his Hellenism made some progress in the army, but at his death the legions selected a Christian successor.

It is almost pathetic to read Julian's accounts of his continual disappointments. He could not find in "all Cappadocia a single man who was a true Hellenist." They did not care to offer sacrifice, and those who did so, did not know how. In Galatia, at Pessinus where stood a famous temple erected to the Great Mother, he had to bribe and threaten the inhabitants to do honour to the goddess. At Beroea he harangued the municipal council on the duty of worshipping the gods. "They all warmly praised my discourse," he says somewhat sadly, "but none were convinced by it save the few who were convinced before hearing." So it was wherever he went. Even pagan admirers like Ammianus Marcellinus were rather bored with the Emperor's *Hellenism* and thought the whole thing a devout imagination not worth the trouble he wasted on it. The senatorial circle at Rome had no sympathy with Julian's Hellenic revival. No one shewed any enthusiasm but the narrow circle of Neoplatonist sophists, and they had no influence with the people.

Yet Julian's attempt to stay the progress of Christianity and to drive back the tide which was submerging the Empire, was, with all its practical faults, by far the ablest yet conceived. It provided a sub_ stitute and presented an alternative. The substitute was pretentious and artificial, but it was probably the best that the times could furnish. *Hellenism*, Julian called it; but where in that golden past of Hellas into which the Imperial dreamer peered, could be found a puritan strictness of conduct, a prolonged and sustained religious fervour, and a religion independent of the State? The three strongest parts of his scheme had no connexion with Hellenism. Religions may be used, but cannot be created by statesmen, unless they happen to have the prophetic fire and inspiration — and Julian was no prophet. He may be credited with seizing and combining in one whole the strongest anti-Christian forces of his generation — the passion of Oriental religion, the patriotic desire to retain the old religion under which Greece and Rome had grown great, the glory of the ancient literature, the superstition which clung to magic and divinations, and a philosophy which, if it lacked independence of thought, at least represented that eclecticism which was the intellectual atmosphere which all men then breathed. He brought them together to build an edifice which was to be the temple of his Empire. But though the builder had many of the qualities which go to make a religious reformer — pure in heart and life, full of sincere piety, manly and with a strong sense of duty — the edifice he reared was quite artificial, lacked the living principle of growth, and could not last. Athanasius gave its history in four words when he said "It will soon pass." The world had outgrown paganism.

Whatever faults the Christianity of the time exhibited, whatever ills had come to it from Imperial patronage and conformity with the world, it still retained within it the original simplicity and profundity of its message. Nothing in its environment could take that from it. It proclaimed a living God, Who had made man and all things and for Whom man was made. *That* God had manifested Himself in Jesus Christ and the centre of the manifestation was the Passion of our Lord — the Cross. Whatever special meanings attach themselves to the intellectual apprehension of this manifestation, it contains two plain thoughts which can be grasped as easily by the simplest as by the most cultured intelligence, and was therefore universal as no previous religion had ever been. It gave a new revelation of God — a personal Deity, whose chiefest manifestation was a sympathy with all who were beneath Him and a yearning to deliver them at all costs to Himself. It gave, at the same time, a new revelation of man, made in the image of God and therefore capable of a far-off imitation; his life no longer ruled by the precepts of a calculating utilitarianism nor curbed by a statutory morality, freed from the chains of all taboos and rituals, inspired by the one principle "Thou shalt love thy neighbour as thyself," and this

CH. IV.

thought made vivid by the vision of a pure active Divine Life which spent itself in the service of mankind.

. Some of the Oriental religions, notably those of Mithras and Isis, were groping after this idea of "brother man"; the Imperial world was, in a vague way, advancing towards it; but the Cross of Christ shewed its highest and clearest manifestation. Therefore Christianity teaching that every follower of Christ, in so far as he was really a disciple, should imitate the Master, could set the stamp of the Cross on every portion of human life and on every social institution. It was the religion of the Cross, the religion whose watchword was "brother man." It was therefore universal and to it the future belonged.

If such things can be dated, the death of Julian marks the triumph of Christianity in the Roman world, eastern and western. The exclamation, "Galilaean, Thou hast conquered," is a fable which clothes a fact. Yet it would be a grave mistake to say that paganism disappeared suddenly either from the East or from the West.

In the East it never recovered its position as a state religion, but it existed as a private cult practised by no inconsiderable proportion of the people. It did not offer the strenuous resistance to Imperial anti-pagan legislation which was to be seen in the West. The number of Christians had always been much larger and it is more than probable that many of the laws against pagans were supported by public opinion. Julian's immediate successors practised a policy of toleration for all religions, and contented themselves with professing and favouring Christianity. It was the religion of the Imperial household and of the great majority of the population — nothing more. Pagans lived on free to worship what divinities they pleased. Even when Valens and emperors who came after him renewed and enforced laws against pagan worship no traces are to be found of anything like a general persecution. Accusations were listened to and procedure taken against numbers of wealthy persons in the hope of filling the Imperial treasury; but the mass of the people remained untouched. Whole districts, which were notoriously poor, were exempted from the operation of the laws. During the reign of Valens a large number of temples fell into ruins, but probably it was not the operation of the law which caused their destruction. The more celebrated temples were often in possession of large yearly revenues derived from lands and other endowments and in charge of the hereditary priesthood who presided over the worship. As paganism decayed these priesthoods frequently secularised the revenues, took possession of them, and were content to see the edifices fall into ruin. Still, paganism remained rooted in many of the old noble families of the East, and in such aristocratic households the place of private chaplain was filled by a Neoplatonic philosopher. As many of the members of this nobility were called to occupy high places in the civil administration of the Empire, they were able to protect their co-religionists and took care to

see that the anti-pagan laws were not enforced within their jurisdic-
tions. Optatus, praefect of Constantinople in 404 was a pagan. In
A.D. 467 Isokasios, the quaestor of Antioch, was accused of paganism.
Phocas took poison to prevent himself being obliged to embrace
Christianity as late as the time of Justinian. Many of the more famous
literary men — Eunapius, Zosimus, perhaps Procopius — were strongly
anti-Christian. Pamprepius, a Neoplatonist, famed for his power of
divination, an avowed pagan, drew a salary from the public revenues
and, along with distinguished generals like Marsus and Leontius, aided
Illus in his revolt against the Emperor Zeno in 484. But by the
end and indeed throughout the whole of the fifth century thoughtful
paganism had become a sort of Quietism and exercised no influence on
the public life of the population. When Theodosius the Great succeeded
in uniting the orthodox Church with the Imperial administration, when
the great bishops were placed in possession of powers almost equal to
those of the governors of provinces, the Church became the guardian of
the rights of the people and the interpreter of its wishes. The Church,
in that age of bureaucracy, had a popular constitution; its clergy came
from the people; the services were in the language of the district; its
bishops were the natural and sympathetic leaders of the people; and
the whole population gradually became included within the Christian
Church.

Athens and Achaia long remained the last stronghold of paganism
in the East. The Eleusinian and other mysteries, the great heathen
festivals celebrated in Athens and in other cities of Hellas, attracted crowds
of strangers from all parts of the Empire. Religious beliefs, patriotic
associations, thoughts of material prosperity, combined to make the
people of the towns and districts resolute to maintain and defend them.
So strong were the popular feelings that it would have led to riots, probably
to attempted insurrection, to enforce the Imperial legislation against
temples, sacrifices, and the celebration of pagan ceremonies by night.
The emperors found it necessary either to exempt Hellas from the
operation of these laws altogether or to suffer their non-enforcement.
The Eleusinian Mysteries continued until the famous temple was
destroyed by the Goths under Alaric. The Olympic Games were
celebrated until the reign of Theodosius I (394). The great and
venerated statue of Minerva remained to protect the city of Athens
until about 480. The great temple of Olympia remained open until its
destruction — whether by the Goths or by command of Theodosius II is
unknown.

In the fourth and fifth centuries Athens remained the most distinguished intellectual centre of the time. The teachers in its schools, for
the most part Neoplatonists who resolutely refused to accept Christianity,
maintained the old pagan traditions. Their influence was recognised
and feared. Theodosius II forbade private teachers to give public

lectures under pain of banishment. Justinian, determined to crush the
last remains of paganism, confiscated the funds which furnished the
salaries of the professors, seized on the endowments of the Academy
of Plato, and closed the schools. The persecuted philosophers fled to
Persia to avoid imprisonment or death and remained there until King
Chosroes obtained from the Emperor a promise that they would be
unmolested if they returned to their homes.

In the West paganism shewed itself much stronger. It displayed its
greatest tenacity in Rome itself, and there were many reasons why it
should do so. The old paganism had been closely connected with the
State and when it ceased to be the privileged religion it had no common
centre round which to rally. In Rome it was otherwise. Its stronghold
was the Senate, and all the elements of opposition to Christianity could
group themselves round that venerable assembly. The Senate had lost
its powers but its prestige remained, and the Emperors were chary of
attacking its dignity. It represented the ancient grandeur of Rome and
was the heir and defender of old Roman traditions. The city was full
of monuments of Rome's past greatness. They were, for the most part,
temples built to commemorate signal victories, and were visible signs of
the old religion under which Rome had grown to greatness. The Senate
took pride in preserving these witnesses of the past splendours of the
Imperial city and in seeing that the old ceremonial rites were duly
performed in spite of anti-pagan legislation. During the second half of
the fourth century and into the fifth, the pagan senators of Rome
flaunted their religion in the face of the world. They were at pains to
record on their family tombstones and other private monuments that
they had been hierophants of Hecate, had been initiated at Eleusis,
had been priests of Hercules, Attis, Isis, or Mithras. In spite of the
edicts and efforts of the sons of Constantine and of successors of
Julian paganism was the *state* religion of Rome down to 383. Its
worship was performed according to the old rites. The days consecrated
to the old gods, and others added in honour of the newer Oriental
deities, were the Roman holidays. Every year on 27 January the
Praefectus urbi went down to Ostia and presided over "games" in honour
of Castor and Pollux. All these costly ceremonies, sacrifices, and shows
were provided for out of the Imperial treasury. They were part of the
state religion, and the Senate were determined that they should be so
regarded. The Emperor might be a Christian, but he was nevertheless Pontifex Maximus, the official head of the old pagan religion,
and they believed themselves justified in performing its rites in his
name.

The Emperor Gratian delivered the first effectual blow against this
state of matters. He refused to assume the office of Pontifex Maximus,
probably in 375. In 382 he ordered that the great pagan ceremonies
and sacrifices should no longer be defrayed out of the Imperial treasury,

and saw that he was obeyed. He took from the ancient priesthoods of Rome the emoluments and immunities which they had enjoyed for centuries. He removed from the Senate House the statue of Victory and its altar on which incense had been duly burnt since the days of Octavius. The last great battle for the official recognition of paganism raged over these decrees. It lasted about ten years. Symmachus and Ambrose, both representatives of old Roman patrician families, were the leaders on the pagan and on the Christian side. The pagan party in the Senate fought every inch of ground against the advancing tide of Christianity. Its leading members enrolled themselves in the ancient priesthoods and assumed the dignities of the *sacra peregrina*. They provided for the sacrifices and other sacred rites at their own expense. They spent their means in restoring ancient temples and in building new ones. They had high hopes of a pagan reaction under Maximus, who had defeated and slain Gratian; under the short-lived Emperor Eugenius, who promised on his leaving Milan to meet Theodosius in battle that, on his return, he would stable his horses in Christian basilicas. The victory of Theodosius (394) on the Frigidus ended these hopes. They revived again for the last time when Alaric made Attalus a rival emperor to Honorius and when that ruler gathered round him counsellors who were for the most part pagans professed or secret. But paganism was not destined to obtain even a temporary victory. Perhaps, as Augustine said, it only desired to die honourably. Its political defeats did not quench the zeal of its lessening number of votaries. They engaged in polemical contests with their opponents. They wrote books to prove that the invasions of the barbarians and the weakness of the Empire were punishments sent by the gods for the abandonment of the ancient religion, and called forth such replies as the *Historia adversus paganos* of Paulus Orosius and the *De Civitate Dei* of St Augustine.

The tenacity of paganism in the West was not confined to Rome. The poems of Rutilius, the Homilies of Maximus of Turin and of Martin of Bracara, the Epistles of St Augustine, the history of Gregory of Tours, and the series of facts collected in the *Anecdota* of Caspari, all shew that paganism lingered long in Italy, Gaul, Spain, and North Africa, and that neither the persuasions of Christian preachers nor the penalties threatened by the State were able to uproot it altogether. The records of district ecclesiastical councils tell the same tale.

Literature may almost be called the last stronghold of paganism for the cultivated classes all over the Empire. It is hard for us to sympathise with the feelings of Christians in the fifth century for whom cultivated paganism was a living reality possessed of a seductive power; who could not separate classical literature from the religious atmosphere in which it had been produced; and who regarded the masterpieces of the Augustan age as beautiful horrors from which they might hardly escape. Jerome had fears for his soul's salvation because he could not conquer

CH. IV.

his admiration for Cicero's Latin prose, and Augustine shrank within himself when he thought on his love for the poems of Vergil. Had not his classical tastes driven him in youth from the uncouth latinity of the copies of the Holy Scriptures when he tried to read them? Christianity had mastered their heart, mind, and conscience, but it could not stifle fond recollection nor tame the imagination. In some respects paganism ruled over literature. The poet Claudian, whether he was heathen or Christian, lived and moved and had his being in the world of pagan thought. Sidonius Apollinaris could not string verses without endless mythological allusions. Rutilius, a hater of Christians and of their religion, adored with heart and soul the Dea Roma, Urbs Aeterna. Perhaps the dread of the power which seemed to lurk in literature was heightened by the courteous and kindly intercourse of Christians with pagans during the years of the last struggle. The Church owed much to the schools and was almost afraid of the debt. Basil and Gregory had been fellow-students with Julian at Athens. Chrysostom had been a pupil of Libanius, and acknowledged how much he owed to the great anti-Christian leader. Synesius had sat in the class-room of Hypatia at Alexandria, and never forgot some of the lessons he had learned there. And paganism never shewed itself to greater advantage than during its last years of heroic but unavailing struggle. Its leaders, whether in the Schools of Athens or among the Senatorial party at Rome, were for the most part men of pure lives with a high moral standard of conduct — men who commanded esteem and respect. Immorality abounded, but the pagan standard had become much higher. Christians and heathen were full of mutual esteem for each other. The letters exchanged between Symmachus and Ambrose reveal the intimacy in which the nobler pagans and earnest-minded Christians lived. Even the caustic Jerome seems to have a lurking but sincere affection for some of the leaders of the pagan Senatorial party. It is curious too to find that many of those stalwart supporters of the old religion of Rome were married to Christian wives, and that their daughters were brought up as Christians while the sons followed the father's faith. Jerome has drawn no more charming picture than that of the old heathen pontiff Albinus, the leader of the anti-Christian party in Rome, sitting in his study with his small grand-daughter on his knees, listening to the child while she repeated to him a Christian hymn she had just been taught by her mother. Theodosius II, most theological of emperors, married the daughter of a pagan who had taught philosophy in the Schools of Athens.

Yet however near pagans and Christians might approach each other in life and standard of conduct, a great gulf separated them. In the grey twilight of that fifth century, when men whose sight seemed furthest looked forward to the coming of a night of chaos, the Christian whisper of consolation was better than the pagan thought of destiny. The difference went further than ideals. If it be strange to find practical statesmen like Ambrose and Augustine, able to see that the pressing need of the times was upright citizenship, defending that ascetic life which threw aside all civic duties and responsibilities, surely it is stranger still to find those pure-minded, noble pagans forced by religious partizanship to be the zealous defenders of the bloody gladiatorial spectacles and the untiring opponents of all attempts to better the unhappy lot of actors and actresses condemned to life-long slavery in a calling which then could not fail to be disgraceful. If the dying world was to be requickened, it was not paganism that could bring salvation. So it slowly, almost unconsciously, passed away before the advancing tide of Christianity.

Means were found of reconciling many festivals to which the populace was devoted, both in town and in country, with the prevailing Christian sentiment. It was evil to fête Bacchus or Ceres, but there could be no harm in rejoicing publicly over the vintage and the harvest. The Lupercalia themselves were changed into a Christian festival by Pope Gelasius. Many a tutelary deity became a patron saint. The people retained their rustic processions, their feasts, and their earthly delights. The temples were left standing. They became public halls where the citizens could meet, or exchanges where the merchants could congregate, while the statues of the gods looked down from their niches undisturbed and unheeded.

So when the Teutonic invasion seemed to overwhelm utterly the ancient civilisation, the Church with its compact organisation was strong enough to sustain itself amid the wreck of all things, and was able to teach the barbarian conquerors to assimilate much of the culture, many of the laws and institutions of the conquered, and in the end to rear a new and Holy Roman Empire on the ruins of the old.

CHAPTER . V

ARIANISM

ARIANISM finds its place in history as one of the four great controversies which have done so much to shape the growth of Christian thought. They all put the central question — *das Wesen des Christentums* — but they put it from different points of view. For Gnosticism — Is the Gospel history; or is it an edifying parable? For Arianism — Is it the revelation of a divine Son, which must be final; or is it something short of this, which cannot be final? For the Reformation — Is its meaning to be declared by authority; or is it to be investigated by sound learning? The scientific (or more truly philosophical) scepticism of our own time accepts the decision of the Reformation, but raises afresh the issues of Gnosticism and Arianism as parts of the deeper question, whether the reign of law leaves any freedom to either God or man.

The Arian controversy arose on this wise. Both Greece and Israel had long been tending in different ways to a conception of God as purely transcendent. If the Stoics made him the immanent principle of reason in the world, they only helped the forces which made for transcendence by their utter failure to shew that the things in the world are according to reason. As the Christians also accepted any current beliefs which did not evidently contradict their doctrine of a historic incarnation, all parties were so far generally agreed by the end of the second century. In times of disillusion God seems far from men, and in the deepening gloom of the declining Empire he seemed further off than ever. But a transcendent God needs some sort of mediation to connect him with the world. There was no great difficulty in gathering this mediation into the hand of a Logos, as was already done by Philo the Jew in our Lord's time, and to assign him functions as of creation; and of redemption, as Christians and Gnostics added. But then came the question, Is the Logos fully divine, or not? If no, how can he create — much less redeem? If yes, then the purely transcendent God acts for himself, and ceases to be transcendent. The dilemma was hopeless. A transcendent God must have a mediator, and yet the mediator cannot be either divine or undivine. Points were cleared up, as when Tertullian shifted the stress of Christian thought from the Logos doctrine to the

Sonship, and when Origen's theory of the eternal generation presented the Sonship as a relation independent of time: but the main question was as dark as ever at the opening of the fourth century. There could be no solution till the pure transcendence was given up, and the Sonship placed inside the divine nature: and this is what was done by Atha_ nasius. There was no other escape from the dilemma, that if the Son is from the divine will, he cannot be more than a creature; if not, God is subject to necessity.

The controversy broke out about 318. Arius was no bustling heresiarch, but a grave and blameless presbyter of Alexandria, and a disciple of the learned Lucian of Antioch; only — he could not under_ stand a metaphor. Must not a son be later than the father, and inferior to him? He forgot first that a divine relation cannot be an affair of time, then that even a human son is essentially equal to his father. However, he concluded that the Son of God cannot be either eternal or equal to the Father. On both' grounds then he cannot be more than a creature — no doubt a lofty creature, created before all time to be the creator of the rest, but still only a creature who cannot reveal the fulness of deity. "Begotten" can only mean created. He is not truly God, nor even truly man, for the impossibility of combining two finite spirits in one person made it necessary to maintain that the created Son had nothing human but a body. Arius had no idea of starting a heresy: his only aim was to give a commonsense answer to the pressing difficulty, that if Christ is God, he is a second God. But if the churches did worship two gods, nothing was gained by making one of them a creature without ceasing to worship him, and something was lost by tampering with the initial fact that Christ was true man. As Athanasius put it, one who is not God cannot create — much less restore — while one who is not man cannot atone for men. In seeking a *via media* between a Christian and a Unitarian interpretation of the Gospel, Arius managed to combine the difficulties of both without securing the advantages of either. If Christ is not truly God, the Christians are convicted of idolatry, and if he is not truly man, there is no case for Unitarianism. Arius is condemned both ways.

The dispute spread rapidly. At the first signs of opposition, Arius appealed from the Church to the people. With commonsense doctrine put into theological songs, he soon made a party at Alexandria; and when driven thence to Caesarea, he secured more or less approval from its learned bishop, the historian Eusebius, and from other conspicuous bishops, including Constantine's chief Eastern adviser, Eusebius of Nicomedia, who was another disciple of Lucian. As it appeared later, few agreed with him; but there were many who saw no reason for turning him out of the Church. So when Constantine became master of the East in 323, he found a great controversy raging, which his own interests compelled him to bring to some decision. With his view of

CH. V.

Christianity as essentially monotheism, his personal leaning might be to the Arian side: but if he was too much of a politician to care greatly how the question was decided, he could quite understand some of its practical aspects. It was causing a stir in Egypt: and Egypt was not only a specially important province, but also a specially troublesome one — witness the eighty years of disturbance from Caracalla's massacre in 216 to the suppression of Achillaeus in 296. More than this, Arianism imperilled the imposing unity of the Church, and with it the support which the Empire expected from an undivided Church. The State could deal with an orderly confederation of churches, but not with miscellaneous gatherings of schismatics. So he was quite sincere when he began by writing to Arius and his bishop Alexander that they had managed to quarrel over a trifle. The dispute was really childish, and most distressing to himself.·

This failing, the next step was to invite all the bishops of Christendom to a council to be held at Nicaea in Bithynia (an auspicious name !) in the summer of 325, to settle all the outstanding questions which troubled the Eastern churches. If only the bishops could be brought to some decision, it was not likely to be disobeyed; and the State could safely enforce it if it was. Local councils had long been held for the decision of local questions, like Montanism or Paul of Samosata; but a general council was a novelty. As it could fairly claim to speak for the churches generally, it was soon invested with the authority of the ideal Catholic Church; and from this it was an easy step to make its decisions *per se* infallible. This step however was not taken for the present: Athanasius in particular repudiates any such idea.

As we have already discussed the council as sealing the alliance of Church and State, we have now to trace only its dealings with Arianism. Constantine was resolved not only to settle the question of Arianism, but to make all future controversies harmless; and this he proposed to do by drawing up a test creed for bishops, and for bishops only. This was a momentous change, for as yet no creed had any general authority. The Lord's Baptismal Formula (Mt. xxviii. 19) was variously expanded for the catechumen's profession at Baptism, and some churches further expanded it into a syllabus for teaching, perhaps as long as our Nicene Creed; but every church expanded it at its own discretion. Now however bishops were to sign one creed everywhere. Whatever was put into it was binding; whatever was left out remained an open question. The council was to draw it up.

The bishops at Nicaea were not generally men of learning, though Eusebius of Caesarea is hardly surpassed by Origen himself. But they had among them statesmen like Hosius of Cordova, Eusebius of Nicomedia, and the young deacon Athanasius from Alexandria; and men of modest parts were quite able to say whether Arianism was or was not what they had spent their lives in teaching. On that question they had no doubt at all. The Arianisers mustered a score or so of bishops out of about 300 — two from Libya, four from the province of Asia, perhaps four from Egypt, the rest thinly scattered over Syria from Mount Taurus to the Jordan valley. There were none from Pontus or from any part of Europe or Africa north of Mount Atlas. The first act of the council was the summary rejection of an Arian creed presented to them. The deity of Christ was not an open question in the churches. But was it needful to put the condemnation of Arianism into the creed? Athanasius had probably but few decided supporters. Between them and the Arianisers floated a great conservative centre party, whose chief aim was to keep things nearly as they were. These men were not Arians, for the open denial of the Lord's true deity shocked them: but neither would they go with Athanasius. Arianism might be condemned in the creed, if it could be done without going beyond the actual words of Scripture, but not otherwise. As they would have said, Arianism was not all false, though it went too far. It maintained the Lord's pre-mundane and real personality, and might be useful as against the Sabellianism which reduced him to a temporary appearance of the one God. Athanasius and Marcellus of Ancyra were mistaken in thinking Arianism a pressing danger, when it had just been so decisively rejected. Only five bishops now supported it. So the conservatives hesitated. Then Eusebius of Caesarea presented the catechetical creed of his own church, a simple document couched in Scripture language, which left Arianism an open question. It was universally approved: Athanasius could find nothing wrong in it, and the Arians were glad now to escape a direct condemnation. For a moment, the matter seemed settled.

Never was a more illogical conclusion. If the Lord's full deity is false, they had done wrong in condemning Arianism: if true, it must be vital. The one impossible course was to let every bishop teach or disown it as he pleased. So Athanasius and his friends were on firm ground when they insisted on revising the Caesarean creed to remove its ambiguity. After much discussion, the following form was reached:

We believe in one God, the Father all-Sovereign,
    maker of all things, both visible and invisible:
And in one Lord Jesus Christ,
    the Son of God,
  begotten of the Father, an only-begotten —
    that is, from the essence (οὐσία) of the Father —
    God from God,
    Light from light,
    true God from true God,
  begotten, not made,
    being of one essence (ὁμοούσιον) with the Father;
by whom all things were made,
  both things in heaven and things on earth;

CH. V.

who for us men and for our salvation came down and was made flesh,
>   was made man, suffered, and rose again the third day,
>   ascended into heaven,
>   cometh to judge quick and dead :
And in the Holy Spirit.
But those who say
>   that "there was once when he was not,"
>   and "before he was begotten he was not,"
>   and "he was made of things that were not,"
or maintain that the Son of God
>   is of a different essence,[1]
>   or created or subject to moral change or alteration —
These doth the Catholic and Apostolic Church anathematize.

It will be seen at once that the creed of the council differs a good deal from the "Nicene Creed" now in use, which is a revision of the catechetical creed of Jerusalem, made about 362.[2]   That is not the work of the Council of Constantinople in 381, but displaced the genuine Nicene Creed partly by its merits, and partly through the influence of the capital.   However, it will be noted further that (apart from the anathemas) the stress of the defence against Arianism rests on the two clauses *from the essence of the Father,* and *of one essence with the Father;* to which we may add that *begotten, not made* contrasts the words which the Arians industriously confused, and that the clause *was made man* meets the Arian denial that he took anything human but a body. Now the *essence* (οὐσία) of a thing is that by which it is — whatever we are supposing it to be.   It is not the general ground of all attributes, but the particular ground of the particular supposition we are making. As we are here supposing that the Father is God, the statement will be first that the Son is from that essence by which the Father is God, then that he shares the possession of it with the Father, so that the two together allow no escape from the confession that the Son is as truly divine and as fully divine as the Father.   The existence of the Son is not a matter of will or of necessity, but belongs to the divine *nature.* Two generations later, under Semiarian influences, a similar result was reached by taking *essence* in the sense of *substance,* as the common ground of all the attributes, so that if the Son is *of one essence with the Father,* he shares all the attributes of deity without exception.[3]

The conservative centre struggled in vain.   The decisive word (ὁμοούσιον, *of one essence with*) is not found in Scripture.   But there was no dispute about the Canon, so that the Arians had their own

---

[1] ἐξ ἑτέρας οὐσίας ἤ ὑποστάσεως.   The two words are used here as synonyms.

[2] A comparison of our "Nicene" Creed, first with the Jerusalem Creed, then with that of the Council, shews that it is the Jerusalem Creed with a few clauses from that of the Council, and differs entirely in structure from the latter.   It even omits the central clause ἐκ τῆς οὐσίας.

[3] Mr Bethune Baker (*Texts and Studies,* VII. 1) endeavours to shew that ὁμοούσιον was practically a Latin word, and underwent no change of meaning.

interpretations for all words that are found in Scripture. Thus to, The Son is eternal, they replied, "So are we, for We which live are alway" (2 Cor. iv. 11, delivered unto death). The bishops were gradually forced back on the plain fact that no imaginable evasion of Scripture can be forbidden without going outside Scripture for a word to define the true sense: and ὁμοούσιον was a word which could not be evaded. No doubt it was a revolution to put such a word into the creed: but now that the issue was fairly raised by Constantine's summons, they could not leave the Lord's full deity an open question without ceasing to be Christians. Given the unity of God and the worship of Christ — and even the Arians agreed to this — there was no escape from the dilemma, ὁμοούσιον or creature-worship. So they yielded to necessity. Eusebius of Caesarea signed with undisguised reluctance, though not against his conscience. To his mind the creed was not untrue, though it was revolutionary and dangerous, and he was only convinced against his will that it was needed. The emperor's influence counted heavily in the last stage of the debates — for Constantine was too shrewd to use it before the question was nearly settled — and in the end only two bishops refused to sign the creed. These he promptly sent into exile along with Arius himself; and Eusebius of Nicomedia shared their fate a few months later. If he had signed the creed at last, he had opposed it too long and been too intimate with its enemies.

Let us now look beyond the stormy controversies of the next half century to the broad issues of the council. The two fundamental doctrines of Christianity are the deity of Christ and the unity of God. Without the one, it merges in philosophy or Unitarianism; without the other, it sinks into polytheism. These two doctrines had never gone very well together; and now the council reconciled them by giving up the purely transcendental conception of God which brought them into collision with each other and with the historical facts of the Incarnation. The question was ripe for decision, as we see from the prevalence of such an unthinkable conception as that of a secondary God: and if the conservatives had been able to keep it unsettled, one of the two fundamental doctrines must before long have overcome the other. Had the unity of God prevailed, Christianity would have sunk into a very ordinary sort of Deism, or might possibly have become something like Islam, with Jesus for the prophet instead of Mahomet. But it is much more likely that the deity of Christ would have effaced the unity of God, and in effacing it have opened a wide door for polytheism, and itself sunk to the level of heathen hero-worship. As a matter of history, the churches did sink into polytheism for centuries, for common people made no practical difference between the worship of saints and that of the old gods. But because the Council of Nicaea had made it impossible to think of Christ simply as one of the saints, the Reformers were able to drop the saint-worship without falling into Deism.

CH. V.

Further, the recognition of eternal distinctions in the divine nature establishes within that nature a social element before which despotism or slavery in earth or heaven stands condemned. It makes illogical the conception of God as inscrutable Power in whose acts we must not presume to seek for reason — a conception common to Rome, Islam, and Geneva. Yet more, if God himself is not a despot, but a constitutional sovereign who rules by law and desires his subjects to see reason in his acts, this is an ideal which must profoundly influence political thought. True, there was little sign for centuries of any such influence. The Empire did not grow less despotic, and such ideas of freedom as the Teutons brought in did not come out of the Gospel: and if Islam and the Papacy lean to despotism, the Unitarians have done honourable work in the cause of liberty. But thoughts which colour the whole of life may have to work for ages before they are clearly understood. The Latin Church of the Middle Ages was not a mere apotheosis of power like Islam; and when Teutonic Europe broke away from Latin tutelage, the way was prepared for the slow recognition of a higher ideal than power, and our own age is beginning to see better the profound and far-reaching significance of the Nicene decision, not for religion only, but for political, scientific, and social thought.

The victory won at Nicaea was decisive. Arianism started vigorously, and seemed for awhile the winning side; but the moment it faced the council, it collapsed before the all but ananimous reprobation of the Christian churches. Only two bishops from the edge of the African desert ventured to deny that it contradicts essentials of the Gospel. The decision was free, for Constantine would not risk another Donatist controversy by putting pressure on the bishops before he could safely crush the remnant; and it was permanent, for words deliberately put into a creed cannot be removed without admitting that the objection to them is valid on one ground or another. Thus Arianism was not only condemned, but condemned in the most impressive way by the assembly which comes nearer than any other in history to the stately dream of a concrete catholic church speaking words of divine authority. No later gathering could pretend to rival the august assembly where Christendom had once for all pronounced the condemnation of Arianism, and no later movements were able definitely to reverse its decision.

But if the conservatives (who were the mass of the Eastern bishops) had signed the creed with a good conscience, they had no idea of making it their working belief. They were not Arians — or they would not have torn up the Arianising creed at Nicaea; but if they had been hearty Nicenes, no influence of the Court could have kept up an Arianising reaction for half a century. Christendom as a whole was neither Arian nor Nicene, but conservative. If the East was not Nicene, neither was it Arian, but conservative: and if the West was not Arian, neither was it Nicene, but conservative also. But conservatism was not the same in East and West.   Eastern conservatism inherited its doctrine from the age of subordination theories, and dreaded the Nicene definition as needless and dangerous.   But the Westerns had no great interest in the question and could scarcely even translate its technical terms into Latin, and in any case their minds were much more legal than the Greek; so they simply fell back on the authority of the Great Council. Shortly, "East and West were alike conservative; but while conservatism in the East went behind the council, in the West it was content to start from it." [1]

The Eastern reaction was therefore mainly conservative.   The Arians were the tail of the party; they were not outcasts only because conservative hesitation at the Nicene Creed kept open the back door of the Church for them.   For thirty years they had to shelter themselves behind the conservatives.   It was not till 357 that they ventured to have a policy of their own; and then they broke up the anti-Nicene coalition at once. The strength of Arianism was that while it claimed to be Christian, it brought together and to their logical results all the elements of heathenism in the current Christian thought.   So the reaction rested not only on conservative timidity, but on the heathen influences around.   And heathenism was still a living power in the world, strong in numbers, and still stronger in the imposing memories of history.   Christianity was still an upstart on Caesar's throne, and no man could yet be sure that victory would not sway back to the side of the immortal gods.   So the Nicene age was pre-eminently an age of waverers; and every waverer leaned to Arianism as a *via media* between Christianity and heathenism.   The Court also leaned to Arianism.   The genuine Arians indeed were not more pliant than the Nicenes; but conservatives are always open to the influence of a Court, and the intriguers of the Court (and under Constantius they were legion) found it their interest to unsettle the Nicene decisions — in the name of conservatism forsooth.   To put it shortly, the Arians could have done nothing without a formidable mass of conservative discontent behind them, and the conservatives would have been equally helpless if the Court had not supplied them with the means of action.   The ultimate power lay with the majority, which was at present conservative, while the initiative rested with the Court, which leaned on Asia, so that the reaction went on as long as both were agreed against the Nicene doctrine.   It was suspended when Julian's policy turned another way, became unreal when conservative alarm subsided, and came to an end when Asia went over to the Nicenes.

The contest (325–381) falls into two main periods, separated by the Council of Constantinople in 360, when the success of the reaction seemed complete.   We have also halts of importance at the return of Athanasius in 346 and the death of Julian in 363.

The first period is a fight in the dark, as Socrates calls it, but upon

[1] *Studies of Arianism*, p. 57.

CH. V.

the whole the conservative coalition steadily gained ground till 357, in spite of Nicene reactions after Constantine's death in 337 and the detection of Stephen's plot in 344. First the Arianising leaders had to obtain their own restoration, then to depose the Nicene chiefs one after another. By 341 the way was open for a series of attempts to replace the Nicene Creed by something that would let in the Arians. But this meant driving out the Nicenes, for they could not compromise without complete surrender; and the West was with the Nicenes in refusing to unsettle the creed. Western influence prevailed at Sardica in 343, and Western intervention secured an uneasy truce which lasted till Constantius became master of the West in 353. Meanwhile conservatism was softening into a less hostile Semiarian form, while Arianism was growing into a more offensive Anomoean doctrine. So the conservatives were less interested when Constantius renewed the contest, and took alarm at the open Arianism of the Sirmian manifesto in 357. This brought things to a deadlock, and gave rise to a Homoean or professedly neutral party supported by the Anomoeans and the Court. They were repulsed at Seleucia by a new alliance of Semiarians and Nicenes, and at Ariminum by the conservative West; but their command of the Court enabled them to exile the Semiarian leaders after the Council of Constantinople in 360.

The second period of the reaction opens with a precarious Homoean supremacy. It was grievously shaken at the outset by Julian's restoration of the exiles. The Nicenes were making rapid progress, and might have restored peace if Julian had lived longer. But Valens, with a feebler character and a weaker position, returned to the policy of Constantius. For the moment it may have been the best policy; but the permanent forces were for the Nicenes, and their issue was only a question of time. There were misunderstandings in abundance, but a fairly united party hailed in Theodosius (379) an orthodox emperor from the West. The Arians were first put out of the churches, then formally condemned by the Council of Constantinople in 381. Henceforth Arianism ceased to be a power except among its Teutonic converts. Now we return to the morrow of the great council.

When the bishops returned home, they took up their controversies just where the summons to the council had interrupted them. The creed was signed and done with, and we hear no more of it. Yet both sides had learned caution at Nicaea. Marcellus disavowed Sabellianism and Eusebius avoided Arianism, and even directly controverted some of its main positions. Before long however a party was formed against the council. Its leader was Eusebius of Nicomedia, who had returned from exile and recovered his influence at Court. Round him gathered the bishops of the school of Lucian, and round these again all sorts of malcontents. The conservatives in particular gave extensive help. Charges of heresy against the Nicene chiefs were sometimes more than plausible.   Marcellus was practically Sabellian, and Athanasius at least refused to disavow him.   Some even of the darker charges may have had truth in them, or at least a semblance of truth.

So in the next few years we have a series of depositions of Nicene leaders.   By 335 the Church was fairly cleared of all but the two chief of them, Marcellus of Ancyra, and Athanasius of Alexandria (since 328). Marcellus was already in middle life when he refuted the Arians at Nicaea; and in a diocese full of the strife and debate of endless Gaulish sects and superstitions he had learned that the Gospel is wider than Greek philosophy, and that simpler forms may better suit a rude flock. So his system is an appeal from Origen to St John.   He begins with the Logos as impersonal — as at once the thinking principle which is in God and the active creating principle which comes forth from God, and yet remains with God.   Thus the Logos came forth from the Father for the work of creation, and in the fulness of time descended into human flesh, becoming the Son of God in becoming the Son of Man.   Only in virtue of this humiliating separation did the Logos acquire personality for a time: but when the work is done, the human flesh will be thrown aside, and the Logos will return to the Father and be immanent and impersonal as before.   Marcellus has got away from Arianism as far as he can: but he is involved in much the same difficulties.   If for example the idea of an eternal Son is polytheistic, nothing is gained by transferring the eternity to an impersonal Logos; and if the work of creation is unworthy of God, it matters little whether it is delegated to a created Son or to a transitory Logos.   Marcellus misses as completely as Arius the Christian conception of the Incarnation.

Then they turned to a greater than Marcellus.   Athanasius was a Greek by birth and education; Greek also in subtle thought and philosophic insight, in oratorical power and skilful statesmanship.   Of Coptic influence he scarcely shows a sign.   His very style is clear and simple, without a trace of Egyptian involution and obscurity.   Athanasius was born about 297, so that he must have well remembered the last years of the Great Persecution, which lasted till 313.   He may have been a lawyer for a short time, and seems to have known Latin; but his main training was Greek and scriptural.   As a man of learning or a skilful party-leader Athanasius was not beyond the reach of rivals.   But he was more than this.   His whole spirit is lighted up with vivid faith in the reality and eternal meaning of the Incarnation.   His small work *de Incarnatione*, written before the rise of Arianism, ranks with the *Epistle to Diognetus* as the most brilliant pamphlet of early Christian times.   Even there he rises far above the level of Arianism and Sabellianism; and throughout his long career we catch glimpses of a spiritual depth which few of his contemporaries could reach.   And Athanasius was before all things a man whose life was consecrated to a simple purpose. Through five exiles and fifty years of controversy he stood in defence

CH. V.

of the great council. The care of many churches rested on him, the pertinacity of many enemies wore out his life; yet he is never soured but for a moment by the atrocious treachery of 356. At the first gleam of hope he is himself again, full of brotherly consideration and respectful sympathy for old enemies returning to a better mind. Even Gibbon is awed for once before "the *immortal* name of Athanasius."

Marcellus had fairly exposed himself to a doctrinal attack, but against Athanasius the most convenient charge was that of episcopal tyranny. In 335 the Eastern bishops gathered to Jerusalem to dedicate the splendid church which Constantine had built on Golgotha. First however a synod was held at Tyre to restore peace in Egypt. The Eusebians had the upper hand, and they used their power shamelessly. Scandal succeeded scandal, till the iniquity culminated in the despatch of an openly partizan commission (including two young Pannonian bishops, Ursacius and Valens) to get up evidence in Egypt. Moderate men protested, and Athanasius took ship for Constantinople. The council condemned him by default and the condemnation was repeated at Jerusalem, where also proceedings were commenced against Marcellus. They also restored Arius; but his actual reception was prevented by his sudden death the evening before the day appointed. Meanwhile Athanasius had appealed to Constantine in person, who summoned the bishops at once to Constantinople. They dropped the charges of sacrilege and tyranny, and brought forward a new charge of political intrigue. Athanasius was allowed no reply, but sent into exile at Trier in Gaul, where he was honourably received by the younger Constantine. The emperor seems as usual to have been aiming at peace and unity. Athanasius was evidently a centre of disturbance, and the Asiatic bishops disliked him: he was therefore best kept out of the way for the present.

Constantine died 22 May 337, and his sons at once restored the exiles. Presently things settled down in 340 with the second son Constantius master of the East, and Constans the youngest holding the three Western praefectures. So Eusebian intrigues were soon resumed. Constantius was essentially a little man, weak and vain, easy-tempered and suspicious. He had also a taste for church matters, and without ever being a genuine Arian, he hated first the Nicene Council, and then Athanasius personally. The intriguers could scarcely have desired a better tool.

They began by raising troubles at Alexandria, and deposing Athanasius afresh (late in 338) for having allowed the civil power to restore him. In Lent 339 Athanasius was expelled, and Gregory of Cappadocia installed by military violence in his place. The ejected bishops — Athanasius, Marcellus and others — fled to Rome. Bishop Julius at once took up the high tone of impartiality which became an arbiter of Christendom. He received the fugitives with a decent reserve, and invited the Easterns to the council they had asked him to hold. After long delay, it was plain that they did not mean to come; so a council of fifty bishops met at Rome in the autumn of 340, by which Athanasius and Marcellus were acquitted. As Julius reported to the Easterns, the charges against Athanasius were inconsistent with each other and con. tradicted by evidence from Egypt, and the proceedings at Tyre were a travesty of justice. It was unreasonable to insist on its condemnation of Athanasius as final. Even the great council of Nicaea had decided (and not without the will of God) that the acts of one council might be revised by another: and in any case Nicaea was better than Tyre. As for Marcellus, he had denied the charge of heresy and presented a sound confession of his faith (our own Apostles' Creed, very nearly) and the Roman legates at Nicaea had borne honourable witness to the part he had taken in the council. If they had complaints against Athanasius, they should not have neglected the old custom of writing first to Rome, that a legitimate decision might issue from the apostolic see.

The Eusebians replied in the summer of 341, when some ninety bishops met to consecrate the Golden Church of Constantine at Antioch. Hence it is called the Council of the Dedication. Like the Nicene, it seems to have been in the main conservative; but the active minority was Arianising, not Athanasian; and it was not quite so successful. The bishops began as at Nicaea by rejecting an Arian creed. They next approved a creed of a conservative sort, said to be the work of Lucian of Antioch, the teacher of Arius. The decisive clause however was rather Nicene than conservative. It declared the Son "morally unchangeable, the unvarying image of the deity and essence of the Father." The phrase declares that there is no change of essence in passing from the Father to the Son, and is therefore equivalent to *homoousion*. Athanasius might have accepted it at Nicaea, but he could not now; and the conservatives did not mean ὁμοούσιον — only the illogical ὁμοιούσιον, of like essence. So they were satisfied with the Lucianic creed: but the Arianisers endeavoured to upset it with a third creed, and the council seems to have broken up uncertainly, though without revoking the Lucianic creed. A few months later, another council met at Antioch and adopted a fourth creed, more to the mind of the Arianisers. In substance it was less opposed to Arianism than the Lucianic, its form is a close copy of the Nicene. In fact, it is the Nicene down to the anathemas, but the Nicene with every sharp edge taken off. So well did it suit the Arianisers that they reissued it (with ever-growing anathemas) three times in the next ten years.

Western suspicion became a certainty, now that the intriguers were openly tampering with the Nicene faith. Constans demanded a general council, and Constantius was too busy with the Persian war to refuse him. So it met at Sardica, the modern Sofia, in the summer of 343. The Westerns were some 96 in number "with Hosius of Cordova for their father." The Easterns, under Stephen of Antioch, were about 76. They demanded that the condemnation of Athanasius and Marcellus should be taken as final, and retired across the Balkans to Philippopolis when the Westerns insisted on reopening the case. So there were two contending councils. At Sardica the accused were acquitted, while the Easterns confirmed their condemnation, denounced Julius and Hosius, and reissued the fourth creed of Antioch with some new anathemas.

The quarrel was worse than ever. But next year came a reaction. When the Western envoy Euphrates of Cologne reached Antioch, a harlot was let loose upon him; and the plot was traced up to bishop Stephen. The scandal was too great: Stephen was deposed, and the fourth creed of Antioch reissued, but this time with long conciliatory explanations for the Westerns. The way was clearing for a cessation of hostilities. Constans pressed the decrees of Sardica, Ursacius and Valens recanted the charges against Athanasius, and at last Constantius consented to his return. His entry into Alexandria (31 Oct. 346) was the crowning triumph of his life.

The next few years were an interval of suspense, for nothing was decided. Conservative suspicion was not dispelled, and the return of Athanasius was a personal humiliation for Constantius. But the mere cessation of hostilities was not without influence. The conservatives were fundamentally agreed with the Nicenes on the reality of the Lord's divinity; and minor jealousies abated when they were less busily encouraged. The Eusebian phase of conservatism, which dreaded Sabellianism and distrusted the Nicenes, was giving place to the Semiarian, which was coming to see that Arianism was the more pressing danger, and slowly moving towards an alliance with the Nicenes. We see also the rise of a more defiant Arianism, less patient of conservative supremacy, and less pliant to imperial dictation. The Anomoean leaders emphasised the most offensive aspects of Arianism, declaring that the Son is *unlike* the Father, and boldly maintaining that there is no mystery at all in God. Their school was presumptuous and shallow, quarrelsome and heathenising, yet not without a directness and firm conviction which compares well with the wavering and insincerity of the conservative chiefs.

Meanwhile new troubles were gathering in the West. Constans was deposed (Jan. 350) by Magnentius. After a couple of minor claimants were disposed of, the struggle lay between Magnentius and Constantius. The decisive battle was fought (28 Sept. 351) near Mursa in Pannonia, but the destruction of Magnentius was not completed till 353. Constantius remained the master of the world. The Eusebians now had their opportunity. Already in 351-2 they had reissued the fourth creed of Antioch from Sirmium, with its two anathemas grown into twenty-seven. But as soon as Constantius was master of Gaul, he determined to force on the Westerns an indirect condemnation of the Nicene faith in the person of Athanasius. A direct approval of Arianism was out of the question, for Western conservatism was firmly set against it by the Nicene and Sardican councils. The bishops were nearly all resolute against it. Liberius of Rome followed in the steps of Julius, Hosius of Cordova was still the patriarch of Christendom, and the bishops of Trier, Toulouse and Milan proved their faith in exile. So doctrine was kept in the background. Constantius came forward personally before a council at Arles (Oct. 353) as the accuser of Athanasius, while all the time he was giving him solemn and repeated promises of protection. The bishops were not unwilling to take the emperor's word, if the Court party would clear itself of Arianism; and at last they gave way, the Roman legate with the rest. Only Paulinus of Trier had to be exiled. For the next two years Constantius was busy with the barbarians, so that it was not till the autumn of 355 that he was able to call another council at Milan, where Julian was made Caesar for Gaul. It proved quite unmanageable, and only yielded at last to open violence. Three bishops were exiled, including Lucifer of Calaris in Sardinia.

Lucifer's appearance is a landmark. The lawless despotism of Constantius had roused an aggressive fanaticism. Lucifer had all the courage of Athanasius, but nothing of his wary self-respect and moderation. He scarcely condescends to reason, but revels in the pleasanter work of denouncing the fires of damnation against the disobedient emperor. A worthier champion was Hilary of Poitiers, the noblest representative of Western literature in the Nicene age. Hilary was by birth a heathen, coming before us in 355 as an old convert and a bishop of some standing. In massive power of thought he was a match for Athanasius; but he was rather student and thinker than orator and statesman. He had not studied the Nicene Creed till lately; but when he found it true, he could not refuse to defend it. He was not at the council, but was exiled to Asia a few months later, apparently on the charge of immorality, which the Eusebians usually brought against obnoxious bishops.

When Hosius of Cordova had been imprisoned, there remained but one power in the West which could not be summarily dealt with. The grandeur of Hosius was personal, but Liberius claimed the universal reverence due to the apostolic and imperial see of Rome. Such a bishop was a power of the first importance, when Arianism was dividing the Empire round the hostile camps of Gaul and Asia. Liberius was a staunch Nicene. When his legates yielded at Arles, he disavowed their action. The emperor's threats he disregarded, the emperor's gifts he cast out of the Church. It was not long before the world was scandalised by the news that Constantius had arrested and exiled the bishop of Rome.

Attempts had already been made to dislodge Athanasius from Alexandria, but he refused to obey anything but written orders from the

CH. V.

emperor. As Constantius had given his solemn promise to protect him in 346, and three times written to repeat it since his brother's death, duty as well as policy forbade him to credit officials. The most pious emperor could not be supposed to mean treachery; but he must say so himself if he did. The message was plain enough when it came. A force of 5000 men surrounded the church of Theonas on a night of vigil (8 Feb. 356). The congregation was caught as in a net. Athanasius fainted in the tumult: yet when the soldiers reached the bishop's throne, its occupant had somehow been conveyed away.

For six years Athanasius disappeared from the eyes of men, while Alexandria was given over to military outrage. The new bishop George of Cappadocia (formerly a pork-contractor) arrived in Lent 357, and soon provoked the fierce populace of Alexandria. He escaped with difficulty from one riot in 358, and was fairly driven from the city by another in October. Constantius had his revenge, but it shook the Empire to its base. The flight of Athanasius revealed the power of religion to stir up a national rising, none the less real for not breaking out in open war. In the next century the councils of the Church became the battlefield of nations, and the victory of Hellenic orthodoxy at Chalcedon implied sooner or later the separation of Monophysite Egypt and Nestorian Syria.

Arianism seemed to have won its victory when the last Nicene champion was driven into the desert. But the West was only terrorised, Egypt was devoted to its patriarch, Nicenes were fairly strong in the East, and the conservatives who had won the battle would never accept Arianism. However, this was the time chosen for an open declaration of Arianism, by a small council of Western bishops at Sirmium, headed by Ursacius and Valens. They emphasise the unity of God, condemn the words οὐσία (essence), ὁμοούσιον and ὁμοιούσιον, lay stress on the inferiority of the Son, limit the Incarnation to the assumption of a body, and more than half say that he is only a creature. This was clear Anomoean doctrine, and made a stir even in the West, where it was promptly condemned by the Gaulish bishops, now partly shielded from Constantius by the Caesarship of Julian. But the Sirmian manifesto spread dismay through the ranks of the Eastern conservatives. They had not put down Sabellianism only in order to set up the Anomoeans; and the danger was brought home to them when Eudoxius of Antioch and Acacius of Caesarea convened a Syrian synod to approve the manifesto. The conservative counterblow was struck at Ancyra in Lent 358. The synodical letter is long and clumsy, but we see in it conservatism changing from its Eusebian to a Semiarian phase — from fear of Sabellianism to fear of Arianism. They won a complete victory at the Court, and sent Eudoxius and the rest into exile. This however was too much. The exiles were soon recalled, and the strife began again more bitterly than ever.

Here was a deadlock. All parties had failed. The Anomoeans were active enough, but pure Arianism was hopelessly discredited throughout the Empire. The Nicenes had Egypt and the West, but they could not overcome the Court and Asia. The Eastern Semiarians were the strongest party, but such men of violence could not close the strife. In this deadlock nothing was left but specious charity and colourless in_ definiteness; and this was the plan of the new Homoean party, formed by Acacius and Eudoxius in the East, Ursacius and Valens in the West.

A general council was decided on; but it was divided into two — the Westerns to meet at Ariminum, the Easterns at Seleucia in Cilicia, the headquarters of the army then operating against the Isaurians. Mean_ while parties began to group themselves afresh. The Anomoeans went with the Homoeans, from whom alone they could expect any favour, while the Semiarians drew closer to the Nicenes, and were welcomed by Hilary of Poitiers in his conciliatory *de Synodis*. The next step was a small meeting of Homoean and Semiarian leaders, held in the emperor's presence on Pentecost Eve (22 May 359) to draw up a creed to be laid before the councils. The dated creed (or fourth of Sirmium) is conservative in its appeals to Scripture, in its solemn reverence for the Lord, in its rejection of *essence* (οὐσία) as not found in Scripture, and in its insistence on the mystery of the eternal generation. But its central clause gave a decisive advantage to the Homoeans. "We say that the Son is like the Father in all things as the Scriptures say and teach." Even the Anomoeans could sign this. "Like the Father as the Scriptures say — and no further; and we find very little likeness taught in Scripture. Like the Father if you will, but not like God, for no creature can be. Like the Father certainly, but not in essence, for likeness which is not identity implies difference — or in other words, likeness is a question of degree." Of these three replies, the first is fair, the third perfectly sound.

The reception of the creed was hostile in both councils. The Westerns at Ariminum rejected it, deposed the Homoean leaders, and ratified the Nicene Creed. In the end however they accepted the Sirmian, but with the addition of a stringent series of anathemas against Arianism, which Valens accepted — for the moment. The Easterns at Seleucia rejected it likewise, deposed the Homoean leaders, and ratified the Lucianic creed. Both sides sent deputies to the emperor, as had been arranged; and after much pressure, these deputies signed a revision of the dated creed on the night of 31 Dec. 359. The Homoeans now saw their way to final victory.

By throwing over the Anomoeans and condemning their leader Aëtius, they were able to enforce the prohibition of the Semiarian ὁμοιούσιον: and then it only remained to revise the dated creed again for a council held at Constantinople in Feb. 360, and send the Semiarian leaders into exile.

The Homoean domination never extended beyond the Alps. Gaul

CH. V.

was firmly Nicene, and Constantius could do nothing there after the mutiny at Paris in Jan. 360 had made Julian independent of him. The few Western Arians soon died out. But in the East, the Homoean power lasted nearly twenty years. Its strength lay in its appeal to the moderate men who were tired of strife, and to the confused thinkers who did not see that a vital question was at issue. The dated creed seemed reverent and safe; and its defects would not have been easy to see if the Anomoeans had not made them plain. But the position of parties was greatly changed since 356. First Hilary of Poitiers had done something to bring together conservatives and Nicenes; then Athanasius took up the work in his own *de Synodis*. It is a noble overture of friendship to his old conservative enemies. The Semiarians, or many of them, accepted *of the essence* (ἐκ τῆς οὐσίας) and the Nicene anathemas, and doubted only of the ὁμοούσιον. Such men, says he, are not to be treated as enemies, but reasoned with as brethren who differ from us only in the use of a word which sums up their own teaching as well as ours. When they confess that the Lord is a true Son of God and not a creature, they grant all that we are contending for. Their own *homoiousion* without *of the essence* does not shut out Arianism, but the two together amount to *homoousion*. Moreover, *homoiousion* is illogical, for likeness is of properties and qualities, whereas the essence must be the same or different, so that the word rather suggests Arianism, whereas *homoousion* shuts it out effectually. If they accept our doctrine, sooner or later they will find that they cannot refuse its necessary safeguard. But if Nicenes and Semiarians drew together, so did Homoeans and Anomoeans. Any ideas of conciliating Nicene support were destroyed by the exile of Meletius, the new bishop of Antioch, for preaching a sermon carefully modelled on the dated creed, but substantially Nicene in doctrine. A schism arose at Antioch; and henceforth the leaders of the Homoeans were practically Arians.

The mutiny at Paris implied a civil war: but just as it was beginning, Constantius died at Mopsucrenae beneath Mount Taurus (3 Nov. 361) and Julian remained sole emperor. We are not here concerned with the general history of his reign, or even with his policy towards the Christians — only with its bearing on Arianism. In general, he held to the toleration of the Edict of Milan. The Christians are not to be persecuted — only deprived of special privileges — but the emperor's favour must be reserved for the worshippers of the gods. So the administration was unfriendly to the Christians, and left occasional outrages unpunished, or dismissed them with a thin reproof. But these were no great matters, for the Christians were now too strong to be lynched at pleasure. Julian's chief endeavour was to put new life into heathenism: and in this the heathens themselves hardly took him seriously. His only act of definite persecution was the edict near the end of his reign, which forbade the Christians to teach the classics; and this is disapproved by "the cool and impartial heathen" Ammianus.

Every blow struck by Julian against the Christians fell first on the Homoeans whom Constantius had left in power; and the reaction he provoked against Greek culture threatened the philosophical postulates of Arianism. But Julian cared little for the internal quarrels of the Christians, and only broke his rule of contemptuous impartiality when he recognised one greater than himself in "the detestable Athanasius." Before long an edict recalled the exiled bishops, though it did not replace them in their churches. If others were in possession, it was not Julian's business to turn them out. This was toleration, but Julian had a malicious hope of still further embroiling the confusion. If the Christians were left to themselves, they would "quarrel like beasts." He got a few scandalous wranglings, but in the main he was mistaken. The Christians only closed their ranks against the common enemy: the Arians also were sound Christians in this matter — blind old Maris of Chalcedon came and cursed him to his face.

Back to their cities came the survivors of the exiled bishops, no longer travelling in pomp and circumstance to their noisy councils, but bound on the nobler errand of seeking out their lost or scattered flocks. It was time to resume Hilary's interrupted work of conciliation. Semiarian violence had discredited in advance the new conservatism at Seleucia: but Athanasius had things more in his favour, for Julian's reign had not only sobered partisanship, but left a clear field for the strongest moral force in Christendom to assert itself. And this force was with the Nicenes. Athanasius reappeared at Alexandria 22 Feb. 362, and held a small council there before Julian drove him out again. It was decided first that Arians who came over to the Nicene side were to retain their rank on condition of accepting the Nicene council, none but the chiefs and active defenders of Arianism being reduced to lay communion. Then, after clearing up some misunderstandings of East and West, and trying to settle the schism at Antioch by inducing the old Nicenes, who at present had no bishop, to accept Meletius, they took in hand two new questions of doctrine. One was the divinity of the Holy Spirit. Its reality was acknowledged, except by the Arians; but did it amount to co-essential deity? That was still an open question. But now that attention was fully directed to the subject, it appeared from Scripture that the theory of eternal distinctions in the divine nature must either be extended to the Holy Spirit or abandoned. Athanasius took one course, the Anomoeans the other, while the Semiarians tried to make a difference between the Lord's deity and that of the Holy Spirit: and this gradually became the chief obstacle to their union with the Nicenes. The other subject of debate was the new system of Apollinarius of Laodicea — the most suggestive of all the ancient heresies. Apollinarius was the first who fairly faced the difficulty, that if all men are sinners, and the Lord was not a sinner, he cannot have been truly man. Apollinarius replied that sin lies in the weakness of the human

CH. V.

spirit, and accounted for the sinlessness of Christ by putting in its place
the divine Logos, and adding the important statement that if the human
spirit was created in the image of the Logos (Gen. i. 28) Christ would
not be the less human but the more so for the difference.   The spirit in
Christ was human spirit, although divine.   Further, the Logos which in
Christ was human spirit was eternal.   Apart then from the Incarnation,
the Logos was archetypal man as well as God, so that the Incarnation
was not simply an expedient to get rid of sin, but the historic revelation
of that which was latent in the Logos from eternity.   The Logos and
man are not alien beings, but joined in their inmost nature, and in a
real sense each is incomplete without the other.   Suggestive as this is,
Apollinarius reaches no true incarnation.   Against him it was decided
that the Incarnation implied a human soul as well as a human body — a
decision which struck straight enough at the Arians, but quite missed
the triple division of body, soul, and spirit (1 Thess. v. 23) on which
Apollinarius based his system.

Athanasius was exiled again almost at once: Julian's anger was
kindled by the news that he had baptised some heathen ladies at
Alexandria.   But his work remained.   At Antioch indeed it was
marred by Lucifer of Calaris, who would have nothing to do with
Meletius, and consecrated Paulinus as bishop for the old Nicenes.   So
the schism continued, and henceforth the rising Nicene party of Pontus
and Asia was divided by this personal question from the older Nicenes
of Egypt and the West.   But upon the whole the lenient policy of the
council was a great success.   Bishop after bishop gave in his adhesion
to the Nicene faith.   Friendly Semiarians came in like Cyril of Jerusalem, old conservatives followed, and at last (in Jovian's time) the
arch-enemy Acacius himself gave in his signature.   Even creeds were re-
modelled in all directions in a Nicene sense, as at Jerusalem and Antioch,
and in Cappadocia and Mesopotamia.   True, the other parties were not
idle.   The Homoean coalition was even more unstable than the Eusebian,
and broke up of itself as soon as opinion was free.   One party favoured
the Anomoeans, another drew nearer to the Nicenes, while the Semiarians
completed the confusion by confirming the Seleucian decisions and re-
issuing the Lucianic creed.   But the main current set in a Nicene
direction, and the Nicene faith was rapidly winning its way to victory
when the process was thrown back for nearly twenty years by Julian's
death in Persia (26 June 363).

Julian's death seemed to leave the Empire in the gift of four barbarian generals: but while they were debating, a few of the soldiers
outside hailed a favourite named Jovian as emperor.   The cry was taken
up, and in a few minutes the young officer found himself the successor
of Augustus.   Jovian was a decided Christian, though his personal
character did no credit to the Gospel.   But his religious policy was one
of genuine toleration.   If Athanasius was graciously received at Antioch,

the Arians were told with scant courtesy that they could hold meetings as they pleased at Alexandria. So all parties went on consolidating themselves. The Anomoeans had been restive since the condemnation of Aëtius at Constantinople, but it was not till now that they lost hope of the Homoeans, and formed an organised sect. But all these movements came to an end with the sudden death of Jovian (16–17 Feb. 364). This time the generals chose; and they chose the Pannonian Valentinian for emperor. A month later he assigned the East from Thrace to his brother Valens.

Valentinian was a good soldier and little more, though he could honour learning and carry forward the reforming work of Constantine. His religious policy was toleration. If he refused to displace the few Arian bishops he found in possession, he left the churches free to choose Nicene successors. So the West soon recovered from the strife which Constantius had introduced. It was otherwise in the East. Valens was a weaker character — timid and inert, but not inferior to his brother in scrupulous care for the interests of his subjects. No soldier, but more or less good at finance. For awhile events continued to develop naturally. The Homoean bishops held their sees, but their influence was fast declining. The Anomoeans were forming a schism on one side, the Nicenes were recovering power on the other. On both sides the simpler doctrines were driving out the compromises. It was time for even the Semiarians to bestir themselves. A few years before they were beyond question the majority in the East; but this was not so certain now. The Nicenes had made a great advance since the Council of Ancyra, and were now less conciliatory. Lucifer had compromised them in one direction, Apollinarius in another, and even Marcellus had never been disavowed; but the chief cause of suspicion to the Semiarians was now the advance of the Nicenes to a belief in the deity of the Holy Spirit.

It was some time before Valens had a policy to declare. He was only a catechumen, perhaps cared little for the questions before his elevation, and inherited no assured position like Constantius. It was some time before he fell into the hands of the Homoean Eudoxius of Constantinople, a man of experience and learning, whose mild prudence gave him just the help he needed. In fact, a Homoean policy was really the easiest for the moment. Heathenism had failed in Julian's hands, and an Anomoean course was even more hopeless, while the Nicenes were still a minority outside Egypt. The only alternative was to favour the Semiarians; and this too was full of difficulties. Upon the whole, the Homoeans were still the strongest party in 365. They were in possession of the churches and had astute leaders, and their doctrine had not yet lost its attraction for the quiet men who were tired of controversy.

In the spring of 365 an imperial rescript commanded the municipalities to drive out from their cities the bishops who had been exiled by Constantius and restored by Julian. At Alexandria the populace

CH. V.

declared that the rescript did not apply to Athanasius, whom Julian had not restored, and raised such dangerous riots that the matter had to be referred back to Valens. Then came the revolt of Procopius, who seized Constantinople and very nearly displaced Valens. Athanasius was restored, and could not safely be disturbed again. Then after the Procopian revolt came the Gothic war, which kept Valens occupied till 369 : and before he could return to church affairs, he had lost his best adviser, for Eudoxius of Constantinople was ill replaced by the rash Demophilus.

The Homoean party was the last hope of Arianism. The original doctrine of Arius had been decisively rejected at Nicaea, the Eusebian coalition was broken up by the Sirmian manifesto, and if the Homoean union also failed, its failure meant the fall of Arianism. Now the weakness of the Homoean power is shewn by the growth of a new Nicene party in the most Arian province of the Empire. Cappadocia was a country district : yet Julian found it incorrigibly Christian, and we hear very little of heathenism from Basil. But it was a stronghold of Arianism; and here was formed the alliance which decided the fate of Arianism. Serious men like Meletius had only been attracted to the side of the Homoeans by their professions of reverence for the Person of the Lord, and began to look back to the Nicene council when it appeared that Eudoxius and his friends were practically Arians after all. Of the old conservatives also, there were many who felt that the Semiarian position was unsound, and yet could find no satisfaction in the indefinite doctrine professed at Court. Thus the Homoean domination was threatened with a double secession. If the two groups of malcontents could form a union with each other and with the older Nicenes of Egypt and the West, they would be much the strongest of the parties.

This was the policy of the man who was now coming to the front of the Nicene leaders. Basil of Caesarea — the Cappadocian Caesarea — was a disciple of the Athenian schools, and a master of heathen eloquence and learning, and man of the world enough to secure the friendly interest of men of all sorts. His connexions lay among the old conservatives, though he had been a decided opponent of Arianism since 360. He succeeded to the bishopric of Caesarea in 370. The crisis was near. Valens moved eastward in 371, reaching Caesarea in time for the great midwinter festival of Epiphany 372. Many of the lesser bishops yielded, but threats and blandishments were thrown away on their metropolitan, and when Valens himself and Basil met face to face, the emperor was overawed. More than once the order was prepared for his exile, but it was never issued. Valens went forward on his journey, leaving behind a princely gift for Basil's poorhouse. Thenceforth he fixed his quarters at Antioch till the disasters of the Gothic war called him back to Europe in 378.

Armed with spiritual power which in some sort extended over

Galatia and Armenia, Basil was now free to labour at his plan. Homoean malcontents formed the nucleus of the league, but old conservatives came in, and Athanasius gave his patriarchal blessing to the scheme. But the difficulties were enormous. The league was full of jealousies. Athanasius might recognise the orthodoxy of Meletius, but others almost went the length of banning all who had ever been Arians. Others again were lukewarm or sunk in worldliness, while the West stood aloof. The confessors of 355 were mostly gathered to their rest, and the Church of Rome cared little for troubles that were not likely to reach herself. Nor was Basil quite the man for the work. His courage indeed was indomitable. He ruled Cappadocia from a sick-bed, and bore down opposition by sheer force of will; and to this he joined an ascetic fervour which secured the devotion of his friends, and often the respect of his enemies. But we miss the lofty self-respect of Athanasius. The ascetic is usually too full of his own purposes to feel sympathy with others, or even to feign it like a diplomatist. Basil had worldly prudence enough to dissemble his belief in the Holy Spirit, not enough to shield his nearest friends from his imperious temper. Small wonder if the great scheme met with many difficulties.

The declining years of Athanasius were spent in peace. Heathenism was still a power at Alexandria, but the Arians were nearly extinct. One of his last public acts was to receive a confession presented on behalf of Marcellus, who was still living in extreme old age at Ancyra. It was a sound confession so far as it went; and though Athanasius did not agree with Marcellus, he had never thought his errors vital. So he accepted it, refusing once again to sacrifice the old companion of his exile. It was nobly done; but it did not conciliate Basil.

The school of Marcellus expired with him, and if Apollinarius was forming another, he was at any rate a resolute enemy of Arianism. Meanwhile the churches of the East seemed in a state of universal dissolution. Disorder under Constantius became confusion worse confounded under Valens. The exiled bishops were so many centres of strife, and personal quarrels had full scope. When for example Basil's brother Gregory was expelled from Nyssa by a riot got up by Anthimus of Tyana, he took refuge under the eyes of Anthimus at Doara, where another riot had driven out the Arian bishop. Creeds were in the same confusion. The Homoeans had no consistent principle beyond the rejection of technical terms. Some of their bishops were substantially Nicenes, while others were thoroughgoing Anomoeans. There was room for all in the happy family of Demophilus. Church history records no clearer period of decline than this. The descent from Athanasius to Basil is plain; from Basil to Cyril it is rapid. The victors of Constantinople are but the Epigoni of a mighty contest.

Athanasius passed away in 373, and Alexandria became the prey of Arian violence. The deliverance came suddenly, and in the confusion

CH. V.

of the greatest disaster that had ever yet befallen Rome. When the Huns came up from the Asiatic steppes, the Goths sought refuge beneath the shelter of the Roman eagles. But the greed and peculations of Roman officials drove them to revolt: and when Valens himself with the whole army of the East encountered them near Hadrianople (9 Aug. 378) his defeat was overwhelming. Full two-thirds of the Roman army perished in the slaughter, and the emperor himself was never heard of more. The blow was crushing: for the first time since the days of Gallienus, the Empire could place no army in the field.

The care of the whole world now rested on the Western emperor, Gratian the son of Valentinian, a youth of nineteen. Gratian was a zealous Christian, and as a Western he held the Nicene faith. His first step was to proclaim religious liberty in the East, except for Anomoeans and Photinians — a small sect supposed to have pushed the doctrine of Marcellus too far. As toleration was still the general law of the Empire (though Valens might have exiled individual bishops) the gain of the rescript fell almost entirely to the Nicenes. The exiles found little difficulty in resuming the government of their flocks, or even in sending missions to the few places where the Arians were strong, like that undertaken by Gregory of Nazianzus to Constantinople. The Semiarians were divided. Numbers of them joined the Nicenes, while the rest took an independent position. Thus the Homoean power in the provinces collapsed of itself, and almost without a struggle, before it was touched by persecution.

Gratian's next step was to share his heavy burden with a colleague. The new emperor came from the far West of Cauca near Segovia, and to him was entrusted the Gothic war, and with it the government of all the provinces east of Sirmium. Theodosius was therefore a Western and a Nicene, with a full measure of Spanish courage and intolerance. The war was not very dangerous, for the Goths could do nothing with their victory, and Theodosius was able to deal with the Church long before it ended. A dangerous illness early in 380 led to his baptism by Acholius of Thessalonica; and this was the natural signal for a more decided policy. A law dated 27 Feb. 380 commanded all men to follow the Nicene doctrine, "committed by the apostle Peter to the Romans, and now professed by Damasus of Rome and Peter of Alexandria," and threatened heretics with temporal punishment. In this he seems to abandon Constantine's test of orthodoxy by subscription to a creed, returning to Aurelian's requirement of communion with the chief bishops of Christendom. But the mention of St Peter and the choice both of Rome and Alexandria, are enough to shew that he was still a stranger to the state of parties in the East.

Theodosius made his formal entry into Constantinople 24 Nov. 380, and at once required the bishop either to accept the Nicene faith or to leave the city. Demophilus honourably refused to give up his heresy, and adjourned his services to the suburbs. But the mob of Constan_tinople was Arian, and their stormy demonstrations when the cathedral of the Twelve Apostles was given up to Gregory of Nazianzus made Theodosius waver. Not for long. A second edict in Jan. 381 forbade all heretical assemblies inside cities, and ordered the churches everywhere to be given up to the Nicenes. Thus was Arianism put down as it had been set up, by the civil power. Nothing remained but to clear away the wrecks of the contest.

Once more an imperial summons went forth for a council of the Eastern bishops to meet at Constantinople in May 381. It was a sombre gathering: even the conquerors can have had no more hopeful feeling than that of satisfaction to see the end of the long contest. Only 150 bishops were present — none from the west of Thessalonica. The Semiarians however mustered 36, under Eleusius of Cyzicus. Meletius of Antioch presided, and the Egyptians were not invited to the earlier sittings, or at least were not present. Theodosius was no longer neutral as between the old and new Nicenes. After ratifying the choice of Gregory of Nazianzus as bishop of Constantinople, the next move was to sound the Semiarians. They were still a strong party beyond the Bosphorus, so that their friendship was important. But Eleusius was not to be tempted. However he might oppose the Anomoeans, he could not forgive the Nicenes their doctrine of the Holy Spirit. Those of the Semiarians who were willing to join the Nicenes had already done so, and the rest were obstinate. They withdrew from the council and gave up their churches like the Arians.

Whatever jealousies might divide the conquerors, the contest with Arianism was now at an end. Pontus and Syria were still divided from Rome and Egypt on the question of Meletius, and there were germs of future trouble in the disposition of Alexandria to look to Rome for help against the upstart see of Constantinople. But against Arianism the council was united. Its first canon is a solemn ratification of the Nicene creed in its original form, with an anathema against all the Arianising parties. It only remained for the emperor to complete the work of the council. An edict in the middle of July forbade Arians of all sorts to build churches even outside cities; and at the end of the month Theodosius issued an amended definition of orthodoxy. The true faith was henceforth to be guarded by the demand of communion, no longer with Rome and Alexandria, but with Constantinople, Alexandria, and the chief sees of the East: and the choice of cities is significant. A small place like Nyssa might be included for the personal eminence of its bishop; but the omission of Hadrianople, Perinthus, Ephesus and Nicomedia shews the determination to leave a clear field for the supremacy of Constantinople.

So far as numbers went, the cause of Arianism was not hopeless even yet. It was fairly strong in Asia, could raise dangerous riots in Constantinople, and had on its side the Western empress-mother Justina. But its fate was only a question of time. Its cold logic generated no fiery enthusiasm, its recent origin allowed no venerable traditions to grow up round it, and its imperial claims cut it off from any appeal to provincial feeling. So when the last overtures of Theodosius fell through in 383, Arianism soon ceased to be a religion in the civilised world. Such existence as it kept up for the next three hundred years was due to its barbarian converts.

CHAPTER VI

THE ORGANISATION OF THE CHURCH

CHRISTIAN organisation was the means of expressing that which is behind and beneath all its details, namely the underlying and pene. trating consciousness of the oneness of the Christian body and the Christian life. It was the process by which the separate *charismata* could be developed and differentiated, while at the same time the unity of the whole was safeguarded. Looked at in this light, the history of organisa-tion in the Christian Church is, in its main stream, the history of two processes, partly successive, partly simultaneous, but always closely related: the process by which the individual communities became complete in themselves, sufficient for their own needs, microcosms of the Church at large; and the process by which the communities thus organised as units proceeded to combine in an always more formal and more ex-tensive federation. But these two processes were not merely successive. Just as there never had been a time when the separate communities, before they became fully organised, were devoid of outside ministration or supervision, so there never came a period when the fully organised communities lived only to themselves : unity was preserved by informal means, till the growing size and number of the communities, and the increasing complexity of circumstances, made informal means inadequate and further formal organisation imperative. And again, though the formal self-expression of the individual community necessarily preceded the formal self-expression of the federation of communities, yet the history of organisation within the single community does not come to an abrupt end as soon as the community becomes complete in itself: all functions essential for the Christian life are henceforth there, but as numbers increase and needs and duties multiply, the superabundant vitality of the organism shews itself in the differentiation of new, though always subordinate, functions. And therefore, side by side with the well-known history of the federation of the Christian churches, it will be our business to trace also the obscurer and less recognised, but perhaps not less important, processes which were going on, simultaneously with the larger processes of federation, in the individual churches and especially in those of them which were most influential as models to the rest.

(A) In the early days of Christianity the first beginnings of a new community were of a very simple kind : indeed the local organisation had at first no need to be anything but rudimentary, just because the community was never thought of as complete in itself apart from its apostolic founder or other representatives of the missionary ministry. "Presbyters" and "deacons" no doubt existed in these communities from the first : "presbyters" were ordained for each church as it was founded on St Paul's first missionary journey ; "bishops and deacons" constitute, together with the "holy people," the church of Philippi. These purely local officials were naturally chosen from among the first converts in each district, and to them were naturally assigned the duties of providing for the permanently recurring needs of Christian life, especially the sacraments of Baptism — St Paul indicates that baptism was not normally the work of an apostle — and the Eucharist. But the evidence of the earlier epistles of St Paul is decisive as to the small relative importance which this local ministry enjoyed : the true ministry of the first generation was the ordered hierarchy, "first apostles, secondly prophets, thirdly teachers," of which the apostle speaks with such emphasis in his first epistle to the Corinthians. Next in due order after the ranks of the primary ministry came the gifts of miracles — "then powers, then gifts of healing" — and only after these, wrapped up in the obscure designation of "helps and governments," can we find room for the local service of presbyters and deacons. Even without the definite evidence of the Acts and the Pastoral Epistles and St Clement of Rome it would be already clear enough that the powers of the local ministry were narrowly limited, and that to the higher ministry, the exercise of whose gifts was not confined to any one community but was independent of place altogether, belonged not only the general right of supervision and ultimate authority over local churches, but also in particular the imparting of the gift of the Spirit, whether in what we call Confirmation or in what we call Ordination. In effect the Church of the first age may almost be said to have consisted of a laity grouped in local communities, and a ministry that moved about from place to place to do the work of missionaries to the heathen and of preachers and teachers to the converts. Most of St Paul's epistles to churches are addressed to the community, the holy people, the brethren, without any hint in the title of the existence of a local clergy : the apostle and the Christian congregation are the two factors of primary account. The *Didache* shews us how right down to the end of the first century, in remoter districts, the communities depended on the services of wandering apostles, or of prophets and teachers, sometimes wandering sometimes settled, and how they held by comparison in very light esteem their presbyters and deacons. Even a well-established church, like that of Corinth, with half a century of history behind it, was able, however unreasonably, to refuse to recognise in its local ministry any right of tenure other than the will of the community: and when the Roman church intervened to point out the gravity of the blow thus struck at the principle of Christian order, it was still the community of Rome which addressed the community of Corinth. And this custom of writing in the name, or to the address, of the community continued, a relic of an earlier age, well into the days of the strictest monarchical episcopacy: it was not so much the bishop's headship of the community as the multiplication of the clergy which (as we shall see) made the real gap between the bishop and his people.

Most of our documents then of the first century shew us the local churches neither self-sufficient nor self-contained, but dependent for all special ministries upon the visits of the superior officers of the Church. On the other hand most of our documents of the second century — in its earlier years the Ignatian letters, and an ever-increasing bulk of evidence as the century goes on — shew us the local churches complete in themselves, with an officer at the head of each who concentrates in his hands both the powers of the local ministers and those also which had at first been reserved exclusively for the "general" ministry, but who is himself as strictly limited in the extent of his jurisdiction to a single church as were the humbler presbyter-bishops from whom he derived his name. When we have explained how the supreme powers of the general ministry were made to devolve on an individual who belonged to the local ministry, we have explained the origin of episcopacy. With that problem of explanation we have not here to deal in detail: we have only to recognise the result and its importance, when in and with the bishop the local church sufficed in itself for the extraordinary as well as for the ordinary functions of church government and Christian life.

In those early days of episcopacy, among the diminutive groups of Christian "strangers and sojourners" which were dotted over the pagan world of the second century, we must conceive of a quite special closeness of relation between a bishop and his people. Regularly in all cities — and it was in the provinces where city life was most developed that the Church made quickest progress — a bishop is found at the head of the community of Christians: and his intimacy with his people was in those primitive days unhindered by the interposition of any hierarchy of functionaries or attendants. His flock was small enough for him to carry out to the letter the pastoral metaphor, and to "call his sheep by name." If the consent of the Christian people had always been, as Clement of Rome tells us, a necessary preliminary to the ordination of Christian ministers, in the case of the appointment of their bishop the people did not consent merely, they elected: not till the fourth century did the clergy begin to acquire first a separate and ultimately a predominant share in the process of choice. Even though the "angel of the church" in the Apocalypse may not have been, in the mind of the seer, at all intended to refer to the bishop, yet this quasi-identification of the community with its representative exactly expresses the ideal of second century writers. "The whole number of you I welcome in God's Name in the person of Onesimus," "in Polybius I beheld the whole multitude of you," writes Ignatius to the Christians of Ephesus and Tralles : "be subject to the bishop and to one another" is his injunction to the Magnesians : the power of Christian worship is in "the prayer of the bishop and the whole church." So too to Justin Martyr, "the brethren as we are called" and "the president" are the essential figures in the portraiture of the Christian society. If it is true that in the first century the apostle-founder and the community as founded by him are the two outstanding elements of Christian organisation, it is no less true that in the second century the twin ideas of bishop and people attain a prominence which throws all subordinate distinctions into the background. Even as late as the middle of the third century we see Cyprian — who is quite misunderstood if he is looked on only as an innovator in the sphere of organisation — maintaining and emphasising at every turn the intimate union, in normal church life, of bishop and laity, while he also recognises the duty of the laity, in abnormal circumstances, to separate from the communion of the bishop who had proved himself unworthy of their choice : "it is the people in the first place which has the power both of electing worthy bishops and of spurning the unworthy." Similar witness for the East is borne in the same century by the *Didascalia Apostolorum*, where bishop and laity are addressed in turn, and their mutual relations are almost the main theme of the writer.

But this personal relation of the bishop to his flock, which was the ideal of church administrators and thinkers from Ignatius to Cyprian, could only find effective realisation in a relatively small community : the very success of the Christian propaganda, and the consequent increase everywhere of the numbers of the Christian people, made some further development of organisation imperative. Especially during the long peace between Severus and Decius (211–249) did recruits pour in. In the larger towns at least there could be now no question of personal acquaintance between the president of the community and all its members. No doubt it might have been possible to preserve the old intimacy at the cost of unity, and to create a bishop for each congregation. But the sense of civic unity was an asset of which Christians instinctively availed themselves in the service of religion. If practical convenience sometimes dictated the appointment of bishops in villages, these χωρεπίσκοποι were only common in districts where, as in Cappadocia, cities were few, and where consequently the extent of the territory of each city was unduly large for supervision by the single bishop of the πόλις. Normally, even in days before there was any idea of the formal demarcation of territorial jurisdiction, the πόλις or *civitas* with all its dependent lands was the natural sphere of the individual bishop's authority. And within the walls of the city it was never so much as conceivable that the *ecclesia* should be divided. When the Council of Nicaea was making provision for the reinstatement in clerical rank of Novatianist clergy willing to be reconciled with the Church, the arrangement was subject always to the maintenance of the principle that there should not be "two bishops in the city." The very rivalries between different claimants of one episcopal throne serve to bring out the same result — witness the earliest instances of pope and anti-pope of which we have documentary know_ ledge, those of Cornelius and Novatian in 251, and of Liberius and Felix about 357. In the latter case Constantius, with a politician's eye to compromise, recommended the joint recognition of both claimants: but the Roman people — Theodoret, to whose *History* we owe the details, is careful to note that he has recorded the very language used — saluted the reading of the rescript in the circus with the mocking cry that two leaders would do very well for the factions at the games, but that there could be only "one God, one Christ, one bishop." Exactly the same reason had been given a century earlier in almost the same words, by the Roman confessors when writing to Cyprian, for their abandonment of Novatian and adhesion to Cornelius: "we are not unaware that there is one God, and one Christ the Lord whom we have confessed, one Holy Spirit, and therefore only one true bishop in the communion of the Catholic Church." Both in East and West, in the largest cities as well as in the smallest, the society of the faithful was conceived of as an indivisible unit; and its oneness was expressed in the person of its one bishop. The παροικία of Christians in any locality was not like a hive of bees, which, when numbers multiplied inconveniently, could throw off a part of the whole, to be henceforward a complete and independent organism under separate control. The necessity for new organisation had to be met in some way which would preserve at all costs the oneness of the body and its head.

It followed that the work and duties which the individual bishop could no longer perform in person must be shared with, or deputed to, subordinate officials. New offices came into being in the course especially of the third century, and the growth of this *clerus* or clergy, and its gradual acquisition during the fourth and fifth centuries of the character of a hierarchy nicely ordered in steps and degrees, is a feature of ecclesiastical history of which the importance has not always been adequately realised.

Of such a hierarchy the germs had no doubt existed from the beginning; and indeed presbyters and deacons were, as we have seen, older component parts of the local communities than were the bishops themselves. In the Ignatian theory bishop, presbyters, and deacons are the three universal elements of organisation, "without which nothing can be called a church" (*ad Trall.* 3). And the distinction between the two subordinate orders, in their original scope and intention, was just the distinction between the two sides of clerical office which in the bishop were in some sort combined, the spiritual and the administrative:

CH. VI.

presbyters were the associates of the bishop in his spiritual character, deacons in his administrative functions.

Our earliest documents define the work of presbyters by no language more commonly than by that which expresses the "pastoral" relation of a shepherd to his flock: "the flock in which the Holy Ghost hath set you as overseers to shepherd the Church of God," "the presbyters I exhort . . . shepherd the flock of God among you . . . not as lords of the ground but as examples of the flock, until the Great Shepherd shall appear." But in proportion as the local oragnisation became episcopal, the pastoral idea, and even the name of ποιμήν, concentrated itself upon the bishop. To Ignatius the distinctive function of the presbyters is rather that of a council, gathered round the bishop as the apostles were gathered round Christ — an idea not unconnected perhaps with the position of the presbyters in the Christian assembly; for there is no reason to doubt that primitive tradition underlies the arrangement of the early Christian basilicas, where the bishop's chair stood in the centre of the apse behind the altar, and the *consessus presbyterorum* extended right and left in a semicircle, as represented in the Apocalypse. So too in the *Didascalia Apostolorum* (Syriac and Latin) the one definite function allotted to presbyters is that of "consilium et curia ecclesiae." Besides pastoral duties, however, the Pauline epistles bring presbyters into definite relation also with the work of teaching. If "teachers" were originally one grade of the general ministry, they would naturally have settled down in the communities earlier than the itinerant apostles or prophets: "pastors and teachers" are already closely connected in the epistle to the Ephesians: and the first epistle to Timothy shews us that "speaking and teaching," λόγος καὶ διδασκαλία, was a function to which some at least of the presbyters might aspire. It is probable enough that the second-century bishop shared this, as all other functions of the presbyterate: St Polycarp is described by his flock as an "apostolic nd prophetic teacher": but, as differentiation progressed, teaching was one of the duties less easily retained in the bishop's hands, and our third-century authorities are full of references to the class known in Greek as οἱ πρεσβύτεροι καὶ διδάσκαλοι, in Latin as *presbyteri doctores*.

If presbyters were thus the bishop's counsellors and advisers where counsel was needed, his colleagues in the rites of Christian worship, his assistants and representatives in pastoral and teaching duties, the proto-types of the diaconate are to be found in the Seven of the Acts, who were appointed to disburden the apostles of the work of poor relief and charity and to set them free for their more spiritual duties of "prayer and ministering of the Word." Quite similarly in the διάκονοι or "servants" of the local church, the bishop found ready to hand a personal staff of clerks and secretaries. The Christian Church in one not unimportant aspect was a gigantic friendly society: and the deacons were the relieving officers who, under the direction of the ἐπίσκοπος or "overseer," sought out the local members of the society in their homes, and dispensed to those who were in permanent or temporary need the contributions of their more fortunate brethren. From their district-visiting the deacons would derive an intimate knowledge of the circumstances and characters of individual Christians, and of the way in which each was living up to his profession: by a very natural develop‐ ment it became part of their recognised duties, as we learn from the *Didascalia*, to report to the bishop cases calling for the exercise of the penitential discipline of the Church. Throughout all the early centuries the closeness of their personal relation with the bishop remains: but what had been spread over the whole diaconate tends to be concentrated on an individual, when the office of archdeacon — *oculus episcopi*, according to a favourite metaphor — begins to emerge: the earliest instances of the actual title are *c.* 370–380, in Optatus (of Caecilian of Carthage) and in the *Gesta inter Liberium et Felicem* (of Felix of Rome).

Originally, as it would seem, deacons were not ministers of worship at all: the earliest subordinate office in the liturgy was that of reader. We need not suppose that ὁ ἀναγινώσκων in the New Testament means a distinct official in the Church any more than in the Synagogue: but the same phrase in Justin's *Apology* has more of a formal sound, and by the end of the second century the first of the minor orders had obviously an established place in church usage. While Ignatius names only bishop, presbyters, and deacons, Tertullian, contrasting the stable orders of Catholics with the unsettled arrangements of heretics, speaks of bishop, presbyter, deacon, and reader: "alius hodie episcopus, cras alius; hodie diaconus qui cras lector; hodie presbyter qui cras laicus." And in remote churches or backwardly organised provinces the same four orders were the minimum recognised long after Tertullian, as in the so-called *Apostolic Church Order* (third century, perhaps for Egypt) and in the canons of the Council of Sardica (343, for the Balkan peninsula: the canon is proposed by the Spaniard Hosius of Cordova).

But the process of transformation by which the diaconate became more and more a spiritual office began early, and one of its results was to degrade the readership by ousting it from its proper functions. It was as attendants on the bishop that the deacons, we may well suppose, were deputed from the first to take the Eucharist, over which the bishop had offered the prayers and thanksgivings of the Church, to the absent sick. In Rome, when Justin wrote, soon after 150, they were already dis‐ tributing the consecrated "bread and wine and water" in the Christian assembly. Not very much later the reading of the Gospel began to be assigned to them: Cyprian is the last writer to connect the Gospel still with the reader; by the end of the third century it was a constant function of the deacon, and the reader had sunk pro‐ portionately in rank and dignity.

CH. VI.

But this development of the diaconate is only part of a much larger movement. In the greater churches at least an elaborate differentiation of functions and functionaries was in course of process during the third century. Under the pressure of circumstances, and the accumulation of new duties which the increasing size and importance of the Christian communities thrust upon the bishop, much which he had hitherto done for himself, and which long remained his in theory, came in practice to be done for him by the higher clergy. As they moved up to take his place, they in turn left duties to be provided for: as they drew more and more to the spiritual side of their work, they left the more secular duties to new officials in their place. Evidence for Carthage and Rome in the middle of the third century shews us that, besides the principal orders of bishop, presbyters, and deacons, a large community would now complete its *clerus* by two additional pairs of officers, subdeacon and acolyte, exorcist and reader, making seven altogether. The church of Carthage, we learn from the Cyprianic correspondence, had exorcists and readers, apparently at the bottom of the clergy (*ep.* xxiii. "praesente de clero et exorcista et lectore [the words are no doubt ironical] Lucianus scripsit"); and it had also *hypodiaconi* and *acoliti*, who served as the bearers of letters or gifts from the bishop to his correspondents. Subdeacons and acolytes were now in fact what deacons had earlier been, the personal and secretarial staff of the bishop, while exorcists and readers were the subordinate members of the liturgical ranks. The combination of all these various officers into a single definitely graduated hierarchy was the work of the fourth century: but it is at least adumbrated in the enumeration of the Roman *clerus* addressed by Pope Cornelius, Cyprian's contemporary, to Fabius of Antioch in 251. Besides the bishop, there were at Rome forty-six presbyters, seven deacons, seven subdeacons, forty-two acolytes; of exorcists and readers, together with doorkeepers, there were fifty-two; of widows and afflicted over fifteen hundred: and all this "great multitude" was "necessary in the church."

Promotion from one rank of the ministry to another was of course no new thing. In particular the rise from the diaconate to the presbyterate, from the more secular to the more spiritual office, was always recognised as a legitimate reward for good service. "They that have served well as deacons," wrote St Paul, "purchase for themselves an honourable step"; though when the *Apostolic Church Order* interprets the βαθμὸς καλός as τόπος ποιμενικός, it is a question whether the place of a presbyter or that of a bishop is meant. But it was a serious and far-reaching development when, in the fourth century, the idea grew up that the Christian clergy consisted of a hierarchy of grades, through each of which it was necessary to pass in order to reach the higher offices. The Council of Nicaea had contented itself with the reasonable prohibition (canon 2) of the ordination of neophytes as bishops or presbyters. The Council of Sardica in 343 prescribes for the episcopate a "prolixum tempus" of promotions through the "munus" of reader, the "officium" of deacon, and the "ministerium" of presbyter. But it was in the church of Rome that the conception of the *cursus honorum* — borrowed, we may suppose, consciously or unconsciously from the civil magistracies of the Roman State — took deepest root. Probably the oldest known case of particular clerical offices held in succession by the same individual is the record, in an inscription of Pope Damasus, of either his own or his father's career — there are variant readings "pater" and "puer," but even the son's career must have begun early in the fourth century — "exceptor, lector, levita, sacerdos." Ambrosiaster, a Roman and younger contemporary of Damasus, expresses clearly the conception of grades of order in which the greater includes the less, so that not only are presbyters ordained out of deacons and not *vice versa*, but a presbyter has in himself all the powers of the inferior ranks of the hierarchy: "maior enim ordo intra se et apud se habet et minorem, presbyter enim et diaconi agit officium et exorcistae et lectoris." The earliest of the dated disciplinary decretals that has come down to us, the letter of Pope Siricius to Himerius of Tarragona in 385 (its prescriptions are repeated with less precision in that of Zosimus to Hesychius of Salona in 418), emphasizes the stages and intervals of a normal ecclesiastical career. A child devoted early to the clerical life is made a reader at once, then acolyte and subdeacon up to thirty, deacon for five years, and presbyter for ten, so that forty-five is the *minimum* age for a bishop: even those who take orders in later life must spend two years among the readers or exorcists, and five as acolyte and subdeacon. But the requirements of Siricius and Zosimus are moderate when brought into comparison with the pseudo-papal documents which came crowding into being at the beginning of the sixth century: of the apocryphal councils fathered on Pope Sylvester the one gives a *cursus* of 52 years, the other of 55, before the episcopate.

Two considerations indeed must be borne in mind which qualify the apparent rigour of the fourth and fifth century *cursus*. In the first place we have already traced the beginning of the depreciation of the readership. In days when liturgical formulae were still unwritten, the reader's office was the only one that was mechanical: what it had necessarily implied was a modicum of education, and all who had passed through the office had at least learned to read. Thus it came about, from the fourth century onwards, that the readers were the boys who were receiving training and education in the schools of the Church: according to the canons, for instance, of the Council of Hippo in 393 readers on attaining the age of puberty made choice between marriage and permanent readership on the one hand, celibacy and rise through the various grades of clerical office on the other. And the second thing to be remembered is that all these prescriptions of canons or decretals represented a theoretical standard rather than a practice regularly carried out. Canon Law in the fourth century could still be put aside, by bishop or people, when need arose, without scruple. Minor orders might be omitted. St Hilary of Poitiers wanted to ordain Martin a deacon straight off, and only made him an exorcist instead because he reckoned that Martin's humility would not allow him to refuse so low an office. Augustine and Jerome were ordained presbyters direct. Even the salutary Nicene rules about neophytes were on emergency violated: Ambrose of Milan and Nectarius of Constantinople were both elected as laymen (the former indeed as a catechumen), and were rushed through the preliminary grades without appreciable delay; St Ambrose passed from baptism to the episcopate in the course of a week.

But in spite of any occasional reassertions of the older freedom, it did nevertheless remain true that the *cursus* and all it stood for was gradually establishing itself as a real influence: and it stood for a body continually growing in size, in articulation, in strength, in dead weight, which drove in like a wedge between bishop and people, and fortified itself by encroachments on both sides. Doubtless it would have been natural in any case that bishop and people, no longer enjoying the old affectionateness of personal intercourse, should lose the sense of community and imperceptibly drift apart: but the process was at least hastened and the gap widened by the interposition of the *clerus*. It was no longer the laity, but the clergy alone, who were in direct touch with the bishop. Even the fundamental right of the people to elect their bishop slipped gradually from their hands into the hands of the clergy. Within the clerical class a continual and steady upward pressure was at work. The minor orders take over the business of the diaconate: deacons assert themselves against presbyters: presbyters in turn are no longer a body of counsellors to the bishop acting in common, but, having of necessity begun to take over all pastoral relations with the laity, tend as parish priests to a centrifugal independence. The process of entrenchment within the parochial freehold was still only in its first beginnings: but already in the fourth century — when theologians and exegetes were feeling after a formal and scientific basis for what had been natural, instinctive, traditional—we find presbyters asserting the claim of an ultimate identity of order with the episcopate.

Such are the summary outlines of the picture, which must now be filled in, here and there, with more detail. And the details will serve to reinforce the conclusion that the principal features of the history of church organisation in the fourth and fifth centuries are not unconnected accidents, but are to a large extent just different aspects of a single process, the multiplication and development of the Christian clergy.

1. The people had originally chosen their bishop without serious possibility of interference from the clergy. Voting by orders in the modern sense was hardly known: in so far as any check existed on the

unfettered choice of the laity, it lay in the hands of the neighbouring bishops from whom the bishop-elect would naturally receive consecration. Cyprian, it is clear from his whole correspondence, was made bishop of Carthage by the laity against the decided wishes of his colleagues in the presbyterate. After the death of Anteros of Rome in 236, we learn from the story in Eusebius that "all the brethren were gathered together for the appointment of a successor to the bishopric." And this was still the practice after the middle of the fourth century: the description of the election of St Ambrose in 374 by his biographer mentions the people only, "cum populus ad seditionem surgeret in petendo episcopo . . . quia et Arriani sibi et Catholici sibi episcopum cupiebant superatis alterutris ordinari." Another biography, that of St Martin of Tours by Sulpicius Severus, depicts a similar scene about the same date: Martin was elected, in the face of opposition from some of the assembled bishops, by the persistent vote of the people. The laity too, at least in some churches, still selected even the candidates for the priesthood. Possidius, the biographer of St Augustine, relates how Valerius of Hippo put before the "plebs dei" the need for an additional presbyter, and how the Catholic people, "knowing Saint Augustine's faith and life," seized hold of him, and, "ut in talibus consuetum est," presented him to the bishop for ordination. In Rome however the influence of the clergy was already predominant. The episcopal elections, during the troubled decade that followed the exile of Liberius in 355, are described in the *Gesta inter Liberium et Felicem*: the clergy — "clerus omnis, id est presbyteri et archidiaconus Felix et ipse Damasus diaconus et cuncta ecclesiae officia" — first pledge their loyalty to Liberius and then accept Felix in his place: the opposition, who clung all through to Liberius and after his death elected Ursinus as his successor, are represented as mainly a lay party — "multitudo fidelium," "sancta plebs," "fidelis populus," "dei populus" — yet even in their electoral assembly the clergy receive principal mention, "presbyteri et diacones . . . cum plebe sancta." And though there are some indications that the party of Ursinus had strong support in the local episcopate, it was Damasus, the candidate of the majority of the clergy, who secured recognition by the civil power. At the end of the fourth century a definite place is accorded to the clergy in the theory of episcopal appointments. The eighth book of the *Apostolic Constitutions* distinguishes the three steps of election by the people, approval by the clergy, consecration by the bishops. Siricius of Rome, in his decretal letter to Himerius, puts the clergy before the people, "si eum cleri ac plebis edecumarit electio": the phrase "cleri plebisque" became normal in this connexion, and ultimately meant that it was for the clergy to elect and for the people to approve.

Fundamental as these changes were, no doubt each stage of them seemed natural enough at its time. Indirect election was an expedient unknown as yet: real election by the laity, in view of the dimensions of the Christian population, became more and more difficult, and the pretence of it tumultuous and unsatisfactory. The members of the clergy on the other hand were now considerable enough for a genuine electing body, yet not too unwieldy for control: and the people were gradually ousted from any effective participation. So far as the influence of the laity still continued to make itself felt, it was through the interference of the State. Under either alternative Christian feeling had to content itself with a grave deflection from primitive ideals.

2. The earlier paragraphs of this chapter have already given us reason to anticipate the developments of the diaconate in the fourth century. We have seen how the intimate relations of the deacons with the bishop as his personal staff caused the business of the churches to pass more and more, as numbers multiplied, through their hands; we have seen also how from their attendance on the bishop, in church as well as outside of it, they gradually acquired what they did not originally possess, a status in Christian worship. It is just on these two lines that their aggrandisement still proceeded. In Rome and in some of the Eastern churches (witness the last canon of the Council of Neocaesarea in Pontus, *c.* 315), the deacons were limited, on the supposed model of the Acts, to seven, while the presbyterate admitted of indefinite increase, and the mere disproportion in numbers exalted the individual deacon: "diaconos paucitas honorabiles, presbyteros turba contemptibiles facit," says Jerome bitterly. But if complaint and criticism focused itself on the affairs of the church of Rome, where everything was on a larger scale and on a more prominent stage than elsewhere, the indications all suggest that the same thing was in lesser measure happening in other churches.

The legislation of the earliest councils of the fourth century supplies eloquent testimony to the ambition of deacons in general and Roman deacons in particular. The Spanish canons of Elvira, *c.* 305, shew that a deacon might be in the position of "regens plebem," in charge, no doubt, of a village congregation: he might (exceptionally) baptize, but he might not do what "in many places" the bishops of the Council of Arles, in 314, learnt that he did, namely "offer" the Eucharist. By a special canon of the same Council of Arles, the deacons of the (Roman) City are directed not to take so much upon themselves, but to defer to the presbyters and to act only with their sanction. Both these canons of Arles are combined and repeated in the 18th canon of Nicaea: but the reference to Rome is omitted, and the presumptions of the diaconate — we must suppose that existing conditions in the Eastern churches are now in view — take the form of administering the Eucharist to presbyters, receiving the Eucharist before bishops, and sitting down among the presbyters in church. Later on in the century we find the Roman deacons wearing the vestment called "dalmatic," which elsewhere was reserved to the bishop: and one of them — probably the Mercury who is mentioned in one of Pope Damasus' epigrams — had asserted the absolute equality of deacons and priests. Ambrosiaster, who may be confidently identified with the Roman ex-Jew Isaac, the supporter of the Anti-pope Ursinus, treats in the hundred and first of his *Quaestiones* "de iactantia Roma_norum levitarum": Jerome, in his epistle *ad Evangelum presbyterum*, appropriates the arguments of Ambrosiaster and clothes them with his own incomparable style. The Roman deacons, they tell us, arrogate to themselves the functions of priests in saying grace when asked out to dinner, and in getting responses made to themselves in church instead of to the priests : and this arrogance is made possible because of their influence with the laity and in the administration of ecclesiastical affairs, "adsiduae stationes domesticae et officialitas." But the mind of the Church is clear : "si auctoritas quaeritur, Orbis maior est Urbe" : even at Rome presbyters sit, while deacons stand, and if at Rome deacons do not carry the altar and its furniture or pour water over the hands of the priest — as they do in every other church — that is only because at Rome there is a "multitude of clerks" to undertake these offices in their place. We do not know that these indignant remonstrances of Ambrosiaster and Jerome had any practical results : we do know that in the second half of the fourth and the beginning of the fifth century three deacons, Felix, Ursinus, and Eulalius, made vain attempts upon the papal throne — the successful rivals of the two latter were priests, Damasus and Boniface — while by the middle of the fifth century, as illustrated in the persons of St Leo and his successor Hilarius, the archdeacon almost naturally became pope.

3. As the deacon thus pressed hard on the heels of the presbyter, so the presbyter in turn put himself into competition with the bishop. Ambrosiaster and Jerome not only deny any parity of deacon and presbyter, but assert in opposition a fundamental parity of order between presbyter and bishop. Both were commentators on St Paul. Exegesis was one of the most fertile forms of that astonishing intellectual efflorescence, which, bursting out at the beginning of the fourth century in the schools of Origen and of Lucian, and in the West fifty years later, produced during several generations a literary harvest unequalled throughout the Christian centuries. And the two Latin presbyters found in the Pastoral Epistles just the historical and scriptural basis for the establishment of the claims of the presbyterate, that the instinct of the times called for. The apostle had distinguished clearly enough between deacons and presbyters or bishops : but he had used — so they rightly saw — the terms πρεσβύτερος and ἐπίσκοπος for the same order of the ministry, and it was an easy deduction that presbyter and bishop must be still essentially one. So Ambrosiaster (on 1 *Timothy*) "post episcopum tamen diaconatus ordinationem subiecit; quare, nisi quia episcopi et presbyteri una ordinatio est? uterque enim sacerdos est, sed episcopus primus est; ut omnis episcopus presbyter sit, non tamen

CH. VI.

omnis presbyter episcopus, hic enim episcopus est qui inter presbyteros primus est." And so Jerome (on *Titus*) explains that in the apostolic age presbyters and bishops were the same, until as a safeguard against dissensions one was chosen out of the presbyters to be set over the rest: consequently bishops should know "se magis consuetudine quam dispositionis dominicae veritate presbyteris esse maiores, et in commune debere ecclesiam regere." The exegesis of Ambrosiaster and Jerome was undeniably sound: their historical conclusions were, if the picture given in the earlier pages of this chapter is correct, not so just to the facts as those of another commentator of the time, perhaps the greatest of them all, Theodore of Mopsuestia. No doubt the New Testament bishop was a presbyter: but "those who had authority to ordain, the officers we now call bishops, were not limited to a single church but presided over a whole province and were known by the title of apostles. In this way blessed Paul set Timothy over all Asia, and Titus over Crete, and doubtless others separately over other provinces ... so that those who are now called bishops but were then called apostles bore then the same relation to the province that they do now to the city and villages for which they are appointed": Timothy and Titus "visited cities, just as bishops to-day visit country parishes."

"Uterque enim sacerdos est." In these words lies perhaps the real inwardness of the movement for equating presbyters with bishops and of its partial success: "Priesthood" was taking the place of "Order." In the first centuries, to St Ignatius for instance and to St Cyprian, the essential principle was that all things must be done within the Unity of the Church, and of that unity the bishop was the local centre and the guardian. That alone is a true Eucharist, in the language of Ignatius, which is under the authority of the bishop or his representative. No rite or sacrament administered outside this ordered unity had any reality. Baptism or Laying on of hands schismatically conferred, whether without the Church among the sects or without the bishop's sanction by any intruder in his sphere, were simply as though they had not been. Under the dominance of this conception the position of the bishop was unique and unassailable. But, as time went on, the single conception of Order, intense and overmastering as to those early Christians it had been, was found insufficient: other considerations must be taken into account, "lest one good custom should corrupt the world." Breaches were made in the theory first at one point, then at another. Christian charity rebelled against the thought of wholly rejecting what was intended, however imperfectly, to be Christian Baptism: iteration of such Baptism was felt, and nowhere more clearly than at Rome, to be intolerable. As with Baptism, so, though much more gradually and uncertainly, with Holy Orders. The distinction between validity and regularity was hammered out: "quod fieri non debuit, factum valet" was the expression of the newer point of view: Augustine, in his writings against the

Donatists, laid down the principles of the revised theology, and later ages have done little more than develop and systematise his work.

It is obvious that in this conception less stress will be set on the circumstances of the sacrament, more on the sacrament itself: less on the jurisdiction of the minister to perform it, more on his inherent capacity: less, in other words, on Order, more on Priesthood. We are not to suppose that earlier thought necessarily differed from later on the question, for instance, to what orders of the ministry was committed the conduct of the characteristic action of Christian worship, or as to its sacrificial nature, or as to the priestly function of the ministrants. But earlier language did certainly differ from later as to the direction in which sacerdotal terminology was most freely employed. In the general idea of primitive times the whole congregation took part in the priestly office: when a particular usage of ἱερεύς or "sacerdos" first came in, and for several generations afterwards, it meant the bishop and the bishop only. The prhaseology in this respect of St Cyprian is repeated by a whole chain of writers down to St Ambrose. No doubt the hierarchical language of the Old Testament was applied to the ministry of the Church long before the fourth century: but it was either transferred in quite general terms from the one hierarchy to the other as a whole, or it was concentrated upon the bishop. Thus in the *Didascalia Apostolorum* it is the bishops who inherit the Levites' right to material support, the bishops who are addressed as "priests to your people and levites who serve in the house of God, the holy catholic Church," the bishop again who is "the levite and the high priest" (contrast the language of the *Didache*). But the detailed comparison of the three orders of the Jewish ministry and the Christian was so obvious that it can only have been the traditional use of "sacerdos" for the bishop that retarded the parallelism. We find "levita" for deacon in the egiprams of Damasus and in the *de Officiis* of St Ambrose: but the complete triad of "levita, sacerdos, summus sacerdos" for deacon, presbyter, and bishop meets us first in the pages of the ex-Jew Ambrosiaster. And while Ambrose employs the Old Testament associations of the levite to exalt the dignity and calling of the Christian deacon, Ambrosiaster contrasts the "hewers of wood and drawers of water" with the priests, and paraphrases the titles "sacerdos" and "summus sacerdos" as "presbyter" and "primus presbyter." "Summus sacerdos" is freely used of bishops by Jerome, though the title was forbidden even to metropolitans by an African canon. But in any case the new extension of "sacerdos" to the Christian presbyter was too closely in harmony with existing tendencies not to take root at once. It is common in both St Jerome and St Augustine: Pope Innocent speaks of presbyters as "secundi sacerdotes": and from this time onward bishop and priest tend more and more to be ranked together as joint possessors of a common "sacerdotium."

This new emphasis on the "sacerdotium" of Christian presbyters is perhaps to be connected with the new position which in the fourth and following centuries they were beginning to occupy as parish priests. It was the necessity of the regular administration of the Eucharist which dictated the commencements of the parochial system. While the custom of daily Eucharists was neither universal nor perhaps earlier than the third century—it arose partly out of Christian devotion, partly out of the allegorical interpretation of the "daily bread"—the weekly Eucharist was both primitive and universal, and the needs in this respect of the Christian people could ultimately be met only by a wide extension of the independent action of the presbyterate. Though in the larger cities it can never have been possible, even at the first, for the Christian people to meet together at a single Eucharist, the bishop, as Ignatius tells us, kept under his own control all arrangements for separate services, and the presbyters, like the head-quarters staff of a general, were sent hither and thither as occasion demanded. It may have been as definite localities came to be permanently set apart for Christian worship, that the custom grew up of attaching particular presbyters to particular churches.

Probably it was during the long peace 211–249 that ground was first acquired for churches within the walls at Rome: cemeteries were constructed by the ecclesiastical authorities as soon as the beginning of the third century, but the earliest mention of church property in the City is when the Emperor Alexander Severus (222–235), as we learn from Lampridius, decided a question of disputed ownership of land between the "christiani" and the "popinarii" in favour of the former, because of the religious use which they were going to make of it. Certainly by the time of Diocletian Christian churches throughout the Empire were of sufficient number and prominence to become, with the sacred vessels and the sacred books, a special mark for the edict of persecution in 303. And just as the restoration of peace produced an outburst of calligraphic skill devoted to the Bible, of which the Vatican and Sinaitic codices are the enduring monuments, so, too, the ruined buildings were replaced by others more numerous and more magnificent. Constantine erected churches over the graves of the Apostles on the Vatican hill and the Ostian Way, while inside the walls the Lateran basilica of the Saviour and the Sessorian basilica of the Holy Cross testified further to the policy of the emperor and the piety of his mother. When Optatus wrote, fifty years later, there were over forty Roman basilicas, all of them open to the African Catholics and closed to the Donatists: "inter quadraginta et quod excurrit basilicas locum ubi colligerent non habebant." But this number perhaps includes the cemetery churches, for the parish churches or "tituli" of the City appear to have been exactly twenty-five under Pope Hilary (461–468), in its life of whom the *Liber Pontificalis* enumerates a service of altar vessels for use within the City, one golden bowl for the "station" and twenty-five silver bowls (with twenty-five "amae" or cruets, and fifty chalices) for the parish churches,

"scyphus stationarius," "scyphi per titulos." The "station thus opposed
to the "parishes" is the reunion, on certain days of the year, of the
whole body of the Roman clergy and faithful under the pope at some
particular church: it was a corrective to the growth of parochial separatism, like the custom of sending round every Sunday, from the pope's
mass to the mass of every church within the walls, the "fermentum"
or portion of the consecrated bread. So Innocent writes, in 416, in
his decretal letter to Decentius of Gubbio: "presbyteri quia die ipso
propter plebem sibi creditam nobiscum convenire non possunt, idcirco
fermentum a nobis confectum per acolythos accipiunt, ut se a nostra
communione maxima illa die non iudicent separatos; quod per parochias"
[=in other dioceses] "fieri debere non puto, quia non longe portanda
sunt sacramenta, nec nos per coemeteria diversa constitutis presbyteris
destinamus."

It was part of the same careful guard against the over-development
of parochial independence, that, though there were parish clergy at Rome
in the fourth and fifth centuries, there was as yet no parish priest.
When Ambrosiaster wrote, it was the custom to allot two priests to
each church (*in* 1 *Tim.* iii. 12, 13) "septem diaconos esse oportet, et
aliquantos presbyteros ut bini sint per ecclesias, et unus in civitate
episcopus." At a council under Pope Symmachus in 499, sixty-seven
priests of the City subscribe, each with his "title," "Gordianus presbyter
tituli Pammachii" and so on: but the "tituli" are not more than thirty,
some of them having as many as four or five priests attached to them.
Indeed, thirty is perhaps too high a figure, for some "tituli" may appear
under more than one name — an original name from the donor or the
reigning pope, and a supplementary name in honour of a saint. Of the
fourth century popes Damasus had named a church after St Lawrence,
and Siricius after St Clement: the basilica built under Pope Liberius
became St Mary Major under Xystus III (432–440), and the two
basilicas founded under Pope Julius (337–352) became in time the
Holy Apostles and St Mary across Tiber.

But if the parochial system with its single rector was thus no part of
Roman organisation as late as the end of the fifth century, it was in full
vigour at Alexandria two centuries earlier. Epiphanius tells us that,
though all the churches belonging to the catholic body in Alexandria
(he gives the names of eight) were under one archbishop, presbyters were
appointed to each of them for the ecclesiastical necessities of the inhabitants
in the several districts. The history of Arius takes the parochial system
fifty or sixty years behind Epiphanius: it was as parish priest of the
church and quarter named Baucalis that he was enabled to organise his
revolt against the theology dominant at head-quarters under the bishop
Alexander. The failure of the presbyter and victory of the bishop
may have reacted unfavourably upon the position of the Alexandrine
presbyters generally; the historian Socrates expressly tells us that after

the Arian trouble presbyters were not allowed to preach there. At any rate it is just down to the time of Alexander and his successor, Athanasius, that those writers who testify to peculiar privileges of the Alexandrine presbyterate in the appointment of the patriarch suppose them to have survived. The most precise evidence comes from a tenth century writer, Eutychius, who relates that by ordinance of St Mark twelve presbyters were to assist the patriarch, and at his death to elect and lay hands upon one of themselves as his successor, Athanasius being the first to be appointed by the bishops. Severus of Antioch, in the sixth century, mentions that "in former days" the bishop was "appointed" by presbyters at Alexandria. Jerome (in the same letter that was cited above, but independent for the moment of Ambrosiaster) deduces the essential equality of priest and bishop from the consideration that the Alexandrine bishop "down to Heraclas and Dionysius" (232–265) was chosen by the presbyters from among themselves without any special form of consecration. Earlier than any of these is the story told in connexion with the hermit Poemen in the *Apophthegms* of the Egyptian monks. Poemen was visited one day by heretics who began to criticise the archbishop of Alexandria as having only presbyterian ordination, ὡς ὅτι παρὰ πρεσβυτέρων ἔχοι τὴν χειροτονίαν. Unfortunately the hermit declined to argue with them, gave them their dinner, and promptly dismissed them.

It is clear that an Alexandrine bishop of the fourth century slandered by heretics can be no one but Athanasius; and therefore this, the earliest evidence for presbyterian ordination at Alexandria, is just that which is most demonstrably false. For Athanasius was neither elected nor consecrated by presbyters: not more than ten or twelve years after the event, the bishops of Egypt affirmed categorically that the electors were "the whole multitude and the whole people" and that the consecrators were "the greater number of ourselves." Yet this very emphasis on the part of the supporters of Athanasius reveals one line of the Arian campaign against him; and the conjecture may be therefore hazarded that it was by Arian controversialists that the allegations of Alexandrine "presbyterianism" were first circulated, and that their real origin lay in the desire to turn the edge of any argument that might be based upon the solidarity of the episcopate. If the Catholics called upon the bishops of the East not to champion a rebellious presbyter, their opponents would, on this view, "go one better" in their enthusiasm for episcopacy, and answer that Athanasius was no more than a presbyter himself. It is difficult for us, who have to reconstruct the history of the fourth century out of Catholic material, to form any just conception either of the mass of the lost Arian literature — exegetical and historical, as well as doctrinal and polemical — or of its almost exclusive vogue for the time being throughout the East, and of the influence which, in a thousand indirect ways, it must have exerted upon Catholic writers of the next generations. Jerome, writing amid Syrian surroundings, would eagerly accept the there current presentation of the Alexandrine tradition, though his knowledge of the later facts caused him to throw back the dates from the known to the unknown, from Athanasius and Alexander to Dionysius and Heraclas. Of course there is no smoke without fire; and presumably the Alexandrine presbyterate, in the generations immediately preceding the Council of Nicaea, must have possessed some unusual powers in the appointment of their patriarch. But it seems as likely that these were the powers which elsewhere belonged to the people as that they were the powers which elsewhere belonged to the bishops.

The explanation here offered would no doubt have to be disallowed, if it were true, as has sometimes been alleged, that Arianism all the world over stood for the rights of presbyters, while the cause of Athanasius was bound up with the aggrandisement of the episcopate. But the connexion was purely adventitious at Alexandria, or at any rate local, and the conditions did not reproduce themselves elsewhere. There is no reason at all to suppose any general alliance between presbyters and Arianism, or between the episcopate and orthodoxy: on the contrary, all the evidence goes to shew that in Syria and Asia Minor, and perhaps elsewhere, the bishops were less Catholic than their flocks. At Antioch, for instance, where Arian bishops were dominant during half a century, orthodox zeal was kept alive by the exertions of Flavian and Diodorus, originally as laymen, afterwards as priests. In so far as the doctrinal issue affected the development of organisation at all, it must on the whole, both because of the general confusion of discipline and also because of the ill repute which the tergiversations of so many bishops earned for their order, have enhanced the tendency towards the emancipation of presbyters from episcopal control.

Whatever special conditions may have affected the course of development at Rome or Alexandria, it may be taken as generally true that, by the end of the fourth century the Christian presbyter's right to celebrate the Eucharist was coming to be regarded as inherent in his *sacerdotium* rather than as devolved upon him by the bishop. With this right went also the right to be served by deacons as *ministri* or ὑπηρέται, and ultimately the right to preach. While the 18th canon of Nicaea still regards the deacons as "ministers"of the bishop only, later in the fourth century the eighth book of the *Apostolic Constitutions* speaks of τῆς πρὸς ἀμφοτέρους διακονίας, "their service to both bishops and priests," and Ambrosiaster is aghast at the audacity of trying to put presbyters and their servants on a par, "presbyteris ministros ipsorum pares facere." The right to preach had never been formally associated with any order of the Christian ministry: Ambrosiaster was certainly interpreting the documents on his own account, rather than recording tradition, when he asserts (*in Eph.* iv. 11, 12) "omnibus inter initia concessum est et evangelizare et baptizare et scripturas in ecclesia explanare," but it is clear that in early times even a layman, like Origen, might at the bishop's request expound Scripture to the congregation.   Nevertheless, though the right might be thus deputed, the sermon (ὁμιλία, *tractatus*) was part of the Eucharistic service, and Justin Martyr no doubt describes the normal practice when he makes the president of the assembly in person expound and apply the lections just read from Prophets or Gospels.   In the fourth century it was treated as axiomatic that the right to preach, as part of the liturgy, could not even be deputed save to those to whom could also be deputed the right to offer the Eucharist itself.   It is true that in many parts of the West the archdeacon did compose and pronounce a solemn thanksgiving once a year, at the lighting of the Paschal candle on Easter Even: but even this extra-liturgical sermon *de laudibus cerei* was unknown at Rome, and Jerome, or whoever was the author of the letter addressed in 384 to a deacon of Piacenza (printed in the appendix to Vallarsi's edition), finds in it a gross violation of Church order, "tacente episcopo, et presbyteris quodam-modo in plebeium cultum redactis, levita loquitur docetque quod paene non didicit, et festivissimo praedicans tempore toto dehinc anno iusti-tium vocis eius indicitur."   Even the rights of presbyters in this respect were inchoate and still strictly circumscribed.   In the Eastern churches it was customary for some of them to preach in the presence of the bishop and for the bishop to preach after them: and Valerius of Hippo was consciously introducing an Eastern use into Africa — he was himself a Greek, and therefore unable to speak fluently to his Latin flock — when he commissioned his presbyter Augustine "against the custom of the African churches" to expound the Gospel and preach frequently in his presence.   To Jerome, familiar with the Eastern custom, it was "pessimae consuetudinis" that in some (doubtless Western) churches presbyters kept silence in the presence of their bishop: their right to preach at-tached directly to the pastoral office which they held, according to him, in common with the bishop.

But because presbyters might preach in the bishop's church, where he could note and correct at once any defects in their teaching, it does not necessarily follow that they might preach in the parish churches, and there does not seem to be any clear indication in the fourth and fifth centuries that they did in fact do so.   For Rome indeed this is hardly surprising: we have seen how jealously parochial independence was there limited, and even at the bishop's mass, if we may believe the historian Sozomen, there were no sermons either by priest or bishop. In fact St Leo's sermons — he became pope just about the time that Sozo-men published his *Church History* — are the first of which we hear after Justin's time in Rome.   But in Gaul too, and as late as the beginning of the sixth century, only the city priests, the priests, that is, who served in the bishop's church, had the right to preach: the second canon of the second Council of Vaison in 529 extends the right, apparently for the first time, to country parishes, "placuit ut non solum in civitatibus sed etiam in omnibus parrociis verbum faciendi daremus presbyteris potestatem"; if the priest is at any time unable to preach through illness, the deacon is to read to the people "homilies of the holy fathers."

It is perhaps surprising at first sight to find that in the fourth and fifth centuries presbyters are establishing a new independence in face of the bishop, rather than bishops exerting a new and stricter authority over presbyters. The conclusion has been reached by direct evidence; but it is also the conclusion clearly indicated by the analogy of the whole upward movement which we have seen at work in respect both to the minor orders and to the diaconate.

But if this movement exerted so powerful an influence on the one hand upon minor orders and diaconate, and on the other hand upon the priesthood, we could not expect that bishops should be exempt from it. How and where it led in their case it will be part of our business, in the second half of this chapter, to trace. It was outside their own borders that the bishops of the great churches were tempted to look for a wider field of activity and a more commanding position. From the very first the bishop of each community had represented it in its relation to other Christian communities, had been, so to say, its minister for foreign affairs. The *Visions* of Hermas were to be communicated to "the cities outside" by Clement, "for that function belongs to him," ἐκείνῳ γὰρ ἐπιτέτραπται. The complex developments of this function, from the second century to the fifth, must now engage our attention.

(B) So far we have been dealing only with the internal development of the individual Christian community. But there is an external as well as an internal development to trace; the separate communities were always in intimate touch with one another, and the common feeling of the mass of them formed an authority which, from the beginning, the law of Christian brotherhood made supreme. "If one member suffer, all the members suffer," "we have no such custom, neither the churches of God:" the principles are laid down in our earliest Christian documents, and the organisation of the Catholic Church was an attempt to work them out in practice. No doubt the result only imperfectly embodied the idea, and in the process of translation into concrete form the means came sometimes to appear of more value than the end.

The history of the second century shews how naturally the formal processes of federation grew out of what was at first the spontaneous response to the calls of membership of the great Society, the natural effort to express the reality of Christian union and fellowship. The Roman community, under the leadership of St Clement, writes a letter of expostulation when the traditions of stability and order are threatened by the dissensions between the Corinthian community and its presbyters.

CH. VI.

St Ignatius addresses separate epistles to the churches of several cities in Asia Minor, on or near his road to Rome, exhorting them to hold fast to the traditional teaching and world-wide organisation of the Christian Society. The church of Smyrna announces to the church of Philomelium the martyrdom of its bishop Poylcarp: the churches of Lyons and Vienne send to their brethren in Asia and Phrygia an account of the great persecution of 177, and the confessors from the same cities intervene with Pope Eleutherus in favour of a sympathetic treatment of the Montanist movement. Correspondence was reinforced by personal intercourse: Polycarp journeyed to Rome to discuss the Easter difficulty with Pope Anicetus; Hegesippus, Melito and Abercius travelled widely among different churches; Clement of Alexandria had sat at the feet of half-a-dozen teachers. Never was the impulse to unity, the desire to test the doctrine of one church or of one teacher by its agreement with the doctrine of the rest, stronger than in the days when formal methods of arriving at the general sense of the scattered communities had not as yet been hammered out. The Christian statesmen of the age of the councils were only attempting to provide a more scientific means of attaining an end which was vividly before the minds of their predecessors in the sub-apostolic generations.

The crucial step in the direction of organised action was taken when the bishops of neighbouring communities began to meet together for mutual counsel. Such σύνοδοι or *concilia* were no doubt, in the first instance, called for specific purposes and at irregular times. Tertullian alludes to decisions of church councils unfavourable to the canonicity of the *Shepherd* of Hermas, and makes special mention on another occasion of councils in Greece: "illa certis in locis concilia ex universis ecclesiis, per quae et altiora quaeque in commune tractantur, et ipsa repraesentatio totius nominis christiani magna veneratione celebratur." The earliest notice of separate councils held simultaneously to discuss a pressing problem of the day is also the earliest indication of the sort of area from which any one of such councils would naturally be drawn; for when, about 196, tension became acute in regard to the attitude of the bishops of proconsular Asia, who refused to come into line with the Paschal observances of other churches, councils were held, as we learn from Eusebius, of the bishops in Palestine and in Pontus and in Gaul and in Osrhoene. During the course of the third century these local or provincial councils became more and more a regular and essential feature of church life and government. But there was as yet very little that was stereotyped about the system. It was Cyprian beyond all others who succeeded, during his brief ten years of episcopate, 248–258, in forging a very practical weapon for the needs of the time out of the conciliar movement: and of Cyprian's councils some represented (proconsular) Africa alone, some Africa and Numidia, some Africa, Numidia, and Mauretania combined; the meetings were more or less annual, but the extent of the area from which the bishops were summoned depended apparently upon the gravity of the business to be dealt with. Again, if the civil province was in ordinary cases the natural model to follow, there was no necessary dependence upon its boundary lines, where these were artificial or arbitrary. For reasons of State the senatorial province of proconsular Africa and the imperial province of Numidia were so arranged that the more civilised districts and the seaboard belonged to the one, the more backward interior to the other: but the Numidia of ecclesiastical organisation was the ethnic Numidia, the country of the Numidians, not the Numidia of political geography. Perhaps it was just for this reason, because ethnic and ecclesiastical Numidia was shared between two civil provinces, that in assemblies of the Numidian bishops the president was not, as elsewhere, the bishop of the capital or μητρόπολις of the province, but the bishop senior by consecration.

Not the least important result of the new direction given by Constantine to the relations of Church and State was the authorisation and encouragement of episcopal assemblies on a larger scale than had in earlier days been possible. Where difficulties, disciplinary or doctrinal, proved beyond the power of local effort to resolve, councils were planned of a more than provincial type. The Council of Arles in 314 was a "general council," *concilium plenarium*, of the Western Church, summoned by Constantine as lord of the Western Empire, to terminate the quarrel in Africa between the partisans of Caecilian and the partisans of Donatus. Judgment went in favour of Caecilian, whose party, because they alone now remained in communion with the churches outside Africa, were henceforward the Catholics, while the others became a sect known after the name of their leader as the Donatists. The dispute between Alexander and Arius at Alexandria was in its beginning as purely local as that between Caecilian and Donatus, but the issue soon came to involve the comparison of the fundamental theologies of the two great rival schools of Alexandria and Antioch. From a council such as Arles it was but a step to the conception of a general council of the whole Church, where bishops from all over the world should meet for comparison of the forms which the Christian tradition had taken in their respective communities, for open ventilation of points of controversy, and for the removal of misunderstanding by· personal intercourse. Constantine, now master of an undivided empire, organised the first oecumenical council at Nicaea in 325. The great experiment was not an immediate success: the Nicene council rather opened than closed the history of Arianism on the larger stage, and it was not till after the lapse of half a century that wisdom was seen to be justified of its works, though the very keenness of the struggle made the long delayed and hardly won triumph more complete in the end. No council ever fastened its hold on Christian imagination in quite the same way as the Council of Nicaea.

CH. VI.

Not that there was ever any quarrel between the supporters and the opponents of the *Homoousion* as to the rightness of the procedure which had been called into being. The weapons with which the council and the creed were fought were rival councils and rival creeds : the verdict of the court was to be set aside by renewed trials and multiplied appeals in the hope of modifying somehow the original judgment. Of all these supplementary councils none was strictly general, though on three occasions — at Sardica and Philippopolis in 343, at Ariminum and Seleucia in 359, at Aquileia and Constantinople in 381 — councils representing separately the Greek and the Latin episcopate were held more or less at the same time in East and West. Others, like that of Sirmium in 351, were held, wherever the emperor happened to be in residence, by the bishops attached at the moment to the court, the σύνοδος ἐνδημοῦσα as it was later called at Constantinople : others again were local and provincial. The atmosphere of Rome was never perhaps quite congenial to councils : yet even the Roman Church was swept into the movement, and the pronouncements of Pope Damasus (366–384) came before the world under the guise of conciliar decisions.

The experience of the fifty years that followed the Council of Tyre in 335 taught the lesson that it was possible to have too much even of a good thing. Pagan historian and Christian saint from different starting-points arrived at the same conclusion. Ammianus Marcellinus, criticising the character and career of the Emperor Constantius, noted caustically that he threw the coaching system quite out of gear because so many of the relays were employed in conveying bishops to and from their councils, "per synodos quas appellant," at the expense of the State. And Gregory of Nazianzus, in the year 382, refused to obey the summons to a new council, because, he says, he never saw "any good end to a council nor any remedy of evils, but rather an addition of more evil as its result. There are always contentions and strivings for dominion beyond what words can describe."

Perhaps it was partly by a natural reaction against councils, in those districts especially where they had followed most quickly upon one another, that the tendency to aggrandise the important sees at the expense of other bishops — and at the expense therefore of the conciliar movement, since in a council all bishops had an equal vote — seems about this time to take a sudden leap forward. Valens the Arian and Theodosius the Catholic alike made communion with some leading bishop the test of orthodoxy for other bishops. A first edict of Theodosius on his way from the West to take up the Eastern Empire in 380 expresses Western conceptions by naming in this connexion only Damasus of Rome and Peter of Alexandria : a later edict from Constantinople in 381 places Nectarius of Constantinople before Timothy of Alexandria, and adds half-a-dozen bishops in Asia Minor and a couple in the Danube lands as centres of communion for their respective districts.

Here then we must pause for a moment to take into account the second main element in the history of the federation of the Christian churches. Every federation has to face this primary problem — the reconciliation of the equal rights of all participating bodies with the proportional rights of each according to their greater or less importance. The difficulty which modern constitutions have tried to solve by the expedient of a dual organisation, the one part of it giving to all constituent units an equal representation, the other part of it a proportionate representation according to population (or whatever other criterion of value may be selected), was a difficulty which lay also before the early Church. The unit of the Christian federation was the community, whose growth and development is described in the first half of this chapter; and that description has shewn us that the necessary and only conceivable representative of the individual community was its bishop. But some communities were small and insignificant and unknown in history, others were larger in numbers, or more potent in influence, or more venerable in traditions: were the bishops of these diverse communities all to enjoy equal weight?

Such a question was no doubt not consciously put until the scientific and reflective period of Christian thought began, nor before the complex process of federation was approaching completeness: that is to say, not before the end of the fourth century. But in so far as it was put, it could receive but one answer. In the theory of Christian writers from St Irenaeus and St Cyprian onwards, all bishops were equal, for they were all appointed to the same order and invested with the same powers, whether the sphere in which they exercised them were great or small; and this theory was given its sharpest expression in Jerome's assertion (in the same 146th letter) that the bishop of Gubbio had the same dignity as the bishop of Rome, seeing that both were equally successors of the Apostles, "ubicumque fuerit episcopus, sive Romae sive Eugubii, sive Constantinopoli sive Rhegii sive Alexandriae sive Tanis, eiusdem meriti eiusdem est sacerdotii...omnes apostolorum successores sunt." But in fact, and side by side with the fullest recognition of this theoretical equality, the bishops of the greater or more important churches were recognised, as the rules of the federation were gradually crystallised, to hold positions of privilege, so that the ministry of the Church came to consist not only of a hierarchy within each local community, at the head of which stood the bishop, but of a further hierarchy among the bishops themselves, at the head of which, in some sense, stood the bishop of Rome. The first steps towards such a hierarchy were on the one hand the traditional influence and privileges which had grown up unnoticed round the greater sees, and on the other hand the position acquired by metropolitans in the working out of the provincial system.

The canons of the same councils which first provide for regular meetings of the bishops of each ἐπαρχία or province, reveal also the

CH. VI.

rapid aggrandisement of the μητροπολίτης, or bishop of the metropolis, who presided over them.   If at Nicaea the "commonwealth of bishops," τὸ κοινὸν τῶν ἐπισκόπων, is the authority according to one canon, by another the "ratification of the proceedings" belongs to the metropolitan. The canons of Antioch, sixteen years later, lay it down that the completeness of a synod consists in the presence of the metropolitan, and, while he is not to act without the rest, they in turn must recognise that the care of the province is committed to him and must be content to take no step of any sort outside their own diocese apart from him. Traditional sanction is already claimed for these prerogatives of the metropolitan : they are "according to the ancient and still governing canon of the fathers."

Things were not so far advanced in this direction, it is true, in the West.   At any point in the first five centuries the Latin Church lagged far behind the pitch of development attained by its Greek contemporaries. Christianity had had a century's start in the East, and at the conversion of Constantine it is probable that if the proportion of Christians in the whole population was a half, or nearly a half, among Greek-speaking peoples, it was not more than a fifth, in many parts not more than a tenth, in the West.   The Latin canons of Sardica in 343 shew how little was as yet known of metropolitans.   Although many of the enactments deal with questions of jurisdiction and judicature, the bishop of the metropolis is mentioned only once, and then in general terms, "coepiscopum nostrum qui in maxima civitate, id est metropoli, consistit."   The name "metropolitan" is as foreign to these canons as to the earliest versions of the Nicene canons, where we meet with just the same paraphrases, "qui in metropoli sit constitutus," "qui in ampliori civitate provinciae videtur esse constitutus, id est in metropoli."

With this backwardness of development among the Latins went also a much smaller degree of subservience to the State : and it resulted from these two causes combined that their church organisation in the fourth and fifth centuries reflected the civil polity much less closely than was the case in the East.   The "province" of the Nicene or Antiochene canons is the civil province, its metropolitan is the bishop of the civil metropolis, and it is assumed that every civil province formed also a separate ecclesiastical unit.   It followed logically that the division of a civil province involved division of the ecclesiastical province as well. When the Arian emperor Valens, about 372, divided Cappadocia into *Prima* and *Secunda*, it was with the particular object of annoying the metropolitan of Caesarea, St Basil, and of diminishing the extent of his jurisdiction by raising Anthimus of Tyana to metropolitan rank; and though Basil resisted, Anthimus succeeded in the end in establishing his claim. Before the end of the fourth century not only every province but every group of provinces formed an ecclesiastical as well as a civil unit : the provinces of the Roman Empire had by subdivision become so numerous that Diocletian had grouped them into some dozen διοικήσεις or *dioeceses* with an exarch at the head of each, and the Council of Constantinople in 381 forbids the bishops of one *dioecese* or exarchate to interfere with the affairs of "the churches beyond their borders." So wholly modelled upon civil lines was the ecclesiastical organisation throughout the East, that in the middle of the fifth century the canons of Chalcedon assume an absolute correspondence of the one with the other. Every place which by imperial edict might be raised to the rank of a city, gained *ipso facto* the right to a bishop (canon 17). Every division for ecclesiastical purposes of a province which remained for civil purposes undivided was null and void—even if backed up by an imperial edict — the "real" metropolis being alone entitled to a metropolitan (canon 12). Civil and public lines must be followed in the arrangement of ecclesiastical boundaries, τοῖς πολιτικοῖς καὶ δημοσίοις τύποις καὶ τῶν ἐκκλησιαστικῶν παροικιῶν ἡ τάξις ἀκολουθείτω.

This conception summed itself up in the claim put forward on behalf of the see of Constantinople at the councils of 381 and 451. The bishops of these councils, deferring, perhaps not unwillingly, to the pressure of the local authorities, civil and ecclesiastical, gave to the bishop of Constantinople the next place after the bishop of Rome, on the ground that Constantinople was "New Rome," and that "the fathers had assigned precedence to the throne of Old Rome because it was the Imperial City."

Nothing was better calculated than such a claim to bring out the latent divergences of East and West. Both in Church and State the rift between the Latin and the Hellenic element had begun to widen perceptibly during the course of the fourth century. Diocletian's drastic reorganisation of the Imperial government gave the first official recognition to the bipartite nature of the Roman realm, and after the death of Julian in 363 the two halves of the Empire, though they lived under the same laws, obeyed with rare and brief exceptions separate masters. Parallel tendencies in the ecclesiastical world were working to the surface about the same time. The Latinisation of the Western Churches was complete before Constantine: no longer clothed in the medium of a common language, the ideas and interests of Latin-speaking and Greek-speaking communities grew unconsciously apart. The rival ambitions of Rome and Constantinople expressed this antinomy in its acutest form.

The right of the civil government to be in its own sphere the accredited representative of Divine power on earth, the duty of the Christian Society to preserve at all costs its separateness and independence as the salt of mankind, the city set upon a hill — these were fundamental principles which could both appeal to the sanction of the Christian Scriptures. To hold the balance evenly between them has been, through the long centuries since Christianity began to play a leading part upon the political stage, the worthy task of philosophers and statesmen. That one scale should outweigh the other was perhaps inevitable in the first attempts, and it was at least instructive for future generations that the experiment of an over-strained allegiance to each of the two theories should have been given full trial in one part or another of Christendom.

To Byzantine churchmen the vision of the Christian State and the Christian Emperor proved so dazzling that they transferred to them something of the religious awe with which their ancestors had venerated the genius of Rome and Augustus. The memory of Constantine was honoured as of an ἰσαπόστολος, a "thirteenth apostle." The resentment of the native Monophysite churches of Syria and Egypt against such of their fellow-countrymen as remained in communion with Constantinople concentrated itself in the scornful epithet of Melkite or "King's man."

The Latins were more moved by the sentiment of the Roman name, and less by its incarnation in the Emperor. As Romans and Roman citizens, they felt the majesty of the Roman *Respublica* to attach to place even more than to person. If Rome was no longer the abode of emperors, it was in their eyes not Rome but emperors who lost thereby. The event which stirred men in the West to the depths of their being was not the conversion of Constantine but the fall of Rome. When Alaric led his Goths to the storm of the City in 410, there seemed to be need for a new theory of life and for revision of first principles. The great occasion was greatly met. St Augustine wrote his twenty-two books *de Civitate Dei* to answer the obvious objection that Rome, inviolate under her ancestral gods, perished only when she turned to Christ. True it was that the City of the World had fallen: but it had fallen in the Divine providence, when the times were ripe for a new and higher order of things to take its place. The reign of the City of God had been ushered in.

It was a natural corollary of the principles of Western churchmen that the Divine Society could not possibly be bound to imitate the organisation of the earthly society which it was to supplant. Pope Innocent, in direct opposition to the practice of the East, wrote to Alexander of Antioch in 415 that the civil division of a province ought not to carry ecclesiastical division with it; the world might change, not so the Church, and therefore it was not fitting "ad mobilitatem necessitatum mundanarum Dei ecclesiam commutari." Pope Leo refused his assent to the so-called 28th "canon" of Chalcedon, not merely as an innovation, but because its deduction of the ecclesiastical primacy of Rome from her civil position was quite inconsistent with the doctrine cherished by the popes upon the subject since at least the days of Damasus.

Here then we have a bifurcation of Eastern and Western ideas, leading to a clear-cut issue, in which both sides appealed to the truth of facts. Which of them represented the genuine Christian tradition? Certainly the case of provincial organisation favoured the Eastern view, for it was taken over bodily from the State. But then it was relatively modern; a far higher antiquity attached to the privileged position of the greater sees, and it was upon the origin and history of their privileges that the answer really turned.

Of course there never had been a time when some churches had not stood out above the rest, and the bishops of those churches above other bishops. The Council of Nicaea, side by side with the canons that prescribed the normal organisation by provinces and metropolitans, recognised at the same time certain exceptional prerogatives as guaranteed by "ancient custom," τὰ ἀρχαῖα ἔθη. In Egypt especially, Alexandria eclipsed its neighbour cities to a degree unparalleled elsewhere in the East; and while it might not have been easy to sanction the authority, ἐξουσία, of the Alexandrine bishop over the whole of "Egypt Libya and Pentapolis," if it had been quite unique in its extent, the Nicene fathers could shelter themselves under the plea that "the same thing is customary at Rome." A gloss in an early Latin version of the canons interprets the Roman parallel to consist in the "care of the suburbicarian churches," that is to say, the churches of the ten provinces of the Vicariate of Rome — central and southern Italy with the islands of Sicily and Sardinia. Over these wider districts the Roman and Alexandrine popes respectively exercised direct jurisdiction, to the exclusion in either case of the ordinary powers of metropolitans. The further prescription of the Nicene canon that "in the case of Antioch and in the other provinces" the churches were to keep their privileges, τὰ πρεσβεῖα, was understood by Pope Innocent to cover similar direct jurisdiction of Alexander of Antioch over Cyprus; and a version of the canons "transcribed at Rome from the copies" of the same pope defines the sphere of Antioch as "the whole of Coele-Syria."

What was it then that had given these three churches of Rome, Alexandria, and Antioch the special position to the antiquity of which the Nicene council witnesses? Roman theologians from Damasus onwards would have answered unhesitatingly that the motive was deference to the Prince of the Apostles, who had founded the churches of Rome and Antioch himself, and the church of Alexandria through his disciple Mark. But this answer is open to two fatal retorts: it does not explain why Alexandria, the see of the disciple, should rank above Antioch, a see of the master, and it does not explain why our earliest authorities, both Roman and non-Roman, so persistently couple the name of St Paul with the name of St Peter as joint patron of the Roman Church. Cyprian is the first writer to talk of the "chair of Peter" only.

Therefore we are driven back upon the secular prominence of the three cities as the obvious explanation of their ecclesiastical dignity. Yet if the appeal to history of the two councils which elevated

Constantinople to the second place was thus not without a large measure of justification, their bald expression of Byzantine theory does not really, any better than the contemporary Roman view, cover the whole of the facts.   If rank and influence in the ecclesiastical sphere depended, more than on anything else, on rank and influence in the civil sphere, it did not depend on it entirely.   The personality and memory of great churchmen went for something.   Carthage was no doubt the civil capital of the *dioecese* of Africa, and Milan of the *dioecese* of Italy: but it would be rash to assert that the inheritance which St Cyprian left to Carthage and St Ambrose to Milan was quite worthless or ephemeral.   And if this was true of the great bishops of the third and fourth centuries, it was still more true of the apostles whom the whole Church united in venerating.   Legends of apostolic foundation were often baseless enough, but their very frequency testified to the value set upon the thing claimed.   Throughout the course of the long struggle with Gnosticism, the teaching of the apostles was the unvarying standard of Christian appeal: and evidence of that teaching was found not only in the written Creed and Scriptures but in the unwritten tradition of the churches and episcopal successions founded by apostles.   "Percurre ecclesias apostolicas" cries Tertullian confidently to his adversary: "habemus adnumerare eos qui ab apostolis instituti sunt episcopi in ecclesiis et successiones eorum usque ad nos" is Irenaeus' rendering of the same argument.   And both the Gallican and the African writer go on to select among apostolic churches the church of Rome — "ista quam felix ecclesia," "maximae et antiquissimae et omnibus cognitae ecclesiae traditionem et fidem" — as for themselves the obvious witness of this teaching.   From the second century onwards a catena of testimony makes and acknowledges the claim of the Roman Church to be, through its connexion with St Peter and St Paul, in a special sense the depository and guardian of an apostolic tradition, a type and model for other churches.

The pontificate of Damasus (366–384) has been more than once mentioned in the preceding pages as the period of the first definite self-expression of the papacy.   The continuous history of Latin Christian literature does not commence till after the middle of the fourth century; the dogmatic and exegetical writings of Hilary in Gaul (*c.* 355) and Marius Victorinus in Rome (*c.* 360) are the first factors in a henceforward unbroken series.   On the beginnings of this new literary development followed quickly the movement, of which we have already noticed symptoms in other directions, for interpreting existing conditions and constructing out of them a coherent and scientific scheme.   These conditions had grown up gradually, naturally, and almost at haphazard: it now seemed time to try to put them on to a firm theological basis, and in the process much that had been fluid, immature, tentative, was crystallised into a hard and fast system.   It fell to the able and masterful Damasus, in the last years of a long life and a troubled pontificate, to attempt what his predecessors had not yet attempted, and to formulate in brief and incisive terms the doctrine of Rome upon Creed and Bible and Pope. A council of 378 or 379, after reciting the Nicene symbol, laid down the sober lines of Catholic theology as against the various forms of one-sided speculation, Eunomian and Macedonian, Photinian and Apollinarian, to which the confusions of the half-century since Nicaea had given birth; and the East could do no better than accept the Tome of Damasus, as seventy years later it accepted the Tome of Leo. Another council in 382 published the first official Canon of Scripture in the West — the influence of Jerome, at that time papal secretary, is traceable in it — and the first official definition of papal claims. Roman primacy ("ceteris ecclesiis praelata," "primatum obtinuit") is grounded, with obvious reference to the vote of the council of 381 in favour of Constantinople, on "no synodal decisions" but directly on the promise of Christ to Peter recorded in the Gospel. Respect for Roman tradition imposes next a mention of "the fellowship of the most blessed Paul"; but the dominant *motif* reappears in the concluding paragraph, and the three sees whose prerogative was recognised at Nicaea are transformed into a Petrine hierarchy with its "prima sedes" at Rome, its "secunda sedes" at Alexandria, and its "tertia sedes" at Antioch.

St Augustine's theory of the *Civitas Dei* was, in germ, that of the medieval papacy, without the name of Rome. In Rome itself it was easy to supply the insertion, and to conceive of a dominion still wielded from the ancient seat of government, as world-wide and almost as authoritative as that of the Empire. The inheritance of the imperial traditions of Rome, left begging by the withdrawal of the secular monarch, fell as it were into the lap of the Christian bishop. In this connexion it is a significant coincidence that the first description which history has preserved to us of the outward habit of life of a Roman pontiff belongs to the same period, probably to the same pope, as the formulation of the claim to spiritual lordship. Ammianus was a pagan, but not a bigoted one. He professes, and we need not doubt that he felt, a genuine respect for simple provincial bishops, whose plain living and modest exterior "commended them to the Deity and His true worshippers." But the atmosphere of the capital, the "ostentatio rerum Urbanarum," was fatal to unworldliness in religion. After relating that in the year 366 one hundred and thirty-seven corpses were counted at the end of the day in the Liberian basilica, on the occasion of the fight between the opposing factions of Damasus and Ursinus, the historian grimly adds that the prize was one which candidates might naturally count it worth any effort to obtain, seeing that an ample revenue, showered on the Roman bishop by the piety of Roman ladies, enabled him to dress like a gentleman, to ride in his own carriage, and to give dinner-parties not less well appointed than the Caesars.

CH. VI.

Some forty or fifty years after Damasus the Roman author of the original form of the so-called Isidorian collection of canons, incorporating in his preface the substance of the Damasine definition on the subject of the three Petrine sees, adds to Rome, Alexandria, and Antioch mention also of the honour paid, for the sake of James the brother of the Lord and of John the apostle and evangelist, to the bishops of Jerusalem and Ephesus. Mere veneration of the "pillars" of the apostolic Church is not enough to account for this modification of the original triad; the reasons must be sought in the circumstances of the day. If Ephesus is said to "have a more honourable place in synod than other metropolitans," it may be merely that Ephesus, the most distinguished church of those over which Constantinople, from the time of St John Chrysostom, asserted jurisdiction, was a convenient stalking-horse for the movement of resistance to Constantinopolitan claims; but it is also possible that the phrase was penned after the oecumenical Council of Ephesus in 431, where Memnon of Ephesus was seated next after the bishops of Alexandria and Jerusalem. If the bishop of Jerusalem is "accounted honourable by all for the reverence due to so hallowed a spot," and nevertheless "the first throne," *sedes prima*, "was never by the ancient definition of the fathers reckoned to Jerusalem, lest it should be thought that the throne of our Lord Jesus Christ was on earth and not in heaven," we cannot help suspecting that at the back of the writer's mind hovers an uneasy consciousness that the apostolic traditions of Rome, which were so readily brought into play against Constantinople, might find an inconvenient rival in Jerusalem. Not that at Jerusalem, apart from a certain emphasis on the position of James the Lord's brother, there was ever any conscious competition with Rome: but it was true that, about the time that this canonical collection was published, the see of Jerusalem was just pushing a campaign of aggrandisement, carried on for over a century, to a triumphant conclusion.

The claims of Jerusalem were comparatively modest at the start, and it did not occur to Damasus for instance that they need be taken into serious consideration. Two initial difficulties hampered their early course. Although Jerusalem was the mother church of Christendom, and the home and centre of the first apostolic preaching, Aelia Capitolina, the Gentile city founded by Hadrian, had no real continuity with the Jewish city on the ruins of which it rose. The church of Jerusalem had been a church of Jewish Christians, the church of Aelia was a church of Gentile Christians, and for a couple of generations too obscure to have any history. A probably spurious list of bishops is all the record that survives of it before the third century. Then came the taste for pilgrimages — in A.D. 333 a pilgrim made the journey all the way from Bordeaux — and the growing cult of the Holy Places: Jerusalem was the scene of the most sacred of Christian memories, and locally at any rate Aelia was Jerusalem. From the time of Constantine onwards the identification was complete. The second difficulty was of a less archaic kind, and took longer to circumvent. Aelia-Jerusalem did not even dominate its own district, but was quite outshone by its near neighbour at Caesarea. Politically Caesarea was capital of the province: ecclesiastically it was the home of the teaching and the library of Origen, and the Origenian tradition was kept alive by Pamphilus the confessor and by Eusebius, bishop of the church at the time of the Nicene council. It was hardly likely that the council would do anything derogatory to the friend of Constantine, the most learned ecclesiastic of the age: and in fact all the satisfaction that the bishop of Jerusalem obtained at Nicaea was the apparent right to rank as the first of the suffragans of the province — like Autun in the province of Lyons, or London in the province of Canterbury. Local patriotism felt the sop thus thrown to it to be quite unsatisfying, and for a hundred years the sordid strife "for the first place," περὶ πρωτείων as Theodoret calls it, went on between the bishop of Jerusalem and the bishop of Caesarea. In the confusion of the doctrinal struggle it was easy enough for an orthodox bishop to refuse allegiance to an Arianising metropolitan: and Caesarea being in close relations with Antioch, it was natural for the bishops of Jerusalem to turn to their neighbours at Alexandria, nor, we may suppose, was Alexandria disinclined to favour encroachment upon the territory of its Antiochene rival. Western churchmen, with their profound belief in the finality of every decision of Nicaea, looked coldly on the movement, and it is one of the counts in Jerome's catalogue of grievances against John of Jerusalem. But at the first Council of Ephesus, with Cyril of Alexandria in the chair and John of Antioch absent, Juvenal of Jerusalem secured the second place, though he still failed to abrogate the metropolitical rights of Caesarea. At the Latrocinium of Ephesus in 449, again under Alexandrine presidency, he managed to sit even above Domnus of Antioch. The business of the Council of Chalcedon was to reverse the proceedings of the Latrocinium, and it might have been anticipated that with the eclipse of Alexandrine influence the fortunes of Jerusalem would also suffer. But a timely tergiversation on the doctrinal issue saved something for Juvenal and his see: the council decreed a partition of patriarchal rights over the "East" between the churches of Antioch and Jerusalem.

Very similar were the proceedings which established the "auto-cephalous" character of the island church of Cyprus. The Cypriots too began by renouncing the communion of the Arian bishops of Antioch: they too espoused the cause of Cyril against John at the Council of Ephesus, and were rewarded accordingly: and just as the Empress Helena's discovery of the Cross served the claims of the church of Jerusalem, so the discovery of the coffin containing the body of Barnabas the Cypriot, with the autograph of St Matthew's Gospel, was held to demonstrate finally the right of the Cypriots to ecclesiastical isolation.

CH. VI.

With this evidence before us, it is hard to deny that the history of the generations which first experienced the "fatal gift" of Constantine supplied only too good ground for St Gregory's complaint of contentions and strivings for dominion among Christian bishops. But though these contentions disturbed the work of councils, councils did not create them and Gregory was hardly fair if he laid on councils the responsibility for them : rather, in this direction lay the remedy and counterpoise, seeing that councils represented the parliamentary and democratic side of church government — stood, that is to say, in idea at least, for free and open discussion as against the untrammelled decrees of authority, and for the equality of churches as against the preponderance of metropolitan or patriarch or pope. No more grandiloquent utterance of these principles could indeed possibly be found than the words with which the Council of Ephesus concludes its examination of the Cypriot claim. "Let none of the most reverend bishops annex a province which has not been from the first under the jurisdiction of himself and his predecessors; and so the canons of the fathers shall not be overstepped, nor pride of worldly power creep in under the guise of priesthood, nor we lose little by little, without knowing it, that freedom which our Lord Jesus Christ, the Liberator of all men, purchased for us with his blood."

And councils really were, at any rate in two main departments of their activity, the organ through which the mind of the federated Christian communities did arrive at some definite and lasting self-expression, namely in the Creed and in the Canon Law. In both directions, it is true, East and West moved only a certain part of the way together : in both too, while the impulse was given by councils, the influence of the great churches added something to the completeness of the work : in the case of the Creed, what became a universal usage in the liturgy was at first only a usage of Antioch and Constantinople; in the case of the Canon Law the collective decisions of councils were supplemented by the individual judgments of popes or doctors before the *corpus* of either Western or Eastern Law was complete. Nevertheless it remains the fact that it was from and out of the conciliar movement that Church Law, as such, came into being at all; that the canons of certain fourth and fifth century councils are the only part of this Law common to both East and West; and that again the only common formulation of Christian doctrine was also the joint work of councils, which for that very reason enjoy the name of oecumenical, Nicaea, Constantinople, and Chalcedon.

1. The origins of the Christian Creed or *Symbolum* are lost in the obscurity which hangs over the sub-apostolic age. We know it first in a completed form as used in the Roman church about the middle of the second century. From Rome it spread through the West, taking the shape ultimately of our Apostles' Creed; and one view of its history would make this Roman Creed the source of all Eastern Creeds as well.

But a summary statement of Christian belief for the use of catechumens must have been wanted from very early times, and it is possible that what St Paul "handed over at the first" to his Corinthian converts (1 Cor. xv. 3) was nothing else than a primitive form of the Creed. Anyhow, from whatever source it was derived, a common nucleus was expanded or modified to meet the needs of different churches and different genera_ tions, so that a family likeness existed between all early Creeds, but identity between none of them.

At the Council of Nicaea the Creed was for the first time given an official and authoritative form, and was at the same time put to a novel use. The baptismal Creed of the church of Palestinian Caesarea, itself a much more technically theological document than any corresponding Creed in the West, was propounded by Eusebius: out of this Creed the Council constructed its own confession of faith, no longer for baptismal and general use, but as the "form of sound words" by acceptance of which the bishops of the churches throughout the world were to exclude the Arian conception of Christianity. The example of the Creed of Nicaea on the orthodox side was followed in the next generation by numerous conciliar formularies expressing one shade or another of opposing belief. When the Nicene cause finally triumphed, the Nicene Creed was received all the world over as the expression of the Catholic Faith; and the Council of Ephesus condemned as derogatory to it the composition of any new formula, however orthodox.

The Council of Ephesus represented the Alexandrine position: at Constantinople, however, a new Creed was already in use, which was like enough to the Nicene Creed to pass as an expanded form of it, and was destined in the end to annex both its name and fame. This Creed of Constantinople had been developed out of some older Creed, probably that of Jerusalem, by the help of the test phrases of the *Nicaenum* and of further phrases aimed at the opposite heresies of the semi-Sabellian Marcellus and the semi-Arian Macedonius. It may be supposed that this Creed had been laid before the fathers of the council of 381: for at the Council of Chalcedon, where of course Constantinopolitan influences were dominant, it was recited as the Creed of the 150 fathers of Constantinople, on practically equal terms with the Creed of the 318 fathers of Nicaea. In another fifty years the two Creeds were beginning to be hopelessly confused, at least in the sphere of Constantinople, and the *Constantinopolitanum* was introduced into the liturgy as the actual Creed of Nicaea. In the course of the sixth century it became not only the liturgical but also the baptismal Creed throughout the East. In the West it never superseded the older baptismal Creeds — except apparently for a time under Byzantine influence in Rome — but as a liturgical Creed it was adopted in Spain on the occasion of the conversion of King Reccared and his Arian Visigoths in 589, and spread thence in the course of time through Gaul and Germany to Rome.

2. Canon Law, even more clearly than the Creed, owed its development to the work of councils.

The conception of a Church Law, *ius ecclesiasticum, ius canonicum,*
was not matured till the fourth century, and then largely as a result of
the new position of the Church in relation to the State, and in conscious
or unconscious imitation of the Civil Law. Down to the close of the
era of persecutions the discipline of the Church was administered under
consensual jurisdiction without any written code other than the Scriptures, in general subordination to the unwritten κανών or *regula*, the
"rule of truth," "the ecclesiastical tradition." Primitive books like the
Didascalia Apostolorum and the *Apostolic Church Order* give us a naive
picture of the unfettered action of the bishop as judge with his presbyters
as assessors. But as time went on the questions to be dealt with grew
more and more complex; it became no longer possible to keep the world
at arm's length, and the relations of Christians with the heathen society
round them required an increasingly delicate adjustment; the simplicity
of the rigorist discipline, by which in the second century all sins of
idolatry, murder, fraud, and unchastity were visited with lifelong
éxclusion from communion, yielded at one point after another to the
demands of Christian charity and to the need of distinctions between case
and case. The problem became pressing when the persecution of Decius
suddenly broke up the long peace, and multitudes of professing
Christians were tempted or driven to a momentary apostasy. The
Novatianist minority seceded rather than hold out to these unwilling
idolaters the hope of any readmission to the sacraments: the Church
was forced to face the situation, and it was obviously undesirable that
individual bishops should adjudicate upon similar circumstances in
wholly different ways. It was here that St Cyprian struck out his
successful line: his first councils were called to deal with the disorganisation which the persecution left behind it, and the bishops at
least of Africa were induced to agree upon a common policy worked out
on a uniform scale of treatment.

There is, however, nothing to shew that at Cyprian's councils any
canons were committed to writing, to serve as a permanent standard
of church discipline. That crucial step was only taken fifty years
later, as the persecution initiated by Diocletian relaxed and the bishops
of various localities could meet to take common counsel for the repair
of moral and material damage. During the decade 305–315 the
bishops of Spain met at Elvira, the bishops of Asia Minor at Ancyra
and at Neocaesarea, the Western bishops generally at Arles; and the
codes of these four councils are the earliest material preserved in later
Canon Law.

The decisions of such councils had however no currency, in the first
instance, outside their own localities, and even the Council of Arles was a
concilium plenarium only of the West; but the feeling was already gaining

strength, and it was quite in accordance with the ecclesiastical policy of Constantine, that uniformity was desirable even in many matters where it was not essential, and an oecumenical council offered unique oppor_ tunities of arriving at a common understanding. So we find the Council of Nicaea issuing, side by side with its doctrinal definition, a series of disciplinary regulations, among which are incorporated, often in a greatly modified form, some canons of the Eastern Council of Ancyra and some canons of the Western Council of Arles.

These Nicene canons are the earliest code that can be called Canon Law of the whole Church, and at least in the West they enjoyed something like the same finality in the realm of discipline that the Nicene Creed enjoyed in the realm of doctrine. "Other canon than the Nicene canons the Roman church receives not," "the Nicene canons alone is the Catholic Church bound to recognise and to follow," writes Innocent of Rome in the cause of St Chrysostom. Leo does not exclude quite so rigorously the possibility of additions to the Church's code: but the Nicene fathers still exercise an authority unhampered by time or place, "mansuras usque in finem mundi leges ecclesiorum ca- nonum condiderunt, et apud nos et in toto orbe terrarum."

The principle was simplicity itself, but it came to be worked out with a naive disregard of facts. On the one hand the genuine Nicene code was not accepted quite entire, and where Western tradition and Nicene rules were inconsistent, it was not always the tradition that went under: the canon against kneeling at Eastertide is, in all early versions that we can connect with Rome, entirely absent; the canon against the validity of Paulianist baptism was misinterpreted to mean that the Paulianists did not employ the baptismal formula. On the other hand many early codes that had no sort of real connexion with the Nicene councils sheltered themselves under its name and shared its authority. The canons of Ancyra, Neocaesarea and Gangra, possibly also those of Antioch, were all included as Nicene in the early Gallican collection. The canons of Sardica, probably because of the occurrence in them of the name of Hosius of Cordova, are in most of the oldest collections joined without break to the canons of Nicaea: and a rather acrimonious controversy was carried on between Rome and Carthage in the years 418 and 419, because Pope Zosimus cited the Sardican canons as Nicene, and the Africans neither found these canons in their own copies nor could learn anything about them in the East. The original form of the collection known as Isidore's was apparently translated from the Greek under Roman auspices at about this time: the canons of Nicaea are those "quas sancta Romanâ recipit ecclesia," the codes of the six Greek councils Ancyra, Neocaesarea, Gangra, Antioch, Laodicea, and Constantinople follow, and then the Sardican canons under the heading "concilium Nicaenum xx episcoporum, quae in graeco non habentur sed in latino inveniuntur ita." A Gallican editor of this version, later in the fifth century, combines the newer material with the older tradition in the shape of a canon proposed by Hosius, giving the sanction of the Nicene or Sardican council to the three codes of Ancyra, Neocaesarea, and Gangra.

We must not suppose that all this juggling with the name Nicene was in the strict sense fraudulent: we need not doubt the good faith of St Ambrose when he quoted a canon against digamous clergy as Nicene, though it is really Neocaesarean, or of St Augustine when he concludes that the followers of Paul of Samosata did not observe the "rule of baptism," because the Nicene canons ordered them to be baptized, or for that matter of popes Zosimus and Boniface because they made the most of the Sardican prescriptions about appeals to Rome, which their manuscripts treated as Nicene. The fact was that the twenty canons of Nicaea were not sufficient to form a system of law: the new wine must burst the old bottles, and by hook or by crook the code of authoritative rules must be enlarged, if it was to be a serviceable guide for the uniform exercise of church discipline. The spurious canon which the Gallican Isidore fathers on Hosius puts just this point; "quoniam multa praetermissa sunt quae ad robur ecclesiasticum pertinent, quae iam priori synodo . . . constituta sunt," let these other acts too receive sanction. In the fourth century the councils had committed their canons to writing. In the fifth century came the impulse to collect and codify the extant material into a *corpus* of Canon Law.

The first steps were taken, as might be expected, in the East. Somewhere about the year 400, and in the sphere of Constantinople-Antioch, the canons of half-a-dozen councils, held in that part of the world during the preceding century, were brought together into a single collection and numbered continuously throughout. The *editio princeps*, so to say, of this Greek code contained the canons of Nicaea (20), Ancyra (25), Neocaesarea (14), Gangra (20), Antioch (25), and Laodicea (59): it was rendered into Latin by the Isidorian collector, and it was used by the officials of the church of Constantinople at the Council of Chalcedon, for in the fourth session canons 4 and 5 of Antioch were read as "canon 83" and "canon 84," and in the eleventh session canons 16 and 17 of Antioch as "canon 95" and "canon 96." The canons of Constantinople were the first appendix to the code: they are translated in the Isidorian collection, and they are cited in the acts of Chalcedon, but in neither case under the continuous numeration. When Dionysius Exiguus, early in the sixth century, made a quasi-official book of Canon Law for the Roman church, he found the canons of Constantinople numbered with the rest, bringing up the total to 165 chapters: his two other Greek authorities, the canons of the Apostles and the canons of Chalcedon, were numbered independently. The earliest Syriac version adds to the original nucleus only those of Constantinople and Chalcedon, with a double system of numeration, the one separate for each council, the other continuous throughout the whole series. And in the digest of Canon Law, published about the middle of the sixth century by John Scholasticus of Antioch (afterwards intruded as patriarch of Constantinople), the "great synods of the fathers after the apostles" are ten in number—*i.e.* not counting the Apostolic Canons the councils proper are brought up to ten by the inclusion of Sardica, Constantinople, Ephesus, and Chalcedon — and "besides these, many canonical rules were laid down by Basil the Great."

Two features in the work of John the Lawyer illustrate the transition from earlier to later Canon Law. In the first place the list of authorities is no longer confined strictly to councils, to whose decrees alone canonical validity as yet attached in the fourth and fifth centuries: a new element is introduced with the Canons of St Basil, and by the time we arrive at the end of the seventh century, when the constituent parts of Eastern Canon Law were finally settled at the Quinisextine council *in Trullo*, the enumeration of Greek councils is followed by the enumeration of individual doctors of the Greek Church, and an equal authority is attributed to the rules or canons of both. In the second place John represents a new movement for the arrangement of the material of Church Law, not on the older historical and chronological method, by which all the canons of each council were kept together, but on a system of subject-matter headings, so that in every chapter all the appropriate rules, however different in date or inconsistent in character, would be set down in juxtaposition. Three of John's contemporaries were doing the same sort of thing for Latin Church Law that he had done for Greek — the deacon Ferrandus of Carthage in his *Breviatio Canonum*, Cresconius, also an African, in his *Concordia Canonum*, and Martin, bishop of Braga in north-western Spain, in his *Capitula*. But the day of the great medieval systematisers was not yet: these tentative efforts after an orderly system seem to have met at most with local success, and the business of canonists was still directed in the main to the enlargement of their codes, rather than to the co-ordination of the diverse elements existing side by side in them.

Early Greek Church Law was simple and homogeneous enough, for it consisted of nothing but Greek councils: even the first beginnings of the *corpus* of Latin Church Law were more complex, because not one element but three went to its composition. We have seen that its nucleus consisted in the universal acceptance of the canons of Nicaea, and in the grafting of the canons of other early councils on to the Nicene stock. Thus, whereas Greek canon law admitted no purely Latin element (and in that way had no sort of claim to universality), Latin canon law not only admitted but centred round Greek material. Of course, as soon as the idea of a *corpus* of ecclesiastical law took shape in the West, a Latin element was bound to add itself to the Greek; and this Latin element took two forms. The natural supplement to Greek councils were Latin

CH. VI.

councils : and every local collector would add to his Greek code the councils of his own part of the world, Gallic, Spanish, African, as the case might be. But just about the same time with the commencement of the continuous series of councils whose canons were taken up into our extant Latin codes, commences a parallel series of papal decretals : the African councils begin with the Council of Carthage in 390 and the Council of Hippo in 393, the decretals with the letter of Pope Siricius to Himerius of Tarragona in 385. Such decretal letters were issued to churches in most parts of the European West, Illyria included, but not to north Italy, which looked to Milan, and not to Africa, which depended on Carthage. As their immediate destination was local, not one of them is found in the early Western codes so universally as the Greek councils; on the other hand their circulation was larger than that of any local Western council, and some or others of them are found in almost every collection. It would even appear that a group of some eight decretals of Siricius and Innocent, Zosimus and Celestine, had been put together and published as a sort of authoritative handbook before the papacy of Leo (441–461). Outside Rome, there were thus three elements normally present in a Western code, the Greek, the local, and the papal. In a Roman collection, the decretals were themselves the local element: thus Dionysius Exiguus' edition consists of two parts, the first containing the Greek councils (and by exception the Carthaginian council of 419), the second containing papal letters from Siricius down to Gelasius and Anastasius II. But even the code of Dionysius, though superior to all others in accuracy and convenience, was made only for Roman use, and for more than two centuries had only a limited vogue elsewhere. Each district in the West had its separate Church Law as much as its separate liturgy or its separate political organisation; and it was not till the union of Gaul and Italy under one head in the person of Charles the Great, that the collection of Dionysius, as sent to Charles by Pope Hadrian in 774, was given official position throughout the Franklin dominions.

CHAPTER VII

EXPANSION OF THE TEUTONS

THE race which played the leading part in history after the break-up of the Roman Empire was the race known as the Teutons. Their early history is shrouded in obscurity, an obscurity which only begins to be lightened about the end of the second century of our era. Such information as we have we owe to Greeks and Romans; and what they give us is almost exclusively contemporary history, and the few fragmentary statements referring to earlier conditions, invaluable as they are to us, do not go far behind their own time. Archaeology alone enables us to penetrate further back. Without its aid it would be vain to think of attempting to answer the question of the origin and original distribution of the Germanic race.

The earliest home of the Teutons was in the countries surrounding the western extremity of the Baltic Sea, comprising what is now the south of Sweden, Jutland with Schleswig-Holstein, the German Baltic coast to about the Oder, and the islands with which the sea is studded as far as Gothland. This, not Asia, is the region which, with a certain extension south, as far, say, as the great mountain chain of central Germany, may be described as the cradle of the Indo-Germanic race. According to all appearance, this was the centre from which it impelled its successive waves of population towards the west, south, and south-east, to take possession, in the end, of all Europe and even of a part of Asia. A portion of the Indo-Germanic race, however, remained behind in the north, to emerge after the lapse of two thousand years into the light of history as a new people of wonderful homogeneity and remarkable uniformity of physical type, the people which we know as the Teutons. The expansion of the Indo-Germanic race and its division into various nations and groups of nations had in the main been completed during the Neolithic Period, so that in the Bronze Age — roughly, for the northern races, B.C. 1500–500 — the territories which we have indicated above belonged exclusively to the Teutons who formed a distinct race with its own special characteristics and language.

The distinctive feature of the civilisation of these prehistoric Teutons is the working of bronze. It is well known that in the North —

a region where the Bronze Age was of long duration — a remarkable degree of skill was attained in this art. The Northern Teutonic Bronze Age forms therefore in every respect a striking phenomenon in the general history of human progress. On the other hand, the advance in culture which followed the introduction of the use of iron was not at first shared by the Northern peoples. It was only about B.C. 500, that is to say quite five hundred years later than in Greece and Italy, in the South of France and the upper part of the Danube basin, that the use of iron was introduced among the Teutons. The period of civilisation usually known as the Hallstatt period, of which the latter portion (from about B.C. 600 onwards) was not less brilliant than the Later Bronze Age, remained practically unknown to the Teutons.

The nearest neighbours of the Teutons in this earliest period were, to the south the Kelts, to the east the Baltic peoples (Letts, Lithuanians, Prussians) and the Slavs, in the extreme north the Finns. How far the Teutonic territories extended northward, it is difficult to say. The southern extremity of Scandinavia, that is to say the present Sweden up to about the lakes, certainly always belonged to them. This is put beyond doubt by archaeological discoveries. The Teutons therefore have as good a claim to be considered the original inhabitants of Scandinavia as their northern neighbours the great Finnish people. It is certain that even in the earliest times they were expanding in a northerly direction, and that they settled in the Swedish lake district, as far north as the Dal Elf, and the southern part of Norway, long before we have any historical information about these countries. Whether they found them unoccupied, or whether they drove the Finns steadily backward, cannot be certainly decided, although the latter is the more probable. The *Sitones* whom Tacitus mentions along with the *Suiones* as the nations dwelling furthest to the north were certainly Finns.

On the east, the Teutonic territory, which as we saw did not originally extend beyond the Oder, touched on that of the Baltic peoples who were later known collectively, by a name which is doubtless of Teutonic derivation, as Aists (*Aestii* in Tacitus, *Germ.* 45). To the south and east of these lay the numerous Slavonic tribes (called *Venedi* or *Veneti* by ancient writers). The land between the Oder and the Vistula was therefore in the earliest times inhabited, in the north by peoples of the Letto-Lithuanian linguistic group, and southward by Slavs. On this side also the Teutons in quite early times forced their way beyond the boundaries of their original territory. In the sixth century B.C., as can be determined with considerable certainty from archaeo-logical discoveries, the settlement of these territories by the Teutons was to a large extent accomplished, the Baltic peoples being forced to retire eastward, beyond the Vistula, and the Slavs towards the south-east. It is likely that the conquerors came from the north, from Scandinavia; that they sought a new home on the south coast of the Baltic and towards the east and south-east. To this points also the fact (otherwise hard to explain) that the tribes which in historic times are settled in these districts, Goths, Gepidae, Rugii, Lemovii, Burgundii, Charini, Varini and Vandals, form a separate group, substantially distinguished in customs and speech from the Western Teutons, but shewing numerous points of affinity, especially in language and legal usage, to the Northern Teutons. When, further, a series of Eastern Teutonic names of peoples appear again in Scandinavia, those for instance of the Goths: *Gauthigoth* (Ταῦτοι, Gautar, Gothland); Greutungi: *Greotingi*; Rugians: *Rugi* (Rygir, Rogaland); Burgundiones: *Borgundarholmr*; and when we find in Jordanes the legend of the Gothic migration asserting that this people came from Scandinavia (*Scandza insula*) as the *officina gentium aut certe velut vagina nationum* the evidence in favour of a gradual settlement of eastern Germany by immigrants from the north seems irresistible. .

By the year B.C. 400, at latest, the Teutons must have reached the northern base of the Sudetes.[1] It was only a step further to the settlement of the upper Vistula; and if the Bastarnae, the first Germanic tribe which comes into the light of history, had their seat here about B.C. 300, the settlement of the whole basin of the upper Vistula, right up to the Carpathians, must have been carried out by the Teutons in the course of the fourth century B.C.

It was with Kelts that the Teutons came in contact towards the sources of the Oder in the mountains which form the boundary of Bohemia. Now there is no race to which the Teutons owe so much as to the Kelts. The whole development of their civilisation was most strongly influenced by the latter — so much so that in the centuries next before the Christian era the whole Teutonic race shared a common civilisation with the Kelts, to whom they stood in a relation of intellectual dependence; in every aspect of public and private life Keltic influence was reflected. How came it then that a people whose civilisation shews such marked characteristics as that of the Teutons of the Later Bronze Age could lose these with such surprising rapidity — perhaps in the course of a single century?

The earliest habitat of the Teutons extended, as we have seen, on the south as far as the Elbe. This river also marks the northern boundary of the Kelts. All Germany west of the Elbe from the North Sea to the

---

[1] This is shewn by the name borrowed from the Keltic for the great central German range, the Hercynian Forest of the Greeks and Romans, called in Old High German Fergunna from the Teutonic *Fergunjo (*Fergunia) from the Early Teutonic= Early Keltic *Perkunia (borrowed, therefore, before the loss of the *p*-sound, which took place in Keltic at latest in the fifth century B.C., and before the Teutonic sound-shifting), and also by the name for the Kelts in general *Walchen* or Walhâs or Walhôs from the Keltic *Wolkoi (Lat. Volcae), borrowings which can only be explained by contact with the Kelts who lived on the southern skirts of the range.

Alps was in the possession of the Kelts, at the time when the Teutons occupied the western shores of the Baltic basin. The vigorous power of expansion which this race displayed in the last thousand years of the prehistoric age has left its traces throughout Europe, and even in Asia; and that is what gives it such importance in the history of the world. The whole of Western Europe — France with Belgium and Holland, the British Isles and the greater part of the Pyrenaean peninsula, in the south the region of the Alps and the plains of the Po — has been at one time or another subject to their rule. Eastward, migratory swarms of Kelts pushed their way down the Danube to the Black Sea and even into Asia Minor.

The starting-point of this movement was probably in what is now north-western Germany and the Netherlands, and this region is therefore to be regarded as the original home of the Keltic race. Place-names and river-names, the study of which is a most valuable means of elucidating prehistoric conditions, enable us to prove the existence in many districts of this original Keltic population.[1] They are scattered over the whole of western Germany and as far as Brabant and Flanders, but occur with especial frequency between the Rhine and the Weser. In the north the Wörpe-Bach (north-east of Bremen) marks the limits of their distribution, in the east the course of the Leine, down to Rosoppe; in the south they extend as far as the Main where the Aschaff (anciently Ascapha) at Aschaffenburg forms the last outpost of their territory. They are not found on the strip of coast along the North Sea, occupied later by the Chauci and Frisians, nor on the western side of the Elbe. From this we may safely conclude that these districts were abandoned by their original Keltic population earlier, indeed considerably earlier, than those to the west of the Weser, and also that the expansion of the Teutons westwards proceeded along two distinct lines, though doubtless almost contemporaneously — one westward along the North Sea and one in a more southerly direction up the Elbe along both its banks.

With this view the results of prehistoric archaeology are in complete agreement. We have determined the area of distribution of the Northern Bronze Age — which we saw to be specifically Teutonic — as consisting, in the earlier period (up to c. B.C. 1000), of Scandinavia and the Danish islands, and also Schleswig-Holstein, Mecklenburg and West-

---

[1] Among Keltic river-names are the Rhine (Keltic Rēnos from an older *Reinas, *Rainas), the Main (Old-High-Germ. Moin, in which the Keltic diphthong is preserved), the Embscher (Embiscara from an older Ambiscara) and the Lippe, also perhaps the Lahn, Sieg, Ruhr, Leine and even the Weser.. The mountain-names Taunus, Finne and Semana (the old name for the Thuringian Forest) also betray a Keltic origin. With these must be classed numerous names of places and rivers which have, sometimes even now, the archaic termination -apa or in High German -afa, -affa (-epa, -efa, -ipa, -ifa, -upa, -ufa), which is absolutely inexplicable from the Teutonic but has its parallels in Keltic and points clearly to a Keltic origin.

Pomerania, and therefore bounded on the south-west by the Elbe. But in the Later Bronze Age (*c*. B.C. 1000–600) this territory is enlarged in all directions. On the south and west especially, to judge from the evidence of excavations, it extends from the point at which the Wartha flows into the Oder, in a south-westerly direction through the Spreewald and Fläming districts to the Elbe; then further west to the Harz, and from there northwards along the Oker and Aller to about the estuary of the Weser, and finally along the coast-line as far as Holland. In Thuringia the Keltic peoples maintained their hold somewhat longer. The northern part of it — above the Unstrut — may have received a Teutonic population in the course of the fifth century B.C.; the southern in the course of the fourth. On the other hand, the whole region westward from the Weser and the Thuringian Forest as far as the Rhine was still in the possession of the Kelts about the year B.C. 300, and was only conquered by the Teutons in the course of the following century.[1] It may be taken as the assured result of all the linguistic and archaeological data, that only about the year B.C. 200 the whole of north-western Germany was held by the Teutons, who had now reached the frontier-lines formed by the Rhine and the Main.

About the close of the fifth century B.C., a new civilisation appears in the Keltic domain, a civilisation which, from the fine taste and technical perfection of its productions, deserves in more than one respect to rank with that of the classical nations. This is the so-called La Tène Civilisation, which takes its name from a place on the north side of the Lake of Neuchâtel where especially numerous and varied remains of it have come to light. Where its centre is to be located we do not know — somewhere, we may conjecture, in the South of France or in Switzerland. Starting from this point it spread through all the parts of Europe, which were not under the sway of the Greek and Roman civilisation. Following the course of the Rhone, of the Rhine, and of the Danube, it rapidly conquered all the countries in which Gallic tongues were spoken and maintained its supremacy until the Graeco-Roman civilisation deposed it from its primacy.

It was with this highly developed civilisation — so far superior, especially in its highly advanced knowledge of the working of iron, to the Northern, which still only made use of bronze — that the Teutons came in contact in their advance towards the south-west. It is quite intelligible that the Teutons in the course of their two hundred years of struggle with the Kelts for the possession of north-western Germany, should have eagerly adopted the higher civilisation of the Kelts.

[1] The Keltic local names in -*apa* — which lie mainly in the country between the Weser and the Rhine — were unaffected by the Teutonic sound-shifting, therefore must have been already adopted into the vocabulary of the advancing Teutons. Then, too, prehistoric remains in this region down to the "Middle La Tène Period" (*c*. B.C. 300), and in its southern parts even later, are so distinctively Keltic that there can be no doubt it was still in Keltic occupation.

CH. VII.

Vague reminiscences of the former supremacy of the Keltic race survived into historic times. *Ac fuit antea tempus cum Germanos Galli virtute superarent, ultro bella inferrent, propter hominum multitudinem agrique inopiam trans Rhenum colonias mitterent*, writes Caesar — a piece of information which he must have derived from Gaulish sources. Here belongs also the Gallic tradition reported by Timagenes [1] according to which a part of the nation was said *ab insulis extimis confluxisse et tractibus Transrhenanis crebritate bellorum et adluvione fervidi maris sedibus suis expulsos*. Caesar himself mentions a Keltic tribe, the Menapii, on the right bank of the lower Rhine.

It is impossible to avoid the conclusion that the Keltic Teuriscans of northern Hungary were originally settled in south-central Germany between the Erzgebirge and the Harz, but later (about B.C. 400) were forced out of this district by the pressure of the advancing Germans, and retired in two sections towards the south and south-east.

About the year B.C. 200 the Teuton occupation of north-west Germany was, as we have seen, completed, having reached the Rhine on the west and the Main on the south. But the great forward movement towards the south-west was not to be stayed by these rivers. Vast waves of population kept pressing downward from the north, and giving fresh impetus to the movement. The whole Germanic world must at that time have been in constant ferment and unrest. Nations were born and perished. Everywhere there was pressure and counter-pressure. Any people that had not the strength to maintain itself against its neighbours, or to strike out a new path for itself, was swept away. The tension thus set up first found relief on the Rhenish frontier. About the middle of the second century B.C. Teutonic hordes swept across the river and occupied the whole country westward of the lower Rhine as far as the Ardennes and the Eifel. These hordes were the ancestors of the later tribes and clans which meet us here in the first dawn of history, the *Eburones, Condrusi, Caeroesi, Paemani, Segni, Nervii, Grudii*, and also of the *Texuandri, Sunuci, Baetusii, Caraces*, who appear later, as well as of the *Tungri*, who after the annihilation of the *Eburones* by Caesar succeeded to their territory and position of influence. The *Treveri*, on the other hand, who had their seat further to the south beyond the Eifel, were doubtless Kelts.[2]

The Teutonic invasion of Gaul must have taken place mainly in the second half of the second century B.C., but it was still in progress in Caesar's time. It may suffice briefly to recall in this connexion the successful campaign of Ariovistus; the incursion immediately before

---

[1] Ammianus, xv. 9. 4.

[2] That the other tribes which we have just named were of Teutonic origin there can be no doubt, and the attempt of Müllenhoff to prove that these tribes were Keltic (*Deutsche Altertumskunde*, II². pp. 194 ff.) must be pronounced to have completely failed, as is shewn by R. Much (*Deutsche Stammsitze*, pp. 162 ff.).

Caesar entered upon his province, of 24,000 Harudi into the country of
the Sequani; the invasion of the Suebi under Nasua and Cimberius in
the year 58; and of the Usipetes and Tencteri at the beginning of the
year B.C. 55.   That there were even later immigrations of Teutonic hosts
into north-eastern Gaul may be conjectured from the absence of any
mention by Caesar of several of the tribes which were settled here in the
time by the Empire, and this conjecture is raised almost to a certainty
by the known instance of the Tungri.

It was only later, in the time of the migrations of the Cimbri, and
doubtless in connexion therewith, that the frontier formed by the Main
was crossed.   It was — to the best of our information — a portion of the
Suebi, previously settled on the northern bank of this river, who were the
first to push across it, and after driving out the Helveti, established
themselves firmly to the south of the river, and were here known under
the name of Marcqmanni (Men of the Marches) — the name first meets
us in Caesar, in the enumeration of the peoples led by Ariovistus.
Their country, the *Marca*, extended south to the Danube.   That the
Tulingi (mentioned by Caesar as *finetini* of the Helveti) were of Germanic
origin is put beyond doubt by their name, which is good German and
forms a pendant to that of the Thuringi.   But it will doubtless be
near the truth to see in them not the whole nation of the Marcomanni,
but only a tribe or *local division* of it, and doubtless its advance-guard
towards the south.   In any case it is evident from Caesar's account that
numbering as they did a round 36,000 (*B.G.* I. 29. 2), of whom about
8000 were warriors, they formed a united whole with a definite territory
and were not merely a migratory body of Marcomanni gathered together
ad hoc.

A remnant of the old Marcomanni of South Germany, who in the
year B.C. 9 migrated to Bohemia, is doubtless to be found in the *Suebi
Nicretes* whom we meet with in the time of the Empire on the lower
Neckar.   Further to the north, on the southern bank of the Main, near
Mittenberg, we find the name of the *Toutoni* in an inscription which
came to light in the year 1878.[1]   Hereupon certain scholars[2] have
arrived at the conviction that this locality was the original home of the
Teutones whom we hear of in association with the *Cimbri*, and so that
they were not of Germanic but of Keltic origin, being of Helvetic race
and identified with the Helvetic local clan of the Τωυγεν of Strabo.
This hypothesis must be absolutely rejected.   There must have been
some connexion between those *Toutoni* and the *Teutoni* of history.   But
to conclude without more ado that the *Teutoni* were Helveti, South-
German Kelts, is to do direct violence to the whole body of ancient

---

[1] *C.I.L.* XIII. 6610, dating perhaps from about the beginning of the second
century A.D.: *inter* | *Toutones* | *C*... | *A*... | *H*... | *F*....

[2] G. Kessima, *Westdeutsche Zeitschrift*, IX. (1890), p. 213; R. Much, *Deutsche
Stammsitze*, p. 5.

CH. VII.

tradition, which consistently represents the *Teutoni* as a people whose original home was in the North. The simplest solution of the difficulty is that the Mittenberg *Toutoni* were a fragment which split off from the Teutonic peoples during their migration southward, and settled in this district, just as in north-eastern Gaul a portion of the Cimbri and Teutones maintained itself as the tribe of the Aduatuci.

The whole process of the expulsion of the Kelts from South Germany must have been accomplished between B.C. 100 and 70, for Caesar knows of no Gauls on the right bank of the upper Rhine, and the Helveti had been living for a considerable time to the south of the head-waters of the river which, as Caesar tells us, divides Helvetic from German territory.

The first collision between the Teutons and the Graeco-Roman world took place far to the east of Gaul. It resulted from a great migration of the eastern Teutonic tribes in the neighbourhood of the Vistula, which had carried some of them as far as the shore of the Black Sea. The chief of these tribes was that of the Bastarnae. Settled, it would seem, before their exodus near the head-waters of the Vistula they appear, as early as the beginning of the second century B.C., near the estuary of the Danube. The whole region north of the Pruth, from the Black Sea to the northern slope of the Carpathians, was in their possession and remained so during all the time that they are known to history. Another Germanic tribe, doubtless dependent upon them, meets us in the same district, namely the Sciri from the lower Vistula. The well-known and much discussed "psephisma" of the town of Olbia in honour of Protogenes mentions them as allied with the Galatai, and there has been much debate as to what nation is to be understood by these Γαλάται, and they have sometimes been conjectured to be Illyrian Kelts (Scordisci), sometimes Thracian, sometimes the — also Keltic — Britolages, or the Teutonic Bastarnae, or even the Goths. The majority of scholars has however decided that these "Galatians" are the Bastarnae,[1] whose presence in the neighbourhood of Olbia in the year B.C. 182 is attested by Polybius. There is, indeed, much in favour of this hypothesis and nothing against it. The inscription then, which is proved by the character of the writing to be one of the oldest found in this locality, would have been written about the time of the arrival of the Bastarnae at the estuary of the Danube, that is to say, about B.C. 200 –180, and would therefore be the earliest documentary evidence for the entrance of the Germanic tribes on the field of general history.

As early as the year B.C. 182 we find the Bastarnae in negotiations with Philip of Macedon. Philip's plan was to get rid of the Dardanians, and after settling his allies on the territory thus vacated to use it as a base for an expedition against Italy. After long negotiations, the Bastarnae in 179 abandoned their lately-won territory, crossed the

[1] So Zeuss and Staehelin.

Danube and advanced into Thrace.   At this point King Philip died, and after an unsuccessful battle with the Thracians the Bastarnae began a re_ treat to the settlement which they had abandoned; but a detachment of some 30,000 men under Clondicus pressed on into Dardania.   With the aid of the Thracians and Scordiscans and with the connivance of Philip's successor, Perseus, he pressed the Dardanians hard for a time, but at last in the winter of 175 he also decided to retire.   In Rome the intrigues of the Macedonian kings had been watched with growing mistrust and displeasure, which found expression in the despatch of a commission to investigate the situation in Macedonia and especially on the Dardanian border.   This, therefore, is the first occasion on which the Roman State had to concern itself with Teutonic affairs.   At that time, it is true, the racial difference between Kelts and Teutons was not yet recognised and the Bastarnae were therefore supposed to be Gauls.   Before very long (168), we find the Bastarnae again in relations with the King of Macedon. Twenty thousand men, again under the command of Clondicus, were to join him in his struggle with the Romans in Paeonia.   But Perseus was blinded by avarice, and failed to keep his promises.   Clondicus therefore, who had already reached the country of the Maedi, promptly turned to the right-about and marched home through Thrace.   From this point they disappear from history for a time, only to reappear in the Mithradatic wars as allies of that King, and they consequently appear also in the list of the nations over whom Pompey triumphed in the year 61.

In the East, on the frontiers of Europe and Asia, the Germanic race attracted little notice; but in the West, about the close of the second century B.C., it shook the edifice of the Roman State to its foundations and spread the terror of its name over the whole of Western Europe.   It was the Cimbri, along with their allies the Teutones and Ambrones, who for half a score of years kept the world in suspense.   All three peoples were doubtless of Germanic stock.[1]   We may take it as established that the original home of the Cimbri was on the Jutish peninsula, that of the Teutones somewhere between the Ems and the Weser, and that of the Ambrones in the same neighbourhood, also on the North Sea coast.   The cause of their migration was the constant encroachment of the sea upon their coasts, the occasion being an inundation which devastated their territory, great stretches of it being engulfed by the sea.   This is the account given by ancient writers and

[1] The arguments which have been alleged in favour of the Keltic origin of the Teutones, and sometimes also of the Ambrones, and even of the Cimbri, are quite untenable.   Not only the unanimous witness of antiquity which always represents the Cimbri and Teutones as having their original home on the German North Sea coast, but also the very names of these peoples which, despite all the contrary assertions of the Keltic enthusiasts, can be naturally and convincingly explained from the Teutonic, put their Germanic character beyond doubt.

CH. VII.

we have no reason to doubt its truth.   The exodus of all three peoples
took place about the same time, and obviously in such a way that from
the first they went forward in close touch with one another. First they
turned southwards, probably following the line of the Elbe, crossed the
Erzgebirge and pressed on into Bohemia, the land of the Boii.   Driven
back by the latter, they seem to have made their way along the valley of
the March, southwards to the Danube, and then through Pannonia into
the country of the Scordisci.   Here, too, they encountered (in the year
114) such vigorous opposition that they preferred to turn westwards.
That brought them into contact with the Taurisci who had just (B.C.
115) formed a close alliance with the Romans.   In the Carnic Alps was
stationed a Roman army under the command of the Consul Cn. Papirius
Carbo, which immediately advanced into Noricum.   Carbo's attempt by
means of a treacherous attack to annihilate the Teutons ended in a
severe defeat.   The way into Italy now lay open to the victors.   But
so great was the awe in which they still held the Roman name, that they
promptly turned away towards the north.   Their route led them to the
territory of the Helveti, which then extended from the Lake of Constance
as far as the Main.   The Helveti do not seem to have offered any
resistance; indeed a considerable section of the Helveti — the Tigurini
and Toygeni — attached themselves to the Teutonic migrants.   The
Germanic hosts then crossed the Rhine and pressed on southwards,
plundering as they went.

In B.C. 109 they halted in the valley of the Rhone, on the frontier
of the Roman province of Transalpine Gaul, for the protection of
which a strong army under the Consul M. Junius Silanus had taken
the field.   The Romans attacked, but were defeated for the second
time.   Again the Germans shrank from invading Roman territory
and preferred to plunder and ravage the Gallic districts, which they
completely laid waste.   Finally, in the year 105 they appeared once
more on the frontier of "the Province," this time resolved to attack the
Romans.   Of the three armies which opposed them that of the Legate
M. Aurelius Scaurus was first defeated in the territory of the Allobroges.
On 6 October followed the bloody battle of Arausio in which the other
two armies, under the Consul Cn. Mallius Maximus and the Proconsul Q.
Servilius Caepio, in all some 60,000 troops, were completely annihilated.
But instead of marching into Italy, the barbarians once again let the
favourable moment slip, and thus lost the fruits of their victory.   They
divided their forces.   The Cimbri marched away westwards, first into
the country of the Volcae, then on over the Pyrenees into Spain where
they carried on a desultory and indecisive struggle with the Celtiberi;
the Teutons and Helveti turned northwards to continue the work of
plundering Gaul.   In 103 the Cimbrian hosts made their way back to
Gaul and reunited, in the territory of South-Belgic Veliocasses, with
their comrades who had remained behind.

Now at last they prepared a march upon Italy. In the spring of 102 the main mass of the united hordes began to move southwards. Only one section, of about 6000 men — the nucleus of the later tribe of the Aduatuci — remained behind in Belgica to guard the spoils. Doubtless with a view to the difficulties of the passage of the Alps, especially in the matter of supply, the invading host was before long divided into three columns. The plan was that the Teutones and Ambrones should make their way into the plain of the Po from the western side, crossing the Maritime Alps, while the Cimbri and the Tigurini should make a wide flanking movement and enter from the north, the former by way of the Tridentine, the latter by way of the Noric Alps. But the attempt was planned on too vast a scale, and was wrecked by the military skill of Marius. The Ambrones and Teutones were annihilated in the double battle near Aquae Sextiae (summer 102), while the fate of the Cimbri overtook them in the following year. They had already reached the soil of Italy, into which they had forced their way after a victorious encounter with Quintus Lutatius Catulus on the Adige, when (30 July 101), on the plains of Vercellae, the so-called *Campi Raudii*, they were utterly routed by the united forces of Marius and Catulus. The Tigurini, who were to form the third invading force, received the news of the defeat of the Cimbri when they were still on the Noric Alps, and immediately turned round and retired to their own country. Thus the great invasion of the northern barbarians was defeated, and Western Europe could once more breathe freely.

We saw above that about B.C. 100, doubtless in connexion with the appearance of the Cimbri and Teutones in South Germany, the line of the Main was crossed by the Germanic peoples, and the settlement of the territory between that and the Danube began. Less than a generation later there was another attempt to extend the Germanic sphere of influence westward over Gaul. About the year B.C. 71, on the invitation of the powerful tribe of the Sequani, Ariovistus chief of the Suebi crossed the Rhine with 15,000 warriors to serve as mercenaries to the Sequani against their neighbours the Aedui. But after the victory was won, the strangers did not return to their own land but remained on the western side of the Rhine and established themselves in the territory of their employers, taking possession of about a third of it, presumably at its northern extremity. Strengthened by large accessions from the home-land this Germanic settlement on Gaulish territory — it consisted of the Vangiones, Nemetes and Tribocci, and finally extended over the whole of the left side of the Rhine valley, eastward of the Vosges — soon became a menace to all the surrounding tribes. A united attempt, in which the Aedui took a leading part, to expel the intruders by force of arms ended after months of indecisive fighting in a crushing defeat of the Gauls (at Admagetobrgia), apparently in the year B.C. 61. Gaul lay defenceless at the feet of the victors, and they did not fail to make the most of their success. The Aedui and all their adherents were forced to give hostages and to pay a yearly tribute. None dared to oppose the conquerors, who already regarded the whole of Gaul as their prey. They pursued their work deliberately and systematically, constantly bringing in new swarms of their compatriots, chiefly Suebi and Marcomanni, and assigning them lands in the territories which they had subjugated. Settlers came even from Jutland, Endusi and Harudes 24,000 strong, and on their arrival the Sequani were forced to give up another third of their territory to the new-comers. Thus the power of Ariovistus became very formidable. The establishment of a great Germanic Empire over the whole of Gaul seemed not far distant.

At other points also the Teutons were preparing to cross the Rhine. It seemed as if the example set by Ariovistus would lead to a general invasion of Gaul, flood the whole country with Germans, and overwhelm the Gaulish race. The movement began on the upper Rhine, on the Helvetic border. The Helveti had been obliged, as we have already seen, to retire further and further before the pressure of the Germans, until finally all the country north of the Lake of Constance was lost to them, and the Rhine became their northern frontier. Even here they were not allowed to rest. A short time after the appearance of Ariovistus the Teutons had again endeavoured to enlarge their border towards the south, and there ensued a long struggle upon the Rhine frontier. It was only by their utmost efforts that the Helveti were able to beat off the attacks of their opponents. Weary of the constant struggle, they at last resolved (B.C. 61) to leave their territory. This, as we have seen, they did three years later, when some smaller tribes, among them the Germanic Tulingi (p. 189 *sup.*), threw in their lot with them. The Jura region, the entrance to southern Gaul, thus lay open to the Teutons. In the same year there appeared on the middle Rhine, probably in the Taunus region, a powerful Suebian army — a hundred "gau's" under the leadership of two brothers named Nasua (perhaps Masua) and Cimberius — and threatened to invade from this point the territory of the Treveri on the opposite bank. Finally, there was great restlessness also on the lower Rhine, among the tribes inhabiting the right bank, especially among the Usipetes and Tencteri, in consequence especially of the repeated aggressions of the warlike Suebi.

This was the condition of affairs when Caesar (B.C. 58) took up his command in Gaul. He was well aware of the danger to the Roman occupation which lay in these wholesale immigrations of Germanic hordes into Gaulish territory, and it was consequently his first care to take prompt measures to meet the Teutonic peril. It is well known how he performed this task, how he removed the haunting dread of a general irruption of the Germanic peoples into Keltic territory, and at the same time established security and order upon the Rhine frontier. The restoration of the conquered Helveti to their abandoned territory in order that they might continue to serve, but now in the Roman interest, as a buffer-state, secured Gaul, and especially the valley of the Rhone, against incursions from the direction of the upper Rhine. His victory over Ariovistus destroyed the latter's vast levies and with them his ascendancy, but not — and herein we see again the far-sighted policy of the conqueror — the work of colonisation begun by the Germanic ruler. The tribes of the Vangiones, Nemetes and Tribocci which he had settled in Gaul were allowed to remain where they were, and, like the Helveti, were placed under the Roman suzerainty while retaining their racial independence — *ut arcerent, non ut custodirentur.* But while Caesar allowed these settlements to remain, he repressed with all the greater energy all further efforts of expansion on the part of the dwellers on the upper Rhine. True, the Suebian bands which in 58 had mustered on the right bank of the river, had retired on receiving news of the defeat of Ariovistus, so that there was no fighting with them, but the attempt of Usipetes and Tencteri, in the following year, to find a new home for themselves in Gaul led to a battle, in which a large portion of them perished, and the rest were flung back across the Rhine.

Augustus assumed the offensive against the Teutons. Even though the extension of the Roman dominion as far as the Elbe effected by the brilliant military successes of the two step-sons of the Emperor was of short duration — the year A.D. 9 witnessed the loss of the territory won by the expenditure of so much blood, of which it had been proposed to make a new province of Germania Magna — yet the Rhine frontier was secured for a considerable time to come by a belt of fortresses garrisoned by an army of nearly 80,000 men. This frontier was not seriously threatened for two hundred years thereafter. Throughout that period, except for a few insignificant raids, Gaul's eastern neighbour remained quiescent. It was only in the third century that unrest shewed itself again, thereafter steadily increasing as time went on. And the cause of this was the appearance of two powerful confederacies which thenceforward dominated the history of the Rhineland — the Alemans and the Franks.

While the expansion of the Teutons towards the west was thus barred by the Romans, it proceeded the more vigorously in a southward and south-eastward direction. It is true that but little certain information has come down to us. The movements of population, implied by the appearance of the Marcomanni in Bohemia, of the Quadi in Moravia, of the Naristi between the Böhmer-Wald and the Danube, of the Buri, Lacringi, Victovali in the north of the Hungarian lowlands, are all more or less shrouded in obscurity, and it is but rarely possible to find a clue to their relations. About B.C. 60 the Boii had been forced by the advance of the Germanic races from the north to abandon their ancestral possessions. A portion of them found a dwelling-place in Pannonia, another portion, on its way from Noricum, joined the Helvetic migra-

CH. VII.

tion. The north of the country thus left unoccupied was immediately taken up by Hermunduric, Semnonic, and Vandalic bands, offshoots of the three great tribes which flanked Bohemia on the north. From them were doubtless sprung the peoples who at a later time are met with here at the southern base of the Sudetes, the *Sudini, Bativi,* and *Corconti.* They were followed by the Marcomanni, who, doubtless in consequence of the military successes of Drusus in Germany, made their way, under the lead of their chief Marbod, to the further side of the Böhmer-Wald and occupied the main portion of the former country of the Boii.

The powerful kingdom which this Germanic prince established by bringing in further masses of settlers and by subjugating the surrounding tribes — even the powerful Semnones, the Langobards, the Goths, and the Lugi (Vandals) are said to have acknowledged his suzerainty — had no rival in northern Europe, and with its trained army of 70,000 footmen and 4000 horse soon became a menace to the Roman Empire. The importance which was attached to it, and to the commanding personality of its ruler by the Romans themselves, is evident from the extraordinary military preparations which Tiberius set on foot (A.D. 6). As is well known, the intervention of the Roman arms was not in the end called for. But what even they might not have been able to accomplish was effected by inner dissension. In the struggle for the supremacy of Germany against Arminius at the head of the Cherusci, and of all the other peoples who flocked to the standard of the *liberator Germaniae,* Marbod was defeated, and the fate of his kingdom was thereby decided. First the Semnones and Langobards ranged themselves on the side of his adversaries, then one tribe after another, so that he found his dominions in the end reduced to their original extent, the country of the Marcomanni. With the ruin of his Empire his own fate overtook him. Treachery in his own camp forced him to seek the protection of the Romans. The fall of its founder did not, however, affect the stability of the Bohemian kingdom of the Suebi. Although the Marcomanni were never afterwards able to regain their ascendancy, they held their own far on into the decline of the ancient world, in the country which they had occupied under Marbod's leadership. Indeed after a time their power was so far revived that, in alliance with the Quadi, they were able to dominate the upper Danube frontier for fully a century.

The earliest mention of the Quadi occurs in the geographer Strabo. He names them among the Suebian tribes who settled within the Hercynian Forest, the mountains which form the frontier of Bohemia. The country which they inhabited is nearly the present Moravia. Its eastern frontier was formed by the March, the ancient Marus. That they were of Suebian origin is clear from the express testimony of Strabo, as well as on linguistic grounds. The only point which remains doubtful is whether even before their coming into Moravia they had formed a political unit, or whether they were a migratory band sent out by one of the great Suebian peoples, perhaps the Semnones, which only developed into a united and independent national community after settling in Moravia.   The former, however, is the more probable.

Like their western neighbours the Marcomanni, the Quadi were the successors of a Keltic people.   As the Boii had been settled in Bohemia, so in Moravia, from a remote period and down to Caesar's day had been settled the *Volcae Tectosages*.   Seeing that about B.C. 60, the advance of the Teutons from the north over the Erzgebirge and Sudetes caused the Boii to leave their territory, it is probable that at the same time, or a little later, the peoples further to the east became involved in a struggle with the invaders.   But whereas the Boii by their prompt retirement escaped the danger, the Tectosages, it would appear, were utterly destroyed.   We find the Quadi soon after in possession of their territory, and since we get no hint of the fate of the Moravian Tectosages, the Romans cannot yet have been in possession of the neighbouring country of Noricum.   Their destruction must therefore have fallen before B.C. 15, when Noricum passed under the dominion of Rome.   If this hypothesis is correct the irruption of the Quadi into Moravia took place shortly after the Boii had left Bohemia; in any case a considerable time before the occupation of that country by the Marcomanni.

To the west of the Marcomanni, between the Böhmer-Wald and the Danube as far up as the river Naab, were settled the Naristi.   It is equally uncertain whence they came and when they appeared in this region.   It is possible, though that is the most that can be said, that like their eastern neighbours they belonged to the Suebian confederacy — Tacitus certainly counts them as members of it — and that they are to be numbered among those peoples which, according to Strabo, Marbod had settled in the region of the *Hercynia Sylva*.

Guarding the flanks, as it were, of the southern territories of the Teutons lay two settlements planted by the Romans; in the west the Hermunduri between the upper Main and the Danube, and in the east the Vannianic kingdom of the Suebi.   The former came into being B.C. 6–2, the Roman general, L. Domitius Ahenobarbus, having assigned to a band of Hermunduri the eastern part of the territory left free by the migration of the Marcomanni into Bohemia; the latter was created by the settlement of bands of Suebian warriors belonging to the following of the fallen Suebian leaders, Marbod and Casvalda.

The *Marus* is of course the March, the *Cusus*, as this Suebian settlement cannot have been very extensive, was probably the Waag, though it may have been the Gran, which lies further to the east.   The Βαῖμοι of Ptolemy are probably identical with these Suebians of northern Hungary, who come into notice several times in the course of the first century.   As they disappear later, they were probably absorbed by the Quadi.   Further towards the north-east, in the Hungarian Erzgebirge, and beyond in the upper region of the Vistula, we find in the first·

CH. VII.

century of our era the Buri and Sidones. The former, who are mentioned as early as Strabo, were probably of Bastarnian, and the latter of Lugian origin; further still, abutting on the eastern flank of the Sidones, were the Burgiones, Ambrones, and Frugundiones, doubtless also Bastarnian.

If we now review the ethnographic situation in ancient Germany about the close of the first century A.D., we find on its western frontier, in the eastern basin of the lower Rhine, the Chamavi, the Bructeri, the Usipii, the Tencteri, the Chattuarii and Tubantes; further in the interior, on both sides of the Weser, the great tribes of the Chatti and Cherusci; further to the north, the Angrivarii; and, on the North Sea coast, the Chauci and Frisians. In the heart of the country three powerful Suebian populations have their seat: on the western bank of the middle Elbe, extending as far south as the Rhaetian frontier, the Hermunduri; north of them, on the western bank of the lower Elbe, the Langobards, and beyond that river, in the basins of the Havel and the Spree, the Semnones, who were held to be the primitive stock of the Suebi. The eastern part of the country was mainly occupied by the Lugii. The tribes too which appear later, in the wars of the Marcomanni (the Victovali, Asdingi, and Lacringi), were doubtless also Vandalic. Northward in the region of the Wartha and Netze, dwelt the Burgundiones or Burgundi; further north still, on the Pomeranian Baltic coast, the Rugii and Lemovi, next to whom on the western side came (with some other smaller tribes) the Saxons. North of these again, on the Jutish peninsula, lay the Anglii and Varini. Turning back to the Vistula again, we find on its eastern bank the Goths, who, apparently by the beginning of our era, had spread from the shores of its estuary to its upper waters. In the south, the portion of the Hermunduri which had its seat between the Main and the Danube formed the first link in a long chain consisting of Naristi, Marcomanni, Quadi, Buri, and finally, beyond the *confinium Germanorum*, the numerous branches of the Bastarnae.

It was therefore a vast territory which the Germanic races claimed for their own, and yet, as was soon to appear, it was too narrow for the energies of these young and vigorous nations. On their north foamed the sea, to the east yawned the desert steppes of southern Russia: thus any further expansion could only take a westward or southward direction. But on the one side as on the other lay the unbroken line of the Roman frontier. Any attempt at expansion in either of these directions must inevitably lead to an immediate collision with the Roman Empire.

The storm which lowered upon the Bohemian mountains was soon to burst. Mighty forces were doubtless at work in the interior of Germany which shortly after the accession of Marcus Aurelius stirred up the whole mass of nations from the Böhmer-Wald to the Carpathians, and let loose a tempest such as the Roman Empire had never before encountered on its frontiers. In the summer of 167 hosts of barbarians mustered along the line of the Danube, ready to make an inroad into Roman territory. The Praetorian Praefect, Furius Victorinus, was defeated, and slain with most of his troops; and the invading flood poured forward over the unprotected provinces. Not until the two Emperors reached the seat of war (spring 168) was the plundering and ravaging stopped. The bar. barians then withdrew to the further side of the Danube and declared their readiness to enter into negotiations.[1] There, in the winter of 168-9 the plague broke out with fearful violence in the Roman camp, and at once the complexion of events changed for the worse. In the spring, in the absence of the Emperors, who on the outbreak of the epidemic had returned to the capital, the army, weakened and disorganised by disease, suffered another severe defeat, and the Praetorian Praefect, Macrinius Vindex, met his death. Following up their victory, the Teutons assumed the offensive all along the line. A surging mass of peoples — Hermunduri, Naristi, Marcomanni, Quadi, Lacringi, Buri, Victovali, Asdingi and other tribes Germanic and Iazygic — swept over the provinces of Rhaetia, Noricum, Pannonia, and Daeid. Some detached bands even pushed their way into North Italy, laid siege to Aquileia, and destroyed Opitergium, further to the west.

But the danger passed as quickly as it had arisen. Effective measures were instantly taken. The flood of invasion was stemmed, and as it receded the Romans, led by the Emperor in person, took the aggressive. All the Teutons and Iazyges who remained on the south bank were forced back across the river. So successful were the Roman arms that by the year 171 the Quadi sued for peace. In the following year the Roman army crossed the Danube, and laid waste the country of the Marcomanni. Thus the two most dangerous adversaries had been subdued and the war seemed over. But by the year 174 the Emperor again found himself obliged to return to Germany. Scarcely had he entered the country of the Quadi, when the army was placed in a highly dangerous position by an enveloping movement of the enemy, and by want of water. Suddenly a torrent of rain descended,[2] and legionaries saw in the "miracle" a proof of the favour of the gods, and were inspired to fight with splendid valour, and gained a complete victory. This broke the resistance of the Quadi, and the Marcomanni also were forced

---

[1] I refer to the fragment of Petrus Patricius (6) which Mommsen, *Ges. Schriften*, IV. p. 492 n. 1, assigns to the time of Pius.

[2] There is no reason to doubt either the event itself, or the fact that it appeared to the minds of contemporaries, especially of Marcus Aurelius himself, as a miracle. See Harnack, *Sitzungsber. der Berl. Akad.* 1894, p. 835, and Th. Mommsen, *Hermes*, 30 (1895), p. 90 = *Ges. Schriften*, IV. p. 498 (against E. Petersen, *Mitt. des Arch. Inst. röm.* Abt. 9 (1894), p. 78 and A. von Damaszewski, *Rhein. Mus. f. Philol.* 49 (1894), p. 612); cf. also J. Geffcken, *N. Jahrbuch f. d. Klass. Altertum,* 3 (1899), p. 253. Further literature in Schanz, *Gesch. d. röm. Literatur,* III². § 644.

to make peace. In 176 the Emperor returned to Rome, and there celebrated, along with his son Commodus, a well-deserved triumph. In 177 Marcus rejoined his army with the purpose of completing the work of conquest. Two new provinces, Marcomania and Sarmatia, were to be added to his Empire and were to round off his northern boundary. The war began (apparently before the end of 177) with an attack upon the Quadi, after which the Marcomanni were to be dealt with. In the course of the three-years' war both peoples were so thoroughly exhausted that when the Emperor suddenly died (17 March 180) their military strength was already broken.

One of the first acts of Commodus, an unworthy successor of his father, was to make peace which surrendered to the all but beaten enemy every advantage that had been wrested from them. The struggle for the lands to the north of the Danube was at an end. Meanwhile the Romans were confronted, about the close of the century, with a new and dangerous enemy in the west, in the angle between the Main and the frontier of upper Germany and Rhaetia—by the Alemans. As their name indicates,[1] the Alemans were not a single tribe but a union of tribes—a confederacy. We hear (somewhat later) the names of several of the component tribes, the *Juthungi*, the *Brisigavi*, the *Bucinobantes*, and the *Lentienses*. Whence did they come? No doubt the nucleus of this confederacy was formed by the southern divisions of the Hermunduri. To these there may have attached themselves various fragments of peoples which had split off before and after the Marcomannic war, just as later, towards the middle of the third century, the Semnones, in the course of a migration southward, probably joined this confederacy and were absorbed by it.

Before long—as early as 213—the new nation came in contact with the Romans. So far as can be made out from the confused account which is given us of their first appearance [2] they had invaded Rhaetia, whereupon the Emperor Caracalla took the field against them, flung them back across the frontier and advanced into their territory carrying all before him.[3] Before twenty years had passed the Teutons—presumably the Alemans again — renewed the attack upon the Roman frontier defences. So threatening was the situation that the Emperor Severus Alexander felt

---

[1] Alemanni (Gothic *alamans* from the Old Teutonic **alamannez*) means "all people," "all men," and therefore designates an aggregate of peoples. So the historian Asinius Quadratus (in Agathias, I. 6, p. 17): οἱ Ἀλαμανοὶ . . . ξύνηλυδές εἰσιν ἄνθρωποι καὶ μιγάδες, καὶ τοῦτο δύναται αὐτοῖς ἡ ἐπωνυμία.

[2] Dio, LXXVII. 13-15, on which see Bang, *Hermes*, 41 (1906), p. 623; cf. Herodian, IV. 7. 2-3; *Vita Carac.* 5. 4. 6; 10. 6.

[3] According to the records of the Arval College for the year 213 (*C.I.L.* VI. 2086) the members made an offering on 11 August *quod dominus n[oster] . . . per limitem Raetiae ad hostes extirpandos barbarorum [terram] introiturus est, ut ea res ei prospere feliciterque cedat,* and on 6 October *ob salute[m] victoriamque Germanicam* of the sovereign. *Ob victoriam Germanicam* is also the cause of the setting up of the inscription in *C.I.L.* XIII. 6459 and the same *victoria Germanica* appears on the coins of the year 213 (Cohen, IV². p. 210 n. 645-6).

himself obliged to break off his campaign against the Persians, and take over in person the direction of the operations on the Rhine. Negotia_ tions had already begun before his assassination (March 235), but his successor, the rough and soldierly Maximin, brought new life into the campaign. Advancing by forced marches into the country of the Alemans he drove the barbarians before him without serious resistance, laid waste their fields and dwellings far and wide, and finally defeated them far in the interior of their territory.

The result of this campaign, the last war of offence on a large scale which the Romans waged on the Rhine, was the restoration of security to the frontier for a period of twenty years. Under Gallienus—probably about the year 258—the storm broke. With irresistible force the armies of the Alemans broke through the great chain of frontier fortifications between the Main and the Danube, and after overpowering the scattered Roman garrisons, poured like a flood across the whole of the *Agri Decumates*, and established themselves permanently in the conquered territory. At the same time Rhaetia became a prey to them; nay more, a strong force even crossed the Alps and penetrated as far as Ravenna. The invaders were, it is true, defeated by Gallienus near Milan, and forced to retreat, but the country at the northern base of the Alps was lost, and its loss threw open to the Germanic hordes the gates of Italy.

In addition to the Alemans of the upper Rhine, there now appeared, on the lower course of that river, another dangerous enemy, namely the Franks. The frontier had scarcely ever been seriously threatened at this point since the days of Augustus, but now under Gallienus the situation was altered. Here also there had quietly grown up a confederacy which, under the name of *Franci*, the Free, presumably comprised the tribes formerly met with in these regions, the Chamavi, Sugambri, and other smaller clans. Their name, first heard in the time of Gallienus, was soon to become even more terrible in the ears of the Romans than that of the Alemans. The first attack of the new league of peoples upon the Rhine frontier occurred in 253. The districts on the Gaulish bank of the Rhine soon fell into the hands of the enemy. With great difficulty Gallienus succeeded in forcing them back across the Rhine. But others followed them, and there ensued a series of desperate struggles which lasted till 258. On the whole the Romans had the best of it, even though their army was not large enough to prevent isolated bands of Franks from establishing themselves upon the left bank of the Rhine.

In 258 Gallienus was called away to the lower Danube, which urgently demanded his presence. The confusion which was created in the Rhine district by the assassination in the following year of the Emperor's son Valerian who had been left behind as Imperial Resident at Cologne, by the ambitious general Cassianus Postumus, gave the Franks a welcome opportunity to make a new inroad into Gaul. Their bands ranged almost unresisted through the whole country from the Rhine to

CH. VII.

the Pyrenees, devastating as they went. Then they pushed on, as the Cimbri had done before them, across the mountains into Spain, and made havoc of that country for several years, reducing to subjection even great cities like Tarraco, while, like the Vandals after them, they also made a foray into Africa. As at the time of the Cimbrian war, the terror of the Germans spread through all the countries of Western Europe. Only after a considerable time Postumus — a capable soldier and a well-intentioned administrator — was able to force the Germanic hordes out of Gaul and restore peace and security. But the Rhine became the frontier of the Empire and remained so as long as the Empire lasted.

From this time onward begins a period of incessant fighting with the Teutons of the Rhine-country : with the Alemans in the south and the Franks in the north. The weakness and exhaustion of the Empire caused by inner dissensions becomes manifest. If Postumus succeeded in keeping the Roman possessions on the Gaulish bank of the Rhine essentially intact, his immediate successors were less successful. The country was left defenceless, and large portions of it were plundered and drained of their resources. Probus indeed, whose short reign (276–282) is a ray of light in these gloomy times, succeeded in clearing them out of Gaul, and even ventured to assume the offensive on the upper Rhine, in a brilliant campaign forcing the Alemans back to the further side of the Neckar. But such successes were but temporary. Only in the time of Diocletian does a durable improvement on the Rhine frontier set in, an improvement which was maintained for the next two or three generations. During this period a third set of invaders, in addition to the Franks and Alemans, appeared towards the close of the century in the Saxons, the terror of the British and Gaulish coasts. In the main, however, Gaul was suffered to enjoy peace ; and with peace returned prosperity.

Meanwhile on the shores of the Euxine, there emerges a people with whose name the world was to ring for centuries, the Goths. Their original home had been, it would appear, in Scandinavia, and after their migration to the German Baltic coast they had at first established themselves about the estuary of the Vistula,[1] then in course of time they had moved further southward along the right bank of that river, so that at the beginning of our era they appear as far south as the neighbourhood of the Bohemian kingdom of the Marcomanni. How long they remained in this region we do not know, but it is not unlikely that their eastward migration falls about the time of the great Marcomannic war. We are equally ignorant of the time occupied by this migration and the details of its progress ; the only thing certain is that it reached its close not later than *c.* 230–240.

[1] The *Gutones* on the North Sea coast mentioned by Pytheas in the fourth century B.C. may have been a branch of this people which had wandered westward, and were absorbed probably by the Frisians.

The territory where the Goths at last took up their abode embraced the whole of the northern coast of the Black Sea. In the east it was separated by the Don from that of the Alani, in the west it bordered on the tract of country northward of the Danube Delta and the Dacian frontier which had been settled four hundred years earlier by the Bastarnae and the Sciri. Here the Goths divided into two sections soon after their immigration, that dwelling more to the west being known as the Tervingi, "the inhabitants of the forest region," while the eastern division was known as the Greutungi, "the inhabitants of the Steppes." For the former the name Visigoths (Vesegoti) came into use,[1] at latest *c.* 350, for the latter the name Ostrogoths, designations however of which the meaning is not absolutely certain, although "the western Goths" and "the eastern Goths" was an interpretation already known to Jordanes. The boundary between them was formed by the Dniester. Before long there appear alongside of them other Germanic peoples, the Gepidae, Taifali, Borani, Urugundi, and Heruli. The two first of these had some original link of connexion with them. The Gepidae indeed appear in the Gothic legend of their migrations as an actual part of the Gothic nation. Whether they migrated to the Black Sea region at the same time as the Goths, or followed them later, must remain an open question.

Towards the end of the reign of Severus Alexander (222–235) the first indications of the appearance on the northern shores of the Black Sea of a new and powerful barbarian race, of a most warlike temper, had already become manifest, when the Greek towns of Olbia and Tyras fell victims to the sudden descent of an unknown enemy from the North. A little later, under Gordian III (238–244), its name is found. In the spring of 238 Gothic war-bands marched southwards, crossed the Danube with the connivance of the Dacian Carpi and broke into the province of Lower Moesia, where they captured and plundered the town of Istrus. The Procurator of the province, Tullius Menophilus (238–241), being unable to repel the invasion by force of arms, induced the Goths to retire by the promise of a yearly subsidy. But by 248 they had renewed their attacks on the Roman frontier in alliance with the Taifali, Asdingi, and Bastarnae. Under the leadership of Argaith and Gunterich their bands again broke into Lower Moesia, assailed without success the fortified town of Marcianople and plundered the unfortunate province again.

But these first exploits of the Goths were completely thrown into the shade by the great invasion of Roman territory made at the beginning of 250 by the half-legendary King Kniwa at the head of a powerful army. While the Carpi flung themselves upon Dacia, the Gothic attack was directed as before upon Moesia. Thence a strong

---

[1] These names, like the division of the race which they express, may have been considerably older, and as the occurrence of Greutungi in Scandinavia suggests, brought by the Goths from their original home.

detachment pressed onward over the undefended passes of the Balkans into Thrace, laid siege to Philippopolis, and even despatched a plundering party into Macedonia. One division of the Gothic army, after vainly assaulting Novae and Nicopolis, was defeated in the neighbourhood of the latter town by the Emperor Decius in person, but this success was immediately counterbalanced by a reverse. The Goths, while retiring southwards by way of Beroë (Augusta Traiana), the present Eski-Zaghra, on the southern slope of the Balkans, defeated the Roman troops who were pursuing them. After this battle the victorious Goths effected a junction with their countrymen who were investing Philippopolis, and that city fell into their hands. The Romans, however, were now making extensive preparations, in view of which the barbarians began their retreat. Decius, eager to wipe out the failure at Beroë, sought to bar their path, and, in the hope of inflicting a crushing defeat upon them, engaged them near Abrittus, about 30 miles south-east of Durostorum (Silistria) in June 251. The day, which began well for the Romans, ended in a fearful disaster, a great part of their army was destroyed, and the Emperor himself and one of his sons were among the slain. The country from which the barbarians had just retired now lay once more defenceless before them. They were finally bought off by the promise of a yearly subsidy.

The Gothic war of 250–251 had revealed in its full extent the danger which had lain hidden behind the mountains of Dacia. Later events did little to remove the terrible impression which the invasion of Kniwa had left behind. On the contrary, the history of the eastern half of the Empire in the reigns of Valerian and Gallienus, Claudius, Aurelian, and Probus is filled with incessant struggles against the Goths and their allies. For even Asia Minor was not exempt from their ravages; besides the bands which swept down by the Balkans and back again there were now others which came by sea from the Crimea and Lake Maeotis to ravage a constantly widening area of the coasts of Asia Minor and which even penetrated to the inland districts. Especially prominent in these piratical raids were the Borani and Heruli, two peoples who here appear in history for the first time side by side with the Goths. The first of these expeditions, made by the Borani in 256 against the town of Pityus (on the eastern shore of the Black Sea), ended in failure, but by the following year these same Borani succeeded in capturing and sacking Pityus and Trapezus. Even more destructive was the expedition which (spring 258) was undertaken by the West Goths, starting by sea and land from the port of Tyras. The whole western coast of Bithynia with the cities of Chalcedon, Nicomedia, Nicaea, Apamea, and Prusa was ravaged. The years 263, 264, and 265 also witnessed the vasting of the coast lands of Asia Minor by similar expeditions of the Pontic Teutons. Ilium, Ephesus with its renowned temple of Artemis, and Chalcedon were this time the victims of the barbarians.

But all these exploits were far surpassed in importance by the great plundering expedition of the Heruli in the year 267. From Lake Maeotis a fleet, said to have been five hundred strong, sailed along the western shore of the Euxine, then through the Bosphorus, where they made a successful *coup-de-main* against Byzantium, through the Propontis, where Cyzicus was captured, and the Hellespont, and onward past Lemnos and Scyros across the Aegean to Greece. Here on the classic soil of Attica, Argolis, and Laconia the wild hosts of these barbarians made fearful havoc, and it was long enough before the bewildered provincial government ventured to oppose them. The defenders, in whose ranks the historian Dexippus of Athens played a leading part, gradually gained confidence, and when they had succeeded in destroying the ships, the invaders were obliged to retreat by the land route. Beaten by the Roman troops their hosts rolled northwards through Boeotia, Epirus, Macedonia, towards their home, which they succeeded in reaching although hard pressed by their pursuers and at the very last compelled by the Emperor Gallienus to fight a battle, in which they incurred heavy losses, at the river Nestus, on the boundary between Macedonia and Thrace.

We have seen above how the Danube had been constantly threatened since the appearance of the Goths on the Black Sea, how invasion after invasion had descended on Dacia and Moesia. Soon after the accession of Gallienus (probably 256–7),[1] Dacia with the exception of the narrow strip between the Temes and the Danube, which continued to be held down to the time of Aurelian, together with the portion of Lower Moesia which lay to the north of the Danube (the present Great Wallachia), became the prey of the barbarians. Some of the West Goths settled in Great Wallachia and the Taifali in the Banat; the northern districts, especially Transylvania, were occupied by the Victovali and Gepidae, who at this time make their appearance among the enemies of Rome. The consequence of the loss of Dacia and Trans-Danubian Moesia was that the Teutons now became on the lower Danube as well as elsewhere the immediate neighbours of the Empire, their territory being divided from it only by the river.

Only once in this whole period of inward decay did the imperial power succeed in winning a decisive victory. That was the achievement of the Emperor Claudius, whom his grateful contemporaries and successors have rightly adorned with the honourable title of "Gothicus." In the spring of 269 the Teutons made yet another attack upon the Empire, surpassing all former ones in violence. East Goths and West Goths, whom tradition here first distinguishes, Bastarnae (Peucini), Gepidae, and Heruli united their forces and advanced with a mighty army and fleet — estimated in the sources at 300,000 fighting-men and 2000

---

[1] In this year the minting of coins for the province of Dacia breaks off. The inscriptions found in this country too do not come down beyond the first year of the reign of Valerian.

CH. VII.

ships — against the Danubian frontier. Once more the province of Lower Moesia bore the brunt of their attack. The land army of the Teutons, in which lay their main strength, first made an unsuccessful attempt to take Tomi and Marcianople, then swept like a flood over the interior of the country, wasting and plundering as they went. Meanwhile the fleet, which was manned chiefly by Heruli, sailed past Byzantium and Cyzicus into the Aegean, and appeared before Thessalonica. Part of it remained there and blockaded the city; the remainder made a great plundering expedition which bears eloquent testimony to the seamanship and daring of these Teutons, along the coasts of Macedonia, Greece, and Asia Minor, extending even as far as Crete and Cyprus.

This was the situation when the Emperor Claudius reached the scene of war. At his approach the besiegers of the hard-pressed Thessalonica had hastily drawn off northwards and effected a junction with their kinsmen in Upper Moesia. The hostile forces met near Naissus. In the desperate struggle which ensued the Teutons suffered a crushing defeat. What remained of their army was in part cut to pieces in the pursuit, in part driven into the inhospitable recesses of the Balkans, where the survivors surrendered. They were partly enrolled in the Roman army, partly, in pursuance of a policy initiated by the Emperor Marcus, settled as *coloni* in the devastated frontier districts.

Thus the danger was averted from the Empire, and the desire of its restless neighbours beyond the Danube to make expeditions on the great scale was damped for nearly a hundred years. No doubt the inroads and piratical voyages of smaller Gothic war-bands continued; indeed, in the next fourteen years (270-284), there was fighting with bands of this kind under Quintillus, Aurelian, Tacitus, and Probus, but all these incursions were easily repelled by the imperial government, which gained strength under Aurelian and Probus. Just at this time, too, there broke out a severe internal struggle between the Teutons of the Euxine and those of the Danube. The first aid called in by the Goths against the Tervingi was that of the Bastarnae, but the outcome of the struggle was that the Bastarnae were defeated and compelled to abandon the territory which they had held so tenaciously for more than five hundred years. The expelled Bastarnae, said to have numbered 100,000 men, were taken under his protection by the Emperor Probus and settled in Thrace. After that the Tervingi, supported by the Taifali, made war on the allied Gepidae and Vandals, while the East Goths fought with their eastern neighbours the Urugundi, who on their defeat were taken under the protection of the Alani.[1] We can see that the whole of the eastern Germanic world was in a state of wild uproar.

On the middle Danube there had been no fighting worth mention

---

[1] *Mamert. genethl. Maxim.* 17 (p. 114 Baehrens) where 'the impossible *Alamanni* is doubtless to be corrected to *Alani*; the *Burgundii* are of course the *Urugundi*. Cf. L. Schmidt, *Gesch. der Wandalen*, p. 14.

since the Marcomannic war. We hear indeed of an incursion of the Marcomanni in the reign of Valerian, but, broadly speaking, the name of this once so warlike nation may be said to disappear from history. Their old comrades the Quadi often appear in association with the Iazyges, from the time of Gallienus, when they made a descent upon Pannonia. There was further fighting with them in 283, as is proved by a coin of Numerian.[1] However, they are in this period thrown into the shade by the other more dangerous assailants of the Empire; indeed, with the appearance of the Goths the main struggle between the Roman and Germanic powers had shifted from the middle to the lower Danube.

Shortly after the death of Probus (Oct. 282), the Alemans on the upper Rhine, and the Franks and Saxons on the lower Rhine, had begun their forays again. The eastern districts of Gaul were again overrun, while the coasts of the Channel were harried by Saxon pirates. The Burgundians also had left their home between the Oder and the Vistula, and forced their way through the heart of Germany to the Main. When the government had been taken over by Diocletian, his colleague and (after April 286) co-Emperor Maximian entered Gaul in the beginning of that year; it was his first care, so soon as he had suppressed the insurrection of the Bagaudae, to put a stop to the piracy of the Saxons and Franks. He first cleared the left bank of the Rhine, drove the Heruli and Chaivones, two Baltic tribes who had invaded Gaul, right out of the country, and, basing himself on Mainz, conducted a successful defensive campaign against Alemans and Burgundians. The defence of the coasts was entrusted to a capable officer, Carausius the Menapian, with a strong command and extensive authority. But when Carausius set up for Emperor in Britain towards the end of 286 the Teutons found a fresh opportunity. The usurper even made common cause with the enemies of the Empire and openly helped them. Maximian, indeed, repeatedly (287 and 291) gained successes against them, but the first decided improvement on the Rhine frontier was due to a new development of imperial organisation by which Gaul and Britain became a distinct administrative department with a governor of their own in the person of the general Flavius Constantius (March 293), who was at the same time appointed Caesar. The Franks were decisively defeated within their own borders (summer 293), Britain was reconquered for the Empire (spring 296) — Carausius himself had fallen a victim to a conspiracy in 293 — and finally by two great victories over the Alemans on the upper Rhine peace was at length restored (298-9), and the Rhine was made secure, especially as regards the upper part of its course, by the building of forts and the restoration of the defensive works which had been destroyed by the enemy or had fallen into decay. Following the example of Maximian, Constantius settled large numbers of prisoners

---

[1] Cohen, VI[2]. p. 378 n. 91, with the inscription *triumfu[s] Quador[um]*.

of war, Franks, Frisians, and Chamavi, as *laeti* and *coloni*, in the wasted and depopulated districts of north-east Gaul. Here they were to cultivate the fields that had been lying fallow, to supply the labour that was sorely needed, and to aid in the defence of the frontier. The country rapidly recovered, trade and commerce began to flourish again, and the ancient prosperity returned.

It was in this hopeful condition that the Western provinces came into the hands of Constantine when (25 July 306) he was called by the will of the army to take up the reins of government. During a reign of thirty-one years he thoroughly fulfilled the promise of his youth. From the first day of his rule he devoted all his efforts to the securing and well-being of the provinces. The Franks who were again on the move were energetically repressed; in the process two of their chiefs were taken prisoners, and given to the beasts. Similarly four years later a combined attack of the Bructeri, Chamavi, Cherusci, Lanciones, Alemans, and Tubantes was repulsed with heavy loss. These were the only occasions during Constantine's long reign on which the Germanic peoples of the Rhine-district made any expeditions on a large scale.

As regards the actual defence of the frontier, the number of troops was increased, the flotilla on the Rhine was reorganised and raised to a considerable strength, and the belt of fortresses along the frontier was improved. In this connexion took place the reoccupation and refortification of Divitia (Deutz), the old bridge-head of Cologne, which once more gave the Romans a firm foothold on the right bank of the Rhine on what had now become Frankish soil.

The coast defence of Gaul and Britain likewise underwent further improvements. The establishment of a special military command in the latter country, mentioned in the *Notitia Dignitatum* under the title *comes litoris Saxonici per Britanniam*, most probably goes back to Constantine. When the Emperor towards the end of 316 left Gaul for the last time, the land was in the enjoyment of complete peace, and this happy state of affairs continued so long as the internal peace of the Empire was preserved. The enemy on the further side of the Rhine was thoroughly overawed, and ventured on nothing more than small violations of the frontier.

Nevertheless the peace did not endure. When Magnentius, a Frank by race, set himself up as Emperor (350), the security of the Rhine was immediately imperilled, since the eastern Emperor Constantius himself incited the Teutons to attack the usurper and so to invade the Empire. All that had been accomplished by Constantine was rapidly lost in the disastrous years of civil war between 351 and 353. The left bank of the Rhine was again overrun by the Teutons, the fortified positions, denuded of their garrisons, were almost all captured and destroyed and the open country far into the interior of the province was plundered till there was nothing left to plunder. Although Constantius, after the suppression of the *pestifera tyrannis*, himself made two campaigns against the

Alemans, in the first (spring 354) against the kings Gundomad and
Vadomar, in the second (summer 355) against the Lentienses, he effected
practically nothing. It was only when the young Caesar Julian took
up the command in Gaul that the situation began to improve. The
whole year 356 was taken up in fighting against the Alemans, who were
driven back on all sides. A great number of towns, including Cologne,
which had been captured by the Franks, were won back again. A
serious defeat incurred in 357 by the *magister peditum* Barbatio was
retrieved by the brilliant victory of the Caesar over the united forces
of Chnodomar, Serapio, Vestralp, and other kings — in all 35,000 men
under seven "kings" (*reges*) and ten "sub-kings" (*regales*) — at Argentoratum (Strassburg). Two further campaigns against the Alemans, in
359 and 361, were equally successful. On the lower Rhine also Julian
defeated the Franks, the Chauci, and the Chamavi (358–360); the
tracts between the Scheldt and the Meuse were cleared of the enemy,
seven towns, among them the old fortresses of Bingium, Antunnacum,
Bonna, Novaesium, and Vetera (all on the Rhine) were retaken, and
again put in a state of defence. Thus the young Caesar seemed in the
way of bringing about a complete pacification of the Rhine country, when
he was compelled to leave Gaul by the outbreak of the conflict with
Constantius (361).[1]

Once again the country was left defenceless before the barbarians, who
did not fail to profit by the situation. It was indeed high time when,
after the death of Jovian (Feb. 364), the new Emperor Valentinian entered
the threatened province in the late autumn of 365, and took up his
headquarters at Paris. So much had the situation altered for the worse
since the departure of Julian that the Alemans could venture in January
366 to cross the frozen Rhine, and penetrate to the neighbourhood of
Châlons-sur-Marne. Here, indeed, they were defeated by the general
Jovinus who had hastened from Paris to intercept them, and were
compelled to beat a retreat. But the danger was not done with. The
guerrilla warfare continued on the frontier, with its forays and surprises.
Several years of vigorous action were needed before any change was
apparent. Following the old and well-tried maxim that attack is the
best defence, Valentinian in 368 himself crossed the Rhine at the head of
a considerable army reinforced by contingents of Illyrian and Italian
troops. Advancing into the country of the Alemans he came upon the
enemy at Solicinium (Sulz on the upper Neckar?)[2] and defeated them

---

[1] Fuller accounts of these campaigns and of the Gothic War are given in the
next chapter.

[2] If this identification is correct, Valentinian started from Trier, and marched
to the Rhine by the great military road through Metz-Zabern-Strassburg, and from this
point advanced in a south-easterly direction, using the old military road which led
upwards from Offenburg in the Kinzig Valley and on which also lies Sulz, formerly
the site of a Roman fortress.

in a bloody battle. Two smaller expeditions beyond the Rhine followed in the years 371 and 374. The result of this successful assumption of the aggressive by the Romans was, broadly speaking, the recovery of the Rhine frontier, which remained for the present exempt from serious attack.

During this time of military activity the defences along the whole line of the Rhine were strengthened. The existing castles and watch-towers were improved and many new ones were built; indeed a vigorous development of this old and well-tried system of frontier defence is the special merit of Valentinian. Taken generally, his reign marks a revival of the strength of the Empire, inward as well as outward, and the results of his work upon the Rhine could be felt for a generation after his death. Thus his son and successor, Gratian (375–383), found for the most part his ways made plain and a more peaceful situation obtaining on his arrival in Gaul than that which had confronted his father ten years earlier. Nevertheless he too had to draw the sword against the Alemans, who — mainly the tribe of the Lentienses — in the spring of 378 crossed the Rhine with a considerable force. A battle took place near Argentaria (Horburg near Colmar) in which the Romans gained a complete victory, destroying the greater part of the enemy. Thus, here on the Rhine frontier the year 378 brought the Romans once more a complete success — the same year which in the East witnessed the break-down of the Roman military power and the disastrous fall of the Emperor Valens.

In contrast to the Rhine countries, the Danubian provinces had, since the death of the Emperor Probus, enjoyed comparative peace. The power of the most dangerous neighbour of the Empire, the Goths, had been crippled for a long time, as we have seen, by Claudius and Aurelian, and more especially by the dissensions and struggles between the different tribes. The East Goths in particular had, since the close of the third century, been fully occupied with their own affairs, and com-pletely disappear for nearly a century. In the fourth century it is always the western division, the Tervingi, of whom we hear; as is indeed natural, seeing that their conquest of Trans-Danubian Moesia under Gallienus had made them the immediate neighbours of the Empire.

No events of any great importance on the Danubian frontier are recorded down to the time of Constantine. True, an inscription of Diocletian and his colleagues of a date shortly before 301, celebrates a victory over hostile tribes on the lower Danube,[1] which doubtless means the Goths, but these battles can hardly have been of any considerable importance. On the other hand Constantine frequently had trouble with the Goths. After some inroads in 314 the frontier defences were strengthened by the building of the fortress Tropaeum Traiani

[1] *C.I.L.* III. 6151.

(Adamelissi).[1] The removal of troops from the frontier during preparations of Licinius for another civil war gave the signal at the beginning of
323 for a new incursion of the Goths.   Thanks to the rapid advance
of Constantine — which brought him into his colleague's territory — the
invaders were intercepted before they had done any great damage, and
after severe losses, including the death of their leader, Rausimod, were
forced back across the Danube.

After the end of the civil war Constantine strove with unwearying
zeal to improve the defences of the frontier.   The line was protected by
castles, and although the number of the frontier troops to whom was
especially assigned the duty of garrisoning them — the *milites limitanei* or
riparienses — was considerably reduced, there was no diminution, but,
on the contrary, a distinct increase of military security, gained by
the creation at the same time of a mobile field force.   So strong did
the Roman Empire feel itself at this period that towards the close of the
reign of Constantine it even ventured to interfere in events on the
further side of the Danube where the Goths and Taifali were encroaching
on the Sarmatians who occupied the tract between the Theiss and the
Danube.   In response to an appeal of the Sarmatians for help, the
Emperor's eldest son Constantine crossed the river at the head of an
army and, in conjunction with the Sarmatians, thoroughly routed the
Teutons (20 April 332).

Doubtless in consequence of this defeat, which clearly brought home
to them the military superiority of the Empire, the warlike ardour of the
Tervingi and Taifali was extinguished for a long time.   Their impulse to
expand, the driving force of all their undertakings, was exhausted for
the present.   The barbarians began to busy themselves with agriculture
and cattle-raising.   As regards their relation to the Empire, former
conditions were reversed.   By the treaty of peace concluded after their
defeat they nominally surrendered their independence and recognised the
suzerainty of the Roman government, being pledged as *foederati*, in
return for yearly subsidies (*annonae foederaticae*), to share in the defence
of the frontier, and in case of war to serve as auxiliary troops.   The
peace continued for more than thirty years.   From time to time there
may have been slight disturbances of the peace — of this, indeed, there
is inscriptional evidence from the period of the joint rule of the three sons
of Constantine (337–340),[2] but on the whole both sides strictly observed
their compact.

---

[1] The only record of these events is contained in *C.I.L.* III. 13734 (presumably
from the year 316): *Romanae securitatis libertatisque vindicibus dd. nn. Fl. Val.
Constantino et V [al. L i c i n] i a [n o L i c i n i o] piis felicibus aeternis Augg. quorum virtute
et providentia edomitis ubique barbararum gentium populis ad confirmandam limitis
tutelam etiam Tropeensium civitas auspicato · a fundamentis feliciter opere constructa
est.*

[2] *C.I.L.* III. 12483.

CH. VII.

During this long period of peace the West Goths underwent a revolution, primarily religious but one which in its consequences affected the whole mental, social, and political life of the people — the introduction of Christianity. As early as the second half of the third century Christian teaching had obtained an entrance among them through Cappadocian prisoners, taken in the sea-expeditions against Asia Minor. There is no reason to doubt this fact; and it is equally certain that a century later there were among the Goths representatives of the most various schools of belief, Catholics, Arians, and (since about 350) Audians. Accordingly, the beginnings of Christianity among the Goths of the Danube reach far back, and its diffusion among them took place under the most various and independent influences. Of a conversion of the nation there can be no question, at least as far down as the middle of the fourth century. Their conversion only begins with the appearance of Ulfila.[1]

Born of Christian parents about the year 310–11 in the country of the Goths, he grew up as a Goth among the Goths, although Greek blood flowed in his veins. One or other of his parents came of a Christian family from the neighbourhood of Parnasus in Cappadocia which had been carried into captivity by the Goths in the time of Gallienus (264 ?). First employed as a Reader, he was, at the age of about 30, that is to say about the year 341, consecrated as bishop of the Christian community in the land of the Goths, by Eusebius (of Nicomedia), the famous leader of the Arian party, at that time bishop of Constantinople. Equally efficient as missionary and as organiser, Ulfila gathered and united the scattered confessors of the Christian faith, and, by his enthusiastic preaching of the Gospel he won for it many new adherents. For seven years he worked with great success among his fellow-countrymen, and then he was suddenly obliged (c. 348) to interrupt his work. A "godless and impious prince," probably Athanarich, inflicted cruel persecution on the Christians who dwelt within his dominion, by which the newly organised church was scattered and its bishop compelled to leave his home. Ulfila gathered together his adherents or as many of them as had escaped the persecution and fled with them across the Danube into Roman territory, where the Emperor Constantius gave him shelter. Here he lived and worked (in the neighbourhood of Nicopolis) as the priestly, and also as the political, head of the Goths who had accompanied him in his flight, until 380 or 381 — in very truth the apostle of the Goths, and not least so in virtue of his great work of translating the Bible, by which he transmitted to his people the knowledge of the Holy Scriptures for all time; and although

[1] On the form of the name cf. G. Kaufmann in his very thorough dissertation on the sources of the history of Ulfila (*Zeitschr. f. deutsch. Altert.* 27, N. F. 15, pp. 243 f.). According to him the bishop of the Goths was named Ulfila not Vulfila, the latter form having only come into use later, alongside of the former.

his missionary activity in his native land had early been brought to a close, yet the conversion of the whole Gothic race to Arian Christianity was nothing else than the harvest of that seed which he had sown in those first years of his work among them.

Soon after the death of Constantius (361) the friendly relations between the West Goths and the Empire began to change. Scarcely had Valentinian and Valens ascended the throne when there was an open rupture. First, towards the end of 364, predatory bands of Goths devastated Thrace — at the same time there was an incursion of the Quadi and Sarmatians into Pannonia — then in the spring of 365 the whole Gothic nation prepared for a great expedition against the Roman territory. Once more the danger was averted; Valens, although he was on the march for Syria and had already reached Bithynia, at once took vigorous measures to cope with it. Two years later however came the long-expected collision. Valens himself advanced to the attack. He found a pretext in the ambiguous attitude of the Goths in recent years, especially in their having aided the usurper Procopius with a contingent of 3000 men (winter of 365–6). In the summer of 367 the Roman army crossed the Danube. Yet no events of decisive importance took place, either in this or the two following years—for the war lasted till 369. The Goths, who had chosen as their leader Athanarich, skilfully avoided a pitched battle, and they withdrew into the fastnesses of the Transylvanian highlands.[1] In the end both sides were weary of the war and negotiations were set on foot, which resulted in a treaty of peace whereby the alliance with the Tervingi was formally annulled and the Danube was established as the boundary between the two powers.

Immediately after the war, which had restored the *status quo* of the beginning of the century,— and therewith the complete liberty of the Goths,[2] — the Romans set to work on a thorough restoration of the frontier defences. Numerous *burgi* (barrier-forts) were erected along the line of the Danube, as we learn in part from the evidence of inscriptions. Yet at first the frontier remained undisturbed. Internal dissensions and strife (chiefly due to a general persecution of the Christians stirred up by Athanarich about the year 370) withdrew his attention from external affairs. The Gothic prince shewed the utmost

---

[1] The statement of Ammianus (XXVII. 5. 6) that Athanarich nevertheless towards the close of the war finally offered battle and was beaten and put to flight, is open to grave doubt, since it is not obvious why the Gothic leader should suddenly abandon the strategic method which had hitherto served him so well; and, moreover, neither Zosimus (IV. 11) nor Themistius in his oration on the peace in 370 (*Or.* x.) makes any mention of a battle in which the Romans had been successful.

[2] As the well-known inscription of Hissarlik, *C.I.L.* III. 7494 (cf. Mommsen, *Hermes*, XVII. 1882, pp. 523 ff. = *Ges. Schriften*, vi. pp. 303 ff.) expressly emphasises: *(Valens)* ... [*in fidem recepto rege Athan]arico, victis superatisque Gothis* ··· [*hunc burgum] ad defensionem rei publicae extruxit.* ...

ferocity against all Christians, without distinction of high or low, Arian, Catholic, or Audian, with the avowed intention of extirpating Christianity as dangerous to the State and deleterious to the strength and vigour of the nation.

Probably in connexion with this, there arose (*c.* 370) a violent conflict between the two most influential chiefs, Athanarich and Fritigern, which finally led to an open schism between two portions of the race. Fritigern was worsted, retired with his whole following into Roman territory, and placed himself under the protection of the Emperor, who readily accorded him all possible succour and support. This step had an important result for the cause of the persecuted Christians, inasmuch as Fritigern with all his followers went over to Christianity and adopted the Arian creed. This conversion of Fritigern to Christianity, and, moreover, to Arian Christianity, powerfully influenced the further development of events, since, on the one hand, it prepared the way for the wider extension and final victory of Christianity among the Goths, and on the other hand it became a serious danger to the political existence of the nation when Arianism had been suppressed among the Romans, for it had acquired a virtually national significance for the Goths.

The sojourn of Fritigern in Roman territory was not of long duration. Confident in the support of the Roman government, he returned with his followers to his own country and succeeded in maintaining his position against Athanarich; there seems indeed to have been a reconciliation between the rivals. Alongside of them, though doubtless inferior to them in power and influence, a whole series of important chiefs are mentioned by name in this period, among them Alavio, Munderich, Eriwulf, and Fravitta. At the same time, however, Athanarich continued to exercise a certain primacy, although his position was not in any sense constitutionally defined — among the Romans he always bears the title of *judex* not *rex.*

The East Goths, of whom we have so long lost sight, had in the meantime extended their dominions far and wide. A mighty empire extending from the Don to the Dniester, from the Black Sea to the marshes of the Pripet and the head-waters of the Dnieper and the Volga, had emerged from their continual wars of conquest against their neighbours, Germanic (such as the Heruli), Slavonic, and Finnish. The main portion of these conquests is doubtless to be ascribed to King Ermanarich, who had ruled over the Greutungi since the middle of the century. In contrast with the West Goths who, as we have seen, down to the end of their residence on the Danube, were ruled according to ancient Germanic custom by *principes* or local chiefs, the East Goths had early developed a monarchy embracing the whole nation. It is doubtless to the inner strength which belongs to a firm and undivided exercise of authority, that we are to attribute the rapid rise of the young Ostrogothic State under its kings from Ostrogotha to Ermanarich, a monarch under whose vigorous rule it enjoyed its period of greatest prosperity __ and also met its fall.

Such was the state of affairs when a nation of untamed savages, horrible in aspect and terrible from their countless numbers and ferocious courage, broke forth from the interior of Asia and threatened the whole of the West with destruction. These were the Huns. They were doubtless of Mongolian race, and were probably natives of the great expanse of steppes which lies to the north and east of the Caspian Sea. Soon after 370 they penetrated into Europe, and threw themselves with irresistible fury upon the peoples which came in their way. The Alani, who had to bear the first brunt of their attack, were soon overpowered, and com_ pelled to join their conquerors, and the same fate befell the smaller peoples whose settlements lay further north, on the right bank of the Volga.

The fate of the Ostrogothic Empire was now imminent. For a con_ siderable time they succeeded in holding the enemy at the sword's point, but finally their strength broke down before the weight of the Asiatic hordes. Ermanarich himself died by his own hand rather than live to see the downfall of his kingdom; his successor, Withimir, after several bloody defeats, met his death on the field of battle. All resistance ceased, and the whole people surrendered itself to the Huns.

The invading flood rolled westward to encounter the Tervingi (375). At the first tidings of the events in the neighbouring country, Athanarich called his people to arms and marched with a part of his forces to meet the Huns. The Gothic leader took his stand on the bank of the Dniester; but finding himself compelled to abandon this position by a crafty turning-movement of the enemy, Athanarich gave up thenceforward all thought of resistance in the field, and betook himself to the impenetrable ravines of the Transylvanian highlands. But only some of the Goths followed him thither. The mass of the people, weary of hardship and privation, separated themselves and resolved to abandon their country. Under the leadership of their local chiefs Alavio and Fritigern they mustered their forces in the spring of 376 on the north bank of the Danube and besought permission to enter the Roman Empire, in the hope of finding a dwelling-place in the rich plains of Thrace. The Emperor Valens graciously received their request and gave orders to the commanders on the frontier to take measures for the shelter and provisioning of this huge mass of people. The Goths passed the river. In boats, and rafts, and hollowed tree-trunks they made their way across and covered all the country round "like the rain of ashes from an eruption of Etna." At first all went well. The new-comers maintained an exemplary attitude: not so the Roman officials — the chief of whom was the Thracian *comes* Lupicinus. They used the precarious position of the barbarians to their own profit, taking advantage of them in every

CH. VII.

possible way. It was not long before their shameless injustice aroused the deep resentment of the Teutons, among whom famine had already set in.

Things soon came to open rupture. In the immediate neighbourhood of Marcianople a bloody battle was fought between the infuriated Teutons and the soldiers of Lupicinus. The Romans were almost annihilated, their leader took refuge behind the strong walls of the town, which was immediately invested by the main body of the Tervingian forces. Other divisions scattered over the plains, plundering as they went. All attempts of the barbarians failed to take the town by storm. So Fritigern "made his peace with stone walls." A strong force remained before the place as an army of observation, while the main body turned, as detachments of it had done before, to the plundering of the adjoining districts of Moesia. Once more the country suffered fearfully, and to complete its misery other bands of plunderers now joined the Goths. Taifali, Alani, and even Huns were drawn across the Danube by the hope of plundering and ravaging these fertile provinces. This was in the summer of 377.

Troops were hurried up from all sides for the defence of the threatened provinces; even Gratian sent aid from the West. Meanwhile the Goths had overrun all Moesia. Not only had the bloody battle fought at a place called Salices (late summer 377) been indecisive and cost the Romans heavy losses, but a strong detachment of Roman troops under the tribune Barzimeres, a Teuton by race, had been cut to pieces at Dibaltus. A success which the *dux* Frigeridus, likewise of Teutonic birth, gained over the Taifali and a company of the Greutungi under their chief Farnobius was not much to balance this and did not alter the fact that Thrace, which after the battle of Salices had been overrun by the Teutons, remained a prey to them.

Finally (30 May 378) Valens arrived at Constantinople. As soon as Fritigern, who lay in the neighbourhood of Hadrianople, heard of the Emperor's arrival, he gave the order for the widely scattered Gothic forces to unite. From this point onward events followed in quick succession. At first the fortune of war seemed to smile upon the Romans. Making Hadrianople his base, Sebastianus, the commander of reinforcements sent by Gratian, succeeded in inflicting a reverse upon the Goths. Fritigern thereupon retired to the neighbourhood of Cabyle and there concentrated his forces. Thereupon Valens, on his part, advanced to Hadrianople, resolved to venture upon a decisive stroke. He had set his heart upon meeting his nephew Gratian, who was hastening up from the West, with the news of a great victory. And so (9 Aug. 378) battle was joined near Hadrianople. It resulted in a terrible defeat of the Romans, in which the Emperor himself was slain. More than two-thirds of his army, the flower of the military forces of the East, was left upon the field of battle.

It was in truth a second Cannae. The Empire rocked to its foundations. Sheer panic fell upon all that bore the name of Rome. The power and glory of the Empire seemed stamped into the dust by the barbarian hordes. The struggle between Rome and the Teutons which we have followed through five centuries was drawing to a close. The battle of Hadrianople introduces the last act of the great drama, the most pregnant with consequences which the history of the world has ever seen.

CHAPTER VIII

THE DYNASTY OF VALENTINIAN AND
THEODOSIUS THE GREAT

THE imperial throne was once more vacant (16–17 February 364), but the army had learned the danger of a tumultuous election, and after the troops had advanced by an eight days' march to Nicaea, both the civil and military authorities weighed with anxious deliberation the rival claims of possible candidates. Aequitius, tribune of• the first regiment of the *scutarii*, men knew to be harsh and uncultured, Januarius, a relative of Jovian in supreme command in Illyricum, was too far distant, and at length one and all agreed to offer the diadem to Valentinian. The new Emperor had not marched from Ancyra with the army, but had received orders to follow in due course with his regiment, the second *schola* of *scutarii*; thus, while messengers hastened his journey, the Roman world was for ten days without a master. Valentinian was a native of Pannonia; his father Gratian, a peasant rope-seller of Cibalae, had early distinguished himself by his strength and bravery. Risen from the ranks he had become successively *protector*, tribune, and general of the Roman forces in Africa; accused of peculation, he remained for a time under a cloud, only to be given later the command of the legions of Britain. After his retirement, hospitality shewn to Magnentius led to the confiscation of Gratian's property by Constantius, but the services of the father made advancement easy for Valentinian. In Gaul, however, when acting under Julian's orders he was dismissed from the army by Barbatio, but on Julian's accession he re-enlisted. Valentinian's military capacity outweighed even in the eyes of an apostate emperor his pronounced Christianity, and an important command was given him in the Persian War. Later he had been sent on a mission to the West, bearing the news of Jovian's election, and from this journey he had but recently returned. The life story of Gratian and Valentinian is one of the most striking examples of the splendid career which lay open to talent in the Roman army. The father, a peasant unknown and without influence, by his ability rises to supreme command over Britain, while his son becomes Emperor of Rome. It is

218

hardly surprising that barbarians were ready to enter a service which offered to the capable soldier such prospects of promotion. It may also be noticed in passing that in the council at Nicaea only military officers were considered as successors of Jovian: we do not hear of any civil administrator as a possible candidate for the vacant throne.

From the very day of his accession the character of Valentinian was declared. When the crowd bade him name at once a co-Augustus, he replied that but an hour before they had possessed the right to command, but that right now belonged to the Emperor of their own creation. From the first the stern glance and majestic bearing of Valentinian bowed men to his will. Through Nicomedia he advanced to Constantinople, and here in the suburb of the Hebdomon on 28 March 364 he created his brother Valens co-Emperor; he looked for loyal subjection and personal dependence, and he was not disappointed; with the rank of Augustus, Valens was content in effect to play the part of a Caesar. At Naissus the military forces of the Empire were divided, and many Pannonians were raised to high office. The new rulers were, however, careful to retain in their posts men who had been chosen both by Julian and Jovian; they wished to injure no susceptibilities by open partisanship. But even though Valentinian remained true to his constant principle of religious toleration and refused to favour the nominees either of a Christian or a Pagan Emperor, yet men traced a secret distrust and covert jealousy of those who had been Julian's intimates; Sallust, the all-powerful praefect, was removed, and accusations were brought against the philosopher Maximus. When both Emperors were attacked with fever, a commission of high imperial officials was appointed to examine whether the disease might not be due to secret arts. No shred of evidence of any unholy design was discovered, but the common rumour ran that the only object of the inquiry was to bring into disrepute the memory and the friends of Julian. Those who had been loyal to the old dynasty began to seek a leader.

At Sirmium the brothers parted, Valentinian for Milan, Valens for Constantinople; they each entered on their first consulship in the following year (365), and as soon as the winter was past Valens travelled with all speed for Syria; it would seem that already the terms of the Thirty Years' Peace were giving rise to fresh difficulties; too many questions remained open between Rome and Persia.

But as yet it was not foreign invasion but domestic rebellion which was to endanger the life and throne of Valens. When Procopius had laid the corpse of Julian to rest in Tarsus, he himself discreetly vanished from the sight of kings and courtiers: it was a perilous distinction to have enjoyed the peculiar favour of the dead Emperor.[1] Before long however he grew weary of his fugitive existence: life as a hunted exile in the Crimea was too dearly bought. In desperation he sailed secretly

[1] Cf. p. 85.

CH. VIII.

for the capital where he found shelter in the friendly house of a senator Strategius, while a eunuch, Eugenius by name, recently dismissed from the imperial service, put unlimited funds at his disposal. As he wandered unrecognised through the streets, on every hand he heard men muttering of the cruelty and avarice of Petronius, the father-in-law of Valens. The Emperor himself was no longer in Constantinople, and popular discontent seemed only to need its champion. The regiments of the Divitenses and the Tungritani Juniores, on their march from Bithynia for the defence of Thrace, were at the moment in the city. For two days Procopius negotiated with their officers; his gold and promises won their allegiance and in their quarters at the Anastasian Baths the soldiers met under cover of night and swore to support the usurpation. "Leaving the inkpot and stool of the notary," so ran the scornful phrase of the Court rhetorician, this stage figure of an emperor, hesitating to the last, assumed the purple and with stammering tongue harangued his followers. Any sensation was grateful to the populace, and they were content to accept without enthusiasm their new ruler. Those who had nothing to lose were ready enough to share the spoils, but the upper classes generally held aloof or fled to the Court of Valens; none of them met Procopius as he entered the deserted senate house. He relied for support upon men's devotion to the family of Constantine; as reinforcements bound for Thrace reached the capital, he came before them with Faustina, the widow of Constantius, by his side, while he himself bore her little daughter in his arms. He pleaded his own kinship to Julian and the troops were won. Gumoarius and Agilo who had served Constantius well were recalled from retirement and put at the head of the army, while to Julian's friend Phronemius was given the charge of the capital. Valentinian had advanced Pannonians, Procopius chose Gauls, for the Gallic provinces had most reason to remember Julian's services to the Empire. Nebridius, recently created praetorian praefect through the influence of Petronius, was held a prisoner and forced to write despatches recalling Julius who was in command in Thrace; the stratagem succeeded and the province was won without a blow. The embassy to Illyricum, however, bearing the newly minted coinage of Procopius, was defeated by the vigilance of Aequitius, every approach, whether through Dacia, Macedonia, or the pass of Succi, being effectually barred.

The news of the revolt reached Valens as he was leaving Bithynia for Antioch, and he was only recalled from abject despair by the counsels of his friends. Procopius with the Divitenses and a hastily collected force had advanced to Nicaea, but before the approach of the Jovii and Victores he retreated to Mygdus on the Sangarius. Once more the soldiers yielded when he appealed to their loyalty to the house of Constantine: the troops of Valens deserting "the degenerate Pannonian," "the drinker of miserable barley beer," went over to the usurper. One success followed another: Nicomedia was surprised by the tribune Rumitalca, who forth_ with marched to the north; Valens who was besieging Chalcedon was taken unawares and forced to fly for his life to Ancyra. Thus Bithynia was won for Procopius. His fleet under Marcellus attacked Cyzicus and when once the chain across the harbour's mouth was broken the garrison surrendered. With the fall of Cyzicus, Valens had lost the mastery of the Hellespont, while he could expect no help from his brother, since Valentinian had determined that the safety of the whole Roman Empire demanded his presence on the western frontier. Thus during the early months of 366, while Procopius endeavoured to raise funds for the future conduct of the war, Valens could only await the arrival of Lupicinus. The Emperor's final victory was indeed mainly due to an ill-considered act of his rival. Arbitio, the retired general of Constantius, had supported the usurper, but had declined an invitation to his court, pleading the infirmities of old age and ill-health. Procopius replied by an order that the general's house should be pillaged, thereby turning a friend into a bitter foe. Arbitio on the appeal of Valens joined the camp of Lupicinus; his arrival at once inspired the Emperor with fresh hope and courage, and gave the signal for wholesale defections from the usurper's forces. In an engagement at Thyatira, Gumoarius procured his own capture and carried with him many of his men. After the march of Valens into Phrygia, Agilo in his turn deserted when the armies met at Nacolia. The soldiers refused to continue the struggle (26 May 366). Procopius was betrayed to the Emperor by two of his own officers and was immediately put to death. Imperial suspicion and persecution had once again goaded a loyal subject to treason and to ruin. His severed head was borne beneath the walls of Philippopolis, and the city surrendered to Aequitius. The ghastly trophy was even carried to Valentinian through the provinces of Gaul, lest loyalty to the memory of Julian should awake treason in the West. Valens could now avenge his terror and sate his avarice. The suppression of the rebellion was followed by a train of executions, burnings, proscriptions, and banishments which caused men to curse the victory of the lawful Emperor.

The plea of kinship with the family of Constantine had induced some thousands of the Gothic tribesmen on the Danube to cross the Roman frontier in support of Procopius. Valens refused to recognise their defence, and depriving them of their weapons settled them in the cities along the northern boundaries of the Empire. When discontent declared itself, in fear of a general attack he acted on his brother's advice, and marched in person to the Danube, and for the three succeeding years (367–369) the Gothic campaign absorbed his attention. With Marci⁻ anople as his base of operations, he crossed the river in 367 and 369; in the latter year he conquered Athanarich, and during the autumn concluded an advantageous peace. The Emperor and the Gothic *judex*

CH. VIII.

met on a ship in mid-stream, for Athanarich professed himself bound by
a fearful oath never to set foot upon Roman soil.   During these years
Valens, pursuing in the East his brother's policy, strengthened the whole
of the Danube frontier line with forts and garrisons.

Valentinian may indeed be styled the frontier Emperor; his title to
fame is his restoration of the defences of Rome in the West against the
surging barbarian hordes.   He was a hard-worked soldier prince, and
the one purpose which inspires his reign is his fixed determination never
to yield an inch of Roman territory.   He had always before his eyes the
terrible warning of his predecessor.   In the year 364, when the Emperor
was still at Milan, ambassadors from the Alemanni came to greet him on
his accession, and to receive the tribute which Roman pride disguised
under the fairer name of gifts.   Valentinian would not squander state
funds in bounty to barbarians; the presents were small, while Ursatius,
the *magister officiorum*, who took his cue from his master, treated the
messengers with scant courtesy.   They returned indignant to their homes,
and in the early days of the new year, A.D. 365, the Alemanni burst
plundering and ravaging across the frontier.   Charietto, the count
commanding in both Germanies, and the aged general Servianus,
stationed at Cabillona (Châlons-sur-Saône), both fell before the
barbarian onset.   Gaul demanded Valentinian's presence; the Emperor
started for Paris in the month of October; and while on the march,
news reached him of the revolt of Procopius.   The report gave no details —
he did not know whether Valens were alive or dead.   But with that strong
sense of imperial duty which dignifies the characters of the fourth
century emperors, he subordinated utterly the personal interest to the
common weal: "Procopius is but my brother's enemy and my own," he
repeated to himself; "the Alemanni are the foes of the Roman world."

Arrived at Paris, it was from that city that he despatched Dagalaiphus
against the Alemanni.   Autumn was fast giving place to winter, the
tribesmen had scattered, and the new general was dilatory and inactive;
he was recalled to become consul with the Emperor's son Gratian
(Jan. 366) and Jovinus, as *magister equitum*, took his place at the
head of the Roman troops.   Three successive victories virtually concluded
the campaign; at Scarponna (Charpeigne) one band of barbarians was
surprised and defeated, while another was massacred on the Moselle.   In
negligent security the Alemanni on the river bank were drinking,
washing, and dyeing their hair red, when from the fringe of the forest
the Roman legionaries poured down upon them.   Jovinus then undertook a further march and pitched his camp at Châlons-sur-Marne; here
there was a desperate engagement with a third force of the enemy.   The
withdrawal during the battle of the tribune Balchobaudes seriously
endangered the army's safety, but at length the day was won.   The
Alemanni lost six thousand killed and four thousand wounded; of the
Romans two hundred were wounded and twelve hundred killed; in

the pursuit Ascarii in the Roman service captured the barbarian king, and in the heat of the moment he was struck dead. After a few lesser encounters resistance was for the time at an end. It was probably his interest in this campaign which had led Valentinian to spend the early months of 366 at Rheims. He now returned to Paris and from the latter city advanced (end of June 366 ?) to meet his successful general, whom he nominated for the consulship in the succeeding year. At the same time the head of Procopius reached him from the East. But in the high tide of success he was struck down with a serious illness (winter 366–7). The Court was already considering possible candidates for the purple when Valentinian recovered, but, realising the dangers for the West which might arise from a disputed succession, at Amiens on 24 August 367 he procured from the troops the recognition of the seven year old Gratian as co-Augustus. It may well have been the necessity for defending the northern coast against raids of Franks and Saxons which had summoned Valentinian to Amiens; and now on his way from that town to Trier tidings reached him of a serious revolt in Britain. Fullofaudes, the Roman general, together with Nectaridus, the commander of the coast line (count of the Saxon shore ?), had both met their deaths. In the autumn of 367 Severus, count of the imperial guards, was despatched to the island only to be recalled. Jovinus, appointed in his place, sent Provertides in advance to raise levies, while in view of the constant reports of fresh disasters the Count Theodosius (the father of Theodosius the Great) was ordered to sail for Britain at the head of Gallic reinforcements. From Boulogne he landed at Rutupiae (Richborough: spring 368) and was followed by the Batavi, Heruli, Jovii, and Victores. Scenes of hopeless confusion met him on his arrival; Dicalydones and Verturiones (the two divisions of the Picts), Attacotti and Scotti (Irish) all ranged pillaging over the countryside, while Frank and Saxon marauders swept down in forays on the coast. Theodosius marched towards London, and it would seem made this city his head-quarters. Defeating the scattered troops of spoil-laden barbarians, he restored the greater part of the booty to the harassed provincials, while deserters were recalled to the standard by promises of pardon. From London, where he spent the winter, Theodosius prayed the Emperor to appoint men of wide experience to govern the island—Civilis as pro-praefect and Dulcitius as general; in this year too, he probably co-operated with imperial troops on the continent in the suppression of Frank and Saxon pirates in the Low Countries and about the mouths of the Rhine and Waal. Valentinian himself advanced as far north as Cologne in the autumn of 368. In the year 369 Theodosius everywhere surprised the barbarians and swept the country clear of their robber bands. Town-fortifications were restored, forts rebuilt, and frontiers regarrisoned, while the Areani, a treacherous border militia, were removed. Territory in the north was recovered, and a new fifth province of Valentia or Valentinia created. The revolt of Valentinus,

CH. VIII.

who had been exiled to Britain on a criminal charge, was easily crushed
by Theodosius, who repressed with a strong hand the treason trials which
usually followed the defeat of an unsuccessful usurper.   When he sailed
for Gaul, probably in the spring of 370, he left the provincials "leaping
for very joy."   On his return to the Court he was appointed to succeed
Jovinus as *magister equitum* (before end of May 370).

While his lieutenant had been restoring order in Britain, Valentinian
had been actively engaged in Gaul.   The winter of 367-8 the Emperor
spent at Rheims preparing for his vengeance upon the disturbers of the
peace in the West.   But the new year opened with a disaster, for while
the Christian inhabitants of Mainz were keeping festival (Epiphany ? 368)
the Aleman prince Rando surprised and sacked the town.   The Romans,
however, gained a treacherous advantage by the murder of King Withicab,
and in the summer of the same year the Emperor together with his son invaded the territory between Neckar and Rhine.   Our authorities give us
no certain information as to his route, perhaps he advanced by the Rhine
road and then turned off by Ettlingen and Pforzheim.   Solicinium (near
Rottenburg on the left bank of the Neckar) was the scene of the decisive
struggle.   The barbarians occupied a strong position on a precipitous
hill; the Romans experienced great difficulty in dislodging them but
were at length successful, and the enemy fled over the Neckar by
Lopodunum towards the Danube.   The advantage thus gained was
secured by the building of a strong fort, apparently at Altrip, and for its
erection it seems possible that the ruins of Lopodunum were employed.
The Emperor spent the winter in Trier, and with the new year (369)
began his great work of frontier defence extending from the province of
Rhaetia to the ocean.   Valentinian even sought to plant his fortresses
in the enemy's territory.   This was regarded by the Alemanni as a breach
of treaty rights, and the Romans suffered a serious reverse at the Mons
Piri (Heidelberg ?).   The Emperor accordingly entered into negotiations
with the Burgundians, who were to attack the Alemanni with the support
of the Roman troops.   The Burgundians, long at feud with their neighbours over the possession of some salt springs on their borders, gladly
accepted the Emperor's overtures and appeared in immense force on the
Rhine: the confederate seemed more terrible than the foe.   Valentinian
was absent superintending the building of his new forts, and feared either
to accept or refuse the assistance of such dangerous allies.   He sought to
gain time by inaction, and the Burgundians, infuriated at this betrayal,
were forced to withdraw, since the Alemanni threatened to oppose their
homeward march.   Meanwhile Theodosius, newly arrived in Gaul from
Britain, swept upon the distracted Alemanni from Rhaetia, and after a
successful campaign was able to settle his captives as farmers in the valley
of the Po.   Macrian, king of the Alemanni, had been the heart and soul
of his people's resistance to Rome; with the intention therefore of
capturing this dangerous enemy by a sudden surprise, in September 371

Valentinian accompanied by Theodosius left Mainz for Aquae Mattiacae, but with the troops the opportunities for pillage outweighed the Emperor's strictest orders. The smoke of burning homesteads betrayed the Roman approach; the army advanced some fifty miles, but the purpose of the expedition was defeated and the Emperor returned disappointed to Trier.

Meanwhile in the East time only served to shew the futility of Jovian's peace with Persia. Rome had sacrificed much but had settled nothing. Sapor claimed that under the treaty he could do as he would with Armenia, which still remained the apple of discord as before, and that Rome had relinquished any right to interfere. But it was precisely this claim that Rome could never in the last resort allow — Armenia under Persian rule was far too great a menace. The chronology of the events which followed the treaty must remain to some extent a matter of conjecture, but from the first Sapor seems to have enforced his conception of his rights, seeking in turn by bribes and forays to reduce Armenia to Persian vassalage. Valens as early as 365 was on his way to the Persian frontier when he was recalled by the revolt of Procopius. At the close of the year 368, or at the beginning of 369, Sapor got possession of King Arsaces, whom he put to death some years later. In 369, it would appear, Persia interfered in the affairs of Hiberia: Sauromaces, ruling under Roman protection, was expelled, and Aspacures, a Persian nominee, was made king. In Armenia the fortress of Artagherk (Artogerassa) where the queen Pharrantsem had taken refuge was besieged (369), while her son Pap, acting on his mother's counsel, fled to the protection of Valens; in his flight he was assisted by Cylaces and Artabannes, Armenian renegades, who now proved disloyal to their Persian master. The exile was well received, and accorded a home at Neocaesarea. But when Mushegh, the Armenian general, prayed that the Emperor would take effective action and stay the ravages of Persia, Valens hesitated: he felt that his hands were tied by the terms of the peace of Jovian. Terentius, the Roman *dux*, accompanied Pap on his return to Armenia, but without the support of the legions the prince was powerless. Artagherk fell in the fourteenth month of the siege (winter 370), Pharrantsem was hurried away to her death, and Pap was forced to flee into the mountains which lay between Lazica and the Roman frontier. Here he remained in hiding for five months; Persian pillage and massacre proceeded unchecked, until Sapor could leave his generals in command of the army, while two Armenian nobles were entrusted with the civil government of the country and with the introduction of the Magian religion. At length Valens took action, and the Count Arinthaeus, acting in concert with Terentius and Addaeus, was sent to Armenia to place Pap upon the throne and to prevent the commission of further outrage by Persia. In May 371 the Emperor himself left Constantinople, slowly journeying towards Syria. Sapor's next move was an attempt to win Pap by promises of alliance, counseling him to be no longer the puppet of his ministers; the ruse was successful and the king put to death both Cylaces and Artabannes. Meanwhile a Persian embassy complained that the protection of Armenia by Rome was a breach of her obligations under the treaty. In April 372 Valens reached Antioch. His answer to Persia was further interference in Hiberia. While Muschegh invaded Persian territory, Terentius with twelve legions restored Sauromaces as ruler over the country bordering on Lazica and Armenia, Sapor on his side making great preparations for a campaign in the following spring, raising levies from the surrounding tribes and hiring mercenaries. In 373 Trajan and Vadomar marched to the East with a formidable army, having strict orders not to break the peace but to act on the defensive. The Emperor himself moved to Hierapolis in order to superintend the operations from that city. At Vagobanta (Bagavan) the Romans were forced to engage and in the result were victorious. A truce was concluded at the end of the summer, and while Sapor retired to Ctesiphon, Valens took up his residence in Antioch.

Here in the following year 374, so far as we can judge from the vague chronology of our authorities, a widespread conspiracy was discovered in which Maximus, Julian's master, Eutropius the historian, and many other leading philosophers and heathens were implicated. Anxious to discover who was to succeed Valens, some daring spirits had suspended a ring over a consecrated table upon which was placed a round metal dish; about the rim of the dish was engraved the alphabet. The ring had spelt out the letters THEO — when with one voice all present exclaimed that Theodorus was clearly destined for empire. Born in Gaul of an old and honourable family, he had enjoyed a liberal education and already held the second place among the imperial notaries; distinguished for his humanity and moderation, in every post alike his merits outshone his office. Absent from Antioch at the time, he was at once recalled, and the enthusiasm of his friends seems to have shaken his loyalty. The life of Valens had previously been threatened by would-be assassins, and when the conspirators' secret was betrayed the Emperor's vengeance knew no bounds; he swept the whole of the Roman East for victims and, as at the fall of Procopius, so now his avarice ruled unchecked. If the accused's life was spared, proscription in bitter mockery posed as clemency and the banishment of the innocent as an act of royal grace. For years the trials continued: "We all crept about as though in Cimmerian darkness," writes an eyewitness, "the sword of Damocles hung suspended over our heads."

Of Western affairs during those years when the long drawn game of plot and counterplot was being played between Valens and Sapor we know but little. Valentinian remained in Gaul (autumn 371 — spring 373), doubtless busied with his schemes for the maintenance of security upon the frontiers, but detailed information we have none. Where Valentinian governed in person we hear of no rebellions: the constitu-tions even shew that a limited relief was granted from taxation and that measures were taken to check oppression, but elsewhere on every hand the Emperor's good intentions were betrayed by his agents. In Britain a disorganised army and a harassed population could offer no effective resistance to the invader: gross misgovernment in the Pannonian provinces made it doubtful whether the excesses of imperial offices or the forays of the barbarian enemy were more to be dreaded, while the story of the woes of Africa only serves to shew how terrible was the cost which the Empire paid for its unscrupulous bureaucracy. Under Jovian (363–4) the Austoriani had suddenly invaded the province of Tripolis, intending to avenge the death of one of their tribesmen who had been burned alive for plotting against the Roman power. They laid waste the rich countryside around Leptis, and when the city appealed for help to the commander-in-chief, Count Romanus, he refused to take any action unless supplied with a vast store of provisions and four thousand camels. The demand could not be met, and after forty days the general departed, while the despairing provincials at the regular annual assembly of their city council elected an embassy to carry statues of victory to Valentinian and to greet him upon his accession. At Milan (364–5) the ambassadors gave (as it would seem) a full report of the sufferings of Leptis, but Remigius, the *magister officiorum*, a relative and confederate of Romanus, was forewarned and contradicted their assertions, while he was successful in securing the appointment of Romanus upon the commission of inquiry which was ordered by the Emperor. The military command was given for a time to the governor Ruricius, but was shortly after once more put into the hands of Romanus. It was not long before news of a fresh invasion of Tripolis by the barbarians reached Valentinian in Gaul (A.D. 365). The African army had not yet received the customary donative upon the Emperor's accession; Palladius was accordingly entrusted with gold to distribute amongst the troops, and was instructed to hold a complete and searching inquiry into the affairs of the province. Meanwhile for the third time the desert clansmen had spread rapine and outrage through Roman territory, and for eight days had·laid formal siege to the city of Leptis itself. A second embassy consisting of Jovinus and Pancratius was sent to the Emperor who was found at Trier (winter 367). On the arrival of Palladius in Africa, Romanus induced the officers to relinquish their share of the donative and to restore it to the imperial commissioner, as a mark of their personal respect. The inquiry then proceeded; much evidence was taken and the complaints against Romanus proved up to the hilt; the report for the Emperor was already prepared when the Count threatened, if it were not withdrawn, to disclose the personal profit of Palladius in the matter of the donative. The commissioner yielded

CH. VIII.

and went over to the side of Romanus; on his return to the Court he found nothing to criticise in the administration of the province. Pancratius had died at Trier but Jovinus was sent back to Africa with Palladius, the latter being directed to hold a further examination as to the truth of the allegations made by the second embassy. Men who on the shewing of the Emperor's representative had given false witness on the inquiry were to have their tongues cut from their mouths. By threats, trickery, and bribes Romanus once more achieved his end. The citizens of Leptis denied that they had ever given any authority to Jovinus to act on their behalf, while he, endeavouring to save his life, was forced to confess himself a liar. It was to no purpose: together with Ruricius the governor and others he was put to death by order of the Emperor (369 ?).

Not even this sacrifice of innocent lives gave peace to Africa. Firmus, a Moorish prince, on the death of his father Nebul, had slain his brother; that brother however had enjoyed the favour of Romanus, and the machinations of the Roman general drove Firmus into rebellion. He assumed the purple, while persecuted Donatists and exasperated soldiers and provincials gladly rallied round him. Theodosius, fresh from his successes in Britain and Gaul, was despatched to Africa by Valentinian as commander-in-chief, charged with the task of reasserting imperial authority. On examining his predecessor's papers, a chance reference caused the discovery of the plots of the last eight years, but it was not till the reign of Gratian that the subsequent inquiries were concluded. Palladius and Remigius both committed suicide, but the arch-offender Romanus was protected by the influence of Merobaudes. The whole story needs no comment: before men's eyes the powerlessness of the Emperor and the might of organised corruption stood luridly revealed.

For at least two years Theodosius fought and struggled against odds in Africa; at length discipline was restored amongst the troops, the Moors were defeated with great loss, and the usurper driven to take his own life: the Roman commander entered Sitifis in triumph (374 ?). Hardly however was his master Valentinian removed by death when Theodosius fell a victim to the intrigues of his enemies (at Carthage, A.D. 375-6); baptised at the last hour and thus cleansed of all sin, he walked calmly to the block. We do not know the ostensible charge upon which he was beheaded, nor do our authorities name his accuser. But the evidence points to Merobaudes, the all-powerful minister of Gratian. Theodosius had superseded Romanus and disclosed his schemes, and Romanus was the friend and *protégé* of Merobaudes, while it is clear that Gratian held in his own hands the entire West including Africa, for as yet (376) the youthful Valentinian II was not permitted to exercise any independent authority.[1] Possibly Merobaudes may have

[1] Rauschen, *Jahrbücher*, p. 23.

been assisted in the attainment of his ends by timely representations from the East, for the general's name began with the same letters which had only recently (374 ?) proved fatal to Theodorus.

In 373 Valentinian had left Gaul for Milan, but returned in the following year (May 374), and after a raid upon the Alemanni, while at the fortress of Robur near Basel, he learned in late autumn that the Quadi and Sarmatae had burst across the frontier. The Emperor with his passion for fortress-building had given orders for a garrison station to be erected on the left bank of the Danube within the territory of the Quadi, while at the same time the youthful Marcellianus through the influence of his father Maximinus, the ill-famed praefect of Illyricum,[1] had succeeded the able general Aequitius as *magister armorum.* Gabinius, king of the Quadi, came to the Roman camp to pray that this violation of his rights might cease. The newly appointed general treacherously murdered his guest, and at the news the barbarians flew to arms, poured across the Danube upon the unsuspecting farmers, and all but captured the daughter of Constantius who was on her journey to meet Gratian her future husband. Sarmatae and Quadi devastated Moesia and Pannonia, the praetorian praefect Probus was stupefied into inactivity, and the Roman legionaries at feud between themselves were routed in confusion. The only successful resistance was offered by the younger Theodosius — the future Emperor — who compelled one of the invading Sarmatian hosts to sue for peace. Valentinian desired to march eastward forthwith, but was dissuaded by those who urged the hardships of a winter campaign and the danger of leaving Gaul while the leader of the Alemanni was still unsubdued. Both Romans and barbarians were, however, alike weary of the ceaseless struggle, and during the winter Valentinian and Macrian concluded an enduring peace. In the late spring of 375 the Emperor left Gaul; from June to August he was at Carnuntum, endeavouring to restore order within the devastated province, and thence marched to Acincum, crossed the Danube, and wasted the territory of the invading tribesmen. Autumn surprised him while still in the field: he retired to Sabaria and took up his winter quarters at Bregetio. The Quadi, conscious of the hopelessness of further resistance, sent an embassy excusing their action and pleading that the Romans were in truth the aggressors. The Emperor, passionately enraged at this freedom of speech, was seized in the paroxysm of his anger with an apoplectic fit and carried dying from the audience hall (17 November 375).

High-complexioned, with a strong and muscular body cast in a noble and majestic mould, his steel-blue eyes scanning men and things with a gaze of sinister intensity, the Emperor stands before us as an imposing and stately figure. Yet his stern and forbidding nature awakes but little sympathy, and it is easy to do less than justice to the character and

---

[1] For his cruelty when acting as praefect of Rome, cf. Ammianus, XXVIII. 1. 5.

work of Valentinian. With a strong hand Diocletian had endeavoured by his administrative system and by the enforcement of hereditary duties to weld together the Roman Empire which had been shattered by the successive catastrophes of the third century; to Valentinian it seemed as though the same iron constraint could alone check the process of dissolution. If it were possible, he would make life for the provincials worth the living, for then resistance to the invader would be the more resolute: he would protect them with forts and garrisons upon their frontiers, would lighten (if he dare) the weight of taxation, would accord them liberty of conscience and freedom for their varied faiths, and would to the best of his power appoint honest and capable men as his representatives: but a spirit of dissatisfaction and discontent among his subjects was not merely disloyalty, it was a menace to the Empire, for it tended to weaken the solidarity of governors and governed: to remove an official for abusing his trust was in Valentinian's eyes to prejudice men's respect for the State, and thus the strain of brutality in his nature declared itself in his refusal to check stern measures or pitiless administration: to save the Roman world from disintegration it must be cowed into unity. Without mercy to others he never spared himself; as a restless and untiring leader with no mean gifts of generalship and strategy it was but natural that he should give preferment to his officers, till contemporaries bitterly complained that never before had civilians been thus neglected or the army so highly privileged. It could indeed hardly be otherwise, for with every frontier threatened it was the military captain who was indispensable. The Emperor's efforts to suppress abuses were untiring; simplicity characterised his Court and strict economy was practised. His laws in the Theodosian Code are a standing witness to his passion for reform. He regulated the corn supply and the transport of the grain by sea, he made less burdensome the collection of the taxes levied in kind on the provincials, he exerted himself to protect the curials and the members of municipal senates, he settled barbarians as colonists on lands which were passing out of cultivation, he endeavoured to put a stop to the debasement of the coinage, while in the administration of justice he attempted to check the misuse of wealth and favour by insisting upon publicity of trial and by granting greater facilities for appeals. As a contemporary observes, Valentinian's one sore need was honest agents and upright administrators, and these he could not secure: men only sought for power in order to abuse it. Had the Emperor been served by more men of the stamp of Theodosius, the respect of posterity might have given place to admiration. Even as it was, in later days when men praised Theodoric they compared him with two great Emperors of the past, with Trajan — and Valentinian.

At the time of the Emperor's death, Gratian was far distant at Trier, and there was a general fear that the fickle Gallic troops now encamped on the left bank of the Danube might claim to raise to the throne some candidate whom they themselves had chosen, perhaps Sebastianus — a man by nature inactive but high in the favour of the army. Merobaudes, the general in command, was therefore recalled as though by order of Valentinian on a pretext of fresh disturbances upon the Rhine, and after prolonged consultation it was decided to summon the late Emperor's four year old son Valentinian. The boy's uncle covered post-haste the hundred Roman miles which lay between Bregetio and the country house of Murocincta, where the young prince was living with his mother Justina. Valentinian was carried back to the camp in a litter, and six days after his father's death was solemnly proclaimed Augustus. Gratian's kindly nature soon dispelled any fear that he would refuse to recognise this hurried election: the elder brother always shewed towards the younger a father's care and affection. No partition of the West however took place at this time, and there could as yet be no question of the exercise of independent power by Valentinian II; Gratian ruled over all those provinces which had been subject to Valentinian I, and his infant colleague's name is not even mentioned in the constitutions before the year 379. Of the government of Gratian however we know but little; its importance lies mainly in the fact that he was determined to be first and foremost an orthodox Christian Emperor, and even refused to wear the robe or assume the title of Pontifex Maximus (probably 375).

Meanwhile in the East the fidelity of Pap grew suspect in the eyes of Rome. The unfavourable despatches of Terentius, the murder of the Katholikos Nerses, and the consecration of his successor by the king without the customary appeal to Caesarea (Mazaca) led Valens to invite Pap to Tarsus, where he remained virtually a prisoner. Escaping to his own country he fell a victim to Roman treachery (375 ?). Still Rome and Persia negotiated, and at length (376) Valens despatched Victor and Arbicius with an ultimatum; the Emperor demanded that the fortresses which of right belonged to Sauromaces should be evacuated by the beginning of 377. The claims of Rome were ignored, and Valens was planning at Hierapolis (July — August 377) a great campaign against Persia when the news from Europe made it imperative to withdraw the Roman army of occupation from Armenia. For several years the European crisis engaged all the Emperor's energies, and he was unable to interfere effectually in Eastern affairs. The Huns had burst into Europe, had conquered the Alans, subjected the East Goths (Ostrogoths) and driven the West Goths (Visigoths) to crave admission within the territory of Rome. Athanarich and Fritigern had become leaders of two distinct parties among the West Goths; Athanarich, driven before the Huns, had lost much of his wealth, and, as he was unable to support his followers, the greater number deserted their aged leader and joined Fritigern. It seems possible too that religious differences may have

CH. VIII.

played their part in these dissensions: Athanarich may have stood at the head of those who were loyal to the old religion, Fritigern may have been willing to secure any advantage which the profession of the Christian faith might win from a devout Emperor. Whether this be so or not, it was the tribesmen of Fritigern who appealed to Valens. It was no unusual request: the settling of barbarians as colonists on Roman soil was of frequent occurrence, while the provision of barbarian recruits for the Roman army was a constant clause in the treaties of the fourth century. Valens and his ministers congratulated themselves that, without their seeking, so admirable an opportunity had presented itself of infusing new life and vigour into the northern provinces of the Empire. The conditions for the reception of the Goths were that they should give up their arms and surrender many of their sons as hostages. The church historians add the stipulation that the Goths should adopt the Christian faith, but this would seem to have been only a pious hope and not a condition for the passage of the Danube, although it was only natural that the Goths should affect to have assumed the religion of their new fellow-countrymen. The conditions were stern enough, but the fate which threatened the barbarians at the hands of the Huns seemed even more unrelenting. The Goths accepted the terms: but for the Romans the enforcement of their own requisitions was a work which demanded extraordinary tact and unremitting forethought.

In face of this immense and sobering responsibility, which should have summoned forth all the energy and loyalty of which men were capable, the ministers of Valens (so far as we can see) did nothing — they left to chance alone the feeding of a multitude which none could number. It is not in their everyday peculations, nor in their habitual violence and oppression of the provincials, that the degradation of the bureaucracy of the Empire is seen in its most hideous form : the weightiest count in the indictment is that when met by an extraordinary crisis which imperilled the existence of the Empire itself the agents of the State, with the danger in concrete form before their very eyes, failed to check their lust or bridle their avarice. Maximinus and Lupicinus kept the Goths upon the banks of the Danube in order to wring from them all they had to give — except their arms. Provisions failed utterly : for the body of a dog a man would be bartered into slavery. As for the Goths who remained north of the river, Athanarich, remembering that he had declined to meet Valens on Roman soil, thought it idle to pray for admission within the Empire and retired, it would seem, into the highlands of Transylvania; now however that the imperial garrisons had been withdrawn to watch the passage of the followers of Fritigern, the Greutungi under Alatheus and Saphrax crossed the Danube unmolested, although leave to cross the frontier had previously been refused them. Meanwhile Fritigern slowly advanced on Marcianople, ready if need be to join his compatriots who were now encamped on the south bank of the river. Still the Goths took no hostile step, but their exclusion from Marcianople led to a brawl with Roman soldiers out. side the walls; within the city the news reached Lupicinus who was entertaining Alavio and Fritigern to a feast. Orders were hurriedly given for the massacre of the Gothic guardsmen who had accompanied their leaders. Fritigern at the head of his men fought his way back to camp, while Alavio seems to have fallen in the fray, for we hear of him no more.

The peace was at an end: nine miles from Marcianople Lupicinus was repulsed with loss; the criminal folly of the authorities of Hadria. nople forced into rebellion the loyal Gothic auxiliaries who were stationed in the town; barbarians bartered as slaves rejoined their comrades, while labourers from the imperial gold mines played their part in spreading havoc throughout Thrace. Thus at last the Goths took their revenge, and only the walls of cities could resist their onset. From Asia Valens despatched Profuturus and Trajan to the province, and they at length succeeded in driving back the barbarian host beyond the Balkans. The Roman army occupied the passes. Gratian had sent reinforcements from the West under Frigeridus and Richomer, and the latter was associated with the generals of Valens; the barbarians drawing together their scattered bands formed a huge wagon laager (*carrago*) at a spot called Ad Salices, not far from Tomi. The Romans were still much inferior in numbers, and anxiously awaited an opportunity to pour down upon the enemy while on the march. For some time however the Goths made no move; when at length they attempted to seize the higher ground the battle began. The Roman left wing was broken and the legionaries were forced to retreat, but neither side gained any decisive advantage: the Goths remained for seven days longer within the shelter of their camp while the Romans drove other troops of barbarians to the north of the mountain chain (early autumn 377). At this time Richomer returned in order to secure further help from Gratian, while Saturninus arrived from Asia with the rank of *magister equitum*, in command, it would seem, of reinforcements. But the tide of fortune which had favoured the Romans during the previous months now ebbed. The Goths, despairing of breaking the cordon or piercing the Balkan passes, by promises of unlimited booty won over hordes of Huns and Alans to their side. Saturninus found that he could hold his position no longer, and was thus forced to retire on the Rhodope chain. Save for a defeat at Dibaltus near the sea-coast he successfully masked his retreat, while Frigeridus, who was stationed in the neighbourhood of Beroea, fell back before the enemy upon Illyricum, where he captured the barbarian leader Farnobius and defeated the Taifali; as in Valentinian's day the captives were settled in the depopulated districts of Italy. The help however which was expected from the West was long delayed; in February 378 the Lentienses chanced to hear from one of their fellow-tribesmen who

CH. VIII.

was serving in the Roman army that Gratian had been summoned to the East. Collecting allies from the neighbouring clans, they burst across the border some 40,000 strong (panegyrists said 70,000). Gratian was forced to recall the troops who had already marched into Pannonia, and in command of these as well as of his Gallic legionaries he placed Nannienus and the Frankish king Mallobaudes. At the battle of Argentaria, near Colmar in Alsace, Priarius the barbarian king was slain and with him, it is said, more than 30,000 of the enemy : according to the Roman estimate only some 5000 escaped through the dense forests into the shelter of the hills. Gratian in person then crossed the Rhine and after laborious operations among the mountains starved the fugitives into surrender ; by the terms of peace they were bound to furnish recruits for the Roman army. The result of the campaign was a very real triumph for the youthful Emperor of the West.

Meanwhile Sebastian, appointed in the East to succeed Trajan in the command of the infantry, was raising and training a small force of picked men with which to begin operations in the spring. In April 378 Valens left Antioch for the capital at the head of reinforcements drawn from Asia : he arrived on 30 May. The Goths now held the Schipka Pass and were stationed both north and south of the Balkans at Nicopolis and Beroea. Sebastian had successfully freed the country round Hadrianople from plundering bands, and Fritigern concentrating the Gothic forces had withdrawn north to Cabyle. At the end of June Valens advanced with his army from Melanthias, which lay some 15 miles west of Constantinople. Against the advice of Sebastian the Emperor determined upon an immediate march in order to effect a junction with the forces of his nephew, who was now advancing by Lauriacum and Sirmium. The eastern army entered the Maritza Pass, but at the same time Fritigern would seem to have despatched some Goths southwards. These were sighted by the Roman scouts, and in fear that the passes should be blocked behind him and his supplies cut off, the Emperor retreated towards Hadrianople. Fritigern himself meanwhile marched south over the pass of Bujuk-Derbent in the direction of Nike, as though he would intercept communication between Valens and his capital. Two alternative courses were now open to the Emperor : he might take up a strong position at Hadrianople and await the army of the West (this was Gratian's counsel brought by Richomer who reached the camp on 7 August), or he might at once engage the enemy. Valens adopted the latter alternative ; it would seem that he under-estimated the number of the Goths, and it is possible that he desired to shew that he too could win victories in his own strength as well as the western Emperor ; Sebastian, who had at his own request left the service of Gratian for that of Valens, may have sought to rob his former master of any further laurels. At dawn on the following morning (9 August) the advance began ; when about midday the armies came in sight of

each other (probably near the modern Demeranlija) Fritigern, in order
to gain time, entered into negotiations, but on the arrival of his cavalry
he felt sure of victory and struck the first blow. We cannot reconstruct
the battle: Valens, Trajan, and Sebastian all fell, and with them two-
thirds of the Roman army. In the open country no resistance could be
offered to the victorious barbarians, but they were beaten back from the
walls of Hadrianople, and a troop of Saracen horsemen repelled them
from the capital. Victor bore the news of the appalling catastrophe
to Gratian.

In the face of hostile criticism Valentinian had chosen Valens as his
co-Augustus, intending that he should carry out in the East the same
policy which he himself had planned for the West. His judgment was
not at fault, for in the sphere of religion alone did the two Emperors
pursue different ends. Like an orderly, with unfailing loyalty Valens
obeyed his brother's instructions. He too strengthened the frontier
with fortresses and lightened the burden of taxation, while under
his care magnificent public buildings rose throughout the eastern
provinces. But Valentinian's masterful decision of character was alien
to Valens: his was a weaker nature which under adversity easily yielded
to despair. Severity, anxiously assumed, tended towards ferocity, and
a consciousness of insecurity rendered him tyrannical when his life or
throne was threatened. His subjects could neither forget nor forgive
the horrible excesses which marked the suppression of the rebellion of
Procopius or of the conspiracy of Theodorus. He was hated by the
orthodox as an Arian heretic and by the Pagans as a Christian zealot,
while it was upon the Emperor that men laid the responsibility for the
overwhelming disaster of Hadrianople. Thus there were few to judge
him with impartial justice, and it is probable that even later historians
have been unduly influenced by the invectives of his enemies. His
imperious brother had made of an excellent civil servant an Emperor
who was no match for the crisis which he was fated to meet.

On the news of the defeat at Hadrianople Gratian at once turned
to the general who had shewn such brilliant promise a few years before
in the defence of Moesia. The young Theodosius was recalled from his
retirement in Spain and put in command of the Roman troops in
Thrace. Here, it would appear, he was victorious over the Sarmatians,
and at Sirmium in the month of January 379 (probably 19 January 379)
Gratian created him co-Augustus. It was only after long hesitation
that Theodosius accepted the heavy task of restoring order in the
eastern provinces, but the decision once taken there was no delay.
Before the Emperors parted company their joint forces seem to have
defeated the Goths; Gratian then relinquished some of his troops in
favour of Theodosius and himself started with all speed for Gaul, where
Franks and Vandals had crossed the Rhine. After defeating the
invaders Gratian went into winter quarters at Trier. Theodosius was

left to rule the Eastern praefecture, while it must perhaps remain a doubtful question whether eastern Illyricum was not also included within his jurisdiction.

The course of events which led up to the final subjection of the Gothic invaders by Theodosius is for us a lost chapter in the story of East Rome. Some few disconnected fragments can, it is true, be recovered, but their setting is too often conjectural.   Many have been the attempts to unravel the confused tangle of incidents which Zosimus offers in the place of an ordered history, but however the ingenuity of critics may amaze us, it rarely convinces.   Even so bald a statement as that of the following paragraphs is, it must be confessed, in large measure but a hypothetical reconstruction.

A pestilence had broken out among the barbarians besieging Thessalonica, and plague and famine drove them from the walls.   The city could therefore be occupied without difficulty by Theodosius, who chose it for his base of operations.   Its natural position made it an admirable centre: from it led the high roads towards the north to the Danube and towards the east to Constantinople.   Its splendid harbour offered shelter to merchant ships from Asia and Egypt, and thus the army's stores and provisions could not be intercepted by the Goths; while from this point military operations could be undertaken alike in Thrace and in Illyricum.   The first task to which Theodosius directed his commanding energy was the restoration of discipline among his disorganised troops; no longer did the Emperor hold himself aloof — an unapproachable being hedged about with awe and majesty: the conception which had since Diocletian become a court tradition gave place to the liberality and friendliness of a captain in the midst of his men. Early in June Theodosius reached Thessalonica, and despatched Modares, a barbarian of royal blood, to sweep the Goths from Thrace.   Falling upon the unsuspecting foe, the Romans massacred a host of marauders laden with the booty of the provinces.   The legionaries recovered confidence in themselves, and the main body of the invaders was driven northwards.   The Emperor himself, with Thessalonica secured and garrisoned, marched north towards the Danube to Scupi (Uskub: 6 July 379) and Vicus Augusti (2 August).   From the first he was determined to win the victory, if it were possible, rather by conciliation than armed force.   It would seem probable that even in the year 379 he was enrolling Goths among his troops and converting bands of pillagers into Roman subjects. But in his winter quarters at Thessalonica the Emperor was struck down by disease, and for long his life hung in the balance (February 380). He prepared himself for his end by baptism — the magical sacrament which obliterated all sin and was therefore postponed till the hour when life itself was ebbing.   Military action was paralysed, and the fruits of the previous year's campaign were lost.   The Goths took fresh courage; Fritigern led one host into

Thessaly, Epirus, and Achaia, another under Alatheus and Saphrax devastated Pannonia, while Nicopolis was lost to the Romans. Gratian hastened perforce to the help of his disabled colleague; Bauto and Arbogast were despatched to check the Goths in the north, and in the summer Gratian himself marched to Sirmium, where he concluded a truce with the barbarians under which the Romans were to supply pro_ visions, while the Goths furnished recruits for the army. It is probable that Gratian and Theodosius met in conference at Sirmium in September. The danger in the south was averted by the death of Fritigern; without a leader the Gothic host turned once more northwards. In the autumn Theodosius was back in Thessalonica, and in November he entered Constantinople in triumph. This fact of itself must signify that the immediate peril was past.

Fortune now favoured Theodosius: Fritigern his most formidable opponent was dead, and, at length, the pride of the aged Athanarich was broken. Wearied out by feuds among his own people he, together with his followers, sought refuge amongst his foes. On 11 January 381 he was welcomed beyond the city walls by Theodosius and escorted with all solemnity and kingly pomp into the capital. Fourteen days later he died, and was buried by the Emperor with royal honours. The magnanimity of Theodosius and the respect paid to their great chieftain did more than many military successes to subdue the stubborn Gothic tribesmen. We hear of no more battles, and in the following year peace was concluded. Saturninus was empowered to offer the Goths new homes in the devastated districts of Thrace, and the victors of Hadrianople became the allies of the Empire,[1] pledged in the event of war to furnish soldiers for the imperial army. Themistius, the Court orator, could express the hope that when once the wounds of strife were healed Rome's bravest enemies would become her truest and most loyal friends.

Peace was hardly won in the East before usurpation and murder threw the West into turmoil. In the early years of the reign of Gratian Christian and Pagan alike had been captivated by the grace and charm of their youthful ruler. His military success against the Lentienses, his heroic efforts to bring help to the East in her darkest hour and the loyal support which he had given to Theodosius only served to heighten his popularity. The orthodox found in him a fearless champion of their cause: the incomes of the vestal virgins were appropriated in part for the relief of the imperial treasury and in part for the purposes of the public post; in future the immemorial sisterhood was to hold no real property whatever. The altar and statue of Victory which Julian had restored to the senate house and which the tolerance of Valentinian had permitted to stand undisturbed were now ordered to be removed (382). Damasus, bishop of Rome, and Ambrose, bishop of Milan, claiming to represent a Christian majority in the senate, prevailed upon the Emperor

---

[1] The actual word *foederati* first occurs in a document of A.D. 406.

CH. VIII.

to refuse to receive an embassy, headed by Symmachus, of the leading Pagans in Rome, and the church was overjoyed at the uncompromising zeal of their Emperor. But the radiant hopes which men had formed of Gratian were not fulfilled; his private life remained blameless, and he was still liberal and humane, but affairs of state failed to interest him and he devoted his days to sport and exercise. His love for the chase became a passion, and he would take part in person in the wild-beast hunts of the amphitheatre. Emergencies which, in the words of a contemporary, would have taxed the statesmanship of a Marcus Aurelius were disregarded by the Emperor; he alienated Roman sentiment by his devotion to his German troops, and although he might court popularity amongst the soldiers by permitting them to lay aside breastplate and helm and to carry the *spiculum* in place of the weighty *pilum*, yet the favours shewn to the Alans outweighed all else and jealousy awoke disaffection amongst the legionaries. The malcontents were not long in finding a leader. Magnus Clemens Maximus, a Spaniard who claimed kinship with Theodosius and had served with him in Britain, won a victory over the Picts and Scots. In spite of his protests the Roman army in Britain hailed him as Augustus (early in 383?) and leaving the island defenceless he immediately crossed the Channel, determined to strike the first blow. From the mouth of the Rhine where he was welcomed by the troops Maximus marched to Paris, and here he met Gratian. For five days the armies skirmished, and then the Emperor's Moorish cavalry went over to the usurper in a body. Gratian saw his forces melting away, and at length with 300 horsemen fled headlong for the Alps; nowhere could he find a refuge, for the cities of Gaul closed their gates at his approach. The accounts of his death are varied and inconsistent, but it would seem that Andragathius was sent by Maximus hot-foot after the fugitive; at Lugdunum by a bridge over the Rhone Gratian was captured by means of a stratagem and was murdered within the city walls. Assured of his life by a solemn oath and thus lulled into a false security, he was treacherously stabbed by his host while sitting at a banquet (25 August 383). The murderer (who was perhaps Andragathius himself) was highly rewarded by Maximus.

Forthwith the usurper sent his chamberlain to Theodosius to claim recognition and alliance. The historian notices as a remarkable exception to the customs of the time that this official was not a eunuch, and further states that Maximus would have no eunuchs about his court. Theodosius had planned a campaign of vengeance for the death of the young ruler to whom he owed so much, but on the arrival of the embassy he temporised. It would be dangerous for him to leave the East: in Persia Ardaschir (379–383) had just died and the policy of the new monarch Sapor III (383–388) was quite unknown; troubles had arisen on the frontier: the nomad Saracens had broken their treaty of alliance with Rome, and Richomer had marched on a punitive expedition. Although the Goths

were now peacefully settled on Haemus and Hebrus and had begun to
cultivate their allotted lands, although it was once more safe to travel
by road and not only by sea, yet for many years the Scyri, the Carpi, and
the Huns broke ever and again across the boundaries of the Empire and
gave work to the generals of Theodosius; the newly won quiet and
order in Thrace might easily have been imperilled by the absence of
the Emperor. With the deliberate caution that always characterised
his action save when he was seized by some gust of passion, Theodosius
acknowledged his co-Augustus and ordered statues to be raised to him
throughout the East. Africa, Spain, Gaul, and Britain, it would seem,
acknowledged Maximus, while even in Egypt the mob of Alexandria
shouted for the western Emperor.

Meanwhile upon his brother's death Valentinian II began his personal
rule in Italy. For the next few years Ambrose and Justina fight a long-
drawn duel to decide whether mother or bishop shall frame the young
Emperor's policy : on Justina's death there remained no rival to challenge
the influence of Ambrose. The latter was indeed throughout Valentinian's
reign the power behind the throne; born probably in 340, the son of a
praetorian praefect of Gaul, he had been educated in Rome until in the
year 374 he was appointed *consularis* of Aemilia and Liguria. In this
capacity he was present at the election (autumn 374) of a new bishop
in Milan; while he was taking anxious precautions lest the contest
between Arian and orthodox should end in bloodshed, a child's cry (says
the legend) of "Bishop Ambrose !" suggested a candidate whom both
factions agreed to accept. The city would take no refusal : against his
will the statesman governor became the statesman bishop. Thus in the
winter of 383–4, although Valentinian looked to Theodosius for help
and counsel, Constantinople seemed to the Court at Milan to lie at
a hopeless distance, while Maximus in Gaul was perilously near. The
Emperor instinctively turned to Ambrose, his one powerful protector,
while even Arianism forgot its feud with orthodoxy. At Justina's
request the bishop started on an embassy to secure peace between Gaul
and Italy. Maximus, however, desired that Valentinian should leave
Milan and that together they should consider the terms of their agreement. Ambrose objected that it was winter : how in such weather
could a boy and his widowed mother cross the Alps ? His own authority
was only to treat for peace — he could promise nothing. Accordingly
Maximus sent his son Victor (shortly afterwards created Caesar) to
Valentinian to request his presence in Gaul. But the net had been
spread in the sight of the bird, and Victor returned from his mission
unsuccessful; when he arrived at Mogontiacum, Ambrose left for Milan
and met on the journey Valentinian's envoys bearing a formal reply
to the proposals of Maximus. If the bishop's diplomacy had achieved
nothing else, precious time had been gained, for Bauto had occupied the
Alpine passes and thus secured Italy from invasion.

CH. VIII.

In the year 384 the Pagan party in Rome had taken fresh heart; the Emperor had raised two of their number to high office — Symmachus had been made urban praefect and Praetextatus praetorian praefect. Men began to hope for a repeal of the hostile measures of Gratian, and a resolution of the senate empowered Symmachus to present to Valentinian their plea for toleration and in especial for the restoration of the altar of Victory. Gratian had thought (the praefect contended) that he was fulfilling the senate's own desires, but the Emperor had been misled; the senate, nay Rome herself, prayed to retain that honoured symbol of her greatness before which her sons for countless generations had pledged their faith. It was the loyalty to their past and to that Godhead before whom their ancestors had bowed that had made the Romans masters of the world and had filled their lands with increase. It was a high and noble argument, but it availed nothing before the scornful taunts of Ambrose, and Valentinian dismissed the ambassadors with a refusal.

At this time a Persian embassy arrived in Constantinople (384) announcing the accession of Sapor III (383–388), and bringing costly gifts for Theodosius — gems, silk, and even elephants — while in 385 the Emperor secured the submission of the revolted eastern tribes. In the following years the disputed question of predominance in Armenia was revived: Stilicho was sent to represent Rome at the Persian Court and in 387 a treaty between the two great powers was concluded, whereby Armenia was partitioned. Some districts were annexed by Rome and some by Persia, while two vassal kings were in future to govern the country, some four-fifths of which was to acknowledge the supremacy of Persia, and the remaining one-fifth the lordship of Rome. Modern historians have condemned Theodosius for his acceptance of these terms, but he needed peace on the eastern frontier if he were to march against his western rival, and his predecessors had all experienced the extreme difficulty of retaining the loyalty of Armenian kings: better a disadvantageous partition with security, he may have argued, than an independent State in secret alliance with the enemy. The Emperor was, in fact, forced to recognise the strength of Persia's position.[1] In the West Ambrose once more travelled to Gaul at Valentinian's request upon a diplomatic mission probably at the end of 385 or in 386.[2] He sought the consent of Maximus to the burial of Gratian's corpse in Italian soil, but permission was refused. Maximus was heard to regret that he had not invaded Italy on Gratian's death: Ambrose and Bauto, he muttered, had foiled

---

[1] It is thus highly improbable that Persia should have agreed to pay tribute to Rome: *ipse ille rex . . . etsi adhuc nomine foederatus, iam tamen tuis cultibus tributarius est* (Pacatus, c. 22 s.f.) are the words of a court orator addressing the Emperor in Rome when a Persian embassy announcing the accession of Bahram IV was in the city. If Persia had really agreed to the payment of tribute the language of the panegyric would have been less studiously vague.

[2] Cf. Rauschen, *Jahrbücher*, Appendix x. p. 487.

his schemes. When the bishop returned to Milan he was convinced
that the peace could not endure.

Indeed, events shewed the profound suspicion and mistrust which
underlay fair-seeming concord. Bauto was still holding the Alpine
passes when the Juthungi, a branch of the Alemanni, entered Rhaetia
to rob and plunder. Bauto desired that domestic pillage should recall
the tribesmen to their homes. And at his instigation the Huns and
Alans who were approaching Gaul were diverted and fell upon the
territory of the Alemanni. Maximus complained that hordes of
marauders were being brought to the confines of his territory, and
Valentinian was forced to purchase the retreat of his own allies.

Preparations for the coming struggle with Maximus absorbed the
attention of Theodosius in the East, and the exceptional expenditure
placed a severe strain upon his resources. In one and the same year,
it would seem (January 387), the Emperor celebrated his own decennalia
and the quinquennalia of his son Arcadius who had been created
Augustus in the year 383. On the occasion of this double festival
heavy sums in gold were needed for distribution as donatives among
the troops. In consequence, an extraordinary tax was laid upon the
city of Antioch, and the magnitude of the sum demanded reduced the
senators and leading citizens to despair. But with the inherited
resignation of the middle classes of the Roman Empire they yielded
to inexorable fate. Not so the populace: turbulent spirits with little
to lose and led by foreigners clamoured round the bishop Flavian's
house; in his absence, their numbers swollen by fresh recruits from the
city mob, they burst into the public baths intent on destruction, and
then overturning the statues of the imperial family dashed them to
pieces. One house was already in flames and a move had been made
towards the imperial palace when at length the authorities took action,
the governor (or *comes orientis*) interfered and the crowd was dispersed.

Immediately the citizens were seized with hopeless dismay as they
realised the horror of their crime. A courier was forthwith despatched
with the news to the Emperor, while the authorities, attempting to
atone by feverish violence for past neglect, began with indiscriminate
haste to condemn to death men, women, and even children: some were
burned alive and others were given to the beasts in the arena. The
glory of the East saw her streets deserted and men awaited in shuddering
terror the arrival of the imperial commissioners. While Chrysostom
in his Lenten homilies endeavoured to rouse his flock from their
anguish of dread, while Libanius strove to stay the citizens from
headlong flight, the aged Flavian braving the hardships of winter
journeyed to Constantinople to plead with Theodosius. On Monday
of the third week of the fast the commissioners arrived — Caesarius
magister officiorum and Hellebicus *magister militiae* — bearing with
them the Emperor's edict: baths, circus, and theatres were to be closed,

the public distribution of grain was to cease, and Antioch was to lose her proud position and be subjected to her rival Laodicea. On the following Wednesday the commission began its sittings; confessions were wrung from the accused by torture and scourgings, but to the unbounded relief of all no death sentences were passed, and judgment upon the guilty was left to the decision of Theodosius. Caesarius himself started with his report for the capital: sleepless and unresting, he covered the distance between Antioch and Constantinople in the incredibly short space of six days. The prayers of Flavian had calmed the Emperor's anger and the passionate appeal of Caesarius carried the day: already the principal offenders had paid the forfeit of their lives, the city in its agony of terror had drained its cup of suffering: let Theodosius have mercy and stay his hand! The news of a complete amnesty was borne hot-foot to Antioch, and to the joy of Easter were added the transports of a pardoned city.

At length in the West the formal peace was broken, and in 387 the army of Gaul invaded Italy. Of late Justina's influence had gained the upper hand in Milan, and the Arianism of Valentinian afforded a laudable pretext for the action of Maximus; he came as the champion of oppressed orthodoxy — previous warnings had produced no effect on the heretical Court; it must be chastened by the scourge of God. It would seem that Valentinian's opposition to Ambrose had for the time alienated the bishop, and the Emperor no longer chose him as his ambassador. Domninus sought to strengthen good relations between Trier and Milan, and asked that help should be given in the task of driving back the barbarians who threatened Pannonia. The cunning of Maximus seized the favourable moment; he detached a part of his own army with orders to march to the support of Valentinian. He himself however at the head of his troops followed close behind, and was thus able to force the passes of the Cottian Alps unopposed. This treacherous attack upon Valentinian was marked by the murder of Merobaudes, the minister who had carried through the hasty election at Bregetio (autumn 387). From Milan Justina and her son fled to Aquileia, from Aquileia to Thessalonica, where they were joined by Theodosius, who had recently married Galla, the sister of Valentinian II. Here it would seem that the Emperor of the East received an embassy from Maximus, the latter doubtless claiming that he had only acted in the interests of the Creed of Nicaea, of which his co-Augustus was so staunch a champion. The action of Theodosius was characteristic; he gave no definite reply, while he endeavoured to convert the fugitive Emperor to orthodoxy. The whole winter through he made his preparations for the war which he could no longer honourably escape. Goths, Huns, and Alans readily enlisted; Pacatus tells us that from the Nile to the Caucasus, from the Taurus range to the Danube, men streamed to his standards. Promotus, who had recently annihilated a host of Greutungi under Odothaeus upon the Danube (386), commanded the cavalry and Timasius the infantry; among the officers were Richomer and Arbogast. In June Theodosius with Valentinian marched towards the West; he could look for no support from Italy, for Rome had fallen into the hands of Maximus during the preceding January, and the usurper's fleet was cruising in the Adriatic. Theodosius reached Stobi on June 14 and Scupi (Uskub) on June 21. It would seem that emissaries of Maximus had spread disaffection among the Germans in the eastern army, but a plot to murder Theodosius was disclosed in time and the traitors were cut down in the swamps to which they had fled for refuge. The Emperor advanced to Siscia on the Save; here, despite their inferiority in numbers, his troops swam the river and charged and routed the enemy. It is probable that in this engagement Andragathius, the foremost general on the side of Maximus, met his death. Theodosius won a second victory at Poetovio, where the western forces under the command of the usurper's brother Marcellinus fled in wild disorder. Many joined the victorious army, and Aemona (Laibach), which had stubbornly withstood a long siege, welcomed Theodosius within its walls. Maximus retreated into Italy and encamped around Aquileia. But he was allowed no opportunity to collect fresh forces wherewith to renew the struggle. Theodosius followed hard on the fugitive's track. Maximus with the courage of despair fell upon his pursuers, but was driven back into Aquileia and forced to surrender. Three miles from the city walls the captive was brought into the Emperor's presence. The soldiers anticipated the victor's pity and hurried Maximus off to his death (probably 28 July 388). Only a few of his partisans, among them his Moorish guards, shared their leader's fate. His fleet was defeated off Sicily, and Victor who had been left as Augustus in Gaul was slain by Arbogast. A general pardon quieted unrest in Italy, and Theodosius remained in Milan during the winter. Valentinian was restored to power, and with the death of his mother Justina his conversion to orthodoxy was completed.

Maximus had fallen, and for a court orator his character possessed no redeeming feature. But from less prejudiced authorities we seem to gain a picture of a man whose only fault was his enforced disloyalty to Theodosius, and of an Emperor who shewed himself a vigorous and upright ruler, and who could plead as excuse for his avarice the pressure of long-threatened war with his co-Augustus. From these exactions which were perhaps unavoidable Gaul suffered severely, and on his departure from the West, while Nannienus and Quintinus were acting as joint *magistri militum*, the Franks burst across the Rhine under Genobaudes, Marcomir, and Sunno and threatened Cologne. After a Roman victory at the Silva Carvonaria (near Tournai?) Quintinus invaded barbarian territory from Novaesium, but the campaign was a disastrous failure. On the fall of Victor Arbogast remained, under the

vague title of *Comes* or Count, the virtual ruler of Gaul, while Carietto
and Syrus succeeded as *magistri militum* the nominees of Maximus.
Arbogast on his arrival counselled a punitive expedition, but it would
seem that Theodosius did not accept the advice. A peace was concluded,
Marcomir and Sunno gave hostages, and Arbogast himself retired to
winter quarters in Trier.

Valentinian remained with Theodosius in Milan during the winter
of 388–9 and was with him on 13 June 389 when he made his solemn
entry into Rome, accompanied by his five year old son Honorius. On
this, apparently his only visit to the western capital he anxiously
endeavoured to weaken the power and influence of Paganism, while he
effected reforms both in the social and municipal life of the city. To
the stern and haughty Diocletian the familiarity of the populace had
been insufferable: Theodosius was liberal with his gifts, attended the
public games, and won all hearts by his ready courtesy and genial
humanity. In the autumn of 389 he returned to Milan, and there he
remained during 390 — that memorable year in which Church and State
met as opposing powers and a righteous victory lay with the Church.
In fact, he who would write of affairs of state during the last years of the
fourth century must ever go borrowing from the church historians; he
dare not at his peril omit the figure of the counsellor of Emperor after
Emperor, the fearless, tyrannous, passionate, and loving bishop of Milan.
Though the conduct of Ambrose may at times be arbitrary and repellent,
the critic in his own despite admits perforce that he was a man worthy
of a sovereign's trust and confidence. The facts of the massacre of
Thessalonica are well known. Popular discontent had been aroused
by the billeting upon the inhabitants of barbarian troops, and resentment sought its opportunity. Botherich, captain of the garrison,
imprisoned a favourite charioteer for gross immorality and refused to
free him at the demand of the citizens. The mob seized the occasion:
disappointed of its pleasure, it murdered Botherich with savage brutality.
The anger of Theodosius was ungovernable, and the repeated prayers
of Ambrose for mercy were of no avail. The court circle had long
been jealous of the bishop's influence and had endeavoured to exclude
him from any interference with state policy. Ambrose knew well that
he no longer enjoyed the full confidence of the Emperor. Theodosius
listened to his ministers who urged an exemplary punishment, and the
order was issued for a ruthless vengeance upon Thessalonica. The
message cancelling the imperial command arrived too late to save the
city. The Emperor had decreed retribution and his officers gave rein
to their passions. Upon the people crowded in the circus the soldiers
poured and an indiscriminate slaughter ensued; at least 7000 victims
fell before the troops stayed their hand. Ambrose, pleading illness,
withdrew from Milan and refused to meet Theodosius. With his own
hand he wrote a private letter to the Emperor, acknowledging his zeal

and love for God, but claiming that for such a crime of headlong passion there must be profound contrition: as David listened to Nathan, so let Theodosius hear God's minister; until repentance he dare not offer the sacrifice in the Emperor's presence. The letter is the appeal of undaunted courage to the essential nobility of the character of Theodosius. The gusts of fury passed and remorse issued in penitence. With his subjects around him in the Cathedral of Milan the Emperor, stripped of his royal purple, bowed himself in humility before the offended majesty of Heaven. Men have sought to heighten the victory of the Church and fables have clustered round the story, but the dignity of fact in its simplicity is far more splendid than the ornate fancies of any legend. Bishop and Emperor had proved each worthy of the other.

In 391 Theodosius returned to Constantinople by way of Thessalonica and Valentinian was left to rule the West. He did not reach Gaul till the autumn of 391; it was too late. Three years of undisputed power had left Arbogast without a rival in Gaul. It was not the troops alone who looked to their unconquered captain with blind admiration and unquestioning devotion: he was surrounded by a circle of Frankish fellow-countrymen who owed to him their promotion, while his honourable character, his generosity, and the sheer force of his personality had brought even the civil authorities to his side. There was one law in Gaul, and that was the will of Arbogast, there was only one superior whom Arbogast acknowledged, and he was the Emperor Theodosius who had given the West into his charge. From the first Valentinian's authority was flouted: his legislative power was allowed to rust unused, his orders were disobeyed and his palace became his prison: not even the imperial purple could protect Harmonius, who was slain by Arbogast's orders at the Emperor's very feet. Valentinian implored support from Theodosius and contemplated seeking refuge in the East; he solemnly handed the haughty Count his dismissal, but Arbogast tore the paper in pieces with the retort that he would only receive his discharge from the Emperor who had appointed him. A letter was despatched by Valentinian urging Ambrose to come to him with all speed to administer the sacrament of baptism; clearly he thought his life was threatened. He hailed the pretext of barbarian disturbances about the Alpine passes and himself prepared to leave for Italy, but mortification and pride kept him still in Vienne. The Pagan party considered that at length the influence of Arbogast might procure for them the restoration of the altar of Victory, but the disciple of Ambrose refused the ambassador's request. A few days later it was known that Valentinian had been strangled. Contemporaries could not determine whether he had met his death by violence or by his own hand (15 May 392). Ambrose seems to have accepted the latter alternative, and the guilt of Arbogast was never proven; with the longed-for rite of baptism so near at hand suicide certainly appears improbable, but perhaps the strain and stress of those days of waiting broke down the Emperor's endurance, and the mockery of his position became too bitter for a son of Valentinian I. His death, it must be admitted, did not find Arbogast unprepared. He could not declare himself Emperor, for Christian hatred, Roman pride, and Frankish jealousy barred the way; thus he became the first of a long line of barbarian king-makers: he overcame the reluctance of Eugenius and placed him on the throne.

The first sovereign to be at once the nominee and puppet of a barbarian general was a man of good family; formerly a teacher of rhetoric and later a high-placed secretary in the imperial service, the friend of Richomer and Symmachus and a peace-loving civilian — he would not endanger Arbogast's authority. Himself a Christian, although an associate of the Pagan aristocrats in Rome, he was unwilling to alienate the sympathies of either party, and adopted an attitude of impartial tolerance; he hoped to find safety in half measures. Rome saw a feverish revival of the old faith with strange processions of oriental deities, while Flavianus, a leading pagan, was made praetorian praefect. The altar of Victory was restored, but Eugenius sought to respect Christian prejudices, and the temples did not recover their confiscated revenues; these were granted as a personal gift to the petitioners. But in the fourth century none save minorities would hear of toleration, and men drew the inference that he who was no partisan was little better than a traitor. The orthodox Church in the person of Ambrose withdrew from Eugenius as from an apostate. The new Emperor naturally recognised Theodosius and Arcadius as co-Augusti, but in all the transactions between the western Court and Constantinople the person of Arbogast was discreetly veiled; his name was not suggested for the consulship, and it was no Frankish soldier who headed the embassy to Theodosius: the wisdom of Athens in the person of Rufinus and the purity of Christian bishops attested the king-maker's innocence, but the ambiguous reply of Theodosius hardly disguised his real intentions. The nomination of Eugenius was, it would seem, disregarded in the East, while in West and East alike diplomacy was but a means for gaining time before the inevitable arbitrament of war. To secure Gaul during his absence Arbogast determined to impress the barbarians with a wholesome dread of the power of Rome; in a winter campaign he devastated the territories of Bructeri and Chamavi, while Alemanni and Franks were forced to accept terms of peace whereby they agreed to furnish recruits for the Roman armies. Thus freed from anxiety in the West, Arbogast and Eugenius left with large reinforcements for Italy, where it seems that the new Emperor had been acknowledged from the time of his accession (spring 393 ?). In the following year Theodosius marched from Constantinople (end of May 394); Honorius, who had been created Augustus in January 393, was left behind with Arcadius in the capital. The Emperor appointed Timasius as general-in-chief with Stilicho for his subordinate; immense preparations had been made for the campaign— of the Goths alone some 20,000 under the leadership of Saul, Gaïnas, and Bacurius had been enlisted in the army. Arbogast, either through the claim of kinship or as virtual ruler of the West, could bring into the field large forces of both Franks and Gauls, but he was outnumbered by the troops of ʻTheodosius. Eugenius did not leave Milan till 1 August. Flavianus, as augur, declared that victory was assured; he had himself undertaken the defence of the passes of the Julian Alps, where he placed gilded statues of Jupiter to declare his devotion to Paganism. Theodosius overcame all resistance with ease and Flavianus, discouraged and ashamed, committed suicide. At about an equal distance between Aemona and Aquileia, on the stream of the Frigidus (Wipbach), the decisive battle took place. The Western army was encamped in the plain, awaiting the descent of Theodosius from the heights; Arbogast had posted Arbitio in ambush with orders to fall upon the unsuspecting troops as they left the higher ground. The Goths led the van and were the first to engage the enemy. Despite their heroic valour, the attack was unsuccessful; Bacurius was slain and 10,000 Goths lost their lives. Eugenius, as he rewarded his soldiers, considered the victory decisive, and the generals of Theodosius counselled retreat. Through the hours of the night the Emperor prayed alone and in the morning (6 September) with the battle-cry of "Where is the God of Theodosius?" he renewed the struggle. Arbitio played the traitor's part and leaving his hiding-place joined the Eastern army. But it was no human aid which decided the issue of the day. A tempestuous hurricane swept down upon the enemy: blinded by clouds of dust, their shields wrenched from their grasp, their missiles carried back upon themselves, the troops of Eugenius turned in panic flight. Theodosius had called on God, and Heaven had answered. The moral effect was overwhelming. Eugenius was surrendered by his own soldiers and slain; Arbogast fled into the mountains and two days later fell by his own hand.

Theodosius did not abuse his victory; he granted a general pardon — even the usurper's ministers lost only their rank and titles, which were restored to them in the following year. But the fatigues and hardships of the war had broken down the Emperor's health; Honorius was summoned from Constantinople and was present in Milan at his father's death (17 January 395).

From the invective of heathen critics and the flattery of court orators it is no easy task rightly to estimate the character and work of Theodosius. To the Christians he was naturally ʻfirst and foremost the founder of an orthodox State and the scourge of heretics and pagans, while to the worshippers of the older faith it was precisely his religious views and the legislation inspired by them which inflamed their furious resentment. The judgment of both parties on the Emperor's policy

¹ as a whole was determined by their religious preconceptions. Rome at least was his debtor; in the darkest hour after the disaster at Hadrianople he had not despaired of the Empire, but had proved himself at once statesman and general. The Goths might have become to the provinces of the East what the Alemanni had long been to Gaul; the fact that it was otherwise was primarily due to the diplomacy of Theodosius. Retrenchment and economy, a breathing space in which to recover from her utter exhaustion, were a necessity for the Roman world; a brilliant and meteoric sovereign would have been but an added peril. To the men of his time the unwearying caution of Theodosius was a positive and precious virtue. His throne was supported by no hereditary dynastic sentiment, and he thus consciously and deliberately made a bid for public favour; he abandoned court tradition and appealed with the directness of a soldier to the sympathies of his subjects. In this he was justified: throughout his reign it was only in the West that usurpers arose, and even they would have been content to remain his colleagues, had he only consented. But this was not the only result of his refusal to play the demigod; Valentinian had often been perforce the tool of his ministers, but Theodosius determined to gather his own information and to see for himself the abuses from which the Empire suffered. His legislation is essentially detailed and practical: the accused must not be haled off forthwith on information laid against him, but must be given thirty days to put his house in order; provision is to be made for the children of the criminal, whether he be banished or executed, for they are not to suffer for their father's sins, and some share of the convict's property is to pass to his issue; men are not to be ruined by any compulsion to undertake high-priestly offices, as that of the high-priesthood of the province of Syria which entailed the holding of costly public games; provincials should not be driven to sell corn to the State below its market price, while corn from sea-coast lands is to be shipped to neighbouring sea-coast towns and not to distant inland districts, in order that the cost of transport may not ruin the farmer. Fixed measures in metal and stone must be used by imperial tax collectors, that extortion may be made more difficult, while *defensores* are to be appointed to see to it that through the connivance of the authorities robbers and highwaymen shall not escape unpunished. Theodosius himself had superintended the work of clearing Macedonia from troops of brigands, and he directed that men were to be permitted to take the law into their own hands if robbed on the high-roads or in the villages by night, and might slay the offender where he stood. Examples might be increased at will, but such laws as these suffice to illustrate the point. In a word, Theodosius knew where the shoe pinched, and he did what he could to ease the pain. Even when claims of Church and State conflicted, he refused to sacrifice justice to the demands of orthodox intolerance; in one case the tyrannous insistence

of Ambrose conquered, and Christian monks who had at Callinicum destroyed a Jewish synagogue were at last freed from the duty of making reparation; but even here the stubborn resistance of the Emperor shews the general principles which governed his administration. Though naturally merciful, so that contemporaries wondered at his clemency towards the followers of defeated rivals, yet when seized by some sudden outburst of passion he could be terrible in his ferocity. He himself was conscious of his great failing, and when his anger had passed, men knew that he was the readier to pardon: *Praerogativa ignoscendi erat indignatum fuisse.* But with every acknowledgment made of his weaknesses he served the Empire well; he brought the East from chaos into order; and even if it be on other grounds, posterity can hardly dispute the judgment of the Church or deny that the Emperor has been rightly styled "Theodosius the Great."

CHAPTER IX

THE TEUTONIC MIGRATIONS, 378–412

THE enormous force of the onrush made by the Huns upon the Ostrogoths had been decisive for the fate of the Visigoths also. A considerable part of Athanarich's army under their leaders Alavio and Fritigern had asked for and obtained from the Emperor Valens in the year 376 land for settlements on the right bank of the Danube. From that time these Goths were *foederati* of the Empire, and as such were obliged to render armed assistance and supply recruits. A demand for land made by bands of Ostrogoths under Alatheus and Saphrax was refused; nevertheless these bold Teutons effected the crossing of the river and followed their kinsmen. Quarrels between Romans and Goths led to Fritigern's victory of Marcianople, which opened the way to the Goths as far as Hadrianople. They were pushed back indeed into the Dobrudscha by Valens' army, and the troops under Richomer sent from the West by Gratian to assist the Eastern Empire were able to join the Eastern forces. After this however the success of arms remained changeable, especially when a section of Huns and Alani had joined the Goths. Thrace was left exposed to the enemy's raids, which extended as far as Macedonia. Now it was time for the Emperor to intervene in person, the more so as Gratian had promised to come quickly to his assistance. At first the campaign was successful. The Goths were defeated on the Maritza near Hadrianople, and Valens advanced towards Philippopolis to effect a junction with Gratian. But Fritigern hastened southward to cut Valens off from Constantinople. The Emperor was forced to turn back, and whilst at Hadrianople was asked by Gratian in a letter delivered by Richomer to postpone the final attack until his arrival. At a council of war however Valens complied with his general Sebastian's opinion to strike without delay, as he had been informed that the enemy numbered but ten thousand. In any case they would have had to wait a long time for Gratian, who was hurrying eastward from a remote field of war. After rejecting a very ambiguous message from Fritigern, Valens led the Romans against the Goths, and (9 Aug. 378) a battle took place to the north-east of Hadrianople, probably near Demeranlija. The Goths were fortunate in receiving timely assistance (from the Ostrogoths and Alani under Alatheus and Saphrax) after they had already defeated a body of Roman cavalry, which had attacked them prematurely. The Roman infantry also met with defeat at the hands of the Goths, and two-thirds of their army perished. The Emperor himself was killed by an arrow, and his generals Sebastian and Trajan also lost their lives. When he heard the news from Richomer, Gratian withdrew to Sirmium, and now the Eastern Empire lay open to the attacks of the barbarians.

On 10 August the Goths advanced to storm Hadrianople, as they had been informed that there, in a strongly fortified place, the Emperor's treasure and the war-chest were kept. But their efforts to seize the town were in vain. The municipal authorities of Hadrianople had not even admitted within its walls those Roman soldiers who during the night after their defeat had fled there and found shelter in the suburbs under the ramparts. At ten o'clock in the morning the long-protracted struggle for the town began. In the midst of the turmoil three hundred Roman infantry formed a wedge and went over to the enemy, by whom, strange to say, all were killed. At last a terrible storm put an end to the fight by bringing the besieged the much needed supply of water, for want of which they had suffered the utmost distress. After this the Goths made several fruitless attempts to take the town by stratagem. When in the course of the struggle it became evident that many lives were being sacrificed to no purpose the Goths abandoned the siege from which the prudent Fritigern had from the beginning tried to dissuade them. Early on 12 August a council of war was held, in which it was decided to march against Perinthus on the Propontis, where, according to the report of many deserters, great treasures were to be found.

When the Goths had left Hadrianople the Roman soldiers gathered together and during the night one part of them, avoiding the high-roads, marched by lonely forest-paths to Philippopolis and thence to Sardica, probably to effect a junction with Gratian; whilst another part conveyed the well-preserved imperial treasures to Macedonia, where the Emperor, whose death was as yet unknown, was supposed to be. It will be observed that at this time the position of the Eastern Empire seemed hopeless. It could no longer defend itself against those robbing and plundering barbarians who, now that the battle was won, actually thought themselves strong enough to advance southward as far as the Propontis, and on their march could also rely on the assistance of the Huns and Alani. But here again the Goths had trusted too much to their good fortune. For, though on their arrival in the environs of Perinthus they encamped before the town, they did not feel strong enough for an attack, and carried on the war by terrible and systematic devastations only. In these circumstances it is surprising that they next marched upon Constantinople itself, the treasures of which greatly excited their covetousness. Apparently they hoped to surprise and take the capital at one blow. This time, however, through fear of hostile attacks they decided to approach the town in close array. They had almost reached Constantinople when they encountered a body of Saracens, who had come out in its defence. It is reported that by a monstrous deed one of these, a hairy, naked fellow, caused them to turn back. He threw himself with wild screams on one of the Goths, pierced his throat with a dagger, and greedily drank the blood which welled forth. For a time the struggles seem to have continued, but soon the Goths saw that they were powerless against the large and strongly fortified town and that they suffered greater loss than they inflicted. They therefore destroyed their siege engines on the Bosphorus, and bursting forth in single detachments, moved in a north-westerly direction through Thrace, Moesia, and Illyricum as far as the foot of the Julian Alps, plundering and devastating the country as they went. Every hand in the Eastern Empire was paralysed with horror at the unrestrained ferocity of the barbarians. Only Julius, the *magister militum*, who held the command in the province of Asia, had courage enough for a terrible deed, which shews the boundless hatred felt by the Romans for the Goths, as well as the cruelty practised in warfare at that time. He announced that on a certain day all Gothic soldiers in the towns and camps of Asia should receive their pay; instead of which all of them were at his command cut down by the Romans. In this manner he freed the provinces of the East from future danger. At the same time this incident shews clearly the straits to which the Eastern Empire was reduced. There was need of a clear-headed and determined ruler, if peace was ever to be restored to the Empire. With regard to this, however, everything depended upon the decision of Gratian, of whose doings we shall now have to give a short account.

We know that Gratian had made efforts long before the catastrophes to come to his uncle's aid against the Goths. From this he was prevented by a war with the Alemanni. An Aleman from the country of the Lentienses (afterwards the Linzgau on the Lake of Constance) who served in the Roman Guard had returned to his country with the news that Gratian was shortly going to render assistance to his uncle in the East. This news had induced his tribesmen to make a raid across the Rhine in February 378. They were at first repulsed by frontier troops; but when it became known that the greater part of the Roman army had marched for Illyricum they prevailed upon their tribesmen to join in a big campaign. It was rumoured in Gaul that 40,000 or even as many as 70,000 Alemanni were on the war-path. Gratian at once called back those of his cohorts which were already on the way to Pannonia and put the *comes Brittanniae* Nannienus in command of his troops, together with the brave Mallobaudes, king of the Franks. A battle was fought at Argentaria (near Colmar), in which the Romans, thanks to the skill of their generals, won a complete victory, and Priarius, the chieftain of the Lentienses, was killed.   Gratian now attacked the Alemanni, crossed the Rhine, and sent the Lentienses flying to their mountains.   There they were completely hemmed in and had to surrender, promising to supply recruits to the Romans.   After this Gratian marched from Arbor Felix (near St Gallen) eastwards along the high-road, passing Lauriacum on the way.   As we have already seen, he did not reach Thrace in time, and on hearing of the defeat at Hadrianople he withdrew to Sirmium.   Here, at the beginning of 379, a great political event took place.   It must be mentioned that Theodosius, who. had formerly been the commander-in-chief in Upper Moesia, and had since been living in a kind of exile in Spain, had been recalled by Gratian and entrusted with a new command.   Before the end of 378 Theodosius had already given a proof of his ability by the defeat of the Sarmatians, who appear to have invaded Pannonia.   The success was welcome in a time so disastrous for the Romans.   This is most probably one of the reasons why Gratian (19 Jan. 379) at Sirmium raised him to be Emperor of the East and enlarged his dominions by adding to them Dacia, Upper Moesia, Macedonia, Epirus 'and Achaia, *i.e.* Eastern Illyricum.

The Visigoths under Fritigern had without doubt been the moving spirit in the war, although the Ostrogoths had played a valiant part in it.   After Ermanarich had committed suicide, Withimir had become king of the Ostrogoths.   He lost his life fighting against the Alani, and seems to have been succeeded by his infant son, in whose name the princes Alatheus and Saphrax reigned supreme.   These, as we saw, joined forces later on with the Visigoths and contributed largely to the victory at Hadrianople.   It appears that for some time after this, both tribes of the Goths made common cause against the Romans.   At first the two Emperors were successful in some minor campaigns against the Goths, and while Gratian went westward against the Franks and perhaps against the Vandals who had made an invasion across the Rhine, Theodosius succeeded in creating at Thessalonica, a place which he chose as a strong and sure base for his further operations, a new and efficient army, into which he admitted a considerable number of Goths.   Before the end of 379 he and his forces gained important successes over the enemy, who found themselves almost entirely confined to Lower Moesia and, owing to a lack of supplies, were compelled to renew the war in 380.   The Visigoths under Fritigern advanced in a south-westerly direction towards Macedonia, whilst the Ostrogoths, Alani, and Huns went to the north-west against Pannonia.   Theodosius, who hurried to meet the Visigoths, suffered a severe defeat in an unexpected night-attack.   The Goths, however, did not follow up their victory, but contented themselves with pillaging Macedonia and Thessaly, whilst the Emperor Theodosius lay a prey to a protracted illness at Thessalonica.   During this period Macedonia suffered terribly from the barbarians.   At last when Gratian, whose assistance Theodosius had implored, sent an army under Bauto and Arbogast, two Frankish generals, the Goths were compelled to retreat into Lower Moesia.   Gratian himself was at the same time forced to take command of an army again; for his general Vitalianus had been unable to prevent the Ostrogoths, Alani, and Huns from invading Pannonia.   As this barbarian invasion was a great danger to the Western Empire, it was highly important for Gratian to make peace with the enemy before suffering great losses.   This he accomplished by assigning Pannonia and Upper Moesia to the Ostrogoths and their allies as *foederati*.   This settlement of the barbarians at its eastern frontier guaranteed the peace of the Western Empire in the immediate future.   For the Eastern Empire also peace seemed now ensured.   When Theodosius, who as an orthodox ruler commanded greater sympathy from his subjects than his predecessor, the Arian Valens, had recovered from his illness, he made a triumphal entry into Constantinople (24 Nov. 380), and here (11 Jan. 381) the Visigoth Athanarich arrived with his followers.   He had been banished by the Goths whom he had led into Transylvania, and not desiring to ally himself with Fritigern on account of an old feud, asked to be admitted into the Empire.   He was received with the greatest honours by Theodosius, but only survived his entrance by a fortnight.   The high honour shewn to Athanarich was evidently intended to create the impression among the inhabitants of the capital that war with the Goths was at an end; perhaps it was also hoped to promote more peaceful feelings among Fritigern's followers.   We are also led to believe that Theodosius soon commenced negotiations with this dreaded prince, which were brought to a conclusion in 382 by the *magister militum* Saturninus.   A treaty of peace was concluded at Constantinople (3 Oct. 382) by which permission was given to Fritigern and all his Goths to settle as allies in Lower Moesia.   They were also to retain their domestic legislation and the right to elect their own princes.   It was their duty in return to defend the frontier and to furnish troops, which, however, were to be led by their own chiefs.   They obtained the districts assigned to them free of tribute, and moreover the Romans agreed to pay them annually a sum of money.

This treaty was, without doubt, at the time a triumph for Theodosius, and as such it was loudly praised by the Emperor's flatterers. But on closer examination we shall see that the Romans had only gained a momentary peace.   From the outset it was impossible to accustom the Goths, proud conquerors of the Roman armies as they were, to the peaceful occupation of tilling the ground, and, as they had doubtless been allowed to settle in Moesia in a compact mass, retaining their domestic government, all efforts to Romanise them could but prove vain.   Besides this the Danube, with the exception of the Dobrudscha, was stripped of Roman troops, and the ever-increasing number of Goths who entered the Roman army was naturally a considerable danger to it.

Moreover the majority of the Goths were Arians, and the rest still heathens. A year previously, however, Theodosius had not only attacked heathenism, but had issued a law against heretics, especially Arians. He had even sent his general Sapor into the East to expel the Arian bishops from their churches; only bishops professing the Nicene faith were to possess the churches. Thus the peace could not possibly be of long duration.

How greatly political questions excited the Goths, and how passionately their national feeling would sometimes break forth is shewn by an event which occurred at Constantinople soon after 382. One day at the royal table two Gothic princes, who were specially honoured by Theodosius, gave free utterance to their opposed political convictions. Eriwulf was the leader of the national party among the Goths, which considered the destruction of the Roman Empire their ultimate object; he was an Arian by confession. Fravitta, on the other hand, was the head of that party which saw their future salvation in a close union with the Empire. He had married a Roman lady, and had remained a heathen. The quarrel between the two party-leaders ended by Fravitta drawing his sword and killing his opponent just outside the palace. The attempts of Eriwulf's followers to take immediate revenge were met with armed resistance on the part of the imperial palace-guards. This incident doubtless helped to strengthen Fravitta's position at the Emperor's Court, whilst he had made himself impossible to the Goths.

At this time a new danger to the Empire arose from those Goths who had remained at home and had been conquered by the Huns. As early as the winter of 384 or 385 they had taken possession of Halmyris (a town to the south of the estuary of the Danube) which however they left again, only to return in the autumn of 386 to ask for admission into the Empire together with other tribes. But the *magister militum* Promotus, commander of the troops in Thrace, forbade them to cross the river. He had the frontier carefully guarded, and met their attack with a ruse, cleverly conceived and successfully executed, by sending some of his men to the Ostrogoths under the pretence of betraying the Roman army to them. In reality however those soldiers of his reported to Promotus the place and time of the proposed night-attack, and when the barbarians, led by Odothaeus, crossed the river, the Romans, who were posted on a large number of anchored boats, made short work of them. This time the better strategy of the Romans gained a complete victory over the Goths. To commemorate this victory the Emperor, who subsequently appeared in person on the battle-field, erected a huge column ornamented with reliefs in the quarter of the town which is called Taurus.

Meanwhile (25 Aug. 383) Gratian had been killed at Lyons at the instigation of the usurper Maximus, who had been proclaimed Emperor by the army in Britain and had found followers in Gaul. At first Theodosius pretended to accept Maximus for a colleague; but in 388 he led his army against him and defeated him at Liscia and Pettau. In the end the usurper was taken prisoner and killed at Aquileia. Theodosius now appointed Valentinian II, Gratian's youthful brother, Emperor of the West, only reserving for himself the co-regency of Italy. He then sent his experienced general Arbogast into Gaul, where the Teutons from the right bank of the Rhine had seized the occasion offered by the quarrel for the throne to extend their power beyond the frontier. Three chiefs of the Ripuarian Franks, Genobaudes, Marcomir, and Sunno, had indeed crossed the Rhine in the neighbourhood of Cologne and made a raid upon the Roman territory. When the Roman generals Nannienus and Quintinus went to meet the raiders at Cologne, one part of them left the borderland of the province, whilst the others continued their march into the country, till they were at last beaten back in the Carbonarian forest (to the east of Tournai). Quintinus now proceeded to attack the enemy and crossed the Rhine at Novaesium (Neuss). But after pushing forward for three days into the wild and pathless regions on the right bank of the Rhine, he was decoyed into an ambush, in which almost the whole of his army perished. Thus it appeared likely that the Roman rule in the Rhenish provinces would before long be completely overthrown; for the generals Carietto and Syrus, whom Maximus had left behind, found it impossible to put a stop to the barbarian raids. At this juncture Arbogast was sent by Theodosius to save the West. His first act was to capture Flavius Victor, the infant son of Maximus, and to have him put to death. Then he reinforced his army with those troops which Maximus had left stationed in Gaul, and which together with their generals Carietto and Syrus were easily won over to his side. Last of all he turned against his former tribesmen, the Franks, and demanded from them the restitution of the booty and surrender of the originators of the war. When these demands were refused, he hesitated to begin war by himself. He found it difficult to come to a decision, for the fate of Quintinus' troops was still fresh in his memory. In these straits he wrote to the Emperor Valentinian II, who seems to have urged a friendly settlement of the feuds; for in the autumn of 389 Arbogast had an interview with Marcomir and Sunno. The Franks, possibly fearing the mighty Theodosius, gave hostages, and a treaty of peace was concluded which cannot have been unfavourable to the barbarians.

In this way the Western Empire shewed considerable indulgence in its treatment of the Teutons. The Eastern Empire on the contrary, and especially the Emperor, was soon directly and indirectly exposed to serious troubles from the Visigoths. We know that the Goths had extended their raids as far as Thessalonica. In this large town, the second in importance in the Balkan peninsula, there existed a certain amount of ill-feeling against the barbarians, which was greatly increased by the fact that the highest offices, both civil and military, were chiefly held by Teutons; moreover the town was garrisoned by Teuton soldiers.

The innate pride of Greeks and Romans alike was deeply wounded by this situation, and a very insignificant occurrence in the year 390 sufficed to make their hatred burst into flames. It happened in the following way. Botherich, the commandant of the town, had imprisoned a very popular charioteer and refused to set him free, when the people clamoured for his deliverance because of the approaching circus-games. This caused a rising against the obnoxious barbarian in which he lost his life. At the time of this incident the Emperor Theodosius was at Milan where he had frequent intercourse with the influential bishop Ambrose; this was not without its effect upon him, though in his innermost heart the Emperor as a secular autocrat could not but be opposed to ecclesiastical pretensions. Although Theodosius inclined by nature to leniency, or at any rate made a show of that quality, in this case at least wrath overcame every human feeling in him, and he resolved to chastise the town in a way so cruel, that nothing can be put forward in defence of it. When the people of Thessalonica were assembled in the circus and absorbed in contemplation of the games soldiers suddenly broke in and cut down all whom their swords could reach. For three hours the slaughter went on, till the victims numbered 7000. The Emperor himself, urged perhaps to mercy by Ambrose, had at the last hour revoked his order, but it was too late. Probably Theodosius had been led to this unspeakable cruelty by persons of his intimate acquaintance, among whom Rufinus played a prominent part. It seems that Rufinus had been *magister officiorum* since 382; in 392 he rose to the position of *Praefectus Praetorio*. When the news of this massacre reached Milan, the Christian population of the town was paralysed with terror. Ambrose left the town and addressed a letter of the utmost gravity to Theodosius. He explained to him that his deed called for penitence and warned him not to attend at church. The proud sovereign perceived that he would have to submit to the penitence imposed on him, and obeyed the bishop's will. He did not leave Milan till the following year; but before returning to the Eastern capital he had to sustain a dangerous attack from the Goths in Thrace.

In 390 the Visigoths broke the peace to which they had sworn, and invaded Thrace; Huns and other tribes from beyond the Danube had thrown in their lot with them. They were commanded by Alaric, a prince of the Visigoths, belonging to the family of the Balti. This is the first appearance of Alaric, who was then about twenty years of age, and whose great campaigns subsequently excited such terror throughout the Roman Empire. But even then the Thracians appear to have been in great distress: for (1 July 391) Theodosius issued an edict at Aquileia, by which the inhabitants of the endangered district received permission to carry arms and to kill anybody found marauding in the open country. After Theodosius had entered the province, he took great pains to destroy the bands of marauders, and himself assisted in their pursuit. On the Maritza, however, he fell into an ambush and was completely defeated. Even his life seems to have been in danger, but he was rescued by his general Promotus. The latter continued the war against the Goths till the end of 391, though he had apparently fallen into disfavour at Court. He lost his life in the war, and public opinion at the capital attributed his death to Rufinus. Stilicho the Vandal now became commander of the troops in Thrace. He was born about 360, and had at an early age been attached to an embassy to Persia. Afterwards Theodosius had given him his niece Serena in marriage and promoted him step by step. He was considered to be one of the ablest statesmen in the Eastern Empire, and the military command entrusted to him in 392 was destined to increase the importance of his position. For he succeeded at length in defeating the enemy, who for so long a time had been the terror of the Empire. The Goths were surrounded on the Maritza. But again the Emperor shewed mercy and gave orders that the enemy should be permitted to go free. Theodosius' policy may probably be attributed to a certain fear of revenge, and it was doubtless influenced by Rufinus, who did not wish Stilicho to become too powerful. Thus a treaty with the vanquished Goths was concluded.

Meanwhile Arbogast had embarked upon a most ambitious course of politics. His aim was to get rid of the young and irresolute Valentinian II. Not indeed that he himself wished for the imperial crown, for he very likely felt its possession to be undesirable. His idea was to get Valentinian II out of the way, and then assist to the imperial throne some one of his ardent devotees, under whose name he himself hoped to wield the supreme power. For the attainment of this end, his first requisite was a trustworthy army. He therefore levied a large number of Teuton troops, in whose loyalty he could place the utmost confidence. When Valentinian took up his abode in Gaul, the relations between him and the powerful Frank became more and more strained, till finally the Emperor from his throne handed to his rival a written order, demanding that he should resign his post. Arbogast tore the document in pieces before the eyes of the Emperor, whose days were thenceforth numbered. On 15 May 392 the youthful sovereign was assassinated at Vienne; but whether Arbogast was directly responsible for this deed remains uncertain. The way was now clear for the Frank's ambitious plans. A short time previously the Frank Richomer had recommended to his tribesman Arbogast the head of the imperial chancery, the *magister scriniorum* Eugenius. This Roman, formerly a rhetorician and grammarian, was the man whom Arbogast intended to raise to the imperial throne. Eugenius could not but yield to the mighty man's wish. He therefore sent an embassy to Theodosius in 392 to obtain his recognition. But Theodosius gave an evasive answer; and as there was every prospect of a war, Arbogast deemed it necessary to make provision for a safe retreat. We know that the neighbourhood of the Franks formed a very vulnerable

point of the Roman government in Gaul. For this reason in the winter
of 392 Arbogast undertook a campaign against these dangerous
neighbours. He probably hoped at the same time to reinforce his army
with Frankish troops, should he be successful in this war. He pushed
on through Cologne and the country along the river Lippe into the
territory of the Bructeri and Chamavi, after which he turned eastward
against the Ampsivarii, who had joined forces with the Chatti under
Marcomir. Apparently he met with but little resistance, for in the spring
of 393 Eugenius succeeded in concluding treaties with the Franks and
even the Alemanni, on condition that they supplied him with troops.
The ensuing period was spent in preparations for war in both Empires,
Eugenius having been, thanks to Arbogast's influence, recognised as
Emperor in Italy also. Theodosius had reinforced his army more
especially with Teutons; the Visigoths were again commanded by Alaric,
whilst the leaders of the other *foederati* were Gaïnas, Saul, and the
comes domesticorum Bacurius, an Armenian. The meeting of the two
armies took place 5 Sept. 394 on the Frigidus, a tributary of the
Isonza, probably the Hubel. As the Gothic troops formed the vanguard
and opened the attack on the enemy, who were posted very favourably,
they suffered severe losses on the first day of the battle, which greatly
elated the Westerns. On the second day the battle would in all
probability have been decided in favour of Arbogast, had not his
general Arbitrio, who commanded the Frankish troops, gone over to
Theodosius. It is related besides, that a violent storm from the north-
east — the *Bora*, as it is called — wrought such havoc in the ranks of
Eugenius' army, that it helped Theodosius to gain a complete victory.
Eugenius was taken prisoner and put to death, and Arbogast escaped
into the mountains, where he died by his own hand (8 Sept.). But whilst
the relations and followers of Eugenius and Arbogast were pardoned,
Alaric waited in vain for the post in the Roman army which Theodosius
had promised him; and when (17 Jan. 395) Theodosius died at Milan,
still in the prime of life, the Goths were sent home by Stilicho, who had
been second in command during the war. To make matters worse, the
yearly payments which had hitherto been made to the Goths were now
injudiciously held back. These various causes combined to disturb the
peace between the Romans and Goths, which had so far been tolerably
well preserved, and the Goths once more commenced hostilities.

The time for a general rising seemed to be well chosen. Theodosius,
whose strong hand had endeavoured to maintain the peace within the
Empire, was now no more, and his sons were yet of tender age. The
late Emperor had been the last to reign over the whole Empire. And
even he, powerless to stay its decline, had been obliged to cede to the
Goths an extensive district within its borders. How important the
Teutonic element had grown can best be understood from the fact that
the Teutons not only furnished the best part of the troops, but also

CH. IX.

commanded the armies and held the highest appointments, both civil and military.   Now that Theodosius was dead, the Empire was divided for ever.   At an age of hardly eighteen years his son Arcadius received the Empire of the East under the guidance of Rufinus, who had in 394, during the absence of Theodosius, been entrusted with the regency as well as with the supreme direction of Arcadius.   On 27 April 395, to Rufinus' great vexation, the young Emperor married Eudoxia, who had been brought to him by Eutropius, the eunuch of the palace.   She was the daughter of Bauto, the Frank who had played an important part under Gratian and Valentinian. In the course of the same year Rufinus was most cruelly slain by the soldiers whom Gaïnas had but recently led back to Constantinople.   After his death Eutropius stood in high favour with the Emperor.   He received the office of High Chamberlain (*praepositus sacri cubiculi*) and later on the title *patricius*.   The younger son Honorius, who was in his eleventh year, received the Western Empire. Stilicho was appointed his guardian and also regent.   He had been raised to the rank of *magister utriusque militiae* by Theodosius before his death, and, as we saw, had married a niece of the Emperor.   This capable man was no doubt better fitted than any other to rule the Empire in the spirit of Theodosius, and when the Emperor died it was he who without delay hurried to the Rhine to receive homage for Honorius from the Teuton tribes, even as far as the Batavi.   Apparently on this journey King Marcomir was delivered into his hands, and was sent into exile to Tuscany.   After this Stilicho immediately returned to Italy.

Meanwhile the Visigoths had broken loose from Moesia.   Those of their tribesmen who had formerly accompanied Alaric to Transylvania had joined them and chosen Alaric, whose power at that time, however, was still limited, as leader in the coming war.   This war was fraught with danger for the Eastern Empire, for it appears that in the early spring of 395 the whole mass of the Visigoths marched south towards Constantinople.   As before, there could of course be no question of capturing the city, but the surrounding country was mercilessly devastated.   It is most probable that Rufinus, who paid repeated visits to the hostile camp, bribed the enemy to retire.   Alaric now made his way along the coast to Macedonia and Thessaly.   Near Larissa he encountered Stilicho, who had left Italy with strong forces.   These were the victorious East-Roman soldiers, whom he was leading home to their own country, hoping at the same time to win back Illyria for the Western Empire. This province, though given to Theodosius by Gratian, was said to have been restored by the former a short time before his death.   Apparently the Goths had first of all tried to gain the valley of the Peneus, the Vale of Tempe; but meeting with resistance, they had pushed on across the eastern slopes of Olympus into Thessaly, where they barricaded themselves behind their wagons.   Stilicho was on the point of attacking them when he received a message from Arcadius, ordering him to dismiss the army of the Eastern Empire, and himself return to Italy. If at first sight this order seems strange, it is because we have long been accustomed to see in Stilicho a disinterested statesman and general, who dedicated his labour and personality to the family of Theodosius. This disposition of Eastern Illyria, which Theodosius was supposed to have made shortly before his death, is however very doubtful, and it is certain that Stilicho had entertained personal ambitions with regard to that province. Viewed in the light of these circumstances, the order from Arcadius appears in a very different light, especially if to this is added the fact that in the same year the Huns had broken through the gates of the Caucasus at Baku on the Caspian Sea and reached Syria by way of Armenia. There they laid siege to Antioch and proceeded thence to Asia Minor. Ravages of every kind marked their way. In this situation it was an absolute necessity for the welfare of the State that the army should return to its own country. Stilicho obeyed the order, because, as has justly been remarked, he was probably uncertain about the future conduct of the East-Roman troops, a section of whom remained in Greece under Gerontius' command to cover Thermopylae. Alaric, however, assisted perhaps by treachery, took possession of this famous pass without difficulty. After this the Goths marched through Boeotia into Attica. Here Alaric succeeded in seizing the Piraeus, and forced Athens to capitulate by cutting off her supplies. It is probable that she escaped pillage by the payment of a sum of money; Alaric stayed for a short time peacefully within her walls. From Athens the march of the Goths was continued to Eleusis, where they ransacked the temple of Demeter, and further to Megara, which was quickly taken. Gerontius had left the entrance to the Peloponnesus undefended, and the Gothic hordes, meeting with no resistance, broke like a torrent upon Corinth and thence on Argos and Sparta. Many an ancient work of art must have perished in this rush, but no mention is made of any systematic and wilful destruction of the ancient monuments.

It is a curious fact, that after all this the East-Roman government seems neither to have made war against the Huns, who had invaded Asia, nor to have lent assistance to the Greeks, when Gerontius had so utterly failed to do his duty at Thermopylae and the Isthmus. Help came rather from another quarter, and primarily, it must be owned, with a different purpose in view. Though Stilicho had returned to Italy, he had been kept well informed about events in Greece. As he himself had designs on East-Illyria, to which Epirus and Achaia belonged, and as Alaric was to all appearances endeavouring to create an independent sovereignty in these provinces, it was imperative for the vicegerent of the West to interfere. In 397 he transported an army to Greece, and, landing on the south side of Corinth, expelled the Goths from Arcadia and surrounded them at Elis near the Alpheus on the

plateau of Pholoe. But no decisive battle was fought, for Stilicho was
not sufficiently master of his own troops, and just then the revolt of the
Moorish prince Gildo threatened to become a serious danger to the
Western Empire. Gildo had formerly been praefect of Mauretania and
had subsequently been raised to the office of *magister utriusque militiae.*
In the year 394 he began his revolt, whereby he intended to secure the
North coast of Africa as a dominion of his own, and in 397 he offered
Africa as a feudal province to the Eastern Empire, hoping thereby to
kindle war between the two Empires. In this predicament Stilicho
avoided a decisive encounter with the Goths. For the second time he
allowed his adversary to escape. He even concluded a treaty with
Alaric, which doubtless contained an alliance against the Eastern
Empire; for in these precarious circumstances the chief of the brave
Goths might possibly prove of great service to Stilicho in his ambitious
private policy. The effect of these conditions on the mutual relations
of the two Empires was soon apparent. At Constantinople Stilicho was
declared an enemy of the State, whilst in the Western Empire the
consulship of Eutropius, who had been nominated for 399 and had
entirely won the favour of Arcadius, was not acknowledged. Before his
death Theodosius had so arranged the division of the Empire that the
cohesion of the whole might for the future be firmly and permanently
secured. Thus the first deep cleft had been made in a union which
was already difficult to maintain. Neither Empire had a permanent
diplomatic representation; only special embassies were sent from time
to time, so that unfounded suspicions were very likely to arise on either
side.

At this time, while Stilicho was sailing back in haste from Greece to
Italy to prepare for war against Gildo, the Goths made a raid into
Epirus, which they devastated in a terrible manner. At last the
government at Constantinople was roused sufficiently to make proposals
of peace to Alaric. In return for a sum of money and the position of
magister militum in Illyria, Alaric withdrew from the alliance with
Stilicho, made peace with the Eastern Empire, and occupied Epirus,
which had been assigned to him, with his Gothic troops. Another
trouble for the Eastern Empire at this time arose from the large number
of Goths who served in the army, and more especially through their
leader Gaïnas. At his command they had killed Rufinus in 395.
When Eutropius did not reward him for his services with the high
military office he coveted, he joined a rebellion of his compatriot
Tribigild in Phrygia, against whom he had been sent out with an army.
For after the fall and execution of the powerful favourite Eutropius in
the summer of 399' a national movement was set on foot at Constantinople, having for its object the abolition of foreign influence in the
high government offices; Aurelianus, Eutropius' successor, was at the
head of this movement. But the Roman supremacy was not destined to

be revived. The Gothic rebellion in Asia Minor grew more and more alarming, and Arcadius was soon obliged to negotiate with Gaïnas. During an interview with the Emperor, the Goth succeeded in obtaining his nomination to the post of *magister militum praesentalis* and the extradition of the three leaders of the national party, one of whom was Aurelianus. On his subsequent return to the capital, Gaïnas could consider himself master of the Empire, and as such demanded of the Emperor a place of worship for the Arian Goths. But the famous theologian and bishop, John Chrysostom, contrived to avert this danger to the orthodox Church. But the power of Gaïnas was not to be of long duration. When in July 400 he left the town with the majority of the Goths, owing to a feeling of insecurity, the inhabitants rose against those who had been left behind. At last no refuge remained to them except the church they had lately been given. In its ruins they were burned, as Gaïnas failed to come to their rescue in time to storm the city. Gaïnas was declared a public enemy, and the pursuit was entrusted to his tribesman Fravitta, who so far carried out his order that he followed Gaïnas to Thrace and the Hellespont, and prevented him from crossing to Asia. Eventually, at the end of the year 400, Gaïnas was killed on the further side of the Danube by a chief of the Huns, called Uldin, who sent his head to Constantinople.

Nothing is more characteristic of the impotence of the Eastern Empire, than the revolt of this Gothic general, whose downfall was only secured by a combination of favourable circumstances. The clever and valiant Goth succumbed only to strangers; the Empire itself had no means to overthrow him.

Such were the conditions at the dawn of the new century; the last twenty-five years of the old having brought nothing but war, poverty, and depopulation to the Eastern Empire. It is true that for the Western Empire the century had closed more favourably; the campaign against Gildo especially had been prepared by Stilicho with characteristic ability. This Moorish prince, after putting to death the sons of his brother Mascezel, who had gone to Italy, had proceeded to conquer the North of Africa. Only the large and fortified towns could resist his ever-increasing power. He created great anxiety in Rome by cutting off her African corn-supply; but the danger of a famine was averted by Stilicho, who succeeded in having corn brought by sea from Gaul and Spain. When his preparations for war were completed, Stilicho did not at this critical time put himself at the head of the army, but resigned the supreme command to Mascezel. The army was not large, but it seems that Stilicho relied upon the skill of its commander for entering into secret relations with the leaders of the enemy. Mascezel departed for Africa, where the campaign was decided between Tebeste and Ammedera on the Ardalio, a tributary of the Bagradas. Apparently no real battle was fought, but Gildo's troops went over to the enemy or fled into the mountains.   Gildo himself first tried to escape by sea, but returned to land and soon after met his death at Tabraca.   These wars against the two rebels Gaïnas and Gildo so excited the imagination of the contemporary world, that they formed the subject of many poetical productions.   Of these "The Egyptians or On Providence," a novel by Synesius of Cyrene, and Claudian's "War against Gildo" are preserved.

With the year 401, however, there began for the Western Empire a period similar to that which the Eastern Empire had already so long endured.   The Teutons began to press forward in dense masses against the provinces of the Western Empire, which they had so long spared, and finally effected the complete dissolution of that once so mighty realm.   But this time the disturbance did not proceed from the Goths only; other tribes also were involved in the movement, which could no longer be restrained, and the danger to the Empire grew in proportion.   In the first place Alaric had made use of the short time of his alliance with the Eastern Empire to increase his power, chiefly by re-arming his Goths from the Roman arsenals.   His plan of founding an independent kingdom for himself in Greece had failed, and it probably seemed most tempting to him to transfer his attentions to Italy, whose resources were not yet so completely drained by the Goths.   No doubt Stilicho ruled there with a firm hand.   He had in 398 created for himself an unassailable position by giving his daughter Maria, a mere child, in marriage to the Emperor Honorius, who was then fourteen years of age.   But apparently Alaric did not fear the power of Stilicho, who had twice allowed him to escape from a most critical position; furthermore the Western Empire was just now engaged in a different direction.   In the year 401, the Vandals, who had long ago settled in the regions between the Danube and the Theiss, began to grow restless. On account of their increasing population the majority of them had resolved to emigrate with their king Godigisel, retaining at the same time the right of possession over their old dominions.   They were joined by Alani from Pannonia, and in the same year this new wave of migration reached Rhaetia by way of Noricum.   Stilicho at first opposed them, but was eventually obliged to grant them territories in Noricum and Vindelicia under the suzerainty of Rome, in return for which they bound themselves to serve in the Roman army.

By this time Alaric had already left Epirus far behind and reached Aquileia by way of Aemona and the Birnbaum forest.   This invasion of Italy by the barbarians caused great consternation; the fortifications of Rome were repaired and strengthened, and the young Emperor Honorius even contemplated an escape into Gaul.   Venetia was already in the enemy's hands, and the road to Milan was occupied by the Goths.   As Honorius was staying in this city, Alaric naturally desired above all to take possession of it.   But Stilicho came to the rescue.   He had reinforced his army with the Vandals and Alani with whom he had just made peace, and Alaric was forced to abandon the siege of Milan. He now tried to gain the coast in order to reach Rome. With Stilicho at his heels he turned to Ticinum and Hasta and thence to Pollentia. Here (6 April 402) a battle was fought in the early stages of which it seemed likely that the Romans would be defeated, as Saul, the Roman general of the Alani, had begun the battle prematurely. But the appear-ance of Stilicho with the main body of infantry changed the aspect of affairs. The fight was continued until nightfall, but though the Romans were left in possession of the field and took numerous prisoners, Stilicho can hardly be said to have gained a victory. For Alaric's forces retreated in perfect order and were able to continue their march on Rome. In this crisis Stilicho was obliged to come to terms with Alaric. The Gothic chief was raised to the rank of *magister militum* and promised to evacuate Italy. For the future the two generals arranged to conquer Eastern Illyria for the Western Empire. This treaty, which put a considerable check on the movements of the Goths, is explained not only by the state of affairs at that time, but also by the fact that Alaric's wife and children had been made prisoners during the battle. The Goths now left Italy, but remained close to the frontier, and made a fresh invasion in 403. This time Alaric tried to lay siege to Verona, but was defeated by Stilicho, and on trying to gain Rhaetia by way of the Brenner again found himself in a very dangerous plight, from which he could only extricate himself by concluding a new treaty with Stilicho against the Eastern Empire. Probably it was at this juncture that Sarus the Visigothic prince with his followers went over to Stilicho, a desertion which must be ascribed to Stilicho's diplomatic skill. The uncertainty of the situation may account for the very remarkable fact that Stilicho suffered the enemy to escape so often from his fatal embrace. Be that as it may, the Goths withdrew, and Stilicho could celebrate a brilliant triumph with Honorius. Alaric, however, does not appear to have returned to Epirus till much later, but remained for some time in the neighbourhood of Illyria.

In the following year (405) the Ostrogoths and Vandals, the Alani and the Quadi under the leadership of Radagaisus left their homes, crossed the Alps, and descended into Italy. Their number, though much exaggerated by contemporary historians, must have been considerable; for the hostile army marched through the North of the peninsula in several divisions. Stilicho seems to have collected his troops at Pavia; the invasion happened at a very inopportune moment, as he was about to carry out his designs on Eastern Illyria. This time, however, he quickly succeeded in ridding himself of the enemy. He surrounded Radagaisus who had attacked Florence, in the narrow valleys of the Apennines near Faesulae, and destroyed a large part of his army. Radagaisus himself was captured with his sons whilst trying to escape, and was shortly afterwards executed. For this victory Stilicho's thanks were chiefly due to two foreign generals, Sarus the Goth and Uldin the Hun. In this manner Italy had indeed been speedily saved from great danger, but at the end of the next year (406) hostile hordes broke into Gaul with so much the greater violence. It is very probable that this invasion, which was undertaken by the Vandals, had some connexion with that of Radagaisus. In conjunction with the Vandals were the Alani, who had recently formed an alliance with them, and the Suevi, by whom we must understand the Quadi, who had formerly dwelt north of the Vandals. This great tribal migration, following the road along the Roman frontier (*limes*), reached the river Main, where they met the Silingi, a Vandal tribe which had gone westward with the Burgundians in the third century. These now helped to swell the Vandal hordes, whilst a part of the Alani under the leadership of Goar enlisted in the Roman army on the Rhine. Near this river the Vandals were attacked by some Frankish tribes, who were keeping guard on the frontier, in accordance with their treaty with Stilicho. In the ensuing fight the Vandals suffered severe losses, their king Godigisel being among the slain. On receiving this news the Alani immediately turned about, and, led by their king Respendial, they completely routed the Franks. On the last day of 406 this mass of people crossed the Rhine at Mainz, which they invested and destroyed. The march was continued by Trèves to Rheims, where the bishop Nicasius was slain in his own church; thence to Tournai, Terouenne, Arras, and Amiens. From this point the journey proceeded through Gallia Lugdunensis to Paris, Orleans, and Tours, and, passing through Aquitania into Novempopulana, by Bordeaux to Toulouse, which the bishop Exuperius saved from falling into the enemies' hands. But the fortified passes of the Pyrenees put a step to their further advance. Thus Spain remained unconquered for the present, and the Vandals now made their way into the rich province of Narbonensis. The devastation of the extensive provinces and the conquered cities of Gaul was terrible; contemporary writers of prose and verse alike complain bitterly of the atrocities committed by the barbarians in this unhappy country. The oldest people could not remember so disastrous an invasion., The weakness of the Empire is revealed by the absence of a Roman army to oppose the Germans. Stilicho's policy was at that time directed towards Illyria, and for this reason he probably found it impossible to come to the assistance of Gaul.

This first great danger was soon followed by a second. The migration of the Vandals had very likely caused the Burgundians along the middle course of the Main to become restless; they now began to bear down upon the Alemanni on the lower Main. A part of the Burgundians had perhaps intended to join the great migration of 406, for shortly after we meet with them on the west side of the Rhine. The most important result, however, was, that the Alemanni now entered on a campaign against Roman Upper Germany, and conquered Worms, Speier, and

Strassburg. Here again the Empire failed to send help, and the allied Franks remained quiet. Stilicho meanwhile collected an army in 406 and arranged a plan with Alaric, by which he could carry out his Illyrian projects from Epirus. Already a *Praefectus Praetorio* for Illyria had been nominated in the person of Jovius, when in the year 407 an event occurred which threw everything else into the background. A new emperor appeared on the scene. When a rumour had spread, that Alaric was dead, the legions in Britain after two unsuccessful attempts[1] proclaimed Constantine emperor. According to Orosius, he was a common soldier, but his name excited hopes for better times. The new Emperor crossed over to Gaul without delay, where he was recognised by the Roman troops throughout the country. He immediately pushed forward into the districts along the Rhone, where, though he probably concluded treaties with the Alemanni, Burgundians, and Franks, he made but little impression on the Teutons who had invaded the land. But Stilicho had already sent the experienced general Sarus with an army against him. In the neighbourhood of Valence, which Constantine had made his temporary abode, his general Justinian was defeated and killed in battle by Sarus. Another of the usurper's generals met his death soon afterwards during an interview with the crafty Goth. When, however, Constantine sent against him his newly appointed generals, the Frank Edobic and the Briton Gerontius, Sarus abandoned the siege of Valence and effected a passage into Italy by paying a sum of money to the fugitive peasants called Bagaudae, who at that time held the passes of the Western Alps. Stilicho joined Honorius at Rome to discuss the serious situation. Constantine, however, directed his attention towards Spain, evidently with a view to protect his rear before attacking Italy. At the passes across the Pyrenees he met with energetic resistance from Didymus, Verenianus, Theodosius, and Logadius, all relatives of the Emperor. But Constantine's son Constans soon overcame the enemy; he captured Verenianus and Didymus, whilst Theodosius and Logadius fled, the former to Italy, the latter to the East. After this, when Constans had returned to Gaul in triumph, he entrusted the passes to Gerontius, who was in command of the Honorians, a troop of barbarian *foederati*. These, it appears, fulfilled their duty but indifferently, for during the quarrels which ensued in the borderlands the Vandals, Alani and Suevi, who had pushed on as far as southern Gaul, saw an opportunity of executing their design on Spain.

With these disturbances in Spain is generally connected a great rising of the Celts in Britain and Gaul, which was directed against the advancing Teutonic tribes as well as against the Roman rule, and in which the Gaulish district of Armorica was specially concerned. Thus

---

[1] First a man named Marcus and after him Gratian, a British official, had been declared emperors; both however were after a short time put to death by the soldiers.

was prepared in these provinces the separation from the Roman government which had lasted for centuries, and at the same time Teutonic rule superseded that of the Romans in Spain.

Meanwhile Alaric had not failed to profit by the violent disturbances within the Western Empire. As Stilicho had neither undertaken the campaign against Illyria nor met the demands of the Gothic soldiers for their pay, Alaric believed himself entitled to deal a powerful blow at the Western Empire. Stilicho had recently strengthened his relations with the imperial house by a new link. The Empress Maria had died early, still a virgin as rumour went, and Stilicho succeeded in persuading the Emperor to marry his second daughter Thermantia. Now Alaric tried to force his way into Italy. He had left Epirus and reached Aemona. There he probably found the roads to the South barred; he therefore crossed the river Aquilis and made his way to Virunum in Noricum, whence he sent an embassy to Stilicho at Ravenna. The ambassadors demanded the enormous sum of four thousand pounds of gold as compensation for the long delay in Epirus and the present campaign of the Goths. Stilicho went to Rome to discuss the matter with the Emperor and the Senate. The majority of the Senate was opposed to the concession of this demand and would have preferred war with the Goths, but Stilicho's power in the assembly was still so great that his opinion prevailed and the huge sum was paid. At this juncture the rumour spread that the Emperor of the East was dead. Arcadius had indeed died (1 May 408). This greatly altered the situation, for Theodosius II, the heir to the Eastern throne, was but a child of seven. Honorius now decided to go to Ravenna, but was opposed by Stilicho, who wanted himself to inspect the troops there. But neither did Stilicho succeed in dissuading Honorius nor could a mutiny among the soldiers at Ravenna, which Sarus had promoted, induce the Emperor to desist from his plan. Nevertheless he eventually diverged from the route to Ravenna, and went to Bologna, where he ordered Stilicho to meet him for the purpose of discussing the situation in the East.

Stilicho's first concern at Bologna was to calm the agitation amongst the soldiers and recommend the ringleaders to the Emperor's mercy; then he took counsel with Honorius. It was the Emperor's wish to go in person to Constantinople and settle the affairs of the Eastern Empire, but Stilicho tried to turn him from this purpose, pointing out that the journey would cause too much expense, and that the Emperor could not well leave Italy whilst Constantine was as yet powerful and residing at Arles. Honorius bent his will to the prudent counsel of his great statesman, and it was resolved that Stilicho should go to the East, whilst Alaric was sent with an army to Gaul against Constantine. Stilicho, however, neither departed for the East nor did he gather together the troops which remained assembled at Pavia, and were ill-disposed towards him. Meanwhile a cunning Greek, the chancellor Olympius, profited by the change in the Emperor's feelings towards his great minister. Under the mask of Christian piety he secretly intrigued against Stilicho in order to undermine his position. Thus Olympius accompanied the Emperor to Pavia and on this occasion spread the calumnious report, that Stilicho intended to kill the child Theodosius and put his own son Eucherius on the throne. The storm now gathered over Stilicho's head. The prelude to the catastrophe, however, took place at Pavia.

When the Emperor had arrived with Olympius at this town, the latter made an exhibition of his philanthropy by visiting the sick soldiers; probably his real object was to gather the threads of the conspiracy which he had already spun and to weave them further. On the fourth day Honorius himself appeared among the troops and tried to inspire them with enthusiasm for the fight against Constantine, At this moment Olympius gave a sign to the soldiers, and, in accordance with a previous arrangement, they threw themselves upon all the high military and civil officers present, who were supposed to be Stilicho's adherents. Some of them escaped to the town, but the soldiers rushed through the streets and killed all the unpopular dignitaries. The slaughter continued under the very eyes of the Emperor, who had withdrawn at first but reappeared without his royal robes and tried to check the mad fury of the soldiers. When the Emperor, fearing for his own life, had a second time retired, Longinianus, the *Praefectus Praetorio* for Italy, was also slain. News of this horrible mutiny reached Stilicho at Bologna. He at once summoned all the generals of Teutonic race in whose loyalty alone he could still trust. It was decided to attack the Roman army, should the Emperor himself have been killed. When, however, Stilicho learned that the mutiny had not been directed against Honorius, he resolved to abstain from punishing the culprits, for his enemies were numerous and he was no longer sure of the Emperor's support. But to this the Teuton generals would not agree, and Sarus even went so far as to have Stilicho's Hunnic body-guard killed during the night. Stilicho now betook himself to Ravenna, and to this town Olympius despatched a letter from the Emperor, addressed to the army, with the order to arrest Stilicho and keep him in honourable custody. During the night Stilicho took refuge in a church to secure the right of sanctuary; but in the morning the soldiers fetched him away, solemnly assuring him that his life was safe. Then a second letter from the Emperor was read, which condemned Stilicho to death for high-treason. The fallen man might still have saved his life by appealing to the Teuton soldiers, who were devoted to him, and would readily have fought for him. But he made no attempt to do so, probably to preserve the Empire from a civil war, which would have been fatal at this time. Without resistance he offered his neck to the sword. In him the Roman Empire (23 August 408) lost one of its most prominent statesmen, and at the same time one of its ablest generals, one who had been in command of the army for twenty-three years.

Without doubt we should consider the fall of Stilicho as a manifestation of a national Roman reaction against the ever-increasing Teutonic influence within the Empire, a reaction proceeding from the political party which saw in the removal of the barbarians the salvation of Rome. Whether this party was right or not, they certainly had acted most unwisely, for Olympius, the successor to Stilicho's position, turned his power to very foolish account. Even the severest tortures could not wring from Stilicho's friends and followers the confession desired by Olympius, that the executed minister had aspired to the imperial throne. And still more injudicious was the edict by which all those who had attained high office under Stilicho's administration forfeited their property to the State. But most incomprehensible of all was the fact that the Roman soldiers were allowed to wander about murdering and robbing the families of the Teuton troops in Italy. The consequence was that thousands of these soldiers deserted, and went over to Alaric. Thermantia was sent back to her mother Serena by Honorius, who also sentenced Eucherius to death. But as the latter had escaped to Rome and taken refuge in a church, he was left unmolested for a time. Shortly afterwards, however, he was murdered by two eunuchs who were rewarded by high offices in the State.

Alaric's opportunity had arrived, now that the Empire had of its own free will lost the services of its great leader. At first the Gothic chief tried to maintain the peace. He sent ambassadors to the Emperor with the message that he would adhere to the treaties made with Stilicho, if he received a moderate payment of money, and that if an exchange of hostages were effected, he would withdraw his troops from Noricum to Pannonia. Although Honorius rejected Alaric's proposals for a peaceful arrangement, he did not take any active steps to ensure success in the campaign which had now become inevitable. Instead of entrusting to Sarus the command of the troops against Alaric, Olympius bestowed it on two men who were faithfully devoted to him but absolutely devoid of merit. This time Alaric did not tarry long. However, as the campaign promised to assume greater dimensions, he sent for reinforcements from his brother-in-law Ataulf, who was stationed in Upper Pannonia with Hunnic and Gothic troops. Without waiting for Ataulf's arrival, Alaric marched to Aquileia and thence westward to Cremona, where he crossed the Po, without meeting with the slightest resistance. Then the Goths proceeded south-east from Placentia to Ariminum, leaving Ravenna unmolested, and through Picenum, until they arrived before Rome without opposition. When Alaric surrounded the city the Senate believed Serena, Stilicho's widow, to be in connivance with him, and as Placidia, the sister of Honorius, was of the same opinion, Serena was put to death. This act of violence had, of course, no influence upon Alaric's policy; on the contrary the investment of the city was carried on with greater vigour than before. As the Goths also blockaded the Tiber, the city was cut off from all supplies, and soon famine broke out. No help came from Ravenna, and when the distress in the city was at its highest ambassadors were sent to the hostile camp to ask for moderate terms. At first Alaric demanded the surrender of all the gold and silver in the city, inclusive of all precious movable goods, and the emancipation of all Teuton slaves, but in the end he lowered his demand to an imposition, which, however, was still so heavy that it necessitated the confiscation of the sacred treasures stored in the temples. After this he withdrew his troops from Rome and went into the neighbouring province of Tuscany where he collected around his standard a great number of slaves, who had escaped from Rome. But even in this situation Honorius declined the negotiations for peace which were now urged by Alaric and the Senate alike.

This temporising policy could not but bring ruin upon Italy, the more so, as at the beginning of 409 ambassadors came to treat with Honorius about the recognition of Constantine. The usurper had raised his son Constans, who had returned from Spain to Gaul, to the dignity of a co-emperor, and had had the two cousins of Honorius put to death. The Emperor, who entertained hopes that they were still alive and counted upon assistance from Constantine against Alaric, no longer withheld his recognition, and even sent him an imperial robe. During this time Olympius did not shew himself in any way equal to the situation, but continued to persecute those whom he believed to be Stilicho's adherents. Honorius now ordered a body of picked troops from Dalmatia to come to the protection of Rome. These six thousand men, however, under their leader Valens were on their way surprised by Alaric, and all of them but one hundred were cut down. A second Roman embassy, in which the Roman bishop Innocent took part, and which was escorted by troops furnished by Alaric, was now sent to the Emperor. In the meantime Ataulf had at last made his way from Pannonia across the Alps, and although an army sent by the Emperor caused him some loss, probably near Ravenna, his junction with Alaric could not be prevented. Now at last a general outcry against Olympius, who had shewn himself so utterly incompetent, arose at the imperial Court. The Emperor was forced to give in and depose his favourite, and after this he at length inclined his ear to more peaceful proposals. When, however, the Gothic chief in an interview with the *Praefectus Praetorio* Jovius at Ariminum demanded not only an annual subsidy of money and corn, but also the cession of Venetia, Noricum, and Dalmatia, and when moreover the same Jovius in a letter to the Emperor proposed that Alaric should be raised to the rank of a *magister utrisque militae*, because it was hoped that this would induce him to lower his terms, Honorius refused everything and was determined to go to war.

CH. IX.

Apparently this bellicose mood continued, for shortly afterwards a fresh embassy from Constantine appeared at the Court, promising Honorius speedy support from British, Gaulish, and Spanish soldiers. Even Jovius had allowed himself to be persuaded by the Emperor and together with other high officials had taken an oath on pain of death never to make peace with Alaric.

At first all seemed to go well; Honorius levied 10,000 Huns for his army, and to his great satisfaction found that Alaric himself was inclined to peace and was sending some Italian bishops as ambassadors to him. Of his former conditions he only maintained the cession of Noricum and a subsidy of corn, the amount of which was to be left to the Emperor's decision. He requested Honorius not to allow the city of Rome, which had ruled the world for more than a thousand years, to be sacked and burnt by the Teutons. There can be no doubt that the Goths were forced by the pressure of circumstances to offer these conditions. But Honorius was prevented from complying with them by Jovius, who is said to have pleaded the sanctity of the oath which he and others had taken. Alaric now had recourse to a simple device in order to attain the object of his desires. As he could not out of consideration for the Goths aspire to the imperial crown himself, he caused an emperor to be proclaimed. In order to put this proclamation into effect he marched to Rome, seized the harbour of Portus, and told the Senate of his intention to divide among his troops all the corn which he found stored there, should the city refuse to obey his orders. The Senate gave in, and in compliance with Alaric's wish was Attalus raised to the throne. He was a Roman of noble descent, who had been given a high government post by Olympius and shortly afterwards made praefect of the city by Honorius. Attalus thereupon raised Alaric to the rank of *magister militum praesentalis*, and Ataulf to that of *comes domesticorum;* but he gave them each a Roman colleague in their office, and Valens was made *magister militum*, while Lampadius, an enemy of Alaric, became praefect of the city. On the next day Attalus delivered a high-flown oration in the Senate, boasting that it would be a small matter for him and the Romans to subjugate the whole world. Soon, however, his relations with Alaric became strained. Formerly he had been a heathen, but though he now accepted the Arian faith and was baptised by the Gothic bishop Sigesar, he not only openly slighted the Goths but also, disregarding Alaric's advice to send a Gothic army under Druma to Africa, despatched the Roman Constans with troops ill-prepared for war to that country. Africa was at that time held by Heraclian, one of Honorius' generals, the murderer of Stilicho, and the province required the Emperor's whole attention, as the entire corn supply of Rome depended upon its possession.

Attalus himself now marched against Honorius at Ravenna. The latter, who had already contemplated an escape to the East, sent Attalus a message to the effect that he would consent to acknowledge him as co-emperor. Attalus replied, through Jovius, that he would order Honorius to be mutilated and banish him to some remote island, besides depriving him of his imperial dignity. At this critical moment, however, Honorius was saved by four thousand soldiers of the Eastern Empire, who disembarked at Ravenna and came to his assistance. When the news arrived that the expedition against Heraclian in Africa had proved a complete failure and that Rome was again exposed to a great famine, owing to this victory of Honorius' arms, Attalus and Alaric abandoned the siege of Ravenna. Alaric turned against Aemilia where he took possession of all the cities except Bologna, and then advanced in a north-westerly direction towards Liguria. Attalus on the other hand hastened to Rome to take counsel with the Senate about the pressing African question. The majority of the assembly decided to send an army of Gothic and Roman troops to Africa under the command of the Goth Druma, but Attalus opposed the plan. This brought about his fall; for when Alaric heard of it he returned, stripped Attalus of the diadem and purple at Ariminum, and sent both to Honorius. He did not, however, leave the deposed Emperor to his fate, but kept him and his son Ampelius under his protection till peace had been concluded with Honorius. Placidia, Honorius' sister, was also in Alaric's keeping. If we may believe Zosimus, she was brought from Rome as a kind of hostage by Alaric, who, however, granted her imperial honours.

The deposition of Attalus in May or June 410 was the starting-point for renewed negotiations for peace between Alaric and the Emperor, in the course of which the former perhaps claimed a part of Italy for himself. But the peaceful propositions were nipped in the bud by the Goth Sarus. He was hostile to Alaric and Ataulf; at that time he lay encamped in Picenum. Under pretence of being menaced by Ataulf's strong body of troops, he went over to the Emperor and violated the truce by an attack on the Gothic camp. Alaric now marched for the third time against Rome, doubtless firmly resolved to punish the Emperor for his duplicity by thoroughly chastising the city, and to establish at last a kingdom of his own. The investment by the Goths caused another terrible famine in the city, and at last, during the night preceding 24 August 410, the Salarian gate was treacherously opened. Then followed a complete sack of the city, which did not, however, degenerate into mere wanton destruction, especially as it only lasted three days. The deeds of violence and cruelty which are mentioned more particularly in the writings of contemporary Christians were probably for the greater part committed by the slaves, who, as we know, had flocked to the Goths in great numbers. As early as 27 August the Goths left Rome laden with enormous spoil, and marched by Capua and Nola into southern Italy. For Alaric, who had probably borne the title of king already for a considerable time, had resolved to go to Africa by way of Sicily, and gain the dominion of Italy by the possession of that rich province. But when part of the army had embarked at Rhegium, his ships were scattered and destroyed by a storm. Alaric, therefore, turned back; but on the way north was seized by an illness which proved fatal before the end of the year 410. He was laid to rest in the river Basentus (Busento) near Cosentia. A large number of slaves were employed in first diverting the course of the river and then bringing it back into its former channel after the dead king and his treasures had been buried. In order that nobody might ever know the burial place, all the slaves who had been employed in the labour were killed. Ataulf was now elected king. He seems at first to have thought of carrying out the plans of his brother-in-law, Alaric; but on further consideration of the great power of Heraclian in Africa, he abandoned them and resolved rather to lead the Goths against Gaul. It is possible that on his march northward he again sacked Rome, and he certainly married Placidia before he withdrew from Italy. He invaded Gaul in 412, and in that year commenced the war which was waged so long by the Teutons against the Roman supremacy in that country.

A little earlier a similar struggle had begun in Spain, which resulted in the victory of the barbarians. In the autumn of 409 the Vandals, Alani, and Suevi had penetrated into Spain, tempted thither no doubt by the treasures of that rich country and by the greater security of a future settlement there. The course followed by those tribes was towards the west of the peninsula, first of all passing through Galicia and Lusitania. Constans, on leaving Spain, had certainly made an unfortunate choice in appointing Gerontius praefect; for not only did this official allow the Teutons to enter the country but he tried at the same time to put an end to Constantine's rule, by deserting him and causing one of his own followers, Maximus, to be proclaimed emperor. Circumstances even forced Gerontius into an alliance with the barbarians. For when Constans returned to Spain, the usurper could only drive him out of the country by making common cause with the Teutons. Gerontius followed Constans to Gaul, invested him at Vienne, and put him to death at the beginning of 411. He then turned his attention to Constantine, who concentrated his forces at Arles. But Honorius had by now recovered sufficiently to make war against Constantine. For that purpose he sent the Roman Constantius and a Goth named Wulfila with an army to Gaul. When Gerontius advanced to meet them, his soldiers deserted him and joined the imperial troops. He himself met his death shortly afterwards in a burning house, whilst Maximus succeeded in escaping. This sealed the fate of Constantine; for Constantius and Wulfila defeated the army of the Frank Edobic, who came to render him assistance. Constantius then proceeded to besiege Arles, which for a considerable time withstood his efforts, but eventually surrendered on conditions to the general of Honorius. The reason for this was that Constantius had heard that Guntiarius, king of the Burgundians, and Goar, king of the Alani, had raised the Gaulish noble Jovinus to the imperial throne at Mainz, and in these circum. stances he deemed it necessary to offer easy terms of capitulation to Constantine. The usurper submitted; but on the way to Ravenna he and his youngest son were killed by Honorius' command. His head was brought to Ravenna (18 Sept. 411). Meanwhile Jovinus with an army consisting of Burgundians, Franks, and Alemanni had marched south. ward, apparently in the belief that the critical situation of the Empire, which was at war with both Goths and Vandals, would facilitate a rapid extension of his power.

In these circumstances it was an easy matter for the Teutons who had invaded Spain to spread over a large part of the peninsula. For two years they scoured the west and south of the country, devastating and plundering as they went, until the alteration in the political situation, caused by the victories of Constantius, induced them to join the united Empire as *foederati*. In 411 they concluded a treaty with the Emperor, which imposed upon them the duty of defending Spain from foreign invasions. In return the Asdingi and Suevi received landed property for settlements in Galicia, the Silingi in Baetica, and the Alani in Lusitania and Carthaginensis. The larger Roman landowners probably ceded a third part of the land to them.

It was a time of the gravest convulsions for the Western Empire; for during these years were laid the foundations, on which the first important Teutonic States on Roman soil were built. Stilicho seems to have thought it possible for a kind of organic whole to develop out of the Roman and Teutonic nationalities; at least, that great statesman had always promoted peaceful relations between Romans and Teutons. But the change in politics after his death, as well as the immense size of the Empire, made a fusion of those two factors impossible. Now the time of the Teutonic conquests begins, though the name of *foederati* helped for a while to hide the real state of affairs. The very foundation of the Western Empire were shaken; but, above all, the future of Italy as the ruling power of the West was endangered by violent agitations in Africa, the country from which she drew her food-supplies. Just as here, in the heart of the Empire, so too on its borders, could serious danger be foreseen. Throughout the provinces the dissolution of the Empire was threatening. It had probably only been delayed so far by the lack of system in the Teutonic invasions and by the immense prestige of the Empire. But in respect of this the last generation had wrought a very perceptible change. During the long-continued warfare the Teutons had had time to become familiar with the manners of the Romans, their strategy, diplomacy, and political institutions, and it was owing to this that the great coalitions of tribes in 405 and 406 had already taken place. They are probably to be explained by the ever‾

increasing political discernment of the Teutons.   Another result of those years of war was that under Alaric's rule the principle of monarchy was evolved out of military leadership; for the continuous warlike enterprises could not but develop an appreciation of a higher and more comprehensive supreme power.   Thus Alaric was no longer the mere adviser of his tribe.   His actions however do not shew that he abused his high rank in his behaviour towards his tribesmen, while at the same time he ever displayed towards the Romans a humane and generous spirit which was remarkable in those times.   On the other hand the Teutonic tribes, and especially the Visigoths, had seen enough of the internal weakness of the great Empire and of the impotence of its rulers to encourage them to make more serious attacks on the Western half, although Alaric in 410 would willingly have saved from pillage the capital of the world — that capital which, according to his own words in a message brought to Honorius by an embassy of bishops, had ruled the world for more than a thousand years.   The fact that he nevertheless led his army to the sack of the city proves that he did not shrink from extreme measures when it was important to display the superiority of the Gothic army over the Roman mercenaries.

Thus it is evident that the Teutonic tribes, and more especially the Visigoths, were at this time passing through a transition stage.   They had not yet forgotten their native customs and manner of living, whilst at the same time the foreign influences to which they had been exposed had been sufficiently strong to modify to some extent their original disposition and mode of viewing things.   But as far as may be gathered from contemporary sources, their policy had not been influenced by Christian principles, and Christianity altogether played an unimportant part in the history of these migrating Teutons.   It is true that, owing to the scantiness of contemporary evidence, we have in many decisive cases to trust to conjecture, and it is a cause for much regret that the moving political forces and even more the real conditions of life among the migrating Teutons are wrapt in impenetrable darkness, which is only dispersed as they begin to live a more settled life, and in particular after the establishment of the Visigoths in Gaul and Spain, the Vandals in Africa, and the Ostrogoths in Italy.

CHAPTER X

(A)

THE VISIGOTHS IN GAUL, 412-507

KING ATAULF had no intention of establishing a permanent dominion in Italy. As an occupation of Africa seemed hopeless he turned towards Gaul in the year 412, probably making use of the military road which crossed Mt Genèvre via Turin to the Rhone. Here he at first joined the anti-emperor Jovinus (set up in the summer of 411) who had a sure footing, especially in Auvergne, but was little pleased by the arrival of the Visigoths, which interfered with his plans of governing the whole of Gaul. Hence the two rulers soon came to open strife, especially as Jovinus had not named the Gothic king co-ruler, as he had hoped, but his own brother Sebastian. Ataulf went over to the side of the Emperor Honorius and promised, in return for the assurance of supplies of grain (and assignments of land), to deliver up the heads of both usurpers and to set free Placidia, the Emperor's sister, who was held as a prisoner by the Goths. He certainly succeeded without much trouble in getting rid of the usurpers. As, however, Honorius kept back the supply of grain and Ataulf, exasperated by this, did not give up Placidia, hostilities once more began between the Goths and the Romans. After an unsuccessful attempt to surprise Marseilles, Ataulf captured the towns of Narbonne, Toulouse, and Bordeaux by force of arms (413). But a complete alteration took place in the king's intentions, obviously through the influence of Placidia, whom he took as his (second) wife in January (414). As he himself repeatedly declared, he now finally gave up his original cherished plan of converting the Roman Empire into a Gothic one, and rather strove to identify his people wholly with the Roman State. His political programme was therefore just the same as that of the Ostrogoth king Theodoric, later on, when he accomplished the founding of the Italian kingdom. In spite of these assurances the Emperor refused him every concession; influenced by the general Constantius, who himself desired the hand of the beautiful princess, Honorius looked upon the marriage of his sister with the Barbarian as a grievous disgrace to his house. In consequence Ataulf was again compelled to turn his arms against the Empire. He first appointed an anti-emperor in the person of Attalus, without however achieving any success by this

move, since Attalus had not the slightest support in Gaul. When Constantius then blockaded the Gallic ports with his fleet and cut off
supplies, the position of the Goths there became quite untenable, so
that Ataulf decided to seek a place of retreat in Spain. He evacuated
Gaul, after terrible devastation, and took possession of the Spanish
province of Tarraconensis (in the beginning of 415), but without quite
giving up the thought of a future understanding with the imperial
power. In Barcelona, Placidia bore him a son, who received the name
of Theodosius at his baptism, but he soon died. And not long afterwards death overtook the king from a wound which one of his followers
inflicted out of revenge (in the summer of 415).

After Ataulf's death the anti-romanising tendencies among the
Visigoths, never quite suppressed, became active again. Many Pretenders contended for the throne, but all, as it seems, were animated by
the thought of governing independently of Rome and not in subjection
to it. At length Sigerich, brother of the Visigoth prince Sarus,
murdered by Ataulf, succeeded in getting possession of the throne.
Sigerich at once had the children of Ataulf's first marriage slaughtered,
and Placidia suffered the most shameful treatment from him. However,
after reigning for one week only he was murdered; certainly by the
instigation of Wallia, who now became head of the Goths (autumn
415).

Wallia, although no less an enemy to Rome than his predecessor,
at once granted the imperial princess a more humane treatment, and
first tried to develop further the dominion already founded in Spain.
But as the imperial fleet again cut off all supplies, and famine broke
out, he determined to take possession of the Roman granary in Africa.
But the undertaking miscarried because of the foundering in the Straits
of Gibraltar of a detachment sent on in advance, which was looked upon
as a bad omen (416). The king, obliged by necessity, concluded a treaty
with Constantius in consequence of which the Goths pledged themselves,
in return for a supply of 600,000 measures of grain from the Emperor, to
deliver up Placidia, to free Spain from the Vandals, Alans, and Sueves,
and to give hostages. After fierce protracted fighting the Gothic army
overcame first the Silingian Vandals and then the Alans (416–418).
But when Wallia also wanted to advance against the Asdingian Vandals
and the Sueves in Galicia he was suddenly called back by Constantius,
who did not wish the Goths to become too powerful, and land for his
people to settle upon was assigned to him in the province of Aquitanica
Secunda and in some adjoining districts by the terms of a treaty of
alliance (end of 418). Shortly after Wallia died, and was succeeded on
the Visigoth throne by Theodoric I, chosen by the people.

Historical tradition is silent over the first years of Theodoric's
reign; they were taken up with the difficulties of devising and executing the partition of the land with the settled Roman population.

The Goths kept their national constitution and were pledged to give military assistance to the Empire. Their king was under the supreme command of the Emperor; he only possessed a real power over his own people, while he had no legal authority over the Roman pro. vincials. Such an indeterminate situation, after the endeavours so long directed towards the attainment of political independence, could not last long.

In 421 or 422 Theodoric fulfilled his agreement by sending a con. tingent to the Roman army which was marching against the Vandals; but in the decisive battle these troops fell upon the Romans from behind and so helped the Vandals to a brilliant victory. In spite of this base breach of faith the Goths came off unpunished, and even dared to advance southwards to the Mediterranean coast. In the year 425 a Gothic corps was before the important fortress of Arles, the coveted key of the Rhone valley; but it was forced to retreat by the rapid approach of an army under Aëtius. After further fighting, about which unfortunately nothing detailed is known to us, peace was made and the Goths were granted full sovereignty over the provinces which had originally been assigned to them for occupation only — Aquitanica Secunda and the north-west corner of Narbonensis Prima — while they restored all their conquests (c. 426).

This peace continued for a considerable period and was only interrupted by the unsuccessful attempt of the Goths to surprise Arles (430). But when in 435 fresh disturbances broke out in Gaul, Theodoric took up once more his plans for the conquest of the whole of Narbonensian Gaul. In 436 he appeared with a strong force before the town of Narbonne, which however after a long siege was relieved by Roman troops (437). The Goths went on fighting, but without success, and were at last driven back as far as Toulouse. But in the decisive battle which was fought before the walls of this town (439) the Romans suffered a severe defeat, and only the heavy loss of life which the Goths themselves sustained could decide the king to agree to the provisional restoration of the *status quo*.

Theodoric was certainly not disposed to be satisfied with the narrow territory surrendered to him. Therefore (c. 442) we find him again on the side of Rome's enemies. First he entered into close relations with Gaiseric, the dreaded king of the Vandals; but this coalition, which would have been so dangerous for the Roman Empire, was broken up by the ingenious diplomacy of Aëtius. He next tried to attach himself to the powerful and rising kingdom of the Sueves by giving King Rechiar one of his daughters in marriage, and by furnishing troops to assist his advance into Spain (449). It was only when danger threatened the whole of the civilised West by the rise of the power of the Huns under Attila, that the Goths again allied themselves with the Romans.

In the beginning of the year 451 Attila's mighty army, estimated at half a million, set out from Hungary, crossed the Rhine at Easter-time, and invaded Belgica. It was only now that Aëtius, who had been deceived by the false representations of the king of the Huns, thought of offering resistance; but the standing army at his command was absolutely insufficient to hold the field against such a formidable opponent. He found himself, therefore, obliged to beg for help from the king of the Visigoths, who although he had at first intended to keep himself neutral and await the development of events in his territory, thought, after long hesitation, that it would be to his own interest to obey the call. Theodoric joined the Romans with a fine army which he himself led, accompanied by his sons Thorismud and Theodoric. Attila had in the meantime advanced as far as Orleans, which Sangiban, the king of the Alans who were settled there, promised to betray to him. The proposed treachery, however, was frustrated, for the allies were already on the spot before the arrival of the Huns, and had encamped in strength before the city. Attila thought he could not venture an attack on the strong fortifications with his troops, which principally consisted of cavalry, so he retreated to Troyes and took up a position five miles before that town on an extensive plain near the place called Mauriacus, there to await a decisive battle with the Gotho-Roman army which was following him. Attila occupied the centre of the Hun array with the picked troops of his people, while both the wings were composed of troops from the subjected German tribes. His opponents were so arranged that Theodoric with the bulk of the Visigoths occupied the right wing, Aëtius with the Romans, and a part of the Goths under Thorismud formed the left wing of the army, while the untrustworthy Alans stood in the centre. Attila first tried to get possession of a height commanding the battlefield, but Aëtius and Thorismud were beforehand and successfully repulsed all the attacks of the Huns on their position. The king of the Huns now hurled thimself with great force on the Visigothic main body commanded by Theodoric. After a long struggle the Goths succeeded in driving the Huns back to their camp; great losses occurred on both sides; the aged king of the Goths was among the slain, as was also a kinsman of Attila's.

The battle however remained drawn, for both sides kept the field. The moral effect, which told for the Romans and their allies, was, however, very important, inasmuch as the belief that the powerful king of the Huns was invincible had suffered a severe shock. At first it was decided to shut up the Huns in their barricade of wagons and starve them out. But when the body of Theodoric, who had been supposed up till then to be among the survivors, had been found and buried, Thorismud, who was recognised as king by the army, called upon his people to revenge and to take the enemy's position by storm. But Aëtius, who did not wish to let the Goths become too powerful, succeeded in persuading Thorismud to relinquish his scheme, advising his return to

Toulouse, to prevent any attempt on his brother's part to get possession of the crown by means of the royal hoard there. Thus were the Goths deprived of the well-earned fruits of their famous exploit; the Huns returned home unmolested (451).

Thorismud proved himself anxious to develop the national policy adopted by his father, and in the same spirit. After he had succeeded, for the time being, in keeping possession of the throne, he subdued the Alans who had settled near Orleans and thereby made preparations for extending the Gothic territory beyond the Loire. Then he tried to bring Arles under his power, but without having attained his object he returned once more to his country, where in the meanwhile his brothers Theodoric (II) and Friedrich had stirred up a rebellion. After several armed encounters Thorismud was assassinated (453).

Theodoric II succeeded him on the throne. The characteristic mark of his rule is the close though occasionally interrupted connexion with Rome. The treaty broken under Theodoric I — which implied the supremacy of the Empire over the kingdom of Toulouse — was renewed immediately after his accession to the throne. For the rest, this connexion was never taken seriously by Theodoric but was principally used by him as a means towards the attainment of that end which his predecessors had vainly striven for by direct means — the spread of the Visigoth dominion in Gaul and more especially in Spain. Already, in the year 454, Theodoric found an opportunity for activity in the interest of the Roman Empire; a Gothic army under Friedrich marched into Spain and pacified the rebellious Bagaudae *ex auctoritate Romana*. After the murder of Valentinian III (March 455) Avitus went as *magister militum* to Gaul to win over the most influential powers of the country for the new Emperor, Petronius Maximus. In consequence of his personal influence — he had formerly initiated Theodoric into the knowledge of Roman literature — he succeeded in bringing the king of the Goths to recognise Maximus. When, however, soon after this, the news of the murder of the Emperor arrived (31 May), Theodoric requested him to take the *imperium* himself. On 9 July, Avitus, who had been proclaimed Emperor, accompanied by Gothic troops marched into Italy where he met with universal recognition. The close relations between the Empire and the Goths came again into operation against the Sueves. As the latter repeatedly made plundering expeditions into Roman territory, Theodoric, with a considerable force to which the Burgundians also added a contingent, marched over the Pyrenees in the summer of 456, decisively defeated them, and took possession of a large part of Spain, nominally for the Empire, but actually for himself.

But the state of affairs changed at one stroke when Avitus, in the autumn of the year 456, abdicated the purple. Theodoric had now no longer any interest in adhering to the Empire. He had in fact required the promotion of Avitus because he enjoyed a great reputation in Gaul and possessed there a strong support among the resident nobility. Friendship with him could only be of use to the king of the Goths in respect to the Roman provincials living in Toulouse. But the elevation of the new Emperor Majorian, on 1 April 457, had occurred in direct opposition to the wishes of the Gallo-Roman nobility to place one of themselves upon the imperial throne. Taking advantage of the consequent discord in Gaul, Theodoric appeared as the open foe of the imperial power of Rome. He himself marched with an army into the Gallic province of Narbonne and once more began with the siege of Arles; he also sent troops to Spain which, however, only fought with varying success. But in the winter of 458 the Emperor appeared in Gaul with considerable forces, quieted the rebellious Burgundians, and obliged the Visigoths to raise the blockade of Arles and again conclude peace (spring 459).

Although in the year 461 yet another change took place on the imperial throne, Theodoric thought it more advantageous for the time being to maintain, at least formally, the imperial alliance. On the other hand the chief general Aegidius, a faithful follower of Majorian, supported by a fine army, marched against the new imperial ruler. In the conflict which then ensued Theodoric found a favourable opportunity for resuming his policy of expansion in Gaul. At the call of Count Agrippinus, who was commanding in Narbonne and was hard pressed by Aegidius, he marched into the Roman territory and quartered upon that important town Gothic troops under the command of his brother Friedrich (462). Driven out of southern Gaul, Aegidius turned northwards whither a Gothic army led by Friedrich followed him. A great battle took place near Orleans in which the Goths suffered a severe defeat, chiefly through the bravery of the Salian Franks, who were opposed to them and lost their leader in the battle (463). Taking advantage of the victory, Aegidius now began to press victoriously into the Visigoth territory, but sudden death prevented him from carrying out his purposes (464).

Theodoric, freed from his most dangerous enemy, did not delay making good the losses he had suffered; but he died in the year 466 at the hand of his brother Euric, who was a champion of the anti-Roman national party and now ascended the throne. Contemporaries agree in describing the new king as characterised by great energy and warlike ability. We may venture to add from historical facts that he was also a man of distinguished political talent. The leading idea in his policy — the entire rejection of even a formal suzerainty of the Roman Empire — came into operation on his accession to the throne. The embassy which he then sent off to the Emperor of Eastern Rome can only have had for its object a request for the recognition of the Visigoth sovereignty. As no agreement was arrived at he tried to bring about an alliance with the Vandals and the Sueves, but the negotiations came to nothing when a strong East-Roman fleet appeared in African waters (467). Euric at first pursued a neutral course, but as the Roman expedition, set on foot with such considerable effort against the Vandal kingdom, resulted so lamentably (468), he did not hesitate to come forward as assailant, while he simultaneously pushed forward his troops into Gaul and Spain (469). He opened hostilities in Gaul with a sudden attack on the Bretons whom the Emperor had sent to the town of Bourges; at Déols, not far from Chateauroux, a battle took place in which the Bretons were overthrown. Yet the Goths did not succeed in pushing forward over the Loire to the north. Count Paulus, supported by Frankish auxiliaries, successfully opposed them here. Euric therefore concentrated his whole strength partly on the conquest of the province of Aquitanica Prima, partly on the annexation of the lower Rhone valley, especially the long-coveted Arles. The provinces of Novempopulana and (for the most part) Narbonensis Prima had been probably already occupied by the Goths under Theodoric II. An army which the West-Roman Emperor Anthemius sent to Gaul for the relief of Arles was defeated in the year 470 or 471, and for the time being a large part of Provence was seized by the Goths. In Aquitanica Prima, also, town after town fell into the hands of Euric's general Victorius; only Clermont, the capital city of Auvergne, obstinately defied the repeated attacks of the barbarians for many years. The moving spirits in the resistance were the brave Ecdicius, a son of the former Emperor Avitus, and the poet Sidonius Apollinaris, who had been its bishop from about 470. The letters of the latter give us a clear picture of the struggle which was waged with the greatest animosity on both sides. Euric is said to have stated that he would rather give up the much more valuable Septimania than renounce the possession of that town. The wholly impotent Western Empire was unable to do anything for the besieged. In the year 475 peace was at last made between the Emperor Nepos and Euric by the intervention of Bishop Epiphanius of Ticinum (Pavia). Unfortunately the conditions are not more accurately known, but there can be no doubt that, besides the previously conquered territory in Spain, the district between the Loire, the Rhone, the Pyrenees, and the two seas was relinquished to Euric in sovereign possession. Thus Auvergne, so fiercely contended for, was surrendered to the Goths.

But in spite of this important success the king of the Goths had by no means reached the goal of his desires; it may be seen from the line of policy he followed later that the present moment seemed to him fit for carrying out that subjection of the whole of the West which had long since been the aim of Alaric I.

For this reason peace only lasted for a year, which was spent in settling internal affairs. The most important event under Euric's government at this time is the publication of a Code of Law which was

CH. X.

intended to settle the legal relations of the Goths, both amongst themselves and with the Romans who had come under the Gothic dominion.
The deposition of the last West-Roman Emperor, Romulus, by the
leader of the mercenaries, Odovacar (Sept. 476), gave the king a welcome
reason for renewing hostilities, as he looked upon the treaty made with
the Empire as dissolved.   A Gothic army crossed the Rhone and obtained final possession of the whole of southern Provence as far as the
Maritime Alps, together with the cities of Arles and Marseilles, after
a victorious battle against the Burgundians, who had ruled over this
district under Roman suzerainty.   But when Euric also marched a
body of troops into Italy it suffered defeat from the officers of Odovacar.
Consequently a treaty was concluded by the East-Roman Emperor
Zeno and the king of the Burgundians whereby the newly conquered
territory in Gaul (between the Rhone and the Alps south of the
Durance) was surrendered by Odovacar to the Goths, while Euric
evidently pledged himself to undertake no further hostilities against
Italy (c. 477).

Euric was incessantly harassed by the difficulties of defending this
mighty conquest from foes without and within.   In particular, very
frequent cause for interference was given by the conduct of the Catholic
clergy, who openly shewed their disloyalty, and in the Vandal kingdom
did not shrink from the most treacherous actions.   Yet they seem only
in rare instances to have been answered by violence and cruelty.   The
Saxon pirates who, according to old custom, infested the coast of Gaul
were vigorously punished by a fleet sent out against them.   In the
same way it seems that an invasion of the Salian Franks was warded
off successfully.   It is not strange that, owing to the prestige of the
Visigoth power, Euric's help was repeatedly requested by other peoples,
as by the Heruli, Warni, and Tulingi who, settled in the Netherlands,
found themselves threatened by the overwhelming might of the Franks
and owed to the intervention of the Gothic king the maintenance of
their political existence.   The poet Sidonius Apollinaris has left behind
a vivid description of the way in which, at that time, the representatives
of the most diverse nations pressed round Euric at the Visigoth Court,
even the Persians are said to have formed an alliance with him against the
Eastern Empire.   It seems that envoys from the Roman population of
Italy also appeared at Toulouse to ask the king to expel Odovacar, whose
rule was only reluctantly endured by the Italians.

We do not know if Euric intended gratifying this last request, in
any case he was prevented from executing any such designs through
death, which overtook him in Arles in December 484.   Under his son
Alaric II the Visigoth power fell from its height.   To be sure, the
beginning of the decline originated at a time further back.   Ataulf's
political programme, as already observed, had originally contemplated
the establishment of a national Gothic State in the place of the Roman

Empire.   Yet not one of the Visigoth rulers, in spite of honest purpose, could accomplish this task.   It is to their credit that they succeeded at last, after severe fighting, in freeing themselves from the suzerainty of the Emperor and obtaining political autonomy, but the State which thus resulted resembled a Germanic National State no more than it did a Roman Imperium, and it could not contain the seeds of life because it was in a great measure dependent on foreign obsolescent institutions.   The Goths had entered the world of Roman civilisation too suddenly to be able either to resist or to absorb the foreign influences which pressed on them from all sides.   It was fortunate for the progress of Romanisation that the Goths, cut off from the rest of the German world, could not draw thence fresh strength to recuperate their nationality or to replace their losses, and moreover that through the immense extension of the kingdom under Euric the numerical proportion between the Roman and Gothic population had altered very much in favour of the former.   So under the circumstances it was a certainty that the Gothic kingdom in Gaul must succumb to the rising and politically creative power of the Franks.   Neither the personality of Alaric, who was little fitted for ruling, nor the antagonism between Catholicism and Arianism caused the downfall, they only hastened it.

Alaric ascended the throne on 28 December 484.   The king was of an indolent weak nature, altogether the opposite of his father, and without energy or warlike capacity, as immediately became evident. For example, he submitted to give up Syagrius, whom he had received into his kingdom after the battle of Soissons (486), when the victorious king of the Franks threatened him with war.   The inevitable settlement by arms of the rivalry between the two principal powers in Gaul was of course only put off a little longer by this compliance.   About 494 the war began.   It lasted for many years and was carried on with varying success on both sides.   Hostilities were ended through the mediation of the Ostrogoth king Theodoric — who in the meanwhile had become Alaric's father-in-law — by the conclusion of a treaty of peace on the terms of *Uti possidetis* (c. 502), but this condition could not last long, for the anatagonism was considerably aggravated by the conversion of Clovis to the Catholic Church in the year 496 (25 Dec.).   Consequently the greatest part of Alaric's Roman subjects, with the clergy of course at their head, adhered to the Franks, and jealously endeavoured to bring about the subjection of the Visigoth kingdom to their rule. Alaric was obliged to adopt severe measures in some instances against such treasonable desires, but usually he tried by gentleness and the granting of favours to win over the Romans to his support, an attempt which, in view of the prevalent and insurmountable antagonism, was of course quite ineffectual and even defeated its own ends, being regarded only as weakness.   Thus he permitted the bishoprics kept vacant under Euric to be again filled, he moreover permitted the Gallic bishops to

CH. X.

hold a Council at Agde in September 506, and — indication of the ambiguous attitude of the clergy — it was opened with a prayer for the prosperity of the Visigoth kingdom. The publication of the so-called *Lex Romana Visigothorum*, also named *Breviarium Alaricianum*, represented the most important act of conciliation. This Code of Law, which had been composed by a commission of lawyers together with prominent laymen and even clergy, and was drawn from extracts and explanations of Roman law, was sanctioned by the king at Toulouse, 2 Feb. 506, after having received the approval of an assembly of bishops and distinguished provincials, and was ordered to be used by the Roman population in the Gothic kingdom.

Why the explosion was delayed until the year 507 is unknown. That the king of the Franks was the aggressor is certain. He easily found a pretext for beginning the war as champion and protector of Catholic Christianity against the absolutely just measures which Alaric took against his treacherous orthodox clergy. Clovis had sufficiently appreciated the by no means despicable power of the Visigoth kingdom, and had summoned a very considerable army, one contingent of which was furnished by the Ripuarian Franks. His allies, the Burgundians, approached from the east in order to take the Goths in the flank. Among his allies Clovis probably also counted on the Byzantines, who placed their fleet at his disposal. On his part Alaric had not looked upon coming events idly, but his preparations were hampered by the bad state of the finances of his kingdom. In order to obtain the necessary funds he was obliged to coin gold pieces of inferior value, which were soon discredited everywhere. Apparently the fighting strength of the Gothic army was inferior to the army of Clovis, but if the Ostrogoth troops, who had held out prospects of coming, should arrive at the right time Alaric could hope to oppose his foe successfully. The king of the Franks had to endeavour to bring about a decisive action before the arrival of these allies. In the spring of 507 he suddenly crossed the Loire and marched towards Poitiers, where he probably joined the Burgundians. On the Campus Vocladensis, ten miles from Poitiers, the Visigoths had taken up their position. Alaric put off beginning battle because he was waiting for the Ostrogoth troops, but as they were hindered by the appearance of a Byzantine fleet in Italian waters he determined to fight instead of beating a retreat, as it would have been wise to do. After a short engagement the Goths turned and fled. In the pursuit the king of the Goths was killed, it was said by Clovis' own hand (507). With this overthrow the rule of the Visigoths in Gaul was ended for ever.

The principal town of the Gothic kingdom was Toulouse, where the royal treasure was also kept; Euric from time to time also held court in Bordeaux, Alaric II in Narbonne. The Gothic rule originally stretched, as has been already mentioned, as far as the province of Aquitanica

Secunda and some bordering municipalities, among which was the district of Toulouse, but later on it extended not only over the whole territory of the Gallic provinces, but in addition to several parts of the provinces Viennensis, Narbonensis Secunda, Alpes Maritimae, and Lugdunensis Tertia. The Gothic possessions included also the greater part of the Iberian peninsula, *i.e.* the provinces of Baetica, Lusitania, Tarraconensis, and Carthaginensis. The provinces named were in Roman times, in so far as it was a question of civil administration, governed by *consulares* or *praesides*, and they were again divided into city-districts (*civitates* or *municipia*). Under the sovereignty of the Goths this constitution was maintained in its chief features.

The inhabitants of the kingdom of Toulouse were composed of two races — the Goths and the Romans. The Goths were regarded by the Romans as foreigners so long as the federal connexion remained in force, yet both peoples lived side by side, each under its own law and jurisdiction: intermarriage was forbidden. This rigid line of separation was adhered to even when the Goths had shaken off the imperial suzerainty and the Gothic king had become the sovereign of the native population of Gaul. Theoretically, the Romans had equal privileges in the State; thus they were not treated as a conquered people without rights, as the Vandals and Langobards (Lombards) dealt with the inhabitants of Africa and Italy. That the Goths were the real rulers was clearly enough made manifest to the Romans.

The domestic condition of the Visigoths before the settlement in Gaul was undoubtedly on the same level as in their original home; private property in land was unknown, agriculture was comparatively primitive, and cattle-rearing provided the principal means of subsistence. A national change began with the settlement in Aquitaine. This was done on the principle of the Roman quartering of troops, so that the Roman landowners were obliged to give up to the Goths in free possession a portion of their total property together with the *coloni*, slaves, and cattle appertaining to it. According to the oldest Gothic codes of law the Goth received two-thirds of the tilled land and, it seems, one-half of the woods. The wood and the meadow land which was not partitioned belonged to the Goths and the Romans for use in common. The parcels of land subjected to partition were called *sortes*, the Roman share, generally, *tertia*, their occupants *hospites* or *consortes*. The Gothic *sortes* were exempt from taxation. As the invaders were very numerous compared with the extent of the province to be apportioned, there is no doubt that not only the large estates, but also the middle-sized and smaller properties were partitioned. Nevertheless it is evident that not every Goth can have shared with a Roman possessor, because there would certainly not have been estates enough; we must rather assume that in the share given up larger properties were split up among several families, as a rule among kinsmen. As the apportionment of the

CH. X.

single lots undoubtedly took place through the decisive influence of the king, it is natural that the nobility (*i.e.* nobility by military service) was favoured in the partition above the ordinary freemen. The landed property of the monarch's favourites must have gained considerably in extent, as elsewhere, through assignments from state property. The very considerable imperial possessions, both crown and private property, as a rule fell to the share of royalty.

Land partition in the districts conquered later followed the same plan as in Aquitaine; seizures of entire Roman estates certainly occurred, but they were exceptions and happened under special circumstances. As a rule the Romans were protected by law in the possession of their *tertiae*, even if it were only for fiscal reasons. The considerably extended range of the Gothic kingdom offered the people ample space for colonisation, so it was not necessary to encroach on the whole of the Roman territory as had been the case in Aquitaine. It is to be assumed that in the newly won territories only the superfluous element of the population had to be provided for; we are not to suppose a general desertion of the home-land.

The social economy proceeded, on the whole, on the same lines as before, *i.e.* through *coloni* and slaves, from whose toil the owners derived their principal support, at least in so far as it was a question of food. For the Goths, whose favourite occupations were warfare and the chase, had no inclination to devote themselves to arduous agricultural toil. They only wanted to control directly the rearing of cattle, as they did of old; animal food seems to have been provided principally by means of large herds of swine. The revolution which the partition of land brought about in the habits of the Goths was too powerful not to exert the deepest influence on all the conditions of life. The rich revenues led to the display of a wanton and indolent way of living; the close contact with the Romans, who were for the most part morally decadent, was bound to affect injuriously a people so famous in earlier times for its austere manners. The old national bonds of union, besides having been relaxed through the migration, now from the scattering of the mass in colonisation lost more and more of their original importance, since kinsmen need no longer be companions on the farmstead in order to obtain a living. The adoption of the Roman conditions of land-holding obliged the Goths to accept numerous legal arrangements which were foreign to their national law and altered its principles considerably. Nevertheless the national consciousness was strong enough to prevent it from merging itself quickly and completely in the Roman system; in contrast to the Ostrogoths who did nothing but carefully conserve the Roman institutions which they found, the Visigoths are remarkable for an attitude in many respects independent towards the foreign organisation.

The entire power of government lay in the hands of the king, but the several rulers did not succeed in making their power absolute. Outwardly the Visigoth king was only slightly distinguished from the other freemen; like them he wore the national skin garment, and long curly hair. The raised seat as well as the sword appear as tokens of royal power, the insignia such as the purple mantle and the crown do not come till later. The succession to the throne follows the system peculiar to the old German constitution of combined election and inheritance. After the death of Alaric I his brother-in-law Ataulf was chosen king; thus a kindred connexion played an important part in this choice. Ataulf's friendliness to Rome had placed him in opposition to the great mass of the people; therefore his successor was not his brother, as he had wished, but first Sigerich and then Wallia, who both belonged to other houses. The elevation of Theodoric I is also an instance of free election; the royal dignity remained in his house for over a century. Thorismud was appointed king by the army; the succession of Theodoric II, Euric, and Alaric II, on the other hand, was only confirmed by popular recognition.

Just as the people regularly took a part in the choice of the successor to the throne, so their influence was often brought to bear on the sovereign's conduct of government. After the settlement in Gaul there could certainly no longer be any question of a national assembly in the old sense of the word, especially after the great expansion of territory under Euric. Meetings of all the freemen had become impossible on account of the expansion of the Gothic colonies. The circle of those who could obey the call to assemble became, therefore, smaller and smaller, while in carrying out the principal public functions, such as the coronation of the king, only those of the people who happened to be present at the place of election or who lived in the immediate neighbourhood, could as a rule take part. The importance which the commonalty hereby lost was gained by the nobility, an aristocracy founded on personal service to the king. It was only in the army that the greater part of the people found opportunity of expressing its will. It is certain that among the Visigoths, as among the Franks, regular military assemblies were held, which at first served the purpose of reviews and were under the command of the king. In these assemblies important political questions were discussed; but the decision of the people was not always for the welfare of the State.

The kingdom was subdivided very nearly on the lines of the previous Roman divisions into *provinciae*, and these again into *civitates (territoria)*. At the head of the province was the *dux* as magistrate for Goths and Romans. He was also, as his title implies, in the first place the commander of the militia in his district, and he provided also the final authority and appeal in matters of government, corresponding to the *Praefectus Praetorio* or *vicarius* of imperial times. The centre of gravity of the government lay in the municipalities whose rulers were *comites civitatum.* They took exactly the place of the Roman provincial governors, so that the city-districts also appear under the title of *provinciae.* Their authority extended even to the exercise of jurisdiction with the exception of such cases as were reserved to the civic magistrates, and included control of the police and the collection of taxes. The *dux* could at the same time be *comes* of a *civitas* in his district. At the head of the towns themselves were the *curiales* who, as hitherto, were bound by oath to fill their offices; and they were personally responsible for collecting the taxes. The most important official was the *defensor,* who was chosen from among the *curiales* by the citizens and only confirmed by the king. He exercised, in the first instance, jurisdiction in minor matters, but his activity extended over all the branches of municipal administration. Side by side with this Roman magistrature existed the national system which the Goths had brought with them. The Gothic people formed themselves into bodies of thousands, five hundreds, hundreds, and tens, which also remained as personal societies after the settlement. The *millenarius,* as of old, led the thousand in war and ruled over it jointly with the heads of the hundreds both in war and in peace. The *comes civitatis* and his vicar originally only possessed jurisdiction over the Romans of his own circuit, but in Euric's time that had so far changed that he now possessed authority to judge the Goths as well in civil suits in conjunction with the *millenarius:* thus the later condition was prepared in which the *millenarius* appears only as military official. On the other hand the *defensor* remained a judiciary solely for the Romans.

We know but little about the officers of the central government. The first minister of Euric and of Alaric II was Leo of Narbonne, a distinguished man of varied talents. His duty comprised a combination of the functions of the *quaestor sacri palatii* and of the *magister officiorum* at the imperial Court; he drew up the king's orders, conducted business with the ambassadors, and arranged the applications for an audience. A higher minister of the royal chancery was Anianus, who attested the authenticity of the official copies of the *Lex Romana Visigothorum* and distributed them; he seems to have answered to the Roman *primicerius notariorum* or *referendarius.*

The organisation of the Catholic Church was not disturbed by the Visigoth rule: rather it was strengthened. The ecclesiastical subdivision of the land as it had developed in the last years of the Roman sway corresponded on the whole with the political: the bishoprics, which coincided in extent with the town districts, were grouped under metropolitan sees, which corresponded with the provinces of the secular administration. Since the middle of the fifth century the authority of the Roman bishop over the Church had been generally recognised. Next to the Pope the bishop of Arles exercised over the Gallic clergy a theoretically almost unlimited disciplinary power. A bishop was chosen by the laity and the clergy of his see, and was ordained by the metropolitan bishop of the province together with other bishops. Although the boundaries of the Visigoth kingdom now in no way coincided with the old provincial and metropolitan boundaries, the hitherto existing metropolitan connexion was nevertheless not set aside, nor were the relations of the bishops with the Pope interfered with. The Gothic government as a rule shewed great indulgence and consideration to the Catholic Church, which only changed to a more severe treatment when the clergy were guilty of treasonable practices, as happened under Euric. No organised and general persecution of the Catholics from religious fanaticism ever took place. The Catholic Church enjoyed particularly favourable conditions under Alaric II, who in consideration of the threatening struggle with Clovis acknowledged the formal legal position of the Roman Church according to the hitherto existing rules.

Hardly anything is known of the ecclesiastical organisation of the Arians in the kingdom of Toulouse. Probably in all the larger towns there were Arian bishops as well as orthodox ones, and no doubt in earlier times they had been appointed by the king. Under the several bishops were the different classes of subordinate clergy; presbyters and deacons are mentioned as in the orthodox Church. The endowment of the Arian Church was probably as a rule allowed for out of the revenue; now and then confiscated Catholic churches as well as their endowments were also made over to it. The church service was of course held in the vernacular as it was in other German churches; the greater number of the clergy were therefore of Gothic nationality. The opposition between the two creeds was also certainly a very sharp one. Both sides carried on an active propaganda, which on the Arian side not unfrequently seems to have been urged by force, but such ebullitions scarcely had the support and approval of the Gothic government.

Very scanty indeed is our knowledge of the civilisation of the kingdom of Toulouse. That the Romance element was foremost in almost every department has already been observed. The Goths however held to their national dress until a later period; they wore the characteristic skin garment which covered the upper part of the body, and laced boots of horse-hide which reached up to the calf of the leg; the knee was left bare. There is no doubt that the Gothic tongue was spoken by the people in intercourse with each other; unhappily no vestiges remain of it except in proper names. It is certain however that a great part of the nobility, especially the higher officials, understood Latin well. Most of the Arian clergy undoubtedly were also masters of both languages. Latin was the language of diplomatic intercourse and of legislation. Theodoric II was trained in Roman literature by Avitus; Euric however understood so little of the foreign language that he was obliged to use an interpreter for diplomatic correspondence. Yet this king was in no way opposed to the knowledge and significance of classical culture. The Visigothic Court therefore formed a haven of frequent resort for the last representatives of Roman literature in Gaul. And the kings, from various motives, but especially from a fondness for Roman models, would employ the art of these men to celebrate their own deeds. Here may be named in the first place the poet Sidonius Apollinaris who for a long time lived, first in the Court of Theodoric II and then in that of Euric. Euric's minister Leo also is said to have distinguished himself as a poet, historian, and lawyer, but no more of his writings have been preserved than of the rhetorician Lampridius, who sang the fame of the Gothic royal house at the Court of Bordeaux. But the decay of literature and of culture in general, which had been for so long in progress in spite of the support of the still existent schools of rhetoricians, could assuredly not be stayed by the patronage of the Gothic kings.

(B)

THE FRANKS BEFORE CLOVIS

Tacitus, in the *de Moribus Germanorum*, tells us that the Germans claimed to be descended from a common ancestor, Mannus, son of the earth-born god Tuisco. Mannus, according to the legend, had three sons, from whom sprang three groups of tribes: the Istaevones, who dwelt along the banks of the Rhine; the Ingaevones, whose seat was on the shores of the two seas, the *Oceanus Germanicus* (North Sea) and the *Mare Suevicum* (the Baltic), and in the Cimbric peninsula between; and, lastly, more to the east and south, on the banks of the Elbe and the Danube, the Herminones. After indicating this general division, Tacitus, in the latter part of his work, enumerates about forty tribes, whose customs presented, no doubt, a strong general resemblance, but whose institutions and organisation shewed differences of a sufficiently marked character.

When we pass from the first century to the fifth, we find that the names of the Germanic peoples given by Tacitus have completely disappeared. Not only is there no mention of Istaevones, Ingaevones, and Herminones, but there is no trace of individual tribes such as the Chatti, Chauci, and Cherusci; their names are wholly unknown to the writers of the fourth and fifth centuries. In their place we find these writers using other designations: they speak of Franks, Saxons, Alemans.

The writers of the Merovingian period not unnaturally supposed that these were the names of new peoples, who had invaded Germany and made good their footing there in the interval. This hypothesis found favour especially with regard to the Franks. As early as Gregory of Tours, we find mention of a tradition according to which the Franks had come from Pannonia, had first established themselves on the right bank of the Rhine, and had subsequently crossed the river. In the chronicler known under the name of Fredegar the Franks are represented as descended from the Trojans. "Their first king was Priam; after_ wards they had a king named Eriga; later, they divided into two parts, one of which migrated into Macedonia and received the name of Macedonians. Those who remained were driven out of Phrygia and wandered about, with their wives and children, for many years. They chose for themselves a king named Francion, and from him took the name of Franks. Francion made war upon many peoples, and after devastating Asia finally passed over into Europe, and established himself between the Rhine, the Danube and the sea." The writer of the *Liber Historiae* combines the statements of Gregory of Tours and of the pseudo-Fredegar, and, with a fine disregard of chronology, relates that, after the fall of Troy, one part of the Trojan people, under Priam and Antenor, came by way of the Black Sea to the mouth of the Danube, sailed up the river to Pannonia, and founded a city called Sicambria. The Trojans, so this anonymous writer continues, were defeated by the Emperor Valentinian, who laid them under tribute and named them Franks, that is wild men (*feros*), because of their boldness and hardness of heart. After a time the Franks slew the Roman officials whose duty it was to demand the tribute from them, and, on the death of Priam, they quitted Sicambria, and came to the neighbourhood of the Rhine. There they chose themselves a king named Pharamond, son of Marcomir. This *naïf* legend, half-popular, half-learned, was accepted as fact throughout the Middle Ages. From it alone comes the name of Pharamond, which in most histories heads the list of the kings of France. In reality, there is nothing to prove that the Franks, any more than the Saxons or the Alemans, were races who came in from without, driven into Germany by an invasion of their own territory.

Some modern scholars have thought that the origin of the Franks, and of other races who make their appearance between the third century and the fifth, might be traced to a curious custom of the Germanic tribes. The nobles, whom Tacitus calls *principes*, attached to themselves a certain number of comrades, *comites*, whom they bound to fealty by a solemn oath. At the head of these followers they made pillaging expeditions, and levied war upon the neighbouring peoples, without however involving the community to which they belonged. The *comes* was ready to die for his chief; to desert him would have been an infamy. The chief, on his part, protected his follower, and gave him a war-horse, spear, etc. as the reward of his loyalty. Thus there were formed, outside the regular State, bands of warriors united together by the closest ties. These bands, so it is said, soon formed, in the interior of Germany, what were virtually new States, and the former *princeps* simply took the title of king. Such, according to the theory, was the origin of the Franks, the Alemans, and the Saxons. But this theory, however ingenious, cannot be accepted. The bands were formed exclusively of young men of an age to bear arms; among the Franks we find from the first old men, women, and children. The bands were organised solely for war; whereas the most ancient laws of the Franks have much to say about the ownership of land, and about crimes against property; they represent the Franks as an organised nation with regular institutions.

The Franks, then, did not come into Germany from without; and it would be rash to seek their origin in the custom of forming bands. That being so, only one hypothesis remains open. From the second century to the fourth the Germans lived in a continual state of unrest. The different communities ceaselessly made war on one another and destroyed one another. Civil war also devastated many of them. The ancient communities were thus broken up, and from their remains were formed new communities which received new names. Thus is to be explained why it is that the nomenclature of the Germanic peoples in the fifth century differs so markedly from that which Tacitus has recorded. But neighbouring tribes presented, despite their constant antagonisms, considerable resemblances. They had a common dialect and similar habits and customs. They sometimes made temporary alliances, though holding themselves free to quarrel again before long and make war on one another with the utmost ferocity. In time, groups of these tribes came to be called by generic names, and this is doubtless the character of the names Franks, Alemans, and Saxons. These names were not applied, in the fourth and fifth centuries, to a single tribe, but to a group of neighbouring tribes who presented, along with real differences, certain common characteristics.

It appears that the peoples who lived along the right bank of the Rhine, to the north of the Main, received the name of Franks; those who had established themselves between the Ems and the Elbe, that of Saxons (Ptolemy mentions the Σάξονες as inhabitants of the Cimbric peninsula, and perhaps the name of this petty tribe had passed to the whole group); while those whose territory lay to the south of the Main and who at some time or other had overflowed into the *agri decumates* (the present Baden) were called Alemans. It is possible that, after all, we should see in these three peoples, as Waitz has suggested, the Istaevones, Ingaevones, and Herminones of Tacitus.

But it must be understood that between the numerous tribes known under each of the general names of Franks, Saxons, and Alemans there was no common bond. They did not constitute a single State but groups of States without federal connexion or common organisation. Sometimes two, three, even a considerable number of tribes, might join together to prosecute a war in common, but when the war was over the link snapped and the tribes fell asunder again.

Documentary evidence enables us to trace how the generic name *Franci* came to be given to certain tribes between the Main and the North Sea, for we find these tribes designated now by the ancient name which was known to Tacitus and again by the later name. In Peutinger's chart we find *Chamavi qui et Pranci* and there is no doubt that we should read *qui et Franci*. The Chamavi inhabited the country between the Yssel and the Ems; later on, we find them a little further south, on the banks of the Rhine in Hamaland, and their laws were collected in the ninth century in the document known as the *Lex Francorum Chamavorum*. Along with the Chamavi we may reckon among the Franks the Attuarii or Chattuarii. We read in Ammianus Marcellinus (xx. 10) *Rheno transmisso, regionem pervasit* (Julian in A.D. 360) *Francorum quos Atthuarios vocant*. Later, the *pagus Attuariorum* will correspond to the country of Emmerich, of Cleves, and of Xanten. We may note that in the Middle Ages there was to be found in Burgundy, in the neighbourhood of Dijon, a *pagus Attuariorum*, and it is very probable that a portion of this tribe settled at this spot in the course of the fifth century. The Bructeri, the Ampsivarii, and the Chatti were, like the Chamavi, reckoned as Franks. They are mentioned as such in a well-known passage of Sulpicius Alexander which is cited by Gregory of Tours (*Historia Francorum*, II. 9). Arbogast, a barbarian general in the service of Rome, desires to take vengeance on the Franks and their chiefs — *subreguli* — Sunno and Marcomir. Consequently in midwinter of the year 392 *collecto exercitu transgressus Rhenum, Bructeros ripae proximos, pagum etiam quem Chamavi incolunt depopulatus est, nullo unquam occursante, nisi quod pauci ex Ampsivariis et Catthis Marcomere duce in ulterioribus collium jugis apparuere*. It is this Marcomir, chief of the Ampsivarii and Chatti, whom the author of the *Liber Historiae* makes the father of Pharamond, though he has nothing whatever to do with the Salian Franks.

Thus it is evident that the name Franks was given to a group of tribes, not to a single tribe. The earliest historical mention of the name may be that in Peutinger's chart,[1] supposing, at least, that the words *et Pranci* are not a later interpolation. The earliest mention in a literary source is in the *Vita Aureliani* of Vopiscus, cap. 7. In the year 240, Aurelian, who was then only a military tribune, immediately after defeating the Franks in the neighbourhood of Mainz, was marching against the Persians, and his soldiers as they marched chanted this refrain :

Mille Sarmatas, mille Francos semel et semel occidimus ;
Mille Persas quaerimus.

It would be in any case impossible to follow the history of all these

[1] The date of the chart is very uncertain.

Frankish tribes for want of evidence, but even if their history was known it would be of quite secondary interest, for it would have only a remote connexion with the history of France. Offshoots from these various tribes no doubt established themselves sporadically here and there in ancient Gaul, as in the case of the Attuarii. It was not however by the Franks as a whole, but by a single tribe, the Salian Franks, that Gaul was to be conquered; it was their king who was destined to be the ruler of this noble territory. It is therefore to the Salian Franks that we must devote our attention.

The Salian Franks are mentioned for the first time in A.D. 358. In that year Julian, as yet only a Caesar, marched against them. *Petit primos omnium Francos, eos videlicet quos consuetudo Salios appellavit* (Ammianus Marcellinus, XVII. 8). What is the origin of the name? It was long customary to derive it from the river Yssel (Isala), or from Saalland to the south of the Zuiderzee; but it seems much more probable that the name comes from *sal* (the salt sea). The Salian Franks at first lived by the shores of the North Sea, and were known by this name in contradistinction to the Ripuarian Franks, who lived on the banks of the Rhine. All their oldest legends speak of the sea, and the name of one of their earliest kings, Merovech, signifies sea-born.

From the shores of the North Sea the Salian Franks had advanced little by little towards the south, and at the period when Ammianus Marcellinus mentions them they occupied Toxandria, that is to say the region to the south of the Meuse, between that river and the Scheldt. Julian completely defeated the Salian Franks, but he left them in possession of their territory of Toxandria. Only, instead of occupying it as conquerors, they held it as *foederati*, agreeing to defend it against all other invaders. They furnished also to the armies of Rome soldiers whom we hear of as serving in far distant regions. In the *notitia Dignitatum*, in which we find a sort of Army List of the Empire drawn up about the beginning of the fifth century, there is mention of *Salii seniores* and *Salii juniores*, and we also find *Salii* figuring in the *auxilia palatina*.

At the end of the fourth and beginning of the fifth century the Salian Franks established in Toxandria ceased to recognise the authority of Rome, and began to assert their independence. It was at this period that the Roman civilisation disappeared from these regions. The Latin language ceased to be spoken and the Germanic tongue was alone employed. Even at the present day the inhabitants of these districts speak Flemish, a Germanic dialect. The place-names were altered and took on a Germanic form, with the terminations *hem, ghem, seele,* and *zele,* indicating a dwelling-place, *loo* wood, *dal* valley. The Christian religion retreated along with the Roman civilisation, and those regions reverted to paganism. For a long time, it would seem, these Salian Franks were held in check by the great Roman road which led, by way of Arras, Cambrai, and Bavay, to Cologne, and which was protected by numerous forts.

The Salians were subdivided into a number of tribes each holding a *pagus*. Each of these divisions had a king who was chosen from the most noble family, and who was distinguished from his fellow_ Franks by his long hair — *criniti reges*. The first of these kings to whom we have a distinct reference bore the name of Clogio or Clojo (Clodion). He had his seat at Dispargum, the exact position of which has not been determined — it may have been Diest in Brabant. Desiring to extend the borders of the Salian Franks he advanced southwards in the direction of the great Roman road. Before reaching it, however, he was surprised, near the town of Helena (Hélesmes-Nord), when engaged in celebrating the betrothal of one of his warriors to a fair-haired maiden, by Aëtius, who exercised in the name of Rome the military command in Gaul. He sustained a crushing defeat; the victor carried off his chariots and took prisoner even the trembling bride. This was about the year 431. But Clodion was not long in recovering from this defeat. He sent spies into the neighbourhood of Cambrai, defeated the Romans, and captured the town. He had thus gained command of the great Roman road. Then, without encountering opposition, he advanced as far as the Somme, which marked the limit of Frankish territory. About this period Tournai on the Scheldt seems to have become the capital of the Salian Franks.

Clodion was succeeded in the kingship of the Franks by Merovech. All our histories of France assert that he was the son of Clodion; but Gregory of Tours simply says that he belonged to the family of that king, and he does not give even this statement as certain; it is maintained, he says, by certain persons — *De huius stirpe quidam Merovechum regem fuisse adserunt.* We should perhaps refer to Merovech certain statements of the Greek historian Priscus, who lived about the middle of the fifth century. On the death of a king of the Franks, he says, his two sons disputed the succession. The elder betook himself to Attila to seek his support; the younger preferred to claim the protection of the Emperor, and journeyed to Rome. "I saw him there," he says; "he was still quite young. His fair hair, thick and very long, fell over his shoulders." Aëtius, who was at this time in Rome, received him graciously, loaded him with presents, and sent him back as a friend and ally. Certainly, in the sequel the Salian Franks responded to the appeal of Aëtius and mustered to oppose the great invasion of Attila, fighting in the ranks of the Roman army at the battle of the Mauriac Plain (A.D. 451). The *Vita Lupi*, in which some confidence may be placed, names King Merovech among the combatants.

Various legends have gathered round the figure of Merovech. The pseudo-Fredegar narrates that as the mother of this prince was sitting by the sea-shore a monster sprang from the waves and overpowered her;

CH. X.

and from this union was born Merovech. Evidently the legend owes its origin to an attempt to explain the etymology of the name Merovech, son of the sea. In consequence of this legend some historians have maintained that Merovech was a wholly mythical personage and they have sought out some remarkable etymologies to explain the name Merovingian, which is given to the kings of the first dynasty; but in our opinion the existence of this prince is sufficiently proved, and we interpret the term Merovingian as meaning descendants of Merovech.

Merovech had a son named Childeric. The relationship is attested in precise terms by Gregory of Tours who says *cujus filius fuit Childericus.* In addition to the legendary narratives about Childeric which Gregory gathered from oral tradition, we have also some very precise details which the celebrated historian borrowed from annals now no longer extant. The legendary tale is as follows. Childeric, who was extremely licentious, dishonoured the daughters of many of the Franks. His subjects therefore rose in their wrath, drove him from the throne, and even threatened to kill him. He fled to Thuringia — it is uncertain whether this was Thuringia beyond the Rhine, or whether there was a Thuringia on the left bank of the river — but he left behind him a faithful friend whom he charged to win back the allegiance of the Franks. Childeric and his friend broke a gold coin in two and each took a part. "When I send you my part," said the friend, "and the pieces fit together to form one whole you may safely return to your country." The Franks unanimously chose for their king Aegidius, who had succeeded Aëtius in Gaul as *magister militum.* At the end of eight years the faithful friend, having succeeded in gaining over the Franks, sent to Childeric the token agreed upon, and the prince, on his return, was restored to the throne. The queen of the Thuringians, Basina by name, left her husband Basinus to follow Childeric. "I know thy worth," said she, "and thy great courage; therefore I have come to live with thee. If I had known, even beyond the sea, a man more worthy than thou art, I would have gone to him." Childeric, well pleased, married her forthwith, and from their union was born Clovis. This legend, on which it would be rash to base any historical conclusion, was amplified later, and the further developments of it have been preserved by the pseudo-Fredegar and the author of the *Liber Historiae.*

But alongside of this legendary story we have some definite information regarding Childeric. While the main centre of his kingdom continued to be in the neighbourhood of Tournai, he fought along with the Roman generals in the valley of the Loire against all the enemies who sought to wrest Gaul from the Empire. Unlike his predecessor Clodion and his son Clovis, he faithfully fulfilled his duties as a *foederatus.* In the year 463 the Visigoths made an effort to extend their dominions to the banks of the Loire. Aegidius marched against them, and defeated them at Orleans, Friedrich, brother of King Theodoric II, being slain in the battle.

Now we know for certain that Childeric was present at this battle. A short time afterwards the Saxons made a descent, by way of the North Sea, the Channel, and the Atlantic, under the leadership of a chief named Odovacar, established themselves in some islands at the mouth of the Loire, and threatened the town of Angers on the Mayenne. The situation was the more serious because Aegidius had lately died (October 464), leaving the command to his son Syagrius. Childeric threw himself into Angers and held it against the Saxons. He succeeded in beating off the besiegers, assumed the offensive, and recaptured from the Saxons the islands which they had seized. The defeated Odovacar placed himself, like Childeric, at the service of Rome, and the two adversaries, now reconciled, barred the path of a troop of Alemans who were returning from a pillaging expedition into Italy. Thus Childeric policed Gaul on behalf of Rome and endeavoured to check the inroads and forays of the other barbarians.

The death of Childeric probably took place in the year 481, and he was buried at Tournai. His tomb was discovered in the year 1653. In it was a ring bearing his name, CHILDIRICI REGIS, with the image of the head and shoulders of a long-haired warrior. Numerous objects of value, arms, jewels, remains of a purple robe ornamented with golden bees, gold coins bearing the effigies of Leo I and Zeno, Emperors of Constantinople, were found in the tomb. Such of these treasures as could be preserved are now in the Bibliothèque Nationale at Paris. They serve as evidence that these Merovingian kings were fond of luxury and possessed quantities of valuable objects. In the ensuing volume it will be seen how Childeric's son Clovis broke with his father's policy, threw off his allegiance to the Empire, and conquered Gaul for his own hand. While Childeric was reigning at Tournai, another Salian chief, Ragnachar, reigned at Cambrai, the town which Clodion had taken; the residence of a third, named Chararic, is unknown to us.

The Salian Franks, as we have said above, were so called in contradistinction to the Ripuarians. The latter doubtless included a certain number of tribes, such as the Ampsivarii and the Bructeri. Julian, in the year 360, checked the advance of these barbarians and forced them to retire across the Rhine. In 389 Arbogast similarly checked their inroads and conquered all their territory in 392, as we have already said. But in the beginning of the fifth century, when Stilicho had withdrawn the Roman garrisons from the banks of the Rhine, they were able to advance without hindrance and establish themselves on the left bank of the river. Their progress however was far from rapid. They only gained possession of Cologne at a time when Salvian, born about 400, was a man in middle life; and even then the town was retaken. It did not finally pass into their hands until the year 463. The town of Trèves was taken and burned by the Franks four times before they made themselves masters of it. Towards 470 the Ripuarians had founded a fairly compact kingdom, of which the

CH. X.

principal cities were Aix-la-Chapelle, Bonn, Juliers, and Zülpich. They had advanced southwards as far as Divodurum (Metz), the fortifications of which seem to have defied all their efforts. The Roman civilisation, the Latin language, and even the Christian religion seem to have disappeared from the regions occupied by the compact masses of these invaders. The present frontier of the French and German languages, or a frontier drawn a little further to the south — for it appears that in course of time French has gained ground a little — indicates the limit of their dominions. In the course of their advance southwards, the Ripuarians came into collision with the Alemans, who had already made themselves masters of Alsace and were endeavouring to enlarge their borders in all directions. There were many battles, between the Ripuarians and Alemans, of one of which, fought at Zülpich (Tolbiacum), a record has been preserved. Sigebert, king of the Ripuarians, was there wounded in the knee and walked lame for the rest of his life; whence he was known as *Sigebertus Claudus*. It appears that at this time the Alemans had penetrated far north into the kingdom of the Ripuarians. This kingdom was destined to have but a transient existence; we shall see in the following volume how it was destroyed by Clovis, and how all the Frankish tribes on the left bank of the Rhine were brought under his authority.

While the Salian and Ripuarian Franks were spreading along the left bank of the Rhine, and founding flourishing kingdoms there, other Frankish tribes remained on the right bank. They were firmly established, especially to the north of the Main, and among them the ancient tribe of the Chatti, from whom the Hessians are derived, took a leading place. Later this territory formed one of the duchies into which Germany was divided, and took from its Frankish inhabitants the name of Franconia.

If we desire to make ourselves acquainted with the manners and customs of the Franks, we must have recourse to the most ancient document which has come down from them — the Salic Law. The oldest redaction of this Law, as will be shewn in the next volume, probably dates only from the last years of Clovis (507–511), but in it are codified much more ancient usages. On the basis of this code we can conjecture the condition of the Franks in the time of Clodion, of Merovech, and of Childeric. The family is still a very closely united whole; there is solidarity among relatives even to a remote degree. If a murderer could not pay the fine to which he had been sentenced, he must bring before the *mâl* (court) twelve comprobators who made affirmation that he could not pay it. That done, he returned to his dwelling, took up some earth from each of the four corners of his room, and cast it with the left hand over his shoulder towards his nearest relative; then, barefoot and clad only in his shirt, but bearing a spear in his hand, he

leaped over the hedge which surrounded his dwelling. Once this cere.
mony had been performed, it devolved upon his relative, to whom he
had thereby ceded his house, to pay the fine in his place. He might
appeal in this way to a series of relatives one after another; and if,
ultimately, none of them was able to pay, he was brought before four
successive *mâls*, and if no one took pity on him and paid his debt, he
was put to death. But if the family was thus a unit for the payment of
fines, it had the compensating advantage of sharing the fine paid for
the murder of one of its members. Since the solidarity of the family
sometimes entailed dangerous consequences, it was permissible for an
individual to break these family ties. The man who wished to do so
presented himself at the *mâl* before the *centenarius* and broke into
four pieces, above his head, three wands of alder. He then threw the
pieces into the four corners, declaring that he separated himself from his
relatives and renounced all rights of succession. The family included the
slaves and *liti* or freedmen. Slaves were the chattels of their master; if
they were wounded, maimed, or killed, the master received the compensation; on the other hand, if the slave had committed any crime the
master was obliged to pay, unless he preferred to give him up to bear
the punishment. The Franks recognised private property, and severe
penalties were denounced against those who invaded the rights of ownership; there are penalties for stealing from another's garden, meadow,
corn-field, or flax-field, and for ploughing another's land. At a man's
death all his property was divided among his sons; a daughter had no
claim to any share of it. Later, she is simply excluded from Salic
ground, that is from her father's house and the land that surrounds it.

We find also in the Salic Law some information about the organisation of the State. The royal power appears strong. Any man who
refuses to appear before the royal tribunal is outlawed. All his goods
are confiscated and anyone who chooses may slay him with impunity;
no one, not even his wife, may give him food, under penalty of a very
heavy fine. All those who are employed about the king's person are
protected by a special sanction. Their *wergeld* is three times as high
as that of other Franks of the same social status. Over each of the
territorial divisions called *pagi* the king placed a representative of his
authority known as the *grafio*, or, to give him his later title, the *comes*.
The *grafio* maintained order within his jurisdiction, levied such fines as
were due to the king, executed the sentences of the courts, and seized
the property of condemned persons who refused to pay their fines. The
pagus was in turn subdivided into "hundreds" (*centenae*). Each "hundred" had its court of judgment known as the *mâl*; the place where it met
was known as the *mâlberg*. This tribunal was presided over by the
centenarius or *thunginus* — these terms appear to us to be synonymous.
Historians have devoted much discussion to the question whether this
official was appointed by the king or elected by the freemen of the

CH. X.

"hundred." At the court of the "hundred" all the freemen had a right to be present, but only a few of them took part in the proceedings — some of them would be nominated for this duty on one occasion, some on another. In their capacity as assistants to the *centenarius* at the *mâl* the freemen were designated *rachineburgi*. In order to make a sentence valid it was required that seven *rachineburgi* should pronounce judgment. A plaintiff had the right to summon seven of them to give judgment upon his suit. If they refused, they had to pay a fine of three sols. If they persisted in their refusal, and did not undertake to pay the three sols before sunset, they incurred a fine of fifteen sols.

Every man's life was rated at a certain value; this was his price, the *wergeld*. The *wergeld* of a Salian Frank was 200 sols; that of a Roman 100 sols. If a Salian Frank had killed another Salian, or a Roman, without aggravating circumstances, the Court sentenced him to pay the price of the victim, the 200 or 100 sols. The *compositio* in this case is exactly equivalent to the *wergeld*; if, however, he had only wounded his victim he paid, according to the severity of the injury, a lower sum proportionate to the *wergeld*. If, however, the murder has taken place in particularly atrocious circumstances, if the murderer has endeavoured to conceal the corpse, if he has been accompanied by an armed band, or if the assassination has been unprovoked, the *compositio* may be three times, six times, nine times, the *wergeld*. Of this *compositio*, two thirds were paid to the relatives of the victim; this was the *faida* and bought off the right of private vengeance; the other third was paid to the State or to the king: it was called *fretus* or *fredum* from the German word *Friede* peace, and was a compensation for the breach of the public peace of which the king is the guardian. Thus a very lofty principle was embodied in this penalty.

The Salic Law is mainly a tariff of the fines which must be paid for various crimes and offences. The State thus endeavoured to substitute the judicial sentences of the courts for private vengeance, part of the compensation being paid to the victim or his family to induce them to renounce this right. But we may safely conjecture that the triumph of law over inveterate custom was not immediate. It was long before families were willing to leave to the judgment of the courts serious crimes which had been committed against them, such as homicides and adulteries; they flew to arms and made war upon the guilty person and his family. The forming in this way of armed bands was very detrimental to public order.

The crimes mentioned most frequently in the Salic Law give us some grounds on which to form an idea of the manners and characteristics of the Franks. These Franks would seem to have been much given to bad language, for the Law mentions a great variety of terms of abuse. It is forbidden to call one's adversary a fox or a hare, or to reproach him with having flung away his shield; it is forbidden to call a woman *meretrix*, or to say that she had joined the witches at their revels. Warriors who are so easily enraged readily pass to violence and murder. Every form of homicide is mentioned in the Salic Law. The roads are not safe, and are often infested by armed bands. In addition to murder, theft is very often mentioned by the code — theft of fruits, of hay, of cattle-bells, of horse-clogs, of animals, of river-boats, of slaves, and even of freemen. All these thefts are punished with severity and are held by all to be base and shameful crimes. But there is a punishment of special severity for robbing a corpse which has been buried. The guilty person is outlawed, and is to be treated like a wild beast.

The civilisation of these Franks is primitive; they are, above all else, warriors. As to their appearance, they brought their fair hair forward from the top of the head, leaving the back of the neck bare. On their faces they generally wore no hair but the moustache. They wore close-fitting garments, fastened with brooches, and bound in at the waist by a leather belt which was covered with bands of enamelled iron and clasped by an ornamental buckle. From this belt hung the long sword, the hanger or *scramasax*, and various articles of the toilet, such as scissors and combs made of bone. From it too was hung the single-bladed axe, the favourite weapon of the Franks, known as the *francisca*, which they used both at close quarters and by hurling it at their enemies from a distance. They were also armed with a long lance or spear (Lat. *framea*) formed of an iron blade at the end of a long wooden shaft. For defence they carried a large shield, made of wood or wattles covered with skins, the centre of which was formed by a convex plate of metal, the boss (*umbo*), fastened by iron rods to the body of the shield. They were fond of jewellery, wearing gold finger-rings and armlets, and collars formed of beads of amber or glass or paste inlaid with colour. They were buried with their arms and ornaments, and many Frankish cemeteries have been explored in which the dead were found fully armed, as if prepared for a great military review. The Franks were universally distinguished for courage. As Sidonius Apollinaris wrote of them: "from their youth up war is their passion. If they are crushed by weight of numbers, or through being taken at a disadvantage, death may overwhelm them, but not fear."

CH. X.

CHAPTER XI

THE SUEVES, ALANS, AND VANDALS IN SPAIN, 409–429
THE VANDAL DOMINION IN AFRICA, 429–533

THANKS to its geographically strong position, the Iberian peninsula had up till now escaped barbarian invasions; when however the Roman troops stationed to protect the passes of the Pyrenees gave way to negligence, the Asdingian and Silingian Vandals, the (non-German) Alans, and the Sueves availed themselves of the favourable opportunity to cross the mountains (autumn 409). For two whole years the four peoples wandered about devastating the flourishing country, especially the western and southern provinces, without settling anywhere; it was only when famine and disease broke out and menaced their own existence that they were persuaded to more peaceful relations. They concluded a treaty in the year 411 with the Emperor, according to which they received land to settle on as *foederati, i.e.* as subjects of the Empire with the duty of defending Spain against attacks from without. The assignment of the provinces in which the different peoples should settle was decided by lot; Galicia fell to the Asdingians and the Sueves, while the Silingians received Baetica (southern Spain), and the Alans, numerically the strongest people, Lusitania (Portugal) and Carthaginensis (capital Carthagena). Probably they divided the land with the Roman proprietors. The peace brought about in this way did not however last long; the Imperial Government had professed only to regard the arrangement as a temporary expedient. As early as the year 416 the Visigoth king, Wallia, appeared in Spain with a considerable army to free the land from the barbarians in the name of the Emperor. First of all the Silingians were attacked and, after repeated combats, completely destroyed (418), their king, Fredbal, being carried to Italy as prisoner. As a tribal name the name of Asdingians disappears: it only survived as the appellation of members of the royal family. The Alans also, against whom Wallia next marched, were severely beaten and so much weakened that after the death of King Addac the people decided not to choose another head but to join the Asdingian Vandals, whose kings from that time bore the title *Reges Vandalorum et Alanorum* (418). Only the recall of Wallia (end of 418) saved the Asdingians and the Sueves from the extermination which menaced them. The former rallied wonderfully: they first of all turned against their Suevian neighbours, then under the rule of Hermeric, who had once more made overtures to the Emperor, and pressed them back into the Cantabrian Mountains from which they were only extricated by a Roman army which hurriedly came to their assistance (419). Obliged to retreat to Baetica, the Vandals encountered in 421 or 422 a strong Roman army under Castinus, but owing to the treachery of the Visigoth troops who were fighting on the Roman side they gained a brilliant victory. This success immensely stimulated the power of the Vandals and their desire for expansion. They then laid the foundation of their maritime power, afterwards so formidable; we understand that they infested the Balearic Isles and the coast of Mauretania in the year 425. At that time Carthagena and Seville, the last bulwarks of the Romans in southern Spain, also fell into their power.

Three years later died Gunderic who had ruled over the Vandals since 406. He was succeeded on the throne by his brother Gaiseric[1] (born about 400), one of the most famous figures in the Wandering of the Nations (428). A year after his accession Gaiseric led his people over to Africa. This undertaking sprang from the same political considerations as had earlier moved the Visigoth kings, Alaric and Wallia: the rulers of that province, whose main function it was to supply Italy with corn, had the fate of the Roman Empire in their hands, but they were themselves in an almost unassailable position so long as a good navy was at their disposal. The immediate occasion was furnished by the confusion which then reigned in Africa — the revolt of the Moors, the revolutionary upheaval of the severely oppressed peasantry, the revolt of the ecclesiastical sects, particularly the Donatists (Circumcelliones), the manifest weakness of the Roman system of defence everywhere, and, finally, a quarrel between the military governor of Africa, Bonifacius, and the Imperial Government. The well-known story that Bonifacius himself had called the Vandals into the land to revenge the wrongs he had suffered is a fable, which first appeared in Roman authorities of a later time and was invented to veil the real reason. The crossing took place at Julia Traducta, now Tarifa, in May 429. Shortly before embarking the Vandal king turned back with a division of his army and totally defeated the Sueves in a bloody fight near Merida. The Sueves had taken advantage of the departure of their enemies to invade Lusitania. According to a trustworthy account, Gaiseric's people numbered at that time about 80,000 souls, *i.e.* about 15,000 armed men; their numbers were made up of Vandals, Alans, and Visigoth stragglers who had remained behind in Spain.

The Germans first met with the sternest resistance when they entered Numidia in the year 430: Bonifacius opposed them here with

---

[1] Correctly Gaisarix. The frequent form Genseric is philologically impossible.

some hurriedly collected troops, but was defeated. The open country was then completely given over to the enemy; only a few forts — Hippo Regius (now Bona), Cirta (Constantine), and Carthage — were kept by the Romans, Hippo mainly through the influence of St Augustine who died during the siege 28 August 430. As it was impossible for the barbarians to take these strongholds owing to their inexperience in siege-work, and as the Romans in the meantime sent reinforcements under Aspar into Carthage by sea, Gaiseric, after heavy losses, resolved to enter into negotiations with the Emperor. On 11 Feb. 435, at Hippo Regius, a treaty was concluded with the imperial agent Trigetius, according to which the Vandals entered the service of the Empire as *foederati* and were settled in the proconsulate of Numidia (capital Hippo), probably in the same way as earlier in Spain, for here too no formal cession of territory took place.

Gaiseric, however, no doubt regarded the situation thus produced as only temporary. After he had again to some extent united his forces, he posed as a perfectly independent ruler in the district assigned to him. The arbitrary actions in which he indulged comprised the deposition of a number of orthodox clergy who had tried to hinder the performance of the Arian service. Vandal pirates scoured the Mediterranean and even plundered the coasts of Sicily in 437. But on 19 Oct. 439, Gaiseric unexpectedly attacked Carthage and captured the city without a stroke. The occupation was followed by a general pillage which naturally did not end without deeds of violence, even if we are not told of any deliberate destruction or damage to particular buildings. The Catholic clergy and the noble inhabitants of Carthage experienced the fate of banishment or slavery. All the churches inside the town as well as some outside were closed for orthodox services and given over to the Arian clergy together with the ecclesiastical property.

Gaiseric must have expected that after these proceedings the Imperial Government would use every possible means of chastising the bold raiders of its most valuable province. To prevent this and to reduce the Western Empire to a state of permanent helplessness by continuously harassing it, he fitted out a powerful fleet in the harbour of Carthage in the spring of 440 with the special aim of attacking Sardinia and Sicily, which were now primarily relied upon to supply Italy with corn. Although extensive preparations for defence had been arranged the Vandals landed in Sicily without encountering any resistance and moved to and fro, burning and laying waste, but returned to Africa in the same year, 440, on hearing tidings of the approach of powerful Byzantine succours. The expected Greek fleet certainly appeared in Sicilian waters in 441, but the commanders wasted their time there in useless delay, and when the Persians and the Huns invaded the borderlands which had been denuded of troops, the whole fighting force was called back without having effected anything. Under these circumstances the

Emperor of Western Rome found himself obliged to conclude a peace with Gaiseric, whose rule was officially recognised as *independent*, 442. It is stated by some authorities that Africa was divided between the two powers. The best parts of the country: Tingitian Mauretania (by which the Straits of Gibraltar were controlled), Zeugitana or Proconsu_laris, Byzacena and Numidia proconsularis fell to the Vandals, whilst Mauretania Caesariensis and Sitifensis, Cirtan Numidia and Tripolis remained to the Roman Empire.

This treaty forms an important epoch in the history of the Vandals and marks the end of their migration. A final settlement of the conditions for colonisation now took place. The Vandals settled down definitely in the country districts of Zeugitana in the neighbourhood of Carthage. Military reasons, which made a settlement of the people desirable, especially in the neighbourhood of the capital city, as well as the circumstance that the most fertile arable land lay there, were of principal weight in this step. The former landowners — as many as had not been slain or exiled during the conquest — had to choose whether, after the loss of their property, they would make their home as freemen elsewhere or remain as servants, *i.e.* probably as *coloni*, on their former estates. The Catholic clergy, if they resided within the so-called Vandal allotment, met with the same fate as the landowners, a measure which was principally directed against their suspected political propaganda. In the other provinces and especially in the towns the Roman conditions of property remained as a rule undisturbed, although the Romans were considered as a subject people and the land the property of the State or the king. In order to deprive his enemies, internal or external, of every possible gathering-point, Gaiseric next had the fortifications of most of the towns demolished, with the exception of the Castle Septa in the Straits of Gibraltar, and the towns Hippo Regius and Carthage. The last was looked upon as the principal bulwark of the Vandal power. The sovereign position which Vandal power had now attained found expression in the legal dating of the regnal years from 19 Oct. 439, the date of the taking of Carthage, which was reckoned as New Year's Day. There is no trace here of any reckoning according to the consular years or indictions, as was the custom, for example, in the kingdom of the Burgundians, who continued to consider themselves formally as citizens of the Roman Empire.

How powerful the kingdom of Gaiseric was at this epoch is seen from the fact that the Visigoth king, Theodoric I, sought to form alliance with him by marrying his daughter to the king's son Huneric, the heir-presumptive to the throne. This state of affairs however did not last long, for Gaiseric, under the pretext that his daughter-in-law wanted to poison him, sent her back to her father after having cut off her nose and her ears. Probably the dissolution of this coalition, so menacing to Rome, was brought about by a diplomatic move on the part

CH. XI.

of the West-Roman minister Aëtius, who held out prospects to the king of the Vandals of a marriage between his son and a daughter of the Emperor Valentinian III. Although the projected wedding did not take place, friendly relations were begun between the Vandals and the Romans which lasted until the year 455. Gaiseric was even induced to allow the see of Carthage, which had been vacant since 439, to be again filled.

But this friendly connexion ceased at once when the Emperor Valentinian, the murderer of Aëtius, was himself slain by that general's following (16 March 455). Gaiseric announced that he could not recognise the new Emperor Maximus, who had had a hand in the murders of Aëtius and Valentinian and had forced the widowed Empress Eudoxia to marry him, as a fit inheritor of the imperial throne. Under this pretext he immediately sailed to Italy with a large fleet, which seems to have been long since equipped in readiness for coming events. That he came in response to an appeal from Eudoxia cannot be for a moment supposed. Without meeting with any resistance the Vandals, amongst whom also were Moors, landed in the harbour of Portus, and marched along the Via Portuensis to the Eternal City. A great number of the inhabitants took to flight; when Maximus prepared to do likewise he was killed by one of the soldiers of his body-guard (31 May). On 2 June Gaiseric marched into Rome. At the Porta Portuensis he was received by Pope Leo I, who is said to have prevailed upon the king to refrain at least from fire and slaughter and content himself merely with plundering.

The Vandals stayed a fortnight (June 455) in Rome, long enough to take all the treasures which had been left by the Visigoths in the year 410 or restored since. First of all the imperial palace was fallen upon, all that was there was brought to the ships to adorn the royal residence in Carthage, among other things the insignia of imperial dignity. The same fate befell the Temple of Jupiter Capitolinus, of which even the half of the gilded roof was taken away. Among the plundered treasure the vessels of Solomon's Temple, formerly brought to Rome by Titus, took a conspicuous place. On the other hand, the Christian churches as a rule were spared. Murder and incendiarism also, as has been certainly proved, did not take place, neither was there any wanton destruction of buildings or works of art. It is therefore very unjust to brand Gaiseric's people with the word "Vandalism," which indeed came into use in France no earlier than the end of the eighteenth century. Besides the enormous spoil which the Vandals carried away were numerous prisoners, in particular the widowed Empress Eudoxia with her two daughters, Eudoxia and Placidia, as well as Gaudentius, the son of Aëtius. The Vandals and the Moors divided the prisoners between them on their return; nevertheless Bishop Deogratias raised funds to ransom many of them by selling the vessels of the churches.

The capture of the Empress Eudoxia and her daughters gave the king valuable hostages against the hostile invasion of his kingdom which might now be expected. He was now fully master of the situation; his personality is from this time the centre of Western history. The Vandal fleet ruled the Mediterranean and cut off all supplies from Italy, so that a great famine broke out. In order to put an end to this intolerable state of affairs, Avitus the new Emperor of Western Rome (from 9 July 455) sent an embassy to Byzantium to induce the Emperor to take part in a joint attack against the Vandal Empire, for in an attack on Africa he could not dispense with the East-Roman fleet. But Marcian, probably influenced by the chief general Aspar, all-powerful in the East, still clung to inactivity and contented himself with asking Gaiseric to refrain from further hostilities towards Italy and to deliver up the prisoners of the imperial house, a proceeding which of course was quite ineffectual.

The result of this lethargy on the part of both empires was that the Vandals were in a position to seize the rest of the African provinces belonging to Rome; even the Moorish tribes seem to have acknowledged the Vandal sovereignty without positive resistance. Moreover Gaiseric made an alliance with the Spanish Sueves who had invaded and plundered the province of Tarraconensis (456) which belonged to the Roman Empire. At the same time a Vandal fleet laid waste Sicily and the bordering coast territory of South Italy. It is true that on land the Romans succeeded, under Ricimer, in defeating a hostile division at Agrigentum, as well as one at sea in Corsican waters, but these successes had no lasting effect, for the Vandals still commanded the Mediterranean as before. The populace, furious from the continued famine, compelled Avitus to fly to Gaul, where he died at the end of the year 456.

His successor on the imperial throne, Majorian (from 1 April 457), at once began in real earnest to consider schemes for the destruction of the Vandal Empire. It might be looked upon as auspicious that not long after his accession a body of Roman troops succeeded in defeating a band of Vandals and Moors, led by Gaiseric's brother-in-law, who were engaged in desultory plunder in South Italy. The Emperor himself marched with a large army, which he had not got together without difficulty, from Italy to Gaul, in November 458, in order to exact recognition of his authority from the Visigoths and Burgundians who had seceded from Rome, and his success in this task at once rendered nugatory Gaiseric's conclusion of a Visigoth, Suevian, and Vandal alliance. In May 460 Majorian crossed the Pyrenees and moved upon Zaragoza to Carthagena in order to cross from thence to Africa. The force that had been raised was so impressive that the king of the Vandals did not feel himself a match for it and sent messengers to sue for peace. When peace was refused he laid waste Mauretania and poisoned the wells in order to delay the advance of the enemy as much as possible. The

CH. XI.

Roman attack, however, could not be carried out, for the Vandals managed by means of treachery to seize a great number of the Roman ships which were lying outside the naval harbour near the modern Elche. Majorian had no alternative but to make peace with Gaiseric; his authority, however, was so shaken by this failure that he was divested of his dignity by Ricimer in August 461.

The result of the elevation of a new Emperor, Libius Severus, was that Gaiseric once more declared the agreement he had but just made to be at an end. He again began his naval attacks on Italy and Sicily. The embassies sent to him by the West-Roman as well as by the Byzantine Emperor Leo had no further result than the deliverance of Valentinian's widow and her daughter Placidia, for he had previously given the elder princess Eudoxia to his son Huneric in marriage. The king received as ransom a part of the treasure of Valentinian. It also seems that an agreement was come to with the East-Roman Empire. On the other hand the hostile relations with West-Rome continued, for Ricimer refused to comply with Gaiseric's principal demand, the bestowal of the imperial throne of the West upon Olybrius, Huneric's brother-in-law. Every year in the beginning of spring detachments of the Vandal fleet left the African harbours to infest the Mediterranean coasts. Unprotected places were plundered and destroyed, while the garrisoned places were carefully avoided.

The danger threatening the Western Empire reached its height when the commander Aegidius, who maintained an independent position in Gaul, made an alliance with Gaiseric and prepared to attack Italy in conjunction with him. This scheme was not carried out, for Aegidius died prematurely (464), but the situation still remained dangerous.

These miserable conditions lasted until the end of 467. The energetic Emperor Leo had by this time succeeded in overcoming the influence of Aspar, who had always been a hindrance to hostile measures against the Vandals. He despatched a fleet under the command of Marcellinus to convey the newly-created Western Emperor Anthemius to Italy and afterwards proceed to Africa. But first he sent an embassy to Gaiseric to inform him of the accession of Anthemius and to threaten him with war unless he would relinquish his marauding expeditions. The king instantly refused the demand and declared the agreements made with Byzantium at an end. His ships no longer sought Italy, but the coasts of the Eastern Empire: Illyria, the Peloponnesus, and all the rest of Greece felt his powerful arm, and even Alexandria felt itself menaced. But when the attempt of Marcellinus to advance against Africa miscarried on account of contrary winds, Leo determined to make great warlike preparations and to destroy his terrible opponent at one blow. Eleven hundred ships were got together and an army of 100,000 men raised. The plan of campaign was to attack the Vandal Empire on three sides. The main army was to march under Basiliscus direct to Carthage, another body under Heraclius and Marsus was to advance overland from Egypt to the West, while Marcellinus with his fleet was to strike at the Vandal centre in the Mediterranean.   But once more fortune favoured the Vandals.   They succeeded under cover of night in surprising Basiliscus' fleet, which was already anchored at the Promontorium Mercurii (now Cape Bon), and destroyed a part of it by fire.   The rest took to flight and scarcely one-half of the fine armada managed to escape to Sicily (468).   The not unimportant successes which the other Byzantine generals had in the meantime achieved could not balance this catastrophe, and as a crowning misfortune the able Marcellinus when on the point of sailing for Carthage was murdered (August 468).   Leo was therefore obliged to relinquish further undertakings and make peace once more with Gaiseric.

The peace, however, only lasted a few years.   After Leo's death (Jan. 474) the Vandals again devastated the coast of Greece in frequent expeditions.   The Emperor Zeno, who was not prepared to punish the marauders, was obliged to sue for peace, and sent the Senator Severus to Carthage to superintend negotiations.   It was agreed that the two empires from that time should not be hostile to each other.   The king promised to guarantee freedom of worship to the Catholics in Carthage and to permit the return of the clergy who had been banished for political intrigues, although he could not be prevailed upon to allow a new appointment to the Carthaginian bishopric, vacant since Deogratias' death (457).   Besides this he restored without ransom the Roman prisoners who had been allotted to him and his family, and gave Severus permission to buy back the slaves allotted as booty among the Vandals with the goodwill of their owners.   In return the Byzantine Emperor, as the overlord of both halves of the Empire, no doubt formally recognised the Vandal kingdom in its then extent — it comprised the entire Roman province of Africa, the Balearic Isles, Pithyusae, Corsica, Sardinia, and Sicily (autumn 476).   Gaiseric soon afterwards made over Sicily to Odovacar in return for the payment of a yearly tribute, only reserving for himself the town of Lilybaeum, which had a strategical importance as a starting-point for Africa.

On 25 January 477, Gaiseric died at a very great age after he had · raised the Vandal Empire to the height of its power.   What he accomplished, as general and politician, in his active life is beyond praise and is unreservedly acknowledged by contemporaries.   On the other hand, a less favourable verdict must be pronounced on his statesmanship. The Empire he established was a hybrid State and therefore bore from the beginning the seeds of decay in itself.   The nations under his rule were kept strictly separate from each other, and the possibility of an amalgamation, which might have been the foundation of a new political organisation, was thus prevented.   Herein is seen the truth found by experience, that the existence of all kingdoms erected by conquest is

CH. XI.

bound up with the life of their creator unless the latter can succeed in creating a united organism on a national, constitutional, or economic basis.

The decline was already noticeable under Gaiseric's eldest son and successor, Huneric, the husband of the imperial princess Eudoxia. The Moorish tribes living in the Aures mountains, after fighting for some time with varying fortune, succeeded at last in shaking off the Vandal rule. In a quarrel with the Eastern Empire over the surrender of Eudoxia's fortune, Huneric early gave in; he was even willing to permit the episcopal see at Carthage to be filled again (481) and grant the Catholics in his Empire still greater freedom of movement. Only when he learned that he had not to fear hostilities from Byzantium did he shew himself in his true colours, a tyrant of the worst, most blood-thirsty type. Then he raged against the members of his own house and against his father's friends. Some of them he banished, others he murdered in a horrible manner in order to secure the succession to his son Hilderic. When nothing more remained for him to do in this direction he proceeded to oppress his Catholic subjects. Among some of the measures taken by him the most important is the notorious Edict of 24 January 484, in which the king ordered that the edicts made by the Roman Emperors against heresy should be applied to all his Catholic subjects unless they adopted Arianism by 1 June in that year. Next, orthodox priests were forbidden to hold religious services, to possess churches or build new ones, to baptise, consecrate, and so forth, and they were especially forbidden to reside in any towns or villages. The property of all Catholic churches and the churches themselves were bestowed on the Arian clergy. Laymen were disabled from making or receiving gifts or legacies; court officials of the Catholic creed were deprived of their dignity and declared infamous. For the several classes of the people graduated money-fines were established according to rank; but in case of persistence all were condemned to transportation and confiscation of property. Huneric gave the execution of these provisions into the hands of the Arian clergy, who carried out the punishments threatened with the most revolting cruelty, and even went beyond them. Repeated intervention on the part of the Emperor and the Pope remained quite ineffectual, for they confined themselves to representations. Perhaps Catholicism might have been quite rooted out in Africa if the king had not died prematurely on 23 December 484.

Under his successor Gunthamund, better times began for the oppressed orthodox Church. As early as the year 487 most of the Catholic churches were opened again and the banished priests recalled. The reason for these changed circumstances lay partly in the personal character of the king, partly in the Emperor's separation from the Roman Church which appeared to debar Gunthamund's Catholic subjects from conspiring with Byzantium, and partly in the now ever-increasing dimensions of Moorish rebellion. Gunthamund was very fortunate in driving back these last to their haunts, but he did not succeed in com-pletely defeating them. He absolutely failed when he attempted to regain possession of Sicily during the struggle between Odovacar and Theodoric the Great. The expedition sent thither was expelled by the Ostrogoths, and the king was compelled even to relinquish the tribute which had hitherto been paid to him (491).

Gunthamund died 3 September 496; Thrasamund his brother, distinguished for his beauty, amiability, wisdom, and general culture, succeeded him on the throne.   He pursued yet a different course from that of his predecessors with regard to the Catholics. He tried, like Huneric, to spread Arianism in his kingdom, yet as a rule he avoided the violent measures to which that king had recourse.   Thus several bishops, among whom was the bishop of Carthage, were once more banished, but they were well treated in their exile. His action was mainly due to religious fanaticism, for there was no ground for political suspicion, at least during the greater part of his reign; the king was on friendly terms with the schismatical Emperor Anastasius.   After the accession of the orthodox Emperor Justin (518) Thrasamund's aversion to the Catholics is easier to understand, especially when the Emperor took steps to improve the position of the orthodox episcopate in Africa.   The Vandal kingdom found a real support in the alliance with the Ostrogoths in Italy.   Theodoric the Great, swayed by the desire to bring about an alliance of all German princes of the Arian faith, wedded his widowed sister Amalafrida to Thrasamund, whose first wife had died childless; she came to Carthage with a retinue of 1000 distinguished Goths as her body-guard as well as 5000 slaves capable of bearing arms, and brought her royal husband a dowry of the part of the island of Sicily round Lilybaeum (500).   A temporary interruption occurred in the alliance between the two States in 510–511, because Thrasamund gave pecuniary support to Gesalech the pretender to the Visigothic throne, who was not recognised by Theodoric; but on the representation of his brother-in-law he repented and apologised. Serious difficulties occurred in the Vandal kingdom once more through the Moors.   The tribes of Tripolis really succeeded in making them-selves independent.   At the end of his reign the king himself took the field against them, but suffered defeat.

Thrasamund died on 6 May 523; he was succeeded by the al-ready aged, utterly effeminate son of Huneric and Eudoxia, Hilderic, who was averse from warfare.   Thrasamund, having a presentiment of future events, had exacted an oath from him not to restore to the banished Catholics either their churches or their privileges, but Hilderic evaded his pledge, for even before his formal accession, he recalled the exiled clergy and ordered fresh elections in the place of those who had died.   In foreign politics also the new king turned entirely from the system

CH. XI.

hitherto followed, of alliance with the Ostrogoth kingdom, and entered into a close connexion with the Byzantine Empire where Justinian, the nephew of the ageing Emperor Justin, already practically wielded the sceptre. Inasmuch as he had coins struck bearing the effigy of Justin I, Hilderic formally gave the impression of recognising a kind of suzerainty of the Byzantine Empire. To the opposition of Amalafrida and her following he replied by slaughtering the Goths and flinging the sister of Theodoric into prison. To avenge this insult the Gothic king fitted out a strong fleet, but his death (526) prevented the despatch of the expedition, which would probably have been fatal to the Vandal kingdom. Theodoric's grandson and successor Athalarich, or rather his mother Amalasuntha, was content with making remonstrances, which of course received no attention.

Though there was nothing to fear from the Ostrogoths, the danger from the Moors waxed ever greater. After the year 525 it appears that they had acquired control over Mauretania Caesariensis with the exception of its capital city, of the Sitifensis Province, and of southern Numidia as well — Mauretania Tingitana had already been given up. But especially momentous in its wide-spread results was the rise of Antalas who at the head of some tribes in the southern part of Byzacene infested this province more and more, and at last severely defeated the relieving Vandal troops commanded by Oamer, a cousin of Hilderic. The dislike of the Vandals to their king, which had been existent long before this event, shewed itself fully at this failure. Hilderic was deposed by the defeated army on its return home and was imprisoned together with his followers, and in his stead the next heir to the throne Gelimer,[1] a great-grandson of Gaiseric, was called upon to rule (19 May 530). Doubtless this usurpation was mainly the result of Gelimer's ambition and love of power, but on the whole it was sustained by the will of the people. They were discontented with the policy hitherto pursued towards the Catholics and Byzantium as well as with the unwarlike, inconsistent character of Hilderic, who was to Teutonic ideas utterly unworthy of royalty.

This course of events was most welcome to the Byzantine Emperor, who in any case had for some time past harboured some idea of the plan which later he definitely announced for joining all the lands belonging to the old Roman Empire under his own sceptre. Just as he afterwards posed as the avenger of Amalasuntha, so he now became the official protector of the rights of the deposed king of the Vandals. He asked Gelimer in the most courteous manner not openly to violate the law regarding the succession to the throne, which had been decreed by Gaiseric and had been always hitherto respected, but to be satisfied with the actual exercise of power and to let the old king, whose death

---

[1] More correctly Geilamir as the name reads in inscriptions and on coins.

might shortly be expected, remain as nominal ruler. Gelimer did not deign at first to answer the Emperor; when, however, the latter took a sharper tone and demanded the surrender of the prisoners he haughtily rejected the interference, emphatically claimed validity for his own succession and declared that he was ready to oppose with the utmost vigour any attack which might occur. Justinian was now firmly resolved to bring matters to an armed decision, but first took steps to end the war which had been begun against the Persians. In the year 532 peace was concluded with them.

The scheme directed against the Vandal kingdom found no approval from the body of crown councillors before whom Justinian laid it for an opinion. They objected to the chronic want of money in the state treasury and that the same fate might easily be prepared for the Byzantines as had befallen Basiliscus under Gaiseric. The troops, too, which had just sustained the fatigues of the Persian campaign, were little fit to be again sent to an uncertain conflict against a powerful and famous kingdom on the other side of the sea. Justinian was almost persuaded to give up the undertaking when a fresh impulse, that of religion, made itself felt. An oriental bishop appeared at Court and declared that God himself had, in a dream, commanded him to reproach the Emperor on account of his indecision and to tell him that he might count on the support of Heaven if he would march forth to liberate the Christian (that is, the orthodox) people of Africa from the dominion of the heretics.

Through this kind of influence on the part of the Catholic clergy, and through the endeavours of the Roman nobility who had been reinstated by Hilderic but driven forth again by Gelimer, Justinian was entirely brought round. Belisarius, previously commander-in-chief in the Persian war, was placed at the head of the expedition with unlimited authority. It was very fortunate for the Emperor that, in the first place, the Ostrogoth queen Amalasuntha declared for him and held out prospects of supplying provisions and horses in Sicily, and, further, that the Vandal governor of Sardinia, Godas, rose against Gelimer and asked for troops to enable him to hold his own, and, finally that the population of Tripolis, led by a distinguished Roman, Prudentius, declared itself in favour of union with Byzantium.

In June 533 the preparations for war were completed. The army mustered reckoned 10,000 infantry under Johannes of Epidamnus and about 5000 cavalry, also the 5000 men of Belisarius' powerfully mounted guard, 400 Heruls, and 600 Huns. The fleet was composed of 500 transport vessels and 92 battleships under the command of Kalonymus. Among Belisarius' attendants was the historian Procopius of Caesarea, to whom we owe the vivid and trustworthy description of the campaign. The departure of the ships took place at the end of July, and the last hour of the kingdom which was once so powerful had struck.

It is only in Africa that we are well acquainted with the internal
circumstances of the Vandal kingdom; for of the parallel conditions in
the Spanish communities of the Sueves, Alans, and the Silingian and
Asdingian Vandals we only know, at the present time, that they were
under monarchical rule. The centre of Vandal rule in Africa was Carthage;
here all the threads of the government converged, here the king also
held court. The Roman division of the land into provinces (Mauretania:
Tingitana, Caesariensis, Sitifensis; Numidia; Proconsularis or Zeugitana;
Byzacene; Tripolitana) remained the same. The districts assigned to
the Vandals, the so-called "Sortes Vandalorum," were separated as
especial commands. The governing people were the Vandals of the
Asdingian branch which now alone survived, with whom were joined the
Alans and contingents from different peoples, among whom in particular
were Goths. The Alans, who probably were already Germanised at the
time of the transference to Africa, seem to have maintained a kind of
independence for a while, but in Procopius' time these foreign elements
had become completely merged in the Vandals. The Romans were by
far more numerous. These were by no means looked upon as having
equal privileges, but were treated as conquered subjects according to the
usages of war. Marriages between them and the Vandals were forbidden,
as they were in all the German States founded on Roman soil except
among the Franks. If, however, the hitherto existing arrangements
outside the Vandal settlements remained the same in the main — and
indeed even the high offices were left in the hands of the Romans — this
only happened because the Vandal kings proved themselves incapable of
providing a fresh political organisation. On the other hand, the numerous
Moorish tribes were to a great extent held in only slight subjection.
They retained their autonomy, as they did in the time of the Romans,
but their princes received from the hands of the Vandal kings the
insignia of their dignity. Under Gaiseric's stern government they
conducted themselves quietly and completely left off their raids into
civilised districts, which had occurred so frequently in the last years of the
Roman rule, but even under Huneric they began with ever-increasing
success to struggle for their independence. The destruction which befell
the works of ancient civilisation in Africa must be placed to the account
of the Moors, not of the Vandals.

The first settlement of the Vandals in Africa was on the basis of a
treaty with the Roman Empire, when the people were settled among the
Roman landowners and as an equivalent became liable to land tax and
military service. The land settlement which took place after the
recognition of the Vandal sovereignty was carried out as by right of
conquest; the largest and most valuable estates of the country landowners in the province of Zeugitana were taken possession of and given
to individual Vandal households. Further particulars of the details are
wanting, yet it is certain that the Roman organisation arranged on the

basis of landed property grants was not disturbed. The property only changed hands, otherwise the conditions were the same as they had been under Roman government. Of the villa, the manor-house on the Roman estate, a Vandal with his family now took possession, and the *coloni* had to pay the necessary dues to the landed proprietor or his representative and render the usual compulsory service. The profits of the single estates were in any case on an average not insignificant, for they made the development of a luxurious mode of life possible even after an increase in the number of the population. The management of the estate was, as formerly, directed only in a minority of cases by the new masters themselves, for they lacked the necessary knowledge, and service in the Court and in the army compelled them to be absent frequently from their property. More often the management was entrusted to stewards or farmers (*conductores*) who were survivals from the earlier state of things. Nevertheless the position of the dependents of the manor, wherever they were directly under the Vandal rule, must have been materially improved in comparison with what it had been formerly, for we know from various authorities that the country people were in no way content with the reintroduction of the old system of oppression by the Byzantines after the fall of the Vandal kingdom.

The Vandals like the other German races were divided into three classes — slaves, freemen, and nobles. The nobleman as he now appears is a noble by service who derives his privileged position from serving the king, not as earlier from birth. The freemen comprised the bulk of the people, nevertheless they had, in comparison with earlier times, lost considerably in political importance while the rights of the popular assembly had devolved in the strengthened monarchy. The slaves were entirely without rights, they were reckoned not as persons but as alienable chattels. The position of the *coloni* who were taken over from the Roman settlement was wholly foreign to the Vandals; they remained tied to the soil but were personally free peasants who kept their former constitutional *status*.

At the head of the State was the King, whose power had gradually become unlimited and differed but little from that of the Byzantine Roman Emperor. His full official title was *Rex Vandalorum et Alanorum*. His mark of distinction and that of his kindred was, as with the Merwings, long hair falling to the shoulders. While the earlier rulers dressed in the customary Vandal costume, Gelimer wore the purple mantle, like the Emperor.

The succession to the throne was legally settled by Gaiseric's so-called testament. Gaiseric, who himself had obtained the throne through the choice of the people, ignoring probably the sons of his predecessor Gunderic, who were still minors, considered himself after he had fully grasped monarchical power as the new founder of the Vandal kingship, as the originator of a dynasty. The sovereignty was looked upon as an inheritance for his family over which no right of disposal belonged to the people. As however the existence of several heirs threatened the by no means solidly established kingdom with the risk of subdivision into several portions, Gaiseric established the principle of individual succession; moreover he provided that the crown should pass to the eldest of his male issue at the time being. By this last provision the government of a minor, unable to bear arms, was made, humanly speaking, impossible. The Vandal kingdom was the first and for a long time the only State in which the idea of a permanent rule of succession came to be realised — and rightly is Gaiseric's family statute reckoned in history among the most remarkable facts relating to public law. It remained valid until the end of the kingdom. Gaiseric himself was succeeded by his eldest son Huneric who was succeeded in turns by two of his nephews Gunthamund and Thrasamund, and only after the death of the latter came Huneric's son Hilderic. Gelimer obtained the throne, on the other hand, in a direct and irregular way, and his endeavours to represent himself to Justinian as a legitimate ruler did not succeed.

The scope of the royal power comprised the national army, the convening of the assembly, justice, legislation and executive, the appointments to the praefecture, the supreme control of finance, of police, and of the Church. · Of any co-operation in the government by the people — by the Vandals (not of course by the Romans) such as obtained in olden times, there is no sign whatever.

The development of absolute government seems to have been completed in the year 442; according to the brief but significant statements of our authorities several nobles, who had twice risen against the king because he had overstepped the limits of his authority, were put to death with a good many of the people. The origin of the royal power is traceable to God; the dominant centre of the State is the king and his court.

In war the king is in chief command over the troops and issues the summons to the weapon-bearing freemen. The arrangement of the army was, like that of the nation, by thousands and hundreds. Larger divisions of troops were placed under commanders appointed especially by the monarch and generally selected from the royal family. The Vandals had been even in their settlements in Hungary a nation of horsemen, and they remained so in Africa. They were chiefly armed with long spears and swords, and were little suited to long campaigns. Their principal strength lay in their fleet. The ships they commanded were usually small, lightly built, fast sailing cruisers which did not hold more than about 40 persons. In the great mobility of the army as well as of the navy lay the secret of the surprising successes which the Vandals achieved. But immediately after Gaiseric's death, a general military decline began. Enervated by the hot climate and the luxury into which they had been allured by the produce of a rich country, they lost their warlike capacity more and more, and thus sank before the attack of the Byzantines in a manner almost unique in history.

The king is the director of the whole external polity. He sends forth and receives envoys, concludes alliances, decides war and peace. On single and peculiarly important questions he may take counsel beforehand with the chiefs of his following, but the royal will alone is absolute.

The Vandals were judged according to their national principles of jurisprudence in the separate hundred districts by the leaders of the thousands. Sentences for political offences were reserved for the king as executor of justice in the national assembly. Legal procedure for the Romans remained the same as before. Judgment was passed on trivial matters by the town magistrates, on greater by provincial governors according to Roman law but in the name of the king. Quarrels between Vandals and Romans were of course settled only in the Vandal court of justice according to the law of the victor. That the king often interfered arbitrarily in the regular legal proceedings of the Romans is not surprising, considering the state of affairs, but a similar arbitrary interference among the Vandals is a circumstance of political importance: treason, treachery against the person of the king and his house, apostasy from the Arian Church come into prominence, so that the life and freedom of individuals were almost at the mercy of the monarch's will.

The laws which the Vandal kings enacted were, as far as we know, for the most part directed against the Romans and the Catholics. In addition to the numerous edicts concerning religion the regulations issued against the immorality so wide-spread in Africa are especially worthy of remark, but like all regulations of the kind only possessed a temporary efficiency. On the other hand, the law of royal succession which we have already alluded to possessed universal validity.

The officials in the service of the Court and State as also those in the Church are all subject to the royal power; they are nominated by the monarch or at least confirmed by him, and can be deprived of their functions by peremptory royal decree. The members belonging to the household of the king represent different elements, spiritual and lay, German and Roman, free and unfree together. The highest official in the Vandal Court was the *praepositus regni*, whose importance lay entirely in the sphere of the government of the kingdom; his position corresponded to that of a prime minister. As holders of this office appear, so far as is known, only persons of Teutonic nationality. An important post was also that of head of the Chancery of the Cabinet, who had to draw up the king's written edicts and was besides frequently entrusted with different missions of especial political importance. The existence of a special Arian court clergy is to be inferred from the fact that at the princely courts house chaplains are mentioned. Besides these there

CH. XI.

lived permanently at the Vandal Court a supernumerary class of men who without holding any definite office enjoyed the favour of the king and were employed by him in different ways. A number of them seem to have borne the title *comes* as among the Franks, Ostrogoths, and others ; from among them were taken, for example, the envoys sent to foreign nations. Together with the provincial officials, who might be temporarily present at the Court, and the Arian bishops, the persons of principal position in the king's circle frequently co-operated in the decision of important questions of state affairs. As a general designation for these persons when they belonged to the laity the expression *domestici* appears. Admittance into the royal household required an oath of fealty.

From among the king's circle were drawn the greater part of the higher officials in the provincial government, especially over the Vandals. The most important officers of the Vandals were the heads of the thousands (the chiliarchs, *millenarii*), on whom devolved the management of the districts, *i.e.* the settlements of a thousand heads of families, in judicial, military, administrative, and fiscal respects. Outside the Vandal allotments the organisation of the Roman system in Africa still remained, with the exception of the military, and the duties of the separate offices were discharged by the Romans themselves. The only exceptions were the islands in the Mediterranean; Sardinia, Corsica, and the Balearic Isles were united into one province and placed under a governor of German nationality who resided in Sardinia and exercised both military and civil functions.

The ruler has by virtue of his position absolute right over the revenue of the State; state property and royal private property are identical. A principal source of revenue is provided by the produce of royal domains, which in Roman Africa occupy a particularly important place. To this was added the taxes paid by the provincials, from which the Vandals themselves were entirely exempt. The burdens, however, cannot as a rule have been so oppressive as they were under the Roman rule, for later on, under the government of the Byzantines, the former more lenient conditions were regretted. Besides the taxes were to be taken into account the proceeds from the tolls, the right of coinage, fines, dues from mines and manufactures, and other unusual receipts.

The Arian as well as the Catholic Church is subject to the royal power; the appointment of bishops is dependent on the consent of the sovereign, the synods are convoked by the king and can only meet with his permission. The Asdingian Vandals in their seats in Hungary had clearly been already converted to Arianism, while the Silingians, Alans, and Sueves in the first phase of their Spanish career were still adherents of paganism. After the occupation of Africa the Catholic clergy were entirely expelled from the country districts in the province of Zeugitana as well as from Carthage, and the vacant places were given over to the Arian clergy with the whole of the church property. In the other parts of the kingdom few or no Arian priests were to be found; only under Huneric who presented the whole of the Catholic churches to the Arians (a measure which certainly was never wholly carried out) were they installed in greater numbers. The bishop residing in Carthage bore the title of Patriarch and exercised as metropolitan a supreme power over the whole of the Arian clergy. Since the Arian church-service was held in the vernacular as among the other Germans, the clergy were mostly of German nationality.

The position of the Catholic Church was, as has been already remarked, very varied under the different rulers and very largely dependent on the state of foreign politics. In Africa, after the tumult of the conquest had passed over and the endowment of the Arian Established Church was put into effect, Gaiseric only proceeded against those adherents of orthodoxy from whom danger to the State was to be feared. The clergy beyond the Vandal allotment were closely supervised, but they were not molested if they did not oppose the royal will but confined themselves to the execution of their pastoral duties. The real persecutions began first under Huneric and were continued, after an interval of peace, by Gunthamund and Thrasamund, though in a milder form. Hilderic gave the Catholic Church its complete freedom again; his successor Gelimer, an ardent Arian, was too much occupied with political complications to be able to be active in that sphere. Ecclesiastical conditions suffered therefore only temporary not permanent disturbance and sustained no material hurt; rather, the persecutions contributed largely to temper the inner strength of the African Church.

When the Vandals occupied Africa they were undoubtedly still in the same primitive stage of civilisation in which they had lived in their homes in Hungary. Their political position as conquerors, the settlement in an enclosed district, the sharp religious opposition must certainly have hindered a rapid acceptance of the Roman influence. But under Gelimer they quite adopted the luxurious mode of life of the Romans, *i.e.* of the rich nobility; they lived in magnificent palaces, wore fine clothes, visited theatres, gave themselves up to the pleasures of an excellent table and did homage with great passion to Aphrodite. Roman literary culture had just made its appearance in the royal Court and among the nobility. Gaiseric was himself certainly, at least at first, not skilled in Latin, but one of his grandsons was famous for having distinguished himself in the acquisition of manifold knowledge. The same is said of Thrasamund, and we may assume it of Hilderic.

Latin was the language of diplomatic intercourse and legislation, as it was in the other German kingdoms; the Vandal language was quite supplanted, and only remained in use in popular intercourse and in

the church-service. So in the last years of the Vandal dominion
Roman literature in Africa produced a tiny harvest. The poet Dracontius
is to be remembered in this connexion, and the poets preserved in the
anthology of the Codex Salmasianus, and Bishop Fulgentius of Ruspe.
The art of architecture found in Thrasamund an eager patron; mention
is made of splendid buildings which were raised under this king. There
is certainly no authentic trace extant of any artistic capacity among the
Vandals themselves.

CHAPTER XII

(A)

THE ASIATIC BACKGROUND

The Asiatic background has its basis in the immense zone of steppes and deserts which stretches from the Caspian Sea to the Khin-gan Mountains, and is divided into two regions by the Pamir and the Thian Shan ranges. The western region, like the whole lowland district of West Asia, even to the extreme north, is a deserted sea-bed; the eastern (Tarim basin and Gobi) seems formerly to have been covered with great fresh-water lakes. The water-basins began to evaporate and to shrink to inland seas, while the intervening country became a desert. The largest remains of former enormous water-basins are the salt Caspian Sea and the sweet-water Aral Sea. In both regions all the moisture that falls evaporates, so that no rivers reach the open sea; most of them ooze away in the sand, and only the greatest, such as the Syr, Amu, Ili, Chu, Tarim, flow into large inland seas. The fact that the evaporation is greater than the fall of moisture, and that the latter takes place chiefly in the cold season, has important consequences, which account for the desert nature of the land. All the salt which is released by the weathering and decomposition of the soil remains in the ground, and only in the higher regions with greater falls of moisture, and by the banks of rivers is the soil sufficiently lixiviated to be fit for cultivation. Everywhere else is steppe and desert absolutely uncultivable. The surface of the land can be divided into six categories: sand-deserts, gravel-deserts, salt-steppes, loam-steppes, loess-land, and rocky mountains.

Of these the sand-deserts form by far the greatest part. They consist of fine drift-sand, which the driving storm wind forms into sickle-shaped shifting dunes (*barkhans*). The loose drift-sand is waterless, and for the most part without vegetation; the *barkhans*, however, here and there display a few poor saxaul and other shrubs; human life is impossible. The gravel-deserts, also very extensive, which form the transition between the sand deserts and the steppes, have a sparse vegetation and serve the nomads as grazing-grounds in their wanderings to and from winter quarters and summer pastures.   The adjoining salt-steppes, consisting of loam and sand, are so impregnated with salt that the latter settles down on the surface like rime.   In spring they bear a scanty vegetation, which, on account of its saline nature, affords excellent pasture for numerous flocks of sheep.   During the rain of autumn and spring the loam-steppes, consisting of loess-soil mixed with much sand, are covered with luxuriant verdure and myriads of wild flowers, especially tulips, and, on the drier ground, with camel-thorn (*Alhagi camelorum*), without which the camel could not exist for any length of time.   These steppes form the real pastures of the nomads.   In the loess-land agriculture and gardening are only possible where the soil has been sufficiently softened by rainfall and artificial canals, and is constantly irrigated.   It forms the sub-soil of all cultivable oases.   Without irrigation the soil becomes in summer as hard as concrete, and its vegetation dies completely.   The oases comprise only two per cent. of the total area of Turkestan.   As a rule the rocky mountains are quite bare; they consist of black gleaming stone cracked by frost and heat, and are waterless.

Roughly speaking these differences of vegetation follow one another from south to north, viz. the salt-, the sand-, and the grass-steppes. A little below 50° N. latitude the landscape of West Asia changes in consequence of a greater fall of moisture.   The undrained lakes become less frequent, the rivers reach the sea (Ishim, Tobol, etc.), and trees appear.   Here begins, as a transition to the compact forest-land, the tree-steppe on the very fertile "black earth."   On the Yenisei are park-like districts with splendid grass plains, and luxuriant trees.   Northward come endless pine-forests, and beyond them, towards the Arctic Sea, is the moss-steppe or tundra.

The climate is typically continental, with icy cold winters, hot summers, cold nights, and hot days with enormous fluctuations of temperature.   The warmth increases quickly from winter to spring and decreases just as quickly from summer to autumn.   In West Turkestan, the summer is almost cloudless and rainless, and at this time the steppes become deserts.   On account of the dryness little snow falls; as a rule it remains loose and is whirled aloft by the north-east storm wind (*buran*). These storm *burans* are just as terrible as the summer storms of salt-dust in Trans-Caspia at a temperature of 104° to 113° Fahr.   Considering that in summer the temperature sometimes reaches 118° in the shade, exceeding body-heat by 20°, and that in winter it sinks below −31°, and further that the heat, especially in the sand-deserts, reaches a degree at which the white of egg coagulates, the climate, even if not deadly, should be very injurious to man; Hindustan, which is far less hot, enervates the European on account of the greater moisture, and has changed the Aryan, once so energetic, to the weak and cowardly Hindu.   Nevertheless the contrary is the case.   The climate of Turkestan is wholesome, and its people are long-lived and healthy, and that especially in the hot summer, on account of the un_paralleled dryness of the air. Once acclimatised, one bears the heat very well, and likewise the extreme cold of winter. The climate of Central Asia furthers a rapid bodily and mental development and premature ageing, as well as corpulence, especially among the Altaians. Obesity is even regarded as a distinction, and it became so native to the mounted nomads that it accompanied them to Europe; it is characteristic of all the nomads who have invaded Europe; and Hippocrates mentions it expressly as a characteristic of the Scythians. The climate of Turkestan also influences the character, leading to an apathy which creates indifference to the heaviest blows of fate, and even accompanies the condemned to the scaffold.

The entire West Asiatic region from the salt-steppes to the compact forest-land forms one economic whole. The well-watered northern part, which remains green throughout the summer, feeds countless herds in the warm season, but affords no pasturage in winter owing to the deep snow. On the other hand, the southern part, which is poor in water — the grass-, sand-, and salt-steppes — is uninhabitable in summer. Thus the northern part provides summer pastures, the southern — the Aral-Caspian basin — winter pastures to one and the same nomad people.

The nomad then is the son and product of the peculiar and variable constitution — which nevertheless is an indivisible economic whole — of the Asiatic background. Any agriculture, worthy of the name, is impossible in the steppes and deserts — the few oases excepted — on account of the dryness of the summer, when animals also find no food. Life on the steppes and deserts is only possible in connexion either with the Siberian grass-region or with the mountains. This life is necessarily extremely hard and restless for man and beast and it creates a condition of nomadism, which must at the same time be a mounted nomadism, seeing that a wagon would be an impossibility in the long trackless wanderings over mountain and valley, river and swamp, and that goods and chattels, together with the disjoinable dwellings, can only be carried on the backs of beasts of burden.

Setting aside the Glacial Period and the small Brückner cycle of 35 years or so, the climatic changes of Central Asia, according to Huntington,[1] fall into cycles of several hundred years' duration within which the aridity rises and sinks considerably. "All Central Asia has undergone a series of climatic pulsations during historic times. There seems to be strong evidence that at the time of Christ or earlier the climate was much moister and more propitious than it now is. Then during the first few centuries of the Christian era there appears to have been an epoch of increasing aridity. It culminated

[1] Huntington, *Pulse*, p. 359.

about A.D. 500, at which time the climate appears to have been drier than at present. Next came an epoch of more propitious climate which reached its acme about A.D. 900. There is a little evidence of a second epoch of aridity which was especially marked in the twelfth century. Finally, in the later Middle Ages, a rise in the level of the Caspian Sea and the condition of certain ruins render it probable that climatic conditions once again became somewhat favorable, only to give place ere long to the present aridity." [1]

But Central Asia has not been, since the beginning of historic records, in a state of desiccation. The process of "geological" desiccation was already ended in prehistoric times, and even the oldest historic accounts testify to the same climatic conditions as those of to-day. The earliest Babylonian kings maintained irrigation works, and Hammurabi (23rd cent. B.C.) had canals made through the land, one of which bore his name. Thus, as at present, without artificial irrigation agriculture was not possible there 4200 years ago. Palestine's climate too has not changed in the least since Biblical times : its present waste condition is the result of Turkish mismanagement, and Biot has proved from the cultivated plants grown in the earliest times that the temperature of China has remained the same for 3300 years. Curtius Rufus and Arrian give similar accounts of Bactria.

Amid the enormous wastes there are countless sand-buried ruins of populous cities, monasteries, and villages and choked-up canals standing on ground won from the waste by systematic canalisation; where the system of irrigation was destroyed, the earlier natural state, the desert, returned. The causes of such destruction are manifold.[2] 1. Earthquake. 2. Violent rain-spouts after which the river does not find its former bed, and the canals receive no more water from it. 3. On the highest edge of the steppe, at the foot of the glacier, lie enormous flat heaps of débris, and here the canalisation begins. If one side of this heap rises higher than the other, the direction of the current is shifted, and the oases nurtured by the now forsaken stream become derelict. But the habitable ground simply migrates with the river. If, for example, a river altered its course four times in historic times, three series of ruins remain behind; but it is erroneous simply to add these ruins together, and to conclude from them that the whole once formed a flourishing land which has become waste, when in reality the three series of settlements did not flourish side by side but consecutively. This fallacy vitiates all accounts which assume a progressive or periodic desiccation as the chief cause of the abandonment of oases. 4. Continuous drought in consequence of which the rivers become so waterless that they cannot

---

[1] The view of Huntington (in *Explorations in Turkestan*, 1904, ed. by Pumpelly, Washington, 1908, p. 231 note).

[2] Cholnoky in *Geogr. Zeitschr.* xv. pp. 249 ff.

feed the canals of the lower river-basin, and thus the oases affected must become parched, and are not always re-settled in more favourable years.
5. Neglect of the extreme care demanded in the administration of the canal system. If irrigation is extended in the district next the mountain from which the water comes, just so much water is taken from the lower oases. But in this case too nothing is lost which cannot be replaced in another direction: *vice versâ* if an oasis on the upper course of the river disappears through losing its canal system, the lower river course thus becomes well watered and makes possible the formation of a new oasis.
6. The most terrible mischief is the work of enemies. In order to make the whole oasis liable to tribute they need only seize the main canal; and the nomads often blindly plundered and destroyed everything. A single raid was enough to transform hundreds of oases into ashes and desert. The nomads moreover not only ruined countless cities and villages of Central Asia, but they also denuded the steppe itself, and promoted drift-sand by senseless uprooting of trees and bushes for the sake of firewood. But for them, according to Berg, there would be little drift-sand in Central Asia, for, in his opinion, all sand-formations must in time become firm. All the sand-deserts which he observed on the Aral Sea and in Semiryechensk were originally firm, and even now most of them are still kept firm by the vegetation.

With the varied dangers of irrigation systems it is impossible to decide in the case of each group of ruins what causes have produced them; it is therefore doubtful whether we can place in the foreground the secular changes of climate. It is not even true that the cultivation of the oases throve better in the damper and cooler periods than in the arid and hot ones. Thus the oases of Turfan in Chinese Turkestan, which is so extremely arid and so unendurably hot in summer, are exceptionally fertile. We may therefore conclude that the cultivation of the oases was considerably more extended in the damper and cooler periods, but considerably less productive than in the arid and hot ones of to-day. Changes in the volume of water of single rivers and lakes are clearly apparent within short periods, and these lead to frequent local migrations of the peasant population and to new constructions as well as to the abandonment of irrigation canals. Thus there is here a continual local fluctuation in the settlements, but history knows nothing of regular migrations of agriculturists.

Still less is an unfavourable climatic change the cause of the nomad invasions of Europe. The nomad does not remain at all during the summer in the parched steppe and desert; and in the periods of increasing aridity and summer heat South Siberia was warmer and the mountain glaciers retreated, and hence the pastures in both these directions were extended. The only consequence of this was that the distance between summer and winter pastures increased and the nomad had to wander further and quicker. The computation is correct in itself, that the number of animals that can be reared to the square mile depends on and varies with the annual rainfall;[1] but the nomad is not hampered by square miles; the poorer or richer the growth of grass the shorter or longer time he remains, and he is accustomed from year to year to fluctuations in the abundance of his flocks. Moreover a shifting of the winter pastures is not impossible, for their autumn and spring vegetation is not destroyed by a progressive aridity, and if the water current changes its bed, the nomad simply follows it. Further, the effect of a secular progressive aridity is spread over so many generations that it is not catastrophic for any one of them. The nomad invasions of China and Europe must therefore have had other causes; and we know something about the invasions of several nomad hordes — of the Avars, Turks (Osmans), and Cumans, for example.

Since the second half of the fifth century A.D. — that is, the time to which Huntington assigns the greatest aridity — there had existed in the Oxus basin the powerful empire of the Ephthalite horde, on the ruins of which the empire of the West Turks was founded in the middle of the sixth century. Had Central Asia been at that time so arid and therefore poor in pasture, the then victorious horde would have driven out the other hordes in order to secure for themselves more pasture land. Yet exactly the opposite took place; the Turks enslaved the other hordes, and when the Avars fled to Europe, the Turkish Khagan claimed them back at the Byzantine Court. In like manner the Turks (Osmans) fled from the sword of the Mongols in 1225 from Khorasan to Armenia, and in 1235 the Cumans fled to Hungary. The violence of the Mongols is strikingly described by Gibbon: "from the Caspian to the Indus they ruined a tract of many hundred miles which was adorned with the habitations and labours of mankind, and five centuries have not been sufficient to repair the ravages of four years." Therefore the main cause of the nomad invasions of Europe is not increasing aridity but political changes.

There remains the question: How did the nomads originate? On the theory of a progressive desiccation it is assumed that the Aryan peasantry of Turkestan were compelled to take to a nomad life through the degeneration of their fields to steppes and wastes. But the peasant bound to the soil is incapable of a mode of life so unsettled, and requiring of him much new experience. Robbed of his corn-fields and reduced to beggary, could he be at the same time so rich as to procure himself the herds of cattle necessary to his existence, and so gifted with divination as suddenly to wander with them in search of pasture over immeasurable distances? A decrease of cultivable soil would bring about only a continual decrease in the number of inhabitants. The peasant as such disappeared, emigrated, or perished, and his home became a desert,

[1] Huntington, *Pulse*, p. 382.

and was occupied by another people who knew from experience how to make use of it in its changed state, *i.e.* as winter grazing-ground. This new people must have been already nomadic, and have made their way from the pastures of the North and therefore they must have belonged to the Altaian race.[1]

The delta oases have been the home of man from early prehistoric time, throughout Turkestan and northern Persia. The two oldest culture-strata of Anau[2] prove that the settlers of the first Culture cultivated wheat and barley, had rectangular houses of air-dried bricks, but only wild animals at first, out of which were locally domesticated the long-horned ox, the pig, and horse, and successively two breeds of sheep. The second Culture had the domestic ox, both long- and short-horned, the pig, and the horse. The domestic goat, camel, and dog appear, and a new hornless breed of sheep. The cultivation of cereals was discovered in Asia long before B.C. 8000. The domestication of cattle, pigs, and sheep, and probably of the horse, was accomplished at Anau between B.C. 8000 and 6800. Consequently, the agricultural stage preceded the nomadic shepherd stage in Asia. It follows, therefore, that before domestication of animals was accomplished, mankind in Central Asia was divided sharply into two classes — settled agriculturists on the one hand, and hunters who wandered within a limited range on the other hand. When the nomadic hunters became shepherds, they necessarily wandered between ever-widening limits as the seasons and pasturage required for increasing herds. The establishment of the first domestic breeds of pigs, long-horned cattle, large sheep and horses, was followed by a de-teriorating climate which may have — as Pumpelly, though questionably, assumes — changed these to smaller breeds. Dr Duerst identifies the second breed of sheep with the turbary sheep (*Torfschaf*), and the pig with the turbary pig (*Torfschwein*), which appear as already domesti-cated in the neolithic stations of Europe. They must therefore have been descendants of those domesticated on the oases of the Anau district. They make their appearance in European neolithic stations apparently contemporaneously with an immigration of a people of a round-headed Asiatic type which seems to have infiltrated gradually among the pre-vailing long-headed Europeans. The presumption is, therefore, that these animals were brought from Asia by this round-headed people, and that we have in this immigration perhaps the earliest post-glacial factor in the problem of Asiatic influence in European racial as well as cultural origins, for they brought with them both the art of cattle-breeding and some knowledge of agriculture.

The skulls of the first and second cultures in Anau are all dolichocephalic or mesocephalic, without a trace of the round-headed element. We are therefore justified in assuming that the domestication

[1] Peisker, *Beziehungen*, p. 21.
[2] Pumpelly, in *Explorations*, 1904, pp. 38 ff., 67 ff.

CH. XII.

and the forming of the several breeds of domestic animals were effected by a long-headed people. And since the people of the two successive cultures were settled oasis-agriculturists and breeders, we may assume as probable that agriculture and settled life in towns on the oases originated among people of a dolichocephalic type. Since Dr Duerst identifies the second breed of sheep established during the first culture of Anau, with the turbary sheep in Europe, contemporaneously with skulls of the round-headed Galcha type, it should follow that the domestic animals of the European neolithic stations were brought thither, together with wheat and barley, by round-headed immigrants (of an Asiatic type). Since the original agriculturists and breeders were long-headed, it seems probable that the immigrants were broad-headed nomads who, having acquired from the oasis people domestic animals and rudimentary agriculture of the kind still practised by the shepherd nomads of Central Asia, infiltrated among the neolithic settlements of Eastern and Central Europe, and adopted the stone-implement culture of the hunting and fishing peoples among whom they came. In this connexion it is not without significance that throughout the whole historical period, the combination of settled town life and agriculture has been the fundamental characteristic of the Aryan-speaking Galchas, and of the Iranians inhabit-. ing Western Central Asia and the Persian plateau, while the peoples of pure Asiatic mongoloid type have been essentially shepherd nomads, who, as already shewn, could have become shepherds only after the settled agriculturists of the oases had established domesticated breeds of cattle.

The origin of the taming of wild into domestic animals is one of the most difficult problems of economic history. What was its aim? The use that we make of domestic animals? Certainly not, for adaptability thereto could only gradually be imparted to the animals and could not be foreseen; it could not be anticipated that the cow and the goat would ever give more milk than their young needed, and that beyond the time of lactation; nor could it be anticipated that sheep not woolly by nature would develop a fleece. Even for us it would be too uneconomical to breed such a powerful animal and such a large consumer of fodder as the ox merely for a supply of meat; and besides beef is not readily eaten in Central Asia. Moreover the wild ox is entirely unsuitable for draught, for it is one of the shyest as well as strongest and most dangerous of animals. And it should be specially emphasised that a long step lies between taming individual animals and domesticating them, for as a rule wild animals, however well tamed, do not breed in captivity. Consequently the domestication was not produced simply by taming or for economic ends. It is the great service of Eduard Hahn[1]

[1] Hahn, *Haustiere*, pp. 26 ff., *Alter*, pp. 91 ff., *Entstehung*, pp. 57 ff., 93; Jevons, *Hist. of Religion*, pp. 113–118. On the contrary, Hildebrand, *Recht u. Sitte*, p. 23.

to have laid down the theory that the domestication — involuntary and unforeseen — was the result of forcing for religious purposes certain favourite animals of certain divinities into reservations where they remained reproductive, and at the same time gradually lost their original wildness through peaceful contact with man. The beasts of sacrifice were taken from these enclosures. Thus originated the castrated ox which quietly let itself be yoked before the sacred car; and by systematic milking for sacrificial purposes the milk-secretion of the cow and the goat was gradually increased. Lastly, when man perceived what he had gained from the animals, he turned to his own use the peculiarities thus produced by enclosure and gradual domestication.

In general, cattle-rearing is unknown to the severest kind of nomadism.[1] The ox soon dies of thirst, and it has not sufficient endurance or speed for the enormous wanderings; its flesh has little value in the steppe. The animals actually employed for rearing and food are consequently the sheep (to a less extent the goat as leader of the sheep flocks), the horse, and here and there the ass; also, in a smaller number, the two-humped camel (in Turan the one-humped dromedary as well) as a beast of burden. Where the district admits of it, and long wanderings are not necessary (*e.g.* in Mongolia, in the Pamir, in the Amu-delta, in South Russia, etc.), the Altaian has engaged in cattle-breeding from the remotest times.

A wealthy Mongolian possesses as many as 20,000 horses and still more sheep. Rich Kirghiz sometimes have hundreds of camels, thousands of horses, tens of thousands of sheep. The minimum for a Kirghiz family of five is 5 oxen, 28 sheep, and 15 horses. Some have fewer sheep, but the number of horses cannot sink below 15, for a stud of mares, with their foals, is indispensable for the production of *kumiz*.

The Turkoman is poorest in horses. However, the Turkoman horse is the noblest in the whole of Central Asia, and surpasses all other breeds in speed, endurance, intelligence, faithfulness, and a marvellous sense of locality; it serves for riding and milk-giving only, and is not a beast of burden, as are the camel, the dromedary, or the ox. The Turkoman horse is tall, with long narrow body, long thin legs and neck, and a small head; it is nothing but skin, bones, muscles, and sinews, and even with the best attention it does not fatten. The mane is represented by short bristly hairs. On their predatory expeditions the Turkomans often cover 650 miles in the waterless desert in five days, and that with their heavy booty of goods and men. Their horses attain their greatest speed when they have galloped from 7 to 14 miles, and races over such a distance as that from London to Bristol are not too much for them. Of course they owe their powers to the training of

---

[1] Under *nomad* and *nomadism*, *mounted-nomad* (Ger. *Reiternomade*), etc., is henceforth to be understood.

CH. XII.

thousands of years in the endless steppes and deserts, and to the continual plundering raids, which demanded the utmost endurance and privation of which horse and rider were capable. The least attractive to look at in Turkestan is the Kirghiz horse, which is small, powerful, and strong-maned. During snow-storm or frost it often does without food for a long time. It is never sheltered under a roof, and bears — 40° Fahr. in the open air, and the extremest summer heat, during which it can do without water for from three to four days. It can easily cover 80 miles a day, and never tastes barley or oats in its life.

The Altaian rides with a very short stirrup, and thus trotting would be too exhausting both for man and horse, so as a rule he goes at a walk or a gallop. Instead of the trot there is another more comfortable movement in which the horse's centre of gravity moves steadily forward in a horizontal line, and shaking and jolting is avoided. The horse advances the two left feet one after the other, and then the two right feet (keeping the time of four threshers); in this way it can cover ten miles per hour. The most prized horses are the "amblers," which always move the two feet on one side simultaneously, and are sometimes so swift that other horses can scarcely keep up with them at a gallop. Spurs are unknown to the Altaian, and in the steppe horseshoes are not needed. The nomad spends the greater part of his life in the saddle; when he is not lying inactive in the tent he is invariably on horseback. At the markets everybody is mounted. In the saddle all bargains are struck, meetings are held, *kumiz* is drunk, and even sleep is taken. The seller too has his wares — felt, furs, carpets, sheep, goats, calves — before, behind, and beneath him on his horse. The riding-horse must answer promptly to the bridle, and must not betray his master by neighing during a raid. Therefore the young stallion — for mares are not ridden — is taken from the herd with a lasso, and castrated.

The nomads of the Asiatic background all belong to the Altaian branch of the Ural-Altaian race. The Altaian primitive type displays the following characteristics: body compact, strong-boned, small to medium-sized; trunk long; hands and feet often exceptionally small; feet thin and short, and, in consequence of the peculiar method of riding (with short stirrup), bent outwards, whence the gait is very waddling; calves very little developed; head large and brachycephalic; face broad; cheek-bones prominent; mouth large and broad; jaw mesognathic; teeth strong and snow-white; chin broad; nose broad and flat; forehead low and little arched; ears large; eyes considerably wide apart, deep-sunken, and dark-brown to piercing black; eye-opening narrow, and slit obliquely, with an almost perpendicular fold of skin over the inner corner (Mongol-fold), and with elevated outer corner; skin wheat-colour, light-buff (Mongols) to bronze-colour (Turks); hair coarse, stiff as a horse's mane, coal-black; beard scanty and bristly, often

entirely wanting, generally only a moustache; bodily strength consider.
able; sensitiveness to climatic influences and wounds slight; sight and
hearing incredibly keen; memory extraordinary.

The Ural-Altaian languages branch off as follows:

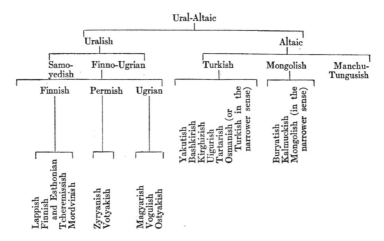

Six to ten blood-related tents (Mongol. *yúrta*) — on the average,
families of five to six heads — form a camp (Turk. *aul*, Mongol. *khoton*,
khotun, Roumanian *catun*) which wanders together; even the best
grazing-ground would not admit of a greater number together.
The leader of the camp is the eldest member of that family which
possesses most animals. Several camps make a clan (Turk. *tire*,
Mongol. *aïmak*). Hence there are the general interests of the clan
and also the individual interests of the camps, which latter frequently
conflict. For the settlement of disputes an authority is necessary, a
personality who through wealth, mental capacity, uprightness, bravery,
and wide relationships is able to protect the clan. As an election of
a chief is unknown to nomads, and they could not agree if it were
known, the chieftainship is usually gained by a violent usurpation, and
is seldom recognised generally. Thus the judgment of the chieftain
is mostly a decision to which the parties submit themselves more or less
voluntarily.

Several clans form a tribe (*uruk*), several tribes a folk (Turk. *il*,
Mongol. *uluss*). Conflicts within the tribes and the folks are settled
by a union of the separate clan chieftains in an arbitration procedure in
which each chieftain defends the claims of his clan, but very often the
collective decision is obeyed by none of the parties. In times of unrest
great hordes have formed themselves out of the folks, and at the head of

these stood a Khagan or a Khan. The hordes, like the folks and tribes, form a separate whole only in so far as they are opposed to other hordes, folks, and tribes. The horde protects its parts from the remaining hordes, just as does the folk and the tribe. Thus all three are in a real sense insurance societies for the protection of common interests.

The organisation based on genealogy is much dislocated by political occurrences, for in the steppe the peoples, like the drift-sand, are in constant motion. One people displaces or breaks through another, and so we find the same tribal name among peoples widely separated from one another. Moreover from the names of great war-heroes arose tribal names for those often quite motely conglomerations of peoples who were united for a considerable time under the conqueror's lead and then remained together, for example the Seljuks, Uzbegs, Chagatais, Osmans, and many others. This easy new formation, exchange, and loss of the tribal name has operated from the earliest times, and the numerous swarms of nomads who forced their way into Europe under the most various names are really only different offshoots of the same few nations.

The organisation of the nomads rests on a double principle. The greater unions caused by political circumstances, having no direct connexion with the life and needs of the people in the desert, often cease soon after the death of their creator; on the other hand the camps, the clans, and in part the tribes also, retain an organic life, and take deep root in the life of the people. Not merely the consciousness of their blood-relationship but the knowledge of the degree of relationship is thoroughly alive, and every Kirghiz boy knows his *jeti-atalar*, that is, the names of his seven forefathers. What is outside this is regarded as the remoter relationship. Hence a homogeneous political organisation of large masses is unfrequent and transitory, and to-day among the Turks it is only the Kara-Kirghiz people of East Turkestan — who are rich in herds — that live under a central government — that of an hereditary *Aga-Manap*, beneath whom the *Manaps*, also hereditary, of the separate tribes, with a council of the "gray-beards" (*aksakals*) of the separate clans, rule and govern the people rather despotically. What among the Turks is the exception, was from the earliest times known to history the rule among the Mongols, who were despotically governed by their princes. The *Khan* wielded unlimited authority over all. No one dared to settle in any place to which he had not been assigned. The Khan directed the princes, they the "thousand-men," the "thousand-men" the "hundred-men," and they the "ten-men." Whatever was ordered them was promptly carried out; even certain death was faced without a murmur. But towards foreigners they were just as barbarous as the Turks. The origin of despotism among the Altaians is to be traced to a subjugation by another nomad horde, which among the Turkish Kazak-Kirghiz and the Mongol Kalmucks of the Volga developed into a nobility ("white bones," the female sex "white flesh") in contrast with the common people ("black bones," "black flesh").

The transitoriness of the wider unions on the one hand, and the indestructibility of the clans and camps on the other, explain why exten_sive separations, especially among the Turko-Tartars, were of constant occurrence. The desert rears to independence and freedom from restraint small patriarchally-directed family alliances with "gray-beards" (ak_sakals) from families of aristocratic strain at their head. These families boast of their direct descent from some Sultan, Beg, or famous *Batyr* ("hero," *recte* robber, cattle-thief). But the "gray-beards" mostly exercise the mere shadow of dominion. The Turkomans say : "We are a people without a head, and we won't have one either; among us each is Padishah;" as an appendage to this, "Sahara is full of Sheikhs."

The wanderings of the nomads are incorrectly designated when they are called "roaming" wanderings, for not even the hunter "roams." He has his definite hunting-grounds, and always returns to his accustomed places. Still more regular are the wanderings of the nomads, however far they extend. The longest are those of the Kirghiz who winter by the Aral Sea and have their summer pastures ten degrees of latitude further north in the steppes of Troitsk and Omsk. The distance, allowing for the zig-zag course, comes to more than 1000 miles, so that each year the nomad must cover 2000 miles with all his herds and other goods.

During the winter the nomad in the desert is, so to speak, a prisoner in his tent, practical, neat, and comfortable as this is. It is a rotunda 15 feet high, and often over 30 feet broad. Its framework consists of a wooden lattice in six to ten separable divisions, which can be widened out, or pushed together for packing. Above this comes the roof-frame of light rafters which come together in a ring above. This is the opening for air, light, and smoke, and is only covered at night and during severe cold. Inside a matting of steppe-grass runs round the framework, and outside is a felt covering bound round with ropes of camel's hair. Tent-pegs and ropes protect the tent from being overturned by the violent north-east *orkan*, during which the hearth-fire must be put out. As the felt absorbs and emits very little heat, the tent is warm in winter, and cool in summer. Inside the tent the sacks of victuals hang on the points of the wall-lattice; on the rafters above are the weapons, harness, saddles, and, among the heathen tribes, the idols. Behind the hearth, the seat of honour for guests and old men is spread with the best felt and carpets; in front of the hearth is the place for drinking-vessels and sometimes for fuel, the latter consisting of camel- and cattle-dung, since firewood is found only in a few places in the steppes and deserts. The nomad-life admits of only the most

CH. XII.

necessary and least breakable utensils : for preparing food for all in the tent there is a large cast-iron caldron, acquired in Chinese or Russian traffic, with tripod and tongs ; a trunk-like *kumiz*-vat of four smoked horse-hides thickened with fat ; *kumiz*-bottles, and water-bottles of leather ; wooden chests, tubs and cans hollowed out of pieces of wood, or gourds ; wooden dishes, drinking-bowls, and spoons ; among the slave-hunting Turkomans short and long chains, manacles, fetters, and iron collars also hung in the tent to the right of the entrance.

The accommodation provided by the tent, and the economising of space is astonishing ; from long past times everything has had its assigned place ; there is room for forty men by day, and twenty by night, notwithstanding the many objects hanging and lying about. The master of the household, with the men, occupies the place of honour ; left and right of the hearth are the sleeping-places (felt, which is rolled up in the daytime) ; left of the entrance the wife and the women and children, to the right the male slaves, do their work. For anyone to leave his wonted place unnecessarily, or without the order of the master, would be an unheard-of proceeding. In three-quarters of an hour a large tent can be put up and furnished, and it can be taken to pieces and packed just as quickly ; even with movables and stores it is so light that two camels suffice to carry it. The Nogai-Tartars carry their basket-like felt tents, which are only 8 to 10 feet in diameter, on two-wheeled carts drawn at a trot by small-sized oxen. In the thirteenth century, under Chinghiz and his followers, the Mongols also made use of such cart-tents, drawn by one camel, as store-holders, but only in the Volga-district and not in their own country in Mongolia. They also put their great tents — as much as thirty feet in diameter —.on carts drawn by twenty-four oxen twelve in a line.[1] The nature of the ground admitted of this procedure and consequently the tent had not to be taken to pieces at each stopping-place (as must be done in the steppes and deserts), but only where a considerable halt was made. In South Russia such wagon-tents date from the oldest times, and were already in use among the Scythians.

Among a continually wandering pastoral people the interests of neighbours often collide, as we know from the Bible-story of Abraham and Lot. Thus a definite partition of the land comes about. A folk, or a section of a folk — a tribe — regards a certain stretch of land as its special property, and tolerates no trespass from any neighbour whatsoever. The tribe, again, consists of clans and the latter of camps, which, in their turn, regard parts of the whole tribal district as their own. This produces a very confused medley of districts, over which the individual camps wander. In spring and autumn the nomad can find abundant fodder almost everywhere, in consequence of the greater moisture and luxuriant grass crop. The winter and summer abodes

[1] Rubruquis in *Recueil*, iv. p. 220 ; Marco Polo, i. p. 255.

demand definite conditions for the prosperity of the herds. The winter settlement must not have too severe a climate, the summer grazing-ground must be as exempt as possible from the terrific plague of insects. Since many more conditions must be satisfied for the winter than for the summer pastures, it is the winter quarters which determine the density of the nomad population. Thus the wealth of a people accords with the abundance of their winter quarters, and all internal encounters and campaigns of former centuries are to be regarded as a constant struggle for the best winter settlements.

In winter, whenever possible, the same places as have been used for long times past are occupied; in the deep-lying valley of a once-existing river, not over-exposed to the wind, with good water, and grazing-places where the snow settles as little as possible, and the last year's dung makes the ground warmer and, at the same time, provides fuel. Here at the end of October the tent, made warmer by another covering, is pitched, protecting the nomad from the raging winter *buran* and the numbing cold. The herds, however, remain in the open air without a sheltering roof, and must scrape for themselves the withered shrubs, stalks, and roots from the snow. They get terribly thin; indeed sheep, camels, and oxen perish when the snow falls deep, and the horses in scraping for fodder trample down the plants and make them uneatable, or when ice forms and shuts out sustenance entirely. But in early spring the situation improves, especially for the sheep, which, from mere skeletons, revive and get fat on the salt-steppes where a cursory inspection reveals no vegetation on the glittering crust of salt. The salt-pastures are incomparably more nourishing than the richest Alpine meadows, and without salt there would be no sheep-rearing nomads in Central Asia. To freshen the spring-pasturage the steppe is burnt off as soon as the snow has melted, as the dry last year's steppe-grass gets matted under the snow, and would retard the sprouting of the new grass; the ground manured by the ashes then gets luxuriantly green after a few days.

In the middle or at the end of April, during the lambing of the sheep, and the foaling of the mares, preparations for striking the winter tent are made. At this time the animals yield most milk, and a stock of hard cheese (*kurut*) is made. At the beginning of May the steppe begins to dry up, and the intolerable insects appear. Now the goods which are superfluous for the summer are secretly buried, the tent is struck, and loaded with all necessary goods and chattels on the decorated camels. It is the day of greatest rejoicing for the nomad, who leaves his inhospitable winter quarters in festal attire.

The winter quarters are regarded as the fixed property of the individual tent owners, but the summer pastures are the common property of the clan. Here each member of the clan, rich or poor, has in theory the right to settle where he likes. But the wealthy and illustrious always know how to secure the best places. To effect this each camp keeps the time of departure to the summer pastures and the direction to be taken as secret as possible; at the same time it makes an arrangement with the nearest-related camps, in conformity with which they suddenly depart in order to reach their goal as quickly as possible. If the place chosen is already occupied, the next which is still free is taken. At the beginning of spring, when the grass is still scanty, the camps can remain only a very short time — often one day or even only half a day — in one place; later on in their more distant wandering—from well to well — they can stay for weeks in the same place. At midsummer movement is more rapid, and in autumn, with an increasing abundance of water, it is again slower. In the sand-desert the nomad finds the wells covered by drift-sand, and he must dig down to them afresh, if necessary daily. The regulation of these wanderings is undertaken by the *aksakals*, not always according to justice.

The cattle can easily be taken off by a hostile neighbour, for the steppe is free and open. Therefore the nomads of the steppes, unlike the nomads of the mountains, do not split themselves into single families. They constantly need a small war-band to recover the stolen booty from the enemy. On the other hand, the instinct of self-preservation often drives a whole people to violate their neighbours' rights of property. When there is dearth of fodder the cattle are ruined, and the enterprise and energy of the owner cannot avert calamity. The impoverished nomad infallibly goes to the wall as a solitary individual, and only seldom is he, as a former wanderer (*tshorva*), capable of becoming a despised settler (*tshomru*). For he feels it to be the greatest misfortune and humiliation when he must take to the plough, somewhere by a watercourse on the edge of the desert; and so long as the loss of all his herds has not hopelessly crushed him, he does not resign himself to that terrible fate which Mahomet has proscribed with the words: "wherever this implement has penetrated, it has always brought with it servitude and shame."

In spring, when severe frost suddenly sets in after the first thaw, and the thin layer of snow is covered in a single night with a crust of ice an inch thick, the cattle cannot scrape food out of the snow, and the owner cannot possibly supply a substitute. When the frost continues hundreds of thousands of beasts perish, and whole districts previously rich in herds become suddenly poor. So as soon as ice appears the people affected leave their winter quarters, and penetrate far into their neighbours' territory until they find food for their herds. If they are successful a part at least of their cattle is saved, and when the weather changes they return home. But if all their cattle perish entirely, they must starve if they are unwilling to rob their wealthy neighbour of a part of his herds. Bloody feuds occur too in autumn on the return from the summer pastures, when the horses have become fat and powerful and the longer nights favour and cover long rides. The nomad now carries out the raids of robbery and revenge resolved upon and skilfully planned in the summer, and then he goes to his winter quarters.

But how can these barbarous robbers live together without exter_ minating each other ? They are bridled by an old and tyrannical king, invisible to themselves, the *deb* (custom, wont). This prohibits robbery and murder, immorality and injustice towards associates in times of peace; but the strange neighbour is outlawed; to rob, enslave, or kill him is an heroic deed. The nomads' ideas of justice are remarkably similar to those of our ancestors. Every offence is regarded as an injury to the interests of a fellow-man, and is expiated by indemnification of the loser. Among the Kazak-Kirghiz anyone who has killed a man of the plebs (a "black bone"), whether wilfully or accidentally makes no differ_ ence, must compensate the relations with a *kun* (*i.e.* 1000 sheep or 100 horses or 50 camels). The slaughter of a "white bone" costs a sevenfold *kun*. Murder of their own wives, children, and slaves goes unpunished, since they themselves are the losers. If a Kirghiz steals an aninfal, he must restore it together with two of the same value. If a wrong-doer is unable to pay the fine, his nearest relations, and failing them the whole camp, must provide it.

The principal food consists of milk-products — not of the fresh milk itself, which is only taken by children and the sick. A special Turko-Tartar food is *yogurt*, prepared with leaven from curdled milk. The Mongols also eat butter — the more rancid the more palatable — dripping with dirt, and carried without wrapping in their hairy greasy coat-pockets. From mare's milk, which yields no cream, *kumiz* (Kirghiz), *tshegan* (Mongolish) is fermented,[1] an extremely nutritious drink which is good for consumption, and from which by itself life can be sustained. How- ever, it keeps only a few hours, after which it becomes too sour and efferves- cent, and so the whole supply must be drunk at once. In summer, with an abundance of mares, there is such a superfluity of *kumiz* that hospitality is unlimited, and half Altai is always drunk. The Turkomans and Kara- Kalpaks, who possess few horses and no studs, drink *kumiz* seldom. The much-drunk *airan* from fermented unskimmed camel, cow, and sheep milk quenches thirst for hours, just as does the *kefir* of the Tartars from cow's milk. The *airan*, after being condensed by boiling, and dried hard as stone into little balls in the sun, is made into *kurt, kurut*, which can be kept for months and is the only means of making bitter salt-water drinkable. According to Marco Polo it formed the provision of the Mongol armies, and if the horsemen could not quench his thirst in any other way, he opened one of his horse's veins and drank the blood. From *kumiz* and also from millet a strong spirit (Kirghiz *boza*) is distilled,

---

[1] Zemarchos (A.D. 568) mentions the drink *kosmos* at the Turkish Khan's Court, Rubruquis (A.D. 1253) *cosmos* (variant *comos*) among the Mongols, and the prince's drink *cara-cosmos*, Marco Polo, *kemiz*; all corruptions of the word *kumiz*.

CH. XII.

which produces dead-drunkenness followed by a pleasant Nirvana-sensation.

A comparison of Rubruquis' account with that of Radloff[1] shews that the dairying among the Altaians has remained the same from the earliest times. A late acquisition from China, and only available for the wealthier, is the "brick-tea," which is also a currency, and a substitute for money.

Little meat is eaten, notwithstanding the abundance of the herds; it is only customary on festive occasions or as a consequence of a visit of special honour. In order not to lessen the stock of cattle, the people content themselves with the cattle that are sick beyond recovery, or dead and even decaying. The meat is eaten boiled, and the broth drunk afterwards. Only the Volga-Kalmucks and the Kara-Kirghiz, who are very rich in flocks, live principally on sheep and horse meat. That the Huns and Tartars ate raw meat softened by being carried under the saddle, is a mistake of the chroniclers. At the present time the mounted nomads are accustomed to put thin strips of salted raw meat on their horses' sores, before saddling them, to bring about a speedy healing. But this meat, impregnated with the sweat of the horse and reeking intolerably, is absolutely uneatable.[2]

From the earliest times, on account of the enormous abundance of game, hunting has been eagerly practised for the sake of food and skins, or as sport, either with trap and snare, or on horseback with falcon and eagle. From Persia came the long-haired greyhound in addition. Fishing cannot be pursued by long-wandering nomads, and they make no use even of the best-stocked rivers. But by the lakes and the rivers which do not dry up, fishing is an important source of food among short-wandering nomads.

For grain the seeds of wild-growing cereals are gathered; here and there millet is grown without difficulty, even on poor soil. A bag of millet-meal suffices the horseman for days; a handful of it with a drink of water appeases him well enough. Thus bread is a luxury for the nomad herdsman, and the necessary grain can only be procured in barter for the products of cattle-rearing and house-industry. But the Kirghiz of Ferghana in their short but high wanderings on the Pamir and Alai high above the last agricultural settlements, which only extend to 4600 feet, carry on an extensive agriculture (summer-wheat, millet, barley) by means of slaves and labourers at a height of 8500 feet, while they themselves climb with their herds to a height of 15,800 feet, and partly winter in the valleys which are free from snow in winter.[3] The nomads eat vegetables seldom, as only carrots and onions grow in the steppes. The half-settled agricultural half-nomads of to-day

[1] Rubruquis, pp. 227 ff.; Radloff, I. pp. 425 ff.
[2] Schwarz, *Turkestan*, p. 89 (note).
[3] Middendorff, pp. 329 f.

can be left out of consideration.[1] According to Plano Carpini the Mongols had neither bread nor vegetables nor leguminous food, nor anything else except meat, of which they ate so little that other peoples could scarcely have lived on it. However, in summer they consumed an enormous quantity of milk, and that failing in winter, one or two bowls of thin millet boiled in water in the morning, and nothing more except a little meat in the evening.

We see that from the earliest times the Altaian nomad has lived by animal-rearing, and in a subsidiary degree by hunting and fishing, and here and there by a very scanty agriculture. As among some hordes, especially the old Magyars, fishing and hunting are made much of, many believe that they were originally a hunting and fishing folk, and took to cattle-rearing later. This is an impossibility. The Magyars, just as were the others, were pure nomads even during winter, otherwise their herds would have perished. Hunting and fishing they pursued only as stop-gaps when milk failed. A fishing and hunting people cannot so easily become mounted nomads, and least of all organised in such a terribly warlike way as were the Magyars.

The innate voracity of the Turko-Tartars is the consequence of the climate. The Bedouin in the latitude of 20° to 32°, at a mean temperature of 86° F., can easily be more abstinent and moderate with his single meal a day (meat, dates, truffles) than the Altaian in the freezing cold, between the latitudes of 38° and 58°, with his three copious meals. The variable climate and its consequences — hunger in winter, superfluity in summer — have so hardened the Altaian that he can without difficulty hold out for days without water, and for weeks (in a known case forty-two days) in a snowstorm without any food; but he can also consume a six-months'-old wether at one sitting, and is ready to repeat the dose straight off !

Originally the Altaian clothed himself in skins, leather, and felt, and not till later in vegetable-stuffs acquired by barter, tribute, or plunder. To-day the outer-coat of the Kazak-Kirghiz is still made of the shining skin of a foal with the tail left on for ornament. The Tsaidan-Mongols wear next their bare skin a felt gown, with the addition of a skin in winter only, and leather breeches. All Central Asiatics wear the high spherical sheep-skin cap (also used as a pillow), the *tshapan* (similar to a dressing-gown and consisting of fur or felt in winter), leather boots, or felt stockings bound round with rags. Among many tribes the hair of the men is worn long or shaved off entirely (Herodotus tells of a snub-nosed, shaven-headed people in the lower Ural), and the Magyars, Cumans, and others were shorn bare, but for two pigtails.

The wife occupies a very dependent position. On her shoulders falls the entire work of the household, the very manifold needs of which are to be satisfied almost entirely by home industry. She must take down

[1] For the transition from the nomad to the half-nomad state *v.* Vámbéry, *Türkenvolk*, p. 171.

. CH. XII.

the tent, pack it up, load it on camels, and pitch it; she must prepare leather, felt, leather-bottles, cords, .waterproof material, and colours from various plants; she must spin and weave wool and hair.; she must make clothes, collect camel- and cattle-dung, knead it with dust into tough paste, and form and dry it into cakes; she must saddle and bridle horses and camels, milk the sheep, prepare *kumiz*, *kurut*, and *airan*, and graze the herds of sheep in the night — for the husband does this only by day, and in addition only milks the mares; his remaining occupation is almost entirely war and plundering.   To share the domestic work would be for an Altaian paterfamilias an unheard-of humiliation.

Originally the choice of a wife was as unrestricted among all the Altaians as among the Mongols, who, according to Plano Carpini and Marco Polo, might marry any relative and non-relative except their own mothers and daughters, and sisters by their own mothers. But to-day several nomad peoples are strictly exogamic.   The bride was chosen by the father, when still in her childhood; her price (*kalym*) was twenty-seven to a hundred mares, and her dowry had roughly the same value.   Polygamy was consequently only possible among tribes rich in herds, but it was a necessity, as one wife alone could not accomplish the many duties.   Virgin purity and conjugal fidelity are among the Turko-Tartars, and especially among the Kirghiz, somewhat rare virtues; on. the other hand, Marco Polo agrees with Radloff in praising the absolute fidelity of the Mongol women.

The upbringing of the children entails the extreme of hardening. During its first six weeks the new-born child is bathed daily, summer and winter alike, in the open air; thenceforward the nomad never washes, his whole life long.   The Kalmuck in particular is absolutely shy of water.   Almost to puberty the children go naked summer and winter; only on the march do they wear a light *khalat* and fur-cap. They are suckled at the breast to their fifth year.   At three or four they already sit free with their mother on horseback, and a six-year-old girl rides like a sportsman.   The education of the boys is limited to riding; at the most falconry in addition.   On the other hand, the girls are put to most exhausting work from their tenderest years, and the value of a bride is decided by the work she can discharge.   Among nearly all Altaian peoples the son thinks little of his mother, but towards his father he is submissive.

Hereditary right is purely agnatic.   As soon as the married son is able to look after himself, he is no longer under the authority of his father, and if he likes he can demand as inheritance a part of the herds adequate to establishing a separate household.   Then however he is entirely settled with, and he cannot inherit further on the death of his father when there are younger sons — his brothers — still unportioned. If impoverished the father has the right to take back from his apportioned sons every fifth animal from the herds (Kalmucks).   The daughters are never entitled to inherit, and on marrying receive merely a suitable dowry from their brothers, who then receive the *kalym*. If only daughters survive, the inheritance goes to the father's brothers or cousins, who in that case receive the *kalym* as well.

Speedy as the Altaian is on horseback, on foot he is helpless and unwieldy; and so the dance is unknown to him. All games full of dash and excitement are played on horseback. His hospitality is marvellous; for weeks at a time he treats the new arrival to the best he has, even when it is the despised and hated Shiitish Persian. He possesses many sagas and songs — mostly in the minor key, and monotonous as the steppes — which are accompanied on a two-stringed guitar. Tenor and mezzo-soprano predominate, and the gait of the horse and the stride of the camel mark the rhythm.

The surplus of the female house-industry and of the herds is, as a rule, exchanged in barter for weapons and armours, metal and wooden articles, clothing material, brick-tea, and grain. Instead of our gold and silver coinage they have — *sit venia verbo* — a sheep coinage, in which all valuations are made. Of course they were acquainted with foreign coins from the earliest times, and obtained countless millions of pounds from tribute, plunder, and ransom of prisoners, and they used coins, now and then, in external trading, but among themselves they still barter, and conclude all their business in sheep, cattle, horses, and camels. Rubruquis says of the Mongols in 1253: "We found nothing purchasable for gold and silver, only for fabrics, of which we had none. When our servant shewed them a Hyperpyron (Byzantine gold coin), they rubbed it with their fingers and smelt it to see if it were copper." They have no hand-workers except a few smiths.

The Altaian, and especially the Turko-Tartar barbarian, considered only the advantage of the moment; the unlimited plundering was hostile to any transit-trade. But when and so long as a strong hand controlled the universal plundering spirit, a caravan trade between north and south, and especially between east and west was possible, and, with high duties, formed a considerable source of income for the Central-Asiatic despots.

The religious conceptions of a group of primitive people inhabiting such an enormous district were of course never uniform. To-day the greatest part of the Altaians is Buddhist, or Islamitic, and only a few Siberian Turkish tribes remain true to the old-Altaian Shamanism.

The characteristic feature of Shamanism is the belief in the close union of the living with their long dead ancestors; thus it is an uninterrupted ancestor worship. This faculty however is possessed only by a few families, those of the Shamans (Mong. *shaman*, Turk. *kam*), who pass on their power from father to son, or sometimes daughter — with the visible symbol of the Shaman drum by means of which he can call up the spirits through the power of his ancestors, and compel them to active assistance, and can separate his own soul from his body and send it into

CH. XII.

the kingdoms of light and of darkness. He prepares the sacrifice, conjures up the spirits, leads prayers of petition and thanksgiving, and in short is doctor, soothsayer, and weather prophet. In consequence he is held in high regard, but is less loved than feared, as his ceremonies are uncanny, and he himself dangerous if evil inclined. The chosen of his ancestors attains to his Shaman power not by instruction but by sudden inspiration; he falls into a frenzy, utters inarticulate cries, rolls his eyes, turns himself round in a circle as if possessed, until, covered with perspiration, he wallows on the ground in epileptic convulsions; his body becomes insensible to impressions; according to accounts he swallows automatically, and without subsequent injury, red-hot iron, knives, and needles, and brings them up again dry. These passions get stronger and stronger, till the individual seizes the Shaman drum and begins "shamaneering." Not before this does his nature compose itself, the power of his ancestors has passed into him, and he must thenceforth "shamaneer." He is moreover dressed in a fantastic garb hung with rattling iron trinkets. The Shaman drum is a wooden hoop with a skin, painted with gay figures, stretched over both sides, and all kinds of clattering bells and little sticks of iron upon it. In "shamaneering" the drum is vigorously struck with one drum-stick, and the ancestors thus invoked interrogated about the cause of the evil which is to be banished, and the sacrifice which is to be made to the divinity in order to avert it. The beast of sacrifice is then slaughtered and eaten, the skin together with all the bones is set aside as the sacrificial offering. Then follows the conjuration-in-chief, with the most frantic hocus-pocus, by means of which the Shaman strives to penetrate with his soul into the highest possible region of heaven in order to undertake an interrogation of the god of heaven himself.

From the great confusion of local creeds some such Shaman system as the following can be constructed; though the people themselves have only very vague conceptions of it.

The universe consists of a number of layers separated one from another by a certain something. The seventeen upper layers form the kingdom of light, seven or nine the underworld of darkness. In between lies the surface of man's earth, constantly influenced by both powers. The good divinities and spirits of heaven protect men, but the bad endeavour to destroy them. Originally there was only water and neither earth nor heaven nor sun nor moon. Then *Tengere Kaira Khan* ("the kind heaven") created first a being like himself, *Kishi*, man. Both soared in bliss over the water, but Kishi wished to exalt himself above the creator, and losing through his transgression the power to fly, fell headlong into the bottomless water. In his mercy Kaira Khan caused a star to rise out of the flood, upon which the drowning Kishi could sit; but as he could no longer fly Kaira Khan caused him to dive deep down and bring up earth, which he strewed upon the surface of the water.

But Kishi kept a piece of it in his mouth in order to create a special country out of it for himself. This swelled in his mouth and would have suffocated him had he not spat it out so that morasses formed on Kaira Khan's hitherto smooth earth. In consequence Kaira Khan named Kishi *Erlik*, banished him from the kingdom of light, and caused a nine-branched tree to grow out of the earth, and under each branch created a man as first father of each of the nine peoples of the present time. In vain Erlik besought Kaira Khan to entrust to him the nine fair and good men; but he found out how to pervert them to evil. Angered thereat Kaira Khan left foolish man to himself, and condemned Erlik to the third layer of darkness. But for himself he created the seventeen layers of heaven and set up his dwelling in the highest. As the protector and teacher of the now deserted race of man he left behind *Mai-Tärä* (the Sublime). Erlik too with the permission of the Kaira Khan built himself a heaven and peopled it with his own subjects, the bad spirits, men corrupted by him. And behold, they lived more comfortably than the sons of the earth created by Kaira Khan. And so Kaira Khan caused Erlik's heaven to be shattered into small pieces, which falling on the earth formed huge mountains and gorges. But Erlik was doomed until the end of the world to everlasting darkness. And now from the seventeenth layer of heaven Kaira Khan controls the destiny of the universe. By emanation from him the three highest divinities came into being: *Bai Ülgön* (the Great) in the sixteenth, *Kysagan Tengere* (the Mighty) in the ninth, and *Mergen Tengere* (the All-wise) in the seventh layer of heaven, where "Mother Sun" dwells also. In the sixth is enthroned "Father Moon," in the fifth *Kudai Yayutshi* (the highest Creator). Ülgön's two sons *Yayik* and *Mai-Tärä*, the protecting patrons of mankind, dwell in the third on the milk-white sea Süt-ak-köl, the source of all life; near it is the mountain Sürö, the dwelling of the seven *Kudai*, with their subjects the *Yayutshi*, the guardian angels of mankind. Here is also the paradise of the blessed and righteous ancestors of living men, who mediate between the divinities of heaven and their own descendants, and can help them in their need. The earth is personified in a community of spirits (*Yer-su*) beneficent to man, the seventeen high Khans (princes) of the seventeen spring districts, whose abodes lie on the seventeen snow peaks of the highest mountains, by the sources of the seventeen streams which water the land In the seven layers of the dark underworld prevails the dismal light of the underworld sun peculiar to them. This is the dwelling of all the evil spirits who waylay men at every turn: misshapen goblins, witches, *Körmös*, and others ruled by Erlik-Khan the dreadful prince on the black throne. Still deeper lies the horrible hell, *Kasyrgan*, where the sinners and criminals of mankind suffer just punishment. All evil comes from Erlik, cattle-disease, poverty, illness, and death. Thus there is no more important duty for man than to hold him steadfastly in honour, to call him "father Erlik," and to appease him with rich sacrifices.   If a man is to be born, Ülgön, at the request of the former's ancestors, orders his son Yayik to give a Yayutshi charge of the birth, with the life-force from the milk-white sea.   This Yayutshi then watches over the newly-born during the whole of his life on earth.   But at the same time Erlik sends forth a Körmös to prevent the birth or at least to hamper it, and to injure and misguide the newly-born his whole life long.   And if Erlik is successful in anni-hilating the life-forces of a man, Körmös drags the soul before Erlik's judgment-seat.   If the man was more good than bad, Erlik has no power over him, Körmös stands aside, and the Yayutshi brings the soul up to paradise,   But the soul of the wicked is abandoned by its Yayutshi, dragged by its Körmös to hell in the deepest layer of the underworld, and flung into a gigantic caldron of scalding tar.   The worst sinners remain for ever beneath the surface of the tar, the rest rise gradually above the bubbling tar until at last the crown of the head with the pigtail comes to view.   So even the sinner's good works are not in vain.   The blessed in heaven reflect on the kindnesses once done by him, and they and his ancestors send his former Yayutshi to hell, who grasps him by the pigtail, pulls him out of the tar, and bears the soul up to heaven.   For this reason the Kalmucks let their pigtails grow, as did many of the nomad peoples of history.

However, there is no absolute justice.   The gods of light, like the spirits of darkness, allow themselves to be won over by sacrificial viands, and, if rich offerings are forthcoming, they willingly wink at trans-gression; they are envious of man's wealth and demand gifts from all, and so it is advisable to stand well with both powers, and that can only be done through the medium of the Shamans.   So long as Erlik is banished in the darkness, a uniform ordering of the universe exists till the last day when everything created comes to an end, and the world ceases to be.[1]

With Shamanism fire-worship was closely associated.   Fire purifies everything, wards off evil, and makes every enchantment ineffective. Hence the sick man, and the strange arrival, and everything which he brings with him must pass between two fires.   Probably fire-worship was originally common to all the Altaians, and the Magyars also of the ninth century were described by the Arabian geographer as fire-worshippers.

In consequence of the healthy climate, the milk diet, and the Spartan hardening, the Altaian enjoys excellent health, hence the saying "Healthy as a Kirghiz."   There are not a few old men of eighty, and some of a hundred years.   Infectious diseases are almost unknown, chiefly because the constant smoke in the tent acts as a disinfectant, though combined with the ghastly filthiness it promotes the very frequent eye-complaints, itch, and eruptions of the skin.   In consequence of the constant wandering

[1] Radloff, II. pp. 1 ff.

on camel-back, and through the Shaman hocus-pocus, illness and death at home are vexatious, and sudden death on the field of battle is preferred. In order not to be forgotten, the Turko-Tartar — in contrast to the Mongol — likes to be buried in a conspicuous place, and, as such places do not exist on the steppes, after a year there is heaped over the buried corpse an artificial mound which, according to the wealth of the dead man, rises to a hill-like tumulus. At the same time an ostentatious funeral festival lasting seven days is held, with races, prize combats, and other games on horseback. Hundreds of horses, camels, and sheep are then consumed.

The nomad loves his horses and weapons as himself. The principal weapon is the lance, and in European warfare the Uhlans and Cossacks survive from the armies of the steppes. The nomad-peoples who invaded Europe were all wonderfully sure bowmen The value of the bow lies in the treacherous noiselessness of the arrow, which is the best weapon for hunting and ambush, and is therefore still in use to-day together with the rifle. In addition there have always been long-handled iron hatchets and pick-shaped battle-axes for striking and hurling, and the bent sabre. The warrior's body was often protected by a shirt of armour made of small polished steel plates, or by a harness of ox-leather plates, the head by a helmet; all mostly Persian or Caucasian work.

The hard restless life of the mounted nomad is easily disturbed by pressure from his like, by the death of his cattle from hunger and disease, and by the prospect of plunder, which makes him a professional robber. Of this the Turkoman was long a type. The leading features in the life of a Turkoman are the *alaman* (predatory expedition) or the *tchapao* (the surprise). The invitation to any enterprise likely to be attended with profit finds him ever ready to arm himself and to spring to his saddle. The design itself is always kept a profound secret even from the nearest relative; and as soon as the *serdar* (chief elect) has had bestowed upon him by some *mollah* or other the *fatiha* (benediction), every man betakes himself, at the commencement of the evening, by different ways, to a certain place indicated before as the rendezvous. The attack is always made either at midnight, when an inhabited settlement, or at sunrise, when a caravan or any hostile troop is its object. This attack of the Turkomans, like that of the Huns and Tartars, is rather to be styled a surprise. They separate themselves into several divisions, and make two, hardly ever three, assaults upon their unsuspecting prey; for, according to a Turkoman proverb, "Try twice, turn back the third time." The party assailed must possess great resolution and firmness to be able to withstand a surprise of this nature; the Persians seldom do so. Very often a Turkoman will not hesitate to attack five or even more Persians, and will succeed in his enterprise. Often the Persians, struck with a panic, throw away their arms, demand the cords, and bind each other mutually; the Turkomans have no occasion to dismount except for the

CH. XII.

purpose of fastening the last of them. He who resists is cut down; the coward who surrenders has his hands bound, and the horseman either takes him up on his saddle (in which case his feet are bound under the horse's belly), or drives him before him: whenever from any cause this is not possible, the wretched man is attached to the tail of the animal and has for hours and hours — even for days and days — to follow the robber to his desert home. Each captive is then ill-treated until his captor learns from him how high a ransom can be extracted from his kinsmen. But ransoming was a long way from meaning salvation itself, for on the journey home the ransomed were not seldom captured again and once more enslaved. Poor captives were sold at the usual price in the slave-markets at Bokhara, Khiva, etc.; for example, a woman of fifty for ten ducats. Those that could not be disposed of and were retained as herdsmen, had the sinews of their heels cut, to hinder them from flight. Until their overthrow by Skobelev in 1881 more than 15,000 Tekke-Turkomans contrived such raids day and night; about a million people in Persia alone were carried off in the last century, and made on the average certainly not less than £10 per head.[1]

In the ninth century the Magyars [2] and their nomadic predecessors in South Russia, according to Ibn Rusta's Arabian source, behaved exactly as the Turkomans in Persia; they provided for the slave-markets on the Pontus so many Slav captives that the name *slave* finally became the designation in the West of the worst servitude.

With man-stealing was associated cattle-stealing (*baranta*), which finally made any attempt at cattle-rearing impossible for the systematically plundered victim, and drove him to vegetarianism without milk nourishment. And what a vegetarianism, when agriculture had to suffer from the ever-recurring raids, and from bad harvests! And where the predatory herdsman settled for the winter in the midst of an agricultural population and in his own interests allowed them a bare existence as his serfs, there came about a remarkable connexion of two strata of people different in race and, for a time, in speech also.

A typical land in this respect is Ferghana, the former Khanate of Khokand, on the southern border of the Great Kirghiz horde. The indigenous inhabitants of this country, the entirely vegetarian Tadjiks and Sarts, from immemorial times passed from the hands of one nomad people to another in the most frightful servitude. In the sweat of their brows they dug canals for irrigation, cultivated fields, and put into practice a hundred arts, only to pay the lion's share to their oppressors who, in the full consciousness of their boundless power, indulged the most bestial appetites. But the majority of the dominant horde could not turn from their innate and uncontrollable impulse to wander; in the spring they were drawn irresistibly to the free air of the high-lying steppes, and only a part of them returned to winter among the enslaved peasantry.

---

[1] Vámbéry, *Travels*, pp. 99 ff., 276 ff., 364 ff.   [2] Marquart, pp. 466 ff.

This hopeless state of affairs continued to the Russian conquest in 1876, for the directly adjoining deserts always poured forth wild hordes afresh, who nipped in the bud any humaner intercourse of herdsmen and peasants. For rapine and slavery were inevitable wherever the nomads of the vast steppes and deserts made their abode in the immediate neighbourhood of more civilized lands. What their own niggardly soil denied them, they took by force from the fruitful lands of their neighbours. And because the plundered husbandman could not pursue the fleet mounted nomad into the trackless desert, he remained unprotected. The fertile districts on the edge of the Sahara and the Arabian desert were also in this frightful position, and Iran felt this calamity all the harder, because the adjoining deserts of Turan are the most extensive and terrible, and their inhabitants the wildest of all the nomads of the world.

No better fared the peoples inhabiting East Europe, on the western boundaries of the steppe-zone. As early as the fourth century B.C. Ephorus stated that the customs, according to the individual peoples, of the Scythians and the Sarmatians (both names covered the most medley conglomerations of nomads and peasants) were very dissimilar. Some even ate human beings (as the Massagetae ate their sick or aged parents), others abstained from all animals. A thousand years later Pseudo-Caesarius of Nazianzus tells of a double people, that of the Sklavenes (Slavs) and Phisonites on the lower Danube, of whom the Sklavenes abstained from meat eating. And Constantine Porphyrogenitus in the year 952 stated that the Russians ('Ρῶς, North Germanic Varangians, who coming from Scandinavia held sway over the Slavs of Russia) bought horses, cattle, and sheep from their terrible nomadic neighbours the Patzinaks, because they had none of these animals themselves (*i.e.* in the Slav lands which they dominated). In certain districts of East Europe therefore vegetarianism was permanent among the peasant folk, who for more than two thousand years had been visited by the Altaians with rapine and murder; this can be proved from original sources to have been the case from the fourth century B.C. to the tenth century A.D. — that is, for 1400 years ! It is exactly the same state of things as in Ferghana in modern times.

As long as a nomad horde finds sufficient room in the steppe it does not think of emigration, and always returns home from its raids richly laden with the plunder. But if the steppe-zone is thrown into a ferment by struggles for the winter pastures or by other causes, the relatively weakest horde gets pushed out of the steppe, and must conquer a new home outside the zone. For it is only weak against the remaining nomad hordes, but against any other State upon which it falls it is irresistible. All the nomads of history who broke into Europe, the Scythians, Sarmatians, Huns, Bulgarians, Avars, Magyars, Cumans, were the weakest in the steppes and had to take to flight, whence they became assailants of

CH. XII.

the world, before whom the strongest States tottered. With an energetic Khan at their head, who organised them on military lines, such a horde transformed itself into an incomparable army, compelled by the instinct of self-preservation to hold fast together in the midst of the hostile population which they subjugated; for however superfluous a central government may be in the steppe, it is of vital importance to a conquering nomad horde outside it. Consequently, while that part of the people which remained in the steppe was split up into loose clan associations, the other part, which emigrated, possessed itself of immense territories, exterminated the greater part of entire nations and enslaved the rest, scattered them as far as they pleased, and founded a despotically governed State with a ridiculously small band of horsemen.

The high figures in the chronicles are fictions exaggerated by terror and imagination, seeing that large troops of horsemen, who recklessly destroyed everything around them, would not have found in a narrow space even the necessary pasture for their many horses. Each Mongol under Chinghiz Khan, for example, was obliged to take with him 18 horses and mares,[1] so as always to have a fresh steed and sufficient mare's milk and horse's blood for food and drink. Two corps under the command of Sabutai and Chebe sufficed this great conqueror for the overthrow of West Asia.[2] In four years they devastated and in great part depopulated Khorasan, North Persia, Azerbaidjan, Georgia, Armenia, Caucasia, the Crimea, and the Volga territories, took hundreds of towns, and utterly defeated in bloody engagements the large armies of the Georgians, Lesghians, Circassians, and Cumans, and the united forces of the Russian princes. But they spared themselves as much as possible, by driving those of the subjugated people who were capable of bearing arms into the fight before them (as the Huns and Avars did previously), and cutting them down at once when they hesitated.

But what the Altaian armies lacked in numbers was made up for by their skill in surprises, their fury, their cunning, mobility, and elusiveness, and the panic which preceded them and froze the blood of all peoples. On their marvellously fleet horses they could traverse immense distances, and their scouts provided them with accurate local information as to the remotest lands and their weakness. Add to this the enormous advantage that among them even the most insignificant news spread like wildfire from *aul* to *aul* by means of voluntary couriers surpassing any intelligence department, however well organised. The tactics of the Mongols are described by Marco Polo in agreement with Plano Carpini and all the other writers as follows: "They never let themselves come to close quarters, but keep perpetually riding round and shooting into the enemy. And as they do not count it any shame to run away in

[1] Marco Polo (Ramusio's edition), I. p. 48
[2] Vámbéry, *Türkenvolk*, p. 180; Bretschneider, I. p. 294.

battle, they will sometimes pretend to do so, and in running away they turn in the saddle and shoot hard and strong at the foe, and in this way make great havoc. Their horses are trained so perfectly that they will double hither and thither, just like a dog, in a way that is quite astonishing. Thus they fight to as good purpose in running away as if they stood and faced the enemy, because of the vast volleys of arrows that they shoot in this way, turning round upon their pursuers, who are fancying that they have won the battle. But when the Tartars see that they have killed and wounded a good many horses and men, they wheel round bodily and return to the charge in perfect order and with loud cries; and in a very short time the enemy are routed. In truth they are stout and valiant soldiers and inured to war. And you perceive that it is just when the enemy sees them run, and imagines that he has gained the battle, that he has in reality lost it; for the Tartars wheel round in a moment when they judge the right time has come. And after this fashion they have won many a fight." The chronicler, Peter of Zittau, in the year 1315, described the tactics of the Magyars in exactly the same way.

When a vigorous conqueror like Attila or Chinghiz arose among the mounted nomads and combined several hordes for a cyclonic advance, they swept all before them on the march, like a veritable avalanche of peoples. The news of the onward rolling flood scared the bravest people, and compelled them to fly from their homes; thus their neighbours, too, were set in tumultuous motion, and so it went on until some more powerful State took defensive measures and stemmed the tide of peoples. Now the fugitives had to face the assailant. A battle of nations was fought, the flower of famous peoples strewed the field, and powerful nations were wiped out. The deserted or devastated territories were occupied by peoples hitherto often quite unknown, or settled by nations forcibly brought there by the conqueror; States, generally without duration and kept together only by the one powerful hand, were founded. The giant State, having no cohesion from within, fell to pieces at the death of the conqueror or shortly after; but the sediment of peoples, together with a stratum of their nomad oppressors which remained from the flood, could not be pushed back again, and immense areas of a continent received once again an entirely new ethnography — the work of one single furious conqueror.

Oftener and longer than in Europe successive Altaian empires held together in Asia, where the original population had long become worn out by eternal servitude and the central zone of the steppes supplied a near and secure base for plundering hordes. That some of these Asiatic empires attained to a high degree of prosperity is not due to the conquerors, who indeed quickly demongolised themselves by marriage with aliens, but was the consequence of the geographical position, the productivity of the soil, and the resigned tractableness and

CH. XII.

adaptability of the subjugated who, in spite of all the splendour of their masters, were forced to languish in helpless servitude.

Out of Central Asia from time immemorial one nomad horde after another broke into the steppes of South Russia and of Hungary, and after exterminating or pushing out their predecessors and occupying their territories, used this new base to harry and enslave the surrounding peoples far and wide, forcibly transforming their whole being, as in Ferghana.

But the bestial fury of the nomads not only laid bare the country, recklessly depopulated enormous tracts, dragged off entire peoples and forcibly transplanted and enslaved them, but where their sway was of any duration they brought their subjects down to the level of brutes, and extirpated every trace of nobler feeling from their souls. Central Asia of to-day, as Vámbéry states from personal observation, is a sink of all vices. And Franz von Schwarz draws the following cheerless picture of the Turkestan Sarts, among whom he lived for fifteen years: With respect to character they are sunk as low as man possibly can be. But this is not at all to be wondered at, as for thousands of years they were oppressed and enslaved by all possible peoples, against whom they could only maintain themselves by servility, cunning, and deceit. The Sart is cowardly, fawning, cringing, reticent, suspicious, deceitful, revengeful, cruel, and boastful. At the same time he shews in his appearance and manner a dignity and bearing that would compel the uninitiated to regard him as the ideal of a man of honour. In the former native States, as in Bokhara and Khiva to-day, the entire system of government and administration was based exclusively on lying, deceit, and bribery, and it was quite impossible for a poor man to get justice.

The opposite of the Sart is his oppressor the Kirghiz, who is shy, morose, and violent, but also honourable, upright, good-hearted, and brave. The terrible slave-hunting Turkoman is distinguished from all other Central Asiatics by his bold and piercing glance and proud bearing. In wild bravery no other race on earth can match itself with him, and as a horseman he is unsurpassed. He has an unruly disposition and recognises no authority, but his word can be asbolutely relied upon.[1]

What a tragic fate for an enslaved people. Although its lowest degradation is already behind it, how long yet will it be the object of universal and not unnatural contempt, while its former oppressor, void of all humane feeling, a professional murderer and cattle-thief, remains as a hero and ideal super-man?

So long as the dominant nomad horde remains true to its wandering life, it lives in the midst of the subjugated only in winter, and proceeds in spring to the summer pastures. But it is wise enough to leave behind overseers and guards, to prevent revolts. The individual nomad has no need to keep many slaves; besides, he would have no occupation and no

[1] Schwarz, *Turkestan*, pp. 25 ff.

food for them, and so an entire horde enslaves entire peoples, who must provide food for themselves. In so far as he does not winter directly among them, the nomad only comes to plunder them regularly, leaving them nothing but what is absolutely indispensable.

The peasantry had to supply the nomads and their herds who wintered among them with all that was demanded. For this purpose they stored up grain and fodder during the summer, for in Central and East Europe the snow falls too deep for the herds to be left to scrape out fodder alone. During the winter the wives and daughters of the enslaved became a prey to the lusts of the yellow-skins, by whom they were incessantly violated, and thus every conjugal and family tie and as a further consequence the entire social organisation was seriously loosened. The ancient Indo-European patriarchal principle, which has exclusively prevailed among the Altaians also from the earliest times, languished among the enslaved just because of the violation and loosening of the conjugal bond, which often continued for hundreds of years. The matriarchal principle came into prominence, for the Altaian adulterer repudiated bastards, and still more did the husband where there was one, so the children followed the mother. Where therefore matriarchal phenomena occur among Indo-Europeans, usually among the lower strata of population, they are not survivals of pre-patriarchal times, but probably arose later from the corruption of married life by systematic adultery. Thus the subjugated Indo-Europeans became — here more, there less — mongolised [1] by the mixture of races, and in places the two superimposed races became fused into a uniform mixed people.

Indo-European usage and law died out, and the savage wilfulness of the Altaians had exclusive sway. Revolutions among the people driven to despair followed, but they were quelled in blood, and the oppression exercised still more heavily. Even if here and there the yoke was successfully shaken off, the emancipated, long paralysed and robbed of all capability of self-organisation, were unable to remain independent. Commonly they fell into anarchy and then voluntarily gave themselves up to another milder-seeming servitude, or became once more the prey of an if possible rougher conqueror.

In consequence of the everlasting man-hunting and especially the carrying off of women in foreign civilised districts there ensued a strong mixing of blood, and the Altaian race-characteristics grew fainter, especially to the south and west. The Greeks by the time of Alexander the Great were no longer struck by the Mongol type — already much obliterated — of the nomads pasturing in the district between the Oxus and the Jaxartes. This led to the supposition that these nomads had belonged to the Indo-European race and had originally been settled peasants, and that they had been compelled to limit themselves to animal rearing and to become nomads only after the conversion

[1] The Mongol type of features extends westward to Bavaria and Württemberg.

of their fields to deserts through the evaporation of the water-basins.[1]
This supposition is false, as we have seen before.

The steppes and deserts of Central Asia are an impassable barrier
for the South Asiatics, the Aryans, but not for the North Asiatic,
the Altaian; for him they are an open country providing him with the
indispensable winter pastures.   On the other hand, for the South Asiatic
Aryan these deserts are an object of terror, and besides he is not
impelled towards them, as he has winter pastures near at hand.   It is
this difference in the distance of summer and winter pastures that makes
the North Asiatic Altaian an ever-wandering herdsman, and the grazing
part of the Indo-European race cattle-rearers settled in limited
districts.   Thus, while the native Iranian must halt before the trackless
region of steppes and deserts and cannot follow the well-mounted robber-
nomad thither, Iran itself is the object of greatest longing to the nomadic
Altaian.   Here he can plunder and enslave to his heart's delight, and if
he succeeds in maintaining himself for a considerable time among the
Aryans, he learns the language of the subjugated people, and by mingling
with them loses his Mongol characteristics more and more.   If the
Iranian is now fortunate enough to shake off the yoke, the dispossessed
iranised Altaian intruder inflicts himself upon other lands.   So it was
with the Scythians.

Leaving their families behind in the South Russian steppes, the
Scythians invaded Media c. B.C. 630 and advanced into Mesopotamia
and Syria as far as Egypt.   In Media they took Median wives and learned
the Median language.   After being driven out by Cyaxares, on their
return some twenty-eight years later, they met with a new generation,
the offspring of the wives and daughters whom they had left behind,
and slaves of an alien race.   A thorough mixture of race within
a single generation is hardly conceivable.   A hundred and fifty years
later Hippocrates found them still so foreign, so Mongolian, that he
could say that they were "very different from the rest of mankind, and
only like themselves, as are also the Egyptians."   He remarked their
yellowish-red complexion, corpulence, smooth skins, and their consequent
eunuch-like appearance — all typically Mongol characteristics.   Hippocrates was the most celebrated physician and natural philosopher of
the ancient world.   His evidence is unshakable, and cannot be in-
validated by the Aryan speech of the Scythians.   Their Mongol type
was innate in them, whereas their Iranian speech was acquired and is no
refutation of Hippocrates' testimony.[2]   On the later Greek vases from
South Russian excavations they already appear strongly demongolised
and the Altaian is only suggested by their hair, which is as stiff as a
horse's mane — hence Aristotle's epithet εὐθύτριχες — the characteristic
that survives longest among all Ural-Altaian hybrid peoples.

---

[1] Ukert, *Geographie*, III. 2, p. 275; Schwarz, *Sintflath*, pp. 346, 489 ff.
[2] Peisker, *Beziehungen*, pp. 22 ff.

If a nomad army is obliged to take foreign non-nomadic wives, there occurs at once a dualism, corresponding to the two sexes, in the language and way of living of each individual household. The new wives cannot live in the saddle, they do not know how to take down the tent, load it on the beasts of burden, and set it up again, and yet they must share the restless life of the herdsman. Consequently, where the ground admits of it, as in South Russia, the tent is put on wheels and drawn by animals. Thus the Scythian women were hamaxobiotic (wagon-inhabiting), the men however remained true to their horse-riding life and taught their boys too, as soon as they could keep themselves in the saddle. But the dualism in language could not maintain itself; the children held to the language of the mother, the more easily because even the fathers understood Medish, and so the Altaian Scythian people, with their language finally iranised, became Iranian. But their mode of life remained unchanged : the consumption of horse-flesh, soured horse's milk (*kumiz*) and cheese of the same, the hemp vapour bath for men (the women bathed differently), singeing of the fleshy parts of the body as a cure for rheumatism, poisoning of the arrow-tips, wholesale human offerings, and slaughter of favourite wives at the burials of princes, the placing on horseback of the stuffed bodies of murdered warriors round the grave, etc. — all such customs as are found so well defined among the Mongols of the Middle Ages.

The modern Tartars of the Crimea, whose classical beauty sometimes rivals that of the Greeks and Romans, underwent, in the same land, the same change to the Aryan type.

The same is the case with the Magyars whose mounted nomadic mode of life and fury, and consequently their origin, was Turkish, but their language was a mixture of Ugrian and Turkish on an Ugrian basis.[1] Evidently a Magyar army, Turkish in blood, formerly advanced far to the north where it subdued an Ugrian people and took Ugrian wives; the children then blended the Ugrian speech of their mothers with the Turkish speech of their fathers. But they must also once have dominated Indo-European peoples and mixed themselves very strongly with them, for Gardēzī's original source from the middle of the ninth century describes them as "handsome, stately men." At that time they were leading the nomad existence in the Pontic Steppe — the old Scythia — whence they engaged in terrible slave-hunting among the neighbouring Slavs; and as they were notorious women-hunters, they must have assimilated much Slav, Alan, and Circassian blood, and thus became "handsome, stately men." [2] However the change did not end there. At the end of the ninth century their army, on its return from a predatory expedition, found their kindred at home totally exterminated by their deadly enemies, the Patzinaks, a related stock.

[1] *v.* the table of languages above, p. 333.
[2] Marquart, pp. 144 ff., 466 ff.

CH. XII.

Consequently the whole body had again to take foreign wives, and they occupied the steppes of Hungary. Before this catastrophe the Magyars are said to have mustered 20,000 horsemen — an oriental exaggeration, for this would assume a nomad people of 200,000 souls. Consequently only a few thousand horsemen could have fled to Hungary. There they mixed themselves further with the medley race-conglomeration settled there, which had formed itself centuries before, and assimilated stragglers from the related Patzinak stock.[1] By this absorption the Altaian type asserted itself so predominantly that the Frankish writers were never tired of depicting their ugliness and loathsomeness in the most horrifying colours. Their fury was so irresistible that in sixty-three years they were able with impunity to make thirty-two great predatory expeditions as far as the North Sea, and to France, Spain, Italy, and Byzantium. Thus the modern Magyars are one of the most varied race-mixtures on the face of the earth, and one of the two chief Magyar types of to-day — traced to the Árpád era by tomb-findings — is dolichocephalic with a narrow visage. There we have before us Altaian origin, Ugrian speech, and Indo-European type combined.

Such metamorphoses are typical for all nomads who, leaving their families at home, attack foreign peoples and at the same time make war on one another. In the furious tumult in which the Central Asiatic mounted hordes constantly swarmed, and fought one another for the spoils, it is to be presumed that nearly all such people, like the Scythians and Magyars, at least once sustained the loss of their wives and children. The mounted nomads could, therefore, remain a pure race only where they constantly opposed their own kin, whereas to the south and west they were merged so imperceptibly in the Semitic and Indo-European stock, that no race-boundary is perceivable.

The most diversified was the destiny of those mounted nomads who became romanised in the Balkan peninsula (Roumanians or Vlakhs, (Βλάχοι), but, surprising as it may be outside the steppe region, remain true to this day to their life as horse and sheep nomads wherever this is still at all possible. During the summer they grazed on most of the mountains of the Balkan peninsula, and took up their winter quarters on the sea-coasts among a peasant population speaking a different language. Thence they gradually spread, unnoticed by the chroniclers, along all the mountain ranges, over all the Carpathians of Transylvania, North Hungary, and South Galicia to Moravia; towards the north-west from Montenegro onwards over Herzegovina, Bosnia, Istria, as far as South Styria; towards the south over Albania far into Greece. In the entire Balkan peninsula there is scarcely a span of earth which they have not grazed. And like the peasantry among which they wintered (and winter) long enough, they became (and become) after

[1] Vámbéry, *Ursprung*, pp. 128 ff., 320 ff., 407 ff.; *A Magyarság*, pp. 152 ff.

a transitory bilingualism, Greeks, Albanians, Servians, Bulgarians, Ruthenians, Poles, Slovaks, Chekhs, Slovenes, Croatians, seeing that they appeared there not as a compact body, but as a mobile nomad stratum among a strange-tongued and more numerous peasant element, and not till later did they gradually take to agriculture and themselves become settled. In Istria they are still bilingual. On the other hand they maintain themselves in Roumania, East Hungary, Bukovina, Bessarabia for the following reasons: the central portion of this region, the Transylvanian mountain belt, sustained with its rich summer pastures such a number of grazing-camps (Roumanian *catun*, Mongol. *khotun*), that the nomads in the favourable winter quarters of the Roumanian plain were finally able to absorb the Slav peasantry, already almost wiped out by the everlasting passage through them of other wild nomad peoples. In Macedonia, too, a remainder of them still exists. Were they not denationalised, the Roumanians to-day would be by far the most numerous — but also the most scattered — people of South Europe, — not less than twenty million souls.

The Roumanians were not descendants of Roman colonists of Dacia left behind in East Hungary and Transylvania.[1] Their nomadic life is a confutation of this, for the Emperor Trajan (after A.D. 107) transplanted settled colonists from the entire Roman Empire. And after the removal and withdrawal of the Roman colonists (c. A.D. 271) Dacia, for untold centuries, was the arena of the wildest international struggles known to history, and these could not have been outlived by any nomad people remaining there. To be sure, some express the opinion that the Roumanian nomad herdsmen fled into the Transylvanian mountains at each new invasion (by the Huns, Bulgarians, Avars, Magyars, Patzinaks, Cumans successively) and subsequently always returned. But the nomad can support himself in the mountains only during the summer, and he must descend to pass the winter. On the other hand, each of these new invading nomad hordes needed these mountains for summer grazing for their own herds. Thus the Roumanians could not have escaped, and their alleged game of hide-and-seek would have been in vain. But south of the Danube also the origin of the Roumanians must not be sought in Roman times, but much later, because nomads are never quickly denationalised. For in the summer they are quite alone on the otherwise uninhabited mountains, having intercourse with one another in their own language, and only in their winter quarters among the foreign-speaking peasantry are they compelled in their dealings with them to resort to the foreign tongue. Thus they remain for centuries bilingual before they are quite denationalised, and this can be proved from original sources precisely in the case of the Roumanians (Vlakhs) in the old kingdom of Servia. Accordingly the romanising of the Roumanians presupposes a Romance peasant population already

---

[1] Hunfalvy. On the contrary, Jorga, Ghergel, etc.

existing there for a long time and of different race, through the influence of which they first became bilingual and then very gradually, after some centuries, forgot their own language. In what district could this have taken place? For nomads outside the salt-steppe the sea-coast offers — precisely on account of the salt, and the mild winter — the most suitable winter quarters, and, as a matter of fact, from the earliest times certain shores of the Adriatic, the Ionian, Aegean, and Marmora, were crowded with Vlakhian *catuns*, and are partly so at the present time. Among all these sea-districts, however, only Dalmatia had remained so long Romanic as to be able entirely to romanise a nomad people.[1] From this district the expansion of the Roumanians had its beginning, so that the name Daco-Roumanians is nothing but a fiction.

The Spanish and Italian nomad shepherds too can have had no other origin. Alans took part in Radagaisus' invasion of Italy in 405, and, having advanced to Gaul, founded in 411 a kingdom in Lusitania which was destroyed by the Visigoths. The remainder advanced into Africa with the Vandals in 429. Traces of the Alans remained for a long time in Gaul. Sarmatian and Bulgarian hordes accompanied Alboin to Italy in 568, and twelve places in northern Italy are still called Bolgaro, Bolgheri, etc. A horde of Altaian Bulgars fled to Italy later, and received from the Lombard Grimoald (662–672) extensive and hitherto barren settlements in the mountains of Abruzzi and their neighbourhood. In the time of Paulus Diaconus (797) they also spoke Latin, but their mother tongue was still intact, for only on their winter pastures in Apulia and Campania, in contact with Latin peasants in whose fields they encamped, were they compelled to speak Latin. The old Roman sheep-rearing pursued by slaves has no connexion with nomadism.

Therefore neither the non-Mongol appearance, nor the Semitic, Indo-European, or Finno-Ugrian language of any historical mounted nomad people can be held as a serious argument for their Semitic, Indo-European, or Finno-Ugrian origin. Everything speaks for one single place of origin for the mounted nomads, and that is in the Turanian-Mongol steppes and deserts. These alone, by their enormous extent, their unparalleled severity of climate, their uselessness in summer, their salt vegetation nourishing countless herds, and above all by their indivisible economic connexion with the distant grass-abounding north — these alone give rise

---

[1] Jireček (*Denkschriften Acad. Wien*, XLVIII. pp. 20, 34) assigns the centre of the oldest Roumanians to Servia and its neighborhood where the district in which the Latin language was spoken was most extended) because the Roumanian language is very different from the dialect of the ancient Dalmatians. But because these central lands offer few suitable winter pastures on account of their raw climate and heavy snowfall, it must be assumed that the district in which the Romanic speech adopted by the ancestors of the Roumanians was spoken, somewhere reached notwithstanding to the Adriatic Sea.

to a people with the ineradicable habits of mounted nomads. The Indo-European vocabulary reveals no trace of a former mounted nomadism; there is no ground for speaking of Indo-European, Semitic, Finno-Ugrian nomads, but only of nomads who have remained Altaic or of indo-europeanised, semiticised, ugrianised nomads. The Scythians became Iranian, the Magyars Ugrian, the Avars and Bulgarians Slavic, and so on.

The identical origin of all the mounted nomads of historic and modern times is also demonstrated by the identity of their entire mode of life, even in its details and most trivial particulars, their customs, and their habits. One nomad people is the counterfeit of the other, and after more than two thousand years no change, no differentiation, no progress is to be observed among them. Accordingly we can always supplement our not always precise information about individual historical hordes, and the consequences of their appearance, by comparisons with the better known hordes. We are best informed about the Mongols of the thirteenth century, and that by Rogerius Canon of Varad, Thomas Archdeacon of Spalato, Plano Carpini, Rubruquis, Marco Polo and others, whose accounts are therefore indispensable for a correct estimation of all earlier nomadic invaders of Europe.

This is the *rôle* of nomadism in the history of the world: countries too distant from its basis it could only ravage transitorily, with robbery, murder, fire, and slavery, but the stamp which it left upon the peoples which it directly dominated or adjoined remains uneffaceable. The Orient, the cradle and chief nursery of civilisation, it delivered over to barbarism; it completely paralysed the greater part of Europe, and it transformed and radically corrupted the race, spirit, and character of countless millions for incalculable ages to come. That which is called the inferiority of the East European is *its* work, and had Germany or France possessed steppes like Hungary, where the nomads could also have maintained themselves and thence completed their work of destruction, in all probability the light of West European civilisation would long ago have been extinguished, the entire Old World would have been barbarised, and at the head of civilisation to-day would be stagnant China.

(B)

ATTILA

The Huns, who were divided into numerous distinct tribes ruled by separate princes, had since the beginning of the fifth century begun to draw together into a closer political union. King Rua (Rugilas) had already united a large part of the nation under his sceptre; he ruled especially over the tribes that inhabited the plains of Hungary. Numerous alien barbaric peoples (Slavs, Germans, Sarmatians, etc.) were under his sway. The Eastern Empire paid him a yearly tribute. He was on friendly terms with Aëtius, the general of the Western Empire, who on this account gave up to him a part of Pannonia, the province of Savia. Rua's successors were his nephews, Bleda and Attila, the sons of Mundzuk (*c.* 433).

They first of all reigned jointly, each ruling over a definite number of tribes but maintaining the unity of their empire, while in questions of foreign politics both rulers co-operated. Bleda's personality traditionally fades into obscurity beside Attila's. Attila was hideous to look upon, little, broad-shouldered, with big head, flat nose, and scanty beard. He was covetous, vain, and, like all despots, careful in the preservation of the outward appearance of dignity; he was superstitious, unable to read or write, but of penetrating intellect; he was cunning, audacious, and skilled in all the arts of diplomacy. He is most fitly compared to the formidable Mongol king, Chinghiz Khan; like him he was a mere conqueror who aimed at destruction and plunder; his supremacy had therefore only the effect of a devastating tornado, not that of a purifying thunderstorm which wakes Nature to new life. Certainly he did not rival the Mongol in cruelty and violence; a wise calculation prevented him from totally laying waste the territory given over to him; he respected the law of nations and could be just and magnanimous towards his enemies. Though surrounded by great pomp he remained simple and moderate in his manner of life; he would sit at meals with a stern and earnest countenance, without taking any part in the revelry going on around him.

The policy of concentrating authority within the nation and extending it externally which was introduced by Rua was consciously developed by Bleda and Attila, especially by the latter after he had in 444 or 445 attained to exclusive dominion by setting aside his brother and co-ruler. About the year 435 the Sorasgi, possibly a people of Turkish origin domiciled in South Russia, as well as other "Scythian" races, were subdued. The Akatziri, living in the district to the north of the Black Sea, who hitherto had been in alliance with the Huns, were obliged to acknowledge Attila's rule, and he placed his eldest son Ellak at their head as sub-king (*c.* 447). The king of the Huns even thought of extending the eastern frontier of his empire to Media and Persia. Among the barbarians tributary to him were, besides, the Alani (on the Don), numerous Slav tribes, some of which lived east of the Vistula while others, driven out by the Huns, had settled in the Danubian lands, as had in particular, the Teutons of the Danube basin: Gepidae, Ostrogoths, Heruli, Rugii, Sciri, Turcilingi, Suevi (Quadi). Certainly other names of German tribes are mentioned as under Attila's dominion: Marcomanni, Bastarnae, Burgundians, Bructeri, Franks (Ripuarii), and perhaps Alemanni on the Neckar, but it is doubtful to whom they were subject. The Burgundians (on the east Rhine) who had previously in the year 430 successfully repelled a Hunnic host, the Bructeri (between the Lippe and the Ruhr), the Franks and Germans on the Neckar must have voluntarily joined the Huns during the great march to Gaul (451), so that we are scarcely justified in advancing the western frontier of the Huns as far as the Rhine. The Germans occupy a conspicuous place in the circle around Attila; it is related of Ardaric, the king of the Gepidae, that he enjoyed especial consideration from Attila on account of his fidelity, and that his advice was not without influence on the decisions of the king of the Huns. Among his trusted counsellors is mentioned, besides, the famous warrior prince of the Sciri, Edeco (Edica), Odovacar's father, who in the year 449 was sent to Constantinople as ambassador. The Ostrogoth king Walamir also is said — though by a biassed and not unimpeachable authority (Jordanes) — to have enjoyed Attila's favour. Thus the German peoples mostly maintained their autonomy and were generally only obliged to serve in the army, while other inferior subject races, in particular the Slavs, forfeited their independence and were compelled to feed their rulers with the produce of their farms and cattle. Yet Attila looked upon all subjugated peoples as his slaves and asserted an absolute right of disposing of their life and property. All attempts to withdraw from his sovereignty he punished with terrible cruelty; the demand for the delivery of fugitives therefore played an important part in his negotiations with the Romans.

We are, as is natural, most accurately informed of his relations with the two halves of the Roman Empire. Like Rua Attila maintained a friendship with Aëtius, at whose disposal he repeatedly placed Hunnish mercenaries. This relationship was partly brought about by personal conditions, partly by the endeavour of Attila to divide the Roman power. With such auxiliaries the general of the Western Empire destroyed at Worms (435-436) the Burgundian kingdom of legendary fame — an event which later tradition and saga have turned into an expedition of Attila's against the Burgundians. Numbers of Huns served in the Roman Army which, in the same way, in 436-439 fought against the

CH. XII.

Visigoths. On his side Aëtius sent to the king a learned Roman scribe, Constantius, as private secretary and gave him his own son, Carpilio, as hostage, for which in return he was honoured with gifts. The office, also, of a *magister militum* which Attila held he seems to have obtained through the Western Empire. The tribute which was paid to him from thence was disguised under the name of a salary as Roman General-in-chief. But at the end of the year 440 serious troubles already disturbed these relations, because Attila repeatedly annoyed the Western Empire and terrified it with threats under the pretext that fugitives from his dominion had found refuge there.

The same degrading treatment must have befallen the Eastern Roman Empire which was under the sovereignty of the incapable Emperor Theodosius II. A complete overthrow and destruction of the Eastern Empire was not Attila's intention. His policy on the contrary aimed at keeping it, by continual extortions of money and actual depredations, in a state of permanent weakness and incapacity to resist. And as he insisted that all deserters should be given up to him he deprived the Romans of the means of strengthening their army by recruiting among the barbaric peoples of the Danube lands. These leading ideas came clearly to light at once in the first treaty which the two kings of the Huns concluded with the Emperor soon after their accession (*c.* 433). It was agreed that the Romans should no longer receive fugitives from the Huns and that these, as well as the Roman prisoners of war who had escaped from the country of the Huns, should be given up unless a ransom was paid for each of the latter. Besides, the Emperor must not assist any barbarian people that was fighting against the Huns; between both the kingdoms there was to be free commercial intercourse; the tribute of the Romans was doubled and raised to 700 lbs. of gold. It was clear that the Huns would not be contented with success so easily gained; if they nevertheless kept the peace for eight years, it was only because they were occupied with the subjection of the various Scythian peoples to the north of the Danube. In the year 441 they were on the war-path and slaughtered the Romans who had come on account of a market to the bank of the Danube. A direct reason for the opening of hostilities was given to them by the East Roman expedition against the Vandals which had occasioned a withdrawal of frontier troops. This coincidence of events has given rise to the groundless supposition that Gaiseric and Attila had at that time formed an alliance. To the Emperor's expostulation the kings replied that the Romans had not paid the tribute regularly, had sheltered deserters, and also that the bishop of Margus (Pussarovitz) had robbed the Hunnish royal graves of their treasures, and they threatened him with a continuation of the war unless the fugitives and the bishop were handed over to them. As the imperial envoys refused everything the Huns captured the Danube forts Ratiaria, Viminacium,

Singidunum (Belgrade) and Margus (the last through the treachery of the bishop, who was afraid of being delivered up) and pressed, devastating as they went, into the interior of the Balkan lands as far as the neighbourhood of Constantinople, where they conquered cities like Naissus (Nisch), Philippopolis and Arcadiopolis. Other Hunnish bands joined with the Persians made an inroad at the same time over the Caucasus into the frontier lands of the Eastern Empire. The Roman army which had in the meantime been called from Sicily by Theodosius was decisively beaten in the Thracian Chersonesus. The kings of the Huns dictated peace; and its conditions were still more disgraceful than before: — the yearly tribute was raised to 2100 lbs. of gold besides the stipulation of the payment of an indemnity of 6000 lbs. of gold, and the surrender of fugitives was insisted upon (443).

Already in the year 447 the Huns invaded once more, and again brought the most terrible calamities upon the Balkan lands. Arnegisclus, the general who opposed the enemy, was beaten and killed after valiant resistance on the river Utus (Wid) in Lower Moesia, after which the Hunnish cavalry pressed up the valley of the river Margus (Morava) and through Thessaly as far as Thermopylae. Some 70 cities and fortresses are said to have fallen victims to them at that time. When in the year 448 peace was again concluded, Attila demanded that besides the usual money payments a broad tract of a five days' journey on the right bank of the Danube from Singidunum to Novae (Šistova) should be left waste; the boundary was placed at Naissus. But even now Attila would not leave the Emperor at peace. Embassy after embassy went to Constantinople and, on the standing pretext that not all deserters had yet been delivered up, continually asserted fresh humiliating claims, the king being however chiefly desirous of giving his messengers an opportunity of enriching themselves with the customary gifts. The Eastern Empire was near a financial collapse; as it could not exert itself to armed resistance the thought came to the Imperial Government, that is to say to the court eunuch Chrysaphius in particular, of getting rid of the king of the Huns by murder. For this deed the co-operation of the Scirian prince Edeco was sought: he declared himself ready to assist but immediately betrayed the plan to Attila. The king revenged himself only by scorning the despicable enemy; the Roman envoys who had come with Edeco to him, amongst whom was the historian Priscus, he allowed to withdraw, respecting the law of nations; he promised besides to maintain the peace and give up the waste frontier territory on the Danube, and he did not once press the demand, made in his first anger, that Chrysaphius should be put to death. But he sent word to the Emperor that as Attila was a king's son so was Theodosius an emperor's son, but that as the latter had rendered himself tributary to the former he thus became his slave and that it was a shameful action that he, as such, should aim at the life of his master

CH. XII.

(449 ?). Attila might rightly consider himself the lord of the whole Roman Empire. His authority had been considerably enhanced among his own people by the discovery, about that time, of a sword buried in the ground which was regarded as the weapon of the god of war.

It was not until Theodosius died (28 July 450) that these wretched conditions altered. His successor, the efficient Emperor Marcian, refused, as soon as he succeeded to the throne, to continue the payment of the tribute to the king of the Huns, and the Western Empire followed his example. The outbreak of war was also due to the conduct of Gratia Justa Honoria, the sister of the Western Emperor Valentinian. She secretly offered herself as wife to the king of the Huns, but the fulfilment of the offer was refused because Attila demanded that half of the Western Empire should be given up to her as her inheritance from her father. Attila hereupon determined to take possession of the Western Empire and of Gaul first of all, for here he might reckon with certainty on the support of the (Ripuarian) Franks who, being split up into two sections on account of dynastic hostilities, called for his intervention, and he could in all probability count on at least the benevolent neutrality of the Visigoths. The story that Gaiseric, out of fear of Theodoric's vengeance, stirred up Attila to make war against the Visigoths, is certainly a fable, for the African kingdom had nothing to fear from an attack on this side; nevertheless the Vandal king may have had a hand in the matter in order to weaken the West Roman Empire still further. Supposing, however, an agreement between the Goths and the Romans to be possible, Attila wrote to Theodoric as well as to the Western Emperor that he was not going to take the field against them but against their enemies. The history of the Hunnic expedition which ended in Attila's defeat on the Campus Mauriacus near Troyes (451) has already been told in another connexion, p. 280. Without being followed by the victors the Hunnic army returned to Hungary. Attila did not venture to repeat the expedition into Gaul; on the contrary, in the following year after having made good his losses he turned towards Italy where he had not to fear Germanic heroism.

Without encountering any resistance the Hunnic army crossed the Julian Alps in the spring of 452. After a long siege Aquileia was taken by storm and destroyed; after which the most important fortresses of Upper Italy, with the exception of Ravenna, easily fell into the hands of the enemy. A great many of the inhabitants of the terribly devastated country sought refuge on the unassailable islands of the lagoons along the Adriatic coast. Yet the real foundation of Venice which tradition has connected with the Hunnic invasion can only be traced back to the invasion of the Lombards (568). After this Attila bethought himself of marching against Rome, but famine and disease, which broke out in his army, and the arrival in Italy of succour from the Eastern Empire, as well as superstitious fear, since the Visigoth king Alaric had died shortly after his capture of the Eternal City, kept him from carrying out his plan. When therefore an embassy of the Romans led by Pope Leo I appeared in his camp on the Mincio to induce him to withdraw, he willingly shewed himself ready to conclude peace and retire. A contemporary, the chronicler Prosper Tiro, who at that time was living in the papal service at Rome, has ascribed the retreat of the "scourge of God" to the influence of Leo's powerful personality, and later ecclesiastical tradition has naturally further enhanced the holy man's ostensible service and adorned it with all manner of supernatural circumstances. But a dispassionate historical inspection will not allow us to ascribe the saving of Italy solely to the influence of the Pope. Having returned home Attila demanded of Marcian the tribute paid by Theodosius, and on the refusal of the Emperor prepared for war against Eastern Rome. But his sudden death prevented the realisation of his scheme: he died of hemorrhage when he was celebrating his wedding (453) with a maiden named Ildico, the Kriemhild of the Nibelungenlied (the name is a diminutive of Hilde). The inheritance was divided among his sons, those mentioned by name being Ellak, Dengisich, and Ernac the youngest, Attila's favourite. But with this was foreshadowed the downfall of the Hunnic power, which was too much dependent on the personal quality of its leader to be able to endure.

Of the domestic life and polity of the Huns we have also accurate knowledge through the genuine fragment of Priscus. The king's head-quarters were on the Hungarian steppe between the Theiss and Körös and covered a large area which was enclosed by a circular wooden fence. In the middle stood the royal residence also fenced round, a wooden erection consisting of one single hall, Attila's private and public dwelling, of ingenious architecture and furnished within with great magnificence.[1] Among the king's circle the *logades* were prominent, a nobility founded on birth and service; these enjoyed the highest consideration with the ruler and the right to choose from the booty the best spoils and the richest prisoners, and they formed a kind of council of state. Out of their midst the body-guard, the military leaders, and the envoys were taken. The highest position amongst them was occupied by Onegesius, Attila's right hand and first minister, who lived in a palace at the entrance to the court residence. Besides Huns there were also Germans and Romans among the *logades*, who on account of their intelligence and culture enjoyed especial consideration. At the king's Court therefore the Latin and Gothic tongues were in predominant use together with the Hunnic. Attila ruled over his people in a wholly patriarchal manner; the administration of justice was executed through him personally in the simplest way, always just without respect of persons.

---

[1] Stephani gives a plan of the encampment. *Der älteste deutsche Wohnbau und seine Einrichtung*, Leipsic, 1902, I. pp. 172 ff.

CH. XII.

The freedom and legal protection which every subject enjoyed caused many a Roman to leave his home and settle with the uncivilised barbarians who knew no kind of taxation. The Huns kept, as before, their character as nomadic horsemen; they were in their element on the steppes; life in towns was repugnant to them. Justly appreciating these conditions Attila had made no attempt to effect a change in the mode of life of his people, and never thought of removing to civilised districts and setting up there a new State. His object was fully attained by keeping the Romans in subjection and making them fill his treasury.

CHAPTER XIII

(A)

ROMAN BRITAIN

THE character and history of Roman Britain, as of many other Roman provinces, were predominantly determined by the facts of its geography. To that cause, or set of causes, more than to any other, we must attribute alike the Roman desire to conquer the province and the actual stages of the conquest, the distribution of the troops employed as permanent garrison, the quality and extent of the Romanised civilisation, and, lastly, a great part of the long series of incidents by which the island was lost to Rome and Roman culture.

Geologically, Britain forms the north-west side of a huge valley which had its south-east side in northern and central France. Down the centre of this valley ran two rivers, the one flowing south-west along a bed now covered by the English Channel, the other flowing north-east through a region now beneath the German Ocean. From these rivers, the land sloped upwards, south-east to Vosges, Alps, and Cevennes, north-west to Cornwall, Wales and northern Britain. The two rivers have long vanished. But the configuration of their valleys has lasted. Though unquiet seas now divide England from north-western Europe, the two areas, that were once the two sides of the valleys, still look to each other. Their lowlands lie opposite; their main rivers flow out into the intervening sea; their easiest entrances face; each area lies open by nature to the trade or the brute force of the other; each has its most fertile, most habitable, and least defensible districts next to those of the other.

Hence comes the peculiar configuration of our island. In south-east Britain there is little continuous hill-country that rises above the 600 foot contour line. Instead, wide undulating lowlands, marked by no striking physical feature and containing little to arrest or even divert the march of ancient armies or of traders, stretch over all the south and east and midlands. For hills, we must go north of Trent and Humber or west of Severn and Exe. There we shall find almost the converse of the south-east. Throughout a large, scattered region, extending from Cornwall to the Highlands, the land lies mostly above, and much of it high above, the 600 foot line; its soil and climate are ill-suited to agriculture; its deep valleys and gorges and wild moors and high peaks oppose alike the soldier and the citizen.   Behind this upland lies the Atlantic, and an Atlantic which meant of old the reverse of what it does to-day.   To the ancients, this hill-country was the end of the world; for us — since Columbus — it is the beginning.

These physical features are reproduced plainly in the early history of Britain.   It was natural that about B.C. 50–A.D. 50 southern Britain should be occupied by Keltic tribes and even families which had close kindred in Gaul, and that a lively intercourse should exist between the two.   It was no less natural that, even before Rome had fully conquered Gaul, Caesar's troops should be seen in Kent and Middlesex (B.C. 55–54) and Roman suzerainty extended over these regions; and when the annexation of Gaul was finally complete, that of Britain seemed the obvious sequel.   The sequel was, indeed, delayed awhile by political causes.   Augustus (B.C. 43–A.D. 14) had too much else to do : Tiberius (14–37) saw no need for it, just as he saw no need for any wars of conquest.   But after 37 it became urgent.   Changes in southern Britain had favoured an anti-Roman reaction there and had even perhaps produced disquiet in northern Gaul; Caligula (37–41) had made some fiasco in connexion with it; when Claudius succeeded, there was need of vigorous action and, as it chanced, the leading statesmen of the moment favoured a forward policy in many lands.   The result was a well-planned and deservedly successful invasion (A.D. 43).

The details of the ensuing war of conquest do not here concern us. It is enough to say that the lowlands offered little resistance.   In one part of them, near the south-east coast, Roman ways had become familiar since Caesar's raids.   In another part — the midlands — the population was then, as now, thin.   Nowhere (despite the theories of Guest and Green) were there physical obstacles likely to delay the Roman arms.   By 47 the invaders had subdued almost all the lowlands, as far west as Exeter and Shrewsbury and as far north as the Humber.   Then came a pause.   The difficulties of the hill-country, the bravery of the hill-tribes, political circumstances at Rome, combined not indeed to arrest but seriously to impede advance.   But the decade 70–80 saw the final conquest of Wales and the first subjugation of northern England, and in the years 80–84 Agricola was able to cross the Tyne and the Cheviots and gradually advance into Perthshire.   Much of the land which he overran was but imperfectly subdued and the northern part of it — everything, probably, north of the Tweed — was abandoned when he was recalled (85).   Thirty years later (115–120) an in-surrection shook the whole Roman power in northern Britain, and when Hadrian had restored order, he established the frontier along a line from Tyne to Solway, which he fortified by forts and a continuous wall (about 122–124).   Fifteen or twenty years later, about A.D. 140, his successor Pius, for reasons not properly recorded, made a fresh advance; he annexed Scotland up to the narrow isthmus between Forth and Clyde and fortified that with a continuous wall, a series of forts along it variously estimated at 12 or (more probably) at 18 or 20, and some outposts along the natural route through the Gap of Stirling to the north-east. This wall was not meant as a substitute for Hadrian's Wall, but as a defence to the country north of it.

Rome had now reached her furthest permanent north. But the advance was not long accepted quietly by the natives. Twenty years after Pius had built his wall, a storm broke loose through all northern Britain from Derbyshire to Cheviot or beyond (about 158–160). A second storm followed 20 years later (about 183); the Wall of Pius was then or soon after definitely lost, and disorder apparently continued till the Emperor Septimius Severus came out in person (208–211) and rebuilt the Wall of Hadrian to form, with a few outlying forts, the Roman frontier. With this step ends the series of alternating organisation and revolt which make up the external history of the earlier Roman Britain. Henceforward the Wall was the boundary until the coming of the barbarians who ended Roman rule in the island.

The force which garrisoned this fluctuating frontier and kept the province quiet consisted of three (till A.D. 85, of four) legions and an uncertain number of troops of the second grade, the so-called *auxilia*, in all perhaps some 35–40,000 men, mostly heavy infantry. The three legions were disposed in three fortresses, Isca Silŭrum (Caerleon on Usk, *legio ii Augusta*), Deva (Chester, *legio xx Valeria Victrix*) and Eburācum (York, *legio vi Victrix*): from these centres detachments (*vexillationes*) were sent out to form expeditionary forces, to construct fortifications and other military works, and generally to meet important but occasional needs. Outside these three main fortresses, the province was kept quiet and safe by a network of small forts (*castella*), varying in size from two or three to six or seven acres and garrisoned by auxiliary *cohortes* (infantry) or *alae* (cavalry), some 500 and some 1000 strong. These forts were planted along important roads and at strategic points, 10 or 15 or 20 miles apart. Their distribution is noteworthy. In the lowlands there were none. During the early years of the conquest we can, indeed, trace garrisons at one or two places, such as Cirencester. But, as the conquest advanced, it was seen that the lowlands needed no force to ensure their peace, and the troops were pushed on into the hills, beyond Severn and Trent. Eighteen or twenty forts were dotted about Wales, though many of these seem to have been abandoned in the course of the second century, as having become superfluous through the growing pacification of the land. A much larger number can be detected in Derbyshire, Lancashire, the hill-country of Yorkshire, and northwards as far as Cheviot: Hadrian's Wall, in particular, was principally defended by a series of such forts. We cannot, however, give precise statistics of these forts until exploration has advanced further: it is doubtful not only how far the known examples provide us with a fairly full list of them, but, still more, to what extent all the forts were in occupation at the same time and to what extent one succeeded another.

The troops which garrisoned these military posts were Roman, in the sense that they not only obeyed the Roman Emperor but were in theory and to a great extent in practice, even in the later days of Roman Britain, recruited within the Empire. The legionaries came from Romanised districts in the Western Empire; the auxiliaries, naturally less civilised to begin with but drilled into Roman ways and speech, were largely drawn from the Rhine and its neighbourhood: some probably were Kelts, like the native Britons, others (as their names on tombstones and altars prove) were Teutonic in race. To what extent Britons were enrolled to garrison Britain, is not very clear; certainly, the statement that British recruits were always sent to the Continent (chiefly to Germany), by way of precaution, seems on our present evidence to be less sweepingly true than was formerly supposed.

From the standpoints alike of the ancient Roman statesman and of the modern Roman historian the military posts and their garrisons formed the dominant element in Britain. But they have left little permanent mark on the civilisation and character of the island. The ruins of their forts and fortresses are on our hill-sides. But, Roman as they were, their garrisons did little to spread Roman culture here. Outside their walls, each of them had a small or large settlement of womenfolk, traders, perhaps also of time-expired soldiers wishful to end their days where they had served. But hardly any of these settlements grew up into towns. York may form an exception (see below): it is a pure coincidence, due to causes far more recent than the Roman age, that Newcastle, Manchester, and Cardiff stand on sites once occupied by Roman "auxiliary" forts. Nor do the garrisons appear to have greatly affected the racial character of the Romano-British population. Even in times of peace, the average annual discharge of time-expired men, with land-grants or bounties, cannot have greatly exceeded 1000, and, as we have seen, times of peace were rare in Britain. Of these discharged soldiers by no means all settled in Britain, and some of them may have been of Keltic or even of British birth. Whatever German or other foreign elements passed into the population through the army, cannot have been greater than that population could easily and naturally absorb without being seriously affected by them. The true contribution which the army made to Romano-British civilisation was that its upland forts and fortresses formed a sheltering wall round the peaceful interior regions.

Behind these formidable garrisons, kept safe from barbarian inroads and in easy contact with the Roman Empire by short sea passages from Rutupiae (Richborough, near Sandwich in Kent) to Boulogne or from Colchester to the Rhine, stretched the lowlands of southern, midland,

and eastern Britain. Here Roman culture spread and something ap-proximating to real Romanisation took place. The process began probably before the Claudian invasion of 43. The native British coinage of the south-eastern tribes and other indications suggest that, in the 100 years between Julius Caesar and Claudius, Roman ways and perhaps even Roman speech had found admission to the shores of Britain, and this infiltration (as I have said) may have made easier the ultimate conquest. After the conquest, the process continued in two ways. In part it was definitely aided by the government which established here, as in other provinces, municipalities peopled by Roman citizens, for the most part discharged legionaries, and known as *coloniae*: these, however, were comparatively few in Britain. Far greater was the automatic movement. Italians flocked to the newly opened regions — traders, as it seems, rather than the labourers who form the emigrants from Italy to-day: how numerous they were, we can hardly tell, but such commerical emigrations are always more important commercially than for their mere numbers. Certainly a far more notable movement was the automatic acceptance of Roman civilisation by the British natives.

We can to some extent trace this movement. Quite early in the period A.D. 43–80, the British town Verulamium, just outside St Albans in Hert-fordshire, was judged to have become sufficiently Romanised to merit the municipal status and title of *municipium* (practically equivalent to that of the *colonia* manned by veteran soldiers). The great revolt of Boudicca (less correctly called Boadicea) in A.D. 60 was directed not only against the supremacy of Rome but also against the spread of Roman civilisation, and one incident in it was the massacre of many thousands of "loyal" natives along with actual Romans. Romanisation, it is plain, had been spreading apace. Nor did this massacre check it for long. The Flavian period (A.D. 70–96) saw in Britain, as indeed in other provinces, a serious development of Roman culture and in particular of Roman town life, the peculiar gift of Rome to her western provinces. In the decade A.D. 70–80, the Britons began, as Tacitus tells us, to speak Latin and to use Latin dress and the material fabric of Latin civilised life. Now towns sprang up, such as Silchester (Calleva Atrebatum) and Caerwent (Venta Silurum), laid out on the model approved by Roman town-planners, furnished with public buildings (*forum, basilica*, etc.) of Roman style, and filled with houses which were Roman in their internal fittings (baths, hypocausts, wall-paintings) if not in ground-plan. Now the baths of Bath (Aquae Sulis) were equipped with civilised buildings suited to their new visitors: the earliest datable monument there belongs to .about 77. Two *coloniae* also were planted. Hitherto there had only been one, established by Claudius at Colchester (Camulodunum): now one was added at Lincoln (Lindum) and in 96 a third at Gloucester (Glevum). A new Civil Judge (*legatus iuridicus*) begins to make his appearance beside the regular *legatus Augusti pro praetore* who was at once commander of

CH. XIII.

the troops and judge of the chief court and governor of the province, and the appointment is doubtless due to increasing civil business in the law courts.   When Tacitus praises Agricola because he encouraged the provincials to adopt Roman culture, he praises him for following the tendency of his age, not for striking out any novel line of his own.   It is probable that by the end of the first century, Roman civilisation was laying firm hold on all the British lowlands.

Subsequent progress was slower, or at least less showy.   Little advance was made beyond the lowlands.   Towns and "villas" were rare west of the Severn, and save in the vale of York they were equally rare north of the Trent.   The uplands remained comparatively unaffected. Their population, as recent excavations in Cumberland and in Anglesey have shewn, used Roman objects and came to some extent within range of Roman culture.   But it seems impossible to speak of them as fully civilised, even if, in the later years of the Roman occupation, they did not remain wholly barbarian.   In the lowlands we may ascribe to the second and third centuries the development of the rural system and the building of farmhouses and country residences contructed in Roman fashion.   It is very difficult to date these houses.   But the evidence of coins seems to shew that the end of the third and the first half of the fourth century were the periods when they were most numerous and most fully occupied, and when, as we may fairly argue, the countryside of Roman Britain was most fully permeated with Roman culture.   For such a conclusion we shall have the support of a neighbouring parallel in Gaul.

The administration of the civilised part of Britain, while of course subject to the governor of the whole province, was in effect entrusted to the local authorities.   Each Roman *municipium* and *colonia* ruled itself, including a territory which might be as long and broad as a small English county.   Some districts probably belonged to the Imperial Domains and were ruled by local agents of the Emperor; such, probably, were the lead-mining districts, as on Mendip or in Derbyshire or Flintshire.   The remainder of the country, by far its largest part, was divided up, as before the Roman conquest, among the native cantons or tribes, now organised in more or less Roman fashion: each tribe had its council (*ordo*) and tribal magistrates and its capital where the tribal council met.   Thus, the tribe or canton of the Silures, the *civitas Silurum*, as it learnt to call itself, had its capital at Venta Silurum, Caerwent (between Chepstow and Newport); there its council met and *decreto ordinis*, by decree of the council, measures were taken for the government of the tribal area which probably covered much of Monmouthshire and some of Glamorgan.   This, we know by epigraphic evidence, occurred at Caerwent and we shall not be rash in assuming, on slighter evidence, that the same system obtained in other tribal areas in Britain.   It is just the system which Rome applied also to the local government of Gaul north of the Cevennes: it illustrates well the Roman method of entrusting local government to a restricted form of Home Rule.

In the social fabric of Romano-British life, the two chief elements were the town and the country house or "villa." Both are mainly Roman importations. The Kelts do not appear to have reached any definite urban life, either in Gaul or in Britain, before the coming of the Romans, though they no doubt had, even in Britain, agglomerations of houses which came near to being towns. But with the Roman conquest a real town life arose. In part, this was directly created by the government under the Roman forms of *municipium* and *colonia*, noticed above. Colchester (Camulodunum), Lincoln (Lindum), Gloucester (Glevum), York (Eburācum), were *coloniae*; the first three were founded in the first century by drafts of time-expired soldiers and the fourth, York, probably grew out of the "civil settlement" on the west bank of the Ouse which confronted the legionary fortress under the present Cathedral and its precincts. One town Verulamium (St Albans) was a *municipium*, ranking with the four *coloniae* in privilege and standing but different (as explained above) in origin. All these five towns attained considerable prosperity, and in particular Camulodunum, Eburācum, and Verulamium, but none can vie with the more splendid municipalities of other provinces.

Besides them, Roman Britain could shew a larger number — some ten or fifteen, according to the standard adopted — of country-towns which varied much in size but possessed in their own way the essential features of urban life. The chief of these seem to be the following: (1) Isurium Brigantum, captial or *chef-lieu* of the Brigantes, now Aldborough, some twelve miles N.W. of York and the most northerly Romano-British town properly so called, (2) Ratae, capital of the Coritani, now Leicester, (3) Viroconium — so best spelt, not Uriconium — capital of the Cornovii, now Wroxeter, on the Severn, five miles below Shrewsbury, (4) Corinium, capital of the Dobuni, now Cirencester, (5) Venta Silurum, already mentioned, (6) Isca Dumnoniorum, capital of the Dumnonii, now Exeter, (7) Durnovaria, capital of the Durotriges, now Dorchester in Dorsetshire, (8) Venta Belgarum, capital of the Belgae, now Winchester, (9) Calleva Atrebatum, capital of the Atrebates, close to Silchester, (10) Durovernum Cantiacorum, capital of the Cantii, now Canterbury, (11) Venta Icenorum, capital of the Iceni, now Caister by Norwich, and perhaps — for the limits of the list are not easily drawn with rigidity — Chesterford (Roman name unknown) in Essex, Kenchester (Magna) in Herefordshire, Chesterton (Durobrivae?) on the Nen, Rochester (also Durobrivae) in Kent, and even one or two which have perhaps less right to inclusion. Many of these town are indicated by the Ravenna Geographer as holding some special rank and nearly all are declared by their remains to be the sites of really Romanised town‾ life. What exactly their status or government was, has yet to be

CH. XIII.

defined. But it is fairly probable — especially from the Caerwent monument erected by the *ordo civitatis Silurum* — that the authorities of town and tribe were one. .

The general fashion of these towns has been revealed to us by excavations at Silchester and Caerwent. At Silchester, the whole 100 acres within the walls have been systematically uncovered during the last twenty years and the buildings studied with especial care. At Caerwent, a smaller area (39 acres) has been excavated so far as the buildings of the present village permit. Both shew much the same features, with certain differences in detail which are both natural and instructive: (i) Both have been *planned* according to the Roman method, which obtained in many parts of the Empire: that is, the streets run at right angles, so as to form a chessboard pattern with square plots for the houses. At Silchester, where space was obviously abundant, the sanctity of the street frontages seems to have been in general observed: at Caerwent, which is of smaller size and more thickly crowded with buildings, the street plan has suffered some encroachments, but not so much as to obliterate its character. (ii) Both towns had near their centre the Town Buildings known as *Forum* and *Basilica*. At Silchester the Forum was a rectangular plot of two acres, with streets running along all its four sides. It contained a central open court, nearly 140 feet square, surrounded on three sides by corridors or cloisters with rooms — presumably shops and lounges — opening into them; on the fourth side was a pillared hall, 270 by 58 feet in floor space, decorated with Corinthian columns, marble lined walls, statues, and the like, and behind this hall a row of rooms which probably served as offices for the town authorities and the like. The Caerwent Municipal Buildings were very similar: so (as far as we can tell from imperfect finds) were those at Cirencester and Wroxeter. They are indeed examples of a type which was represented in most large towns of the western Empire and in Italy itself. (iii) Both towns had in addition small temples in different quarters within the walls and at Silchester a small building close to the Forum is so similar in every detail to the early Christian church of the western "basilican" type, that we can hardly hesitate to call it a church. (iv) Both towns, again, seem to have had Public Baths: those at Silchester covered an area of 80 by 160 feet in their earliest form and in later times were much extended. Both again had more direct provision for amusements. At Silchester an earthen amphitheatre stood outside the walls: at Caerwent there are traces of the stone walls of one inside the ramparts. (v) Of dwelling-houses and shops and the like both towns had naturally no lack. The private houses are built like most of the private houses in the Keltic part of the Empire, in fashions very dissimilar from anything at Pompeii or Rome, but are fitted in Roman style with mosaics, hypocausts, painted wall-plaster, and the like. They are specially noteworthy as being properly "country houses," brought together to form a town perforce, and not "town houses" such as could be used to compose regular rows or terraces or streets. Even the architecture thus declares that the town life of these cantonal *chef-lieux*, though real, was incomplete.

The civilisation of the towns appears to have been of the Roman type. Not only do the buildings declare this: inscriptions, and, in particular, casual scratchings on tiles or pots which can often be assigned to the lower classes, prove that Latin was both read and written and spoken easily in Silchester and Caerwent. Whether Keltic was also known, is uncertain: here evidence is totally lacking. But it may be observed that if Keltic was understood, one would expect to meet it, quite as much as Latin, on casual *sgraffiti*, while the total disappearance of a native tongue can be paralleled from southern Gaul and southern Spain and is not incredible in towns. Nor do the smaller objects found at Silchester and Caerwent shew much survival of the Late Keltic art which prevailed in Britain in the pre-Roman age and which certainly survived here and there in the island. But while Romanised, these towns are not large or rich. It has been calculated that Silchester did not contain more than eighty houses of decent size, and the industries traceable there — in particular, some dyers' furnaces — do not indicate wealth or capital. The Romano-British towns, it seems, were assimilated to Rome. But they were not powerful enough to carry their Roman culture through a barbarian conquest or impose it on their conquerors.

From the town we pass to the country. This seems to have been divided up among estates commonly (though perhaps unscientifically) styled "villas." Of the residences, etc. which formed the buildings of these estates many examples survive. Some are as large and luxurious as any Gaulish nobleman's residence on the other side of the Channel. Others are small houses or even mere farms or cottages. It is difficult, on our present evidence, to deduce from these houses the agrarian system to which they belonged, save that it was plainly no mere slave system. But it is clear from the character of the residences and the remains in them that they represent the same Romanised civilisation as the towns, while a few chance *sgraffiti* suggest that Latin was used in some, at least, of them. A priori, it is not improbable that, while the towns were Romanised, the countryside remained to some extent Keltic or bilingual. But all that is certain as yet is that scanty evidence proves some knowledge of Latin. These country houses were very irregularly distributed over the island. In some districts they abounded and included splendid mansions: such districts are north Kent, west Sussex, parts of Hants, of Somerset, of Gloucestershire, of Lincolnshire. Other districts, notably the midlands of Warwickshire or Buckingham-shire, contained very few "villas" and indeed, as it seems, very few inhabitants at all. The Romans probably found these latter districts thinly peopled and they left them in the same condition.

CH. XIII.

Besides country houses and farms, the countryside also contained occasional villages or hamlets inhabited solely by peasants; such have been excavated in Dorsetshire by the late General Pitt-Rivers. These villages testify, in their degree, to the spread of Roman material civilisation. However little their inhabitants understood of the higher aspects of Roman culture, the objects found in them — pottery, brooches, etc. — are much the same as those of the Romanised towns and "villas" and are widely different from those of the Keltic villages, such as those lately excavated near Glastonbury, which belong to the latest pre-Roman age.

The province was, on the whole, well provided with roads, some of them constructed for military purposes, some obviously connected with the various towns: whether any of them follow lines laid out by the Britons before A.D. 43 is more than doubtful. In describing them, we must put aside all notion of the famous "Four Great Roads" of Saxon times. That category of four roads was a medieval invention, probably dating from the eleventh or twelfth century antiquaries, and the names of the roads composing it are Anglo-Saxon names, some of which the inventors of the "Four Roads" plainly did not understand. If we examine the Roman roads actually known to us, we discern in the English lowlands four main groups of roads radiating from the natural geographical centre, London, and a fifth group crossing England from north-east to south-west. The first ran from the Kentish ports and Canterbury through the populous north Kent to London. The second took the traveller west by Staines (Pontes) to Silchester and thence by various branching roads to Winchester, Dorchester, Exeter, to Bath, to Gloucester and south Wales. A third, known to the English as Watling street, crossed the Midlands by Verulam to Wall near Lichfield (Letocetum), Wroxeter, Chester (Deva) and mid and north Wales: it also, by a branch from High Cross (Venonae) gave access to Leicester and Lincoln. A fourth, running north-east from London, led to Colchester and Caister by Norwich and (as it seems) by a branch through Cambridge to Lincoln. The fifth group, unconnected with London, compromises two roads of importance. One, named "Fosse" by the English, ran from Lincoln and Leicester by High Cross to Cirencester, Bath and Exeter. Another, probably called Ryknield street by the English, ran from the north through Sheffield and Derby and Birmingham (of which Derby alone is a Roman site) to Cirencester and in a fashion duplicated the Fosse. There were also other roads — such as Akeman street, which crossed the southern Midlands from near St Albans by way of Alchester (near Bicester) to Cirencester and Bath — which must be considered as independent of the main scheme. But, judged by the places they served and by the posts along them, the five groups above indicated seem the really important roads of southern or non-military Roman Britain.

The road systems of Wales and of the north were military and can best be understood from a map. In Wales, roads ran along the south and north coasts to Carmarthen and Carnarvon, while a road (Sarn Helen) along the west coast connected the two, and interior roads — especially one up the Severn from Wroxeter and one down the Usk — connected the forts which guarded the valleys: these roads, however, need further exploration before they can be fully set out. In the north, three main routes are visible. One, starting from the legionary fortress at York, ran north, with various branches, to places on the lower Tyne, Corbridge, Newcastle (Pons Aelius), Shields. Another, diverging at Catterick Bridge from the first, ran over Stainmoor to the Eden valley and the Roman Wall near Carlisle. A third, starting from the legionary fortress at Chester (Deva) passed north to the Lake country and by various ramifications served all that is now Cumberland, Westmorland and west Northumberland. Several of these roads appear, as it were, in duplicate leading from the same general starting-point to the same general destination, and no doubt, if we knew enough, we should find that one of the two routes in question belonged to an older or a later age than the other.

Communications with the Continent seem to have been conducted chiefly between the Kentish ports and those of the opposite Gaulish littoral, and in particular between Rutupiae (Richborough, just north of Sandwich) and Gessoriacum, otherwise called Bononia, now Boulogne. There was also not infrequent intercourse between Colchester and the Rhine estuary, to which we may ascribe various German products found in Roman Colchester, though not elsewhere in Roman Britain. On occasion men also reached or left the island by long sea passages. Troops, it appears, were sometimes shipped direct from Fectio (Vechten, near Utrecht), the port of the Rhine, to the mouth of the Tyne in Northumberland, while traders now and then sailed direct from Gaul to Ireland and to British ports on the Irish Channel. The police of the seas was entrusted to a *classis Britannica*, which intermittent references in our authorities shew to have existed from the middle of the first century (that is from the original conquest or soon after) till at least the end of the third century. Despite its title, the principal station of this fleet was not in Britain but at Boulogne, and its work was the preservation of order on either coast of the Straits of Dover. This fleet appears to have been a police flotilla rather than a naval force, but for once it emerged into the political importance which fleets often assume. About 286 a Menapian (*i.e.* probably, Belgian) by name Carausius became commandant, possibly with extended powers to cope with the increasing piracy; he set himself up as colleague to the two reigning emperors, Maximian and Diocletian, enlarged his fleet, allied himself with the searobbers, and in 289 actually extorted some kind of recognition at Rome. But in 293 he was murdered and his successor Allectus was crushed by the Emperor Constantius Chlorus in 296. Carausius was apparently an

able man. But in his aims he differed little from many other pretenders
to the throne whom the later third century produced : his object was
not an independent Britain but a share in the government of the
Empire. His special significance is that he shewed, for the first time in
history, how a fleet might detach Britain from its geographical connexion
with the north-western Continent. Twelve centuries passed before this
possibility was again realised.

The preceding paragraphs have described the main features of
Roman Britain, civil and military, during the main part of its existence.
In the fourth century, change was plainly imminent. Barbarian sailors,
Saxons and others, began, as we have seen, rather earlier than 300
to issue from the other shores of the German Ocean and to vex the
coasts of Gaul and probably also those of Britain. Carausius in 286
or 287 was sent to repress them. After his and his successor's deaths,
some change, the nature of which is not yet quite clear, was made
in the *classis Britannica*, and we now hear hardly anything more of it.
A system of coast defence was established from the Wash to the Isle
of Wight. It consisted of some nine forts, each planted on a harbour
and garrisoned by a regiment of horse or foot. The "British Fleet,"
so far as Britain was concerned, may have been divided up amongst
these forts or may have been entirely suspended. But it is difficult to
make out (owing to the general obscurity) whether the change was
made in the interests of coast defence or as a preventive against another
Carausius. The new system was known — from the name of the chief
assailant — as the Saxon Shore (*Litus Saxonicum*).

Whatever the step and whatever the motive, Britain appears for
a while to have escaped the Saxon pillages. During the first years of
the fourth century, it enjoyed indeed considerable prosperity. But no
Golden Age lasts long. Before 350, probably in 343, the Emperor
Constans had to cross the Channel and drive out the raiders — not Saxons
only, but Picts from the north and Scots (Irish) from the north-west.
This event opens the first act in the Fall of Roman Britain (343–383).
In 360 further interference was needed and Lupicinus, *magister armorum*,
was sent over from Gaul. Probably he effected little : certainly we read
that in 368 all Britain was in evil plight and Theodosius (father of
Theodosius I), Rome's best general at that time, was despatched with
large forces. He won a complete success. In 368 he cleared the invading
bands out of the south : in 369 he moved north, restoring towns and forts
and *limites*, including presumably Hadrian's Wall. So decisive was his
victory that one district — now unfortunately unidentifiable — which he
rescued from the barbarians, was named Valentia in honour of the then
Emperor of the West, Valentinian I. . For some years after this Britain
disappears from recorded history, and may be thought to have enjoyed
comparative peace.

Such is the account given us by ancient writers of the period *circa*

343–383. It sounds as though things were already "about as bad as they could be." But a similar tale is told of many other provinces, and yet the Empire survived. When Ausonius wrote his *Mosella* in 371, he described the Moselle valley as a rich and fertile and happy countryside. Britain had no Ausonius. But she can adduce archaeological evidence, which is often more valuable than literature. The coins which have been found in Romano-British "villas," ill-recorded as they too often are, give us a clue. They suggest that some country houses and farms were destroyed or abandoned as early as 350 or 360, but that more of them remained occupied till about 385 or even later. It is not surprising to read in Ammianus that about 360 Britain was able to export corn regularly to northern Germany and Gaul. The first act in the Fall of Roman Britain contained trouble and disturbance, no doubt, but few disasters.

The second act (383 to about 410) brought greater evils and of a new kind. In 383 an officer of the British army, by birth a Spaniard, by name Magnus Maximus, proclaimed himself Emperor, crossed with many troops to Gaul and conquered western Europe: in 387 he seized Italy: in 388 he was overthrown by the legitimate Emperors. Later British tradition of the sixth century asserted that his British troops never returned home and that the island was thus left defenceless. We cannot verify this tradition. But we have proof, both that Britain was sore pressed and that the central government tried to help it. Claudian alludes to measures taken by Stilicho, prime minister to the then Emperor Honorius, about 395–8. Archaeological evidence shews that the coast-fort of Pevensey (Anderida) was repaired under Honorius, and that a fort was built high on the summit of Peak, overhanging the Yorkshire coast half-way between Whitby and Scarborough, by an officer of the same period who is known to have been in Britain a little after 400. These efforts were in vain. Troops — not necessarily legionaries though Claudian calls them *legio* — had to be withdrawn for the defence of Italy in 402. Finally, the Great Raid of barbarians who crossed the Rhine on the winter's night which divided 406 from 407 and the subsequent barbarian attack on Rome itself cut Britain off from the Mediterranean. The so-called "departure of the Romans" speedily followed. This departure did not mean any great departure of persons, Roman or other, from the island. It meant that the central government in Italy now ceased to send out the usual governors and other high officials and to organise the supply of troops. No one went: some persons failed to come.

How far the British themselves were responsible for, or even agreeable to, this sundering of an ancient tie is, even after the latest inquiries, not very certain. The old idea that Britons and Romans were still two distinct and hostile racial elements has, of course, been long abandoned by all competent inquirers — for reasons which the preceding pages will have made evident. But we have the names of three usurpers who tried to seize the imperial crown in Britain (406–11), Marcus, Gratian, and Constantine, and it seems that, as Constantine went off to seek a throne on the Continent, the Britons left to themselves set up a local autonomy for self-protection. Unfortunately, our ancient authorities are less clear than could be wished, especially on the chronology of these events. One thing which seems certain is that Britain did not conceive herself as breaking loose from the Empire and that in the years to come the Britons considered themselves "Romans." If we may believe Gildas, they even appealed for help to Aëtius, the Roman minister, in 446.

The attacks of the "Saxons" had begun before 300 and though at first their brunt fell more heavily on the Gaulish than on the British coasts, they were felt seriously in Britain from about 350 onwards. At first, they were the attacks of mere pillagers: later, like the later attacks of the barbarians elsewhere, they became invasions of settlers. When exactly the change took place, is unknown, nor is it clear what incident gave the stimulus. It seems probable, however, that the Britons of the early fourth century, harassed by attacks of all kinds, adopted the common device — even more familiar in that age than in any other — and set a thief to catch a thief. The man who set is named in the legends Vortigern of Kent; the thieves who were set, are called Hengest and Horsa. We need not attach much weight to these names, nor can we hope to fix a precise date. But the incident is sufficiently well attested and sufficiently probable to find acceptance, and it obviously occurred early in the fifth century. It had the natural result. The English, called in to protect, remained to rule: they formed settlements on the east coast and began the English invasion. But they began it under conditions altogether different from those which attended the barbarian conquests on the Continent. The English were more savage and hostile to civilisation than most of the continental invaders; on the other hand, they were far less overwhelmingly numerous. The Romano-British culture was less strong and coherent than the civilisation of Roman Gaul, but the Britons themselves — at least those in the hills — were no less ready to fight than the bravest of the continental provincials. The sequel was naturally different in the two regions.

The course of the invasion is a matter for English historians. But part of it depends on Romano-British archaeology. This seems to contradict violently the chronology which the Anglo-Saxon Chronicle sets out in suspiciously precise detail. We know that Wroxeter was burnt and we have evidence that the burning occurred soon after (if indeed it was not before) A.D. 400. We must treat this evidence cautiously, since not a fiftieth part of the site has yet been explored. But at Silchester, which has been all uncovered, the spade has told us that the town was abandoned (not burnt), and as a limit for the date, we find no coins which need be later than about A.D. 420. The same absence of fifth century coins may be noted on other sites which have been sufficiently explored to yield trustworthy testimony. It would seem as if the invaders, entering Britain on its eastern and least defensible side, were able, like the Romans four centuries earlier, rapidly to sweep over the lowlands, but were not able to maintain their hold. Thus for several generations this region became a debatable land, where neither Romano-British city life could safely endure nor the English take firm hold and settle. In the long confusion, the Romano-British civilisation of the lowlands perished. The towns, burnt or abandoned, lay waste and empty. Even Durovernum (Canterbury), presumably the capital of Vortigern, whom the legend mates with a Saxon wife, ceased to exist, and at the healing springs of Aquae Sulis (Bath) the wild birds built their nests in the marsh which hid the ruins. The country houses and farms perished even more easily: not one is known in which we can trace English inhabitants succeeding to British. The old native tribal areas and the Roman administrative boundaries were alike lost: to-day we have no certain knowledge of any of them. The Roman speech vanished; the Romano-British material civilisation, and the house-plans and house-furniture, hypocausts and mosaics, even the fashions of brooches and pottery, vanished with it. Only the solid *aggeres* of the roads remained still in use, and in these, too, there were gaps and intervals. All else was but the scattered débris of a ruined world.

Meanwhile the Romanised Britons, in losing the lowlands, lost their towns and all the apparatus of town life. They retired into the hills, to Wales and to the north — the later Strathclyde — and there, in a region where Roman civilisation had never established itself in its higher forms, they underwent an intelligible change. The Keltic element, never quite extinct in those hills and reinforced perhaps by immigrations from Ireland, reasserted itself afresh. Gradually, the remnants of Roman civilisation were worn down: the Keltic speech reappeared and, as a sequel, the Late Keltic art was strong enough to pass on an artistic legacy to the Middle Ages.

(B)

TEUTONIC CONQUEST OF BRITAIN

According to Bede, who wrote his Ecclesiastical History about A.D.731, the Teutonic invasions of Britain began during the joint reign of Marcian and Valentinian III, that is, between the years A.D. 450 and 455. Bede states that the invaders came from three powerful nations, the Saxons, Angles, and Jutes. From the Jutes came those who occupied Kent and the Isle of Wight with the adjacent coast of Hampshire, from the Saxons came the people of Essex, Sussex, and Wessex, and from the Angles the East Anglians, Middle Anglians, and Northumbrians. He adds that the Saxons were sprung from the Old Saxons and that the Angles came from a district called Angulus, which lay between the territories of the Jutes and those of the Saxons, and was said to be still unoccupied in his day. The leaders of this invasion, according to Bede, were two brothers named Hengest and Horsa, from the former of whom the Kentish royal family claimed to be descended. They were summoned in the first place by the British king Wyrtgeorn (Vortigern) to defend him against the assaults of his northern foes, and received a reward in territory in return for their assistance, but a quarrel soon broke out on account of the alleged failure of the king to redeem his promises. The Saxon Chronicle amplifies Bede's account by mentioning certain battles, the result of which was to transfer Kent to the possession of the invaders. Of these events, however, a far more detailed account is furnished by the *Historia Brittonum* known by the name of Nennius, which narrates that the British nobles were treacherously massacred by Hengest at a conference, and that the king himself was captured and only released on the cession of certain provinces. After this a heroic resistance was offered to the invaders by the king's son Vortemir.

The Saxon Chronicle is our only authority for two stories dealing with the early history of the kingdoms of Sussex and Wessex. The foundation of the former kingdom is attributed to a certain Aelle, who is said to have landed in 477. This person is mentioned by Bede as the first king who gained a hegemony (*imperium*) over the neighbouring English kings, though he gives no account of his exploits and assigns no date for his reign. The foundation of the kingdom of Wessex is attributed in the Chronicle to a certain Cerdic and his son Cynric, who are said to have arrived about forty years after Hengest and to have eventually established their position after a number of conflicts with the Britons. This story is connected, according to the same authority, with the occupation of the Isle of Wight, which is said to have been given by Cerdic to his nephews Stuf and Wihtgar (530).

It is difficult to determine how much historical fact underlies these stories. Little value can be attached to the dates given in the Saxon Chronicle. It is clear too that we have to deal with an aetiological element, especially in the West Saxon story. Indeed this story is the most suspicious of the three. In making Cynric the son of Cerdic the account is at variance even with the genealogy contained in the Chronicle itself, while it is also very curious that Cerdic, the founder of the kingdom, bears what appears to be a Welsh name.

The only reference to the invasion which can be regarded as in any way contemporary occurs in an anonymous Gaulish Chronicle [1] which comes to an end in the year 452. It is there stated that in 441–2 after many disasters the provinces of Britain were subdued by the Saxons. This date would appear to be irreconcilable with that given by Bede for the arrival of Hengest, and the discrepancy has given rise to a good deal of discussion. Yet another date 428–9 is given by an entry in the *Historia Brittonum*, the source of which cannot be traced.

The difference in all these cases is of comparatively little moment. Some scholars however hold that the invasions began at a much earlier time, during the latter half of the fourth century. The authority of the passage in the *Historia Brittonum* which states that the Saxons came in 375 can hardly be upheld. More importance is perhaps to be attached to the fact that part of the coast of Britain is called *Litus Saxonicum* in the *Notitia Dignitatum*, which was drawn up in the early years of the fifth century; as this may indicate that Saxon settlements had already taken place in this island. Yet if this be so these Saxons must have been subject to the Roman authorities. Whether they had any connexion with Hengest's invasion we have no means of determining.

The first reference to the Saxons occurs in a work dating from the middle of the second century A.D., namely the Geography of Ptolemy (II. 11. §8), in which they are said to occupy the neck of the Cimbric Peninsula (presumably the region which now forms the province of Schleswig), together with three islands off its west coast. The Angles are mentioned half a century earlier by Tacitus in his *Germania* (cap. 40). No precise indication is given of their position, but they are clearly represented as a maritime people and the connexion in which their name

---

[1] This Chronicle is printed by Mommsen in *M. G. H.* Tom. IX. He ascribes its authorship to a monk of the south of France, perhaps of Marseilles, owing to the commendation of Bishop Proculus contained in it. There are other references to Britain in this Chronicle, which are apparently original, including a notice of victories won by Maximus over the Picts and Scots.

occurs would suggest the Baltic coast, though Tacitus appears to have little knowledge of that region.   Such indications as are given are perfectly compatible with the traditions of later times, which place the original home of the Angles on the east coast of Schleswig.   To the Jutes we have no reference earlier than the sixth century.

The Saxons no doubt belonged to the same stock as the Old Saxons of the Continent.   In the fourth century we find this people settled in the district between the lower Elbe and the Zuiderzee.   According to their own traditions they had come thither by sea, and certainly we have no evidence of their presence in that region during the first century, when it was well known to the Romans and frequently traversed by their armies.   Whether the Saxons who invaded Britain came from the peninsula or from the region west of the Elbe cannot be decided with certainty, but since they appear to have been practically indistinguishable from the Angles the former alternative seems more probable.   In any case they were a maritime people and their piratical ravages are frequently mentioned from the close of the third century onwards.

The Angles, on the other hand, are never mentioned by Roman writers from the time of Tacitus until the sixth century, when they were settled in Britain.   In their case however we have certain heroic traditions which appear to have been preserved independently both in England and Denmark.   These traditions centre round an old king named Wermund and his son Offa, of whom the latter is said to have won great glory in a single combat, the scene of which was fixed by Danish tradition at Rendsburg on the Eider.   From him the Mercian royal family traced their descent, while the royal family of Wessex claimed to derive their origin from a certain Wig the son of Freawine, both of whom according to Danish tradition were governors of Schleswig under the kings above mentioned.   The date indicated by the genealogies for the reigns of these kings is the latter half of the fourth century.

It is a much debated question whether the Jutes who settled in Britain came from Jutland.   In the course of the sixth century we hear twice of a people of this name which came into conflict with the Franks, probably in western Germany, but it is by no means impossible that this also was a case of invasion from Jutland.   The same name probably occurs also in connexion with the heroic story of Finn and Hengest, with regard to which our information is unfortunately very defective.

We have no satisfactory evidence of any linguistic differences between the Angles, Saxons, and Jutes.   The divergencies of dialect which appear in our earliest records are at first only slight and such as may very well have grown up after the invasion of Britain.   The language as a whole must be pronounced homogeneous, its nearest affinities being with the Frisian dialects.   Nor with regard to customs or institutions have we any evidence of a distinction between the Angles and Saxons.   On the other hand the Kentish laws exhibit a marked divergence from those of the other kingdoms, in respect of the constitution of society, a diver. gence which can scarcely have come into existence subsequent to the invasion. We have no information with regard to the characteristics of the Hampshire Jutes.

It may be doubted whether all those who took part in the invasion of Britain belonged to the three nationalities which we have been discussing. The attempts made from time to time to trace the presence of settlers belonging to other peoples cannot be pronounced successful, and when Procopius speaks of Frisians inhabiting our island together with Angles and Britons it is possible that he may mean either the Jutes or the Saxons. Yet considering the numbers which must have been required for such an undertaking, it is highly probable that the invading forces were augmented by adventurers from all the regions bordering on the North Sea, perhaps even from districts more remote.

With regard to the state of civilisation attained by the maritime Teutonic peoples at the period when these settlements took place, a good deal of information is afforded by their earliest cemeteries in this country as well as by others on the opposite side of the North Sea. Amongst the latter perhaps the most important is that of Borgstedterfeld near Rendsburg, where the remains found shew much affinity to those discovered in this country. Much is also to be learnt from the great bog-deposits at Thorsbjaerg and Nydam in the east of Schleswig, the latter of which appears to be only slightly earlier than the cemetery of Borgstedterfeld. In a district slightly more remote, at Vi in Fyen, a still larger deposit has been found dating from about the same period. Among the most interesting objects found at Nydam were two clinker-built boats about seventy feet long which are preserved practically complete. A very large number of weapons were also found in this and the other deposits. At Nydam were found 550 spears and 106 swords, a large number of which bear the marks of Roman provincial workshops. At Vi was discovered a complete coat of mail containing twenty thousand rings. Fragments of such articles together with silver and bronze helmets were found at Thorsbjaerg. This deposit also yielded some articles of clothing in a fair state of preservation, among them cloaks, coats, long trousers, and shoes. Taken together the evidence of the various deposits shews conclusively not only that the warriors of the period were armed in a manner not substantially improved upon for many centuries afterwards, but also that certain arts, such as that of weaving, had been carried to a high degree of perfection.

The form of writing employed by the invaders of Britain was the Runic alphabet. The origin of this is uncertain, but it was widely used by the inhabitants of Scandinavian countries from perhaps the fourth century A.D. until late in the Middle Ages. A few early inscriptions have been found in Germany. In England itself we have scarcely any inscriptions dating from the first two centuries after the invasion, but in the seventh century the Mercian kings engraved their coins with it, and about the same time and perhaps down to the end of the eighth century it was used on sepulchral monuments in Northumbria as well as on various small articles found in different parts of the country.

It may be noted that inscriptions in the same alphabet were found in the deposits at Thorsbjaerg and Nydam and also on one of the two magnificent horns found at Gallehus in Jutland, which perhaps represent the highest point reached by the art of the period.

Apart from this archaeological evidence a considerable amount of information may be derived from the remains of ancient heroic poetry. For although these poems, as we have them, date only from the seventh century, there is no reason for supposing that the civilisation which they portray differs substantially from that of a century or two earlier. The weapons and other articles which they describe appear to be identical in type with those found in the deposits already mentioned, while the dead are disposed of by cremation, a practice which apparently went out of use during the sixth century. The poems are essentially court works, and scanty as they unfortunately are, they give us a vivid picture of the court life of the period with which they deal. This period is substantially that of the Conquest of Britain, namely, from the fourth to the sixth century, but it is a remarkable fact that these works never mention Britain itself and very seldom persons of English nationality. The scene of *Beowulf* is laid in Denmark and Sweden and the characters belong to the same regions, while *Waldhere* is concerned with the Burgundians and their neighbours. Many of these characters can be traced in German and Norse literature, and the evidence seems to point to the existence of a widespread court poetry which we may perhaps almost describe as international.

Concerning the religion of the invading peoples little can be stated with certainty. Almost all that we know of Teutonic mythology comes from Icelandic sources, and it is difficult to determine how much of this was peculiar to Iceland and how much was common to Scandinavian countries and to the Teutonic nations in general. The English evidence unfortunately is particularly scanty. However there is little doubt that the chief divinity among the military class was Woden, from whom most of the royal families claimed to be descended. Thunor, presumably the Thunder-God, may be traced in many place-names and Ti (Tiw) is found in glosses as a translation of Mars. All these deities together with Frig have left a record of themselves in the names of the days of the week. The East Saxon royal family claimed descent from a certain Seaxneat who appears to have been a divinity. There is evidence also of belief in elves, valkyries, and other supernatural beings.

On their forms of worship we have scarcely any more information. In Northumbria at any rate there seems to have been a special class of priests who were not allowed to bear arms or to ride except on mares. Sanctuaries are occasionally mentioned, but we do not know whether these were temples or merely sacred groves.   A number of religious festivals are also recorded by Bede, especially during the winter months. It may be remarked in passing that the calendar appears to have been of the "modified lunar" type with an intercalary month added from time to time.   The year is said to have begun — approximately, we must presume — at the winter solstice.   There are some indications however which suggest that at an earlier period it may have begun after the harvest.

There is no doubt that the invading peoples possessed a highly developed system of agriculture long before they landed in this country. Many agricultural implements have been found among the bog-deposits in Schleswig.   Representations of ploughing operations occur in rock-carvings in Bohuslän (Sweden) which date from the Bronze Age, at least a thousand years earlier than the invasion.   All the ordinary cereals were well known and cultivated, though on the other hand the system of cultivation followed in this country was probably a continuation of that which had previously been employed here.   There is no evidence that the heavy plough with eight oxen was used before the invasion by the conquerors.   The water-mill doubtless first became known to them in Britain, and for ages afterwards it failed to oust the quern.   In horticulture the advance made was very great: the names of practically all vegetables and fruits are derived from Latin, and though the knowledge of a few of their names may have filtered through from the Rhine provinces, there can be little doubt that the great bulk were first acquired in this country.

These considerations bring us to the much disputed question as to what became of the native population.   The insignificance of the British element in the English language is scarcely explicable unless the invaders came over in very large numbers.   On the other hand, many scholars have probably gone too far in supposing that the native population was entirely blotted out.   British records say that they were massacred or enslaved.   In later times, *i.e.* in the eleventh century, the number of slaves in England was not great, but it is not safe to infer that such was the case four or five centuries earlier.   Indeed the little evidence that we have on this question suggests that in some districts at least they were a very numerous class.   There can be little doubt at all events that the first invasions were essentially of a miltary character.   Attempts have been made to trace in various quarters settlements of kindreds especially from the occurrence of place-names with the suffixes *-ingas*, *-ingatun*, etc., but the evidence is at best exceedingly ambiguous. Among the Scandinavians who took part in the great invasion of 866 we can trace various grades of officials (*eorlas, holdas*, etc.) between whom the land appears to have been partitioned, and although we have no

CH. XIII.

contemporary evidence of what took place in the Saxon invasion, there is a *prima facie* probability that a similar course was followed. To the present writer it seems incredible that so great an undertaking as the invasion of Britain should have been accomplished without the employment of large and organised forces. The earliest records we possess furnish abundant evidence for the existence of a very numerous military class of different grades, while the provincial government appears to have been vested in the hands of royal officials and not in popular bodies.

From archaeological evidence and from the character of local nomenclature we can to a certain extent determine the area occupied by the invaders at various periods, although very much remains to be done in these fields of investigation. Thus the practice of cremation is found in early cemeteries in the valley of the Trent and in various parts of the Thames valley as far west as Brighthampton in Oxfordshire, but there is scarcely any evidence for its employment further to the west. In local nomenclature again changes may be observed — thus the proportion of place-names ending in the suffix -*ham* to those ending in the suffix -*ton* decreases as we proceed from east to west. So far as the evidence is at present collected it would seem to indicate that the eastern and south-eastern counties, together with the banks of the large rivers for some distance inland, shew an earlier type of Saxon nomenclature than the rest of the country. But it is highly probable that as in the case of the invasion of 866 a much larger area was ravaged by the invaders than was actually settled by them at first.

The account of the invasion given by Gildas, vague as it unfortunately is, points distinctly to the same conclusion. He speaks in the first place of a time when the country was harried far and wide, when the cities were spoiled, and the inhabitants slain or enslaved. Then came a time when the natives under Ambrosius Aurelianus began to offer a more effective resistance, from which time forward war continued with varying success until the siege of Mons Badonicus. From the time of that siege until the date when Gildas wrote, the Britons had had no serious trouble from the invaders, though faction was rife among themselves. Unfortunately he supplies us with no means of dating the course of events with certainty except that apparently the period of comparative peace had lasted forty-four years. The Cambrian Annals date the siege of Mons Badonicus in 518, but they also date in 549 the death of Maelgwn king of Gwynedd who is mentioned by Gildas as alive. The majority of scholars accept the latter of these dates and reject the former, placing the date of the siege towards the end of the fifth century. The evidence of Gildas then on the whole leads us to conclude that the Conquest of Britain may be divided into two distinct periods. The first occupied some fifty years from the beginning of the invasion, while the second can hardly have begun much before the middle of the sixth century.

Among the invaders themselves a number of separate kingdoms

arose. It is commonly held that these kingdoms were the outcome of separate invasions, but no evidence is forthcoming in favour of such a view, and it seems at least as likely that several of them arose out of subsequent divisions, as was the case after the Scandinavian invasion in the ninth century. The kingdoms which we find actually existing in our earliest historical records are ten in number: (1) Kent, (2) Sussex, (3) Essex, (4) Wessex, (5) East Anglia, (6) Mercia, (7) Hwicce, (8) Deira, (9) Bernicia, (10) Isle of Wight. There are traces also of a kingdom in the district between Mercia, Middle Anglia, East Anglia, and Essex —perhaps Northamptonshire and Bedfordshire—while from Lindsey we have what appears to be the genealogy of a royal family. There is no clear evidence that Middlesex and Surrey were separate kingdoms at any time, though (if certain disputed charters are genuine) the latter was under a ruler who styled himself *subregulus* in the latter part of the seventh century. The balance of probability is in favour of the view that both these provinces originally formed part of Essex.

We have already mentioned that little value is to be attached to the dates given for the foundation and early progress of the kingdom of Wessex. They are apparently quite incompatible with the testimony of Gildas. Moreover that part of the story which relates to the Isle of Wight is difficult to reconcile with Bede's account, since it altogether ignores the existence of Jutish settlements in this quarter. According to Bede the Isle of Wight retained a dynasty of its own until the time of Ceadwalla (685–688), by whom it was mercilessly ravaged. The Chronicle states, as we have seen, that the island was given by Cerdic to his nephews Stuf and Wihtgar and barely mentions the devastations of Caedwalla. Further, according to Bede, the greater part of the coast of Hampshire was occupied by Jutes. These likewise are ignored by the Chronicle, which seems to imply that the West Saxon invasion started from this quarter. In view of these difficulties some scholars have been inclined to suspect that the annals dealing with the early part of the West Saxon invasion are entirely of a fictitious character, and that the West Saxon invaders really spread from a different quarter, perhaps the valley of the Thames, and at a later date than that assigned by the Chronicle. It is to be hoped that in the future archaeological research may throw light on this difficult question.

The difficulties presented by Gildas cease when we reach the middle of the sixth century. From this time onwards, although we have no means of checking them, the entries in the Chronicle may be records of real events which took place approximately at the times assigned to them. The first entry of this series is the account of a fight between Cynric and the Britons at Salisbury in 552: the second records a similar conflict in 556 at Beranburg, which has been identified with Barbury Camp near Swindon. In 560 Cynric is said to have been succeeded by Ceawlin, who in 568 had a successful encounter with

CH. XIII.

Aethelberht king of Kent.   In 571 another prince apparently West
Saxon, by name Cuthwulf, fought with the Britons at a place called
Bedcanford, commonly supposed to be Bedford, and gained possession
of Bensington, Aylesbury, Eynsham, and perhaps Lenborough.   If we are
to trust this entry it would seem to mean that Buckinghamshire and
Oxfordshire were conquered by the West Saxons at this time.   In 577
Ceawlin and another West Saxon prince named Cuthwine are said to
have fought against the Britons at Deorham (identified with Dyrham
in Gloucestershire) and gained possession of Bath, Cirencester, and
Gloucester.

Ceawlin is the first West Saxon king mentioned by Bede.   The same
historian states that he was the first English king after Aelle, whose
overlordship (*imperium*) was recognised by the other kings.   We need
not doubt that the records of his victories have some solid foundation.
About a century later we find in the basins of the Severn and Avon, in
Gloucestershire, Worcestershire, and part of Warwickshire, the kingdom
of the Hwicce with a dynasty of its own which lasted down to the time
of Offa.   This kingdom can hardly have come into existence before
Ceawlin's successful westward movements, but we have no information
as to its origin, as to the date when it was separated from Wessex, or
whether its dynasty was a branch of the West Saxon royal family.

In the basin of the Trent both north and south of that river lay the
Mercian kingdom, the name of which seems to imply that it grew out
of frontier settlements.   Its royal family traced its descent from the
ancient kings of Angel, but we do not know whether the kingdom
itself was due to an independent movement, or whether like that of the
Hwicce it was an offshoot from one or more eastern kingdoms.   The
first king of whom we have any definite record is a certain Cearl who
flourished early in the seventh century and married his daughter to the
Northumbrian king Edwin.   Eventually the kingdom of Mercia absorbed
all its immediate neighbours, Lindsey, Middle Anglia, and Hwicce,
together with parts of Essex and Wessex.   In the sixth century however
it was probably of comparatively limited extent.   Chester appears to
have remained in possession of the Britons until about the year 615,
and it is scarcely probable that the western districts of the Wreocensaete
and Magasaete, corresponding to the present counties of Shropshire and
Herefordshire, were occupied until still later.

To the north of the Humber we find the two kingdoms of Deira and
Bernicia.   Concerning the former, which appears to have coincided with
the eastern half of Yorkshire, we have very little information.   The first
king of whom we have record is a certain Aelle who was reigning at the
time when Gregory met with English slave-boys in Rome (585-8).   The
date given for his reign by the Chronicle (560-588) cannot be trusted.
Eventually this kingdom came into the hands of the Bernician king
Aethelfrith, who married Aelle's daughter.   If we are to believe the

account given in the *Historia Brittonum* that Aethelfrith reigned twelve years in Deira, the date of this event would be about 605. The western part of Yorkshire appears to have been known as Elmet and to have remained in British hands until the reign of Edwin.

The northernmost kingdom founded by the invaders in Britain was that of Bernicia. Ida, from whom subsequent kings claimed descent, is said to have begun to reign in 547. After his death, which took place twelve years later, he was followed by several of his sons in swift succession. Of these the most important was Theodric, who according to ancient chronological computation reigned from about 572 to about 579. The *Historia Brittonum* relates that he fought against several British kings, amongst them Urien who appears in ancient Welsh poetry, and Rhydderch Hen, who as we know from Adamnan's Life of St Columba reigned at Dumbarton. On one occasion the Britons are said to have besieged Theodric in Lindisfarne. The chief centre of the Bernician kingdom appears to have been Bamborough, but we have no occasion to suppose that it attained to any great dimensions or significance until the reign of Aethelfrith. He seems to have become king in 592–3, and is said by Bede to have harried the Britons more than any other English prince. The chief exploits for which his name has been handed down are firstly his encounter with the Dalriadic king Aedan who came against him probably in support of the Britons in 603, and secondly the massacre of the Britons at Chester about twelve years later. The former of these events is said to have occurred at a place called Degsastan. If this place is rightly identified with Dawston in Liddesdale, it would seem that the Bernician kingdom had already extended some distance into what is now Scotland; but its northern and western boundaries must be regarded as very uncertain at the time of which we are speaking.

Aethelfrith's successes had the effect of placing the later Northumbrian kings in a position of superiority to their southern rivals. At the close of the sixth century however the chief English ruler was Aethelberht of Kent, whose authority was recognised by all the more southern kings. The precise nature of the *imperium* which he exercised has been much disputed, but we can hardly doubt that it implied some such recognition of personal overlordship as we find in later times, for example, in the relations of the northern princes with Edward the Elder. His power too was sufficient to guarantee a safe conduct to foreign missionaries as far as the western border of Wessex. He married the Christian Berhta (Bertha), daughter of the Frankish prince Chariberht, and shortly before the close of the century was confronted by Augustine who had been sent to Britain by Gregory the Great. This event had far-reaching conse‐quences in the history of the Anglo-Saxon kingdoms, which will be described in a later chapter of this work.

CHAPTER XIV

ITALY AND THE WEST, 410–476

THE process of history in the Western Empire, during the period which lies between the death of Alaric (410) and the fall of Romulus Augustulus (476), is towards the establishment of Teutonic kingdoms, partly displacing and partly embracing the old local administration within their boundaries, but as a rule remaining in some sort of nominal connexion with the imperial system itself. In the course of this process, therefore, the imperial scheme, in which the invading barbarians take a regular place under the name of *foederati*, still survives, along with much of the old provincial machinery, which they find too useful to be disturbed; but while much that is old survives, much is also added which is new. Germanic tribes, with their kings and their dooms, their moots and their fyrds, settle bodily on the soil, as new forces in the domain of politics and economics, of religion and of law. The Latinised provincial pays a new allegiance to the tribal king: the Roman *possessor* has to admit the tribesmen as his "guests" on part of his lands; the Catholic priest is forced to reconcile himself to the Arianism, which these tribes had inherited from the days of Ulfila; and the Roman jurist, if he can still occupy himself by reducing the Codex Theodosianus into a Breviarium Alaricianum, must also admit the entrance of strange Leges Barbarorum into the field of jurisprudence.

This process of history may be said to have entered on its effective stage in the West with Alaric's invasion of Italy. But it had been present, as a potentiality and a menace, for many years before Alaric heard the voice that drew him steadily towards Rome. The frontier war along the *limes* was as old as the second century. The pressure of the population of the German forests upon the Roman world was so ancient and inveterate, and so much of that population had in one way or another entered the Empire for so long a period, that when the barrier finally broke, the flood came as no cataclysm, but as something which was almost in the natural order of things. There may have been movements in Central Asia which explain the final breach of the Roman barriers; but even without invoking the Huns to our aid, we can see that at the beginning of the fifth century the Germans would finally have passed the *limes*, and the Romans at last have failed to stem their advance, owing to the simple operation of causes which had long been at work on either side. Among the Germans population had grown by leaps and bounds, while subsistence had increased in less than an arith_ metical ratio ; and the necessity of finding a *quieta patria*, an unthreatened territory of sufficient size and productivity, with an ancient tradition of more intensive culture than they had themselves attained, had become for them a matter of life and death. Among the Romans population had decayed for century after century, and the land had gone steadily out of cultivation, until nature herself seemed to have created the vacuum into which, in time, she inevitably attracted the Germans. The rush begins with the passage of the Danube by the Goths in 376, and is continued in the passage of the Rhine by the Vandals, Alans, and Sueves in 406. A hundred years after the passage of the Danube the final result of the movement begins to appear in the West. The praefecture of Gaul now sees in each of its three former dioceses Teutonic kingdoms established — Saxons and Jutes in the Britains; Visigoths (under their great king Euric) in the Seven Provinces of Gaul proper; Sueves (along with Visigoths) in the Spains. In the praefecture of Italy two of the three dioceses are under powerful barbarian rulers : Odovacar has just made himself king of Italy, and Gaiseric has long been king of Africa; while the diocese of Illyricum is still in the melting-pot.

, If we regard the movement of events from 410 to 476 internally, and from a Roman point of view, we shall find in the domestic politics of the period much that is the natural correlative of the *Völkerwanderung* without. Already, in the very beginning of this period, and indeed long before, the barbarian has settled in every part of the Empire, and among every class of society. Masses of barbarians have been attached to the soil as cultivators (*inquilini*), to fill the gaps in the population and reclaim the derelict soil : masses, again, have entered the army, until it has become almost predominantly German. Barbarian cultivators and soldiers thus formed the basis of the pyramid; but barbarians might also climb to the apex. Under Theodosius I, who had made it his policy to cultivate the friendship of the barbarians, the Frank Arbogast already appears as *magister militiae*, and attempts, like Ricimer afterwards, to use his office for the purpose of erecting a puppet as emperor. He fell before Theodosius in the battle of the Frigidus (394); but the Vandal Stilicho (to whom he is said to have commended the care of his children and the defence of the Empire) was the heir of his position, and Stilicho had for successor Aëtius — the "last of the Romans," but also the friend of the Huns — as Aëtius was succeeded in turn by Ricimer the Sueve. It is these barbaric or semi-barbaric figures, vested with the office of commander-in-chief of the troops of the West, which form the landmarks in the history of the fifth century; and we should be most true to reality if we distinguished the divisions of this period not by the *regna* of an Honorius or a Valentinian, but by the *magisteria* of Constantius, Aëtius, and Ricimer. These "empire-destroying saviours of the Western Empire" were in reality the prime ministers of their generation, prime ministers resting not on a parliament (though they might, like Stilicho, affect to rely on the Senate), but on their control of a barbarian soldiery. Their power depended, partly on their influence with this wild force, which the Empire at once needed and dreaded, partly on the fact that the nominal representatives of imperial rule were weaklings or boys, whose court was under the influence of women and eunuchs; but the *de facto* position which they held was also sanctioned, since the time of Theodosius, by something of a legal guarantee. Treating the West, after the battle of the Frigidus, as a conquered territory, whose main problem was certain to be that of military defence, Theodosius had left it under the nominal rule of his son, but under the real government of Stilicho; and in his hands he had combined the two commands of infantry and cavalry, which in the East continued to remain distinct. In this position of *magister utriusque militiae* (already anticipated for a time by Arbogast), Stilicho, and his successors who inherited the title, controlled at once the imperial infantry and cavalry, along with the fleets on seas and on rivers: they supervised the barbaric settlements within the Empire; and they nominated the heads of the staffs of subordinate officers. As imperial generalissimo, in an age of military exigencies, the barbarian *magister militiae* was the ultimate sovereign; and the title of *patricius*, sometimes united with the name of *parens*, which in the fifth century came to be applied peculiarly to the "master of the troops," proclaimed his sovereignty to the world.[1]

Dependent upon barbarian troops, and himself often of barbarian origin, the policy of the "master of the troops" towards the barbarians outside the pale, who sought to enter the Empire, was bound to be dubious. Orosius practically accuses Stilicho of complicity with Alaric, and certainly charges him with the invitation of the Vandals, Alans, and Sueves into Gaul in 406: Aëtius was for years the friend of the Huns: Ricimer was apparently not averse to inciting the Visigoths to war against a Roman commander in Gaul. Inevitably, therefore, a Roman party formed itself in opposition to the master of the troops, a party curiously uniting within its ranks the senate, the eunuchs of the court, and some jealous soldier with his followers. The result would be a *coup d'état*, such as those of 408 or 454; but inevitably a new *magister* succeeds to the assassinated Stilicho or Aëtius, and if the struggle still continues to be waged (as for instance between Anthemius and Ricimer), its predestined end — the foundation of a kingdom of Italy by some real

---

[1] Priscus, as Freeman noticed in his article on *Aëtius and Boniface*, speaks of "Aëtius and the emperor of the West" as sending an embassy to the Huns — recognising the *de facto* sovereignty of the *magister militum* (Müller, *Fragm. Hist. Graec.* IV. p. 85).

or virtual generalissimo — draws constantly nearer. In the course of this struggle religious motives apparently intertwine themselves with the underlying motive of racial feeling. Stilicho would seem to have stood for toleration: and a Catholic reaction, headed by the Court, followed upon his fall, and gave to the episcopate an increase of jurisdiction, while it banished all enemies of the faith from the imperial service. Yet Litorius, the lieutenant of Aëtius, put his trust in the responses of seers and the monitions of demons" as late as 439: Ricimer, though no pagan, was an Arian. The extreme orthodoxy of the Court of Ravenna, contrasted with the dubious faith of the soldiery and its leaders, must thus have helped to whet the intensity of party strife.

In the period which we are to consider, it would thus appear that the great feature, from an external point of view, is the occupation of successive portions of the Western Empire by barbaric kings, of whom the greatest is Gaiseric, the hero of the last scene of the Wandering of the Nations, who links by his subtle policy the various enemies of the Empire into one system of attack; while internally the dominant factor is the transmutation of the Diocletian autocracy into a quasi-constitutional monarchy, in which the last members of the Theodosian house sink into *empereurs fainéants*, and the commander-in-chief becomes, as it were, a mayor of the palace. Yet another feature in external policy is the relation of the Western Emperors to those of the East, and other features deserving of notice in internal development are the growth of the Papacy, and the new importance from time to time assumed by the Senate.

Upon the Eastern Empire the West is again and again forced to rely. The Eastern Emperors give the West its rulers — Valentinian III, Anthemius, Nepos; or in any case they give a legitimate title to the rulers whom the West, in one way or another, has found for itself. Not only so, but upon occasion they give to the West the succour, which again and again it is forced to beg in the course of its struggle with the Vandals. Theoretically, as always, the unity of the Empire persists: there is still one Empire, with two joint rulers. But in practice, after 395, there are two separate States with separate policies and separate lines of development; and both Priscus in the East, and Sidonius Apollinaris in the West, acknowledge the fact of the separation.[1] In these separate States there is, indeed, much that is parallel. The East has to face the Huns and the Goths equally with the West; like the West, it has its barbarian *magistri militiae* (with the great difference, however, that there are generally two concurrent *magistri* to weaken each other by their rivalry) and the Eastern Emperor has to deal with Aspar in 471, as Valentinian III had dealt with Aëtius in 454. In both Empires, again, the house of Theodosius became extinct at much

[1] See Priscus, frag. 30 in Müller (*F.H.G.* IV. p. 104); Sidon. Apoll. *Carm.* II. 65.

the same time. But here the parallel ends. In the West the death of Valentinian III was followed by the rule of the emperor-makers (Ricimer, Gundobad, and Orestes), and by a succession of nine emperors in twenty-one years: in the East new and powerful emperors arose, who found the office of "master of the troops" far weaker than in the West, and were able, by the alliance they formed with the Isaurians, to discover in their own realms a substitute and an antidote for barbaric auxiliaries, and thus to prolong the existence of their Empire for a thousand years. Meanwhile ecclesiastical development confirmed the separation and widened the differences between the two Empires. While Eastern theologians pursued their metaphysical inquiries into the unity of the Godhead, a new school of churchmanship, of a legal rather than a metaphysical complexion, arose in the West under the influence of St Augustine; and the growth of the Papacy, especially under the rule of Leo I (440–461), gave to this new school a dogmatic arbiter and an administrative ruler of its own.

The development of the papacy, like the new vigour which the Senate occasionally displays, is largely the result of the decadence of the Western Emperors and of their seclusion in the marshes of Ravenna. The pietism of the Court, under the influence of Placidia, helped to confirm a power, which its withdrawal to Ravenna had already begun to establish; while the victories of Pope Leo over heresies in Italy, his successful interference against Monophysitism in the East, and the prestige of his mission to Attila in 451 and his mediation with Gaiseric in 455, contributed to the increase both of his ecclesiastical power and of his political influence. Meanwhile the bishops, everywhere in the West, tended to become the leading figures in their dioceses. The constitutions of 408 gave them civil jurisdiction in their dioceses and the power of enforcing the laws against heresy. In the chief town of his diocese each bishop gradually came to discharge the duties, even if he did not assume the office, of the *defensor civitatis*; and wherever a barbarian kingdom was established, the bishop was a natural mediator between the conquerors and their subjects.

The new importance assumed by the Senate in the course of the fifth century is evident both at Constantinople and at Rome. During the minority of Theodosius II it is chiefly the Senate of Constantinople which aids the regent Pulcheria and her minister Anthemius, the praetorian praefect, in the conduct of affairs; and though the Roman Senate hardly exerts any continuous influence, again and again in times of crisis it helps to determine the course of events. The autocracy consolidated by Diocletian begins to revert to the original dyarchy of *princeps* and *senatus* which Augustus had founded. In the early years of the fifth century, partly in the later years of Stilicho, who made it his policy to favour the Senate, and partly during the interregnum in the effective exercise of the office of *magister militiae*, which lasted from the fall of

Stilicho till the appearance of Constantius (411), it had shewn considerable activity; but the period of its greatest influence covers the last twenty-five years of the Western Empire. It was with two of the chief senators that Pope Leo went to meet Attila in 451: it was before the Senate that Valentinian defended himself for the assassination of Aëtius in 454. The assassination of Valentinian himself was followed by the accession of Maximus, a member of the great senatorial family of the Anicii; and it has even been suggested that the accession of Maximus perhaps indicates an attempt of the Anicii to establish a new government in the West, independent of Constantinople and resting on the support of the Senate. Maximus fell; but his successor, Avitus, who came to the throne by the support of a Gallo-Roman party, was resisted by the Senate, and fell in his turn. The accession of the next emperor, Majorian, is at any rate in form a triumph for the Senate; in his first constitution Majorian thanks the Senate for letting its choice fall upon him, and promises to govern by its advice. But the reign of Anthemius (467–472) seems tō mark the zenith of senatorial power. It was the appeal of the Senate to Constantinople which led to his accession; during his reign the Senate is powerful enough to try and condemn Arvandus, the praetorian praefect of Gaul, on a charge of treason; and in the civil war which precedes his fall, the Senate takes his side against his adversary Ricimer. Thus, in the paralysis of the imperial authority, the Senate stands side by side, and sometimes face to face, with the military power, as the representative of public authority and civil order. Its effective power is indeed little; the sword is too strong and too keen for that; but at any rate, in the agonies of the Empire, it behaves not unworthily of its secular tradition. And indeed in still other ways one cannot but feel that the end of Rome was not unworthy of herself. Her last work in her age-long task of ruling the peoples was to give into the hands of the Teutonic tribes her structure of law and her system of administration: to the one, as late as 438, the Codex Theodosianus had just been added, while the other was being reformed and purified as late as the days of the last real Emperor of the West, Majorian. So Rome handed on the torch, as it were, newly trimmed; and though we must admit that in fact the imperial government of the fifth century suffered from the impotence of over-centralisation, we must also allow that she was in intention, as Professor Dill has well said, "probably never so anxious to check abuses of administration, or so compassionate for the desolate and the suffering, as in the years when her forces were being paralysed."

The figures in the drama of the last years of the Western Empire, which have perhaps had the greatest appeal for the imagination of the historian, are those of Galla Placidia and of Attila. Both figures have, indeed, a significance, which deserves some little consideration. Ravenna still testifies to-day to the fame of Placidia; and her name suggests the names of many others, her kinswomen and contemporaries, Pulcheria, Eudocia, Eudoxia, and Honoria, whose influence appears, in the pages of the Byzantine historians, to have largely determined the destinies of their age. "It is indeed," writes Gregorovius, "a remarkable historic phenomenon, that in periods of decadence some female figure generally rises into prominence"; and Professor Bury has also remarked that the influence of women was a natural result of the new mode of palatial life — a result which is obviously apparent in the attribution of the title of Augusta to Eudoxia in the East and to Placidia in the West. Yet one cannot but feel that the Byzantine historians have been led by a certain "feminism," if it may be so called, which is characteristic of their historiography, to attribute to women, at any rate as regards the West, an excessive influence on the politics of the period. The fifth century was the age of the erotic novel — of *Daphnis and Chloe*, of *Leucippe and Cleitophon*; and it would almost appear as if Byzantine historians had infused into their history the eroticism of contemporary novels.[1] It is therefore permissible to doubt whether Honoria was really responsible for the attack of Attila upon the West, or Eudoxia for the sack of Rome by Gaiseric: whether Olympiodorus' account of the relations of Honorius and Placidia after the death of Constantius is not a play of fancy, and the story given by Joannes Antiochenus[2] and Procopius of the seduction of the wife of Maximus by Valentinian III, which led Maximus to compass his death, is not equally fanciful.

The figure of Attila owes much of its fascination to the vivid descriptions which Priscus gives of his court and Jordanes of the great battle of the Mauriac plain; and the Nibelungenlied has added the attraction of legend to the appeal of history. Attila has, indeed, his significance in the history of the world. It matters little that he was vanquished in one of the so-called "decisive battles of the world": if he had been the victor on the Mauriac plain, and had lived for twenty years afterwards, instead of two, he would none the less have fallen at last, if only the allies who stood together in that battle had continued their alliance. The real significance of Attila lies in the fact, that the pressure of his Huns forced the Romans and the Teutons to recognise that the common interest of civilisation was at stake, and thus drove them to make the great alliance, on which the future progress of the world depended. The fusion of Romans and Teutons, of which the marriage of Ataulf and Placidia, as it is described in the pages of Olympiodorus, may seem to be a harbinger, is cemented in the bloodshed of the Mauriac plain.

[1] Most striking is the fragment of Malchus (Müller, *F. H. G.* IV. p. 117) describing the armour of Harmatius and Zenonis. It reads like the passage in Dante which tells the story of Paolo and Francesca.

[2] The fragment of Joannes Antiochenus in which this story occurs (Müller, *F. H. G.* IV. p. 614) contradicts another fragment, in which a totally different version is given; and it is rejected as spurious by Bury, *History of the Later Roman Empire*, I. p. 181 n. 4.

Between the death of Alaric and the fall of Romulus Augustulus, the progress of events may be arranged in three definite stages. A period, which is marked by the patriciate of Constantius, begins in 410 and ends with the death of Honorius in 423; during this period there takes place the Visigothic settlement in the South of France. A second period, marked by the patriciate of Aëtius, covers the reign of Valentinian III, and ends in 455: it is the period of the Vandal settlement in Africa, and of Hunnish inroads into Gaul and Italy. A final period, in which the patriciate is held by Ricimer, follows upon the extinction of the Theodosian house in the West: it ends, in the phrase of Count Mar- cellinus, who alone seems to have realised the importance of the event, with the "extinction of the Western Empire of the Roman race," and the settlement of Odovacar in Italy.

At the end of 410 Rufinus, as he wrote the preface to his translation of the homilies of Origen in a Sicilian villa which looked across to Reggio, saw the city in flames, and witnessed the gathering of the ships with which Alaric was preparing to invade Africa. A little later, and he may have seen the ships destroyed by a tempest; a little later still, and he may have heard of Alaric's death and of his burial in the bed of the Busento. The Gothic king was succeeded by his brother-in-law Ataulf; and upon the doings of Ataulf, for the next two years, there rests a cloud of darkness. We know, indeed, that he stayed in Italy till the spring of 412; we learn from the Theodosian Code that he was in Tuscany in 411; and we are told by Jordanes that at this time he was spoiling Italy of public and private wealth alike, and that his Goths stripped Rome once more, like a flock of locusts, while Honorius sat powerless behind the walls of Ravenna — the one rock left to the Emperor in the deluge which at this time covered Italy, Gaul, and Spain. But the story of Jordanes is probably apocryphal. Orosius and Olympiodorus, who are excellent contemporary authorities, both remark on the prosperity of Rome in the years that followed on the sack of 410: "recent as is the sack, we would think, as we look at the multitude of the Roman people, that nothing at all had happened, were it not for some traces of fire." In the face of this evidence, a second plundering of Rome by Ataulf is improbable; and it appears equally improbable, when we consider the character of the new Gothic king and the natural line of his policy. A Narbonese citizen, who had perhaps witnessed the marriage of Ataulf to Galla Placidia in 414 at Narbonne and heard the shouts of acclamation, from Romans and Goths alike, which hailed the marriage festivities, reported to St Jerome at Bethlehem, in the hearing of Orosius, the words which he had often heard fall from the lips of Ataulf. "I have found by experience, that my Goths are too savage to pay any obedience to laws, but I have also found, that without laws a State is never a State; and so I have chosen the glory of seeking

CH. XIV.

to restore and to increase by Gothic strength the name of Rome. Wherefore I avoid war and strive for peace." In 411 Ataulf had indeed already[1] strong motives for seeking peace. He had abandoned the African expedition of Alaric, but he needed the supplies which that expedition had been meant to procure, and which he could now only gain from the Emperor; and he had in his train the captive Placidia, the sister of Honorius, whose hand would carry the succession to her brother's throne. To negotiate with Honorius for supplies and for formal consent to his marriage with Placidia was thus the natural policy of Ataulf; and in such negotiations the year 411 may have passed. But if there were negotiations, there was no treaty.[2] Honorius had been strengthened by the arrival of a Byzantine fleet with an army on board; and he shewed himself obdurate. When Ataulf was driven from Italy into Gaul, apparently by lack of supplies, in the spring of 412, he did not come as the friend and ally of Honorius.

In 412 Gaul was beginning to emerge from a state of whirling chaos. The usurper within, and the barbarian from without, had divided the country since 406. There had been two swarms of invaders, and two different "tyrants." In 406 the Vandals, Alans, and Sueves had poured into Gaul, surged to the feet of the Pyrenees, and falling back for a while had then, with the aid of treachery, poured over the mountains and vanished into Spain, which henceforth became the prey of "four plagues — the sword, and famine, and pestilence, and the noisome beast" (409). In the wake of this tide had followed an influx of Franks, Alemanni, and Burgundians; and in 411 these three peoples were still encamped in Gaul, along the western bank of the Rhine, preparing for a permanent settlement. The usurpation of Constantine in 406 had synchronised with the invasion of Gaul by the Vandals, Alans, and Sueves; and indeed, the invasion was probably the result of the usurpation, for Stilicho would seem to have invited these people into Gaul, in the hope of barring the usurper's way into Italy. In 409 a second tyrant had arisen in Spain: Gerontius, one of Constantine's own officers, had created a rival emperor, called Maximus; and it was this usurpation which had caused the invasion of Spain by the Vandals and their allies, Gerontius having invited them into Spain, as Stilicho had before invited them into Gaul, in order to gain their alliance in his struggle with Constantine. In 411 Gerontius had advanced into Gaul,

---

[1] L. Schmidt (*Geschichte der deutschen Stämme*, p. 225) thinks that Ataulf's policy of peace was only conceived towards 414, under the influence of Placidia. But did not Ataulf think of marrying Placidia, and therefore of "Romanising," from the very first?

[2] F. Martroye (*Genséric*, pp. 92–3) is inclined to believe that there was a treaty: otherwise, he thinks, Ataulf would not have had sufficient supplies to maintain himself in Italy for the year, and Honorius would not have been able to despatch Constantius with an army into Gaul. But the fact remains that Ataulf entered Gaul as a free-lance, and *not* as a man under treaty.

and was besieging Constantine in Arles, while Constantine was hoping
for the arrival of an army of relief from the barbarians on the Rhine.
At this moment Constantius, the new "master of the troops," arrived in
Gaul to defend the cause of the legitimate emperor, Honorius. He
met with instant success. Gerontius was overwhelmed and perished;
Constantine's barbarian reinforcements were attacked and defeated;
Constantine himself was captured, and sent to Italy for execution. By
the end of 411 Gaul was clear of both usurpers; and the Roman general
stood face to face with the Franks, Alemanni, and Burgundians, who had
meanwhile, during the operations round Arles, created a new emperor,
Jovinus, to give a colour of legality to their position in Gaul. Without
attacking Jovinus, however, Constantius seems to have left Gaul at the
end of the year, perhaps because the northward march of Ataulf was
already causing unrest at Ravenna.

When Ataulf's march finally conducted him over Mont Genèvre
into Gaul, somewhere near Valence, in the spring of 412, it seemed
probable that he would throw himself on the side of Jovinus, now
encamped in Auvergne, and acquire from the usurper a settlement in
southern Gaul. It was his natural policy: it was the course which was
advised by the ex-Emperor Attalus, who still followed in the train of
the Goths. But Jovinus and Ataulf failed to agree. Ataulf seems to
have occupied Bordeaux in the course of 412, and Jovinus regarded him
as an intruder, whose presence in Gaul threatened himself and his
barbarian allies; while on his side Ataulf attacked and killed one
of Jovinus' supporters, with whom he had an ancient feud. Dardanus,
the loyal praefect of the Gauls, was able to win Ataulf over to the side
of his master, and some sort of treaty was made (413), by which Ataulf
engaged to send to Honorius the heads of Jovinus and his brother
Sebastian, in return for regular supplies of provisions, and the recognition of his position in Bordeaux and (possibly) the whole of Aquitanica
Secunda.[1] Ataulf fulfilled his promise with regard to Jovinus and
Sebastian; but by the autumn of 413 he had already quarrelled with
Honorius, and the Goths and the Romans were once more at war. Two
causes were responsible for the struggle. In the first place the government of Honorius had failed to provide the Goths with the promised
supplies. The failure is evidently connected with the revolt of Heraclian,
the Count of Africa, in the course of the year 413. Heraclian, influenced
by the example of the many usurpations in Gaul, and finding a basis in

---

[1] The date of the treaty is taken from Olympiodorus (Müller, *F. H. G.* IV.
p. 61). That Ataulf had occupied Bordeaux in 412 is a suggestion of Seeck
(article on Ataulf in Pauly-Wissowa): that the occupation was recognised in the
treaty of 413 is suggested by the entry in *Chronica Gallica* (no. 73), *Aquitania Gothis
tradita* — an entry which is best dated under the year 413. Seeck and Schmidt,
however, both think that the cession of Aquitaine was made by Attalus, when
acting as Emperor at Ataulf's behest, in 414.

the anti-imperial sentiment of the persecuted Donatists of Africa, had prepared for revolt in 412; and in 413 he prohibited the export of corn from his province, the great granary of Rome, and had sailed for Italy with an armada which contained, according to Orosius, the almost incredible number of 3700 ships. He was beaten at Otricoli in Umbria with great slaughter, and flying back to Africa perished at Carthage; but his revolt, however unsuccessful in its issue, exercised during its course a considerable effect on the policy of Honorius. On the one hand, it must have been largely responsible for the treaty with Ataulf in 413: the imperial Government needed Constantius in Italy to meet Heraclian, and, destitute of troops of its own in Gaul, it had to induce the Goths to crush the usurper Jovinus on its behalf. At the same time, however, the revolt had also exercised an opposite effect; it had prevented the imperial Government from furnishing the Goths with supplies, and had made it inevitable that Ataulf should seek by war what he could not get by peace.

There was however a second and perhaps more crucial cause of hostilities between the Goths and the Romans. Placidia still remained with the Goths; and the question of the succession, which her marriage involved, had still to be settled. Again and again, in the course of history, the problem of a dubious succession has been the very hinge of events; and the question of the succession to Honorius, as it had influenced the policy and the fate of Stilicho, still continued to determine the policy of Ataulf and the history of the Western Empire. In this question Constantius, the "master of the troops," was now resolved to interfere. Sprung from Naissus (the modern Nisch), he was a man of pure Roman blood, and stood at the head of the Roman or anti-barbarian party. "In him," says Orosius, "the State felt the utility of having its forces at last commanded by a Roman general, and realised the danger it had before incurred from its barbarian generals." As he rode, bending over his horse's mane, and darting quick looks to right and left, men said of him (Olympiodorus writes) that he was meant for empire; and he had resolved to secure the succession to the throne by the hand of Placidia — the more, perhaps, as such a marriage would mean the victory of his party, and the defeat of the "barbarian" Ataulf.

In the autumn of 413 hostilities began. Ataulf passed from Aquitanica Secunda into Narbonensis: he seized Toulouse, and "at the time of the gathering of the grapes" he occupied Narbonne. Marseilles (which, as a great port, would have been an excellent source of supplies) he failed to take, owing to the stout resistance of Boniface, the future Count of Africa; but at Narbonne, in the beginning of 414, he took the decisive step of wedding Placidia. By a curious irony, the bridegroom offered to the bride, as his wedding gift, part of the treasures which Alaric had taken from Rome; and the ex-Emperor Attalus joined in singing the epithalamia. Yet Romans and Goths rejoiced together; and the marriage, like that of Alexander the Great to Roxana, is the symbol of the fusion of two peoples and two civilisations. "Thus was fulfilled the phrophecy of Daniel," Hydatius writes, "that a daughter of the King of the South should marry the King of the North." Meanwhile in Italy Constantius had been created consul for the year 414, and was using the confiscated goods of the rebel Heraclian to celebrate his entry upon office with the usual public entertainments, in the very month of the marriage festivities at Nar_ bonne. In the spring he advanced into Gaul. Here he found that Ataulf, anxious for some colour of legitimacy, and seeking to maintain some connexion with the "Roman name," had caused Attalus once more to play the part of emperor, excusing thereby his occupation of Narbonensis, as the Franks and their allies had sought to excuse their position on the west of the Rhine by the elevation of Jovinus in 412. An imperial Court arose in Bordeaux in the spring of 414; and Paulinus of Pella was made procurator of the imaginary imperial domain of the actor-emperor Attalus, who once more, in the phrase of Orosius, "played at empire" for the pleasure of the Goths. But on the approach of Constantius, Ataulf set the city on fire, and leaving it smoking behind him, advanced to defend Narbonensis. Constantius, however, used his fleet to prevent the Goths from receiving supplies by sea; and the pressure of famine drove Ataulf from Narbonne. He retreated by way of Bazas, which he failed to take, as the procurator Paulinus induced the Alans to desert from his army; and, having no longer a base in Bordeaux, he was forced to cross the Pyrenees into Spain, where along with the Emperor Attalus, he occupied Barcelona (probably in the winter of 414–415). In devastated Spain famine still dogged the steps of the Goths: the Vandals nicknamed them *Truli*, because they paid a piece of gold for each *trula* of corn they bought. This of itself would naturally drive Ataulf to negotiate with Honorius, but the birth of a son and heir, significantly named Theodosius, made both Ataulf and Placidia tenfold more anxious for peace, and for the recognition of their child's right of succession to the throne of his childless uncle. The Emperor, Attalus, was thrown aside as useless; Ataulf was ready to recognise Honorius, if Honorius would recognise Theodosius. But his hopes shipwrecked on the resistance of Constantius, who had now been rewarded with the title of *patricius* for his success in expelling the Goths from Gaul. Soon afterwards the child Theodosius died, and was buried in a silver coffin with great lamentations at Barcelona. In the same city, in the autumn of 415, Ataulf himself was assassinated in his stables[1] by one of his followers. With him died his dream of "restoring by

---

[1] It may be suggested here that the phrase in Prosper and Hydatius (*inter familiares fabulas jugulatur*, followed by Isidore of Seville) should read *inter familiares stabulis jugulatur*. Olympiodorus speaks of Ataulf as killed while εἰς ἐπιτήρησιν τῶν οἰκείων ἵππων . . . διατρίβων ἐν τῷ ἱππῶνι (Müller, *F. H. G.* IV. p. 63).

Gothic strength the Roman name"; yet with his last breath he commanded his brother to restore Placidia and make peace with Rome.

The Goths, however, were not minded for peace. On the death of Ataulf (after the week's reign of Sigerich, memorable only for the humiliation he inflicted on Placidia, by forcing her to walk twelve miles on foot before his horse), there succeeded a new king, Wallia, "elected by his people," Orosius says, "to make war with Rome, but ordained by God to make peace." Harassed by want of supplies, Wallia resolved to imitate the policy of Alaric, and to strike at Africa, the great granary of the West.[1] The fate of Alaric attended his expedition: his fleet was shattered by a storm during its passage, twelve miles from the Straits of Gibraltar, at the beginning of 416. Wallia now found that it was peace with Rome, which alone would give food to his starving army; and Rome was equally ready for peace, if it only meant the restoration of Placidia. In the course of 416 the treaty was made. The Romans purchased Placidia by 600,000 measures of corn; Wallia became the ally of the Empire, and promised to recover Spain from the Vandals, Alans, and Sueves. In January 417 Constantius was once more created consul: in the same month he became the husband of the unwilling Placidia. She bore him two children, Honoria and Valentinian; and thus the problem of the succession was finally settled by the victory of the Roman Constantius, and the name of Rome was renewed by Roman strength. It was no undeserved triumph which Constantius celebrated in 417. The turmoil which had raged since Alaric's entry into Greece in 396 seemed to have ceased: the loss of the whole of the Gauls, which had seemed inevitable since the usurpation and the barbarian influx of 406, was, at any rate in large measure, averted. Constantius had recovered much of the Seven Provinces: Wallia was recovering Spain.

Constantius too was finally destined to settle the problem of the Goths, and to give them at last the *quieta patria*, in search of which they had wandered for so many years. For a time Wallia fought valiantly in Spain (416–418): he destroyed the Silingian Vandals, and so thoroughly defeated the Alans, that the broken remnants of the tribe merged themselves into the Asdingian Vandals. In the beginning of 416 the Romans had only held the east coast and some of the cities of Spain: by 418 the Asdingian Vandals and the Sueves had been pushed back into the north-west of the peninsula, and Lusitania and Baetica had been recovered. In 419 Wallia had his reward; Constantius summoned the Goths into Gaul, and gave them for a habitation the Second Aquitaine. Along with it went Toulouse,

---

[1] It is possible that Wallia first attempted to move northward again into Gaul. In the *Chronica Gallica* (no. ¦78) there is mention of a movement by the Goths on the death of Ataulf, and of its being repelled by Constantius, who would naturally be encamped in southern Gaul. It is unlikely that Constantius entered Spain, as Seeck thinks.

which became their capital, and other towns in the Narbonese province; and thus the Visigoths acquired a territory of their own, with an Atlantic seaboard, but, as yet, without any outlet to the Mediterranean. We can only conjecture the reasons which dictated this policy. It may be, as Professor Bury suggests, that Honorius did not wish to surrender Spain, because it was the home of the Theodosian house and the seat of the gold mines: it may be that the imperial Government wished to in-vigorate with the leaven of Gothic energy the declining population of south-western Gaul. In any case the policy is of great importance. For the first time the imperial Government had, of its own motion, given a settlement within the Empire to a Teutonic people living under its own king.[1] But the policy becomes doubly important, when it is con-sidered in connexion with the constitution of 418, which gave local government to Gaul, and enacted that representatives of all its towns should meet annually at Arles. Honorius was endeavouring to throw upon Gaul the burden of its own government, and in the new municipal federation which he had thus instituted he sought to find a place for the Goths. On the one hand, the council at Arles would contain representatives from the towns in Gothic territory, and would thus connect the Goths with the Roman name: on the other, the Goths, as *foederati* of the council, defending its territory, and supplying its troops, would give weight to its deliberations. The policy of decentralisation thus enunciated in 418, and the combination of that policy with the settlement of the Visigoths in 419, indicate that the Empire was ceasing to be centralised and Roman, and was becoming instead Teutonic and local.

The years that elapse between the settlement of the Goths and the death of Honorius in 423 are occupied by the affairs of Italy and the court history of Ravenna. In 421 Constantius, who had been virtual ruler of the West since 411, was elevated by Honorius, somewhat reluctantly, to the dignity of Augustus and the position of colleague. Placidia, to whose instance the elevation of her husband was probably due, had her own ambition satisfied by the title of Augusta, and began actively to exercise the influence on events, which she had already exercised more passively during the struggle between Ataulf and Constantius. The elevation of Constantius and of Placidia to the imperial dignity led to friction with the Eastern Empire, which refused to ratify the action of Honorius, and in 421 a war seemed imminent between East and West. But Constantius, whose rough soldier tastes made him chafe at the restrictions of imperial etiquette, fell ill and died

---

[1] It is, however, possible that Ataulf had already, as was suggested above, received the Second Aquitaine in 412. It is also possible that, as von Wietersheim suggests, the imperial Government had recognised the Burgundians in the district round Worms as early as 413 (cf. Prosper Tiro, *s. a.* 413: *Burgundiones partem Galliae . . . optinuerunt*).

CH. XIV.

in the autumn of 421, and with his death the menace of war disappeared.
The influence of Placidia remained unshaken after her husband's death:
the weak Honorius shared his affection between his beloved poultry and
his sister; and scandalmongers even whispered tales about his excessive
affection for Placidia.   But by 422 the affection had yielded to hatred;
and a struggle raged at Ravenna between the party of Honorius, and a
party gathered round Placidia, which found its support in the retinue
of barbarians she had inherited from her marriages with Ataulf and
Constantius.   The struggle would appear to be the old struggle of the
Roman and the barbarian parties; and it is perhaps permissible to conjecture that the question at issue was the succession to the office of *magister
militum*, which Constantius had held.   If this conjecture be admitted,
Castinus may be regarded as the candidate of Honorius, and Boniface as
the candidate of Placidia; and the quarrel of Castinus and Boniface, on
the eve of a projected expedition against the Vandals of Spain, which is
narrated by the annalists, may thus be connected with the struggle between
Honorius and Placidia.   The issue of the struggle was the victory of
Honorius and Castinus (422).   Castinus became the *magister militum* and
took command of the Spanish expedition, in which he allowed himself to
be signally defeated by the Asdingian Vandals, now settled in Baetica:
Boniface fled from the Court to Africa, and established himself, at the head
of a body of *foederati*, as a semi-independent governor of the African diocese, where he had before been serving as the tribune of barbarian *auxilia*.
The flight of Boniface was followed by the banishment of Placidia and
her children to Constantinople (423); but in her exile she was supported
by Boniface, who sent her money from Africa.   This was the position
of affairs when Honorius died (423).   One of the weakest of emperors,
he had had a most troubled reign; yet the last years of his rule had
been marked by peace and success, thanks to the valour and policy of
Constantius, who had defeated the various usurpers and recovered much
of the Transalpine lands.   The one virtue of Honorius was a taste
for government on paper, such as his nephew Theodosius II also
shewed; he issued a number of well-meant *constitutiones*, alleviating
the burden of taxation on Italy after the Gothic ravages, and seeking
to attract new cultivators to waste lands by the offer of advantageous
terms.

The death of Honorius marks the beginning of a new phase in the
history of the Western Empire.   For the next thirty years a new
personality dominates the course of events within the Empire:
Aëtius, ὕστατος Ῥωμαίων fills the scene with his actions; while without
the barbaric background is peopled by the squat figures of the Huns.
Aëtius was a Roman from Silistria, born about the year 390, the son of
a certain Gaudentius, a *magister equitum*, by a rich Italian wife.   In his
youth he had served in the office of the praetorian praefect; and twice

he had been a hostage, once with Alaric and his Goths, and once with
the Huns. During the years in which he lived with the Huns, some
time between 411 and 423, he formed a connexion with them, which
was to exercise a great influence on the whole of his own career and on
the history of the Empire itself. The Huns themselves, until they
were united by Attila under a single government after the year 445,
were a loose federation of Asiatic tribes, living to the north of the
Danube, and serving as a fertile source of recruits for the Roman army.
They had already served Stilicho as mercenaries in his struggle with
Radagaisus, and some time afterwards Honorius had taken 10,000 of them
into his service. After 423 they definitely formed the bulk of the
armies of the Empire, which was now unable to draw so freely on the
German tribes, occupied as these were in winning or maintaining their
own settlements in Gaul, in Spain, and in Africa. Valentinian III may
thus almost be called Emperor "by the grace of the Huns"; and to them
Aëtius owed both his political position and his military success.

On the death of Honorius the natural heir to the vacant throne
was the young Valentinian, the son of Constantius and Placidia. But
Valentinian was only a boy of four, and he was living at Constantinople.
When the news of Honorius' death came to the ears of Theodosius II,
he concealed the intelligence, until he had sent an army into Dalmatia;
and he seems to have contemplated, at any rate for the moment, the
possibility of uniting in his own hands the whole of the Empire. But
meanwhile a step was taken at Ravenna — either in order to anticipate
and prevent such a policy on the part of the Eastern Emperor, or
independently and without any reference to his action — which altered
the whole position of affairs. A party, with which Castinus, the new
magister militum, seems to have been connected, determined to assert
the independence of the West, and elevated John, the chief of the
notaries in the imperial service, to the vacant throne. Aëtius took
office under the usurper as *Cura Palatii* (or Constable), and was sent
to the Huns to recruit an army; while all the available forces were
despatched to Africa to attack Boniface, the foe of Castinus and the
friend of Placidia and Valentinian. Theodosius found himself compelled
to abandon any hopes he may have cherished of annexing the Western
Empire, and to content himself with securing it for the Theodosian
house, while recognising its independence. He accordingly sent
Valentinian to the West in 424, with an army to enforce his claims;
and as John was weakened by the despatch of his forces to Africa, and
Aëtius had not yet appeared with his Huns, the triumph of Valentinian
was easy. His succession was a vindication of the title of the Theodosian
house; and, when we consider the anti-clerical policy pursued by John,
who had attacked the privileges of the clergy, it may also be regarded
as a victory of clericalism, a cause to which the Theodosian house was
always devoted. A closer connexion between East and West may also

be said to be one of the results of the accession of Valentinian, even if it finally prevented the union of the two which had for a moment seemed possible; and the hostile attitude which had characterised the relations of Byzantium and Rome during the reign of Honorius, both in the days of Stilicho and in those of Constantius, now disappears.

Three days after the execution of the defeated usurper, Aëtius appeared in Italy with 60,000 Huns. Too late to save his master, he nevertheless renewed the fight; and he was only induced to desist, and to send his Huns back to the Danube, by the promise of the title of *comes* along with a command in Gaul. Here Theodoric, the king of the Visigoths, had taken advantage of the confusion which had followed on the death of Honorius to deliver an attack upon Arles. Aëtius relieved the town, and eventually made a treaty with Theodoric, by which, in return for the cession of the conquests they had recently made, the Visigoths ceased to stand to the Western Empire in the dependent relation of *foederati*, and became autonomous. Meanwhile in Italy Castinus, who appears to have been the chief supporter of John, had been punished by exile; and a certain Felix had taken his place at the head of affairs, with the titles of *magister militum* and *patricius*. Inheriting the position of Castinus, Felix seems to have inherited, or at any rate to have renewed, his feud with Boniface, the governor of Africa.[1] Possibly Boniface, the old friend and supporter of Placidia, may have hoped for the position of regent which Felix now held, and he may have been discontented with the reward which he actually received after Placidia's victory — the title of *comes* and the confirmation of his position in Africa; possibly the situation in Africa itself may have forced Boniface, as it had before forced Heraclian, into disloyalty to the Empire. Africa was full of Donatists, and the Donatists hated the central government, which, under the influence of clericalism, used all its resources to support the orthodox cause. Religious schism became the mother of a movement of nationalism; in contrast with loyal and imperialist Gaul, Africa, in the early years of the fifth century, was rapidly tending to political independence. At the same time a certain degeneration of character seems to have affected Count Boniface himself. The noble hero celebrated by Olympiodorus, the pious friend and correspondent of St Augustine, who had once had serious thoughts of deserting the world for a monastery, would appear — if it be not a calumny of orthodox Catholics — to have lost all moral fibre after his second marriage to an Arian wife. He shewed himself slack at once in his private life and in his government of Africa; and the result was a summons from Felix, recalling him to Italy, in 427. Boniface shewed himself

[1] The Procopian story, which also appears in Joannes Antiochenus, of the intrigues of Aëtius against Boniface, is here ignored, as mere fable. Felix was in control of affairs, and Aëtius absent in Gaul, at the date at which these intrigues are supposed to have taken place.

contumacious, and a civil war began.   In the course of the war Boniface defeated one army sent against him by Felix; but when a second army came, largely composed of mercenaries hired from the Visigoths, and under the command of a German, Sigisvult, he found himself hard pressed.

At this moment, if we follow the accounts of Procopius and Jordanes, Boniface made his fatal appeal to the Vandals of Spain, and thereby irretrievably ruined his own reputation and his province.   But Procopius and Jordanes belong to the sixth century; and the one contemporary authority who writes of this crisis with any detail —- Prosper Tiro — definitely says that the Vandals were summoned to the rescue by *both contending parties* (*a concertantibus*), and thus implies, what is in itself most probable, that the imperial army under Sigisvult and the rebel force of Boniface both sought external aid.   It may well have been the case that the Vandals were already pressing southward from Spain towards Africa, and that, perhaps impelled by famine, or attracted by the fertility of Africa, the El Dorado of the Western Germans of this century, they were following the line of policy already indicated by Alaric, and unsuccessfully attempted from Spain itself by Wallia. Spain and Northern Africa have again and again in history been drawn together by an inevitable attraction, alike in the days of Hamilcar and Hannibal, in the times of the Caliphate of Cordova, and during the reigns of the Spanish monarchs of the sixteenth century. So the Vandals, who in 419 had moved down from their quarters in the north-west of Spain, and again occupied its southernmost province (Baetica), already appear as early as 425 in Mauretania (probably the western province of Mauretania Tingitana, which lay just across the Straits of Gibraltar and counted, for administrative purposes, as part of Spain).   Their pressure would naturally increase, when the civil war in Africa opened the doors of opportunity; and we may well imagine that the incoming bands, whose numbers and real intentions were imperfectly apprehended in the African diocese, would naturally be invited to their aid by both sides alike.   In any case Gaiseric came with the whole of the Vandal people in the spring of 429, and evacuating Spain he rapidly occupied the provinces of Mauretania.[1]   The Romans at once awoke to their danger: the civil war abruptly ceased; and the home government quickly negotiated first a truce, and then a definite treaty, with the rebel Boniface.   Uniting all the forces he could muster, including the Visigothic mercenaries, Boniface, as the recognised governor of Africa, attacked the Vandals, after a vain attempt to induce them to depart by means of negotiations.   He was defeated; the Vandals advanced from

---

[1] Hydatius, the Spanish chronicler, says never a word of any invitation to Gaiseric.   He chronicles under 425 the attack on Mauretania; and under 429 he enters the invasion of that year, as if it were a natural sequel of the previous attack.

CH. XIV.

Mauretania into Numidia; and he was besieged in Hippo (430). A new army came to his aid from Constantinople, under the command of Aspar; but the combined troops of Aspar and Boniface suffered another defeat (431). After the defeat Aspar returned to Constantinople, and Boniface was summoned to Italy by Placidia; Hippo fell, and Gaiseric pressed onwards from Numidia into Africa Proconsularis.

It was Aëtius who was the cause of the recall of Boniface to Italy in 432; for the summons of Placidia was dictated by the desire to find a counterpoise to the influence which Aëtius had by this time acquired. After his struggle with the Goths, and the treaty which ended the struggle (? 426), Aëtius had still been occupied in Gaul by hostilities with the Franks. While Africa was being lost, Gaul was being recovered; Tours was relieved; the Franks were repelled from Arras, and, in 428, driven back across the Rhine. Aëtius even carried his arms towards the Danube, and won success in a campaign in Rhaetia and Noricum in the year 430, in the course of which he inflicted heavy losses on the Juthungi, a tribe which had crossed the Danube from the north. Like Julius Caesar five centuries before, he now acquired, as the result of his Transalpine campaigns, a commanding position at Rome. In 429 he became *magister equitum per Gallias*, but Felix, with the title of *patricius*, still stood at the head of affairs. In 430, however, Felix was murdered on the steps of one of the churches at Ravenna, in a military tumult which was apparently the work of Aëtius. Felix had been plotting against his dangerous rival, and Aëtius, forewarned of his plots, and forearmed by the support of his own Hunnish followers, saved himself from impending ruin by the ruin of his enemy. He now became *magister utriusque militiae*, at once generalissimo and prime minister of the Empire of the West; and in 432 (after a new campaign in Noricum, and a second defeat of the Franks) he was created consul for the year.

It was at this juncture that Placidia (who, according to one authority, had instigated the plots of Felix in 430) summoned Boniface to the rescue, and sought to recover her independence, by creating him "master of the troops" in Aëtius' place. The dismissed general took to arms; and a great struggle ensued. Once more, as in the days of Caesar and Pompey, two generals fought for control of the Roman Empire; and as the earlier struggle had shewn the utter decay of the Republic, so this later struggle attests, as Mommsen remarks, the complete dissolution of the political and military system of the Empire. The fight was engaged near Rimini; and though one authority [1] speaks of Aëtius as victor, the bulk of evidence and the probabilities of the case both point to the victory of Boniface. Boniface died soon after the

---

[1] Joannes Antiochenus (Müller, *F. H. G.* IV. frag. 201 § 2), followed by Professor Bury (*op. cit.* I. p. 169). But earlier authorities like Prosper Tiro and the *Chron. Gall.* speak of Aëtius as defeated; and his subsequent flight to the Huns surely implies defeat.

victory, but his son-in-law, Sebastian, succeeded to his position; and the defeated Aëtius, after seeking in vain to find security in retirement on his own estates, fled to his old friends the Huns. Here he was received by King Rua, and found welcome support. Returning in 433 with an army of Huns, he was completely victorious. It was in vain that Placidia attempted to get the support of the Visigoths; she had to dismiss and then to banish Sebastian, and to admit Aëtius not only to his old office of master of the troops, but also to the new dignity of *patricius*. Once more, as in 425 and in 430, Aëtius had forced Placidia to use his services; and henceforward till his death in 454 he is the ruler of the West, receiving in royal state the embassies of the provinces, and enjoying the honour, unparalleled hitherto under the Empire for an ordinary citizen, of a triple consulate.

The policy of Aëtius seems steadily directed towards Gaul, and to the retention of a basis for the Empire along the valleys of the Rhine, the Loire, and the Seine. Loyal Gaul seemed to him well worth defence; nationalist Africa he apparently neglected. One of the first acts of the government, after his accession to power, was the conclusion of a treaty with the Vandals and their king, whereby the provinces of Mauretania and much of Numidia were ceded to Gaiseric, in return for an annual tribute and hostages. In this treaty Aëtius imitated the policy of Constantius towards the Visigoths, and gave the Vandals a similar settlement in Africa, as tributary *foederati*. Peace once made in Africa, he turned his attention to Gaul. Here there were several problems to engage his attention. The Burgundians were attacking Belgica Prima, the district round Metz and Trèves; a Jacquerie of revolted peasantry and slaves (the Bagaudae, who steadily waged a social war during the fourth and fifth centuries) was raging everywhere; and, perhaps most dangerous of all, the Visigoths, taking advantage of these opportunities to pursue their policy of extension from Bordeaux towards the Mediterranean, were seeking to capture Narbonne. Aëtius, with the aid of his Hunnish mercenaries, proved equal to the danger. He defeated the Burgundians, who were shortly afterwards almost annihilated by an attack of the Huns (the remnant of the nation gaining a new settlement in Savoy); his lieutenant Litorius raised the siege of Narbonne, and he himself, according to his panegyrist Merobaudes, defeated a Gothic army, during the absence of Theodoric, *ad montem Colubrarium* (436); while the Jacquerie came to an end with the capture of its leader in 437. Encouraged by their successes, the Romans seem to have carried their arms into the territory of the Visigoths, and in 439 Litorius led his Hunnish troops to an attack upon Toulouse itself. Eager to gain success on his own hand, and rashly trusting the advice of his pagan soothsayers, he rushed into battle, and suffered a considerable defeat. Aëtius now consented to peace with the Goths, on the same terms as before in 426; and he sought to ensure the continuance of the

CH. XIV.

peace by planting a body of Alans near Orleans, to guard the valley of the Loire. Then, leaving Gaul at peace — a peace which continued undisturbed till the coming of Attila in 451 — he returned once more to Italy.

During the absence of Aëtius in Gaul, Valentinian III had gone to the East, and married Eudoxia, the daughter of Theodosius II, thus drawing closer that new connexion of East and West, which had begun on the death of Honorius, and had been testified by the despatch of Eastern troops to the aid of the Western Empire against the Vandals in 431. One result of Valentinian's journey to the East was the reception at Rome by the senate in 438 (the reception is described in an excerpt from the acts of the Senate which precedes the Code) of the Codex Theodosianus, a collection of imperial constitutions since the days of Constantine, which had just been compiled in Byzantium at the instance of Theodosius.[1] Another result was the final cession by the Western Empire of part of Dalmatia, one of the provinces of the diocese of Illyricum, the debatable land which Stilicho had so long disputed with the East. The cession was perhaps the price paid by the West in order to gain the aid of the East against the Vandals of Africa, and, more especially, to secure the services of the fleet which was still maintained in Eastern waters. In spite of the treaty of 435, the croachments of the Vandals in Africa had still continued, and they had even begun to make piratical descents on the coasts of the Western Mediterranean. In the first years of his conquest of Africa, Gaiseric must have put himself in possession of a small fleet of swift cruisers (*liburnae*), which was maintained in the diocese of Africa for the defence of its coasts from piracy. To these he would naturally add the numerous transports belonging to the *navicularii*, the corporation charged with the duty of transporting African corn to Rome. In 439 he was able, by the capture of Carthage, to provide himself with the necessary naval base; and henceforth he enjoyed the maritime supremacy of the Western Mediterranean. Like many another sovereign of Algeria since his time, Gaiseric made his capital into a buccaneering stronghold. Even before 435, he had been attacking Sicily and Calabria: in 440 he resumed the attack, and not only ravaged Sicily, but also besieged Panormus, from which, however, he was forced to retire by the approach of a fleet from the East. In the face of this peril Italy, apparently destitute of a fleet, could do no more for itself than repair the walls of its towns, and station troops along

---

[1] Though the reception of the Codex Theodosianus in the West may be taken as a symptom of the connexion of East and West at this date, its issue nevertheless marks an epoch in the history of the separation of the two. After 438 the East and the West legislate independently; the validity of a law made in the East is restricted to the East, unless it has been specifically adopted, after due communication, by the ruler of the West. The independence vindicated for the West in 425 was thus maintained in 438.

the coasts — measures which are enjoyed by the novels of Valentinian III for the years 440 and 441; but Theodosius II determined to use the Eastern fleet to attack Gaiseric in his own quarters. The expedition of 441 proved, however, an utter failure, as indeed all expeditions against the Vandals were destined to prove themselves till the days of Belisarius. Gaiseric, a master of diplomacy, was able to use his wealth to induce both the Huns of the Danube and the enemies of the Eastern Empire along the Euphrates to bestir themselves; and Theodosius, finding himself hard pressed at home, was forced to withdraw his fleet, which Gaiseric had managed to keep idle in Sicily by pretence of negotiation. The one result of the expedition was a new treaty, made by Theodosius and confirmed by Valentinian in 442, by which Gaiseric gained the two rich provinces of Africa Proconsularis and Byzacena, and retained possession of part of Numidia (possibly as full sovereign and no longer as *foederatus*), while he abandoned to the Empire the less productive provinces of Mauretania on the west. But the treaty could not be permanent; and the two dangers which had shewn themselves between 439 and 442 were fated to recur. On the one hand the piratical inroads of Gaiseric were destined to sap the resources and hasten the fall of the Western Empire; on the other, Gaiseric was to continue with fatal results the policy, which he had first attempted in 441, of uniting the enemies of the Roman name by his intrigues and his bribes in a great league against the Empire. It is of these two themes that the history of the Western Empire is chiefly composed in the few remaining years of its life.

The loss of Africa thus counterbalanced, and indeed far more than counterbalanced, Aëtius' arduous recovery of Gaul. Elsewhere than in Gaul and Italy, the Western Empire only maintained a precarious hold on Spain. Britain was finally lost: a Gaulish chronicler notes under the years 441–442 that "the Britains, hitherto suffering from various disasters and vicissitudes, succumb to the sway of the Saxons." The diocese of Illyricum was partly ceded to the Eastern Empire, partly occupied by the Huns. Gaul itself was thickly sown with barbarian settlements: there were Franks in the north, and Goths in the south-west; there were Burgundians in Savoy, Alemanni on the upper Rhine, and Alans at Valence and Orleans; while the Bretons were beginning to occupy the north-west. In Spain the disappearance of the Vandals in 429 left the Sueves as the only barbarian settlers; and they had for a time remained entrenched in the north-west of the peninsula, leaving the rest to the Roman provincials. But the accession of Rechiar in 438 marked the beginning of a new and aggressive policy. In 439 he entered Merida, on the southern boundary of Lusitania; in 441 he occupied Seville, and conquered the provinces of Baetica and Carthagena. The Roman commanders, who in Spain, as in Gaul, had to face a Jacquerie of revolted peasants as well as the barbarian enemy,

CH. XIV.

were impotent to stay his progress; by his death in 448 he had
occupied the greater part of Spain, and the Romans were confined to
its north-east corner.

Such was the state of the Western Empire, when the threatening
cloud of Huns on the horizon began to grow thicker and darker, until in
451 it finally burst. Till 440 the Huns, settled along the Danube, had
not molested the Empire, but had, on the contrary, served steadily as
mercenaries in the army of the West; and it had been by their aid that
Aëtius had been able to pursue his policy of the reconquest of Gaul. But
after 440 a change begins to take place. The subtle Gaiseric, anxious
to divert attention from his own position in the south, begins to induce
the Huns to attack the Empire on the north; while at the same time a
movement of consolidation takes place among the various tribes, which
turns them into a unitary State under a single ambitious ruler. After
the death of King Rua, to whom Aëtius had fled for refuge in 433, two
brothers, Attila and Bleda, had reigned as joint sovereigns of the Huns;
but in 444 Attila killed his brother, and rapidly erecting a military
monarchy began to dream of a universal empire, which should stretch
from the Euphrates to the Atlantic. It was against the Eastern Empire
that the Huns, like the Goths before them, first turned their arms.
Impelled by Gaiseric, they ravaged Illyria and Thrace to the very gates
of Constantinople, in the years 441 and 442; and the "Anatolian
Peace" of 443 had only stayed their ravages at the price of an annual
Hungeld of over 2000 pounds of gold. But it was an uneasy peace
which the Eastern Empire had thus purchased; and in 447 Attila swept
down into its territories as far as Thermopylae, plundering 70 cities on
his way. After this great raid embassies passed and repassed between
the Court of Attila and Byzantium, among others the famous embassy
(448) of which the historian Priscus was a member, and whose fortunes
in the land of the Huns are narrated so vividly in his pages. Still the
Hungeld continued to be paid, and still Theodosius seemed the mere
vassal of Attila; but on the death of Theodosius in 450 his successor
Marcian, who was made of sterner stuff, stoutly refused the tribute. At
this crisis, when the wrath of Attila seemed destined to wreak itself in
the final destruction of the Eastern Empire, the Huns suddenly poured
westward into Gaul, and vanished for ever from the pages of Byzantine
history.

It has already been seen that under the influence of Aëtius the
relations of the Western Empire to the Huns had been steadily amicable,
and indeed that Hunnish mercenaries had been the stay and support not
only of the private ambitions of the *patricius* but also of his public
policy. The new policy of hostility to the Empire, on which Attila had
embarked in 441, seems for the next ten years to have affected the East
alone. During these ten years, the history of the Western Empire is
curiously obscure: we hear nothing of Aëtius, save that he was consul for

the third time in 446, and we know little, if anything, of the relations of Valentinian III to the Huns. We may guess that tribute was paid to the Huns by the West as well as by the East; we hear of the son of Aëtius as a hostage at the Court of Attila. We know that, during the campaign of 441–442, the church plate of Sirmium escaped the clutches of Attila, and was deposited at Rome, apparently with a government official; and we know that in 448 Priscus met in Hungary envoys of the Western Empire, who had come to attempt to parry Attila's demand for this plate. To this motive, which it must be confessed appears but slight, romance has added another, in order to explain the diversion of Attila's attention to the West in 451.

In 434 the princess Honoria, the sister of Valentinian III, had been seduced by one of her chamberlains, and banished to Constantinople, where she was condemned to share in the semi-monastic life of the ladies of the palace. Years afterwards, embittered by a life of compulsory asceticism, and snatching at any hope of release, she is said (but our information only comes from Byzantine historians, whose tendency to a "feminine" interpretation of history has already been noticed) to have appealed to Attila, and to have sent him a ring. Attila accepted the appeal and the ring; and claiming Honoria as his betrothed wife, he demanded from her brother the half of the Western Empire as her dowry. The story may be banished, at any rate in part, as an instance of the erotic romanticism which occasionally appears in the Byzantine historiography of this century. We may dismiss the episode of the ring and the whole story of Honoria's appeal, though we are bound to believe (on the testimony of Priscus himself, confirmed by a Gaulish chronicler) that when Attila was already determined on war with the West, he demanded the hand of Honoria and a large dowry, and made the refusal of his demands into a *casus belli*. But there are other causes which will serve to explain why Attila would in any case have attacked the West in 451. The Balkan lands had been wasted by the raids of the previous ten years; and Gaul and Italy offered a more fertile field, to which events conspired to draw Attila's attention about 450. A doctor in Gaul, who had been one of the secret leaders of the Bagaudae, had fled to his Court in 448, and brought word of the discontent among the lower classes which was rife in his native country. At the same time a civil war was raging among the Franks; two brothers were contending for the throne, and while one of the two appealed to Aëtius, the other invoked the aid of Attila. Finally, Gaiseric was instigating the Huns to an expedition against the Visigoths, whose hostility he had had good reason to fear, ever since he had caused his son Huneric to repudiate his wife, the daughter of Theodoric I, and send her back mutilated to her father, some years before (445). The reason here given for hostility between the Vandals and the Visigoths, which only comes from Jordanes, is perhaps dubious;

the fact of such hostility, resting as it does on the authority of Priscus, must be accepted.[1]

When the Huns poured into Gaul in 451, the position of the Western Empire seemed desperate. It was perhaps a little thing that a terrible famine (*obscenissima fames*) had devastated Italy in 450. Far more serious was the absence of any army with which Aëtius might confront the enemy. For the last twenty-five years he had relied on Hunnish mercenaries to fight his battles; and now, when he had to fight the Huns themselves, he was practically powerless. Everything depended on the line which the Visigoths would take. If they would combine with Rome in the face of a common danger, Rome was saved: if they stood aloof, and waited until they were themselves attacked, Rome could only fall. Attila was cunning enough to attempt to sow dissension between the Visigoths and the Romans, writing to assure either, that the other alone was the object of his attack; but his actions were more eloquent than his words. After crossing the Rhine, somewhere to the north of Mainz, he sacked the Gallo-Roman city of Metz. The Romans now awoke to the crisis: Aëtius hastened to Gaul, and collected on the spot a motley army of mercenaries and *foederati*. Meanwhile, as the Romans looked anxiously to the Visigoths, Attila moved on Orleans, in the hope of acquiring possession of the city from the Alans who were settled there, and so gaining a base of operations against the Goths. The move shewed Theodoric I his danger; he rapidly joined his forces with those of Aëtius, who now at last could draw breath; and the two together hastened to the defence of Orleans. Finding Orleans too strongly guarded, Attila checked his advance, and retired eastwards; the allies followed, and near Troyes, on the Mauriac plain,[2] was engaged *bellum atrox multiplex immane pertinax*. The great battle was drawn; but its ultimate result was the retreat of the Huns, after they had stood their ground in their camp for several days. We are assured by more than one of our authorities, that the camp might have been stormed, and the Huns annihilated, but for the astute policy of Aëtius. Perhaps he desired to keep his hands free to renew once more his old connexion with the Huns; perhaps he feared the predominance of the Visigoths, which would have followed on the annihilation of the Huns. At any rate he is said to have induced the new Gothic king Thorismud — Theodoric I had been killed in the battle — to with-

---

[1] Resting on the authority of Priscus, I have refused to follow Martroye (*Genséric*, pp. 142–3) in rejecting the whole story of Honoria, or Schmidt (*Geschichte der deutschen Stämme*, p. 244) in refusing to believe in the hostility between Vandals and Visigoths.

[2] The battle is often called the battle of Châlons. Contemporaries speak of it as engaged *in campis Catalaunicis*, but this means in the plains of Châlons (Champagne), not at Châlons itself. The battle was actually fought at a point on the road between Sens and Troyes, a few miles in front of Troyes.

draw at once to his territories, by representing forcibly to him the need of securing his succession against possible rivals at home. A bridge was thus built for Attila's retreat; and Aëtius was able to secure for himself the booty, which the retreating Huns were forced to relinquish in the course of their long march.

The significance of the repulse of Attila from Gaul by the joint forces of the Romans and the Goths has already been discussed at the beginning of this chapter. The repulse was no decisive crisis in the history of the world: the Empire of Attila was of too ephemeral a nature to be crucially dangerous; and his attack on the West was like the passing of a transitory meteor, which affected its destinies far less than the steady and deliberate menace of the policy of Gaiseric. But the meteor was not yet exhausted; and Italy had to feel in 452, what Gaul had experienced in 451. Attila now marched from Pannonia over the Julian Alps: Aquileia fell, and the whole of the province of Venetia was ravaged.[1] Passing from Venetia into Liguria, the Huns sacked Milan and Pavia; and the way seemed clear across the Apennines to Rome itself. Aëtius, with no troops at his command, was powerless; a contemporary writer, Prosper Tiro, failing to understand that the successes of the previous years had only been won by the aid of Goths, blames the Roman general "for making no provision according to the manner of his deeds in the previous year; failing even to bar the Alpine passes, and planning to desert Italy together with the Emperor." In truth the position was desperate; and it remains one of the problems of history why 'the Huns refrained from attacking Rome, and retired instead to the Danube. Tradition has ascribed the merit of diverting Attila from Rome to Pope Leo I; the *Liber Pontificalis* tells how Leo "for the sake of the Roman name undertook an embassy, and went his way to the king of the Huns, and delivered Italy from the peril of the enemy." It is indeed true that the Emperor, now resident in Rome, joined with the senate in sending to Attila an embassy of three persons, one of whom was Pope Leo, and that soon after the coming of this embassy Attila gave the signal for retreat. It may be that the embassy promised Attila a tribute, and even the hand of Honoria with a dowry; and it may be that Attila was induced to listen to these promises, by the unfavourable position in which he began to find himself placed. His army was pressing for return, eager perhaps to secure the spoils it had already won, and alleging the fate of Alaric as a warning against laying hands on Rome. His troops, after all their ravages, were suffering from famine, and an Italian summer was infecting them with fever; while the Eastern Emperor, who had been occupied by the Council of Chalcedon and the problem of Eutychianism in the year 451,

---

[1] It was at this date, and as a result of this march of Attila, that, according to tradition, fugitives from Padua fled to Rialto and Malamocco, and founded a set⁻tlement which afterwards grew into the city of Venice.

was now despatching troops to the aid of Aëtius. Swayed, perhaps, by these considerations, Attila listened to the offers of the embassy, and re- turned home; and there he died, in the year after his Italian campaign.

The death of Attila was followed, in the next year, by the assassina- tion of Aëtius (454); and the assassination of Aëtius was followed, a year afterwards, by the assassination of his master, Valentinian III. The death of Attila, and the subsequent collapse of the Hunnish Empire, which had rested entirely on his personality, deprived Aëtius of any prospect of support from the Huns, if his position were once again challenged. Nor was there, after the end of the war with Attila, any pressing danger which made the services of the great soldier indispensable. He had never enjoyed the confidence of the Theodosian house: he had simply forced himself on Placidia and her son Valentinian, both in 425 and in 433. Placidia, a woman of ambitious temper, must have chafed under his domination; and she must equally, as a zealous Catholic and the friend of the Roman party in the Empire, have resented the supremacy of a man who rested on barbarian support and condoned, if he did not share, the paganism of supporters like Litorius and Marcellinus. She had died in 450; but the eunuch Heraclius had succeeded to her policy and influence, and in conjunction with the senator Maximus he instigated his master to the ruin of Aëtius. The ambition of Aëtius made Valentinian the more ready to consent to his ruin. No son had been born to Valentinian from his marriage with Eudoxia; and Aëtius apparently aspired to secure the succession for his own family, by gain- ing the hand of one of the two imperial princesses for his son Gaudentius. One of the few things, however, which stirred the pusillanimity of the Theodosian house to action was a dynastic question; and as Theodosius II had been ready to go to war rather than admit the elevation of Constantius to the dignity of Augustus in 419, so Valentinian III nerved himself to assassinate Aëtius with his own hand, rather than permit the marriage of one of his daughters to the son of a subject. At the end of September 454, as the minister and his master sat together over the accounts of the Empire, Valentinian suddenly sprang up from the table, and after hot words drew his sword on Aëtius. Heraclius hurried to his aid, and the two together cut him down. Thus he fell, *atque cum ipso Hesperium cecidit regnum.* Of his character and real magnitude we know little. Gregory of Tours preserves a colourless eulogy from the pages of a contemporary prose-writer; and the panegyrics of Merobaudes are equally colourless. That he was the one prop and stay of the Western Empire during his life is the unanimous verdict of his contemporaries; but whether or no he was really great as a general or a statesman we cannot tell. He was beaten by Boniface; and it was not he, but the Goths and their king, who really triumphed on the Mauriac plain; yet he recovered Gaul in a series of campaigns, and he kept the Visigoths in check. As a statesman he may be blamed for neglect of

Africa, and a too ready acquiescence in its occupation by Gaiseric; yet it may be doubted whether the Roman hold on the allegiance of Africa was not too weak to be maintained, and in any case he kept Italy comparatively free from the ravages of the Vandals so long as he lived. If he was less Roman than his predecessor Constantius, he was far more Roman than his successor Ricimer; and if he had occasionally used the arms of the Huns for his own ends, he had also used them to maintain the Empire. One merit he had which must count for much — the merit of recognising and encouraging men of ability. Majorian and Marcellinus, two of the finest figures in the history of the falling Empire, were men of his training.

A wit at Court, when asked by Valentinian III what he thought of the death of Aëtius, replied — "Sir, you have used your left hand to cut off your right." In truth, Valentinian signed his own death warrant, when he joined in the murder of his minister. He had hastened, immediately after the murder, to send explanations to the barbarian *foederati*, with whom Aëtius had been allied; but vengeance was to come upon him within his own Court. Maximus, the senator who had joined with Heraclius in compassing the ruin of Aëtius, had hoped to succeed to the position and office of his victim. Disappointed in his hopes, he resolved to procure the assassination of Valentinian, and to seize for himself the vacant throne.[1] Two of Aëtius' followers, whose names, Optila and Thraustila, suggest a Hunnish origin, were induced to revenge their master; and in March 455 Valentinian was assassinated on the Campus Martii, in the sight of his army, while he stood watching the games. Heraclius fell with him; but not a hand was raised to punish the assassins. With Valentinian III the Theodosian house was extinguished in the West, as it had already come to an end in the East on the death of Theodosius II in 450. Though he had ruled for thirty years, Valentinian had influenced the destinies of his Empire even less than his uncle Honorius. Procopius, if his evidence is worth consideration, tells us that Valentinian had received an effeminate education from his mother Placidia, and that, when he became a man, he consorted with quacks and astrologers, and practised immorality. He only once flashed into action, when, piqued by the presumption of Aëtius in aspiring to connect himself with the imperial family, he struck him down. He thought he had slain his master; he found that he had slain his protector; and he fell a helpless victim to the first conspiracy which was hatched against his throne.

The twenty-one years which precede the utter extinction of the Roman Empire in the West are distinguished in several respects from the preceding thirty years in which Aëtius had ruled and Valentinian III

---

[1] I have dismissed, as a Byzantine invention based on the erotic motive, the story that Valentinian was murdered in revenge for his seduction of the wife of Maximus.

had reigned. The "master of the troops" is still the virtual ruler of the Empire; and after a short interval Ricimer proves himself the destined successor of Aëtius. But the new master of the troops, in the absence of any legitimate representative of the Theodosian house, shews his power more openly: he becomes a king-maker instead of a prime minister, and ushers on and off the stage a rapid succession of puppet emperors. And while Aëtius had rested on the support of the Huns, Ricimer uses instead the support of new German tribes. The death of Attila in 453 had been followed by a great struggle between the Huns and the various Germanic tribes whom they had subdued — the Ostrogoths and the Gepidae, the Rugii, the Heruli, and the Sciri. At the battle of Nedâo the Huns had been vanquished, and the German tribes had settled down in the Danubian provinces either as independent powers, or as *foederati* of the Western Empire. It was from these tribes, and particularly from the Rugii, Heruli, and Sciri that the army of the Western Empire was drawn for the last twenty years of its existence. The Rugii were settled to the north of the Danube, in what is now Lower Austria: they appear in the history of the time now as sending troops to Italy (for instance in 458), and now as vexing with their inroads the parts of Noricum which lay immediately south of the river. The Life of St Severinus, one of the most trustworthy and valuable authorities which we possess, describes their depredations, and the activity of the Saint in protecting the harassed provincials. The Sciri had settled after 453 in the north-west corner of modern Hungary; but shattered in a struggle with the Ostrogoths in 469, they had either merged themselves with the Heruli, or passed into Italy to serve under the Roman standards. The Heruli had also settled in Hungary, close to the Sciri: they were a numerous people, and they supplied the bulk of the German mercenaries who served in the legions. Herulian troops were the leaders in the revolt of 476, which overthrew the last emperor; and Odovacar is styled *rex Herulorum*. It was the steady influx of these tribes which led to their demand for a regular settlement in Italy in 476; and when that settlement took place, it involved the disappearance of the Empire from Italy, and the erection in its place of a barbarian kingdom, similar to the kingdoms established by the Vandals and Visigoths, except that it was a kingdom resting not on one people, but on a number of different if cognate tribes.

Apart from these new factors, the play of forces remains in many ways much the same. The Gallo-Romans still form the loyalist core of the Empire; but the advance of the Visigoths threatens, and finally breaks, their connexion with Rome. There is still an intermittent connexion with the East; and the policy of Gaiseric still contributes to determine the course of events. It was Gaiseric who, after the catastrophe of 455, first struck at the derelict Empire. The assassination of Valentinian had been followed by the accession of Maximus. The head of the great family of the Anicii, Maximus was the leader of the senatorial and Roman party; and his accession would seem to indicate an attempt by that party to institute a new government, independent at once of the *magister militiae* at home and of the Eastern Emperor at Constantinople. But it was an age of force; and in such an age such a government had no root. Gaiseric saw his opportunity, and with no Aëtius to check his progress, he launched his fleet at Rome. Byzantine tradition ascribes the attack once more to the influence of a woman; Eudoxia, the wife of the murdered Valentinian, whom Maximus had married to support his title, is said to have invited Gaiseric to Rome, as Honoria is said to have invited Attila, in order to gain her revenge. In reality Gaiseric simply came because the riches of Rome were to be had for the coming. As his ships put into the Tiber, the defenceless Maximus fled from the city, and was killed by the mob in his flight, after a brief reign of 70 days. The Vandals entered Rome unopposed, in the month of June. Once more, as in the days of Attila, the Church shewed itself the only power which, in the absence of an army, could protect the falling Empire, and at the instance of Pope Leo Gaiseric confined himself to a peaceful sack of the city. For a fortnight the Vandals plundered at their leisure, *secura et libera scrutatione*: they stripped the roof of the Temple of Jupiter of its gilded bronze, and laid their hands on the sacred vessels of the Temple, which Titus had brought to Rome nearly four hundred years before. Then they sailed for Africa with their spoils, and with valuable hostages, destined for the future to be pawns in the policy of Gaiseric — Gaudentius the son of Aëtius, and Eudoxia the widow of Valentinian, with her two daughters, Eudoxia and Placidia.

The next Emperor, Avitus, came from Gaul. Here Thorismud, the new king of the Visigoths, who had succeeded to his crown on the Mauriac plain, had been killed by his brothers in 453, for pursuing a policy "contrary to Roman peace." Theodoric II, his successor, owing his succession to a Roman party, was naturally friendly to Rome. He had learned Latin from Avitus, a Gallo-Roman noble, and he shewed his Latin sympathies by renewing the old *foedus* of the Visigoths with Rome, and by sending an army to Spain to repress the Bagaudae in the interest and under the authority of the Empire. Avitus, who had been despatched to Gaul during the brief reign of Maximus as master of the troops of the diocese, came to Toulouse in the course of his mission, during the summer of 455; and here, on the death of Maximus, he was induced to assume the imperial title. The new Emperor represented an alliance of the Gallo-Roman nobility with the Visigothic kingdom; and the fruits of his accession rapidly appeared, when Theodoric, in the course of 456, acting under an imperial commission, invaded and conquered the Suevic kingdom in Spain, which had shewn itself of late inimical to the Empire, and had taken advantage of the troubles of 455 to pursue a policy of expansion into the Roman territory in the north-east of the peninsula.

CH. XIV.

But Avitus, strong as was his position in Gaul and Spain, failed to conciliate the support of Rome. He was indeed recognised by the Senate, when first he came to Rome, at the end of 455; and he was adopted by the Eastern Emperor, Marcian, as his colleague in the government of the Empire. But difficulties soon arose. One of his first acts had been the despatch of an embassy to Gaiseric, who seems to have annexed the province of Tripolitana and reoccupied the Mauretanias during the course of 455. Avitus demanded the observance of the treaty of 435, and sent into Sicily an army under Ricimer the Sueve to support his demand, Gaiseric at once replied by launching his fleet against Italy; but Ricimer, in 456, was able to win a considerable victory over the Vandal fleet near Corsica. The victory might seem to consolidate the position of Avitus; but Ricimer determined to use his newly won influence against his master, and he found a body of discontent in Rome to support his plans. Avitus had come to Rome with a body of Gothic troops; but famine had compelled him to dismiss his allies, and in order to provide them with pay before they departed he had been forced to strip the bronze from the roofs of public buildings. In this way he succeeded at once in finally alienating the Romans, who had always disliked an emperor imposed upon them by Gaul, and in leaving himself defenceless; and when Ricimer revolted, and the Senate, in conjunction with Ricimer, passed upon him the sentence of deposition, he was forced to fly to Gaul. Returning with an insufficient army, in the autumn of 456, he was defeated by Ricimer near Piacenza; and his short reign was ended by his compulsory consecration to the office of bishop, and shortly afterwards by his death. It is curious to notice that the two things which seemed most in his favour had proved his undoing. The Gothic invasion of Spain, successful as it was, had left him without the aid of the Gothic king at the critical moment; while Ricimer's victory over the Vandals had only impelled the victor to attempt the destruction of his master.

Ricimer, now virtual ruler of the West, was a man of pure German blood — the son of a Suevic noble by a Visigothic mother, the sister of Wallia. *Magister militum*, he is the successor of Stilicho and Aëtius; but unlike his predecessors, he has nothing Roman in his composition and little that is Roman in his policy. Stilicho and Aëtius had wished to be first in the State, but they had also wished to serve the Theodosian house; Ricimer was a jealous barbarian, erecting puppet after puppet, but unable to tolerate even the rule of his puppets. His power rested nakedly on the sword and the barbarian mercenaries of his race; and one only wonders why he tolerated the survival of an emperor in Italy throughout his life, and did not anticipate Odovacar in making a kingdom of his own instead. It may be that his early training among the Visigoths, and his subsequent service under Aëtius, had given him the Roman tincture which Odovacar lacked; in any case his policy towards the Vandals and the Visigoths shews something of a Roman motive.

For some months after the disappearance of Avitus there was an interregnum. Ricimer apparently took no steps to fill the vacancy, and Marcian, the Eastern Emperor, was on his death-bed. At last Leo, who had eventually succeeded to Marcian by the grace of Aspar, the "master of the troops" in the East, elevated Ricimer to the dignity of *patricius* (457), and named Majorian, who had fought by Ricimer's side in the struggle of 456, as *magister militum* in his stead. A few months afterwards the election of the Senate and the consent of the army united to make Majorian emperor. Majorian belonged to an old Roman family with administrative traditions. His grandfather had been *magister peditum et equitum* on the Danube under Theodosius the Great; his father had been a fiscal officer under Aëtius; and under Aëtius he had himself served with distinction. If we can trust the evidence of his constitutions and the testimony of Procopius, Majorian has every title to be considered one of the greatest of the later Roman Emperors. Not only is the rescript in which he notifies his accession to the senate full of pledges of good government; he sought in the course of his reign to redeem his pledges, and by strengthening, for instance, the office of *defensor civitatis* to repeople and reinvigorate the declining *municipia* of the Empire. The constitution by which he sought to protect the ancient monuments of Rome is in marked contrast with the vandalism to which Avitus had been forced, and bears witness to the conservative and Roman policy which he sought to pursue. In his foreign policy he addressed himself manfully to the problems which faced him in Africa, in Gaul, and in Spain.

His first problem lay naturally in Gaul. The party which had stood for Avitus, and the Visigoths who had been its allies, were both inevitably opposed to the man who had joined in Avitus' deposition; and the reconciliation of Gaul to the new *régime* was thus of primary importance. After issuing a number of constitutions for the reform of the Empire in the course of 458, Majorian crossed the Alps at the end of the year, with a motley army of Rugians, Sueves, and Ostrogoths. The Gallo-Roman party received him without a struggle, and the *littérateur* of the party, Sidonius Apollinaris, pronounced a eulogy on the Emperor at Lyons. With the Visigoths, who had been attacking Arles, there was a short but apparently decisive struggle: Theodoric II was beaten, and renewed his alliance with Rome. It remained for Majorian to regulate the affairs of Spain, and, using it as a base, to equip a fleet in its ports for a final attack on Gaiseric. In 460 he moved into the province. His victory over the Visigoths, themselves in occupation of much of Spain since 457, had made his path easy; and a fleet of 300 vessels, which had long been under preparation, was assembled at the port of Alicante for the expedition against the Vandals. But Gaiseric, aided by treachery, surprised the fleet and captured a number of ships; the projected expedition collapsed, like every expedition against Gaiseric, and Majorian had to acknowledge defeat. He seems to have made a treaty with Gaiseric, recognising the new acquisitions which Gaiseric had made since 455; but the failure of the expedition proved nevertheless his ruin.   Ricimer was jealous of an emperor who shewed himself too vigorous; and though Majorian had sought to conciliate him, as the language of his constitutions shews, he had failed to appease his jealousy.   When he moved into Italy, in the summer of 461, perhaps to forestall an attack by Ricimer, he only came to meet with defeat and death in a battle near Tortona.   With him indeed died the "Roman name," and in his fall the barbarian party triumphed.   His reign had been filled by a manly attempt at the *renovatio imperii*, both by administrative reforms within, and a vigorous policy without; but his reforms had aroused the opposition of a corrupt bureaucracy; his foreign policy had been defeated by the cunning of Gaiseric; and he fell before the jealousy of the barbarian whom he overshadowed.

The death of Majorian advanced the dissolution of the Western Empire a step further.   The Visigoths and the Vandals both regarded themselves as absolved from the treaties which they had made with Majorian; and Gaiseric, hating Ricimer as the nephew of Wallia, the destroyer of part of his people, directed his piratical attacks once more against Sicily and Italy.   Not only so, but when Ricimer raised to the imperial throne Severus (a puppet-emperor, on the reverse of whose coins he significantly placed his own monogram), two of the provincial governors of the Empire refused him allegiance, and ruled as independent sovereigns within their spheres — Aegidius in central Gaul, and Marcellinus in Dalmatia.   Ricimer was almost powerless: he could only attempt an alliance with the Visigoths against Aegidius, and send his petitions to the Eastern Emperor Leo to keep Marcellinus and the Vandals in check.   The policy had some success: Aegidius and Theodoric checked each other, until the death of the former in 464; and Marcellinus was induced by the Eastern Emperor to keep the peace. But Gaiseric, though he consented to restore Eudoxia and one of her daughters to Leo, refused to cease from his raids upon Italy, until he had received the inheritances of Aëtius and Valentinian III, which he claimed in the name of his captives — Gaudentius, the son of Aëtius, and Eudoxia, the elder daughter of Valentinian, now married to his son Huneric.   To these claims he soon added another.   Placidia, the younger daughter of Valentinian, was married at Constantinople to a Roman senator, Olybrius; and Gaiseric demanded that Olybrius, now the brother-in-law of his own son, and therefore likely to be a friend of the Vandals, should be acknowledged as Emperor of the West.   As Attila had demanded the church plate of Sirmium and the hand of Honoria, so Gaiseric now demanded the two inheritances and the succession of Olybrius; and it was to give weight to these demands that he continued to direct his annual raids against Italy.

It is perhaps the positions held by Aegidius and Marcellinus in Gaul and Dalmatia which shew most clearly the ruin of the Empire.   The flagging brain ceases to control the limbs and members of the State; the Roman scheme of an organised world-community falls into fragments. Marcellinus, one of the young men trained by Aëtius, had been promoted to the office of *magister militiae* in Dalmatia.   On the murder of Aëtius, he had refused obedience to Valentinian III; but on the succession of Majorian, who was also one of Aëtius' men, he resumed his allegiance to the Empire, and was given the task of defending Sicily.   The fall of Majorian drove him once more into rebellion, and though he was forced to leave Sicily, owing to the intrigues of Ricimer among his troops, he maintained himself as the independent ruler of Dalmatia.   In the great expedition of 468 he joined with the Eastern and Western Emperors as a practically independent sovereign, and though he was assassinated in the course of the expedition, possibly at the instigation of Ricimer, he seems to have left his nephew, Nepos, the future Emperor, to succeed to his position.   A pagan, and a friend of philosophers, with whom he held high converse in his Dalmatian palace, Marcellinus stands, alike in his character and in his political position, as one of the most interesting figures of his age.   His contemporary, Aegidius, is a man of more ordinary type.   A lieutenant of Majorian, he had been created *magister militum per Gallias*; and on the death of his master, he had assumed an independent position in central Gaul, with the aid of the Salian Franks, who, in revolt against their own king, had, if Gregory of Tours may be trusted, accepted him for their chief.   In 463 he had defeated the Visigoths in a battle near Orleans, and put himself into touch with Gaiseric for a combined attack on Italy; but in 464 he died.   His power descended to his son Syagrius, who maintained his independence as "Roman King of Soissons" until he was overthrown by Clovis in 486.   Parallel in some ways to the position of Marcellinus and Aegidius is the beneficent theocracy which St Severinus established about the same time in Noricum, a masterless province unprotected by Rome, and harassed by the raids of the Rugii from the north of the river.   The Saint mediated for his people with the Rugian kings Flaccitheus and his successor Feletheus; he used his influence among the provincials of Noricum to secure the regular payment of tithes for the use of the poor; in famine and flood he helped his flock, and kept the lamp of Christianity alight in a dark land.

The death of the nominal Emperor, Severus, in 465, made little difference in the history of the West.   For two years after his death the West had no emperor of its own, and the whole Empire was nominally united under Leo I.   Ricimer was content to prolong an interregnum, which left him sole ruler; Gaiseric was still pressing for the succession of Olybrius; and Leo was at once unwilling to create an emperor who was likely to be a vassal of Gaiseric, and anxious to maintain the peace which existed between the Vandals and the Eastern Empire.   Accordingly he delayed the creation of a successor to Severus until Gaiseric, in 467, impatient of the delay, delivered an attack on the Peloponnesus. Leo now felt himself free to act : he listened to the prayers of. the Roman Senate, and appointed as Emperor Anthemius, a son-in-law of the Emperor Marcian, and a man of large experience, who had held the highest offices of the Eastern Empire. The gift of Anthemius' daughter in marriage was intended to conciliate the support of Ricimer; and East and West, thus united together on a firm basis, were to deliver a final and crushing attack on the Vandals, and to punish Gaiseric for the reign of terror he had exercised in the West ever since 461.

In April 467, Anthemius came to Italy, escorted by Count Marcellinus and an army. By 468 a great armada had been collected, to be launched against Carthage. The expenses were enormous : one office supplied 47,000 pounds of gold, another 17,000 pounds of gold and 700,000 pounds of silver; and this vast sum, which seems incredibly large, was furnished partly from the proceeds of confiscations, and partly by the Emperor Anthemius. A triple attack was projected. On the side of the East Basiliscus was to command the armada, and to deliver an attack on Carthage, while Heraclius marched by land through Tripoli to deliver a simultaneous attack on the flank of the Vandals. On the side of the West Marcellinus (conciliated by the Eastern Emperor, who was not unwilling to see Dalmatia in the hands of a ruler practically independent of the West) commanded a force which was destined to operate in Sardinia and Sicily. Once more, however, Gaiseric defeated his foes, as in 442 and 461, and once more treachery, perhaps instigated by the subtle Vandal, proved the ruin of an expedition against Carthage. The Alan Aspar, *magister militum per Orientem*, frowned on an expedition which might render his master independent of his support; and already dubious of his ascendancy, he seems to have procured the nomination of Basiliscus, an incapable procrastinator, in order to ruin the success of the expedition. Ricimer, generalissimo of the West, was in a very similar position : he feared the success of the expedition, because it might consolidate the power of Anthemius, and he hated with a personal hatred the Count Marcellinus, who commanded the Western forces. The inevitable result followed. Basiliscus was amused by Gaiseric with negotiations, and not unwillingly delayed, until Gaiseric sent fire-ships among his armada, and destroyed the bulk of his ships; while Marcellinus, after recovering Sardinia, was killed in Sicily by an assassin, in whom it is impossible not to suspect an agent of Ricimer. The success gained by Heraclius, who had won Tripoli and was marching on Carthage, was neutralised; the destruction of Basiliscus' fleet and the assassination of Marcellinus involved the complete failure of the expedition. When one remembers that Aspar, Ricimer, and Gaiseric were all Arians, one almost wonders if the whole story does not indicate an Arian conspiracy against the Catholic Empire; but political exigencies are sufficient to explain the issue, and the real fact would appear to be, that the two generalissimos of East and West were content to purchase their own security at the cost of the Empire they served.

Aspar indeed failed in the event to buy security, even at the price he had been willing to pay. In 471 Leo attempted a *coup d'état*: Aspar fell, and the victorious Emperor, who had already been recruiting Isaurians within his own Empire, in order to counteract and eventually supersede the dangerous influence of the German mercenaries, was able to continue his policy, and thus to preserve the independent existence of the Eastern Empire. With the West it was different. Here there was no substitute for Ricimer and his Germans : here there was no elasticity which would enable the Empire to recover, as it did in the East, from the loss of prestige and of resources involved by the disastrous failure of 468. For a time, indeed, Anthemius, with the support of the Senate which had called him to the throne, and of the Roman party which hated barbarian domination, struggled to make head against Ricimer. The struggle partly turned on the course of events in Gaul. Here Euric, in 466, had assassinated his brother Theodoric II, as Theodoric had before assassinated his brother Thorismud. A vigorous and enterprising king, the most successful of all the Visigothic rulers of Toulouse, Euric immediately began, after the failure of the expedition of 468, to take advantage of the condition of the Western Empire in order to make himself ruler of the whole of Gaul. He may have hoped to gain the aid of the Gallo-Roman nobility, who were by no means friendly to the ascendancy of Ricimer ; and there were certainly Roman officials in Gaul, like Arvandus, the *Praefectus Praetorio*, who lent themselves to his plans. But Anthemius and the Senate saw the danger by which they were threatened. Arvandus was brought to Rome in 469, tried by the Senate, and sentenced to death — a striking instance of the activity which the Senate could still display ; and Anthemius attempted to gain the support of the nobility of Gaul, by giving the title of *patricius* to Ecdicius, the son of Avitus, and the office of praefect of Rome to Sidonius Apollinaris. In spite of these measures, however, he failed to save Gaul from the Visigoths. In 470 Euric took the field, and, defeating a Roman army, gained possession of Arles and other towns as the prize of his victory. Much of Auvergne also fell into his hands, but he failed to take its chief city, Clermont, where the valour of Ecdicius and the exhortations of Sidonius, newly consecrated bishop of the city, inspired a stout resistance. Yet Gaul was none the less really lost ; and failure in Gaul meant for Anthemius ruin in Italy. Already in 471 civil war was imminent. Ricimer, seeing his chance, had gathered his forces at Milan, while Anthemius was stationed at Rome. Round the one was collected the army of Teutonic mercenaries ; round the other, though he was not popular in Catholic Italy, being reputed to be "Hellenic" and a lover of philosophy, there rallied the officials, the Senate, and the people of Rome. Once more the old struggle of the Roman and barbarian parties was destined to be rehearsed. For a moment the mediation of Epiphanius, the saintly bishop of Pavia, procured (if we may trust the account of his biographer Ennodius) a temporary peace ; but in 472 war came. Early in the year Ricimer marched on Rome, and besieged the city with an army, in which the Scirian Odovacar was one of the commanders. For five months the city suffered from siege and from famine. At last an army which had marched from Gaul to the relief of Anthemius, under the command of Bilimer, the master of troops of that province, was defeated by Ricimer, and treachery completed the fall of the beleaguered city. In July Ricimer marched into Rome, now under the heel of a conqueror for the third time in the course of the century ; and Anthemius, seeking in vain to save his life by mingling in disguise with the beggars round the door of one of the Roman churches, was detected and beheaded by Ricimer's nephew, Gundobad. Once more the Empire seemed destroyed : civil war, said Pope Gelasius, had overturned the city and the feeble remnants of the Roman Empire.

The death of Anthemius had already been preceded by the accession of Olybrius, the husband of Valentinian's daughter, and the relative by marriage of Gaiseric. The circumstances of the accession of Olybrius are obscure. A curious story in a late Byzantine writer makes him appear in Italy during the struggle between Anthemius and Ricimer, with public instructions from Leo to mediate in the struggle, but with a sealed letter to Anthemius, in which it was suggested that the bearer should be instantly executed. The letter is said to have fallen into the hands of Ricimer, who replied by elevating Olybrius to the imperial throne. We can only say that Olybrius came to Italy in the spring of 472, whether sent by Leo, or (as is perhaps more likely) invited by Ricimer, and that he was proclaimed emperor by Ricimer before the fall of Rome and the death of Anthemius. The reign of Olybrius, connected as he was with the old Theodosian house and with the Vandal rulers of Africa, seemed to promise well for the future of the West ; but it only lasted for a few months. Short as it was, it saw the death of Ricimer, at the end of August 472, and the elevation in his place of his nephew Gundobad, a Burgundian. But though a nominal successor took his place, the death of Ricimer left a gap that could not be filled. If he was a barbarian, he had yet in his way venerated the Roman name and preserved the tradition of the Roman Empire ; he had sought to be emperor-maker rather than King of Italy, and for sixteen years he had kept the Empire alive in the West. Within four years of his death the last shadow of an emperor had disappeared ; and a barbarian kingdom had been established in Italy.

Olybrius died at the end of October 472. The throne remained vacant through the winter ; and it was not until March of 473 that Gundobad proclaimed Glycerius emperor at Ravenna. But Gundobad soon left Italy, having affairs in Gaul; and Glycerius, deprived of his support, was unable to maintain his position. He succeeded, indeed, in averting one danger, when he induced a body of Ostrogoths, who had entered Italy from the north-east under their king Widimir, to join their kinsmen, the Visigoths of Gaul. His position, however, had never been confirmed by the Eastern Emperor; and at the end of 473 Leo appointed Julius Nepos, the nephew of Marcellinus of Dalmatia, to be emperor in his place. In the spring of 474 Nepos arrived in Italy with an army: Glycerius could offer no resistance; and in the middle of June he was captured at Portus, near the mouth of the Tiber, and forcibly consecrated bishop of Salona in Dalmatia.[1] The accession of Nepos seemed a triumph for the Roman cause, and a defeat for the barbarian party. Once more, as in the days of Anthemius, an emperor ruled at Rome who was the real colleague and ally of the Emperor of Constantinople; and Nepos, unlike Anthemius, had the advantage of having no master of troops at his side. With the aid of the Eastern Empire, and in the absence of any successor to Ricimer, Nepos might possibly hope to secure the permanent triumph of the Roman cause in the West.

But the aid of the Eastern Empire was destined to prove a broken reed, and Ricimer was fated to find his successor. In 475 a revolt, headed by Basiliscus, drove Zeno, who had succeeded to Leo in 474, from Constantinople, and disturbed the East until 477. The West was thus left to its own resources during the crisis of its fate; and taking their opportunity the barbarian mercenaries found themselves new leaders, and under their guidance settled its fate at their will. For the first few months of his reign Nepos was left undisturbed; but even so he was compelled to make a heavy sacrifice, and to buy peace with Euric at the price of the formal surrender of Auvergne, to the great grief of its bishop Sidonius.[2] In 475, however, there appeared a new leader of the barbarian mercenaries. This was Orestes, a Roman of Pannonia, who had served Attila as secretary, and had been entrusted by his master with the conduct of negotiations with the Roman Empire. On the death of Attila, he had come to Italy, and having married a daughter of Romulus, an Italian of the rank of *comes*, who had served under Aëtius as ambassador to the Huns, he had had a successful career in the imperial service. He had risen high enough by 475 to be created *magister militiae* by Nepos; and in virtue both of his official position and of a natural sympathy which his previous career must have inspired he became the leader of the barbarian party. Once at the head of the army he instantly marched upon Rome. Nepos, powerless before his

---

[1] Perhaps the first instance of this method of political extinction.

[2] Schmidt (*Geschichte der deutschen Stämme*, p. 265) believes that the treaty meant the cession to Euric in full sovereignty of all the territories between the Loire on the north, the Atlantic on the west, the Pyrenees and the Mediterranean on the south, and the Rhone on the east.

adversary, fled to Ravenna, and unable to maintain himself there, escaped at the end of August 475 to his native Dalmatia, where he survived as an emperor in exile until he was assassinated by his followers in 480.   At the end of October Orestes proclaimed as emperor his son, a boy named Romulus after his maternal grandfather, and surnamed (perhaps only in derision, and after his fall) Augustulus.   Thus was restored the old *régime* of the nominal emperor controlled by the military dictator, and for nearly a year this *régime* continued.

But the barbarian mercenaries — the Rugii, Sciri, and Heruli — were by no means contented with the old condition of things.   Since the fall of Attila, they had emigrated so steadily into Italy from the north-east, that they had become a numerous people; and they desired to find for themselves, in the country of their adoption, what other Germanic tribes had found in Gaul and Spain and Africa — a regular settlement on the soil in the position of *hospites*.   They would no longer be cantoned in barracks in the Roman fashion : they desired to be free farmers settled on the soil after the German manner, ready to attend the levy in time of need for the defence of Italy, but not bound to serve continually in foreign expeditions as a professional army.   They accordingly asked of Orestes a third of the soil of Italy : they demanded that every Roman possessor should cede a third of his estate to some German *hospes*.   It appears a modest demand, when one reflects that the Visigoths settled by Constantius in south-western Gaul in 418 had been allowed two-thirds of the soil and its appurtenant cattle and cultivators.   But the cession of 418 had been a matter of free grant : the demand of 476 was the demand of a mutinous soldiery.   The grant of south-western Gaul had been the grant of one corner of the Empire, made with the design of protecting the rest : the surrender of Italy would mean the surrender of the home and hearth of the Empire.   Orestes accordingly rejected the demand of the troops.   They replied by creating Odovacar their king, and under his banner they took for themselves what Orestes refused to give.

Odovacar, perhaps a Scirian by birth, and possibly the son of a certain Edeco who had once served with Orestes as one of the envoys of Attila, had passed through Noricum, where St Severinus had predicted his future greatness, and come to Italy somewhere about 470.   He had served under Ricimer in 472 against Anthemius; and by 476 he had evidently distinguished himself sufficiently to be readily chosen as their king by the congeries of Germanic tribes which were cantoned in Italy. His action was prompt and decisive.   He became king on 23 August : by the 28th Orestes had been captured and beheaded at Piacenza, and on 4 September Paulus, the brother of Orestes, was killed in attempting to defend Ravenna.   The Emperor Romulus Augustulus became the captive of the new king, who, however, spared the life of the handsome boy, and sent him to live on a pension in a Campanian villa.   While Odovacar was annexing Italy, Euric was spreading his conquests in Gaul; and when he occupied Marseilles, Gaul, like Italy, was lost.

The success of Odovacar did not, however, mean the erection of an absolutely independent Teutonic kingdom in Italy, or the total extinction of the Roman Empire in the West; and it does not therefore indicate the beginning of a new era, in anything like the same sense as the coronation of Charlemagne in 800. It is indeed a new and important fact, that after 476 there was no Western Emperor until the year 800, and it must be admitted that the absence of any separate Emperor of the West vitally affected both the history of the Teutonic tribes and the development of the Papacy, during those three centuries. But the absence of a separate emperor did not mean the abeyance of the Empire itself in the West. The Empire had always been, and always continued in theory to be, one and indivisible. There might be two representatives at the head of the imperial scheme; but the disappearance of one of the two did not mean the disappearance of half of the scheme; it only meant that for the future one representative would stand at the head of the whole scheme, and that this scheme would be represented somewhat less effectively in that part of the Empire which had now lost its separate head. The scheme itself continued in the West, and its continued existence was acknowledged by Odovacar himself. Zeno now became the one ruler of the Empire; and to him Odovacar sent the imperial insignia of Romulus Augustulus, while he demanded in return the traditional title of *patricius*, to legalise his position in the imperial order. The old Roman administration persisted in Italy: there was still a *Praefectus Praetorio Italiae*; and the Roman Senate still nominated a consul for the West. Odovacar is thus not so much an independent German king, as a second Ricimer — a *patricius*, holding the reins of power in his own hands, but acknowledging a nominal emperor, with the one difference that the emperor is now the ruler of the East, and not a puppet living at Rome or Ravenna. Yet after all Odovacar bore the title of *rex*: he had been lifted to power on the shields of German warriors. *De facto*, he ruled in Italy as its king; and while his legal position looks backwards to Ricimer, we cannot but admit that his actual position looks forward to Alboin and the later Lombard kings. He is a Janus-like figure; and while we remember that he looks towards the past, we must not forget that he also faces the future. We may insist that the Empire remained in the West after 476; we must also insist that every vestige of a Western Emperor had passed away. We may speak of Odovacar as *patricius*; we must also allow that he spoke of himself as *rex*. He is of the fellowship of Euric and Gaiseric; and when we remember that these three were ruling in Gaul and Africa and Italy in 476, we shall not quarrel greatly with the words of Count Marcellinus: *Hesperium Romanae gentis imperium* · · · *cum hoc Augustulo periit* . . . *Gothorum dehinc regibus Romam tenentibus.*

CH. XIV.

CHAPTER XV

THE KINGDOM OF ITALY UNDER ODOVACAR
AND THEODORIC

THE time between the years 476 and 526 is a period of transition from the system of twin Empires which existed from the time of Arcadius and Honorius to the separation of Italy from the rest of the Empire. It is for this reason an interesting period. It marks the surrender by Constantinople of a certain measure of autonomy to that portion of the Empire which, finding that government under the faction set up after the death of Theodosius was impossible, had ended by submission to rulers nominated from Byzantium; it marks too, the progress achieved by the barbarians, who far from wishing to destroy a state of things which had formerly been hostile, adapted themselves to it readily when they had once risen to power, and shewed themselves as careful of its traditions as their predecessors; it marks further, the preponderant part played in the affairs of the time by a growing power — the Church — and the adaptability shewn by her in dealing with kings who were heretics and avowed followers of Arius.

The attempt to found an Italian kingdom was destined to speedy failure. There were too many obstacles in the way of its permanent establishment; Justinian it is true was to shew himself capable of giving effectual support to the claims of Byzantium and of making an end of the Ostrogothic kingdom, but even his authority was powerless to bring about the union of the two portions of the Roman Empire. Another barbarian race, the Lombards, shared with the Papacy — the one authority which emerged victorious from these struggles — the possession of a country which, owing to the irreconcilable nature of the lay and religious elements, was destined to recover only in modern times unity, peace and that consciousness of a national existence which is the sole guarantee of permanence.

Cassiodorus writes in his chronicle: "In the Consulate of Basiliscus and Armatus, Orestes and his brother Paulus were slain by Odovacar;

the latter took the title of king, albeit he wore not the purple, nor assumed the insignia of royalty." We have here in the concise language of an annalist intent on telling much in a few words, the history of a revolution which appears to us, at this distance of time, to have been pregnant with consequences. The Emperor—that Romulus Augustulus whose associated names have so often served to point a moral — is n̶o̶t̶ mentioned. It was left to Jordanes alone, a century later, to make any reference to him. The seizure of the supreme power by military leaders of barbarian origin had become since the time of Ricimer a recognised process; it is moreover Orestes who is attacked by Odovacar, and Orestes was a simple patrician and in no sense clothed with the imperial dignity. The Empire itself suffered no change, it was merely that one more barbarian had come to the front. It was only when Odovacar was to set up pretensions to independent and sovereign authority that annalists and chroniclers were to accord him special mention on the ground that his claim was without precedent. Up to that point his intervention was only one among many similar events which occurred at this period.

Orestes was of Pannonian origin; he had acted as secretary to Attila, and with Edeco had taken a chief part in frustrating the conspiracy organised by Theodosius II against the life of the king of the Huns. After the death of the barbarian king, he entered the service of Anthemius, who appointed him commander of the household troops. He took part — under what circumstances we are ignorant — in the struggles which brought about the fall and the murder of Anthemius, an emperor imposed from Constantinople, the elevation and death of Olybrius, the short-lived rule of the Burgundian Gundobad and the elevation of Glycerius. For the second time the East imposed an Augustus on the West, and Leo appointed Julius Nepos to bear rule at Rome. Under his reign Orestes, who had been promoted to the rank of commander-in-chief, was charged with the task of transferring Auvergne to the Visigoth king Euric, to whom it had been ceded by the Roman government.

How it came about that Orestes, instead of leading his army to Gaul, led it against Ravenna and who induced him to attack Nepos, we have no documentary evidence to shew. Nepos fled and retired to Salona, where he found his predecessor Glycerius, whom he had appointed to be bishop of that place. Having achieved this success Orestes proclaimed as the new Emperor Romulus Augustulus, his son by the daughter of Count Romulus, a Roman noble (475). Even as Orestes had driven out Nepos, another barbarian — Odovacar — was before long to drive out Orestes and his son, and once more the contemporary documents afford no plausible explanation of this fresh revolution.

Odovacar was a Rugian, the son of that Edeco, Attila's general and minister. Odovacar had followed his father's colleague into Italy where he occupied the humble position of spearman in the household troop, from which he gradually rose to higher rank. Whether the ambition which fired him was provoked by the spectacle of the internal conflicts in which he took part, or whether by the prediction of St Severinus the Apostle of Noricum, it is impossible to say. It is, however, certain that in the Lives of the Saints there is a record to the effect that Severinus in his hermitage of Favianum was visited one day by certain barbarians who asked for his benediction before going to seek their fortunes in Italy, and one of them, scantily clad in the skins of beasts, was of so lofty a stature that he was compelled to stoop in order to pass through the low doorway of the cell. The monk observed the movement and exclaimed: "Go, go forward into Italy. To-day thou art clothed in sorry skins but ere long thou shalt distribute great rewards to many people." The man whom Severinus thus designated for supreme rule was Odovacar the son of Edeco. He appears to have enjoyed great popularity among the mercenary troops, and profiting by their discontent at the failure of Orestes to reward their devotion, he induced them to take active measures, and gained to his side the barbarians of Liguria and the Trentino. Orestes declined the combat offered by Odovacar in the plains of Lodi, retreated behind the Lambro with the object of covering Pavia and shortly afterwards shut himself up in that city. Odovacar laid siege to him there, and Pavia, which, as Ennodius tells us, had been pillaged by the soldiers of Orestes, was sacked by the troops of Odovacar; Orestes was delivered up to Odovacar, who had him put to death 28 August, 476. Odovacar next marched on Ravenna which was defended by Paulus the brother of Orestes and where Romulus had taken refuge. In a chance encounter which took place in a pine forest close to the city Paulus was killed and Odovacar, occupied Ravenna, which had taken the place of Rome as the favourite residence of the Caesars of the West.

Romulus who had hidden himself and cast off the fatal purple was brought before him. Odovacar taking pity on his youth and moved by his beauty consented to spare his life. He moreover granted him a revenue of 6000 gold *solidi* and assigned him as his residence the Lucullanum, a villa in Campania near Cape Misenum which had been built by Marius and decorated by Lucullus.

In succession to three Emperors of the West who still survived — Glycerius and Nepos in Dalmatia and Romulus in Campania — Odovacar, styled by Jordanes King of the Rugians, by the Anonymus Valesii King of the Turcilingi, and by other authorities Prince of the Sciri, now wielded supreme power.

At this point certain questions arise as to the nature of the authority which he exercised and to his relations with Byzantium and the established powers in Italy. The documents which supply an answer are scanty. The passages devoted to Odovacar give no details except such as relate to the beginning and end of his reign; it is plain too, that the Latin writers of the time were more intent on pleasing Theodoric than on recording the facts of history.

Cassiodorus has been careful to point out that Odovacar refused altogether to assume the imperial insignia and the purple robe and was content with the "title of king." These events took place when Basiliscus having driven Zeno from power was reigning as Emperor of the East, that is, at a moment of dynastic trouble in the other half of the Empire. The possession of Ravenna, the exile of Romulus, and the death of Orestes did not suffice to secure to Odovacar the lordship of Italy; it was only after his formal entry into Rome and his tacit recognition by the Senate, that he could look upon his authority as finally established.

He was not however satisfied with this, but desired a formal appointment by the Emperor and the recognition of his authority by Constantinople. A palace conspiracy which broke out in 477 having replaced Zeno on the throne of Byzantium, the ex-sovereign Romulus Augustulus, in spite of the fact that never having been formally recognised by the Emperor, he had no legal claim to take such a step, sent certain Senators as an embassy to Zeno.[1] The representatives of the Senate were instructed to inform the Emperor that Italy had no need of a separate ruler and that the autocrat of the two divisions of the Empire sufficed as Emperor for both, that Odovacar moreover, in virtue of his political capacity and military strength, was fully competent to protect the interests of the Italian diocese, and under these circumstances they prayed that Zeno would recognise the high qualities of Odovacar by conferring on him the title of Patrician and by entrusting him with the government of Italy.

The Emperor's reply was truly diplomatic. After severely censuring the Senate for the culpable indifference they had shewn with respect to the murder of Anthemius and the expulsion of Nepos, two sovereigns who had been sent by the East to rule in Italy, he declared to the ambassadors that it was their business to decide on the course to be pursued. Certain members of the legation represented more especially the interests of Odovacar, and to them the Emperor declared that he fully approved of the conduct of the barbarian in adopting Roman manners, and that he would forthwith bestow on him the well-merited title of Patrician if Nepos had not already done so,[2] and he gave them a letter

---

[1] Malchus gives the history of this embassy. *Excerpt de leg. gent.* ap. Müller, *Fragm. Hist. Graec.* iv. 119. Müller quite gratuitously emends the text on the supposition that the embassy was sent by Odovacar and not, as the Byzantine writer states, by Augustulus. The original reading is far more convincing.

[2] This is the first allusion to the promotion of Odovacar to the important office which during the reign of Nepos had been filled by Orestes.

for Odovacar in which he granted him the dignity in question. Zeno in short had to recognise the *fait accompli*, the more so as the ambassadors from Rome to Byzantium had there found themselves in the presence of another mission sent from Dalmatia by Nepos to beg for the deposed sovereign the assistance of the newly restored Emperor. He however could only condole with him on his lot and point out its similarity to that from which he himself had just escaped.

There is yet another proof of the tacit recognition of Odovacar's authority. In 480 Nepos was assassinated by the Counts Victor and Ovida (or Odiva) and in 481, as if he had been the legitimate heir of a predecessor whose death it was his duty to avenge, Odovacar led an expedition against the murderers, defeated and slew Ovida and restored Dalmatia to the Italian diocese. More than this, Odovacar looked upon himself as the formally appointed representative of Zeno, for at the time of the revolt of Illus, he refused to aid the latter, who had applied to him as well as to the kings of Persia and Armenia for assistance against the Emperor. He had already exercised sovereign power in the cession of Narbonne to the Visigoths of Euric and in the conclusion of a treaty with Gaiseric in 477, by the terms of which the king of the Vandals restored Sicily to the Italians, subject to the payment of a tribute and retaining possession of a castle which he had built in the island.

This is all we know, till Theodoric appears upon the scene, of the achievements of Odovacar; with respect to his relations with the inhabitants of Italy we are better informed. In and after 482 the regular record of consuls, interrupted since 477, was resumed. The Roman administration continued to work as in the past; there was a praetorian praefect Pelagius who, like so many of his predecessors, contrived to exact contributions on his own behalf as well as on behalf of the State. The relations between Odovacar and the Senate were so intimate that together and in their joint names they set up statues to Zeno in the city of Rome. Between the Church and Odovacar, albeit he was an Arian, no difficulties arose, the Pope Simplicius (468–483) recognised the authority of Odovacar, and the king preserved excellent relations with Epiphanius, bishop of Pavia, and with St Severinus, whose requests he was accustomed to treat with marked deference and respect. On the death of Simplicius in March 483, a meeting of the Senate and clergy took place and on the proposition of the praetorian praefect and patrician Basilius, it was resolved that the election of a new pope should not take place without previous consultation with the representative of King Odovacar, as he is styled without addition in the report of the proceedings. Further, future popes were bidden in the name of the king and under threat of anathema to refrain from alienating the possessions of the Church.

The picture of Italy under the government of Odovacar is difficult to trace. We have no Cassiodorus to preserve for us the terms of the decrees which he signed. Our only source of information, the works of Ennodius, is by no means free from suspicion. If we are to believe the bishop of Pavia, it was the evil one in person who inspired Odovacar with the ambition to reign, that he was a destroyer — *populator intestinus* — that his fall was a veritable relief and that Theodoric was a deliverer; in short that Odovacar was a tyrant in the full sense of the word.

It must be remembered that it is the panegyrist of Theodoric who speaks in these terms. The word tyrant which he employs must be understood, as the Byzantine historians understood it, in its Greek sense, that is, in the sense of an authority set up out of the ordinary course. The specific charges of tyranny which are made against Odovacar are unconvincing, especially the accusation that he distributed amongst his soldiers a third of the land of Italy. We will deal later with the part played by Theodoric.

It is not among these events that we must look for the cause of the fall of Odovacar; the only possible explanation lies in the fact that the Italians obeyed with alacrity, so soon as they were made clear, the orders of Constantinople on domestic affairs — holding themselves free to disobey them later on — and it was by the formal and specific authority of the Emperor that Theodoric was sent into Italy.

Theodoric, an Amal by birth, was the son of Theodemir king of the Goths and his wife Erelieva. His father had discharged the duties of a paid warden of the marches on the northern frontiers of the Empire of the East. Theodoric having been sent to Constantinople as a hostage spent his childhood and youth in that city; he stood high in the favour of the Emperor Leo and became deeply imbued with Greek civilisation; his education cannot however have advanced very far, as when he reigned in Italy he was unable to sign his name and was compelled therefore to trace with his pen the first four letters cut out for the purpose in a sheet of gold.

On the death of his father, having in his turn become king, Theodoric established his headquarters in Moesia and found himself involved in a chronic struggle with a Gothic chief Theodoric "the Squinter" (Theodoric Strabo), who aspired to the kingly dignity. To accomplish this purpose Theodoric Strabo relied on the good will of the Eastern Emperors. Having thrown in his lot with Basiliscus, he helped him to drive Zeno from the throne and received rewards in the shape of money and military rank; but when Zeno returned to power it was Theodoric the Amal who in virtue of his fidelity stood highest in the imperial favour. Adopted by the Emperor, loaded with wealth and raised to patrician dignity, he enjoyed from 475 to 479 great influence at the Byzantine Court. He was given the command

CH. XV.

of an expedition sent to chastise Strabo who had risen in revolt, and found his rival encamped in the Haemus; the men of each army were of kindred race and Theodoric the Amal was compelled by his soldiers to form a coalition with the enemy. Till the death of Strabo, which occurred in 481, the two Theodorics intrigued together against the Emperor and with the Emperor against each other and there followed a series of reconciliations and mutual betrayals. From that time forward Theodoric the Amal became a formidable power, he held Dacia and Moesia and it was necessary to treat him with respect. Zeno nominated him for Consul in 483 and in 484 he filled that office; it was in this capacity that he subdued the rebels Illus and Leontius, and on this ground he was granted in 486 the honour of a triumph and an equestrian statue in one of the squares of Byzantium.

This accumulation of dignities conferred by Zeno concealed the distrust which he felt, and which before long he made manifest by sending Theodoric into Italy.

Jordanes maintains that it was Theodoric himself who conceived the plan of the conquest of Italy and that in a long speech addressed to the Emperor, he depicted the sufferings of his own nation which was then quartered in Illyria and the advantages which would accrue to Zeno in having as his vicegerent a son instead of a usurper, and a ruler who would hold his kingdom by the imperial bounty. Certain authors such as the Anonymus Valesii and Paulus Diaconus have transformed this permission granted by the Emperor into a formal treaty giving to Theodoric the assurance, says the former, that he should "reign" in the place of Odovacar, and recommending him, says the latter — after formally investing him with the purple — to the good graces of the Senate. The explanation given by Procopius and adopted by Jordanes in another passage is, however, more plausible. Zeno, better pleased that Theodoric should go into Italy than that he should remain close at hand and in the neighbourhood of Byzantium, sent him to attack Odovacar; a similar method had been pursued with Widimir and Ataulf in order to remove them to a distance from Rome. In any case it was in the name of the Emperor that Theodoric acted, and he held his power by grant from him.

The title which he bore when he started from Constantinople, that of Patrician, sufficed in his own opinion and that of Zeno to legalise his power and to clothe him with the necessary authority: it was the same rank as that borne by Odovacar. Later, like Odovacar, he aspired to something higher and like him he was to fail in his attempts to obtain it. Zeno had no intention of yielding up his rights over Italy, and recognised no one other than himself as the lawful heir of Theodosius.

In 488 Theodoric crossed the frontier at the head of his Goths; it was the first step in the conquest which took five years to complete.

Odovacar opposed him at the head of an army not less formidable but less homogeneous than that of his adversary. He was defeated on the Isonzo; he retreated on Verona, was once more beaten and fled to Ravenna. Theodoric profited by this error of tactics to make himself master of Lombardy, and Tufa, Odovacar's lieutenant in that district, came over to his side. This was merely a stratagem, as when Tufa was sent with a picked body of Goths to attack Odovacar, he rejoined him with his Ostrogoths at Faventia. In 490 Odovacar again took the offensive; he sallied from Cremona, retook Milan and shut up Theodoric in Pavia. The latter would have been destroyed if the arrival of the Visigoths of Widimir, and a diversion made by the Burgundians in Liguria, had not left him free to rout Odovacar in a second battle on the Adda and to pursue him up to the walls of Ravenna. In August 490 Theodoric camped in the pine forest which Odovacar had occupied in his campaign against Orestes and a siege began which was to last three years. In 491 Odovacar made a sortie in which, after a first success, he was finally defeated and the siege became a blockade.

Theodoric, while keeping the enemy under observation, proceeded to capture other towns and to form various alliances. He seized Rimini and so destroyed the means of provisioning Ravenna, after which he opened negotiations with the Italians.

Without asserting that Theodoric owed all his success to the Church, the facts shew pretty clearly that she afforded him — Arian though he was, like Odovacar—valuable assistance. It was Bishop Laurentius who opened for him the gates of Milan and it was he who, after the treason of Tufa, held for him that important city; Epiphanius bishop of Pavia acted in similar fashion. In a letter written in 492, Pope Gelasius takes credit to himself for having resisted the orders of Odovacar, and finally it was another bishop, John of Ravenna, who induced Odovacar to treat.

Theodoric like Clovis understood to the full the advantages which would accrue to him from the good offices of the Church. From his first arrival in Italy he shewed in his attitude towards her the greatest consideration and tact. He was lavish in promises, he took pains to conciliate and he did not despise the use of flattery. Thus when he saw Epiphanius for the first time he is said to have exclaimed: "Behold a man who has not his peer in the East. To look upon him is a prize, to live beside him security." Again, he entrusts his mother and his sister to the care of the bishop of Pavia, an act of high policy by which he added to the friendly feelings already exhibited towards him. The conquest of Italy was practically achieved between 490 and 493, and the various members of the nobility such as Festus and Faustus Niger and the chief senators rallied to his cause; with the capitulation of Odovacar, which took place at this latter date, the victory of Theodoric was complete.

On 27 February 493, through the good offices of John bishop of

CH. XV.

Ravenna who acted as official intermediary and negotiated the terms of the treaty, an agreement was concluded between Odovacar and Theodoric. It was arranged that the two kings should share the government of Italy and should dwell together as brothers aṅd consuls in the same palace at Ravenna. Odovacar as a pledge of good faith handed over his son Thela to Theodoric, and on 5 March the latter made his state entry into Ravenna.

Theodoric broke the agreement by an act of the basest treachery. A few days later he invited Odovacar, his son and his chief officers to a banquet in that part of the palace known as the Lauretum. At the end of the feast Theodoric rose, threw himself on Odovacar and slew him together with his son. The chief officers of Theodoric's army followed his example and massacred the Rugian leaders in the banqueting hall, while in the interior of the palace and as far as the outskirts of Ravenna the Gothic soldiery attacked the soldiery of Odovacar. It was clear that all acted on orders from headquarters.

Theodoric had now no rival in Italy: he was not however equally successful in his attempts to obtain recognition as king by the Emperor. He had already, during the first year of the siege of Ravenna, despatched Festus to Constantinople, hoping that his position as chief of the Senate would favour the success of his mission. On the completion of his conquest, Festus having in the meantime failed, Theodoric sent a fresh envoy, Faustus Niger; the second enterprise was however no less abortive than the first. The Anonymus Valesii tells us, indeed, that "peace having been made" (had Theodoric then in the eyes of the Emperor been guilty of disobedience?), "Anastasius sent back the royal insignia which Odovacar had forwarded to Constantinople"; nowhere, however, do we find it stated that the Emperor had authorised Theodoric to assume them. In a letter writteṇ to Justinian to beg for his friendship, Athalaric records the benefits conferred by the Court of Byzantium on his ancestors, he mentions adoption and the consulate and in referring to the question of government he merely recalls that his grandfather had been invested in Italy with the *toga palmata*, the ceremonial robe of *clarissimi* of consuls who triumphed. However that may be, Theodoric took that which was not conferred upon him. He abandoned military dress and assumed the royal mantle in his capacity of "governor of the Goths and the Romans" (Jordanes); but officially he was not, any more than Odovacar had been, king of Italy. Even his panegyrist Ennodius who styles him "our lord the king," refers to the Italians as "his subjects," accepts him as "lord of Italy" and *de facto* "*Imperator*" and speaks of him as clothed with the *imperialis auctoritas*, nowhere calls him king of Italy or king of the Romans. He was at once a Gothic king and a Roman official: Jordanes has called him *quasi Gothorum Romanorumque gubernator*.

We have proof of this double position in the two letters whicḥ he wrote to Anastasius and which are quoted by Cassiodorus (*Var.* I. 1; II. 5). In the first Theodoric expresses to the Emperor the respect which he feels for the latter's counsels and especially for the advice which he had given him to shew favour to the Senate. If he uses the word *regnum* (a word which may also mean nothing more than government) it is to tell the Emperor that his object is to imitate the latter's system of governing. In the second letter, his tone is that of a lieutenant who begs his superior officer to approve the choice of a consul. It is the tone neither of a rebel on the one hand, nor of an independent sovereign on the other.

As the Anonymus Valesii saw very clearly, Theodoric made no attempt to found a new State: he ruled two nations together without seeking to blend them, to allow one to absorb the other, or to make either subordinate. The Goths retained their own rights, their own laws, and their own officials; the Italians continued to be governed as they had been in the past, and the rule of Theodoric offers us the spectacle of a government purely Roman in character.

The Goths had established themselves almost imperceptibly in Italy, as their king had been careful to maintain continuity of government, and Theodoric appears in the pages of contemporary writers as a sovereign whose habits and traditions were altogether Roman. The works of Ennodius abound in evidence of this: his *Panegyric* in particular, in which he represents Italy and Rome as loud in their praise of Theodoric because he had revived the old tradition and because he himself was a Roman prince whose ambition it was to place Italy in harmony with her past; this is the idea which dominates the pages of the famous prosopopoeia of the Adige.

The government of Theodoric was then wholly Roman; he published laws and appointed consuls. He maintained and enforced Roman law and the *edictum Theodorici* was derived exclusively from Roman sources. He even imitated the imperial policy of encouraging barbarians in Italy, as when, for example, he established the Alemanni as guardians of the frontier. He also had a Court, officials and an administrative organisation similar to that of Byzantium; he respected the Senate, restored the consular office, and though himself an Arian intervened as arbitrator, much as a Caesar would have done, in the affairs of the Church. Theodoric had a royal palace at Ravenna and there held his Court (*Aula*) surrounded by the chief men of Italy and his Gothic nobles. To enjoy interest at Court was all-important. No career was open to the man who did not attend there. "He was unknown to his master," says Ennodius. The Court was at once the home of good manners and the source of enlightenment, the centre of state affairs and a school of administration for the younger men.

The Court and the service of the *palatium* entailed certain functions

CH. XV.

nearly all of which were discharged by Romans: the *comes rerum privatarum* (Apronianus held the office in the time of Ennodius) had charge of the privy purse, and in his double capacity of censor and magistrate was responsible for the preservation of tombs and the administration of private justice: the *comes patrimonii* (Julianus) as steward of the royal domains, had under his orders the troublesome band of farmers of the revenue (*conductores*) and inspectors (*chartularii*); he had moreover supreme charge of the royal commissariat. The palace with its magnificent gardens and sumptuously decorated apartments was thronged with Roman nobles who came there in search of preferment. It was guarded by picked troops, and Ravenna was the head-quarters of an important military district where the chief commands were filled by such men as Constantius, Agapitus and Honoratus. There was not a Goth among them.

If from the Court we turn to the officials we find again that they are all Romans. Among the ministers of the Court of Theodoric, as would have been the case under the Roman administration, the most important was the praetorian praefect Faustus, a personage of high consequence who in right of his office enjoyed a considerable police authority and extensive patronage; he was at the head of the postal administration, and to him was the final appeal in all criminal matters which arose in the provinces. His powers were almost legislative in character; in the forum his jurisdiction was supreme and his person sacred. The *comes sacrarum largitionum* discharged the duties of finance minister; the *quaestor*, Eugenetes, was responsible in matters relating to jurisprudence and the framing of laws. Then came the treasury counsel Marcellus, who filled a position coveted by the rising members of the Bar, and who acted as a sort of attorney-general with respect to the estates of intestates and unclaimed assets; next came the *magister officiorum* and then the *peraequator* whose business it was to adjust the incidence of taxation in the royal cities. Finally the *vicarius*, the deputy in each diocese of the praetorian praefect.

We have here only specified some of those officials whose personal characters have been depicted for us in the letters of Ennodius. If we complete — and with the help of Cassiodorus it is possible to do so — the catalogue of government departments, both administrative and provincial, which existed in Italy under Theodoric we might well imagine it to be a record, not of the reign of a barbarian king, but of the times of Valentinian and Honorius. It was the Romans alone who struggled — and they did so with the greatest eagerness — to obtain these posts. Did, for example, the office of Treasury Counsel fall vacant, the whole province was agitated by intrigues, and even bishops joined in the contest. The crowd of candidates for a minor office such as *peraequator* was so great that Ennodius could not refrain from bantering Faustus on the subject.

The *cursus honorum* of the principal officers of state, during the forty years from Odovacar to the death of Theodoric, proves that very little was altered in Italy during that period, except the nationality of the ruler of the country. We find, for instance, that Faustus was successively Consul, Quaestor, Patrician, and Praetorian Praefect, and was moreover entrusted with missions to Anastasius; while Liberius, who had remained faithful to Odovacar, and had even refused to surrender Caesena to Theodoric, was nevertheless employed by the latter sovereign, who made him a Patrician and Praefect of Ligurian Gaul. Senarius, again, was employed first as a soldier, and then as a diplomatist, and Count of the *patrimonium*; Agapitus, another official, obtained the rank of Patrician, held a military appointment at Ravenna, and was in turn Consul, Legate in the East, and Praefect of the city; while Eugenetes, whom Ennodius styles "the honour of Italy," became a *vir illustris*, and was employed as an advocate, a Quaestor, and as Master of the Offices; other examples might also be quoted. The readiness of these Italian noblemen to serve successively under both Odovacar and Theodoric arose from no feeling of indifference on their part, but must rather be attributed to the fact that these rulers were in no sense hostile to tradition, and because they continued the form of administration established by the Roman Empire.

The Senate and the consulate, those two institutions with which the whole history of the past had been so intimately connected, especially engaged the attention of Theodoric. Ever since the time of Honorius, the part played by the Senate in the government of Italy had been growing more and more important. After the death of Libius Severus, it had asked Leo for an emperor; while both Augustulus and Odovacar had entrusted it with a similar mission to Zeno. In a well-known novel, Majorian may be found thanking the Senate for his election, and promising to govern according to its counsels; and when Anthemius was endeavouring to involve Ricimer in the struggle that was to end so fatally for himself, he leant for support upon the Curia. Examples such as these shew that the Senate represented tradition; it was the single authority that remained unchanged through every vicissitude, and to it accordingly Theodoric at once made overtures. He entrusted a mission of considerable importance to two Senators, Festus and Faustus, the former of whom occupied the position of chief of the Senate; and on making his entry into Rome his first visit was to the Senate-house. In fact, to make use of a saying of his own, as recorded by his panegyrist, he adorned the crown of the Senate with countless flowers. He enrolled a few Goths among its members, but he only did this on rare occasions, for he preferred, as a rule, to recruit the senatorial ranks from among the old aristocracy of the country. During his reign men became senators in three ways; they might either be co-opted, or else selected from a list of candidates nominated by the king, or they obtained the rank because they had been advanced to some dignity which conferred the title of "illustrious." In Rome indeed the Senate at this time was the supreme power. In conjunction with the praefect, it had the control of the municipal police; it organised the games in the circus; and exercised authority over the city schools and working men's corporations. Without abandoning any of its legislative power it assumed the functions of the Aediles; nor could a royal edict become law until it had received the senatorial sanction. The *Varia* of Cassiodorus are full of letters from Theodoric to the Senate. Indeed, he never made a nomination of any consequence, or filled up an important office, without immediately communicating the fact to the senators in the most deferential terms, and even soliciting their advice and approbation. A great deal of this deference was no doubt a mere form, but to a certain extent it was also sincere. The king's respect could hardly have been altogether feigned, for he invariably addressed even those senators who held aloof from his government in a kindly manner. Festus, for instance, although he remained in Rome and never visited Ravenna, obtained the rank of Patrician, and received no less than four letters from Theodoric, all expressed in the most flattering terms; while Symmachus, another Patrician who refused to leave his native city, was favoured with a royal letter praising the buildings which he had erected.

In spite of these friendly relations, some opposition was aroused in the Curia by the question of the Arian schism; indeed towards the end of the king's reign, the behaviour of the senators over this matter even provoked against him the hostility of Byzantium. Not only was this opposition a source of serious trouble to Theodoric, but it rendered him suspicious and cruel, and caused him to act with great severity against some of the senatorial families, and several victims, among whom Boethius was the most illustrious, were executed by his command.

In the opinion of Theodoric, the consulship was as valuable as ever, though in reality it had lost a great deal of its former importance. As Justinian justly observes in an *Authenticus*, this office had originally been created to defend the State in time of war, but since the emperors had undertaken the business of fighting, the consulship had deteriorated into a means of distributing largess among the people. Under these circumstances, candidates for the office were not very numerous. Ennodius mentions the small number of aspirants for the consulship; while Marcian, in an official communication, expresses his indignation at the stinginess of the men holding this high office, and obliges them to contribute a hundred pounds weight of gold, for the purpose of repairing the aqueducts. The consulship indeed at this period had degenerated into a mere name. A formula of nomination, which has been preserved for us by Cassiodorus, merely recalls the fame of this magistracy in the past, and then goes on to point out that a consul's sole duty is to be magnanimous, and not to be sparing with his money. However, the consul has no more authority. "By the grace of God," the formula declares, "we govern, while your name dates the year. Your good fortune, indeed, is greater than that of the prince himself, for though endowed with the highest honours, you have been relieved of the burden of power." On the other hand, as if to make up for this loss of authority, the dress of a consul was sumptuous and magnificent; a spreading cloak hung from his shoulders; he carried a sceptre in his hand, and wore gilded shoes. In addition, he possessed the right of sitting in a curule chair, and was allowed to make the seven processions in triumph through Rome of which Justinian speaks in one of his novels.

Theodoric would have liked to restore the consulship to a somewhat more respected position. An eloquent letter on the subject of this magistracy was addressed by him to the Emperor Anastasius, and when Avienus, the son of Faustus, became consul in 501, Ennodius, who shared the opinion of his master, wrote as follows: "If there are any ancient dignities which deserve respect, if to be remembered after death is to be regarded as a great happiness, if the foresight of our ancestors really created something so excellent that by it humanity can triumph over time, it is certainly the consulship, whose permanence has overcome old age, and put an end to annihilation." In his *Panegyric*, moreover, Ennodius praises Theodoric because, during his reign, "the number of consuls exceeded the number of candidates for the office in previous times."

The main outlines of Theodoric's government have now been described, and it will be seen that they were all of Roman origin. We must next inquire in what manner he administered this government. A judicious policy and gentle means had been employed to supplant Odovacar, and at the beginning of his reign he governed by similar methods. He endeavoured to help the Italian officials with whom he had surrounded himself, and to whom he had entrusted the high offices of state, in their task of pacifying and reorganising the country. When Epiphanius described the miserable plight of Liguria to him, and told him in moving terms how the land there lay uncultivated owing to its husbandmen having been carried away captive by the Burgundians, the king replied: "There is gold in the treasury, and we will pay their ransom, whatever it may be, either in money or by the sword." He then suggested that the bishop should himself undertake negotiations for ransoming the captives. Epiphanius accepted this mission; and, the king having placed the necessary funds at his disposal, triumphantly brought home six thousand prisoners, whom he had either ransomed or whose liberty he had obtained by his eloquent pleading in their behalf. The effect produced in Italy by such an act of liberality, followed by so satisfactory a result, can be imagined. The king's aim, indeed, as he told Cassiodorus, was to restore the old power of Italy, to re-establish

CH. XV.

a good government, and to extend the influence of that Roman *civilitas* upon which he desired to model his own administration.

As ministers, he selected men capable of inspiring confidence, such as Liberius, for instance, whose official work had been attended with such excellent results. In his opinion, fidelity to a vanquished patron was a virtue, nor was he afraid of praising it; indeed, in his administration, the value of a post given to a son would be in proportion to the deserts of the father. He attracted young men capable of making good officers of state to his Court; in a word, he acted like a sovereign who desires to be loved by his subjects, and at the same time to give stability to his rule. As Ennodius remarks, "No man was driven to despair of obtaining honours; no man, however obscure, had to complain of a refusal to his demands provided that they rested on substantial foundations; no man, in fact, ever came to the king without receiving liberal gifts"; but at this point we detect the panegyrist.

As we shall see before long, the end of his reign differed from the beginning, but during the chief part of it, at any rate, he governed with singular prudence. When Laurentius begged Theodoric to pardon some rebellious subjects, the king answered him as follows: "Your duty as a bishop obliges you to urge me to listen to the claims of mercy, but the needs of an Empire in the making shut out gentleness and pity, and make punishments a necessity." Nevertheless, we find that he allowed some mitigation to be made in the punishment of the culprits.

Theodoric could be a just as well as a politic ruler, and he shewed his sense of justice when he had to deal with financial questions. At the request of Epiphanius, he remitted two-thirds of the taxes for the current year to the inhabitants of Liguria; levying the remaining third, it is said, "in order that the poverty of his treasury might not impose fresh burdens on the Romans." During his reign, even the Goths were obliged to submit to taxation, and he also made them respect the public finances. At Adria, for instance, he forced them to give back what they had taken from the *fiscus*; in Tuscany he ordered Gesila, the *Sajo*, to make them pay the land tax. Moreover, if in any province the servants of the Gothic Count or his deputy behaved violently to the provincials, we find Severianus giving information against them; while in Picenum and Samnium we find him ordering his compatriots to bring grants made to the king to Court, without keeping back any portion of them.

Nevertheless, contemporary chroniclers have all declared that Theodoric, like Odovacar, distributed a third part of the land in Italy among his soldiers. Their statement appears to have been almost invariably accepted by later historians, who have repeated it one from another. A theory, that the barbarians despoiled the conquered people of their estates, is commonly believed, and indeed has hardly ever been contradicted. But in addition to the fact that such a proceeding would

certainly have led to some disturbance, of which we can find no evidence
in any part of the country, another circumstance renders such a conclusion unreasonable. This is that neither Odovacar's soldiers, nor
Theodoric's, were in reality sufficiently numerous to occupy a third
part of the land in Italy. Greek chronicles, it is true, speak of the
τριτημόριον τῶν ἀγρῶν, Latin writers of the *tertiae*. But what are
we to understand by these expressions? Among the few scholars who
have attempted to dispute the current theory, some, like de Rozière,
believe that the chronicler's words denote an act of confiscation for
which compensation was made to the owners by a tax levied at the rate
of one-third of the annual value. Others, like Lécrivain, consider that
they mean a surrender of unappropriated land, in return for which a
tribute was exacted equal to a third of the annual produce. At no
period, not even during the agrarian troubles in the far away days of
the Republic, had it ever been the custom to eject legal proprietors
from their estates. On the contrary, on every occasion when land had
been required for the purpose of making grants to the plebeians, to
veterans or praetorians, or even to barbarians, it had invariably been
taken from land owned by the community, that is to say from the land
around the temples, from unoccupied land, or from the property of the
Treasury. Whenever indeed a distribution of land took place, it was
made exclusively from the lands belonging to the Treasury, which, at
certain periods, multiplied exceedingly owing to escheated successions
or confiscations. In our own opinion, it was a third of these state lands,
this *ager publicus*, that was assigned to the barbarians during the reigns
of Odovacar and Theodoric. In addition to the fact that not one of the
texts actually contradicts this theory, it appears to be sufficiently proved
by the following words, addressed by Ennodius to Liberius, when the
latter was ordered to allot the land of Liguria to the Goths: "Have
you not enriched innumerable Goths with liberal grants, and yet the
Romans hardly seem to know what you have been doing." Even the
courtier-like Ennodius would not have expressed himself in this manner
in a private letter, or even in an official communication, if private
estates had been attacked for the benefit of the conquerors.

During the early years of the Roman Empire, the annual food
supply of Italy had always been one of the government's chief anxieties;
and the writings of Cassiodorus constantly shew us that Theodoric was
not free from a similar care. His orders to his officials, however, on
this subject, appear to have been attended with excellent results.
During his reign, according to the Anonymus, sixty measures of
wheat might be purchased for a *solidus*, and thirty amphorae of wine
might be had for a like sum. Paul the Deacon has remarked the joy
with which the Romans received Theodoric's order for an annual
distribution of twenty thousand measures of grain among the people.
It was, moreover, with a view to making the yearly food supply more

secure, that the king caused the seaports to be put into good repair; and we find him especially charging Sabiniacus to keep those in the vicinity of Rome in good order.

At the same time, Theodoric gratified the ruling passion of the Italians for games in the circus; and Ennodius, the Anonymus, and Cassodorus, are unanimous in praising him for reviving the gladiators. From their pages, we learn that he provided shows and pantomimes, that he endeavoured to shield the senators from the abusive jests of the comedians, and that he brought charioteers from Milan for the Consul Felix. But, in the eyes of his contemporaries, the most striking of all Theodoric's characteristics seems to have been his taste for monuments, for making improvements at Rome and Ravenna, and for works of restoration of every kind. Such a taste, indeed, was very remarkable in a barbarian. According to the Anonymus he was a great builder. At Ravenna, the aqueducts were restored by his order; and the plan of the palace which he constructed there has been preserved for a mosaic in Sant' Apollinare Nuovo. At Verona, also, he erected baths and an aqueduct. Cassiodorus tells us how the king sought out skilled workers in marble to complete the Basilica of Hercules; how he ordered the Patrician Symmachus to restore the theatre of Pompey; how he bade Artemidorus rebuild the walls of Rome, and how he desired Argolicus to repair the drains in that city. We find him, moreover, requesting Festus to send any fallen marbles from the Pincian Hill to Ravenna; and giving a portico, or piece of ground surrounded by a colonnade, to the Patrician Albinus, in order that he may build houses on it. Count Suna received directions to collect broken pieces of marble, in order that they might be used in wall-building; while the magistrates of a tributary town were required to send to Ravenna columns, and any stones from ruins that had remained unused. In fact, Ennodius' statement that "he rejuvenated Rome and Italy in their hideous old age by amputating their mutilated members," is perfectly correct in spite of its rhetorical style. Not a few of his orders, moreover, bear witness to a care for the future: the Goths of Dertona, for instance, and of Castellum Verruca, were commanded to build fortifications; the citizens of Arles were directed to repair the towers that were falling into decay upon their walls; and the inhabitants of Feltre were ordered to build a wall round their new city. He even looked forward to his own death, building that strange mausoleum now become the Church of Santa Maria della Rotonda, whose monolithic roof is still an object of wonder.

Ennodius also tells us that Theodoric encouraged a revival of learning, nor is this eulogy by any means undeserved, for a real literary renaissance did in fact take place during his reign. In addition to Cassiodorus himself, to Ennodius, who was at once an enthusiastic lover of literature, an orator, a poet, and a letter-writer, and to Boethius, the most illustrious and popular writer of his day, quite a number of other distinguished literary men flourished at that time. Rusticus Helpidius, for instance, the king's physician, has left a poem entitled the *Blessings of Christ*; Cornelius Maximianus wrote idyllic poetry; while Arator of Milan translated the Acts of the Apostles into two books of hexameters. The greatest poet of this period was Venantius Fortunatus, who became bishop of Poitiers; and mention should also be made of the lawyer Epiphanius, who wrote an abridgment of the ecclesiastical histories of Socrates, Sozomen, and Theodoret.

Theodoric was himself an Arian, yet he was always ready to extend his protection to the Catholic Church. Indeed, as we have already noticed, it was his policy to win over the bishops of northern Italy. Accordingly he granted complete liberty of worship to all Catholics; while so long as papal elections were quietly conducted, as in the cases of Gelasius and Anastasius II, he took no part in them. But should a pontifical or episcopal election lead to disturbances of any kind, more especially if such disturbances were likely to end in a schism, Theodoric at once intervened in them, in the character of arbitrator or judge. For he claimed to be *dominator rerum*, that is to say the sovereign, responsible for the maintenance of order in the State; the successor, indeed, of the Caesars, who had always considered the task of maintaining the integrity of the faith as their most especial prerogative. And he assumed such a position at the time of the Laurentian schism.

In the year 498, two priests, Laurentius and Symmachus, had been simultaneously elected by rival parties to the Roman See. As neither prelate was willing to resign his claim to profit by the election, the dispute was referred to the Gothic king, who decided that whichever candidate had obtained a majority of votes should be proclaimed bishop of Rome. This condition being fulfilled by Symmachus, he was accordingly recognised as Pope, while Laurentius was given the bishopric of Nuceria as a compensation. By this arrangement peace, it was believed, was again established; and, in the year 500, Theodoric paid a visit to Rome, where he was enthusiastically received by Pope, Senate and people.

But the schism was by no means at an end. On the contrary, the enemies of Symmachus lost no time in renewing their attack with redoubled vigour; and accusations of adultery, of alienating church property, and of celebrating Easter on the wrong date, were successively brought against the Pope. Theodoric summoned the accused Pontiff to appear before him, and when Symmachus refused to comply with this command, the case was referred to an assembly, over which Peter of Altinum presided as visitor. No less than five synods were convoked for the purpose of settling this question, and it was eventually terminated by the acquittal and rehabilitation of Symmachus.

The debates held in these ecclesiastical assemblies were very stormy. The partisans on both sides appear to have been equally unwilling to give way, nor did they scruple to promote their cause by exciting riots in the streets, or by slanderous libels. Both parties indeed seem to have been mainly occupied with justifying themselves in Theodoric's eyes, in order that they might obtain his support; in fact, from the second Synod onwards, the friends of Laurentius adopted the tactics of attempting to prove that Symmachus and his adherents had disobeyed the orders of the king.

In every phase of this controversy, so full of information respecting the relations of Church and State at that period, Theodoric, it will be seen, occupies an important place. In Rome, troubles were temporarily smoothed over by his presence, while his departure, on the other hand, proved the signal for a fresh outbreak. Appeals for a peaceful settlement, expressed with increasing vigour, and mingled with reproofs of increasing sternness, fill his letters at this time. When the hostile parties, unable to come to any decision on their own account, referred the question to their sovereign, he reminded them of their duty in the following severe words: "We order you to decide this matter which is of God, and which we have confided to your care, as it seems good to you. Do not expect any judgment from us, for it is your duty to settle this question." Later, as a verdict still failed to make its appearance, he writes again: "I order you to obey the command of God." And this time he was obeyed.

The fact that Theodoric was himself an Arian never seems to have limited his influence in any way during this long quarrel, so celebrated in the history of the Church. His prerogative as king gave him a legitimate authority in ecclesiastical matters, nor does that authority ever appear to have been called in question on the ground that he was a heretic. On the contrary, we find him giving his sanction to canons and decrees, exactly in the same manner as his predecessors had done in the days of the dual Empire. But, though his words were sometimes haughty and peremptory, he was careful not to impose his own will in any matters concerning faith or discipline; indeed the most extreme action that can be laid to his charge is the introduction into the Roman Synods of two Gothic functionaries, Gudila and Bedculphas, for the purpose of seeing that his instructions were not neglected.

A similar wise impartiality, mingled with firmness, distinguished his dealings with the clergy. When a priest named Aurelianus was fraudulently deprived of a portion of his inheritance, restitution was made to him by order of the king. He assisted the churches to recover their endowments; he appreciated good priests, and did them honour. Occasionally, indeed, he deposed a bishop for a time, on account of some action having been brought against him, but he always had him reinstated in his see as soon as he had proved his innocence. When he desired to give some compensation to the inhabitants of a country over which his troops had marched, he placed the matter in the hands of Bishop Severus, because that prelate was known to estimate damages fairly; and when a dispute arose between the clergy and the town of Sarsena he ordered the case to be tried in the bishop's court, unless the prelate himself should prefer to refer it to the king's tribunal. Finally, he made it a rule that ecclesiastical cases were only to be tried before ecclesiastical judges.

The foreign policy of Theodoric was conducted in the same masterly manner as his home government, or his dealings with the Church. He appears to have exercised a kind of protectorate over the barbarian tribes upon his frontiers, especially over those of the Arian persuasion, nor did he hesitate to impose his will upon them, if necessary, by force of arms. As he had only daughters he was obliged to consider the question of his successor; and the marriages which he arranged for his children, or other relations, were accordingly planned with a view to procuring political alliances. Of his daughters the eldest, Arevagni, was married to Alaric, king of the Visigoths; the second, Theudegotha, became the wife of Sigismund, son of Gundobad, king of the Burgundians; and the third, Amalasuntha, was given in marriage to one of Theodoric's own race, the Amal Eutharic. Other alliances were formed by the marriage of his sister Amalafrida to Thrasamund, king of the Vandals, and of another sister, Amalaberga, to Hermanfred, king of the Thuringians; while Theodoric himself wedded Childeric's daughter Audefleda, the sister of Clovis.

These alliances were all made with the definite object of extending Theodoric's sphere of action (*sic, per circuitum placuit omnibus gentibus*, says the Anonymus); but when, as for example in the case of the Franks, they failed to attain the end desired by the king, they were never permitted to hamper schemes of an entirely contrary nature.

A simple enumeration of Theodoric's wars is alone sufficient to prove the firmness of his will. When he found that Noricum and Pannonia, two provinces on the Italian frontier, were not to be trusted, he attacked and killed a chieftain of freebooters, named Mundo, in the former province. As the Emperor Anastasius was supporting Mundo, and had recently despatched a fleet to plunder on the coasts of Calabria and Apulia, such an attack gave Theodoric an opportunity of asserting his independence. Moreover, in order to render his demonstration even more effective, he collected a fleet of his own, which he sent to cruise in the Adriatic. At the same time, he took Pannonia from the Gepid chief Trasaric, and thus effectually secured his north-eastern frontiers. Those on the north-west next engaged his attention, and here he protected the Alemanni from the attacks of Clovis, and eventually settled them in the province of Rhaetia. Finally he took advantage of the wars between the Franks and the Burgundians to secure the passes of the Graian Alps.

Theodoric had striven to prevent hostilities from breaking out between the Franks and the Visigoths; but after Alaric's death at the battle of Vouillé (507), he found himself obliged to take the latter people under his own protection. In the war that ensued, Ibbas, one of his generals, defeated the eldest son of Clovis near Arles (511) ; took possession of Provence; secured Septimania for the Visigoths; and established Amalaric in Spain. Among more distant nations we find the Esthonians on the shores of the Baltic paying him a tribute of amber, while a deposed prince of Scandinavia found a refuge at his Court.

History, as may be seen from these events, fully corroborates the legends in which Theodoric is represented as a protector of barbarian interests, and chief patron of the Teutonic races. In the Nibelungenlied, for instance, we find him occupying a distinguished place under the name of Dietrich of Bern (Theodoric of Verona). At the time of his death his dominions included Italy, Sicily, Dalmatia, Noricum, the greater part of what is now Hungary, the two Rhaetias (Tyrol and the Grisons), Lower Germany as far north as Ulm, and Provence. Indeed, if his supremacy over the Goths in Spain be also taken into account, it will be seen that he had succeeded in re-establishing the ancient Western Empire for his own benefit, with the exceptions of Africa, Britain, and two-thirds of Gaul.

So far as we have examined it, Theodoric's government has been found invariably broad-minded and liberal, but it was destined to undergo a complete change during the latter years of his reign. Whether this change was the consequence of a relapse into barbarism, or whether, as seems more probable, it must be attributed to the persecution under which the Arians were suffering in every part of the Empire, is not easy to determine, for no definite information on this point is to be found in any of the texts. In any case, however, there can be no doubt that it was the religious question that produced this complete change of policy. On this point the Anonymus is perfectly clear; and if we disregard the severity and the cruelty of his punishments, and at the same time make due allowance for intrigues of the Byzantine Court, and of the Church itself, the precise nature of which cannot be determined, it does not appear that the king was himself to blame.[1]

During his reign we find the Jews enjoying an extraordinary amount of protection; and, in one of his edicts, he testifies with what obedience this people had accepted the legal position assigned to them by the Roman law. His son-in-law Eutharic, however, appears to have

---

[1] The following saying of Theodoric's should not be forgotten: "We cannot impose a religion by force, since no one can be compelled to believe against his will." Cass. *Var.* ii. 27.

been addicted to persecution; and during his consulship the Christians of Ravenna made an attempt to force all the Jews in their city to submit to the rite of baptism. As the Jews refused to comply, the Christians flung them into the water, and in spite of the king's decrees, and the orders of Bishop Peter, attacked and set fire to the synagogues. Upon this, the Jews complained to the king at Verona, who ordered the Christians to rebuild the synagogues at their own expense. This command was carried out, but not before a certain amount of disturbance had aroused Theodoric's suspicions; and in consequence the inhabitants of Ravenna were forbidden to carry arms of any kind, even the smallest knife being prohibited.

While these events were in progress, in the year 523, the Emperor Justin proscribed Arianism throughout the Empire. Such an action was a direct menace to the Goths, and Theodoric felt it very acutely. The painful impression which it produced on him was probably much increased by the fact that Symmachus' successors in the papal chair had not been as tolerant as their predecessor; while one of them in particular, John I, had shewn a most bitter enmity towards heresy. We have no certain knowledge as to whether the Senate was in sympathy with Theodoric on this occasion, or whether it approved of Justin's measure, but the most probable theory seems to be that the Curia was on Justin's side, and that Theodoric moreover was aware that this was the case. At any rate, when the Senator Albinus was denounced by Cyprian for carrying on intrigues with Byzantium the accusation found ready credence at Court. The Anonymus declares, besides, that the king was angry with the Romans; and it is difficult to see why he should have been thus angry unless the Romans had been approving of Justin's religious decrees. On the other hand, if any plot had existed in the real sense of the term, it is not probable that such a man as Boethius, the master of the offices, that is to say one of the chief officers of the Crown, would have endeavoured to shield Albinus by saying, "Cyprian's accusation is false, but if Albinus has written to Constantinople he has done so with my consent and that of the whole Senate." He might perhaps have spoken in such a manner for the purpose of expressing his own and his colleagues' approval of a religious decree promulgated by a sovereign to whom they owed allegiance. Boethius indeed had himself just published a work against Arianism, entitled *De Trinitate*, but it does not seem likely that he would have talked in this fashion had a conspiracy really been brewing. In any case, he was at once thrown into prison; and is said to have composed his work *De Consolatione* while in captivity. In the end, after a brief trial, he was put to death with every refinement of cruelty, while not long afterwards his father-in-law, Symmachus, met with a similar fate.

Theodoric, indeed, understood very well that his whole life-work was likely to be compromised by this readiness on the part of his subjects to accept Justin's edict. For what would become of his authority if it became the fashion to criticise him on account of his faith ?. It was in the hope of finding some remedy for this situation that he summoned Pope John to Ravenna, and from thence despatched him, accompanied by five bishops and four senators, on an embassy to Constantinople. The king charged this mission, among other things, with the task of requiring the Emperor to reinstate the outcast Arians within the pale of the Church. But the Emperor, though willing enough to make concessions on any other subject, would concede nothing to the Arians, and the mission was forced to leave Constantinople without obtaining any redress on this point. As for Pope John, he died almost immediately after his return to Italy, and as his biographers tell us that he worked numerous miracles after his death, we may conclude that this sectarian quarrel must have been very acute. The failure of this embassy made Theodoric so furious that he allowed an edict to be published during the consulship of Olybrius by Symmachus, the chief official in the *Scholae*, which stated that all Catholics were to be ejected from their churches, on the seventh day of the Kalends of September. But on the very day fixed upon by his minister for the execution of this act of banishment, the king died, apparently from an attack of dysentery, in the year 526.

The Byzantine historian Procopius — though he was himself an opponent of the king's — has summed up Theodoric and his work in the following verdict, which remains true in spite of the errors committed by him during the latter years of his reign. "His manner of ruling over his subjects was worthy of a great Emperor; for he maintained justice, made good laws, protected his country from invasion, and gave proof of extraordinary prudence and valour."

Theodoric's work was not destined to survive his death. He left a daughter, Amalasuntha, the widow of Eutharic, who was not unlike him; and who now became guardian to her son Athalaric, to whom his grandfather had bequeathed the crown on his death-bed. She had been educated entirely on Roman lines, and understood the value of her father's work; but she had to reckon with the Goths. During Theodoric's lifetime this people had done nothing to excite attention, and had lived side by side with the Romans without shewing any desire to obtain the upper hand; but under the regency of a woman we find that they soon aspired to play a more important part. Their first step was to take Athalaric from the guardianship of his mother. He died, however, in 534. Amalasuntha was now confronted once again with her former difficulties; and in the hope of overcoming them, she attempted to share the crown with Theodoric's nephew Theodahad, a man of weak and evil character. The new king's first care was to get rid of Amalasuntha, and he had her shut up on an island, in the lake of

Bolsena. From her prison, she appealed to Justinian for assistance. When this came to Theodahad's ears, he had her strangled.

But her cry for help had not been unheeded. By the death of Anastasius the situation at Constantinople had been completely changed; it was no longer the imperial policy to allow Italy to be governed by a vassal, more especially if that vassal were an Arian; and political and religious motives alike urged Justinian to intervene. A struggle began accordingly which was to last from 536 to 553, which was to devastate Italy with fire and bloodshed, and which ultimately opened the door for a new invasion by the Lombards.

CHAPTER XVI

THE EASTERN PROVINCES FROM ARCADIUS
TO ANASTASIUS

By the death of Theodosius the Eastern throne passed to his incapable elder son, Arcadius, then 17 years old, while the practical administration was in the hands of the praetorian praefect, Rufinus of Aquitaine, a man of vigour and ability who in the pursuit of ambition and avarice was not limited by scruples. Under these circumstances a conflict was likely to arise between Rufinus and Stilicho, who was the guardian of the Western Emperor Honorius, and husband of Theodosius' niece, who also asserted that Theodosius had on his death-bed committed both his sons to his care. Rufinus proposed to counterbalance the advantage which his rival possessed in his connexion with the imperial family by marrying Arcadius to his own daughter; but, unfortunately for him, he had a rival at Court in the eunuch Eutropius, a former slave who had risen to the position of *praepositus sacri cubiculi*; who now profited by the praefect's absence to thwart his scheme. Lucian, whom Rufinus had made count of the East, had refused a request of Eucherius, the Emperor's great-uncle; and, upon Arcadius complaining of this, the praefect, to shew his own loyalty, made a hasty journey to Antioch and put Lucian to a cruel death. Meanwhile Eutropius induced Arcadius to betroth himself to Eudoxia, daughter of Bauto the Frank, who had been brought up by a son of Promotus, an enemy of Rufinus; who thus had the mortification of seeing his master united not to his own daughter but to one who from her upbringing would be bitterly opposed to him (27 Apr. 395).

The inferiority of Rufinus was increased by the fact that the best of the Eastern troops had accompanied Theodosius to the West, and of these only some of the less efficient had been sent back. The Visigothic *foederati* had however returned to Moesia; and their leader Alaric, who was now proclaimed king, was quick to profit by the weakness of the government. Professing indignation at not being appointed *magister militum*, he invaded Thrace and advanced to Constantinople, while Rufinus, having also to meet an incursion of Caucasian Huns into Asia Minor and Syria (July), where Antioch was threatened and Old

Tyre abandoned by its citizens, had no forces to oppose to him. He therefore went to the Gothic camp, and, after some negotiations, Alaric withdrew to Macedonia, and after a check from local forces at the Peneus passed into Thessaly. Stilicho, who, besides desiring to overthrow Rufinus, wished to re-unite eastern Illyricum to the Western power, treated this as a pretext for interference; and, starting in early spring, he marched with considerable forces to Thessaly, and met the Goths in a wide plain. Probably, however, he did not wish to crush them; and, after some months had been spent in skirmishes or negotiations, Rufinus, who feared Stilicho more than Alaric, sent him in the Emperor's name an order to evacuate the dominions of Arcadius and send back the Eastern troops. To break openly with the East at this time did not suit Stilicho's purpose; and, as the Eastern forces, which comprised a large Gothic contingent, were devoted to him, he could attain his primary object in another way. He therefore returned at once, while the Eastern army under Gaïnas the Goth marched to Constantinople. In accordance with custom the Emperor, accompanied by Rufinus, came out to meet the troops, and the soldiers, at a signal from Gaïnas, fell upon the praefect and cut him in pieces (27 Nov.).

The Emperor's chief adviser was now Eutropius, who appropriated a large part of Rufinus' property and procured the banishment of the two most distinguished generals in the East, Abundantius and Timasius (396), while he entrusted positions of power to such obscure men as Hosius the cook and Leo the wool-comber. He also gained much obloquy by selling offices, though as the prices were fixed and there was no system of public loans, this was only a convenient method of raising money. As a eunuch, he could not hold any state office; but for this he partly compensated by transferring some of the powers of the praefect to the master of the offices and by interfering in matters altogether out-side the functions of a chamberlain. Thus he is said to have acted as a judge, probably on a special commission, and to have gone on embassies to the Goths and Huns, from which he returned with military pomp. Finally he was made a patrician and assumed the consulship (399), though his name was not admitted to the Western *Fasti*. At first he was necessarily on good terms with the army, and therefore with Stilicho; but he was no more inclined than Rufinus had been to allow the Western regent to direct Eastern affairs, and the previous position therefore soon recurred.

After Stilicho's retreat Greece lay at Alaric's mercy, for, perhaps because the army was too much under Stilicho's influence, no force was sent against him, and through the unguarded Thermopylae he marched plundering into Boeotia. Thebes indeed was too strong to take, and Athens he entered only under a capitulation. Megara however was taken, and, the Isthmus being left undefended, Corinth, Argos, and Sparta also. During 396 Peloponnesus lay under his heel; but early

CH. XVI.

in 397 ¹ Stilicho, secure in the support of the Eastern army, thought that the time had come for another campaign. This time he came by sea to Corinth, and, marching westwards, blockaded the Goths-at Pholoe in Elis. But Eutropius opened negotiations with Gildo, count of Africa, whose loyalty had long been doubtful, to induce him to transfer his allegiance to Arcadius; and, the threatening state of affairs making it necessary for Stilicho to return, he allowed Alaric to withdraw to Epirus, probably on the understanding that he would keep the Eastern Court occupied. Eutropius however preferred to satisfy him by the post of *magister militum* in Illyricum, and on these terms peace was concluded. Such being the relations between the two Courts, it is not surprising to find that some of the eunuch's enemies conspired with the Gothic soldiers, the allies of Stilicho, against his life, and that, with the fate of Rufinus before him, he tried to prevent such plots by a law of extraordinary severity (4 Sept.). Perhaps for the same reason that no army was sent against Alaric no support was given to Gildo; but his revolt occupied Stilicho's attention during most of 398. The pacification of Africa was however soon followed by Eutropius' fall.

Gaïnas, now *magister militum*, had been strengthening his own position by filling the army with Goths from Moesia; and in spring 399 an opportunity for action presented itself. Tribigild, commander of the Gothic colonists in Phrygia, having been refused a donative by Eutropius, revolted and ravaged the country, upon which Eutropius offered the money; but Tribigild raised his demands and insisted upon the eunuch's deposition. Gaïnas, with Leo, the satellite of Eutropius, was sent against him; but, while Leo advanced toward the disturbed district, Gaïnas remained at the Hellespont. Tribigild on hearing of Leo's approach marched through Pisidia into Pamphylia, where a large part of his army was cut to pieces by a rustic force under Valentinus, a citizen of Selga, and the rest blockaded between the Eurymedon and the Melas. Leo moved to the support of the local force: but, as he was too indolent and dissolute to maintain discipline, Tribigild was able by an unexpected attack to make his way through, while the disorderly force scattered in all directions, Leo himself perishing in the flight. Tribigild then returned to Phrygia, which he again plundered. Nor was he the only enemy with whom the Empire had to contend; for, besides the constant incursions of the desert tribes into Egypt and Libya, the Huns were ravaging Thrace, and Vram Shapuh of Armenia was, at the instigation of the Persian king, attempting to annex the five satrapies north of the Tigris.²

Accordingly Gaïnas with much show of reason represented to Arcadius that his best course was to grant Tribigild's demand; and,

---

¹ I cannot resist Koch's argument for 397 rather than 396. The connexion with Gildo's revolt is then obvious.

² I take this to be the meaning of "Mesopotamia" in Mos. *Chor.* III. 52.

as Eudoxia urged the same, his consent was easily obtained. Eutropius was deposed from his office, and, though he had abolished by legal enactment the right of sanctuary possessed by the churches, fled to the altar of St Sophia, where the bishop, John Chrysostom, who owed his appointment to the eunuch, made use of his presence to preach on the vanity of earthly things, but resisted all attempts to remove him. Finally he left the church on a promise that his life should be spared, but was deprived of property and honours, and banished to Cyprus (July or Aug.).[1] As however Gaïnas insisted upon the necessity of his death, he was, on the pretext that the promise applied only to Con- stantinople, brought back to Chalcedon, tried on a charge of using imperial ornaments, and beheaded (Nov. or Dec.).[2]

The fall of Eutropius had been effected by a combination between Eudoxia and Gaïnas; and during the absence of the Goth, who had returned to Phrygia, the Empress secured the appointment of Aurelianus to the praefecture in preference to his brother Caesarius, who was supported by Gaïnas. After Eutropius' death she further had herself proclaimed Augusta (9 Jan. 400); and by an innovation which called forth a protest from Honorius her busts were sent round the provinces like those of emperors. But Gaïnas had not designed to set Eudoxia in the place of Eutropius; accordingly he sent Tribigild, with whom he had joined forces, to Lampsacus, while he himself returned to Chalcedon, and demanded the surrender of three of the principal supporters of the empress, Aurelianus the praefect, Saturninus an ex-consul, and Count John, her chief favourite. Resistance was useless ; and Aurelianus and Saturninus crossed to Chalcedon, while John hid himself, probably in a church; but his hiding-place was discovered, and the bishop's enemies afterwards asserted that he had betrayed him. The three men were ordered to prepare for death; but, when the executioner's sword was at their necks, Gaïnas stayed his hand and had them conveyed by sea towards the Adri- atic, perhaps intending to place them in the hands of Stilicho or Alaric. He next demanded a meeting with the Emperor; which took place at Chalcedon, where they gave mutual oaths of good faith in the church of St Euphemia. Both the Gothic leaders then crossed to Europe. Caesarius was made praefect, and in consequence of the recent troubles was com- pelled to increase the taxation; but in systematising the sale of offices by limiting the tenure of each he seems to have performed an act of advantage to the State and justice to the purchasers. Meanwhile Gaïnas was so distributing the Roman troops in the city as to place them at the mercy of the Goths; and then, thinking his will law, he asked that a

---

[1] The change in the praefecture, which must be connected with his fall, seems from the dates in the Code to have occurred at this time.

[2] Claudian heard reports of the movements of Yezdegerd (who dated his years from 14 Aug. 399) before hearing of Eutropius' death, while Asterius knew of it on 1 Jan.

church within the walls should be given to the Arians.   This time however the strong orthodoxy of Arcadius and the influence of the bishop
caused the demand to be refused.   The violent hostility aroused by these
events made men believe that the Goths intended to attack the palace;
while they on their side were seized with a panic which led them to
expect an attack from forces which did not exist.   Accordingly Gaïnas,
alleging ill-health, retired to the suburban church of St John, instructing
his men to come out singly and join him.   After the greater part had
left the city, a trivial occurrence brought on a scuffle between the Goths
and the citizens, who attacked the already panic-stricken barbarians with
any weapons they could find, and at last the gates were shut, and the
Goths, enclosed within the city, without cohesion and without leaders,
offered little resistance and were mercilessly massacred, while Arcadius
found courage to declare Gaïnas a public enemy and send his guards to
support the populace.   Next day the survivors, who had fled to a church
that the bishop had given to the orthodox Goths, were surrounded by
the soldiers; and, though none dared to attack them in the church,
the roof was stripped off and burning wood thrown in until all perished,
in spite of the appeals of Caesarius for a capitulation (12 July).

The Roman troops were now collected and placed under Fravitta,
a loyal pagan Goth who had distinguished himself in the time of
Theodosius.   The attempts of Gaïnas on the Thracian cities failed,
Tribigild was killed, and lack of provisions compelled the Goths to
withdraw to the Chersonese in order to cross to Asia; but Fravitta had
already placed a fleet on the Hellespont to intercept them.   They were
however forced to attempt the passage in rafts, and, these being sunk,
most of them were drowned, while Gaïnas with the survivors retreated
across the Danube, where he was attacked and killed by Uldin the Hun
(23 Dec.),[1] who sent his head to Constantinople, where it was carried
through the city (3 Jan. 401).   Shortly before the victory Aurelianus and
the other hostages escaped from their guards in Epirus, and returned to
the capital; and early in 401 Caesarius was deposed and imprisoned, and
Aurelianus restored.   Some deserters and fugitive slaves, who continued
to ravage Thrace, were put down by Fravitta.   But he was accused of
not pressing his advantage against the Goths, and, though acquitted,
incurred Eudoxia's enmity, and afterwards fell a victim to the machinations of her satellites.

Stilicho's hopes of directing Eastern affairs through the army were
thus destroyed; and soon afterwards the government was delivered from
Alaric, who, having exhausted eastern Illyricum, invaded Italy, and
after an indecisive battle at Pollentia (402) was established in western
Illyricum as *magister militum*, probably on the understanding that he
would help Stilicho to annex eastern Illyricum when opportunity arose.

In other directions things went less fortunately. By the annihilation

[1] Seeck in Pauly-Wissowa, ii. 1150.

of the Goths the East was left almost without an army; and the Isaurian robbers terrorised eastern Asia Minor and Syria, where they took Seleucia (Feb. 403), and even crossed to Cyprus. Arbazacius the Armenian indeed gained some successes; but he was suspected of corruption and recalled, though by the influence of the empress he escaped punishment (404).

The chief power in the State was now Eudoxia; but there was one man who dared to oppose her, John Chrysostom. As early as 401 he offended her by complaining of some act of oppression; and not only was he constantly preaching against the prevailing luxury and dissipation among the ladies of fashion of whom she was leader, but he used the names "Herodias" and "Jezebel," and in one of his sermons employed the word ἀδοξία, with an application that could not be mistaken. His popularity was so great that she would hardly have attacked him on this ground alone; but, with the help of the ecclesiastical jealousy of the bishop of Alexandria and the discontent which his high-handed proceedings in the cause of discipline aroused among some of the clergy, she procured his deposition (c. July 403). Popular clamour however and a building collapse in the imperial chamber frightened her into recalling him after a few days and excusing herself by throwing the blame upon others. This reconciliation did not last long. Two months later a statue of Eudoxia was erected on a spot adjoining the church of St Irene during divine service, and John, regarding the festivities as an insult to the church, preached a violent sermon against those responsible for them, which the empress took as an attack upon herself. The bishops were therefore again assembled; but the proceedings were protracted, and Arcadius, who in religious matters had something like a will of his own, was hard to move. On 20 June 404 however the bishop was finally expelled. That night some of his fanatical partisans set fire to St Sophia, which was destroyed with the adjoining Senate-house, in which many ancient works of art perished.

Less than four months afterwards Eudoxia died from a miscarriage (6 Oct.); and the period of active misrule from which the East had suffered since 395 came to an end. The praefecture was now entrusted to the capable hands of Anthemius: but the government had still no force to repress the incursions of the Libyan tribes or the Isaurian brigands, whose raids continued to the end of the reign. The relations with the West had been further embittered by the affair of John Chrysostom; and, while Stilicho lived, a good understanding was impossible. After delays not easy to explain Stilicho prepared to carry out his compact with Alaric, and, as an earnest of his intention, closed the ports against Eastern ships, while Alaric invaded Epirus. But, hearing that the usurper Constantine had crossed to Gaul, Stilicho again postponed his Eastern expedition, and Alaric in anger evacuated the dominions of Arcadius and threatened Italy. At this juncture Arcadius died (1 May

CH. XVI.

408), leaving a son, Theodosius, aged seven, who since 10 Jan. 402 had been his father's colleague, and three (perhaps four) daughters; and Stilicho, thinking the time come to carry out his old project of bringing the East under his rule, proposed to send Alaric to Gaul and go himself to Constantinople as the representative of Honorius; but a hostile party secured the Emperor's ear, and he was put to death (Aug. 408). The ports were then opened and amity restored.

The care of the Emperor's person was in the hands of Antiochus, a eunuch with Persian connexions; but the direction of affairs fell to Anthemius, whose chief adviser was the sophist Troilus; and the period of his administration was one of the most fortunate in the history of the East. The danger from the West had been removed by Stilicho's fall; and on the eastern side the best relations were maintained with Yezdegerd the Persian king, with whom a commercial treaty was made. The military power of the Empire had suffered too much to be quickly restored; but we hear no more of Isaurian raids, and it was found possible to send a small force to support Honorius against Alaric. It was only however by a combination with subject tribes that the Huns were driven across the Danube, while their tributaries the Sciri were captured in vast numbers, and enslaved or settled as *coloni* in Asia Minor (409). To prevent such incursions the fleet on the Danube was strengthened (412). Other salutary measures were the relief given to the taxpayers of Illyricum and the East (413–14), the restoration of the fortifications of the Illyrian cities (412), and the re-organisation of the corn supply of Constantinople (409). But the work for which the name of Anthemius was most remembered is the wall built from the Propontis to the Golden Horn to enclose the portion of the city that had grown up outside the wall of Constantine, a wall which substantially exists to this day (413).

In 414 the administration of Anthemius came to an end, probably by death; and on 4 July Pulcheria, the daughter of Arcadius, was proclaimed Augusta, a title that had not been granted to an emperor's sister since Trajan's time; and henceforth, though only two years older than Theodosius, she exercised the functions of regent, and her bust was placed in the Senate-house with those of the emperors (30 Dec.). At the same time Antiochus was removed from the palace.

The Court of Pulcheria was a strange contrast to her mother's. For political rather than religious reasons she took a vow of perpetual virginity and induced her sisters to do the same, and the princesses spent their time in spinning and devout exercises. She herself was a ready speaker and writer in Greek and Latin; and she had her brother trained in rhetoric, as well as horsemanship and the use of arms, in ceremony and deportment, and the observances of religion. Hence he grew up a strict observer of ecclesiastical rules, a fair scholar with a special interest in natural science and medicine, a keen huntsman, an excellent penman, exemplary in private life, mild and good-tempered; but, as everything likely to make him a capable ruler was excluded from his education, the Emperor remained all his life a puppet in the hands of his sister, his wife, and his eunuchs.

The transference of the regency to a girl of 15 could not be effected without a change in the methods of administration; and it is therefore not surprising to find the government accused of fiscal oppression, while the sale of offices, which was restricted under Anthemius, became again a matter of public notoriety. In Alexandria, which, being almost equally divided between Christians, Jews, and heathens, was always turbulent, the change gave occasion for a serious outbreak. After prolonged rioting between Jews and Christians the bishop Cyril instigated his followers to expel the Jews. This the praefect Orestes reported to the Emperor, while Cyril sent his own account; and, Orestes refusing to yield, some fanatical monks attacked and stoned him. The chief perpetrator was tortured to death, whereupon Cyril treated him as a martyr, and both parties appealed to Constantinople. It now came to be believed among Cyril's partisans that Orestes was acting under the influence of the celebrated mathematician and philosopher, Hypatia, who was in constant communication with him: accordingly a party of *parabolani* (sick-attendants) pulled her from her chariot, dragged her into the church called Caesarium, and beat or scraped her to death with tiles (Mar. 415). At first the government acted with some vigour. No personal punishment was inflicted, but the *parabolani* were limited to 500, and the selection made subject to the approbation of the Augustal and praetorian praefects, while they were forbidden to appear in the council-house or law-courts or at public spectacles (29 Sept. 416). It was not long however before the influence or bribes of Cyril procured the restoration of the freedom of selection (3 Feb. 418). The increase of anti-pagan feeling was also shewn by a law excluding pagans from high administrative office and from the army (7 Dec. 416). Other disturbances were the rebellion of Count Plintha in Palestine (418), an attack on the city praefect Aëtius (23 Feb. 419), and a mutiny in the East (420). In Armenia, Yezdegerd having appointed his brother as king, the Roman portion of the country was definitely annexed and placed under a count (415–16).

It was now time for Theodosius to marry; and it was Pulcheria's object to prevent the choice of a wife with powerful connexions, who would be likely to endanger her ascendancy. She had by some means made the acquaintance of Athenais, daughter of the Athenian sophist Leontius, a woman of high education and literary ability, who had come to Constantinople through a dispute with her brothers about their father's property. As a friendless girl dependent on herself, yet fitted by education for the part of an empress, she seemed exactly suited for the purpose. The Augusta therefore introduced her to Theodosius, who declared himself willing to make her his wife; Athenais made no objection to accepting Christianity, and was baptized under the name of Eudocia, Pulcheria standing sponsor; and on 7 June 421 the marriage was celebrated. The new empress bore no malice against her brothers, but summoned them to Court, where one became praefect of Illyricum and the other master of the offices; in this however she perhaps shewed worldly wisdom rather than Christian charity. After the birth of a daughter she received the title of Augusta (2 Jan. 423).

About the time of the marriage the peace with Persia was broken. Yezdegerd had always shewn himself friendly to the Christians; but at the end of his reign the fanatical act of a bishop drove him to severe measures. Some Christians fled to Roman territory, and when their surrender was refused, the position became so critical that permission was given to the inhabitants of the exposed provinces to fortify their own lands (5 May 420). After Yezdegerd's violent death (late in 420) a more extended persecution was begun by Warahran V; and the Court of Constantinople began the war by sending the Alan Ardaburius through Roman Armenia into Arzanene, where he defeated the Persian Narsai (Aug. or Sept 421), who retreated to Nisibis. Ardaburius with numerous prisoners advanced to Amida to prevent an invasion of Mesopotamia; and here, as the prisoners were starving, Bishop Acacius melted the church plate, ransomed them with the price, gave them provisions, and sent them home. Ardaburius then besieged Nisibis, and Warahran prepared to march to its relief, while he sent Al Mundhir, sheikh of Al Hira, to invade Syria. Many of the Arabs were however drowned in the Euphrates, and the rest defeated by the general Vitianus. On the king's approach Ardaburius burnt his engines and retreated, and the Persians, crossing the frontier, vainly attacked Rhesaina for over a month; but, though the Romans gained some successes, no decisive victory was obtained, and Theodosius thought it best to propose terms. Warahran was also inclined for peace; but, wishing to gain a success first, he ordered an attack upon a Roman force, while he kept the ambassador with him. The Romans were surprised; but during the battle another division under Procopius, the son-in-law of Anthemius, unexpectedly appeared, and the Persians, taken on both sides, were defeated. Warahran then took up the negotiations in earnest; and, on his undertaking to stop the persecution and each party binding itself not to receive the Arab subjects of the other, peace was made for 100 years (422). This victory was celebrated by Eudocia in an epic poem. It was probably a result of the transference of troops from Europe to meet the Persians that the Huns this year invaded Thrace, though in consequence of the prudent measures of Anthemius the Danubian frontier was rarely violated before 441. The provinces had however not recovered from the calamities of Arcadius' time, and constant remissions of taxation were necessary.

The relations with the West were again disturbed through the refusal of Theodosius to recognise the elevation of Constantius (421); and when after the death of Honorius (Aug. 423) the obscure John was proclaimed emperor in prejudice of the claims of the young Valentinian the son of Placidia, there was an open breach. When John's envoys arrived to ask for recognition, Theodosius threw them into prison. Placidia now received anew the title of Augusta (424), which Theodosius had before ignored, Valentinian was declared Caesar at Thessalonica, mother and son were sent to Italy with a large army under Ardaburius, his son Aspar, and Candidianus; and, John having been overthrown, Valentinian was invested with the empire (Oct. 425). The concord between the two divisions of the Empire was confirmed by the betrothal of Valentinian to Theodosius' daughter Eudoxia, and the victory celebrated by the building of the Golden Gate, through which the emperors made their formal entries into Constantinople. In 431, when Placidia needed assistance against the Vandals, an army under Aspar was sent to Africa; but Aspar returned three years later without success, probably after an understanding which made him ever after a friend of the Vandals.

In 427 some Ostrogoths who had seceded from the Huns were settled in Thrace, and other tribes were received in 433; while a raid was made by the Huns, and a more serious attack only prevented by abject submission to their demands (434). At sea a pirate fleet entered the Propontis, but in 438 the pirate Contradis was captured. At home stones were thrown at Theodosius in a riot after a famine in 431, and there were bitter complaints of the extortion of the eunuchs.

Two matters of internal administration deserve special mention—the codification of the law (438), and the foundation of a university at Constantinople as a counterpoise to the schools of Athens (27 Feb. 425). In this university there were 28 professors of Greek and Latin grammar and rhetoric, and two of law, but only one of philosophy, and all other public teaching in the city was forbidden.

Eudocia was at first of necessity subservient to her sister-in-law; but that she would always accept this position was not to be expected. A difference appeared at the time of the synod of Ephesus (431), when Pulcheria was victorious; but afterwards her influence declined, and at last a palace intrigue drove her to retire from court. Under Eudocia's patronage a large share in the administration fell to Cyrus, an Egyptian poet and philosopher, who became city-praefect in 435,[1] and in 439 combined this office with the praetorian praefecture. Cyrus was the first praefect who published decrees in Greek, and he also distinguished himself by renovating the buildings of the city, especially by an extension of the sea-wall to join the wall of Anthemius, which the capture of Carthage by the Vandals had made desirable (439). Antiochus, the emperor's old guardian, was restored to favour and made *praepositus*.

The capture of Carthage caused the despatch of a fleet to Sicily in

[1] I assign *Codex Just.* II. vii. 5 to this year.

441: but in consequence of an irruption of Huns into Illyricum the force was recalled in 442 and peace made; but not before the expedition had led to a war with Persia. Under the capable direction of Anatolius, the *magister militum per Orientem*, the defence of the eastern frontier had been strengthened by stricter rules of discipline in the army (25 Feb. 438) and by the building of the fortress of Theodosiopolis in Armenia. This last the new king, Yezdegerd II, probably considered a menace; and he therefore took advantage of the troubles in the West to begin war, crossing the frontier from Nisibis and sacking several towns, while another force raided Roman Armenia (441). He was however hampered by bad weather and threatened by the Ephthalites beyond the Caspian; hence, though the Romans had no army to oppose to him, Anatolius and Aspar by a large sum of money and a promise to surrender some Christian refugees persuaded him to make a truce for a year. As the troubles with the Ephthalites continued, this was followed by a definite peace on the terms that neither party should build a fort within a certain distance of the frontier, and the Romans should renew an undertaking made by Jovian to contribute to the defences of the Caucasian Gates. One of the last acts of Cyrus was to provide that the Armenian frontier lands should be held on condition of supplying horses, wagons, and pikemen for the army (26 June 441).

After her daughter's marriage (21 Oct. 437), for which Valentinian came to Constantinople, Eudocia went on pilgrimage to Jerusalem (438), and on the way gained much popularity at Antioch by a speech in which she boasted of her Greek blood. She returned in 439; and meanwhile some hostile influence seems to have been at work, for in 440 Paulinus, ex-master of the offices, was beheaded at Caesarea in Cappadocia on suspicion, as was popularly believed, of an intrigue with her, and soon afterwards she asked leave to retire to Jerusalem, and left Constantinople for ever (441?). With her fell Cyrus, who through the popular acclamation, "Constantine founded, Cyrus restored," had incurred the Emperor's jealousy. Being charged with paganism, he took orders to save his head, and was made bishop of Cotyaeum, where four bishops were said to have been murdered. By his discreet conduct he succeeded in retaining his see till the time of Leo, when on some unknown charge he was deprived and came back to Constantinople, where he remained in possession of large property. Antiochus was also deposed and compelled to take orders. Pulcheria returned to Court; but the chief influence was for the rest of the reign exercised by the eunuch Chrysaphius. Eudocia was not left in peace at Jerusalem; but Saturninus, count of the *domestici*, was sent to spy upon her, and for some reason beheaded two clergymen who attended upon her (444). She in revenge assassinated Saturninus and was deprived of her imperial train, though she still disposed of ample revenues, which she spent on the erection of churches and monasteries. She composed several poems, of which large portions are extant, and died in 460 (20 Oct.).

The good administration introduced by Anthemius had been in some measure maintained under the ascendancy of Pulcheria and Eudocia ; but under Chrysaphius the days of Arcadius seemed to have returned. The Huns overran Thrace and Illyricum, and the murder of the *magister militum* of Thrace, John the Vandal (apparently by order of Chrysaphius), did not strengthen the resistance. The Romans suffered a severe defeat (447), and Chrysaphius could only grant Attila's terms and send emissaries to assassinate him. In 447 the walls of Constantinople were shattered by an earthquake, and in consequence of the terror caused by the Huns the praefect Constantine rebuilt them in 60 days, and the Isaurians, who had renewed their raids in 441, were called in under their leader Zeno to defend the city. Zeno afterwards extorted the office of *magister militum per Orientem*, and demanded the surrender of Chrysaphius; and, though this was not granted, the danger from the Huns prevented an intended campaign against the marauders. Bands of Tzani, Saracens, and Caucasian Huns had invaded the Empire during the Persian war, and we hear of Saracen raids again several years later (448), while Yezdegerd shewed signs of a desire to renew hostilities. Libya too was again harrased by the frontier tribes, and the Vandals terrorised the Ionian sea.

On 26 July 450 Theodosius broke his spine by a fall from his horse while hunting, and died two days later. The appointment of a successor was left to the Augusta Pulcheria; and her choice fell upon Marcian, a veteran soldier from Thrace of high character who had held the post of *domesticus* (chief of the staff) to Aspar, to whose influence the selection must be ascribed. Pulcheria crowned Marcian in the presence of the Senate (24 Aug.), and gave him her hand in nominal marriage.

The first act of the new rulers was to put Chrysaphius to death. The sale of offices was prohibited, though it is unlikely that the prohibition was strictly carried out; and attempts were made to lighten the burden of taxation by a remission of arrears, by reducing the number of praetors to three and relieving non-resident senators from the burden of the office (18 Dec. 450), and by enacting that the consuls instead of squandering money on the populace should make a contribution towards the repair of the aqueducts (452), an obligation which was extended to honorary consuls by the Emperor Zeno. Marcian also put an end to a system under which the possessors of certain lands which had been sold by the State in the time of Valens escaped their share of taxation. The popularity of his rule is shewn by the words "Reign like Marcian," with which the citizens in 491 greeted Anastasius.

In external relations the reign was a fortunate one. As Attila was preparing for his western expedition, his demands ˙for money could safely be refused; and, when after his return he repeated them with threats, death prevented him from carrying these out (453). From Zeno, who was appealing to heathen support, the Emperor was delivered by his death following a fall from his horse. Envoys from the Armenian insurgents had come before Theodosius' death to ask for help; but Marcian refused to break the peace with Persia. With the Vandals also peace was maintained; for, though after the sack of Rome (455) Marcian tried to obtain the release of Eudoxia and her daughters, the possession of these hostages as well as Aspar's influence secured Gaiseric from attack. In Syria the *magister militum*, Aspar's son Ardaburius, was in 452 fighting with Arab raiders near Damascus, after which negotiations were begun, but with what result is not known. At the same time Egypt was suffering from incursions of the Blemmyes, who gave hostages to the imperial envoy Maximin, and made peace for 100 years, but on his sudden death recovered the hostages by force and renewed their raids till put down by Florus, praefect and count of Egypt. A more serious position arose on the Danubian frontier, where after the collapse of the Hun empire (454) some of the Huns and other tribes were settled in the north of Illyricum and Thrace as *foederati*. Of these the most important was a body of Ostrogoths, who under three brothers of the Amal family, Walamir, Theodemir, and Widimir, settled in eastern Pannonia, of which they received a grant from Marcian, who did not recognise Valentinian III's successors: they also received pay as *foederati*.

In 453 Pulcheria died, leaving all her property to the poor, a bequest which Marcian faithfully carried out. By a former wife Marcian had a daughter, whom he had given in marriage to Anthemius, grandson of the praefect Anthemius; but, when he died (27 Jan. 457) at the age of 65, he had taken no steps to secure his son-in-law's succession, and the throne lay at the disposal of Aspar the patrician and *magister militum*, who as an Arian and barbarian could not himself assume the crown, but might reign in the name of some puppet-emperor. He therefore chose Leo, a military tribune from Dacia and his own steward, a man of some capacity but little education; and the choice was ratified by the Senate. As there was no elder emperor or Augusta to perform the coronation, Leo was crowned by the patriarch Anatolius (7 Feb.). This precedent was henceforth followed whenever an emperor was not merely being associated with a senior colleague.

One of the first acts of the new reign was the recognition of Majorian (April), after whose death (461) Leo, though not recognising Severus, accepted the Western consuls, and, while sending an embassy to Gaiseric to secure the liberation of the widow and daughters of Valentinian, urged him to cease attacking Italy and Sicily. Gaiseric refused to make peace with the West or to release Eudoxia, whom he married to his son, but on receiving a share of Valentinian's property released his widow and her other daughter Placidia, who came to Constantinople. Some years later Eudoxia escaped (471) and ended her days at Jerusalem. Leo also induced Marcellinus, who had set up an independent power in Dalmatia, to keep peace with the Western Emperor; but further embassies to Gaiseric effected nothing.

About this time the migration of the Avars from the east caused a movement among the Hunnic tribes of the Caucasus, in consequence of which the Saragurs asked for Roman protection, and obtained it, though some trouble with the fugitive peoples followed. But when the Saragurs invaded Persian territory, an embassy arrived from King Piroz to complain of the treatment of Magians in the Empire and the reception of fugitives, and to ask for the stipulated contribution in money or men towards the defence of the Caucasian Gates, and money for the war against the Ephthalites; to which an answer was sent through the ex-praefect Constantine that the complaints were unfounded and the contribution could not be given. Meanwhile Gobazes, king of Lazica (Colchis), had offended the government, and a campaign in his country was undertaken (464), the troops returning to Roman territory for the winter. The coast-road was however so difficult that the Romans were thinking of asking leave to pass through Persian territory; accordingly on receiving an embassy from Gobazes Leo granted peace on the nominal condition that he and his son should not reign conjointly; and Gobazes, having failed to obtain help from Piroz on account of the Ephthalite war, consented to retire in his son's favour. A certain Dionysius, who was known to Gobazes from previous negotiations, was at his request sent to Lazica and brought the king back with him to Constantinople (466), where by plausible words and the wearing of Christian emblems he obtained favour, so that his abdication was not insisted on. His submission drew upon him the enmity of Piroz, and a force under Heraclius was sent to his support; but, as the Persians were occupied elsewhere and the maintenance of the troops was expensive, Gobazes sent them back. Leo was meanwhile negotiating with Piroz through Constantine; but Piroz, having overcome the Ephthalites, sent to announce the fact and turned against Gobazes, who had meanwhile taken some forts from his north-eastern neighbours, the Suani, who were in alliance with Persia. Gobazes asked that part of the Armenian frontier force might be sent to his support; but Leo, being occupied with the African expedition, refused assistance (468).

Meanwhile the relations between Leo and Aspar had become strained. A difference between them had arisen in 459, when Leo appointed Vivianus praefect in preference to Aspar's candidate, Tatianus; and again in 460 Leo expelled the patriarch Timothy of Alexandria in spite of Aspar's opposition. Another dispute arose over the affairs of Illyricum. The Pannonian Ostrogoths, whose subsidy had been withheld by Leo, raided Illyricum and took Dyrrachium (459), but were obliged to give Theodemir's son, the boy Theodoric, as a hostage before obtaining the pay which they claimed. They then turned against the neighbouring tribes, and after a time became involved in a war with the Sciri. Both parties appealed to the Emperor for help, and, though Aspar advised neutrality, Leo insisted on supporting the Sciri, who gained a victory, Walamir falling in the battle.

The Emperor was alarmed by the condition of the West, which after Majorian's death fell under the domination of Ricimer; and he determined, if possible, to save the East from a similar fate: but, as Aspar was surrounded by a large body-guard of Goths and other dependants and the Thracian Goths, whose chief, Theodoric, son of Triarius, was his wife's nephew, were in alliance with him, it was necessary to raise a force from some other quarter to overthrow him. Accordingly Leo turned his eyes towards the Isaurians, who had done so much injury to the Empire in the days of Arcadius and Theodosius, but might now be used to rescue it from more dangerous enemies. His elder daughter, Ariadne, was therefore given in marriage to the Isaurian Tarasicodissa, who in memory of his countryman of the time of Theodosius took the name of Zeno and brought with him an Isaurian body-guard to set against that of Aspar (467 ?).

Meanwhile disturbances had arisen in Thrace. From about 460 the command there was held by Ardaburius, but it was afterwards transferred to Basiliscus, brother of Leo's wife Verina. In 467 trouble arose with Attila's son Dengizic, and a force of Huns crossed the Danube with a large body of Goths; but the two nations were surrounded by a Roman army, and induced by a trick to fight one another, so that a general slaughter followed, from which only a few escaped.

In 467 Ricimer, requiring the Eastern fleet for protection against the Vandals, asked Leo to nominate an emperor; whereupon he chose Marcian's son-in-law, Anthemius, and, having persuaded Marcellinus to submit to the new emperor, prepared a great expedition by land and sea (468): but the fleet was by the mismanagement of Basiliscus almost annihilated; and Aspar, the Vandals' friend, was believed to have induced him to betray his trust. After his return he took refuge in St Sophia, but at Verina's intercession escaped punishment.

Meanwhile Zeno was sent to Thrace; and the soldiers, instigated, as was supposed, by Aspar, tried to murder him, and he with difficulty escaped to Sardica. The command was then given to Anagast, who soon afterwards rebelled (469). Having been persuaded to submit, he accused Ardaburius of prompting his rebellion. Zeno now strengthened the Isaurians in Constantinople by introducing a band of marauders who had been driven from Rhodes (469), and their arrival was, on account of the unpopularity of the Isaurians, followed by a riot. He was then sent to the East, as *magister militum*, and as such was compelled to remove the Isaurian robber Indacus, son of Papirius, from his hereditary stronghold of Cherris.

The rise of Zeno and the strength of the Isaurians forced Aspar to act vigorously if he was not to be altogether ousted from power; and he pressed Leo to make his second son Patricius Caesar and give him his daughter Leontia in marriage. In spite of the opposition of the monks, who were horrified at the prospect of an Arian emperor, Leo thought it best to comply (470), and the new Caesar for some reason went to Alexandria, where he displayed himself with great pomp. Something more than titles was however needed to make Aspar secure; and Ardaburius tried to cut the ground from under the Emperor's feet by tampering with the Isaurians in Constantinople. This was revealed to Zeno, who had returned to Constantinople in the latter half of 471; and it was resolved to make an end of the supremacy of the Alans. Aspar and his two elder sons were accordingly treacherously cut down in the palace, though Patricius is said to have recovered from his wounds (471): the youngest son, Hermanric, had received warning from Zeno and was not there. Some of Aspar's guards under Ostrui broke into the palace, but were expelled by the *excubitores*, a new force instituted by Leo, perhaps for some such purpose. They succeeded however in escaping, and after doing some damage in Thrace joined Theodoric; but an attack on the city by the Goths was repulsed. Leontia was now given in marriage to Marcian the son of Anthemius.

Before the attack on Aspar, Leo had thought it desirable to gain the support of the Goths of Pannonia, and therefore released Theodoric (the Amal), who returned with great gifts to his father. His first act was to defeat the Sarmatians and recover Singidunum, which however he did not restore to the Emperor. So far from assisting Leo, Theodemir, now released from restraint, thought the disturbances in both divisions of the Empire a good opportunity to acquire new territories. Accordingly he sent Widimir to Italy, while he himself marched south-east and occupied Naissus. Leo thereupon sent Hilarianus, master of the offices, to offer him settlements in Lower Moesia. On these terms peace was made; and soon afterwards Theodemir died and was succeeded by Theodoric (471).

As Theodoric the son of Triarius remained in arms, an ambassador was sent to ask his terms (473), and through his envoys whom he sent to Constantinople he demanded Aspar's property, his post of *magister militum*, and a grant of the whole of the province of Thrace. As Leo would only agree to the second of these demands, Theodoric sent a force to Philippi, which however only burned the suburbs, while he himself reduced Arcadiopolis. But, as the Goths were straitened for food, he sent another embassy, and peace was made on the conditions that he was made *magister militum* and paid 2000 lbs. of gold a year, and that Leo recognised him as chief of all the Thracian Goths and did not receive deserters from them, while he undertook to assist the Emperor against all enemies except the Vandals, who had been Aspar's friends.

The reign of Leo was afterwards remembered for the law by which all legal process and all spectacles in the theatre, amphitheatre, and circus were forbidden on Sundays (9 Dec. 469). Similar laws had been passed by Constantine, Theodosius, and Arcadius, but had probably remained little more than dead letters; and it is unlikely that even this law, at least the latter portion, was ever fully carried out. But in spite of the increasing Christian tendency of the government and of laws to the contrary, heathens continued to hold high offices of state and enjoy the favour of the Court. Prominent among these was James the physician, philosopher, and man of letters, son of a Syrian father and Greek mother, whose medical skill made him indispensable. Isocasius also, a Cilician philosopher, was made quaestor. Being deprived of his post and arrested under the law which forbade the tenure of office by a heathen, he was at the intercession of James sent for trial before Pusaeus the praefect, who was known to be in sympathy with him, and allowed to escape by submitting to baptism. The philosopher Eulogius also received a pension.

One of Leo's last acts was to surrender the island of Jotaba at the northern end of the Red Sea to the Arab Amru 'l Kais. This man, coming from Persian territory, had reduced several Arab tribes and occupied the island, driving out the Roman tax-collectors. He then sent the bishop of his tribe to ask for a grant of the island and the chieftainship of the tribes in the province of Palestine III; and, though this was contrary to the treaty of 422, Leo sent for him, treated him with honour, and granted his requests (473). During this year the Emperor was attacked by a serious illness, which made it necessary to settle the succession. Fearing (on account of the unpopularity of the Isaurians) to declare Zeno his successor, he made his grandson, Zeno's son Leo, a boy of five, Caesar, and later crowned him Augustus in the circus (18 Nov.). Less than three months afterwards he died at the age of 63 (3 Feb. 474); and, as it was probably known that the child was unlikely to live, he was directed by Ariadne and Verina to place the crown upon his father's head (9 Feb.). On his death nine months later (10 Nov.) Zeno became sole emperor in the East.

The new government began with a great success, the end of the disastrous Vandal war. One of the last acts in this war was the capture of Nicopolis by the Vandals very soon after Leo's death; and about the same time Zeno sent Severus to treat for peace, who greatly impressed Gaiseric by refusing to accept presents for himself and saying that the most acceptable present would be the release of the captives; whereupon the king gave him all the captives belonging to himself and his sons, and allowed him to ransom as many more as he could. Shortly afterwards a perpetual peace was made (474), which after Gaiseric's death (477) was confirmed by his son. The Vandal danger was at an end.

The peace was the more necessary on account of the disturbances in other quarters. The Arabs were making one of their raids in Syria, the Bulgarians appeared for the first time south of the Danube, and the accession of the Isaurian led to a serious rising of the Thracian Goths, who took prisoner Heraclius, the *magister militum* of Thrace, and held him to ransom. Zeno levied the sum from the general's kinsmen and sent it to the Goths; but after receiving it they killed their captive. Illus, one of the many Isaurians who came to Constantinople after Zeno's accession, a man whose large native following and influence with his countrymen made him a power in the State, was now appointed to the command and succeeded in holding the Goths in check. But the favour with which these Isaurian adventurers were received increased the Emperor's unpopularity; and his son's death was soon followed by a plot. Verina's brother Basiliscus, who was living in retirement at Heraclea, opened negotiations with Illus, and no doubt by large promises induced him to betray his patron; and Verina joined the conspiracy, which the son of Triarius also supported. Verina frightened Zeno into escaping by night with his wife and mother (9 Jan. 475) and fleeing to Isauria; and the conspirators gained possession of the city without fighting. The Empress had been led to believe that she would be allowed to raise Patricius, master of the offices, to the throne, which she intended to share as his wife; but Basiliscus did not intend to act for anyone but himself, and, having the strongest support, was proclaimed emperor, the proclamation being followed by a massacre of Isaurians. Patricius was put to death; and Verina tried to get up a conspiracy for Zeno's restoration. This being discovered, she fled to St Sophia; but her nephew, Armatus, conveyed her away and kept her in safety till Zeno's return. Meanwhile Illus and his brother Trocundes were sent against Zeno, blockaded him in Sbide, and captured his brother Longinus.

But soon things turned again in his favour. In the first place Basiliscus had offended Theodoric by transferring the post of *magister militum* to his own nephew Armatus, a man of fashion who posed as a soldier and was supported by the favour of the Empress Zenonis; and in the second place he favoured the Monophysites, and, not content with abrogating the theological decree of Chalcedon, was induced by Timothy of Alexandria to abolish the patriarchate of Constantinople created by that synod, thereby making a bitter enemy of the bishop Acacius, a man who cared little about theology, but knew well how to stir up popular fanaticism. So threatening was the aspect of affairs that Basiliscus recalled his decrees: but it was too late; Illus and Trocundes went over to Zeno, and the combined force marched on Constantinople while Trocundes with some Isaurian guards was sent to Antioch. Armatus marched to Nicaea to oppose Zeno's advance; but he had no mind to fight in a losing cause, and on receiving the promise of the office of *magister militum* for life and the rank of Caesar for his son Basiliscus, left the road open; and as Theodoric held aloof, Zeno entered Constantinople without opposition (Aug. 476). Basiliscus and his family fled to St Sophia; but they were handed over to some of his enemies, who took them to Cappadocia and beheaded them all. The promise to Armatus was kept; but, as he was entering the circus, where Zeno and the young Caesar were watching the games, he was assassinated by Onoulf, a man

who had received great kindness from him and been raised by his influence
to the military command of Illyricum.   His son was ordained a reader,
and afterwards became bishop of Cyzicus.   Theodoric the Amal, who
from rivalry with his namesake had supported Zeno, was made *magister
militum* and adopted in Teutonic fashion as Zeno's son in arms.   It was
perhaps these commotions which enabled the Samaritans to set up as
emperor the robber Justasa, who took Caesarea, but was defeated and
killed by the duke of Palestine.

Leo left the treasury full; and at the beginning of Zeno's reign the
burdens were considerably lightened by the praefect Erythrius; but, as
the sums wanted for the Isaurian favourites could not be raised without
extortion, he resigned, and his successor Sebastian earned a bad reputation by selling offices to the highest bidder.   His administration was
however distinguished by an act providing that all civil and military
governors should remain in their districts for fifty days after the termination of office, in order that anyone with a grievance might prefer an
accusation against them (9 Oct. 479).

One of Zeno's first tasks after his return was to decide what policy
to follow with regard to the affairs of the West.   The concord between
the Courts had been broken by the murder of Anthemius (472); but
Leo shortly before his death nominated as emperor Nepos, the nephew
and successor of Marcellinus, and gave him Verina's niece in marriage.
The fiction of the unity of the Empire was however in part abandoned,
since Nepos' name does not appear in Eastern laws.   After his expulsion (475) and the dethronement of his successor (476) the Roman
Senate asked Zeno to grant Odovacar the title of patrician, and Nepos
begged for help to recover his throne.   Zeno advised Odovacar to apply
to Nepos for the title, but styled him "patrician" in a letter, while
declining to help Nepos.

The son of Triarius, wishing to obtain pay for his men, sought to
make his peace (477): but the Senate, to which Zeno referred the
matter, said they could not pay both Theodorics and left it to him to
choose between them.   Zeno then made a violent speech to the army
against the son of Triarius.   He did not however immediately break
with him, but protracted negotiations.   At last, finding that his strength
was increasing, while that of his rival was diminishing, he summoned
troops from all quarters and announced the appointment of Illus to the
command; which was however, probably because of his growing jealousy
of Illus, afterwards transferred to Martinianus.   As this change led to
disorder among the Isaurian soldiery, Zeno summoned the Amal to his
aid, promising that, if he would take the field, Martinianus should meet
him at the passes of Mt Haemus and another force at the Hebrus, and
on this understanding Theodoric set out; but either from treachery or
from lack of discipline no army met him, and his Roman guides led
him to a place where he found the heights in front occupied by his rival,

who then easily persuaded him to make common cause against the Emperor. Both sent to Constantinople to state their terms, the Amal demanding land and provisions for his men and the emoluments of his office, and the son of Triarius the terms granted by Leo with the arrears of pay and the restoration of any living members of Aspar's family. Zeno promised the former in case of victory a large sum down, a yearly pension, and the hand of Valentinian's granddaughter Juliana, or any other lady whom he might name, and, this offer being refused, announced that he would lead the army himself. But circumstances now caused a change of plan.

The part played by Illus in 475, together with his retention of Longinus as a hostage and his influence with the Isaurian soldiers, made him something of a thorn in Zeno's side, and the jealous ambition of Verina rendered her his deadly enemy. In the summer of 477 Paul, one of the Emperor's slaves, tried to assassinate him and was surrendered for punishment. In 478 another attempt was made by an Alan, who under torture confessed that he had been instigated by Epinicus the praefect, a client of Urbicius the eunuch-chamberlain and favoured by Verina. Zeno thereupon surrendered Epinicus also to Illus, who sent him to Isauria, and then, having obtained leave on the ground of the death of a brother, withdrew to his native country. Fearing a rebellion on the part of Illus, Zeno now resolved to secure the support of the son of Triarius and renounced his intention of taking the field; and, as this caused disaffection in the army, he on Martinianus' advice recalled it to winter quarters. Peace was then made. The son of Triarius was to receive food and pay for 13,000 men, the command of two regiments of *scholarii*, the office of *magister militum*, and the property that had been taken from him, while any surviving members of Aspar's family were to retain their property and live in any city that Zeno might choose.

The imperial troops succeeded in expelling the Amal from Thrace; but Macedonia was left to his mercy (479). He sacked Stobi; and on his approaching Thessalonica the citizens, thinking themselves betrayed, transferred the keys from the praefect to the bishop. Heraclea he was at first persuaded by large gifts to spare; but on the refusal of a demand for corn and wine burnt the greater part of it. He was repulsed from Lychnidus, but took Scampia, which was deserted, and occupied Dyrrachium, which a confederate had induced the garrison by a trick to abandon. Meanwhile Zeno had again opened negotiations, and the patrician Adamantius, the son of Vivianus, was sent to treat. At Thessalonica he put down a military tumult directed against the praefect; and at Edessa handed to Sabinianus the Emperor's commission as *magister militum* of Illyricum in place of Onoulf. From Lychnidus he invited Theodoric either to come to Lychnidus or to send hostages for his own safety if he went to Dyrrachium. As Sabinianus, who accompanied him, refused to secure the return of the hostages by oath, this plan failed; but

Adamantius went with a small escort to a wild spot near Dyrrachium and invited Theodoric to meet him. Theodoric came and stood on the opposite bank of a river, and Adamantius offered him a settlement in the district of Pautalia in Dardania, where he would act as a check on his namesake and be between the Thracian and Illyrian armies. Theodoric refused to move before spring, but offered, if supported by a Roman army, to destroy the Thracian Goths on condition that he might then be made *magister militum* and live in Constantinople, or, if preferred, to go to Dalmatia and restore Nepos. Adamantius however declined to make terms until he left Epirus. Meanwhile Sabinianus, having received reinforcements, captured 5000 Goths, and Zeno was encouraged to break off negotiations. For the next two years Sabinianus held the Goths in check.

On 25 Sept. 479[1] the walls of Constantinople were greatly damaged by an earthquake; Zeno in fear of the Goths begged Illus to return, in order that his Isaurians might assist in defending the city; and the Emperor and the chief officials came out beyond Chalcedon to meet him. Having learned from Epinicus that Verina was the author of the plot against his life, Illus refused to enter Constantinople unless she was surrendered; and Zeno, who was clearly in fear of him and was perhaps not sorry to be rid of his mother-in-law, complied. She was conveyed by Illus' brother-in-law, Matronianus, to Tarsus, where she was compelled to become a deaconess, and kept in custody at the Isaurian Dalisandus. Illus was made master of the offices, Epinicus was at his request recalled, and his client, Pamprepius the philosopher, who had been expelled on account of his open paganism and the suspicion of inciting his patron to treason, returned with him and was made quaestor.

The predominance of Illus soon led to a vigorous attempt to throw off the Isaurian rule. On the pretext of Verina's banishment Marcian, the son-in-law of Leo, having secured the adhesion of the son of Triarius and the support of a force of barbarians and a large number of citizens, rose against Zeno and claimed the crown for himself on the ground that Leontia was born in the purple while Ariadne was born before Leo's accession (end of 479). During the day the insurgents, aided by the people, who hurled missiles from the houses at the soldiers, carried all before them; but in the night Illus brought some Isaurians over from Chalcedon, and on the next day the rising was suppressed, though Illus' house was burnt. Marcian, who fled to the church of the Apostles, was compelled to take orders and sent to Caesarea in Cappadocia, while his brothers, Procopius and Romulus, escaped to Theodoric's camp, and Leontia sought refuge in a convent. Marcian however escaped and with a rustic force attacked Ancyra, but was captured by Trocundes and confined in the castle of Cherris, whither his wife and daughters were now

[1] Theoph. 477, Marc. 480, or by indictional reckoning 479. The chronology shews 479 to be right.

brought to join him. Immediately after the rising Theodoric the son of Triarius appeared before Constantinople under pretence of assisting the Emperor, thinking that, as the towers and battlements had been overthrown by the earthquake, he could easily take it; but, finding the Isaurians manning the wall and ready to burn the city in case of defeat, he accepted Zeno's gifts and promises and withdrew. He refused however to surrender the fugitives, and was thereupon superseded in the office of *magister militum* by Trocundes. He then plundered Thrace, and Zeno could only call in the Bulgarians against him. Having defeated the Bulgarians, Theodoric again appeared before the capital (481); but, finding the gates strongly guarded by Illus and his Isaurians, tried to cross to Bithynia and was defeated at sea. Receiving news of a conspiracy against him, he returned home and put the conspirators to death; after which he marched towards Greece to seek new territory, but on the way was accidentally killed. His son Rekitach, who by killing his uncles became sole ruler of his people, returned to Thrace and continued to ravage the country. In 481 Sabinianus died a violent death, some said by Zeno's contrivance, and Theodoric (the Amal) plundered Macedonia and Thessaly and sacked Larissa (482). John the Scythian and Moschianus were sent against him; but no great success was obtained. In consequence of the threatened revolt of Illus Theodoric was invited to Constantinople, made patrician and *magister militum*, and designated consul, and received territory in Dacia and Lower Moesia (483). His rival Rekitach, who was in the city at the same time, he was allowed to assassinate, and the Thracian Goths ceased to maintain a separate existence.

Ariadne, urged by her mother, pressed Zeno to recall Verina; but he referred her to Illus, who refused compliance. A third attempt upon the life of Illus was then made by a scholarian, who succeeded in cutting off his ear, while he was going to the palace to receive some barbarian envoys at the Emperor's request. The assassin was put to death, and Zeno denied on oath all knowledge of the matter; but Illus, feeling himself unsafe, asked for leave of absence on the ground of needing change of air. Zeno then made him *magister militum per Orientem* with the right of appointing dukes, and, taking with him Matronianus, Marsus, who had commanded the land force in the expedition against the Vandals, Pamprepius, and other powerful men, and a large military force, he withdrew to Antioch (early in 482), where he set himself to gain popularity by largesses and lavish expenditure on public buildings. The patrician Leontius, who was sent to ask for Verina's release, was induced to remain.[1]

That a civil war was imminent must have been clear to both parties; and after the accommodation with Theodoric Zeno demanded the surrender of Longinus, and on receiving a refusal, sent John the Scythian to

[1] This is now here stated, but I infer it from a comparison of Jo. Mal., Jordanes, and "Joshua."

supersede Illus, expelled his friends, and confiscated their property, which
he gave to the Isaurian cities. Illus now openly revolted, proclaimed
Marcian emperor, and sent envoys to Odovacar, who refused assistance,
and to the Persians and the satraps of the five provinces annexed in 298,
who promised support to any force that appeared in their neighbourhood
(484). It is clear that he did not intend to head a mere Isaurian revolt,
which could not have any lasting success, but to form a powerful combination against the Emperor; for which purpose he held out hopes to
the heathens through Pamprepius, while he was also on friendly terms
with the Chalcedonians, who had been offended by the issue of the
Henoticon, whereby Zeno soon after his departure tried to placate the
Monophysites (482).

At first, to prevent a revolt in Isauria, Zeno sent a small force under
Illus' bastard brother, Linges, and the Isaurian Conon, who had exchanged a military life for the bishopric of Apamea; whereupon Illus
for some reason dropped Marcian, and brought Verina, who as Augusta
might advance some claim to appoint an emperor, to Tarsus, where she
formally crowned Leontius (19 July),[1] who eight days later entered
Antioch. The inhabitants of Chalcis refused to accept the new Emperor's
busts, and he attacked the city for 45 days; while at Edessa the citizens
shut the gates against Matronianus. About the same time the great
victory of the Ephthalites precluded all hope of support from Persia.

Theodoric was now sent with a force of Romans and Goths to join
John the Scythian; but Zeno changed his mind and recalled him, though
his Goths remained with the army; and in his place Hermanric the son
of Aspar, who had once revealed a conspiracy to Zeno and had married
a daughter of his illegitimate son, was sent with a contingent of Rugians.
When the force which Illus sent against the imperial army was defeated,
he hastily summoned Leontius from Antioch (Sept.), and they fled to
the stronghold of Cherris, to which Verina had already been sent. His
confederates then shut themselves up in different fortresses, and many of
his men deserted. Zeno recalled the Goths, who were no longer needed,
and made the Isaurian Cottomenes *magister militum* in place of Theodoric,
while another Isaurian, Longinus of Cardala, was made master of the
offices. Nine days after the beginning of the siege Verina died, and a
month later Marsus, and Illus left the defence to the owner of the
fortress, Indacus, Trocundes' brother-in-law. Trocundes, who had been
sent to collect reinforcements, was captured by John and beheaded, and
Zeno's brother Longinus was allowed to escape (485).

Theodoric had perhaps been occupied during 485 by a Bulgarian
invasion; but in 486 he raided Thrace, and Odovacar in spite of his previous refusal shewed signs of wishing to assist Illus, who now in vain made
proposals for peace, while Zeno stirred up the Rugians against Odovacar.

---

[1] *Rev. de l'instr. publ. en Belgique*, XL. 8. Hence I substitute "July" for the
"June" of Theoph.

In 487 Theodoric advanced close to Constantinople, and an agreement was made under which he set out to wrest Italy from Odovacar,
who had defeated the Rugians, and the East was rid of the Goths
for ever (488).

All hope for the besieged was now at an end; Pamprepius, who had
prophesied success, was put to death, and at last Indacus and others
betrayed the fort. Illus' requests with regard to the burial of his
daughter, who had died during the siege, and the treatment of his
family were granted, and he and Leontius were beheaded, and their heads
exposed at Constantinople (488). The traitors were all killed during
the assault, perhaps by the besieged. Verina's body was taken to Constantinople and buried with Leo's. Most of the Isaurian fortresses were
dismantled. As the satraps of the five provinces had been in communication with Illus, the hereditary tenure of the four most important
satrapies was abolished, though the satraps retained their native
forces.

Zeno had by his first wife a son, Zeno; but he had killed himself by
his excesses at an early age, and the Emperor wished to leave the crown
to his brother Longinus. The infamous character of Longinus and the
unpopularity of the Isaurians hindered him from declaring him Caesar;
but he appointed him *magister militum,* in the hope that his military
authority and the strength of the Isaurians in the army would
secure him the succession. On 9 April 491 Zeno died of dysentery at
the age of 60.

In accordance with the precedent of 450 the choice of a successor
was left to the Augusta Ariadne; and on the next morning, by the
advice of Urbicius, she nominated the silentiary Anastasius of Dyrrachium, a man of 61, who had shortly before been one of the three
candidates selected for the see of Antioch. He was crowned the next day;
and, when he appeared before the people, they greeted him with the acclamation "Reign as you have lived." On 20 May he married Ariadne.

The new Emperor began by the popular measures of remitting arrears
of taxation and refusing facilities to informers, and he is credited with
abolishing the sale of offices; but his reign was constantly disturbed by
serious outbreaks. No immediate opposition was offered to his elevation;
but in Isauria a revolt on a small scale broke out, and at Constantinople
some unpopular action on the part of Julian the city-praefect led to
an uproar; and on an attempt to restore order by force the rioters threw
down the pedestals on which stood the busts of the Emperor and Empress
in front of the circus, and many were killed by the soldiers. To avoid
more bloodshed Anastasius deposed Julian, who had been appointed by
Ariadne on the day of Zeno's death, and named his own brother-in-law
Secundinus to succeed him. Thinking that peace was impossible while
the Isaurians were in the city, he expelled them and deprived them of
the pay assigned by Zeno. Longinus the brother of Zeno was compelled

CH. XVI.

to take orders and exiled to the Thebaid, where he died, it is said, of hunger, eight years later, while his wife and daughter retired to Bithynia and lived the rest of their life on charity. The property of the late Emperor, even his imperial robes, was sold by auction, and the castle of Cherris, which had not yet been occupied by the rebels, was dismantled. Longinus of Cardala and a certain Athenodorus, who were among those who had been expelled from the capital, joined the insurgents in Isauria, among whom were now to be found Linginines, count of Isauria, Conon the ex-bishop, and another Athenodorus. Reinforced by discontented Romans and others who served under compulsion, they advanced to Cotyaeum. Here John the Scythian and John the Hunchback, who had succeeded Longinus as *magister militum in praesenti* met and defeated them. Linginines fell in the battle, and the Isaurians fled to their native mountains (end of 492) : but the generals waited till spring before crossing the Taurus. In 493 Diogenes, a kinsman of Ariadne, took Claudiopolis, but was besieged in it by the Isaurians, and his men were nearly starved. John the Hunchback however forced the passes, and by a sudden attack, aided by a sortie on the part of Diogenes, routed the enemy, Bishop Conon being mortally wounded. The Isaurians were henceforth confined to their strongholds, and a certain Longinus of Selinus, who resided in the strong coast town of Antioch and had a large fleet, supplied them with provisions by sea.

The Emperor's attention was now distracted by an incursion of barbarians, perhaps Slavs, in Thrace, during which Julian, the *magister militum* of Thrace, was killed. Moreover, as his Monophysite opinions made his rule distasteful to the Chalcedonians, who were strong in Constantinople, there was perhaps communication between them and the insurgents, a charge on which the patriarch Euphemius was deprived in 495. At last in 497 Longinus of Cardala and Athenodorus were taken and beheaded by John the Scythian and their heads sent to Constantinople, while the head of the other Athenodorus, who was captured the same year, was exhibited at the gates of Tarsus. Longinus of Selinus held out till 498, and was then made prisoner by Priscus, an officer serving under John the Hunchback, exhibited in chains at Constantinople, and tortured to death at Nicaea. Large numbers of Isaurians were settled in Thrace, and the population of Isauria, which had been greatly thinned by the two wars, was thereby yet further reduced, so that the necessity which had made the mountaineers the terror of Asia Minor no longer existed. The Isaurians had done their work of saving the East from the fate of the West; and, though they still provided useful recruits for the army, their day of political power was over. The importance of looking at home for soldiers instead of trusting to the barbarians had been learned and was never forgotten.

Besides the Isaurian war Anastasius had also been troubled by incursions of Blemmyes in Egypt (491); and in 498 bands of Saracens invaded the eastern provinces. The followers of Nu'man of Al Hira, who owed allegiance to Persia, were after an inroad into Euphratesia defeated by Eugenius, a duke stationed at Melitene, and parties of Taghlibi and Ghassani Arabs under Hugr and Gabala, the latter at least a Roman subject, were routed by Romanus, duke of Palestine, who also recovered Jotaba, which was leased to a company of Roman traders for a yearly tribute. In 502 a more successful raid was made by Hugr's brother, Ma'di Kharb; but the outbreak of the Persian war made it possible to turn the raids in another direction, and peace was made with the Taghlibi chief, Al Harith, father of Ma'di Kharb (503). In 502 the Tzani also raided Pontus.

Immediately after the accession of Anastasius, Kawad, who became king of Persia in 488, demanded a contribution towards the defences of the Caucasian Gates. This was refused; but the Armenian rising prevented further action, though Anastasius refused to aid the insurgents. Kawad took advantage of the Isaurian troubles to repeat his demand, but was soon afterwards deposed (496). Having been restored by the king of the Ephthalites under a promise of paying a large sum of money (499), he again applied to Anastasius for help. The Emperor would only agree to lend the money on a written promise of payment; and Kawad, refusing this, entered Roman Armenia (22 Aug. 502) and took and sacked Theodosiopolis, which was surrendered by the treachery of Constantine, the count of Armenia, who went over to the Persian service. Having occupied Martyropolis, he passed on to Amida (5 Oct.), where, though there was no military force in Mesopotamia except the garrison of Constantina, a stubborn defence was made by the citizens. Anastasius sent Rufinus to offer him money to withdraw, but he kept the ambassador in custody. A Persian force, accompanied by Arabs and Ephthalites, was sent to the district of Constantina, and, after a small party had been cut to pieces (19 Nov.), routed Eugenius of Melitene and Olympius, duke of Mesopotamia, while Nu'man's Arabs plundered the territory of Carrhae (26 Nov.) and advanced to Edessa. Eugenius however retook Theodosiopolis. Meanwhile Kawad, despairing of taking Amida, was willing to retire for a small sum; but the governor and the magistrates refused this and demanded compensation for the crops that had been destroyed. The siege therefore continued, until on a dark night the Persians found access by some aqueducts to a part of the wall which was guarded by some monks who were in a drunken sleep. They thereupon scaled the wall, and after hard fighting made themselves masters of the town (11 Jan. 503), which for three days was given up to massacre. Rufinus was then released, and Kawad at the beginning of spring retreated to the neighbourhood of Singara, leaving 3000 men under Glon in Amida. Further demands for money were rejected by Anastasius (April), who, having immediately after the fall of Amida sent men to defend the fortified places, now despatched a considerable army from Thrace to

Mesopotamia under Patricius, *magister militum in praesenti*, Areobindus, *magister militum per Orientem*, great-grandson of Aspar, and his own nephew Hypatius (May), accompanied by Appion the praefect, who took up his quarters at Edessa to look after the commissariat. Patricius and Hypatius laid siege to Amida, while Areobindus encamped near Dara to stop a new invasion, and for some time prevented an advance on the part of the Persians from Singara, and even drove them in confusion to Nisibis; but, when the enemy, reinforced by Arabs and Ephthalites, prepared to attack him in greater strength under the traitor Constantine (July), he retreated to Harram near Mardin to be near his colleagues: his request for assistance being however disregarded, he was compelled to abandon his camp and flee to Constantina and Edessa. Patricius and Hypatius on hearing of Areobindus' flight raised the siege of Amida and met the Persians under Kawad himself at the neighbouring fort of Apadna (Aug.), but were routed and fled to Samosata. Hypatius was then recalled. Kawad's attempts to take Constantina, Edessa, and Carrhae by assault were unsuccessful, and Patriciolus, who was bringing reinforcements, destroyed a small Persian force at the Euphrates, while the Persian Arabs, having ravaged the country up to the river near Batnae, crossed into Syria. A second attempt upon Edessa fared no better than the first, and Kawad then advanced to the Euphrates.

Anastasius now sent Celer, the master of the offices, with large reinforcements; and, though he had hitherto followed a civil career and was not formally appointed to the chief command, his personal position gave him practical authority over the other generals and replaced division by unity. On his approach Kawad marched down the river to Callinicus, where a detachment was cut to pieces by Timostratus, duke of Osrhoene. Hearing of an invasion of Caucasian Huns, Kawad then returned home, upon which Patricius, who was wintering at Melitene, returned to Amida and routed a force sent against him by Kawad. Celer, and afterwards Areobindus, then joined Patricius before Amida, where Glon had been captured by a stratagem and put to death. Seeing how things were going, Constantine returned to his allegiance (June 504) and was allowed to take orders and live at Nicaea. 'Adid the Arab and Mushel the Armenian also went over to the Romans. The whole army was now no longer needed at Amida; accordingly Areobindus raided Persian Armenia, while Celer crossed into Arzanene, where he cut some cavalry to pieces, and burnt the villages, killing the men and taking the women and children prisoners. Similar raids were made by the Roman Arabs. Kawad then sent his *spahpat* (commander-in-chief) to Celer to propose peace, returning the most important prisoners. Celer at first refused terms in the hope of taking Amida, and an attempt to revictual it failed; but during the winter, which was a severe one, there were many desertions in the army, and he agreed to pay a sum of money for the surrender of the town, a definite peace being postponed till the Emperor's pleasure should be known. Hostilities were however considered to be ended, and some Arab sheikhs on the Persian side who had raided Roman territory were put to death by the Persian *marzban*, and some sheikhs of the Roman Arabs who had raided Persian territory were treated in the same way by Celer, who after a visit to Constantinople had returned to Syria. Anastasius granted remissions of taxes throughout Mesopotamia, gave largesses to the districts which had suffered most, restored the fortifications, and built a new fortified position on the frontier at Dara. As this was contrary to the treaty of 442, the Persians tried to prevent it; but Kawad, being engaged in war with the Huns and the Tamuraye, a tribe of unknown geographical position, was unable to take active steps in the matter. In April 506 Celer came to Edessa on his way to meet the *spahpat*, but, hearing from Persian envoys of his death, he waited till a successor should be appointed, while his Gothic soldiers caused much trouble to the citizens: he then went to Dara (Oct.) and made peace for seven years with the new *spahpat* (Nov.), the Emperor agreeing to pay compensation for the breach of faith involved in the fortification of Dara.

In Thrace and Illyricum the departure of the Goths left the way open to the more savage Bulgarians. In 499 they inflicted a disastrous defeat on Aristus, *magister militum* of Illyricum, at the Tzurta; and in 500 Anastasius thought it wise to give a donative to the Illyrian army. At an unknown date his nephew Pompeius was defeated by some enemy at Hadrianople; and in 507 the long wall across the peninsula on which Constantinople stands was built to secure the city from attack by land. In 512 the Heruli after their defeat by the Lombards were settled in the Empire, but afterwards rebelled and had to be put down by force of arms. In 517 the Slavs plundered Macedonia, Thessaly, and Epirus, and carried off captives, whom Anastasius ransomed. Libya also suffered from the incursions of the Mazices.

Though there was little serious hostility with the Goths, relations were for a large part of the reign unfriendly. In 493 the Emperor refused Theodoric's request for confirmation of his title to Italy, though by accepting his consuls he tacitly recognised him. In 498 however he gave the desired recognition and returned the imperial insignia which Odovacar had sent to Zeno. But in 505 a conflict was brought about by a certain Mundo, who had been expelled by the king of the Gepids and received as a *foederatus* in the Empire, but afterwards became a captain of robbers, and being attacked by Sabinianus, *magister militum* of Illyricum (son of the Sabinianus who held the same office under Zeno), with Bulgarian allies, called in a Gothic force which had been fighting the Gepids. In the battle which followed at Horrea Margi the Romans were routed; but no further fighting seems to have taken place, and Mundo entered Theodoric's service. The assistance given to Mundo caused ill-feeling at Constantinople, and in 508 a fleet raided the coast of Italy, by which Theodoric was hindered from supporting the Visigoths against the Frankish king, on whom Anastasius conferred the insignia of the consulship.   Shortly afterwards peace was restored, no doubt by concessions on the side of Theodoric, who wished to be free to deal with the Franks.

The domestic administration of Anastasius was distinguished by several popular measures.   The most celebrated of these was the abolition of the *chrysargyron* (May 498), a tax on all kinds of stock and plant in trade, instituted by Constantine, which pressed heavily on the poorest classes.   Instead of this he imposed a land-tax called *chrysoteleia*, which he applied to the support of the army, abolishing the right of requisition.   He also attempted by several enactments to ensure that the soldiers received their full pay.   But his chief financial reform was the abolition, by the advice of the Syrian Marinus, of the system under which the *curiales* were responsible for the taxes of the municipalities, and the institution of tax-collectors called *vindices*.   The burdens of the *curiales* were not however wholly removed, for they existed in some form under Justinian.   These measures were no doubt primarily intended to increase the revenue, and at the end of his reign under the administration of Marinus complaints were made of heavy extortion; but the immediate financial success of the policy is proved by the fact that at the time of his death the treasury was full.   His humanity was shewn by the abolition of fights between men and beasts (Aug. 499); but this did not extend to the practice of exposing criminals to beasts, which existed as late as the time of Maurice.

But, although Anastasius is almost universally praised for mildness and good administration, his Monophysite opinions were distasteful to the population of the capital, and the peace was constantly disturbed by serious riots.   In 493 his refusal to release some stone-throwers of the Green faction who had been arrested by the city-praefect produced an outbreak, during which a stone was thrown at the Emperor, part of the circus buildings burnt, and the statues of Anastasius and Ariadne dragged through the streets.   Many of the rioters were arrested and punished, and the thrower of the stone, a Moor, was killed by the *excubitores*; but the Emperor was compelled to appoint a new praefect in the person of Plato.   An occasion for rioting was also provided by the ancient pagan festival of the Brytae, which was celebrated by dancing performances every May.   Such a riot occurred in the praefecture of Constantine (501), when the Greens attacked the Blues in the theatre and many were killed, among them an illegitimate son of Anastasius.   After this an order was issued that the celebration of the Brytae should cease throughout the Empire (502).   In 512 the Monophysite addition to the *Trisagion*, made at the instigation of Marinus, caused the most dangerous outbreak of the reign (6 Nov.).   The rioters killed the Monophysite monks, threw down the Emperor's statues, and

proclaimed emperor the unwilling Areobindus, whose wife Juliana represented the Theodosian house. When Celer and Patricius were sent to
appease them, they drove them away with stones, burnt the houses of
Marinus and Pompeius, and plundered Marinus' property. On the
third day Anastasius shewed himself in the circus without his crown and
begged them to refrain from massacre, whereupon they demanded that
Marinus and Plato should be thrown to the beasts; but the Emperor
by promising concessions persuaded them to disperse. The banishment
of Ariadne's kinsman, Diogenes, and the ex-praefect Appion (510) may,
as they were recalled by Justin, have been caused by religious troubles.
In Alexandria and Antioch also riots were frequent.

In 513 the religious differences culminated in an armed rising. The
military administration of Hypatius (not the Emperor's nephew)[1] had
caused discontent in the Thracian army, especially among the Bulgarian
foederati. These *foederati* were commanded by Vitalianus (son of the
Patriciolus who held a command in the Persian war); who had a grievance
on account of the expulsion of the patriarch Flavianus of Antioch (512),
with whom he was on terms of close friendship. Making use of the
discontent in the army, he murdered two of the general's staff, bribed the
duke of Moesia, and, having seized Carinus, one of the chief confidants
of Hypatius, forced him to place the town of Odessus in his hands. By
means of the money there found he collected a large force of soldiers
and rustics, and, with the cry of justice for the banished patriarchs and
abolition of the addition to the *Trisagion*, marched on Constantinople,
whither Hypatius had fled. Anastasius, having no army at hand, could
only provide for the defence, while he set up crosses on the gates and
announced the remission of one-fourth of the animal-tax in Asia and
Bithynia. Patricius the *magister militum*, to whom Vitalianus in large
measure owed his promotion, was sent to confer with him; and next
day some of Vitalianus' chief officers entered the city; who on receiving
a promise that just grievances should be remedied and the Pope asked
to send representatives to settle the religious differences took the oath of
allegiance, returned to Vitalianus, and compelled him to withdraw. Cyril,
a man of some capacity, was now appointed to succeed Hypatius, and,
having entered Odessus, from which Vitalianus had retired, was believed
to be planning an attack on him. Hearing of this, Vitalianus made his
way into the town by night, surprised Cyril while asleep in his house,
and killed him. He was thereupon declared a public enemy by decree
of the Senate, and a large force collected and sent against him under
Hypatius, the Emperor's nephew, though the office of *magister militum* of
Thrace was given to the barbarian Alathar. Hypatius fought for some
time with varying success, and gained at least one victory (autumn 513).[2]

---

[1] By introducing Anastasius' nephew later as τὸν ἀδελφιδοῦν τὸν ἑαυτοῦ Jo. Ant. shews
that another man is meant here.

[2] Known at Antioch before 18 Nov. (Wright, *Cat. Syr. MSS. Brit. Mus.* 333).

Finally he encamped at Acris on the coast, where, being attacked by the enemy and routed, he was captured in the sea, into which he had fled. Alathar was also captured, and was ransomed by Vitalianus himself from the Bulgarians, whom he permitted to sell the prisoners. Vitalianus occupied all the fortresses in Scythia and Moesia, among them Sozopolis, in which he captured some envoys sent with a ransom for Hypatius. It was now expected that he would be proclaimed emperor; and further rioting occurred at Constantinople, in which the praefect of the watch was killed. Meanwhile he advanced on the capital by land and sea; but on receiving 5000 lbs. of gold, the Thracian command, and a promise of satisfaction upon the religious question, he again retired and released Hypatius, though he refused to disband his army (514). It was clear that neither party was likely to observe the peace; and in 515 Vitalianus, having probably promises of support from inside the city, where another riot had occurred, again appeared before Constantinople, but was defeated by land and sea and retired to Anchialus, though still remaining at the head of his barbarian force. Hypatius was sent to the East as *magister militum*, and in July 517 went on an embassy to Persia.[1]

On 9 July 518 Anastasius died suddenly, Ariadne having died three years before.

[1] Wright, *op. cit.* 536.

CHAPTER XVII

RELIGIOUS DISUNION IN THE FIFTH CENTURY

THE importance of the religious controversies of the fifth century must strike the most casual reader of history: but when we approach the subject closely, we find it a tangled skein. Questions of dogmatic theology and of ecclesiastical authority are intermingled with the conflict of national ideals and the lower strife of personal rivalries. Only later are the lines of separation seen to indicate ancient ethnic differences. Nor does this century, more than any other century, form for our purpose one connected and distinct whole. The antagonistic forces had been gathering to a head during the preceding period and they had to fight the battle out in the days that came after. Nevertheless, it is possible, within limits, to distinguish the more important of the elements making for ecclesiastical disunion, and also to mark the chief acts of the drama that fall within the limits assigned.

First, then, we have to do with the opposition of two rival schools of thought, those of Alexandria and of Antioch, the homes of allegorical and of literal interpretation respectively. Next we have the emphatic assertion of authority; and rejection of external interference, by the great sees, which before the end of our period have obtained the title and status of *patriarchates*. So far, we seem to be concerned with forces already known in the Arian controversy. But in both respects there is a difference. The dogmatic difference between Alexandria and Antioch was, in the fifth century, quite unlike that of Athanasius and Arius in the fourth, though the theologian may discern hidden affinities in the parties severally concerned. The disputants on both sides in the controversies we are to consider were equally ready to accept the creed of Nicaea, and indeed to accuse their opponents of want of loyalty to that symbol. And with regard to spheres of authority, a new complication had arisen. At Nicaea (325), the rights of the great sees of Rome, Alexandria, and Antioch had been maintained. Byzantium counted for nothing. In fact, authorities differ on the question who was bishop at that time, and whether he attended the Council in person or by deputy. But at the Second Council (that of Constantinople in 381) besides a strict injunction against the intervention of bishops in places beyond their jurisdiction, there was an assertion of the prerogative of the bishop of Constantinople next after the bishop of Rome; "because Constantinople is New Rome." The last clause asserted an important principle, that might easily lead to Caesaro-papacy. For the other great sees were supposed to hold their high position in virtue of apostolic tradition, not of coincidence with secular dominion. Constantinople might — and did — discover that it, too, had an apostle for its patron — namely St Andrew. But St Andrew's claims were vague, and the imperial authority and court influence were pressing. The decision was but doubtfully accepted in the East, and the distinction, if allowed at all, was taken as purely honorary. In Rome it was never received at all. We cannot wonder that the bishops of Alexandria, in their far-reaching aims and policy, were unwilling to allow such power or prestige to the upstart see of the "queenly city," and that sometimes the bishops of Old Rome might support their actions.

It is not, of course, to be supposed that all the ecclesiastical dissensions of the period can be comprised in the quarrels between the great sees, although, for our present purpose, that series of conflicts seems the best to choose as our guiding line. Though the Arian heresy lived vigorously all through the century, it had become for the most part a religion of barbarians. It was not so much a source of disunion within the Empire as a serious — perhaps insuperable — obstacle to a good understanding between the Roman and the Teuton. The Arianism of the Ostrogoths was at least one of the most prominent weaknesses of their kingdom in Italy. But the Empire, generally speaking, was Nicene. The only regions which had not adopted or were not soon to adopt the definitions of the First General Council, lay in the far East, beyond the limits of undisputed imperial sway. When these are brought into the general current of church history, they take one side or another in the prevalent controversies, with very conspicuous results. Again, the Pelagian controversy on free will and original sin will not here concern us in proportion to its theological and philosophical interest. Though its roots lay deep, and ever and anon put forth new shoots, it did not result in a definite schism.

Taking then the main lines of controversy as already indicated, we may distinguish four phases or periods within the fifth century. In the first we have an attack on a bishop of Constantinople, a representative of the Antiochene school, by an archbishop of Alexandria. Rome sympathises with Constantinople, but Alexandria triumphs for a time, in great part by court influence. (Chrysostom controversy.)

In the second, Alexandria again advances against Constantinople, the bishop of which is again Antiochene. Rome, in this phase of the conflict, sides with Alexandria, which prevails. Court influence is divided, but gradually comes over to the Alexandrian side. (Nestorian controversy.)

In the third, Alexandria is again aggressive, and prevails over Constantinople by violence. Rome fails at first to obtain a hearing, but helps to get the doctrinal points settled in another Council. (Eutychian or Monophysite controversy.)

In the fourth, the controversy is caused by an abortive attempt, started by an emperor, but manipulated by the bishops of Constantinople and of Alexandria working together, to reunite some at least of the parties alienated by the decision of the last conflict. Rome disapproves strongly, and the result is a serious blow to imperial authority in the West. (*Henoticon* controversy.)

I. The chief persons, then, in the first controversy, are Theophilus of Alexandria and Chrysostom of Constantinople. The doctrinal question is not to the front, and the interest is in great part personal. This is in fact the only one of the controversies in which one side at least — here the one on defence — has an imposing leader. But perhaps it is the one in which it is least possible to find any reasons beyond motives of official ambition or of personal antipathy.

The beginner of the attack, Theophilus, who held the Alexandrian see from 385 to 412, has earned a bad name in history for violence and duplicity. He was probably not more unscrupulous than many leading men among his contemporaries, and excelled most of them in scientific and literary tastes. But he has incurred the odium which attaches to every religious persecutor who has not the mitigating plea of personal fanaticism. Another excuse might be alleged in extenuation of his unjust actions: the excessively difficult position in which he was placed. The peculiar character of the government of Egypt — its close and direct connexion with the imperial authority — and the absence, except in the city itself, of any civic and municipal institutions, always rendered a good understanding between bishop and praefect one of the great desiderata. The history of the see and of its most eminent occupants had given it a prestige which was not easily kept intact without encroachments on the secular power. Alexandria had from the beginning been a city of mixed populations and cults, and at this time the factions were more numerous and the occasions of disturbance as serious as in the days of Athanasius. Arianism may have been quelled, but paganism was still vigorous, and had adherents both in the academies of the grammarians and philosophers and also among the most ignorant of the lower classes, who even anticipated disaster when the measuring gauge was moved from the temple of Serapis to a church. The Jewish element was large, and the broad toleration of Alexander, the Ptolemies, and the pagan Emperors was hardly to be expected in the stormy days which had followed the conversion of Constantine. But more difficult to deal with than praefects, town mobs, philosophers or Jews, though a more powerful weapon to use if tactfully secured, was the vast number of monks that dwelt in the "desert" and other regions within the

CH. XVII.

Alexandrian see. These did not constitute one body, and were very dissimilar among themselves. The rule of those who had a rule will be set forth in the following chapter. Here we have to notice the difficulties which the soaring speculations of some, the crass ignorance of others, and the detachment of all from worldly convention and ordinary constituted authority, placed in the way of any attempt to bring them within the general system of civil and ecclesiastical order.

Theophilus was himself a man of learning and culture, eclectic in tastes, diplomatic in schemes. He had used his mathematical knowledge to make an elaborate table of the Easter Cycle. He favoured, in later days, the candidature of a philosophic pagan (Synesius of Cyrene) for the bishopric of Ptolemais. He could read and enjoy the works of writers whose teaching he was publicly anathematising. He appreciated the force of monastic piety, and endeavoured, by vigorous and even violent means, to impose episcopal consecration on some leading ascetics. He shewed his powers as a pacificator in helping to compose dissension in the church of Antioch (392) and in that of Bostra (394). He obtained from the civil authority powers to demolish the great temple of Serapis, which was done successfully, though not without creating much bitterness of feeling. The great campaign of his life, however, began with an attack on the followers of Origen at the very beginning of the fifth century.

There seems some paradox in the circumstance that the strife between the Alexandrian and the Antiochene should have begun (as far as our present purpose is concerned) by an attack made by an Alexandrian patriarch on the principles of the most eminent of all Alexandrian theologians. Theophilus was, both before and after the controversy, an appreciative student of Origen. He had already aroused a tumultuous opposition from some Egyptian monks who were practically anthropomorphites by insisting on the doctrine laid down by Origen as to the incorporeality of the Divine nature, that God is invisible by reason of His nature, and incomprehensible by reason of the limits of human intelligence. The line he now took up may have been due to the influence of Jerome, at that time organising an anti-Origenistic crusade in Palestine; or else, in his opposition to the philosophic paganism of Alexandria, he may have become nervous of any concessions as to æons and gnosis and final restitution; or again, as seems most probable, he saw a powerful ally in his ambition for his see in the grossest and least enlightened theology of his day — that of the unhappy monk who wept that "they had taken away his God" — when in the earlier stage of the controversy the doctrines of the anthropomorphites were condemned by the man who was now their champion.

Having determined to combat Origenism, Theophilus called a synod to Alexandria, which decreed against it. He followed up the ecclesiastical censure by securing from the praefect the support of the secular arm. An attack was made by night on the settlement of those monks, in the district of Nitria, who were supposed to be imbued with Origenistic doctrine. The leaders of them were the four "tall brethren," monks of considerable repute, formerly treated by Theophilus with great respect. Hounded out by soldiers and by the rival "Anthropomorphite" monks, the Tall Brothers fled for their lives, and after many vicissitudes arrived in Constantinople and appealed to the protection of the bishop, John Chrysostom.

In position and in character Chrysostom bears a marked contrast to his opponent Theophilus. Both, it is true, were men of learning and culture; both were exposed to the caprices of a pleasure-loving and much-divided populace. But Chrysostom had one disadvantage more: he was under the immediate eye of a Court. It was by court influence, unsought on his part, that he had been elevated, and the same influence could easily be turned against him. The Emperor Arcadius was of sluggish temperament, but his wife, Eudoxia, a Frankish lady, was violent in her likes and dislikes, sensitive, ambitious, and inspired by a showy and aggressive piety. John had held the see since 397. In early days he had studied under the pagan Libanius at Antioch, and later he had been trained in the theological school of that city. He was an intimate friend of Theodore of Mopsuestia, the most eminent leader of Antiochene thought, whose principles in the next stage of the controversy came to the front. Himself a practical teacher rather than a theological systematiser, he had devoted his power and eloquence, both in Antioch and Constantinople, to the restraint of violence and the denunciation of vice and frivolity. He had in earlier days followed for some years the monastic life, and was always ascetic in self-discipline, and tactless towards those under his authority. He had been brought into public prominence, during the anxious time in 387 at Antioch, after the riot. On his appointment at Constantinople, he shewed great firmness in resisting the demands made upon him by the minister Eutropius, and subsequently in negotiations with the Gothic general Gaïnas. He preached much, and his sermons were intensely popular, for the people of Byzantium, however mixed, were sufficiently Greek to enjoy good speaking. But John seems to have done more than excite a transient enthusiasm. A good many Constantinopolitans, particularly some well-born women, devoted their lives to the works he commended to them. By his clergy, as might be expected, he was both well beloved and well hated.

Just at the time when Theophilus was beginning his attacks on the Origenistic monks, Chrysostom was starting on an expedition which was the beginning of all his troubles. Complaints had been brought to him of the bad conduct of the bishop of Ephesus. He sent to make inquiries, and though the accused bishop had in the meantime died, Chrysostom was requested by the clergy and people of Ephesus to come and settle their affairs. Accordingly the first three months of the year 401 were spent by him in a visitation of Asia, in the removal of many clergy, and the putting down of much corruption. No doubt he considered that he was acting within his rights, according to the canon of Constantinople and the precedent set by the previous bishop. But he had given a handle to the rival see of Alexandria. Worse than this, his absence had led to difficulties at home, where Severianus, a wandering bishop whom he had left as *locum tenens,* and Serapion, Chrysostom's archdeacon and friend, had quarrelled beyond hope of reconciliation.   On his return, Chrysostom judged Severianus to be in fault, and thereby affronted the Empress, who had taken delight in Severianus' sermons.   With so much of combustible elements about, the arrivals from Egypt were likely to cause a general conflagration.

Chrysostom received the Tall Brethren courteously, and admitted them to some of the church services, though he hesitated to receive them into full communion till the charge of heresy hanging over them had been removed. He seems to have wished to avoid any provocative measures. But the Brothers, anxious to remove the slur, or perhaps stirred up by some sinister interest, appealed to the Empress, as she rode down the streets in her chariot. The result was that Theophilus himself was summoned to Constantinople.to stand a charge of calumny and persecution, with darker accusations in the background. He came, but, though nominally accused, he actually took the rôle of accuser.

Before Theophilus himself arrived in Constantinople, he shewed the measure of respect in which he held that see by inducing his friend Epiphanius, bishop of Constantia in Cyprus, to go thither on the business of Origen. Epiphanius had a reputation for piety and zeal, but seems to have traded on that reputation and on his advanced years in going beyond all bounds of courtesy and even of legality. He came with a large following of bishops and clergy, began his mission by the ordination of a deacon — an act of defiance to Chrysostom's authority — refused the hospitality offered by the bishop, and endeavoured, by colloquies with the clergy and harangues to the people, to obtain the condemnation of Origen which Chrysostom refused to pronounce. He returned baffled, but soon after Theophilus himself appeared at Constantinople, and speedily gathered a party among those who had from any reason a grudge against Chrysostom. Strange to say, the Origenistic question retired into the background. Some of the bishops and clergy at Constantinople were greatly attached to the writings of Origen, with which, as we have seen, Theophilus had a secret intellectual sympathy. The charge of Origenism was brought against some of John's adherents, the charges preferred against himself were either trivial or very improbable. If any of them were founded on fact, the utmost we can safely gather from them is that John may have erred occasionally by severity in discipline, and that his ascetic habits and delicate digestion had proved incompatible with generous hospitality.

It is hardly necessary to say that Theophilus was acting without a shadow of right. He had thirty-six bishops with him and many more were coming from Asia at the Emperor's bidding. Chrysostom had forty who kept by his side. The strange phenomenon of a dual synod will be met again in the next conflict. Theophilus had the support of the Court, but he did not venture to pass judgment within the precincts of the capital. A synod was held in the neighbourhood of Chalcedon, on the Asiatic side of the Bosphorus. Theophilus was present and presided, unless the presidency was held by the old rival see of Heraclea. John refused four times to appear, and judgment was passed against him. As to the Tall Brethren, two had died and the other two made no opposition. A tumultuous scene followed in Constantinople, but John, rather than become a cause of bloodshed, withdrew under protest.

But he did not go far from the city, and in three days he was summoned back. Constantinople suffered at this time from a shock of earthquake, which seems to have alarmed the Empress, and the dislike of Egyptian interference stimulated the desire of the people of Constantinople to recover their bishop. Arcadius sent a messenger to summon John home. John at first prudently declined to come without the resolution of a synod, but his scruples were overcome, and he was reinstated in triumph.

But his return of good fortune was not of long duration. What the Court had lightly given, it might lightly withdraw. The new cause of offence was a remonstrance made by Chrysostom, who objected to the noise and revellings consequent on the erection of a statue of the Empress close to the church where he officiated. Eudoxia's blood was up. Report said that the bishop had compared her to Herodias. He had possibly compared his duty to that of John the Baptist, and his hearers had pressed the analogy further. He had previously made a quite pertinent comparison of her court clergy to the priests of Baal, who "did eat at Jezebel's table," and the inference had seemed to be that the Empress was a Jezebel. A synod was hastily convoked. Theophilus did not appear this time, but John's opponents were now sufficient. He was accused of violating a canon of the Council of Antioch (341) in having returned without waiting for a synodical decree. Insult was here added to injury. The canon had been passed by an Arian council, the violation of it had been due to imperial pressure. But there was no way of escape. Amid scenes of confusion and bloodshed, John was conveyed to Cucusus, on the Armenian frontier, and afterwards to Pityus, in Pontus.

His steadfastness under persecution, the letters by which he sought to strengthen the hands of his friends and disciples, and the efforts of his adherents, besides producing a great moral effect, seemed likely to bring about a reversal of the sentence. Pope Innocent I wrote a letter of

CH. XVII.

sympathy to Chrysostom and one of strong remonstrance to Theophilus, to whom a formal deputation was sent. To the clergy and people of Constantinople he wrote a vigorous protest against the legality of what had been done, and asserted the need of a Council of East and West. But for such a council he could only wait the opportunity in faith and patience. He did all he could by laying the matter before the Emperor Honorius at Ravenna. A deputation of clergy was sent from Emperor and Pope to Constantinople. On the way, however, the messengers had their despatches stolen from them, and they only returned from their bootless errand after many dangers and insults. Meantime the fire was allowed to burn itself out. The sufferings of Chrysostom were ended by his death in exile in September 407. There were still adherents of his in Constantinople, who refused to recognise his successor, as did also many bishops in the West. The breach was healed when Atticus, second bishop after Chrysostom, restored the name of his great predecessor to the diptychs (or tablets, on which the names of lawful bishops were inscribed).

It can hardly be said that this part of the controversy was ecclesiastical in the strict sense of the word. It made no new departure in church doctrine and discipline. But it revealed the more or less hidden forces by which succeeding conflicts were to be decided.

II. In the second period the Alexandrian leader was Cyril, nephew of Theophilus, who had succeeded him as bishop in 412. The Byzantine bishop was Nestorius, who succeeded Sisinnius in 428. Both of these prelates were more distinctly theological controversialists than were the chiefs in the last encounter. But·theology apart, they succeeded to all the difficulties in Church and State that had beset their predecessors, and neither of them was gifted with forbearance and tact. Cyril's episcopate began with violent conflicts between Christians and Jews, in which the ecclesiastical power came into collision with the civil. The story is well known how the bishop canonised a turbulent monk who had met his end in the anti-Jewish brawls, how the praefect Orestes opposed him in this and other high-handed acts, and fell a victim to the Alexandrian mob. The murder of Hypatia in 415 is not, perhaps, to be laid directly to Cyril's charge; but it illustrates the attitude of anti-pagan fanaticism towards the noblest representatives of Hellenic culture. Perhaps we may see here the effects of the policy of Theophilus when he stirred up the more ignorant of the monks to chase away or to destroy those more capable of philosophic views.

The monks were indeed becoming a more and more uncontrollable element in the situation. Cyril allied himself with a very powerful person, the archimandrite Senuti, who plays a large part in the history of Egyptian monasticism and also in the Monophysite schism. At present he was orthodox, or rather his views were those that had not yet been differentiated from orthodoxy, and his zeal was shewn chiefly in organising raids on "idols," temples and pagan priests, and in attacks, less reprehensible perhaps, but no more respectful of private property, on the goods of wealthy landowners who defrauded and oppressed the poor.

Nestorius came from Isauria. His education had been in Antioch, and the doctrines with which his name is associated are those of the great Antiochene school carried to their logical and practical conclusions. But this association has a pathetic and almost a grotesque interest. Much labour has of recent years been devoted to the task of ascertaining what Nestorius actually preached and wrote, and the result may be to acquit him of many of the extravagances imputed to him by his opponents. To put the case rather crudely: experts have contended that Nestorius was not a Nestorian. He seems to have been a harsh and unpleasant man, though capable of acquiring friends, intolerant of doctrinal eccentricities other than his own. He made it his mission to prevent men from assigning the attributes of humanity to the Deity, and boldly took the consequences of his position. Like Chrysostom, he suffered from the proximity and active ecclesiastical interest of the imperial family. When Nestorius became bishop of Constantinople in 428, the Emperor Theodosius II was in the twenty-seventh year of his age and the twentieth of his reign. Though his character and abilities offer in some respects a favourable comparison with those of his father, he suffered, partly through his education, from a too narrowly theological outlook on his empire and its duties. For fourteen years a leading part in all matters, especially ecclesiastical, had been taken by his elder sister Pulcheria, who had superintended his education and seems to have maintained a jealous regard for her own influence. This influence was at times more or less thwarted by her sister-in-law Eudocia, the clever Athenian lady, whom she had herself induced Theodosius to take in marriage. Nestorius had somehow incurred the enmity of Pulcheria. The cause is too deeply buried in the dirt of court scandal to be disinterred. Eudocia, though she is often in opposition to her sister-in-law, does not seem to have had any leanings to the party of Nestorius, and in the end, as we shall see, she took a much stronger line against it than did Pulcheria. But both ladies, in addition to personal feelings, had decided theological leanings, and to these the Alexandrians were able to appeal.

The theological principles of Cyril were those of the Alexandrian school. To him it seemed that the doctrine of the Incarnation of the Logos is impugned by any hesitation to assign the attributes of humanity to the divine Christ. It was this theological principle which was the cause, or at least the pretext, of his first attack on Nestorius. The distinctions between the Alexandrian and Antiochene schools have their roots far back in the history of theological ideas. One of the main differences lies in the preference by the Alexandrians for

allegorical modes of interpreting Scripture, while the Antiochenes preferred — in the first instance, at least — a more literal method.   This is
not unnatural, so far as Alexandria is concerned.   That city had seen
the first attempt at amalgamation of Jewish and Hellenic conceptions,
by the solvent force of figure and symbolism, while underneath there
worked the mind of primeval Egypt.   The speculations of Philo and
his successors, both Christian and Pagan, carried on the tradition into
orthodox theology.   The Christology of Alexandria had produced the
ὁμοούσιος, and now it regarded that term as needing further development — as pointing to an entire union (ἔνωσις) of divine and human in
the nature of Christ, beyond any conjunction (συνάφεια) which seemed
to admit a possible duality.   On the other side, the Antiochene school
is well represented by Theodore of Mopsuestia, the friend of Chrysostom,
and the teacher, whether directly or indirectly, of Nestorius.   He was
a learned man and a great commentator, who insisted on the need of
historical and literary studies in elucidating Holy Scripture.   His
eminence in this respect is to be seen in the fact that we often find him
cited in quite recent commentaries.   In his Christology, he held that the
union of the divine and human in the person of Jesus was moral rather
than physical or dynamical (κατ' εὐδοκίαν rather than κατ' οὐσίαν or
κατ' ἐνέργειαν).   He was, however, very careful to avoid the deduction
that the relation of divine and human was similar in kind though
different in degree, in Christ and in His followers.   The actions and
qualities ascribed to Christ as man, and particularly His birth, sufferings
and death, were not to be attributed to the Deity without some
qualifying phrase.

This question might have seemed to be one of purely academic
interest, if it had not obtained an excellent catchword which appealed to
the popular mind: the title of Θεοτόκος (Mother of God) as applied to
the Virgin Mary, vehemently asserted by the Alexandrians, rejected,
or accepted with many qualifications, by the Antiochenes.   The fierce-
ness of the battle over this word suggests analogies and associations
which are easily exaggerated.   In some sermons preached on behalf of
the Alexandrian view there are remarks which seem to foreshadow the
Virgin cult in medieval and modern times.   And the great glory of
Cyril, as we find in superscriptions of his works, was that of being the
chief advocate of the Θεοτόκος.   Again, and this is a more important
point, and one that will meet us again, both the word and the conception
could be interpreted in harmony with one of the strongest elements
in revived paganism.   The worship of a maternal deity, such as seems
to have prevailed widely in the earliest civilisation of Mediterranean
lands, had again come to the fore in the last conflict of Paganism with
Christianity.   The mysteries of Isis and of Cybele were widespread.
Julian wrote a mystic treatise in honour of the Mother of the Gods;
and as he blames the Christians for applying the term "Mother of God"

to the Virgin Mary, he seems here to be following his ordinary policy of strengthening Hellenism on its devotional side by bringing in such elements from Christianity as might be found compatible with it. The reverse process, by which Christianity among both the educated and the uneducated was assimilating pagan ideas, was of course going on at the same time, consciously in some quarters, unconsciously in others. But it would be a mistake to look on the Nestorian controversy as chiefly, or even as greatly, connected with the honour of the Virgin. Nestorius himself, in one of his sayings, probably uttered in a testy mood, protested "anyhow, don't make the Virgin a Goddess"; but this is, I believe, almost the only utterance of the kind during the controversy.

Generally speaking, on its speculative side, the controversy was Christological. The Nicene Fathers had finally pronounced on the relation of the Father to the Divine Logos, but within the limits of orthodoxy there was room for a difference as to the relation of the Logos to the human Christ. Some — on the Antiochene side — dreaded lest the idea of the humanity should be entirely merged in that of the Logos. Others (leaning towards Alexandria) would avoid any contamination of the Logos by the associations of humanity. Meantime the unphilosophical minds that took part in the dispute imagined in a vague way that it was possible for human beings to commit the crime of literally confusing the nature of the Deity or of cutting Christ in pieces.

The position of Nestorius himself and of those who followed him most closely is summarised in a saying of his that was often quoted and oftener misquoted: "I cannot speak of God as being two or three months old." He regarded it as impiety to attribute to a Person of the Trinity the acts and accidents of human, still more of infant, life. The Alexandrians, on the other hand, considered this view as virtually implying the existence of two Christs, a divine and a human. Naturally the opponents made no efforts to understand one another's position, and if they had their efforts could hardly have been successful. During this unhappy century, the mind of man had gone hopelessly astray as to its limitations. Intellectual courage had survived intellectual contact with facts, but that courage was often directed against chimaeras.

The Pope of Rome at this juncture was Celestine I (422–432). He seems to have been a conscientious and active ruler, a strict disciplinarian, yet averse to extreme rigour in dealing with delinquents. As we have already said, in this conflict Rome is not on the side of Constantinople and Antioch, but on that of Alexandria. Among the many reasons that may be assigned for the change, two considerations are prominent: first, that the relations between the sees of Rome and of Constantinople had been somewhat strained through rival claims to ecclesiastical supremacy in the regions of Illyria; and secondly, that Celestine was a devoted admirer of Augustine and anxious to put down the Pelagian heresy. Nestorius, we may safely say, was not himself a Pelagian. In some, at least, of his extant discourses he strongly opposes that teaching. But it is clear that the most eminent Antiochene theologians were not so pronounced as was Augustine in their doctrine of original sin and of predestination. Theodore of Mopsuestia was accused of the same tendency, though he avoided the heretical deductions from his principles, and Nestorius himself once wrote a sympathetic letter (though the obscurity of the text makes it doubtful as evidence) to Coelestius the notable follower of Pelagius. Again, a few years before our present date (at the Council of Carthage, 426), a monk named Leporius of Marseilles, who has been called a "Nestorian before Nestorius," was condemned as a Pelagian.

The Antiochene see was more definitely than it had previously been on the side of Constantinople. It was now occupied by a certain John, who plays an ambiguous part, but seems to have been favourable to Nestorius. But the most eminent person on this side was Theodoret, bishop of Cyrus, in the province of Euphratensis, a learned theologian, a good fighter, and a man of generous impulses, though he did not keep by his friend Nestorius to the bitter end. In these Eastern bishops we see a growing jealousy of the overweening power of Alexandria. The Church of Edessa, which had, generally speaking, lived a life apart, was drawn into the controversy. The bishop Rabbulas, though not inclined to urge the adoption of the disputed terms, took the anti-Nestorian side. His successor however, Ibas (435), upheld the Nestorian position, and retained for centuries the reverence of the Nestorian Christians of the East.

To take up briefly the main events of the controversy : It was most probably during the Christmas festival of the year 428, or else early in 429, that Proclus, bishop of Cyzicus, but resident at Constantinople, preached a sermon in which he used and expounded the term Θεοτόκος. Nestorius replied to this discourse by another, in which he warned the people to distinguish between the Divine Word and the temple in which the Deity dwelt, and to avoid saying without qualifications, that God was born of Mary. Nestorius seems to have been more guarded in his language than some of his clergy, especially a priest called Anastasius, who condemned the word Θεοτόκος altogether and even denounced as heretics those who used it. It is extremely difficult to determine how widely the Antiochene or Nestorian view prevailed, and whether it had yet reached Egypt, and on this question depends the conviction or acquittal of Cyril in regard to the charge of aggressive violence generally brought against him. In the Easter of 429 he issued an encyclical to the Egyptian monks, warning them against the dangers ahead. Men were teaching doctrines, he said, which would bring Christ down to the level of ordinary humanity.

Soon after, he wrote a long letter to the Emperor, "image of God on earth," against heresies in general and the new one — with which, however, he does not couple the name of Nestorius — in particular. He followed this up by two very long treatises to "the most pious princesses" (Pulcheria and her sisters), in which he cites many Fathers to justify the term Θεοτόκος, and makes out that the new heretics would assert two Christs. The appeal to these ladies does not seem to have pleased Theodosius, who resented Cyril's use of the discord in the imperial family. Cyril, when once he had begun, spared no pains to succeed. He had agents in Constantinople and adherents whom, at much trouble and expense, he had attached to his cause. Especially he had the support of a large following among the monks. We have his letters written both to Nestorius himself and to Celestine, bishop of Rome. In all of them he takes the ground of one having authority, of one also who, in spite of personal affection for Nestorius as a man, is bound to consider the supreme interests of the Truth. Nestorius in return eulogises Christian ἐπιείκεια, a grace in which he does not himself seem to have excelled, but maintains an independent bearing. He somewhat superfluously accuses Cyril of ignorance of the Nicene creed, and reassures him as to the satisfactory state of the Church in Constantinople. Nestorius was meantime in correspondence with Celestine on another matter. Certain bishops from the West, accused of heresy, had come to Constantinople, How was he to deal with them? He had to write a second time before a rather curt answer came; that of course they were heretics and so was Nestorius himself: they are known from other sources to have been Pelagians. Cyril had by this time sent to Rome a Latin translation of the communications that had passed between him and Nestorius with regard to the whole Christological question. A synod was consequently held at Rome which approved of Cyril's action and position, and the Pope wrote to the clergy of Constantinople, as well as to Cyril and to Nestorius himself. Ten days were given to Nestorius to make a satisfactory explanation, after which he and those holding with him were to be held excommunicated. Letters announcing this decision were sent to the bishops of Antioch, Jerusalem, Thessalonica and Philippi. To Cyril the Pope delegated the power to take necessary action against Nestorius and his followers. In a synod held at Alexandria, a series of propositions condemnatory of the doctrine taught by Nestorius and insisting on that of the "physical union" (ἕνωσις φυσική) were drawn up. In consequence of these actions, Nestorius, urged by John of Antioch, Theodoret of Cyrus and others, made certain explanations so as to tolerate the figurative use of the word Θεοτόκος.[1] But he stood his ground as to the main principles, and issued, with the support of his adherents, a list of counter-anathemas to those of Cyril.

[1] *I.e.* in accordance with the union of the two natures in Christ, even during mortal life.

CH. XVII.

It may seem strange that local councils and leading bishops or patriarchs should have gone so far without insisting on a General Council. One person evidently took this view — the Emperor Theodosius himself. The builder of the Theodosian Wall and the promulgator of the Theodosian Code can hardly have been the mere weakling that some historians would paint him. He seems to have been a man of some energy and love of fair play, though he had not the strength to carry out a policy to the end. Now, however, jointly with his cousin Valentinian, he issued a writ summoning Eastern and Western bishops to a Council to be held the following Whitsuntide (431) at Ephesus. He did not attempt to go himself, but he sent as his emissary the count Candidianus, to keep order, by military force if necessary, and especially to prevent monks and laymen from intruding. Pope Celestine sent two deputies, instructed to act along with Cyril. Cyril himself went largely accompanied. Among his monastic followers was the wild ascetic Senuti of Panopolis, already mentioned, though the stories of Senuti's conduct at the Council are not easily brought into accordance with the facts we have. Nestorius and his Constantinopolitan friends went there, but kept at a prudent distance from "the Egyptian." John of Antioch and forty Asiatic bishops came likewise, but at slow pace. Their delay, whether accidental or designed, determined the character and events of the Council. The weak point about the Council of Ephesus was that the presiding judge and the principal prosecutor were one and the same person, in an assembly which, though supposed to be primarily legislative, had also to exercise judicial functions. From the very first, Nestorius had no chance, and he declined to recognise the authority of the Council till all its members were assembled. Cyril was in no mind to allow this plea, and perhaps, in refusing to wait for the Eastern bishops, he overreached himself, and brought subsequent trouble on his own head. Celestine's delegates had not arrived, but there was no reason to wait for them, as it was known that they had been instructed to follow the Alexandrian lead. John of Antioch and the other Eastern bishops were, of course, an essential part of the Council, but a message of excuse which John had sent was tacitly construed into acquiescence with what might be done before his arrival. Accordingly, in spite of remonstrances from Nestorius, from a good many Eastern bishops who had already arrived, and from the imperial Commissioners, the Council was opened sixteen days after the appointed time, without the Antiochenes or those who were in favour of any kind of compromise with Nestorius. Messengers were sent to Nestorius, who refused to attend. It was the work of one day, the first session of the Council, to condemn him and deprive him of his see. This was done on the testimony of his letters, his reported speeches, and his rejection of the messengers from the Council. One hundred and ninety-eight bishops signed these decrees. The populace of Ephesus received the result with wild enthusiasm, and gave the champions of the Theotokes an ovation on their way to their lodgings. Perhaps it is not mere fanciful analogy to recall the two-hours' shouting of an earlier city mob : "Great Artemis of the Ephesians."

Five days afterwards, John of Antioch arrived. He had with him comparatively few bishops, and when he was joined by the Nestorians, the number of his party only amounted to forty-three. There seems a touch of irony in the assertion which he made afterwards that the reason of his scanty numbers was to be found in his strict injunctions to follow out the Emperor's directions. Similarly, when he justifies the delay by the necessity that the bishops should officiate in their churches on the First Sunday after Easter, we may seem to have a covert hit at Cyril's large numbers who found no difficulty in absenting themselves from their flocks.

From the first, John took his stand against the acts of Cyril. He rejected the communications of the Council and joined forces with Nestorius. The imperial officials afforded him protection and support. In the "Conciliabulum," as his assembly was contemptuously called, Cyril and Memnon of Ephesus were in their turn deprived and excommunicated. Meantime the original Council, now joined by delegates from Rome, continued its sessions, deposed John and all his adherents, and continued to pass decrees against the Pelagians and other heretics. Whether or no the precise articles anathematising Nestorius, which had been drawn up at Alexandria, were passed by the Council is a disputed matter and one of inferior importance. Their sense was certainly maintained, and they were answered by counter-anathematisms on the other side.

The situation was becoming intolerable. Two rival assemblies of bitterly hostile factions were sitting in conclave through the sultry days of an Eastern summer, in a city always given to turbulence, and now stirred up by long and eloquent discourses such as a Greek populace ever loved to hear. Count Candidianus and the other imperial delegates had a hard task. He had, after the first session, torn down the placards declaring the deposition of Nestorius. He tried to prevent the Egyptian party from preaching inflammatory sermons, and from communicating the fever of controversy to Constantinople. This, however, he could not do, as Cyril found means of corresponding with the monks of Constantinople.

The Emperor himself was hardly equal to the emergency. The difficulty as to Nestorius was partly removed by the offer of Nestorius himself to retire to a monastery. With regard to the other leaders, Cyril and Memnon were for a time imprisoned. The Emperor received embassies from both sides, and finally decided to maintain the decisions of both councils. Maximian, a priest of Constantinople, was appointed to the vacant see of that city. Then Cyril and Memnon were liberated and restored to their sees, and the remaining members of the council

CH. XVII.

were bidden to return home, unless they could first find some means of accommodation with the Orientals.

The means by which the Emperor's partial change of front and the yet more clearly marked prevalence of anti-Nestorian feeling at Court were brought about can only be brought to light by untangling a most involved skein of ecclesiastical diplomacy. From a letter of one of Cyril's agents, as well as from the recently published account of Nestorius himself, there was a profuse distribution of gratuities among notable persons, including the princesses themselves. But Cyril appealed to zeal as well as to avarice. It would appear that a good many people in Constantinople were favourable to Nestorius, but that the clergy and the monks were generally against him. The union between Egyptians and Orientals was brought to pass sooner than we might have expected. It was based on an explanation not wholly unlike that urged on Nestorius by John of Antioch near the beginning of the difficulties, an acknowledgment of two natures united into one (δύο φύσεων ἕνωσιν; and μίαν τὴν τοῦ Θεοῦ φύσιν σεσαρκωμένην), with a recognition, in virtue of the union, of the propriety of the term Θεοτόκος. It was a triumph for Cyril, but some of the most independent of his opponents still held out. Especially Theodoret, the best theologian of the party, and the most faithful — a slight distinction — to his friends, refused to be included in an arrangement which did not restore all the sees of the dispossessed bishops to their rightful occupants. It was only to a special decree of the Emperor, enforcing ecclesiastical agreement in the East, that he gave at last a qualified assent. But the indignant protest widely raised against Alexandrian ambition was expressed in a playful letter which he wrote after Cyril's death in 444, in which, along with more charitable wishes that we might expect for the final judgment on his soul, he recommends that a large stone be placed over the grave, to keep quiet the disturber who had now gone to propagate strange doctrines among the shades below. The last efforts of Cyril had been towards the condemnation of the great commentator, the father of Antiochene philosophy, Theodore of Mopsuestia. The reverence in which the memory of Theodore was held caused the scheme to fail, only to be renewed, with baneful consequences, by the Emperor Justinian.

We may now narrate the end of Nestorius. For some years he lived in peace in a monastery near Antioch, but his relations with its bishop appear to have cooled. In 435, he was banished to Petra in Arabia, but instead of going thither, he seems to have been sent to one of the oases of Egypt. There a wandering horde of Libyans, the Blemmyes, made him prisoner. Soon after he was released, and fled to Panopolis in Egypt. Thence he wrote a pathetic letter to the Praeses of the Thebaid, begging for protection "lest to all time the evil report should be brought that it is better to be a captive of barbarians than a fugitive suppliant of the Roman Emperor." But Nestorius had fallen into the very hotbed of fanatical monasticism. The Praeses caused him to be removed by "barbarian" soldiers to Elephantine, on the borders of the province. There is some evidence that the blow which put an end to his sufferings was dealt by the hand of Senuti himself. This was however some years later.

Nestorius was not a great leader of men, nor a very striking figure-head for a great cause. His whole story illustrates the perversity and blind cruelty of his opponents, and it is only in comparison with them that he sometimes appears in an almost dignified character. This character is greatly emphasized by the lately discovered writings in which Nestorius was employed shortly before his death. He seems to have approved the final arrangement of Chalcedon, and even to have acquiesced, with a magnanimity hardly to be expected, in the compromise by which his own name was left under the cloud while the principles for which he had striven were in great measure confirmed.

III. The Monophysite or Eutychian Controversy may be regarded as a continuation of the preceding one, yet as some of the leading parties were different, as well as their objects and methods, it may be better to take it apart.

The main difference as to character and issue of this conflict compared with the last lies in the character of the champions of Rome and of Alexandria respectively. Now there was a Pope of commanding character and ability. Leo I stands out in history as a great ruler of the Church, who crushed a premature movement towards Gallicanism; as a moral power in Rome itself in times of demoralising panic; and as the shepherd of his people, who — in ways known and unknown — stopped the Romeward march of Attila the Hun. Here we have to deal with him as a firm and successful assertor of the claims of St Peter's chair over all others, and as a great diplomatic theologian who could mark out a permanent *via media* between opposite dogmatic tendencies.

Dioscorus, the champion of Alexandria, had succeeded Cyril in A.D. 444. The fact that he was subsequently condemned as a here-siarch, whereas Cyril was canonised as a saint, has necessarily led to differences of opinion as to the relations between the two. He may be regarded, with respect to his dogmatic position, either as a deserter of Cyril's position between the heresies of Monophysitism and Dyo-physitism, or else as the real successor of Cyril in pressing the Alexandrian Christology to its natural conclusions. Personally he seems to have dissociated himself from Cyril by making foes of Cyril's family, although according to one account, he was himself of Cyril's kin. The charges made against his morals, both in public and in private life, may have been well founded, but in three respects, at least, he was a real follower of Cyril — in his zeal for the prerogatives of the see of St Mark; in the remarkable pertinacity and unscrupulousness with which he pursued his ends; and in his reliance on the monastic element among his followers, particularly on the part of it that was most violent and fanatical.

Of Flavian, bishop of Constantinople, there is less to be said. He enjoyed a reputation for piety, and seems to have acted with some independence in his relations with the Emperor. But he does not shew enough dignity and moderation in the early stages of the dispute to obtain the sympathy which his cruel treatment at the end might seem to claim.

The premonitory symptoms of the controversy are to be seen in the complaints made by Dioscorus against Theodoret of Cyrus, who, as we have seen, had come into the general agreement without renouncing his hostility to the "Egyptians" and all their ways. On the promotion of Dioscorus, he had written him a congratulatory and conciliatory letter. Since Theodoret almost alone in his generation seems to have had a sense of humour, we may suspect a grain of sarcasm in singling out for commendation a virtue — that of humility — which the dearest friend of Dioscorus could hardly claim for him. Dioscorus soon charged Theodoret with having gone beyond justice in helping to restore an ex-Nestorian bishop in Tyre, of having himself preached a Nestorian sermon in Antioch, and of having, by appending his signature to a document issued by the late patriarch of Constantinople, acknowledged too widespread a jurisdiction in that see. Dioscorus secured an imperial prohibition served on Theodoret against departing from his diocese. Considering the events which followed, he could hardly have conferred on him a greater benefit.

The central controversy, which broke out in 448, may have likewise originated from Dioscorus. Another source assigned is a court intrigue. The eunuch Chrysaphius is said to have found the Patriarch Flavian an obstacle in his way. Flavian had incurred the ill-will of Theodosius by breaking a custom of sending complimentary gifts, and also by refusing or at least avoiding the task of forcing Pulcheria to retire into religious seclusion. The figure-head in the controversy is a poor one. Eutyches, an archimandrite (or abbot of some monastery) in or near Constantinople, was an aged man, who according to his own statements never left his monastery. But he had been a strong opponent of Nestorius, and now he was accused of disseminating errors of the opposite kind — of trying to propagate the doctrine of the One Nature. His accuser, Bishop Eusebius of Dorylaeum, induced Flavian, at first reluctant, to call him to account. This was done at the half-yearly local council of the bishops who chanced to be at Constantinople. The accusations were made, and Eutyches was with difficulty brought from his seclusion to make his defence. He did not shine as a theologian, and wished to fall back on the decisions of Nicaea and of Ephesus. On being hard pressed, he stated his belief in the words that he confessed Christ as being of two natures, *before* the union in the Incarnation, of one nature afterwards, being God Incarnate. On this point he refused to go back, and he was accordingly condemned and degraded. He afterwards tried in vain to prove that the reports of the synod had been falsified. He appealed to the Emperor, to Pope Leo, and to the monks of Constantinople. His friends, especially Chrysaphius, stirred up Dioscorus on his behalf. Suggestions were made of a larger council, to revise the decision recently made at Constantinople, and the Emperor decided that such a council should be held, and that Dioscorus should preside.

But if it was the opportunity of Alexandria, it was likewise the opportunity of Rome. Leo had received the communication of Eutyches with courtesy, and was at first somewhat irritated at Flavian's delay in keeping him informed and asking his counsel. But as soon as he had made inquiries into the whole affair, he became convinced that Flavian was right and Eutyches wrong. He at once urged his views in letters to Flavian, Theodosius, Pulcheria and others. There were three principles which determined his action : first, that it was not a case for a General Council at all. The Emperor however had decided otherwise. Secondly, that if there were a Council, it ought to be called in the West. Here again he failed to secure his point. Thirdly, that it was for him, as successor to St Peter, to draw up for the Church an authoritative statement (or *Tome*) as to the points in controversy. Here he succeeded, though only in part. When the Council was finally decided upon he sent three delegates, a bishop, a priest, and a deacon, to represent him, and to communicate his *Tome* to the fathers present.

The Council was summoned to meet at Ephesus on 1 August 449. Dioscorus, as president, was to have as assessors Juvenal of Jerusalem and Thalassius of Caesarea. Both in composition and in procedure, to say nothing of state interference, it was exceedingly irregular. Many conspicuous bishops, such as Theodoret, were absent. An archimandrite, Barsumas, was allowed to come accompanied by a host of wild Syrian monks. The authority of the Roman see was so far neglected that Leo's *Tome* was not even allowed to be read, and by an unblushing terrorism the signatures of over one hundred and fifteen bishops were obtained. Flavian who had condemned Eutyches, and Eusebius who had accused him, were deposed. Eutyches himself was reinstated and declared orthodox. Several bishops who had been more or less friendly with Nestorius, or who had some grudge against the Alexandrian see, were condemned and deprived on the strength of sayings attributed to them in public or private, and of many improbable moral offences. Among the deprived were Theodoret of Cyrus and Ibas of Edessa. The papal legates were not present during the whole time of the Council; indeed with regard to two of them the question of their presence at all is doubtful. A single protest — *Contradicitur* — was made by the Roman deacon Hilary, who escaped for his life and brought tidings of what had been done to Rome. Many suffered severe treatment. Flavian succumbed and died very soon after. The nominee of Dioscorus, Anatolius, was appointed to succeed him.

CH. XVII.

The violence of Dioscorus and his party may have been somewhat exaggerated by those who afterwards brought him to account. Yet there can be little doubt that the name given to the whole proceeding by Leo, the Robber Council, which has clung to it all through the course of history, was one that it richly deserved. It is difficult to understand how Dioscorus could have so far overshot the mark. Either he must have been an utterly vain and foolhardy man, who could not appreciate the strength of his antagonists, or he must have relied on the forces at his command, especially the monks and the Emperor. The Egyptian and Syrian monks were certainly to be relied on, and Theodosius upheld him and the decisions of his Council to the very end, even after a court revolution in which Chrysaphius had been degraded. (Eudocia had some years previously been obliged to leave the city.) Leo acted with decision and promptitude. He called a synod at Rome, and endeavoured to secure a revision of the acts of the irregular Council by one that should be full and legal. He refused to recognise Anatolius till he should have given satisfaction as to orthodoxy. He wrote to Pulcheria, asking again for her influence. He also used influence with the Western Court, and induced the Emperor Valentinian, his mother Placidia, and his wife Eudoxia — the cousin, the aunt and the daughter respectively of Theodosius — to write to him and urge a new Council. Before the death of Flavian was known, his restoration was also demanded. The council should be held in Italy. At first there was no result. But the whole aspect of affairs was changed when, in July 450, Theodosius died from the effects of a fall from his horse. Pulcheria, with the orthodox husband Marcian, whom ambition or stress of circumstances led her to choose, ascended the imperial throne. She had, as we have seen, disliked Nestorius, but she had no sympathy with the extreme party on the other side. She had always greatly interested herself in theological matters, and was quite ready to avail herself of the opportunity now offered to give power and unity to the Church.

The change in governors necessitated with Leo a modification not of strategy but of tactics. If no new Council was necessary, the calling of one was not, from the Roman point of view, desirable. The memory of Flavian must be rehabilitated, but Pulcheria was quite ready to order the removal of the martyred bishop's bones. Dioscorus must be called to order and his victims reinstated, and the rule of faith must be laid down. But for these objects, again, a Council seemed superfluous, since according to Leo's view of papal authority, which the sufferers, especially Theodoret, were willing to acknowledge, he was competent to revise their cases on appeal, and as to the faith, Leo's *Tome* had been prepared with the express view of making a settlement. Accordingly he wrote to Marcian against the project of a Council. As was natural, Marcian and Pulcheria took a somewhat different view. Some circumstances, it is true, would make them ready to receive Leo's suggestions. Piety apart, they would naturally desire peace and unity, and also freedom from Alexandrian interference. Rumour said that Dioscorus was plotting against them. This may be false, though the friendly relations between the Monophysites and the exiled widow. Empress Eudocia might render such a suggestion not improbable. But on the other hand the Emperor and Empress were not likely to avoid Scylla in order to fall into Charybdis — to liberate their ecclesiastical policy from Alexandrian dictation merely to bow beneath the yoke of Rome. With regard to the appointment of Anatolius, Leo had, by the appointment of a patriarch of Constantinople, attacked the independence of the Emperor as well as the dignity of the patriarch himself. A Council must be called, Leo or his legate might preside, and his *Tome* might serve as basis for a confession of faith. But the Council must be held in the East, not, as Leo now vainly requested, in the West, and measures must be taken in it to secure the prestige of the Byzantine see against that of either St Mark or St Peter. This policy however was not all to be declared at once.

The Council was summoned to assemble at Nicaea, the orthodox associations of that place being of good omen. It was to be larger and more representative than any hitherto held, comprising as many as six hundred and thirty-six bishops (twice as many as those at Nicaea), though the Emperor and Empress took strong measures to exclude a concourse of unauthorised persons, who might come to make a disturbance. Seeing, however, that military and civil exigencies prevented Marcian from attending meetings at a distance from his capital, he adjourned the Council to Chalcedon. The wisdom of this step soon became evident. Chalcedon was sufficiently near to Constantinople to allow a committee of imperial Ministers, with some distinguished members of the Byzantine Senate, to undertake the general control of affairs, and the Emperor and Empress were able, at least once, to attend in state, as well as to watch proceedings throughout.

When we consider the composition of the Council of Chalcedon and the state of parties at the time, we are surprised less at its failure to secure ecclesiastical unity than at its success in accomplishing any business at all. It can hardly be said that anyone wished for unity except on conditions that some others would pronounce intolerable. On the one hand were the ex-Nestorian bishops, Theodoret of Cyrus and Ibas of Edessa, who, though they had repudiated Nestorius himself, were strongly attached to the school from which he had sprung, and had suffered on many occasions, but worst at the Robber Council, from the injustice and violence of the Eutychian party. These, being dispossessed, could not of course take part in the proceedings till they had been reinstated, but they had been summoned to the spot, and their very presence was very likely to inflame the passions of their opponents. At the opposite extreme was Dioscorus, supported but feebly by the bishops

CH. XVII.

who had assisted him at Ephesus, or rather by such as had not already submitted to Rome, yet backed up vigorously by a host of Syrian and Egyptian monks, who had managed to secure admittance in the character of petitioners. Between these parties stood the legates and the party of Leo, determined on urging the Roman solution of the problem and no other. In the church of St Euphemia, where the Council sat, the central position was held by the imperial Commissioners. Immediately on their left were the Roman delegates, who were regarded as the ecclesiastical presidents: the bishops Paschasinus and Lucentius, and the priest Boniface; and near them the bishops of Antioch, Caesarea, and Ephesus; then several from Pontus, Thrace, and some Eastern Provinces. To the right of the Commissioners were the bishops of Alexandria and Jerusalem, with those from Egypt, Illyria, and Palestine. These seem to have been the most conspicuous members of the Council, and were ranged like government and opposition parties in parliament. A certain number walked over from the Egyptian to the Roman side in the course of the first session, and before the whole business was over, the right must have been very much weakened. There were no restraints set to the expression of agitated feelings, and cries of "turn him out," "kill him," as an objectionable person came in sight were mixed with groans of real or feigned penitence for past errors, and imprecations against those who would either "divide" or "confuse" the Divine Nature.

The first and third sessions were devoted to the case of Dioscorus, the second, fourth, and fifth, to the question of Belief, the others chiefly to minor or personal matters. At the very first, the papal legates refused to let Dioscorus take his seat, stating that Leo had forbidden it. The first charge against him was that he had held a Council without the consent of the Roman see. It is difficult to see how this could have been maintained, since Leo had certainly sent his representatives to the Second Council of Ephesus. But other charges were soon brought forward by Eusebius of Dorylaeum as to his behaviour with regard to Flavian and Eutyches. The acts of the Robber Council, as well as those of the synod at Constantinople at which Flavian had condemned Eutyches, were read, a lengthy process which lasted till after night had fallen and candles had been brought in. Theodoret, amid cheers from one side and groans from the other was brought in to witness against his enemy, now at bay. The bishops who had signed the decrees at Ephesus told ugly stories of terrorism and begged for forgiveness. Finally, the secular judges declared Dioscorus deposed. But a further examination was made in the third session, from which, since the subjects to be discussed were of technical theology, the imperial Commissioners were absent. This fact gave Dioscorus an excuse for declining to obey the summons sent him. Charges against his private life were made at some length. After his third refusal to appear, the sentence of deprivation was passed. A similar decree was passed against Thalassius, Juvenal, and others who had assisted him, but on due submission these were not only pardoned but allowed to take part in the business of the Council. A similar indulgence was extended to all who, by force or guile, or possibly of their own will, had joined in the action which they were now ready to condemn.

Yet Dioscorus was not wholly without a following. Perhaps the demand made in the fourth session, by certain Egyptian bishops, that according to usage, they might not be forced to consent to anything important without the consent of the Alexandrian see, may not have shewn much loyalty to the late occupant of that see. But there can be no doubt that the petition presented by a body of monks, chiefly Eutychian, shewed serious disaffection. The request was for a truly oecumenical council, such as this one could hardly be without the presence of an Alexandrian patriarch. It is needless to say that the petitioners were angrily repelled. Yet they alone, of all who had been concerned in the Robber Council, had at least retained something of thieves' honour.

The discussions on the question of the Faith were long and stormy. The practical problem might seem to be comparatively simple, if it consisted in marking out safe ground between dyophysitism and monophysitism. Neither of these forms of belief had advocates in the Council. For we have seen that Nestorius was not an uncompromising dyophysite and Eutyches was not an entire monophysite. Even had it been otherwise, Nestorianism had been trampled in the dust, and Eutychianism might seem to have received its death-blow. Those who said that further definitions were unnecessary, that the doctrines of Cyril and of Leo were in full accord, had some show of reason on their side. But the need for further definition was urged, and nearly led to a collapse of the whole Council. A general agreement was obtained without great difficulty. The creeds of Nicaea and of Constantinople, the letters of Cyril to Nestorius and to John of Antioch, and finally the *Tome* of Leo, were read and approved. It was this last document that the Roman delegates regarded as sufficient to put a stop to all further controversy. It has always remained a classical monument in the history of Christology, and has been far more widely read and studied than the declaration finally made at Chalcedon. Perhaps it seemed insufficient to some because the word Θεοτόκος was not contained in it, though the idea implied in that word is set forth in unmistakable terms. And again, though very many present had subscribed to the *Tome*, it was not unnatural that in many quarters there should be a reluctance to accept as possessing peculiar authority a document emanating from a Western source. Anatolius and certain other bishops accordingly drew up a formula which was presented to the Council. But this only roused fierce opposition from the Roman legates, and even to a threat

CH. XVII.

that they would withdraw altogether, and cause a new Council to be assembled in Italy.

The obnoxious creed has not come down to us, but we gather that it contained the expression: Christ is *of* two natures (ἐκ δύο φύσεων) instead of the phrase *in* two natures (ἐν δύο φύσεσιν). Those who would regard the theological difference as rooted in philosophical distinction may suggest a rational apprehension in the minds of Leo and his supporters, that whatever might be the principle of union or separation in divine and human nature, it could not, as Eutyches supposed, be dependent on a merely temporal relation.

It would, of course, have been fatal to the policy of the Emperor and Empress if Rome had seceded at this juncture. As a compromise, Anatolius and a chosen representative committee of bishops were bidden to retire into the oratory of St Euphemia and prepare a new creed. The document, when produced, proved to be based on that of Leo. But it contained on the one side the word Θεοτόκος, and on the other — there can hardly be any doubt, in spite of what seem to be clerical errors — the phrase ἐν δύο φύσεσιν.

After the question of the Faith had been settled, the Emperor came himself to the Council and congratulated the bishops on the success of their labours in the cause of unity and truth. Sundry matters of local yet not unimportant interest were transacted in the last sessions. Thus Ibas and Theodoret were reinstated in their sees. In the case of Theodoret, a natural reluctance to anathematise the memory of his quondam friend Nestorius was overcome by threats. The only conceivable excuse is that the anathema may have been drifting into a mere *façon de parler*, and that, as shewn above, Nestorius had himself generously expressed a wish that his own reputation might not be preferred to the cause of truth.

Finally, a list of canons, thirty in number, were drawn up, mostly on points of less burning interest, and the imperial authorities undertook to add the force of the secular arm to the decrees of the Council. But before the members dispersed, a stormy discussion arose which might seem to give the lie to the Emperor's pious hopes, especially as it was but the beginning of a fresh breach. This was the dispute as to Canon xxviii. It is certain, from the remonstrance made by the Roman delegates, that neither they nor the imperial Commissioners had been present when the one in question was put to the vote; also that a comparatively small number of bishops had subscribed it. The canon is so important that it had better be given in full:[1]

"Following in all things the decisions of the holy Fathers and acknowledging the canon, which has just been read, of the One Hundred and Fifty Bishops beloved-of-God (who assembled in the Imperial city of Constantinople, which is New Rome, in the time of the Emperor

[1] Nearly Dr Percival's translation, *ap. The Seven Oecumenical Councils.*

Theodosius of happy memory), we also do enact and decree the same things concerning the privileges of the most holy Church of Constanti_nople, which is New Rome. For the Fathers rightly granted privileges to the throne of Old Rome, because it was the imperial city. And the One Hundred and Fifty most religious bishops, actuated by the same consideration, gave equal privileges (ἴσα πρεσβεῖα) to the most holy throne of New Rome, justly judging that the city which is honoured with the Sovereignty and the Senate and enjoys equal privileges with the old imperial Rome, should in ecclesiastical matters also be magnified as she is, and rank next after her; so that in the Pontic, the Asian, and the Thracian Dioceses the metropolitans only, and such bishops also of the Dioceses aforesaid as are among the barbarians, should be ordained by the aforesaid most holy throne of the most holy Church of Constanti_nople; every metropolitan of the aforesaid dioceses, together with the bishops of his province, ordaining his own provincial bishops, as has been declared by the divine canons; but that, as has been above said, the metropolitans of the aforesaid Dioceses should be ordained by the arch_bishop of Constantinople, after the proper elections have been held according to custom and have been reported to him."

It is hardly necessary to say that all the earlier or theoretical part of this document clashed entirely with Leo's views as to the supremacy of Rome and the relations of Church and State, while the latter or practical part seemed to give dangerously wide powers to the see of New Rome. When the Roman delegates objected, they were allowed a hearing, but reminded that it was their own fault that they had not been present when the canon was passed. They lodged a formal protest, supported by a phrase which had been interpolated into the Nicene canons. The result was nugatory. The canon was maintained. Leo supported the action of his delegates, or rather, they had rightly gauged his mind. A long and stormy correspondence which he kept up with Marcian, Pulcheria, and Anatolius led to no final settlement. Leo acknowledged the validity of what had been done at Chalcedon with regard to the Faith, but held out tenaciously against the claims of the Byzantine see. There seems a touch of unconscious irony in his championship of the ancient rights of Alexandria and of Antioch, as well as in his incul-cations on Anatolius to practise the virtue of humility. He only became reconciled to Anatolius three years later, after receiving from him a very apologetic letter, laying the blame on the Byzantine clergy, and stating that the whole case had been reserved for Leo's decision. But Anatolius could not bind the Eastern churches. Canon XXVIII continued to be accepted by the East, though unrecognised by the West.

We may ask which cause, or which party, profited by the Council of Chalcedon. The Papacy had put forth great claims, and in part had realised them, yet it seemed at the last to have been overreached by the East. A certain uniformity of belief had been imposed on a

CH. XVII.

great part of the Christian world, but this belief was not supposed to add anything to the authoritative declarations of former councils, and so far as it wore any semblance of novelty, it served only to embitter party strife in the regions that most required pacification. The most active and ambitious disturber of the peace had been got rid of, but only with the result that his see had become the prey of hostile factions. There was some gain to the far East, in the restoration of learned and comparatively moderate men, like Theodoret and Ibas; but they had still to encounter active opposition. Perhaps the Emperor was the chief gainer; but he had overstrained his authority. The best that can be said for the Council is that things might have been worse if no council had met.

We may take briefly, as Epilogue to the Council of Chalcedon, the disturbances and insurrections consequent on the attempts to enforce its decisions: (a) in Palestine; (b) in Egypt; (c) in Provinces further to the East.

(a) Juvenal, bishop of Jerusalem, had played a sorry part in the whole business. It is not surprising that when he returned, pardoned and rehabilitated, to his bishopric, his flock was not unanimous in welcoming him back. His opponents, the most vigorous of whom came from the monastic bodies, set up in opposition to him a certain Theodosius, a monk who had been at Chalcedon and who had returned full of wrath and of determination to resist the new decisions. Juvenal fled back to Constantinople, while Theodosius acted as patriarch, appointing bishops of Monophysite views, and bidding defiance to imperial as well as to conciliar authority. The recalcitrant monks had the sympathy, if not the active assistance, of the ex-Empress Eudocia, who was still residing in Palestine. Pope Leo, it need scarcely be said, was vigorous with his pen on the other side. Marcian determined on armed intervention. Forces were sent under the count Dorotheus, and Juvenal was reinstated. Theodosius was brought prisoner to Constantinople, and liberated during the next reign. The undercurrent of Monophysitism was, however, only covered for a time, not permanently checked.

(b) In Alexandria, as might be expected, the resistance was more prolonged and more serious. Whatever the faults of Dioscorus, he still had partisans among the monks and the common people. His successor Proterius was chosen, we are told, by the *nobiles civitatis*, and aristocratic management did not always succeed in Alexandria. Here again recourse was had to military force. Proterius had not the art of making himself popular; and when Dioscorus died at Gangra, his place of banishment, a clever schemer came to the force. This was Timothy, a Teuton whose tribal name, the *Herul*, was appropriately twisted into *Aelurus*, the Cat. He is said to have gone by night to the bedsides of those whom he wished to persuade and to have told them, as they lay between sleep and waking, that he was an angel, sent to bid them provide themselves with a bishop and, in particular, to choose Timothy. On the death of Marcian, he obtained his desire and was chosen bishop by the people, and consecrated in the great church of the Caesarium, once the scene of the murder of Hypatia. A fate very much like that of Hypatia befell the bishop Proterius, whose mangled body was dragged through the streets and then committed to the flames. How far the actual murder was instigated by Timothy it is impossible to say. The Emperor Leo, who had succeeded Marcian in 457, could not, of course, sanction the result of such proceedings. One scheme which suggested itself was the calling of a new Council. Any notion of the kind was, however, frustrated by Leo of Rome, who probably thought that an assembly held in the East at that juncture might prove even more antagonistic to Roman authority than the Council of Chalcedon. Accordingly, by his advice, the Emperor sent round circular letters to a large number of bishops and ascetics (Simeon Stylites had a copy) asking for their opinion and advice. The result was a general condemnation of Timothy Aelurus, and a confirmation of the Chalcedonian decrees. One bishop declared against Chalcedon, but even he was opposed to Timothy. Aelurus was accordingly driven out and succeeded by another Timothy, called Salophaciolus. But Aelurus maintained his influence, and on the wave of Monophysite reaction under the pretender Basiliscus he returned to his see. From about this time we may date the practical nullity of the orthodox Alexandrian patriarchate and the rise of the Coptic Church. But, as is seen by the whole course of events from the days of Theophilus and earlier, the causes of disruption were not entirely due to the difference between ἐκ and ἐν. Alexandria itself might be Greek and cosmopolitan, but Egypt had a peculiar and national character, which was chiefly evident in its language and its institutions, particularly its monasticism. If it seems surprising that violent ecclesiastical rivalries and the turbulence of the most unrestrained city mob to be found in all history should have led to the growth of a church which, with all its faults, has maintained itself ever since in the affections of the common people, the clue is to be found in the separation of Greek and Egyptian elements, which were incapable of a satisfactory and wholesome combination. But the separation naturally led in time to the fall of the Roman power in the chief seat of Hellenic civilisation in the East.

(c) In the East, on the other hand, in Syria and Mesopotamia, there was less opposition to the Chalcedonian settlement, but a few years later a latent discontent broke into revolt. Domnus, bishop of Antioch, had played an undignified and unhappy part in the controversy. Though a friend of Theodoret and of Ibas, and an Antiochene in theology, he had been forced to subscribe the decisions of the Robber Council, and even after that humiliation had been deprived of his see. He was therefore pardoned at Chalcedon, but he was pensioned, not restored to office. His successor Maximus had been practically appointed by Anatolius of Constantinople. Leo thought best to confirm the appointment, and Maximus justified the hopes placed in him by proclaiming the decrees of Chalcedon on his return. But a few years after, for some unknown reason, he was deposed. In 461 a violent Monophysite, Peter the Fuller, succeeded in intruding into the see. His contribution to the Monophysite cause was of the kind always more effectual than argument in winning popular sympathy — a change in ritual. He introduced into the *Trisagion* "Holy, holy, holy is the Lord God of Hosts" the phrase: "who was crucified for us." The imputation of suffering to one of the Trinity seemed to go further in the doctrine of One Nature than even the ascription to the Deity of birth in time. The catch-phrase excited the more passion because of the opportunity it afforded for rival singing or shouting in the church services. Peter was twice expelled from Antioch, but returned in triumph, and took an active part in the Henoticon scheme, to which we shall come directly.

Meantime, Ibas had returned to Edessa. The part taken by this city in the next period of the conflict is so interesting and important that it may seem desirable to notice here the circumstances which had made it theologically prominent. Edessa was the capital of the border-province of Osrhoene, belonging to the Empire, but close to the Persian frontier. According to tradition, it had received Christianity at a very early period, and there is no doubt that the people of those regions, speaking a Syrian tongue, and but little acquainted with Greek philosophy, held a theology different in many respects from that of the Catholics or of Greek-speaking heretics of the fourth and early fifth centuries. All this, however, came to be changed by two events: the foundation of a school, chiefly for theological studies, at Edessa (*circ.* A.D. 363) and the active efforts of Bishop Rabbula (d. A.D. 435) to bring the church of Edessa into line with those of the Empire. These two forces, on the present occasion, acted in contrary directions. The school, which had been founded soon after the abandonment of Nisibis to the Persians (363), had become a nursery of Antiochene thought. For some time Ibas had presided over it, and laboured hard at the translation and promulgation of the theology and exegesis of Theodore of Mopsuestia, the real founder (as is sometimes stated) of Nestorianism. Rabbula the bishop was an uncompromising Cyrillian. On his death Ibas was raised to the bishopric, and thence exerted his influence in the same direction as formerly, supported by a faithful and singularly able pupil, Barsumas or Barsauma, who shared his fortunes and returned with him to Edessa after the Council of Chalcedon. On the death of Ibas, however, there came a Monophysite reaction. Nonnus, who had held the see while Ibas was under a cloud, reascended the episcopal throne (457). In his anxiety to purge the city of Nestorianism (though Ibas had anathematised Nestorius more than once), he made an attack on the school, and banished a large number of "Persian" teachers, *i.e.* of the orientals who had kept by Ibas. Barsumas came to Nisibis, now under Persian rule, and there devoted himself to the task of freeing the Syrian Church from the Western yoke, and of combating Monophysite doctrine. It will shortly appear how an unexpected turn of events greatly assisted him in both these objects. What has chiefly to be noticed here is that a few years after the Council of Chalcedon, Nestorians and Eutychians, or those to whom their adversaries would respectively apply these names, were in unstable equilibrium in various parts of the East.

IV. We now come to the fourth stage in the controversy, or series of controversies, which both manifest and also enhance the religious disunion of this century: the attempt of the Emperor Zeno, along with the bishops of Constantinople and Alexandria, to bring about a compromise. A few words about the character and position of each of the three parties in this attempt may fitly precede our examination of their policy and the reason of its failure.

Zeno the Isaurian (history has forgotten his original name — Tarasicodissa the son of Rusumbladestus) was son-in-law of Leo I, and succeeded his own infant son Leo II in 474. As to the part of his policy which concerns us here, we have Gibbon's often-quoted remark that "it is in ecclesiastical story that Zeno appears least contemptible." We shall see directly that this opinion is open to controversy. But there is no doubt that Zeno found himself in a very difficult position. Scarcely was he seated on his throne when Basiliscus, brother of the Empress-dowager, raised an insurrection against him (475), and he went into exile. Basiliscus appealed to the Monophysite subjects of the Empire, anathematised the *Tome* of Leo and the Council of Chalcedon, and recalled the disaffected bishops, including Timothy the Cat and Peter the Fuller. The circular letter in which he stated this decision is a remarkable assertion of the secular power over the Church. It was, however, of no lasting effect. The storm it aroused forced Basiliscus to countermand it. After about two years of banishment, Zeno fought or bought his way back. The bishops who had assented to the Encyclical of Basiliscus made very humble apology, and for a time it seemed as if the Chalcedonian settlement would prevail. The fact that it did not, is to be attributed mainly to the bishops of Constantinople and Alexandria, Acacius and Peter.

Acacius who had succeeded Gennadius (third after Anatolius) on the episcopal throne of Constantinople in 471, was a man of supple character, forced by circumstances to appear as a champion of theological causes rather than in the more congenial character of a diplomatist. He seems to have been drawn into opposition to Basiliscus, to whose measures he had at first assented, then to have headed the opposition to them and to have earned the credit of the Anti-encyclical and of the final surrender of the usurper. In this crisis, Acacius had found his hand forced by the monks of the capital. The monastic element is very strong in all the controversies of the period, but it is not always on one side. In Egypt, as we have seen, the monks were Monophysite. In Constantinople, the great order of the Acoemetae (*sleepless* — so called from the perpetual psalmody kept up in their churches) was fanatically Chalcedonian. Possibly the recent foundation (under the patriarch Gennadius) of their great monastery of Studium by a Roman, may partly account for their devotion to the *Tome* of Leo. In any case, they formed the most vigorous resisting body to all efforts against the settlement of Chalcedon. The policy of Acacius seems to have been determined by the influence acquired over him by Peter Mongus of Alexandria, although, in his earlier days of Chalcedonian orthodoxy, he had regarded Peter as an arch-heretic.

Peter Mongus, or the Stammerer, had been implicated in many of the violent acts of Dioscorus, and had been archdeacon to Timothy the Cat. On the death of Timothy he was, under circumstances somewhat diversely related, chosen as his successor, though the other Timothy (Salophaciolus) was still alive. On the death of Salophaciolus, a mild and moderate man, there was a hotly disputed succession, and Zeno obtained the recognition of Peter as patriarch of Alexandria (A.D. 482). Peter had already sketched out a line of policy with Acacius, which was shortly embodied in the document well known as the Henoticon or Union Scheme of Zeno.

The object of the Henoticon was stated as the restoration of peace and unity to the Church. The means by which such unity was to be obtained were, however, unlikely to satisfy more than one party. We have seen that Gibbon eulogises it, and more recent historians have followed his opinion. But since a theological eirenicon drawn up by men of shifty character and no scruples must be judged by the measure of its success, we may hesitate to congratulate the originators of a document which, though approved by the patriarchs of the East, was certainly *not* so by all their clergy and people, and therefore caused a schism of thirty-five years between Rome and Constantinople, and forced the Church of the far East into counter-organisation under the aegis of the Great King. Like the Emperor Constantius before him, who sought to settle the Arian difficulty by abolishing the ὁμοούσιον, and the Emperor Constans after him, who wished to allay the bad feelings of the Monotheletes and their opponents by disallowing their distinctive terminology, Zeno tried the autocratic short cut out of controversy by the prohibition of technical terms. Like the other would-be pacifiers, he aroused a great storm.

The Henoticon is in the form of a letter from the Emperor to the bishops and clergy, monks and laity, of Alexandria, Egypt, Libya, and Pentapolis. It begins by setting forth the sufficiency of the faith as declared at Nicaea and at Constantinople, and goes on to regret the number of those who, owing to the late discords, had died without baptism or communion, and the shedding of blood which had defiled the earth and even the air. Therefore, the above-mentioned symbols which had also been confirmed at Ephesus are to be regarded as entirely adequate. Nestorius and Eutyches are anathematised and the "twelve chapters" or anathemas of Cyril approved. It declares that Christ is "consubstantial with the Father in respect of the Godhead and consubstantial with our. selves as respects the manhood; that He, having descended and become incarnate of the Holy Spirit and Mary, the Virgin and Mother of God, is one and not two . . . for we do in no degree admit those who make either a division or a confusion or introduce a phantom." It goes on to say that this is no new form of faith, and that if anyone had taught any contrary doctrine, whether at Chalcedon or elsewhere, he was to be anathematised. Finally, all men are exhorted to return into the com- munion of the Church.

On its face, the document may seem reasonable enough. If all men could be brought to an agreement on the basis of the creeds of 325 and 381, the less said about Chalcedon the better. But the very mention of Chalcedon in the document, with the suggestion that it might have erred, destroys the semblance of perfect impartiality. As might naturally be expected, the Alexandrians and Egyptians generally were ready to adopt it, though there was an exception in the "headless" party (*acephali*), the right wing of the anti-Chalcedonians, who were not satisfied because it did not directly condemn the *Tome* of Leo. But these people were extreme. In general, the apparent intention of leaving the authority of Chalcedon an open question was interpreted as giving full liberty to repudiate that authority. This was certainly the view taken by Peter Mongus, and in all probability by Acacius likewise. Certain letters purporting to be from these prelates shew a more compromising spirit, but in a lately discovered correspondence handed down from Armenian sources, we find Peter denouncing the "infamous Leo," and exhorting Acacius, as he celebrates mass, to sub- stitute mentally for the names of Marcian, Pulcheria, and others whom he is bound outwardly to commemorate, those of Dioscorus, Eudocia, and other faithful persons.

As might naturally be expected, the Henoticon policy received strenuous opposition in Rome, where Simplicius, the next pope but one after Leo the Great, was determined to lose none of the ground gained by his predecessors. After a very bitter and unsatisfactory correspondence with Acacius, and two nugatory embassies to Con- stantinople, Simplicius solemnly excommunicated the Patriarch of Constantinople, as favourer of heretics, at a synod in Rome. An Acoemete monk took charge of the notification and fastened it to the mantle of Acacius during service. A similar sentence was passed on Mongus and on Zeno himself.

During the long period of the schism, a good many efforts were made for the restoration of peace, which proved abortive by reason on the one hand of the high demands of the Roman see, which always required the erasure of the name of Acacius from the diptychs, and on the other, the growth in power and assurance of Eastern Monophysitism. Anastasius, Zeno's successor (491–518), generally bore a character for piety and moderation, but towards the end of his life, when he was very aged, appears to have been committed to a Monophysite policy. He seems at least to have been regarded by the Monophysites of later days as friendly to their party. He was influenced in this direction by a refugee of great force of intellect and will, Severus the Pisidian, formerly a pagan and a lawyer, later an uncompromising Monophysite, and head of the once "headless party" to whom the Henoticon seemed not to go far enough. Under his influence, the people of Constantinople were agitated by the singing in church of the *Trisagion* with addition, while their rivals shouted Peter's Theopaschite in its original form. Anastasius shewed some firmness in withstanding the Roman demands, but he was unfortunate in his dealings with his own patriarchs. The first of these, Euphemius, who was eager for peace with Rome, he degraded from office, only to replace him by another advocate (Macedonius) of the same cause, and after Macedonius in turn had been degraded, a patriarch was appointed (Timotheus) who gave no confidence to either party. With a large section of the people, Anastasius, in spite of his conscientious devotion to duty, made himself intensely unpopular. He made a last attempt to come to an agreement with Pope Hormisdas, but it failed in the same way as previous efforts. The task of making terms with Rome was left to his successor Justin, who became emperor in 518. A solemn ceremony was held in rehabilitation of the Council of Chalcedon. Shortly after, legates arrived from the Pope, and union was restored on the condition, formerly refused, of the erasure of Acacius' name from the diptychs. Strange to say the two patriarchs whom Anastasius had displaced for their Romeward inclinations, were, in virtue of their schismatic appointment, struck off likewise. Zeno and Anastasius received a kind of post-mortem excommunication. All the leading members of Monophysite and other heretical sects were anathematised.

The end of the schism can hardly be regarded as terminating the series of controversies which are the subject of this chapter. East and West were never again to be reunited with any cordiality. But now, for a time, the outward dissension ceases, and in the struggle not far distant with Vandals in Africa and Goths in Italy, the Empire represents the side of the Catholic Faith against either persecuting or tolerant Arianism.

Meantime, in the East, the Henoticon and the semi-Monophysite policy of the Emperors had far-reaching results. Mention has already been made of the school of Edessa, once presided over by Ibas, and of the reaction in Osrhoene, after Ibas' death, in a Monophysite direction. In 489 Zeno, regarding Edessa as still a hotbed of Nestorianism, closed the school there. The result was that a good many scholars migrated across the Persian frontier to Nisibis where, as already stated, Barsumas was bishop. In this city a very flourishing school was founded, in which the works of the great Antiochene doctors, Diodorus of Tarsus and Theodore of Mopsuestia, might be studied in peace, and where even the memory of Nestorius himself was honoured. The great episcopal see of the Persian Church had since 410 been fixed at Seleucia-Ctesiphon, and the bishop (*catholicos*) of that see was fairly independent of those who, from his point of view, were regarded as the "western fathers" of the Syrian churches. Christians in Persia enjoyed peace and patronage, with intermittent persecutions, under the great kings of the Sassanid dynasty. It seems to have been part of the Nestorian policy of Barsumas to convince the king that Monophysitism meant inclination to side with the Empire whenever war broke out, while Nestorianism was consistent with loyalty to Persia. Under these circumstances, the Nestorian Church in Persia grew and flourished. Beside its school at Nisibis, it had, in course of time, one at Seleucia. Its character was greatly determined by its monastic institutions. Its missionary zeal made itself felt in India and even in China. Altogether, though the time of its greatness was not of very long duration, it acquired, by its intellectual and religious activity, a very respectable place among the Churches which the dissensions of the fifth century alienated from Catholic Christendom.

While Christianity in Persia was becoming Nestorian, Syria was becoming Monophysite. The whole story of the process does not fall within our present limits, but it may be remarked that the great organiser of the Monophysite communities, both in Egypt and Syria, was Severus the Pisidian who held the see of Antioch from 512 till his deposition in 519, and whose active and productive life ended about 540. The reorganiser of the Monophysite Church after the persecution which followed the reunion of Rome and Constantinople was Jacobus Baradaeus, who died about 578, and from whom the Syrian Monophysites are sometimes called Jacobites. His history, however, does not concern us here.

Historically viewed, the interest of these controversies lies not so much in the motives by which they were inspired as in the dissolutions and combinations to which they gave birth. The alienation of churches seems in many cases to be at bottom the alienation of peoples and nations, the religious difference supplying pretext rather than cause. And sometimes the asserted cause of the dispute is lost sight of when the difference has been made permanent. So it was, apparently, with the Jacobite-Syrian and the Nestorian-Persian Churches. Also we may notice that the Christianity of the Copts has become more like a reversion, with

CH. XVII.

differences, to the popular religion of the old Egyptians than an elaboration of the principles of Cyril and Dioscorus. And again the breach between Greeks and Latins was sure to break out again, however often the ecclesiastical dispute which had served as the occasion of a temporary alienation might be settled. The fruits of the disunion we have been examining became evident enough in the days of the Mahommedan invasions, yet had the actual occasions of the disunion been entirely absent, we can hardly feel sure that a united Christendom would have stood ready to repel the Saracen advance. Even if the Empire had never lost its unity, it could hardly have retained in permanent and loyal subordination the populations of Egypt and of the East. They had been but superficially connected with Byzantium, while, perhaps unconsciously, they remained under the sway of more ancient civilisations than those of Hellas and of Rome.

CHAPTER XVIII

MONASTICISM

CHRISTIAN Monasticism was a natural outgrowth of the earlier Christian asceticism, which had its roots in the gospel. For it is now recognised that such sayings as: "If thou wouldest be perfect, go sell that thou hast, and give to the poor, ... and come, follow me"; and: "There are eunuchs, which made themselves eunuchs for the kingdom of heaven's sake: he that is able to receive it, let him receive it"; and the teaching of St Paul on celibacy, did as a matter of fact give an impetus to the tendency so common in seriously religious minds towards the practice of asceticism. These tendencies are clearly discernible among Christians from the beginning; and not only among the sects, but also in the great Church. Celibacy was the first and always the chief asceticism; but fasting and prayer, and the voluntary surrender of possessions, and also works of philanthropy, were recognised exercises of those who gave themselves up to an ascetical life. This was done at first without withdrawal from the world or abandonment of home or the ordinary avocations of life. At an early date female ascetics received ecclesiastical recognition among the virgins and widows, and there are grounds for believing that at the middle of the third century there already were organised communities of women — for in the Life of Anthony we are told that before withdrawing from the world he placed his sister in a Παρθενών or house of virgins, the name later used for a nunnery. At this date there was nothing of the kind for men; but, at any rate in Egypt, the male ascetics used to leave their homes and dwell in huts in the gardens near the towns. For when, c. 270, St Anthony left the world, it was this manner of life he embraced at first.

St Anthony was born in middle Egypt about the year 250. When he was twenty, on hearing in church the gospel text "If thou wouldest be perfect," as cited above, he took the words as a personal call to himself and acted on them, going to practise the ascetical life among the ascetics who dwelt at his native place. After 15 years so spent, he went into complete solitude, taking up his abode in a deserted fort at a place called Pispir, on the east bank of the Nile opposite the Fayum, now called Der-el-Memun (c. 285). In this retreat Anthony spent twenty years in the strictest seclusion, wholly given up to prayer and religious exercises. A number of those who wished to lead an ascetic life congregated around him, desiring that he should be their teacher and guide. At last he complied with their wishes and came forth from his seclusion, to become the inaugurator and first organiser of Christian monachism.

This event took place about the beginning of the fourth century — 305 is the traditional date; only a few years later did Pachomius found, in the far south, the first Christian monastery properly so called. It will be convenient to trace separately the two streams of monastic tradition that flowed respectively from the two great founders, Anthony and Pachomius.

The form of monachism that drew its inspiration from St Anthony prevailed throughout Lower or Northern Egypt. All along the Nile to the north of Lycopolis (Asyut), and in the adjacent deserts, and on the sea-board near Alexandria, there were at the end of the fourth century vast numbers of monks, sometimes living alone, sometimes two or three together, sometimes in large congregations — but even then the life was semi-eremitical. Antonian monachism reached its greatest and most characteristic development in the deserts of Nitria and Scete, and it is here that we have the most abundant materials for forming a picture of the life of these monks. Palladius and Cassian both lived in this district for many years during the last decade of the fourth century; St Jerome, Rufinus, and the writer of the *Historia Monachorum* visited it; and they have left on record their impressions. Nitria, the present Wady Natron, is a valley round some nitre lakes, lying out in the desert to the west of the Nile, some 60 miles due south of Alexandria. Those who began the monastic life here were Amoun and Macarius of Egypt, himself a disciple of Anthony. A few miles from Nitria was the desert called Cellia from the number of hermits' cells that studded it, and further away still, out in the "utter solitude," was the monastic settlement of Scete. Rufinus and the writer of the *Historia Monachorum* describe Cellia: The cells stood out of sight and out of earshot of one another; only on the Saturday and Sunday did the monks assemble for the services; all the other time was spent in complete solitude, no one ever visiting another except in case of sickness or for some spiritual need. Palladius says that 600 lived in Cellia.

This was a purely eremitical life; but in Nitria it was otherwise. The following is Palladius' account, as he saw it in 390.

"In Mount Nitria 5000 monks dwell following different manners of life, each according to his power and desire; so that anyone could live alone, or with another, or with several. In the mountain there are seven bakeries and a great church by which stand three palm trees, each with a whip hanging from it; one is for the monks who misbehave themselves, one for thieves, and one for chance comers: so that anyone who offended and was judged worthy of stripes, embraced the palm tree and made amends by receiving on the back the fixed number of blows. Close to the church is the guest house, and any guest who comes is entertained until he goes of his own accord, even if he stay for two or three years. For the first week they let him stay, in idleness, but after that they make him work, either in the garden or the bake-house or the kitchen. Or if he be a man of position they give him a book to read, but do not allow him to have intercourse with anyone till noon. Physicians dwell in this mountain, and confectioners; they use wine, and wine is sold. They all make linen with their hands, so that they have no needs. And about three in the afternoon one may stand and hear how the psalmody arises from each habitation, and fancy oneself rapt aloft into Paradise. But they assemble at the church only on Saturday and Sunday." Palladius tells, too, of one Apollonius, a merchant, who became a monk in Nitria, and being too old to learn a handicraft, purchased medicines and stores at Alexandria and cared for all the brotherhood in their sicknesses, for twenty years going the round of the cells from daybreak till three in the afternoon, knocking at the doors to see if anyone was sick: and of another who on becoming a monk retained his money and devoted it wholly to works of hospitality towards the poor, the aged and the infirm, and was judged by the fathers to be equal in merit to his brother, who had dispossessed himself of his belongings and given himself up wholly to a life of strict asceticism.

What has been said will bring out the special feature of this type of monasticism — its voluntariness: even when the monks lived together, there was not any common life according to rule. A large discretion was left to each one to follow his own devices in the employment of his time and the practice of his asceticisms. In short, this form of monachism grew out of the eremitical life, and it retained its eremitical or semi-eremitical character even in the great monastic colonies of Nitria and Scete.

We may now pass to the Pachomian monachism dominant in the southern parts of Egypt. Pachomius was a pagan by birth; he was born about 290, and became a Christian at the age of twenty. He adopted the eremitical life under Palaemon, a hermit who lived by the Nile in the diocese of Tentyra (Denderah). The legend of his call to be the creator of Christian cenobitical life is thus told by Palladius.

"Pachomius was in an extraordinary degree a lover of mankind and a lover of the brotherhood. While he was sitting in his cave an angel appeared unto him and said: 'Thou hast rightly ordered thy own life; needlessly therefore dost thou sit in the cave; come forth and bring together all the young monks and dwell with them, and legislate for them according to the exemplar I will give thee.' And he gave him

CH. XVIII.

a brazen tablet whereon was engraved the Rule." There follows what probably is the most authentic epitome of the earliest Christian Rule for Monks.

St Pachomius founded his first monastery at Tabennisi near Denderah *c.* 315–320, and by the time of his death in 346 his order counted nine monasteries of men and one of women, all situated between Panopolis (Akhmīm) to the north and Latopolis (Esneh) to the south, and peopled by some 3000 monks in all. After his death other monasteries were founded, one at Canopus near Alexandria, and several in Ethiopia; so that by the end of the century Palladius tells us there were 7000 Pachomian or Tabennesiot monks — St Jerome's 50,000 may safely be rejected.

Palladius visited the Pachomian monastery at Panopolis (Akhmīm) and has left us what is by far the most actual and living picture of the daily life. He tells us that there were 300 monks in this monastery, who practised all the handicrafts and out of their superabundance contributed to the support of nunneries and prisons. The servers of the week got up at daybreak and some worked in the kitchen while others laid the tables, getting them ready by the appointed hour, spreading on them loaves of bread, mustard leaves, olive salad, cheeses, herbs chopped up, and pieces of meat for the old and the sick. "And some come in and have their meal at noon, and others at 1 or at 2 or at 3 or at 5, or in the late evening, and others every second day. And their work was in like fashion: one worked in the fields, another in the garden, another in the smithy, another in the bakery, another at carpentry, another at fulling, another at basket-making, another in the tanyard, another at shoe-making, another at tailoring, another at calligraphy"; he mentions also that they keep camels and herds of swine: he adds that they learn by heart all the Scriptures. From the Rule it appears that they assembled in the church four times a day, and approached Communion on Saturday and Sunday.

Here we have a fully constituted and indeed highly organised cenobitical life, the day being divided between a fixed routine of church services, Bible reading, and work seriously undertaken as an integral factor of the life. Herein lies one of the most significant differences between Pachomian and Antonian monachisms. In the latter the references to work are few, and the work is of a sedentary kind, commonly basket-making and linen-weaving, which could be carried on in the cell; and the work was undertaken merely in order to supply the necessaries of life, or to fill up the time that could not be spent in actual prayer or contemplation or the reading of the Bible. Palladius' picture of the Pachomian monastery, on the other hand, is that of a busy, well-organised, self-supporting agricultural colony, in which the daily religious exercises only alternated with, and did not impede, the daily labour that was so large an element of the life: and so this picture is of extraordinary value. Whatever may be thought of the life led by the hermits or quasi-hermits of northern Egypt, there will hardly be two opinions as to the strenuousness and virility of the ideal aimed at by St Pachomius. The Antonian ideal is the one that (even in accentuated forms) has been in all ages dominant in the East, and it was the form of monachism first propagated throughout Western Europe. It was not the least of St Benedict's contributions to Western monachism that he introduced, with the modifications called for by differences of climate and national character, a type of monachism more akin to the Pachomian, in which work of one kind or another, undertaken for its own sake, forms an essential part of the life.

Having thus traced in the briefest manner the external phenomena of the earliest Christian monachism, we must say a word on its inner spirit. The theory or philosophy of primitive Christian monachism finds its fullest expression in Cassian's Collations. These are 24 conferences of considerable length, which purport to be utterances of several of the most prominent of the Nitriot and Scetic monks, made in response to queries and difficulties put by Cassian himself and his friend Germanus, who lived for a number of years in Scete between 390 and 400. The Collations were not written till 25 years later, and the question has been raised how far they reproduce actual discourses uttered by the various monks named; or are compositions of Cassian's, a literary device for presenting the teaching and ideas current in Scete. In any case, there can be no reasonable doubt that they do faithfully represent the substance and spirit of that teaching — and this is all that is of historical importance. Cassian puts into the foreground, in his first Collation, an exposition of the purpose or scope of the monastic life: Abbot Moses declares it to be the attainment of Purity of Heart, so that the mind may rest fixed on God and divine things: for this purpose only are fastings, watchings, meditation of Scripture, solitude, privations to be undertaken: such asceticisms are not perfection, but only the instruments of perfection. This conference supplies the key to the fundamental conception of the monastic state. It is a systematic and ordered attempt to exercise the tendencies symbolised by the terms Mysticism and Asceticism — two of the most deeply rooted religious instincts of the human heart, but which beyond most others need regulation and control. Egyptian monachism was probably at its highest point of development about the year 400, just when Cassian and Palladius came in contact with it. Without accepting the probably apocryphal figures given by some of the authorities, there can be no doubt that there were at that date very many thousands of monks in Egypt. And the original enthusiasms and spirituality of the movement still, on the whole, held sway. But with the fifth century the decay set in, which has gone on progressively till our day. The Egyptian monks, who had been the great adherents of the Catholic faith in the Arian

CH. XVIII.

times, became the chief supporters of Dioscorus in making the Egyptian Church Monophysite. As the Mahommedan invasion swept over Egypt the monasteries were in great measure destroyed, and Egyptian monasticism has ever since been gradually dying out; at the present day only a few monasteries survive, and the institution is in a moribund condition, unless some unlooked-for revival come about.

When we pass from Egypt to the oriental lands, we find that in Palestine monastic life was introduced from Egypt by Hilarion early in the fourth century. He had been a disciple of Anthony, and the life he led in Palestine was purely eremitical. There are traces of cenobitic monasteries in Palestine during the fourth century, especially those established under Western influences — as by St Jerome and Paula, Rufinus and the two Melanias. But the glimpses of Palestinian monachism the end of the century given us by Palladius in the Lausiac History, reveal the fact that it remained in large measure eremitical.

In Syria and Mesopotamia, whether in the Roman or in the Persian territories, there was at the beginning of the fourth century what appears to have been an indigenous growth of asceticism analogous to the pre-monastic asceticism found in Egypt and elsewhere. The institution was known as the "Sons of the Covenant," and the members were bound to celibacy and the usual ascetical practices, but they were not monks properly so called. We hear much of them from Aphraates (c. 330); and Rabbula, bishop of Edessa a century later, wrote a code of regulations for priests and Sons of the Covenant. As he wrote also a Rule for monks, it seems clear that the Sons of the Covenant did not develop into a monastic system, but the two institutions existed alongside of each other till at any rate the middle of the fifth century. The beginnings of monachism proper in the Syrian lands are difficult to trace. It is probable that the story of Eugenius, who was said to have introduced monasticism from Egypt in the early years of the fourth century, must be rejected as legendary. Theodoret opens his *Historia Religiosa*, or lives of the Syrian monks, with an account of one Jacob who lived as a hermit near Nisibis before 325; but as this was a century before Theodoret's time, the facts must remain somewhat doubtful. He gives accounts of a number of Syrian monks in the end of the fourth century and the beginning of the fifth: most of them were hermits; and even when disciples gathered around them, the life continued to be strongly individualistic and eremitical. This has continued to be the tendency of Syrian monachism, both Nestorian and Monophysite. Cenobitical life was commonly only the first stage of a monk's career; the goal aimed at was to be a hermit; after a few years each monk withdrew to a cell at a distance from the monastery, to live in solitude, frequenting the monastic church only on Sundays and feasts. Rabbula's Admonitions for Monks (c. 425) are of great interest: he lays down that no one is thus to become a hermit until he has been proved in a monastery for a considerable time. The following regulation is of special interest: "Those who have been made priests and deacons in the monasteries, and have been entrusted with churches in the villages, shall appoint as superiors those who are able to rule the brotherhood; and they themselves shall remain in charge of their churches." The practice here indicated, of monks serving churches, is probably unique in the East; it has been done in the West in later times, but has always been regarded as abnormal.

Thus while in Egypt the tendency was to abandon the eremitical life for the cenobitical, in Syria the opposite tendency set in. In another respect, too, Syrian monachism developed along lines different from those that prevailed in Egypt. Egyptian monks practised, it is true, austerities and mortifications of the severest kind; but they were what may be called natural, as prolonged abstinence from food and sleep, exposure to heat and cold, silence and solitude, heavy labour and physical fatigue. In Syria on the contrary austerities of a highly artificial character became the vogue: the extraordinary life of the pillar hermits, who abode for years on the summits of pillars, at once presents itself in illustration. Theodoret and the other authorities speak as if it were a common practice that monks should carry continually fastened to their backs great stones or iron weights — Rabbula forbids this except to hermits. Sozomen tells us of a kind of Syrian monk called "Grazers," who used to go out into the fields at meal-times and eat grass like cattle. A good picture of the lines on which Syrian monachism settled down after the sixth century is afforded by Thomas of Marga's "Book of the Governors," or history of the great Nestorian monastery of Beth Abhe in Mesopotamia.

All the evidence shews that the ingrained oriental hankering after asceticism, still found in Hindu fakirs, asserted itself in Syrian monachism from the beginning, and it has there at all times been a characteristic feature of the system.

Monasticism seems to have made its entry into Greek-speaking lands from the East. It first appears in the Roman province of Armenia in connexion with Eustathius of Sebaste, *c.* 330–340. The claim has been made, indeed, that monasteries were established in Constantinople by Constantine, but this must be regarded as legend; there probably were none there before the end of the fourth century. The monasticism of Eustathius was of a highly ascetical character, with strongly developed Manichaean tendencies, which were condemned at the Council of Gangra, *c.* 340. Similar in character, but carrying the same tendencies to still greater extremes, were the Messalians or Euchitae, in Paphlagonia, described by Epiphanius.

The real father of Greek monachism was St Basil. After spending a year in visiting the monks of Egypt and Syria, he retired, *c.* 360, to a lonely spot near Neocaesarea in Pontus, and there began to lead a

CH. XVIII.

monastic life with the disciples who quickly gathered round him. His conception of the monastic life was in many important points a new departure, and it proved epoch-making in the history of mona-chism: it has continued to this day the fundamental conception of Greek and Slavonic monasticism; and St Benedict, though he borrowed more in matter of detail from Cassian, in matter of principles and ideas owed more to St Basil than to any other monastic legislator. Thus in the monasticism of both East and West, St Basil's ideas still live on. For this reason it will be proper to give a somewhat full account of his monastic legislation. The materials are to be found chiefly in the two sets of Rules (the Longer and the Shorter), the authenticity of which is now recognised, and in certain of his Letters, supplemented by letters of St Gregory Nazianzen to him.

St Basil's construction of the monastic life was fully cenobitical, in this respect advancing beyond that of St Pachomius. In the Pachomian system the monks dwelt in different houses within the monastery pre-cincts; the meals were at different hours; and all assembled in the church only for the greater services. But St Basil established a common roof, a common table, a common prayer always; so that we meet here for the first time in Christian monastic legislation the idea of the cenobium, and common life properly so called. Again, St Basil de-clared against even the theoretical superiority of the eremitical life over the cenobitical. He asserted the principle that monks should endeavour to do good to their fellow men; and in order to bring works of charity within reach of his monks, orphanages were established, separate from the monasteries but close at hand and under the care of the monks, in which apparently children of both sexes were received. Boys also were taken into the monasteries to be educated, and not with the view of their becoming monks. Another new feature in St Basil's conception of the monastic life was his discouragement of excessive asceticism; he enunciated the principle that work is of greater value than austerities, and drew the conclusion that fasting should not be practised to such an extent as to be detrimental to work. All this represents a new range of ideas.

The following is an outline of the actual daily life in St Basil's monasteries. A period of novitiate or probation, of indeterminate length, had to be passed, at the end of which a profession of virginity was made, but no monastic vows were taken: Palladius, writing in 420, says in the Prologue to the Lausiac History, that it is better to practise the monastic life freely, without the constraint of a vow. But though there were no vows, St Basil's monks were considered to be under a strict obligation of persevering in the monastic life, and of abiding in their own monastery. Their time was divided between prayer, work, and the reading of Holy Scripture. They rose for the common psalmody while it was still night and chanted the divine praises till the dawn; six times each day did they assemble in the church for prayer. Their work was field labour and farming — St Gregory Nazianzen speaks of the ploughing and vine-dressing, the wood-drawing and stone-hewing, the planting and draining. The food and clothing, too, the housing and all the conditions of life, he describes as being coarse and rough and austere. The monastic virtues of obedience to the superior, of personal poverty, of self-denial, and the cultivation of the spiritual life and of personal religion, are insisted on.

The Basilian form of monachism was the one that spread in the adjacent provinces of Asia Minor and in Armenia; and under the influence of the Council of Chalcedon, which passed several canons regulating the monastic life, and of the civil law, it gradually made its way and became recognised throughout the Greek portion of the Empire as the official form of monastic life. But the Eastern tendency towards the practice of extreme austerity and the eremitical life has always struggled to find expression, and to this day there are hermits on Mount Athos and at other monastic centres of the Orthodox Church.

In the fifth century the Holy Land became the head centre of Greek monachism, and monasteries of two kinds arose in considerable numbers. There were the cenobia, or monasteries proper, where the life was according to the lines laid down by St Basil; and there were the lauras, wherein a semi-eremitical life was followed, the monks living in separate huts within the enclosure. St Sabas, a Cappadocian, was the great organiser of this manner of life — he founded no fewer than seven lauras in Palestine, and drew up a *Typicon* or code of rules for their guidance. Sabas was appointed Exarch of all the lauras of Palestine, while his compatriot and contemporary Theodosius became Archimandrite of all the cenobia of Palestine. Under the stress of the Origenistic controversy and of the Arab invasion Palestinian monachism waned, and in the seventh century the centre of gravity of Greek monasticism shifted to Constantinople, where in the early years of the ninth century it underwent a reorganisation at the hands of Theodore, abbot of the monastery of the Studium. In the eleventh and twelfth centuries the centre of gravity again shifted, this time to Mount Athos, where it has ever since remained.

Since the time of Theodore the Studite Greek and Slavonic monachism has undergone little change: it is still St Basil's monachism, but the elements of hard labour and of works of charity have been almost wholly eliminated from the life, and intellectual work has not, as in the West, taken their place on any large scale — indeed, it has usually been discouraged; so that for the past thousand years Greek and Slavonic monks have been almost wholly given up, in theory at any rate, and in great measure in practice too, to a life of purely devotional contemplation. They do not call themselves Basilians, but simply

Monks, and St Basil's Rules scarcely hold a leading place in the code of monastic legislation that regulates their life.

While the monastic system was in its primitive unorganised state it lent itself to certain obvious abuses. Anyone who chose could become a hermit and live according to his own devices. Impostors and charlatans under the guise of pretended austerities deceived the simple and lived upon alms received on false pretences. These abuses seem to have attained a great magnitude in Syria at the middle of the fifth century, if we may judge from the vigorous protests of Isaac of Antioch; but they existed everywhere. · They led to the gradual regulating of the monastic life and the subjecting of the monks to the authority of the bishops. In this way a body of legislation, both ecclesiastical and civil, grew up, which restricted the voluntariness of the system, and made it an integral part of the general polity of both Church and State. This "ecclesiasticising" of the monks is often deplored; but it was part of the inevitable march of events and a condition of the continued existence of the institution. In the fifth and sixth centuries other tendencies made themselves felt, and the monks in great numbers became embroiled in the ecclesiastical politics and the theological controversies of the time. Sometimes they were on the orthodox side, sometimes on the heterodox; but on whatever side they stood, they were only too often violent and fanatical, and some of the most discreditable episodes of Church history in those days were the work of Eastern monks — as the murder of Flavian at the Robber Synod of Ephesus.

Before we pass to the West, it will be well to speak of the nuns in Egypt and the East. It has already been said at the beginning of this chapter, when speaking of the pre-monastic Christian ascetics, that communities of women existed at an earlier date than communities of men — in Egypt as early as the middle of the third century. The records of Egyptian monachism agree in representing women as taking part in great numbers in every phase of the monastic movement. There were women who lived as hermits and as recluses, shut up in tombs; there are various stories of women disguising themselves as men and living in monasteries, and being discovered only after death. Pachomius founded two nunneries, one, under his sister, at Tabennisi, the other, which numbered 400 nuns, near Panopolis (Akhmīm); and after his death many others were founded in his order. The famous Coptic abbot Senuti of Atripè governed a great community of nuns in addition to the monks of the White Monastery. We learn from Palladius that at the end of the fourth century there were numerous nunneries in all parts of monastic Egypt, and the glimpses he lets us see of their inner life are graphic and interesting. He tells us of one Dorotheus who had the spiritual charge of a nunnery, and used to sit at a window overlooking the convent, "keeping the peace among the nuns"; also of an old nun, Mother Talis, superioress of a convent at Antinoë, so beloved by her nuns that there was no need of a key in that convent, as in others, to keep the nuns from wandering, "as they were fast tied by love of her."

In Syria there were at the beginning of the fourth century "Daughters of the Covenant," analogous to the "Sons of the Covenant," spoken of above. Whether they led a full community life is uncertain; but in one of Rabbula's regulations, at the beginning of the fifth century, it is prescribed that "Sons or Daughters of the Covenant who fall from their estate be sent to the monasteries for penance," which implies the existence of convents of women. In all probability there were in Syria, as elsewhere, fully organised nunneries, though there is not much Syrian evidence concerning them. Certainly in Palestine at this time there were many convents of women, including those established under the influence of the Roman ladies Paula and Eustochium and the Melanias. When St Basil began his monastic life about 360, his mother and sister were already living in a community of nuns in the immediate vicinity, with a river between them; and throughout Greek-speaking Christendom, in Asia Minor and above all in Constantinople, women practised the monastic life hardly less than men. No Eastern nuns, however, have at any time devoted themselves to external works of charity like the modern active congregations of women in the West.

There is a considerable body of evidence shewing that the ascetical life was pursued in the West — notably at Carthage and Rome — as in the East, before the introduction of monasticism proper; but there is no sufficient reason for questioning the tradition that attributes the knowledge of the monastic life in Western Europe to the influence of St Athanasius. In the year 339 he came to Rome, accompanied by two Egyptian monks, and thus spread in the City and its neighbourhood the knowledge of the manner of life that was then being practised in Egypt. Many candidates presented themselves, and we learn from Ambrose, Jerome, and Augustine that in the last quarter of the fourth century there were numerous monasteries of men and of women in Rome. Among the high-born patrician ladies the movement had a great vogue and became so fashionable that an agitation against it arose, of which St Jerome had to bear the brunt. These ladies, brought up in every luxury, gave up all things and surrendered themselves to lives of hardship and devotional exercises. The most famous of them, as Paula and Melania, even left Rome and went to the Holy Land, where they established sisterhoods. Monasteries rapidly spread over Central and Southern Italy, and the islands of the Tyrrhenian Sea were peopled by hermits. In North Italy, too, monasteries existed by the end of the fourth century at the chief cities — at Aquileia, where Rufinus and Jerome were trained in the monastic life; at Milan, where Ambrose had a great monastery of men; at Ravenna and Pavia and many other towns.

Eusebius, bishop of Vercelli (d. 371), introduced a change in the idea of the monastic life that merits for him a more prominent place among monastic legislators than is commonly accorded to him: he combined the clerical and monastic states, making the clerics of his cathedral live together in community according to the monastic rule. This was the starting-point of the practice destined to prevail both in West and East, whereby monks as by ordinary rule become priests, though it was several centuries before the custom was established.

It was in the form initiated by Eusebius at Vercelli that the monastic life was introduced into Africa by St Augustine on his return from Italy in 388. In 391 he was ordained presbyter at Hippo and established a community of clerics living together according to rule; and when in 396 he became bishop of Hippo, he continued to follow the same manner of life along with his clerics. Several bishops went forth from this community to other sees, and in most cases they established similar monasteries of clerics in their episcopal cities. This union of the clerical and monastic lives was widely prevalent in Africa, and it became the exemplar both of the institution of secular canons in the Carolingian reform, and of that of canons regular, or Augustinian canons, in the Hildebrandine.

Monasteries of the type normal in those days also arose in Africa. In the times of Tertullian and Cyprian veiled virgins were recognised; but it is doubtful whether they had developed into a proper monastic system before St Augustine's time. During his episcopate there certainly were many nunneries, one being presided over by his sister; and his Letter 211 — the only authentic "Rule of St Augustine" — was written for the guidance of a nunnery. Thus in the early years of the fifth century monachism was strong and flourishing in the African Church.

The beginnings of Spanish monachism are obscure, and the records scanty. The first reference is a canon of the Council of Zaragoza in 380, forbidding clerics to become monks: this shews that the monastic institute must by that date have spread considerably in Spain; but there seems to be no extant evidence of the existence of a monastery in Spain till the beginning of the sixth century. There is a tradition that then one Donatus carried monasticism from Africa into Spain; but the names to be associated with early Spanish monachism are Martin, bishop of Braga, a Pannonian and the apostle of the Arian Sueves, who died in 580, and Fructuosus, also bishop of Braga, about a century later. The latter was the great organiser and propagator of monachism in the Peninsula, establishing several monasteries and writing (probably) two rules for their guidance. It is chiefly from these rules that we get glimpses of the earlier Spanish monachism. It seems to have been a common practice for a man to call his house a "monastery," and to live in it with his wife, children and servants: against this abuse, and others, St Fructuosus legislates. One feature of his Rule is unique: it contains a pact between the abbot and monks, whereby the latter bind themselves to the performance of the duties of the monastic life under the abbot, and empower him to inflict specified punishments for certain offences; and on the other hand reserve to themselves, in case the abbot should act in an arbitrary or tyrannical way, the right of appeal to other abbots or to the bishop. St Fructuosus lived a century after St Benedict's death; but throughout the Gothic period there is no trace of Benedictine monachism in Spain. In the extant rules of Spanish origin — those of Leander, of Isidore, and of Fructuosus — it is possible to discern certain reminiscences which betray a knowledge of the Benedictine Rule; but Mabillon greatly exaggerates their significance. These rules are in no sense declarations or commentaries on St Benedict's, and Spanish monachism was not at all Benedictine before the time of the Christian Reconquest. Early Spanish monachism was indigenous, and it retained its individuality till the fall of the Gothic kingdom. Our only glimpses of it have to be obtained through these later rules, and so it has been necessary to carry our view forward beyond the strict limits of this survey. It may be doubted whether monasteries were numerous in the Gothic period: the Councils of Toledo throughout the seventh century used to be attended by fifty or sixty bishops; but there were never more than ten abbots present, and often only six, or five, or four.

We have little information concerning the origins of monachism in the Keltic lands, though the system played a prominent part in the Christianising of most of them. It seems that the earliest Keltic monasteries were missionary stations, closely connected with the tribal system. St Patrick, who had passed some years as a monk in Lerins (see below), built up the Irish Church in large measure on a monastic framework, and this initial tendency became more and more accentuated, till the bishops came to be subordinated to the abbots of the great monasteries. Our first definite knowledge of an organised cenobitical life in Ireland comes to us from the sixth century, during the course of which several great monasteries were established in various parts of the island, some of them counting more than a thousand monks. But any full knowledge of early Irish monachism has to be gathered, not on Irish soil, but from the documents connected with St Columba, who towards the end of the sixth century established a great monastery in the island of Iona or Hy, the missionary influence whereof spread over southern Scotland and northern England; and from the documents connected with St Columbanus, who early in the seventh century founded a number of Irish monasteries in Central Europe. St Columbanus' Rule is the only Irish monastic rule, properly so called, that has come down to us from the early period of Irish monachism: it was not composed

CH. XVIII.

in Ireland, but undoubtedly it embodies the Irish traditions of monasticism and ascetical discipline. Irish cenobitical life as seen in these documents, was one of extreme rigor and austerity. At all times the eremitical life had a great vogue in Keltic monachism; and in spite of all difficulties of climate, the Irish hermits successfully rivalled in their extraordinary penances and austerities and vigils, the hermits of Egypt, and even those of Syria. In Ireland, where the population continued purely Keltic, the Irish rules and Irish monasticism maintained themselves throughout the Middle Ages; but in England and on the Continent, where they came into contact with populations Teutonic or teutonised, they succumbed before the Roman Rule of St Benedict.

Gaul is the country of Western Europe in which early monachism was most widely propagated and flourished most, and for which the records of pre-Benedictine monachism are the most abundant. It is said that St Athanasius introduced the knowledge of the monastic life at Trier during his exile there (336–7); and the well-known story of St Augustine's conversion shews that before the end of the century there were monks living an eremitical life there.

But it is with the name of St Martin of Tours that the beginnings of Gallic monachism are rightly associated. A Pannonian by race, born early in the fourth century, he had practised the monastic life for some years before becoming bishop of Tours in 372. Nearly ten years earlier he had established a monastery near Poitiers, and on becoming bishop of Tours he formed one just outside of his episcopal city, at the place afterwards called Marmoutier. Here he gathered together eighty monks, and lived with them a life of great solitude and austerity. They dwelt singly in caves and huts, meeting only for the church services and for meals; they fasted rigorously and prayed long — it was indeed a reproduction of the life of the Egyptian monks. Our information concerning this earliest Gallic monachism is mainly derived from the writings of St Martin's biographer, Sulpitius Severus, and from his correspondence with St Paulinus of Nola. From these sources we learn that by the end of the fourth century monasteries and monks and nuns were already numerous not only in the province of Tours, but in Rouen and the territory that afterwards became Normandy and Picardy.

The beginning of the fifth century witnessed the inauguration of monachism in Provence, at Marseilles under the influence of John Cassian, and in the island of Lerins under that of Honoratus. From Lerins went forth a number of monk-bishops, who throughout the fifth and sixth centuries, by the monasteries they set up in their episcopal cities, and by the monastic rules they composed for their government, spread far and wide through south-eastern Gaul the influence and ideas of Lerins. In other parts of Gaul, too, monasteries arose in the fifth century, the most famous being Condat in the Jura mountains.

After the Frankish conquest of Gaul and under the early Merovingian kings the monastic movement continued throughout the sixth century to spread all over Frankland. A twofold tendency set in — one towards relaxation of life and observance; the other towards the eremitical life and the extremest forms of asceticism, such as are met with among the Syrian hermits. Gregory of Tours gives numerous examples of hermits, especially in Auvergne, who in their fantastic austerities equalled those of Syria; and his evidence is corroborated by other documents. It was not till the seventh century that Benedictine monachism got a foothold in Gaul, and about the same time St Columbanus imported his Rule and manner of life from Ireland. For a time the three forms of monachism — the old Gallic, the Columbanian, and the Benedictine — existed side by side in Gaul. In order to understand why the Benedictine gradually and inevitably supplanted the earlier monachisms in France, in Italy, and in England, and was destined to become the only monachism of Teutonic Europe, it is necessary to survey the character of the earlier types. The early African and Spanish monachisms were swept away by Vandals and Moors; the Irish remained insular and isolated from the great currents of monastic development; so that Italy, France and England are the countries in which the transformation of the earlier types of Western monachism into the Benedictine was worked out.

It has to be remembered that in those days neither in the West nor in the East, outside the Pachomian system, was there anything resembling the present Western idea of different "Orders" of monks — there was only the monastic order. Monasteries were autonomous, each having its own practices and its own rule, or selection of rules, depending mainly on the abbot's choice. Before St Benedict's time there were current in the West translations of certain Eastern rules — that of Pachomius, translated by Jerome; that of Basil, translated by Rufinus; and a rule attributed to Macarius. There was a rule made up out of the writings of Cassian; there was St Augustine's Letter (No. 211) on the government of a nunnery. It is doubtful whether Honoratus of Lerins wrote a rule. The only extant Western rules, properly so called, which are certainly earlier than St Benedict's, are that of Caesarius of Arles for monks and his somewhat longer rule for nuns; but these are quite short, and not one of the rules that came into contact with St Benedict's in his own time, or for a century afterwards, not even the Rule of Columbanus, could claim to be an ordered and practical code of laws regulating the life and working of a monastery. This St Benedict's Rule pre-eminently was; and the fact that it supplied so great a want doubtless was one of the chief reasons why it supplanted all its rivals.

But there was another and still more powerful reason: St Benedict was the man who adapted monasticism to Western ideas and Western needs. Monasticism in Italy and Gaul was an Eastern importation, and up to St Benedict it bore the marks of its origin. The life of the hermits of the Egyptian deserts, with their prolonged fasts and vigils and their other bodily austerities, was looked upon as the highest ideal — the true ideal — of the monastic life; and the monks of Italy and Gaul endeavoured to emulate a manner of life hard enough in oriental climes, but doubly hard in Western Europe. This straining after severe bodily austerities can clearly be discerned in the fragmentary records that have survived of pre-Benedictine monachism in Italy and France, where the practice of a purely eremitical life was very common.

St Benedict, while recognising the eremitical life, says definitely that he legislates for cenobites only; moreover, he did away with the oriental spirit of rivalry in asceticism, whereby the monks used to vie with one another in their mortifications. St Benedict laid down the principle that all should live by the Rule and conform themselves in all things to the life of the community; and even during Lent, when the undertaking of some extra mortification was recommended, it was all to be under the abbot's control. Moreover, the common community life which St Benedict established in his monasteries was not one of great severity: a hard life it was of course, and one of self-denial; but if judged by the ideals and ideas current in his day, his Rule must have appeared to his contemporaries to be in the matter of diet, of sleep, of work, and of hours of prayer, nothing else than what he describes it — "A little rule for beginners." Italian and French monks were at that time trying to live up to ideals that were impossible for most in the Western lands, and the general failure was producing a widespread disorganisation and decay. St Benedict came and eliminated these incongruous Eastern elements, and made a reconstruction of the monastic life admirably suited to Western, and especially to Teutonic, conditions. To this must be attributed in greatest measure the success achieved by his Rule.

St Benedict was born in Nursia, near Spoleto, probably about the year 480; he was of a noble Umbrian family, and he was sent to Rome to follow the courses in the schools. The licentiousness there prevalent made him determine to withdraw not only from Rome, but also from the world, and to become a monk. Full of this idea he fled away from Rome to the Sabine hills, and buried himself in a cave overlooking Nero's artificial lake on the Anio at Subiaco, forty miles from Rome. It is probable that he was not a mere boy, but a youth old enough to have become enamoured with a lady in Rome: consequently the date was within a few years of 500. There can be no doubt that the Sacro Speco at Subiaco is the cave inhabited by St Benedict during the first years of his monastic life; its solitude was complete, and the wild severe grandeur of the surrounding scenery was well calculated to inspire his young heart with deep religious feeling. In this cave he lived for three years, only a single monk of a monastery in the neighbourhood knowing of his existence and supplying him with the necessaries of life. It is not a little remarkable that he who was destined to turn Western monasticism definitely away from the eremitical ideal, should himself, as a matter of course, have gone to live as a hermit on determining to become a monk : it was only after very thorough personal experience of the hermit's life that St Benedict decided it was not to be for his disciples.

In another matter also did he turn his back on his own early ideas : after passing three years of solitude in his cave, his existence gradually became known and disciples flocked to him in such numbers that he was able to establish not only a monastery ruled over by himself, but also twelve others in the neighbourhood, over which he exercised the sort of control which the superior-general of a group or congregation of monasteries would now be said to exercise. But when he was compelled to leave Subiaco, and migrated to Monte Cassino, he confined himself exclusively to the government of his own community there, without continuing to exercise control over the other monasteries he had founded. And so his Rule is concerned with the government of a single monastery only, without any provision for the grouping of monasteries into congregations or orders, as became the vogue later on in the West. This continued the Benedictine practice for many centuries; during the greatest period of Black Monk history the great Benedictine houses stood in isolation, each self-governed and self-contained. It was not till the thirteenth century that, under the inspiration of Cluny and Citeaux, the policy was adopted of federating the Benedictine abbeys of the different ecclesiastical provinces ; and to this day the essential autonomy of each house is the foundation stone and central idea of Black Monk polity.

It is impossible to fix the date at which St Benedict founded his monastery at Monte Cassino — probably about 520. He lived there till his death, and Monte Cassino is the place above all others associated with his name. The rest of his life was quite uneventful; in 543 he was visited by Totila, and he died about the middle of the century.

As Benedictine life soon became, and for well-nigh seven centuries continued to be, the norm of monastic life in the Latin Church, it will be to the point to give a rough picture of the daily life that obtained in St Benedict's monasteries, as it may be reconstructed from the Rule.

St Benedict's monks rose early in the morning — usually about 2, but the hour varied with the season of the year. They had had, however, an ample period of unbroken sleep, usually not less than 8 hours : the midnight office between two periods of sleep, so common a feature of later monasticism in the West, had no place in Benedictine life as conceived by St Benedict. The monks repaired to the church for the night office, which consisted of fourteen psalms, and certain readings from Scripture; it was chanted throughout, and must have taken from an hour to an hour and a half. It was followed by a break, which varied from a few minutes in the summer to a couple of hours at mid-winter, and which was devoted to private reading of Scripture, or

CH. XVIII.

prayer. The Matin office, now called Lauds, was celebrated at dawn, and Prime at sunrise; each took about half an hour. Prime was followed by work — *i.e.* field work for most of the monks — or reading, according to the time of the year; and these exercises filled up the time till dinner, which was at 12 or at 3, the short offices of Tierce, Sext, and None being celebrated in the church at the appropriate hours. In summer, when the night sleep was short, the usual Italian siesta was allowed after dinner. The afternoon was passed in work and reading, like the forenoon. Vespers or Evensong was sung some time before sunset, and in the summer was followed by an evening meal. Before dark, while there yet was enough light to read by, they assembled once again in the church, and after a few pages·had been read, Compline was said, and they retired to rest in the dusk, before there was need of an artificial light. On Sundays there was no work, and the time assigned to the church services and to reading was considerably lengthened.

According to St. Benedict's scheme of the monastic life, work occupied notably more time daily than either the church services or reading; and this work was manual, either in the fields or garden, or about the house. This element of work was intended to be an integral part of the life; not a mere occupation, but a very real factor of the monk's service of God, and from six to seven hours were devoted to it daily. These long hours of manual labour, coupled with the unbroken fast till midday, or 3 p.m., or even till sunset during Lent, and the perpetual abstinence from flesh meat, may convey the impression that, after all, the life in St Benedict's monastery was one of great bodily austerity. But it has to be remembered that though members of patrician families were to be found in his community, still the great majority was recruited from the ranks of the Italian peasantry, or from those of the Goths and other barbarians who were then overrunning Italy. Neither the fasting nor the abstinence from meat would appear to Italian peasants in the present day, and still less in the sixth century, so onerous as they do to us in northern climes.

The other exercise of the monks, outside the direct worship of God, was reading, to which from three to five hours were assigned daily, according to the season. There can be little doubt that this reading was wholly devotional, confined to the Bible and the writings of the fathers, St Basil and Cassian being recommended by name. Out of this germ grew in the course of ages those works of erudition and of historical science with which the Benedictine name in later ages became associated: the first step forward along the path of monastic studies was taken not by St Benedict, but by his younger contemporary Cassiodorus in his Calabrian monastery at Squillace.

But the chief work of the monk was, in St Benedict's eyes, neither field work nor literary work: all the services of Benedictines to civilisation and education and. letters have been but by-products. Their primary and essential work is what St Benedict calls the "Work of God" — *Opus Dei* — the daily chanting of the canonical Office in the choir. To this work he says nothing is to be preferred, and this principle has been the keynote of Benedictine life throughout the ages. The daily "course" of psalmody ordinarily consisted of 40 psalms with certain canticles, hymns, responses, prayers, and lections from Scripture and the fathers. It was divided into the eight canonical hours, the Vigils or night office being considerably the longest. It is probable that this daily common prayer took some 4 to 4½ hours, being chanted throughout, and not merely recited in a monotone. Mass was celebrated only on Sundays and holy-days. Private prayer was taken for granted, and was provided for, but not legislated for, being left to personal devotion.

The abbot governed the monastery with full patriarchal authority. He was elected by the monks, and held office for life. All the officials of the monastery were appointed by him, and were removable at his will. He should take counsel with his monks — in matters of moment with the whole community, in lesser matters with a few seniors. He was bound to listen to what each had to say; but at the end, it rested with him to decide what was to be done, and all had to obey. The great — in a sense it might be said, the only — restraining influence upon the abbot to which St Benedict appeals, was that of religion—the abiding sense, impressed on him again and again by St Benedict, that he was directly and personally responsible, and would have to answer before the judgment seat of God for all his actions, for all his judgments, nay, even for the soul of each one of his monks as well as for his own. But his government must be according to the Rule, and not at his own mere will and pleasure, as had been the case in the earlier forms of monachism; and he is warned not to overburden his monks, or overdrive them, but to be considerate always and give no one cause for just complaint. The chapters specially written for the abbot (2, 3, 27, 64) are the most characteristic in the Rule, and form a body of wise counsel, not easily to be surpassed, for anyone in office or authority of any kind. This formation of a regular order of life according to rule, this provision for the disciplined working of a large establishment, was St Benedict's great contribution to Western monachism, and also to Western civilisation. For as Benedictine abbeys came gradually to be established more and more thickly in the midst of the wild Teutonic populations that were settling throughout Western Europe, they became object-lessons in disciplined and well-ordered life, in organised work, in all the arts of peace, that could not but impress powerfully the minds of the surrounding barbarians, and bring home to them ideals of peace and order and work, no less than of religion.

Another point of far-reaching consequence was that St Benedict laid upon the monk the obligation of abiding till death, not only in the

CH. XVIII.

monastic life, but in his own monastery in which he was professed. This special Benedictine vow of stability cut off what was the very common practice of monks, when they grew dissatisfied in one monastery, going to another. St Benedict bound the monks of a monastery together into a permanent family, united by bonds that lasted for life. This idea that the monks of each Benedictine monastery form a permanent community, distinct from that of every other Benedictine monastery, is a characteristic feature of Benedictine monachism, and a chief distinction between it and the mendicant and other later Orders; without doubt it has also been the great source of the special influence and strength of the Benedictines in history.

Another distinction lies in the fact that St Benedict, in common with the early monastic legislators, set before his monks no special object or purpose, no particular work to be done, other than the common work of monks — the living in community according to the "evangelical counsels," and thereby sanctifying their souls and serving God. "A school of the service of the Lord" is St Benedict's definition of a monastery, and the one thing he requires from the novice is that "in very deed he seek God." Nothing probably was further from his thoughts than that his monks were to become apostles, bishops, popes, civilisers, educators, scholars, men of learning. His idea simply was to make them *good*: and if a man *is* good, he will *do* good. The ascetical side of the training in the Rule lies chiefly in obedience and humility. The very definition of a monk is "one who renounces his own wishes, and comes to fight for Christ, taking up the arms of obedience"; it is the temper of renunciation and obedience rather than the actual obeying that is of value. The chapter on humility (7), the longest in the Rule, has become a classic in Christian ascetical literature; it embodies St Benedict's teaching on the spiritual life. The general spirit of the Rule is beautifully summed up in the short chapter "on the good zeal which monks ought to have" (72): "As there is an evil and bitter emulation which separates from God and leads to hell, so there is a good spirit of emulation which frees from vices and leads to God and life everlasting. Let monks therefore practise this emulation with most fervent love; that is to say, let them in honour prefer one another. Let them bear most patiently with each other's infirmities, whether of body or of character. Let them contend with one another in their obedience. Let no one follow what he thinks most profitable to himself, but rather what is best for another. Let them shew brotherly charity with a chaste love. Let them fear God and love their abbot with sincere and humble affection, and set nothing whatever before Christ, Who can bring us unto eternal life."[1]

In view of the great influence exercised on the course of European history and civilisation in things both ecclesiastical and civil, from the

[1] Abbot Gasquet's translation.

sixth century to the thirteenth, by St Benedict and his sons, it seemed proper to supply the foregoing somewhat detailed account of the Benedictine Rule and life. With an outline sketch of the steps whereby St Benedict's supremacy in Western monachism was achieved, this chapter will be concluded.

Though the Rule was written as a code of regulations for the government of one monastery, it is evident that St Benedict contemplated the likelihood of its being observed in different monasteries, and even in different countries. Besides Monte Cassino, his own monastery at Subiaco, and perhaps the twelve others, continued after he had left them; and there is mention of one founded by him from Monte Cassino, at Terracina. These are the only Benedictine monasteries of which there is any record as existing in St Benedict's lifetime, for the stories of the missions of St Placidus to Sicily and St Maurus to Gaul must be regarded as apocryphal. It is said of Simplicius, the third abbot of Monte Cassino, that "he propagated into all the hidden work of the master"; and this has been understood as indicating that the spread of the Rule to other monasteries began in his abbacy. But the historical determining point was the sacking of Monte Cassino by the Lombards about 580–590, when the monks fled to Rome, and were placed in a monastery attached to the Lateran Basilica, in the heart of Latin Christendom, under the eyes of the Popes. It is now generally agreed by critical students of the period that the monachism which St Gregory the Great established in his palace on the Coelian Hill, wherein he himself became a monk, was in an adequate and true sense Benedictine, being based on that Rule which St Gregory eulogises as "conspicuous for its discretion." From the Coelian Hill it was carried to England by Augustine, the prior of the monastery, and his companions (596), and it is probable that the monastery of SS. Peter and Paul, later St Augustine's, Canterbury, was the first Benedictine monastery out of Italy. As has been said above, it was not till the seventh century that Benedictine monarchism got a foothold in Gaul; but during that century it spread steadily and at last rapidly throughout Gaul and England, and from England it was carried into Friesland and the other Germanic lands by the great English Benedictine missioners, Willibrod, Boniface, and the rest. Being well adapted to the spirit and character of the Teutonic peoples then overrunning Western Europe, the Benedictine Rule inevitably and quickly absorbed and supplanted all those previously in vogue — so completely that Charles the Great could ask the question, if there had ever been any other monastic Rule than St Benedict's? The Benedictines shared fully in the effects of the Carolingian revival, and from that date, for three centuries, St Benedict's spirit ruled supreme throughout Western monachism, Ireland alone excepted.

All through the Benedictine centuries, Benedictine nuns flourished no less than Benedictine monks, and nowhere more than in England.

CH. XVIII.

St Boniface's correspondence with several Anglo-Saxon nuns, both in England and in Germany, reveals the high standards of education and of life that prevailed in the English nunneriès. Communities of Benedictine nuns have in all ages been predominantly ladiës, recruited from the upper classes, and the life is specially adapted for them. Naturally it has been a more secluded life than that of the monks; but the great Benedictine nunneries have always exercised considerable religious and social influence.

In the foregoing pages the ideals of the various phases of early monasticism have been set forth.   It is not pretended that these ideals have always been realised by monks.   But it is right to estimate a system in large measure by its ideals, except where failure adequately to realise them has predominated.   That this has been the case with Christian monachism as a whole will hardly now be contended by any historian.

CHAPTER XIX

SOCIAL AND ECONOMIC CONDITIONS OF THE ROMAN EMPIRE IN THE FOURTH CENTURY

THE ancients saw in the stupendous destiny of the Roman State the clue to the history of the Universe and a revelation of the plans of Providence in regard to the world. "Italy," wrote Pliny the elder in the time of Vespasian, "has been selected by Deity in order to collect dispersed power, to soften customs, and to unite by the communion of one language the various and barbarous dialects of so many nations, to bestow on men the intercourse of ideas and humanity, in a word — that all the races of the world should have one fatherland" (*Hist. Nat.* III. 6). For Christians the conquest of the world by Rome had even a deeper meaning. "Jesus was born in the reign of Augustus, who as it were associated in one monarchy the immense multitude of men dispersed about the earth, because a plurality of kingdoms would have been an obstacle to the diffusion of Christ's doctrine through the whole world" (Origen, *c. Celsum*, II. 30). But Augustus was a heathen and his successors persecuted Christianity, so that the Roman Empire served the Gospel for a long while unconsciously and in spite of its desires. This conception of universal history made a further stride when Constantine the Great proclaimed Christianity the religion of the State. "In ancient times," says Eusebius of Caesarea, "the world was divided according to countries and nations into a multitude of commonwealths, tyrannies, principalities. Hence constant wars and the devastations and depredations following thereon. . . . The origin of these divisions may certainly be ascribed to the diversity of the gods worshipped by men. But when the instrument of salvation, the most holy body of Christ · · · was raised . . . against the demons, forthwith the cause of demons has vanished and states, principalities, tyrannies, commonwealths have passed away. . . . One God has been announced to the whole of mankind, one empire obtained sway over all men — the Roman Empire" (Eusebius, *Panegyric of Constantine,* c. 16).

But the unification of the inhabited world (οἰκουμένη) which forms the meaning and the greatness of the Roman Empire, is a process presenting two different sides to the observer. Kelts, Iberians, Rhaetians, Moors, Illyrians, Thracians were to some extent civilised by the culture of Greece and Rome, and achieved by its help a great advance in economic and civic organisation as well as in education; Syrians, Egyptians, the inhabitants of Asia Minor only modified to a certain extent their manners and views in order to meet the requirements of the Empire. But if the intermixture of tribes and their permeation by Graeco-Roman culture was in one sense a great progress, it was at the same time, but from another point of view, a decline; it was accompanied by a lowering of the level of the culture which exerted the civilising influence. While conquering barbarism and native peculiarities, Graeco-Roman culture assumed various traits from its vanquished opponents, and became gross and vulgar in its turn. In the words of a biographer of Alexander Severus: good and bad were promiscuously thrust into the Empire, noble and base, and numbers of barbarians (*Hist. Aug. Alex. Sev.* 64).

The unification and transformation of tribes standing on low grades of civilisation leads to consequences characterised by one common feature, the simplification of aims — degeneration. This process is concealed for a while by the political and economic advantages following on the establishment of the Empire. The creation of a central authority, upholding peace and intercourse (*Pax Romana*), the conjunction of the different parts of the world into one economic system enlivened by free trade, the spread of citizenship and civil culture in wider and wider circles of population — all these benefits produced for a time a rise of prosperity which counterbalanced the excess of barbarous, imperfectly assimilated elements.

But a series of political misfortunes set in rather rapidly in the third century: invasions of barbarians, conflicts between rival candidates to the throne, competition between armies and provinces put an end to order and prosperity and threatened the very existence of the Empire. In these calamities the barbarisation of Roman culture became more and more manifest, a backward movement began in all directions, a backward movement, however, which was by no means a mere falling back into previous conditions, but gave rise to new and interesting departures.

It suffices to glance at the names of the Roman citizens of the Empire in order to notice that we are in very mixed company. Instead of the *nomina* and *cognomina* of earlier days we find strange barbaric appellations hardly whitewashed by the adjunction of *us* or *er* at the end. A T. Tammonius Saeni Tammoni filius Vitalis, and a Blescius Diovicus do not look very pure "Quirites." Such barbarians had first of all to learn Latin as the common tongue of the Western Empire, and they did learn to use Latin. But what Latin! As St Jerome has it: "Latin language gets transformed according to countries and to epochs." Common speech, the *lingua vulgaris*, with a former Kelt, Iberian, or Rhaetian became gradually a new Romance language, the sounds and forms of which were deflected from the original Latin in consequence of the physiological and intellectual peculiarities of Kelts, Iberians, Rhaetians.

We may be allowed to give a few instances of this curious process of transformation from the well-known history of French phonetics and grammar. The Latin *u* was kept up in Italian but softened into the French *u* (*ü*), *e.g.* durus — duro — dur, and we cannot wonder at that, because the population of Gaul when yet speaking Keltic sounded *u* as *ü* and not somewhat like the English *oo* in "poor." The French "*liaison*," the habit of sounding the otherwise mute consonant at the end of a word before a vowel in order to avoid a "*hiatus*," may be traced to the Keltic habit of joining separate words into compounds. In Keltic dialects the accent makes one or the other syllable so prominent that other syllables become indistinct and may get slurred over. This stress put on the accentuated syllable has called forth in French a characteristic deterioration of unaccentuated parts of words. Sometimes whole groups of sounds disappear, as in "Août" (Augustus), sometimes they are represented only by a mute *e* as in "vie" (vita). The French habit of marking the last syllable by an accent even in the pronunciation of Latin goes back ultimately to this trait. In reading the Latin text of the Salic Law we are struck by the complete dislocation of the system of declensions — the ablative case is constantly used instead of the accusative, the accusative instead of the nominative, etc. But this degeneration was prepared by the practice of vulgar Latin even in the first and second centuries when the genitive case disappeared. The dative followed suit somewhat later.

It is not however to be supposed that Latin was imposed even in its vulgarised forms on the entire population of the Empire. It is needless to remind the reader of the fact that in the whole eastern half Greek was the language of the educated classes. But both in the East and in the West there were many backward regions in which vernacular speech held its own stubbornly against Greek and Latin. The Copts, Arabs, Syrians, Armenians never gave up their native languages, and the oriental undercurrents continued to play an important part in the social life of Asia and Egypt. There are many vestiges of a similar persistency of barbarian custom and speech in the West. Roman law admitted expressly that valid deeds could be executed in Punic and, judging from the story about a sister of Septimius Severus, Punic must have been very prevalent among well-to-do families of knightly rank in Africa: when the lady in question came to visit her brother in Rome, the Emperor had often to blush on account of her imperfect knowledge of Latin. The letters and sermons of St Augustine shew that this state of things had by no means disappeared in romanised Africa in the fifth century: the great African bishop repeatedly urged the necessity for dignitaries of the Church to be acquainted with Punic, and he had recourse himself to illustrations drawn from this language.   In Spain and Gascony one living remnant of pre-Roman civilisation has survived to our days in the "Es-c-aldunac" speech of the Basques, the offspring of the Iberian race, while Brittany exhibits another block of pre-Roman custom in the speech and manners of its Breton population.   St Jerome testifies to the fact that in the neighbourhood of Trèves, one of the mightiest centres of Roman civilisation, a Keltic dialect was spoken by the peasants in the fourth century, so that a person reared there possessed a clue to the speech of the Galatians, the Keltic tribe of Asia Minor.   In the Latinised north-west of the Balkan peninsula the vernacular Illyrian was never driven out or destroyed, and the present speech of the Albanians is directly derived from it in spite of a sprinkling of Latin words and expressions.   In the west of England Keltic speech and custom runs on uninterruptedly through the ages of Roman, Saxon, and Norman conquest.   Not to speak of Welsh, which has borrowed many Latin words, especially technical terms, but remains a purely Keltic language, Cornish was spoken in Cornwall up to the eighteenth century, while in Cumberland and Westmorland the custom of shepherds to count their sheep in Keltic numerals was the last vestige of the separate existence of a "Welsh" population.

These traces of stubborn national life forming a kind of barbarian subsoil to Roman culture are important in many ways : they help us not only to understand the history of dialects and of folklore, but they account for a good many spontaneous outbursts of barbarism in the seemingly pacified and romanised provinces of the Empire at a time when the iron hand of the rulers began to relax its grip over the conquered populations.   Berber, Punic, Iberian, Illyrian, and Keltic tribes come forward again in the calamitous years of the fourth and fifth centuries.   Usurpers, riotous soldiers, and brigands gather strength from national aspirations, and in the end the disruption of the Empire becomes inevitable on account of internal strife as well as of foreign invasions. Nowhere perhaps has this subliminal life of the province to account for so much as in England, where the arts and crafts of Rome were introduced in the course of three centuries and a half of gradual occupation, and Latin itself was widely spoken by the upper classes, but where nevertheless the entire fabric of Roman rule crumbled down so rapidly during the fifth century, and Kelts were left to fight with the Teutons for the remnants of what had been one of the fair provinces of Rome.

A transformation similar to that expressed in language is clearly perceivable in the history of Art.   Christianity introduced into the world a powerful new factor, the strength of which may be gauged in the paintings of the Catacombs and in the rise of new styles of architecture — the Byzantine and the Romanesque.   Thus we have to deal not with mere deterioration and decay, but also with the lowering of the level of culture and the barbarisation of art which make themselves felt in various ways. When Rome had to raise a triumphal arch to the conqueror of Maxentius, a great part of the reliefs for its adornment were carried over from the Arch of Trajan, while some sculptures were added by contemporary artists. And the latter perpetuate the decay of art and of aesthetic taste. The figures are distorted, the faces deformed. On the so-called discus of Theodosius the symbolical figures of the lower part were copied from ancient originals and are handsome. The upper half was filled with representations of living people, and it is evident that the gross, flat, ugly faces, the heavy embroidered uniforms, were reproduced with fidelity, while the handling of the figures strikes the observer by its clumsiness and faulty designs. The chief thing in the pictorial and plastic artś of the third and fourth centuries is not beauty or expression, but size and costly material. Gallienus, whose unfortunate reign was nicknamed the "period of the thirty tyrants," ordered a statue of himself 200 feet in height : it was planned on such a scale that a child was able to ascend by a winding staircase to the top of the Emperor's lance. Instead of marble, precious porphyry, a stone exceedingly difficult to cut, was used for plastic purposes; the contractor and polisher were more important persons than the sculptor for the purpose of making statues of this material.

It is of special importance for us to notice the gradual degeneration or rather transformation of economic life. Towards the beginning of our era a great circuit of industrial and commercial intercourse is formed under the protection of the Empire : it reminds us in some ways of the world-market of the present time. The different provinces exchanged goods and developed specialities fitting into one whole through mutual support; the excellent roads made quick exchanges possible, considerable capital sought employment in productive enterprises, firm political power and mutual confidence fostered the growth of credit. From the third century onwards the picture changes. The subjection of conquered peoples by Roman citizens ceases and the greater part of the population of the Empire is admitted to the rights of citizenship. This meant that masses of people, over whom governors, *publicans* and contractors had exercised almost uncontrolled sway, were enabled to come forward with their interests and legal claims. Provincial forces began to assert themselves, and in husbandry local needs and the requirements of small people made themselves more and more felt. As a consequence, the wide organisation of world intercourse gives way before more direct and modest economic problems — each social group has to look out primarily for itself in regard to food, clothing, housing, furniture. On the other hand the supply of slaves gets more and more hampered by the fact that wars of conquest cease. In the beginning of the third century we hear already of a price of 200 aurei or 500 denarii of full ancient coinage for a slave (*Dig.* IV. 4, 51) — a very high price indeed, which shews indirectly how

CH. XIX.

difficult it was to get slaves. During the protracted defensive wars which had to be fought on all the frontiers prisoners were frequently made, but these Germans, Slavs, Huns were difficult to manage and made clumbsy labourers when settled for agricultural purposes : it was more profitable to leave them a certain independence on their plots, and therefore to cut up large estates into small holdings. Lastly, the rise of provincial and local interests and the change in the condition of the labouring classes coincided with the terrible political calamities which I have already had occasion to mention. The dislocation of the commonwealth rendered all widely extended economic plans insecure and contributed by itself to the tendency of each separate locality to live its own life and to work for its own needs without much help from the outside. As a result of the working of these different causes society falls back from a complicated system of commerical intercourse to the simpler forms of "natural economy." This movement is not arrested by the restoration of the Empire in the fourth century, but rather strengthened by it. Political power is indeed restored, but it has to be maintained by straining every nerve in social life, and this straining hampers free movement and free contract, fastens every one to a certain place and to a certain calling.

In an "Exposition of the whole world and of nations" translated from Greek in the time of Constantius (soon after 345) much attention is still paid to the economic intercourse between the different parts of the Empire. Greece itself is said to be unable to satisfy its own needs, but in regard to many of the other provinces it is expressly noted that they are sufficient unto themselves. Besides, most of them produce goods which are exported to other places. Ascalon and Gaza, for example, are said to provide excellent wine for Syria and Egypt; Scythopolis, Laodicea (in Syria), Byblus, Tyre, Berytus send out linen wares all round the world, while Caesarea, Tyre, Sarepta and Neapolis are famous in the same way for their purple-dyed tissues. Egypt supplies Constantinople and the Eastern provinces with corn and has a monopoly in the production of papyrus. From Cappadocia furs are obtained, from Galatia different kinds of clothing. Laodicea in Phrygia has given a name to garments of a special kind. Asia and the Hellespont produce corn, wine, and oil; in Macedonia and Dalmatia, iron and lead mines are noted; in Dardana (Illyria) pastoral pursuits are prevalent and bacon and cheese are sent to market, while Epirus is distinguished by its large fishing trade. The Western provinces are not described in such a minute way but fine Italian wines are mentioned, the trade of Arles for imports into Gaul is noted, and Spain is extolled on account of its oil, cloth, bacon and mules. Oil is also said to be largely supplied by the African province, while clothing and cattle come from Numidia. Pannonia and Mauretania are the only provinces mentioned as carrying on the slave trade.

. Some forty-five years before this commercial geography of the Empire was drawn up, another curious document shews the imperial authorities engaged in a wearisome struggle in order to protect easy intercourse and to ward off the rise of prices — I mean the famous edict of Diocletian and of his companion emperors establishing maximum prices in the Empire. Such measures are not taken without cogent reasons, and, indeed, we are told that prices had risen enormously, although it is hardly probable that the reason of the dearth had to be sought in the iniquities of the rulers (Lactantius, *de mortibus perse_ cutorum*, c. 7). The enactment itself dilates on the evil greed of avaricious producers and venders, and declares in the name of the "fathers of human kind" that justice has to arbitrate and to intervene. The Emperors are especially incensed at the hard bargains which are extorted from soldiers quartered in the provinces or moving along the roads : prices are screwed up on such occasions not to four or eight times the ordinary value, but to an extent that could not be expressed in words. If such things happen in times of abundance what is to be expected from seasons when actual want is experienced? Without attempting to fix normal prices the Emperors threaten with capital punishment merchants engaged in supplying the different provinces with wares : Lactantius reports that blood flowed and that the impossibility of enforcing cheapness by the hands of executioners was only recognised after fruitless attempts to terrorise tradesmen into submission.

Let us look, however, at some of the details of the edict, fragments of which have been preserved in several copies in the Balkan peninsula, Asia Minor, and Egypt, viz., in the provinces under the direct sway of Diocletian.

Traces of commercial intercourse of the same kind as that described in the *Expositio* frequently meet the eye. We hear again of the high class wines of Italy, of linen vestments from Laodicea, Scythopolis, Byblus, of purple-dyed garments manufactured on the Syrian coast and fetching very high prices, and of somewhat less expensive kinds from Miletus : a piece of purple linen for ornamental stripes (*clavi*) weighing six ounces may be sold for 13,000, 23,000 and even 32,000 denarii, 50,000 of the latter corresponding to one pound of gold.[1] Cloth garments came from Laodicea in Phrygia, from Modena in Italy and in the shape of coarse, warm mantles from Flanders. In a word the lines of commercial intercourse are clearly traced, but the difficulties encountered by trade under new conditions are also very visible. Some comparisons with extant valuations of goods ordered for soldiers enable us to form a judgment as to the fluctuations of prices which Diocletian's enactment tried to moderate. We hear, *e.g.*, that in one case 80

---

[1] Roughly equivalent to £46 present coinage.

pounds of bacon were estimated at 1 solidus (6000 copper denarii) and in another instance 20 pounds at 1000 denarii. According to the tariff of Diocletian the maximum price for bacon of the best kind would have been in the first instance 96,000, and in the second 16,000 copper denarii, the latter being about 16 times more than the ordinary price.

It is important to notice that while the ordinary agricultural labourer is not allowed to receive higher wages than 25 silver denarii (about 120 copper denarii) per day besides board, the maximum price of a double sextarius (roughly, about a quart) of wheat was fixed at 100 silver denarii, and that of a pound of pork at 12 silver denarii.

One cannot wonder at the failure of Diocletian's attempt, which according to contemporary testimony only increased the evils it was meant to suppress, the penalties against the merchants leading to concealment of goods and interruptions of trade. But it is characteristic of the methods of compulsory legislation constantly employed by the emperors of the fourth century that Julian made a similar and quite as unsuccessful attempt to coerce the citizens of Antioch into fair trade.

It is impossible to suppose that such measures were dictated by a kind of "Caesar madness," prompting the rulers of the civilised world to affirm their will and wisdom as against economic laws. However faulty in its conception, the policy indicated by the edicts of Diocletian and Julian had its roots in a well-meaning though ineffectual desire to regulate trade and to protect fair intercourse. It may be likened, as most attempts to impose maximum limits to prices, to the police supervision of trade in necessaries of life practised in besieged cities. The emperors and their bureaucracy had come to look on the whole civilised world subject to their authority as upon a besieged city, in which all civil professions had to conform to military rule.

The same kind of evolution from free intercourse to compulsion may be observed in the legislation on commercial and industrial corporations. Roman law passed through several stages in this respect. At the time of the Republic guilds of artisans and merchants could be formed by private agreement if their statutes and activity did not infringe the laws of the State (Gaius in *Dig.* XLVII. 22, 4). During the civil conflicts of the last years of the Republic and in the early Empire organised corporations were several times dissolved and forbidden on account of the political agitation carried on by their members, and from Augustus' time concession by the Senate and confirmation by the Prince had to be applied for when a new college or guild had to be formed. But police supervision by the State did not alter the main feature of the corporations, namely their spontaneous origin in the needs of society and the wish of private persons to carry on profitable trade and to form unions for mutual support and social intercourse. The imperial Government was often inclined to repress these spontaneous tendencies, as we may gather, *e.g.*, from Trajan's correspondence with Pliny.

The first indication of a further change in the relations between government and corporations may be noticed in the reign of Alexander Severus. This Emperor, instead of restricting the rise of trade guilds, actually favoured the formation of corporations of wine merchants, grocers, shoemakers, and other crafts (Lampridius, *Alexander Severus*, 33). We may suspect that at this time, that is in the second quarter of the third century, the Government began to perceive a slackening in the energy of trade and commerce and chose to exert its authority in patronising trade guilds. The restoration of imperial power under Aurelian brought about another and more powerful attempt in the same direction. One of the measures of this Emperor was the assumption of a wide-reaching guardianship over the alimentation of Rome. The supply of corn from Egypt was increased; lists of paupers (*proletarii*) entitled to be fed by the State were drawn up, and the privilege of living at the cost of the commonwealth was made hereditary; instead of corn, bread was distributed, and along with bread — oil, salt, and pork. In connexion with this system of alimentation of the poorer classes in Rome Aurelian reorganised the service of the merchants responsible for the transport of corn on the Nile and on the Tiber. This throws light on the immediate reason for the transformation of corporations in the ensuing age: trades and crafts which had a bearing on vital needs of social intercourse were taken under the tutelage of the Empire and carried on henceforth, not as free professions but as compulsory services.

This is clearly seen in the legislation of Constantine and remains characteristic of the legal treatment of trade during the whole of the fourth and of the fifth century.

In the *Lex Julia* of 747 u.c. enacted by Augustus the principle was already formulated that a combination of individual workmen or traders into a college had to be warranted not only by their wishes and interests but by public utility. The public element assumes now a preponderating influence. Bakers are authorised to form a craft guild not because they see an advantage in being organised in this way, but because the State wants their services in regulating the trade in bread and providing for the needs of the inhabitants of cities. The result of this enlisting of trades and crafts into public service is a system entirely at variance with our conceptions of supply and demand, and of economic intercourse.

To begin with, all freedom in the choice of professions came to an end. Corporations are required to hold their members to their occupations all through life. All attempts of single members to leave their place of abode and customary work are considered as a flight from duty and severely forbidden. In 395, *e.g.*, Arcadius and Honorius decree heavy fines against powerful people who conceal and protect fugitive

members of *curiae* and *collegia*. For each one of the latter the patron
has to pay a fine of a pound of gold (C. Th. xii. 1, 147). The codices
are full of enactments against fugitives of this kind, and such legislation
would prove, by itself, that a *régime* of caste was being gradually
established in the Empire. It is certain that the invasions of barbarians,
such as those of Alaric for example, contributed powerfully to scatter
the working population, but, apart from these, one of the motives of
flight was the heavy burden of taxation.[1] It is probable that the
initiative in regard to the measures of stern compulsion came not from
the bureaucrats of the Empire, but from the corporations themselves
which were made liable to the requirements of the State in case of the
flight of their members. Of course, the consistent enforcement of such
a policy actually blocked the natural selection of professions and the
development of independent enterprise.

Let us, to take a concrete example, attend somewhat closer to the
discipline imposed on the important college of *navicularii*. During the
first two centuries of our era the term designated all shipowners
engaged in the carrying trade by sea; gradually it came to mean
shippers employed by the State for the transport of goods, especially of
corn. Most of the corn necessary for the population of Rome was
derived from Egypt and Africa, and we hear of a large fleet starting
from Alexandria for the purpose of carrying over the supply. There is
good evidence to shew that during the second century A.D. the college
was composed of men who had joined it as voluntary members and sought
the privileges which were conceded to it in return for its services to the
State. All this appears changed in the fourth century. The *navicularii*
are to devote themselves primarily to the transport of goods belonging
to the State, more particularly corn and oil for Rome and Constantinople, while African *navicularii* were bound to bring wood for fuel to
the public baths of Rome. The Egyptian *navicularii* received their
cargo from the collectors of the *annona*, the corn tribute in the province.
The season for the voyages of their ships was reckoned from the first of
April to the 15th of October, the other months being held free on
account of stormy weather. Each *navicularius* had to send his ships to
the fleet once in two years. When the ship weighed anchor it had to
proceed by the shortest route and not to stop anywhere without absolute
necessity. Should one of the ships of the corn fleet be delayed in a port
the governor and Senate of the place were bound, if necessary, to use
force, in order to send the merchants out to sea again. Outside these
official journeys they had the right to move on their own behalf, but
evidently their right did not outweigh the uncomfortable limitations
imposed on them during their service period, as we find the emperors
endeavouring in every way to keep the *navicularii* to their task and to
prevent them from slipping out of the college. A curious letter of

[1] Ammianus Marcellinus, xxxi. 6, § 6.

St Augustine tells how the bishop refused to accept the bequest of a certain Bonifacius, an African *navicularius*, on behalf of the see of Hippo. Bonifacius had disinherited his son and wanted to pass over his property to the Church. St Augustine refuses to accept the gift, because he does not wish to entangle the Church with the dealings of the *navicularii*. In case of shipwreck the Government would order an inquiry, the sailors rescued from the wreck would be put to torture, the Church would have to pay for the lost cargo, etc. The members of the college evidently had to be rich men and, sometimes, if there were gaps to be filled, the State would compel rich men to join the *corpus naviculari_orum*. The service was hereditary, and if any member absconded, his property was forfeited to the college. These facts may be sufficient to shew to what extent the commerce of those days suffered under the stringent discipline imposed by the requirements of the State, and what a queer mixture of a business man and of an official a shipowner of those days was. I may add that, although we know most about *navicularii*, bakers, purveyors of pork, and similar merchants engaged in supplying the capitals with food. The provisioning of the smaller towns and the management of all crafts and trades were carried on more or less on similar principles.

An important chapter in the history of the decline and fall of the Empire is constituted by the gradual decay of municipal institutions. The ancient world took a long time to exchange its organisation of free cities for that of a great power, governed by a centralised bureaucracy. Even after the conquest of its provinces the Roman commonwealth remained substantially a confederation of cities, and municipal autonomy prospered for a long while. We see the cities of the first and second centuries vying one with the other in local patriotism, in the munificence of leading citizens, in generous contributions of private men towards the welfare of poorer classes, public health, and order. The economic progress brought about by the establishment of the Empire made itself felt primarily in the increased activity and prosperity of city life. But threatening symptoms begin to appear even in the second century A.D. Municipal self-government, bereft of its political significance, restricted to the sphere of local interests and local ambitions, is apt to degenerate into corrupt and spendthrift practices : the wealthier provincial citizens ruin themselves by lavish expenditure on pageants and distributions, municipal enterprise in matters of building and philanthropy often turns out to be extravagant and inefficient. The emperors find no other means of remedying such defects than the institution of curators of different kinds — *curatores rei publicae, curatores kalendarii*, commissioners for the correction of the condition of free cities (*ad corrigendum statum liberarum civitatum*). In the correspondence between Pliny and Trajan the imperial commissioner is already seen to interfere in the most minute questions of city administration and, at the same time, he is constantly applying for direction to his imperial master. The ideal of centralisation is clearly expressed in this intimate intercourse of two well-meaning and talented statesmen : the Emperor appears in the light of an omniscient and all-powerful Providence watching over all the dealings and doings of his innumerable subjects. In order to embody such an ideal the central power had to surround itself with helpers and executive officers, and Hadrian laid the foundations of a Civil Service more comprehensive and better organised than the rudimentary administrative institutions of the Commonwealth and of the early Empire. Later on Diocletian and Constantine multiplied the number of bureaucratic organs and combined them into one whole by the bands of constant supervision and iron discipline. But even before this ultimate completion of bureaucracy in the fourth century, in the very beginnings of the system of central tutelage, a kind of vicious circle formed itself : central authority was called upon to interfere on account of the deplorable defects of municipal administration, while municipal life was disturbed and atrophied by constant interference from above. It is impossible to say precisely what was cause and what was effect in this case : the process was, as it happens in many diseases, a constant flow of action and reaction. The jurists of the third century find already a characteristic formula for corporative town organisation in an analogy with the condition of a minor under tutelage, and this analogy is followed up into all sorts of particulars as to rights and duties. No wonder that for many citizens municipal life loses its interest, that they try to eschew the burdens of unremunerated and costly local administration, and that as early as the time of the Severi compulsion has sometimes to be used to bring together a sufficient number of unwilling magistrates and members of municipal senates (*Dig.*, L. 1, 38, 6 ; L. 2, 2, 8).

A circumstance which in itself would have hardly been sufficient to overthrow municipal organisation, certainly contributed to divert people's minds from the customary trend of local patriotism and to make the performance of certain duties difficult — I mean the spread of Christianity. Municipal institutions were intertwined with cults of Roman and local gods, including religious devotion to the Deity of the Emperors. The new faith, on the other hand, did not admit of sacrifices or prayer to the false gods of heathendom : hence a conflict which did not admit of a ready solution. Let us listen to the somewhat exaggerated statement of Tertullian — "We concede," he says, "that a Christian may without endangering salvation assume the honour and title of public functions — if he does not offer sacrifices nor authorise sacrifices, if he does not furnish victims, if he does not entrust anybody with the upkeep of temples, if he does not take part in the management of their income, if he does not give games either at his own or at the public expense, if he does not preside at them, if he does not announce or arrange any festival, if he avoids all kinds of oath and abstains, while exercising power, from giving sentence in regard to the life or the honour of men, decisions as to money matters being excepted; if he does not proclaim edicts, nor act as a judge, nor put people into prison or inflict torture on them. But is all this possible?" As a matter of fact the heathen State did certainly not go out of its way to make all these exceptions possible, and conflicts between law and religious conviction arose every day. On many occasions Christians of a softer mould submitted to what they considered to be inevitable, and performed most of the duties challenged by the fiery African. The Church had to work out a penitentiary code for those among its members who had sullied themselves by heathen practices (see *e.g.* the canons of the Synod of Elvira in Spain). Sometimes again the more firm among the Christians made a stubborn stand and were martyrised for their protest as enemies of the Roman State. Altogether there can be no doubt that the inherent contradiction between Christian religion and the pagan practices of municipal life did put an extra strain on the latter and could not but increase the disorder which was setting in. The bold step taken by Constantine in recognising Christianity as a state religion saved the situation to some extent, but it could not do away at a stroke with all the pagan elements of municipal life: the strife between religions assumed a new aspect, and as the vital connexion between local self-government and local cults was never restored, that unity of conception which marked antiquity when at its best had to be replaced by a deep dualism tending towards new solutions of political and moral problems. The greatest representative of conquering Christianity, St Augustine, recognises the defeat of the material world of antiquity and has to fashion his ideals according to a scheme of two cities in which only the heavenly one appeals to his devotion and energy.

Apart from this complication arising out of peculiarities of religious history, the middle class of the citizens was undergoing a transformation similar to that of the merchants and craftsmen. When the chaotic conditions of the second half of the third century were arrested by the statesmanship and military power of Aurelian and Diocletian, the policy of compulsion was brought to bear with full weight on the well-to-do inhabitants of cities. They were mostly not only houseowners in our sense, but also owners of lands in the vicinity of the towns, although distinctions which it is somewhat difficult for us at the present time to formulate in detail were drawn between them and the *possessores* or land-owners properly so called. However, the bulk of the well-to-do townsmen was considered as a separate class, the *curiales*, out of which the actual members of city senates, the *decuriones*, as well as its executive officials and justices, were selected. Yet the connexion between the *curiales* group and the actual office-holders was so close, there were so few members of the former who had not to serve in one way or the other, that the enactments of the Codes currently confuse the two distinct terms — *curiales* and *decuriones*. This confusion of itself points to the overburdening of the middle class in the towns with service. And we find indeed that its members are compelled to take over without salary the various personal *munera*, or charges, of local government, to administer the town, to act as petty justices, to take part in deputations, to arrange games, to inspect public buildings, to provide fuel for baths, to superintend postal and transport service (*cursus publicus*), to collect rates, etc.

The most burdensome of their obligations were connected with the collection of taxes. They were chiefly responsible for assessing the town population, and out of their number were selected the inspectors of public stores (*horrea*) and the *decemprimi* (δεκάπρωτοι), who had to collect the land tax and the tribute in kind (*annona*). Both heathen and Christian authors testify to the crushing burden of taxation during the fourth and fifth centuries, and the unfortunate *curiales*, who were made the instruments of collection under the watchful and extortionate supervision of state officials, were not only suffering from the unpopularity of their functions, but had constantly to fall back on their own resources in order to make good deficiencies and arrears. The *decemprimi* were primarily responsible as collectors, and when they vacated their office they had to nominate their successors and to stand security for their good behavior. Not content with this the provincial authorities commonly made the town, that is, primarily the town senate (*curia*), liable for deficiencies in the full sum required. The emperors sometimes intervened to forbid such collective liability (C. Th. xi. 7, 2; C. Just. xi. 59, 16), but on other occasions they enforced it in the most sweeping manner, as for instance when Aurelian, and later on Constantine, decreed that the town senates (*ordines*) should be made responsible for the taxes of deserted estates, and in case they should be unable to support the burden it should be distributed among the various local districts and estates (C. Just. xi. 59, 1).

In consequence of such oppressive burdens laid on the *curiales* we witness the curious spectacle of widely spread attempts on the part of the citizens to escape into more privileged professions — into the clergy or the army — and even of their flight into the country, where they were sometimes glad to live and work as simple *coloni*. The Codex Theodosianus and the Codex Justinianus are full of enactments forbidding the *curiales* to leave the place of their birth, condemning them to a hereditary subjection to municipal charges (*munera*) in fact turning their condition into a kind of serfdom. All the sons of a *curialis* had to follow their father's career, they were deemed *curiales* from the date of their birth (C. Th. xii. 1, 122). If there was not a sufficient number of persons of this class to uphold all its obligations, owners of estates (*possessores*), denizens (*incolae*), well-to-do plebeians, were pressed into it. The wretched townspeople were suspected of wanting to escape by flight from their onerous condition and had to apply to the governor for special leave of absence when they left the place of their birth for the sake of business or travel. If one of them wanted to change permanently his place of abode he was bound to provide a substitute or to leave a great part of his fortune to the *curia*. This epoch of imperial legislation does away, for fiscal and administrative purposes, with some of the fundamental principles of Roman law in its better times. A *curialis*, though a Roman citizen in the exercise of full civil rights, is unable freely to bequeath his fortune to another Roman citizen belonging to a different city : property passing out of the jurisdiction of one *curia* into that of another is charged with a heavy special payment to the former senate, and in fact remains "obnoxious" to it (C. Th. xii. 1, 107) ; a later constitution enacted that at least one-fourth of the property should remain in the hands of the original *curia*. If a *curialis* wanted to sell land or slaves employed in the cultivation of his estate he had to obtain leave from the governor of the province (C. Th. xii. 3, 1). Heiresses were much hampered in the right to marry strangers outside their late father's *curia* and had in such cases to relinquish one-fourth part of their property.

The climax of this legislation of servitude is reached when the emperors actually condemn people for some crime or misdemeanour to be enrolled as members of a *curia* : sons of veterans, *e.g.* who, by chopping off their fingers, had rendered themselves unfit to serve in the army, were stuck into the *curia*, and the same fate awaited unworthy ecclesiastics.

The policy of compulsion and the spread of caste were undoubtedly responsible to a great extent for another social process of great moment, namely, for the formation of the colonate, an institution destined to play an important part in medieval peasant life. Its roots stretch far back into the earlier history of Roman husbandry. Columella, a writer on agriculture of the first century A.D., instructs his readers that it is advantageous for owners of estates of insufficient fertility and difficult cultivation to employ free farmers, *coloni*, instead of slaves. The tenants were sometimes settled on the *métayer* system (*colonia partiaria*), the farmer sharing crops with the owner. Juridically the relation was regulated by the rules of the law of lease (*locatio conductio*) and the Digest often refers to the various problems arising under this contract; custom and tacit agreement played a great part in the treatment of such questions in practice. By the side of contractual relations between private landlords and tenants stood administrative regulations as to the management of vast domains of the Crown and of the private patrimony of the Emperor. Crowds of tenants were settled on these estates who had to look for a guarantee to the possession of their holdings rather to the equity and properly understood interest of their imperial masters than to formal contractual right. Lastly, a good many slaves were put into a position similar to that of the tenants of free birth, and as a matter of fact, it got to be more and more difficult to distinguish between *coloni* by contract and *quasi-coloni* by long usage and customary tenure. One trait which tended to reduce the distance between the different groups was the heavy indebtedness of most free farmers: they had often to take their agricultural outfit from the landowner along with the farm; in case of economic difficulties they turned to him as to their natural protector and a capitalist near at hand, and when once debts had been made, it was exceedingly difficult to pay them off.

Fourth-century legislation approaches these relations in its usual despotic manner. A law of Constantine dated A.D. 332 gives us the first glimpse of a new order of men standing between the free and the unfree and treated, in fact, as serfs of the glebe. It runs thus: "With whomsoever a *colonus* belonging to someone else (*alieni juris*) may be discovered, let the new patron not only restore the *colonus* to the place of his birth (*origini*), but let him also pay the tax for the time of his absence. As for the *coloni* themselves who contemplate flight, let them be put into fetters after the manner of slaves, so that they should perform duties worthy of freemen on the strength of a servile condemnation" (C. Th. v. 17, 1). But from Constantine again we have another en-- actment marking the other side of the condition, namely, the legal protection afforded to the *colonus* against possible exactions. About A.D. 325 the Emperor laid down in a rescript to the *vicarius* of the East that, "a *colonus* from whom a landlord exacted more than it was customary to render and than had been obtained from him in former times, may apply to the judge nearest at hand and produce evidence of the wrong. The person who is convicted of having claimed more than he used to receive shall be prohibited to do so in the future after having given back what he extorted by illegal superexaction" (C. Just. XI. 50, 1).

The legal protection afforded to the *coloni* was not suggested by principles of humanity, but by the necessity of keeping up at least some portion of the previous personal freedom of these peasants in order to safeguard the interest of the State which looked upon this part of the population as the mainstay of its fiscal system. If the emperors made light of the right of free citizens to choose their abode and their occupations as they pleased and did not scruple to attach the *coloni* to their tenures, the absolute right of landowners to do what they pleased with their land was not more sacred to them. Constantine imposed the most stringent limitations on their power of alienating plots of land. "If someone wants to sell an estate or to grant it, he has not the right to retain *coloni* by private agreement in order to transfer them to other places. Those who consider *coloni* to be useful, must either hold them together with the estates or, if they despair of getting profit from these estates, let them also give up the *coloni* for the use of other people" (C. Th. XIII. 10, 3; A.D. 357). In the reign of Valentinian, Valens, and Gratian, about A.D. 375, this principle is characteristically extended to the very slaves. "As born cultivators (*originarii*) cannot be sold without their land, even so it is forbidden to sell agricultural slaves inscribed in the census rolls. Nor must the law be evaded in a fraudulent manner, as has been often practised in the case of *originarii*, namely, that while a small piece of land is handed over to the buyer, the cultivation of the whole estate is made impossible. But if entire estates or portions of them pass to a new owner, so many slaves and 'born cultivators' should be transferred at the same time as used to stay with the former owners in the whole or in its parts" (C. Just. XI. 48, 7). The fiscal point of view is clearly expressed on many occasions. Valentinian and Valens entrust the landowners with the privilege of collecting the taxes of their *coloni* for the State with the exception of those tenants who have besides their farms some land of their own (C. Th. XI. 1, 14). This right and duty might be burdensome, but it certainly gave the landlords a powerful lever in reducing their free tenants to a condition of almost servile subjection. Perhaps the most drastic expression of the process may be seen in the fact that *coloni* lose their right to implead their masters in civil actions except in cases of superexaction. In criminal matters they were still deemed possessed of the full rights of citizens (C. Just. XI. 50, 2).

But it would be wrong to suppose that the condition of the farmers in the fourth and fifth centuries is characterised by mere oppression and deterioration. In the case of rustic slaves it is clearly seen that their fate was much improved by the course of events and by legislation. Their masters lost part of their former absolute authority because the State began to supervise the relations between master and slave for the sake of keeping cultivators to their work and thereby ensuring the coming in of taxes. Considerations of a similar nature exerted an influence on the fate of *coloni*, and they made themselves felt not only in social legislation, but also in husbandry. The tremendous agrarian crisis through which the Empire was passing could not be weathered by mere compulsion and discipline. On a large scale, it was a case like the one described in Columella's advice to landowners: if you want to get your land cultivated under difficult conditions, do not try to manage it by slave labour and direct orders, but entrust it to farmers. The great *latifundia* of earlier times were parcelled up into small plots, because only small cultivators could stand the storm of hostile invasion, of dislocation of traffic, of depopulation. Nor was it possible for the landowner to demand rack-rents and to avail himself of the competition between agricultural labourers. He had to be content if he succeeded in providing his estates with tenants ready to take care of them at moderate and customary rents, and both sides — the lord and the tenant — were interested

CH. XIX.

in making the leases hereditary if not perpetual. Thus there is a second
aspect to the growth of the colonate. The institution was not only one of
the forms of compulsion and caste legislation, but also a "ameliorative"
device, a means for keeping up culture and putting devastated districts
under the plough. Among the earliest roots of the colonate we find the
licence given to squatters and peasants dwelling in villages adjoining
waste land to occupy such land and to acquire tenant right on it by the
process of culture. The Emperor Hadrian published a general enactment protecting such tenants on imperial domains, and the African
inscriptions testify that his regulations did not remain a dead letter.

This feature — cultivation of waste and amelioration of culture — is
seldom expressed in as many words in the enactments of the Codex
Theodosianus and of the Codex Justinianus, because the laws and
rescripts collected there are chiefly concerned with the legal and fiscal
aspects of the situation. The legislators had no occasion to speak
directly of low rents and remissions in their payment. Yet even in
these documents some indications of the "emphyteutic" tendency
may be gleaned. I will just call attention to one of the earliest
"constitutions" relating to the colonate, namely, to the decree of
Constantine of A.D. 319 (C. Just. XI. 63, 1). It is directed against
encroachments of *coloni* on the lands of persons who held their estates
by the technical title of *emphyteutae*, of which we shall have to say more
by and by. It is explained that *coloni* have no right to occupy lands for
the culture of which they have done nothing. "By custom they are
allowed to acquire only plots which they have planted with olives or
vines." This ruling is entirely in conformity with the *Lex Hadriana de
rudibus agris* and testifies to the peculiar right of occupation conceded to
cultivators of waste.

The technical requirement of making plantations of olive trees or
vines corresponds exactly to the Greek expression θυτεύειν which reappears in the term *emphyteusis* so much in use in the later centuries of
the Empire. Of course, cultivation of the waste was not restricted in
practice to the rearing of these two kinds of useful trees, nor can the
view so clearly formulated in this case have failed to assert itself on other
occasions, especially in the relations between landlord and tenant. But
the luxuriant growth of· *emphyteusis* as a widely prevalent contract is
very characteristic of the epoch.

The *emphyteusis* of the later Empire is distinguished from other
leases by three main features: it is hereditary; the rent paid is fixed
and generally slight; the lessee undertakes specific duties in regard to
amelioration on the plot and may lose the tenancy if he does not carry
them out. These peculiarities were so marked that there was considerable doubt whether the relation of *emphyteusis* was originated by the
sale of a plot by one owner to the other with certain conditions as to the
payment of rent, or by a downright lease. A constitution of Zeno,

published between 476 and 484, decided the controversy in the sense that the contract was a peculiar one, standing, as it were, between a sale and a lease (C. Just. IV. 66, 1). The meaning of such a doctrine was, of course, that in many cases rights arose under cover of *dominium* (Roman absolute property), which amounted in themselves to a new hereditary possession, and arising from the labour and capital sunk by the subordinate possessor into the cultivation of the estate, and leaving a very small margin for the claims of the proprietor. Such hybrid legal relations do not come into being without strong economic reasons, and these reasons are disclosed by the history of the tenure in question. Its antecedents go far back into earlier epochs, although the complete institution was matured only towards the end of the fifth century. One of the roots of *emphyteusis* we have already noticed in the occupation of waste land by squatters or cultivators dwelling on adjoining plots. In the fourth and fifth centuries the emperors not only allow such occupation, but make it a duty for possessors of estates in a proper state of cultivation to take over waste plots. This is the basis of the so-called *epibole* (ἐπιβολή), of the "imposition of desert to fertile land," an institution which arose at the time of Aurelian and continued to exist in the Byzantine Empire, It is worth noticing that a law of Valentinian, Theodosius, and Arcadius gives every one leave to take possession of deserted plots; should the former owner not assert his right in the course of two years and compensate the new occupier for ameliorations, his property right is deemed extinguished to the profit of the new cultivator (C. Just. XI. 59, 8). In this case voluntary occupation is still the occasion of the change of ownership, but several other laws make the taking over of waste land compulsory. An indirect but important consequence of the same view may be found in the fact that the right of possessors of estates to alienate portions of the same was curtailed: they were not allowed to sell land under profitable cultivation without at the same time disposing of the barren and less profitable parts of the estate; the Government took care that the "nerves" of a prosperous exploitation should not be cut.

A second line of development was presented by *leases* made with the intention of ameliorating the culture of certain plots. The practice of such leases may be followed back into great antiquity, especially in provinces with Greek or Hellenised population; and it is on such estates that the terms φυτεύειν, *emphyteusis* first appear in a technical sense. A good example is presented by the tables discovered on the site of Heraclea in the gulf of Tarentum, where land belonging to the temple of Dionysos was leased to hereditary tenants about B.C. 400 on the condition of the construction of farm buildings and the plantation of olives and vines.[1] Emphyteutic leases of the same kind, varying in

[1] Dareste, Houssoulier et Reinach, *Recueil d'inscriptions juridiques grecques*, I. pp. 201 ff.

details, but based on the main conditions of amelioration and hereditary tenancy, have been preserved from the second century A.D. in the Boeotian town of Thisbe.[1] Roman jurists, *e.g.* Ulpian, mention distinctly the peculiar legal position of such "emphyteutic" tenancies, and there can be no doubt that as the difficulties of cultivation and economic intercourse increased, great landowners, corporations, and cities resorted more and more to this expedient for ensuring some cultivation to their estates even at the cost of creating tenancies which restricted owners in the exercise of their right.

A third variety of relations making towards the same goal may be observed in the so-called perpetual right (*jus perpetuum*). It arose chiefly in consequence of conquest of territories by the Roman State. The title of former owners was not extinguished thereby but converted into a possession subordinate to the superior ownership of the Roman people and liable to the payment of a rent (*vectigal, canon*). The distinction between Roman land entirely free from any tax and provincial land subject to tax or rent was removed in the second century A.D. when land in Italy was made subject to taxes. But the legal conception of tenant right subject to the eminent domain of the emperor remained and the *jus perpetuum* continued as a special kind of tenure on the estates of cities and of the Crown, as we should say nowadays, until it was merged into the general right of *emphyteusis* together with the two other species already mentioned.

These juridical distinctions are not in the nature of purely technical details. The great need of cultivation and the wide concessions made in its interest in favour of effective farming are as significant as the subdivision of ownership in regard to the same plot of land, one person obtaining what may be called in later terminology the useful rights of ownership (*dominium utile*), while the other detains a superior right nevertheless (*dominium eminens*). In this as in many other points the peculiarities of medieval law are foreshadowed in the declining Empire.

This observation applies even more to the part assumed by great landowners in the fourth and fifth centuries. A great estate in those times comes to form in many respects a principality, a separate district for purposes of taxation, police, and even justice. Already in the first century A.D. Frontinus speaks of country seats of African magnates surrounded by villages of their dependents as if by bulwarks. By the side of the *civitas*, the town forming the natural and legal centre of a district, appears the *saltus*, the rural, more or less uncultivated district organised under a private lord or under a steward of the emperor. The more important of these rural units are extraterritorial — outside the jurisdiction and administration of the towns. By and by the seemingly omnipotent government of the emperor is driven by its difficulties to

---

[1] Dittenberger, Programme of the University of Halle, 1881.

concede a large measure of political influence to the aristocracy of large landowners. They collect taxes, carry out conscription, influence ecclesiastical appointments, act as justices of the peace in police matters and petty criminal cases. The disruptive or rather the disaggregating forces of local interests and local separatism come thus to assert themselves long before the establishment of feudalism, under the very sway of absolute monarchy and centralised bureaucracy.

If the formation of the colonate means the establishment of an order of half-free persons intermediate between free citizens and slaves, if *emphyteusis* amounts to a change in the conception of ownership, the rise of the privileges and power of landowners corresponds to the appearance of a new aristocracy which was destined to play a great part in the history of medieval Europe.

Besides what was directly conceded to these lords by the central authority we must reckon with their encroachments and illegal dealings in regard to the less favoured classes of the population. The State had to appeal to private persons of wealth and influence because it was not able to transmit its commands to the inert masses of the population in any other way. Aristocratic privilege was from this point of view a confession of debility on the part of the Empire. But the inefficiency of the State was recognised by its subjects as well and, as a natural result, they applied for protection to the strong and the wealthy, although such a recourse to private authority led to the infringement of public interests and to the break-up of public order. Private patronage appears as a threatening symptom with which the emperors have to deal. In the time of undisputed authority of the commonwealth it was a usual occurrence that benefactors of a town or village, persons who had erected waterworks, built baths, or founded an alimentary institution for destitutes should be honoured by the title of *patroni* and by certain privileges in regard to precedence and ceremonial rights. The emperors of the fourth and of the fifth century had to forbid patronage because it constituted a menace to law and to public order. We hear of cases of "maintenance"; parties to a trial being protected by powerful *patroni*, who seek to turn the course of justice in favour of their clients. Libanius, a professional orator of the epoch of Valentinian II and Theodosius I, gives a vivid description of the difficulties he had to meet in a suit against some Jewish tenants of his who refused to pay certain rents according to ancient custom. If we are to believe our informant, they had recourse to the protection of a commander of troops stationed in the province, and when Libanius came into court and produced witnesses, he found the judge so prepossessed in favour of his opponents that he could not get a hearing, and his witnesses were thrown into prison or dismissed. In another part of the same speech Libanius inveighs against officers who prevent the collection of taxes and rents and favour brigandage. There may be a great deal of exaggeration in the impassioned account of the Greek rhetor, but the principal heads of his accusation can be confirmed from other sources, especially from imperial decrees.   A company of soldiers gets quartered in a village and when the *curiales* of the next town appear to collect taxes or rents, they are met by violence and may be called fortunate if they escape without grievous injury to life and limbs.   In the Theodosian Code enactments directed against patronage in villages go so far as to forbid the acquisition of property in a rural district by outsiders for fear the strangers should prove powerful people capable of opposing tax collectors.   According to the account of Salvian, a priest who lived in the fifth century in southern Gaul, patronage had become quite prevalent in that region.   People turned to private protection out of sheer despair and surrendered their land to the protector, rather than face the extortions of public authorities.   There can be no doubt that patrons and protectors of the kind described, if they were helpful to some, were dangerous and harmful to others, and the State in the fourth and fifth centuries had good reasons to fight against their influence.   But the constant repetition of the same injunctions and prohibitions proves that the evil was deeply rooted and difficult to get rid of.   The Sisyphean task undertaken by the Government in its struggle against abuses and encroachments is well illustrated by various attempts to create special authorities to repress the exactions of ordinary officers and to correct their mistakes.

One of the principal expedients used by Diocletian and his successors was to institute a special service of supervising commissaries under the names of *agentes in rebus* and *curiosi*. They were sent into the provinces more particularly to investigate the management of the public post, but, as a matter of fact, they were employed to spy on governors, tax collectors, and other officials.   They received complaints and denunciations and sometimes committed people to prison.   A decree of Constantius tries to restrict the latter practice and to impress on these *curiosi* the idea that they are not to act in a wanton manner but have to produce evidence and to communicate with the regular authorities (A.D. 355, C. Th. vi. 29, 1).   But the very existence of such a peculiar institution was an incitement to delation and arbitrary acts, and in 395 Arcadius and Honorius try to concentrate the activity of the *agentes in rebus* on the inspection of the post.   "They ought not to levy illicit toll from ships, nor to receive reports and statements of claims, nor to put people into prison" (C. Th. vi. 29, 8).   The service of the *agentes* and of the *curiosi* was deemed to be as important as it was dangerous, and those who went through the whole career were rewarded by the high rank of counts of the first class.   It is hardly to be wondered at that these extraordinary officials provided with peculiar methods of delation did not succeed in saving the Empire from the corruption of its ordinary officers.   .

And yet the emperors found that the only means of exercising some control over the abuses of the bureaucratic machinery and the oppression of influential people was in pitting extraordinary officials against them. The *defensor civitatis* was designed to act as a protector of the lower orders against such misdeeds. The office originated probably in voluntary patronage bestowed on cities by great men, but it was regularised and made general under Valentinian I. An enactment of Gratian, Valentinian II, and Theodosius lays chief stress on the protection afforded by *defensores* to the *plebs* in regard to taxation. The *defensor* ought to be like a father of the *plebs*, to prevent superexaction and hardships in the assessment of taxes both in regard to the town population and to rustics, to shield them against the insolence of officials, and the impertinence of judges. Not merely fiscal oppression was aimed at, but also abuses in the administration of justice, and the emperors tried to obviate the evils of a costly litigation and inaccessible tribunals by empowering the *defensores* to try civil cases in which poor men were interested. It was somewhat difficult to draw the line between such exceptional powers and ordinary jurisdiction, but the Government of the later Empire had often to meet similar difficulties. An important privilege of the *defensores* was the right to report directly to the emperor, over the governor of the province: this was the only means for making protests effective, at least in some cases. As to the mode of electing the *defensores* we notice some variation: they are meant to represent the population at large and originally the people took part in the election, though it had to be confirmed by the emperors. In the fifth century, however, the office became a burden more than an honour, a quantity of petty police functions and formal supervision was tacked on to it, and the emperors are left no choice but to declare that all notable citizens of the town have to take it in turn. This is certainly a sign of decline and there can be no doubt that the original scope of the institution was gradually lost sight of.

A third aspect of the same tendency to counterbalance the evil working of official administration by checks from outside forces may be noticed in the political influence assigned to the Church. Here undoubtedly the emperors of the fourth and fifth centuries reached firm ground. It was not a mere shuffling of the same pack of cards, not a pitting of one official against the other by the help of devices which at best answered only for a few years. It was an appeal from a defective system to a fresh and mighty force which drew forth the best capabilities of the age and shaped its ideals. If anywhere, one could hope to find disinterested effort, untiring energy, and fearless sense of duty among the representatives of the Church, and it is clear that both government and people turned to them on especially trying occasions. We need not here speak of the intense interest created by ecclesiastical controversies or of the signal evidence of vigorous moral and intellectual life among the clergy. But we have to take these facts into account if

CH. XIX.

we want to explain the part assumed by Church dignitaries in civil administration and social affairs. A significant expression of the confidence inspired in the public by the ecclesiastical authorities may be seen in the custom of applying to them for arbitration instead of seeking redress in the ordinary courts. The custom in question had its historical roots in the fact that before the recognition of Christianity as a state religion by the Empire the Christians tried to abstain as far as possible from submitting disputes and quarrels to the jurisdiction of pagan magistrates. There was a legal possibility of escaping from such interference of pagan authorities by resorting to the arbitration of persons of high moral authority within the Church, especially bishops. When Christianity conquered under Constantine, episcopal arbitration was extended to all sorts of cases and an attempt was made, as is shewn by two enactments of this emperor (Const. Sirmond. xvii.; I.) to convert it into a special form of expeditious procedure, well within reach of the poorer classes. Episcopal awards in such cases were exempted from the ordinary strict forms of compromise accompanied by express stipulation; the procedure was greatly simplified and shortened, the recourse of one party to the suit to such arbitration was held to be obligatory for the other party. At the close of the fourth century Arcadius considerably restricted this wide jurisdiction conceded to bishops and tried to reduce it to voluntary arbitration pure and simple. But the moral weight of their decisions was so great, that the ecclesiastical tribunals continued to be overwhelmed with civil cases brought before them by the parties. Not only Ambrose of Milan, who lived in the time of Theodosius the Great, but also Augustine, who belongs chiefly to the first quarter of the fifth century, complain of the heavy burden of judicial duties which they have to bear.

The bishops had no direct criminal jurisdiction, but through the right of sanctuary claimed by churches and in consequence of the general striving of Christian religion for humanity and charity, they were constantly pleading for grace, mitigation of sentences, charitable treatment of prisoners and convicts, etc. Panic stricken and persecuted persons and criminals of all kinds flocked for refuge to the churches; famous cathedrals and monasteries presented curious sights in those days: they seemed not only places of worship but also caravanserais of some kind. Fugitives camped not only in the churches but at a distance of fifty paces around them. Gangs of these poor wretches accompanied priests and deacons on their errands and walks outside the church, as in such company they were held to be secure from revenge and arrest. The Government restricted the right of fiscal debtors to take sanctuary in order to escape from the payment of taxes, but in other respects it upheld the claims of ecclesiastical authority. Certain compromises with existing law and custom had undoubtedly to be effected. The Church did not attempt, for instance, to proclaim the abolition of slavery. It merely negotiated with the masters in order to obtain promises of better treatment or a pardon of offences. But it coun_tenanced in every way the emancipation of slaves and protected freed_men when once manumitted. The Acts of Councils of the fourth century are full of enactments in these respects (*e.g.* Council of Orange, c. 7; Council of Arles, II. cc. 33, 34).

Another domain in which the authority of the bishops found ample scope for its assertion was the sphere of moral police, if one may use the expression. To begin with, pious Christians were directed by the Gospel to visit prisoners, and this commandment of Christ became the foundation for a supervision of the Clergy over the state of prisons, their sanitary conditions — baths, food, the treatment of convicts, etc. In those times when terrible need and famines were frequent, parents had the legal right to sell their children directly after their birth (*sanguinolenti*) and a person who had taken care of a foundling was considered its owner. It is to ecclesiastical authorities that the emperors turn in order to prevent these rights from degenerating into a ruthless kid_napping of children. The Church enforces a delay of ten days in order that parents who wish to take back their offspring should be able to formulate their claims. If they have not done so within the days of respite, let them never try to vindicate their flesh and blood any more: even the Church will treat them as murderers (Council of Vaison, cc. 9, 10). Again, ecclesiastics are called upon to prevent the sale of human beings for immoral purposes: no one ought to be forced to commit adultery or to offer oneself for prostitution, even if a slave, and bishops as well as secular judges have the power to emancipate slaves who have been subjected by their masters to such ignominious practices. They are also bound to watch that women, either free or unfree, should not be constrained to join companies of pantomime actors or singers against their will (C. Just. i. 4, 10).

In conclusion it may be useful to point out once more that the social process taking place in the Roman Empire of the fourth and fifth centuries presented features of decline and of renovation at the same time. It was brought about to a great extent by the increased influence of lower classes and the influx of barbarous customs, and in so far it expresses itself in an undoubted lowering of the level of culture. The sacrifice of political freedom and local patriotism to a centralised bureaucracy, the rigid state of siege and the caste legislation of the Constantinian and Theodosian era produced an unhealthy atmosphere of compulsion and servility. But at the same time the Christian Church asserts itself as a power not only in the spiritual domain, but also in the legal and economic sphere. Society falls back to a great extent on the lines of local life and of aristocratic organisation, but the movement in this direction is not a merely negative one: germs appear which in their further growth were destined to contribute powerfully towards the formation of feudal society.

CH. XIX.

CHAPTER XX

THOUGHTS AND IDEAS OF THE PERIOD

THE fourth and fifth centuries A.D. were marked by the rise of no new school of metaphysics and were illustrated by only one pre-eminent philosopher. In theology the period can boast great names, perhaps the greatest since the Apostles of Christ, but in philosophy it is singularly barren. Plotinus (A.D. 205–270), the chief exponent and practical founder of that reconstruction of Greek philosophy known as Neo-platonism, had indeed many disciples; but Proclus the Lycian (A.D. 412–485) is the only one of them who can be said to have advanced in any marked degree the study of pure thought. The mind of the age was inclined towards religion, or at least religious idealism, rather than towards metaphysics. Nor is this matter for surprise when we remember the spiritual revival of the centuries preceding, a movement which began under the Flavians and had by no means spent its force when Constantine came to the throne. From an early period in the Empire, and more especially under the Severi, men were turning in disgust and disillusion to religion as a refuge from the evils of the world in which they lived, as a sphere in which they could realise dreams of better things than those begotten of their present discontent. This fact explains the quickening of the older cults and the ready adoption of new ones, which issued in a promiscuous pantheon and a bewildering medley of religious rites and practices. Then came philosophy and sought to bring order out of chaos. It tried, and with some success, to clear away superstition and to raise the believer in gods many to a living communion with the One divine of which they were but different manifestations. There is no doubt that Proclus, who unified to some extent the heterogeneous system of Plotinus, was engaged in the proper business of philosophy, viz. the contemplation of metaphysical truth; there is equally no doubt that in practice the philosophy of the age was addressed to the same human need as its religion. And that need was a better knowledge of God. It is most significant that the final rally of the old religions was under the banner of a philosophy: Julian and his supporters were Neo-platonists.

We may therefore claim that the temper of the times was on the whole religious, concerned chiefly with man's relation to God; and the fact that the Church had recently achieved so signal a victory is in itself an indication that the best intellects had gravitated towards her. Thus the highest thought was Christian, finding expression in those systematised ideas about God which are summed up in the word theology.

It would however be a grave mistake to suppose that the age which saw the triumph of the Christian idea and the establishment of Christianity as the state religion was entirely of one mind and Christian to the core. Side by side with the great current of Christian thought and belief, that was now running free after a long subterranean course, there flowed a large volume of purely pagan opinion or preconception, such interfiltration as took place being carried on by unseen channels. Thus, while eager and courageous spirits were contending for the Faith with all kinds of weapons against all kinds of foes throughout the Empire, men (and some of them Christian men) were writing and speaking as though no such thing as Christianity had come into the world. And the age that witnessed the conversion of Constantine and inherited the benefits of that act was an age that in the East listened to the interminable hexameters of Nonnus' *Dionysiaca*, which contain no conscious reference to Christianity; that laughed over the epigrams of Cyrus; that delighted in many frankly pagan love-stories and saw nothing surprising in the attribution of one of them (the *Aethiopica*) to the Christian bishop Heliodorus; that in the West applauded the panegyrists when they compared emperor and patron to the hierarchy of gods and heroes; and that in extremity found its consolation in philosophy rather than in the Gospel.[1]

This persistence of paganism in the face of obvious defeat was due to a number of co-operating causes. Roman patriotism, which saw in worship of the gods and the secret name of Rome the only safeguard of the eternal city; the cults of Cybele, Isis, Mithra, and Orpheus, with their dreams of immortality; the stern tradition of the Stoic emperor Marcus; the lofty ideals of the Neoplatonists — all these factors helped to delay the final triumph. But probably the strongest and most persistent conservative influence was that of the rhetoric by which European education was dominated then as it was by logic in the Middle Ages, and as it has been since the Renaissance by humane letters. Rhetoric lay in wait for the boy as he left the hands of the grammarian, and was his companion at every stage of his life. It went with him through school and university; it formed his taste and trained or paralysed his mind; but more than this, it opened to him the

---

[1] The most famous instance of such reversion is afforded by Boethius, who died in prison A.D. 525, but who fairly represents the age before him.

CH. XX.

avenues of success and reward. For although by the fourth century oratory had lost its old political power, rhetoric still remained a bread-winning business. It was always lucrative, and it led to high position, even to the consulship, as in the case of Ausonius the rhetor (A.D. 309–392), who was Gratian's tutor and afterwards quaestor, praefect of Gaul, and finally consul. Here is cause enough to account for the long life and paramount influence of rhetoric in the schools. Now the instrument with which both schoolmaster and professor fashioned their pupils was pagan mythology and pagan history. The great literatures of the past supplied the theme for declamation and exercise. Rules of conduct were deduced from maxims that passed under the names of Pythagoras, Solon, Socrates, and Marcus Aurelius. It was inevitable that the thoughts of the grown man should be expressed in terms of paganism when the education of the youth was upon these lines. And this education was for all, not only for the children of unbelievers. Gregory of Nyssa himself informs us that he attended the classes of heathen rhetoricians. So did Gregory of Nazianzus and his brother Caesarius, and so did Basil. John Chrysostom was taught by Libanius, the last of the Sophists, who claimed that it was what he learnt in the schools that led his friend Julian back to the worship of the gods. Even Tertullian, who would not suffer a Christian to teach rhetoric out of heathen books, could not forbid his learning it from them. They were indeed the only means to knowledge. Efforts were made to provide Christian books modelled upon them. Proba, wife of a praefect of Rome, compelled Virgil to prophesy of Christ by the simple means of reading Christianity into a cento of lines from the *Aeneid*. Juvencus the presbyter dared, in Jerome's phrase, to submit the majesty of the Gospel to the laws of metre, and to this end composed four books of Evangelic history. The two Apollinarii turned the O.T. into heroic and Pindaric verse, and the N.T. into Platonic dialogues; Nonnus the author of the *Dionysiaca* rewrote St John's Gospel in hexameters; Eudocia, consort of Theodosius II, composed a poetical paraphrase of the Law and of some of the Prophets. But as soon as Julian's edict against Christian teachers was withdrawn, grammarians and rhetors returned to the classics with renewed zest and a sense of victory gained. Jerome and Augustine, both of them students and teachers, pointed out the educational capacity of the sacred books; but some 80 years after the publication of the *de doctrina christiana*, in which Augustine as a teacher urged the claims of Scripture, we find Ennodius the Christian bishop speaking of rhetoric as queen of the arts and of the world. It was reserved for Cassiodorus (A.D. 480–575), the father of literary monasticism in the West, to attempt the realisation of Augustine's dream.

Like Ennodius his older contemporary, Cassiodorus loved and practised rhetoric, but he had visions of a better kind of education, and in 535–6 he made an abortive attempt to found a school of

Christian literature at Rome, "in which the soul might gain eternal salvation, and the tongue acquire beauty by the exercise of the chaste and pure eloquence of Christians." His project was ill-timed; it was the moment of the invasion of Belisarius, and Rome had other business on hand than schemes of education and reform. The schools were pagan to the end, and it may be said with truth that rhetoric retarded the progress of the Faith, and that Christianity when it conquered the heathen world was captured by the system of education which it found in force. The result of rhetorical training is very plainly seen in all the literature of the period and in the characters of the writers. Even the Fathers are deeply tinged with it, and Jerome himself admits that one must always distinguish in their writings between what is said for the sake of argument (διαλεκτικῶς) and what is said as truth. Though perjury and false witness were heavily punished, lying was never an ecclesiastical offence, and rigid veracity cannot be claimed as a constant characteristic of any Christian writer of the period except Athanasius, Augustine, and (outside his panegyrics) Eusebius of Caesarea.

Reference has already been made to some of the Eastern authors who wrote in the full current of Christianity but with no sensible trace of its influence. Passing West, we find ourselves in better company than that of the novelists and epigrammatists, and among men who even more effectively illustrate the tendencies of the time. By Macrobius we are introduced to a little group of gentlemen who meet together in a friendly way for the discussion of literary, antiquarian, and philosophic matters. Most of the characters of the *Saturnalia* are known to us from the history of the day and from their own writings, which express opinions sufficiently similar to those which Macrobius lends them in his symposium to make it a faithful mirror of fourth century thought and conversation. There is Praetextatus, at whose house the company first assembles to keep the Saturnalia. He is a scholar and antiquary, a statesman and philosopher, the hierophant of half-a-dozen cults, formerly praefect of the city and proconsul of Achaia. His dignity and urbanity, his piety, his grave humour, his overflowing erudition, his skill in drawing out his friends, render him in all respects the proper president of the feast of reason. There is Flavian the younger, a man of action and of greater mark in the real world than Praetextatus, who however plays but a small part on Macrobius' stage. There is Q. Aurelius Symmachus, the wealthy senator and splendid noble, the zealous conservative and patron of letters, who opposed Ambrose in the affair of the Altar of Victory and brought Augustine to Milan as teacher of rhetoric. There are two members of the house of Albinus, chiefly remarkable for their worship of Virgil. There is Servius, the young but erudite critic, who carries his scholarship with so much grace and modesty. There is Evangelus, whose rough manners and uncouth opinions serve as a foil to the strict

correctness of the rest.   There is Disarius the doctor, the friend of
Ambrose, and Horus, whose name proclaims his foreign birth.   These
persons of the *Saturnalia* we know to have been living men.[1]   What
are the topics of their conversation ?   The range is astonishing, from
antiquities (the origin of the Calendar, of the Saturnalia, of the *toga
prætextata*, linguistics (derivations and wondrous etymologies), literature
(especially Cicero and Virgil), science (medicine, physiology and astro-
nomy), religion and philosophy (a syncretism of all the cults), ethics
(chiefly Stoical, *e.g.* the morality of slavery and suicide), down to table
manners and the jokes of famous men.   In a word, everything that a
Roman gentleman ought to know is treated somewhat mechanically but
with elaborate fulness — except Christianity, of which there is no hint.
And yet one of the Albini had a Christian wife and the other was
almost certainly himself a Christian.

This silence on a topic which must have touched all the characters
to whom Macrobius lends utterance is equally felt when we pass to fact
from fiction.   Symmachus in the whole collection of his private letters
refers but rarely to religion and never once to Christianity.   Claudian,
the poet courtier of Christian emperors, has only one passage which betrays
a clear consciousness of the new faith, and that is in a lampoon upon
a bibulous soldier.   It is the same with the panegyrists, the same with
allegorist and dramatist.   Martianus Capella, whose manual of the arts,
entitled *The Nuptials of Mercury and Philology*, represents the best
culture of the epoch and enjoyed an almost unexampled popularity
during the Middle Ages, passes over Christianity without a word.   The
anonymous *Querolus*, an agreeable *comédie à thèse* written for the
entertainment of a great Gallican household and obviously reflecting
the serious thought of its audience, is entirely dominated by the Stoical
and heathen notion of Fate.[2]   This general silence cannot be due to
ignorance.   Rather it is due to Roman etiquette.   The great conservative nobles, the writers who catered for their instruction and amusement,
would seem to have agreed to ignore the new religion.

We must now consider in some detail the character of this persistent paganism, especially as it is presented to us by Macrobius, either
in the *Saturnalia* or in his *Commentary on the Dream of Scipio*, to
which last we owe our knowledge of the treatise of Cicero bearing
that title.

The philosophy or religion of these two works is pure Neoplatonism,
drawn straight from Plotinus.   Macrobius seems to have known the
Greek original; he gives actual citations from the *Enneads* in several

---

[1] The only one about whom there seems to be any doubt is Evangelus, but see
Glover, *Life and Letters*, p. 175.

[2] For the Christian idea of Fate=Providence, see Augustine, *e.g. de civ. Dei*, v. 8:
*ipsam itaque præcipue Dei summi voluntatem, cuius potestas insuperabiliter per
cuncta porrigitur, eos appellare fatum sic probatur.*

places, and one passage (*Comment.* I. 14) contains as good a summary of the Plotinian Trinity as was possible in Latin.

The universe is the temple of God, eternal like Him and filled with His presence. He, the first cause, is the source and origin of all that is and all that seems to be. By the overflowing fertility of His majesty He created from himself Mind (*mens*). Mind retains the image of its author so long as it looks towards him; when it looks backward it creates soul (*anima*). Soul in its turn keeps the likeness of mind while it looks towards mind, but when its turns away its gaze it degenerates insensibly, and, although itself incorporeal, gives rise to bodies celestial (the stars) and terrestrial (men, beasts, vegetables). Between man and the stars there is real kinship, as there is between man and God. Thus all things from the highest to the lowest are held together in an intimate and unbroken connexion, which is what Homer meant when he spoke of a golden chain let down by God from heaven to earth.

·Then Macrobius describes the soul's descent. Tempted by the desire for a body, it falls from where it dwelt on high with the stars its brethren. It passes through the seven spheres that separate heaven from earth, and in its passage acquires the several qualities which go to make up the composite nature of man. As it descends it gradually in a sort of intoxication sheds its attributes and forgets its heavenly home, though not in all cases to the same extent. This descent into the body is a kind of temporary death, for the body σῶμα is also the tomb or σῆμα (an old Platonic play upon words), a tomb from which the soul can rise at the body's death. Man is indeed immortal, the real man is the soul which dominates the things of sense. But although the body's death means life to the soul, the soul may not anticipate its bliss by voluntary act, but must purify itself and wait, for "we must not hasten the end of life while there is still possibility of improvement." Heaven is shut against all but those who win purity, and the body is not only a tomb; it is a hell (*infera*). Cicero promised heaven to all true patriots; Macrobius knows a higher virtue than patriotism, viz. contemplation of the divine, for the earth is but a point in the universe[1] and glory but a transient thing. The wise man is he who does his duty upon earth with his eyes fixed upon heaven.

If beside this pure and lofty idealism, grafted upon Roman patriotic feeling, we set the somewhat crude syncretism of the *Saturnalia*, we have a true reflection of all the higher thought of fourth century Paganism — except dæmonology and its lower accompaniment, magic. Of the former we have no direct indication beyond a doubtful etymology. The latter is present, but only in its least objectionable form, viz. divination. The omission is the more remarkable since dæmonology

---

[1] Cf. Boethius, *de cons. phil.* II. pr. 7.

was a salient feature of the Neoplatonic system, and magic was its inevitable outcome. For the god of Neoplatonism was a metaphysical abstraction, yet a cause, and therefore bound to act, since a cause must have an effect. Being above action Himself, there must be a secondary cause or causes. And the Platonic philosophy provided a host of intermediary beings who bridged the chasm between earth and God, and who interpreted and conveyed on high the prayers of men. The ranks of these divine agents were largely supplied by the old heroes and dæmons, who in the popular imagination were omnipotent, watching over human affairs. All dæmons however were not equally beneficent. At the bottom of the scale of nature lurked evil dæmons, powers of darkness ceaselessly scheming man's destruction. It was to these supernatural beings, good and· bad, that his mind turned in hope or fear. He dreaded the evil dæmons and sought to charm them; he loved the good and addressed to them his prayers and worship. Plotinus indeed forbad but could not prevent the worship of dæmons, for he admitted their real existence. With Porphyry (d. *c.* 305) the tendency towards dæmonological rites is clearly marked; with Proclus the habit is established.

Thus upon a monotheistic basis there arose a new polytheism, in which the Olympian deities, whose credit had been shaken by rationalistic philosophy, were largely replaced by dæmons and demigods. Theology, which is presented on its purer side by Macrobius, degenerated in popular usage into theurgy; the ethical and intellectual aspirations after union with the divine were replaced by mere magic. Yet magic had the countenance of the philosophers, who, distinguishing carefully between white and black magic (to borrow later terms) repudiated the latter while they allowed the former. And although theurgy was a sharp declension from the principles of Platonism, whether old or new, it was very natural. It was extremely venerable and it was able to take the colour of science. The doctrine of the sympathy of the seen and the unseen worlds, together with the gradual recognition of the mighty power of cosmic law, even when controlled by spirits or dæmons, resulted necessarily in an attempt to coerce these beings by means of material things, almost, one might say, by means of chemical reagents. So, the larger the knowledge of nature and its operations, the wider the spread of magical practices. Magic had a living force which Christianity was for ages powerless to break.

Another potent factor in keeping alive the flame of Paganism was the belief in the eternal destiny of Rome. Christian writers in the second century, like Tertullian, held that Rome would last as long as the world and that her fall would coincide with the Day of Judgment. Christian writers before whose eyes the city fell without the coming of the Day, stood bewildered and in part regretful. The news dashed the pen from the hand of Jerome in his cell at Bethlehem : "the human race is included in the ruins," he wrote; and Augustine, while he looks for the founding of an abiding and divine city in the room of that which had disappeared, and taunts the Romans with the poor protection afforded them by their gods, declares that the whole world groaned at the fall of Rome and is himself proud of her great past and of the qualities of Roman endurance and faith that gave her so high a place among the nations. Orosius, again, who carried on the plan and thought of the *de civitate Dei*, to whose mind the Roman Empire was founded upon blood and sin, yet proclaims, as Augustine his master had proclaimed, that Roman peace and Roman culture were greater and would last longer than Rome herself.

If such were the sentiments of Christian writers towards the imperial city, which had been much more of a step-mother than a mother to their faith, what must pagans have felt for the home of their religion, upon which Plutarch had exhausted his store of eulogistic metaphor (cf. *de fortuna Rom.*), which to Julian was θεοφιλή, ἀδαμαντίνη, "dear to the gods, invincible," whose piety might surely claim divine protection? To discover this we have but to turn the pages of Claudian and Rutilius Namatianus. Claudian (fl. A.D. 400) was not a Roman born, but a Greek-speaking native of Egypt. Yet he has Juvenal's contempt for "Greek Quirites" and an unconcealed hatred of New Rome, and he finds his true inspiration in the great city on the Tiber whom he addresses as Roma dea, consort of Jupiter, mother of arts and arms and of the world's peace. "Rise, reverend mother," he cries, "and with firm hope trust the favouring gods. Lay aside old age's craven fear. O city coeval with the sky, iron Fate shall never master thee till Nature changes her laws and rivers run backward." But it is not only the city with her pomp and beauty, her hills and temples, the home of gods and Fortune, that compels his praise. The empire of which she was the visible head, an empire won by bloodshed, it is true, but kept together by the willing love of all the various races that have passed into the fabric — this is Claudian's real theme, the mighty diapason that runs through all his utterance and redeems his panegyric of Roman noble and emperor from the charge of mere servility.

We have said that Claudian hardly ever refers directly to Christianity, and indeed echoes of spiritual language in his verse are faint and uncertain. The hostility which he must have felt against the religion that was sapping the seats of the ancient worship is to be gathered from hints rather than from direct expression. That hostility lies nearer the surface in the *Return from exile* (A.D. 416) of Rutilius Claudius Namatianus, a great Gaulish lord and friend of Roman lords, who betrays more clearly than Claudian the sentiments of the ruling class. But even in Rutilius the allusions to Christianity are veiled. As a high official (he was praefect of the city) he could not openly attack the religion of the emperor, and must content himself with fulminations against Judaism, "the root of superstition," and the monks whose life is a voluntary death to life, its pleasures, and its duties.[1]

It is almost needless to say that Rutilius the Gaul shares the belief of Claudian the Egyptian in the destiny of Rome. The sight of the temples still shining in the sun after the Gothic invasion was to him an earnest of her perennial youth. "Allia did not keep back the punishment of Brennus." Rome will rise more glorious for her present discomfiture. *Ordo renascendi est, crescere posse malis.* This faith in Rome meant of course faith in the gods who had made her great, and good Romans all believed in them and were eager to maintain the national cult with which Rome's welfare was bound up. Roman worship was at all times directed mainly towards the attainment of material blessings, and the material disasters which, despite the optimism of Rutilius and his circle, lay heavy on the city, were attributed to the anger of forsaken deities. How, asked Symmachus, could Rome bring herself to abandon those under whose protection her conquests had been made and her power established? The appeal to the gods was already more than two centuries old, and now the disaster seemed to justify it. In answer to it Augustine took up his pen and wrote the *City of God.* It occupied the spare moments of his episcopal life for thirteen years (A.D. 413–426), and, with all its defects, it remains a noble example of the new philosophy of history, and sets in vivid contrast the two civilisations from whose fusion sprang the Middle Ages. He answers the heathen complaints one by one. Christianity was not responsible for Rome's disaster. The Christian enemy even tried to mitigate it, and Christian charity saved many pagans. Had Rome been really prosperous? Her history is dark with calamity. Had the gods really protected her? Remember Cannae and the Caudine Forks. These boasted gods have ever been but broken reeds, from the fall of Troy onwards. The glory of Rome (which he admits) is due, under the Christian's God, to Roman courage and patriotism. This God has a destiny for Rome and He means her to be the eternal city of a regenerate race. Such is the main subject of the first ten books. The next twelve develop the contrast between the city of men and the city of God, the one built upon love of self to the exclusion of God, the other built upon the love of God to the exclusion of self. The history of the world is briefly sketched, but the elaboration of the historical theme, on which he set great store, was entrusted to his disciple, Orosius, a young Spanish monk who came to Hippo in A.D. 414. Orosius' cue was this: the world, far from being more miserable than before the advent of Christianity, was really more prosperous and happy. Etna was less active than of old, the locusts consumed less, the barbarian invasions

[1] Cf. *de reditu*, ll. 383–398, in the interpretation of which I follow Pichon, *Les derniers écrivains profanes*, p. 266, against Dill and Keene, who hold that the passage is definitely anti-Christian.

were no more than merciful warnings. Here is an optimism as false in
its way as that of Rutilius; but it shews the spirit that carried Europe
safe through the darkness that was coming.

Thirty years later the situation had changed; optimism was difficult,·
it could no longer be said with Orosius that the world was "only tickled
with fleas," and none the worse for it. Under the almost universal
dominion of the barbarian, the old complaints of the heathen against
heaven were now heard on the lips of the Christians. Why had a special
dispensation of suffering accompanied the triumph of the Cross? Salvian
the Gaul takes up the theme and in his treatise *On the Government of the
World* compares Roman vice with barbarian virtue. His brush is too
heavily charged: he protests too much; but he undoubtedly helped his
contemporaries to recover tone, to bear the burdens laid upon them with
resignation, and to see the guiding hand of Providence in their misfortunes.
Salvian has not the faith of Augustine and Orosius in the future of the
Empire; for him the future was with the new races. But Sidonius Apollinaris (*c.* 430–489), who perhaps saw them closer and at any rate describes
them more minutely, is very loth to allow the ascendancy of the "stinking
savages" over Rome, which is still the one city where the only strangers
are slaves and barbarians. Thus even when Roman citizens were
bowing their heads to fate, even seeking help and an emperor from
the hated Greeks, the old love of Rome was strong, the sense of her
greatness hardly dimmed. It is not difficult to see how a city which
could command so much affection even from Christians served as a strong
support to those who for her sake strove to uphold her gods.

Meanwhile the religion which men of letters and Roman patriots
passed over in silent contempt or attacked with covert hatred had been
gathering notions from the very sources which fostered opposition to it.
"Spoil the Egyptians" was Augustine's advice, and not a few distinctive
Neoplatonist tenets were borrowed by Christian theologians and lived
on through the Middle Ages. The Church indeed rejected from her
authoritative teaching the Pantheism and Nihilism to which those
tenets lead if held consistently, and affirmed a personal triune God,
intelligent and free; a world created out of nothing and to return to
nothing; mankind redeemed from evil by one sole mediator; a future
life to be enjoyed without the sacrifice of the soul's individual nature.
But the Neoplatonists supplied illustration of church doctrine and
interpretation of Christian truth, and thinkers who saw danger in
anthropomorphism found support for their metaphysic in the heathen
school of Alexandria. The time is past when men spoke of fourth
century Christianity as a mere copy of Neoplatonism, but the object
and principles of the two systems are so much alike that it is not
surprising to find points of close resemblance in their presentment.
The resemblance is most marked in the writings of the Greek and
Syrian fathers. The Eastern element in Neoplatonism could not but

37

appeal to Eastern theologians; this appeal and its response explain the
large welcome extended to the works of two supposed disciples of St
Paul, "Hierotheus" and "Dionysius the Areopagite," whose rhapsodies
were received as Pauline truth not only by their credulous contemporaries
but by the mystics of the medieval Church. In these writings the
personal existence of God is threatened and the direct road to Him is
closed. "God is the Being of all that is." "The Absolute Good and
Beautiful is honoured by eliminating all qualities, and therefore the
non-existent must participate in the Good and Beautiful." God, who
can only be described by negatives, can only be reached by the surrender
of all personal distinctions and a voluntary descent into uncreated
nothingness. As has been well said, "the name God" came to be little
more than the deification of the word "not." All this is the language
of Brahmanism or Buddhism, and, but for the corrective influence of
Christian experience on the one hand and of Greek love of beauty on
the other, it would have led to Oriental apathy and hatred of the world
which God called good. The Cappadocian fathers — Basil and the two
Gregorys — who were Platonists at heart, and were driven, by the argument that God being simple must be easily intelligible, to assert in
strong terms the essential mystery of the divine being, yet maintained
that imperfection does not render human knowledge untrue, and that
the wisdom displayed in the created universe enables the mind to grasp,
by analogy, the divine wisdom and the uncreated beauty. This habit
of tracing analogies between the seen and the unseen is characteristic of
Platonism, Christian or heathen, and, we may remark in passing, it bears
pleasant fruit in that love for natural beauty that marks the writings
of the Cappadocians.

The mind of Plotinus is seen still more clearly in Synesius of Cyrene
(A.D. 365–412), country gentleman, philosopher, and bishop, who was in
every sense a Neoplatonist first and a Christian afterwards. All his
serious thought is couched in the language of the schools, while his
hymns are merely metrical versions of Neoplatonist doctrine. When
he was chosen bishop he was reluctantly ready to give up his dogs — he
was a mighty hunter — but not his wife, nor his philosophy, although it
contained much that was opposed to current Christian teaching on such
important points as the end of the world and the resurrection of the
body. He probably represents the attitude of many at this transition
period, though few possessed his clearness of mind and boldness of speech.

The influence of Neoplatonism in the West is less marked, but it is
there. Hilary's curious psychology, according to which soul makes body,
is Plotinian, though he may have taken it from Origen; and his own
sketch of his spiritual progress from the darkness of philosophy to the
light gives evidence that he first learnt from Neoplatonism the desire
for knowledge of God and union with Him (cf. *de Trin.* I. 1–13).

Augustine was yet more deeply affected by "the philosophers,"
especially in his early works. It was Plato, interpreted by Plotinus,

whom he read in a Latin version, that, as he himself tells us, delivered him from materialism and pantheism.   Thus the ecstatic illumination recorded in the *Confessions* (VII. 16, 23) was called forth by the perusal of the *Enneads* and is indeed expressed in the very words of Plotinus. Again, in more than one passage there is a distinct approach on his part to the Plotinian Trinity (one, mind, soul), or at least a statement of the Christian Trinity in terms of being, knowledge, and will, that seems to go beyond the limits of mere illustration or analogy.[1]

Again, Augustine accepts and repeats word for word the Neo-platonic denial of the possibility of describing God.   "God is not even to be called ineffable, because to say this is to make an assertion about Him" (*de doctr. christ.* I. 6); but, like the Cappadocians, his feet are kept from the hopeless *via negativa* by an intense personal conviction of the abiding presence of God and by a real vision of the divine.   His mind and heart taught him the real distinction between the old philosophy and the new religion, but all his deepest thoughts about God and the world, freedom and evil, bear the impress of the books which first impelled him "to enter into the inner chamber of his soul and there behold the light."   The appeal away from the illusion of things seen to the reality that belongs to God alone, the slight store set by him on institutions of time and place, in a word, the philosophic idealism that underlies and colours all Augustine's utterance on doctrinal and even practical questions and forms the real basis of his thought, is Platonic.   And, considering the vast effect of his mind and writings on succeeding generations, it is no exaggeration to say with Harnack that Neoplatonism influenced the West under the cloak of church doctrine and through the medium of Augustine.   Boethius, the last of the Roman philosophers and the first scholastic, certainly imitated Augustine's theology, and thought like him as a Neoplatonist.   At the same time it must be remembered that Platonism was the philosophy that commended itself most naturally to Christian or even to heathen thinkers.   Aristotle had had no attraction for Plutarch, while Macrobius deliberately set out to refute him.   The influence of Aristotle is certainly seen in the treatment of particular problems by individual writers, but the only school that deliberately preferred his method to his master's is that of Antioch.   To the mystical and intuitive movement of Alexandria the Antiochenes, especially Diodorus and Theodore of Mopsuestia, opposed a rationalism and a systematic treatment of theological questions which is obviously Aristotelian.

But there were two articles of the old religion that went deeper and spread further into the new than any philosophic method.   These were, first the mediators between God and man that were so prominent in Neo-

---

[1] Cf. *Conf.* XIII. 12;   *de Trin.* XV. §§ 17–20, 41.

platonism, and secondly the magic that was its inseparable accompaniment.

It is mere futility to find a pagan source for every Christian saint and festival, but a study of hagiographic literature reveals a very large amount of heathen reminiscence, and even of formal adoption, in the Church's Calendar. Doubtless there were other factors in the growth of the cultus of the saints and their relics — human instinct, the Jewish theory of merit, the veneration of confessors and martyrs, and the strong confidence which from an early date was placed in the virtue of their intercessions. But the extraordinary development of the cultus between A.D. 325 and 450 can only be explained by the polytheistic or rather the polydæmoniac tendencies of the mass of Gentile converts with the memories of hero and dæmon worship in their minds. Again, Neoplatonism involved the use of magic; the Christianity of the day admitted belief in it; for while the Bible forbade the practice, it did not deny its potency. Closely connected with magic stood divination, whether by astrology and haruspication, or by dreams and oracles. The Neoplatonists, following earlier thinkers, were committed to a theory of inward illumination, and ascribed the various phenomena of divination to the agency of spiritual forces working upon responsive souls. Christians allowed the supernatural inspiration of pagan oracles but held that it came, not from God like the inspiration of the Prophets, but from the fellowship of wicked men with evil dæmons, of whose real existence they had no manner of doubt. The fact that Scripture used the word δαιμόνιον of an evil spirit was immediate evidence of his existence and his wickedness. Philosophers might plead that there were beneficent dæmons. Δαιμόνιον had only one sense in the Bible, and that was enough to condemn all that bear the name. The dæmons, in the worship of whom, as Eusebius said, the whole religion of the heathen world consisted, were the object of the Christian's deepest fear and hate as being the source of all material and spiritual evil, and the avowed enemies of God. To them were due all the errors and sins of men, all the cruelty of nature. Wind and storm fulfilled God's word; but when mischief followed in their train, it was the work of Satan and his angels. Intercourse with these was stringently forbidden, but no one questioned its possibility. Augustine records the various charms and rites by which dæmons can be attracted; he was a firm believer in his mother's dreams and in her power to distinguish between subjective impressions and heaven-sent visions. And Synesius (writing, it is true, before his conversion) states his conviction that divination is one of the best things practised among men. Magic had been the object of penal legislation from the early days of the Empire, but the very violence of the laws passed by Christian emperors against it points to the prevalence of the belief in it, a belief which the lawgiver shared with his subjects. Constantine and Theodosius may have really looked to their anti-magical measures as a means to destroy polytheism and purify the Church, but the former emperor expressly excluded from the scope of his edict rites whose object was to save men from disease and the fields from harm, while his son Constantius, and Valens and Valentinian, were persuaded that magic might be turned against their life or power, and by way of self-defence fell to persecuting the magicians as fiercely as their predecessors had persecuted the Church. The title, "enemies of the human race," formerly applied to Christians was now transferred to the adepts in magical arts.

But present punishment and future warning were powerless to check practices that were the natural results of all-prevailing credulity.   What this was in heathen circles may be learnt from the pages in which Ammianus Marcellinus (A.D. 325–395) describes the Rome of his day; "many who deny that there are powers supernal will not go abroad nor breakfast nor bathe till they have consulted the calendar to find the position of a planet."   In Christian circles the credulity took also another form, that of an easy belief in miracles, not only of serious import such as the discovery of the bodies of Gervasius and Protasius — which is still a problem to the historian — but trivialities such as the winning of a horse race through the judicious use of holy water, the gift of reading without letters, and all the marvels of the Thebaid.   The truth is that amid the universal ignorance of natural laws men were ready to believe anything.   And it must be confessed that what greatly fostered credulity and error among educated Christians was the literal interpretation of Scripture which held the field in spite of Alexandrian allegorism.   The scientific and the common sense of Augustine were alike shocked by the interminable fables of the Manichaeans concerning sky and stars, sun and moon; but it was their sacrilegious folly that finally turned him from the sect.   "The authority of Scripture is higher than all the efforts of the human intelligence," he wrote, and the words exactly express the mind of churchmen whenever there was a conflict between physical theory and the faith.   The erroneous speculations of early philosophers, from whatever source derived, were taken up and readily adopted, provided that they did not contradict the Bible. There are already anticipations in the fourth century of the marvellous scheme of Cosmas Indicopleustes in the sixth, whereof the chief features were a two-storied firmament and a great northern mountain to hide the sun by night — all duly supported by scriptural quotations.   The results to which Greek speculation had by a supreme intellectual effort arrived were cast aside in favour of the wildest Eastern fancies, because these latter had the apparent sanction of Genesis and the Psalms.   The heliocentric theory of the universe, which although not universally admitted had at least been propounded and warmly supported, was deliberately refused, first on the authority of Aristotle, and a system adopted which led the world astray until Galileo.   Genesis demanded that the earth should be the centre, and the sun and stars lights for man's convenience.

CH. XX.

Again, the notion of a spherical earth was favoured in classical antiquity even by geocentricians. But the words of Psalmist, Prophet, and Apostle required a flat earth over which the heavens could be stretched like a tent, and the believers in a globe with antipodes were scouted with arguments borrowed from Lucretius the epicurean and materialist. Augustine denies the possibility not of a rotund earth but of human existence at the antipodes. "There was only one pair of original ancestors, and it was inconceivable that such distant regions should have been peopled by Adam's descendants." The logic is fair enough; the false premiss arises from the worship of the letter. The fact is that while as spiritual teachers the fathers are unrivalled, common sense interpretation is rare enough in our period; it is not often that we find such sober judgment as is shewn by Basil. "What is meant," he writes (*Hom. in Ps. xxviii*), "by the voice of the Lord? Are we to understand thereby a disturbance caused in the air by the vocal organs? Is it not rather a lively image, a clear and sensible vision imprinted on the mind of those to whom God wishes to communicate His thought, a vision analogous to that which is imprinted on our mind when we dream?"

In connexion with the unquestioning trust in the letter of Scripture as the touch-stone for all matters of knowledge some mention must be made of attempts to adjust universal history by the standard of Biblical dates, although the results, in one instance at least, bear witness to no uncritical credulity but to a singular freedom from prejudice and to love of truth.

The science of comparative chronography, so greatly developed by the Byzantines, was really founded by Sextus Julius Africanus in the early third century. The beginning which he made was carried out with far greater knowledge and with the use of much better material by Eusebius, bishop of Caesarea (A.D. 265–338). Former critics were inclined to belittle Eusebius' work and qualify him as a dishonest writer who perverted chronology for the sake of making synchronisms (so Niebuhr and Bunsen). It is certainly true that he manipulates the figures supplied by his authorities and employs conjecture and analogy to control the incredible length of their time-periods. But his reductions are all worked in the sight of the reader, who if he cannot allow the main contention, viz. the infallibility of the Biblical numbers, must confess the honesty of the method and the soundness of the process. In dealing with Hebrew chronology Eusebius shews candour and judgment. There was need of both, for even when the discrepancies between the Hebrew and the LXX texts were removed by claiming for the latter a higher inspiration, there remained contradictions enough between the covers of the Greek Bible. For instance, the time between the Exodus and Solomon's Temple is different in Acts and Judges from what it is in Kings. On this point Eusebius, after a fair and sensible discussion, decided boldly and to the dismay of his contemporaries against St Paul in favour of the shorter period, remarking that the Apostle's business was to teach the way of salvation and not accurate chronology. The effect of this decision is to lessen the antiquity of Moses by 283 years. This was clean against the whole tendency of previous apologists, who desired to establish the seniority of the Hebrew over all other lawgivers and philosophers. Eusebius, although conscious that the reversal of preconceived opinion demands some apology, is content to place Moses after Inachus. The work in which these novel conclusions were set forth consists of two parts, of which the first (*Chronographia*) contains the historical material — extracts from profane and sacred writers — for the synthetic treatment of the second part (*Canones*). Here the lists of the world's rulers are displayed in parallel columns shewing at a glance with whom any given monarch is contemporary. Side-notes accompany the lists, marking the main events of history, and a separate column gives the years of the world's age, reckoned from the birth of Abraham. The choice of this event as the starting-point of the Synchronism distinguishes the work of Eusebius from that of his predecessors and does great credit to his historical sense and honesty. As a Christian he felt that his standard of measurement must be the record of the scriptures; but as a historian he saw that history really begins with Abraham, the earlier chapters of Genesis being intended for edification rather than instruction. At a time when the Jews were a despised race, it was no slight achievement to place their history on a footing with that of proud and powerful monarchies, and although Eusebius' work cannot at all points stand the test of modern science, it is of permanent value to-day both as a source of information and as a model of historical research. The *Canons* were translated by Jerome and thus obtained at once, even in the West, a position of undisputed authority. The Latin medieval chronicle is founded on Eusebius, whose name, together with his translator's, quite overshadowed all other workers in the same field whether earlier or later, such as Africanus or Sulpicius Severus.

But although the learned labours of Eusebius bear witness to a strong individual regard for truth and a vast range of secular knowledge, the solid contributions to thought on the part of Christian writers must be looked for in other directions. The period which we must admit to have been marked by so much credulity and error in matters of science is the period of the oecumenical councils, of the conciliar creeds and the consequent systematisation of Christian doctrine. Councils gathered and expressed in creed and canon the common belief and practice of the churches. Their aim was, not to introduce fresh doctrine, but precisely the reverse, to protect from ruinous innovation the faith once delivered. Nor were the creeds, which served as tests of orthodoxy, intended to simplify or explain the mystery of that faith. Rather

CH. XX.

they reaffirmed in terms congenial to the age the inexplicable mystery of the revelation in Christ.   It was such heretics as the Arians who tried to simplify and explain the difficulties that confronted the Christian believer.   This intellectual effort was met by an appeal to experience, to man's need of redemption and the means by which that need is satisfied. The great advance made by Athanasius was really a return to the simple facts of the Gospel and the words of Scripture.   "He went back from the Logos of the philosophers to the Logos of St John, from the god of the philosophers to God in Christ, reconciling the world to Himself."   In a word, the great victories of the fourth and fifth centuries were the victories of soteriology over theological speculation.   Into the thorny labyrinth of the Arian and Nestorian conflicts there is no need to enter in this chapter.   We have only to consider what contributions to general thought were made by the victorious party.

The process of fixing the terminology in which the results of the Arian controversy were expressed and the doctrine affirmed of One God in three Persons of equal and coeternal majesty and Godhead could not be carried through without a serious attempt to deal with the problem of personality.   Pre-Christian thinkers had no clear understanding, or at least had not formulated a clear view, of human personality in its two most essential features, viz. universality and unity. These were necessarily brought out by Christianity, first in the historic figure of its founder and His unexampled life, and then in the development of the doctrine of His person.   In that development the Cappadocian fathers were pioneers.   The formula in which they declared the eternal relations existing within the Godhead — μία οὐσία τρεῖς ὑποστάσεις — marks a great advance in scientific precision of thought and language.   Up to A.D. 362 οὐσία and ὑπόστασις were interchangeable terms.   Athanasius in one of his latest writings says that they both mean Being.   Misunderstanding and confusion inevitably followed. But after the Synod of Alexandria in A.D. 362 οὐσία in Christian documents means the Being which is shared by several individuals and ὑπόστασις the special character of the individual.   For this happy settlement Basil of Caesarea was largely responsible.   He distinguishes between the terms and defines οὐσία as the general, ὑπόστασις as the particular, in application to both human and divine existence.   "Every one of us both shares in existence by the general term of οὐσία and by his own properties in such and such a one.   Similarly the term οὐσία is common, like goodness or Godhead, while ὑπόστασις is contemplated in the special quality of Fatherhood, Sonship, or the power to sanctify."

The way was thus prepared for Boethius' great definition of person as the individual substance of a rational nature (*persona est naturae rationalis individua substantia, contra Eut. et Nest.* III.), which was accepted by Thomas Aquinas and held good throughout the Middle Ages.   But between the times of Basil and Boethius a great controversy had arisen which carried forward the recognition of the facts of human personality — the controversy concerning the will and its freedom.

To understand this we must know what were the current opinions concerning the origin of the soul. The Platonic doctrine of pre-existence, as taught by Origen, had had its day; the only traces of it within the period are to be found in the pages of Nemesius the philosophic bishop of Emesa, and, less certainly, in those of Prudentius the Spanish poet. Thus the field was divided between Creatianism and Traducianism. The former view, according to which each soul is a new creation, the body alone being naturally begotten, emphasised the essential purity of the spiritual principle, the evilness of matter, and the unity of man's physical nature. Traducianism, on the other hand, maintained the transmission from the first parents through all succeeding generations of both soul and body, and sin therewith. Creatianism left room for the exercise of a free will, enfeebled but not destroyed by the Fall; Traducianism seemed to exclude free will and to posit a total corruption of soul and body. Creatianism was held by most of the Eastern fathers, and by Jerome and Hilary in the West: Traducianism, by the Westerns generally and by Gregory of Nyssa. Augustine, without definitely declaring himself on either side, was so far traducianist that he regarded the Fall as an historical act resulting in such a complete disablement of man's will that a special divine operation was required to start him again on the Godward path from which Adam's sin had driven him. Without Grace man can only will and do evil. To this conclusion Augustine was led in large measure by his own experience. He had undergone a two-fold conversion, first intellectual and then moral. The former brought him a conviction of divine truth and beauty; the latter, a recognition of human weakness. He had seen God, but the cloud of sin obscured the vision, the power of the world still enthralled his will; for the surrender to which he felt himself called meant surrender of all his habits, hopes, and desires. The conflict between his will and his reluctance was terrific. The world must have won, had not God come to his aid and set his will free to serve. Looking back at his life, the long enslavement of his will and the final victory, he is compelled to confess that he himself contributed nothing towards the restoration of his will and the recovery of peace. He had always believed in God's Grace, but once he held that man's own Faith, fruit of Free Will, went forth to meet it. Now he felt, and St Paul confirmed the conviction, that the whole movement was from God, that Faith as much as Grace is His gift, and that both are determined by the inscrutable decree of His predestinating counsel. Henceforth (this conversion took place in A.D. 386) the sense of God's guidance colours all his thought — a guidance unseen at the time but recognisable in a retrospect. What was true for him must be true for all. Augustine's character and circumstances are the clue to his

CH. XX.

later doctrine and his controversies. Thus it was the passionate cry of the *Confessions* for help against self, *da quod jubes et jube quod vis*, that evoked the Pelagian controversy. Pelagius, quiet inmate of the cloister, hardly knew what temptation is, and protested against words that discouraged moral effort and fostered fatalism. "Grace was good and a help; sin was widespread; but the latter was due not to an inherited taint but to the influence of Adam's bad example. Man can overcome temptation, if he sets his will to it." Augustine met the charge of fatalism by a scornful repudiation of the superstitions that attend the system, and of the impiety which confuses blind and undiscriminating Fate with Grace working with infinite wisdom on vessels of choice. But God's Predestination involves necessity, and this he co-ordinates with man's Free Will in a scheme that clearly betrays the influence of Roman jurisprudence. The synthesis is incomplete, the facts are stated scientifically and empirically, but the legal cast given to a purely metaphysical conception clouds rather than clears the issue.

Here was material for debate. The fight began in A.D. 411 and lasted with varying fortune until A.D. 418 when Pelagianism was condemned by Councils in Africa and at Rome, the infirmity of the Will and the vital need of Grace for the fulfilment of God's purposes being affirmed against all compromise. But a strong body of Christian sympathy, due partly to the prevalence of the monastic ideal and partly to a confusion between sin and atrocious sin, remained and still remains on the side of the Pelagians. Attempts were made to mediate between the two extremes by Cassian and Faustus of Riez, both of them monks, who were in great fear of fatalism and who, whilst condemning Pelagius as a heretic, urged the need of man's co-operation in the work of Grace. The predestination of a few they regarded as simple impiety, though they could not deny God's foreknowledge as to who are to be saved. It is plain that Foreknowledge raises more difficulties than it answers. A further and a bold attempt at explanation is offered by Boethius, who saw very clearly the danger of measuring the arm of God by the finger of man. He starts with the thesis, "all things are foreseen but all do not happen by necessity." But how can human freedom be really free if it is already foreseen by God? The answer lies in a recognition of the difference between the divine and human faculties of knowledge. "God's knowledge is a present consciousness of all things, past, present, and to come. Human knowledge as regards things future is called prescience. The divine knowledge of things future is rather called providence than prescience, because, transcending time, it looks down as from a lofty height upon a time-conditioned world. Such knowledge is no more incompatible with human freedom, than human knowledge is incompatible with present free acts" (*de Cons.* v. pr. 6).

The thought of man's fallen nature and consequent alienation from God, which is the starting-point of the Free Will controversy, leads naturally to the thought of Atonement through the death of Christ, and Atonement involves the theory of the Church and its sacraments, whereby the benefits of the Atonement are secured. On all these topics our period throws fresh light.

Two of the main aspects under which the earliest Christian writers regarded the Atonement were those of a sacrifice to God and of a ransom from evil. They did not specify to whom the price was paid. The third century had tried to remedy their indefiniteness by the unfortunate addition of the words "to Satan," and the proposition thus enlarged held its own for nearly 1000 years until it was discredited by Anselm.[1] The notion that the arch-enemy had overreached himself, and, while receiving the ransom, found no advantage in it (inasmuch as Christ's death saved more souls than His life), appealed to the mind of the age, and Gregory of Nyssa's grotesque image of the devil caught by the hook of the Deity, baited with the Humanity, was taken up and repeated with applause. But not by all. The "harrowing of Hell," in the form current in the fourth century, describes deliverance of souls by the triumphant Christ without a word of ransom. Gregory of Nazianzus rejects with scorn the notion of ransom paid to Satan or to God; the views of Athanasius and Augustine are entirely free from bad taste and extravagance. They start from the thought of God's goodness and justice. Goodness required that man should be delivered from the bondage of misery; justice required something more than mere repentance in order to effect that deliverance, nothing less than the offering up of the human nature which contained the sinful principle. This was achieved by Him who assumed human nature and represented man. Thus far Athanasius. Augustine, who is equally insistent on the fact of the sacrifice of Christ, goes deeper than Athanasius into the reason for the particular form that it took and the effects that it wrought. He shares Athanasius' admiration of the divine goodness exhibited in the long-suffering of God and the voluntary humility of the God-man; he is even more jealous for the divine justice. It was just that Satan who had acquired right over the race should be satisfied in respect of his claims. But Satan took more than his due, slaying the innocent. It was therefore just that he should be forced to relinquish the sinners in behalf of whom the sinless suffered.

The controversy concerning Free Will and Grace also affected the idea of the Church and sacraments. Until the rise of Pelagianism a very wide scope was allowed here to Free Will. The Grace conveyed by the sacraments, which were not to be had outside the Church, was considered

---

[1] The idea of *satisfactio per poenam* so often ascribed to the Latin fathers is altogether foreign to Roman Law and belongs to the sphere of Germanic institutions. In Roman Law the alternative is *solvere satisve facere*.

CH. XX.

to be conditioned by the faith and life of the recipient. It was tacitly assumed that these factors were within the control of the will. That is to say, Grace preceded Election. This, according to Augustine's mind matured by reflection and controversy, was an inversion of the truth. His theory of Predestination demanded that Election should precede Grace. And thus side by side with his practical belief in an external society in which good and bad, wheat and tares, were growing together, partaking of the means of grace, *i.e.* the visible church, he conceived the novel idea of a spiritual society of elect, the communion of saints, the invisible church, whose members were known to God alone, whether they were within the fold of the external society or not. Of this body it might be affirmed without a trace of bigotry, *extra ecclesiam nulla salus*. The two conceptions are not kept strictly apart, and the characteristics of the invisible church are constantly transferred by Augustine to the visible church. This body, whose growing nucleus is thus supplied by the invisible church, is the *civitas Dei* on earth. Over against it stands the *civitas terrena*, the earthly polity. The two states, separate in idea, origin, purpose, and practice, are yet dependent the one on the other, giving and taking influence. The *civitas Dei* needs the practical support of the *civitas terrena* in order to be a visible state. The *civitas terrena* needs the moral support of the *civitas Dei* in order to be a real state, for a *civitas* only exists on a basis of love and justice and by participation in the sole source of existence, which is God. The city of God is the only real *civitas*, gradually absorbing the *civitas terrena* and borrowing its authority and power in order to carry out the divine purpose. Magistrate and legislator become the sons and servants of the church, bound to execute the church's objects. We have here the germ of the medieval theory of the church as the kingdom of God on earth, but it must be noted that Augustine does not start with the assumption of identity, does not use church and kingdom of God as interchangeable terms, despite the assertion *ecclesia iam nunc est regnum*, which he is the first of Christian writers to make. Even in this phrase he does not mean that the church is actually the kingdom, but only that it is so potentially. The full and perfect realisation he reserves until the consummation of all things.

From the earliest days of Christianity the words sacrament and mystery were borrowed to denote any sacred secret thing, and especially the means of grace. The number of these was not distinctly specified, for Christians, believing that the Church was the store-house of unlimited grace, were not careful to count the means. Two however stood out pre-eminent, Baptism and the Lord's Supper. With regard to the doctrine underlying these two, it may be said that it was in the fourth and fifth centuries essentially what it had been before. No doubt Christian experience and the struggle with paganism and heresy tended to produce explanations, but the main thought was always simply that of life bestowed and life maintained. The early believers had not asked how, but the question could not but arise, and that rather in connexion with the Eucharist than with Baptism. For the water of Baptism did not invite speculation to the same degree as did the bread and wine, and their relation to the Body and Blood of Christ. Not that Baptism was ever regarded merely as a ceremony of initiation; it was the fear of losing, through post-baptismal sin, the grace conveyed by Baptism that in our period kept many from the font. Other causes such as negligence, reluctance to forgo the world, and various fancies and superstitions, combined to render Baptism, as in Constantine's case, the completion rather than the commencement of Christian life. Such delay was not the intention of the Church, and the necessity of checking slackness, together with the Western doctrine of prevenient grace helping the first step Godward, brought about a strict insistence on the necessity of Baptism and a readiness, in the West at least, to allow the Baptism of heretics, provided the right form of words was used. But both wisdom and generosity were shewn by the refusal to tie down the operation of the Holy Spirit to ritual action, and by the admission of faith, repentance, or martyrdom, as substitutes for formal Baptism when this could not be had. It must not be forgotten however that Augustine, when he found the Donatists proof against persuasion, advocated a resort to violence — *coge intrare*.

The Eucharist was more obviously mysterious, and at a time when the rite was attended by many who were more conscious of its mysterious experience than of any effect it might have upon life, speculation was active, and teachers laboured to assist inquiry by analogy and illustration which often grew to something more. Thus from Gregory of Nyssa came an impulse which finally developed into the doctrine of transubstantiation. Not that Gregory means to teach this; the passage in his works containing the germ is not a definition. His style is highly imaginative and the *Oratio catechetica* is full of similes. One of these is borrowed, but without hesitation, from physiology. Gregory draws a parallel between the change of bread and wine, by digestion, into the human body, and the change of the sacramental elements, by consecration, into Christ's immortal body. Using Aristotelian terms, he says that in each case the constituents are arranged under a fresh form. This is not transubstantiation but transelementation (μεταστοιχείωσις). The image commended itself, and it was repeated and elaborated by other writers until at length the complete identification of the bread and wine with the Body and Blood of Christ became the authoritative doctrine of the Eastern Church. The Roman doctrine of transubstantiation has points of resemblance with Gregory's illustration, but it is expressed in terms of a different and later philosophy. Gregory teaches a change of form; the schoolmen, a change of both material and form, which they explain by the help of the distinction between *substantia* and *accidentia*. The

CH. XX.

great contribution of the age to the doctrine of the Sacraments is the view that in a real sense they continue the process of the Incarnation. Human nature first became divine in the person of Christ by union with the divine Word, and subsequently and repeatedly in the person of the individual believer through union with Christ in the Sacraments. This is the teaching of both East and West as represented by Hilary and Gregory of Nyssa. As in Baptism the soul is joined to Christ through faith, so in the Eucharist is the body, being transformed by the Eucharistic food, joined with the Body of the Lord. Thus the special purpose of the Incarnation, viz. the deification of man, is being constantly fulfilled. The language in which this noble conception is expressed, especially in the East, tends to encourage a superstitious reverence for the outward symbols, which the Greek fathers frequently have occasion to correct.

Augustine earnestly desired that the *civitas terrena* should help to establish the *civitas Dei*, and that the *civitas Dei* should leaven with moral influence the *civitas terrena*. It remains for us to see how far his dream was realised, in other words how far the Christian Empire affected the Church and was in turn affected by it.

The influence of the Empire upon the internal and external structure of the Church had been felt from the first. Thus, the development of the monarchical episcopate was doubtless due in great measure to the example of Roman law, which required all corporate bodies to have a representative. The mark of Roman law is also seen in the Western doctrines of Free Will, Sin and its transmission, and Atonement. The language in which these problems are stated is the phraseology of the courts, and recalls the Roman penal code, theory of contract and delict, debt, universal succession, etc.

The effect of civil order is seen in certain pieces of church administration which though themselves practical are the expression of underlying theory, and therefore call for notice here.

(1) The Church was organised in "dioceses" (with exarchs or patriarchs), provinces (with metropolitans or primates), and cities (with bishops), much in the manner of the Empire. This arrangement was not directly imposed upon the Church by the Empire nor did it exactly correspond to the imperial distribution. But the sudden rise of the see of Byzantium from a subordinate position into the next place of honour after Rome proves that civil importance was a factor in determining ecclesiastical precedence.

(2) The bargain proposed by Nestorius to Theodosius II, "Give me the world free from heretics and I will give thee heaven," was in a fair way of fulfilment. The emperors from being foes became powerful friends to the Church, able to give the material support that Augustine desired. Constantine would no doubt gladly have enjoyed the same controlling relation towards his adopted religion as he held towards the religion of which he and his successors till Valens remained chief pontiffs. But the

Church was too strong for that, and the rescript of A.D. 314, in which he declared that the sentence of the bishops must be regarded as that of Christ Himself, shews what their power was, and hints what they might have done with it. Still, he was allowed to style himself (perhaps in jest) ἐπίσκοπος τῶν ἐκτός, and he set the example of convoking general councils, the decrees of which were published under imperial authority and thus acquired a political importance. Those only who accepted their rulings could enjoy the rights of state favour, and civil penalties were presently threatened in the interest of civic peace against all who declined to acknowledge them.

(3) Pagan teachers, priests, and doctors were already exempt from certain civil charges on the ground of professional usefulness. To this list Constantine added first the African, and later all Christian, clergy; and them he allowed to engage in trade untaxed because they could give their profits to the poor. Clerical families and property were likewise excused all the ordinary responsibilities of *curiales*. Many citizens sought this immunity from taxation, even after the State, fearing the loss of useful service, had forbidden the ordination of curials; and the Church came to welcome the exclusion of the well-to-do from her ministry as a protection against unworthy ministers, as she also did the removal of exemption from trade-taxes, for the age was averse from any interference with the spiritual duties of the clergy. But the fact that privileges were withdrawn from the heathen priesthood and bestowed on the clergy enhanced the position of the latter as a favoured class.

(4) The Church was distinguished as a corporation capable of receiving donations and bequests. Earlier confiscations and restorations prove that the Church had held property long before the time of Constantine. But Constantine bestowed upon it a more extensive privilege than was known to any heathen religious foundation. Whereas the latter could only be endowed under special circumstances, and, with few exceptions, never acquired the right to receive bequests, "the sacred and venerable Christian churches" might be left anything by anybody. Abuse of the privilege gradually led to its withdrawal under Valentinian III, and Christian writers deplore the cause more keenly than the result; but the growing wealth was as a rule generously applied to philanthropic work started by the Church, and Augustine was justified in calling upon churchmen to remember Christ as well as their sons. They were the more likely to listen, since the old Jewish belief that alms win heaven had taken root and sprung up in the doctrine of merit.

(5) The Church secured another prerogative, which was fraught with serious consequences, in the establishment of episcopal courts as an integral part of the secular judicial system with final jurisdiction in civil cases. But it had analogy with the Roman institution of *recepti arbitri*, an extrajudicial arrangement allowing the civil authority to step in and enforce the decision of the arbitrator. At a time when, as we learn from

Salvian and Ammianus, the courts were monuments of justice delayed
and of chicanery, it was no small boon to be allowed to carry a civil suit
to the arbitration of a bishop whose equitable decision had the force of
law.   The early history of this remarkable legislation is obscure and
complicated, but it clearly contained in germ the clerical exemption from
criminal procedure which formed one of the most difficult problems in
medieval politics.   The episcopal jurisdiction underwent considerable
limitations and bishops lost their position of privilege before the law;
but appeal to the episcopal court became a tradition in the Church.

(6)   There are other indications of the great influence acquired by
bishops in the administration of justice.   Into their hands passed the
right of intercession formerly exercised in behalf of clients by wealthy
patrons or hired rhetoricians.   One of their duties, according to Ambrose,
was to rescue the condemned from death, and he himself was active in
its discharge.   So Basil interceded for the unfortunate inhabitants of
Cappadocia at the partition of the province in A.D. 371.   So Flavian of
Antioch, with better success, stood between his flock and the emperor,
not unjustly irritated by the riot of 387.

(7)   Closely connected with episcopal intercession was the right of
asylum, transferred from heathen temples to Christian churches, which
afforded protection to fugitives, pending the interference of the bishops.
One out of many instances, and that the most romantic, is the case of the
miserable Eutropius (A.D. 399), who benefited by the privilege which he
had himself in the previous year sought to circumscribe.

Such are some of the points at which the Empire touched the Church.
The effect of the Church upon the Empire may be summed up in the
word "freedom."   Obedience to authority was indeed required in every
department of public and private life, provided that it did not conflict
with religious duty.   But the old despotic attributes were gradually
removed, the Roman *patria potestas* suffered notable relaxation, and
children were regarded no longer as a *peculium* but as "a sacred charge
upon which great care must be bestowed."   In a word, authority was
seen to be a form of service, according to God's will, and such service
was freedom.   This great principle found expression in many ways,
and first in respect of literal bondage.   The better feeling of the
age was certainly already in favour of kindness towards the slave.
Stoicism, like Christianity, accepted slavery as a necessary institution,
but no one ever more clearly discerned its baneful results than
Seneca.   And Seneca was still listened to.   It is in his words that
Praetextatus in Macrobius' *Saturnalia* pleads the slave's common
humanity, faithfulness, and goodness, against the old feeling of contempt
of which there were still traces in Christian and pagan writers.   It was,
however, not from Seneca but from Christ and St Paul that the fathers
took their constant theme of the essential equality of men, before which
slavery cannot stand.   Not only do they establish the primitive unity

and dignity of man, but, seeing in slavery a result of the Fall, they find in the sacrifice of Christ a road to freedom that was closed to Stoicism. They offered a more effective consolation than the philosophers, for they pointed the slave upward by recognising his right to kneel beside his master in the Lord's Supper. Close upon the Church's victory follows legislation more favourable to the slave than any that had gone before. Constantine did not attempt sudden or wholesale emancipation, which would have been unwise and impossible. Nor is there any sign that he recognised the slave's moral, intellectual, or religious needs. But he sought to lessen his hardships by measures which with all their inequalities are unique in the statute-book of Rome. He tried to prevent the exposing of children, though he could not stop the enslavement of foundlings; he forbade cruelty towards slaves in terms which are themselves an indictment of existing practice; he forbade the breaking up of servile families; he declared emancipation to be "most desirable"; he transferred the process of manumission from pagan to Christian places of worship in a way and with words that testify to his view of it as a work of love belonging properly to the Church. But the Church was not content to influence the lawgiver and preach to master and slave the brotherhood of man and the duties of forbearance and patience. She struck at all the bad conditions that encouraged slavery.

The stage and the arena had always been the objects of her hate as hotbeds of immorality and nurseries of unbelief. Attendance there was forbidden to Christians as an act of apostasy. Julian caught the feeling and forbade his priests to enter theatres or taverns. Yet Libanius, Julian's friend and mentor, defends not only comedy and tragedy but even the dance, exalting it above sculpture as a school of beauty and a lawful recreation. But dancing, as Chrysostom points out, was inseparable from indecency and, far from giving the mind repose, only excites it to base passions. The ban of the Church accordingly was proclaimed against the ministers of these arts upon the public stage; it followed them into private houses when they went to enliven wedding or banquet, forbidding them baptism so long as they remained players. This apparent harshness, which can be matched from civil legislation, was in reality a kindness. The actor's state was at this time incompatible with purity, and the Church sought to deliver a class enslaved to vice. A notable victory was won when it was ruled that an actress who asked for and received the last sacraments should not, if she recovered, be dragged back to her hateful calling. The only way of escape from it in any case lay in the acceptance of Christianity. As the theatre gratified low tastes, so the arena stimulated tigerish instincts. Both Pliny and Cicero apologised for it as being the proper playground of a warrior race; it certainly held the Roman imagination. The story of Alypius (a friend of Augustine) is well known, whom one reluctant look during a gladiatorial show enslaved completely to the lust for blood.

Attempts to suppress the shows were made, doubtless under Christian influence.   They met with little response, except in the East, where the better spirits (like Libanius) repudiated them as a Roman barbarity, unworthy of a Greek.   But the action of Constantine in forbidding soldiers to take part in gladiatorial shows, and of Valentinian in exempting Christians from suffering punishment in the arena, prove that earlier regulations were a dead letter.   The show which Alypius attended was at Rome in A.D. 385.   Symmachus as urban praefect speaks with pride of the games he gave, and when the Saxon captives with whom he had hoped to make a Roman holiday committed suicide in prison he had to turn to Socrates and his example for consolation.   The sums spent on these games is an index to the wealth of noble Romans. The same Symmachus spent £80,000 on the occasion of his son's praetorship; a festival given in the reign of Honorius lasted a week and cost £100,000.   Ammianus Marcellinus and Jerome paint the same picture, and even when their charges have been discounted by the more sober pages of Macrobius, it is still clear that the dying Roman civilisation was marked by general luxury and self-indulgence.   The Church could not stop this waste; sumptuary laws lay outside her competence; but leaders practised and encouraged simplicity and frugality and reproved the tendency towards ecclesiastical display.   Jerome meets the argument that lavish hospitality would strengthen the hand of clerical intercessors by answering that judges will honour holiness above wealth, and simple clergy more than luxurious ones.   "Golden mediocrity" doubtless had its devotees.   There were many Christian men of the world to whom monasticism was a riddle, as it was to Ausonius, whose prayer was, "give me neither poverty nor riches."   But better than moderation was renunciation of the world, and the ascetic element of early Christianity, reinforced by the example of all exponents of high thought, led many to turn their faces from the luxury around them and flee to the desert. To those who remained behind the Christian writers tried to teach the view of poverty as a probation and of wealth as a trust, the mutual dependence of rich and poor, and the lesson that men should be one in heart as they are one in origin — *caritas qua in uno incommunicabili unum sumus.* They frequently recall the communion recorded in the Acts, and now that change of conditions had rendered community of goods impossible, a new means of applying the principle was sought, first in feasts of charity and regular collections for the poor, in the private munificence of the bishop, or in a proportionate and elaborately organised distribution, under the bishop, of church revenues.   These by dint of careful administration and continual accessions grew to an immense property, till by the fifth century the Church had become the greatest landowner in the Empire. In general, promotion to a bishop's stool meant merely entry into a large fortune.   "Make me Bishop of Rome and I will become a Christian," was Praetextatus' reply to Damasus, and it reflects the public opinion.

Ammianus Marcellinus waxes scornful over the episcopal splendour and extravagance at Rome, but he qualifies or points his sarcasm by the admission that there were bishops in the provinces who, "moderate in eating and drinking, simple in dress, shew themselves worthy priests of the Deity." Instances of fine and unselfish philanthropy are equally common in the theory held by great churchmen and in their practice.[1]

Perhaps the most striking justification of the common claim that bishops are the proper and recognised helpers and guardians of the poor, the widow, and the orphan, is found in their readiness to convert the communion plate into money for the distressed. "It is better to save living souls than lifeless metals ... the ornament of the sacraments is the redemption of captives," are the words with which Ambrose defended himself against the charge of sacrilege. Refuge from the tax-burthened world was afforded by the monasteries, which are too often judged, not by the circumstances which called them into being, but by the abuses which attended their decay. And side by side with the strictly religious houses there sprang up innumerable charitable institutions — orphanotrophia, ptochotrophia, nosocomia, gerontocomia, brephotrophia — intended to relieve the wants of every class and every age and not merely those of citizens, as had been the case in heathen Rome and Athens. Not the least of the debts which the world owes to fourth century Christianity is this invention of open hospitals. Julian felt its power and summoned his followers to imitate in this respect the hated Galilaeans. But with superior organisation the old spirit of voluntary charity waned. Individual effort disappeared; a steward discharged the philanthropic activities of the bishops; deaconesses waited less on the poor and more on the worship of the Church. Charity became less discriminating and aped the pagan largesses. Begging now finds a place in the statute-book, and the first law against mendicancy was issued by a Christian Emperor (Valentinian II).[2] Yet the Church sought to meet this evil also by restoring labour to honour. Slavery had degraded it, and commerce had always been despised at Rome. Before the eyes of an idle and unprofitable multitude was now displayed the example of Christ and his apostles, workmen all, an example which was actually followed in the monasteries where the "perfect" life joined prayer with work, both to charitable purposes. The Pachomian houses, as self-sufficing communities, provided regular work, not merely as a penitential exercise, but as an integral part of the life. Basil would have his ascetics despise no form of labour; Augustine reproved African monks who were deserting work for prayer. Sloth was assuredly no

[1] Cf. Ambros. *Ep. 3 contr. Symm.*; Aug. *Ep. 50*; Jerome, *Ep. ad Pammach. 26*; Greg. Nyss. *Or. de paup. amand.*; Basil, *Ep. 151*; Socr. *H. E.* vii. *26*; Soz. *H. E.* iii. *16*; Theodoret, *Epp. 42–45*; Conc. Sardica, c. viii. etc.

[2] Cod. Just. lib. xi. tit. *26 de mendicantibus validis.*

inmate of the cloister then, though the work done cannot be described as always useful or rational.

But the efforts of Christianity in behalf of the weak are nowhere seen more clearly than in the uplifting of women. The Church gave them a place of consideration in her ministry, not however the privilege of preaching or administering the sacraments, though a deaconess was allowed to assist in the baptism of women. Besides the carefully regulated orders of deaconesses, virgins, and widows, there arose towards the end of the fourth century classes of widows and virgins of higher rank who gave themselves to voluntary work under church auspices, without taking regular vows or living in communities. Such were Jerome's friends and correspondents, Paula and Eustochium. In the East, where this class attained a position of greater prominence than in the West (the Roman spirit was averse from the public ministry of women), they approximated to an order and were finally assimilated to the deaconesses.

Outside the ministry of the Church women were made the subject of special legislation. Constantine was austere in morals. The age was loose. The antique ideal of the Roman nation had long since disappeared. Constantine determined to restore it. The severity of his measures against adultery and rape shews his zeal in the cause of morality, while the terms of those which regulate the relations of women to the courts exhibit his care for their good fame and the *matris familiae majestas*. Thus to spare their modesty wives were forbidden to appear in court at all. His tenderness is also seen in his forbidding a son to disinherit his mother, and in the exemption of widows from the penalties visited on coiners. On the other hand there are signs, both in contemporary legislation and literature, of unchristian and brutal contempt for the women who had most need of protection. Tavern-keepers and barmaids are set free from the operation of the laws against adultery, "since chaste conduct is only expected of those who are restrained by the bonds of law, and immunity must be extended to those whose worthless life has set them beyond the pale of the laws." Again, it is difficult to understand the mind of Augustine, who loves his natural son Adeodatus as David loved the child of Bathsheba, and who yet has regret, but no word of pity, for the mother whom he cast off. So Sidonius Apollinaris, the aristocratic bishop of Auvergne, is very lenient towards the irregularities of a young noble, and quite heartless towards the victim. But in the latter case it must be remembered that the Christianity of Sidonius was not very deep, that the girl was a slave, and that for all their good intentions and growing instincts of humanity the Church and churchmen did not yet regard slaves as free; and in the former, that concubinage, *i.e.* the association of one man with one woman, was recognised by Roman law and by the Council of Toledo (A.D. 400) and hardly differed from wedlock except in name. What is astonishing to modern notions in the case of Augustine and his mistresses is not so much his own conduct as the line taken by his friends and the saintly Monnica, and too readily adopted by himself. Something like a *mariage de convenance* was projected for him while he was still attached to a woman whom there is no reason to suppose unworthy to become his wife, in the hope that as soon as he was married he might be washed clean in saving baptism. Monnica was indeed more concerned by his Manichaeism than by his irregular life. The incident reveals a flaw in a great character. But if that were all it would have no place here. It is of value to our purpose as illustrating the view of the relation between the sexes held at this time, and as a witness to the vastness of the task that lay before the Church in purifying and uplifting society.

CH. XX.

CHAPTER XXI

EARLY CHRISTIAN ART

NOT many years ago Greek art seemed to be marked off from Roman, and Roman from Early Christian by wide intervals. The art of Greece was typified by the buildings of the Athenian Acropolis, Roman art by those of the imperial Forum and the Palatine, and Christian art by the catacombs. Unceasing exploration and fruitful discoveries have since brought to light so many works of the transitional periods that art history has become rather the account of a continuous process than of clearly defined epochs and schools.

The art of Rome itself under the new light appears rather as one of the many later Hellenistic schools, than as purely indigenous. Part of the transition from Classical Greek may be traced in the art centres of Asia Minor, and part, again, in the non-Roman city of Pompeii. As to the latter, it is held that the sequences of style which have been distinguished in its wall-paintings were probably fashions imported from Alexandria. The covering of internal walls with thin slabs of rare coloured-marbles and porphyries, and the incrustation ·of vaults with mosaics of gilt and coloured glass, had the same origin.

This process of change in classical art carries us to some point in the early centuries of Christianity, and many groups of facts shew that it was long continued. Not only did Egypt and the East export their porphyry, ivory, glass, bronze, and textiles, but craftsmen were drawn to the Roman capital from every Hellenistic city.

The works used or made by the Early Christians could at first have been differentiated in no obvious way from the current classical works of the time. When anything emerges which we can entitle Christian Art, the change is, for the most part, manifest in a new spirit dealing with old forms. The art was necessarily shaped externally by the modes and codes of expression of the time. In many cases new ideas were expressed under old forms; thus the winged angel derives from the antique Victory; the nimbus is classical as well as Christian; the story of Orpheus is interpreted as a type of Christ; and Amor and Psyche are adopted as symbols of the Divine Love and the soul.

598

In so far as there was novelty it is clear that, as Christianity itself was from the East, so the changed forms must themselves have held in them much that was oriental. Early Christian art is Roman art in the widest sense, purified, orientalised, and informed with a new and epical content which held as seed the possibilities of the mighty cycle of Byzantine and Medieval art.

It is still in Rome and in the catacombs that the best connected series of works of the first three or four centuries of this early art is found. The great roads of approach to Rome were lined by countless tombs of every degree of magnificence: rotundas, pyramids, cellae, and sarco-phagi. Amongst them stood vestibules to underground tomb-chambers where large numbers were buried in common. Along their walls, tier upon tier, urns of ashes were packed like vases in a museum. The Jews and other oriental peoples followed the custom of burying the unburnt body in subterranean galleries, and appropriate sites for these also were obtained round about Rome. The Christians, following the same usage, at first shared such catacombs, and in other cases formed groups of their own. The catacombs were primarily not places of hiding, however much they may have been so used. Frequently there was a space above ground planted as a garden, and made use of as a cemetery. In some were small burial chapels from which access was obtained to the catacombs beneath. The ruins of two or three such chapels have been discovered and described. They agree in having had a central apse and two lateral apses grouped together at one end.

There were also subterranean chapels, the most famous of which is the Capella Graeca of the Catacomb of Priscilla. It has, roughly, the form of a small nave or body, 8 by 25 ft., ended by an apse with lateral apses on each side of it. It opens from a long vaulted apartment or *atrium*. The walls are decorated with paintings of the usual subjects — Daniel, and Lazarus, Moses, Susannah, and the Adoration of the Magi. On the vault over the nave are four heads representing the seasons. Above the central apse is represented the Eucharistic repast. This recently-discovered *Fractio Panis* is not only one of the most interesting, it is also one of the most beautiful of the catacomb paint-ings, as may be seen in the large photogravure published by Wilpert. The forms and features of the seven participants are classic and gracious. It is painted in a masterly way in a few simple colours on a vermilion ground. The inscriptions on the walls are in Greek, hence the name of the chapel. In the apse was an altar-tomb. It belongs to the second century.

Another catacomb church is probably of the third century, and a third, the largest, in the catacomb of St Hermes is probably of the fourth. The catacombs themselves are complexes of subterranean passages and galleries excavated for the disposal of the dead, who rested one above another along the sides. The chambers, more or less square, were

CH. XXI.

roughly vaulted above, and the vaults and walls were for the most part decorated with painting, and occasionally with stucco reliefs. This ornamentation was a branch of the ordinary house and tomb decorator's work of the time, and the painted subjects were clearly executed with the swift mastery which came of long practice in repeating a limited stock of ideas. The vaulted ceilings were usually decorated by some geometrical arrangement of panels, radiating from the centre and bounded by a large circle. In these panels were little figures, groups, birds, and foliage. The colours were reds, greens, and ochres, and a little blue, the whole mellow yet bright.

The subjects of these paintings have been most thoroughly illustrated, and their chronology analysed, in Wilpert's large work. Under the first century he groups several schemes of vault decoration in which the motives consist of the geometrical division of the field, and of little *putti* and foliage. One vault is entirely covered with a branching vine. On others of the same century are landscapes and burial feasts, while the cycle of Biblical subjects begins with Daniel standing between two lions, and the Good Shepherd. To the second century he assigns vaults on which appear the Three Children in the furnace, Moses striking the rock, the Eucharist, Noah and the Ark, scenes from the story of Jonah, and subjects from the life and miracles of Christ; the raising of Lazarus, the cure of the paralytic, the cure of the woman, and the meeting with the Samaritan. The most noticeable and beautiful is in the cemetery of Priscilla, and represents the seated Virgin and Child, with a prophet standing by, and a star or the sun above. This is a small group at the side of a central composition of the Good Shepherd, from which it is divided by a flowering tree. This central subject and the trees on either hand of it were roughly modelled in the plaster before colouring. The modelling of the tree is but a few swift marks of the tool defining the trunk, and the leaves and flowers are painted. The Virgin and Child are beautifully drawn with some remaining tradition of classical feeling. The figures are only about a foot high, and unhappily the lower part is much injured. The whole is very like a sketch by Watts. Belonging to this century are two or three versions of the Baptism. Another subject is the mocking of Christ; others are symbolical, a ship in a storm, Orpheus charming the beasts, and *orantes* who represent souls rather than persons. One beautiful vault is decorated by a series of bands, on the lowest of which, on the four sides, are four typical occupations of the seasons — picking flowers, cutting corn, the vintage, and gathering olives — while the upper bands are ornamented successively with pattern-work of roses, corn, vine, and olive.

Amongst the third century paintings may be noticed Christ enthroned, the Virgin and the Magi, and Amor and Psyche gathering flowers. In the fourth century Christ is represented enthroned amidst the twelve apostles, as in the apses of the early basilicas. In the fifth century the treatment of the figures becomes more rigid and hieratic, while their costumes are much bejewelled, in a manner distinctly Byzantine. There is little in the catacomb paintings which has peculiar application to the grave. The raising of Lazarus or Daniel between the lions belong to a series of "deliverance" subjects which were in general use in all forms of Early Christian art; when we come to the fourth and fifth centuries the decoration resembles that which we are accustomed to in the churches of those centuries, and the decoration of the earlier catacombs would have been equally according to the general custom of the time when they were built. That is, the pre-Constantinian churches and earlier domestic oratories must have been painted in like fashion with the catacombs. The ideas underlying the choice of subjects are of resurrection and salvation, thoughts which are further expressed in the simple epitaphs, which speak of hope, peace, and eternal welfare. Some of the subjects chosen have, indeed, been compared with the ancient prayers for the dying, "Deliver, O Lord, Thy servant as Thou didst deliver Enoch and Elias from the common death, as Thou didst deliver Noah from the Deluge, Job from his torments, Isaac from the Sacrifice, Moses from the hand of Pharaoh, Daniel from the lions, the three young men from the furnace, and Susannah from false accusation. . . . So deign to deliver the soul of Thy servant."

The *orantes*, who were figured with extended arms amidst such scenes, are types of supplication. They are generally feminine, and are symbols of the soul in prayer. Thus understood they go far to explain the scope and meaning of the art of the catacombs.

There is little sculpture in the round extant from our period, but it is almost surprising that there is any. The examples are three or four figures of the Good Shepherd bearing the lamb on His shoulder. The most perfect of these, in the Lateran Museum, is a sweet pastoral figure. They have been compared with statues of Hermes bearing the ram. The composition is clearly derived, but the sentiment is very different. As usual, the Christians were using old symbols in a new spirit.

The early sarcophagi furnish us with a series of relief sculptures parallel in extent and interest to the paintings of the catacombs. Some are so little differentiated from late classical art that it is hardly possible to say whether they are indeed Christian. Others have quite a collection of the usual triumph subjects which appear in the catacombs as paintings. The most noteworthy of all of them is a fragment, now in the Berlin Museum, which was lately brought from Constantinople. On it appear Christ and two apostles, standing in niches, separated by columns. Christ is unbearded and the head has a cruciform nimbus. The figures, which are about four feet high, are draped in a dignified style like classical statues of philosophers. This remarkable work has the closest relation of style with the series of late antique sarcophagi, one of which is in the Mausoleum Room of the British Museum, another in the Cook

Collection at Richmond. The Berlin relief probably belongs to the third century, and had its origin at Constantinople or in Asia Minor.

Another famous sarcophagus is that of Junius Bassus, praefect of Rome, who died in 359. It has several scenes sculptured on it, amongst which are, Christ enthroned, the Entry into Jerusalem, Christ brought before Pilate, and Pilate washing his hands; also Adam and Eve, Daniel, etc. The sculptures are in panels divided by columns, some of which are covered with scrolls of foliage among which climb *amorini*. This ornamentation is noteworthy, as the columns thus decorated resemble the celebrated sculptured columns at St Peter's which are usually thought to be antique. These columns formed a screen in front of the altar of Constantine's basilica; they were saved, and re-used in the new church. The motive of Cupids climbing amidst vines is also found on the mosaics of Santa Costanza (*c.* 360) and on many tombs.

Two more most famous sarcophagi must be spoken of — those of the Empress Helena and of Santa Costanza. Both are of royal porphyry with sculptures in high relief, and they are now in the Vatican. That of the Empress is sculptured with a military triumph, that of Costanza with *amorini* and the vintage, peacocks, and lambs. With the latter Strzygowski has lately compared fragments of other porphyry sarcophagi at Constantinople and Alexandria, and has shewn that they must all have come from Egypt, the land of the porphyry-quarries and the place of origin of other porphyry sculptures such as the well-known group at the south-west corner of St Mark's, Venice.

A class of objects which dates from the time of the catacombs, if not from the apostolic age, is that of engraved gems. Of these the British Museum has a good representative collection. "The use of rings as signets or ornaments was as widely spread among the early Christians as among their Pagan contemporaries. St James speaks of the man who wears a gold ring and goodly apparel, and the Fathers of the Church were obliged to reprimand the community for extravagance in this respect." The devices engraved on these gems are for the most part of a simple symbolic character as befits the small field which they occupy. In the British Museum collection we have anchors and fish, doves and trees, sheep, branches of olive and palm, shepherds' crooks, ships, sacred monograms, the word IXΘYC, and the inscription *Vivas in Deo*. Of more pictorial subjects we have the Good Shepherd bearing the sheep, Adam and Eve, Daniel, Jonah, and the Crucifixion. Two are especially important. One of them contains quite a collection of the favourite subjects brought together on its narrow space. The Good Shepherd with the sheep, Daniel and the lions, the dove with the olive branch, and the story of Jonah, as well as two trees, fish, a star, and a monogram. The other is probably the earliest representation of the Crucifixion known, and must date from the third century at latest. On either side of the Crucified Christ are six much smaller figures, the apostles, and above is the word IXΘYC. M. Brehier in *Les Origines du Crucifix* (1904) suggests that the representation was of Syrian origin and arose in opposition to merely symbolical interpretations. At South Kensington there are several Early Christian, Gnostic, and Byzantine rings, some of which are of importance. One is a ship with the XP monogram on its sail, another has two saints embracing, probably the Visitation. Another has a symbolic composition engraved on silver which has been figured by Garrucci and others. Later writers copy it from Garrucci and seem not to know of its being preserved now at South Kensington. From a pillar resting on a pyramid of steps spring branches of foliage above which, in a circle, is a Lamb with the XP monogram. Below the branches stand two sheep, and two doves fly toward the tree. It is inscribed IANVARI VIVAS.

The elementary symbols which are found on the engraved rings and all the other objects of art are so direct and simple, as has been said, that they are still perfectly obvious and modern. We have the anchor, cross, crook, ship, light-house, fish, and star; the dove, lamb, drinking harts, palms and olive branches, trees, baskets of fruit, lamps and candles, chalice, amphora, bowl of milk; the vintage, harvest, sowing, and fishing; the shepherd, the *orantes*, Eros and Psyche; the Heavenly Sanctuary, the Celestial Banquet, and Garden of Paradise. Out of this alphabet ideas were built up by combination. Thus we have a ship with a cross-mast, and the sacred monogram on its sails; another ship on a stormy sea approaching a light-house; still another ship made fast to land, bearing vessels of wine and with a dove holding a branch of olive perched on the rigging. Or we have a Lamb lying at the foot of the Cross, or another caressing an axe. There are combined anchors and crosses, flowering crosses, crosses with birds perched on their arms, and crosses rising from a mound from which flow four rivers.

Larger objects in metal work must be mentioned, if only that attention may be drawn to the celebrated Casket of Projecta and the excellent collection of bronze candlesticks and hanging lamps at the British Museum. The silver toilet casket is entirely Pagan in style. On the top are the portraits of a husband and bride in a wreath supported by Cupids. On the front is embossed the Toilet of Venus and a lady seated between handmaids who bring to her articles of the toilet. At the ends are nereids; and the smaller spaces are filled by peacocks, doves, and baskets of fruit. The most interesting subject is that on the back, where the bride is being led to her new home, a house of two stories covered above by several domes. The inscription, which is in letters pricked on the plain border, is the only Christian thing about the work, and it is possible, as in the case of some of the sarcophagi with Pagan subjects, that it was shop work, and that the inscription was added for the purchaser. There are many indications that it was made in Alexandria.

CH. XXI.

We have in our English museums a remarkably fine collection of Early Christian Ivories. At South Kensington there is a leaf of a famous diptych, inscribed *Symmachorum*, the companion of which in Paris is inscribed *Nicomachorum*; it is not itself Christian, but it can be associated with other works which are, and it can be accurately dated as of the end of the fourth century. It is of extraordinary beauty both of design and workmanship, and is the most perfect existing example of marriage diptychs. It was made on the occasion of the marriage of Nicomachus Flavianus with the daughter of Quintus Aurelius Symmachus, consul in A.D: 391, or another marriage between the same families in 401.

Now there is an ivory in the Trivulzio Collection at Milan, sculptured with a representation of the Holy Sepulchre and watching soldiers, on which some of the details are identical with the one just spoken of — and a third diptych of the same class, having exactly similar details, and inscribed with the name of Rufinus Probianus is now at Berlin. They are all so much alike in style that it would seem that they must come from one shop and may even be the work of the same hand.

At the British Museum there are some pieces which formed the sides of a casket which are sculptured with scenes from the Passion. Some of the subjects have so much in common with the other ivories just discussed that they may be assigned to the same school. On these panels are represented Pilate washing his hands, St Peter's Denial, Christ bearing the Cross, the Crucifixion, Judas hanged, the Women at the Sepulchre, the incredulity of St Thomas. Pilate washing his hands is a fine classical composition which may be compared with the same subject on the Brescia coffer, which also has the Denial of St Peter, and the Death of Judas. This coffer is acknowledged to be early fourth century work, which is further confirmed by the fact that on the sarcophagus of Junius Bassus the subject of Pilate washing his hands is treated in a similar manner. The Brescia coffer has often been called the most beautiful of Christian Ivories. It has been pointed out that the cycle of subjects from the Passion represented upon it stops before the Crucifixion, and it has been held that this omission was a matter of principle, but the London series, and other still earlier treatments of the Crucifixion which are now known, contradict this view. The Holy Sepulchre as it appears on the British Museum fragments is identical with that on the Trivulzio tablet before mentioned, and the curious costume of the watching soldiers is alike in both. In both the doors of the tomb are burst open, and in both, on the panels of the doors, is carved the raising of Lazarus.

These British Museum panels have been assigned by the Museum authorities to the fifth century, but there can be little doubt that they should be classed with the other fourth century works they so closely resemble. They are distinctly earlier in style than the carved doors of Santa Sabina in Rome which are usually dated about 425.

There are other points which go to shew that these Ivories were wrought in Rome, although possibly by a school of Eastern ivory-carvers. A domed building practically identical with the upper part of the Holy Sepulchre on the British Museum Ivory is found on a fourth century Roman sarcophagus now in the Lateran. While the Trivulzio tablet has the symbols of the four evangelists appearing in the sky, which are remarkably similar to the same symbols in the apse mosaic of Santa Pudentiana, wrought about 390, these symbols hardly appear in Byzantine work, but they do in Egyptian wall-paintings. Another casket at the Museum which is carved with the stories of St Peter and St Paul has much in common with the one last described. Moses striking the Rock seems at first an intrusion amongst these subjects, but it was in fact a favourite Early Christian type of the Gospel, and is frequently found in the catacombs; Christ is the Rock, St Peter is the Moses of the New Law, and the water is that of Baptism. In some cases, indeed, the name of Peter is written over what appears to be the figure of Moses. This treatment occurs again engraved on the glass vessel from Cologne in the Museum. At South Kensington are sides of a casket sculptured with scenes from the Life of Christ, and known as the Werdan casket. The subjects comprise the Annunciation, the Angel appearing to Joseph, the Visitation, the Presentation of the Virgin, the three Shepherds, the Nativity, the Magi, men going out of Jerusalem toward the Jordan, the axe laid to the root of the tree, the Baptism. The Annunciation is represented after a form which appears in the Apocryphal Gospel of St Matthew, according to which the Virgin was drawing water at a fountain when the angel appeared. The Ox and Ass of the Nativity come from the same source, as also does the Presentation in the Temple. On this casket Christ at the Baptism is represented as small and youthful as compared to the Baptist. Mr Cecil Torr has founded on this the conjecture that an account different from that in the Gospels was followed, but it may be suggested that it came about through some stylistic formula like that of the old Egyptian monuments, whereby some persons might be bigger than others. (Compare three Ivories, 373–5, in Cabrol's Dictionary.) It is true that we should expect the Christ to be the dominating figure, but may it not in this instance be the Baptist's office which is magnified?

A famous ivory book-cover at Milan has subjects which resemble those of the Werdan casket so closely that they must have come from the same shop. Except for slight changes called for by the different spaces to be filled, the Nativity, the Wise Men, the Shepherds, and the Annunciation, the Presentation of the Virgin, and the Baptism, are all practically identical. There is also at the Bodleian an Ivory of the same school which contains a Baptism.

The Early Christian "Gilt Glasses" (*Fondi d' oro*) were shallow glass bowls and other vessels decorated with figures, inscriptions, etc., in gold

CH. XXI.

leaf, the detail drawing being made out by removing parts of the gold, and the whole fixed by a film of glass fused over the surface. The subjects shew that vessels so ornamented were used alike by Pagans, Jews, and Christians. They have been more particularly associated with the latter, as a large number of the decorated medallions which formed the bottoms of the glasses have been found in the catacombs, where they were stuck in the plaster, probably as one means of the identification of the *loculus*. In the fine collection at the British Museum is a medallion with a figure of the gladiator Stratonicus which, together with some others, is evidently of pagan origin, and one with the seven-branched candlestick and other ritual objects of the Temple is Jewish.

In the main the Gilt Glasses belong to the third and fourth centuries of our era. They were most popular from *c*. 300 to *c*. 350 and few were made after 400. The method of decoration seems to have originated in the glass-works of Egypt. Many of them are inscribed ΠIE-ZHCAIC which on others is found in the corrupt form PIE-ZESES. This suggests a Greek origin, and there is in the British Museum Christian Collection a fragment of a glass bowl found at Behnésa in Egypt in 1903 which bears part of the earlier form in large engraved letters. In the Slade Collection, in the Glass Room, there are two most beautiful basins with exquisitely refined classical decoration in gold. These it is said were "probably made in Alexandria in the first century, and the method of ornamentation by designs in gold foil enclosed between two thicknesses of glass is similar to that employed in the case of Early Christian Gilded Glasses." Probably the Christian, Jewish, and pagan vessels were sold together in the same shops. Amongst those at the British Museum, for instance, there is one with profile heads of St Peter and St Paul, and Christ between, crowning them. Another has a man and wife with a small figure of Christ offering them garlands, and the inscription "Long life to thee, sweet one." Similar pagan compositions shew a Cupid or a Hercules between the husband and bride. The Jewish glass with the golden candlestick also has the popular inscription "Long Life." The vessels were evidently made use of largely as memorial, anniversary, or wedding gifts, and some were specially made with personal inscriptions. Volpel; in his thorough study of these objects, has shewn that where the names of two saints occur on one piece, the names also come together in the Calendar, as St Agnes and St Vincent of Zaragoza (21 and 22 January). This goes to confirm the view that they were prepared for special festivals.

In the British Museum there are also fragments of a larger glass dish, or paten, decorated with small medallions of such gilded glass which were made apart and fused into it. Glass patens were used in the Office of the Mass during the fourth century. At South Kensington Museum one little medallion, of Christ with the wand of power, is a replica of one of those on the British Museum paten. With the latter may be mentioned two beautiful plain blue glass chalices in the Slade Collection. The Biblical subjects which appear on the Gilt Glasses resemble for the most part those popular in the catacombs: Adam and Eve, Jonah and the Whale, Daniel, and so on. Some of the fragments at the British Museum may be restored by a comparison with other objects. One interesting piece which shews two columns with a lattice between the lower part, and a lamp hanging above, compared with a figure in Pérate's Manual is seen to have been, when complete, a deceased person in the attitude of prayer before the heavenly sanctuary. The inscription, IN DEO, confirms this view. No. 615, which shews the golden candlestick in the lower half, the upper being lost, must have had the Ark and the Cherubim in the upper part like another figured by Garrucci. None of these Gilt Glasses are known to have ever been found in Britain, but fragments of engraved glass, almost certainly Christian, were found at Silchester. The fashion for engraved glasses seems to have followed that for those decorated in gold. Cologne was an important centre for the production of this glass. The paten above mentioned, and another ornate Gilt Glass, were found there. So also was the cup with engraved subjects, no. 625, in our national museum; and others like it are preserved at Cologne.

The small terra-cotta lamps decorated with a cross, monogram, dove, vine, or other symbol, can here be only mentioned. But a small shallow bowl of glazed ware in the British Museum must be referred to as one of the most important of Early Christian works of art. On it appears Christ having a cruciform nimbus, and the face bearded, the earliest example of the kind, which may be compared with heads of the more youthful type on some of the Gilt Glasses in the same gallery. On the bowl there are heads also of Constantine and Fausta on either hand of the chief figure; they are named in an inscription around the rim and shew that it must have been made before the death of Fausta in 326. Following the analogy of the Gilt Glasses where a figure of Christ is placed between the portraits of a husband and wife, may we not suppose that this vessel was made for Constantine himself? Recently Wilpert has argued against its authenticity, but Strzygowski, who formerly doubted, is now entirely convinced. It is generally agreed that it was of Egyptian origin. Most of the objects preserved in our museums shew how freely the Early Christians of the time following the Peace of the Church made use of various materials in ornamental art. A bishop, indeed, complained that the weavers rivalled painters in representing animals, flowers, and figures on their stuffs. Of late years great stores of early textiles have been found wonderfully preserved under the sands of Egypt, and a fine collection has been brought together at South Kensington. Some of the earliest figured linens seem to have been printed. Two of these, at the Museum, are of the Annunciation, and

CH. XXI.

another shews some scenes from the miracles of Christ, and also Moses receiving the Law. These stained linen clothes were sometimes figured with pagan subjects. On the staircase of the Egyptian section at the Louvre there has recently been exhibited an important piece on which is depicted the story of Dionysos. In this classical piece we have the same charàcteristics of style: big eyes, flowing draperies, inscriptions associated with the figures and even the large nimbuses.

We must now turn from these smaller objects to the beginnings of Christian architecture. The first meeting-places of Christians were the private houses where they came together for the breaking of bread. In the Recognitions of Clement (second century) it is told that while St Peter was at Antioch, Theophilus, a leading citizen, turned his house into a basilica, that is, a place of assembly. Some of the early acts of the martyrs tell how they left their houses to the Church, and so it came about that certain churches were associated with the names of their founders, as the churches of Clement, Pudens, and Cecilia in Rome.

Basilica was a word in very general use, very much like our word Hall, and there is no direct relation between the basilicas of justice and Christian churches. More true it is that the greater private houses had *triclinia* and halls which were themselves called basilicas, and it is probable that these were actually used for assemblies of Christians. It is possible, further, that there may be some sympathetic relation between the developed church plan and the basilica of justice, for the scene of the Heavenly Temple in the Apocalypse appears to be cast into the form of such a basilica.

The origins of church fabrics have been worked out in great detail in regard to the possible prototypes found in private dwellings, but so far as architectural arrangement goes it is looking for elaborate explanation where but little is required. The "basilican" type was the appropriate and popular plan for any place of meeting. It is found in temples as those of Apollo at Gortyna, which had an apse and internal pillars. In the isle of Samothrace was the temple of the Cabiri; this was of rectangular plan, it had a portico with an *atrium*, the interior was divided into three aisles and at the end was a semicircular niche. In Rome itself the temples of Venus and Rome are of the same form except that there is no subdivision of their interiors, and they were surrounded entirely by the enclosure instead of having an *atrium*. The temple at Jerusalem and many Hellenistic temples were in the same way isolated in a court surrounded by a colonnade. Several of the Christian churches built after the Peace of the Church were also surrounded by similar colonnaded courts entered through an outer portico. Orientation certainly derives from temple arrangement, and many of the earliest churches were built with their entrances facing the East, as was Herod's temple. Again, the foundations of several synagogues which have been discovered shew a division of the interior into three or five aisles with three entrance doors in the façade. A description of. the synagogue at Alexandria calls it a basilica, and speaks of its colonnades; it probably had an apse as well.

The earliest special places of assembly were the holy sites and the burial chapels of the martyrs. The subterranean chapels in the cata- combs, already mentioned, belong to this class. Probably the first specifically Christian buildings were Martyria — tomb chambers, usually round, which were practically memorial churches. During the course of the third century a large number of churches were built in Syria, Asia Minor, Armenia, and North Africa. An ancient church at Edessa is said on good authority to have existed before 201; but Edessa was then a Christian city. A document of 303 mentions "the house where the Christians assemble," together with its library and *triclinium*, at Cirta in North Africa. And another document of 305 says that, as the "basilicas" had not been repaired, the bishops met in a private house. An episcopal election, however, was held in *area martyrum in casa majore*.

An inscription from the tomb of Bishop Eugenius of Laodicea Combusta has lately been published. He held the see immediately after the cessation of Diocletian's persecution and speaks of *re*-building the whole of his church from its foundations, together with the colon- naded court which surrounded it. Eusebius speaks of such rebuilding as general, but says that the new churches were larger and more splendid than those that had been destroyed. Of the churches built after the imperial adoption of Christianity only a few of the most famous can be mentioned here. In and near Jerusalem three churches were built in association with the sacred sites of the Holy Sepulchre, the Nativity, and the Ascension. All three are mentioned in 333 as basilicas by a pilgrim from Bordeaux. At the Holy Sepulchre there was a memorial above the tomb called the Anastasis; and a basilica called the Great Church, or Martyrium, both included in a precinct called New Jerusalem. According to Eusebius Constantine first adorned the sacred cave, the chief point of the whole, with choice columns and other works. The Great Church rose high within a large court surrounded by porticoes. It was lined within with marble, the ceiling was carved and gilt woodwork, the roof was covered with lead. The body of the church was divided by rows of columns into five aisles. It was entered from the east by three doors; and opposite to these, continues Eusebius, was the Hemisphere, the crown of the whole work, containing twelve columns bearing bowls of silver (probably lamps). This "Hemisphere" would seem to be the dome-building over the tomb, which first was spoken of as the chief point of the whole. That the anastasis and basilica were separate buildings is made clear by the account of Etheria (formerly known as St Sylvia) who, about 380, described the sacred sites. The churches at Bethlehem and the Mount of Olives were, says Eusebius, built over two sacred caves, one church at the scene of the Saviour's birth, the second on the mountain top in memory of His ascension; these two beautiful edifices were dedicated at the two holy caves. At Bethlehem a noble basilican church still exists which many hold to be the original edifice, although there is some conflicting evidence that it was either rebuilt or repaired by Justinian. It is 180 feet long, by 85 feet wide. The head of the church over the grotto of the Nativity is cruciform, and the nave is divided into five aisles. The columns are marble with Corinthian capitals having crosses upon their abaci. The walls above are carried by level beams instead of arches. To the west was an extensive *atrium*. A point in favour of the antiquity of this great church is that the historian Socrates says that the church at the grotto of the Nativity was not inferior to that of the New Jerusalem. Constantine's church on the Mount of Olives is generally understood to be the circular edifice which is known from later descriptions and which occupied the site of the present church. The pilgrim Etheria, however, says that the church was at Eleona, "on the Mount from which the Lord ascended, and in which church is that cave (*spelunca*) in which the Lord taught the apostles." From thence pilgrims ascended with hymns to the Imbomon, the actual place from which the Lord ascended. Now Eusebius, although he speaks of the church as on the summit, says that in it was the cave where Christ taught His disciples the sacred mysteries. St Eucharius, a later pilgrim, about 440, says that there were upon the Mount of Olives *two* celebrated churches, one where Christ taught, and the other on the site of the Ascension. The cave site is known to be below the summit, and remains of buildings have been found there. From this it seems that Constantine built a church at the cave, and probably a memorial on the summit. He also built large churches as martyr memorials at Constantinople, where that of the Apostles is described as high, covered with marble, and adorned with gilding, and situated in a court having porticoes all round and chambers opening from them. It was completed about 337. As rebuilt by Justinian it was a pronounced cross, and there seems to be no doubt that it had this form from the first. Gregory of Nazianzus speaks of the earlier building as "the splendid Church of the Apostles divided in the four parts of the arms of a cross." The account of Eusebius, that it was very high and was covered above with gilded brass which reflected the sun to a distance, suggests a dome or a tower at the crossing. That this church was cruciform in shape is confirmed by the fact that the church of the Apostles built by St Ambrose in 382 at Milan was also a cross. It has been rebuilt and is now St Nazario Grande, but it is still cruciform. An existing building which may represent the whole series is the little church of SS. Nazario and Celso, the Mausoleum of Galla Placidia at Ravenna, which has four equal arms and a tower in the midst. At Antioch Constantine rebuilt the metropolitan church, which Eusebius describes as unique in size and beauty, and built in the form of an octagon. It was very high and decorated with a profusion of gold so that it came to be called the golden church. Around it was an enclosure of great extent.` The great church of Tyre was also built within a large walled enclosure (*peribolos*), having a great fore-gate (*propylon*) toward the east. Within the *atrium* was a fountain, and the church was entered through three doors, the centre one of bronze. The pavement was marble, and it was roofed with cedar. The interior was divided into aisles by rows of columns (*stoai*), the altar-place (*thusiasterion*) was screened by lattice-work.

Other churches were erected at Nicomedia and at Mamre. The former is described as great and splendid. Such, says Eusebius, were the most noble of the sacred buildings erected by the Emperor. He only refers to those at the Holy Sites, at the Emperor's "own city" of Nicomedia, and in the city "which was called after his own name." He does not mention even his own metropolitan church of Caesarea, nor does he mention the churches in Rome, much less those that arose by hundreds all over the Empire. One of these is that of Bishop Eugenius, referred to above, and further evidence as to them is frequently being brought to light. Wiegand has lately uncovered the foundations of an early church at Miletus which may be of Constantine's time.

The Bishop of Rome built the great basilica of St Peter over the tomb of the apostle. The interior had five avenues between colonnades crossed at the end by a transept from which opened the apse raised high above the crypt which contained the apostle's tomb. Screening the apse were twelve most beautiful columns of spiral form carved on the surface with *amorini* climbing amidst vines. In front of the entrances, which were at the east, was the fine *atrium* with a fountain in the centre. The outer gates and the façade, as well as the apse and the triumphal arch of the interior, were subsequently adorned with mosaics. The church of St Paul outside the walls was also of the Constantinian age; but the first church was not of the great scale of that one which still exists in a restored condition to-day. Its foundations were exposed in 1835. It was so small that the length of the church was almost exactly the same as the width of the present transept. It had its entrances towards the east and the *atrium* abutted on the Ostia road. When the great basilica was built later its orientation was reversed, but its altar, as is usually the case, yet stands over the site of the older one.

There are still three buildings in Rome which date from this early period; the Lateran Baptistery, the basilica of Santa Agnese, and the attached tomb-church of Santa Costanza. Santa Agnese is a most beautiful type of church having arcaded galleries within, around the two sides and the end opposite the apse. It is sunk into the ground to the level of the catacombs in which the saint was buried, and these are entered from a door in the side-wall, the descent into the church being by a long flight

CH. XXI.

of steps. The church is nine bays long, and the columns are of marble. The apse is lined with marble and porphyry, and in the midst is the bishop's throne. Above, in the conch, is a fine mosaic, but not so ancient. Close by, but at the higher level of the natural ground, stands Santa Costanza, built about 354. It is circular, with an inner ring of columns which supported a dome. The diameter is about 76 feet, and the columns are only about 18 feet high. They are mostly of grey granite. The walls were sheeted with marble and the annular aisle has its vaults covered with mosaic, chiefly of pattern-work, but in some places there are vintage scenes with *amorini* gathering the grapes and making wine.

The most splendid feature of the early churches was the mosaic work which from the Constantinian age adorned their vaults and especially the conches of their apses. Such mosaics were generally formed of small cubes of glass variously coloured and gilded. At the same time mosaics of marble of the more ordinary Roman kind were used for floors. The glass mosaics and even gilt *tesserae* had been employed under the Roman Empire. Glass is found so far West as Cirencester, where small parts of a floor are of that material. Gold mosaic has been found on the vaults of the Baths of Caracalla and of the Palatine Palace; also in North Africa. Quite recently a mosaic having gilt cubes has been found at Pompeii. It is next to certain that, like the vessels of gilded glass, this kind of mosaic came from the factories of Egypt. There is in the British Museum a small glass plaque, decorated with a flowering plant of several colours fused into its substance. This was found in London, while similar pieces, now at South Kensington, have lately been discovered at Behnésa in Egypt. The earliest existing Christian mosaics are those of the vaults of the round church of Santa Costanza in Rome. Besides the mosaics mentioned above there are two small, much injured, conches which display figure subjects. In one of them God the Father gives the ancient Law to Moses, and in the other St Peter receives the new Law from the hand of Christ. The whole of the central dome was once covered with mosaic, but of this only a slight drawing is now preserved.

The next mosaic in point of date, but more interesting and beautiful as a work of art, fills the apse of the basilica of Santa Pudentiana. This church, not far from the better known Santa Maria Maggiore, is deeply sunk in the ground, itself a mark of a primitive foundation. The apse mosaic forms part of a work undertaken about 390. On it Christ sits enthroned in the midst of a semicircle of apostles, while behind St Peter and St Paul stand two female figures robed in white and holding crowns; these are interpreted as the Churches of the Circumcision and of the Gentiles. Behind Christ on a mountain stands a vast jewelled cross, and on the sky are the four symbolic beasts. This noble work still retains much of classical grace, the fixity characteristic of Byzantine art is entirely absent. The colour, also, is fair and extremely beautiful, gold being used to illuminate the high lights of the draperies and other parts, but not in broad fields as in the later mosaics.

It is desirable to include here some account of Early Christian art in Britain. The discovery, about twelve years ago, of the perfect plan of a small early basilican church at Silchester makes more certain than anything else had done the existence of recognised Christian communities in British cities. The Silchester church occupied an important position near the civil basilica, but in itself was quite small. It had a nave about ten feet wide and aisles five feet; the length, including the apse, which was at the west end, was about thirty feet. The aisles had a small additional projection at the end next the apse, which made the whole plan cruciform. At the east end was a narthex, and in front of that a court with a fountain in the centre. The position of the altar in the apse was marked by a square of pattern-work in the mosaic floor. This pattern, of the chess-board type, is in quarters, what heralds call *quarterly*. A very accurate model of this important relic is now in the Reading Museum.

It is well known that the XP monogram appeared on a mosaic floor found about a century ago at Frampton, and figured by Lysons. The monogram occurred in the centre of a band of ornament which separated an apse from a square compartment. Lysons thought that the general style of the ornaments of the apse seemed "inferior to that of the square part," and spoke of the monogram as "inserted." The last writer on Christian antiquities in Britain, in Cabrol's great Dictionary, says that the monogram must have been "inserted" at some time not earlier than the middle of the fourth century. Lysons tried to suggest, being interested in the Roman art point of view, that the pavement was pre-Constantinian, but he himself remarked that the pattern on a neighbouring area occurred also on the vault mosaics of Santa Costanza at Rome, a work of the second half of the fourth century. This is, probably, the date of the whole of the Frampton mosaics, and a consideration of the sequence of the turns of the scroll ornament in the middle of which the monogram was found shews that the scroll-work and the symbol certainly formed part of one design. The only other subject figured on the floor of the apse, excepting patterns, was a single vase or chalice in the middle. At the Roman villa at Chedworth again the XP monogram has been found cut in the foundation stones of some steps. In the museum on the site there is also a small plain stone cross.

Mr Romilly Allen suggested that "two other Roman pavements found in this country may possibly be Christian"; — that at Harpole which has a circle in the middle divided into eight parts by radial lines so as to resemble one form of the monogram of Christ, and that at Horkstow which has "some small red crosses in the decoration." The latter not only has the crosses, but at the centre is Orpheus playing

CH. XXI.

the lyre, a subject frequently found in Early Christian art. The writer in Cabrol's Dictionary has independently come to the conclusion that this mosaic is Christian. "It has passed unrecognised," he says, "but we have no doubt of its Christian origin." Now, if this mosaic with the catacomb subject of Orpheus and the beasts is Christian, is it not probable that the several other British mosaics which display the same subject are also works of Christian art? All these mosaics probably date from about 350, when the Church must have been a recognised institution in every city, and it is difficult to think that the subject, once Christianised, should have been employed in another sense. An Orpheus pavement was found at Littlecote Park, Ramsbury, at the centre of a triapsidal apartment resembling the Roman Christian burial chapels. Yet another pavement, at Stourton, had a quartered design practically identical with that of the altar space of the Silchester basilica.[1] The subject of Orpheus is known to have occurred four times in the catacombs, but none of these appear to have been later than the third century, and it has indeed been suggested that the subject was taken over in profane art, especially in Gaul and Britain, but this is unproven, and in any case we get the Christian influence. Several British pavements are known in which ornamental cross-forms appear. It has been said that these cannot be Christian, as the cross symbol did not come into general use at so early a time. But the many instances which have now been found contradicting this view reopen the question. With those Roman objects having crosses which have been found in England may be mentioned the chain-bracelet with an attached cross. A comparison with fig. 1606 in Cabrol's Dictionary makes it almost certain that it is Christian. Perhaps the most important Christian documents found in Britain are ingots of pewter found in the Thames at Battersea which are stamped several times over with the XP monogram surrounded by the words, *Spes in Deo*. These look like official marks.

When a full history of Early Christian art in Britain is written it will be seen that it shared in the great movement of the time, although of course it was second to Gaul and third to Italy.

---

[1] In a panel occurred the design of two beasts drinking from a vase, a motive which also appears on the enamelled plate found in London. A similar group of two peacocks drinking formed part of the Orpheus pavement at Withington.

BIBLIOGRAPHIES

ABBREVIATIONS

The following abbreviations are used:

AARAB.	Annales de l'Académie royale d'archéologie de Belgique. Antwerp.
AB.	Analecta Bollandiana. Brussels.
ABe.	Archives belges. Liège.
AHR.	American Historical Review. New York and London.
AKKR.	Archiv für katholisches Kirchenrecht. Mainz.
AM.	Annales du Midi. Toulouse.
AMur.	Archivio Muratoriano. Rome.
ASAK.	Anzeiger für schweizerische Alterthumskunde. Zurich.
ASBoll.	Acta Sanctorum Bollandiana. Brussels. 1643–1894. 60 vols.
ASHF.	Annuaire-Bulletin de la Société de l'histoire de France. Paris.
ASI.	Archivio storico italiano. Florence.
ASL.	Archivio storico Lombardo. Milan.
ASRSP.	Archivio della Società romana di storia patria. Rome.
BCRH.	Bulletins de la Commission royale d'histoire. Brussels.
BEC.	Bibliothèque de l'École des Chartres.
BHisp.	Bulletin hispanique. Bordeaux.
BRAH.	Boletin de la R. Academia de la historia. Madrid.
BZ.	Byzantinische Zeitschrift. Leipsic.
CQR.	Church Quarterly Review. London.
CR.	Classical Review. London.
CRSA.	Comptes rendus des séances de l'Académie des inscriptions et belles-lettres. Paris.
CSEL.	Corpus scriptorum ecclesiasticorum latinorum. Vienna. 1866, in prog.
CSHB.	Corpus scriptorum historiae Byzantinae. Bonn. 1828–97.
DCB.	Dictionary of Christian Biography. Smith, W., and Wace, H. London. 1877–87. 4 vols.
DZKR.	Deutsche Zeitschrift für Kirchenrecht. Leipsic.
EHR.	English Historical Review. London.
HJ.	Historisches Jahrbuch. Munich.
Hm.	Hermes. Berlin.
HVJS.	Historische Vierteljahrsschrift. Leipsic.
HZ.	Historische Zeitschrift (von Sybel). Munich.
JA.	Journal Asiatique. Paris.
JB.	Jahresberichte der Geschichtswissenschaft im Auftrage der historischen Gesellschaft zu Berlin, 1878 ff. Berlin.
JSG.	Jahrbuch für schweizerische Geschichte. Zurich.
JTS.	Journal of Theological Studies. London.
MA.	Le moyen âge. Paris.
MGH.	Monumenta Germaniae Historica. Berlin. Pertz, G. H. 1902, in progress.
MIOGF.	Mittheilungen des Instituts für österreichische Geschichtsforschung. Innsbruck.

MPG.	Migne, J. P. Patrologiae cursus completus. Series graeca. Paris. 1857.
MPL.	Migne, J. P. Patrologiae cursus completus. Series latina.
NAGDG.	Neues Archiv der Gesellschaft für ältere deutsche Geschichtskunde. Hanover.
QFIA.	Quellen und Forschungen aus italianischen Archiven und Bibliotheken. Rome.
RA.	Revue archéologique. Paris.
RBAB	Revue des bibliothèques et des archives de la Belgique. Brussels.
RBén.	Revue bénédictine. Maredsous.
RCel.	Revue celtique. Paris.
RCHL.	Revue critique d'histoire et de littérature. Paris.
RE³	Real-Encyklopädie für protestantische Theologie und Kirche. Herzog and Hauck. Leipsic.
RH.	Revue historique. Paris.
RHD.	Revue d'histoire diplomatique. Paris.
RHE.	Revue d'histoire ecclésiastique. Louvain.
RN.	Revue de numismatique. Paris.
ROC.	Revue de l'Orient chrétien. Paris.
RQCA.	Römische Quartalschrift für christliche Altertumskunde und Kirchen geschichte. Rome.
RQH.	Revue des questions historiques. Paris.
RSH.	Revue de synthèse historique. Paris.
RSI.	Rivista storica italiana. Turin.
RSS.	Rivista di scienze storiche. Pavia.
SPAW.	Sitzungsberichte der k. preussischen Akademie der Wissenschaften. Berlin.
TQS.	Theologische Quartalschrift. Tübingen.
TRHS.	Transactions of the Royal Historical Society. London.
TSK.	Theologische Studien und Kritiken. Gotha.
VV.	Vizantiiskii Vremenik. St Petersburg.
ZCK.	Zeitschrift für christliche Kunst. Düsseldorf.
ZKG.	Zeitschrift für Kirchengeschichte. Gotha.
ZKT.	Zeitschrift für katholische Theologie. Gotha.
ZWT.	Zeitschrift für wissenschaftliche Theologie. Frankfurt-a.-M.

In the case of many other works given in the General Bibliography abbreviations as stated there are used.

GENERAL BIBLIOGRAPHY FOR VOLUME I

I. DICTIONARIES, BIBLIOGRAPHIES AND GENERAL WORKS OF REFERENCE

Bardenhewer, D. Patrologie. Freiburg-i.-B. 1894. Translated by Shahan, T. J. Freiburg-i.-B. and St Louis, Minnesota. 1908.

Biographie universelle, ancienne et moderne. (Michaud.) Paris. 1854–65. 45 vols. [Greatly improved edn. of earlier work, 1811–28, and supplement, 1832–62.] (B. univ.)

Cabrol, F. Dictionnaire de l'archéologie chrétienne et de la Liturgie. Paris. 1901. 2nd edn., 1907, in progress.

Ceillier, R. Histoire générale des auteurs sacrés et ecclésiastiques. 2nd edn. 14 vols. in 15. Paris. 1858–69.

Chevalier, C. U. J. Répertoire des sources historiques du moyen âge. Bio-bibliographie. Paris. 1883–8. Topo-bibliographie. Montbéliard. 1894–1903. Rev. edn. of Bio-bibliographie, 1905–7.

Du Cange, C. du Fresne. Glossarium mediae et infimae Latinitatis. Edns. of Henschel, 7 vols., Paris, 1840–50, and Favre, 10 vols., Niort, 1883–7.

Encyclopædia Britannica. 9th edn. London. 1885–9. Additional vols. (10th edn.) 1902–3. 11th edn. Cambridge. 1911. (Enc. Br.)

Ersch, J. S., and Gruber, J. G. Allegemeine Encyklopädie der Wissenschaften und Künste. Berlin. 1818–50. (Ersch-Gruber.) (Incomplete.)

Fabricius, J. A. Bibliotheca Graeca sive Notitia Scriptorum Veterum Graecorum. 4th edn. Ed. Harles, G. C. 12 vols. Hamburg. 1790–1809. Index. Leipsic. 1837.

Grässe, J. G. T. Lehrbuch einer allgemeinen Litterärgeschichte aller bekannten Völker der Welt von der ältesten bis auf neueste Zeit. Leipsic. 1837–59. (Vols. I, II. Ancient and Medieval Peoples.)

Hastings, Jas. Encyclopaedia of Religion and Ethics. London. 1908, in progress.

Herzog, J. J. and Hauck, A. Real-Encyklopädie für protestantische Theologie und Kirche. Gotha. 1896–1909. (RE³.)

Herre, P. (Hofmeister, A. and Stübe, R.) Quellenkunde zur Weltgeschichte. Leipsic. 1910.

Lichtenberger, Frédéric. Encyclopédie des Sciences religieuses. 13 vols. Paris. 1877–82.

Lorenz, O. Genealogischer Hand-und Schul-Atlas. 3rd edn. Devrient, E. Stuttgart and Berlin. 1908.

Nouvelle Biographie générale, depuis les temps les plus reculés jusqu'à nos jours, avec les renseignements bibliographiques. Sous la direction de J. Ch. F. Höfer. Paris. 1854–66. 46 vols. in 23. (B. Gén.)

Oudin, Casimir. Commentarius de scriptoribus ecclesiae antiquae illorumque scriptis tam impressis quam manuscriptis adhuc extantibus in celebrioribus Europae Bibliothecis a Bellarmino etc. omissis ad annum MCCCCLX. Frankfurt-a.-M. 1722.
Pauly, A. F. von. Real-Encyklopädie der klassischen Alterthumswissenschaft. Vienna. 1837–52. Ed. Wissowa, G. Stuttgart. 1894–1903. New edn. 1904, in progress. (Pauly-Wissowa.)
Potthast, August. Bibliotheca historica medii aevi. Wegweiser durch die Geschichtswerke des Europäischen Mittelalters bis 1500. Berlin. 2nd edn. 2 vols. 1896.
Smith, Wm. and Cheetham, S. Dictionary of Christian Antiquities. 2 vols. London. 1875–80. (DCA.)
Smith, Wm. and Wace, Hy. Dictionary of Christian Biography, Literature, Sects and Doctrines. 4 vols. London. 1877–87. (DCB.)
Vacant, A. Dictionnaire de la Théologie. Paris. 1901 ff.
Wetzer, H. J. and Welte, B. Kirchenlexikon oder Encyklopädie der katholischen Theologie. Freiburg-i.-B. 1847–60. 2nd edn. Kaulen, F. 1882–1901. (Wetzer-Kaulen.) French transl. Goschler, J. 26 vols. 1869.

II. ATLASES AND GEOGRAPHY

Droysen, G. Allgemeiner historischer Handatlas. Bielefeld. 1886.
Freeman, E. A. Historical Geography of Europe (with Atlas). London. 1881. 3rd edn. revised and ed. Bury, J. B., 1903.
Kiepert, H. Atlas Antiquus. 1894 ff. and other edns.
Poole, R. L. (ed.). Historical Atlas of Modern Europe. Oxford. 1902.
Saint-Martin. Nouveau dictionnaire de Géographie Universelle. 7 vols. Paris. 1879–95. Supplement by Rousselet, L. 2 vols. 1895–7. (Contains short bibliographies.)
Schrader, F. Atlas de géographie historique. Paris. New edn. 1907.
Spruner-Menke. Hand-Atlas für die Geschichte des Mittelalters und der neueren Zeit. Gotha. 1880. (3rd edn. of Spruner's Hand-Atlas etc. Ed. by Menke, Th.)

(For place-names : —)

Bischoff, H. T. and Möller, J. H. Vergleichendes Wörterbuch der alten, mittleren und neuen Geographie. Gotha. 1892.
Brunet, J. C. Manuel du Libraire et de l'amateur de livres — Supplément (by Deschamps). Paris. 1870.
Grässe, J. G. T. Orbis Latinus. Dresden. 1861. Ed. Benedict, F. Berlin. 1909. (Vol. ı only.)
Martin, C. T. The Record Interpreter. London. 1892. 2nd edn., 1910 (for British Isles).

III. CHRONOLOGY

Clinton, H. F. Fasti Hellenici. 3 vols. Oxford. 1827–34.
—— Fasti Romani. 2 vols. Oxford. 1845–50. (Clinton, F. R.)
Gams, P. B. Series episcoporum ecclesiae Catholicae (with supplement). Ratisbon. 1873, 1886.

Ginzel, F. K. Handbuch der mathematischen und technischen Chronologie. Vol. I. Leipsic. 1906.

—— Spezieller Kanon der Sonnen und Mondfinsternisse für das Landgebiet der klassischen Altertumswissenschaften und den Zeitraum v. 900 vor Chr. bis 600 nach Chr. [18 charts.] Berlin. 1899.

Goyau, G., ed. Cagnat, R. Chronologie de L'empire romain. Paris. 1891. [Excellent handbook up to A.D. 395.]

Grotefend, H. Taschenbuch der Zeitrechnung des deutschen Mittelalters und der Neuzeit. 3rd enlarged edn. Hanover. 1910.

—— Zeitrechnung des deutschen Mittelalters und d. Neuzeit. 2 vols. Hanover 1891-8.

Ideler, C. L. Handbuch der mathematischen und technischen Chronologie. 2 vols. Berlin. 1825. New edn. Breslau. 1883.

L'Art de vérifier les dates et les faits historiques. 2e partie. Depuis la naiss. de J.-C. 3rd edn. Paris. 3 vols. 1783 ff., and other edns. and reprints. Also 4th edn. by Saint-Allais. 1818-19. 18 vols. (Art. de v.)

Mas Latrie, J. M. J. L. de. Trésor de chronologie, d'histoire et de géographie pour l'étude des documents du moyen âge. Paris. 1889.

Nicolas, Sir H. N. The Chronology of History. London. Best edn. 1838.

Ritter, Carl. Geographisch-Statistisches Lexicon. 2 vols. Leipsic. 1894-5.

Schram, R. Hilfstafeln für Chronologie. Vienna. 1883. New edn. Kalendariographische und chronologische Tafeln. Leipsic. 1908.

Wislicenus, W. F. Astronomische Chronologie. Leipsic. 1895.

Bernheim, Ernst. Lehrbuch der historischen Methode und der Geschichtsphilosophie. Leipsic. (5th and 6th enlarged edn.) 1908. Pp. 312-15.

Grotefend, H. Chronologie *in* vol. I, pp. 267 ff. of Meister, Aloys. Grundriss der Geschichtswissenschaft zur Einführung in das Studium der deutschen Geschichte des Mittelalters und der Neuzeit. Vol. I (1). Leipsic. 1906. Vol. I (2) and II (3). 1907, in progress. (Meister.)

(NUMISMATICS : —)

Cohen, H. (contin. Feuardent). Descriptions des Monnaies frappées sous l'Empire romain communément appelées Médailles impériales. 8 vols. 2nd edn. Paris. 1880-92.

Eckhel, J. H. von. Doctrina Numerorum Veterum. 8 vols. Vienna. 1792-8.

Head, B. F. Corolla Numismatica. London. 1906.

Keary, C. F. Coinages of Western Europe, Honorius to Charles the Great. London. 1879. 3rd edn. 1894.

Maurice, J. Numismatique Constantinienne. Iconographie et chronologie, description historique, etc. Vol. I. Paris. 1908, in progress. [Plates.]

Wroth, W. Catalogue of the Imperial Byzantine coins in the British Museum. 2 vols. London. 1908. [Plates.]

—— Catalogue of the coins of the Vandals, Ostrogoths, Lombards, etc. in the British Museum (in preparation).

IV. COLLECTIONS OF SOURCES

Acta Sanctorum Bollandiana. Brussels. 1643–1894. 60 vols. (ASBoll.)
Codex Theodosianus, Gothofred, J. Ed. Marvillius, A. and Ritter, I. D. 6 vols.
in 3. Leipsic. 1736–45. Ed. Mommsen, Th. and Meyer, P. M. Berlin.
1905.
Corpus Juris civilis. Ed. Beck, I. L. G. Leipsic. 1829–37. 2 vols. 3rd edn.
Berlin. 1877–95. 3 vols.
Corpus scriptorum ecclesiasticorum latinorum. Vienna, 1866, in progress. (CSEL.)
Corpus scriptorum Historiae Byzantinae. Bonn. 1828–97. (CSHB.)
Duchesne, L. Fastes épiscopaux de l'ancienne Gaule. Paris. 1894–, in progress.
Jaffé, Phil. Regesta pontificum Romanorum ab condita ecclesia ad annum post
Christum natum 1198. Berlin. 1851. 2nd edn. Wattenbach, W., Loewen-
feld, S., Kaltenbrunner, F., Ewald, P. Leipsic. 1885–8. 2 vols. Jaffé reg.)
Kehr, P. F. Regesta Pontificum Romanorum, in progress. Vol. I. Rome.
II. Latium. Berlin. 1906–7.
Liber Pontificalis. 3 vols. Rome. 1724–55. Ed. Duchesne, L. 2 vols. Paris.
(Bibl. des écoles d'Athènes et de Rome.) 1886–92. (LP.) Vol. 1 to 795.
Ed. Mommsen, Th. In MGH. 1898.
Mansi, J. D. Sacrorum conciliorum collectio. Florence and Venice. 1759–98.
31 vols. Reprint Martin, J. B. and Petit, L. Paris. 1901, in progress.
Migne, J. P. Patrologiae cursus completus. Series graeca. Paris. 1857–66.
161 vols, in 166. (MPG.)
—— Do. Series latina. 221 vols. Paris. 1844–55. Index, 4 vols. 1862–4.
(MPL.)
Molinier, A. Les Sources de l'histoire de France. 5 vols. Paris. 1901–6.
Monumenta Germaniae Historica. Ed. Pertz, G. H., Mommsen, Th. and others.
Berlin. 1826, in progress. (MGH.)
Müller, C. Fragmenta Historicorum Graecorum. 5 vols. Paris. 1841–83
(vol. v, ii, ed. Langlois, V.). (FHG.)
Muratori, L. A. Rerum Italicarum scriptores. Milan. 1723–51. Indices chronolog.
Turin. 1885. New edn. Carducci, G. and Fiorini, V. Città du Castello.
1900, in progress.
Rerum Gallicarum et Franciscarum scriptores. (Recueil des hist. des Gaules et de
la France.) 23 vols. 1738–1876. Ed. Bouquet, M. and contin. Recueil des
historiens de la France. 1899, in progress.
Turner, C. H. Ecclesiae Occidentalis monumenta juris antiq. Canonum et concil.
Graecorum interpret Latinae. Fasc. I, 1, 2; II, 1. Oxford. 1899–1907, in
progress.

Inscriptions : ——

Corpus Inscriptionum Graecarum. Ed. Böckh and others. Berlin. 1828–77.
(For Christian inscriptions cf. vol. IV, part 2, ed. Kirchhoff.) (CIG.)
Corpus Inscriptionum Latinarum. Ed. Mommsen and others. Berlin. 1862, in
progress. New edn. 1893, in progress. (CIL.)
Hübner, A. E. Exempla Scripturae epigraphicae Latinae a Caesaris morte ad aet.
Justiniani. Berlin. 1884.
Le Blant, E. de. L'épigraphie chrétienne en Gaule et dans l'Afrique romaine.
Paris. 1890.
—— Nouveau recueil des inscript. chrét. de la Gaule ant. au 8ᵉ siècle. (Coll. des
doc. inéd. sur l'hist. de France.) Paris. 1892.
Rossi, G. B. de. Inscriptiones Christianae urbis Romae VII° saeculo antiquiores.
Rome. 1857–88. (2 vols. only published.)

V. MODERN WORKS

Alzog, J. Universalgeschichte der Kirche. Mainz. 1841. Best edn. 10th by Kraus, F. X. 1882. Transl. (from 9th German edn.) Pabisch, F. J. and Byrne, T. S. Manual of Church History. 4 vols. Dublin. 1895–1900.

Bardenhewer. Patrologie (*see* I.).

Baronius, Cæs., Annales Ecclesiasticae una cum critica historica chronologica P. A. Pagii, contin. Raynaldus, O. Ed. Mansi, J. D. Lucca. 34 vols. 1738–46. Apparatus, 1 vol. Index, 4 vols. 1740, 1757–9.

Broglie, J. V. A. duc de. L'église et l'empire au ive siècle. 6 vols. Paris. 1856. And later edns.

Bury, J. B. A History of the later Roman Empire from Arcadius to Irene. (395 A.D. to 800 A.D.) 2 vols. London. 1889.

Dill, S. Roman Society in the last century of the Western Empire. London. 1898.

Döllinger, J. J. Ignatius von. Christenthum und Kirche in der Zeit der Grundlegung. Ratisbon, 1860. Transl. Oxenham, H. N. The first age of Christianity and the Church. 2 vols. London. 1866. 3rd edn. 1877.

—— Geschichte der christl. Kirche. Vol. i. Parts 1, 2 [to A.D. 630]. Landshut. 1833–5. (No more pubd.) Transl. Cox, E. History of the Church. 2 vols. London. 1840–2.

—— Lehrbuch der Kirchengeschichte. (i; ii, 1.) Ratisbon. (2nd improved edn.) 1834. [A shorter work.]

Duchesne, L. Histoire ancienne de l'Église. 3 vols. 2nd edn. Paris. 1906–7, and later edns. Transl. (vol. i) Early Hist. of the Christian Church, etc. from 4th edn. London. 1909.

—— Les Origines du Culte Chrétien. Paris. 1890. 3rd edn. 1903. 4th edn. 1910. Transl. London (from 4th edn.). 1910.

Duruy, V. Histoire des Romains depuis les temps les plus reculés jusqu'à l'invasion des barbares. 1870 ff. Transl. ed. Mahaffy, J. P. History of Rome and of the Roman people. London. 1883 ff.

Ebert, A. Allgemeine Geschichte der Litteratur des Mittelalters im Abendland. 3 vols. Leipsic. 1874–87. 2nd edn. of vols. i and ii. 1889.

Finlay, G. Ed. Tozer, H. F. History of Greece, B.C. 146 to A.D. 1864. 7 vols. Oxford. 1877.

Fleury, Claude. Histoire ecclésiastique. 20 vols. Paris. 1691–1720. Continued to end of 18th century under Vidal, O. Many editions. [Orig. edn. to 1414. 4 add. vols, by Fl. to 1517, pub. Paris, 1840.] Eng. transl. (to 456). 3 vols. Oxford. 1843–4.

Gibbon, Edward. The History of the Decline and Fall of the Roman Empire. 1776–81. Ed. in 7 vols, by Bury, J. B. 1896. Latest edn. 1909 ff. (Bury-Gibbon.) [Notes essential especially for chronology.]

Gieseler, J. C. L. Lehrbuch der Kirchengeschichte. Bonn. 3 vols. 1824 ff. and 6 vols. in 5, 1828–57. Transl. Davidson, S. 5 vols. Edinburgh, 1854, and Cunningham, Text-book of Ecclesiastical History. Philadelphia. 3 vols. 1836.

Glover, T. R. Life and Letters in the Fourth Century. Cambridge. 1901.

—— The Conflict of Religions in the Early Roman Empire. London. 1909.

Gregorovius, F. Geschichte der Stadt Rom im Mittelalter. 8 vols. Stuttgart. 1859–72. (Translated from 4th edition by Miss A. Hamilton. London. 1894–1902. 8 vols. in 13.)

Gwatkin, H. M. The Knowledge of God. (Gifford Lectures.) 2 vols. Edinburgh. 1906.
Harnack, Adolf. Lehrbuch der Dogmengeschichte. Freiburg-i.-B. 1886 ff. Second enlarged edn. 1894–7. 4th edn. 1905 ff. Transl. Buchanan, N. and others. 7 vols. London. 1894–9. *Also* Mitchel, A. London and N.Y. 1893.
Hase, Karl A. Kirchengeschichte auf Grundlage akadem. Vorlesungen. 1885 ff.
—— Kirchengeschichtliche Lehrbuch zunächst für akademischen Vorlesungen. 1834 and often since.
Hefele, C. J., contin. Hergenröther, J. A. G. Conciliengeschichte. 9 vols. Freiburg-i.-B. 1855 ff. 2nd edn. 1873 ff. Transl. of vols. 1–5 [to 800]. History of the Councils of the Church. London. 1871–96. French transl. Delarc, O., new Fr. transl. Leclercq, H. Paris. 1907 ff., in progress.
Hergenröther, J. A. G. Handbuch der allgemeinen Kirchengeschichte. 4th edn. Vols. i, ii, ed. Kirsch, J. P. Freiburg-i.-B. 1892 ff. French transl. by Belet.
Hodgkin, T. Italy and her invaders. 8 vols. Oxford. 1880–99. 2nd edn. Vols. 1–4 in 5. 1892–6.
Kraus, F. X. Ed. Sauer, J. Geschichte der christlichen Kunst. Freiburg-i.-B. and St Louis, Minnesota. 1896–1908. 2 vols. in 3.
Kurtz, J. H. Lehrbuch der Kirchengeschichte. 14th edn. Ed. Bonwetsch, N. and Tschackert, P. Vols. i, ii. Leipsic. 1906. Transl. from 9th edn. Macpherson, J. Church History. 3 vols. London. 1888–93.
Langen, Jos. Geschichte der römischen Kirche. 4 vols. i bis zum Pontifikat Leos I. Bonn. 1881.
Lavisse, Ernest, and Rambaud, Alfred. Histoire genérale du ive siècle jusqu'à nos jours. Paris. 12 vols. 1896.
Lecky, W. E. H. History of European morals from Augustus to Charlemagne. 2 vols. London. 1870. [Very superficial.]
Le Nain de Tillemont, L. S. de. Mémoires pour servir à l'histoire ecclésiastique des six premiers siècles. 15 vols. Brussels. 1693–1707. 2nd edn. 16 vols. Paris. 1701–12.
—— Histoire des Empereurs. 6 vols. 1690–1738.
Loofs, Fr. Leitfaden zum Studium der Dogmengeschichte. Halle. 1889. 2nd edn. enlarged, 1900.
Milman, Henry Hart. History of Latin Christianity. London. 1854–5. Rev. edn. 9 vols. 1867.
—— The History of Christianity from the birth of Christ to the Abolition of Paganism in the Roman Empire. 3 vols. 1840. Rev. edn. 1867.
Möller, W. Lehrbuch der Kirchengeschichte. 3 vols. Tübingen. 1892–1900. 2nd edn. of vol. i [to A.D. 600] by Schubert, H. von. Tübingen and Leipsic. 1902. Transl. Rutherford, A. History of the Christian Church. London. 1898.
Mommsen, Th. Römische Geschichte. Vol. v. Leipsic. 1885. Translated by Dickson, W. P. The Provinces from Caesar to Diocletian. 2 vols. 1886. 2nd edn. London. 1909. Ed. Haverfield, F. J.
—— Römisches Staatsrecht. 3 vols. 1873–8. 3rd edn. Leipsic. 1887–8.
Mosheim, J. L. von. Institutionum historiae ecclesiasticae antiquae et recentioris libri 4. 4 vols. Helmstadt. 1755. Transl. Murdock, J., ed. Soames, H. 1841. Rev. edn. 1850.
Müller, I. E. P. von. Handbuch der klassischen Alterthumswissenschaft. Various edns. New edn. Berlin. 1892, in progress.
Müller, K. Kirchengeschichte. Vols. i, ii. Freiburg-i.-B. 1892.
Neander, August. Allgemeine Geschichte der christlichen Religion und Kirche. 6 vols. in 11. Hamburg. 1825–52. Transl. Torrey, J. General History of the Church. 9 vols. London. 1847–55.

Peter, H. Die geschichtliche Litteratur über die römische Kaiserzeit bis Theo-
dosius I und ihre Quellen. 2 vols. Leipsic. 1897.
Rainy, R. The Ancient Catholic Church. Edinburgh. 1902. [Convenient
handbook.]
Ranke, L. von. Weltgeschichte. 9 vols. Leipsic. 1881-8. Transl. vol. I,
Prothero, G. W. London. 1884.
Reumont, A. von. Geschichte der Stadt Rom. 3 parts. Vol. i. Berlin. 1687-70.
Schiller, Hermann. Geschichte der römischen Kaiserzeit. 2 vols. Gotha. 1883-7.
[Excellent for political, very superficial for religious side.]
Seeck, O. Geschichte des Untergangs der antiken Welt. 3 vols. Berlin. 1895-
1909. 2nd edn. i-ii and 2 supplements. 1898-1901.
Teuffel, W. S. and Schwabe, L. Geschichte der römischen Litteratur. 1891-2.
Transl. Warr, G. C. W. 2 vols. London. 1900.
Tillemont, *see* Le Nain de Tillemont.

CHAPTERS I, II, AND V

I. CONSTANTINE AND HIS CITY
II. THE RE-ORGANIZATION OF THE EMPIRE
V. HERESIES (ARIAN CONTROVERSY TO 381)

1. SPECIAL BIBLIOGRAPHIES

In Select Library of Nicene and Post-Nicene Fathers, ed. Wace, H. and Schaff, P. Oxford, 1890 ff. (Nicene Library). In connexion with:
> Eusebius. *Vita Constantini.* Richardson, E. C. (Extremely full on Constantine.)
> Socrates. *Hist. Eccl.* Zenos, A. C.
> Athanasius. Select Writings and Letters. Robertson, A. (Most recent and best on Arianism.)

2. ORIGINAL DOCUMENTS

In Codex Theodosianus and writers cited below, esp. Eusebius, Lactantius, Athanasius, Julian, Socrates.

3. AUTHORITIES

(a) CONTEMPORARY

Ammianus Marcellinus. *Rerum gestarum libri.* Ed. Gardthausen, V. 2 vols. Leipsic. 1874–5. Wagner, J. O. 3 vols. Leipsic. 1808 (for notes). Baynes, N. H. Transl. with historical notes, introd. and bibliog. London. (Shortly, *see Bibl. to c.* III.)
Anonymus Valesii. Commonly printed with Ammianus.
Athanasius. *Opera.* MPG 25–8.
> *De Incarnatione.* Ed. Robertson, A. London. 1893.
> Select Historical Treatises. Ed. Bright, W. Oxford. 1881.
> Orations against the Arians. Ed. Bright, W. Oxford. 1873.
> Festal Letters. Ed. Cureton, W. London. 1848. Transl. (a) in Oxford Libr. of the Fathers. 1854. (b) Robertson, A., in Nicene Library. Oxford. 1892. (With full and thorough discussions.) (c) *German,* Larsow, F. Berlin. 1852.
Basil. *Opera.* MPG 29–32. Or (better) Ed. Garnier, Dom Jul. Paris. 1839.
> Transl., Letters and Select Works, in Nicene Library. Oxford. 1895.
Epiphanius. *Opera.* MPG 41–3. Ed. Dindorf, G. 5 vols. Leipsic. 1859–62.
Eusebius of Cæsarea. *Opera.* MPG 19–24. Ed. Heinichen, F. A. 3 vols. Leipsic. 1868–70.

Hist. Eccl. Ed. (*a*) Schwartz, E. and Mommsen, Th. 2 vols. Berlin. 1903 ff. and (smaller edn.) 1908. (*b*) Bright, W. Oxford. 1872. 2nd edn. 1881 (text of Burton, E.). Transl. (*a*) Crusè, C. F., last edn. Oxford. 1870. (*b*) McGiffert, A. C., in Nicene Library. 1890.
Vita Constantini and *Panegyricus.* Ed. Heikel, I. A. Berlin. 1902. Transl. Nicene Library, *as above.*
Contra Marcellum. Ed. Gaisford, W. Oxford. 1872. Klostermann, E. Berlin. 1906.
Eutropius. *Breviarium ab urbe condita.* Ed. Droysen, H. MGH. Berlin. 1878. Rühl, Fr. (Teubner) Leipsic. 1887. Wagener, C. Leipsic. 1884.
Gregory of Nazianzus. *Opera.* MPG 35–8. Five Theological Orations. Ed. Mason, A. J. Cambridge. 1899. Transl. in Nicene Library, vol. vii. 1894.
Historia Acephala. MPG 28. But better edn. with notes, Sievers, G., in ZKT 1868; also with transl. in Athanasius, Robertson, as above.
Julian. *Opera.* Ed. Hertlein, F. C. Leipsic. 1875. Contra Christianos. Ed. Neumann, C. J. 1880. Letters, in Rheinisches Museum, xlii, p. 15. 1887 and other edns.
Lactantius. *De mortibus persecutorum.* MPL 7 (for notes). Ed. Brandt, S. and Laubmann, G., in CSEL, 1897.
Macarius Magnes. *Opera.* Ed. Blondel, C. Paris. 1876.
Panegyrici Latini, vi–x. Ed. Bährens. Leipsic. 1874.
Patrum Nicaenorum nomina Latine Graece Coptice Arabice Armeniace sociata opera ediderunt H. Gelzer, H. Hilgenfeld, O. Cuntz. Leipsic. 1898.
Codex Theodosianus. Gothofred, Jac. 6 vols. Lyons. 1665 (for notes). Ed. Hänel, G. Leipsic. 1837. Mommsen, Th., and Meyer, P. M. Berlin. Vol. i. 1905. To be supplemented by Hänel, G. Corpus Legum. Leipsic. 1857.

(*b*) Later

Codinus. *De originibus Constantinopolitanis* in CSHB, or (better) in *Scriptores originum Constantinopolitanarum.* Ed. Preger, Th. Leipsic. 1901–7 (for foundation of Constantinople).
Constantine Porphyrogenitus. *Opera.* 3 vols. In CSHB. Vol. iii, p. 244. (For history of Cherson.)
Philostorgius. *Hist.* MPG 65. Notes ed. Gothofred, Jac. Paris. 1642.
Socrates. *Hist. Eccl.* MPG 67. Ed. Hussey, R. 3 vols. Oxford. 1853. Bright, W. Oxford. 1878.
Sozomen. *Hist. Eçcl.* MPG 67. Ed. Hussey, R. 3 vols. Oxford. 1860.
Theodoret. *Opera.* MPG 80–4. Ed. Schultze, J. L. 10 vols. Halle. 1769. *Hist. Eccl.* Ed. Gaisford, T. Oxford. 1854.
Vita S. Artemii. ASBoll., Oct. 8.
Zosimus. *Historia nova.* Ed. Mendelssohn, L. Leipsic. 1887.

4. MODERN WORKS

(*a*) General

Allen, A. V. G. Christian Institutions. Edinburgh. 1898.
Bardenhewer. Patrologie. *See General bibliography,* i.
Bright, W. Age of the Fathers. 2 vols. Oxford. 1903.
Broglie. L'église et l'empire. *See G. b. v.*
Clinton. Fasti. *See G. b.* iii.
Dill. Roman Society. *See G. b. v.*

DCB. *See G. b.* Articles by Lightfoot [Bp]. Eusebius of Cæsarea.
          Wordsworth, Bp John. Constantine, and cognate arts.
          Bright, Dr Wm. Athanasius.
          Gore [Bp]. Victorinus Afer.
Dorner, I. A. Doctrine of the Person of Christ. Transl. Alexänder, W. E.
          5 vols. Edinburgh. 1868.
Gibbon. Decline and Fall. *See G. b.* v.
Glover. Roman Life and Letters. *See G. b.* v.
Greenwood, Thomas. Cathedra Petri. 7 vols. London. 1856 ff.
Gwatkin, H. M. Studies of Arianism. Cambridge. 1882, 1902.
          Arian Controversy. London. 1889. (Summary) — *See G. b.*
Harnack. Dogmengeschichte. *See G. b.* v.
Hatch, E. The Organization of the Early Christian Churches (Bampton Lectures.)
          Oxford. 1881. (For persecuting laws.)
Hefele. Conciliengeschichte. *See G. b.* v.
Langen. Röm. Kirche. *See G. b.* v. Vol. I, bis zum Pontificat Leos I.
Lecky. European morals. *See G. b.* v.
Le Nain de Tillemont. Hist. des Empereurs. *See G. b.* v.
Löning, Edgar. Das Kirchenrecht in Gallien von Constantin bis Chlodovech.
          Strassburg. 1878.
Loofs, Fr. Leitfaden zum Studium der Dogmengeschichte. Halle. 1889 and
          later edns.
Mommsen. Römische Geschichte. Vol. v. *See G. b.* v.
Neander. Allgem. Geschichte. *See G. b.* v.
Newman, J. H. Arians of the Fourth Century. London. 1833 and later edns.
          (*Tendenzschrift.*)
Pauly-Wissowa. *See G. b.* I. Articles by
                    Benjamin. Constantinus I.
                    Oberhummer, E. Constantinopolis.
Rainy. Catholic Church. *See G. b.* v.
Ranke. Weltgeschichte. *See G. b.* v. Vols. III, IV.
Reumont. Stadt Rom. *See G. b.* v.
RE³. *See G. b.* I. Articles on Arianismus, Christologie, and cognate articles.
Schiller. Röm. Kaiserzeit. *See G. b.* v.
Teuffel and Schwabe. Röm. Litteratur. *See G. b.* v.

(*b*) On Authorities

Ammianus Marcellinus : Bury-Gibbon II, pp. 536–8 (and for further authorities).
Anonymus Valesii :
          Cipolla, C. in Bollettino dell' Istituto storico Italiano, II, pp. 7–98. 1892.
                    (Best study of MSS.)
          Ohnesorge, W. Der Anon. Valesii *de Constantino.* Kiel. 1885. (Best
                    critical discussion.)
Athanasius :
          Atzberger, L. Die Logoslehre d. hl. Athanasius. Munich. 1880.
          Dräseke, Joh. Zur Athanasios-Frage. ZWT, 1895, pp. 238, 516.
                    (Ascribes Ath. *c. Gentes* and *de Inc.* to Eusebius of Emesa.)
          Eichhorn, Alb. Athanasii de vita ascetica testimonia collecta. Halle. 1886
          Fialon, Eugene. Saint Athanase. Étude Littéraire. Paris. 1877.
                              Saint Basile. Étude historique et littéraire. Paris.
                                        1869. (Sketches, but suggestive.)
          Hubert. Jugendschrift d. heiligen Athanasius. ZKG, 1895, p. 561.
                    (Answer to Dräseke's doubts.)

Athanasius (*cont.*) :
Möhler, J. A. Athanasius der Grosse und die Kirche seiner Zeit besonders im Kampfe mit dem Arianismus. Mainz. 1844.
Schwartz, E. Athanasiana. Göttingsche Gelehrte Anzeigen.
Voigt, H. Die Lehre d. Athanasius von Alexandrien. Bremen. 1861.
Eusebius :
Brieger, Th. On Arrangement of Eus. *H. E.*, VIII. ZKG, 1878, p. 586.
Chase, Bp F. H. Authorship of *c. Marcellum* and *de Eccl. Theol.* JTS, VI, 512. (Defends genuineness against Conybeare.)
Conybeare, F. C. The Authorship of the *c. Marcellum*. Z. f. NTliche Theol., 1904. (Ascribes to Eus. of Emesa.)
Gwatkin, H. M. Eusebius of Cæsarea. In Norwich Church History Lectures. London. 1896.
Schultze, V. Quellenuntersuchungen z. *Vita Constantini* d. Eusebius. ZKG, 1894, p. 503.
Violet, Bruno. Die palästinischen Märtyrer des Eusebius von Cäsarea. Leipsic. 1896.
Eutropius : C. Wagener's Jahresbericht on, in Philologus, XLII, p. 521.
Hilary : Dom André Wilmart on, in RBén 1907.
Julian : Bury-Gibbon, II, 534 sq.
Lactantius : Bury-Gibbon, II, p. 531 sq. on date of *De mortibus persecutorum* and critiques thereon.
Philostorgius, Socrates, Sozomen, Theodoret :
Batiffol, Abbé P. H. Quaestiones Philostorgianae. Paris. 1891.
Geppert, Fr. Die Quellen des Kirchenhistorikers Socrates Scholasticus. Leipsic. 1898.
Güldenpenning, A. Die Kirchengeschichte des Theodoret von Kyrrhos. Halle. 1889.
Jeep, L. Quellenuntersuchungen zu den griechischen Kirchen historikern. Leipsic. 1884.

(c) MONOGRAPHS, BIOGRAPHIES, AND SPECIAL TREATISES

Allard, Paul. Julien l'Apostat. 2 vols. Paris. 1900–3.
Antoniades, Crysanthos. Kaiser Licinius, eine historische Untersuchung. Munich. 1884.
On Antony and early Monachism :
Butler, Dom E. C. The Lausiac History of Palladius. Texts and Studies, VI. Cambridge. 1898–1904.
Preuschen, Erw. Palladius u. Rufinus. Beitrag z. Quellenkunde des ältesten Mönchtums. Giessen. 1898.
Weingaten, H. Ursprung des Mönchtums im nach-Constantinischen Zeitalter. Gotha. 1877, and in ZKG.
Batiffol, Abbé P. H. Passion de S. Lucien d'Antioche. Paris. 1891.
Baur, F. C. Lehre von der Dreieinigkeit. 3 Thle. Tübingen. 1841–3.
Boissier, Gaston. La Fin du Paganisme, Étude sur les dernières luttes religieuses en Occident au quatrième Siècle. 2 vols. Paris. 1891.
Brieger, Theodor. Constantin der Grosse als Religionspolitiker. Gotha. 1880.
Bright, Wm. Notes on the Canons of the First Four General Councils. Oxford. 1882.
—— The Roman See in the Early Church. London. 1896.
Burckhardt, Jakob. Die Zeit Constantins des Grossen. Basel. 1853. (Very sceptical.)
Chawner, W. Influences of Christianity on the Legislation of Constantine. Cambridge. 1874.

Draseke, Joh. Apollinarius v. Laodicea, sein Leben u. seine Schriften. Leipsic. 1892.
—— Athanasiana. TSK. 1893.
Firth, J. B. Constantine the Great. New York. 1905.
Funk, F. X. Zeit d. ersten Synode v. Arles. TQS, 1890, p. 296. (Gives date 314; possibly 315, not 316.)
Gardner, Alice. Julian emperor and philosopher and the last struggle of Paganism against Christianity. London. 1895.
Gorres, Fr. D. Verwandtenmord Constantius. ZWT, 1887, p. 343.
Güldenpenning, A. and Ifland, J. Der Kaiser Theodosius. Halle. 1878.
Gummerus, J. Die homöous. Partei (356–61). Leipsic. 1900.
Heisenberg, A. Die Apostelkirche in Konstantinopel. Leipsic. 1908.
Hort, F. J. A. Two Dissertations. Cambridge. 1875. (On the spurious Nicene CR.)
Kaye, Bp J. Council of Nicæa. London. 1853.
Keim, Theodor. Der Übertritt Constantins des Grossen zum Christentum. Zurich. 1862. (Valuable collections of refs.)
Krüger, Gust. Lucifer Bischof v. Calaris. Leipsic. 1886.
Lichtenstein, Ad. Eusebius von Nikomedien. Halle. 1903.
Lietzmann, H. Chronologie d. ersten u. zweiten Verbannung des Athanasius. ZWT, 1901, p. 380.
Loofs, Fr. Eustathius v. Sebaste. Halle. 1898.
—— Arianismus. In RE³.
Maurice, Jules. Numismatique Constantinienne. Iconographie et Chronologie. Vol. I. Paris. 1908.
Millingen, A. van. Byzantine Constantinople, the walls of the City and adjoining historical sites. London. 1899.
Mordtmann, A. D. Esquisse topographique de Constantinople. Lille. 1892.
Mücke, J. F. Alphons. Flavius Claudius Julianus. 2 vols. Gotha. 1867–9.
Neander, Aug. Über den Kaiser Julianus und sein Zeitalter. 1812. Transl. Cox, G. V. Oxford. 1850.
Pears, Edw. The Campaign against Paganism, A.D. 324, in Contemporary Review, January, 1909. (Local knowledge: dates battle of Chrysopolis 324.)
Reinkens, [Bp] J. H. Hilarius von Poitiers. Schaffhausen. 1864.
Rendall, G. H. The Emperor Julian, Paganism and Christianity. Cambridge. 1879.
Rode, Dr. Fr. Gesch. der Reaction Kaiser Julians. Jena. 1877.
Rogala, Th. S. Die Anfänge des Arianischen Streites untersucht. Paderborn. 1907. (Reply to Seeck.)
Schalkhausser, G. Zu den Schriften des Makarios von Magnesia. Leipsic. 1907.
Schmidt, Ch. Essai historique sur la Société Civile dans le Monde Romain, et sur la Transformation par le Christianisme. Strasburg. 1853. Transl. Mrs Thorpe. London. 1885 (Hardly just to heathenism.)
Schultze, V. Geschichte des Untergangs des griechische-römische Heidentums. 2 Bde. 1887–93.
—— Untersuchungen z. Geschichte Constantins. ZKG, 1885, p. 343; 1886, p. 517.
Seeck, O. Das sogenannte Edikt von Mailand (denies that such an edict was issued). ZKG, 1891, p. 381, *and see* Görres, Franz, ZWT, 1892, p. 282. (Answer to Seeck.)
—— Die Urkunden der Vita Constantini. ZKG, 1898, p. 321. (Answer to Crivellucci's doubts.)
—— Quellen u. Urkunden über d. Anfänge des Donatismus. ZKG, 1889, p. 505.
—— Untergang d. antiken Welt. 2 vols. Berlin. 1895, 1901.

Seeck, O. Urkundensfälschungen des 4ⁿ Jahrhunderts. ZKG, June, 1909 (Bd xxx, p. 181) (reply to antagonists).
—— Zur Geschichte des Nicänischen Konzils. ZKG, 1897, pp. 1 and 319. (Very hypercritical.)
Sievers, G. R. Leben des Libanius. Berlin. 1868.
Stanley, Dean A. P. The Eastern Church. 4th edn. London. 1869. (Best account of the externals of the Nicene Council.)
Uhlhorn, G. Die Christliche Liebesthätigkeit in der alten Kirche. Transl. S. Taylor. Edinburgh. 1883.
Ullmann, C. Gregor von Nazianz. Gotha. 1825, 1867. Transl. Cox, G. V. London. 1851.
Völter, Daniel. Der Ursprung des Donatismus. Tübingen. 1883.
Weiss, H. Die drei grossen Cappadocier. Braunsberg. 1872.
Wilmart, Dom André, on Hilary. RBén. 1907.
Zahn, Theodor. Constantin der Grosse und die Kirche. Hanover. 1876.
—— Marcellus von Ancyra. Gotha. 1867.

CHAPTER III

CONSTANTINE'S SUCCESSORS (TO JOVIAN) AND THE STRUGGLE WITH PERSIA

AUTHORITIES

[A more complete critical bibliography will be found in N. H. Baynes' forthcoming translation of Ammianus Marcellinus.]

(a) CONTEMPORARY

Ammianus Marcellinus: Rerum gestarum libri qui supersunt. Recens. rhythmiceque distinxit Carolus U. Clark adjuvantibus L. Traube et G. Heraeo. Vol. I (all pubd.). Libri xiv–xxv. Berlin. 1910.

    [N. H. Baynes' translation (with historical notes and bibliography) of Ammianus Marcellinus awaits the appearance of the second volume of this text.]
    For Gardthausen and Wagner's editions *see Bibl. to cc.* I, II, *and* v.

Aurelius Victor: Sexti Aurelii Victoris de Caesaribus Liber. Ed. F. Pichlmayr. Programm des Ludwigs Gymnasiums in München. 1892.

Basil: *see Bibl. to cc.* I, II, *and* v, esp. his λόγος πρὸς τοὺς νέους ὅπως ἂν ἐξ Ἑλληνικῶν ὠφελοῖντο λόγων.

Bickell, G. Ephraem Syrus. ZKT. II, 2. 1878. pp. 335 sqq.

Codex Theodosianus: *see Bibl. to cc.* I, II, *and* v.

Ephraem Syrus: Carmina Nisibena: additis prolegomenis etc. primus edidit vertit explicavit Gustavus Bickell. Leipsic. 1866.

Eunapius: Vitas Sophistarum et Fragmenta Historiarum recens. notisque illustravit Jo. Fr. Boissonnade, accedit annotatio Dan. Wyttenbachii. 2 vols. Amsterdam. 1822.

    For the fragments also: FHG, ed. C. Müller IV (1868) 7 ff. and L. Dindorf: Hist. Graec. Min. I (1870) 205 ff.

Eutropius. Eutropii Breviarium ab urbe condita recogn. Franciscus Rühl. Leipsic. 1906. Ed. H. Droysen. MGH. 1879.

Gregory of Nazianzus. *See Bibl. to cc.* I, II, *and* v (esp. the orations agt. Julian).

Julian. Opera: ed. Hertlein, F. C. Leipsic. 1875. For the writings against the Christians, Neumann, C. J., in Scriptorum Graecorum qui Christianam impugnaverunt religionem quae supersunt, Fasc. III, Leipsic, 1880; and for the newly found correspondence *see* Largajolli e Parisio *infrà* p. 633 *or* Rheinisches Museum. Frankfurt-a.-M. 1827 ff. *See Bibl. to cc.* I, II, *and* v.

Libanius. Opera rec. R. Förster. Orationes. Vols. I–IV. Leipsic. 1903–8. Epistolae. Ed. J. C. Wolf. Amsterdam. 1738.

Panegyrici Latini. Ed. Bährens. Leipsic. 1874.

Themistius. Ed. Dindorf. Leipsic. 1832.

(b) LATER

Augustine: Confessions. Ed. Gibb and Montgomery. Cambridge. 1908.
Cedrenus. Σύνοψις ἱστοριῶν. Ed. Bekker in CSHB. 1838–9.
Cyril of Alexandria: Contra Julianum. MPG 76.
Faustus of Byzantium: translation by M. Lauer. Cologne. 1879.
Philostorgius. *See Bibl. to cc.* I, II, *and* V.
Prudentius. Carmina. MPL 59, 60.
Socrates. *See Bibl. to cc.* I, II, *and* V.
Sozomen. *See Bibl. to cc.* I, II, *and* V.
Symmachus in MHG. Ed. Seeck.
Theodoret. Church History. Ed. L. Parmentier. Leipsic. 1911. For the
Θεραπευτική (Graecarum affectionum curatio), edn. Räder, J. Leipsic. 1904.
Vita S. Artemii. P. Batiffol: RQCA, III (1889) 252–9, *and see Bibl. to cc.* I, II
and V.
Zonaras in CSHB. Vol. III. Ed. Büttner-Wobst. 1896.
Zosimus. *See Bibl. to cc.* I, II, *and* V.
For the legend of the death of Julian, Faustus of Byzantium, Malalas, the
Pasch. Chron. the pseudo-Amphilochian life of Basil, Nicephorus, Callistus and
many other late authors should be consulted.

MODERN WORKS

On Authorities

Ammianus Marcellinus: O. Seeck: in Pauly-Wissowa. I (ii) [where informa-
tion as to modern literature will be found, cf. M. Schanz: Röm. Litteratur-
geschichte IV (i) pp. 85–98.]
    id. Zur Chronologie und Quellenkritik des Ammianus Marcellinus.
Hm. (1906) XLI, pp. 481–539.
Basil: for the λόγος πρὸς τοὺς νέους. St Basil the Great to Students on Greek
Literature. Ed. E. R. Maloney. Cir. 1901. American Book Company.
    Choix de Discours tirés des Pères grecs, par L. de Sinner. Nouvelle
    édition par E. Sommer. (16th edition.) Paris. 1899. On the
    sources: cf. G. Büttner: Programm d. k. humanistischen Gymnasiums
    Ingolstadt. Munich. 1908.
Cyril of Alexandria. A. Vishnyakov: Imperator Yulian Otstupnik i literaturnaya
polemika s nim cv. Kirlla arkhiepiskopa Alexandriiskago. Simbirsk. 1908.
Julian. Asmus, R. Julian's Galiläerschrift in Zusammenhang mit seinen übrigen
Werken. Ein Beitrag zur Erklärung und Kritik der julianischen Schriften.
Beilage zum Jahresbericht des grossherzoglichen Gymnasiums zu Freiburg i.
Br. 1904.
    Bidez, J. and Cumont, Fr. Recherches sur la Tradition manuscrite des
    Lettres de l'Empereur Julien. Brussels. 1898. pp. 154. (Extrait
    du Tome LVII des Mémoires couronnés et autres Mémoires publiés
    par l'Académie royale de Belgique. 1898.)
    Chinnock, E. J. A few Notes on Julian and a Translation of his Public
    Letters. pp. 82. London. 1901.
    Cumont, Fr. See Bidez, J.
    —— Fragments inédits de Julien. Revue de Philologie, de Littérature et
    d'Histoire anciennes. N. S. XVI. (1892.) 161–6.

Gladis, C. De Themistii Libanii Juliani in Constantium orationibus. Dissertatio inauguralis. Breslau. 1907.

Neumann, K. J. Kaiser Julians Bücher gegen die Christen nach ihrer Wiederherstellung übersetzt. Leipsic. 1880.

Schwarz, G. De Vita et Scriptis Juliani Imperatoris. Bonn. 1888. pp. 43.

Libanius. Gladis, C. *See under* Julian *suprà.*

 Seeck, O. Die Briefe des Libanius. Leipsic. 1906.

 Sievers, G. R. Das Leben des Libanius. Berlin. 1868.

Panegyrici Latini. Pichon, R. Les derniers écrivains profanes. Paris. 1906.

Sozomen. Bidez, J. La tradition manuscrite de Sozomène et la Tripartite de Théodore le Lecteur. Leipsic. 1908. Harnack and Schmidt, Texte und Untersuchungen. 3 series. 3 vols. Pt. 2b. (Vol. xxxii, pt. 2b.)

Themistius. Gladis, C. *See under* Julian *suprà.*

Theodoret. Asmus, J. R. Theodorets Therapeutik und ihr Verhältnis zu Julian. BZ. iii. (1894.) 116–45.

 Güldenpenning, A. Die Kirchengeschichte des Theodoret von Kyrrhos. Halle. 1889.

 Räder, J. De Theodoreti Graecarum affectionum curatione quaestiones criticae. Copenhagen. 1900.

 —— Analecta Theodoretiana. Rhein. Mus. lvii. (1902.) 449–59.

GENERAL WORKS

Boissier, Gaston. La Fin du Paganisme. 4th edn. 2 vols. Paris. 1903.

Delbrück, H. Geschichte der Kriegskunst im Rahmen der politischen Geschichte. Berlin. 1900 ff.

Duruy, V. Histoire romaine. (Vol. vii.) Paris. 1879–85.

Gibbon. Decline and Fall. *See Gen. Bibl.*

Glover. Life and Letters. *See Gen. Bibl.*

Gwatkin, H. M. Studies of Arianism. 2nd edn. Cambridge. 1900.

Hesseling, D. C. Byzantium. Haarlem. 1902. (French translation. Essai sur la civilisation byzantine. Paris. 1907.)

Linsenmayer, A. Die Bekämpfung des Christentums durch den röm. Staat bis zum Tode des Kaisers Julian (363). Munich. 1905. pp. 240–69.

Ranke, L. von. Weltgeschichte. Leipsic. 1881–6.

Schiller. Geschichte der röm. Kaiserzeit. Vol. ii. *See Gen. Bibl.*

Schultze, V. Geschichte des Untergangs des griechisch-römischen Heidentums. Jena. 1887–92. 2 vols.

Seeck. Untergang. *See Gen. Bibl.*

Sievers, G. R. Studien zur Geschichte der römischen Kaiser. Berlin. 1870.

Wietersheim, E. von. (2nd edition by F. Dahn.) Geschichte der Völkerwanderung. Leipsic. 1880–1. 2 vols.

JULIAN: BIBLIOGRAPHY, ETC.

Adler, M. Julian and the Jews. Jewish Quarterly Review. 1893. pp. 615–51, and cf. Campbell, Sir J. M. *infrà*.

Allard, Paul. Julien l'Apostat. 3rd edn. rev. and enlarged. 3 vols. Paris. 1906.

Andersson, H. Quae de numine divino cultuque eius senserit Julianus ex scriptis Imperatoris demonstrat H. A. Lund, Regia Academia Carolina, Acta Universitatis Lundensis. Tom. xxvii. 1891.

Babelon, E. L'iconographie monétaire de Julien l'Apostat. Revue Numismatique. 4ᵐᵉ Sér. vii. 1903. pp. 130–5.

Desjardins, Abel. L'Empereur Julien. Thèse présentée à la Faculté des Lettres de Paris. Paris. 1845.

Förster, R. Kaiser Julian in der Dichtung alter und neuer Zeit. Studien zu vergleich. Litteraturgesch. 1905. pp. 1–120.

Gardner, Alice. The Emperor Julian's View of Christianity. Macmillan's Magazine. Vol. xlviii. pp. 402–13. Sept. 1883.

— Julian. Philosopher and Emperor. London. 1901.

Gildersleeve, Basil L. Julian, in Essays and Studies. Baltimore. 1890. pp. 355–98. (Reprinted from The Southern Review. Baltimore. Vol. iii. No. 5. January, 1868. pp. 179–209.)

Harnack, A. Sub voc. Julianus in Hauck's Realencyklopädie. Leipsic. 1880.

Hecker, Hermann. Zur Geschichte des Kaisers Julianus. Eine Quellenstudie, wissenschaftliche Beilage zum Programm des königlichen Gymnasiums zu Kreuznach, Ostern. 1886. pp. 48.

Holzwarth, Fr. Julian der Abtrünnige. In Sammlung historischer Bildnisse. Freiburg-i.-B. Cir. 1874.

Kellerbauer, Albert. Skizze der Vorgeschichte Julians. Jahrbb. f. class. Phil. Supplementband xi. pp. 81–121.

— Kaiser Julians Regierung, nach den Quellen kurz dargestellt. Programm d. k. Studienanstalt zu Kempten für das Schuljahr 1875–6. Kempten. 1876. pp. 48.

Koch, Wilhelm. Kaiser Julian der Abtrünnige, seine Jugend und Kriegsthaten bis zum Tode des Kaisers Constantius 331–61. Eine Quellenuntersuchung. Besonder Abdruck aus dem fünfundzwanzigsten Supplementband der Jahrbb. f. class. Phil. pp. 333–488. Leipsic. 1899. Contains substance and corrections of

— De Juliano imperatore Scriptorum qui res in Gallia ab eo gestas enarrarunt auctore disputatio. Arnheim. 1890 (now unobtainable). (And cf. Neue Jahrbb. für Phil., vol. cxlvii, pp. 362–8.)

Largajolli, D. Della politica religiosa di Giuliano Imperatore. 1887. Piacenza. pp. 159.

—— e Parisio. Rivista di Filologia, xvii. 1889. pp. 289 sqq.

Mau, G. Die Religionsphilosophie Kaiser Julians in seinen Reden auf König Helios und die Göttermutter, mit einer Übersetzung der beiden Reden. Leipsic and Berlin. 1907.

Mücke, J. F. Alphons. Flavius Claudius Julianus nach den Quellen. 2 Bände. Gotha. 1867, 1869.

Negri, Gaetano. L'Imperatore Giuliano L'Apostata. Studio Storico. 2ⁿᵈᵃ edizione. Milano. 1902. pp. 523. (English translation by Duchess Litta-Visconti-Arese. Introduction by Prof. Pasquale Villari. 2 vols. London. 1905.)

Neumann, K. J. Das Geburtsjahr Kaiser Julians. Philologus. l. 1891. pp. 761–2.

Radinger, C. Das Geburtsdatum des Kaisers Julian. Apostata. Philologus. 1891.
L. p. 761.
Rendall, G. H. The Emperor Julian. Cambridge. 1879.
Reville, Albert. L'Empereur Julien. Annales du Musée Guinet. Revue de l'histoire des Religions. Ann. 7me, vol. XIII, no. 3, pp. 265–91, vol. XIV, no. 1, pp. 1–25, no. 2, pp. 145–67. 1886.
Rode, F. Geschichte der Reaktion Kaiser Julians. Jena. 1877.
Semisch, Carl. Julian der Abtrünnige. Ein Charakterbild. Breslau. 1862.
Strauss, D. F. Der Romantiker auf dem Throne der Cäsaren oder Julian der Abtrünnige. Ein Vortrag. 3te Auflage. Bonn. 1896. pp. 40.
Teuffel. Der Kaiser Julianus und seine Beurtheiler. Allgemeine Zeitschr. für Gesch. herausgegeben von W. A. Schmidt. Fünfter Band der Zeits. für Geschichtswissenschaft. 1846. pp. 405–39.
    Zur Geschichte des Kaisers Julianus. Zeits. für Geschichtswissenschaft. Vol. IV. 1845. pp. 143–61.
Wiggers, G. F. Julian der Abtrünnige. Ein Verfolger des Christentums und ein Verfolger der Christen. Zeits. f. d. hist. Theologie, ed. Illgen. Vol. VII. Leipsic. 1837. N. F. vol. I, Art. III. pp. 115–58.

THE GALLIC WARS

Borries, E. von. Die Örtlichkeit der Alamannenschlacht. Beilage zu dem Jahres bericht der neuen Realschule zu Strassbúrg i. E. 1892.
    Noch einmal die Örtlichkeit der Alamannenschlacht. Westdeutsche Zeitschrift für Geschichte und Kunst. Vol. XII. pp. 242–55. (Adopted in text.)
    Die Quellen zu den Feldzügen Julians des Abtrünnigen gegen die Germanen. Hm. Vol. XXV. (1889.) pp. 173 sqq.
Dahn, F. Die Alamannenschlacht bei Strassburg, 357 n. Chr. Eine Studie. Braunschweig. 1880.
Nissen, H. Die Alamannenschlacht bei Strassburg. Westdeutsche Zeits. für Gesch. und Kunst. Vol. VI. 1887. pp. 319 sqq.
Oberziner, Lodovico. Le guerre Germaniche di Flavio Claudio Giuliano. Rome. 1896. pp. 128.
Wiegand, W. Die Alamannenschlacht vor Strassburg 357. Eine kriegsgeschichtliche Studie. Beiträge zur Landes- und Volkeskunde von Elsass-Lothringen. Heft III. Strassburg. 1887.
    Die Alamannenschlacht bei Strassburg. Westd. Zeitschr. f. Gesch, und Kunst. Vol. VII. 1888. pp. 63 sqq. and see Oberrheinische Zeitschrift. N. F. VIII. Heft I, pp. 134 sqq.

THE PERSIAN WAR

Büttner-Wobst, T. Der Tod des Kaisers Julian. Philologus. LI. 1892. pp. 561–80.
Chesney, F. R. Expedition for the Survey of the Rivers Euphrates and Tigris. Vol. II. London. 1850.
Gleye, C. E. Zu den Nachrichten vom Tode Julians. Philologus. Vol. LIII. 1894. p. 587.
Jurien de la Gravière, J. P. E. La Flotille de l'Euphrate. Paris. 1892.

Nostitz-Rieneck, R.   Vom Tode des Kaisers Julian.   Berichte und Erzahlungen.
   Ein Beitrag zur Legendenforschung.   xvi Jahresbericht des öff.   Privatgymna-
   siums an der Stella matutina zu Feldkirch.   1907.
Reinhardt, G.   Der Tod des Kaisers Julian, nach den Quellen dargestellt.   Köthen.
   1891.
   Der Perserkrieg des Kaisers Julian, in x Jahresbericht des herzoglichen
      Friedrichs Realgymnasiums und der Vorschule des Fridericianum
      für das Schuljahr 1891–2.   Dessau.   1892.
Sachau, E.   Am Euphrat und Tigris : Reisenotizen aus dem Winter 1897–8.
   Leipsic.   1900.
Sudhaus, H.   De Ratione quae intercedat inter Zosimi et Ammiani de Bello a
   Juliano imperatore cum Persis gesto Relationes.   Dissertatio historica.   Bonn.
   1870.   pp. 102.

MONOGRAPHS ON VARIOUS SPECIAL POINTS

Baynes, N. H.   Rome and Armenia in the Fourth Century.   EHR. xxv.   (1910.)
   pp. 625–43.
Bury, J. B.   The date of the Battle of Singara.   Byzantinische Zeitschrift.
   Vol. v.   p. 302.
Campbell, Sir J. M.   Julian and Jerusalem.   Scottish Review.   Vol. xxv.
   pp. 291–306.
Ferrero, Ermanno.   (a)   I Titoli di Vittoria dei Figli di Costantino.   Atti della
   reale Accademia delle Scienze di Torino. Vol. xxxiii.   1897.   pp. 59–63.
      (b)   Ancora dei Figili di Costantino.   *Ibid*. Vol. xxxiv.   1899.   pp. 131–6.
      (c)   Mogli e figli di Costantino.   *Ibid*. Vol. xxxiii.   1898.   pp. 376–88.
Güterbock, Karl.   Römisch-Armenien und die römische Satrapieen im vierten bis
   sechsten Jahrhundert ;   eine rechtsgeschichtliche Studie in Festgabe der
   iuristischen Fakultät zu Königsberg für ihren Senior Johann Theodor Schir-
   merzum 1 August 1900.   pp. 1–58.
Seeck, O.   Die gallischen Steuern bei Ammian.   Rheinisches Museum.   N. F. xlix
   (1894).   pp. 630–2.
—— Zu den Festmünzen Constantins.   Zeitschrift für Numismatik.   xxi.   1898.
   pp. 17–65.

CHAPTER IV

THE TRIUMPH OF CHRISTIANITY

A. ORIGINAL AUTHORITIES

For de Broglie, Bury, Dill, Duruy (*Hist. rom.*), Gibbon, Glover, Gregorovius, Harnack (*D. G.*), Hodgkin (*Italy and Inv.*), Lecky, Seeck (*Untergang*), Le Nain de Tillemont, see *Gen. Bibl.*

Ambrose, Bishop of Milan, Opera Omnia. 8 vols. Venice. 1781. English translation. Select works and letters. Oxford. 1896.

Ammianus Marcellinus. *See Gen. Bibl.*

Apuleius Madaurensis. Opera Omnia ex optimis codicibus edidit. . . Hildebrand, G. F. Leipsic. 1843. Thomas, P. Leipsic. 1908. Transl. The Metamorphoses of Apuleius, Head, Sir G. London. 1851. The Golden Ass, Adlington, W. London. 1566 and 1904. (Chiswick Library.) Butler, H. E. 2 vols. Oxford. 1910.

Arnobius Afer. Adversus nationes; libri septem. CSEL. 1866. Transl. in Clark's Ante-Nicene Library. Edinburgh. 1871.

Augustinus Aurelius. De Civitate Dei. Ed. Dombart, 1st and 3rd edn. 1877–92. Transl. in Dent's Temple Classics. *Also by* Dods, E. M. Edinburgh. 1871–6. And other edns.

—— The Confessions of Augustine. A critical edition by Gibb, J. and Montgomery, W. Cambridge. 1908. Transl. in Dent's Everyman's Library.

—— Epistolae. The 2nd vol. of Opera Omnia. Bassano. 1797.

—— *Works also in* CSEL. 1891–1900. MPL 32–46.

Ausonius, Decimus Magnus. Opera. MPL 19. Paris. 1844.

Cassiodorus Senator. Variae. . .recensuit Mommsen, T. In MGH, auct. ant. Vol. XII.

—— The letters of Cassiodorus. . .with an introduction by Hodgkin, T. London. 1886.

Chronicon Paschale. CSHB. 1832. Cf. JTS, April, 1906.

Claudianus. Carmina. Ed. Birt, T. MGH. 1892. Koch, J. Leipsic. 1893. Ludwich, A. Leipsic. 1897.

—— Opera. Ed. Doullay. Paris. 1845. English transl. Hawkins, A. London. 1817.

Cyrilli, Alexandriae Episcopi, pro sancta Christianorum religione, adversus libros Athei Juliani. Ed. Berbosio, N. and Aubertus, J. Leipsic. 1696.

Ephraim the Syrian. (The four poems of Ephraim against Julian have been translated into German and published, by Bickell, in ZKT for 1878.)

Eunapius. Vitae Sophistarum et Fragmenta Historiarum. MPG. Boissonnade, J. F. 2 vols. Amsterdam. 1822. Another edn. Paris. 1849. Dindorf, L. Historici Graeci Minores. 2 vols. Leipsic. 1870-1.

Eutropius. Breviarium Historiae Romanae. Ed. Havercamp. Leyden. 1729. Rühl, F. Leipsic. 1887. MGH. 1879. Transl. Watson, J. S. London. 1875. And others.

Gregory of Nazianzus. Orationes contra Julianum. MPG 35. Paris. 1857. Mason, A. J. Cambridge. 1899.

Himerii Sophistae Oratio qua laudes urbis Constantinopoleos et Juliani Augusti celebrantur. Ed. Wernsdorf, G. Erlangen. 1785.

—— Declamationes.... Dübner, Fr. Paris. 1849.

Iamblichus. De Mysteriis Egyptiorum Liber. Ed. Parthey, G. Berlin. 1857. Transl. by Taylor, T. Chiswick. 1821.

—— Vita Pythagorica. Leipsic. 1815-16.

Jerome, Eusebii Hieronymi Opera. Venice. 1766, and MPL. English transl. of the Epistles in Nicene Library. 2nd series. Vol. VI. 1893. *See Bibl. to ch. I, II, and V.*

Julianus, Flavius Claudius. Juliani Imperatoris quae supersunt praeter reliquias apud Cyrillum omnia. Ed. Hertlein. (Teubner.) 2 vols. Leipsic. 1875.

—— Juliani Imperatoris librorum contra Christianos quae supersunt. Collected and ed. by Neumann, C. J. Leipsic. 1880. *Also* German transl. Kaiser

—— Julians Bücher gegen die Christen. Neumann, C. J. Leipsic. 1880.

Lactantius, Lucius Coelius Firmianus. Opera Omnia. MPG 6, 7. Ed. Brandt, S. CSEL. 2 vols. 1890-3. Transl. in Ante-Nicene Library.

Libanius. Libanii Opera recensuit Richardus Förster. (Teubner.) 4 vols. Leipsic. 1903-8. (Does not contain the Epistles.)

—— Libanii Epistolae. Ed. Wolff, J. C. Amsterdam. 1738.

Macrobius. Opera. Ed. Eyssenhardt. (Teubner.) Leipsic. 1868.

Mamertinus. Gratiarum actio Juliano Augusto pro consulato. MPG 18. Paris. 1848. Ed. Bährens. (Teubner.) Leipsic. 1874.

Maternus. Julius Firmicus. De errore profanorum religionum. Ed. Halm, C. CSEL. 1867.

Maximus of Turin. Opera Omnia (chiefly homilies). MPL 67.

Minucius Felix. Ed. Halm, C. CSEL. 1868. Transl. in Clark's Ante-Nicene Library. Edinburgh. 1869.

Orosius, Paulus. Historiae adversus paganos libri septem. Ed. Havercamp. Leyden. 1738. Also MPL 31. Paris. 1846. Also ed. Zangemeister. CSEL. 1882. (Teubner.) Leipsic. 1889.

Paulinus Nolanus. Carmina de St Martino. Pressburg (Hungary). 1817. In A. Jordansky's Biographi Veteres Sancti Martini Turonensis Episcopi. MPL 61. CSEL 30. 1894.

Philostorgius. Ecclesiasticae Historiae Libri septem. Ed. Valesius, H. Paris. 1673. *Also* MPG 44.

Plotinus. Opera. Ed. Kirchhoff, A. Leipsic. 1856. Volkmann, R. (Teubner.) 2 vols. Leipsic. 1883-4.

Porphyry. Vita Plotini. Leipsic. 1815-16.

Procopius. Anecdota a Historia Arcana. Ed. Eichel, J. Helmstädt. 1654. CSHB. Muratori. *See Gen. Bibl.*, vol. I. Transl. London. 1672. Another in the Athenian Society's Publication for 1896.

Prudentius, Clemens Aurelius. Prudentii quae exstant Carmina recensuit A. Dressel. Leipsic. 1860. *Also* MPL 59, 60.

Rufinus, Tyrannius. Historia ecclesiastica. MPL 21. Nicene Library. 1892.

Rutilius Claudius Namatianus. Rutilii Claudii Namatiani De Reditu suo libri duo. Ed. Keene, C. H. and Savage-Armstrong, G. F. London. 1907.
—— Édition critique, accompagnée d'une traduction française et d'un index, et suivie d'une étude historique et littéraire sur l'œuvre et l'auteur. Vessereau, J. Paris. 1904.
Salvianus Massiliensis. Opera Omnia. Ed. Pauly, F. Vienna Corpus. 1868. De Gubernation Dei. Ed. Halm, C. Berlin. 1878.
Sidonius Apollinaris, Caius Sollius. Opera Omnia. In Nisard's Collection des auteurs latins. Paris. 1850. Also ed. Krusch, Bruno in MGH. 1887.
Socrates. Historia ecclesiastica. Ed. Hussey, R. Oxford. 1853. Bright, W. Oxford. 1872. MPG 67. English transl. in Select Library of Nicene and Post-Nicene Fathers. . . Wace, H. and Schaff, P. 2nd series. Vol. II. Oxford and New York. 1891.
Sozomen. Historia Ecclesiastica. Ed. Hussey, R. Oxford. 1860. *Also* MPG 67. English translation in Select Library of Nicene and Post-Nicene Fathers. . . Wace, H. and Schaff, P. 2nd series. Vol. II. Oxford and New York. 1891.
Sulpicius Severus. Libri qui supersunt. Ed. Halm, C. CSEL. 1866.
Symmachus, G. Aurelii Symmachi quae supersunt edidit Otto Seeck. 1883. MGH, auctores antiquissimi. VI, pt 1.
Synesius. Opera. In MPG 66.
—— Die Briefe des Bischofs Synesius von Kyrene. Fritz, W. 1898.
Themistius. Πολιτικοὶ Λόγοι. Ed. Dindorf. Leipsic. 1832.
Theodoret. Historia ecclesiastica. Ed. Gaisford, Th. Oxford. 1854. MPG 82.
Zonaras, Joannes. Epitomae Historiarum libri XVIII (books XII and XIII). Ed. Büttner-Wobst, Th. Berlin. 1897. MPG. CSHB.
Zosimus. Historia nova. CSHB. 1837. *Also* ed. Mendelssohn, L. Dorpat. 1887.

Codex Theodosianus. Ed. Hänel. CSHB. 1842. Mommsen, Th. 1905. Vol. I.
CIL. *See Gen. Bibl.*
CIG. *See Gen. Bibl.*
Fabricius. Bibliotheca Graeca. 7th vol.

B. MODERN WORKS

Adler, Hermann. The Emperor Julian and the Jews. Jewish Quarterly Review for July, 1893.
Allard, Paul. Julien l'Apostat. 2 vols. Paris. 1900–3.
—— Le christianisme et l'empire romain de Néron à Théodose. Paris. 1897.
Anrich, Gustave. Das antike Mysterienwesen in seinem Einfluss auf das Christentum. Göttingen. 1894.
Asmus, J. R. Kaiser Julians philosophische Werke übersetzt und erklärt. 1908.
—— Julian's Brief über Pegasius. ZKG. Vol. XXIII. Gotha. 1902.
—— Ist die pseudojustinische Cohortatio ad Graecos eine Streitschrift gegen Julian? ZWT. Leipsic. 1895.
Beugnot, A. Histoire de la destruction du Paganisme en Occident. Paris. 1835.
Biegelmair, Andreas. Die Beteiligung der Christen am öffentlichen Leben in vorconstantinischer Zeit. Munich. 1902.
Bigg, Charles. The Church's Task in the Roman Empire. Oxford. 1905.

Boissier, Gaston. La Religion Romaine d'Auguste aux Antonins. 2nd edn. Paris. 1878.

—— La Fin du Paganisme. Etude sur les dernières luttes religieuses en occident au quatrième siècle. 2 vols. 5th edn. Paris. 1907.

Bouché-Leclercq, A. Histoire de la divination dans l'Antiquité. 4 vols. Paris. 1879–82.

Burckhardt, J. Die Zeit Constantines des Grossen. 2nd edn. Leipsic. 1880.

Capes, W. W. University Life in ancient Athens. London. 1877.

Caspari, C. P. Kirchenhistorische Anecdota. Vol. I. Christiania. 1883.

Chassang, Alexis. Histoire du roman et de ses rapports avec l'histoire dans l'antiquité Grecque et Latine. Paris. 1862.

Chastel, E. Histoire de la destruction du paganisme dans l'Empire de Orient. Paris. 1850.

Clinton. Fasti Romani. *See Gen. Bibl.*

Comparetti, Domenico. Virgilio nel medio evo. 2 vols. 1st edn. Leghorn. 1872. 2nd edn. Florence. 1896. Transl. from first edn, by Benecke, E. F. M. Introd. by Robinson Ellis. London. 1895.

Crawford, W. S. Synesius the Hellene. London. 1901.

Cumont, Franz. Article in Revue de l'instruction publique en Belgique. Vol. XL. Brussels. 1897.

—— Textes et Monuments figurés relatifs aux mystères de Mithra. . . . Brussels. 1899.

—— The Mysteries of Mithra. . . transl. McCormick, J. T. London. 1903.

—— Les Religions orientales dans le Paganisme Romain. Paris. 1907.

Cumont, Franz, and Bidez, F. Recherches sur la tradition manuscrite des lettres de l'empereur Julien. Mémoires couronnés etc. pub. par l'Acad. Royale. Brussels. 1898.

Dautremer, L. Ammien Marcellin. Étude d'histoire littéraire. Lille. 1899.

Desjardins, A. L'Empereur Julien. Paris. 1845.

Dietrich, Alrbecht. Eine Mithrasliturgie. Leipsic. 1903.

Druon, H. Études sur la vie et les œuvres de Synesius. Paris. 1859.

Duruy, Victor. La politique religieuse de Constantin. In the RA. Vol. XLIII. Paris. 1882.

Eckhel, Joseph. Doctrina numorum veterum. 8th vol. Leipsic. 1826.

Finlay. A History of Greece. *See Gen. Bibl.*

Franc, Henri. Nature et caractères de la polémique de l'Empereur Julien contre le Christianisme. Strassburg. 1857.

Friedländer, Ludwig. Darstellungen aus der Sittengesch. Roms in d. Zeit von August bis z. Ausgang d. Antonine. 3 vols. Leipsic. 1862–71. 7th edn. 1901. Transl. from 7th edn. Roman life and manners under the early Empire. Magnus, L. A. London. 1908 ff.

Gardner, Alice. Julian, Philosopher and King, and the last struggle of Paganism against Christianity. London. 1890.

—— Synesius of Cyrene, Philosopher and Bishop. London. 1886.

Gibbon. Decline and Fall. *See Gen. Bibl.*

Gimazane, Jean. Étude sur le quatrième siècle. Ammien Marcellin, sa vie et son œuvre. Toulouse. 1889.

Gollwitzer, I. Observationes criticae in Juliani Imperatoris contra Christianos libros. Erlangen. 1886.

Grätz, H. Die Herrschaft des Christenthums durch Konstantins Bekehrung. In Monatsschrift für Geschichte des Judentums. 1886.

Grindle, G. E. A. The Destruction of Paganism in the Roman Empire. Oxford. 1892.

Gruppe, Otto. Griechische Mythologie und Religionsgeschichte. Munich. 1903.

Gwatkin, H. M. Studies of Arianism. 2nd edn. Cambridge. 1900.

Harnack, Adolf. Die Mission und Ausbreitung des Christentums in den ersten drei Jahrhunderten. 2nd edn. Leipsic. 1906. Transl. The Expansion of Christianity in the first three centuries. Moffat, J. London. 1904.

—— Article on "Julian" in RE³. Vol. ix. Leipsic. 1901.

—— Das Mönchtum, seine Ideale und Geschichte. Giessen. 1881. Transl. from 5th edn. London. 1901.

—— Article on "Neo-Platonism" in Enc. Br. 9th edn. Vol. xii.

Hauck, Albert. Kirchengeschichte Deutschlands. 1st vol. 4th edn. Leipsic. 1904.

Heintze, M. Article on "Neo-Platonism" in RE³.

Hepding, Hugo. Attis, seine Mythen und sein Kult. Giessen. 1903.

Hodgkin, Thomas. The Dynasty of Theodosius. Oxford. 1889.

Holmes, W. G. The Age of Justinian and Theodora. 2 vols. London. 1905–7.

Holzwarth, F.J. Julian der Abtrünnige. Freiburg-im-Breisgau. 1874.

Jeep, L. Zur Überlieferung des Philostorgios. In Texte und Untersuchungen. Neue Folge. Leipsic. 1899.

Jondot, M. Histoire de l'Empereur Julien. Paris. 1817.

Kellerbauer. Kaiser Julians Regierung. Kempten. 1876.

Kleffner, A. D. Porphyrius der Neuplatoniker und Christenfeind. Paderborn. 1896.

Klimek, P. Conjectanea in Julianum et Cyrilli Alexandriae contra illum libros. Breslau. 1883.

La Bleterie, J. P. Vie de l'Empereur Julien. Paris. 1735.

Lasaulx, E. von. Der Untergang des ¡Hellenismus. Munich. 1854.

Madden, W. Christian Emblems on the coins of Constantine the Great, his family and his successors. Numismatic Chronicle. New Series. Vols. xvii, xviii. London. 1877–8.

Marquardt, Joachim. Römische Staatsverwaltung. 3 vols. 2nd edn. Leipsic. 1881.

Mau, G. Die religionsphilosophie Kaiser Julians in seinen Reden auf König Helios und die Götter-Mutter. Leipsic. 1906.

Maury, L. F. La Magie et l'Astologie dans l'antiquité et au moyen âge, ou étude sur les superstitions païennes qui se sont per pétuées jusqu'à nos jours. Paris. 1860.

Mücke, J. F. A. Flavius Claudius Julianus. Julians Kriegsthäten. Gotha. 1867. Julian's Leben und Schriften. Gotha. 1869.

Müller, Eugen. Kaiser Flavius Claudius Julianus. Biographie nebst Auswahl seiner Schriften. . . . Hanover. 1901.

Naville, H. Adrien. Julien l'Apostat et sa philosophie du polythéisme. Paris, Neuchatel, and Geneva. 1877.

Neander, Augustus. Kaiser Julian und sein Zeitalter. Berlin. 1812. Transl. The Emperor Julian and his friends : an historical picture. Cox, G. V. London. 1850.

Negri, Gaetano. L' Imperatore Giuliano l'Apostata. Florence. 1902. Transl. by the Duchess Litta-Visconti-Arese, with introd. by Pasquale Villari. London. 1905.

Nostiz-Rienach, Robert Graf. Vom Tode des Kaisers Julian. (Grauert's Historisches Jahrbuch.) 1907.

Ozanam, A. F. La civilisation au Vᵐᵉ siècle. Paris. 1855. Transl. History of Civilisation in the Fifth Century. London. 1887.

Peter, Hermann. Die geschichtliche Litteratur über die römischen Kaiserzeit bis Theodosius I, und ihre Quellen. 2 vols. Leipsic. 1897.

Rauschen, Gerhard. Jahrbücher der christlichen Kirchen unter dem Kaiser Theodosius dem Grossen. Freiburg-im-Breisgau. 1897.

Rauschen, Gerhard. Das griechisch-römische Schulwesen zur Zeit des ausgehenden Heidentum. Bonn. 1901.

Rendall, G. H. The Emperor Julian. Paganism and Christianity. With genealogical, chronological and biographical appendices. (Hulsean Prize Essay for 1876.) Cambridge. 1879.

Réville, Jean. Religion à Rome sous les Sévères. Paris. 1886.

Richter, Arthur. Neu-Platonische Studien. 5 Pts. Halle. 1864-7.

Rode, Friedrich. Geschichte der Reaction Kaiser Julians gegen die Christliche Kirche. Leipsic. 1877.

Rohde, Erwin. Psyche. Seelencult und Unsterblichkeitsglaube der Griechen. 4th edn. Tübingen. 1907.

Schlosser, F. C. Universitäten, Studirende und Professoren der Griechen zu Julians und Theodosius Zeit...nach Eunapius, Libanius, Julian, Basilius d. Gr., und Gregor v. Naz. Archive für Gesch. u. Litteratur. Vol. I, pp. 217-72. Frankfurt-a.-M. 1830.

Schultze, Victor. Geschichte des Untergangs des griechisch-römischen Heidentums. 2 vols. Jena. 1887-92.

—— Article in RE³, on Constantine and his sons. Vol. X

Schwarz, W. De vita et scriptis Juliani Imperatoris. Bonn. 1888.

Seeck, Otto. Die Briefe des Libanius zeitlich geordnet. Leipsic. 1906. In Texte und Untersuchungen zur Geschichte der altchristlichen Literatur. Neue Folge.

Semisch, C. Julian der Abtrünnige. Ein Characterbild. Breslau. 1862.

Sievers, Gottfried. Das Leben des Libanius. Berlin. 1868.

Sorley, W. R. Article on "Iamblichus" in Encyclopædia Britannica. 9th edn. London. 1883.

Stengel, Paul. Die griechischen Kultusaltertümer. Munich. 1898.

Strauss, D. F. Der Romantiker auf dem Thron der Cäsaren oder Julian der Abtrünnige. 1847. (Pt. v of Ges. Schriften, I, pp. 174-216. Bonn. 1876.)

Teuffel, W. S. Article on "Julian" in Pauly's Realencyklopädie, IV. 1846.

—— De Juliano Imperatore religionis Christianae contemtore et osore. Tübingen. 1844.

—— Zur Geschichte des Kaisers Julian in Schmidt's Zeitschrift für geschichtlichen Wissenschaft. 1845.

Torquati. Studii storico-critici sulla vita et sulle gesta di Flavio Claudio Giuliano sopranominato l' Apostata. Rome. 1878.

Vacherot, Étienne. Histoire critique de l'Ecole d'Alexandrie. 2 vols. Paris. 1846.

Volkmann, R. Synesius von Cyrene. Berlin. 1869.

Vollert, W. Kaiser Julian's religiöse und philosophische Überzeugung. Gütersloh. 1899.

Wissowa, Georg. Religion und Kultus der Römer. Munich. 1902.

Wordsworth, John. Articles on Constantine and his sons and on Julian in DCB. Vols. I and III.

Zahn, Theodor. Skizzen aus dem Leben der alten Kirche. Leipsic. 1908.

Zeidler, E. Julian. 1869.

Zeller, Eduard. Die Philosophie der Griechen. 3rd edn. Leipsic. 1903.

CHAPTER VI

ORGANIZATION OF THE CHURCH

ORIGINAL AUTHORITIES

The New Testament in Greek (especially the Acts; of the Pauline Epistles 1 Cor., Eph., Phil. and the Pastoral Epistles; 1 Peter; Apocalypse).

Commentaries on the Pauline Epistles:

> Ambrosiaster. Sancti Ambrosii Mediolanensis episcopi opera, Benedictine edition, II appendix, col. 25. Paris. 1690. Separate edition in preparation for CSEL by Brewer, H., S. J.
>
> Jerome: on Gal., Eph., Titus, Philemon. Sancti Eusebii Hieronymi Stridonensis presbyteri opera. Ed. Vallarsi, D., VII 367. Verona. 1737.
>
> Theodore of Mopsuestia. Ed. Swete, H. B. 2 vols. Cambridge. 1880–2.

The Apostolic Fathers:

> Collected edition (comprising Clement, Ignatius, Polycarp, the Teaching of the Twelve Apostles, Barnabas, Hermas, etc.): revised texts with short introductions and English translations. Ed. Lightfoot, J. B. and Harmer, J. R. London. 1891.
>
> The Apostolic Fathers. Ed. Lightfoot, J. B. Part 1. S. Clement of Rome. 2 vols. London. 1890. Part 2. S. Ignatius, S. Polycarp. 3 vols. London. 1885. 2nd edn. 1889.

Διδαχὴ τῶν Δώδεκα Ἀποστόλων. Die Lehre der zwölf Apostel nebst Untersuchungen zur ältesten Geschichte der Kirchenverfassung und des Kirchenrechts. Includes the Apostolic Church Order, Die sogenannte apostolische Kirchenordnung. Ed. Harnack, A. Leipsic. 1884.

Didascalia Apostolorum and Apostolic Constitutions. (Latin) Fragmenta Veronensia Latino. Ed. Hauler, E. Leipsic. 1900. (Syriac) Didascalia Apostolorum Syriace. Ed. Lagarde, P. A. de. Leipsic. 1854. (English) The Didascalia Apostolorum in English. Translated from the Syriac by Gibson, M. D. London. 1903. Didascalia et Constitutiones Apostolorum. Ed. Funk, F. X. 2 vols. Paderborn. 1905.

Liber Pontificalis — Duchesne, L. Le Liber Pontificalis. Vol. I. Paris. 1886. [Indispensable.]

Papal Letters:

> Ballerini, P. and G. Sancti Leonis Magni opera. 3 vols. (epistles in vol. I). Venice. 1753–7.
>
> Coustant, P. Epistolae Romanorum Pontificum (down to Xystus III inclusive). Paris. 1721.
>
> Thiel, A. Epistolae Romanorum Pontificum (Hilarus to Hormisdas). Braunsberg. 1868.

Biographies:

> Ambrose by Palladius. Ed. Bened. Vol. II, appendix, col. i.
>
> Augustine by Possidius. Ed. Bened. Vol. x. Appendix. (Antwerp [1700]. col. 164.)
>
> Martin of Tours by Sulpicius Severus. Ed. Halm, C. (CSEL, vol. I.) 1866.

For Ammianus Marcellinus, Socrates, Sozomen, Theodoret *see Bibl. to cc.* I, II, *and* v.

Ambrose (Benedictine edition). 2 vols. Paris. 1686–90.
Ambrosiaster (Pseudo-Augustinus). Quaestiones. Ed. Souter, A. (CSEL, vol. L)
Vienna. 1908.
Apophthegmata Patrum. Greek in Cotelier, Ecclesiae Graecae Monumenta. (4
vols. Paris. 1677–92.) I. 338. MPG·LXV 71: Latin in Rosweyd, H.,
Vitae Patrum. (Antwerp. 1615. 2nd edn. 1628.) Books III, V–VII.
Augustine. De Civitate Dei. Ed. Hoffmann, E. (CSEL, vol. XL.) 1899–1900.
Scripta contra Donatistas. Ed. Petschenig, M. (CSEL, vols. LI–LIII.) 1908–
10.
Cyprian. Opera omnia. Ed. Hartel, W. 3 parts. (Epistles in part II.) 1871
(CSEL, vol. III).
Damasus — Ihm, M. Damasi Epigrammata. In the Teubner series. Leipsic. 1895.
Epiphanius. Opera. Ed. Oehler, F. 4 vols. Berlin. 1859–61.
Eusebius. Historia Ecclesiastica. Ed. Bright, W. 2nd edn. Oxford. 1881. Ed.
Schwartz, E. 3 parts (in the Berlin Griechische Christliche Schriftsteller).
Leipsic. 1903–9. Smaller edn. 1908.
Irenaeus. Adversus haereses. Ed. Stieren, A. 2 vols. Leipsic. 1853. Ed.
Harvey, W. W. 2 vols. Cambridge. 1857.
Jerome. Epistolae. Vol. I of Vallarsi's edition. Verona. 1734. See also the
epistle ad Praesidium de cereo paschali. Vol. XI (1742), part 2, col. 154.
Justin Martyr. Apology. Ed. Otto, J. C. Th. von. Jena. 1842.
Optatus Milevitanus. Ed. Ziwsa, C. (CSEL, vol. XXVI.) 1893.
Severus of Antioch. Select Letters (Syriac and English). Ed. Brooks, E. W.
4 parts. London. 1902–4.
Tertullian. Ed. Oehler, F. 3 vols. Leipsic. 1853, 1854. CSEL, part I [1890],
part III [1906]: (apparently two more parts to follow).

MODERN WRITERS

Bruns, H. T. Canones Apostolorum et Conciliorum saeculorum IV–VII. 2 parts
in one vol. Berlin. 1839.
Günther, O. Collectio Avellana (containing as no. 1 the Gesta inter Liberium et
Felicem). 1895 (CSEL, vol. XXXV).
Hatch, E. Article on "Orders, Holy" in DCA, vol. II. London. 1880.
—— The Organization of the Early Christian Churches (Bampton Lectures for
1880). 2nd edn. London. 1882.
Justellus, C. (Voellus, G. and Justellus, H.) Bibliotheca Iuris Canonici Veteris.
2 vols. Paris. 1661.
Maassen, Fr. Geschichte der Quellen und der Literatur des canonischen Rechts
im Abendlande. Gratz. 1870. [Indispensable.]
Turner, C. H. Ancient and Modern Church Organization. CQR. 1888.
—— The Roman Council under Damasus, A.D. 382. JTS. 1900.

CHAPTER VII

EXPANSION OF THE TEUTONS

1. ORIGINAL DOCUMENTS

In Corpus Inscriptionum Latinarum (CIL), vol. III: Inscr. Orientis et Illyrici, edd. Mommsen, Hirschfeld, v. Domaszewski; vol. XIII: Inscr. trium Galliarum et Germaniarum, edd. Hirschfeld, Zangemeister, v. Domaszewski. *See G. b.* IV.

2. AUTHORITIES

Ammianus Marcellinus. Rerum gestarum libri. *See Gen. Bibl.*
Anonymus Valesii. Origo Constantini imperatoris. Ed. Mommsen, Th., in MGH Chron. min. I, p. 1.
Aurelius Victor. De Caesaribus. Ed. Piehlmayr, Fr. Munich. 1892.
Ausonius. Opuscula. Ed. Schenkl, C., in MGH, auct. ant. v, 2. 1883. Peiper, R. Leipsic. 1886.
Auxentius. Ed. Waitz, G. Über das Leben und die Lehre des Ulfila. Hanover. 1840. Bernhardt, E. Vulfila. Halle. 1875. Kauffmann, Fr. Texte und Untersuchungen zur altgerman. Religionsgesch. I. Strassburg. 1899.
Caesar. Commentarii rerum in Gallia gestarum. Ed. Kübler, B. Leipsic. 1893. Meusel, H. Berlin. 1894.
Cassius, Dio. Historia Romana. Ed. Boissevain, U. Ph. Berlin. 1895–1901.
Eutropius. Breviarium ab urbe condita. Ed. Droysen, H., in MGH, auct. ant. II. 1879. Rühl, Fr. Leipsic. 1886.
Festus Breviarium. Ed. Wagener, C. Leipsic. 1886.
Florus. Epitoma de Tito Livio. Ed. Rossbach, O. Leipsic. 1896.
Herodianus. Ab excessu divi Marci. Ed. Mendelssohn, L. Leipsic. 1883.
Historici Graeci minores. Ed. Dindorf, L. Vol. I. Leipsic. 1870.
Jordanes. Romana et Getica. Ed. Mommsen, Th., in MGH, auct, ant. v, 1. 1882.
Julianus. Opera. Ed. Hertlein, C. F. Leipsic. 1875–6.
Libanius. Ed. Förster, R. Leipsic. 1903–9.
Livius. Ab urbe condita. (XLI–XLV.) Ed. Zingerle, A. Leipsic. 1899–1908.
—— Periochae. Ed. Jahn, O. Leipsic. 1853.
Mela. De chorographia. Ed. Parthey, G. Berlin. 1867. Frick, C. Leipsic. 1880.

Orosius. Historia adv. paganos. Ed. Zangemeister, C. Vienna. 1882.
Panegyrici Latini, xii. Ed. Bährens, E. Leipsic. 1874.
Plinius. Naturalis historia. Ed. Detlefsen, D. Berlin. 1866–82.
Plutarch. Opera. Ed. Reiske, J. J. Leipsic. 1774–82. Döhner, Th. and
    Dübner, F. Paris. 1841–55.
—— Vitae parallelae. Ed. Sintenis, C. Leipsic. 1858–60.
Ptolemaeus. Geographia. Ed. Müller, C. Vol. i. Paris. 1883–1901.
Scriptores historiae Augustae. Ed. Peter, H. 2nd edn. Leipsic. 1884.
Strabo. Geographia. Ed. Karmer, G. Berlin. 1844–52. Meineke, A. Leipsic.
    1852–3.
Tacitus. Opera. Ed. Orelli, J. G. 2nd edn. cur. Orelli, Schweizer-Sidler,
    Andresen, Meiser. Zurich and Berlin. 1859–95. Halm, C. 4th edn.
    Leipsic. 1883 and later edns.
Velleius Paterculus. Hist. Rom. Ed. Halm, C. Leipsic. 1876. Lib. ii. Ed.
    Rockwood, F. E. Boston. 1893. Ed. Ellis, R. Oxford. 1898.
Zonaras. Epitome historiarum. Ed. Pinder, M. and Büttner-Wobst, Th.
    Bonn. 1841–97. Dindorf, L. Leipsic. 1868–75.
Zosimus. Historia nova. Ed. Mendelssohn, L. Leipsic. 1887.
For the Church Historians (Philostorgius, Socrates, Sozomenus, Theodoret) *see*
    Bibliography to cc. i, ii, *and* v.

3. MODERN WORKS

(*a*) GENERAL

Arnold, W. Deutsche Urzeit. Gotha. 1879. 3rd edn. 1881.
Bethmann-Hollweg, M. A. von. Über die Germanen vor der Völkerwanderung.
    Bonn. 1850.
Bremer, O. Ethnographie der german. Stämme. (From Paul's Grundriss d. ger-
    man. Philol.) Strassburg. 1899. 2nd edn. 1904.
Dahn, F. Gesch. der deutschen Urzeit. Pt. i. Gotha. 1883.
Much, R. Deutsche Stammsitze. Halle. 1892.
Müllenhoff, K. Deutsche Altertumskunde. Vols. ii, iii. Berlin. 1887. 1892.
    Vol. ii. 2nd edn. 1906.
Schmidt, L. Gesch. der deutschen Stämme bis zum Ausgange der Völkerwanderung.
    Pt. i, Bks. 1–6. (Sieglius, Quellen u. Forschungen zur alten Gesch. u. Geogr.
    Heft 7, 10, 12.) Berlin. 1904–7.
Usinger, R. Die Anfänge der deutschen Geschichte. Hanover. 1875.
Wietersheim, E. von. Zur Vorgeschichte deutscher Nation. Leipsic. 1852.
—— Gesch. der Völkerwanderung. 4 vols. Leipsic. 1859–64. New edn. by
    Dahn, F. 2 vols. 1880–1.
Wilser, L. Stammbaum und Ausbreitung der Germanen. Bonn. 1895.
Zeuss, K. Die Deutschen und die Nachbarstämme. Munich. 1837. 2nd edn.
    (unaltered). Göttingen. 1904.

(*b*) ON AUTHORITIES (*and see Bibl. to Chapters* i, ii, *and* v)

Ammianus Marcellinus:
    Michael, H. Die verlorenen Bücher des Ammianus. Breslau. 1880.
    Reiche, F. Chronologie der letzten sechs Bücher des Ammianus. Liegnitz.
        1889.
    Schneider, E. Quaestiones Ammianeae. Berlin. 1879.

Anonymus Valesii :
      Ohnesorge, W.   Der Anon. Val. de Constantino.   Kiel.   1885.
Eutropius :
      Ebeling, P.   Quaestiones Eutrop.   Halle.   1881.
      Hartel, W.   Eutropius und Paulus Diaconus.   Vienna.   1872.
      Pirogoff, W.   De Eutropii breviarii indole ac fontibus.   Berlin.   1873.
Festus :
      Jacobi, R.   De Festi breviarii fontibus.   Bonn.   1874.
Herodianus :
      Baaz, E.   De Herodiani fontibus et auctoritate.   Berlin.   1909.
      Kreutzer, J.   De Herodiano rerum Romanarum scriptore.   Pars i.   Bonn.
            1881.
Libanius :
      Seeck, O.   Die Briefe des Libanius zeitlich geordnet.   Leipsic.   1906.
      Sievers, G. R.   Das Leben des Libanius.   Berlin.   1868.
Strabo :
      Dommerich, F. A.   Die Nachrichten Strabos über die zum jetzigen deutschen
            Bunde gehörigen Länder.   Marburg.   1848.
      Wilkins, H.   De Strabonis aliorumque rerum Gallicarum auctorum fonti-
            bus.   Marburg.   1886.
Tacitus :
      Froitzheim, J.   De Taciti fontibus in libro i annalium.   Bonn.   1873.
      Horstmann, W.   Über die Quellen des Tacitus in den ersten sechs Büchern
            der Annalen.   Marburg.   1877.
      Lückenbach, A.   De Germaniae Tacit. fontibus.   Marburg.   1891.
      Schumacher, L.   De Tacito Germaniae geographo.   Berlin.   1886.
Zonaras :
      Sauerbrei, P.   De fontibus Zonarae.   Leipsic.   1881.
      Zander, C. L. E.   Quibus e fontibus Zonaras hauserit suos annales Romanos.
            Ratzeburg.   1849.
Zosimus :
      Leidig, J.   Quaestiones Zosimeae.   Anspach.   1900.
      Martin, R. C.   De fontibus Zosimi.   Berlin.   1866.

(c) Monographs, Biographies, and Special Treatises

Abraham, A. F.   Zur Gesch. der german. u. pannon. Kriege unter Augustus.
      Berlin.   1875.
Bang, M.   Die Germanen im römischen Dienst bis zum Regierungsantritt Con-
      stantins I.   Berlin.   1906.
Bergman, J.   De P. Herennio Dexippo et Gothorum illa in Atticam incursione
      etc.   Stockholm.   1897.
Bessell, W.   Über das Leben des Ulfilas und die Bekehrung der Gothen zum
      Christenthume.   Gottingen.   1860.
Blanchet, A.   Les trésors de monnaies romaines et les invasions germaniques en
      Gaule.   Paris.   1900.
—— Les enceintes romaines de la Gaule.   Paris.   1907.
Böttger, H.   Wohnsitze der Deutschen in dem von Tacitus in seiner Germania
      beschriebenen Lande.   Stuttgart.   1877.
Böhmer-Romundt, H.   Ein neues Werk des Wulfila?   N. Jahrb. f. d. klass.
      Altert. xi, 1903, p. 272.
Borries, E. von.   Die Quellen zu den Feldzügen Julians des Abtrünnigen gegen
      die Germanen.   Hm. xxvii (1892), p. 170.

Borries, E. von. Die Alamannenschlacht des Jahres 357 n. Chr. u. ihre Örtlichkeit. Strassburg. 1892.

Brandes, H. B. Chr. Das ethnographische Verhältnis d. Kelten u. Germanen nach den Ansichten der Alten und den sprachlichen Überresten. Leipsic. 1857.

Buschan, G. Germanen u. Slaven, eine archäol.-anthropol. Studie. Münster. 1890.

Chadwick, H. M. The Origin of the English Nation. Cambridge. 1907.

Conrad, F. R. Mark Aurels Markomannenkrieg. Neu-Ruppin. 1889.

Dederich, A. Jul. Cäsar am Rhein. Paderborn. 1870.

—— Der Frankenbund, dessen Ursprung u. Entwickelung. Hanover. 1873.

Devrient, E. Hermunduren und Markomannen. N. Jahrb. f. d. klass. Altert. VII, 1901, p. 51.

—— Angeln und Warnen. Die Entstehung des thüringischen Stammes. *Ditto*, p. 418.

Domaszewski, A. von. Die Chronologie des bellum Germanicum et Sarmaticum 166–175 n. Chr. N. Heidelb. Jahrb., V, 1895, p. 107.

—— Der Völkerbund des Markomannenkrieges. Serta Harteliana. Vienna. 1896, p. 8.

Erdmann, A. Über die Heimat u. den Namen d. Angeln. Upsala. 1890.

Erhardt, L. Älteste german. Staatenbildung. Leipsic. 1879.

Hahnel, P. Die Bedeutung der Bastarner für das german. Altertum. Leipsic. 1865.

Hecker, H. Die Alamannenschlacht bei Strassburg. N. Jahrb. f. klass. Philol., CXXXIX (1889), p. 59.

Hedinger, A. Die Urheimat d. Germanen. N. Jahrb. f. d. klass. Altert. III, 1899, p. 562.

Helbing, A. Der Zug der Cimbern u. Teutonen. Zurich. 1898.

Helmke, F. Die Wohnsitze der Cherusker und der Hermunduren. Emden. 1903.

Holländer, A. Die Kriege der Alamannen mit den Römern im 3. Jahrh. n. Chr. Carlsruhe. 1874.

Huschberg, J. F. Geschichte der Alamannen und Franken bis zur Gründung der fränkischen Monarchie durch König Chlodwig. Sulzbach. 1840.

Jahn. Gesch. der Burgundionen. Halle. 1875.

Kinkelin, F. Die Urbewohner Deutschlands. Lindau and Leipsic. 1882.

Kirchmayr, H. Der altdeutsche Volksstamm d. Quaden. Vienna. 1888.

—— Bildungsverhältnisse des altdeutschen Volksstammes d. Quaden. Leipsic. 1893.

Köpke, R. Die Anfänge des Königthums bei den Gothen. Berlin. 1859.

Kossinna, G. Die vorgeschichtl. Ausbreitung d. Germanen in Deutschland. Ztschr. d. Ver. f. Volkskunde, VI, 1896, p. 1.

—— Die Grenze der Kelten und Germanen in der La Tène-Zeit. Corrbl. d. Ges. f. Anthropol. XXXVIII, 1907, p. 57.

—— Die ethnologische Stellung d. Ostgermanen. Indogerm. Forschungen, VII, 1897, p. 276.

Králiček. Die Donauvölker Altgermaniens nach Tacitus u. Ptolemaeus. Brünn. 1897.

Löwe, R. Ethnische u. sprachliche Gliederung d. Germanen. Halle. 1899.

Lupi, E. Dei caratteri intrinseci per classificare i Langobardi nelle loro attinenze storiche cogli altri popoli Germanici. Rome. 1879.

Matthias, F. Über die Wohnsitze und den Namen der Kimbern. Berlin. 1904.

Matusiak, S. Namen u. Wohnsitze d. Lugiervölker. Bochnia. 1889.

Merkel, F. Deutschlands Ureinwohner. Rostock. 1873.

Möhring, W. Cäsar im nordöstlichen Gallien u. am Rhein. Kreuznach. 1870.

Mommsen, Th. Der Markomannen-Krieg unter Kaiser Marcus (1896). Gesammelte Schriften, IV, p. 487.
Nicolai, R. Der sächsische Völkerbund vor Karl d. Gr. Part I. Berlin. 1865.
Nissen, H. Die Alamannenschlacht bei Strassburg. Westd. Ztschr. VI (1887), p. 319.
Oberziner, L. Le guerre Germaniche di Fl. Cl. Giuliano. Rome. 1896.
Paape. Über die Heimat der Arier und die der Ostgermanen. Schöneberg. 1906.
Pallmann, R. Die Cimbern u. Teutonen. Berlin. 1870.
Rappaport, B. Die Einfälle der Goten in das röm. Reich bis auf Constantin. Leipsic. 1899.
Rospatt, J. J. Die Verteidigungskriege der Römer am Rhein. Cologne. 1847.
Schiern, F. E. Origines et migrationes Cimbrorum. Copenhagen. 1842.
Schmidt, L. Älteste Gesch. d. Langobarden. Leipsic. 1884.
—— Älteste Gesch. d. Wandalen. Leipsic. 1888.
—— Zur Gesch. des Markomannenkrieges unter Mark Aurel. Hm. XXXIV, 1899, p. 155.
—— Gesch. der Wandalen. Leipsic. |1901.
Scott, Ch. A. A. Ulfilas, apostle of the Goths. Cambridge. 1885.
Sehmsdorf, E. Die Germanen in den Balkanländern bis zum Auftreten der Goten. Leipsic. 1899.
Sepp, B. Die Wanderungen der Cimbern u. Teutonen. Würzburg. 1882.
Stähelin, F. Der Eintritt der Germanen in die Geschichte. Festschr. f. Th. Plüss, Basel, 1908, p. 46.
Stein, Fr. Die Völkerstämme d. Germanen nach röm. Darstellung. Schweinfurt. 1896.
—— Die Stammsage der Germanen und die älteste Geschichte der deutschen Stämme. Erlangen. 1899.
—— Tacitus und seine Vorgänger über german. Stämme. Schweinfurt. 1904.
Tomaschek, W. Die Goten in Taurien. Vienna. 1881.
Vogt, F. Wulfila. Allgem. deutsche Biographie, XLIV, 1898, p. 270.
Waitz, G. Über das Leben und die Lehre des Ulfila. Hanover. 1840.
Watterich. Die Germanen des Rheins, ihr Kampf mit Rom und der Bundesgedanke. Leipsic. 1872.
Weismann, E. De Francorum primordiis. Bonn. 1868.
Wiegand, W. Die Alamannenschlacht bei Strassburg 357. Strassburg. 1887.
Wislicenus, P. Gesch. d. Elbgermanen vor der Völkerwanderung. Halle a. S. 1868.
Wittmann, F. M. Die älteste Geschichte der Markomannen. Abh. d. Münch. Akad., 1855.
Wormstall, J. Ethnographische Forschungen zur Gesch. Nordwestdeutschlands in der Römer-, Sachsen- und Frankenzeit. Münster. 1901.
—— Über die Chamaver, Brukterer u. Angrivarier, mit Rücksicht auf den Ursprung d. Franken u. Sachsen. Münster. 1888.
Zippel, G. Die Heimat d. Kimbern. Königsberg. 1893.
—— Deutsche Völkerbewegungen in der Römerzeit. Königsberg. 1895.

CHAPTER VIII

VALENTINIAN TO THEODOSIUS

AUTHORITIES

These are generally the same as those for ch. III.
To the list there given add:

Ambrose: Opera, MPL 14–17, including the life of Ambrose by Paulinus. The works are being re-edited by Schenkl, K., in CSEL, vol. XXXII, etc. For the letters cf. the translation in A Library of Fathers of the Holy Catholic Church, Oxford, 1881, and Principal Works of S. Ambrose. A Select Library of Nicene and Post-Nicene Fathers of the Christian Church. Series II. Vol. X. Oxford and New York. 1896.

Ausonius. Ed. Schenkl, K. MGH. 1883. Peiper, R. Leipsic. 1886.

Chronica Minora. Ed. Mommsen, T. MGH. 1892–6. 3 vols.

Claudian. Ed. Birt, Th. MGH. 1892. Koch, K. Leipsic. 1893.

Gregory (of Tours). Ed. Krusch, B. MGH. 1889.

John Chrysostom. MPG 47–64 (especially the 21 homilies on the sedition at Antioch: and cf. Rauschen ut infrà, pp. 495–529.)

Jordanes. Romana et Getica. Ed. Mommsen, T. MGH. 1882.

Orosius. Ed. Zangemeister, C. CSEL. Vol. V (1882.) id. Leipsic. 1889.

Rufinus. MPL 21.

MODERN WORKS

I. General

Boissier, G. La Fin du Paganisme. 4th edn. 2 vols. Paris. 1903.

Delbrück, H. Geschichte der Kriegskunst im Rahmen der politischen Geschichte. Berlin. 1900 ff.

Duchesne, L. Histoire ancienne de l'Église. See Gen. Bibl. Vol. II.

Ernst, Paul. Die Sozialen Zustände im römischen Reich vor dem Einfall der Barbaren. Die Neue Zeit. Jahrg. XI, vol. II. (1892–3.) Nos. 34–9.

Gibbon, E. Decline and Fall. Ed. Bury. See Gen. Bibl. and new edition 1909 ff.

Glover, T. R. Life and Letters. See Gen. Bibl.

Hodgkin, Th. Italy and her Invaders. See Gen. Bibl. Vol. I.

Ranke, L. von. Weltgeschichte. See Gen. Bibl.

Rauschen, G. Jahrbücher der christlichen Kirche unter dem Kaiser Theodosius dem Grossen. Freiburg-i.-B. 1897. (Indispensable.)

Rhys, J. Celtic Britain. 3rd edn. London. 1904. (In the series "Early Britain.")

Richter, H. Das weströmische Reich besonders unter den Kaisern Gratianus, Valentinianus II und Maximus. Berlin. 1865.

Scarth, H. M. Roman Britain. (In the series "Early Britain.") London. 1883.
Schiller, H. Geschichte der römischen Kaiserzeit. *See Gen. Bibl.* Vol. ii.
Schultze, V. *Sub voc.* Theodosius in RE³.
—— Geschichte des Untergangs des griechisch-römischen Heidentums. Jena. 1887–92. 2 vols.
Seeck, O. Articles in Pauly-Wissowa.
—— Die Briefe des Libanius. Leipsic. 1906.
—— Geschichte des Untergangs der antiken Welt. (2nd edn. Vols. i, 1897, ii, 1901. 1st edn. Vol. iii, 1909.) *See Gen. Bibl.*
Sievers, G. R. Studien zur Geschichte der römischen Kaiser. Berlin. 1870.
—— Das Leben des Libanius. Berlin. 1868.
Wietersheim, E. von. Geschichte der Völkerwanderung. Ed. by Dahn, F. Leipsic. 1880–1. 2 vols.

II. On Ambrose

Amati, A. A series of studies on Ambrose in Rendiconti : Reale Istituto Lombardo di Scienze e Littere. 2nd ser., vol. xxx, pp. 311–29, 588–612, 764–85, 892–911 ; vol. xxxi, pp. 706–23, 749–60.
Ambrosiana. Scritti varii pubblicati nel xv centenario dalla morte di S. Ambrogio con introduzione di Andrea C. Cardinale Ferrari Arcivescovo di Milano. Milan. 1897.
Barry, A. Life and times of St Ambrose *in* Lectures on Ecclesiastical History delivered in Norwich Cathedral. (pp. 377–414.) London. 1896. (Slight and popular.)
Broglie, J. V. A. duc de. Saint Ambrose, 340–97. 3rd edn. Paris. 1899.
    (In the series Les Saints.) English trans. Maitland, M. with preface by Tyrrel, G. 1899. (*And see* Les Pères Bollandistes et la Pénitence de Théodose. Le Correspondant. 20 August 1900. pp. 645–61, which is included in the present 4th edn.)
Conferenze Santambrosiane. (Gennaio—febbraio 1897.) Milan. 1897.
Förster, T. Ambrosius, Bischof von Mailand. Eine Darstellung seines Lebens und Wirkens. Halle. 1884. (Indispensable.) (Cf. A. Coen in RSI. Ann. 2, fasc. 3. (1885.) Turin. pp. 602–12.)
Ihm, M. Studia Ambrosiana. Leipsic. 1889.
Koch, H. Die Kirchenbusse des Kaisers Theodosius des Grossen in Geschichte und Legende. HJ, xxviii. 1907. Part ii. pp. 257–77.
de Labriolle, P. Saint Ambroise. Paris. 1908.
Ortroy, F. van. Saint Ambroise et l'Empereur Théodose. (1904.) AB. Excerptum ex tomo xxiii, fasc. iv. Brussels. 1904.
—— Les Vies grecques de saint Ambroise et leurs sources, in Ambrosiana, *vide supra.*
Thamin, R. Saint Ambroise et la morale chrétienne au iv siècle. Annales de l'Université de Lyon. Vol. viii. Lyons. 1895.

III. Other Monographs

Baynes, N. H. Rome and Armenia in the Fourth Century. EHR. xxv (1910). pp. 625–43.
Duchesne, L. Les documents ecclésiastiques sur les divisions de l'Empire romain au quatrième siècle. Mélanges Graux. pp. 133–41. Paris. 1884.

Güldenpenning, A. and Ifland, J. Der Kaiser Theodosius der Grosse, ein Beitrag zur römischen Kaisergeschichte. Halle. 1878.

Güterbock, K. Römisch-Armenien und die römische Satrapieen im vierten bis sechsten Jahrhundert; eine rechtsgeschichtliche Studie in Festgabe der juristischen Fakultät zu Königsberg für ihren Senior Johann Theodor Schirmer zum 1 August 1900.

Hassebrauk, G. Zur Geschichte des Kaisers Theodosius I. Jahresbericht über das Herzogliche Gymnasium zu Blankenburg am Harz. (Easter 1893– Easter 1894.) Wissenschaftliche Beilage.

Haverfield, F. J. The Romanization of Roman Britain. Reprint from vol. ii of Proceedings of the British Academy. (1905.) Oxford.

Hug, A. Antiochia und der Aufstand des Jahres 387 n. Chr. Studien aus dem classischen Altertum. Pt. i. Freiburg and Tübingen. 1881. pp. 133–200.

Judeich. Die Schlacht bei Adrianopel am 9. August 378. Deutsche Zeitschrift für Geschichtswissenschaft. 1891. Vol. vi, pp. 1–21.

Kaufmann, G. Kritische Untersuchungen zu dem Kriege Theodosius des Grossen mit den Gothen 378–82. Forschungen zur deutschen Geschichte, vol. xii. Göttingen. 1872. pp. 413–38. [Zos. iv, cc. 26–34. Eunap. Fragm. 6, 7.]

—— Wurde Theodosius von Gratian zunächst zum magister militum und erst nach einem Siege über die Sarmaten zum Kaiser ernannt? Philologus. 1872. Vol. xxxi. pp. 473–80.

Klee, H. De exitu Valentiniani II Augusti et de Eugenii imperii initiis. Monasterii Guestphalorum. 1892.

Léotard, E. Essai sur la condition des Barbares établis dans l'Empire romain au ive siècle. Paris. 1873.

Liebenam, W. Reichsgewalt und Reichsteilungen im 4ten Jahrhundert n. Chr. Festschrift für A. von Bamberg. pp. 150–82. Gotha. 1905.

Löffler, E. F. O. Der Comes Theodosius. Halle. 1885.

Maurer, H. Valentinians Feldzug gegen die Alamannen. Zeits. f. d. Gesch. des Oberrheins, N. F. iii. 1888. pp. 303–28 (for topography).

Mommsen, T. Carmen Codicis Parisini 8084. Hm. Vol. iv. 1870. pp. 350–63.

—— Das römische Militärwesen seit Diocletian. Hm. Vol. xxiv. 1889. pp. 195– 279.

Morel, C. Recherches sur un poème latin du ive siècle. RA. 1868 (June and July), nouvelle série. 9e année, pp. 451–9, pp. 44–55.

Nitzsche, R. Der Gothenkrieg unter Valens und Theodosius. Altenburg. 1871. (Now unobtainable.)

Reiche, F. Chronologie der letzten sechs Bücher des Ammianus Marcellinus. Liegnitz. 1889.

Runkel, F. Die Schlacht bei Adrianopel. Rostock. 1903.

Seeck, O. Preface to Edition of Symmachus, MGH.

—— Zur Chronologie und Quellenkritik des Ammianus Marcellinus. 1906. Hm. Vol. xli. pp. 481–539.

Stephan, C. Kritische Untersuchungen zur Geschichte der Westgoten von 372– 400. i. Der Gothenkrieg unter Theodosius. Jahresb. über das königl. Gymnas. zu Siegburg. 1889.
    ii. Die Friedenszeit von 382–95. Programm des königl. kathol. Gymnas. an Aposteln zu Köln, No. 447. Cologne. 1897.

CHAPTER IX

THE TEUTONIC MIGRATIONS

BIBLIOGRAPHY

I. Original Authorities

Ambrosii Opera. MPL, 15, 16. *See Gen. Bibl.* Ballerini. 5 vols. Milan. 1875 ff.
Ammiani Marcellini rerum gestarum libri. Ed. Gardthausen. Leipsic. 1874, *and see Bibl. to cc.* I, II, *and* V.
Aurelii Prudentii Clementis carmina. Rec. Dressel, A. Leipsic. 1860.
Aurelius Victor. Ed. Schröter, F. Leipsic. 1829–31.
Bedae presbyteri chronicon. MGH. Ed. Mommsen. Chron. minora II, 223. MPL. Plummer, C. Oxford. 2 vols. 1896.
Cassiodori chronicon. Ed. Mommsen. Chron. minora II, 109.
Cl. Marii Victoris oratoris Massiliensis Alethia. Ed. Schenkl, C. CSEL. 1888.
Claudii Claudiani carmina. Ed. Birt, Th. Berlin. 1892. MGH. Rec. J. Koch. Leipsic. 1893.
Codex Theodosianus. Ed. Mommsen, and Meyer. *See Gen. Bibl.*
Consularia Constantinopolitana. Ed. Mommsen. Chron. minora I, 196.
Eunapii fragmenta. *In* Müller, FHG. *See Gen. Bibl.* Tom. IV.
Gregorii Turonensis Histor. Francorum. Ed. Arndt, W. Hanover. 1884. MGH. Ed. Omont, C. 2 vols. Paris. 1886–93 (Collection des Textes).
Hydatii chronicon. Ed. Mommsen. Chron. minora II, 1.
Isidori Historia Gothorum Wandalorum et Sueborum. Ed. Mommsen. Chron. minora II, 241.
Isidori iunioris Hispalensis chronicon. Ed. Mommsen. Chron. minora II, 391.
Jordanis Getica. Ed. Mommsen. MGH. 1882.
Le poème d'Orientius par Bellanger, L. Paris. 1903.
Libanii orationes. Ed. Reiske. Altenburg. 1791–7. *Opera.* Rec. Förster, R. Vol. I–IV. Leipsic. 1903–8.
Marcellini Comitis chronicon. Ed. Mommsen. Chron. minora II, 37.
Pacati penegyricus Theodosio Augusto dictus. Ed. Bährens, Panegyrici veteres. Leipsic. 1874, p. 217.
Pauli Orosii historiarum adv. paganos libri vii. Ex recogn. Zangemeister, C. Leipsic. 1889.
Philostorgius. Ed. Gottfried, J. 1643. MPG 65.
Prosperi Aquitani chronicon. Ed. Mommsen, Th. Chron. minora I, 341.
Q. Aurelii Symmachi quae supersunt. Ed. Seeck, O. MGH, auct. ant. VI.
Salviani presbyteri Massiliensis Opera. Ed. Halm, C. MGH, auct. ant. I.
Socratis Ἐκκλησιαστικὴ ἱστορία. Ed. Hussey, R. Oxford. 1853.
Sozomeni Ἐκκλησιαστικὴ ἱστορία. Ed. Hussey, R. Oxford. 1860.
Sulpicii Severi Opera. Ed. Halm, C. CSEL.
Synesii Cyrenensis Opera. Ed. Krabinger. Landeshut. 1850. MPG, vol. LXVI.
Themistii orationes. Ed. Dindorf. Leipsic. 1832.
Theodoreti historia ecclesiastica. Ed. Valesius, H. Hist. eccl. scriptores. Tom. III. Amsterdam. 1695.
Zosimi Historia nova. Ed. Mendelssohn, L. Leipsic. 1887.

II. General Modern Works

Dahn, F. Deutsche Geschichte ɪ, 1. 2. Leipsic. 1883–8.
—— Urgeschichte der germanischen und romanischen Völker ɪ, 147, 227, 333. Berlin. 1881.
Gibbon. Decline and Fall. *See Gen. Bibl.*
Güldenpenning, A. Geschichte des oströmischen Reichs unter den Kaisern Arcadius und Theodosius II. Halle. 1885.
Le Nain de Tillemont. Mémoires. *See Gen. Bibl.*
Ranke, L. von. Weltgeschichte ɪv, 1, 155–262. *See Gen. Bibl.*
Richter, H. Das weströmische Reich besonders unter den Kaisern Gratianus, Valentinianus II und Maximus. Berlin. 1865.
Schmidt, Ludw. Geschichte der deutschen Stämme bis zum Ausgang der Völkerwanderung ɪ, 2, 114–123, 164–223. Berlin. 1905.
—— Geschichte der Wandalen. Leipsic. 1901, pp. 17–28.
Wietersheim, E. von. Geschichte der Völkerwanderung. 2nd edn. by Dahn, F. ɪɪ, 35–169. Leipsic. 1881.

III. Monographs and Special Treatises

Eicken, H. v. Der Kampf der Westgothen und Römer unter Alarich. Leipsic. 1876.
Güldenpenning, A. and Ifland, J. Der Kaiser Theodosius der Grosse. Halle. 1878.
Kaufmann, G. Forschungen zur deutschen Geschichte xɪɪ, 413. Philologus xxxɪ, 473.
Kaul, L. Abwanderung und Verteilung der Alamannen. Beitr. zur Gesch. der Völkerwanderung. Augsburg. 1907.
Keller, R. Stilicho oder die Geschichte des weströmischen Reichs von 395–408. Berlin. 1884.
Lamprecht, K. Fränkische Ansiedelungen und Wanderungen im Rheinland. Westdeutsche Zeitschr. ɪ (1882), p. 123.
Mommsen, Th. Hm. 24, 195; 38, 101 (*or* Ges. Schriften, ɪv, 516).
Pallmann, R. Geschichte der Völkerwanderung von der Gothenbekehrung bis zum Tode Alarichs. Gotha. 1863.
Rauschen. Jahrbücher der christlichen Kirche unter Theodosius dem Grossen. Freiburg. 1897.
Runkel. Die Schlacht von Adrianopel. Berlin. 1903.
Schmidt, Ludw. Die Ursachen der Völkerwanderung. N. Jahrb. f. d. klass. Altert. xɪ (1903), p. 340.
Stephan, Chr. Kritische Untersuchungen zur Geschichte der Westgoten von 372–400. ɪ. Siegburg. 1889. ɪɪ. Cologne. 1897.
Stähelin. Der Eintritt der Germanen in die Geschichte (Festschrift für Th. Plüss). Basel. 1908. (*Most recent discussion of* CIG 2058 — the inscription at Olbia.)
Thierry, A. Alaric, l'agonie de l'empire. Paris. 1880.
Volz, B. De Vesegothorum cum Romanis conflictionibus post mortem Fl. Theodosii I exortis. Greifswald. 1861.
Westberg, F. Zur Wanderung der Langobarden. (Akad. St Petersburg.) 1904.

CHAPTER X (A)

THE VISIGOTHS IN GAUL, 412-507

I. SOURCES

IN LATIN

Cassiodorus Senator. Variae. Ed. Mommsen, MGH, auct. ant. XII. 1894. Select transl. with introd., Hodgkin, T. London. 1886.

Chronicles: —

    Chronica Gallica a. 452 et 511. Chron. min. I.

    Chronica Regum Visigothorum. MGH, Leges Visigoth. pp. 457–61.

    Chronicorum Caesaraugustanorum reliquiae. Chron. min. II.

    Gregory of Tours, Historia Francorum. Ed. Arndt, MGH. 1884. Vol. I.

    Hydatius, MGH, auct. ant. XI. (Chron. min. II.)

    Isidore of Seville. Chron. min. II. MPL 81–4.

    Jordanes, Getica. Ed. Mommsen, MGH. 1882.

    Marius Aventicensis. Chron. min. II. Ed. Arndt, W. Leipsic. 1878. MPL 72.

    Orosius, Paulus, Historiarum adversum paganos lib. VII. Ed. Zangemeister in CSEL. 1882. *And in* Teubner. 1889.

    Paulus Diaconus, Hist. Romana (in Historia Miscella). MPL 95, and MGH, auct. ant. II. 1879. Muratori, I.

    Prosper Tiro of Aquitaine, MGH, auct. ant. IX (Chron. min. I). *And see* Bury-Gibbon, III. Ap. 1.

Consular Fasti for Italy and the Eastern Empire. MGH, auct. ant. IX. (Chron. min. I.)

Ennodius, Vita Epiphanii episcopi Ticinensis. Ed. Vogel, MGH, auct. ant. VII. CSEL.

Inscriptions in CIL, Vol. XII, and in Le Blant, Inscr. chrétiennes de la Gaule, *see Gen. Bibl.*

Leges Visigothorum. Ed. Zeumer, MGH, Leges sect. I. 1902.

Lex Romana Visigothorum. Ed. Hänel. Leipsic. 1849.

Salvianus, De Gubernatione Dei. MGH, auct. ant. I. CSEL 8.

The Imperial Decrees in Codex Theodosianus and Codex Justinianus, *see Gen. Bibl.*

The Poems of : —

    Apollinaris Sidonius. MGH, auct. ant. VIII. MPL 58.

    Merobaudes. MGH, auct. ant. XIV. CSHB, *and see* Bury-Gibbon, III, Ap. 1.

    Paulinus of Pella. CSEL 16.

    Rutilius Namatianus. Ed. Vessereau. Paris. 1904.

The Synodal Acts *in* Mansi, *see Gen. Bibl.*

IN GREEK

Cedrenus. CSHB. 1838–9.
Chronicon Paschale. Dindorf, L. in CSHB. 2 vols. 1832. MPG.
Ecclesiastical historians : —
    Evagrius. Ed. Bidez, J. and Parmentier, L. London. 1898.
    Sozomen. MPG, *and see Bibl. to cc.* I, II, *and* v.
    Theodorus Lector. MPG 186. *See* Bury-Gibbon, IV, Ap. 1.
John of Antioch. FHG IV. MPG 77.
Pagan historians : —
    Candidus. FHG IV.
    Malchus. FHG IV. Dindorf, L. Hist. Gr. min.
    Olympiodorus. FHG IV.
    Priscus. FHG IV. CSHB.
    Procopius, De Bello Vandalico. CSHB. (Dindorf.) 1833–8. Muratori,
       I. *See* Bury-Gibbon, IV, Ap. 1. *See* Opera omnia, ed. Haury, J., *in*
       progress. Leipsic. 1906 ff.
Theophanes Confessor. Ed. de Boor. 2 vols. Leipsic. 1883–5.
Zonaras. CSHB. 1841–4 and 1896. Dindorf, L. 6 vols. 1868–75. (Teubner.)
    Notes by Du Cange, C.

II. MODERN WORKS

Barrière-Flavy, C. Les arts industriels des peuples barbares de la Gaule. Toulouse.
    1901. pp. 273–324.
Bethmann-Hollweg, M. A. von. Der germanisch-romanische Civilprozess im
    Mittelalter. Vol. I. Bonn. 1868. pp. 173–98.
Brunner, H. Deutsche Rechtsgeschichte. Vol. I. 2nd edn. Leipsic. 1906.
    pp. 74–5, 482–9.
Büdinger, M. Apollinaris Sidonius als Politiker : Sitzungsberichte der Wiener
    Akademie. XCVII. (1880.) pp. 915–54.
Bury, J. B. Later Roman Empire. Vols. I, II (passim). *See Gen. Bibl.*
Dahn, F. Die Könige der Germanen. Vol. v. Würzburg. 1870. VI. 2nd edn.
    Leipsic. 1885.
—— Urgeschichte der germanischen und romanischen Völker. Vol. I. 2nd edn.
    Berlin. 1899. pp. 347–66.
Ebert, A. Allgemeine Geschichte der Literatur des Mittelalters im Abendlande.
    Vol. I. 2nd edn. Leipsic. 1889. pp. 402–28.
Engel, A. and Serrure, R. Traité de numismatique du moyen âge. Vol. I. Paris.
    1891. p. 41.
Freeman, E. A. West-Goths and Burgundians; Wallia and the settlement of
    Aquitaine; Theodoric the West-Goth and Aetius : *in* Western Europe in the
    fifth century, an Aftermath. London. 1904. pp. 171–287.
Gaupp, E. T. Die germanischen Ansiedelungen und Landtheilungen. Breslau.
    1884. pp. 372–414.
Halban, A. von. Das römische Recht in den germanischen Volksstaaten. Pt 1.
    Breslau. 1899. pp. 151–237.
Hodgkin, T. Italy and her Invaders. Vols. I, II, III. *See Gen. Bibl.*
Kaufmann, G. Über die Hunnenschlacht des Jahres 451 : Forschungen zur
    deutschen Geschichte, VIII. 1868. pp. 115–46.
—— Über das Föderatverhältniss des tolosanischen Reiches zu Rom : *ibid.* VI.
    1866. pp. 435–76.

Löning, Edg. Geschichte des deutschen Kirchenrechts. Vol. i. Strassburg.
    1878. pp. 500–48.
Monod, G. Bibl. de l'histoire de France. Paris. 1888.
Pflugk-Harttung, J. von. Zur Thronfolge in den germanischen Stammesstaaten:
    Zeitschrift der Savignystiftung für Rechtsgeschichte. xi, 1. 1890. pp. 186–7.
Roger, M. L'enseignement des lettres classiques d'Ausone à Alcuin. Paris. 1905.
    pp. 48–88.
Schmidt, Ludwig. Allgemeine Geschichte der germanischen Völker. Munich.
    1909. Vol. i. pp. 120–30.
—— Geschichte der deutschen Stämme bis zum Ausgange der Völkerwanderung.
    Berlin. 1910. Vol. i. pp. 233–304.
Werminghoff, A. Geschichte der Kirchenverfassung Deutschlands im Mittelalter.
    Vol. i. Hanover. 1905. pp. 40–4.
Wietersheim, E. von. Geschichte der Völkerwanderung. Vol. ii. 2nd edn.
    by Dahn, F. Leipsic. 1881. pp. 169–320.
Yver, G. Euric roi des Wisigoths: Études d'histoire du moyen âge dédiées à
    G. Monod. Paris. 1896. pp. 11–46.
Zeumer, K. Geschichte der Westgothischen Gesetzgebung: NAGDG. xxiii.
    1898. pp. 419-516. xxiv. 1899. pp. 39–122.

CHAPTER X (B)

THE FRANKS BEFORE CLOVIS

I. CONTEMPORARY AUTHORITIES

Ammianus Marcellinus. Rerum Gestarum libri. *See Bibl. to cc.* I, II, *and* V.
Apollinaris Sidonius. Epistulae et Carmina (ed Luetjohann, Chr.). MGH, auct. ant. t. VIII. 1887.
Chronicarum quae dicuntur Fredegarii Scholastici libri IV (ed. Krusch, Bruno). MGH. Scriptores rerum merovingicarum, t. II. Hanover. 1888.
Gregorius Turonensis. Historiae Francorum libri X (ed. Arndt, W.). MGH. Scriptores rerum merovingicarum, t. I. Hanover. 1884.
Lex Salica. Ed. Hessels, J. H. and Kern, H. London. 1880. Ed. Geffcken, H. Leipsic. 1898.
Liber Historiae Francorum. Ed. Krusch, B. *Ibid.*

II. LATER WORKS

Chiffletius, J. J. Anastasius Childerici I Francorum regis. Antwerp. 1655.
Dahn, F. Urgeschichte der germanischen und romanischen Völker. 4 vols. Berlin. 1880-9. (Oncken's Allgemeine Geschichte.)
—— Deutsche Geschichte, t. I. Gotha. 1883.
Fustel de Coulanges, N. Histoire des institutions politiques de l'ancienne France. t. II. L'invasion germanique et la fin de l'Empire. Paris. 1891.
Gutsche, O., and Schultze, W. Deutsche Geschichte von der Urzeit bis zu den Karolingern. 2 vols. Stuttgart. 1894-6.
Huschberg, J. F. Geschichte der Alamannen und Franken bis zur Gründung der fränkischen Monarchie durch König Chlodwig. Sulzbach. 1840.
Junghans, W. Kritische Untersuchungen zur Geschichte der fränkischen Könige Childeric und Chlodovech. Göttingen. 1857. French transl. Monod, G. Paris. 1878.
Kurth, G. Histoire poétique des Mérovingiens. Paris. 1893.
Lamprecht, K. Fränkische Wanderungen und Ansiedlungen. Aachen. 1882. (Zeitsch. des Aachener Geschichtsvereins, t. IV.)
Lüthgen, E. Die Quellen und der historische Werth der fränkischen Trojasage. Bonn. 1876.
Ricci, F. Notes sur les tarifs de la loi salique. (RH, mars-avril, 1909.)
Schröder, R. Die Ausbreitung der Salischen Franken. (Forschungen zur deutschen Geschichte, t. XIX. 1879.)
Thonissen, J. J. L'organisation judiciaire, le droit pénal et la procédure pénale de la loi salique. 2nd edn. Brussels and Paris. 1882.
Waitz, G. Deutsche Verfassungsgeschichte, t. I and II. 3rd edn. Kiel. 1880-2.
Wietersheim, E. von. Geschichte der Völkerwanderung. 2nd edn. Ed. Dahn, F. 2 vols. Leipsic. 1880-1.

CHAPTER XI

THE SUEVES, ALANS AND VANDALS IN SPAIN 409–29
THE RULE OF THE VANDALS IN AFRICA 429–533

I. SOURCES

For edns. see, except where otherwise stated, bibl. to ch. x (*a*).

1. In Latin

Italian and East-roman Consular Fasti. MGH, auct, ant. IX (chron. min. I).
Chronicles of Prosper Tiro Hydatius, Cassiodorus, Marius Aventicensis, Victor
    Tonnenensis, Marcellinus Comes. MGH IX, XI (chron. min. I, II).
Orosius, Historiarum adversum paganos lib. VII. *See Bibl. to c.* x (*a*).
Salvianus, De Gubernatione Dei. *See Bibl. to c.* x (*a*).
Isidore of Seville, Historia Sueborum et Wandalorum.
Possidius, Vita Augustini. *See Bibl. to c.* VI.
Letters of St Augustine. *See Bibl. to c.* IV.
Jordanes, Romana et Getica. MGH, auct. ant. V.
Paulus Diaconus, Historia Romana. *See Bibl. to c.* x (*a*).
Victor of Vita, Historia persecutionis Africanae provinciae. CSEL.
Laterculus Regum Wandalorum et Alanorum. MGH, auct. ant. XIII (chron. min.
    III).
Life of Bishop Fulgentius (ascribed to Ferrandus). MPL 65, 67, 18.
Poems of Apollinaris Sidonius, Merobaudes, Dracontius, Corippus: MGH, auct.
    ant. VIII; XIV; III, 2, *and in* Codex Salmasianus, Anthologia Lat. ed. Riese
    II, I, pp. 33–296.
The *Varia* of Cassiodorus. *See Bibl. to c.* x (*a*).
Inscriptions in CIL, Vol. VIII. *See Gen. Bibl.*

2. In Greek

Chronicles of Olympiodorus, Priscus, and John of Antioch.
Procopius. De Bello Gothico. De Bello Vandalico. Historia arcana. Opera.
    Ed. Haury. (Vol. I–III.) Leipsic. 1905–6.

II. LITERATURE

Audollent, A. Carthage romaine 146 B.C.–698 A.D. Paris. 1901–4. pp. 95–113,
    541–65, 749–66.
Auler, A. Victor von Vita: Historische Untersuchungen. Dedicated to A. Schäfer.
    Bonn. 1882. pp. 253–75.
Bethmann-Hollweg, M. A. von. Der germanisch-romanische Civilprozess im
    Mittelalter. Vol. I. Bonn. 1868. pp. 129–39.

Bury, J. B. Later Roman Empire. Vols, I, II. *See Gen. Bibl.*

Cagnat, R. L'armée romaine d'Afrique. Paris. 1892.

Dahn, F. Die Könige der Germanen. Vol. I. 2nd edn. Leipsic. 1910.

—— Urgeschichte der germanischen und romanischen Völker. Vol. I. 2nd edn. Berlin. 1899. pp. 147–214.

Ebert, A. Literatur des Mittelalters. *See Gen. Bibl.* Vol. 1. 2nd edn. pp. 429–32, 455–8.

Engel, A. and Serrure, R. Traité de numismatique du moyen âge, Paris. 1891 ff. Vol. I. pp. 17–20.

Freeman, E. A. Aetius and Boniface : *in* Western Europe in the fifth century, an Aftermath. London. 1904.

Friedländer, J. Die Münzen der Vandalen. Leipsic. 1849.

Gaupp, E. T. Die germanischen Ansiedelungen und Landteilungen. Breslau. 1844. pp. 432–54.

Görres, F. Beiträge zur Kirchengesch. des Wandalenreiches. ZWT, XXXVI, 1. (1893.) pp. 494–513.

—— Kirche und Staat im Wandalenreiche : Deutsche Zeitsch, f. Geschichtswissenschaft. X. (1893.) pp. 14–70.

Halban, A. von. Das römische Recht in den germanischen Volksstaaten. Part I. Breslau. 1899. pp. 60–86.

Hodgkin, T. Italy and her Invaders. Vol. II, pp. 241–90. *See Gen. Bibl.*

—— Visigothic Spain. EHR, II, p. 209.

Kaufmann, G. Die Werke des C. Sollius Apollinaris Sidonius als eine Quelle für die Geschichte seiner Zeit. Göttingen. 1864.

Leclercq, H. L'Afrique chrétienne. Vol. II. Paris. 1904. pp. 143–213.

Manitius, M. Geschichte der christlich-lateinischen Poesie bis zur Mitte des 8. Jahrh. Stuttgart. 1891. pp. 326–44.

Papencordt, F. Geschichte der vandalischen Herrschaft in Afrika. Berlin. 1837.

Pflugk-Harttung, J. von. Zur Thronfolge in den germanischen Stammesstaaten : Zeitschr. der Savignystift. für Rechtsgeschichte. XI, 1. (1890.) pp. 182–4.

Pötzsch, W. Victor von Vita und die Kirchenverfolgung im Wandalenreiche. Döbeln. 1887.

Ruinart, T. Historia persecutionis Vandalicae. Venice. 1737.

Schmidt, L. Bonifatius und der Übergang der Wandalen nach Afrika : HVJS. II. (1899.) pp. 450–62.

—— Geschichte der Wandalen. Leipsic. 1901.

—— Zur Geschichte der Wandalen. BZ, XII. (1903.) pp. 601–3.

—— Allg. Geschichte der german. Völker. Munich. 1909. pp. 53–67.

Geschichte der deutschen Stämme bis zum Ausgange der Völkerwanderung. Vol. I. Berlin. 1910. pp. 354–66.

Schulze, H. De testamento Genserici. Jena. 1859.

—— Geschichtliche Entwickelung der fürstlichen Hausverfassung im deutschen Mittelalter : Zeitschr. für Rechtsgeschichte. VII. (1868.) pp. 341–7.

Schwarze, A. Untersuchungen über die äussere Entwicklung der afrikanischen Kirche. Göttingen. 1892.

Shaw, R. Diggles. The Fall of the Visigothic Power in Spain. EHR. XXI. p. 209.

Tissot, Ch. Géographie comparée de la province romaine d'Afrique. Paris. 1884–8. Vols. I, II, passim.

Wietersheim, E. von. Geschichte der Völkerwanderung. Vol. II. 2nd edn. Leipsic. 1880. pp. 185–207.

Wrede, F. Über die Sprache der Wandalen. Strassburg. 1886.

CHAPTER III (A)

THE ASIATIC BACKGROUND

I. SPECIAL BIBLIOGRAPHIES

Mezhov, V. J. Recueil du Turkestan, comprenant des livres et des articles sur l'Asie Centrale....Composé par Méjow, V. J. Petersburg. 1878 ff.

——Сибирская библіографія... Bibliographia Sibirica. 3 vols. Petersburg. 1891–3.

—— Библіографія Азіи... Bibliographia Asiatica. 2de sér. Toute l'Asie excepté la Sibérie. 2 vols. / Petersburg. 1893–4.

Pypin, A. N. Исторія русской этнографіи. 4 vols. Petersburg. 1890–2.

II. ANCIENT AND MEDIEVAL AUTHORITIES

Medieval Authorities on the Nomads in Europe, in Stritter, J. G. Memoriae populorum, olim ad Danubium, Pontum Euxinum, Paludem Maeotidem, Caucasum, Mare Caspium et inde magis ad Septemtriones incolentium, e Scriptoribus historiae Byzantinae erutae et digestae. 4 vols. Petersburg. 1771–9.—Zeuss, K., Die Deutschen u. ihre Nachbarstämme. Munich. 1837, pp. 691 ff.

Sobranie свѣдѣніи о народахъ въ средней Азіи въ древнія времена. Translated by Father Hyacinth [Bichurin]. Petersburg. 1851.

Documents sur les Tou-Kiue (Turcs) occidentaux. Recueillis et commentés par E. Chavannes. In Sbornik trudov Orkhon. ekspeditsii, vol. VI. Petersburg. 1903.

Ammianus Marcellinus. Rerum gestarum libri. Ed. Gardthausen. Translated by Yonge, C. D. London. 1887. *See Bibl. to cc.* I, II *and* V.

Arrianus, F. Anabasis et Indica (in Arriani quae exstant omnia. Edidit Roos, A. D. Leipsic. 1907). Transl. by Chinnock, E. J. London. 1893.

Curtius Rufus, Q. Historiae Alexandri Magni. Ed. Vogel, T. Translated...with original notes...by Pratt, P. Revised edition. 2 vols. London. 1821.

Fredegar. Historia Francorum. Ed. Krusch, B., 1880, in MGH. SS. r. Mer. II.

Gardēzī : Barthold, V. Отчетъ о поѣздкѣ въ среднюю Азію, in Mémoires de l'Acad. Imp. des Sciences de St-Pétersbourg. VIIIe sér. Tome 1er. 1897.

Herodotus. Ed. Blakesley, J. W. London. 1854. Transl. by Macaulay, G. C. London. 1890.

Hippocrates. Περὶ ἀέρων. Ed. Ruder, J. Sulzbach. 1849. Transl. by Adams, F. London. 1849.

Ibn Rusta (Rosteh) : Chwolson, D. Извѣстія о Хозарахъ ... Болгарахъ, Мадьярахъ, Славянахъ и Руссахъ ... Ибнъ-Даста. Petersburg. 1869.

Inschriften, Die alttürkischen, der Mongolei.   Ed. by Radloff, W.   3 vols.
    Petersburg. 1895–9.
John of Plano Carpini.   Historia Mongalorum : in Recueil de voyages et mémoires,
    publ. par la Soc. de Géogr. Tome 4. Paris. 1839, *and see below under* Wm.
    of Rubruck.
Jordanes, De origine actibusque Getarum.   Ed. Mommsen, Th., in MGH.
Marco Polo.   The Book of Ser Marco Polo. . .done in English by Yule, H. 2 vols.
    London. 1871. 2nd edn. 1874. 3rd edn. 1903.
—— Italian version prepared by Ramusio, G. B., in the 2nd volume of the
    Navigationi e viaggi. Venice. 1559. Transl. Engl. London. 1625.
Mauricius.   Arriani Tactica et Mauricii Artis militaris libri. . .ed. . .Scheffer, J.
    Upsala. 1664.
Rogerius canon of Varad.   Carmen miserabile, in MGH. SS. xxix.
Schiltberger, Hans.   Reisen, ed. by Langmantel. Tübingen. 1885.
Strabo. Geographica.   Ed. Meineke, A. Leipsic. 3 vols. 1852–3. Transl. by
    Hamilton, H. C. and Falconer, W. London. 1854–7.
Thomas archdeacon of Spalato.   Historia pontificum Salonitanorum, in MGH.
    SS. xxix.
William of Rubruck (Rubruquis).   Itinerarium Wilhelmi de Rubruk. . .ad partes
    orientales, in Recueil de voyages et mémoires, publ. par la Soc. de Géogr.
    Tome iv. Paris. 1839.
—— Journey to the eastern parts of the world 1253–5. With two accounts of the
    earlier journey of John of Plano Carpini, transl. by Rockhill. London. 1900.

III. MODERN WORKS

(a) GENERAL

Bretschneider, E. Mediaeval Researches from Eastern Asiatic Sources. Fragments
    towards the knowledge of the geography and history of Central and Western
    Asia from the 13th to the 17th century. 2 vols. London. 1888.
Cahun, L.   Introduction à l'histoire de l'Asie. Turcs et Mongols des origines à
    1405. Paris. 1896.
De Guignes, J. Histoire générale des Huns, Turcs, Mogols et des autres peuples
    tartares occidentaux. 5 vols. Paris. 1756–8.
Georgi, J. G.   Beschreibung aller Nationen d. russischen Reichs. 2 vols.
    Petersburg. 1776–80.
Gibbon, E.   Decline and Fall, ed. Bury. *See Gen. Bibl.*
Herbelot, B. d'.   Bibliothèque orientale ou Dictionnaire universel contenant tout
    ce qui fait connaître les peuples de l'Orient. Paris. 1697. 2nd edition with
    "Supplément" by Visdelou, C. and Galland, A. Maestricht. 1776–81. New
    edition. The Hague. 1777–9.
Hruševśkyj, M. Gesch. d. ukrainischen (ruthenischen) Volkes. i. Leipsic.
    1906, pp. 89 ff.: (history of the nomad peoples in Russia.)
Huntington, E.   The Pulse of Asia. London. 1907.
Keane, A. H. Asia. 2 vols. London. 1896. 2nd edn. vol. i. 1906. (Stanford's
    Compendium of Geography.)
Kiepert, H. Lehrbuch d. alten Geographie. Berlin. 1878.
Marquart, J. Osteuropäische u. ostasiatische Streifzüge. Leipsic. 1903.
Pallas, P. S.   Sammlungen hist. Nachrichten ü. d. mongol. Völkerschaften.
    2 vols. Petersburg. 1776–1802.
Ratzel, Fr. History of Mankind. Transl. by Butler, A. J. 3 vols. London.
    1896–8.

Reclus, E. Nouvelle géographie universelle. Vols. VI and VII. Paris. 1876–94.
Richthofen, F. Vorlesungen über Allgemeine Siedelungs- und Verkehrsgeographie. Bearbeitet von O. Schlüter. Berlin. 1908.
Ritter, K. Die Erdkunde. Asien. 9 vols. Berlin. 1832–59. Russian, revised and improved by Semenov, P. P. and Potanin, G. N., Землевѣдѣніе Азіи. Petersburg. 1860–77.
Rossiya. Россія. Полное геогр. описаніе…подъ ред. В. П. Семенова. Petersburg. 1899 sqq.
Schurtz, H. Geschichte von Hochasien u. Sibirien, in Helmolt's Weltgeschichte. Vol. II. Leipsic. 1902.
Semenov, P. P. Азія. Petersburg. 1894.
Sievers, W. Asien. Eine allg. Landeskunde. Leipsic. 1892. 2nd edn. 1904.
Ujfalvy, E. Les migrations des peuples et particulièrement celles des Touraniens. Paris. 1873.
Ukert, F. A. Geographie der Griechen u. Römer. Vol. III. Weimar. 1846.
Wirth, A. Geschichte Asiens u. Osteuropas. Jena. 1905.

(b) Travels, Monographs, and Special Treatises

Atkinson, Th. W. Explor. in Orient. and Western Siberia. London. 1858.
Berg, L. Аральское море. Petersburg. 1908.
—— Высыхает-ли Срелная Азія? (in Izvyestiya of the Russ. Geogr. Soc.). Petersburg. 1905. Transl. German in Geogr. Zeitschrift. XIII. Leipsic. 1907. (Cf. The Geogr. Journal. XXIX. 1907.)
Berlioux, E. F. Les premiers voyages des Européens dans l'Asie Centrale…(Soc. de Géogr. de Lyon, Bulletin 1898.)
Bezold, K. Ninive u. Babylonien. 2nd edn. Bielefeld. 1903.
Biot, E. Recherches sur la température ancienne de la Chine, in: Journal Asiatique. 3rd ser. Tomex. Paris. 1840.
Brückner, E. Klimaschwankungen (Geogr. Abhandlungen IV, 2). Vienna. 1890.
Brunnhofer, H. Arische Urzeit. Forschungen auf dem Gebiete des ältesten Vorder- u. Zentralasiens nebst Osteuropa. Bern. 1910.
Burnes, Sir Alex. Travels into Bokhara… London. 1834. New edition. 1847.
Cholnoky, J. Künstliche Berieselung in Innerasien u. die Völkerwanderung (in Geogr. Zeitschrift xv). Leipsic. 1909. pp. 241 ff.
Clough, H. W. Synchronous Variations in Solar and Terrestrial Phenomena: in Astrophys. Journal. Vol. xxii. 1905.
Brosby, O. T. Tibet and Turkestan. New York. 1905.
Dingelstedt, V. Le régime patriarcal et le droit coutumier des Kirghiz. Paris. 1891.
Dutreil de Rhins, J. L. L'Asie Centrale. (Thibet et régions limitrophes.) Paris. 1890.
Explorations in Turkestan. Expedition of 1904. Ed. by R. Pumpelly. 2 vols. Washington. 1908.
Explorations of Turkestan…Expedition of 1903, under the direction of R. Pumpelly. Washington. 1905.
Franke, O. Beiträge aus chines. Quellen zur Kenntnis der Türkvölker und Skythen Centralasiens: in Abhandlungen d. Preuss. Akademie. Berlin. 1904.
Futterer, K. Durch Asien. 3 vols. Berlin. 1901–3.
Gherghel, J. Zur Frage der Urheimat der Rumänen. Vienna. 1910.

Gilmour, J. Among the Mongols. London. 1883. 2nd edn. 1892.
—— More about the Mongols. London. 1893.
Grenard, F. Mission scientifique (J. L. Dutreil de Rhins) dans la Haute Asie. 3 vols. Paris. 1897–8.
Hahn, E. Das Alter der wirtschaftlichen Kultur der Menschheit. Heidelberg. 1905.
—— Die Entstehung der Pflugkultur (unsres Ackerbaus). Heidelberg. 1909.
—— Die Haustiere u. ihre Beziehungen zur Wirtschaft des Menschen. Leipsic. 1896.
Hedin, S. Central Asia and Tibet. 2 vols. London. 1903.
—— Scientific results of a Journey in Central Asia. 6 vols. London. 1904 ff.
—— Through Asia. 2 vols. London. 1898.
Herman, O. A magyarok nagy ösfoglalkozása. Buda-Pesth. 1909.
Hildebrand, R. Recht und Sitte auf den verschiedenen wirtschaftlichen Kulturstufen. Jena. 1896. 2nd edn. 1907.
Howorth, H. H. History of the Mongols. 3 vols. London. 1876–88.
Huc, E. R. Recollections of a Journey through Tartary...transl. by Sinnett, P. London. 1852.
Hunfalvy, P. Neuere Erscheinungen d. rumän. Geschichtschreibung. Vienna. 1886.
Jevons, F. B. An introduction to the history of religion. London. 1896. 4th edition. 1908. (On domestication of animals.)
Jireček, J. C. Die Romanen in den Städten Dalmatiens während des Mittelalters. (Denkschriften d. Kaiserl. Akademie, phil-hist. Classe. Vol. XLVIII. Vienna. 1902.)
Jorga, N. Geschichte des rumänischen Volkes. I. Gotha. 1905.
Kennan, G. Tent-Life in Siberia and adventures among the Kazaks. 14th edn. London. 1894.
Khanikov, N. Бухара. Petersburg. 1841. Transl.: Bokhara, its Amir and its People. London. 1845.
—— Mém. sur la partie mérid. de l'Asie Centr. Paris. 1863.
Kropotkin, P. A. prince. The desiccation of Eur.- Asia (in Geogr. Journal XXIII). 1904.
Kuropatkin, A. N. Кашгарія... Petersburg. 1879. Transl. Gawan. Kashgaria, Hist. and statist. sketch. Calcutta. 1882.
Lansdell, H. Chinese Central Asia. 2 vols. London. 1893.
—— Russian Central Asia. 2 vols. London. 1885.
Latham, R. G. Russian and Turk form a Geographical, Ethnological, and Historical Point of View. London. 1898.
Lepechin, J. Дневныя записки путешествія по разн. пров. Росс. Государства. Petersburg. 1771. Transl. German by Haase: Tagebuch über seine Reise durch versch. Provinzen d. russ. Reichs. 4 vols. Altenburg. 1774–82.
Levshin, A. J. Описаніе Киргизъ-Кайзацкихъ ордъ и степей. Petersburg. 1832. Transl. French: Levchine, A. de. Description des Hordes et des Steppes de Kirghiz-Kazaks trad. par F. de Pigny. Paris. 1849.
Marvin, Ch. Merw, the Queen of the World. London. 1881.
Meakin, A. M. B. In Russian Turkestan. London. 1903.
Middendorff, A. v. Einblikke in das Ferghana-Thal: in Mémoires de l'Acad. Imp. des Sciences de St-Pétersbourg. VII sér. Tome XXIX. 1881.
Moser, H. Durch Central-Asien. Leipsic. 1888.
O'Donovan, E. The Merw- Oasis. Travels and Adventures. London. 1882.

Ohsson, M. d'. Histoire des Mongols. 4 vols. The Hague. 1834–5.
Pallas, P. S. Reisen durch versch. Provinzen d. russ. Reichs. 3 vols. Peters-burg. 1771–6. Transl. French : Voyages dans plusieurs provinces de l'Empire de Russie. Paris, l'an xi.
Parker, E. H. Thousand years of the Tartars. London. 1895.
Peisker, J. Die älteren Beziehungen der Slawen zu Turkotataren und Germanen. (Reprint of Vierteljahrsschrift f. Soc. u. Wirtschaftsgesch. iii.) Stuttgart. 1905.
Petzholdt, A. Umschau in Russisch Turkestan. Leipsic. 1877.
Pozdnyeev, A. M. Монголія и Монголы. Petersburg. 1897.
Przheval'skij, N. M. Монголія и страны Тангутовъ... Petersburg. 1875–6. Transl. by Morgan : Mongolia, the Tangut Country and the Soli-tudes of Northern Tibet. 2 vols. London. 1876.
Pumpelly, R. *See p.* 662, Explorations.
Radloff, W. Aus Sibirien... 2 vols. Leipsic. 1884. 2nd edn. 1893.
—— Ethnograph. Übersicht d. Türkstämme.... Leipsic. 1883.
—— *See p.* 661, Inschriften.
Richthofen, F. China. Ergebnisse eigener Reisen. Berlin. 1877 ff.
Schott, W. Älteste Nachrichten von Mongolen und Tataren. Berlin. 1846.
Schuyler, E. Turkistan. Notes of a Journey... 2 vols. London. 1876–7.
Schwarz, Fr. von. Sintfluth u. Völkerwanderungen. Stuttgart. 1894.
—— Turkestan. Freiburg-i.-Br. 1900.
Sergi, G. Dalle esplorazioni del Turkestan. Rome. 1907.
Shokal'skij, J. M. Le niveau de lacs de l'Asie Russe et les changements de climat, par J. de Schokalsky (in Annales de Géographie xviii). Paris. 1909.
Stein, M. A. Ancient Khotan. 2 vols. Oxford. 1907.
—— Sand-buried ruins of Khotan. London. 1903.
Ujfalvy de Mezö-Kövesd, C. E. de. Les Aryans au nord et au sud de l'Hindou-Kouch. Paris. 1896.
—— Aus dem westlichen Himalaya... Leipsic. 1884.
Vámbéry, Arm. A magyarság keletkezése és gyarapodása. Buda-Pesth. 1905.
—— Das Türkenvolk. Leipsic. 1885.
—— Der Ursprung der Magyaren. Leipsic. 1882.
—— Die primitive Cultur des turkotatarischen Volkes. Leipsic. 1879.
—— Sketches of Central Asia. London. 1868.
—— The Turkomans. Journal of the Anthropol. Inst., 1880.
—— Travels in Central Asia... London. 1864. New York. 1865.
Venyukov, M. J. Путешествія по окраинамъ русской Азіи. Peters-burg. 1868. Transl. German : Wenjukow, Die russisch-asiatischen Grenz-lande übers. v. Krahmer. Leipsic. 1874.
Watt, A. The climate of Hebron in Syria, in Journal Scott. Meteorol. Soc. 3rd ser. Vol. xiii. 1903.
Weil, M. La Tourkménie et les Tourkmènes. Paris. 1880.
Wright, G. F. Asiatic Russia. 2 vols. London. 1903.
Xénopol, A. D. Histoire des Roumains. Paris. 1896.
Yadrintsev, N. M. Сибирскіе инородцы. Petersburg. 1891.
Yavorskij, J. L. Средная Азія Odessa. 1893.
Zaleski, B. La vie des steppes Kirghises. Paris. 1865.
Zichy, E. count of. Dritte asiatische Forschungsreise. 6 vols. Leipsic. 1900–5.
—— Voyages au Caucase et en Asie Centrale. 2 vols. Buda-Pesth. 1897.

CHAPTER XII (B)

ATTILA

I. SOURCES

Our chief authority is the Byzantine historian Priscus, whose description of the period c. 440–472 is based on his own experiences and on reliable accounts, but whose work has unfortunately only come down to us in fragments (Müller's FHG. *See Gen. Bibl.*, IV, 1851, p. 71 ff.; V [1871], p. 24 ff. De Boor, Excerpta de legationibus, I, p. 121 ff., II, p. 575 ff. Berlin. 1903).

A long fragment (No. 8) contains the description of the journey on which he accompanied an Embassy from the Eastern Empire to the Court of the king of the Huns in Hungary.

Priscus was also the principal source for the later Byzantine historians as well as for Cassiodorus' History of the Goths, which is only preserved in the abstract made by Jordanes (Getica, ed. Mommsen: MGH, auct. ant., V).

Supplementary contemporary accounts independent of Priscus, are given in the Chronicle of Marcellinus Comes (according to the East-Roman Annals) (MGH, auct. ant., XI), the poems of Apollinaris Sidonius (ditto, VIII), the Italian Consular Fasti (ditto, IX), the Chronicles of Prosper Tiro and Hydatius (ditto, IX, XI), as well as the South Gallic Chronicle up to 452 (ditto, IX).

II. LITERATURE

Barthélemy. La campagne d'Attila: RQH. VIII. (1870.) pp. 337–404.
Bury. Later Roman Empire. *See Gen. Bibl.* Vol. I. pp. 161–83.
Girard. Le campus Mauricus: RH, XXVIII. (1885.) pp. 321–31.
Güldenpenning, A. Geschichte des oströmischen Reichs unter den Kaisern Arcadius und Theodosius II. Halle. 1885. pp. 327–73.
Haage. Geschichte Attilas. Celle. 1862.
Hodgkin. Italy and her Invaders. *See Gen. Bibl.*
Kaufmann, G. Über die Hunnenschlacht des Jahres 451: Forschungen zur deutschen Geschichte, VIII. (1868.) pp. 115–46.
Klemm, G. Attila nach der Geschichte, Sage und Legende. Leipsic. 1827.
Schmidt, L. Geschichte der deutschen Stämme. Vol. I. Berlin. 1910. pp. 241–9
Troplong, E. La diplomatie d'Attila. Revue d'hist. dipl. XXII. (1908.) pp. 541–68.
Wiestersheim, E. von. Geschichte der Völkerwanderung. 2nd edn. by Dahn, F. Vol. II. Leipsic. 1880. pp. 217–76.

Compare also the literary accounts in Chevalier, Répertoire; *see Gen. Bibl.*
Bio-Bibliographie, I, col. 360–1; Topo-Bibliogr., II col. 1877.

CHAPTER XIII (A)

ROMAN BRITAIN

(a) GENERAL

Articles by Haverfield, F. J. in Victoria County History, Northamptonshire and
Somerset.

Oman, C. W. C. England before the Norman Conquest, pp. 61–185.

Appendix by Haverfield, to revised English translation of Mommsen's Roman
Provinces (London, 1910), pp. 347 ff. *for* recent literature on Roman Britain.

(b) HISTORY OF THE CONQUEST

Army system : Art. in Victoria County History of Derbyshire (F. J. Haverfield).
Oman, *supra*.
Article in Social England, illustr. edn. 1901, I, 76.

Conquest of Wales : Haverfield, F. J. Proceedings of the Hon. Soc. of Cymmrodorion, 1908–9, pp. 53–187.

Roman Wall in North England (Hadrian's Wall) : Bruce, J. C. Roman Wall (1867).
Haverfield, Archaeologia Aeliana, XXIII, 9, and Cumberland and Westmorland
Arch. Soc. Transactions, vols. XIII, ff.

Roman occupation of Scotland : Haverfield, Antonine Wall Report (Glasgow,
1899), pp. 156 ff., and Proceedings of the Scottish Soc. of Antiquaries,
XXXVIII, 454.
Curle, Jas. A Roman Frontier Post. Glasgow. 1911. On Newstead.
Edinburgh Review, April 1911.
Macdonald, Geo. Roman Wall in Scotland. Glasgow. 1911.

(c) ROMAN ROADS

Codrington, T. Roman Roads in Britain. London. 1913. (Describes some roads
well, but is very unequal.)

Haverfield, Victoria History *supra* and the map for this chapter.

(d) CIVILIZATION

Haverfield, F. J. Romanization of Roman Britain. London. 1905.
—— Victoria County History of Somerset, Northants, Warwick, Norfolk, and
appendix to Mommsen *supra*.
—— Social England (illustr. edn. 1901), I, 136 ff. (On the Art.)
Pitt-Rivers, A. H. L. Fox-. Excavations. 1887 ff. (On the village life.)
Vinogradoff, P. Growth of the Manor. London. 1905. Ch. II.

(e) CHRISTIANITY

Archaeologia, LIII, and Victoria County History of Hampshire, I, 277, 278. (On the Christian Church at Silchester.)

Haverfield, EHR, XI, 427, *and* Oman, *supra*, supplementing Haddan and Stubbs, Councils and Documents. Oxford. 1869. I.

(f) INSCRIPTIONS

Bruce, J. C. Lapidarium Septentrionale. London. 1875.

Haverfield, F. J. *Ibid.* vols. VII, IX (1890–1911).

Hübner, E. Corpus inscriptionum Latinarum, VII, Berlin, 1873; and Ephemeris epigraphica, vols. III, IV (1877–80).

For Christian inscriptions, mostly in Wales, see Hübner, Inscript. Christ. Brit. (Berlin, 1876), now however almost out of date, and many scattered corrections and additions, especially by J. Rhys in Archaeologia Cambrensis. The Christian stones of Cornwall are summarized in the Victoria History of the County, I, 407.

For the so-called Pictish inscriptions, Rhys, Proc. of the Soc. of Antiquaries of Scotland, XXXII, 324.

(g) TRANSITION FROM ROMAN TO ENGLISH AND THE END OF THE ROMAN EMPIRE IN THESE ISLANDS

Bury, J. B. Life of St Patrick. London. 1905.

Haverfield, F. J. Last days of Silchester. EHR, XI, 427.

Oman, *supra*.

Stevenson, W. H. EHR, XX, 474. On an alleged survival of the tribe name Parisii in Lincolnshire.

—— *Ibid.* XIV, 32, XVII, 625. On the character of the English conquest.

Zimmer, H. Nennius Vindicatus. Berlin. 1893.

—— Handelsverbindungen Westgalliens mit Irland im Altertum. Sitzungsberichte der kgl. pr. Akad. Wiss. 1909 (rather fanciful).

Older "standard" works are Camden's Britannia (esp. ed. 1607 and re-edition with add. by Gough, 1806).

Gordon, A. Itinerarium Septentrionale (1726, with add. 1732).

Hodgson, John. Hist. of Northumberland, 1820–40.

Horsley, J. Britannia Romana, 1732.

Lysons, D. and S. Magna Britannia, 1806 ff.

Lysons, S. Woodchester, 1797 ff., and Reliquiae Romano-Britannicae, 1813 ff.

Roach Smith, C. Collectanea Antiqua, 1848 ff., and Roman London, 1859.

Stuckeley, W. Itinerarium Curiosum, 1724–76.

Watkin, W. T. Roman Lancashire, 1883, and Roman Cheshire, 1886.

See also the publications of the Societies of Antiquaries of London, Newcastle, and Scotland, and the Archaeological Journal.

The student needs to be warned that the literature of Roman Britain contains a larger proportion than the literature of any other historical subject, of unsound and unscholarly work. Much of this is valuable as a record of finds, but the interpretation of the finds and the theories based on them are too often worthless, even when they seem to be authoritative. This class of literature, has, as far as possible, not been quoted above.

CHAPTER XIII (B)

TEUTONIC CONQUEST OF BRITAIN

I. PRIMARY AUTHORITIES

(a) ROMAN

Earliest references to Angles and Saxons

Tacitus. Germania. Cap. 40. Transl. Church, A. J. and Brodribb, W. J. (The Agricola and Germany of Tacitus). London. 1868.

Claudius Ptolemaeus. Geographia. Lib. II, cap. 11.

Eutropius. Breviarium. Lib. IX, cap. 21.

Orosius. Historiae. Lib. VII, cap. 25.

Ammianus Marcellinus. Lib. XXVI, capp. 4, 5; XXVII, 8; XXVIII, 2, 5; XXX, 7.

Notitia Dignitatum. Ed. Seeck, O. Berlin. 1876.

(*Editions will be found in Bibl. to c. VII.*)

Most of these passages can be found collected in either

Horsley, John. Britannia Romana. London. 1732. *or*

Elton, C. J. Origins of English History. London. 1882. 2nd edn. 1890.

(b) ENGLISH TRADITIONS

Alfred's Orosius. Lib. I, cap. 1. Ed. Sweet, H. E.E.T.S. *Orig. ser. 79*. Pt. 1. O.E. text and Latin original. London. 1883. *Also* App. to Pauli's Life of Alfred (with literal transl. by Thorpe). London. 1857.

Bede. Historia Ecclesiastica. Lib. I, cap. 15. Ed. Plummer. Oxford. 1896.

Vitae duorum Offarum. (*In* Wats' edn. of Matthew Paris. London. 1640.) On which see Saxo Grammaticus, Gesta Danorum. (Ed. Holder, A. Strassburg. 1886.) pp. 105–50.

Widsith. The Anglo-Saxon poem, vv. 35 ff., and passim. Cf. Beowulf, vv. 1944 ff. *in* Grein-Wülker. Bibliothek der Angelsachsischen Poesie. Vol. I. Cassel. 1881. *Also in* Sedgefield's Beowulf. Manchester. 1910. pp. 139 ff.

William of Malmesbury. II, 116. Ed. Stubbs, W. Rolls Series. London. 1887–9.

(c) REFERENCES TO THE INVASION

Gildas. De excidio et conquestu Britanniae. Ed. Mommsen, T. *in* MGH, auct. ant. XIII, 1–85.

Monumenta Hist. Britannica, *as below*.

Nennius. Historia Brittonum. §§ 31 ff. MGH, auct ant. XIII, 111–98. 1894.

Petrie, H. and Hardy, T. D. Monumenta Hist. Britannica. London. 1848. And with transl. Williams, H. Cymmrodorion Record. Ser. 3. London. 1899. (*Best edn.*) Stevenson, J. (English Hist. Soc.) London. 1838. *And many early edns.*

Prosper Tiro. ed. MGH, IX, pp. 385–499.

Saxon Chronicle. Annals, 449 ff. Ed. Thorpe, B. Rolls series. 2 vols. London. 1861. Earle, J. Two of the Saxon Chronicles parallel. Oxford. 1865. Plummer, C. (based on Earle). 2 vols. Oxford. 1892–9. (Best edn.) Transl. Stevenson, J. (Church historians of England.) London. 1853–8. Gomme, E. F. London. 1909 (based on Plummer). (Cf. Procopius. De Bello Gothico. IV, 20.)

(d) EVENTS OF SIXTH CENTURY

Historia Brittonum. §§ 57 ff.
Saxon Chronicle. *See above.*
See also Liebermann, Felix. Die Gesetze der Angelsachsen. Halle. 1898–9.

II. SECONDARY WORKS

Chadwick, H. M. Origin of the English Nation. Cambridge. 1907.
Engelhardt, C. Denmark in the Early Iron Age (transl.). London. 1866. Also French transl. by Beauvais, E. (Mém. de la Soc. des antiquaires du Nord). Copenhagen. 1883. And other edns.
Guest, E. Origines Celticae. 2 vols. London. 1883. (*For a destructive criticism, see* Stevenson *below.*)
Hodgkin, T. Political History of England. Vol. I. London. 1906.
Hoops, J. Waldbäume und Kulturpflanzen im germanischen Altertum etc. p. 92 ff. Strassburg. 1905.
Kemble, J. M. The Saxons in England. London. 1849. Ed. Birch, W. de G. 2 vols. 1876.
Lloyd, J. E. History of Wales. 2 vols. London. 1911.
Meitzen, August. Siedelung und Agrarwesen der Westgermanen und Ostgermanen etc. Berlin. 1895.
Montelius. The Civilization of Sweden in Heathen Times. London. 1888. And Leipsic. 1906.
Müller, Sophus. Vor Fortid. Nordische Alterthumskunde. Vol. II. Strassburg. 1898.
Oman, C. England before the Norman Conquest. London. 1910.
Round, J. H. The Settlement of the South- and East-Saxons. *In* Commune of London. Westminster. 1899.
Seebohm, F. The English Village Community. London. 1883. 4th edition. 1890. Reprinted 1896.
—— Tribal Custom in Anglo-Saxon Law. London. 1902.
Stevenson, W. H. *on* Dr Guest and the English Conquest of South Britain. EHR, XVII, p. 625.
Victoria History of the Counties of England. 1900. *In progress.*
Vinogradoff, P. The Growth of the Manor. London. 1905.

On Runes : —
Vietor, W. Die Northumbrischen Runensteine. Marburg. 1895.
Winner, L. F. A. Die Runenschrift. 2nd edn. transl. by Holthausen, F. Berlin. 1887.

NOTE ON AUTHORITIES

The date and authorship of the *Historia Brittonum* have long been matter of dispute. Schoell and La Borderie (1851 and 1883) held the view that the work was written in the first quarter of the ninth century A.D., discrediting the alleged authorship of Nennius. Zimmer (1893), Duchesne (1894) and Thurneysen (1895) all claim for Nennius some share in the compilation of the book, which they date between 790 and 830. There is no doubt that it is a highly composite work. Zimmer and Thurneysen agree in dating the composition of the nucleus of the *Historia Brittonum* in 679. The sections with which we are concerned are §§ 31–49 and §§ 56–66. The greater part of the latter appears to be derived from an English genealogical document connected with the genealogies which appear in several early MSS. *e.g.* Cott. Vesp. B 6 (published in Sweet's *Oldest English Texts*, pp. 167–71), C.C.C.C. 183 and the *Textus Roffensis*, to which some notices of Welsh origin have also been added. There is some reason for believing that §§ 31–49 likewise are partly of English origin (cf. Chadwick, *Origin of the English Nation*, pp. 38 ff. and 345).

The *Saxon Chronicle* down to the year 892 is preserved in two recensions, one of which is represented by texts A, B, C, the other by texts D, E, F, for which see Plummer's introduction. The latter or northern recension contains many additions derived chiefly from Bede's *Ecclesiastical History* and from some lost Northumbrian annals, which can be traced also in Simeon of Durham and Roger of Howden. The lost archetype from which all the texts are descended down to 892 was perhaps itself extended from an earlier chronicle composed in the time of Aethelwulf. For the period with which we are concerned, the chief sources of the chronicle are firstly, the Chronological Summary in Bede's *Ecclesiastical History*, v. 24, secondly, a genealogical document intimately related to those mentioned in the preceding note, and thirdly, a series of annals of unknown authorship dealing chiefly with Wessex, which appear to have extended to a time shortly after the middle of the eighth century, though this last section may consist of elements of different date. The value of earlier entries derived from this last source is difficult to estimate, but in any case it is extremely doubtful whether the dates assigned to events before the end of the sixth century can be trusted.

CHAPTER XIV

ITALY TO THE REVOLUTION OF ODOVACAR

I. SPECIAL BIBLIOGRAPHIES

Some account of the original authorities for the period may be found in

Ebert, A. Geschichte der christlich-lateinischen Literatur. Vol. I. Leipsic. 1874.

Gibbon, E. The Decline and Fall of the Roman Empire. Ed. Bury, J. B. Vol. III, Appendix I. Vol. IV, Appendix I. *See Gen. Bibl.*

Hodgkin, T. Italy and her Invaders. Vol. I, Part II, and Vol. II. Second edition. Oxford. 1892 (at the beginning of each chapter).

Schmidt, L. Geschichte der deutschen Stämme. Berlin. 1904. Abteilung 1, Buch 1, pp. 3–25.

II. ORIGINAL DOCUMENTS

Codex Theodosianus. Ed. Mommsen, Th., and Meyer, P. M. Berlin. 1905. (The edition of Gothofredus, Lyons, 1665, is still valuable for its historical notes.)

CIL. *See Gen. Bibl.*

Notitia Dignitatum. Ed. Seeck, O. Berlin. 1876.

Regesta Pontificum Romanorum. Ed. Kehr, P. F. Berlin. 1906–8.

III. AUTHORITIES

(a) CONTEMPORARY

Augustine. Epistolae (referring to Count Boniface). MPL 33.

Candidus. Excerpta. Ed. Müller, C. FHG IV. *See Gen. Bibl.*

Carmen de Providentia divina (falsely attributed to Prosper Tiro). MPL 51. (Valuable as regards the condition of Gaul after the barbarian influx.)

Chronica Gallica. Ed. Mommsen, Th., MGH, auct. ant. IX, ii. (There are two Chronica, one to 452, and one to 511. Both probably spring from Marseilles, and both show imperialist sympathies.)

Consularia Italica. Ed. Mommsen, Th., MGH, auct. ant. IX, ii. (Under this name Mommsen includes Anonymi Valesiani Pars posterior, Fasti Vindobonenses priores *and* posteriores, Paschale Campanum, Continuatio Hauniensis Prosperi, and two sets of Excerpta. The collection is valuable as giving dates, especially for the later part of this period.)

Consularia Constantinopolitana. Ed. Mommsen, Th., MGH, auct. ant. IX, ii. (The Additamentum Hydatii alone bears on this period.)

Ennodius. Vita beatissimi viri Epifani. Ed. Vogel, F., MGH, auct. ant. VII. CSEL. (A verbose life of a bishop of Pavia, of some value for the events of the years 470–6.)

Eugippius. Vita Sancti Severini. Ed. Sauppe, H., MGH, auct. ant. I. CSEL. (A very valuable account of the activity of Severinus in Noricum at the end of this period.)

Hydatius. Continuatio Chronicorum Hieronymianorum. Ed. Mommsen, Th., MGH, auct. ant. xi, ii. (Hydatius, a Spanish bishop, carried his continuation to 468. To him are also attributed an Additamentum to the Cons. Constant., *ut supra* and Fasti, MPL 51.)

Jerome. Epistolae. MPL 22.

Leo the Great. Epistolae. MPL 54.

Malchus. Excerpta de Legationibus. FHG iv. Teubner. (Valuable for the end of the period.)

Merobaudes. Carmina (chiefly panegyrics of Aëtius). Ed. Vollmer, F., MGH, auct. ant. xiv.

Olympiodorus. Excerpta. FHG iv. (A valuable if poetic account of the early part of the period, preserved in Excerpts by Photius.)

Orientius. Commonitorium. Ed. Ellis, R., CSEL xvi. (Deals with the state of Gaul after the barbarian influx.)

Orosius. Historiae (ending about 416). MPL 31. CSEL.

Paulinus of Nola. Epistolae et poemata. MPL 61.

Paulinus of Pella. Eucharisticos. Ed. Brandes, G. CSEL xvi. (Deals with the condition of Gaul between 414 and 416.)

Philostorgius. Excerpta. MPG 65. (Ecclesiastical historian.)

Possidius. Vita Sancti Augustini. MPL 32.

Priscus. Fragmenta. FHG iv. Teubner. 1870. (Very valuable, especially as regards the full account of an embassy to the Huns.)

Profuturus Frigiridus, Renatus. A contemporary historian quoted by Gregory of Tours in his Historia Francorum (see under b).

Prosper Tiro. Chronica. Ed. Mommsen, Th., MGH, auct. ant. ix, ii. (Prosper, an Aquitanian clerk, wrote annals down to 455 A.D. The Copenhagen Continuatio of Prosper is printed by Mommsen in the Consularia Italica, *ut supra*: it is supposed to be of Lombard origin. The first of the two Chronica Gallica has been attributed, but mistakenly, to Prosper. See Hodgkin, Vol. i, Part ii, pp. 703–7 (second edition).)

Rutilius Claudius Namatianus. De Reditu suo. (An account of the writer's return from Gaul to Rome in 416.) Ed. Bährens, Aem. Poetae Latini Minores, v. Leipsic. 1883.

Salvianus. De Gubernatione Dei. (An account and indictment of Roman society and administration in the fifth century.) Ed. Halm, C., MGH, auct. ant. i. CSEL.

Sidonius Apollinaris. Opera. (Letters and poems by a Gaulish noble, at one time praefectus Urbi, and afterwards bishop of Clermont, at the end of this period. Ed. Luetjohann, C., MGH, auct. ant. viii.

Socrates. Historia Ecclesiastica. MPG 67. Ed. Hussey, R. 3 vols. Oxford. 1853. Bright, W. Oxford. 1878.

Sozomen. Historia Ecclesiastica. MPG 67. Ed. Hussey, R. 3 vols. Oxford. 1860.

Theodoret. Historia Ecclesiastica. Ed. Gaisford, T. Oxford. 1834. *And see Bibl. to cc.* i, ii, *and* v.

Victor of Aquitaine. Cursus paschalis. Ed. Mommsen, Th., MGH, auct. ant. ix, ii.

Zosimus. Historia Romana. (Only for the very beginning of the period.) Ed. Mendelssohn, L. Leipsic. 1887.

(b) Later

Agnellus. Liber Pontificalis. (An account of the bishops of Ravenna, composed in the ninth century.) Ed. Holder-Egger, O., MGH, script. rer. Langobard. (See Hodgkin, T., Part ii (second edition), pp. 898–917.)

Antiochenus, Joannes. Fragmenta. FHG IV. (Joannes was a Byzantine historian of the early 7th century. There is a genuine and a spurious Joannes : see Krumbacher, Gesch. der byzant. Lit.², p. 335. The genuine Joannes seems to have used Priscus, and is therefore valuable.)

Avitus, Alcimus Ecdicius. (Bishop of Vienne, †524 circiter.) Opera. Ed. Peiper, R., MGH, auct. ant. VI, ii.

Cassiodorus (6th century). Chronica and Variae. Ed. Mommsen, Th., MGH, auct. ant. XI, i, and XII.

Chronicon Caesaraugustanum. (A Saragossa Chronicle of the 6th century, only a few lines of which bear on the period.) Ed. Mommsen, Th., MGH, auct. ant. XI, ii.

Evagrius (†600 circiter). Historia Ecclesiastica. MPG 86. Bidez, J. and Parmentier, L. Paris. 1898.

Fortunatus, Venantius. Bishop of Vienne, †600 circiter.) Opera. Ed. Leo, F. MGH, auct. ant. IV, i.

Gregory of Tours (6th century). Historia Francorum. Edd. Arndt, W., and Krusch, Br., MGH, script. rer. Merov. XIV. Omont, H. and Collon, G. (Collection des Textes pour servir à l'étude. . .de l'histoire.) 2 vols. Paris. 1886, 1893.

Historia Miscella. Ed. Muratori, L. A., RSI I. (A redaction made by Landulfus Sagax, circiter 1000 A.D., of the Historia Romana of Paulus Diaconus. Of little value.)

Isidorus of Seville (floruit 600). Historia Gothorum, Wandalorum et Suevorum *and* Chronica. MGH, auct. ant. XI, ii.

Jordanes (6th century). Romana and Getica. (The latter is of value.) Ed. Mommsen, Th., MGH, auct. ant. V.

Liber Pontificalis. Ed. Duchesne, L. Paris. 1886.

Malalas. (Byzantine writer of the 6th century.) Chronographia. Ed. Dindorf, L., CSHB 28.

Marcellinus. (A *comes* of the 6th century.) Chronicon. MGH, auct. ant. XI, ii.

Marius Aventicensis. (Gaulish bishop of the 6th century.) Chronica. Ed. Mommsen, Th., MGH, auct. ant. XI, ii.

Procopius. De Bello Vandalico. Ed. Dindorf, L., CSHB 37. (This work seems to be of little value for the 5th century, and to have been too much regarded by historians.)

Theophanes. (Byzantine writer of the 9th century.) Chronographia. Ed. Classen, J., CSHB 43. De Boor, C. 2 vols. Leipsic. 1883.

Victor Tonnennensis. (6th century bishop.) Chronica. MGH, auct. ant. XI, ii.

Victor Vitensis. (African writer of the 6th century.) De Persecutione Vandalica. Ed. Halm, C., MGH, auct. ant. VII, i. CSEL.

IV. MODERN WORKS

(a) GENERAL

Bury. Later Roman Empire. *See Gen. Bibl.*

Clinton. Fasti Romani. *See Gen. Bibl.*

Dahn, F. Die Könige der Germanen. Munich, Würzburg and Leipsic. 1861–71.

—— Urgeschichte der germanischen und römanischen Völker (in Oncken's series). Berlin. 1880–9.

—— Deutsche Geschichte. Gotha. 1883.

Dill. Roman Society. *See Gen. Bibl.*

Fustel de Coulanges. Histoire des instit. pol. de l'ancienne France. L'invasion germanique. Paris. 1897.

Gibbon, Bury-Gibbon. *See Gen. Bibl.*
Gregorovius. Geschichte der Stadt Rom in Mittelalter. Transl. Hamilton from 4th German edition, Rome in the Middle Ages. London. 1894 ff.
Güldenpenning, A. Geschichte des oströmischen Reichs unter den Kaisern Arcadius und Theodosius II. Halle. 1885.
Hodgkin, T. Italy and her Invaders. Vols. I and II. (Second edn.) *See Gen. Bibl.*
Lavisse, E. Histoire de France. Vol. II. Paris. 1903.
Le Nain de Tillemont, L. S. Histoire des Empereurs. Paris. 1693 ff.
Ozanam, A. F. History of Civilisation in the fifth century. Transl. London. 1868.
Pallmann, R. Die Geschichte der Völkerwanderung. Gotha. 1863.
Ranke, von. Weltgeschichte. *See Gen. Bibl.*
Schmidt, L. Geschichte der deutschen Stämme. Berlin. 1904 ff.
Sievers, G. R. Geschichte der römischen Kaiser. Berlin. 1870.
Thierry, A. Récits de l'histoire romaine au v⁰ siècle. Paris. 1860.
Wietersheim, E. von. Geschichte der Völkerwanderung. 2nd edn. by Dahn, F. Leipsic. 1880–1.

(b) On Authorities

Paulinus of Nola :
    Baudrillart, A. Saint Paulin de Nole. Paris. 1904.
Sidonius Apollinaris :
    Chaix, L. A. St. Sid. Ap. et son siècle. Clermont-Ferrand. 1866.
    Fertig, M. Sidonius und seine Zeit. Würzburg and Passau. 1845–8.
    Germain, A. Essai littéraire et historique sur Ap. Sid. Montpellier. 1840.

(c) Monographs, Biographies, and Special Treatises

Bury, J. B. A note on the reign of Olybrius : EHR. Vol. I (1886), p. 507.
Freeman, E. A. Tyrants of Britain, Gaul, and Spain, A.D. 406–11 : EHR. Vol. I (1886), p. 53. *See also* Western Europe in the Fifth Century. London. 1904. (Less complete but with quotations in notes.)
—— Aëtius and Boniface : EHR II (1887), p. 417, *repr. in* Western Europe in the Fifth Century. London. 1904. Appendix I.
Goyau, G. Sainte Mélanie. Paris. 1908.
Lecrivain, F. Le sénat romain depuis Dioclétien. Paris. 1888.
Martroye, F. Genséric. Paris. 1907.
Mommsen, Th. Gesammelte Scriften, IV. Berlin. 1906. (Articles on Aëtius, and on Stilicho und Alarich.)
Pauly-Wissowa. Articles by Seeck on Aëtius, Ataulf, Boniface, and Constantius.
Rampolla, M. A. Santa Melania giuniore, senatrice Romana. Rome. 1905.
Schmidt, L. Geschichte der Wandalen. Leipsic. 1901.
Thierry, A. Histoire d'Attila. Paris. 1873. (4th edition.) For a brief bibliography of monographs on Attila's campaign of 451, see Lavisse, Histoire de France, II, 76 note.

The following may also be mentioned :

Cantarelli, L. L'imperatore Maioriano. ASRSP VI.
Tamassia. Egidio e Siagrio. RSI. 1886.
Yver. Euric, Roi des Visigoths. (In Etudes d'histoire du Moyen Age. Paris. 1896.)

CHAPTER XV

THE KINGDOM OF ITALY UNDER ODOVACAR AND THEODORIC

Authorities for this period abound, but neither for the government of Odoacer nor for that of Theodoric is there anything in the shape of a continuous history nor of a collection of official documents such as letters or papers of authentic character.

ORIGINAL AUTHORITIES

Ennodius bp. of Pavia (a contemporary of the two kings and panegyrist of Theodoric). Best edn. Vogel in MGH, auct. ant. vii, CSEL.
Cassiodorus. Varia. (An inexhaustible source of information as to the details of the administration and the chronology of Theodoric), MGH. 1894. English summary by Hodgkin, T. London. 1886.
Anonymus Valesii (Chronica Theodoriciana). Usually appended to the editions of Ammianus Marcellinus, *see Bibl. to cc.* i, ii, *and* v.
Chronicle of Count Marcellinus (Justinian's chancellor). *See Bibl. to c.* xiv.
Epistolae pontificum Romanorum. Ed. Thiel, CSEL.
Malchus (a page). Ed. Dindorf, L. Hist. Graeci Minores. Leipsic. 1870–1. FHG. Teubner. 1870.
And certain passages of Jordanes, Procopius, and Paulus Diaconus.

LATER WORKS

Among the most important are:

Bertolini, F. Studi critici intorno all' regno di Odoacro. Ant. st. Ital. 1869.
Dahn, F. Die Könige der Germanen. Leipsic. 1861 ff. Part ·ii.
Dumoulin, Maurice. Le gouvernement de Théodoric et la domination des Ostrogoths en Italie. RH. 1902.
Freeman, E. A. The Goths at Ravenna *in* Historical Essays, Ser. iii. London. 1879.
Gaudenzi, A. Rapporti tra l' Italia e l' impero d' Oriente fra gli anni 476 e 554 (D.C. studio storico e giuridico). Bologna. 1888.
Hodgkin, T. Italy and her Invaders. Vol. iii. *See Gen. Bibl.*
Lécrivain, Ch. Le Sénat romain depuis Dioclétien. Paris. 1888.
Magani, F. Ennodio. 3 vols. Pavia. 1888.
Malfatti, B. Imperatori e Papi. Milan. 1876. Vol. i.
Pflugk-Harttung, J. von. Der erste König von Italien. Deutsche Revue. 1886.
Stöber, E. Quellenstudien zur laurentianischen Schisma. Vienna. 1886.
Thierry, Am. Récits de l'histoire romaine au vᵉ siècle. Paris. 1860–80.

CHAPTER XVI

THE EASTERN PROVINCES

1. SPECIAL BIBLIOGRAPHIES

Gibbon. Decline and Fall. Ed. Bury, see Gen. Bibl., vols. III, IV, App.
Hodgkin, T. Italy and her Invaders, see Gen. Bibl., 2nd edn.; vol. I, introd. to
  chs. 12, 13; vol. III, introd. to chs. 2, 3.
Krumbacher, K. Geschichte der byzantinischen Litteratur, 2nd edn. (See under
  each author and pp. 1068 ff.) Munich. 1897.
  For contemporary authorities, Christ, W., Gesch. der griech. Litteratur, 3rd
  edn. Munich. 1898.

2. ORIGINAL DOCUMENTS

Acta Synodi ad Quercum, ap. Photium, Bibl., Cod. LIX, in MPG 103.
Codex Justinianus. Ed. Krüger, P. (Corpus juris civilis, vol. II.) 4th edn.
  Berlin. 1888.
Codex Theodosianus. See Bibl. to c. I. Vol. II of Mommsen and Meyer's edn.
  (1906) contains the Novellæ ad Theodosianum pertinentes.
CIL, vol. III. No. 734. Berlin. 1873. (For the walls of Constantinople.)
Epistolæ Imperatorum, Pontificum, aliorum, inde ab a. CCCLXVII usque ad a. DLIII
  datæ, Avellana quæ dicitur collectio. Ed. Günther, O. (CSEL, vol. XXXV.,
  2 pts. Vienna. 1895–8.

3. AUTHORITIES

(a) CONTEMPORARY

Asterius. Homiliæ. MPG 40.
Candidus. Fragmenta. Ed. Müller, C. FHG, vol. IV, p. 135. Paris. 1851.
  Ed. Dindorf, L. (Hist. Gr. Min., vol. I, p. 441). Leipsic. 1870.
Claudian. Carmina. Ed. Birt, Th., in MGH, auct. ant., x. Ed. Koch, J.
  Leipsic. 1893.
Damascius. Vita Isidori (fragments). Ed. Westermann, A. (Vitæ Philosophorum,
  p. 119). Paris. 1850.
Elisha Vardapet. History of Vardan (Armen.). Ed. Calfa, Kh. Kaffa. 1861.
  Ed. Mekhitarists. Venice. 1864. Ed. Isaiah, patr. Jerusalem. 1865.
  Transl. English, Neumann, C. F. (Oriental Translation Fund.) London.
  1830. Transl. French, Langlois, V. (Coll. des historiens de l'Arménie, t. II.)
  Paris. 1869.

Eunapius. *Fragmenta.* Ed. Müller, C. (*op. cit.*, p. 7). Ed. Dindorf, L. (*op. cit.*, p. 205). Ed. Boissevain, U. P. (Exc. Hist. jussu Imp. Const. Porph. confecta, vol. IV, p. 71). Berlin. 1906.

Hydatius. *Continuatio Chronicorum Hieronymianorum.* Ed. Mommsen, Th., in MGH, auct. ant., XI.

Jerome. *Epistolæ.* MPL 22.

John Chrysostom. *Opera.* MPG 47–64.

Joshua the Stylite (so called). *Chronicle* (Syr.). Ed. and transl. Wright, W. Cambridge. 1882.

Lazarus of Pharp. *History of Armenia* (Armen.). Ed. Mekhitarists. Venice. 1793 and 1807. Transl. French. Ghésarian, P., in Langlois, V., *op. cit.*

Liber de promissionibus. MPL 51. (For Eutropius' fall and Aspar's African expedition.)

Malchus. *Fragmenta.* Ed. Müller, C. (*op. cit.*, p. 111). Ed. Dindorf, L. (*op. cit.*, p. 383). Ed. De Boor, C. (Exc. Hist. etc., vol. I, p. 155; p. 568). Berlin. 1903.

Marcus diaconus. *Vita Porphyrii ep. Gazensis.* Ed. Soc. Phil. Bonn. Sodales. Leipsic. 1895.

Marinus. *Vita Procli.* Ed. Boissonnade, J. F., in Westermann, A., *Vitæ Philosophorum*, p. 149. Paris. 1850.

Moses of Chorene. *History of Armenia* (Armen.); authenticity doubtful. Ed. Mekhitarists (Coll. des anciens écrivains, tom. XXI). Venice. 1843. Ed. and transl. French, Levaillant de Florival, P. E. 2 vols. Venice. 1844. Transl. Ital., by the Mekhitarists. Venice. 1849 and 1850. Transl. Fr., Langlois, V. *op. cit.*

Notitia Dignitatum. Ed. Böcking, E. 2 vols. and index. Bonn. 1839–53. (For notes.) Ed. Seeck, O. Berlin. 1876.

Palladius. *Dial. de vita S. Joannis Chrysostomi.* MPG 47.

Philostorgius. *See Bibliography to c.* I.

Priscian. *Panegyricus.* CSHB, pt. VI.

Priscus. *Fragmenta.* Ed. Müller, C., *op. cit.*, vol. IV, p. 69; vol. v. p 24 (1870). Ed. Dindorf, L., *op. cit.*, p. 275. Ed. De Boor, C., *op. cit.*, p. 121; p. 575.

Procopius of Gaza. *Panegyricus.* CSHB, pt. VI.

Prosper. *Epitoma Chronicon.* Ed. Mommsen, Th., in MGH, auct. ant., t. IX.

Socrates. *See Bibl. to c.* I.

Sozomen. *Do.*

Synesius. *Opera.* MPG 66.

Theodoret. *See Bibl. to c.* I *and to c.* III.

Vita Melaniæ junioris. Ed. Rampolla del Tindaro, M. (With notes.) Rome. 1905.

(b) LATER

Anonymus Valesii, pars 2ª. Ed. Mommsen, Th., in MGH, auct. ant., IX, p. 306.

Chronicon Edessenum (Syr.). Ed. and trans. German, Hallier, L. (Texte u. Untersuchungen zur Gesch. d. altchristlichen Litt., Bd. 9.) Leipsic. 1892. Ed. and transl. Latin, Guidi, I. (Corp. Script. Orient. Christian., Script. Syr. ser. 3, t. IV.) Paris. 1903.

Chronicon Paschale in CSHB and MPG 92. The portions derived from a Constantinopolitan chronicle are edited by Mommsen, Th., in MGH, auct. ant., XI, p. 64.

Constantine Porphyrogenitus. *De Cærim. Aulæ Byzantinæ.* In CSHB. (For accession ceremonies of Leo and Anastasius.)

Cyril of Scythopolis. *Vita Sabæ.* Ed. Cotelerius, J. B. (Eccl. Græcæ Monu-

CH. XVI.

menta, t. iii.) Paris. 1686. Reprinted with an Old Slavonic Version by Pomyalovskiy, I. Petersburg. 1890. (Obshtshestvo Liubiteley Drevney Pismennosti.)

Evagrius. *Historia Ecclesiastica.* Ed. Bidez, J. and Parmentier, L. London. 1898.

John of Antioch. *Fragmenta.* Ed. Müller, C. (Fragm. Hist. Gr., vol. iv, p. 355; vol. v, p. 27). Paris. 1851–70. Constantinian excerpts ed. Büttner-Wobst, Th. and De Boor, C. (Exc. Hist. jussu Imp. Const. Porph. confecta, vol. ii, p. 164 and vol. iii, p. 58.) Berlin. 1905. (Fragments of two or more authors are combined under this name.)

John the Lydian. *De magistratibus populi Romani.* Ed. Wünsch, R. Leipsic. 1903.

John Malala. Chronographia. In CSHB. Constantinian excerpts ed. Büttner-Wobst, Th. and De Boor, C., *op. cit.*, vol. ii, p. 187 and vol. iii, p. 151. Other fragments in MPG 85, p. 1806.

Jordanes. *Romana et Getica.* Ed. Mommsen, Th., in MGH, auct. ant., v.

Marcellinus. *Chronicon.* Ed. Mommsen, Th., *ibid.*, t. xi.

Procopius of Cæsarea. *Opera.* Ed. Haury, J. 3 vols. Leipsic. 1905 ff.

Suidas. *Lexicon.* Ed. Bernhardy, G. Halle. 1853.

Theodore the Reader. *Exc. ex Ecclesiastica Historia.* MPG 86, pt. i. Further fragments ed. Miller, E., in Rev. Arch., xxvi (1873), p. 273; p. 396.

Theophanes. *Chronographia* (with the Latin version of Anastasius). Ed. De Boor, C. 2 vols. Leipsic. 1883.

Victor Tonnennensis. *Chronica.* Ed. Mommsen, Th., in MGH, auct. ant., xi.

Vita Danielis Stylitæ. MPG 116.

—— *Marcelli Archimandritæ.* Ibid.

Zacharias Rhetor (so called). *Historia Miscellanea* (Syr.). Ed. Mai, A. (Script. Vet. Nova Coll., t. x.) Rome. 1838. (Vatican fragments.) Ed. Land, J. P. N. (Anecd. Syriaca, t. iii.) Leiden. 1870. (Text of Brit. Mus. MSS.) Trans. German with commentary, Krüger, G. and Ahrens, K. Leipsic. 1899. Trans. English with new collation of MSS., Hamilton, F. J. and Brooks, E. W. London. 1899.

Zonaras. *Annales.* In CSHB.

Zosimus. *See Bibl. to c. i.*

4. MODERN WORKS

(a) GENERAL

Bury, J. B. History of the Later Roman Empire. 2 vols. London. 1889.

Dahn, F. Die Könige d. Germanen. 12 vols. Munich and Würzburg. 1861–1909.

Gelzer, H. Abriss der byzantinischen Geschichte. In Krumbacher's Gesch. d. byz. Litteratur, 2nd edn. Munich. 1897.

Gibbon, E. Decline and Fall. *See Gen. Bibl.*

Grosvenor, E. A. Constantinople. 2 vols. London. 1895.

Hertzberg, G. F. Gesch. Griechenlands unter d. Herrsch. d. Römer. 3 vols. Halle. 1866–75.

Hodgkin, Th. Italy and her Invaders. *See Gen. Bibl.*

Hopf, C. Griechische Geschichte vom Beginn des Mittelalters bis auf unsere Zeit. In Ersch-Gruber, Sect. 1, pt. 85, 86. *See Gen. Bibl.*

Lampros, S. P. Ἱστορία τῆς Ἑλλάδος. 3 vols. Athens. 1886–92.

Lebeau, Ch. Histoire du Bas-Empire. 1757 ff. Ed. Saint-Martin, J. A. de. 21 vols. Paris. 1824–36. (Still the fullest history of the period. S.-M.'s additions specially useful for eastern affairs.)

Muralt, E. de. Essai de Chronographie byzantine pour servir à l'examen des annales du Bas-Empire. Petersburg. 1855. (Very inaccurate.)

Paparrhegopoulos, K. Ἱστορία τοῦ Ἑλληνικοῦ Ἔθνους. Athens. 1853. 3rd edn. ed. Konstantinides, A. 5 vols. and maps. 1885–7. 4th edn. ed. Karolides, P. 5 vols. 1903.

Sievers, G. Studien zur Geschichte der römischen Kaiser. Berlin. 1870.

(b) On Authorities

Claudian:

    Crees, J. H. E. Cl. as an historical authority. Cambridge. 1908. (With a critical account of the administrations of Rufinus and Eutropius and a summary of the opinions of other writers.)

    Koch, J. Cl. u. die Ereignisse; d. Jahre 395 bis 398. Rh. Mus., 1889, p. 575.

Damascius:

    Asmus, J. B. Zur Rekonstruktion von Damascius' Leben Isidorus. BZ, 1909, p. 424; 1910, p. 265.

John of Antioch:

    Patzig, E. Joh. Antiochenus u. Joh. Malalas. Leipsic. 1892.

    Soteriadis, G. Zur Kritik des Joh. v. Antiochia. Neue Jahrb. f. Philologie u. Pädagogik, Supplem. Bd. xvi (1888), p. 1.

John the Lydian:

    Zachariä v. Lingenthal, E. Joannes, des Philadelphiers Laurentius Sohn, genannt Lydus. Zeitschr. d. Savigny-Stiftung f. Rechtsgesch., Romanistische Abth. 12 (1891), p. 77.

John Malala:

    Brooks, E. W. The date of the historian J. Mal. EHR, 1892, p. 291.

    Bury, J. B. J. Mal.: the text of the Cod. Baroccianus. BZ, 1897, p. 219.

    Gleye, C. E. Beiträge zur Johannesfrage. BZ, 1896, p. 422.

    Mommsen, Th. Bruchstücke d. Joh. v. Ant. u. d. Joh. Mal. Hm. vi (1872), p. 323.

    Patzig, E. Unerkannt u. unbekannt gebliebene Malalasfragmente. | Leipsic. 1891.

    —— Joh. Antiochenus u. Joh. Mal. Leipsic. 1892.

Marcellinus:

    Holder-Egger, O. Die Chronik d. Marc. u. die oströmische Fasten. NAGDG, 1877, p. 47.

Sozomen:

    Bidez, J. La tradition manuscrite de Sozomène. (Texte u. Untersuchungen, etc., Bd. xxxii.) Leipsic. 1908.

Synesius:

    Mommsen, Th. Die Diokletianische Reichspräfectur. Hm. 1901, p. 210. (Denies Seeck's identification of "Typhos" with Cæsarius.)

    Seeck, O. Studien zu Synesios. Philologus, 1894, p. 442.

Zosimus:

    Rühl, F. Wann schrieb Zosimos? Rh. Mus., 1891, p. 146.

Greek authorities to 527:

    Christ, W. Gesch. d. griechischen Litteratur. 2 pts. (Müller's Handb. d. klass. Altertumswissenschaft, vol. viii.) 3rd edn. Munich. 1898.

Do. from 527:

    Krumbacher, K. Gesch. d. byz. Litt. (Müller's Handb., vol. ix, pt. 1.) 2nd edn. Munich. 1897.

(c) MONOGRAPHS, BIOGRAPHIES, AND SPECIAL TREATISES

Articles in Pauly-Wissowa, especially
    Seeck, O.: Alaricus. Anatolius. Antiochos. Ardabur. Arkadios. Collatio lustralis. Eudokia. Eudoxia.
    Oehler: Anastasios.
Barth, W. Kaiser Zeno. Basel. 1894.
Brooks, E. W. The emperor Zenon and the Isaurians. EHR, 1893, p. 209. ´
Gregorovius, F. Athenais, Gesch. einer byzantinischen Kaiserin. Leipsic. 1882.
Güldenpenning, A. Gesch. d. oström. Reiches unter d. Kaisern Arcadius u. Theodosius II. Halle. 1885.
Haury, J. Review of above (taking opposite view). BZ, 1906, p. 291.
Holmes, W. G. The age of Justinian and Theodora. 2 vols. London. 1905–7. (With a description of the empire under Anastasius.)
Ludwig, E. Der hl. Johannes/Chrysostomus in seiner Verhältniss zum byzantinischen Hof. Braunsberg. 1883.
Merten, E. De bello Persico ab Anastasio gesto (Comm. phil. Jenenses, tom. VII, fasc. 2). Leipsic. 1905.
Mommsen, Th. Epinikos./ Hm. 1897, p. 660.
Nöldeke, Th. Gesch. d. Perser u. Araber zur Zeit d. Sassaniden, aus d. arab. Chronik d. Tabari übersetzt u. mit ausführlichen Erläuterungen versehn. Leyden. 1879. (For Sassanid chronology.)
Rose, A. Kaiser Anastasius I. Halle. 1882.
Sauerbrei, P. König Yazdegerd, d. Sünder, d. Vormund d. byz. Kaisers Theodosius d. Kleinen (Festschr. Alb. v. Bamberg gewidmet, p. 90). Gotha. 1905. (Rejects Procopian story.)
Schmidt, L. Gesch. d. Wandalen. Leipsic. 1901.
—— Gesch. d. deutschen Stämme bis zum Ausgange d. Völkerwanderung. 4 pts. (Quellen u. Forschungen zur alten Gesch. u. Geogr. herausg. v. W. Sieglin, Heft 7, 10, 12.) Berlin. 1904–10. Repr. as sep. work. (1st pt. Die Gesch. d. Ostgermanen.) With Addenda. Berlin. 1910. (Important for history of the Ostrogoths in the East.)
Sickel, W. Das byz. Krönungsrecht bis zum 10en Jahr. BZ, 1898, p. 511.
Thierry, A. S. D. Nouveaux recits de l'histoire romaine aux ive et ve siècles. Trois ministres des fils de Théodose. Paris. 1865.
—— Recits de l'hist. rom. au ve siècle. St Jean Chrysostome et l'impératrice Eudoxie. Paris. 1872.

CHAPTER XVII

RELIGIOUS DISUNION IN THE FIFTH CENTURY

ANCIENT SOURCES

Documents in: Mansi, Historia Conciliorum. Florence. 1769.
    Labbé and Cousart. Sacrosancta Concilia. 15 vols. in 16, Apparatus
    2 vols. Paris. 1671–2.
    Hefele. Hist. of the Councils. (Eng. Translation.) London. 1871–6.
    Perry. Second Council of Ephesus. Dartford. 1881.
    Percival, H. R. The Seven Oecumenical Councils. Oxford. 1900.
    Letters of Chrysostom. MPG.
    Life of Chrysostom by Palladius. MPG 47.
CSHB, esp. Theophanes. (Chronographia, new edn. by De Boor, C. 2 vols.
    Leipsic. 1883.)
Fragments of Theodorus Lector. MPG 86.
Tome of Leo and other documents *in* Heurtley; De Fide et Symbolo. Oxford and
    London. 1902.
Zacharias of Mitylene. Translated by Brooks, E. London. 1899.
Ecclesiastical Histories of Socrates. London. 1880.
                Sozomen. London. 1855. All these have been trans-
                Theodoret. London. 1854. lated into English. Bohn.
                Evagoras. London. 1854.
Assemanus, B. Bibliotheca Orientalis. Rome. 1719–28.
Nestorius apud (i) Loofs. Nestoriana (containing a great many fragments of
        Nestorius and a full discussion of documents). Halle. 1905.
    (ii) Marius and Mercator (containing many important documents relating
        to the Nestorian controversy). MPL 48.
    (iii) Bethune-Baker (see below) for portions of Bazaar of Heraclidas.
Cyril. Works. MPG 68–77.
Theodoret. Works. MPG 80–4.
Leo the Great. Works. MPL 54–6.
Liberati Breviarium. MPL 68.

MODERN BOOKS

Amélineau, E. Le christianisme des anciens Coptes. Rev. de l'hist. des Rel. xiv,
    xv.
—— Les Moines d'Égypte etc. Paris. 1904.
—— Résumé de l'Hist. de l'Égypte. Paris. 1894.
Beet, W. E. The Rise of the Papacy, 385–461. London. 1910.
Bethune-Baker, J. F. Theology of the First Six Centuries.
                Nestorius and his Teaching. Cambridge. 1908.
Böhringer, F. Die Kirche Christi und ihre Zeugen, esp. Leo I. Th. xii. Zurich.
    1841–57.

Burkitt, F. C. Early Eastern Christianity. London. 1904.
Bury. Later Roman Empire. *See Gen. Bibl.*
Conybeare, F. C. Anecdota Monophysitarum *in* American Journal of Theology.
    Chicago. Oct. 1905.
DCB *passim* esp. : —
              Chrysostom by Venables.
              Coptic Church by Fuller.
              Cyrillus by Bright.
              Dioscorus by Bright.
              Leo by Gore.
              Pelagius by Ince.
              Petrus Mongus by Bright.
              Severus by Venables.
              Theodoretus by Venables.
Dorner, J. A. History of Development of the Doctrine of the Person of Christ,
    trans. Alexander, W. E. and Simon, D. W. (Clark's Foreign Theolog.
    Library.) 5 vols. (Div. ii, vol. iii, ed. Fairbairn, P.) Edinburgh. 1861-3.
Duchesne, L. Hist. ancienne de l'Église. Vol. iii. Paris. 1910. (To 5th
    century inclusive.)
Duval, R. Hist. d'Édesse. Paris. 1892.
Finlay. Hist. of Greece, ed. Tozer. *See Gen. Bibl.*
Gfrörer, A. T. Allgemeine Kirchengeschichte. Stuttgart. 1841 seq.
Gibbon. Decline and Fall. *See Gen. Bibl.*
Gieseler. History of the Church (transl.). *See Gen. Bibl.*
Güldenpenning, A. Das oströmische Reich unter Arcadius und Theodosius II.
    Halle. 1885.
Harnack. Hist. of Dogma, tr. Mitchell. *See Gen. Bibl.*
Hastings. Encyclopædia of Religion and Ethics. *See Gen. Bibl.* Articles on : —
    Alexandrian Theology by Inge (does not go down to Cyril).
    Antiochene Theology by Srawley.
Hergenröther, J. Photius. Introduction on "die Byzantinischen Patriarchen."
    Ratisbon. 1867.
Hodgkin. Italy and her Invaders. *See Gen. Bibl.*
Labourt, J. Le Christianisme dans l'empire Perse sous la dynastie sassanide.
    Paris. 1904.
Leipoldt, W. J. Geschichte der Koptischen Litteratur, 1907, *and* review by Crum.
    JTS, January, 1908.
—— Schenute von Atripe *in* Texte u. Untersuchungen zur Gesch. der altchristl.
    Literatur (ed. Harnack and Gebhardt). Neue Folge, vol. x, 1903, *and* review
    by Crum. JTS, Oct. 1903.
Le Nain de Tillemont. *See Gen. Bibl.*
Milne, J. G. Hist. of Egypt under Roman Rule. London. 1898.
Möller. History of the Church. *See Gen. Bibl.*
Neander. History of the Church. *See Gen. Bibl.*
Püch, A. Vie de S. Chrysostom. Paris. 1891.
RE³ articles Monophysitismus etc.
              Koptische Kirche by Crum.
Révillout, E. Sénuti le Prophète. Revue de l'histoire des Religions. 1883.
Stephens, W. R. W. Chrysostom, his Life and Times. London. 1872.
Thierry, A. Nestorius et Eutyches. (Récits d'hist. Romaine au 5ᵉ siècle.) Paris.
    1878.
Walch, C. W. F. Historie der Ketzereien. Leipsic. 1762-85.
Wigram, W. A. History of the Assyrian Church. London. 1910.

CHAPTER XVIII

MONASTICISM

No unprinted sources have been utilized for this Chapter. It will be convenient to deal with the Bibliography under the following headings : —
I. General; II. Egyptian; III. Oriental and Greek; IV. Pre-Benedictine European; V. Benedictine.

I. GENERAL

A. Bibliography Proper

Berlière, Dom U. Bulletin d'histoire Bénédictine, appearing 3 or 4 times a year since 1893, in the RBén. (Maredsous, Belgium) : all current literature covering the subject-matter of the Chapter is indicated, the original title "Monastique" being more correct than "Bénédictine."

Heimbucher ⎫
Zöckler   . ⎭ *See under I, B.*

　　(Their books contain the best general bibliographies for all aspects of monastic history.)

Leclercq. *See under II, B.*

RE³ contains excellent bibliographies in general article, "Mönchtum" (Grützmacher), and special articles as "Pachomius," "Benedikt von Nursia," etc.

B. General History

Helyot, H. Histoire des Ordres religieux. 8 vols. Paris. 1714–19.

Le Nain de Tillemont. *See Gen. Bibl.*

　　(The sections of the Mémoires that deal with the prominent monks probably make up the best general account of early monasticism.)

Montalembert, C. Les Moines d'Occident. 7 vols. Paris. 1860–77. Transl. Mrs Oliphant. Edinburgh. 1861–79. (Vols. I, II.)

Of more recent general accounts may be named :

Eckenstein, Lina. Woman under Monasticism. Cambridge. 1896.

Hannay, J. O. Spirit and Origin of Christian Monasticism. London. 1903.

Harnack, A. Das Mönchtum. Giessen. 1881, and later edns. Reprinted in Reden und Aufsätze. Giessen. 1903. Transl. Kellett, E. E. London. 1901.

Heimbucher, M. Die Orden und Kongregationen der Kath. Kirche. 2nd edn. 3 vols. Paderborn. 1907–8.

　　(Vol. I contains, both in regard to materials and to bibliography, by far the most useful general account of the subject.)

Zöckler, O. Askese und Mönchtum. 2 vols. Frankfurt-a.-M. 1897.

II. EGYPTIAN

A. ORIGINAL SOURCES

Historia Monachorum in Aegypto. Ed. Preuschen, E. In Palladius und Rufinus. Giessen. 1897.

Palladius. Historia Lausiaca. Ed. Butler, E. C. Cambridge. 1904.
  (The only critical edn., and the only one that can be used with safety for historical purposes.)

Vita Antonii (among the Works of Athanasius). Transl. Robertson, [Bp] A., in Nicene Library. Oxford. 1892.

Vita Pachomii (Greek). Acta SS. Tom. III. Maii (App.).
  The foregoing works in Latin in H. Rosweyd's Vitae Patrum. Antwerp. 1615.

MPL 72, 73. English translation (from Syriac) by Budge, E. W., "The Paradise of the Fathers." London. 1907.

The foregoing are the principal sources for the facts of the external history of early Egyptian monachism. / For the theory or philosophy of the movement the chief authorities are :

Apophthegmata Patrum seu Verba Seniorum. Greek MPG 65 ; Latin MPL 73.
  On these and the oriental versions, see Butler (below). Transl. from Syriac by Budge, E. W. (above). Selections, by Hannay, J. O. "Wisdom of the Desert." London. 1904.

Cassianus, Joannes. Instituta Coenobiorum and Collationes Patrum. Ed., with learned commentary, by Gazet, Alard. Doway. 1616 (reprinted in MPL 49). Critical edn. by Petschenig in the Vienna Corpus. 2 vols. 1886–8. Transl. Gibson, [Bp] E., in Nicene Library. Oxford. 1894.

Egyptian Rules, in early Latin translation, in Holsten, L. Codex Regularum. Rome. `1661` Paris. 1663. Enlarged edn. by Brockie. 6 vols. Vienna. 1759. (Vol. I.) (MPL 103.)

B. LITERATURE

Discussion of Sources :

Butler, E. C. The Lausiac History of Palladius. Texts and Studies VI. Cambridge. 1898–1904.
  (Part I goes over the whole discussion fully ; and § 1 of Part II summarizes the attitude of expert critical opinion in 1904 : the outcome of the controversy is the substantial rehabilitation of the documents as historical sources. The best general survey in English is an art. by C. H. Turner, reviewing this work in JTS, April, 1905.)

Ladeuze, P. Le Cénobitisme Pakhomien. Louvain. 1898.

Lucius, P. E. Die Quellen der älteren Geschichte des ägyptischen Mönchtums. *Ibid.* 1885.

Preuschen, E. Palladius und Rufinus. Giessen. 1897.

Weingarten, H. Ursprung des Mönchtums. Gotha. 1877.
  (From Brieger's ZKG, 1876.)

Other works are :

Besse, J. M. Les Moines d'Orient. Paris. 1900.

Duchesne, L. Histoire ancienne de l'Église. Paris. 1907. (Vol. II, cap. 14 : an excellent sketch.)

Leclercq, H. Article "Cénobitisme," in Dictionnaire d'Archéologie Chrétienne, Paris. 1910. (An exhaustive treatise of 200 columns on the whole subject-matter of this chapter.)

Leipoldt, J.　Schenute von Atripè.　Texte u. Untersuchungen.　Leipsic.　1903.
Lejay, P.　Ancienne Philologie chrétienne: Monachisme Oriental, in Revue
　d'Histoire et de Littérature religieuses, xi.　Paris.　1906.　(An admirable
　survey of the most recent literature on Egyptian monachism.)
Schiwietz, S.　Das morgenländische Mönchtum.　Mayence.　1904.　(A series of
　articles reprinted without revision.)

III.　ORIENTAL AND GREEK

A. Syriac and Persian

Rabbula.　Admonitions for Priests and Sons of the Covenant; also Admonitions for
　Monks.　Transl. Connolly, R. H. in Downside Review, 1906.
Sozomen.　Hist. Eccl. vi.　cc. 32–4.
Theodoret.　Historia Religiosa.
The "Sons of the Covenant."　Aphraates, Discourses vi, vii.　Transl. Latin, in
　Parisot's ed., Patrologia Syriaca, i.　Paris.　1894.　English of vi by Gwynn, J.,
　in Nicene Library, xiii.　Oxford.　1898.　Thereon: Burkitt, F. C.　Early
　Eastern Christianity.　London.　1904.　Connolly, R. H. in JTS, July, 1905.
Thomas of Marga.　Book of the Governors.　Ed. and transl. by Budge, E. W.
　2 vols.　London.　1893.
Vita Simeonis Stylitae.　Ed. Lietzmann, H.　Texte u. Untersuchungen, 3rd Series,
　ii, 4.　1908.　(Also a cheap edn.)

　The above are sources; the following are the best works thereon:

Assemani, J. S.　Bibliotheca Orientalis.　3 vols.　Rome.　1719.　(The Disserta-
　tions in iii, ii include copious information on Syrian monachism.)
Labourt, J.　Le Christianisme dans l'Empire perse.　Paris.　1904.
　For Isaac of Antioch see Connolly, R. H. in Downside Review xxv, p. 161. 1906.

B. Greek

St Basil:
　(1) The Rules, Longer and Shorter;
　(2) Five "ascetical" sermons;
　(3) Epp. 2, 14, 22, 23, 42–6, 173;
　(4) Epp. Greg. Naz. ad Bas. 1, 2, 4, 5, 6.
　　(All to be found in the works of Basil and of Gregory Naz.　The Monastic
　　Constitutions are not by Basil.　For translations of most important
　　portions of the letters, see Newman, Church of the Fathers "Basil
　　and Gregory," §§ 4, 5.)
Cyril of Scythopolis.　Lives of Euthymius, Sabas, and others.
John Moschus.　Leimonarion, or Paradise.
　　(For editions, etc. of these two writers, see Ehrhard apud Krumbacher, as
　　below; or Bardenhewer, Patrologie.)
Petrakakos, D.　Οἱ μοναχικοὶ Θεσμοί.　Leipsic.　1907.
　　(Useful bibliography for Greek monachism prefixed.)
Theodore Studita.　Constitutiones.　MPG 99.

　As literature may be cited:

Bulteau, L.　Essai de l'histoire monastique d'Orient.　Paris.　1678.
Ehrhard, A.　The best survey and bibliography of the literature of the whole
　subject is in the section "Theologie," supplied by Ehrhard to Krumbacher's
　Geschichte der byzantinischen Litteratur, Munich, 1897, subheadings C
　(Asketik und Mystik) and E (Hagiographie) (i, 139 and 176).
Gardner, Alice.　Theodore of Studium.　London.　1905.

Lake, K. Early Days of Monasticism on Mount Athos. Oxford. 1909.
(See also accounts of visits to Athos, *e.g.* by Curzon, Riley, Gelzer, de
Meester.)
Marin, Eug. De Studio Coenobio Constantinopolitano. Paris. 1897. Les
Moines de Constantinople. Paris. 1898. (He antedates by nearly a century
the establishment of monasteries there. See Pargoire, I. Les débuts du
monachisme a Constantinople, in RQH, LXV. 1899.)
Meyer, Ph. Die Haupturkunden für die Geschichte der Athosklöster. Leipsic.
1864.

IV. PRE-BENEDICTINE EUROPEAN

Lives in collections of Vitae SS., especialy Mabillon's Acta SS. Ben., and vols.
of MGH.

(a) ITALY

Spreitzenhofer, E. Die Entwicklung des alten Mönchtums in Italien. Vienna.
1894.

(b) AFRICA

St Augustine:
De Opere Monachorum.
De Moribus Clericorum (Sermons 355, 356).
Ep. 211.
Besse, J. M. Le Monachisme Africain. Ligugé. 1900.
Leclercq, H. L'Afrique Chrétienne. Paris. 1904.

(c) SPAIN

Gams, P. B. Kirchengeschichte Spaniens. 3 vols. Ratisbon. 1862–79.
Herwegen, I. Das Pactum des hl. Fruktuosus. Stuttgart. 1907.
Rules of Isidore, Fructuosus and Leander in Holsten's Codex Regularum (above
II, A).

(d) IRELAND

Bellesheim, A. Geschichte der Kath. Kirche in Irland. 3 vols. Mayence.
1890–1.
Colgan, J. Acta SS. Hiberniae. Louvain. 1645.
de Smedt, C. Acta SS. Hiberniae. 1888.
Lanigan, J. Ecclesiastical History of Ireland. 4 vols. Dublin. 1822 and 1829.
Loofs, F. Antiqua Britonum Scotorumque Ecclesia. London. 1882.
Plummer, C. Acta SS. Hiberniae. Oxford. 1910.
Regula Columbani. (Holsten; MPL 80; best edn. by Seebass in series of arts. in
Brieger's ZKG, XIII to XVIII: cf. RE³, "Columba der Jüngere.")
Vita S. Columbae, by Adamnan. Ed. Reeves, W. Irish Archaeological Soc.
Dublin. 1857. Also in "Scottish Historians." Edinburgh. 1874. (Intro-
duction and Notes of great value.)
Vitae Columbani et Sociorum, by Jonas. Ed. Krusch, B., in MGH, Script.
Merov. IV, 1902. Also separately, "in usum scholarum." Hanover. 1905.
Willis-Bund, J. W. Celtic Church in Wales. London. 1897.
Zimmer, H. RE³, "Keltische Kirche." Transl. Kuno Meyer. London. 1902.
(See thereon Bury, J. B. Life of St Patrick. London. 1905.)

(*e*) Gaul and Frankland

St Martin of Tours: Sulpitius Severus, Life of Martin and Dialogues II and III; his correspondence with Paulinus of Nola.

Lerins.
    Arnold, C. F. Caesarius von Arelate. Leipsic. 1894.
    Malnory, A. Saint Césaire Éveque d'Arles. Paris. 1894.
    Rules of Caesarius, Aurelian, and Ferreolus (Holsten).
    Writings of Hilary of Arles, Eucherius, Faustus of Reji, Caesarius.

Jura and Auvergne.
    Gregory of Tours.
        Historia Francorum.
        Liber Vitae Patrum.
        Liber in Gloria Confessorum.

Other parts of Gaul.
    Lives of Merovingian Saints in MGH.

For survey of whole subject:
Besse, J. M. Les Moines de l'ancienne France. Paris. 1906.

V. BENEDICTINE

(*a*) St Benedict

Life: Liber II Dialogorum S. Gregorii Magni.
Rule: Editio critico-practica, with Sources, etc., by Butler, E. C., Freiburg-i.-B., 1911. Also reproduction of cod. S. Gall 914, Monte Cassino, 1900, Wölfflin's ed., Leipsic, 1895, may also be mentioned.
    Transl. Hunter Blair, D. O., London, 1906; Gasquet, F. A., London, 1908.
Commentaries: Martène, Paris, 1690 (MPL 66); Calmet, Paris, 1732.

(*b*) Early History

Mabillon, J.
    Annales. (Vol. I.)
    Prefaces to Acta SS. Ben. (Vols. I, II.)

(*c*) Literature

Brewer, J. S. Preface to Works of Giraldus Cambrensis. Rolls Ser. (Vol. IV.) London. 1861 ff.
Butler, E. C. Articles on: Benedict; Benedictines; Monasticism *in* Enc. Br. 11th edn. *See Gen. Bibl.*
—— The Lausiac History of Palladius. (Part I, pp. 251–6.) (Vol. VI of Texts and Studies.) 2 vols. Cambridge. 1898–1904.
Dudden, F. H. Gregory the Great. London. 1905. (Contains the best summaries in English of St Benedict's Rule, life, and personality: I 109–115; II 161–9.)
Gasquet, F. A. Sketch of Monastic Constitutional History, being Introduction to reprint of transl. of Montalembert. London. 1896.
Montalembert (as I, B).
Tosti, L. San Benedetto. Monte Cassino. 1892. Transl. Woods, W. R. London. 1896.

CHAPTER XIX

SOCIAL AND ECONOMIC CONDITIONS

I. SOURCES

Augustinus. Epistolae. Vol. II of Opera. 11 vols. Paris. 1836–9.
CIL. *See Gen. Bibl.* III and Suppl. II, 1902. VII, 1873.
Codex Theodosianus. Ed. Mommsen, Th. and Meyer, P. 2 vols. Berlin. 1905.
Corpus juris civilis. Ed. Mommsen, Th. and Krüger, P. 2 vols. 8th edn.
Berlin. 1906.
Eusebius. Vita Constantini et Panegyricus. Ed. Heikel, I. A. Berlin. 1902.
Fontes juris romani antiqui. Ed. Bruns, C. G., Mommsen, Th. and Gradenwitz,
O. 6th edn. Freiburg-i.-B. 1893.
Gai Institutiones. Ed. Poste, E. and Whittuck, E. A., with an introduction by
Greenidge, A. H. J. 4th edn. Oxford. 1904.
Geographi latini minores. Ed. Riese, A. Heilbronn. 1878.
Girard, P. F. Textes de droit romain. 3rd edn. Paris. 1903.
Imperatorio Justiniani institutionum libri quattuor. Ed. Moyle, J. B. 4th edn.
Oxford. 1903.
Lactantius. De mortibus persecutorum. Ed. Brandt, S. Vienna. 1897.
Notitia dignitatum. Ed. Böcking, E. 2 vols. Bonn. 1839–53.
Salvianus. De gubernatione Dei. MGH, auct. ant. Vol. I. Berlin. 1877–9.
Wilmanns. Exempla inscriptionum latinarum. 2 vols. Berlin. 1873.

II. LITERATURE

Articles on colonatus, defensor civitatis, emphyteusis, in Pauly-Wissowa, *see
Gen. Bibl.*
Beaudouin, Ed. Les grands domaines dans l'Empire romain. *In* Nouvelle rev. hist.
de droit français et étranger, 1897, 1898. Paris.
Bethmann-Hollweg, M. von. Der Civilprozess des gemeinen Rechts in geschicht-
licher Entwicklung. Vols. II, III. Bonn. 1864–6.
Blumenstock, A. H. Entstehung des deutschen Immobiliareigenthums. Inns-
bruck. 1894.
Burckhardt, Jacob. Die Zeit Constantins des Grossen. 2nd edn. Leipsic. 1880.
Bury, J. B. The Later Roman Empire. 2 vols. London. 1889.
Chénon, Émile. Le defensor civitatis. *In the* Nouvelle revue historique de droit
français et étranger, 1889. Paris.
Daremberg and Saglio. Dictionnaire des antiquités grecques et romaines. Paris.
1873 ff.
Declareueil, J. Institutions municipales dans l'Empire romain. *In the* Nouvelle
revue historique de droit français et étranger, 1902, 1904, 1907. Paris.
Dill, S. Roman society in the last century of the Western Empire. London.
1898.

Duruy, V. Histoire des Romains. Vols. v, vi, vii. 2nd edn. Paris. 1850. *See Gen. Bibl.*

Fustel de Coulanges. Le colonat romain. Part i of Recherches sur quelques problèmes d'histoire. Paris. 1885.

—— Histoire des institutions politiques de l'ancienne France. 6 vols. Paris. 1888–92.

    Vol. ii. L'Invasion Germanique et la fin de l'Empire. 1891.

    Vol. iv. L'Alleu et le domaine rural pendant l'époque mérovingienne. 1889.

Garsonnet, Eugène. Histoire des locations perpétuelles et des baux à longue durée. Paris. 1878.

Gibbon, E. Decline and Fall of the Roman Empire. Ed. Bury, J. B. 7 vols. London. 1905–6.

Gierke, O. Das deutsche Genossenschaftsrecht. i. 3 vols. Berlin. 1868–81.

Girard, P. F. Manuel élémentaire de droit romain. 3rd edn. Paris. 1901.

Gothofredus, Jac. Paratitla et Commentarii to the Codex Theodosianus. 6 vols. Lyons. 1665.

Gröber, G. Grundriss der romanischen Philologie. 4 pts. Strassburg. 1886–1901. Part i. 1886–8. Die Quellen der romanischen Philologie. Die romanischen Sprachen. See especially Die französische u. provenzalische Sprache und ihre Mundarten.

Haverfield, F. J. The Romanisation of Britain. Proceedings of the British Academy. ii. London. 1906.

Jung, J. Die romanischen Landschaften des römischen Reiches. Innsbruck. 1881.

Karlowa, O. Römische Rechtsgeschichte. 2 vols. Leipsic. 1885, 1892.

Kuhn, E. Die städtische und bürgerliche Verfassung des römischen Reichs. 2 vols. Leipsic. 1864–5.

Le Nain de Tillemont, L. B. Histoire des Empereurs. 6 vols. Paris. 1700–38.

Liebenam, W. Zur Geschichte und Organisation des römischen Vereinswesen. Drei Untersuchungen. Leipsic. 1890.

—— Städteverwaltung im römischen Kaiserreiche. Leipsic. 1900.

Löning, E. Geschichte des deutschen Kirchenrechts. Leipsic. 1878 ff.

Marquardt, J. Römische Staatsverwaltung. ii. Vols. iv–vi of Handbuch der römischen Alterthümer. Marquardt, J. and Mommsen, Th. Leipsic. 1873–8.

Mitteis. Zur Geschichte der Erbpacht im Alterthum. *In the* Abhandlungen der philologisch-historischen Klasse der Königl. Sächsischen Gesellschaft der Wissenschaften. iv. 1901.

Mommsen, Th. Römisches Staatsrecht. 3 vols. 4 pts. 3rd edn. Leipsic. 1887–8.

—— Über das Edikt Diocletians "de pretio rerum venalium." Nachtrag zu dem Edikt Diocletians. Das Diocletianische Edikt über die Waarenpreise. Juristische Scriften. ii, 292 ff.

—— Zur Lehre von den römischen Korporationen. Juristische Schriften. iii, 53 ff.

—— Decret des Commodus für den Saltus Burunitanus. Juristische Schriften. iii, 153 ff.

—— Die Erblichkeit des Decurionats. Juristische Schriften. iii, 43 ff.

—— Römische Geschichte. Vol. v. *See G. b. v.*

Mounier, H. Études sur le droit byzantin. *In the* Nouvelle revue historique de droit français et étranger. 1900.

Muirhead, J. Historical introduction to the private law of Rome. 2nd edn. Ed. Goudy, H. London. 1899.

Pelham, H. F. The Imperial domains and the Colonate. London. 1890.

Preuss, Th. Kaiser Diocletian und seine Zeit. Leipsic. 1869.

Rodbertus. Zur Geschichte der agrarischen Entwicklung Roms unter den Kaisern : die Adscriptitier, Inquilinen und Colonen. *In* Jahrbücher für National-ökonomie und Statistik. Vol. II. Jena. 1864.

Rostowtzew, M. Studien zur Geschichte des römischen Kolonates. Leipsic. 1910.

Roth, P. Feudalität und Unterthanverband. Weimar. 1863.

Ruggiero, E. de. Dizionario epigrafico di antichità romane. Rome. 1886.

Savigny, F. C. von. Über den römischen Colonat. Vermischte Schriften. II. Berlin. 1850.

Schiller, Hermann. Gesch. der römischen Kaiserzeit. *See Gen. Bibl.*

Schulten, A. Die römischen Grundherrschaften. Weimar. 1896.

—— Libello dei Coloni d' un domanio imperiale in Asia. *In* Mittheilungen des deutschen archäologischen Instituts in Rom. XIII.

Seeck, O. Die Pachtbestimmungen eines römischen Guts in Afrika. *In the* Zeitschrift für Social- und Wirtschaftsgeschichte. Vol. VI. Part IV. Weimar. 1898.

—— Untergang. *See Gen. Bibl.* 2nd edn.

Vinogradoff, P. The Growth of the Manor. pp. 37 ff. London. 1905.

Waltzing, J. P. Étude historique sur les corporations professionnelles chez les Romains. Brussels. 1895–1900.

Weber, M. Die römische Agrargeschichte. Stuttgart. 1891.

CHAPTER XX

THOUGHT AND IDEAS OF THE AGE

See Bibl. to cc. i, ii, *and* v *for —*

Ammianus Marcellinus.
Anonymus Valesii.
Athanasius.
Basil.
Eusebius of Caesarea.
Gregory of Nazianzus.

Julian.
Lactantius.
Panegyrici Latini.
Codex Theodosianus.
Socrates.
Sozomen.

ORIGINAL AUTHORITIES

Augustine. *Opera.* Ed. Gaume. 11 vols. Paris. 1836. MPL 32–46. Transl. Dods, M. Edinburgh. 1871.
    De civitate Dei. Edd. Hoffmann, E. 2 vols. in CSEL. 1899–1900. Dombart, B. 2 vols. Leipsic. 1877–92. (New edn. in progress.)
    Confessions. Edd. Knöll, P. in CSEL. 1896. Gibb, J. and Montgomery, W. Cambridge. 1908. (With notes.)
Ausonius. *Opera.* MPL 19. Edd. Schenkl, C. in MGH. 1883. Peiper, R. Leipsic. 1886.
Boëthius. *Opera.* MPL 63, 64.
    De consolatione philosophiae and *Opuscula sacra.* Ed. Peiper, R. Leipsic. 1871.
Capella, Martianus. *De nuptiis Philologiae et Mercurii.* Edd. Kopp, U. F. Frankfort. 1836. (With notes.) Eyssenhardt, F. Leipsic. 1866.
Cassianus. *Opera.* MPL 49, 50. Ed. Petschenig, M. 2 vols. in CSEL. 1886–8. Transl. Gibson, E. C. S. (Bp). Oxford. 1894. (With prolegomena.)
Cassiodorus. *Variae.* MPL 69. Ed. Mommsen, Th. in MGH. 1894. Transl. Hodgkin, T. London. 1886.
Chrysostom. *Opera.* MPG 47–63.
Claudian. *Carmina.* Ed. Birt, Th. in MGH. 1892.
Cosmas Indicopleustes. *Topographia christiana.* MPG 88. Transl. McCrindle, J. W. London. 1897.
Diodorus of Tarsus. *Fragmenta.* MPG 33.
Ennodius. *Epistolae.* MPL 63. Edd. Hartel, W. in CSEL. 1882. Vogel, F. in MGH. 1885.
Erotici Scriptores Graeci. Ed. Hirschig, W. A. Paris. 1856.
Eusebius. *Chronica.* Ed. Schöne, A. 2 vols. Berlin. 1875–6.
Faustus of Riez. *Opera.* MPL 58. Ed. Engelbrecht, A. in CSEL. 1891.
Gregory of Nyssa. *Opera.* MPG 44–6. *The Catechetical Oration.* Ed. Srawley, J. H. Cambridge. 1901.
Hilary of Poitiers. *Opera.* MPL 9, 10. Transl. Watson, E. W. in Nicene Library. Oxford. 1899. (With valuable introduction.)

Jerome. *Opera.* MPL 22–30. *Principal Works.* Transl. Fremantle, W. H. in Nicene Library. Oxford. 1893.
Julius Africanus, Sextus. *Chronographiae.* MPG 10. Transl. Salmond, S. D. F. in Ante-Nicene Library. Edinburgh. 1869.
Juvencus. *Evangelia.* MPL 19. Ed. Hümer, J. in CSEL. 1891.
Libanius. *Opera.* Ed. Förster, R. Leipsic. 1903 ff. (5 vols. publ.)
Macrobius. *Opera.* Edd. Jan, L. 2 vols. Quedlinburg. 1848. Eyssenhardt, F. 2 vols. Leipsic. 1868 and 1893. Transl. (French) Mahul, A. J. in Nisard's Collection des auteurs latins. Paris. 1850.
Nemesius. De natura hominis. MPG 40. Transl. Wither, G. London. 1636.
Nonnus. *Paraphrasis.* Ed. Scheindler, A. Leipsic. 1881.
  Dionysiaca. Ed. Köchly, A. 2 vols. Leipsic. 1857–8.
  Transl. (French) Marcellus, Comte de (in Nisard's Collection des auteurs latins). Paris. 1856.
Orosius. *Historiae.* MPL 31. Ed. Zangemeister, C. in CSEL. 1882. And Leipsic, 1889.
Plotinus. *Enneads.* Ed. Volkmann, R. 2 vols. Leipsic. 1883–4.
  Transl. (French) Bouillet, L. 3 vols. Paris. 1857–61 (with excellent excursuses).
  Transl. (German) Müller, H. F. 2 vols. Berlin. 1878.
Porphyry. *Opuscula selecta.* Ed. Nauck, A. Leipsic. 1886.
  De vita Pythagorae. Ed. Holsten, L. Leipsic. 1815.
  De philosophia ex oraculis. Ed. Wolff, G. Berlin. 1856.
Proclus. *Opera.* Ed. Cousin, V. 6 vols. Paris. 1820–7.
Prudentius. *Carmina.* MPL 59, 60. Ed. Dressel, A. Leipsic. 1860. Transl. Morison, G. Cambridge. 1887–9.
Querolus. Edd. Peiper, R. Leipsic. 1875. Havet, L. Paris. 1880. (With introduction.)
Rutilius Namatiänus. *De reditu suo.* Edd. Müller, L. Leipsic. 1870. Vessereau, J. Paris. 1904. (With French transl.) Keene, C. H. London. 1907. (With verse transl. by Savage Armstrong, G. F.) German transl. by Itasius Lemniacus (A. von Reumont). Berlin. 1872. (With notes.)
Salvian. *Opera.* MPL 53. Edd. Pauly, F. in CSEL. 1883. Halm, C. in MGH. 1877.
Sidonius. *Epistolae et Carmina.* Ed. Luetjohann, C. in MGH. 1887.
Symmachus. *Opera.* MPL 18. Ed. Seeck, O. in MGH. 1882.
Synesius. *Opera.* MPG 66.
Theodore of Mopsuestia. *Opera.* MPG 66.

MODERN WORKS

(a) General

See Bibl. to cc. i, ii, and v for —
  Dill, Dorner, Glover, Gwatkin, Harnack, Lecky, Teuffel, and Schwabe.
Arnold, E. V. Roman Stoicism. London. 1911.
Bethune Baker, J. F. Introduction to the early history of Christian doctrine. London. 1903.
Bigg, C. The Christian Platonists of Alexandria. London. 1886.
—— Neoplatonism. London. 1895.
Bury, J. B. History of the later Roman Empire. 2 vols. London. 1889.
Chassang, A. Histoire du roman. Paris. 1862.
Davidson, W. L. The Stoic creed. Edinburgh. 1907.
Delehaye, H. Les légendes hagiographiques. Brussels. 1906.

Dill, S. Roman Society. *See Gen. Bibl.*
Hicks, R. D. Stoic and Epicurean. London. 1910.
Inge, W. R. Christian mysticism. London. 1901.
Lecky, W. E. H. History of Rationalism in Europe. London. 1868.
Littré, E. Études sur les barbares et le moyen-âge. Paris. 1874.
Maine, H. S. Ancient Law. London. 1906.
Maury, L. F. A. La magie et l'astrologie. Paris. 1877.
Monnier, A. Histoire de l'assistance. Paris. 1866.
Ozanam, A. F. La civilisation au vᵉ siècle. Paris. 1855. Transl. A. C. Glyn.
   2 vols. London. 1868.
RE³, esp. Loofs, Fr., Augustinus, and Neuplatonismus.
Rendall, G. H. The Emperor Julian. Cambridge. 1879. (Account of his religion.)
Robertson, A. [Bp]. Regnum Dei. London. 1901.
Rohde, E. Der griechische Roman. Leipsic. 1900.
Vacherot, E. Histoire critique de l'école d'Alexandrie. 3 vols. Paris. 1846–51.
Villemain, A. F. Tableau de l'éloquence chrétienne au ivᵉ siècle. Paris. 1876.
Wallon, H. Histoire de l'esclavage dans l'antiquité. Paris. 1879.

(*b*) ON AUTHORITIES

Codex Theod. :
   Boyd, William K. The ecclesiastical edicts of the Theod. code. N.Y.
      1905.
Amphilochius:
   Holl, K. Amphilochius von Ikonium. Tübingen. 1904.
Augustine:
   Angus, S. The sources of Aug.'s *de civ. Dei*. Princeton. 1906.
   Becker, Hans. Augustin. Leipsic. 1908. (Deals with his conversion.)
   Cunningham, W. St Austin. London. 1886. (Paradoxical.)
   Grandgeorge, L. Saint Augustin et le Néoplatonisme. Paris. 1896.
   Mozley, J. B. The Augustinian Doctrine of Predestination. London. 1878.
   Reuter, H. Augustinische Studien. Gotha. 1887.
Boëthius:
   Rand, E. K. On the composition of B.'s *cons. phil.* in Harvard Studies in
      Class. Phil. vol. xv.
   Usener, H. Anecdoton Holderi. Bonn. 1887. (Deals with the external
      evidence for the theological tracts.)
Claudian:
   Hodgkin, T. Claudian, the last of the Roman poets. London. 1875.
Cosmas Indicopleustes:
   Marinelli, G. La geografia e i padri della chiesa. Rome. 1882.
Eusebius:
   Gelzer, H. Sextus Julius Africanus und die byzantinische Chronographie.
      2 vols. Leipsic. 1885–98. (Includes a careful study of the *Chronica*.)
Libanius:
   Seeck, O. Die Briefe des Libanius zeitlich geordnet. Leipsic. 1906.
   Sievers, G. R. Das Leben des Libanius. Berlin. 1868.
Plotinus:
   Whittaker, T. The Neo-Platonists. Cambridge. 1901. (Strongly anti-
      Christian.)
Symmachus:
   Seeck, O. Die Reden des Symmachus und ihre kritische Grundlage.
      Berlin. 1877.

Synesius :
    Crawford, W. S.   Synesius the Hellene.   London.   1901.
    Gardner, A.   Synesius of Cyrene: in The Fathers for Engl. Readers.
       London.   1886.
    Nicol, J. C.   Synesius of Cyrene.   Cambridge.   1887.   Volkmann, R.
       Synesius von Cyrene.   Berlin.   1869.

     (c) Monographs, Biographies, and Special Treatises

See Bibl. to cc. i, ii, and v for —
    Boissier, Chawner, Hort, and Seeck (Quellen u. Urkunden, Untergang).
Abt, A.   Die Apologie des Apuleius von Madaura und die antike Zauberei.
    Giessen.   1908.
Cumont, F.   Le manichéisme.   Paris.   1908.
Pichon, R.   Les derniers écrivains profanes.   Paris.   1906.
Püch, A.   St. Jean Chrysostome et les mœurs de son temps.   Paris.   1891.
Roger, M.   L'enseignement des lettres classiques d'Ausone à Alcuin.   Paris.   1905.
Stephens, W. R. W.   St John Chrysostom, his life and times.   London.   1883.
Stewart, H. F.   Boëthius, an Essay.   Edinburgh.   1891.

CHAPTER XXI

EARLY CHRISTIAN ART

1. BIBLIOGRAPHY

Complete list of books given in the work of Leclerq (*see* below).

2. ADDITIONAL, CHIEFLY MODERN WORKS

Butler, H. C. Architecture and other Arts etc., in Syria etc. New York. 1902.
Cabrol, le R. P. dom. Dictionnaire d'Archéologie Chrétienne etc. Paris. 1902, still in progress. (A very comprehensive account of every branch of the subject.)
Dalton, O. M. British Museum, Catalogue of Early Christian Antiquities etc. London. 1901.
   Guide to the Christian Antiquities in the British Museum. (The best small book on the subject in English.) (Also many other works and articles by the same writer.)
Frothingham, A. L. The Monuments of Christian Rome etc. New York. 1908.
Leclercq, H. M. Manuel d'Archéologie Chrétienne etc. Paris. 1907. (One of the best general accounts of the subject.)
Lowries, W. Christian Art etc. London. 1901.
Marrucchi. Éléments d'Archéologie Chrétienne etc. Paris. 1900.
Michel, A. Histoire de l'Art etc. Paris. 1905.
Peraté, A. L'Archéologie Chrétienne. Paris. 1892. (An excellent small handbook.)
Ramsay, Sir W. and Miss G. L. Bell. The Thousand and One Churches. (Asia Minor.) 1909.
Smith and Cheetham. A Dictionary of Christian Antiquities. London. 1876–90.
Strzygowski, J. Orient oder Rom. Leipsic. 1901. Also many other works.
Venturi, A. Storia dell' Arte Italiana etc. Milan. 1901.
   (And more recent works.)
Wilpert, J. Die Malereien der Katakomben etc. Freiburg-i.-B. 1900. (A finely illustrated work on Early Christian Paintings.)

CHRONOLOGICAL TABLE

OF

LEADING EVENTS MENTIONED IN THIS VOLUME

284   Election of Diocletian (17 Sept.).
297   Peace with Persia: acquisition of the five provinces.
303   The Great Persecution (24 Feb.).
305   Abdication of Diocletian (1 May).
306   Elevation of Constantine at York.
309–380   Reign of Sapor II in Persia.
311   Edict of Toleration and death of Galerius.
312   Battle of Saxa Rubra (28 Sept.).
      Edict of Milan.
323   Battle of Chrysopolis (Sept.).
325   Council of Nicaea.
328–373   Athanasius Bishop of Alexandria.
330   Foundation of Constantinople.
337   Death of Constantine (22 May).
      War with Persia.
339   Second Exile of Athanasius.
341   Council of the Dedication at Antioch.
343   Council of Sardica.
346   Return of Athanasius.
350   Revolt of Magnentius.
352   Battle of Mursa.
355   Julian made Caesar for Gaul.
356   Third Exile of Athanasius.
357   Battle of Argentoratum.
359   Councils of Ariminum and Seleucia.
360   Mutiny at Paris: Julian proclaimed Augustus.
      Council of Constantinople.
361–363   Julian Emperor.
363–364   Jovian Emperor. Peace with Persia: cession of the five provinces.
364   Valentinian and Valens Emperors.
369   Count Theodosius in Britain.
374–397   Ambrose Bishop of Milan.
375–383   Gratian Emperor in the West.
376   Passage of the Danube by the Goths.
378   Battle of Hadrianople (9 Aug.).
379–395   Reign of Theodosius.

381 Council of Constantinople.
383–388 Usurpation of Maximus.
386 Execution of Priscillian.
390 Destruction of the Serapeum.
392 Revolt of Arbogast.
394 Battle of the Frigidus (6 Sept.).
395 Arcadius and Honorius Emperors.
400 Revolt of Gaïnas.
402 Battle of Pollentia.
406 Passage of the Rhine by the Germans (31 Dec.).
407 Withdrawal of the legions from Britain.
408–450 Reign of Theodosius II in the East.
408 Mutiny at Pavia. Execution of Stilicho.
410 Sack of Rome by Alaric (23 Aug.).
412 The Visigoths in Gaul.
418 Rescript of Honorius to Agricola.
425–455 Valentinian III Emperor in the West.
429 The Vandals in Africa.
430 Death of Augustine.
431 Council of Ephesus.
438 *Codex Theodosianus.* Legal separation of East and West.
439 Capture of Carthage by the Vandals.
440–461 Pope Leo I.
445 Edict of Valentinian III.
449 The *Latrocinium* at Ephesus.
c. 449 Traditional date of Hengest and Horsa.
450–458 Marcian Emperor in the East.
451 Council of Chalcedon.
      Battle of the Mauriac Plain.
452 Destruction of Aquileia by Attila. Embassy of Pope Leo.
454 Assassination of Aëtius.
455 Sack of Rome by Gaiseric.
457–461 Reign of Majorian in the West.
468 Failure of Basiliscus before Carthage.
472 Capture of Rome by Ricimer.
474–491 Zeno Emperor in the East.
476 Deposition of Romulus Augustulus.
      Odovacar master of Italy till 493.
481 The *Henoticon* of Zeno. Schism in the Church.
481–511 Reign of Clovis.
486 Clovis defeats Syagrius.
491–518 Anastasius Emperor.
493–526 Reign of Theodoric in Italy.
507 Battle of Vouglé. Clovis conquers Aquitaine.
518 Justin Emperor. End of the Schism.
533 Conquest of Africa by Belisarius.
597 Landing of Augustine.
      Death of Columba (9 June).

INDEX

Aachen. *See* Aix-la-Chapelle

Abercius, Bishop of Hierapolis, 164

Ablabius, favourite of Constantine, 21 sq.; murder of, 55

Aboras (Khabūr), River, 22; Julian crosses, 82

Abraham, patriarch, story of, 336; 583

Abrittus, battle of, 204

Abruzzi, Altaian Bulgars settle in mountains of, 358

Abundantius, general, banished, 457

Acacius, Bishop of Amida, helps the Persian prisoners, 464

Acacius, Bishop of Caesarea in Palestine, convenes a Syrian synod, 132; 133; assents to Nicene faith, 136

Acacius, Bishop of Constantinople, opposes Basiliscus, 473; character, 515; alliance with Peter of Alexandria, 516; and the Henoticon, 517; excommunicated by Simplicius, *ib.*; erasure of name from diptychs, 518

Achaia, 30 sq.; last stronghold of paganism, 113; Goths in, 237; under Theodosius, 253; 261

Achillaeus, usurper, revolt of, 120

Acholius, Bishop of Thessalonica, baptises Theodosius I, 140

Acincum, Valentinian at, 229

Acoemetae, order of monks at Constantinople, 516

Aconia Paulina, wife of Praetextatus, pagan rites of, 93

Acris, Hypatius captured at, 485

Acropolis at Athens, the, 598

Acts of the Apostles, the, cited, 148; 154; translated into verse by Arator of Milan, 449

Adamantius, son of Vivianus, treats with Theodoric, 475 sq.

Adamelissi, fortress of Tropaeum Traiani built at, 210 sq.

Adamnan, his Life of St Columba cited, 391

Adda, River, battle on, 439

Addac, King of the Alani, death of, 304

Addaeus, Roman officer, employed in Armenia, 225

Adeodatus, son of Augustine, 596

ad Evangelum presbyterum of Jerome, 155

'Adid the Arab, joins Romans, 482

Adige, River, 193, 441

Admagetobriga (Montbéliard), Gauls defeated at, 193

Admonitions for Monks, of Rabbula, cited, 526

Adria, Goths at, 446

Adriatic Sea, fleet of Maximus in, 243; nomads find winter quarters by, 358 *and note*; 364; Theodoric's fleet in, 451; 459

Aduatuci, Teutonic tribe, in Gaul, 190; in Belgica, 193

Aedan, Dalriadic King, encounters Aethelfrith, 391

Aedesius, philosopher, 64, 99

Aedui, Keltic tribe, at war with the Sequani, 193; subdued, 194

Aegean Sea, 16 sq., 19, 205 sq.; nomads winter near, 358

Aegidius, general of Majorian, victorious near Orleans, 282, 298; death, 299, 310; makes alliance with Gaiseric, 310; independent ruler in Gaul, 424 sq.; defeats Visigoths, 425; death, *ib.*

Aegina, pagan worship at, 93

Aelia Capitolina. *See* Jerusalem

Aelle, King of Deira, 390

Aelle, reputed founder of the kingdom of Sussex, 382, 390

Aemilia, 239; Alaric in, 273

Aemona (Laibach), Theodosius at, 243; 247; Alaric at, 264, 268

Aequitius, Roman general, 218, 220 sq., 229

Aeruli. *See* Heruli.

Aesculapius, Julian revives worship of, 107

Aestii. *See* Aists

Aethelberht, King of Kent, and Ceawlin, 389 sq.; importance of, 391

Aethelfrith, King of Bernicia, obtains Deira by marriage, 390; encounters Aedan, 391; massacres the Britons, *ib.*

Aethiopica, attributed to Heliodorus, 569

Aëtius, Roman general, forms alliance with Visigoths, 279, 416; defeats the Huns, 280, 416; and the Salian Franks, 297; 298; and the Vandals, 308; and the Huns, 360 sqq., 407; 394; Britons appeal for help to, 380; 393; and Valentinian III, 395, 397, 399; birth and parentage, 406; supports usurper John, 407 sq.; promoted, 408; successes of, 410; struggle

ROMAN EMPIRE

EASTERN DIVISION

At the end of the 4ᵗʰ Century
Natural Scale 1:13,250,000

0 50 100 150 200 250 Miles

NOTE

The colours indicate the seven Dioceses the names of
which are shown thus............. **D. OF ASIA**
The names of the Provinces are shown thus LYCIA

PONTUS EUXINUS

INOPLE (Byzantium)

Pityus

Trapezu

(DACIA
TRAIA A)
Ulpia Traiana
Sarmizeget

SIA SUPE
D. OF
ACIA
DARDANIA
MACEDONIA
SALUTARIS
MACEDONIA
MACEDONIA

DAC
RI
DACIAMEDI

onae

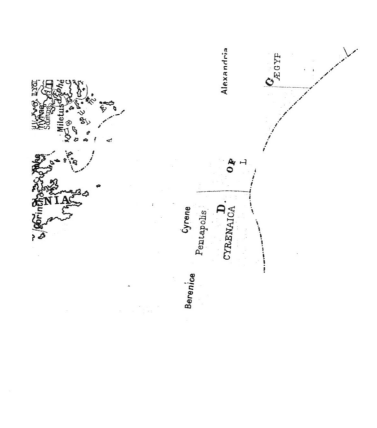

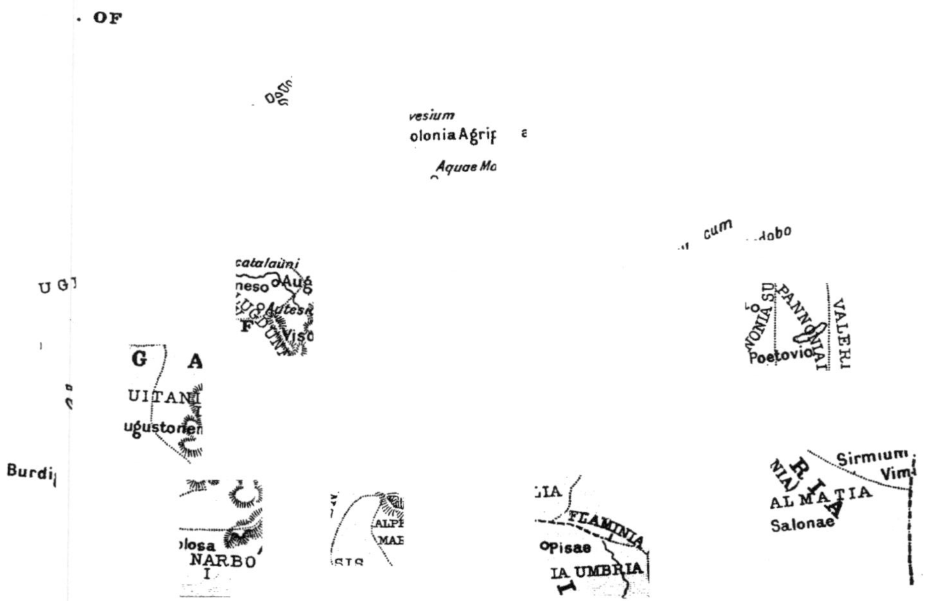

VALERI

PANNONIA

PANNONIA SU

Poetovio

cum

odor.

Sirmium

Vimi

R
NIA
AL MA TIA
Salonae

FLAMINIA

opisae

IA UMBRIA

I

IA

vesium
olonia Agrip

Aquae Ma

ALPE
MAE

BIS

catalauni

neso

Aug

FORUM

G
A

UITANI

ugustofen

losa

NARBO

I

Burdi

U G

OF

OF

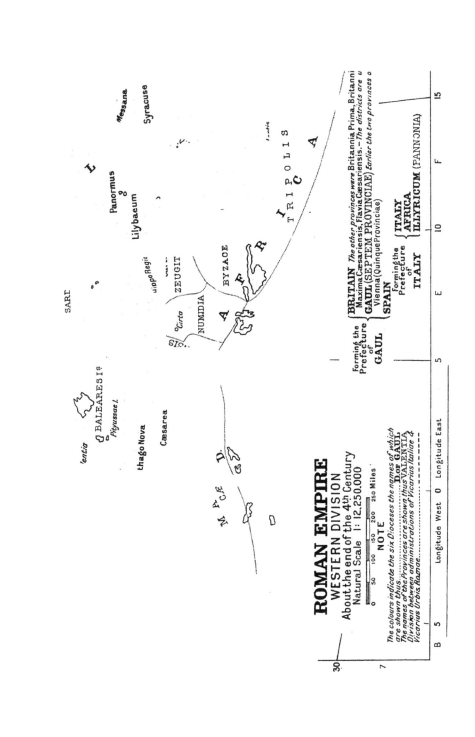

ROMAN EMPIRE
WESTERN DIVISION
About the end of the 4th Century
Natural Scale 1: 12,250,000

0 50 100 150 200 250 Miles

NOTE

The colours indicate the six Dioceses the names of which
are shown thus........D OF GAUL
The names of the Provinces are shown thus VALENTIA
Division between administrations of Vicarius Italiae &
Vicarius Urbis Romae..................

Longitude West 0 Longitude East

Forming the
Prefecture
of
GAUL

BRITAIN The other provinces were Britannia Prima, Britanni
Maxima Caesariensis, Flavia Caesariensis.—The districts are u
GAUL (SEPTEM PROVINCIAE) Earlier the two provinces o
SPAIN Vienna (Quinque Provinciae)

Forming the
Prefecture
of
ITALY

ITALY
AFRICA
ILLYRICUM (PANNONIA)

SARI

BALEARES Is
Pityussae I.

thago Nova

Caesarea

MACÆD.

SIS

NUMIDIA

Cirta

ZEUGIT

BYZAOE

A F R

C

TRIPOLIS

Messana

Syracuse

Panormus

Lilybaeum

Regit

G R

(S A L

(ian)

Seistan L.

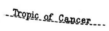

Tropic of Cancer

Mts
IA

ASIA
(PHYSICAL)
to illustrate migrations
Natural Scale 1:30,000,000

0   100   200   300   400   500 Miles

NOTE

Approximate extent of Caspian & Aral Seas
(A) until at least I*st* Century A.D. & possibly
................(C) again about 900 to 1200 A.D.
Approximate extent during (B) period of
...greatest drought about 200 to 600 A.D.
Presumed river or lake channels dur-
....=ing periods (A) or (C)
Desert, mostly sand.................................
Highest mount.ⁿ grass region & north-
...=ern grass steppe - *Summer Pasture*
Mountain slopes & upper valleys among
high m.ᵗ.ˢ (only indicated) also gravel
......................belt - *Spring Pasture*
Zone of thicker vegetation and of
lower mountain slopes - *Autumn Pas-
ture*
Winter shelter (not shown) reed thickets among
lake & river beds e.g. Aral & Ala Kul regions.
Northern forest belt.................................
Northern fir tree limit.............................
Isotherms for January,   for July.

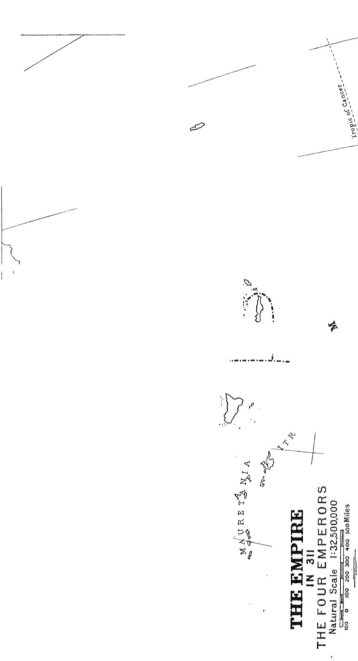

THE EMPIRE
IN 311
THE FOUR EMPERORS
Natural Scale 1:32,500,000
100 0 100 200 300 400 500 Miles

Tropic of Cancer

MAURETANIA

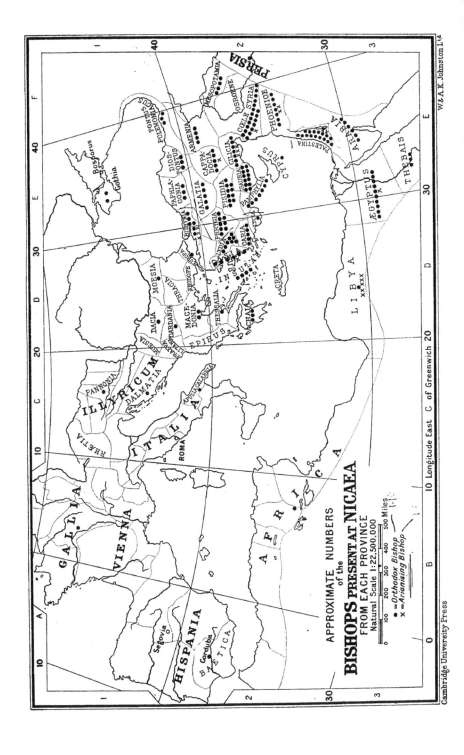

APPROXIMATE NUMBERS
of the
BISHOPS PRESENT AT NICAEA
FROM EACH PROVINCE
Natural Scale 1:22,500,000

0 100 200 300 400 500 Miles

● = Orthodox Bishop
× = Arianising Bishop

Cambridge University Press

W.&A.K.Johnston Lᵗᵈ

Map 6

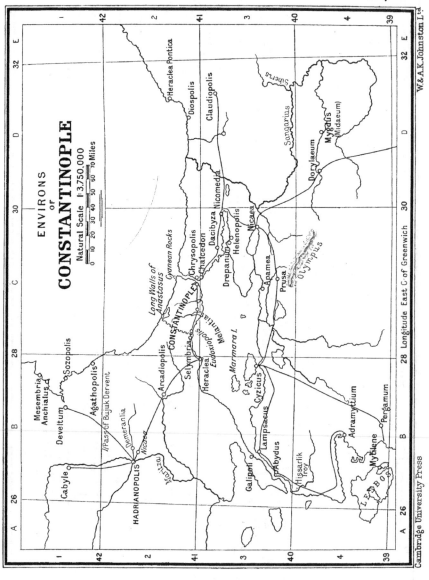

ENVIRONS
OF
CONSTANTINOPLE
Natural Scale 1:3,750,000
0 10 20 30 40 50 60 70 Miles

W&A.K.Johnston Ltd.

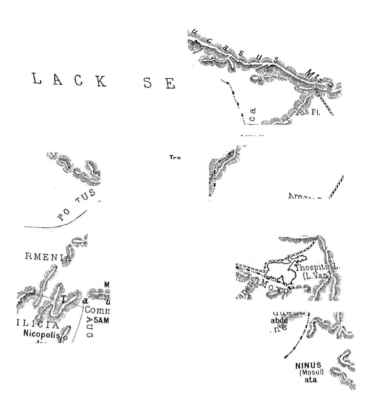

LACK SE

Caucasus Mts

ca

us Fl.

Tra

Arax

PO TUS

RMENI

Thospiti L.
(L.Van)

T a Comm
M
U SAM
U
G

ILICIA
Nicopolis

anegh Mou

abd
n

NINUS
(Mosul)
ata

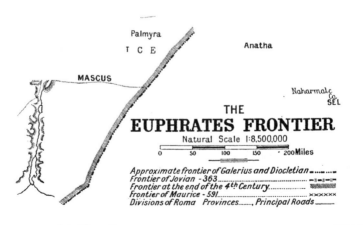

Palmyra

ICE

Anatha

MASCUS

Naharmal
SEL

THE
EUPHRATES FRONTIER
Natural Scale 1:8,500,000

| 0 | 50 | 100 | 150 | 200 Miles |

Approximate frontier of Galerius and Diocletian — ··· —
Frontier of Jovian - 363
Frontier at the end of the 4th Century
Frontier of Maurice - 591
Divisions of Roma Provinces, *Principal Roads*

Cambridge University Press.

W & A K Johnston Ltd

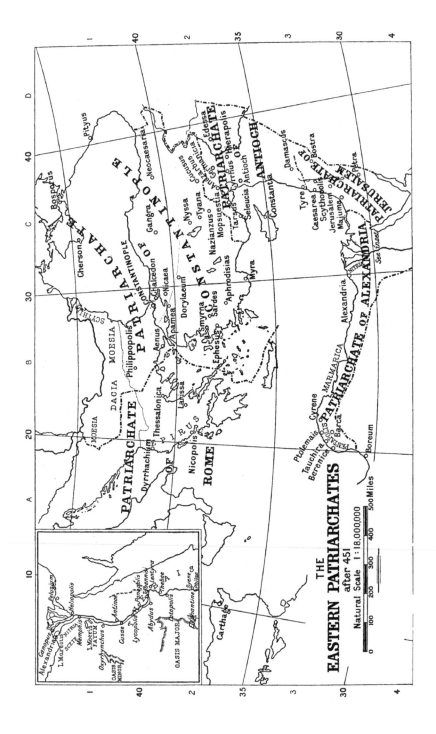

THE
EASTERN PATRIARCHATES
after 451
Natural Scale 1 : 18,000,000

0   100   200   300   400   500 Miles

Gothl

olm   A E S T

II
RGUNDIAN   T H S
VANDAL

Danube
M   o

idge University Press

THE
TEUTONIC   TRIBES
in the 1st & 4th. Centuries A. D.
Natural Scale   1 : 12,500,000

0   50   100   150   200   250 Miles

NOTE

The names of Roman Provinces are shown thus. Dacia
The names of the Tribes in the 1st Century A.D. are
shown thus..FRISII
The names of the Tribes towards the close of the
4th century are shown thus.........................**SAXONS**

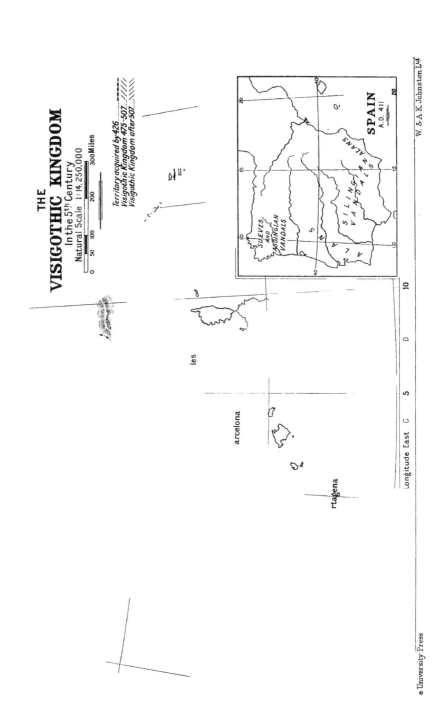

THE
VISIGOTHIC KINGDOM

In the 5th Century
Natural Scale 1:14,250,000

0   50   100   200   300 Miles

Territory acquired by 426
Visigothic Kingdom 475-507
Visigothic Kingdom after 507

SPAIN

A.D. 411

SUEVES AND ASDINGIAN VANDALS

SILINGIAN VANDALS

ALANS

les

arcelona

rtagena

Longitude East   C   D   5   10

e University Press

W. & A K Johnston Lᵗᵈ

G A U L
in the 5th Century
Natural Scale 1:5,000,000

0 10 20 30 40 50   100 Miles

LugdunBatavo

Bononia

Hele

forur

assi ıa

⌒
Aǧde)

(Béziers)
Narbo˙

ıusta

Bruso
Nuceri
anorm s
rtana
Syracus
THS
0
es

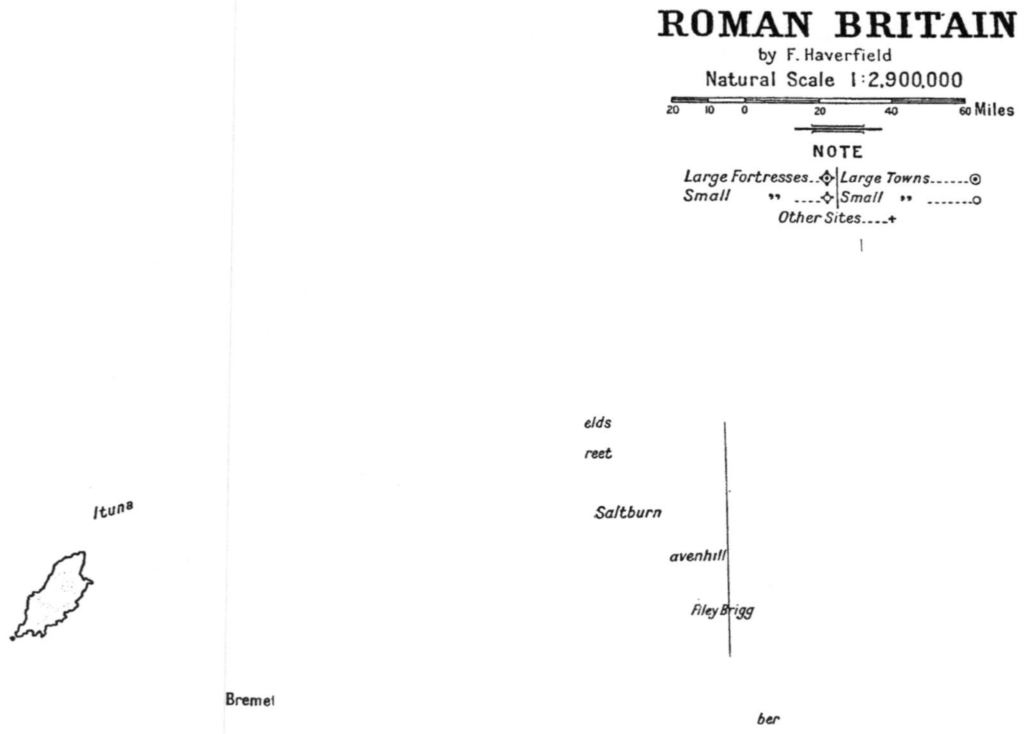

ROMAN BRITAIN

by F. Haverfield

Natural Scale 1:2,900,000

20 10 0   20   40   60 Miles

NOTE

Large Fortresses..◈|Large Towns......◉
Small   " ....◇|Small " ....○
        Other Sites....+

56

elds

reet

Saltburn

avenhill

filey Brigg

ber

Bremei

Ituna

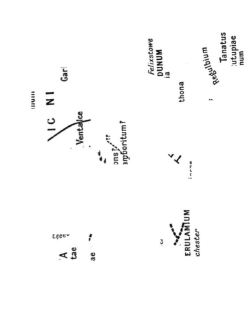

IC NI

Gari

VentaIce

ons?
Emporitum?

Felixstowe
DUNUM
ia

thona

Regulbium
Tanatus
Rutupiae
num

A
tae
ae

ERULAMIUM
chester

the 4th and 5th

Pontus Euxinus

Odessus

ambria
ialus
ilonia
zopolis)

Alpheus

THE following pages contain a prospectus and contents table of the Cambridge Medieval History and the Cambridge Modern History

The Cambridge Medieval History

PLANNED BY

J. B. BURY, M.A.

Regius Professor of Modern History in the University of Cambridge

EDITED BY

H. M. GWATKIN, M.A.

Dixie Professor of Ecclesiastical History in the University of Cambridge
Late Gifford Lecturer, Edinburgh

AND

J. P. WHITNEY, B.D.

Professor of Ecclesiastical History, King's College, London

In Eight Volumes   8vo   Buckram   Gilt Top   Maps

Price, $5.00 net per volume   Expressage extra

The Syndics of the Cambridge University Press, on the completion of *The Cambridge Modern History*, undertook to publish a comprehensive history of medieval times, drawn up on similar lines. The work covers the period from Constantine to the close of the Middle Ages, and is to appear in eight volumes.

The principles which have guided the conception of this work are those laid down by the late Lord Acton for *The Cambridge Modern History*, though experience has suggested some improvements of detail in the mode of carrying these principles out. The scheme for the work was laid down by Mr. J. B. Bury, Lord Acton's successor as Regius Professor of Modern History. The editorship was entrusted to the Rev. H. M. Gwatkin, Dixie Professor of Ecclesiastical History in the University of Cambridge, and the Rev. J. P. Whitney, of King's College, Cambridge, Professor of Ecclesiastical History in King's College, London.

The need of some such work is evident, for there is nothing resembling it in the English language. Gibbon deals mainly with the Empire, and with the Teuton, the Slav, the Magyar, the Turk, and even the Saracen, chiefly in their connection with the Empire. Even the great French work of Lavisse and Rambaud deals with the Middle Ages on a much smaller scale than is here contemplated. The present work covers the entire field of European medieval history and in every chapter sums up recent research upon the subject. Foreign specialists as well as English have given their assistance; America, France, Germany, Spain, Italy, Russia, and Hungary are represented in the list of contributors.

CONTENTS

Vol. III. GERMANY AND THE WESTERN EMPIRE

Vol. IV. THE EASTERN ROMAN EMPIRE

Vol. V. THE CRUSADES

1125–1152. 10. Italy, 1125–1152. 11. Frederick Barbarossa and Germany.
12. (a) Frederick Barbarossa and the Lombard League; (b) South Italy in
the twelfth century. 13. England: Norman kings (William II to Stephen).
14. England: Henry II. 15. France and the Angevin dominion. 16.
France and the Communal movement. 17. The Jews. 18. Scholasticism.
19. Effects of the Crusades on Western Europe.

Vol. VI. THE ROMAN THEOCRACY

1. Henry VI. 2. Growth of the Papal power: Innocent III. 3. The
struggle for the Empire (Philip II and Otto IV). 4. Frederick II: Germany.
5. Frederick II: Italy and Sicily. 6. The Fall of the Hohenstaufens (a)
(Germany); (b) Italy. 7. Philip Augustus (and Louis VIII). 8. Louis IX.
9. England: Richard and John. 10. England: Henry III. 11. Spain.
12. Scandinavia (from middle of eleventh to end of thirteenth century).
13. Poland and Hungary (from middle of eleventh to end of thirteenth century). 14. Heresies and inquisition. 15. The Mendicant Orders. 16.
Universities and learning. 17. Commerce and Industry in the Middle
Ages. 18. Chivalry. 19. Architecture (a) Ecclesiastical; (b) Military.
20. Legendary cycles in the Middle Ages.

Vol. VII. DECLINE OF THE EMPIRE AND PAPACY

1. The Empire (1272–1313). 2. Italy in the time of Dante. 3. Lewis the
Bavarian. 4. Charles IV and Bohemia. 5. Switzerland. 6. The Hansa.
7. The Teutonic order, Poland and Lithuania. 8. The Popes at Avignon
and the Great Schism. 9. France: the last Capetians. 10. France: Hundred Years' War (First part). 11. France: Armagnacs and Burgundians.
12. England: Edward I and Edward II. 13. England: Edward III and
Richard II. 14. Scotland, Wales, and Ireland. 15. (a) Wyclif (b) Hus.
16. The Councils of Constance and Basel. 17. Spain. 18. Assemblies
of Estates. 19. Italian States in the fourteenth century. 20. Early Renaissance. 21. Mysticism. 22. Growth of towns in Western Europe.

Vol. VIII. GROWTH OF THE WESTERN KINGDOMS

1. The Hussite Wars. 2. The Empire in the 15th century. 3. Hungary.
4. The Papacy in the 15th century. 5. Italy. 6. Florence under the Medici.
7. Spain and Portugal. 8. France: Hundred Years' War (Second period).
9. France: Louis XI. 10. Burgundy. 11. Low Countries. 12. England:
Lancastrians. 13. England: New Monarchy. 14. The Scandinavian Kingdoms. 15. Russia. 16. The Renaissance. 17. New theories of education.
18. Political theory. 19. Warfare 20. Magic, witchcraft, astrology in the
Middle Ages.

THE MACMILLAN COMPANY

Publishers   64-66 Fifth Avenue   New York

The Cambridge Modern History

ROYAL OCTAVO   GILT TOPS
TWELVE VOLUMES   CLOTH

$4.00 net per volume   *$48.00 the set in box*   *Carriage extra*

PLANNED BY

The Late LORD ACTON, LL.D.
Regius Professor of Modern History

EDITED BY

A. W. WARD, Litt.D.   G. W. PROTHERO, Litt.D.
STANLEY LEATHES, M.A.

What Critics say of The Cambridge Modern History:

" A work of great value. It may justly claim to have no rival in English."
— *The Atlantic Monthly*, Boston.

" There can be no question about the great value of the work — in fact, it is invaluable to every historical student." — *Philadelphia Public Ledger*.

" As this great work, now nearing completion, goes steadily on its way, it gathers in each successive volume fresh contributors. Some of them are comparatively new to us, and probably to most readers, but all are pervaded by the business-like attention to careful statement which characterized their predecessors in earlier volumes." — *The Nation*.

" Attention has been called more than once or twice in the *Eagle's* book pages to the consummate scholarship displayed in the preparation of the monographs composing these volumes, the thoroughness of treatment, the breadth of the historical perspective, and the even-handed liberality with which all questions have been discussed. It is a wonderful history." — *Brooklyn Eagle*.

" A work of such lasting value and solid scholarship must become a standard authority." — *Athenaeum*.

WS - #0022 - 050123 - C0 - 229/152/44 [46] - CB - 9780331962888 - Gloss Lamination